September 27–30, 2015
Northampton, MA, USA

I0047459

Association for Computing Machinery

Advancing Computing as a Science & Profession

ICTIR'15

Proceedings of the 2015 International Conference on

Theory of Information Retrieval

Sponsored by:

ACM SIGIR

Supported by:

Google, Microsoft Research, Oracle Labs, and Lexalytics

Association for Computing Machinery

Advancing Computing as a Science & Profession

The Association for Computing Machinery
2 Penn Plaza, Suite 701
New York, New York 10121-0701

Notice to Past Authors of ACM-Published Articles
ACM intends to create a complete electronic archive of all articles and/or other material previously published by ACM. If you have written a work that has been previously published by ACM in any journal or conference proceedings prior to 1978, or any SIG Newsletter at any time, and you do NOT want this work to appear in the ACM Digital Library, please inform permissions@acm.org, stating the title of the work, the author(s), and where and when published.

ISBN: 978-1-4503-3833-2 (Digital)

ISBN: 978-1-4503-4030-4 (Print)

Additional copies may be ordered prepaid from:

ACM Order Department
PO Box 30777
New York, NY 10087-0777, USA

Phone: 1-800-342-6626 (USA and Canada)
+1-212-626-0500 (Global)
Fax: +1-212-944-1318
E-mail: acmhelp@acm.org
Hours of Operation: 8:30 am – 4:30 pm ET

Printed in the USA

ICTIR 2015 General Chairs' Welcome

Welcome to ICTIR 2015, the 5th International Conference on the Theory of Information Retrieval and the first conference with that name to be fully sponsored by the ACM Special Interest Group on Information Retrieval (SIGIR). Becoming part of the SIGIR family, along with the well-known SIGIR conference and the new CHIIR conference, will improve both the coordination between these venues and the availability of resources such as student scholarships. We believe that ICTIR is a natural complement to the SIGIR conference, with a stronger emphasis on theory and formal approaches, and less emphasis on large-scale experimentation and practice.

Given that ICTIR has generally been a smaller, more discussion-oriented conference than SIGIR, we felt that the Pioneer Valley, and Northampton in particular, would be an ideal venue for a September meeting. We hope to provide a relaxing small-town setting, beautiful Fall colors, and enough restaurants and bars to satisfy attendees used to living in large cities. The Center for Intelligent Information Retrieval and the University of Massachusetts are just on the other side of the Connecticut River in Amherst, and Noah Webster and Melvil Dewey did some of their best work at Amherst College, so there is a strong association with information retrieval. Given the quality of research that will be presented at ICTIR 2015, this should be another milestone in this local IR history. Enjoy the conference!

James Allan
College of Information and
Computer Sciences
University of Massachusetts
Amherst

Bruce Croft
College of Information and
Computer Sciences
University of Massachusetts
Amherst

Program Chairs' Welcome

The program chairs are excited to welcome you to the ACM SIGIR International Conference on the Theory of Information Retrieval (ICTIR); a new episode in the history of ICTIR where the conference has been embraced by ACM SIGIR and now runs for the first time under their flag.

The conference aims to provide a forum for the presentation and discussion of research related to the *foundational* aspects of Information Retrieval (IR), including, for example, new or improved models of relevance, ranking, representation, information needs, and evaluation. Norbert Fuhr helped define foundation precisely as *a scientific result that others can build upon and use for their own research*. The class of scientific works solicited in the call for papers thus covers both purely theoretical contributions as well as reproducible experimental results; where reproducibility is emphasized (e.g., through sharing the data sets and/or software implementations).

The conference has been very successful in attracting high quality contributions, helping us compose a strong and varied program. In response to the call for contributions, the conference received a healthy number of submissions: 4 tutorials out of which we accepted 2 (or 50%), 43 short paper submissions where we accepted 22 (51%), and, 57 long paper submissions out of which 29 have been included in the final program (51%). (As an aside, due to the high quality of the submission pool, we would like to emphasize that acceptance rate is obviously not an indicator of quality!)

We thank all the program committee members for their effort and excellent reviews, the Tutorial Chair, Peter Bruza, and his committee for the selection of tutorials, and the General Chairs, James Allan and Bruce Croft, for their guidance. We invite you to enjoy the scientific program with exciting novel results in our field!

Arjen de Vries and ChengXiang Zhai
(Long paper PC Chairs)

Norbert Fuhr and Yi Zhang
(Short paper PC Chairs)

Table of Contents

Session T3: Language Models for IR

Session T4: Entity Analysis

Session W1: IR Applications

Session W2: NLP and IR

Session W3: Learning-based Retrieval Models

Short Papers

2015 ACM SIGIR International Conference on the Theory of Information Retrieval (ICTIR) Organization

General Chairs: James Allan *(University of Massachusetts Amherst, USA)*
Bruce Croft *(University of Massachusetts Amherst, USA)*

Program Chairs: Arjen de Vries *(CWI Amsterdam, The Netherlands)*
Chengxiang Zhai *(University of Illinois at Urbana-Champaign, USA)*

Program Chairs, Short Papers: Norbert Fuhr *(University Duisburg-Essen, Germany)*
Yi Zhang *(University of California, Santa Cruz, USA)*

Tutorial Chair: Peter Bruza *(Queensland University of Technology, Australia)*

Program Committee: Eugene Agichtein *(Yahoo Labs and Emory University, USA)*
Robin Aly *(University of Twente, The Netherlands)*
Giambattista Amati *(Fondazione Ugo Bordoni, Italy)*
Jaime Arguello *(University of North Carolina at Chapel Hill, USA)*
Leif Azzopardi *(University of Glasgow, UK)*
Krisztian Balog *(University of Stavanger, Norway)*
Alejandro Bellogin *(Universidad Autónoma de Madrid, Spain)*
Michael Bendersky *(Google, USA)*
Peter Bruza *(Queensland University of Technology, Australia)*
Katriina Byström *(Oslo and Akershus University College of Applied Sciences, Norway)*
Jamie Callan *(Carnegie Mellon University, USA)*
Mark Carman *(Monash University, Australia)*
Claudio Carpineto *(Fondazione Ugo Bordoni, Italy)*
Ben Carterette *(University of Delaware, USA)*
Pablo Castells *(Universidad Autónoma de Madrid, Spain)*
Yi Chang *(Yahoo! Labs, USA)*
Tat-Seng Chua *(National University of Singapore, Singapore)*
Kevyn Collins-Thompson *(University of Michigan, Ann Arbor, USA)*
Fabio Crestani *(University of Lugano (USI), Switzerland)*
Ronan Cummins *(Cambridge University, UK)*
Jeffrey Dalton *(Google, USA)*
Arjen P. de Vries *(CWI, The Netherlands)*
Gianluca Demartini *(University of Sheffield, UK)*
Thomas Demeester *(Ghent University - iMinds, Belgium)*
Fernando Diaz *(Microsoft, USA)*
Laura Dietz *(Mannheim University, Germany)*
Miles Efron *(University of Illinois, USA)*
Hui Fang *(University of Delaware, USA)*
Ingo Frommholz *(University of Bedfordshire, UK)*

Program Committee (continued):	Mark Smucker *(University of Waterloo, Canada)*
	Dawei Song *(The Open University, UK)*
	Benno Stein *(University of Weimar, Germany)*
	Theodora Tsikrika *(CERTH, Greece)*
	Howard Turtle *(Syracuse University, USA)*
	Olga Vechtomova *(University of Waterloo, Canada)*
	Jun Wang *(University College London, UK)*
	Grace Hui Yang *(Georgetown University, USA)*
	Chengxiang Zhai *(University of Illinois, USA)*
	Yi Zhang *(University of California Santa Cruz, USA)*
	Guido Zuccon *(Queensland University of Technology, Australia)*
Local Arrangements:	Jean Joyce *(University of Massachusetts Amherst, USA)*
	Kate Moruzzi *(University of Massachusetts Amherst, USA)*
Steering Committee Chair:	Oren Kurland *(Technion - Israel Institute of Technology, Israel)*
Steering Committee:	Leif Azzopardi *(University of Glasgow, UK)*
	Peter Bruza *(Queensland University of Technology, Australia)*
	Susan Dumais *(Microsoft Research, USA)*
	Jaap Kamps, SIGIR representative *(University of Amsterdam, The Netherlands)*
	Birger Larsen *(Aalborg University, Denmark)*
	Donald Metzler *(Google, USA)*
	Stefan Rueger, BCS-IRSG representative *(The Open University, UK)*
	Keith van Rijsbergen, Honorary Chair *(University of Glasgow, UK)*
Additional reviewers:	Zhuyun Dai *(Carnegie Mellon University, USA)*
	Kyle Yingkai Gao *(Carnegie Mellon University, USA)*
	Parantapa Goswami *(University J. Fourier/Grenoble 1, France)*
	Savvas Karagiannidis *(University College London, UK)*
	Kleanthis Malialis *(University College London, UK)*
	Stefania Marrara *(Universita degli Studi di Milano Bicocca, Italy)*
	Daan Odijk *(University of Amsterdam, The Netherlands)*
	Ridho Reinanda *(University of Amsterdam, The Netherlands)*
	Anne Schuth *(University of Amsterdam, The Netherlands)*
	Marc Sloan *(University College London, UK)*
	Marco Viviani *(Universita degli Studi di Milano Bicocca, Italy)*
	Weinan Zhang *(University College London, UK)*
	Xiaoxue Zhao *(University College London, UK)*

ICTIR 2015 Sponsor & Supporters

Sponsor:

Association for Computing Machinery

Advancing Computing as a Science & Profession

SIGIR
Special Interest Group on Information Retrieval

Organizer:

Supporters:

Silver

Google™

Microsoft® Research

Oracle Labs

Bronze

LEXALYTICS
Read   Between The Lines

Embedded Representations of Lexical and Knowledge-Base Semantics

Andrew McCallum

Professor, College of Information and Computer Sciences
University of Massachusetts Amherst
mccallum@cs.umass.edu

BIO

Andrew McCallum is a Professor, Director of the Center for Data Science, and Director of the Information Extraction and Synthesis Laboratory in the College of Information and Computer Sciences at University of Massachusetts Amherst. He has published over 250 papers in many areas of AI, including natural language processing, machine learning, data mining and reinforcement learning, and his work has received over 40,000 citations.

He obtained his PhD from University of Rochester in 1995 with Dana Ballard and a postdoctoral fellowship from CMU with Tom Mitchell and Sebastian Thrun. In the early 2000's he was Vice President of Research and Development at at WhizBang Labs, a 170-person start-up company that used machine learning for information extraction from the Web.

He is an AAAI Fellow, the recipient of the UMass Chancellor's Award for Research and Creative Activity, the UMass Amherst Samuel F. Conti Faculty Fellowship, the UMass Amherst NSM Distinguished Research Award, the UMass Amherst Lilly Teaching Fellowship, and research awards from Google, IBM, Yahoo, and Microsoft. He was the General Chair for the International Conference on Machine Learning (ICML) 2012, and is a member and the current president of the International Machine Learning Society, as well as a member of the editorial board of the *Journal of Machine Learning Research*. He and co-authors received the ICML Test-of-Time Award in 2011.

For the past ten years, McCallum has been active in research on statistical machine learning applied to text, especially information extraction, entity resolution, semi-supervised learning, topic models, word embeddings, and social network analysis. Work on open peer review can be found at http://openreview.net. Work on search and bibliometric analysis of open-access research literature can be found at http://rexa.info.

ICTIR '15, September 27–30, Northampton, MA, USA.
ACM 978-1-4503-3833-2/15/09. DOI: http://dx.doi.org/10.1145/2808194.2808195

Theory of Retrieval: The Retrievability of Information

Leif Azzopardi
School of Computing Science, University of Glasgow
Glasgow, United Kingdom
Leif.Azzopardi @glasgow.ac.uk

ABSTRACT

Retrievability is an important and interesting indicator that can be used in a number of ways to analyse Information Retrieval systems and document collections. Rather than focusing totally on relevance, retrievability examines what is retrieved, how often it is retrieved, and whether a user is likely to retrieve it or not. This is important because a document needs to be retrieved, before it can be judged for relevance. In this tutorial, we shall explain the concept of retrievability along with a number of retrievability measures, how it can be estimated and how it can be used for analysis. Since retrieval precedes relevance, we shall also provide an overview of how retrievability relates to effectiveness - describing some of the insights that researchers have discovered thus far. We shall also show how retrievability relates to efficiency, and how the theory of retrievability can be used to improve both effectiveness and efficiency. Then we shall provide an overview of the different applications of retrievability such as Search Engine Bias, Corpus Profiling, etc., before wrapping up with challenges and opportunities. The final session will look at example problems and ways to analyse and apply retrievability to other problems and domains. Participants are invited to bring their own problems to be discussed after the tutorial. This half-day tutorial is ideal for: (i) researchers curious about retrievability and wanting to see how it can impact their research, (ii) researchers who would like to expand their set of analysis techniques, and/or (iii) researchers who would like to use retrievability to perform their own analysis.

Categories and Subject Descriptors

H.3.4 [**Information Storage and Retrieval**]: Systems and Software:Performance Evaluation

General Terms

Theory, Experimentation

ICTIR'15, September 27-30, Northampton, MA, USA.
ACM 978-1-4503-383 -2/15/09.
DOI: http://dx.doi.org/ 0.1145/2808194.2809444.

Keywords

Retrievability; Effectiveness; Evaluation; Simulation

1. INTRODUCTION

This half day tutorial will be broken into five main parts: (i) Definition, Theory and Measures of Retrievability (ii) The Estimation of Document Retrievability, (iii) The Relationship between Retrievability and Effectiveness, (iv) Applications of Retrievability and (v) Applying Retrievability to your own research. Finally, we will conclude with a summary of the challenges and directions of future research.

1.1 Definitions and Measures

In this part of the tutorial, we will introduce the different "abilities" in IR, which affect how findable a document is, either from a user's perspective or a system's perspective. And importantly how they related and are dependent upon each other. For example,a document needs to be indexed before it can be retrieved, and to be indexed a document needs to be crawled, etc. Once this context is set, we shall explicitly define retrievability explaining how it can be derived from first principles and how it can be derived through an analogy with Transportation Planning. This session is then concluded with an introduction to the different measurements that can be obtained. The following topics will be covered:

1. The -abilities of Information Retrieval

   - Findability [30]
   - Navigability [44, 19, 21]
   - Accessibility [27, 9]
   - Searchability [36]
   - Crawlability [29]
   - Discoverability [20]
   - Usability [33]
   - Retrievability [11]

2. What is retrievability? How easily can a document be found? What is the probability of finding a document? [11]

3. How Information Retrieval relates Transportation Planning [9]

   - Transportation planning, Land Use and Accessibility Measures [26, 25]

- Information Spaces vs. Physical Spaces
- An analogy between IR and Transportation Planning

4. Measure of Retrievability

- Cumulative based measures
- Gravity based measures

5. Retrievability Bias

- The Lorenze Curve [23]
- Gini Co-efficient [23]
- Other inequality measure (Hoover, Theil, Palma, etc)

1.2 Estimating Retrievability

The second part of the tutorial will focus on how to estimate the retrievability of a particular document (i.e. a page-centric approach) and how the retrievability of all the documents can be estimated (i.e. a collection-centric approach). The pragmatic problems of obtaining such estimates shall be discussed along with how to generate/simulate the queries required to formulate a reasonable estimate (thus we shall provide an overview of various ways to simulate queries). The type of estimate depends on how the measure will be used - so we shall describe how depending on the type of analysis to be performed which estimation techniques will be more appropriate. Also, we shall describe retrievability can be efficiently estimated depending on how it will be used. A summary of the topics we shall cover here are:

1. Page-Centric estimates versus Collection-Centric Estimates

2. The Universe of all Possible Queries

3. Absolute estimates versus Relative estimates

4. Generating Queries to estimate retrievability [5, 6, 1, 24]

   - Single Term
   - Bigram / Biterm
   - n-grams
   - Title based
   - Query Logs

5. Efficient estimations and approximation of retrievability and bias [41, 28]

6. Relationship between Cumulative and Gravity based measures

7. Relationship between inequality measures [43]

8. Analysis of documents and collections using Retrievability and how document collections can be analysed using retrievability? [10, 13, 15, 32]

1.3 Relationships with Retrievability

Part three will focus in on the relationship between retrievability and various retrieval effectiveness measures. Here we will describe and discuss the various efforts that have tried to understand the relationship between retrievability and effectiveness [17, 16, 40, 4, 39, 42]. Firstly, from a theoretical point of view, we will discuss the different possible relationships and how retrievability can impact upon both effectiveness and efficiency. Then we will consider the relationship with effectiveness between different retrieval models (i.e. how well do the retrievability scores of various systems correlate to system effectiveness or system rankings) and within a retrieval model (i.e. how well does the retrievability of a particular retrieval model, given its different parameter settings, correlate to system effectiveness). Specifically, we shall show how retrievability can be used to rank systems and tune retrieval models.

1. The conceptual / hypothesised relationship between retrievability and performance [4]

2. Retrievability and Efficiency

3. The empirical relationship between retrievability [4, 39] and:

   - Mean Average Precision,
   - Precision and MRR,
   - Recall,
   - NDCG, etc.

4. The empirical relationship between retrievability and new user oriented gain based measures [38]

5. Retrievability and Retrieval Models when ranking systems [18]

1.4 Applications of Retrievability

Part four will describe the research conducted by a growing number of research groups who have applied retrievability, or the theory of, to gain improvements in effectiveness and/or efficiency, or to gain other insights. Some of the research directions covered will include:

1. Search Engine Bias: how systems influence user populations [7, 37, 31].

2. Improving Recall: the highs and lows of affect retrievable patents [12, 17].

3. The Reverted Index: how retrievability turns retrieval on its head to produce improvements in both effectiveness and efficiency [34].

4. Psuedo Relevance Bias: how Pseudo Relevance is biased, and addressing that bias leads to performance improvements [16].

5. Findability: games that make you find while measuring how easily documents can be found [8, 35]. As part of this session, participants will be invited to play test out the games developed to measure how easily people can find pages given a search engine.

To wrap up, we will then outline the future directions and research challenges associated with retrievability. There are numerous research opportunities in how to use and apply retrievability research, as well as more basic research in terms of the estimation, relationships, theory and applications of retrievability. The final part of the tutorial will be dedicated to questions and answers about retrievability, and going through in groups, how to apply retrievability in the domains that are of interest to the participants. In fact, participants will be invited to bring along and share their research problems and during the course of this session focus on designing a retrievability analysis along with the necessary experiments to undertake such an analysis.

2. INTENDED LEARNING OUTCOMES

By the end of the tutorial, students should be able to:

- Define and describe retrievability and retrievability bias

- Explain the relationship between retrievability, accessibility, findability, navigability, and other -abilities.

- Estimate the retrievability of documents within a collection

- Design a retrievability experiment to detect/monitor retrieval bias

- Describe the relationships between retrievability, effectiveness and efficiency

- Evaluate an application using retrievability measures

3. BIOGRAPHY

Leif Azzopardi is a Senior Lecturer within the School of Computing Science at the University of Glasgow, unofficial leader of the legendary Glasgow Information Retrieval Group, and pioneer of the theory of retrievability. His research focuses on building formal models for Information Retrieval - usually drawing upon different disciplines for inspiration, such as Quantum Mechanics, Operations Research, Microeconomics, Transportation Planning and Gamification. Central to his research is the theoretical development models for Information Seeking and Retrieval, where his research interests include:

- Models for the retrieval of documents, sentences, experts and other information objects [14, 22];

- Probabilistic models of user interaction and the simulation of users for evaluation [1, 5, 6];

- Microeconomic models of information interaction, specifically how cost and effort affect interaction and performance with search systems [2];

- Methods which assess the impact of search technology on society in application areas such as, search engine bias and the accessibility of e-Government information [11] and;

- Searching for fun (i.e. the SINS of users) [3].

He received his Ph.D. in Computing Science from the University of Paisley in 2006, and he received a First Class Honours Degree in Information Science from the University of

Newcastle, Australia, 2001. In 2010, he received a Post-Graduate Certificate in Academic Practice and has been lecturing at the University of Glasgow since then.

4. REFERENCES

[1] L. Azzopardi. Query side evaluation: an empirical analysis of effectiveness and effort. In *Proceedings of the 32nd international ACM SIGIR conference on Research and development in information retrieval*, pages 556–563. ACM, 2009.

[2] L. Azzopardi. The economics in interactive information retrieval. In *Proceedings of the 34th International ACM SIGIR Conference on Research and Development in Information Retrieval*, SIGIR '11, pages 15–24, 2011.

[3] L. Azzopardi. Searching for unlawful carnal knowledge. In *Proceedings of the SIGIR Workshop: Search for Fun*, volume 11, pages 17–18, 2011.

[4] L. Azzopardi and R. Bache. On the relationship between effectiveness and accessibility. In *Proc. of the 33rd international ACM SIGIR*, pages 889–890, 2010.

[5] L. Azzopardi and M. de Rijke. Automatic construction of known-item finding test beds. In *Proceedings of SIGIR '06*, pages 603–604, 2006.

[6] L. Azzopardi, M. de Rijke, and K. Balog. Building simulated queries for known-item topics: an analysis using six european languages. In *Proceedings of the 30th annual international ACM SIGIR conference on Research and development in information retrieval*, pages 455–462. ACM, 2007.

[7] L. Azzopardi and C. Owens. Search engine predilection towards news media providers. In *Proc. of the 32nd ACM SIGIR*, pages 774–775, 2009.

[8] L. Azzopardi, J. Purvis, and R. Glassey. Pagefetch: a retrieval game for children (and adults). In *Proceedings of the 35th international ACM SIGIR conference on Research and development in information retrieval*, SIGIR '12, pages 1010–1010, 2012.

[9] L. Azzopardi and V. Vinay. Accessibility in information retrieval. In *Proc. of the 30th ECIR*, pages 482–489, 2008.

[10] L. Azzopardi and V. Vinay. Document accessibility: Evaluating the access afforded to a document by the retrieval system. *Workshop on Novel Methodologies for Evaluation in Information Retrieval*, pages 52–60, 2008.

[11] L. Azzopardi and V. Vinay. Retrievability: An evaluation measure for higher order information access tasks. In *Proc. of the 17th ACM CIKM*, pages 561–570, 2008.

[12] R. Bache. Measuring and improving access to the corpus. In *Current Challenges in Patent Information Retrieval*, volume 29 of *The Information Retrieval Series*, pages 147–165. 2011.

[13] R. Bache and L. Azzopardi. Transactions on large-scale data- and knowledge-centered systems ii. chapter Improving access to large patent corpora, pages 103–121. Springer-Verlag, 2010.

[14] K. Balog, L. Azzopardi, and M. de Rijke. Formal models for expert finding in enterprise corpora. In *Proceedings of the 29th Annual International ACM*

SIGIR Conference on Research and Development in Information Retrieval, SIGIR '06, pages 43–50, 2006.

[15] S. Bashir and A. Rauber. Analyzing document retrievability in patent retrieval settings. In *Proceedings of the 20th International Conference on Database and Expert Systems Applications*, DEXA '09, pages 753–760. Springer-Verlag, 2009.

[16] S. Bashir and A. Rauber. Improving retrievability of patents with cluster-based pseudo-relevance feedback documents selection. In *Proc. of the 18th ACM CIKM*, pages 1863–1866, 2009.

[17] S. Bashir and A. Rauber. Improving retrievability of patents in prior-art search. In *Proc. of the 32nd ECIR*, pages 457–470, 2010.

[18] S. Bashir and A. Rauber. On the relationship bw query characteristics and ir functions retrieval bias. *J. Am. Soc. Inf. Sci. Technol.*, 62(8):1515–1532, 2011.

[19] E. H. Chi, P. Pirolli, K. Chen, and J. Pitkow. Using information scent to model user information needs and actions and the web. In *Proceedings of the SIGCHI Conference on Human Factors in Computing Systems*, CHI '01, pages 490–497. ACM, 2001.

[20] A. Dasgupta, A. Ghosh, R. Kumar, C. Olston, S. Pandey, and A. Tomkins. The discoverability of the web. In *Proc. of the 16th ACM WWW*, pages 421–430, 2007.

[21] X. Fang, P. Hu, M. Chau, H.-F. Hu, Z. Yang, and O. Sheng. A data-driven approach to measure web site navigability. *J. Manage. Inf. Syst.*, 29(2):173–212, Oct. 2012.

[22] R. T. Fernández, D. E. Losada, and L. A. Azzopardi. Extending the language modeling framework for sentence retrieval to include local context. *Information Retrieval*, 14(4):355–389, 2011.

[23] J. L. Gastwirth. The estimation of the lorenz curve and gini index. *The Review of Economics and Statistics*, 54:306–316, 1972.

[24] M. Hagen, M. Michel, and B. Stein. What was the query? generating queries for document sets with applications in cluster labeling. In *Natural Language Processing and Information Systems*, pages 124–133. 2015.

[25] S. L. Handy and N. D. A. Measuring accessibility: An exploration of issues and alternatives. *Environemnet and Planning A*, 29(7):1175–1194, 1997.

[26] W. Hansen. How accessibility shape land use. *Journal of the American Institute of Planners*, 25(2):73–76, 1959.

[27] S. Lawrence and L. Giles. Accessibility of information on the web. *Nature*, 400:101–107, 1999.

[28] A. Lipani, M. Lupu, A. Aizawa, and A. Hanbury. An initial analytical exploration of retrievability. In *To appear in the Proceedings of the International Conference on the Theory of Information Retrieval*, 2015.

[29] A. Marchetto, R. Tiella, P. Tonella, N. Alshahwan, and M. Harman. Crawlability metrics for automated web testing. *International Journal on Software Tools for Technology Transfer*, pages 131–149, 2011.

[30] P. Morville. *Ambient Findability: What We Find Changes Who We Become*. O'Reilly Media, Inc., 2005.

[31] A. Mowshowitz and A. Kawaguchi. Assessing bias in search engines. *Information Processing and Management*, pages 141 – 156, 2002.

[32] S. Noor and S. Bashir. Evaluating bias in retrieval systems for recall oriented documents retrieval. *The International Arab Journal of Information Technology*, 2013.

[33] J. W. Palmer. Web site usability, design, and performance metrics. *Info. Sys. Research*, 13(2):151–167, June 2002.

[34] J. Pickens, M. Cooper, and G. Golovchinsky. Reverted indexing for feedback and expansion. In *Proc. of the 19th ACM CIKM*, pages 1049–1058, 2010.

[35] J. Purvis and L. Azzopardi. A preliminary study using pagefetch to examine the searching ability of children and adults. In *Proceedings of the 4th Information Interaction in Context Symposium*, IIIX '12, pages 262–265, 2012.

[36] T. Upstill, N. Craswell, and D. Hawking. Buying bestsellers online: A case study in search & searchability. In *7th Australasian Document Computing Symposium*, Sydney, Australia, 2002.

[37] L. Vaughan and M. Thelwall. Search engine coverage bias: evidence and possible causes. *Information Processing and Management*, pages 693 – 707, 2004.

[38] C. Wilkie and L. Azzopardi. An initial investigation on the relationship between usage and findability. In *Advances in Information Retrieval*, pages 808–811. Springer, 2013.

[39] C. Wilkie and L. Azzopardi. Relating retrievability, performance and length. In *Proc. of the 36th ACM SIGIR conference*, SIGIR '13, pages 937–940, 2013.

[40] C. Wilkie and L. Azzopardi. Best and fairest: an empirical analysis of retrieval system bias. In *Proceedings of the European Conference in Information Retrieval*, ECIR '2014, 2014.

[41] C. Wilkie and L. Azzopardi. Efficiently estimating retrievability bias. In *Proceedings of the European Conference in Information Retrieval*, pages 720–726. Springer International Publishing, 2014.

[42] C. Wilkie and L. Azzopardi. Query length, retrievability bias and performance. In *To appear in the Proceedings of the 24th ACM CIKM*, pages 561–570, 2015.

[43] C. Wilkie and L. Azzopardi. Retrievability and retrieval bias: A comparison of inequality measures. In *Proceedings of the European Conference in Information Retrieval*, pages 209–214, 2015.

[44] Y. Zhang, H. Zhu, and S. Greenwood. Web site complexity metrics for measuring navigability. In *Proc. of the 4th QSIC.*, pages 172–179, 2004.

Statistical Significance Testing in Information Retrieval: Theory and Practice

Ben Carterette, University of Delaware, USA
carteret@udel.edu

ABSTRACT

The past 20 years have seen a great improvement in the rigor of information retrieval experimentation, due primarily to two factors: high-quality, public, portable test collections such as those produced by TREC (the Text REtrieval Conference [28]), and the increased practice of statistical hypothesis testing to determine whether measured improvements can be ascribed to something other than random chance. Together these create a very useful standard for reviewers, program committees, and journal editors; work in information retrieval (IR) increasingly cannot be published unless it has been evaluated using a well-constructed test collection and shown to produce a statistically significant improvement over a good baseline.

But, as the saying goes, any tool sharp enough to be useful is also sharp enough to be dangerous. Statistical tests of significance are widely misunderstood. Most researchers and developers treat them as a "black box": evaluation results go in and a p-value comes out. But because significance is such an important factor in determining what research directions to explore and what is published, using p-values obtained without thought can have consequences for everyone doing research in IR. Ioannidis has argued that the main consequence in the biomedical sciences is that most published research findings are false [12]; could that be the case in IR as well?

Categories and Subject Descriptors

H.3.4 [**Information Storage and Retrieval**]: Systems and SoftwarePerformance evaluation (efficiency and effectiveness)

Keywords

information retrieval; evaluation; statistical significance testing; reproducibility

ICTIR'15, September 27–30, Northampton, MA, USA.
ACM 978-1-4503-383-2/15/09.
DOI: http://dx.doi.org/10.1145/2808194.2809445 .

1. OVERVIEW & OBJECTIVES

The past 20 years have seen a great improvement in the rigor of information retrieval experimentation, due primarily to two factors: high-quality, public, portable test collections such as those produced by TREC (the Text REtrieval Conference [28]), and the increased practice of statistical hypothesis testing to determine whether measured improvements can be ascribed to something other than random chance. Together these create a very useful standard for reviewers, program committees, and journal editors; work in information retrieval (IR) increasingly cannot be published unless it has been evaluated using a well-constructed test collection and shown to produce a statistically significant improvement over a good baseline.

But, as the saying goes, any tool sharp enough to be useful is also sharp enough to be dangerous. Statistical tests of significance are widely misunderstood. Most researchers and developers treat them as a "black box": evaluation results go in and a p-value comes out. But because significance is such an important factor in determining what research directions to explore and what is published, using p-values obtained without thought can have consequences for everyone doing research in IR. Ioannidis has argued that the main consequence in the biomedical sciences is that most published research findings are false [12]; could that be the case in IR as well?

This tutorial will help researchers and developers gain a better understanding of how tests work and how they should be interpreted so that they can both use them more effectively in their day-to-day work as well as better understand how to interpret them when reading the work of others. It will be appropriate for researchers and practitioners who are new to IR and wish to learn the standards of the community for significance testing and reporting, but also for experienced IR researchers and practitioners who already perform tests but desire a deeper understanding of what they are and how to interpret the information they provide. We aim to bridge the gap between the statistical theories of testing and how they are actually used in IR—a gap that is larger than is commonly understood.

2. PROPOSER BIOGRAPHY

Ben Carterette is an Associate Professor of Computer and Information Sciences at the University of Delaware in Newark, Delaware, USA. His research primarily focuses on evaluation in Information Retrieval, including test collection construction, evaluation measures, and statistical testing. He has published over 60 papers in venues such as ACM

TOIS, SIGIR, CIKM, WSDM, ECIR, and ICTIR, winning three Best Paper Awards for his work on evaluation. In addition, he has co-organized four workshops on IR evaluation and co-coordinated five TREC tracks. In addition to the ICTIR tutorial mentioned above, he has presented two SIGIR tutorials (one on low-cost evaluation and one on evaluation measures) and one summer course for RUSSIR on evaluation in general, all in collaboration with Evangelos Kanoulas and Emine Yilmaz.

Contact information: Ben Carterette, 101 Smith Hall, University of Delaware, Newark, DE, USA 19716. Phone: +1 302-831-3185. E-mail: carteret@cis.udel.edu. E-mail preferred.

3. OUTLINE

The tutorial will be organized and presented in three parts. The first part will consist of an introduction to the reasons for testing significance and a guide to the most common tests used in IR. (Depending on the background of the audience, this section could be shorter or longer.) The second part will dig into the theory of tests, with the goal of providing a deeper understanding about exactly what significance tests tell us, what their limitations are, and how misunderstanding them can lead us astray. The third part will take a broader view, looking at how significance tests are used by scientists & engineers in the field and by the reviewers and editors of conferences and journals.

1. Introduction to testing significance in IR (45 min (or less depending on audience))

   (a) Why test significance?
   (b) Common tests used in IR
      i. Wilcoxon signed rank test
      ii. t-test (including ANOVA and the linear model)
      iii. randomization and bootstrap tests
      iv. meta-analysis
      v. multiple comparisons corrections

2. Theory of significance testing (and what it means for you) (90 min)

   (a) Terms and definitions—a test-independent foundation
      i. null hypothesis and alternate hypothesis
      ii. paired (one-sample) and unpaired (two-sample); one-tailed and two-tailed
      iii. test statistic; confidence interval; p-value; critical value; effect size
      iv. power and accuracy; false positives and false negatives in testing
      v. sources of variance; within-group and between-group variance
   (b) Myths and misconceptions
      i. statistical significance has an intrinsic meaning
      ii. when data violates the assumptions of a test, the test cannot be used
      iii. the p-value has an intrinsic meaning
      iv. smaller p-values indicate greater significance
      v. a p-value less than 0.05 indicates significance
      vi. there is no harm in performing multiple tests at a time
      vii. there is no harm in reusing test collections

3. How significance testing affects us all (45 min)

   (a) Three classes of scientist engineers and how they make use of significance tests:
      i. as readers of research papers: to guide choice of baseline systems
      ii. as working scientists/engineers: to guide experimentation and determine what to publish or deploy
      iii. as reviewers and editors: to guide publication recommendations and decisions
   (b) Reproducibility and generalizability
   (c) How adherence to the misconceptions listed above can set back research and development in IR
   (d) Specific recommendations for using and interpreting tests

4. MATERIALS

Tutorial materials, including presentation slides, R labs, and worksheets, are available on the web at `http://ir.cis.udel.edu/ICTIR15tutorial`.

5. REFERENCES

[1] Timothy G. Armstrong, Alistair Moffat, William Webber, and Justin Zobel. Improvements that don't add up: ad-hoc retrieval results since 1998. In *Proceedings of CIKM*, pages 601–610, 2009.

[2] James O. Berger. Could Fisher, Jeffreys and Neyman have agreed on testing? *Statistical Science*, 18(1):1–32.

[3] Leonid Boytsov, Anna Belova, and Peter Westfall. Deciding on an adjustment for multiplicity in IR experiments. In *Proceedings of SIGIR*, 2013.

[4] Ben Carterette. Model-based inference about ir systems. In *Proceedings of ICTIR*, 2011.

[5] Ben Carterette. Multiple testing in statistical analysis of systems-based IR experiments. *ACM TOIS*, 2012.

[6] Ben Carterette, Evangelos Kanoulas, Virgil Pavlu, and Hui Fang. Building reusable test collections through experimental design. In *Proceedings of SIGIR*, 2010.

[7] Ben Carterette, Evangelos Kanoulas, and Emine Yilmaz. Simulating simple user behavior for systems effectiveness evaluation. In *Proceedings of CIKM*, 2011.

[8] Ben Carterette, Evangelos Kanoulas, and Emine Yilmaz. Incorporating variability in user behavior into systems based evaluation. In *Proceedings of CIKM*, 2012.

[9] Ben Carterette and Mark D. Smucker. Hypothesis testing with incomplete relevance judgments. In *Proceedings of the 16th ACM International Conference on Information and Knowledge Management*, pages 643–652, 2007.

[10] G. V. Cormack and T. R. Lyman. Statistical precision of information retrieval evaluation. In *Proceedings of SIGIR*, pages 533–540, 2006.

[11] John P. A. Ioannidis. Contradicted and initially stronger effects in highly cited clinical research. *Journal of the American Medical Association*, 294(2):218–228, 2005.

[12] John P. A. Ioannidis. Why most published research findings are false. *PLoS Medicine*, 2(8), 2005.

[13] Douglas H. Johnson. The insignificance of statistical significance testing. Technical Report 225, USGS Northern Prairie Wildlife Research Center, 1999.

[14] Karen Sparck Jones, editor. *Information Retrieval Experiment*. Buttersworth, 1981.

[15] Karen Sparck Jones and Peter Willett, editors. *Readings in Information Retrieval*. Morgan Kaufmann Publishers, 1997.

[16] Alistair Moffat and Justin Zobel. What does it mean to "measure performance"? In *Proceedings of WISE*, pages 1–12, 2004.

[17] Regina Nuzzo. Statistical errors. *Nature News*, 506, 2014.

[18] Mark Sanderson. Test collection based evaluation of information retrieval systems. *Foundations and Trends in Information Retrieval*, 4(4):247–375, 2010.

[19] Mark Sanderson and Justin Zobel. Information retrieval system evaluation: effort, sensitivity, and reliability. In *Proceedings of SIGIR*, pages 162–169, 2005.

[20] Mark D. Smucker, James Allan, and Ben Carterette. A comparison of statistical significance tests for information retrieval evaluation. In *Proceedings of CIKM*, pages 623–632, 2007.

[21] Mark D. Smucker, James Allan, and Ben Carterette. Agreement among statistical significance tests for information retrieval evaluation at varying sample sizes. In *Proceedings of SIGIR*, pages 630–631, 2009.

[22] Jean Tague. The pragmatics of information retrieval evaluation. In Jones [14], pages 59–102.

[23] Jean Tague-Sutcliffe. The pragmatics of information retrieval evaluation revisited. In Jones and Willett [15], pages 205–216.

[24] Jean Tague-Sutcliffe and James Blustein. A statistical analysis of the TREC-3 data. In *Proceedings of the 3rd Text REtrieval Conference (TREC)*, pages 385–399, 1994.

[25] Julián Urbano, Mónica Marrero, and Diego Martín. A comparison of the optimality of statistical significance tests for information retrieval evaluation. In *Proceedings of SIGIR*, 2013.

[26] Ellen Voorhees. Variations in relevance judgments and the measurement of retrieval effectiveness. In *Proceedings of SIGIR*, pages 315–323, 1998.

[27] Ellen M. Voorhees and Chris Buckley. The effect of topic set size on retrieval experiment error. In *Proceedings of SIGIR*, pages 316–323, 2002.

[28] Ellen M. Voorhees and Donna K. Harman. *TREC: Experiments and evaluation in information retrieval*. The MIT Press, 2005.

[29] William Webber, Alistair Moffat, and Justin Zobel. Statistical power in retrieval experimentation. In *Proceedings of CIKM*, pages 571–580, 2008.

[30] Justin Zobel. How reliable are the results of large-scale information retrieval experiments? In *Proceedings of SIGIR*, pages 307–314, 1998.

An Axiomatically Derived Measure for the Evaluation of Classification Algorithms

Fabrizio Sebastiani*
Qatar Computing Research Institute
Hamad bin Khalifa University
PO Box 5825, Doha, Qatar
fsebastiani@qf.org.qa

ABSTRACT

We address the general problem of finding suitable evaluation measures for classification systems. To this end, we adopt an axiomatic approach, i.e., we discuss a number of properties ("axioms") that an evaluation measure for classification should arguably satisfy. We start our analysis by addressing binary classification. We show that F_1, nowadays considered a standard measure for the evaluation of binary classification systems, does not comply with a number of them, and should thus be considered unsatisfactory. We go on to discuss an alternative, simple evaluation measure for binary classification, that we call K, and show that it instead satisfies all the previously proposed axioms. We thus argue that researchers and practitioners should replace F_1 with K in their everyday binary classification practice. We carry on our analysis by showing that K can be smoothly extended to deal with single-label multi-class classification, cost-sensitive classification, and ordinal classification.

1. INTRODUCTION

Classification is an enabling technology of capital importance in nowadays' data science, and plays a central role in countless tasks of practical importance, including text classification, spam filtering, word sense disambiguation, Web search, data mining and knowledge discovery, and others. As in all data-related endeavours, experimental evaluation plays a central role in classification, and the mathematical measure that we adopt is the cornerstone of this evaluation. In the last 20 years the F_1 measure (the harmonic mean of precision and recall – sometimes colloquially termed the "F-score" or "the F-measure") has progressively replaced "accuracy" (the fraction of classification decisions that are correct, which corresponds to the complement of "Hamming distance" or "0-1 loss") as the standard evaluation measure of binary classification in information retrieval, machine learning, data mining, and NLP.

In this paper we challenge F_1 and its suitability for evaluating binary classification. To this end we adopt an *axiomatic* approach, i.e., one based on arguing in favour of a number of properties ("axioms") that an evaluation measure for classification should intuitively satisfy. The benefit of this axiomatic approach (which has a rich history in IR – see Section 7) is that it shifts the discussion from the evaluation measures to the axioms, which is like shifting the discussion from a complex combination to its building blocks: once the scientific community has agreed on a set of axioms (the building blocks), it then follows whether a given measure (the combination) is satisfactory or not. After discussing these axioms, we study F_1 and a few other existing measures for binary classification, and find them to be unsatisfactory, in the sense that they all fail to satisfy some of the properties we have argued for. We carry on to propose K, a new evaluation measure for binary classification, which actually consists of a variant of measures ("balanced accuracy", "Youden's index") which have surfaced in the past in classification or related endeavours; we formally prove that K satisfies all the properties we have previously argued for.

Since K can deal with binary classification it can also deal with *multi-label multi-class classification* (MLMCC), i.e., the case in which zero, one, or several from a set $\mathcal{C}$ of available classes (with $|\mathcal{C}| > 1$) can be attributed to a given item. We then go on to show that K can smoothly be extended to deal with *single-label classification* (SLC – i.e., when exactly one class must be chosen from set $\mathcal{C}$, with $|\mathcal{C}| > 1$), with *cost-sensitive classification* (CSC – i.e., when different types of misclassification may have different costs), and with *ordinal classification* (OC – i.e., when such costs are constrained by a linear order defined on $\mathcal{C}$). This shows that K can be used as a unifying measure for all types of classification (binary, MLMC, SL, cost-sensitive, ordinal).

Note that in this paper we only deal with the problem of evaluating "hard" classification (i.e., the crisp assignment of classes to items), and not with evaluating systems that rank items according to their degree / probability of membership in a class ("soft" classification)[1]. For the same reason we disregard (a) measures (such as "precision as a function of recall") that do not depend on the choice of a classification threshold, and (b) measures (such as "precision-recall breakeven point" – see also Section 4) in which the threshold is chosen not by the system but (cryptically enough) by the evaluation software.

---

*Fabrizio Sebastiani is currently on leave from Consiglio Nazionale delle Ricerche, Italy.

ICTIR '15, September 27-30, 2015, Northampton, MA, USA
© 2015 ACM. ISBN 978-1-4503-3833-2/15/09 ...$15.00.
DOI: http://dx.doi.org/10.1145/2808194.2809449.

---

[1]Hard and soft classification are sometimes referred to as "autonomous" and "interactive" classification, respectively; see e.g., [15].

The rest of the paper is organised as follows. Section 2 discusses some known measures for evaluating binary classification. In Section 3 we argue in favour of a series of properties ("axioms") that we claim binary classification measures should satisfy, while in Section 4 we show that F_1 and some existing measures for binary classification do not satisfy some of them. Section 5 is devoted to discussing the K measure, and to showing that it does satisfy all of the axioms proposed in Section 3. Section 6 deals instead with extending K to the SLC case, to the cost-sensitive case, and to the ordinal case. Section 7 discusses related work, while Section 8 concludes.

2. KNOWN MEASURES OF CLASSIFICATION EFFECTIVENESS

2.1 Preliminaries

In Sections 2 to 5 we restrict our discussion to binary classification. Let $\mathcal{D}$ be a domain of items, let c be a class, and let $\mathcal{Y}_c : \mathcal{D} \rightarrow \{-1, +1\}$ be the *target function* for c, where -1 and $+1$ indicate non-membership and membership in c, respectively. We denote by $D \subseteq \mathcal{D}$ a nonempty set of items on which the effectiveness of classifiers needs to be evaluated. A pair $\langle D, \mathcal{Y}_c \rangle$ will be called a *ground truth* for c. We denote by $h_c : \mathcal{D} \rightarrow \{-1, +1\}$ a *classifier* (or *hypothesis*, or *predictor*) for c. We will thus call $\mathcal{Y}_c(d)$ and $h_c(d)$ the *actual label* and the *predicted label* of d for c, respectively.

We will also denote

- by $\bar{c}$ the complement of class c;

- by $\overline{\mathcal{Y}_{\bar{c}}}$ the complement of target function $\mathcal{Y}_c$, defined as the target function for $\bar{c}$ such that $\mathcal{Y}_c(d) = -\overline{\mathcal{Y}_{\bar{c}}}(d)$;

- by $\overline{h_{\bar{c}}}$ the complement of classifier h_c, defined as the classifier for $\bar{c}$ such that $h_c(d) = -\overline{h_{\bar{c}}}(d)$.

Note that $\mathcal{Y}_c$ and $\overline{\mathcal{Y}_{\bar{c}}}$ are essentially the same function, although the former is framed in terms of c and the latter is framed in terms of $\bar{c}$. For instance, if c stands for ProRepublican and $\bar{c}$ stands for ProDemocrat, the same items that belong to ProRepublican according to $\mathcal{Y}$ also belong to ProRepublican according to $\overline{\mathcal{Y}}$, but according to $\mathcal{Y}$ they are positive examples (of ProRepublican, which is the "positive class" for $\mathcal{Y}$) while according to $\overline{\mathcal{Y}}$ they are negative examples (of ProDemocrat, which is the "positive class" for $\overline{\mathcal{Y}}$). The same we have said of target functions $\mathcal{Y}$ and $\overline{\mathcal{Y}}$ applies to classifiers h_c and $\overline{h_{\bar{c}}}$ too.

Some special classifiers that we will refer to are

- the *trivial acceptor* h_c^{acc} (i.e., the classifier that attributes class c to every item);

- the *trivial rejector* h_c^{rej} (i.e., the classifier that attributes class $\bar{c}$ to every item);

- the *perfect classifier* h_c^{perf} (i.e., the classifier that attributes the correct label to every item);

- the *pervert classifier* h_c^{perv} (i.e., the classifier that attributes the wrong label to every item);

- the *random classifier* h_c^{rand} (i.e., the classifier which only takes random classification decisions)[2].

By TP, FP, FN, TN, we denote the numbers of true positives, false positives, false negatives, and true negatives for class c, as determined by the triple $\langle D, \mathcal{Y}_c, h_c \rangle$. By $AP = TP + FN$ and $AN = TN + FP$ we denote the number of *actual positives* and *actual negatives*, while by $PP = TP + FP$ and $PN = TN + FN$ we denote the number of *predicted positives* and *predicted negatives*, respectively.

We will denote by $M(D, \mathcal{Y}_c, h_c)$ a measure for evaluating the effectiveness of a classifier h_c as applied to a dataset D labelled according to target function $\mathcal{Y}_c$. Note that $M(D, \mathcal{Y}_c, h_c)$ is essentially a function of the two variables TP and TN, since AP and AN are constants for a given pair $\langle D, \mathcal{Y}_c \rangle$, i.e., they are not under the control of the experimenter, and since $FP = (AN - TN)$ and $FN = (AP - TP)$. In this paper we will take M to be a measure of accuracy, and not of inaccuracy, so we will always assume that higher values are better.

One assumption we will make in the rest of this work is that, for each ground truth $\langle D, \mathcal{Y}_c \rangle$, a *cost vector* $\Lambda(D, c) = (\lambda_1, \ldots, \lambda_{|D|})$ is known in advance, where $\lambda_i > 0$ denotes the cost of misclassifying item d_i for class c, and where $\sum_{i=1}^{|D|} \lambda_i = |D|$. This assumption is not restrictive. For instance, we might want to impose that $\lambda_i = 1$ for all $d_i \in D$, which covers the most frequent case in which all items have the same importance, an assumption which underlies common evaluation measures such as accuracy, F_1, and many others; but other choices are possible, in which different documents are deemed of different importance[3]. Note that, as we have specified, λ_i must be strictly higher than zero for all items d_i; this formalizes the intuition that, when it comes to evaluation, "no item is worthless". In the rest of this paper we will only address measures of the first type, i.e., characterized by the "$\lambda_i = 1$ for all $d_i \in D$" assumption; anything we say can be straightforwardly extended to the case in which this assumption is relaxed.

2.2 Measures for evaluating classification

Table 1 lists a number of "simple" evaluation measures for binary classification that have been proposed or talked about over the years, while Table 2 lists a number of "combined" such measures.

"Simple" measures (called "partial measures" in [3]) involve only two (adjacent) cells of the contingency table and only one between FP and FN. "Combined" measures involve more than two cells of the contingency table and both FP and FN, and often result from the combination of two simple measures, one involving FP and the other involving FN. All of them are expressed as ratios, where the denominator is a certain population of items and the numerator is the part of that population that bears some significance to the behaviour of the system. Since any plausible evaluation measure must come to terms with the ability of the system to avoid *both* false positives and false negatives, simple measures are usually not employed on their own but only as building blocks of combined measures. Note that the same measure may have several alternative names, due to the fact that it may have independently originated in several fields

---

[2]"The random classifier" is actually an abstraction, since there is no unique such classifier; when speaking of h_c^{rand} we will thus be interested in the "average behaviour" of all possible classifiers, i.e., in the expected value of h_c^{rand}.

[3]In order to implement *cost-sensitive classification* [10] we might want to impose, e.g., that $\lambda_i = k_p$ for all $d_i \in AP$ and $\lambda_i = k_n$ for all $d_i \in AN$, where k_p and k_n are two different constants (normalized in such a way that $\sum_{i=1}^{|D|} \lambda_i = |D|$). However, in Section 6.2 we will see a different method of dealing with CSC, which does not require setting different values of λ_i for the items in AP and AN.

Symbol	Name	Formula	Note
ρ	Recall (aka "Sensitivity", "True Positive Rate", "Hit Rate")	$\frac{TP}{TP+FN}$	$(1\text{-}FNR)$
FNR	False Negative Rate (aka "Miss Rate")	$\frac{FN}{TP+FN}$	$(1\text{-}\rho)$
π	Precision (aka "Positive Predicted Value")	$\frac{TP}{TP+FP}$	$(1\text{-}FDR)$
FDR	False Discovery Rate (aka "False Alarm Rate")	$\frac{FP}{TP+FP}$	$(1\text{-}\pi)$
ϕ	Fallout (aka "False Positive Rate")	$\frac{FP}{FP+TN}$	$(1\text{-}\sigma)$
σ	Specificity (aka "True Negative Rate", "Inverse Recall")	$\frac{TN}{FP+TN}$	$(1\text{-}\mathcal{Y}_c)$
NPR	Negative Predicted Value (aka "Inverse Precision")	$\frac{TN}{FN+TN}$	$(1-\epsilon)$
ϵ	Elusion [20, p. 55]	$\frac{FN}{FN+TN}$	$(1\text{-}NPR)$

Table 1: "Simple" measures computed from a contingency table (alternative names common in disciplines other than IR are also given).

Symbol	Formula
Acc	$\dfrac{TP+TN}{|D|}$
DOR	$\dfrac{TP\ TN}{FN\ FP}$
$LAM\%$	$\dfrac{1}{\log\dfrac{\frac{1}{2}\log\dfrac{FP\ FN}{TP\ TN}}{1-\frac{1}{2}\log\dfrac{FP\ FN}{TP\ TN}}}$
ASP	$\dfrac{TP^2}{AP\ PP}$
MCC	$\dfrac{(TP\ TN)-(FP\ FN)}{(AP\ AN\ (TP+TN)\ (FP+FN))^{\frac{1}{2}}}$
F_1	$\dfrac{2TP}{2TP+FP+FN}$

Table 2: Common "combined" measures computed from a contingency table.

far from each other (e.g., information retrieval, signal detection, diagnostic testing).

2.2.1 "Simple" measures

Among the simple measures listed in Table 1, precision (π), recall (ρ), fallout (ϕ), and specificity (σ) are historically the most important. Recall has been the universally adopted way to measure the ability of the system to avoid false negatives. Instead, the ability of the system to avoid false positives has been measured in various ways (precision, fallout, specificity); in IR fallout was the measure of choice in the '60s, but was gradually replaced by precision, while other fields such as e.g. epidemiology, have instead always relied on specificity, the complement of fallout. Note that, while fallout and specificity are independent of recall (since they use non-overlapping parts of the contingency table), precision is not.

2.2.2 "Complex" measures

Accuracy (Acc), the fraction of classification decisions that are correct, has been for many years the measure of choice in machine learning and statistics, mostly because of its simplicity. Accuracy is little used in text classification and other endeavours characterised by high imbalance (typically meaning that $AP \ll AN$), since in this case the trivial rejector trivially obtains high values; F_1 is usually the measure of choice in these cases. As a measure of binary classification performance in diagnostic testing, Glas et al. [13] proposed *diagnostic odds ratio* (DOR), defined as $DOR = (TP \cdot TN)/(FP\ FN)$; the same measure is then used in [7] for measuring spam filtering performance. Actually, one binary classification measure popular in the spam filtering community is the *logistic average misclassification percentage* ($LAM\%$ – see e.g., [8]); differently from other measures discussed in this paper, $LAM\%$ is a measure of ineffectiveness, and not one of effectiveness, i.e., low $LAM\%$ values are better. Other measures that have been put forward in the past are *average set precision* (ASP; see [14]), originally proposed in the context of the TREC filtering track; the *Matthews Correlation Coefficient* (MCC; see [18]), which originated within biochemistry; and, of course, F_1.

3. AXIOMS FOR CLASSIFICATION

We approach the issue of how to evaluate binary classification in an *axiomatic* way, i.e., by (a) arguing for a number of properties that an evaluation measure for binary classification should satisfy, (b) studying existing evaluation measures in terms of whether they satisfy these properties or not, and possibly (c) synthesizing new measures that do satisfy them. An advantage of this method is that research on evaluation measures may proceed, rather than by challenging previously proposed measures, by challenging previously proposed *axioms*, and by possibly arguing in favour of new ones. Once the scientific community has converged on a given set of axioms thanks to this process, the suitability of existing measures is immediate to ascertain, and the synthesis of measures that satisfy this set is made easier.

3.1 The axioms

We argue that a function $M(D, \mathcal{Y}_c, h_c)$ that measures the effectiveness of binary classifiers h_c should obey the following axioms. We will often write $M(\mathcal{Y}_c, h_c)$ instead of $M(D, \mathcal{Y}_c, h_c)$ when the first argument is clear from the context.

AXIOM 1. *Strict Monotonicity (**MON**). For any ground truth $\langle D, \mathcal{Y}_c \rangle$, and for all classifiers h_c and h'_c such that h'_c differs from h_c only for the label attributed to a single item $d \in D$, wrong for h_c and correct for h'_c, it holds that $M(\mathcal{Y}_c, h_c) < M(\mathcal{Y}_c, h'_c)$.* □

MON enforces the notion that in no case the evaluation measure can be indifferent to the fact that a given classification decision is correct or wrong; that is, the monotonicity of M should be *strict*. **MON** is a direct consequence of the assumption (see Section 2.1) that for no item d_i the cost of misclassifying d_i can be zero.

Note that what **MON** says in practice is that, given D and $\mathcal{Y}_c$, the measure should be sensitive to *both* the number FP of false positives and the number FN of false negatives. It does *not* state that it should be sensitive to the values of precision and recall; these latter are *derived* notions (i.e., functions of the contingency table), while FP and FN are *primitive* elements of the same table.

In [3] **MON** is called the "growing quality constraint". A consequence of **MON** is that M can achieve its maximum value *only* when the predicted label equals the actual label for all $d_i \in D$ (i.e., when h_c is the "perfect classifier"). [3] calls this the "best system constraint"; we do not list this as a separate axiom since it is a direct consequence of **MON**, and since we deem **MON** mandatory anyway. Analogously, a consequence of **MON** is that M can achieve its minimum value *only* when the predicted label is different from the actual label for all items in the set (i.e., when h_c is the "pervert classifier").

AXIOM 2. ***Continuity (CON)***. *For any ground truth* $\langle D, \mathcal{Y}_c \rangle$, *M is a continuous function of* TP *and* TN. □

We have argued in Section 2.1 that M is essentially a function of TP and TN. The continuity requirement means that, should TP and TN be real-valued arguments, M should be differentiable everywhere. In other words, imagine that TP and TN were "masses" instead of "counts"; this requirement has the goal of ensuring that M should behave "reasonably", i.e., respond minimally (i.e., smoothly) to minimal variations of TP and TN, throughout the domain on which it is defined. The intuition behind this axiom is that we want small variations in the contingency table to bring about variations in the value of M that are small themselves.

AXIOM 3. ***Strong Definiteness (SDE)***. *M is defined for any ground truth* $\langle D, \mathcal{Y}_c \rangle$ *and for any classifier* h_c. □

The rationale of **SDE** is fairly obvious, i.e., we want our evaluation measure to always return an answer insofar as the situation being evaluated (the ground truth, the classifier) is a legitimate one.

AXIOM 4. ***Weak Definiteness (WDE)***. *For any ground truth* $\langle D, \mathcal{Y}_c \rangle$, *and for any classifiers* h_c *and* h'_c, *M is defined for* h_c *iff it is defined for* h'_c. □

This is a weaker definiteness requirement than **SDE**, which acknowledges the fact that sometimes M might not be defined (e.g., because the measure is defined as a ratio and the denominator is zero). The rationale of **WDE** is that, when and if the evaluation function is not defined, it must be such because of the problem itself, and not because of the classifier we want to evaluate. That is, if the function is defined for one classifier, it must be defined for all classifiers, since we cannot afford to comparatively evaluate classifiers defined on the same class c and find out that they are incomparable. This is well explained by Robertson in the context of binary retrieval [22]:

> (...) Such difficulties are almost bound to occur if ratios are used, and there is no hope of comparing results if ratios are not used. (...) But I would like to distinguish between the two cases. The case [in which there are no actual positives] refers to a particular type of question, and does not depend on the test results. If such questions are used to test systems, they can be treated separately from the rest. But the case [in which there are no predicted positives] might occur in answer to any question; to leave such cases out of the averages would be to distort the results.

AXIOM 5. ***Fixed Range (FIX)***. *The set of values* $[\alpha, \beta]$ *on which M ranges is fixed, and independent of the ground truth* $\langle D, \mathcal{Y}_c \rangle$. □

The rationale of **FIX** is that, in order to be able to intuitively judge whether a given value of M means high accuracy or low accuracy, we need to known what values M ranges on, and these values must be independent of the problem setting; if this range is constant regardless of item set D and class c, we may *immediately* interpret the meaning of a given value of M.

AXIOM 6. ***Robustness to Chance (CHA)***. *It holds that* $E[M(\mathcal{Y}_c, h_c^{rand})] = \gamma$, *where* $E[\cdot]$ *indicates "expected value" and* γ *is a constant independent of the ground truth* $\langle D, \mathcal{Y}_c \rangle$. □

CHA says that the expected value of M for the random classifier should always be the same, irrespective of class frequency and other factors. Its rationale is allowing the experimenter to fully appreciate a result by correctly placing it into the context of what the random classifier is expected to return. In other words, once that for a given classifier h_c we are told that $M(\mathcal{Y}_c, h_c) = a$, we should be in a position to know how much of a is due to the chance agreement between ground truth and prediction, and how much is instead due to the true insight of h_c. **CHA** says that a good measure should allow to easily factor out, or discount, the chance effect from one's results.

AXIOM 7. ***Robustness to Imbalance (IMB)***. *It holds that* $M(\mathcal{Y}_c, h_c^{acc}) = k_1$ *and* $M(\mathcal{Y}_c, h_c^{rej}) = k_2$ *for any ground truth* $\langle D, \mathcal{Y}_c \rangle$ *such that* $AP > 0$ *and* $AN > 0$, *where* k_1 *and* k_2 *are two constants independent of* $\langle D, \mathcal{Y}_c \rangle$. □

The rationale of **IMB** is similar to that of **CHA**: trivial classifiers should obtain the same fixed values k_1 and k_2 for all ground truths, so that the effectiveness $M(\mathcal{Y}_c, h_c)$ of a given classifier is actually determined by where it falls in the $[\max(k_1, k_2), \beta]$ interval, rather than in the $[\alpha, \beta]$ interval discussed for **FIX**. If k_1 and k_2 are the same for all grounds truths, the results returned by M are immediately interpretable, and the experimenter may more easily appreciate the real effectiveness of a classifier.

That k_1 and k_2 are the same for all grounds truths means in particular that they are the same for every level of imbalance. Therefore, a measure that satisfies **IMB** can be meaningfully used *for balanced and imbalanced datasets alike*, and the experimenter can use it without worrying what the level of imbalance in the test set is. This is a striking contrast to the current situation, in which accuracy tends to be considered *the* measure for balanced sets, while F_1 tends to be considered *the* measure for imbalanced sets, a dichotomy that seems unscientific, since it dodges the question as where the threshold between balance and imbalance lies.

The case in which $AN = 0$ is obviously excluded from consideration in this axiom, since in this case the trivial acceptor h_c^{acc} is indeed the perfect classifier h_c^{perf}, and thus needs (see the discussion for the **MON** axiom) to be given the highest possible score. By the same token, when $AN = 0$ the trivial rejector h_c^{rej} is the pervert classifier h_c^{perv}, and thus needs to be given the lowest possible score. Analogous arguments apply to the $AP = 0$ case.

AXIOM 8. ***Symmetry (SYM)***. *For any ground truth* $\langle D, \mathcal{Y}_c \rangle$ *and for any classifier* h_c, $M(\mathcal{Y}_c, h_c) = M(\overline{\mathcal{Y}_c}, \overline{h_c})$ *holds.* □

SYM enforces the notion that the evaluation measure should be invariant with respect to switching the roles of the class c and its complement $\bar{c}$. This is desirable because it is not always the case that binary classification is naturally understood as the choice between a class and "its complement" (e.g., webpages about nuclear waste disposal vs. webpages not about it), where members of the first are naturally interpreted as "the positives". Sometimes the natural interpretation is a choice between two classes of equal standing (e.g., Shakespeare vs. Marlowe; Endorsements vs. Rebuttals; ProDemocrat vs. ProRepublican; FakeReviews vs. AuthenticReviews; Spam vs. Legitimate; etc.). In this case, it would be undesirable for the measure to return different results depending on which of the two is taken to be "the class" and which is taken to be "the complement of the class".

3.2 Discussion

SDE, **WDE** and **CON** deserve some comment, as they are mutually dependent. In a sense, all measures can be made to satisfy **SDE** and **WDE** by stipulating, for the cases in which they are (strongly or weakly) undefined, specific values that they should take up. For instance, the equation that defines F_1 (see Table 2) is such that F_1 is undefined when all of TP, FP, FN are 0, which means that F_1 would satisfy neither **SDE** nor **WDE**; in this case we may simply stipulate that, say, when $TP = FP = FN = 0$ then $F_1 = 1$, so that **SDE** and **WDE** are satisfied. The problems with this approach are that (a) when researchers propose or use an evaluation measure, they often omit to say what its output values are meant to be for the input values that make the function undefined, and (b) even when these output values are specified, they may generate points of discontinuity, i.e., make **CON** unsatisfied (see the discussion on F_1 and **CON** in Section 4). For the reasons above, in the next sections we will mostly concentrate on axioms other than **SDE** and **WDE**, since these other axioms do not have easy "fixes" as **SDE** and **WDE**.

One might think that the emphasis on axioms such as **SDE**, **WDE**, **CON** is excessive, since failure to satisfy them usually derives from the behaviour of the function in limiting cases, e.g., when $TP = FP = FN = 0$ and $TN = |D|$. We think that this emphasis is not excessive, since these limiting cases occur quite frequently in practice. For instance, in the well-known MLMCC Reuters-21578 collection[4], out of the 115 classes normally used for experimentation by researchers, no less than 25 are such that $AP = 0$. When results are macroaveraged (i.e., expressed as an unweighted average across the classes), Reuters-21578 results are determined for $\approx 21.7\%$ (since $25/115 \approx 21.7$) by classes such that $AP = 0$. In this, Reuters-21578 is not an exception, since large classification schemes usually exhibit a power-law behaviour, i.e., they typically consists of a few high-frequency classes and very many low- or very-low-frequency classes.

Another aspect that deserves mentioning is that not all axioms are equally desirable, since the motivations that lie behind these axioms are not all equally compelling. For instance, Axiom 4 (**SYM**) is desirable but probably not of fundamental importance, while Axiom 1 (**MON**) is of so fundamental importance as to invalidate, in our opinion, a measure that does not satisfy it. However, we will not attempt any classification of these axioms as "important vs. unimportant", since this is arguably a matter of degree.

4. PROPERTIES OF THE F1 MEASURE

The F_1 measure is the most widely adopted evaluation metric for binary classification. In binary *text* classification F_1 has been the dominant measure ever since the recall-precision breakeven measure was deprecated in the late '90s [5]. The use of F_1 in text classification was first proposed in [16] (see also [15] for more on F_1 in text classification).

F_1 is based on the E_α measure, introduced by van Rijsbergen [27] and defined as

$$E_\alpha = 1 - \frac{1}{\alpha \frac{1}{\pi} + (1 - \alpha) \frac{1}{\rho}} \qquad 0 \le \alpha \le 1 \qquad (1)$$

where α is a parameter whose role is to specify the relative importance of precision and recall; a value $\alpha = 1/2$ attributes them equal importance. Note that E_α is a measure of error, not of accuracy, so lower values of E_α are better. F_1 is defined as

$$F_1 = 1 - E_{\frac{1}{2}} = \frac{2\pi\rho}{\pi + \rho} = \frac{2TP}{2TP + FP + FN}$$
$$= \frac{2TP}{AP + AN + TP - TN} \qquad (2)$$

where the last passage makes explicit the dependence of F_1 on the two variables (TP and TN) and two constants (AP and AN) of our problem.

We will now discuss how F_1 copes with respect to some of the axioms of Section 3.

PROPERTY 4.1. F_1 *does not satisfy Axiom 1* (**MON**).

PROOF. Let us examine the case in which $TP = 0$ and $FN > 0$. In this case $F_1 = 0$ regardless of the values of FP; e.g., $TN = AN$ and $FP = 0$ (all the actual negatives have been classified correctly) and $TN = 0$ and $FP = AN$ (all the actual negatives have been misclassified) return the same result, i.e., $F_1 = 0$. This shows that F_1 fails to comply with Axiom 1. □

PROPERTY 4.2. F_1 *does not satisfy Axiom 2* (**CON**).

PROOF. The partial derivatives of F_1 with respect to variables TP and TN are

$$\frac{\partial F_1}{\partial TP} = \frac{2(AP + AN - TN)}{(AP + AN + TP - TN)^2}$$
$$\frac{\partial F_1}{\partial TN} = \frac{2(AP + AN + TP)}{(AP + AN + TP - TN)^2} \qquad (3)$$

These two derivatives are both undefined when $(AP + AN + TP - TN) = 0$, i.e., when $TP = AP = 0$ and $TN = AN = |D|$, which shows that F_1 is not continuous at $\langle TP = 0, TN = |D| \rangle$. □

This lack of continuity is reflected in the fact that what should F_1 be taken to return when $TP = FP = FN = 0$ and $TN = |D|$ is controversial. Some researchers (see e.g., [11]) maintain that in this case F_1 should evaluate to 1, since the classifier has classified all items correctly; incidentally, unless this is the case, F_1 does not satisfy **MON**. Other researchers have F_1 evaluate to 0 (e.g., [17]), likely on the

---

[4] http://bit.ly/1F8AFc0

[5] See Footnote 19 of [23] for a discussion of this point.

grounds that, when $\rho = 0$, F_1 returns 0 for all other values of TN; note that this latter is a "continuity argument", applied to a situation in which (as we have seen) F_1 is not continuous. Yet other researchers (e.g., [15]) maintain that more than one value could be legitimate. To make matters worse, most other researchers do not actually specify, when using F_1, how they handle this case, which makes the results they report (especially those framed in terms of "macroaveraged F_1" in MLMCC) difficult to interpret and to compare with other results on the same datasets.

PROPERTY 4.3. F_1 does not satisfy Axiom 6 (**CHA**).

PROOF. It is easy to check that different ground truths generally give rise to different values of $E[F_1(\mathcal{Y}_c, h_c^{rand})]$. For instance, assume that $\langle D, \mathcal{Y}_c \rangle$ is such that $AN = 0$; if $|D| = 1$ then $E[F_1(\mathcal{Y}_c, h_c^{rand})] = 0.500$, while if $|D| = 100$ then $E[F_1(\mathcal{Y}_c, h_c^{rand})] \approx 0.612$. □

PROPERTY 4.4. F_1 does not satisfy Axiom 7 (**IMB**).

PROOF. Assume $AP > 0$ and $AN > 0$. For the trivial acceptor h_c^{acc} it holds that $TP = AP$, $FP = AN$, $FN = 0$, which means that $F_1(\mathcal{Y}_c, h_c^{acc}) = 2AP/(2AP + AN)$; this is not constant across all ground truths, since it depends on the relative cardinalities of AP and AN[6]. □

The fact that F_1 does not satisfy **IMB** has undesirable consequences in terms of the interpretability of its results. For instance, is an F_1 value of 0.70 "good"? Most practitioners would answer "Yes", and this is indeed a good result if the relative frequency of class c is, say, 0.01 (in this case, $F_1(\mathcal{Y}_c, h_c^{acc}) = 2AP/(2AP + AN) \approx 0.01$), but cannot be considered a good result when the prevalence (i.e., relative frequency) of c is, say, 0.60, since in this case $F_1(\mathcal{Y}_c, h_c^{acc}) = 2AP/(2AP + AN) = 0.75$; i.e., in the latter case $F_1 = 0.70$ is well below the value obtained by a trivial classifier on the same data! Note that cases in which the prevalence of the class is 0.60 are not uncommon (as in all the cases mentioned at the end of Section 3.1), and that a perfectly balanced problem (i.e., when the relative frequency of c is 0.5) gives rise to $F_1(\mathcal{Y}_c, h_c^{acc}) \approx 0.666$.

The fact that F_1 does not satisfy **IMB** is extremely surprising, since F_1 is usually considered robust to imbalance, and is indeed the measure of choice for imbalanced binary classification. The reason of this apparent contradiction is that F_1 is considered robust to imbalance simply because, in the presence of imbalanced data, h_c^{acc} and h_c^{rej} return "low" values. However, (i) this occurs only when c is the minority class (see below about F_1 not satisfying Axiom 8), (ii) the values returned by h_c^{acc} and h_c^{rej} are not constant, and strongly depend on the prevalence of c, and (iii) these values increase steeply as the prevalence of c increases. In imposing **IMB** we are stating that, for a measure to be robust to imbalance, it is not enough that h_c^{acc} and h_c^{rej} return low values when the prevalence of c is low: the most important fact is that these values must *always be the same*, and independent of the prevalence of c.

PROPERTY 4.5. F_1 does not satisfy Axiom 8 (**SYM**).

PROOF. In switching from h_c to $h_{\overline{c}}$ and from $\mathcal{Y}_c$ to $\overline{\mathcal{Y}_c}$, TP and TN switch their roles, as do FP and FN. That F_1 does

---

[6] $F_1(\mathcal{Y}_c, h_c^{rej})$ is instead a constant independent of $\langle D, \mathcal{Y}_c \rangle$, since it is always 0 whenever $AP > 0$; in fact, when $TP = FP = 0$ and $FN = AP$ then $F_1 = \frac{0}{AP} = 0$.

not satisfy **SYM** is thus shown by simply observing that

$$\frac{2TP}{2TP + FP + FN} \neq \frac{2TN}{2TN + FN + FP} \qquad \square$$

4.1 Other measures for classification

Like F_1, all of the measures listed in Table 2 fail to satisfy some fundamental axiom. Some examples are listed below.

PROPERTY 4.6. *ASP, DOR, LAM% do not satisfy Axiom 1 (**MON**).*

PROOF. Similarly to F_1, if $TP = 0$ and $FN > 0$ then ASP, DOR, $LAM\%$ take up values that are independent of how the actual negatives distribute across the false positives and the true negatives. While this suffices to prove our statement, note that for DOR and $LAM\%$ the same also holds when $TN = 0$; $LAM\%$ is also such that, when either FP or FN are 0, its value is the same irrespective of the value of the other among FP and FN. □

PROPERTY 4.7. *ASP, MCC and LAM% do not satisfy Axiom 2 (**CON**).*

PROOF. The partial derivatives of ASP with respect to variables TP and TN are

$$\frac{\partial ASP}{\partial TP} = \frac{TP(2AP + 2AN - 2TN + TP)}{(AP + AN + TP - TN)^2}$$
$$\frac{\partial ASP}{\partial TN} = \frac{TP^2}{(AP + AN + TP - TN)^2} \qquad (4)$$

These two derivatives are both undefined when $(AP + AN + TP - TN) = 0$, i.e., when $TP = AP = 0$ and $TN = AN = |D|$, which shows that ASP is not continuous at $\langle TP = 0, TN = |D| \rangle$.

Concerning $LAM\%$, both derivatives $\partial LAM\%/\partial TP$ and $\partial LAM\%/\partial TN$ (not reported here since they are too complex) are undefined for both $TP = 0$ and $TN = 0$, which shows that $LAM\%$ is not continuous at any point of type $\langle TP = 0, TN = x \rangle$ or $\langle TP = x, TN = 0 \rangle$, for any $x \in [0, |D|]$.

Concerning MCC, both $\partial MCC/\partial TP$ and $\partial MCC/\partial TN$ (also not reported here since they are too complex) are undefined for $TP + TN = |D|$, which shows that MCC is not continuous at any point of type $\langle TP = x, TN = |D| - x \rangle$. □

PROPERTY 4.8. *ASP and MCC do not satisfy Axiom 3 (**SDE**).*

PROOF. ASP is undefined for $TP = AP = 0$, since in this case it evaluates to $\frac{0}{0}$. MCC is undefined for either $AP = 0$ or $AN = 0$, since in this case it evaluates to $\frac{0}{0}$. □

PROPERTY 4.9. *DOR and LAM% do not satisfy Axiom 4 (**WDE**).*

PROOF. Assume we deal with a certain $\langle D, \mathcal{Y}_c \rangle$ such that $AP > 0$ and $AN > 0$. In this case (a) DOR is defined for any classifier h_c such that $FP > 0$ and $FN > 0$, but is not defined for all classifiers h_c' such that $FP = 0$ or $FN = 0$; and (b) $LAM\%$ is defined for most cases in which both $TP > 0$ and $TN > 0$ but is undefined for all cases in which either $TP = 0$ and $TN = 0$. □

PROPERTY 4.10. *Accuracy and ASP do not satisfy Axiom 7 (**IMB**).*

PROOF. For the trivial acceptor h_c^{acc}, since $AP = TP$ and $TN = 0$, then $Acc = \frac{TP + TN}{|D|} = \frac{AP}{|D|}$, and since it is also true that $PP = |D|$, then $ASP = \frac{TP^2}{AP \cdot PP} = \frac{AP}{|D|}$. So, in this case both accuracy and ASP coincide with the relative class frequency $\frac{AP}{|L|}$ of the class; therefore, in general they are different for different ground truths. $\square$

Note that, concerning DOR and $LAM\%$, we cannot even say whether they satisfy **IMB** or not, since for h_c^{acc} and h_c^{rej} they are not even defined.

5. PROPERTIES OF THE K MEASURE

In the previous sections we have seen that all of the measures listed in Table 2, including F_1, are unsatisfactory, since they all fail to satisfy one or more fundamental axioms among the ones we have argued for. As a measure of effectiveness for binary classification we then discuss K, which we define as

$$K = \begin{cases} \rho - \sigma - 1 & \text{if } AP > 0 \text{ and } AN > 0 \\ 2\sigma - 1 & \text{if } AP = 0 \\ 2\rho - 1 & \text{if } AN = 0 \end{cases} \quad (5)$$

where $\rho = TP/AP$ denotes recall and $\sigma = TN/AN$ denotes specificity. That is, when recall and specificity are both defined, K is a rescaled sum of recall and specificity; when one of them is not defined, K coincides with a rescaled version of the other. K is not entirely new, since it is a variant of

- *Youden's index* [29], or *informedness* [21], defined as $(\rho + \sigma - 1)$;

- *balanced accuracy* [4, 12, 24], defined as $(\rho + \sigma)/2$.

The main difference between K and these measures is that the proposers of the latter do not discuss exactly how to extend them to the cases in which either ρ or σ are undefined; how these extensions are accomplished impacts on the axioms that the measure does or does not satisfy.

Let us analyse the behaviour of K in the three cases listed in Equation (5). When $AP > 0$ and $AN > 0$ we have

$$K = \rho + \sigma - 1 = \frac{TP\ AN + TN\ AP}{AP\ AN} - 1 \quad (6)$$

When there are no positives ($AP = 0$) recall is obviously undefined; in this case we let K default to specificity, since when there are no positives the ability of the system to avoid false negatives is a non-problem, and the best the system can do is to correctly recognize all the negative examples as such, i.e., maximize specificity. Similarly, when there are no negatives ($AN = 0$) specificity is undefined, and we let K default to recall.

An evaluation measure for binary classification must reward the ability of the system to avoid false positives *and* the ability of the system to avoid false negatives. Similarly to F_1, K measures the ability of the system to avoid false negatives by means of recall; differently from F_1, K measures the ability of the system to avoid false positives by means of specificity (F_1 measures it by means of precision).

Let us now check how K behaves with respect to the axioms laid out in Section 3.1.

PROPERTY 5.1. *K satisfies Axiom 1 (**MON**).*

PROOF. Assume that h_c' differs from h_c only for the label attributed to a single item $d \in D$, wrong for h_c and correct for h_c'. If d is a false negative for h_c then it is a true positive

for h_c', which means that $\rho(h_c) < \rho(h_c')$ and $\sigma(h_c) = \sigma(h_c')$; if d is a false positive for h_c then it is a true negative for h_c', which means that $\rho(h_c) = \rho(h_c')$ and $\sigma(h_c) < \sigma(h_c')$. In both cases it derives that $K(\mathcal{Y}_c, h_c) < K(\mathcal{Y}_c, h_c')$. $\square$

PROPERTY 5.2. *K satisfies Axiom 2 (**CON**).*

PROOF. If $AP = 0$ (resp., $AN = 0$), then $K = (2\sigma - 1)$ and $\partial K / \partial TN = 2/AN$ (resp., $K = (2\rho - 1)$ and $\partial K / \partial TP = 2/AP$), which is a constant. If $AP > 0$ and $AN > 0$, then $\partial K / \partial TP = 1/AP$ and $\partial K / \partial TN = 1/AN$, both also constants. This proves that K is continuous everywhere. $\square$

PROPERTY 5.3. *K satisfies Axiom 3 (**SDE**).*

PROOF. Trivial. $\square$

PROPERTY 5.4. *K satisfies Axiom 4 (**WDE**).*

PROOF. Follows from **SDE**, since **SDE** strictly implies **WDE**. $\square$

PROPERTY 5.5. *K satisfies Axiom 5 (**FIX**).*

PROOF. If $AP = 0$ (resp., $AN = 0$), then $K = (2\sigma - 1)$ (resp., $K = (2\rho - 1)$) ranges on the $[-1,+1]$ interval. If $AP > 0$ and $AN > 0$, then $K = \rho + \sigma - 1$ ranges on $[-1,+1]$ since both ρ and σ range on $[0,1]$ and are independent. In particular, the perfect classifier has a value of $K = 1$, since $\rho = 1$ and $\sigma = 1$, and the pervert classifier has a value of $K = -1$, since $\rho = 0$ and $\sigma = 0$. So, K always ranges on $[-1,+1]$ irrespectively of the ground truth $\langle D, \mathcal{Y}_c \rangle$. $\square$

PROPERTY 5.6. *K satisfies Axiom 6 (**CHA**).*

PROOF. For every ground truth $\langle D, \mathcal{Y}_c \rangle$, for every classifier h_c there is a unique classifier h_c' such that $h_c(d) = -h_c'(d)$; this latter is such that $K(\mathcal{Y}_c, h_c) = -K(\mathcal{Y}_c, h_c')$, so the mean of the K scores of h_c and h_c' is 0. Since h_c and h_c' are equiprobable, it derives that $E[M(\mathcal{Y}_c, h_c^{rand})] = 0$ for each ground truth $\langle D, \mathcal{Y}_c \rangle$. $\square$

PROPERTY 5.7. *K satisfies Axiom 7 (**IMB**).*

PROOF. If $AP > 0$ and $AN > 0$, then $K(\mathcal{Y}_c, h_c^{acc}) = 0$, since $\rho(h_c^{acc}) = 1$ and $\sigma(h_c^{acc}) = 0$, while $K(\mathcal{Y}_c, h_c^{rej}) = 0$, since $\rho(h_c^{rej}) = 0$ and $\sigma(h_c^{rej}) = 1$. $\square$

PROPERTY 5.8. *K satisfies Axiom 8 (**SYM**).*

PROOF. This is shown by noting that $\sigma(h_c) = \rho(\overline{h_c})$ and $\rho(h_c) = \sigma(\overline{h_c})$, and by noting that K is symmetric with respect to ρ and σ. $\square$

5.1 Discussion

We have seen that, while F_1 fails to comply with a number of axioms (**MON**, **CON**, **CHA**, **IMB**, **SYM**), K satisfies all the eight axioms we have argued for in Section 3. While this shows the superiority of K over F_1, there are additional reasons why the former should be preferred to the latter:

1. K is based on two *independent* quantities (recall and specificity), while F_1 is based on two dependent quantities, precision and recall (one cannot increase recall without also increasing precision[7]), which is odd. That

---

[7] Assume a classifier h_c' identical to h_c except it has one less false negative and one more true positive; in moving from h_c to h_c', recall has increased, but precision has also increased, since TP has increased and FP is unmodified.

recall and specificity are independent can be seen by the fact that they are computed on two non-overlapping halves of the contingency table (TP and FN for recall, TN and FP for specificity), while recall and precision are computed on two *overlapping* halves (TP and FN for recall, TP and FP for precision).

2. K takes all the elements of the contingency table into account, while this is not true for F_1, which seems especially unsuitable when c and $\bar{c}$ are two classes of equal standing (e.g., ProDemocrat vs. ProRepublican). For instance, given two contingency tables $t_1 = \langle TP, FP, FN, TN \rangle$ and $t_2 = \langle TP, FP, FN, 1000000 * TN \rangle$, F_1 is the same for both t_1 and t_2 (which is odd), while this is not true for K.

3. It is linear. It is thus easy (much easier than, say, F_1 or $LAM\%$) to use as a loss function that gets explicitly minimized within supervised learning algorithms.

4. It is extremely simple. This means it can be easily understood even by people with little mathematical background (e.g., company managers), for whom even the very notion of "harmonic mean" present in the definition of F_1 is esoteric.

6. EXTENDING K TO SLC, CSC, AND OC

We now turn our attention to classification problems other than binary classification. Classification problems may be ordered according to a "specialization hierarchy", where

- *Binary classification* (BC) is a special case of *single-label classification* (SLC). SLC is defined as the task of assigning to each item exactly one class from a set $\mathcal{C} = \{c_1, ..., c_{|\mathcal{C}|}\}$, where $|\mathcal{C}| > 1$. BC corresponds to the $|\mathcal{C}| = 2$ case[8], while *single-label multi-class classification* (SLMCC) corresponds to the $|\mathcal{C}| > 2$ case.

- Both SLC and *ordinal classification* (OC) are special cases of *cost-sensitive classification* (CSC), defined as the task of assigning to each item exactly one class from a set of classes $\mathcal{C} = \{c_1, ..., c_{|\mathcal{C}|}\}$, where $|\mathcal{C}| > 1$ and where a set of pairwise *distances* (or *costs*) $\Delta(c_i, c_j) \geq 0$ between classes is defined such that

  - $\Delta(c_i, c_i) = 0$ for all $c_i \in \mathcal{C}$
  - $\Delta(c_i, c_j)$ quantifies the cost of misclassifying into c_i an item which actually belongs to c_j.

The set of $\Delta(c_i, c_j)$ values is usually referred to as the *cost matrix*. Accordingly,

  - SLC is the case in which $\Delta(c_i, c_j) = 1$ for all $c_i, c_j \in \mathcal{C}, i \neq j$;
  - OC is the case in which $|\mathcal{C}| > 2$ and, for all $c_i, c_j \in \mathcal{C}$ such that $i < j$, it holds that

$$\Delta(c_i, c_j) = \Delta(c_j, c_i)$$

$$\Delta(c_i, c_j) = \sum_{k=i}^{j-1} \Delta(c_k, c_{k+1}) \quad (7)$$

---

[8] *Multi-label multi-class classification* (MLMCC) is defined as the task of assigning to each item zero, one, or several classes from a set of classes $\mathcal{C} = \{c_1, ..., c_{|\mathcal{C}|}\}$, where $|\mathcal{C}| > 1$. As such, MLMCC is equivalent to BC (at least from the standpoint of evaluation), since it corresponds to performing BC independently for each of the classes in $\mathcal{C}$. We will thus not consider it a separate task.

A problem with current evaluation measures for classification is that they do not reflect the specialization hierarchy of classification problems. For instance, while F_1 is a standard measure used for evaluating binary classification, there is no known equivalent of F_1 for CSC or OC. In the following we define such equivalent for K, i.e., extend K to cover the general CSC case (hence the SLMCC and OC cases too); this means that K can be used as a unifying evaluation measure for all types of classification.

6.1 The SLC case

We start by addressing SLC. In order to discuss this case, let's fix some notation. By TP_j, FP_j, FN_j, and TN_j we will indicate the numbers of true positives, false positives, false negatives, and true negatives, *for class c_j*; for instance, FN_j will indicate the number of items that belong to class c_j and were instead predicted to belong to some class different from c_j. AP_j and AN_j are defined accordingly.

Let us define the indicator variable

$$\xi_j = \begin{cases} 1 & \text{if } AP_j > 0 \\ 0 & \text{if } AP_j = 0 \end{cases} \quad (8)$$

and let us define *recall for c_j* (indicated as ρ_j) as

$$\rho_j = \begin{cases} \dfrac{TP_j}{AP_j} & \text{if } AP_j > 0 \\ undefined & \text{if } AP_j = 0 \end{cases} \quad (9)$$

Note that, in the binary case, $\sigma(h_c)$ is equivalent to $\rho(\overline{h_{\bar{c}}})$, hence K may be viewed as (a rescaled version of) the sum of the recall values for the two binary classes c and $\bar{c}$. This suggests a natural extension of K to the SLC case, as

$$K = \frac{|\mathcal{C}|}{|\mathcal{C}| - 1} \frac{\sum_{c_j \in \mathcal{C}, \xi_j = 1} \rho_j}{\sum_{c_j \in \mathcal{C}} \xi_j} - \frac{1}{|\mathcal{C}| - 1} \quad (10)$$

which is a rescaled variant of *macroaveraged recall*. It is easy to observe that, when $|\mathcal{C}| = 2$, Equation (10) defaults to Equation (5). It is also easy to check that all the axioms discussed in Section 3, that we proved to hold for the "binary" version of K, also hold for this "multiclass" version.

6.2 The CSC case and the OC case

We may extend K to the general cost-sensitive classification case (and hence to the ordinal classification case). CSC (see e.g., [9, 10]) is important in many real-life applications (e.g., spam filtering, medical diagnosis) in which some classification errors have more serious consequences than others. OC (also known as *ordinal regression* – see e.g., [6, 26]) is also important due to its key role in the social sciences, where ordinal (i.e., discrete) scales are often used to elicit human judgments and evaluations from respondents or interviewees.

We extend K to deal with cost-sensitive classification by defining a notion of recall that is sensitive to the error $E(d_i)$ made in misclassifying an item d_i into a class $h_c(d_i)$ that has a certain distance $\Delta(h_c(d_i), \mathcal{Y}_c(d_i))$ from its true class $\mathcal{Y}_c(d_i)$. $E(d_i)$ may be one of the metrics popular in ordinal classification, such as absolute error

$$AE = \Delta(h_c(d_i), \mathcal{Y}_c(d_i))$$

or squared error

$$SE = \Delta(h_c(d_i), \mathcal{Y}_c(d_i))^2$$

Let us define recall on class c_j as

$$\rho_j = \begin{cases} \dfrac{\sum\limits_{i=1}^{AP_j}(1 - \dfrac{E(d_i)}{\max(E_j)})}{AP_j} & \text{if } AP_j > 0 \\ undefined & \text{if } AP_j = 0 \end{cases} \quad (11)$$

Here, $\max(E_j)$ is the maximum possible error that could be made in misclassifying an item whose true class is c_j (i.e., the error that we make in picking the class most distant from true class c_j). It can be easily checked that ρ_j is 1 if and only if all items belonging to c_j are correctly classified into c_j, and is 0 if and only if all items belonging to c_j are misclassified with the maximum possible error, i.e., into the class most distant from c_j. As such, ρ_j is a natural extension of the notion of recall as we know it from binary classification.

EXAMPLE 6.1. Assume that absolute error AE is our measure of error E. Assume that $C = \{c_1, ..., c_5\}$, that $\Delta(c_i, c_{i+1}) = 1$ for all $i \in \{1, 2, 3, 4\}$, that items d_1, d_2, and d_3 all have true class c_3, that d_1 is correctly classified into c_3, that d_2 is misclassified into c_2, and that d_3 is misclassified into c_1. Assume also that item d_4 has true class c_4 and is misclassified into c_3.

The contribution of d_1 to ρ_3 is $(1 - 0) = 1$, while the contribution of d_2 is $(1 - \frac{1}{2}) = \frac{1}{2}$ and the contribution of d_3 is $(1 - \frac{2}{2}) = 0$; the contribution of d_4 to ρ_4 is $(1 - \frac{1}{3}) = \frac{2}{3}$.

Note that, while both d_2 and d_4 are misclassified into a class that has distance 1 from their true class, the error made for d_2 is considered more severe than that made for d_4, since error is evaluated relative to the maximum possible error $\max(E_j)$ that could in principle be made, which is different for different classes c_j. $\square$

For CSC we stick to the definition of K, unchanged, as given in Equation (10): the difference with the SLC case is thus in the notion of recall adopted (Equation (11) instead of Equation (9)), and not in the way of summing the class-specific values of recall, which remains the same as in standard SLC.

It is immediate to check that if distances have all the same magnitude, i.e., $\Delta(c_i, c_j) = 1$ for all $c_i, c_j \in C, i \neq j$, as in standard SLC, Equation (11) defaults to Equation (9). It is also easy to check that all the axioms that we have shown to hold for the binary and SLC versions of K, also hold for the CSC version (and, as a consequence, for the OC version).

7. RELATED WORK

This axiomatic approach to evaluating evaluation measures is not new in information retrieval. For instance, [2] studies measures for evaluating clustering systems in an axiomatic way, while [19] does the same for measures for evaluating ad hoc search. Sokolova and Lapalme [25] discuss properties of classification measures, but focus on properties of invariance across ground truths characterised by different sets $|D|$, which is hardly of relevance to the present context.

More recently, in discussing where the "Frontiers, Challenges, and Opportunities for Information Retrieval" lie, the SWIRL 2012 participants [1, p. 20] called for the development of axiometrics for information retrieval (see also [5]), i.e., axiomatically defined evaluation metrics. It is exactly axiometrics for classification that we are looking at here. The effort closest in spirit to the present one is [3], which proposes axiomatic studies of evaluation measures for filtering systems (especially focusing on cost-sensitive measures); since filtering is an instance of classification, [3] is relevant

to the present work. In [3] the authors claim that the main difference between metrics is how the trivial acceptor, trivial rejector, and random classifiers are evaluated, and only identify two axioms that they argue should be complied with by any evaluation measure; these axioms are **MON** plus another weaker axiom, strictly entailed by **MON**, which says that only the perfect classifier can obtain the highest M score. One further difference between [3] and the present work is that [3] has a *descriptive* intent, i.e., describes a number of axioms but does not necessarily argue that a measure should satisfy them; our work has a *normative* character instead, i.e., we describe a number of axioms *and* argue that a worthwhile measure should satisfy them.

We should also recall that an early mention of the axiomatic approach to evaluating binary retrieval is to be found in van Rijsbergen's work [27, 28], in which the author discusses a number of formal properties (that collectively characterize "additive conjoint structures") that, as he argues, combinations of precision and recall should satisfy. The author goes on to propose one such combination (the E_α measure of Equation 1) but does not prove that it indeed satisfies the said formal properties. Binary retrieval and binary classification are strongly related, so van Rijsbergen's work is indeed relevant to our quest. However, our approach is more general than his, since he focuses on properties that a combination of two simple measures (precision and recall, in his case) should satisfy, while the properties we study view the evaluation measure as a direct function of the contingency table, without postulating (actually: without lending importance to) the presence of intermediate simple measures.

8. CONCLUSIONS

We have proposed K (a variant of "Youden's index" and "balanced accuracy") as an evaluation measure for binary classification. K has a number of interesting properties. The perfect classifier obtains $K = 1$, the pervert classifier obtains $K = -1$, the trivial acceptor and the trivial rejector both obtain $K = 0$, and the expected value of the random classifier is always $K = 0$; all of these hold irrespectively of class prevalence, which makes classification results expressed in terms of K easily interpretable. K is defined on all the cells of the contingency table, which makes it suitable for addressing both balanced and imbalanced test sets; in particular, this avoids the problem of defining what counts as a "balanced" test set. One advantage of K is that it smoothly extends to multi-label multi-class classification, single-label multi-class classification, cost-sensitive classification, and ordinal classification. K has the additional virtues of simplicity, which makes it easily interpretable by non-initiates, and linearity, which makes it easy to directly optimize by supervised learning algorithms.

We have obtained K as the result of an "axiomatic" study of the properties that a measure for classification should have. This study has also shown that F_1, the currently standard evaluation measure for binary classification, is flawed, since it does not satisfy several properties that should intuitively hold for any satisfactory measure; of particular importance is the fact that F_1 is not monotonic and is not continuous. This hints at the power of the axiomatic approach, which we argue should be used more and more for scrutinizing the accepted wisdom in effectiveness evaluation.

Acknowledgments

I am grateful to Andrea Esuli, Tiziano Fagni, Donna Harman, David Lewis, Stefano Mizzaro, Steve Robertson, and Keith van Rijsbergen for interesting discussions about the subject of this paper. I am also indebted to one of the reviewers for spotting a problem with a previous formulation of Axiom 8.

9. REFERENCES

[1] J. Allan, B. Croft, A. Moffat, and M. Sanderson. Frontiers, challenges, and opportunities for information retrieval. Report from SWIRL 2012. *SIGIR Forum*, 46(1):2–32, 2012.

[2] E. Amigó, J. Gonzalo, J. Artiles, and F. Verdejo. A comparison of extrinsic clustering evaluation metrics based on formal constraints. *Information Retrieval*, 12(4):461–486, 2009.

[3] E. Amigó, J. Gonzalo, and F. Verdejo. A comparison of evaluation metrics for document filtering. In *Proceedings of the 2nd International Conference of the Cross-Language Evaluation Forum (CLEF 2011)*, pages 38–49, Amsterdam, NL, 2011.

[4] K. H. Brodersen, C. S. Ong, K. E. Stephan, and J. M. Buhmann. The balanced accuracy and its posterior distribution. In *Proceedings of the 20th International Conference on Pattern Recognition (ICPR 2010)*, pages 3121–3124, Istanbul, TR, 2010.

[5] L. Busin and S. Mizzaro. Axiometrics: An axiomatic approach to information retrieval effectiveness metrics. In *Proceedings of the 4th International Conference on the Theory of Information Retrieval (ICTIR 2013)*, Copenhagen, DK, 2013.

[6] W. Chu and S. S. Keerthi. Support vector ordinal regression. *Neural Computation*, 19(3):145–152, 2007.

[7] G. V. Cormack and A. Kołcz. Spam filter evaluation with imprecise ground truth. In *Proceedings of the 32nd ACM Conference on Research and Development in Information Retrieval (SIGIR 2009)*, pages 604–611, Boston, US, 2009.

[8] G. V. Cormack and T. Lynam. TREC 2005 Spam Track overview. In *Proceedings of the 14th Text Retrieval Conference (TREC 2005)*, Gaithersburg, US, 2005.

[9] P. M. Domingos. MetaCost: A general method for making classifiers cost-sensitive. In *Proceedings of the 5th ACM SIGKDD International Conference on Knowledge Discovery and Data Mining (KDD 1999)*, pages 155–164, San Diego, US, 1999.

[10] C. Elkan. The foundations of cost-sensitive learning. In *Proceedings of the 17th International Joint Conference on Artificial Intelligence (IJCAI 2001)*, pages 973–978, Seattle, US, 2001.

[11] A. Esuli and F. Sebastiani. Active learning strategies for multi-label text classification. In *Proceedings of the 31st European Conference on Information Retrieval (ECIR 2009)*, pages 102–113, Toulouse, FR, 2009.

[12] V. García, R. A. Mollineda, and J. S. Sánchez. Index of balanced accuracy: A performance measure for skewed class distributions. In *Proceedings of the 4th Iberian Conference on Pattern Recognition and Image Analysis (IbPRIA 2009)*, pages 441–448, Póvoa de Varzim, PT, 2009.

[13] A. S. Glas, J. G. Lijmer, M. H. Prins, G. J. Bonsel, and P. M. Bossuyt. The diagnostic odds ratio: A single indicator of test performance. *Journal of Clinical Epidemiology*, 56(11):1129–1135, 2003.

[14] D. Hull. The TREC-6 filtering track: Description and analysis. In *Proceedings of the 6th Text Retrieval Conference (TREC 1997)*, pages 33–56, 1997.

[15] D. D. Lewis. Evaluating and optimizing autonomous text classification systems. In *Proceedings of the 18th ACM International Conference on Research and Development in Information Retrieval (SIGIR 1995)*, pages 246–254, Seattle, US, 1995.

[16] D. D. Lewis and W. A. Gale. A sequential algorithm for training text classifiers. In *Proceedings of the 17th ACM International Conference on Research and Development in Information Retrieval (SIGIR 1994)*, pages 3–12, Dublin, IE, 1994.

[17] D. D. Lewis, Y. Yang, T. G. Rose, and F. Li. RCV1: A new benchmark collection for text categorization research. *Journal of Machine Learning Research*, 5:361–397, 2004.

[18] B. Matthews. Comparison of the predicted and observed secondary structure of T4 phage lysozyme. *Biochimica et Biophysica Acta*, 405(2):442–451, 1975.

[19] A. Moffat. Seven numeric properties of effectiveness metrics. In *Proceedings of the 9th Conference of the Asia Information Retrieval Societies (AIRS 2013)*, pages 1–12, Singapore, SN, 2013.

[20] D. W. Oard and W. Webber. Information retrieval for e-discovery. *Foundations and Trends in Information Retrieval*, 7(2/3):99–237, 2013.

[21] D. M. Powers. Evaluation: From precision, recall and F-factor to ROC, informedness, markedness, and correlation. *Journal of Machine Learning Technologies*, 2(1):37–63, 2011.

[22] S. E. Robertson. The parametric description of retrieval tests. Part I: The basic parameters. *Journal of Documentation*, 25(1):1–27, 1969.

[23] F. Sebastiani. Machine learning in automated text categorization. *ACM Computing Surveys*, 34(1):1–47, 2002.

[24] M. Sokolova, N. Japkowicz, and S. Szpakowicz. Beyond accuracy, F-score and ROC: A family of discriminant measures for performance evaluation. In *Proceedings of the 19th Australian Joint Conference on Artificial Intelligence (AJCAI 2006)*, pages 1015–1021, Hobart, AU, 2006.

[25] M. Sokolova and G. Lapalme. A systematic analysis of performance measures for classification tasks. *Information Processing and Management*, 45(4):427–437, 2009.

[26] B.-Y. Sun, J. Li, D. D. Wu, X.-M. Zhang, and W.-B. Li. Kernel discriminant learning for ordinal regression. *IEEE Transactions on Knowledge and Data Engineering*, 22(6):906–910, 2010.

[27] C. J. van Rijsbergen. Foundations of evaluation. *Journal of Documentation*, 30(4):365–373, 1974.

[28] C. J. van Rijsbergen. *Information Retrieval*. Butterworths, London, UK, second edition, 1979.

[29] W. J. Youden. Index for rating diagnostic tests. *Cancer*, 3:32–35, 1950.

Towards a Formal Framework for Utility-oriented Measurements of Retrieval Effectiveness

Marco Ferrante
Dept. Mathematics
University of Padua, Italy
ferrante@math.unipd.it

Nicola Ferro
Dept. Information Engineering
University of Padua, Italy
ferro@dei.unipd.it

Maria Maistro
Dept. Information Engineering
University of Padua, Italy
maistro@dei.unipd.it

ABSTRACT

In this paper we present a formal framework to define and study the properties of utility-oriented measurements of retrieval effectiveness, like AP, RBP, ERR and many other popular IR evaluation measures. The proposed framework is laid in the wake of the representational theory of measurement, which provides the foundations of the modern theory of measurement in both physical and social sciences, thus contributing to explicitly link IR evaluation to a broader context. The proposed framework is minimal, in the sense that it relies on just one axiom, from which other properties are derived. Finally, it contributes to a better understanding and a clear separation of what issues are due to the inherent problems in comparing systems in terms of retrieval effectiveness and what others are due to the expected numerical properties of a measurement.

Categories and Subject Descriptors

H.3.4 [**Information Search and Retrieval**]: Systems and Software—*Performance evaluation (efficiency and effectiveness)*

General Terms

Experimentation, Measurement, Performance, Theory

Keywords

Representational Theory of Measurement; Omomorphism; Swap; Replacement; Balancing Index

1. INTRODUCTION

Information Retrieval (IR) has been deeply rooted in experimentation since its inception and we often hear quotes like "*To measure is to know*" or "*If you cannot measure, you cannot improve it*", attributed to Sir William Thompson first baron of Kelvin, to remark the importance of experimental evaluation as a means to foster research and innovation in the field.

ICTIR'15, September 27–30, Northampton, MA, USA.
© 2015 ACM. ISBN 978-1-4503-3833-2/15/09 ...$15.00.
DOI: http://dx.doi.org/10.1145/2808194.2809452.

However, even if evaluation has greatly contributed to the advancement of IR, we still lack a deep comprehension about what the evaluation measures we daily employ are and this, somehow, hinders the "*to measure*" part in Lord Kelvin's quotes. This is witnessed by the fact that our understanding of evaluation measures is mostly tied to empirical evidence: for example, we use different kinds of correlation analysis [19, 35] to see how close two evaluation measures are, we adopt different pool downsampling techniques to study the robustness of measures to incomplete information [7, 34], we analyse their sensitivity, stability and discriminative power [6, 28], and so on.

We, as others [3, 8, 16, 26], think that a better comprehension of evaluation measures is needed and that the development of a formal theory to define what an evaluation measure is and to derive and study its properties can be the way to address this need.

In this paper, we start to lay the foundations for a formal framework for utility-oriented measurements of retrieval effectiveness. In particular, we place our work in the broader framework of the *representational theory of measurement* [21], which provides the foundations of the modern theory of measurement in both physical and social sciences.

Our work differs from previous attempts to formalize IR evaluation measures in three main aspects: (i) for the first time, it explicitly puts IR measures in the wake of the measurement theory adopted in other branches of science; (ii) it provides a deeper understanding of what issues are due to the intrinsic difficulties in comparing runs rather than attributing them to the expected numerical properties of a measure; (iii) it is minimal, basically consisting of just one axiom (Definition 5.1), which makes the framework easy and intuitive to grasp and from which the other needed properties are (and will be) derived.

The paper is organized as follows: Section 2 explains the basic concepts of the representational theory of measurement and how our framework will lay on it; Sections 3 to 6 introduce our framework; finally, Section 7 wraps up the discussion and outlooks some future work.

2. MEASUREMENT AND MEASURE

2.1 Representational Theory of Measurement

Measurement is the process by which numbers or symbols are assigned to attributes of entities in the real world in such a way as to describe them accordingly to clearly defined rules [12].

The *representational theory of measurement* [21] aims at providing a formal basis to our intuition about the way the world works. According to the above definition of measurement, the numbers or symbols we collect as measures about the attributes of the entities we examine should be such that their processing and manipulation maintain the relationships among the actual entities under examination in the real world. Therefore, at the basis of measurement, there are the relationships among entities and how we empirically observe them [14].

Consider, for example, the attribute "height" of a tree: in the real world, we are easily able to recognize that some trees are "taller than" others. "Taller than" is an *empirical relation* for height (of a tree) and we can think at it as a *mapping* from the real world to a formal mathematical one, namely from the set of trees to the set of real numbers, provided that, whenever a tree is "taller than" another one, any measure of height assigns a higher number to that tree.

This is the so called *representation condition* which ensures that a measurement must map attributes of entities into numbers (symbols) and empirical relations into numerical (symbolic) ones so that the empirical relations imply and are implied by the numerical (symbolic) ones.

More formally [21, 24], a *relational structure* is an ordered pair $\mathbf{X} = \langle X, R_X \rangle$ of a domain set X and a set of relations R_X on X, where the relations in R_X may have different arities, i.e. they can be unary, binary, ternary relations and so on. Given two relational structures $\mathbf{X}$ and $\mathbf{Y}$, a *homomorphism* $\mathbf{M} : \mathbf{X} \to \mathbf{Y}$ from $\mathbf{X}$ to $\mathbf{Y}$ is a mapping $\mathbf{M} = \langle \mathrm{M}, \mathrm{M}_R \rangle$ where:

- M is a function that maps X into $\mathrm{M}(X) \subseteq Y$, i.e. for each element of the domain set there exists one corresponding image element;

- M_R is a function that maps R_X into $\mathrm{M}_R(R_X) \subseteq R_Y$ such that $\forall r \in R_X$, r and $\mathrm{M}_R(r)$ have the same arity, i.e. for each relation on the domain set there exists one (and it is usually, and often implicitly, assumed: and only one) corresponding image relation,

with the condition that $\forall r \in R_X, \forall x_i \in X$, if $r(x_1, \ldots, x_n)$ then $\mathrm{M}_R(r)\big(\mathrm{M}(x_1), \ldots, \mathrm{M}(x_n)\big)$, i.e. if a relation holds for some elements of the domain set then the image relation must hold for the image elements.

Note that we talk about a homomorphism rather than an isomorphism because M is generally not one-to-one; in general $M(a) = M(b)$ does not mean that two trees are identical but merely of equal height.

A relational structure $\mathbf{E}$ is called *empirical* if its domain set E spans over the entities under consideration in the real world, e.g. the set of trees; a relational structure $\mathbf{S}$ is called *symbolic* if its domain set S spans over a given set of symbols, e.g. the set of positive real numbers $\mathbb{R}_0^+ = \big\{ x \in \mathbb{R} \mid x \geq 0 \big\}$.

We can now provide a more precise definition of measurement on the basis of the just introduced concepts

> **measurement** is a homomorphism $\mathbf{M} = \langle \mathrm{M}, \mathrm{M}_R \rangle$ from the real world to a symbolic world. Consequently, a **measure** is the number or symbol assigned to an entity by this mapping in order to characterize an attribute [12].

As an example, consider a set of rods R [21] where an order relation $\preceq$ and a concatenation operation $\circ$ among

rods exist. Note that $\preceq$ is a binary relation on the set of rods R while $\circ$ is a ternary one which assigns to each pair of rods a third rod representing their concatenation. Then, the empirical relational structure $\mathbf{E} = \langle A, \preceq, \circ \rangle$ can be mapped into the symbolic relational structure $\mathbf{S} = \langle \mathbb{R}_0^+, \leq, + \rangle$, using as mapping function $M(\cdot)$ the length of a rod so that $a \preceq b \Leftrightarrow M(a) \leq M(b)$ and $M(a \circ b) = M(a) + M(b)$. Note that this example covers also the basics of the classical measure theory [4, 15], where the order relation among sets is given by $A \preceq B \Leftrightarrow A \subseteq B$ and the concatenation operation among two disjoint sets $A \cap B = \varnothing$ is given by $\circ = A \cup B$; a measure is then requested to be *monotonic* $A \subseteq B \Rightarrow M(A) \leq M(B)$ and *additive* $A \cup B \Rightarrow M(A) + M(B)$ when two sets are disjoint $A \cap B = \varnothing$.

2.2 Our Framework

The core of our framework is to start individuating an empirical relational structure $\mathbf{E} = \langle IRS, \preceq \rangle$ which allows us to compare and order different IR systems on the basis of the utility they provide to their users [9, 11, 29]. Clearly, being an empirical relational structure, it is assumed to exist in the real word, i.e. users have their own intuitive notion of when a system is better than another one. In Section 4 we will make this intuitive notion explicit, at least for the cases where it is possible to determine a commonly shared agreement about when a system is better than another one, thus leading to a partial ordering among systems.

We will then individuate a suitable symbolic relational structure $\mathbf{S} = \langle \overline{\mathbb{R}}_0^+, \leq \rangle$ with $\overline{\mathbb{R}}_0^+ = \mathbb{R}_0^+ \cup \{\infty\}$ and, in Section 5, we will provide a definition of IR utility-oriented measurement as a homomorphism between these two relational structures, i.e. we will provide a representation condition. We will also provide an equivalence theorem which allows us to easily verify the representation condition in terms of two simple properties, *swap* and *replacement*, i.e. to check in practice when an evaluation measure like AP or nDCG is actually a measurement in the previous sense. Note that according to the above definition AP or nDCG are called *measurement* while the actual numerical value computed by AP or nDCG for a given run and topic is called *measure*.

Finally, we will also introduce the concept of *balancing* meant to explore the behaviour of a measurement when, in the empirical relational structure, the ordering between two systems is not a priori known. We will show that balancing accounts for the top heaviness of a measurement and we will conduct a preliminary experiment to validate the meaningfulness of its numerical value.

The problem of grounding IR evaluation measures into a broader approach to measuring is a longstanding and crucial one [16]. C. J. van Rijsbergen was early pointing out the issues we encounter with IR evaluation measures [31]:

> In the physical sciences there is usually an empirical ordering of the quantities we wish to measure [...] Such a situation does not hold for information retrieval. There is no empirical ordering for retrieval effectiveness and therefore any measure of retrieval effectiveness will by necessity be artificial

We are not claiming to have fully addressed this hard problem in the present work but rather to have started laying foundations which can contribute to its solution. Moreover, to the best of our knowledge, this is the first attempt to systematically apply the representational theory of measurement in the context of IR evaluation.

Indeed, [3, 26] stated numerical properties and constraints IR evaluation measures should comply on a case-by-case basis, e.g. when a system retrieves one more relevant document than another one, but they did not build up on an explicit relational structure among systems. [8, 22] built their formal framework for IR evaluation measures on the notion of measurement scale [12, 30], which somehow comes after the definition of measurement; here, we prefer to start from the definition of what IR utility-oriented measurements are and we leave for future work a throughout study of the issues concerning the scales for such measurements. [2] provided a formal framework concerning measures for clustering rather than for IR, even it has been extended in [3] to include also IR measures. Finally, [5] sought for two axioms which allowed him to define when an IR evaluation measure could be expressed as a linear combination of the number of relevant retrieved documents and the number of not-relevant not retrieved documents, which is a different problem from the one of the present paper.

3. PRELIMINARY DEFINITIONS

We stem from [1, 13] for defining the basic concepts of topics, documents, ground-truth, run, and judged run. To the best of our knowledge, these basic concepts have not explicitly defined in previous works [3, 8, 22, 26].

Note that we need to define the same concepts for both set-based retrieval and rank-based retrieval and, to keep the notation compact and stress the similarities between these two cases, we will use the same symbols in both cases – e.g. r_t for run, $D(n)$ for set of retrieved documents by a run, $\mathcal{D}$ for universe set of documents and so on – being clear later on from the context whether we will refer to the set-based or rank-based version.

3.1 Topics, Documents, Ground-truth

Let us consider a set of **documents** D and a set of **topics** T; note that D and T are typically finite sets but we can account also for countable infinite ones.

Let $(REL, \preceq)$ be a totally ordered set of **relevance degrees**, i.e. they are defined on an ordinal scale [30], where we assume the existence of a minimum that we call the **non-relevant** relevance degree $nr = \min(REL)$. Note that REL is typically a finite set but we can account also for an infinite one. In the former case, we can represent both binary relevance[1] $REL = \{nr, r\}$ (non relevant and relevant) and graded relevance [18], e.g. $REL = \{nr, pr, hr\}$ (non-relevant, partially relevant, highly relevant); in the latter case, we can represent both continuous relevance [18] and relevance assigned using unbounded scales, e.g. by using magnitude estimation [23]. Note that the definition of the REL set can accomplish both a notion of "immutable" relevance, as the one somehow adopted in evaluation campaigns, and a notion of relevance dependent on users and their context. In the latter case, we will have different REL sets corresponding to each user/context.

In the following, and without any loss of generality, we consider $REL \subseteq \mathbb{R}_0^+$ with the constraint that $0 \in REL$

and the order relation $\preceq$ becomes the usual ordering $\leq$ on real numbers, which ensures that a higher number corresponds to a higher relevance degree; the non-relevant degree is therefore given by $\min(REL) = 0$. Note that most of the algebraic operations we typically perform on numbers, like addition and multiplication, will be in general senseless on REL, since we take for granted only its order property. As above, this choice allows us to represent the most common cases, i.e. both binary relevance with $REL = \{0, 1\}$ and graded relevance, either discrete with $REL \subseteq \mathbb{N}_0$ or continuous with $REL \subseteq \mathbb{R}_0^+$ in general.

For each pair $(t, d) \in T \times D$, the **ground-truth** GT is a map which assigns a relevance degree $rel \in REL$ to a document d with respect to a topic t. Note that, in the case of more complex situations like crowdsourcing for relevance assessment, we can define different GT maps, one for each crowd-worker.

The **recall base** is the map RB from T into $\mathbb{N}$ defined as the total number of relevant documents for a given topic $t \mapsto RB_t = \left| \{d \in D : GT(t, d) > 0\} \right|$. The recall base is a quantity often hard to know in reality and, in some applications, it may be preferable to substitute it with a family of random variables $(t, \omega) \mapsto RB_t(\omega)$ which represents the unknown number of relevant documents present in the collection for every topic, that we will be able at most to estimate. For simplicity, in the sequel we will denote by RB_t the recall base in both the cases, omitting in the latter the dependence on ω.

3.2 Set-based Retrieval

Given a positive natural number n called the *length of the run*, we define the **set of retrieved documents** as $D(n) = \{\{d_1, \ldots, d_n\} : d_i \in D\}$ and the **universe set of retrieved documents** as $\mathcal{D} := \bigcup_{n=1}^{|D|} D(n) = 2^D$, which is the power set of D, i.e. the set of all the subsets of D.

A **run** r_t, retrieving a set of documents $D(n)$ in response to a topic $t \in T$, is a function from T into $\mathcal{D}$

$$t \mapsto r_t = \{d_1, \ldots, d_n\}$$

Note that, since D can be an infinite set, we can have runs retrieving infinite documents.

A multiset (or bag) is a set which may contain the same element several times and its multiplicity of occurrences is relevant [20]. A **set of judged documents** is a (crisp) multiset $(REL, m) = \{rel_1, rel_2, rel_1, rel_2, rel_2, rel_4, \ldots\}$, where m is a function from REL into $\overline{\mathbb{N}}_0 = \mathbb{N}_0 \cup \{\infty\}$ representing the multiplicity of every relevance degree rel_j [25]; if the multiplicity is 0, a given relevance degree is simply not present in the multiset, as in the case of rel_3 in the previous example. Note that the multiplicity function m can lead to infinite multisets, when needed. Suppose $\mathcal{M}$ is the infinite set of all the possible multiplicity functions m, then the **universe set of judged documents** is the set $\mathcal{R} := \bigcup_{m \in \mathcal{M}}(REL, m)$ of all the possible sets of judged documents (REL, m).

We call **judged run** the function $\hat{r}_t$ from $T \times \mathcal{D}$ into $\mathcal{R}$, which assigns a relevance degree to each retrieved document

$$(t, r_t) \mapsto \hat{r}_t = \{GT(t, d_1), \ldots, GT(t, d_n)\} = \{\hat{r}_{t,1}, \ldots, \hat{r}_{t,n}\}$$

3.3 Rank-based Retrieval

Given a positive natural number n called the *length of the run*, we define the **set of retrieved documents** as

---

[1] Binary relevance is often thought to be on a categorical scale but, since the scale consists only of two categories one of which indicates the absence of relevance, we can safely consider it as an ordinal scale in fact.

$D(n) = \{(d_1, \ldots, d_n) : d_i \in D, d_i \neq d_j \text{ for any } i \neq j\}$, i.e. the ranked list of retrieved documents without duplicates, and the **universe set of retrieved documents** as $\mathcal{D} := \bigcup_{n=1}^{|D|} D(n)$.

A **run** r_t, retrieving a ranked list of documents $D(n)$ in response to a topic $t \in T$, is a function from T into $\mathcal{D}$

$$t \mapsto r_t = (d_1, \ldots, d_n)$$

We denote by $r_t[j]$ the j-th element of the vector r_t, i.e. $r_t[j] = d_j$. Note that, since the cardinality of D may be infinite, we can model also infinite rankings, as those assumed by [27, 33]. We define the **universe set of judged documents** as $\mathcal{R} := \bigcup_{n=1}^{|D|} REL^n$.

We call **judged run** the function $\hat{r}_t$ from $T \times \mathcal{D}$ into $\mathcal{R}$, which assigns a relevance degree to each retrieved document in the ranked list

$$(t, r_t) \mapsto \hat{r}_t = \big(GT(t, d_1), \ldots, GT(t, d_n)\big)$$

We denote by $\hat{r}_t[j]$ the j-th element of the vector $\hat{r}_t$, i.e. $\hat{r}_t[j] = GT(t, d_j)$.

4. EMPIRICAL RELATIONAL STRUCTURE

As discussed in Section 2, a key point in defining a measurement is to start from a clear empirical relational structure among the attributes of the entities you would like to measure, in our case the effectiveness of IR systems in terms of the utility they provide to their users [9, 11, 29]. Therefore, $\mathbf{E} = \langle T \times \mathcal{D}, \preceq \rangle$ is our empirical relational structure, i.e. the set of all the runs with an ordering relation where the utility systems provide to their users is roughly expressed in terms of the "amount" of relevance: the more relevance is retrieved by a run, the greater it is.

This is an especially critical point since, as highlighted out by [31], "there is no empirical ordering for retrieval effectiveness". The hardness of this problem clearly emerges also when you consider the actual properties of the set $\mathcal{D}$.

Typically, when you define a measurement, you start from sets having very good properties. For example, in the case of the theory of measure [4, 15], σ-algebras are closed under countable unions, intersections, and complements and the inclusion relation among sets leads to a natural partial ordering. All these nice properties are then reflected in measures and probabilities: since a σ-algebra is closed under countable union, a measure is then requested to be σ-*additive*, i.e. if $\{A_n\}_{n \in \mathbb{N}}$ is a family of disjoints subsets, then $M(\bigcup_{n \in \mathbb{N}} A_n) = \sum_{n \in \mathbb{N}} M(A_n)$ and from this property one obtains that is also *monotone* $A \subseteq B \Rightarrow M(A) \leq M(B)$, since $B = A \cup (A^C \cap B) \Rightarrow M(B) = M(A) + M(A \cup (A^C \cap B)) \geq M(A)$, which in turn reflects the ordering induced by the inclusion relation on the σ-algebra.

Unfortunately, the set $\mathcal{D}$ lacks many of these desirable properties. For example, inclusion and union on $\mathcal{D}$ would not be as intuitive and agreeable as they are in the case of σ-algebras and this hampers the possibility of requiring additivity as a property of an IR utility-oriented measurement.

Let us consider inclusion: we could say that $r_t \subseteq s_t$ if s_t appends one more document to r_t. Differently from σ-algebras, inclusion would not induce an ordering on $\mathcal{D}$, since you may think that a run retrieving one more relevant document is greater than another one not retrieving it [3, 26] but you may also think that a run retrieving one more not-

relevant document is smaller than another one not retrieving it [3], or it should stay equal [26].

The above inclusion can be seen also as a form of union, i.e. as concatenating a run with another one constituted by just a single document, i.e. somehow $s_t = r_t \cup \{d_j\}$. Almost no one would require additivity, i.e. $M(s_t) = M(r_t) + M(d_j)$, and as discussed above there is neither agreement on monotonicity, i.e. when it should be $M(s_t) > M(r_t)$ and when $M(s_t) < M(r_t)$. This is even more evident if you think at data fusion, a kind of much more complicated union: no one would quest for additivity, even in the case of runs without any common document, and consider the performance of the fused run as the sum of the performances of the composing runs, nor they could a priori guarantee monotonicity, ensuring that the performance of the fused run is always greater than or equal to the the performances of the composing runs.

The above mentioned issues with inclusion and union of runs make it difficult also to deal with runs of different length, e.g. constraining the behaviour of a measurement in the symbolic relational structure $\mathbf{S}$ when runs of different length are somehow contrasted, as it is done in [3, 8, 22, 26], since we basically do not know how to unite and compare them in the empirical relational structure $\mathbf{E}$.

Therefore, in this paper, we will focus on a partial ordering among runs of the same length in the empirical relational structure $\mathbf{E}$, leading to monotonicity in the symbolic relational structure $\mathbf{S}$, and we leave for future work a deeper investigation of inclusion, union, additivity and their implications. In particular, we will restrict ourselves only to those cases where the ordering is intuitive and it is possible to find a commonly shared agreement. Examples of very basic cases are: a run retrieving a relevant document in the first rank position is greater than another one retrieving it in the second position or a run retrieving a more relevant document in a given rank position is greater than another one retrieving a less relevant document in the same position.

The above discussion points out one key contribution of this paper, i.e. highlighting that the core problem in defining an IR measurement is not to constraint its numerical properties (symbolic world) but rather our quite limited understanding of the operations and relationships among runs (empirical world). Indeed, if we better clarify how runs behave in the empirical relational structure, a measurement, intended as a homomorphism between the empirical and symbolic worlds, has to comply with them by construction.

Note that this vision is somehow implicitly present in [8, 22]. Their framework is based on the idea that there must be an agreement between two distinct "relevance measurements", one made by assessors and the other by systems, i.e. how assessors and systems rank documents on the basis of their relevance to a query. Then, they constrain what they call "metric" to the behaviour of the similarity between these two "relevance measurements", but without actually defining what this similarity is . In relation to our work, we could say that the assessor and system "relevance measurements" may somehow resemble the notion of relational structures in the empirical world and the "metric" may in some way approximate the notion of measurement as homomorphism between empirical and symbolic worlds. However, we think that framing the problem in the context of the representational theory of measurement provides more advantages than an ad-hoc approach: it streamlines the core concepts, helps to discuss and address issues at the proper level either in the empirical or symbolic worlds, and better links IR evaluation to other sciences. Moreover, we provide an actual partial ordering among runs in the empirical world, from which we derive properties for a measurement, while the concept of similarity is not actually defined by [8, 22].

4.1 Set-based Retrieval

Let us consider two runs r_t and s_t with the same length n. We introduce a **partial ordering among runs** as

$$r_t \preceq s_t \Leftrightarrow |\{j : \hat{r}_{t,j} \geq rel\}| \leq |\{j : \hat{s}_{t,j} \geq rel\}| \quad \forall rel \in REL$$

which counts, for each relevance degree, how many items there are above that relevance degree and, if a run has higher counts for each relevance degree, it is considered greater than another one.

For example, if we have four relevance degrees $REL = \{0, 1, 2, 3\}$, the run $\hat{r}_t = \{0, 1, 1, 2, 2\}$ is smaller than the run $\hat{s}_t = \{0, 1, 1, 2, 3\}$ but the run $\hat{r}_t = \{0, 1, 1, 2, 2\}$ is not comparable to the run $\hat{w}_t = \{0, 1, 1, 1, 3\}$ because, relying just on an ordinal scale for the relevance degrees, it is not a priori known whether the decrease from a document with relevance degree 2 to one with relevance degree 1 is compensated or not by the increase from a document with relevance degree 2 to one with relevance degree 3, actually we cannot even say if the two runs are equal.

If we have the relevance grades $REL = \{0, 1, \cdots, q\}$, among all the runs with a fixed number of relevant documents, the run $\{1, \ldots, 1, 0, \ldots, 0\}$ is the smallest, while $\{q, \ldots, q, 0, \ldots, 0\}$ is the greatest one.

In the case of binary relevance, i.e. $REL = \{0, 1\}$, we obtain an intuitive total ordering

$$r_t \preceq s_t \Leftrightarrow |\{j : \hat{r}_{t,j} \geq 1\}| \leq |\{j : \hat{s}_{t,j} \geq 1\}|$$

where r_t is less than s_t if it retrieved less relevant documents than s_t.

If REL relies on a more powerful scale, e.g. a ratio scale where we can know, for example, that a highly relevant document is twice as relevant as a partially relevant one, the above definition becomes a total ordering also in the case of graded relevance, by basically summing up how many "relevance units" there are in each run.

4.2 Rank-based Retrieval

Let us consider two runs r_t and s_t with the same length n. We introduce a **partial ordering among runs** as

$$r_t \preceq s_t \Leftrightarrow |\{j \leq k : \hat{r}_t[j] \geq rel\}| \leq |\{j \leq k : \hat{s}_t[k] \geq rel\}|$$
$$\forall rel \in REL \text{ and } k \in \{1, \ldots, n\}$$

which counts, for each relevance degree and rank position, how many items there are above that relevance degree and, if a run has higher counts for each relevance degree and rank position, it is considered greater than another one.

For example, if we have four relevance degrees $REL = \{0, 1, 2, 3\}$, the run $\hat{r}_t = (0, 1, 1, 2, 2)$ is smaller than the run $\hat{s}_t = (0, 1, 1, 2, 3)$ but the run $\hat{r}_t = (0, 1, 1, 2, 2)$ is not comparable to the run $\hat{w}_t = (0, 1, 1, 1, 3)$ because, relying just on an ordinal scale for the relevance degrees, it is not a priori known whether the decrease from a document with relevance degree 2 to one with relevance degree 1 at rank 4 is compensated or not by the increase from a document with relevance degree 2 to one with relevance degree 3 at rank 5, as it happens in the set-based retrieval case. On the other

hand, the run $\hat{r}_t = (0, 1, 1, 2, 2)$ is not comparable with the run $\hat{v}_t = (2, 0, 1, 2, 1)$ because, even if the document with relevance degree 2 moves forward from rank 5 to rank 1, the backward movement of the document with relevance degree 1 from rank 2 to rank 5 may or may not compensate for it. This latter case points out the effect of ranking with respect to the previous case of set-based retrieval, which would have considered these two runs as equal.

Note that in rank-based retrieval, we cannot achieve a total ordering even in the case of binary relevance. Indeed the run $\hat{r}_t = (0, 1, 0, 1, 0)$ is not comparable to the run $\hat{s}_t = (1, 0, 0, 0, 1)$ because you cannot a priori say whether the forward movement of the relevant document from rank 2 to rank 1 is compensated or not by the backward movement of the relevant document from rank 4 to rank 5.

A possible segmentation of all the runs can be performed in terms of the total number of relevant documents, where a minimum and maximum run can be found. Taking for simplicity $REL = \{0, 1, \ldots, q\}$ and considering a run r_t retrieving just one relevant document, we have that it lays between the minimum and maximum below:

$$(0, \ldots, 0, 1) \preceq \hat{r}_t \preceq (q, 0, \ldots, 0)$$

More in general, for any run r_t retrieving k relevant documents, it holds:

$$(0, \ldots, 0, 1, \ldots, 1) \preceq \hat{r}_t \preceq (q, \ldots, q, 0, \ldots, 0) \quad (1)$$

Summing up, differently from the case of set-based retrieval, this partial ordering cannot become a total order neither in the case of binary relevance nor in the case of relevance degrees on more powerful scales, e.g. ratio ones. Indeed, the presence of the ranking adds a further dimension which makes impossible to compare every run pair because it is not a priori known how much each rank position influences the ordering.

5. UTILITY-ORIENTED MEASUREMENTS OF RETRIEVAL EFFECTIVENESS

We define an **utility-oriented measurement of retrieval effectiveness** as an homomorphism between the empirical relational structure $\mathbf{E} = \langle T \times \mathcal{D}, \preceq \rangle$, discussed in the previous section, and the symbolic relational structure $\mathbf{S} = \langle \overline{\mathbb{R}}_0^+, \leq \rangle$, that is a mapping which assigns to any sequence of documents $D(n)$ retrieved by a system for a given topic t, a non negative number, i.e. a **utility-oriented measure of retrieval effectiveness**.

More in detail, a utility-oriented measurement of retrieval effectiveness is the composition of a judged run $\hat{r}_t$ with a **scoring function** μ from the universe set of judged documents $\mathcal{R}$ into $\overline{\mathbb{R}}_0^+$ which assigns to any sequence of judged documents a non negative number, ensuring that the ordering $\preceq$ among the runs is properly mapped in the ordering $\leq$ among real numbers.

DEFINITION 5.1. *A function*

$$M : T \times \mathcal{D} \to \overline{\mathbb{R}}_0^+$$

defined as $M = \mu(\hat{r}_t)$, *i.e. the composition of a judged run* $\hat{r}_t$ *with a scoring function* $\mu : \mathcal{R} \to \overline{\mathbb{R}}_0^+$ *is a* **utility-oriented measurement of retrieval effectiveness** *if and only if for any two runs* r_t *and* s_t *with the same length* n *such that* $r_t \preceq s_t$, *then* $\mu(\hat{r}_t) \leq \mu(\hat{s}_t)$.

Any utility-oriented measurement of retrieval effectiveness is indeed the specification of the scoring function μ and that the property which ensures a proper mapping between the empirical and symbolic relational structures is the *monotonicity* of μ. In this respect, an utility-oriented measurement of retrieval effectiveness is not a "measure" in the classical sense of the measure theory [4, 15], since it lacks the additivity property, but shares with fuzzy measures [32] the fact of relying just on monotonicity.

Note that the monotonicity requested in the definition above differs from the notion of monotonicity in [26], since this latter one applies to runs of different length, which is not our case for the motivations we discussed in the previous section. Similar considerations hold for the notion of document/query monotonicity in [22] which applies to unions of documents/queries.

Even if the previous definition fits our purposes, it could be difficult to check it in practice. Therefore, we introduce two "monotonicity-like" properties, called **replacement** and **swap**, which we will prove to be equivalent to the required monotonicity but are easier to check.

Replacement If we replace a less relevant document with a more relevant one in the same rank position, a utility-oriented measurement of retrieval effectiveness should not decrease. More formally, if

$$r_t = (d_1, \ldots, d_{i-1}, \mathbf{d_i}, d_{i+1}, \ldots, d_n)$$

and

$$s_t = (d_1, \ldots, d_{i-1}, \tilde{\mathbf{d_i}}, d_{i+1}, \ldots, d_n)$$

with $\mathbf{d_i} \neq \tilde{\mathbf{d_i}}$ and $\hat{r}_t[i] \leq \hat{s}_t[i]$, then

$$M(r_t) \leq M(s_t)$$

Swap If we swap a less relevant document in a higher rank position with a more relevant one in a lower rank position, a utility-oriented measurement of retrieval effectiveness should not decrease. More formally, if

$$r_t = (d_1, \ldots, d_{i-1}, \mathbf{d_i}, d_{i+1}, \ldots, d_{j-1}, \mathbf{d_j}, d_{j+1}, \ldots, d_n)$$

and

$$s_t = (d_1, \ldots, d_{i-1}, \mathbf{d_j}, d_{i+1}, \ldots, d_{j-1}, \mathbf{d_i}, d_{j+1}, \ldots, d_n)$$

with $\hat{r}[i] \leq \hat{r}[j]$, then

$$M(r_t) \leq M(s_t)$$

The above definitions of replacement and swap are formulated in the case of rank-based retrieval; clearly, in the set-based retrieval case only replacement makes sense while swap does not apply since there is no ranking among documents.

Note that the swap property somehow recalls the idea of priority constraint in [3] and of convergence in [26].

THEOREM 5.2 (EQUIVALENCE). *A scoring function μ defined from $\mathcal{R}$ into $\overline{\mathbb{R}}_0^+$ leads to a utility-oriented measurement of retrieval effectiveness M if and only if it satisfies the Replacement and the Swap properties.*

PROOF. : If μ leads to a utility-oriented measurement of retrieval effectiveness, the Replacement property is clearly a special case of the monotonicity of μ.

Let us now define

$$A(r_t, k, p) = |\{i \leq k : \hat{r}_t[i] \geq p\}|$$

and assume that

$$r_t = (d_1, \ldots, d_{i-1}, \mathbf{d_i}, d_{i+1}, \ldots, d_{j-1}, \mathbf{d_j}, d_{j+1}, \ldots, d_n)$$

and

$$s_t = (d_1, \ldots, d_{i-1}, \mathbf{d_j}, d_{i+1}, \ldots, d_{j-1}, \mathbf{d_i}, d_{j+1}, \ldots, d_n)$$

with $\hat{r}_t[i] \leq \hat{r}_t[j]$.

It is clear that $A(r_t, k, p) = A(s_t, k, p)$ for any $k \leq i - 1$ and $p \in \mathbb{R}_0^+$. If $k = i, i+1, \ldots, j-1$, we have $A(r_t, k, p) = A(s_t, k, p)$ for $p < \hat{r}_t[j]$ and $A(r_t, k, p) < A(s_t, k, p)$ for $p \geq \hat{r}_t[j]$, while for $k > j$ again $A(r_t, k, p) = A(s_t, k, p)$ for any $p \in \mathbb{R}_0^+$. This implies that $r_t \preceq s_t$: by the monotonicity we get that $\mu(\hat{r}_t) \leq \mu(\hat{s}_t)$ and the Swap property is proved.

Let us now assume that the Replacement and the Swap properties are satisfied by M. Taken $r_t \preceq s_t$, our aim is to prove that we are able to construct an increasing sequence of runs

$$r_t = r_t^0 \preceq r_t^1 \preceq r_t^2 \preceq \ldots \preceq r_t^h = s_t$$

such that $\mu(\hat{r}_t^j) \leq \mu(\hat{r}_t^{j+1})$ for any $j = 0, \ldots, h-1$, which proves the monotonicity of μ. Let us start from the last term in both the collections of judged runs. If $\hat{r}_t[n] = \hat{s}_t[n]$, we define $r_t^1 = r_t$ and pass to the $n-1$-th element. If $\hat{r}_t[n] < \hat{s}_t[n]$, we replace the last document in r_t with a document of relevance degree $\hat{s}_t[n]$ and define this new run as r_t^1. We have that $r_t^0 = r_t \preceq r_t^1$, by the replacement that $\mu(\hat{r}_t^0) \leq \mu(\hat{r}_t^1)$ and we pass to consider the $n-1$-th element. If $\hat{r}_t[n] > \hat{s}_t[n]$, we swap the last document in r_t with the closest document of minimum relevance grade of the same run. For example, if

$$\hat{r}_t = (1, 0, 1, 0, 1, 1) \quad \text{and} \quad \hat{s}_t = (1, 1, 0, 1, 1, 0)$$

we define $\hat{r}_t^1 = (1, 0, 1, 1, 1, 0)$. It is immediate to see that the new last element of r_t has a relevance degree smaller than or equal to $\hat{s}_t[n]$. Indeed, if on the contrary we assume that $\hat{r}_t[k] > \hat{s}_t[n]$ for any $k < n$ and we define $p = \min\{\hat{r}_t[i], 0 \leq i \leq n\}$, we have that

$$A(r_t, n, p) > A(s_t, n, p)$$

which is in contradiction with the hypothesis that $r_t \preceq s_t$. We have that $r_t^0 = r_t \preceq r_t^1$ and by the swap property that $\mu(\hat{r}_t^0) \leq \mu(\hat{r}_t^1)$. Proceeding now as before in the case that $\hat{r}_t^1[n] = \hat{s}_t[n]$ or $\hat{r}_t^1[n] < \hat{s}_t[n]$, we (possibly) define a new run r_t^2 such that $r_t^1 \preceq r_t^2$ and we pass to consider the $n-1$-th element. Repeating this procedure to the $n-1$-th element, the $n-2$-th element and so on we construct the desired sequence of runs and the monotonicity is proved. $\square$

The same theorem can be proved in the case of set-based retrieval by using just the Replacement property.

As a final remark, note that for any two runs r_t and s_t such that $r_t \preceq s_t$, Definition 5.1 ensures that any two utility-oriented measurements M_1 and M_2 will order r_t below s_t, i.e. $M_1(r_t) \leq M_1(s_t)$ and $M_2(r_t) \leq M_2(s_t)$. On the contrary, when two runs are not comparable, i.e. when they are outside the partial ordering $\preceq$ and we cannot say which one is the greater, we can find two utility-oriented measurements M_1 and M_2 which order them differently.

Consider, for example the following runs

$$r_t = (1, 0, 0, 1, 0) \quad \text{and} \quad s_t = (0, 1, 1, 0, 1),$$

We obtain that

$$Prec(r_t)[5] = \frac{2}{5} < Prec(s_t)[5] = \frac{3}{5}$$

while

$$AP(r_t) = \frac{1}{RB_t}\frac{3}{2} > AP(s_t) = \frac{1}{RB_t}\frac{53}{30}$$

Therefore, Precision judges preferable s_t, while *Average Precision (AP)* r_t.

5.1 Examples of Application of the Equivalence Theorem

In this section, we use the equivalence Theorem 5.2 to show how to demonstrate that an existing IR evaluation measure is an utility-oriented measurements of retrieval effectiveness.

The proof is trivial in the case of *Average Precision (AP)*, *Rank-Biased Precision (RBP)* [27], and *Normalized Discounted Cumulated Gain (nDCG)* [17] and not reported here due to space reasons. Here, we present the case of *Expected Reciprocal Rank (ERR)* [10], which is more interesting.

Given a run r_t of length n, the ERR is defined as

$$ERR(x_1,\ldots,x_n) = \sum_{i=1}^{n}\frac{1}{i}\prod_{k=1}^{i-1}(1-x_k)x_i$$

with the convention that $\prod_{i=1}^{0} = 1$ and x_i represents the probability that a user leaves his search after considering the document at position i. An additional assumption is that the map $\hat{r}_t[i \mapsto x_i(\hat{r}_t[i])$ is increasing and $x_i(0) = 0$.

Let us consider the **Replacement property** and to avoid trivial cases, take $\hat{r}_t[i] < \hat{s}_t[i]$. The property is satisfied if the function $(x_1,\ldots,x_n) \mapsto ERR(x_1,\ldots,x_n)$ is non-decreasing in any variable. With this aim, we will prove that the partial derivatives $\frac{\partial}{\partial x_k}ERR > 0$ for any $k \leq n$ and $(x_1,\ldots,x_n) \in [0,1]^n$. It is immediate that $\frac{\partial}{\partial x_n}ERR = \frac{1}{n}\prod_{k=1}^{n-1}(1-x_k) > 0$. Let us now consider $\frac{\partial}{\partial x_{n-1}}ERR$. Denoting $A(x_i,\ldots,x_j) = \prod_{k=i}^{j}(1-x_k)$, we get $\frac{\partial}{\partial x_{n-1}}ERR = A(x_1,\ldots,x_{n-2})\left(\frac{1}{n-1} - \frac{x_n}{n}\right) > 0$ since $\frac{1}{n-1} - \frac{x_n}{n} > \frac{1}{n-1} - \frac{1}{n} > \frac{1}{(n-1)n} > 0$.

The general case follows similarly: take $k < n-1$ and consider $\frac{\partial}{\partial x_k}ERR$. This partial derivative will be positive if and only if

$$S(x_{k+1},\ldots,x_n) = \frac{1}{k} - \frac{1}{k+1}x_{k+1}$$

$$-\frac{1}{k+2}A(x_{k+1},x_{k+2}) - \ldots - \frac{1}{n}A(x_{k+1},\ldots,x_{n-1})x_n > 0.$$

Considering the last two terms, we get

$$\frac{1}{n-1}A(x_{k+1},\ldots,x_{n-2})x_{n-1} + \frac{1}{n}A(x_{k+1},\ldots,x_{n-1})x_n$$

$$\leq A(x_{k+1},\ldots,x_{n-2})\frac{1}{n-1}\ .$$

This implies that

$$S(x_{k+1},\ldots,x_n) > \frac{1}{k} - \ldots - \frac{1}{n-2}A(x_{k+1},\ldots,x_{n-3})x_{n-2}$$

$$-\frac{1}{n-1}A(x_{k+1},\ldots,x_{n-2})$$

Applying the previous computation with the new last two terms and repeating this procedure on and on, at the end we obtain that

$$S(x_{k+1},\ldots,x_n) > \frac{1}{k} - \frac{1}{k+1} > 0$$

and the replacement is proved for ERR.

The **Swap property** is a little more challenging. We have

$$ERR = F(x_1,\ldots,x_{i-1}) + \frac{1}{i}\prod_{k=1}^{i-1}(1-x_k)\mathbf{x_i}$$

$$+\frac{1}{i+1}\prod_{k=1}^{i-1}(1-x_k)(1-\mathbf{x_i})x_{i+1} + \ldots$$

$$\ldots + \frac{1}{j-1}\prod_{k=1}^{i-1}(1-x_k)(1-\mathbf{x_i})(1-x_{i+1})\cdots(1-x_{j-2})x_{j-1}+$$

$$+\frac{1}{j}\prod_{k=1}^{i-1}(1-x_k)(1-\mathbf{x_i})\cdots(1-x_{j-1})\mathbf{x_j} + G(x_1,\ldots,x_n)\ ,$$

where F and G are suitable functions, while $ERR(s)$ has the same expression with the $\mathbf{x_i}$'s and $\mathbf{x_j}$'s interchanged. It is immediate that $ERR(r_t) \leq ERR(s_t)$ if $j = i+1$. Indeed, we have that the previous inequality holds if and only if

$$\frac{1}{i}\mathbf{x_i} + \frac{1}{i+1}(1-\mathbf{x_i})x_{i+1} \leq \frac{1}{i}\mathbf{x_{i+1}} + \frac{1}{i+1}(1-\mathbf{x_{i+1}})x_i$$

which is equivalent to $\frac{1}{i(i+1)}\mathbf{x_i} \leq \frac{1}{i(i+1)}\mathbf{x_{i+1}}$. If $|i-j| > 1$, $ERR(r_t) \leq ERR(s_t)$ if and only if

$$\mathbf{x_i}D(x_{i+1},\ldots,x_{j-1}) \leq \mathbf{x_j}D(x_{i+1},\ldots,x_{j-1})$$

where

$$D(x_{i+1},\ldots,x_{j-1}) = \frac{1}{i} - \frac{1}{i+1}x_{i+1} - \frac{1}{i+2}(1-x_{i+1})x_{i+2} - \ldots$$

$$\ldots - \frac{1}{j-1}(1-x_{i+1})\cdots(1-x_{j-2})x_{j-1}$$

$$-\frac{1}{j}(1-x_{i+1})\cdots(1-x_{j-2})(1-x_{j-1})$$

It will be therefore sufficient to prove that $D(x_1,\ldots,x_k) > 0$ for any $(x_1,\ldots,x_k) \in [0,1]^k$, where $k = j-i-1 > 0$. Let us prove this by induction on k: if $k = 1$ we get

$$D(x_1) = \frac{1}{i} - \frac{x_1}{i+1} - \frac{(1-x_1)}{i+2} \geq \frac{1}{i(i+1)}$$

for any $x_1 \in [0,1]$. Let us now assume that $D(x_1,\ldots,x_i) > 0$ for any $i \leq k-1$ and $(x_1,\ldots,x_i) \in [0,1]^i$. It holds

$$D(x_1,\ldots,x_k) = D(x_1,\ldots,x_{k-1})$$

$$+\tfrac{1}{(i+k-1)(i+k)}(1-x_1)\cdots(1-x_{k-1}) > 0$$

for any $(x_1,\ldots,x_k) \in [0,1]^k$ and the property is proved.

6. BALANCING

In this section, we explore the behaviour of utility-oriented measurements when two runs r_t and s_t are not comparable according to the the partial ordering $\preceq$.

Let n be the length of a run, let r_t and s_t be two runs, $q_{min} = \min\{rel \in REL : rel > 0\}$ be the minimum relevance degree above not relevant and $q_{max} = \max\{rel \in REL\}$ be the maximum relevance degree, and $M(\cdot)$ a utility-oriented measurement. We assume here that $0 < q_{min} \leq q_{max} < \infty$.

We define the **Balancing Index** as

$$B(n) = \max\Big\{b \in \mathbb{N}\colon M\big(r_t : \hat{r}_t[1] = q_{max}, \hat{r}_t[j] = 0,\ 1 < j \leq n\big)$$
$$\leq M\big(s_t : \hat{s}_t[i] = 0,\ 1 \leq i < b, \hat{s}_t[j] = q_{min},\ b \leq j \leq n\big)\Big\}$$

As an example, let us consider the case of four relevance degrees $REL = \{0,1,2,3\}$ and runs of length 5. The balancing index seeks the maximum rank position b for which $M\big((3,0,0,0,0)\big)$ is balanced by $M\big((0,0,0,0,1)\big)$ or $M\big((0,0,0,1,1)\big)$ or $M\big((0,0,1,1,1)\big)$ or $M\big((0,1,1,1,1)\big)$, i.e. it determines when the greatest run possible with just one maximally relevant document (3 in this case) is scored "the same" as the smallest run possible with an increasing number of minimally relevant documents (1 in this case).

The balancing index exploits the Replacement and Swap properties in a way, different from the one used in the equivalence theorem, that allows us to move among runs not comparable for the empirical ordering $\preceq$.

In the above example, we have that

$$(3,0,0,0,0) \xrightarrow[\succeq]{\text{Swap}} (0,0,0,0,3) \xrightarrow[\succeq]{\text{Replacement}} (0,0,0,0,1)$$
$$\xrightarrow[\preceq]{\text{Replacement}} (0,0,0,1,1) \xrightarrow[\preceq]{\text{Replacement}} (0,0,1,1,1)$$
$$\xrightarrow[\preceq]{\text{Replacement}} (0,1,1,1,1)$$

where every two adjacent run pairs in the chain are comparable according to the empirical ordering $\preceq$ but not the first run with the last ones, e.g. $(3,0,0,0,0)$ is not a priori comparable to $(0,0,0,1,1)$ because neither you know whether the loss of a document with relevance degree 3 is compensated or not by two documents with relevance degree 1 nor you know the effect of ranking.

The balancing index allows us to explore cases that fall outside the empirical ordering $\preceq$ and to characterize the behaviour of the measurements in those circumstances where Definition 5.1 cannot ensure they will a priori act in a homogeneous way.

In particular, a measurement with $B(n) \to n$ behaves like a binary set-based measure, being extremely sensitive to the presence of additional relevant documents in the lowest ranks. On the contrary, a measurement with $B(n) \to 1$ is not sensitive to the presence of additional relevant documents after a relevant one in the top rank.

The balancing index models the concept of *top heaviness*, an important and somehow desired characteristic of a measurement, as highlighted also in previous works. The closeness threshold constraint [3] resembles it, even if it is formulated as a constraint stating that relevant documents in top ranks should count more rather than as an index you can actually compute to characterize a measurement; similar considerations hold for the notion of top-weightedness [26]. However, it should be noted that, instead of requesting top heaviness to be an a-priori propriety as in [3, 26], the balancing index explicitly points out that top heaviness is a property of the measurements that concerns the area where

runs are not a priori comparable, i.e. outside the empirical ordering $\preceq$, and this, in turn, causes measurements to possibly behave differently one from another, being more or less top heavy.

With respect to other empirical indexes for quantifying top heaviness, the balancing index has the advantage that it can be derived analytically. Below, some example of balancing indexes for some popular measurements are reported:

AP

$$B(n) = \max\left\{b \in \mathbb{N}\colon \sum_{k=1}^{n-b+1} \frac{k}{k+b-1} \geq 1\right\}$$

RBP

$$B(n) = \max\left\{b \in \mathbb{N}\colon b \geq \log_p(1 - p + p^n) + 1\right\}$$

where p is the persistence parameter of RBP.

ERR

$$B(n) = \max\left\{b \in \mathbb{N}\colon x_{min} \sum_{k=b}^{n} \frac{(1-x_{min})^{k-1}}{k} \geq x_{max}\right\}$$

where x_{min} represents the probability that a user leaves his search after considering a document of relevance q_{min} and x_{max} represents the probability that a user leaves his search after considering a document of relevance q_{max}.

nDCG

$$B(n) = \max\{b_1, b_2\}$$

where

$$b_1 = \max\left\{b > a \in \mathbb{N}\colon \sum_{k=0}^{n-b} \frac{q_{min}}{\log_a(k+b)} \geq q_{max}\right\},$$

$$b_2 = \max\left\{b \leq a \in \mathbb{N}\colon (a-b+1)q_{min} + c \geq q_{max}\right\},$$

$$c = \sum_{k=0}^{n-a-1} \frac{q_{min}}{\log_a(k+a+1)}$$

and a is the base of the logarithm in nDCG. Recall that $\max\{\varnothing\} = -\infty$.

It can be noted that some of the above formulas depend explicitly on the length of the run under consideration, as in the case of RBP, while others have an implicit dependence on it and might be more complex to be computed.

Therefore, we defined an algorithm which allows us to compute the balancing index numerically. The complexity of the algorithm is $O(n)$, since, assuming that the computation of the measurement M requires a constant number of operations, the while loop carries out at most $n-1$ iterations and at any iterations it performs a constant number of operations.

Note that, even if we compute the balancing index in a numerical way, it is not an empirical indicator, as for example the discriminative power [28] is, whose computation depends on a given experimental collection and a set of runs and whose value may change from dataset to dataset.

Figure 1.(a) reports the balancing index for several evaluation measurements at different run lengths. It can be noted that for AP and nDCG we have $B(n) \to n$ since it is close

Algorithm 1 Algorithm for computing the balancing index.

Require: n, the length of the run; q_{min} and q_{max} the minimal and maximal relevance degrees
Ensure: b, the balancing index for a run of length n

    procedure BALANCING(n, q_{min}, q_{max})
        $refValue \leftarrow M(r : \hat{r}_t[1] = q_{max}, \ldots$
            $\hat{r}_t[j] = 0 \ 1 < j \leq n)$
        $cmpValue \leftarrow M(r : \hat{r}_t[j] = 0 \ 1 \leq j < n, \ldots$
            $\hat{r}_t[n] = q_{min})$
        $b \leftarrow n$
        while $refValue > cmpValue$ **do**
            $b--$
            $cmpValue \leftarrow M(r : \hat{r}_t[j] = 0 \ 1 \leq j < b, \ldots$
              $\hat{r}_t[j] = q_{min} \ b \leq j \leq n)$
        end while
        return b
    end procedure

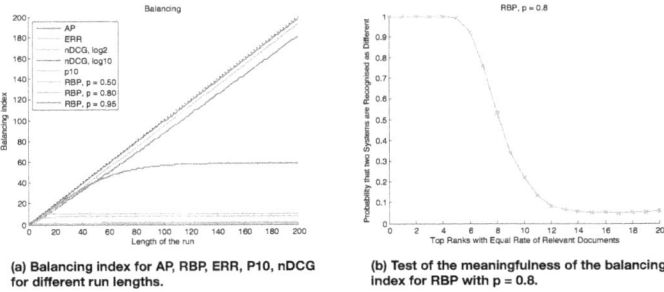

(a) Balancing index for AP, RBP, ERR, P10, nDCG for different run lengths.

(b) Test of the meaningfulness of the balancing index for RBP with p = 0.8.

Figure 1: (a) Balancing index for various measures and (b) its evaluation for RBP.

to the bisector, indicating that they are not strongly top-heavy measurements and that they are sensitive to relevant documents in the lower ranks. On the other hand, ERR is the most top-heavy measurement since its balancing index is $b = 1$ for any run length, meaning that missing a relevant document in the first rank position can not be compensated even by a run filled in with relevant documents from the second rank position to the end. RBP falls somehow in-between, still being a quite top-heavy measurement; it can be noted as for $p = 0.8$ the balancing index saturates to $b = 8$ for run lengths greater than 20 while, as p increases, it tends to be less top-heavy with almost $b = 60$ for $p = 0.95$.

In order to assess the meaningfulness of the balancing index, we conducted a preliminary experiment with RBP and $p = 0.8$. We simulated two runs of length $n = 1000$ consisting of 50 topics each, generated as shown in Figure 2.

In the top ranks up to rnk they have the same proportion (20%) of relevant documents; in the ranks from rnk to 20 they have different proportions of relevant documents 70% for r_t and 30% for s_t; in the ranks from 21 to $n = 1000$ they have still different proportions of relevant documents 10% for r_t and 70% for s_t. Then, we increased rnk from 0 to 20: when $rnk = 0$, r_t contains more than twice relevant documents in the top ranks than s_t and much less relevant documents in the very long tail; when $rnk = 20$, r_t and s_t have the same proportion of relevant documents in the top ranks but r_t has much less relevant documents than s_t in all

the other rank positions. For each increasing value of rnk, we performed a Student's t test with $\alpha = 0.05$ to assess whether r_t and s_t were significantly different. We repeated this experiment 10,000 times and, for each value of rnk, we computed the probability that the two runs are considered significantly different as the ratio among the number of times the Student's t test rejects the null hypothesis and 10,000, the total number of trials.

Figure 1.(b) shows the results of this experiment. It can be noted that, as far as rnk grows up the balancing index $b = 8$, the fact that r_t contains a bigger proportion of relevant documents than s_t in the top ranks almost always leads to consider the two runs as significantly different. On the other hand, as soon as rnk passes the balancing index $b = 8$ and the proportion of relevant documents in the top ranks of r_t and s_t starts to get more and more similar, the probability of considering the two runs significantly different gets lower and lower, completely ignoring the long tail where they are actually quite different. This is a clear indicator of top-heaviness, well reflected by the balancing index.

7. CONCLUSIONS AND FUTURE WORK

In this paper we have laid the foundations of a formal framework for defining what a utility-oriented measurement of retrieval effectiveness is, on the basis of the representational theory of measurement, putting IR evaluation in the wake of other physical and social sciences as far as measuring is concerned. A core contribution of the paper is to address the problem by clearly separating what are the issues in dealing with comparable/not comparable runs in the empirical world from what are the expected properties of a measurement in the symbolic world.

We proposed a minimal definition of measurement, based on just one axiom (Definition 5.1), and provided an equivalence theorem (Theorem 5.2) to check it in practice, as well as examples of its application.

Finally, we proposed the balancing index as an indicator of the top-heaviness of a measurement, providing both formulas and an algorithm to compute it. We have also conducted a preliminary experiment to show that its numerical value is a meaningful indicator of top-heaviness.

Future work will concern a deeper exploration of the core problems such measurements have, as for example additivity. We will also exploit the theory of scales of measurement in order to study the scales actually adopted by common measurements like AP, RBP, ERR, nDCG and others.

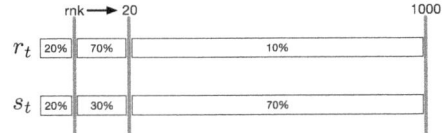

Figure 2: Creation of the simulated runs for assessing the meaningfulness of the balancing index in the case of RBP. Note that the percentages are not referred to the whole run but to each segment separately. Therefore, they do not need to sum up to 100% but to be between 0% and 100% within each segment.

Furthermore, we will consider the application of the proposed framework to other cases, such as measures based on diversity. This will lead to a different definition of the partial ordering $\preceq$ in the empirical relational structure **E** to capture the notion of diversity but Definition 5.1 of IR measurement of retrieval effectiveness will remain the same. Moreover, this may also require to individuate properties different from Swap and Replacement to provide an equivalence theorem in the vein of Theorem 5.2 suitable for this case.

8. REFERENCES

[1] M. Angelini, N. Ferro, G. Santucci, and G. Silvello. VIRTUE: A visual tool for information retrieval performance evaluation and failure analysis. *JVLC*, 25(4):394–413, 2014.

[2] E. Amigó, J. Gonzalo, J. Artiles, and M. F. Verdejo. A comparison of extrinsic clustering evaluation metrics based on formal constraints. *IR*, 12(4):461–486, 2009.

[3] E. Amigó, J. Gonzalo, and M. F. Verdejo. A General Evaluation Measure for Document Organization Tasks. In SIGIR 2013, pp. 643–652.

[4] P. Billingsley. *Probability and Measure*. John Wiley & Sons, New York, USA, 3rd edition, 1995.

[5] P. Bollman. Two Axioms for Evaluation Measures in Information Retrieval. In SIGIR 1984, pp. 233–245.

[6] C. Buckley and E. M. Voorhees. Evaluating Evaluation Measure Stability. In SIGIR 2000, pp. 33–40.

[7] C. Buckley and E. M. Voorhees. Retrieval Evaluation with Incomplete Information. In SIGIR 2004, pp. 25–32.

[8] L. Busin and S. Mizzaro. Axiometrics: An Axiomatic Approach to Information Retrieval Effectiveness Metrics. In ICTIR 2013, pp. 22–29.

[9] B. A. Carterette. System Effectiveness, User Models, and User Utility: A Conceptual Framework for Investigation. In SIGIR 2011, pp. 903–912.

[10] O. Chapelle, D. Metzler, Y. Zhang, and P. Grinspan. Expected Reciprocal Rank for Graded Relevance. In CIKM 2009, pp. 621–630.

[11] W. S. Cooper. On Selecting a Measure of Retrieval Effectiveness. *JASIS*, 24(2):87–100, 1973.

[12] N. E. Fenton and J. Bieman. *Software Metrics: A Rigorous & Practical Approach*. Chapman and Hall/CRC, USA, 3rd edition, 2014.

[13] N. Ferro, G. Silvello, H. Keskustalo, A. Pirkola, and K. Järvelin. The Twist Measure for IR Evaluation: Taking User's Effort Into Account. *JASIST*, 2015.

[14] L. Finkelstein. Widely, Strongly and Weakly Defined Measurement. *Measurement*, 34(1):39–48, 2003.

[15] G. B. Folland. *Real Analysis: Modern Techniques and Their Applications*. John Wiley & Sons, New York, USA, 2nd edition, 1999.

[16] N. Fuhr. IR between Science and Engineering, and the Role of Experimentation. In CLEF 2010, p. 1. LNCS 6360.

[17] K. Järvelin and J. Kekäläinen. Cumulated Gain-Based Evaluation of IR Techniques. *TOIS*, 20(4):422–446, 2002.

[18] J. Kekäläinen and K. Järvelin. Using Graded Relevance Assessments in IR Evaluation. *JASIST*, 53(13):1120—1129, 2002.

[19] M. G. Kendall. *Rank correlation methods*. Griffin, Oxford, England, 1948.

[20] D. E. Knuth. *The Art of Computer Programming – Volume 2: Seminumerical Algorithms*. Addison-Wesley, USA, 2nd edition, 1981.

[21] D. H. Krantz, R. D. Luce, P. Suppes, and A. Tversky. *Foundations of Measurement. Additive and Polynomial Representations*, volume 1. Academic Press, New York, USA, 1971.

[22] E. Maddalena and S. Mizzaro. Axiometrics: Axioms of Information Retrieval Effectiveness Metrics. In EVIA 2014, pp. 17–24.

[23] E. Maddalena, S. Mizzaro, F. Scholer, and A. Turpin. Judging Relevance Using Magnitude Estimation. In ECIR 2015, pp. 215–220. LNCS 9022.

[24] L. Mari. Beyond the Representational Viewpoint: a New Formalization of Measurement. *Measurement*, 27(2):71–84, 2000.

[25] S. Miyamoto. Generalizations of Multisets and Rough Approximations. *International Journal of Intelligent Systems*, 19(7):639–652, 2004.

[26] A. Moffat. Seven Numeric Properties of Effectiveness Metrics. In AIRS 2013, pp. 1–12. LNCS 8281.

[27] A. Moffat and J. Zobel. Rank-biased Precision for Measurement of Retrieval Effectiveness. *TOIS*, 27(1):2:1–2:27, 2008.

[28] T. Sakai. Evaluating Evaluation Metrics based on the Bootstrap. In SIGIR 2006, pp. 525–532.

[29] T. Sakai. Metrics, Statistics, Tests. In *Bridging Between Information Retrieval and Databases - PROMISE Winter School 2013, Revised Tutorial Lectures*, pp. 116–163. LNCS 8173, 2014.

[30] S. S. Stevens. On the Theory of Scales of Measurement. *Science, New Series*, 103(2684):677–680, 1946.

[31] C. J. van Rijsbergen. Retrieval effectiveness. In K. Spärck Jones, editor, *Information Retrieval Experiment*, pp. 32–43. Butterworths, London, United Kingdom, 1981.

[32] Z. Y. Wang and G. J. Klir. *Fuzzy Measure Theory*. Springer-Verlag, New York, USA, 1992.

[33] W. Webber, A. Moffat, and J. Zobel. A Similarity Measure for Indefinite Rankings. *TOIS*, 4(28):20:1–20:38, 2010.

[34] E. Yilmaz and J. A. Aslam. Estimating average precision when judgments are incomplete. *Knowledge and Information Systems*, 16(2):173–211, 2008.

[35] E. Yilmaz, J. A. Aslam, and S. E. Robertson. A New Rank Correlation Coefficient for Information Retrieval. In SIGIR 2008, pp. 587–594.

Bayesian Inference for Information Retrieval Evaluation

Ben Carterette
Department of Computer and Information Sciences
University of Delaware
Newark, DE, USA
carteret@udel.edu

ABSTRACT

A key component of experimentation in IR is *statistical hypothesis testing*, which researchers and developers use to make inferences about the effectiveness of their system relative to others. A statistical hypothesis test can tell us the likelihood that small mean differences in effectiveness (on the order of 5%, say) is due to randomness or measurement error, and thus is critical for making progress in research. But the tests typically used in IR—the t-test, the Wilcoxon signed-rank test—are very general, not developed specifically for the problems we face in information retrieval evaluation. A better approach would take advantage of the fact that the atomic unit of measurement in IR is the *relevance judgment* rather than the effectiveness measure, and develop tests that model relevance directly. In this work we present such an approach, showing theoretically that modeling relevance in this way naturally gives rise to the effectiveness measures we care about. We demonstrate the usefulness of our model on both simulated data and a diverse set of runs from various TREC tracks.

Categories and Subject Descriptors
H.3.4 [**Information Storage and Retrieval**] Performance Evaluation (Efficiency and Effectiveness)

Keywords: information retrieval; evaluation; statistical testing; bayesian inference

1. INTRODUCTION

Arguably the fundamental problem in IR is modeling the relevance of information to users. Vast amounts of effort have gone into developing features, model families, and optimization methods that can model relevance in a way that produces systems that are useful to users. Nearly as important is modeling the actual usefulness of these systems to the users that are supposed to benefit from them. This is the *effectiveness evaluation* problem, and it is traditionally based on the use of effectiveness measures and statistical hypothesis testing to make inferences about the relative ef-

ICTIR'15, September 27–30, Northampton, MA, USA.
© 2015 ACM. ISBN 978-1-4503-3833-2/15/09 ...$15.00.
DOI: http://dx.doi.org/10.1145/2808194.2809469.

fectiveness of different systems. But while IR research on relevance modeling looks into all aspects of the problem, much of the IR literature on hypothesis testing defers to basic work on statistics that is written conservatively, with the goal of providing solutions that make the fewest and weakest assumptions so as to be applicable to the widest range of cases rather than providing the solution that is right for the particular case at hand. We argue that better inference is possible if we tailor our tests to the particular challenges of evaluating IR.

Others have considered this problem. There have been tests developed for specific scenarios in IR [1, 9]. In addition, general techniques such as the bootstrap and randomization have been used to create statistical hypothesis tests for IR [15, 14]. For the most part, applications of these techniques to IR are based on the same basic assumption as the application of the t-test and other tests to IR: that measures like AP or nDCG accurately measure something about effectiveness, and that over a sample of topics we can use variability in those measures to determine whether a difference between two systems is likely to be "due to chance".

In earlier work, we proposed an explicitly model-based Bayesian framework for hypothesis testing and evaluation in general [2]. The advantage of that framework over techniques based on the bootstrap or randomization is that it models relevance directly rather than relying on an effectiveness measure's abstraction of relevance judgments. This means that it can be tailored to what we really care about in IR: modeling relevance to users.

The work in this paper builds on that work. We develop a deeper theoretical justification for our models, explaining in more detail how effectiveness measures emerge from models. This theoretical discussion provides a deeper framework for other researchers to adapt our work. We also extend the work to graded judgments and nDCG, an important contribution due to the importance of graded judgments in modern IR. Finally, we perform deeper empirical evaluations of our models on both simulated data and real data.

We begin in Section 2 by describing the use of models in traditional IR evaluation, both in effectiveness measures and in statistical significance tests. In Section 3 we present the case for why IR requires a different approach. We then present our Bayesian approach in Section 4, with Bayesian versions of the t-test along with new Bayesian methods for direct inferences about system effectiveness using relevance generated by a user model, and analysis on simulated data. In Section 5 we empirically analyze the Bayesian framework applied to TREC data, and we conclude with Section 6.

2. MODELS IN EVALUATION

In this section we summarize some previous work on models in evaluation. Broadly speaking, models come into play at two points in evaluation: first, in effectiveness measures that model user utility or satisfaction, and second, in statistical tests of the significance of mean differences in effectiveness. A third way models come into play is in the use of data mined from interaction logs for evaluation, but that is currently outside the scope of this work.

2.1 Model-based evaluation measures

There has long been interest in using effectiveness measures to model usefulness to users. Recent work along these lines often involves constructing an explicit probabilistic model of a user browsing a ranked list of results, then combining that model with relevance judgments to evaluate effectiveness [3]. Some widely-known examples include rank-biased precision (RBP) [10], discounted cumulative gain (DCG) [8], expected reciprocal rank [5], expected browser utility (EBU) [17], α-nDCG [6], and others [13]. In addition, traditional measures have had user models backfit to their mathematical expression [12, 18], showing that most measures at least suggest a user model.

In this work we will focus on three measures: precision at rank K, rank-biased precision (RBP), and nDCG. We will use x_k to indicate the relevance of the document at rank k; for precision and RBP x_k is binary, but for nDCG x_k may be a numeric grade (for example, $x_k \in \{0, 1, 2, 3, 4\}$).

$$\text{prec@K} = \frac{1}{K}\sum_{k=1}^{k} x_k \qquad \text{RBP} = \sum_{k=1}^{\infty} x_k \theta^{k-1}(1-\theta)$$

$$\text{nDCG@K} = \frac{1}{Z}\sum_{k=1}^{K} \frac{2^{x_k}-1}{\log_2(k+1)}$$

In RBP, θ is a free parameter representing the probability that a user scanning down a ranked list of results will decide to continue scanning to the next rank; $\theta^{k-1}(1-\theta)$ is the probability that they will encounter the document at rank k. In nDCG@K, Z is the "ideal" DCG@K, that is, the maximum possible value DCG@K could be, had the system ranked documents perfectly. It is used as a normalization to keep the measure bounded between 0 and 1.

2.2 Statistical hypothesis tests

Statistical hypothesis testing is meant to evaluate the likelihood that a difference in effectiveness between two systems is "real" and not due to randomness or measurement error. Many different tests are used by IR researchers; the most common are the sign test, the Wilcoxon signed rank test, the t-test, ANOVA, the randomization (exact) test, and the bootstrap test [15, 19].

For this work we will focus on the t-test. We assume the basics of the t-test are well-known and will not reiterate them here. Instead we want to focus on the model behind the t-test: it is actually based on a model of the effectiveness y_{ij} of system j on topic i as a linear combination of an intercept μ, a "system effect" β_j, a "topic effect" α_i, and random error ϵ_{ij} that is assumed to be normally distributed with variance σ^2 [11]. The model underlying the t-test is therefore:

Model 1 Linear model for the t-test

$$y_{ij} = \mu + \beta_j + \alpha_i + \epsilon_{ij}$$
$$\epsilon_{ij} \sim N(0, \sigma^2)$$

In this model notation y_{ij} is equal to a sum of effects, three of which are fixed, and one of which (the error ϵ_{ij}) is assumed to be drawn randomly from a normal distribution with mean zero and variance σ^2 (as indicated by the $\sim N(0, \sigma^2)$ notation). We can equivalently express this model as:

$$y_{ij} \sim N(\mu + \beta_j + \alpha_i, \sigma^2)$$

which says that the effectiveness of system j on topic i is drawn from a normal distribution centered at $\mu + \beta_j + \alpha_i$ (i.e. biased by the system, topic, and population of topics) with variance σ^2.

To fit a linear model like the one above, we maximize a likelihood function w.r.t. model parameters $\mu, \beta_j, \alpha_i, \sigma$:

$$\arg\max L_{M_1} = \prod_{i=1}^{N}\prod_{j=1}^{M} P(y_{ij}|\mu, \beta_j, \alpha_i, \sigma)$$

Since y_{ij} is normally distributed, L_{M_1} can be maximized using ordinary least squares.

Note that this is identical to the multiple linear regression model; the t-test is essentially just a special case of linear regression. This is not well-known among IR practitioners; we refer to Carterette [4], Monahan [11], Gelman et al. [7], and Venables & Ripley [16] for deeper treatment of linear models from different perspectives.

Strictly speaking, performing a t-test involves estimating parameters $\mu, \beta_j, \alpha_i, \sigma^2$. In practice, getting a p-value from a paired t-test only requires estimates of the magnitude of the difference between two system effects ($\beta_1 - \beta_2$) and the error variance σ^2. The maximum likelihood estimates of $\beta_1 - \beta_2$ and σ^2 are the mean difference and variance of differences in measure values respectively. Thus it is easy to perform inference in the linear model without actually fitting the full linear model; this is part of the appeal of the t-test, but also part of the risk of using it.

3. SIGNIFICANCE TESTING IN IR

Generally speaking, in experimental science, one performs an experiment by defining a measurement of some property of a subject, then measuring multiple subjects in multiple conditions or "treatments". That measurement may have sources of error: properties of the subject, treatment, or environment that affect it; imprecision in the measurement device; human error; etc. These sources of error are what motivate significance testing: we would like to know how likely it is that the observed measured difference is "real" in the presence of possible errors.

This translates to batch IR experimentation as follows: we define effectiveness measures such as precision at 10 or nDCG and, using human relevance judgments to retrieved documents, compute them over a sample of topics. There is a subtle but important difference between what we do in IR and the general scientific experiment case: our effectiveness measures can be viewed not only as measures in the measure-theoretic sense, but also as *statistics* computed from relevance judgments—that is, summaries of more "atomic" measures of the relevance of individual documents.

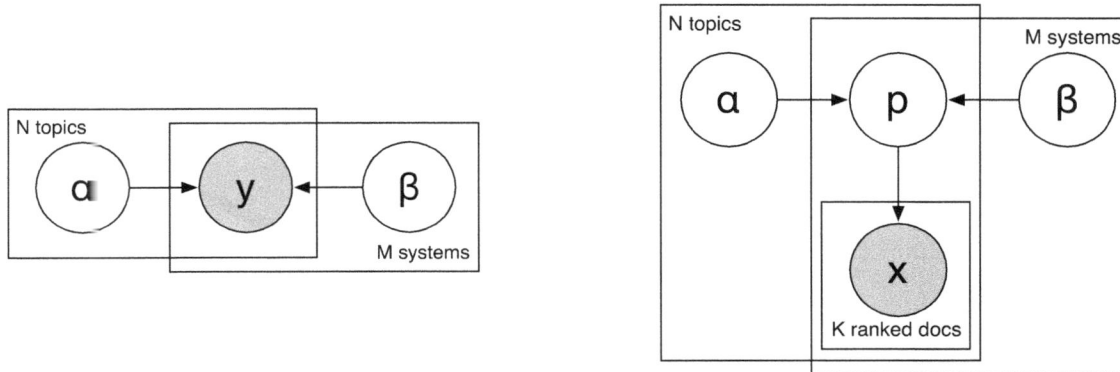

Figure 1: Graphical representations of two evaluation models. The left depicts the traditional t-test and our Model 2 (minus nuisance parameters): the effectiveness measure y is a linear function of a topic effect α and a system effect β; we use our observations of the measure y to fit β for inferences about systems. The right depicts more complex models that are tailored to IR: the relevance judgments x are determined by a hidden variable p, which is a function of a topic effect α and a system effect β; we use our observations of the relevance of documents x to fit β for inferences about systems.

Information retrieval can be seen as involving a hierarchical experimental design: we measure the relevance of individual documents (using human assessors as our measuring device), aggregate those measurements into a statistic (such as precision at 10, average precision, or nDCG) for each topic in the experiment then further aggregate those aggregations into a statistic for each system in the experiment (mean P10, MAP, mean NDCG). In practice, this means that by using standard techniques, we are ignoring data that might tell us something interesting about systems. Specifically, we are ignoring individual relevance judgments by abstracting them into an aggregate measure of effectiveness. But these individual judgments might actually convey important information, particularly if assessors disagree about them, or if the system has been designed (whether intentionally or not) in a way to find specific types of documents, or how users will encounter them.

Figure 1 illustrates the difference between the two. The first approach says that there are factors that influence the effectiveness measure y, one of which is the quality of the system β; significance tests like the t-test are designed to draw inferences about that. The second says that there are factors that influence relevance x, but not directly. Rather, they influence relevance by exerting influence on a hidden variable p that determines relevance. One of those factors, too, is the quality of the system β. But as we will see, it is the hidden variable that represents the most important determinant of relevance: the user.

4. BAYESIAN INFERENCE

We begin by describing a fully Bayesian version of the linear model we presented above, the same as that we described in previous work [2]. We then build on this model to present a full model of IR evaluation that includes the hidden variable in Figure 1.

4.1 Bayesian linear model

As discussed above, the t-test is based on a linear model with population, system, and topic effects, plus normally-distributed error. For our Bayesian version, we will start

with the same two assumptions. We will also introduce *prior distributions* for each model parameter. These prior distributions can be used to model any information we already have about the experiment. If we do not wish to make any strong assumptions, we can use non-informative priors. An example non-informative prior might be a uniform distribution over the entire real line. Better is a normal distribution with uncertain variance—i.e. the variance itself is a parameter with a prior distribution.

Thus a Bayesian version might look like this:

Model 2 Bayesian linear model for evaluation

$y_{ij} \sim N(\mu + \beta_j + \alpha_i, \sigma^2)$	$\sigma \sim 1/\sigma$
$\mu \sim N(0, \sigma_\mu^2)$	$\sigma_\mu \sim 1/\sigma_\mu$
$\beta_j \sim N(0, \sigma_\alpha^2)$	$\sigma_\alpha \sim 1/\sigma_\alpha$
$\alpha_i \sim N(0, \sigma_\beta^2)$	$\sigma_\beta \sim 1/\sigma_\beta$

As in the t-test, each measure of system effectiveness on a topic is a sum of a population effect μ, a system effect β_j, and a topic effect α_i. But now, in order to not assume anything about them, we put prior normal distributions over them. Since we further do not know anything about the variances of those prior distributions, we use improper flat priors on the log scale (the non-informative Jeffreys prior, denoted as σ distributed as its own reciprocal).

To make inferences about systems, we need the posterior distribution of system effects: $P(\beta_j | y_{ij})$, where y_{ij} is the observed effectiveness evaluation of system j on topic i. Obtaining the posterior distributions is best done by simulation, iteratively sampling parameters from their prior distributions, then updating posteriors based on the likelihood of the data. The likelihood function is:

$$L_{M_2} = \prod_{i=1}^{N} \prod_{j=1}^{M} P(y_{ij} | \mu, \beta_j, \alpha_i, \sigma, \sigma_\mu, \sigma_\beta, \sigma_\alpha)$$

$$= \prod_i \prod_j P(y_{ij} | \mu, \beta_j, \alpha_i, \sigma) P(\mu | \sigma_\mu) P(\beta_j | \sigma_\beta) P(\alpha_i | \sigma_\alpha) P(\sigma) P(\sigma_\mu) P(\sigma_\beta) P(\sigma_\alpha)$$

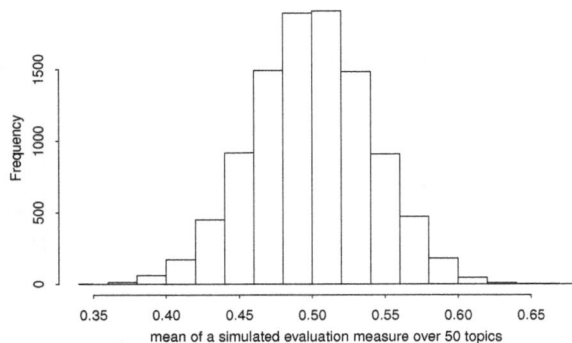

Figure 2: Distribution of a mean evaluation over 50 topics for 10,000 randomly-generated systems.

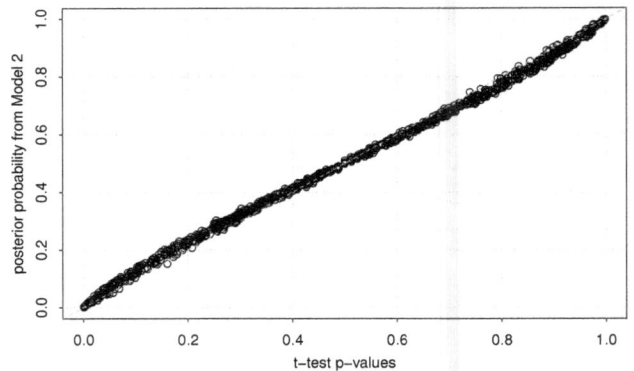

(a) Full range of x and y axes

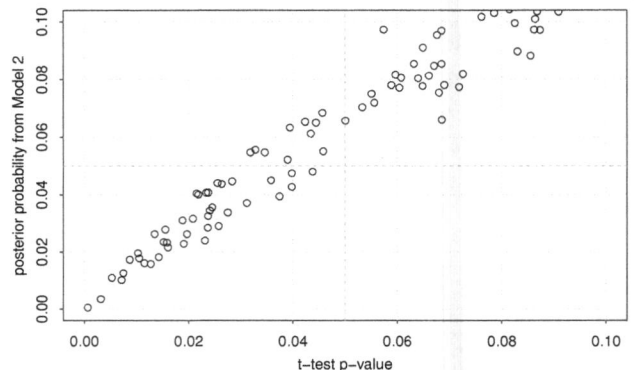

(b) Axes limited to 0–0.1

Figure 3: Comparison between t-test p-values and posterior probabilities from Model 2 for simulated systems.

Monte Carlo Markov Chain simulation is a standard technique for computing posterior distributions. We do not provide details here, as there are packages for general MCMC computation of posteriors available.[1]

Once the posteriors have been computed, making inferences about the systems is relatively simple: we estimate the probability of a hypothesis such as $S_1 \leq S_2$ by estimating $P(\beta_1 \leq \beta_2)$ from our simulation data. Note that the Bayesian approach actually estimates the probability that a hypothesis is true (conditional on the model and the data) rather than the probability of observing the data under a null model (like the t-test and other traditional tests).

Also note that this is *not* the same as the procedure called "Bayesian hypothesis testing". We are not computing a Bayes factor, for instance. Our goal is not to bring Bayesian hypothesis testing to IR, but to use explicit models to understand retrieval systems and their usefulness to users. It just so happens that Bayesian methods are well-suited to fitting those models.

4.1.1 Comparison to t-test

We can demonstrate the validity of this approach by comparing its results to the results of a standard t-test. For this experiment we use completely simulated data; we will show results for actual TREC runs in Section 5.

To simulate a system evaluation over 50 topics, we randomly draw 50 values from a uniform distribution between 0 and 1. We can do this thousands of times to generate random systems. Since all values are sampled identically, all systems are "equal" in theory, but because of randomness some will have a higher mean evaluation than others. Figure 2 shows a histogram of mean evaluation values; most simulated systems are between 0.45 and 0.55 (with the mean/median/mode at 0.5), but a substantial number are outside that range.

To compare the two, we first generate two random systems, then set up a standard one-sided null hypothesis:

$$H_0 : S_1 \leq S_2$$
$$H_a : S_1 > S_2$$

We then compare the t-test p-value to the marginal posterior distribution $P(\beta_1 \leq \beta_2)$ after fitting our model. Because of

---

[1]We use JAGS (an open-source implementation of BUGS) and its R interface `rjags`.

the identical sampling we used for all systems, S_1 is always equal to S_2 in the population (so H_0 is always true), but because of randomness we may incorrectly reject H_0.

Figure 3(a) shows the results. Clearly there is a very high correlation between the two—in fact, the linear correlation is over 0.999. This is actually higher than the correlations reported by Smucker et al. [15] between the t-test and bootstrap and randomization tests. This suggests that our proposed Bayesian approach *is* a valid alternative to the traditional t-test.

The region of the figure we care most about is the region around $p = 0.05$—the standard threshold for rejecting the null hypothesis in traditional testing. Figure 3(b) shows that region. We can see that in this region, the Bayesian probabilities are a bit higher than the t-test p-values, leading to a lower rejection rate. Since H_0 is true by definition in this experiment, that also means a lower false positive rate: 0.05 for the t-test compared to about 0.037 for the Bayesian procedure. It is remarkable how close the two values are, however, considering they are based on totally different distributions: the t-test p-value is the likelihood of the data given H_0 (i.e. $P(y|H_0)$), while our posterior probability is the probability that the null hypothesis is true (i.e. $P(H_0|y)$).

Figure 4(a) shows a comparison of density plots of the posterior distribution of the β parameter for three different

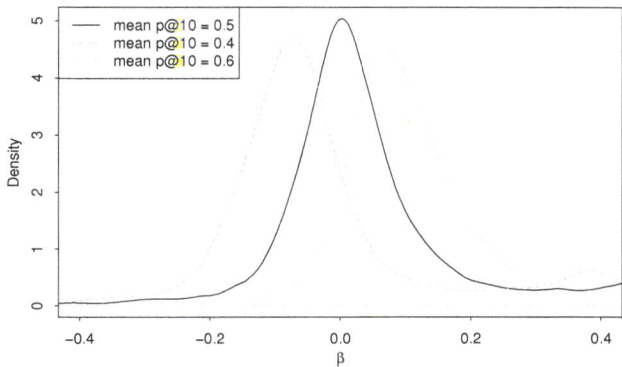

(a) Posterior distributions of β parameters from Model 1.

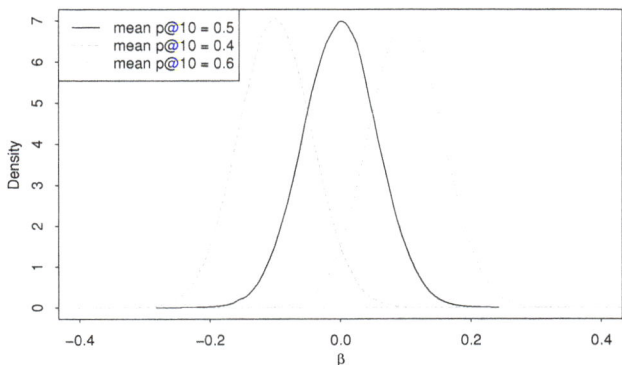

(b) Distributions of β parameters assumed by the t-test.

Figure 4: Comparisons of distributions of β parameters used to make inferences about differences between systems.

simulated systems: one with a mean precision@10 of 0.4, one with a mean precision@10 of 0.5, and one with a mean precision@10 of 0.6. The middle system has a sharper peak to its distribution than the other two, reflecting that its per-topic scores tend to be closer to the mean. All three have heavier tails to the right, because in this particular simulation there turned out to be "easy" topics on which all three systems perform well.

Contrast Figure 4(a) with Figure 4(b), which shows the distributions of the β parameter as assumed by the t-test. While these are much "nicer-looking"—symmetric, with shorter, well-behaved tails and identical caps—they do not reflect the reality of the evaluation data.

4.2 Direct inference about relevance

As discussed in Section 3, effectiveness measures are essentially summaries of individual measurements on documents—that is, summaries of relevance judgments. Instead of testing a hypothesis about a summarization of judgments by an effectiveness measure, the Bayesian framework allows us to model relevance *directly* according to some user model.

Let x_{ijk} be a binary relevance judgment to the document retrieved by system j at rank k for topic i. We will model the judgment as a Bernoulli trial with parameter p_{ij}, essentially a coin flip biased by the system and topic. We will model

p_{ij} using the linear model with a population effect, a system effect, and a topic effect, just as we modeled effectiveness measures y_{ij} above.

Model 3 Bayesian relevance model for evaluation	
$x_{ijk} \sim \text{Bernoulli}(p_{ij})$	
$\text{logit } p_{ij} \sim N(\mu + \beta_j + \alpha_i, \sigma^2)$	$\sigma \sim 1/\sigma$
$\mu \sim N(0, \sigma_\mu^2)$	$\sigma_\mu \sim 1/\sigma_\mu$
$\beta_j \sim N(0, \sigma_\alpha^2)$	$\sigma_\alpha \sim 1/\sigma_\alpha$
$\alpha_i \sim N(0, \sigma_\beta^2)$	$\sigma_\beta \sim 1/\sigma_\beta$

In this model, we have replaced the effectiveness measure y_{ij} with a probability p_{ij}, and by using the logit (log-odds) function on p_{ij} we ensure that it will always have a value between 0 and 1 (thereby correcting a problem with the linear model that it allows y_{ij} to take on values outside that range, something that most IR measures cannot do). Then the relevance judgment x_{ijk} is modeled as a coin flip with probability p_{ij}.

4.2.1 Comparison to t-test and Bayesian t-test

Now we compare this new model to both the traditional t-test and the Bayesian version we introduced in Section 4.1. Since we are now modeling the evaluation at a much finer granularity (individual judgments rather than an effectiveness measure computed over many judgments), we cannot expect that results will be correlated as highly as they were before. We still expect to see a strong correlation though.

This time, to generate a random system, we sample 50 values from a uniform distribution between 0 and 1. These values represent the probability that a randomly-chosen document is relevant to that topic; we then generate the actual binary relevance judgments by flipping a coin with that probability. For each topic we generate 10 random relevance judgments, for a total of 500 per simulated system.

Again, the null hypothesis is true by definition, but it may be falsely rejected by any of the three models due to randomness. We will again compare p-values to marginal posterior probabilities as well as rejection rates by each procedure.

Figure 5(a) compares t-test p-values and marginal posterior probabilities from Model 3. Figure 5(b) compares marginal posterior probabilities from Models 2 and 3. In both cases the correlation is very high (over 0.98), though Model 3 is more conservative in its estimates than either the t-test or Model 2. This is in part because it needs to estimate many more parameters than the other two: while Model 2 has $O(NM)$ parameters, Model 3 has $O(NMK)$ parameters to estimate. In this case, its greater conservatism means its false positive rate is also much lower at only 0.002 (on the other hand, this means its false negative rate will likely be much higher—we defer this to Section 5, where there is a possibility of false negatives).

4.2.2 Hidden effectiveness measures

As discussed, Model 3 does not include an effectiveness measure; it models document relevance directly. But, as we previously argued [2], effectiveness measures emerge naturally as a side effect of using the model.

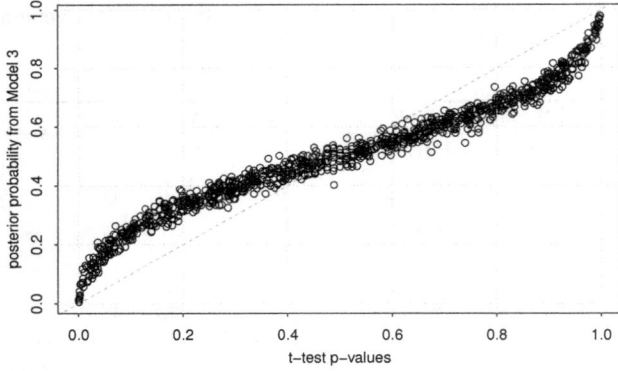

(a) t-test p-values versus posterior probabilities from Model 3.

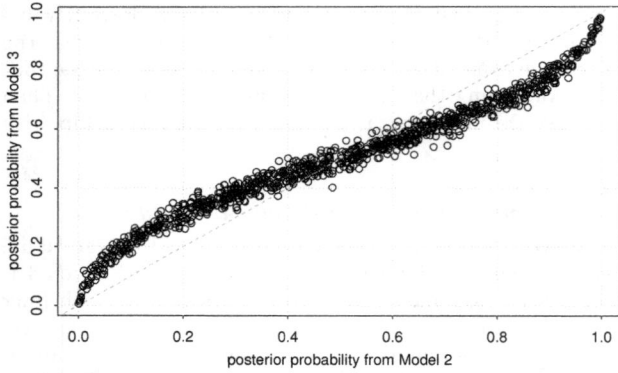

(b) Posterior probabilities from Model 2 vs. Model 3.

Figure 5: Comparisons between t-test p-values and posterior probabilities for simulated systems.

The likelihood function for Model 3 is:

$$L_{M_3} = \prod_{i=1}^{N} \prod_{j=1}^{M} \prod_{k=1}^{K} P(x_{ijk}|\mu, \alpha_i, \beta_j)$$

Since x_{ijk} is a coin flip, its probability density is $p_{ij}^{x_{ijk}}(1 - p_{ij})^{x_{ijk}}$. Then the likelihood is:

$$L_{M_3} = \prod_{i=1}^{N} \prod_{j=1}^{M} \prod_{k=1}^{K} p_{ij}^{x_{ijk}}(1 - p_{ij})^{1-x_{ijk}}$$

The value of p_{ij} that maximizes L_{M_3} is exactly the precision at rank K of system j on topic i. In words, since x_{ijk} is the result of a coin flip, and the best estimate for the probability that a coin flip comes up heads is the historical rate of observing heads, and the historical rate of observing heads for system j on topic i is its observed precision at rank K for that topic, then p_{ij} should be precision at K. The only question is how close it is possible to get to that ideal when p_{ij} is determined in the model by other parameters such as μ, β_j, α_i and various σs.

Figure 6 compares actual precision at 10 to the p_{ij} estimate of precision at 10 for one simulated system. The correlation is only slightly less than perfect due to jitter in estimates, which is expected from using MCMC sampling to fit the model. Also, the estimates themselves are not

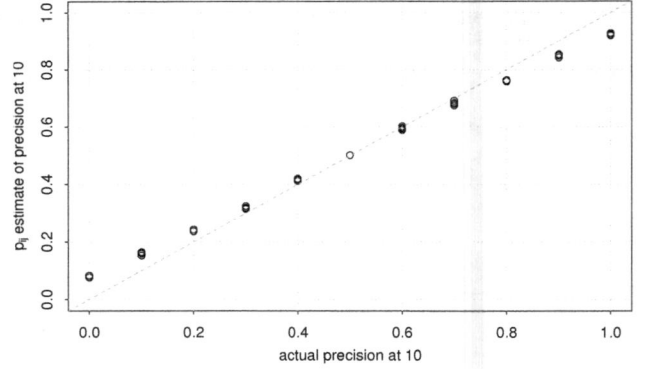

Figure 6: Comparison of actual precision at 10 to estimated values of precision at 10 from Model 3.

perfect; they are high at the low end of precision and low at the high end of precision. This is because the priors in the model act to regularize estimates, pulling them closer to the mean. The "step function" property of precision is still clearly visible however.

So precision at K is a natural consequence of building a proper evaluation model for the type of data we have in information retrieval. But precision at K is hardly the only measure IR researchers are interested in. Is it possible to derive other measures from this model?

This is where the user models described in Section 2.1 come into play. Instead of modeling x_{ijk} as a Bernoulli trial, suppose we model it as a Bernoulli trial *and* a probability that a user would encounter the document at rank k according to some user model:

$$P(x_{ijk}) = p_{ij} \times u_k$$

Here u_k will be defined as the probability that a user sees the document at rank k. Using RBP's geometric model of browsing described in Section 2.1, we set $u_k = \theta^{k-1}(1 - \theta)$, where θ is a fixed value chosen by the researcher ($\theta = 0.2, 0.5, 0.8$ are common values).

Then the likelihood function is:

$$L_{M_4} = \prod_{i=1}^{N} \prod_{j=1}^{M} \prod_{k=1}^{K} p_{ij}^{x_{ijk} \times u_k}(1 - p_{ij})^{(1-x_{ijk}) \times u_k}$$

This function is maximized when p_{ij} is equal to the RBP of system j on topic i (assuming K large enough to compute RBP). To see this, we take the log and perform some basic algebra:

$$\log L_{M_4} = \sum_i \sum_j \left(\log p_{ij} \sum_k x_{ijk} u_k + \log(1 - p_{ij}) \sum_k (1 - x_{ijk}) u_k\right)$$

Then $\sum_k x_{ijk} u_k = \sum_k x_{ijk} \theta^{k-1}(1 - \theta) = RBP_{ij}$, so:

$$\log L_{M_4} = \sum_i \sum_j RBP_{ij} \log p_{ij} + (1 - RBP_{ij}) \log(1 - p_{ij})$$

Functions of the form $x \log y + (1 - x) \log(1 - y)$ are maximized when $x = y$, so L_{M_4} is maximized when $p_{ij} = RBP_{ij}$. This essentially proves the assertion that p_{ij} emerges as an effectiveness measure.

Since p_{ij} depends on μ, β_j, α_i, and variance parameters, the fitted values will not necessarily exactly match the corresponding RBPs; they will only be estimates. Figure 7

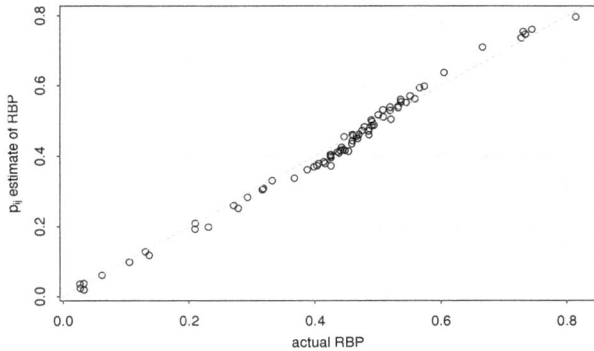

Figure 7: Comparison of actual RBP values and estimates produced by fitting Model 4.

compares actual values of RBP to p_{ij} estimates; clearly the estimates are very close.

We conclude this section with Model 4, in which a user browsing model is explicitly incorporated into Model 3. The difference is that x_{ijk} is drawn from a quasi-binomial distribution of size 1, which means that there is a Bernoulli trial that, when successful, returns the probability u_k that the user encounters the document at rank k. The values u_k must sum to 1 over the range $k = 1$ to K.

Model 4 Bayesian user+relevance model for evaluation

$x_{ijk} \sim$ Quasi-Binomial$(1, p_{ij}, u_k)$	$\Sigma_{k=1}^{K} u_k = 1$
logit $p_{ij} \sim N(\mu + \beta_j + \alpha_i, \sigma^2)$	$\sigma \sim 1/\sigma$
$\mu \sim N(0, \sigma_\mu^2)$	$\sigma_\mu \sim 1/\sigma_\mu$
$\beta_j \sim N(0, \sigma_\alpha^2)$	$\sigma_\alpha \sim 1/\sigma_\alpha$
$\alpha_i \sim N(0, \sigma_\beta^2)$	$\sigma_\beta \sim 1/\sigma_\beta$

This model is not restricted to RBP; it works for any measure that can be defined as a sum over a binary relevance judgment times a probability of a user encountering rank k.

4.2.3 Graded relevance judgments

Models 3 and 4 both assume binary relevance judgments. Graded judgments are now widely considered practically necessary for web search and other tasks. A method that cannot adapt to graded judgments will not find wide use.

Fortunately, we can incorporate graded judgments fairly easily by modeling x_{ijk} with a multinomial distribution. Let $\mathcal{G}$ be a set of numeric grades, e.g. $\mathcal{G} = \{0, 1, 2, 3, 4\}$. Let $x_{ijkg} = 1$ if the relevance of x_{ijk} is grade g and 0 otherwise. Then x_{ijk} has a multinomial distribution with size 1 and $|\mathcal{G}|$ probability parameters, one for each grade. In our model, those probabilities will be a function of p_{ij}, the user model u_k, and a probabilistic model of the gain of the grade g.

Robertson et al. [13] introduced a user model for graded judgments that essentially converts grades to binary judgments by defining a probability that a user considers grade g the *minimum* grade required for the document to be relevant. We use a similar idea, defining a probability mass function $P_{\text{gain}}(x = g) \propto 2^g - 1$ if x has grade g, and 0 otherwise. Thus if there are 5 grades numbered 0 through 4,

and a document $x_{ijk} = 4$, then $P_{\text{gain}}(x_{ijk} = 4) \propto 15$ while $P_{\text{gain}}(x_{ijk} = 1) = P_{\text{gain}}(x_{ijk} = 2) = P_{\text{gain}}(x_{ijk} = 3) = 0$. Normalizing by $2^{|\mathcal{G}|} - 1 - (|\mathcal{G}| + 1)$ makes it a probability distribution.

If we use $u_k \propto 1/\log_2(k + 1)$ and $P_{\text{gain}}(x = g)$ as defined above, then the value of p_{ij} that maximizes likelihood is proportional to the DCG of system j on topic i. It is straightforward to include an "ideal" or maximum possible DCG in u_k to obtain nDCG.

For the sake of simplicity, in the full model specification we will decompose the multinomial distribution into $|\mathcal{G}|$ quasi-binomial distributions, one for each grade. These are like the ones in Model 4, except now including a gain probability as well as a user browsing probability.

Model 5 Bayesian user+graded relevance model

$x_{ijkg} \sim$ Quasi-Binomial$(1, p_{ij},$	$\Sigma_{k=1}^{K} u_k = 1$
$\qquad u_k \cdot P_{\text{gain}}(x_{ij} = g))$	$\Sigma_{g \in \mathcal{G}} P_{\text{gain}}(x_{ij} = g) = 1$
logit $p_{ij} \sim N(\mu + \beta_j + \alpha_i, \sigma^2)$	$\sigma \sim 1/\sigma$
$\mu \sim N(0, \sigma_\mu^2)$	$\sigma_\mu \sim 1/\sigma_\mu$
$\beta_j \sim N(0, \sigma_\alpha^2)$	$\sigma_\alpha \sim 1/\sigma_\alpha$
$\alpha_i \sim N(0, \sigma_\beta^2)$	$\sigma_\beta \sim 1/\sigma_\beta$

Once again, it is possible to write out the full likelihood function and show that it is maximized when p_{ij} is equal to the nDCG@10 of system j on topic i (assuming all distributions are properly normalized). We do not show it only due to space limitations.

5. EXPERIMENTS ON TREC DATA

Our proposal in this work is that Bayesian models are a powerful alternative to traditional tools for evaluation and statistical analysis such as the t-test. We cannot prove that Bayesian versions are superior: empirically, there is no gold standard against which we can compare the inferences from different approaches to show that one is more accurate on average; theoretically, both are valid. We can only show when the two approaches agree and when they disagree, and argue from principles about the relative cost of the disagreements.

5.1 Experimental set-up

Our data consists of retrieval systems submitted to TREC tracks over the years. We focus on three TREC tracks:

- the TREC-8 (TREC 1999) ad hoc track, with 129 submitted runs and over 80,000 binary relevance judgments to 50 topics;

- the TREC 2004 Robust track, with 110 submitted runs and over 310,000 graded relevance judgments (on a three-grade scale) to 249 topics;

- the TREC 2012 Web track, with 48 submitted runs and over 16,000 graded relevance judgments (on a five-grade scale) to 50 topics.

This gives us a variety of tasks, topics, corpora, participants, and relevance grade systems to work with.

In all of our analyses below we test a one-sided hypothesis about two systems. The null hypothesis is that the system

S_1 is better than S_2 by some measure.

$$H_0 : S_1 \leq S_2$$
$$H_a : S_1 > S_2$$

The one-sided null hypothesis is generally the hypothesis practitioners are interested in, and we argue it is more "natural" than the two-sided point null hypothesis of $S_1 = S_2$. We test these hypotheses with three measures: precision at rank 10, rank-biased precision (RBP) with $\theta = 0.8$, and nDCG at rank 10. We compare the p-value for rejecting H_0 to the Bayesian posterior probability of H_0 being false.

We use JAGS (Just Another Gibbs Sampler, an open-source implementation of BUGS for MCMC sampling to compute posteriors in Bayesian models) and its R interface `rjags` to implement the models we describe above. JAGS allows a user to write a "model file", a programmatic description of the model which is parsed into a full simulation program. `rjags` executes the simulation, computing posterior distributions conditional on data objects in R. All of our model files and R code can be downloaded from `http://ir.cis.udel.edu/~carteret/downloads.html`.

Because it requires simulation, Bayesian testing is much more computationally-intensive than classical testing. Rather than test all pairs of runs from each collection, we sampled a subset of 1,000 pairs to test. For the MCMC sampling, we used a burn-in period of 10,000 samples followed by 50,000 samples to estimate the posterior.

5.2 Evaluation

We are looking for the following:

- high correlations between the three approaches (t-test p-values, Model 1 posterior probabilities, Models 2–5 posterior probabilities);
- high agreement about "significance" between the three approaches;
- potentially novel conclusions about systems or collections of systems.

To evaluate the first, we will measure linear correlation between t-test p-values and posterior probability distributions. Even though these represent different things, they should correlate highly as they did for simulated data.

To evaluate the second, we will measure the proportion of pairs for which approaches agree about "significance", i.e. the proportion for which the t-test rejects H_0 and the Bayesian model posterior probability of H_0 is less than 0.05. Again, these are very different things; in fact, Bayesian inference generally does not make statements about "significance". Nevertheless, we should see high agreement.

The third is highly subjective. We will try to identify some pairs of systems for which the Bayesian approach, particularly Model 3, suggests something about the systems that is not suggested by the t-test, or some property of the collection and/or measure that causes the resulting relationships.

5.3 Model comparisons

5.3.1 Classical t-test vs. Model 2

Figure 8 compares t-test p-values to posterior probabilities from the Bayesian linear model we presented in Section 4.1, Model 2. We elected to show three comparisons:

TREC-8 using precision@10, Robust 2004 using RBP (converting the graded judgments to binary), and Web 2012 using nDCG@10 (keeping the graded judgments). In all three cases the linear correlation is 1. The agreement about significance is 0.99 for all three, though all disagreements reflect cases where the t-test found significance while the Bayesian posterior probability was slightly above 0.05.

There is one noticeable outlier: a pair of systems in the Web 2012 collection for which the t-test p-value is around 0.42, while the posterior probability is close to 0.5. This is a case where the two systems have skewed evaluation results, performing very well on a handful of topics but poorly on the rest. The t-test is unable to capture the distribution effectively, so we believe the Model 2 result to be more accurate in this case.

5.3.2 Classical t-test vs. Models 3, 4, and 5

Figure 9 compares p-values from the one-sided paired t-test to posterior probabilities from the Bayesian direct inference models we presented in Section 4.2, Models 3, 4, and 5. We chose six combinations of corpus and evaluation measure to present.

We now see that tailoring the model to the particular data we have in IR and a particular user model has a stronger effect on inferences. The posterior probabilities are much more conservative than the t-test p-values. In addition, the collection and measure we use both have some effect on the relationship: while TREC-8 has a relatively tight relationship (Figs. 9(a), 9(d)), Web 2012 is more dispersed (Figs. 9(c), 9(f)), and Robust 2004 is even more dispersed (Figs. 9(b), 9(e)). Likewise, precision@10 results in a tighter relationship than RBP, which in turn is tighter than nDCG.

This is likely due to two factors: first, that each successive measure has more parameters to estimate and therefore more noise; and second, that TREC-8 is more homogeneous across both topics and participant systems than Robust 2004 (with more variability across topics) and Web 2012 (with more variability across systems). These are not factors that could be revealed in a simple t-test or linear model fit.

Despite the more conservative estimates and wider dispersion, the correlations are still very high: the lowest is the 0.91 correlation for Web 2012 with nDCG@10. Agreement about significance is high as well, with almost all disagreements due to our model producing a posterior probability higher than 0.05 while the t-test p-value was below 0.05.

5.3.3 Model 2 vs. Models 3, 4, and 5

Figure 10 compares posterior probabilities from the Bayesian linear Model 2 to the direct inference models we presented in Section 4.2, Models 3, 4, and 5. We chose the same six combinations of corpus and evaluation measure to present.

Since the correlation between the t-test and Model 2 is so high, it is not surprising that these figures are not substantially different from those in Figure 9. We would like to point out the three outliers in Fig. 10(a), also present in Fig. 9(a), which are particularly surprising because the TREC-8 precision@10 relationship is otherwise so close. Like the outlier in Figure 8(c), these are cases where the t-test was unable to fit the data well, so we believe the Bayesian result to be more accurate.

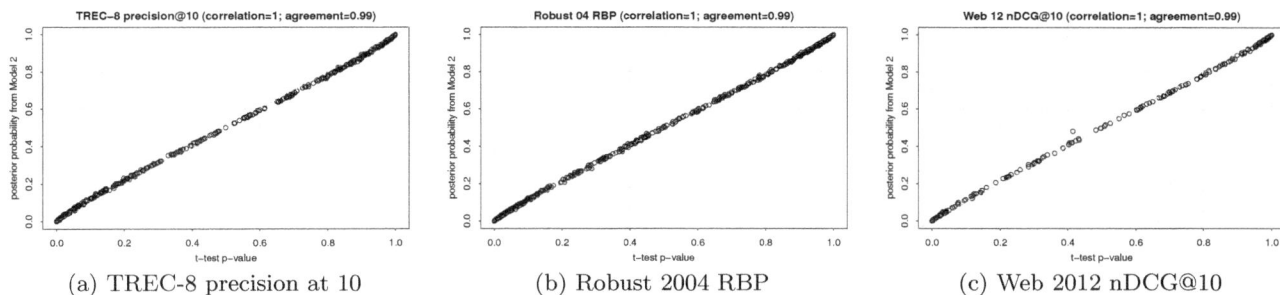

(a) TREC-8 precision at 10   (b) Robust 2004 RBP   (c) Web 2012 nDCG@10

Figure 8: Comparison of t-test p-values and posterior probabilities from Model 2 for three different collections and three different evaluation measures.

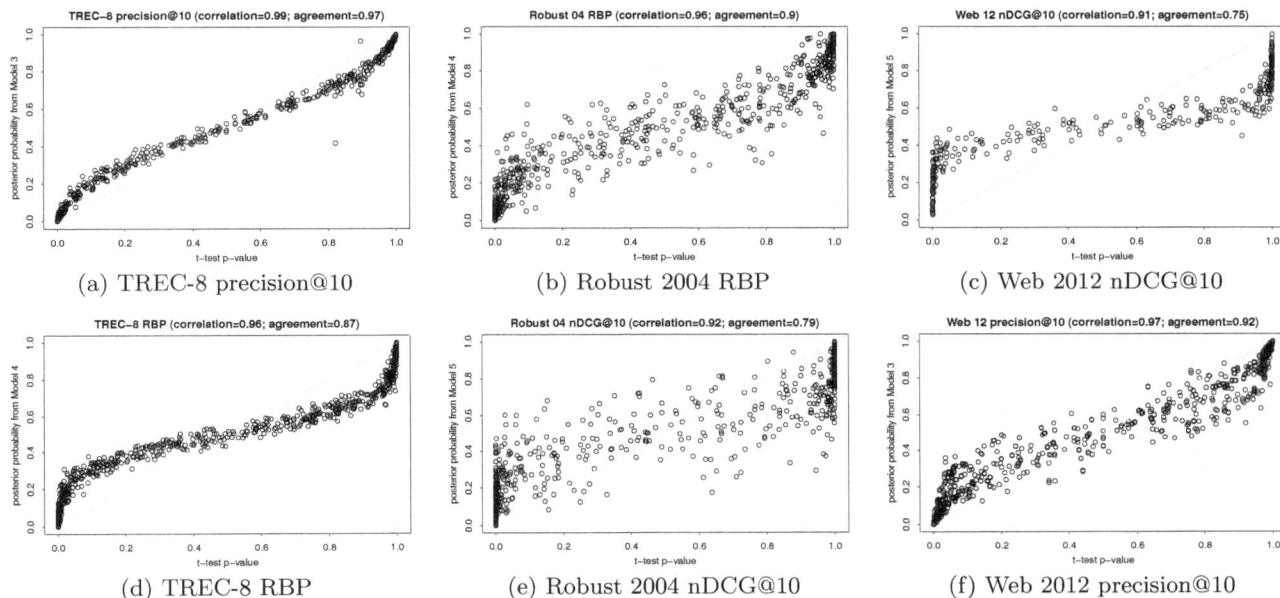

(a) TREC-8 precision@10   (b) Robust 2004 RBP   (c) Web 2012 nDCG@10

(d) TREC-8 RBP   (e) Robust 2004 nDCG@10   (f) Web 2012 precision@10

Figure 9: Comparison of t-test p-values and posterior probabilities from Models 3, 4, and 5 for three different collections. Model 3 captures precision@10, Model 4 RBP, and Model 5 nDCG@10.

5.4 Failures of the t-test

We were able to take our observations about the outliers described above and simulate a family of runs for which the t-test consistently does not match our approach. We generated random systems that performed very poorly on 45 topics and very well on 5, then compared t-test p-values to the probabilities from our Model 2. This time we found *no* correlation between the two, in stark contrast to the very high correlations seen above. This strongly suggests that there are cases that the t-test cannot handle due to its assumptions (e.g. Fig. 4(a)).

6. CONCLUSION

In this paper, we have extended our previous model-based framework [2] for testing differences in IR systems with both deeper theory about how it incorporates user models and naturally produces evaluation measures as well as to the important practical case of graded relevance judgments. Additionally, we have presented more empirical evidence—with simulated data and in TREC collections—of its similarities to and differences from the t-test.

The framework sits alongside standard hypothesis tests like the t-test and the Wilcoxon signed-rank test, but also other general techniques used to create hypothesis tests such as the bootstrap or randomization. We have shown that the inferences from our model correlate well with inferences from the t-test; since it is known that the t-test correlates close to perfectly with bootstrap and randomization tests [15] based on similar assumptions, we can conclude our methods correlate equally well with those.

But while those are more general techniques than the t-test, it is still unclear how to adapt them to the specific nature of IR discussed in Section 3. Relevance judgments cannot simply be randomly reordered or resampled as effectiveness measures can be. But they can be modeled—and as IR researchers we know a great deal about modeling relevance! In this work we only modeled them as a function of a generalized system effect, a topic effect, and a user model, but the framework is general enough to incorporate other factors. In particular, by decomposing the system effect into

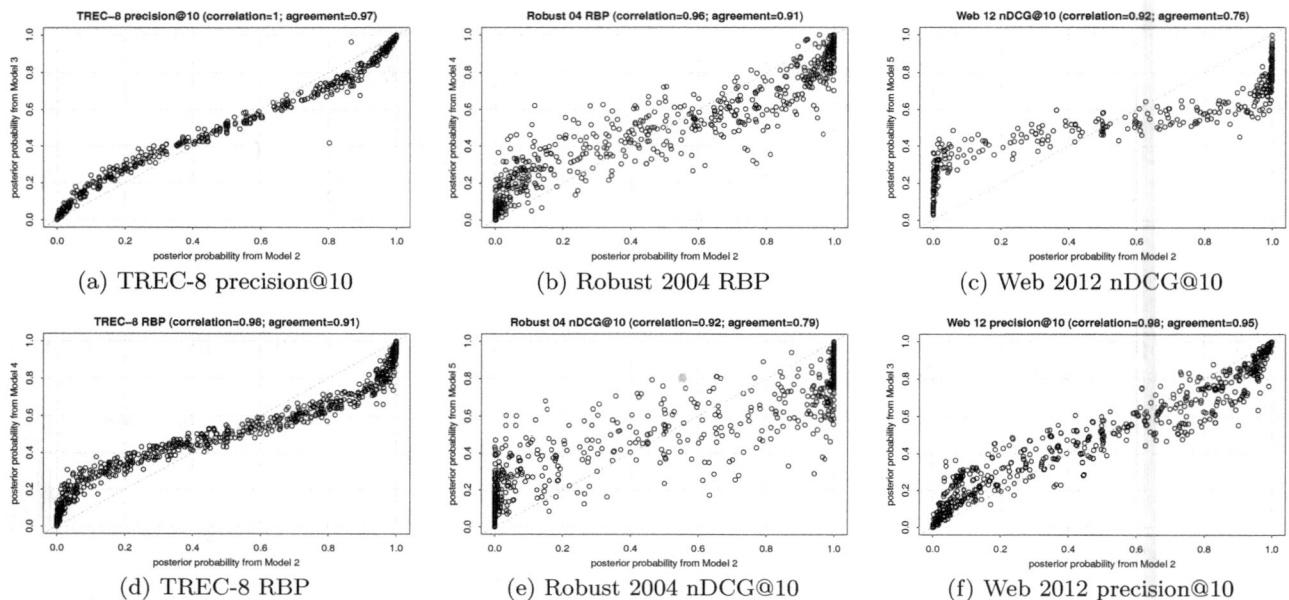

Figure 10: Comparison of posterior probabilities from Model 2 and posterior probabilities from Models 3, 4, and 5 for three different collections. Model 3 captures precision@10, Model 4 RBP, and Model 5 nDCG@10.

multiple factors representing different system components (such as the tokenizer, the stemmer, the retrieval function, etc), we could potentially learn a great deal about the effect of these components on user-perceived relevance.

Acknowledgments This work was supported in part by the National Science Foundation (NSF) under grant number IIS-1350799. Any opinions, findings and conclusions or recommendations expressed in this material are the authors' and do not necessarily reflect those of the sponsor.

7. REFERENCES

[1] Ben Carterette. On rank correlation and the distance between rankings. In *Proceedings of the 32nd Annual International ACM SIGIR Conference on Research and Development in Information Retrieval*, pages 436–443, 2009.

[2] Ben Carterette. Model-based inference about IR systems. In *Proceedings of ICTIR*, 2011.

[3] Ben Carterette. System effectiveness, user models, and user utility: A conceptual framework for investigation. In *Proceedings of SIGIR*, 2011.

[4] Ben Carterette. Multiple testing in statistical analysis of systems-based information retrieval experiments. *ACM TOIS*, 30(1), 2012.

[5] Olivier Chapelle, Donald Metzler, Ya Zhang, and Pierre Grinspan. Expceted reciprocal rank for graded relevance. In *Proceedings of the Annual International ACM Conference on Knowledge and Information Management (CIKM)*, 2009.

[6] Charles L. A. Clarke, Maheedhar Kolla, Gordon V. Cormack, Olga Vechtomova, Azin Ashkan, Stefan Büttcher, and Ian MacKinnon. Novelty and diversity in information retrieval evaluation. In *Proceedings of SIGIR '08*, pages 659–666.

[7] Andrew Gelman, John B. Carlin, Hal S. Stern, and Donald B. Rubin. *Bayesian Data Analysis*. Chapman & Hall/CRC, 2004.

[8] Kalervo Jarvelin and Jaana Kekalainen. Cumulated gain-based evaluation of ir techniques. *ACM Trans. Inf. Syst.*, 20(4):422–446, 2002.

[9] Gaya K. Jayasinghe, William Webber, Mark Sanderson, Lasitha S. Dharmasena, and J. Shane Culpepper. Evaluating non-deterministic retrieval systems. In *Proc. SIGIR*, 2014.

[10] Alistair Moffat and Justin Zobel. Rank-biased precision for measurement of retrieval effectiveness. *ACM Trans. Info. Sys.*, 27(1):1–27, 2008.

[11] John F. Monahan. *A Primer on Linear Models*. Chapman and Hall/CRC, 1st edition, 2008.

[12] Stephen E. Robertson. A new interpretation of average precision. In *Proceedings of the 31st Annual International ACM SIGIR Conference on Research and Development in Information Retrieval*, pages 689–690, 2008.

[13] Stephen E. Robertson, Evangelos Kanoulas, and Emine Yilmaz. Extending average precision to graded relevance judgments. In *Proceedings of the 33rd International ACM SIGIR Conference on Research and Development in Information Retrieval*, pages 603–610, 2010.

[14] Tetsuya Sakai. Evaluating evaluation metrics based on the bootstrap. In *SIGIR '06: Proceedings of the 29th annual international ACM SIGIR conference on Research and development in information retrieval*, pages 525–532, New York, NY, USA, 2006. ACM.

[15] Mark Smucker, James Allan, and Ben Carterette. A comparison of statistical significance tests for information retrieval evaluation. In *Proceedings of CIKM*, pages 623–632, 2007.

[16] W. N. Venables and B. D. Ripley. *Modern Applied Statistics with S*. Springer, 4th edition, 2002.

[17] Emine Yilmaz, Milad Shokouhi, Nick Craswell, and Stephen Robertson. Expected browsing utility for web search evaluation. In *Proceedings of the ACM International Conference on Knowledge and Information Management*, 2010.

[18] Yuye Zhang, Laurence A. Park, and Alistair Moffat. Click-based evidence for decaying weight distributions in search effectiveness metrics. *Inf. Retr.*, 13:46–69, February 2010.

[19] Justin Zobel. How reliable are the results of large-scale information retrieval experiments? In *Proceedings of SIGIR*, pages 307–314, 1998.

Transferring Learning To Rank Models for Web Search

Craig Macdonald[1], B. Taner Dinçer[2], Iadh Ounis[1]

[1] University of Glasgow, Glasgow G12 8QQ, UK
[2] Dept of Statistics & Computer Engineering, Mugla University, Mugla, Turkey

{craig.macdonald, iadh.ounis}@glasgow.ac.uk[1], dtaner@mu.edu.tr[2]

ABSTRACT

Learning to rank techniques provide mechanisms for combining document feature values into learned models that produce effective rankings. However, issues concerning the transferability of learned models between different corpora or subsets of the same corpus are not yet well understood. For instance, is the importance of different feature sets consistent between subsets of a corpus, or whether a learned model obtained on a small subset of the corpus effectively transfer to the larger corpus? By formulating our experiments around two null hypotheses, in this work, we apply a full-factorial experiment design to empirically investigate these questions using the ClueWeb09 and ClueWeb12 corpora, combined with queries from the TREC Web track. Among other observations, our experiments reveal that ClueWeb09 remains an effective choice of training corpus for learning effective models for ClueWeb12, and also that the importance of query independent features varies among the ClueWeb09 and ClueWeb12 corpora. In doing so, this work contributes an important study into the transferability of learning to rank models, as well as empirically-derived best practices for effective retrieval on the ClueWeb12 corpus.

Categories and Subject Descriptors: H.3.3 [Information Storage & Retrieval]: Information Search & Retrieval
Keywords: Learning-to-rank, Web Search

1. INTRODUCTION

Learning to rank [18], a means of utilising machine learning techniques in information retrieval (IR), provides a way to combine various features - such as query dependent weighting models and query independent document features - into effective *learned models*, based on learning from existing queries and associated relevance judgments. For the purposes of effective retrieval, a learned model can then be used to effectively (re)rank the documents retrieved for any given new query, by measuring the same features on the given query and the retrieved documents [22].

A learning to rank technique is typically trained on the same corpus for which the learned model is to be applied.

However, there are situations when there may be a need to *transfer* the learned model to another (e.g. newer) corpus, or if the learned model obtained from a *subset* of the target corpus can be applied on the target corpus. Both situations arise within participations to the TREC Web track [5]: for example, do learned models obtained when training upon the category B subsets generalise to the larger category A sets of the ClueWeb09 or ClueWeb12 corpora; orthogonally, do learned models obtained using ClueWeb09 transfer to the newer ClueWeb12? Next, the features that can be employed by a learning to rank technique can vary greatly in kind, as well as in number (e.g. 44 query dependent and independent features are used by the LETOR datasets [19], while the MSLR datasets released by Microsoft[1] have 136 features per document). Hence, it is important to understand the role of the types of features present in the learned model, and how these learned models encapsulating different features transfer between corpora.

In this study, we consider a state-of-the-art learning to rank technique, namely LambdaMART [3], in comparison with another technique based on linear learning for experimental purposes [24], and examine two null hypotheses of interest through an empirical study conducted upon the ClueWeb09 and ClueWeb12 document corpora, as used by the TREC Web tracks 2009-2012 and 2013-2014.

Indeed, this paper contributes the first large-scale study in transfer learning for Web search, by means of a full-factorial experiment design, to provide empirically supported observations concerning three aspects: within-corpus training, cross-corpus training, and choice of feature set. Among many results, we show the importance of query independent quality features for the ClueWeb09 corpus – in contrast to ClueWeb12 – which is due to the high prevalence of spam documents within the older ClueWeb09. Hence, our experiments and analysis provide new insights for researchers and practitioners into the transfer of learning to rank models between corpora and how the corpus used to train/test can impact upon the choice of effective features (c.f. field-based query dependent weighting model features), while also providing empirically derived best practices for effective retrieval upon the TREC ClueWeb12 corpus.

The remainder of this paper is structured as follows: In Section 2, we introduce the necessary background concerning learning to rank; Section 3 defines our experimental setup and evaluation methodology; Our experimental results are described in Section 4; We provide concluding remarks in Section 5.

ICTIR'15, September 27–30, 2015, Northampton, MA, USA.
© 2015 ACM. ISBN 978-1-4503-3794-6/15/10 ...$15.00.
DOI: http://dx.doi.org/10.1145/2808194.2809463.

---

[1] http://research.microsoft.com/en-us/projects/mslr/

2. BACKGROUND

Learning to rank techniques have become an oft-deployed technology that can combine many feature values into an effective ranking of documents. The output of the (offline) learning phase is a *learned model*, which defines how feature values should be combined to make the final predicted relevance scores for each ranked document. Learned models may take the form of the weights for a linear combination of feature values (e.g. AFS [24]) or of regression trees defined on feature values (e.g. GBRT [33] or LambdaMART [3]). When ranking documents for an unseen query, the learned model is applied on the computed feature values to produce the final ranking of documents for the query.

The *candidate document set*[2] is an important aspect during learning to rank: typically, a single standard weighting model selects a number of top-ranked documents for each query to later re-rank. These documents then have feature values computed. Liu [18] suggests that a single standard weighting model such as BM25 is sufficient, but not the most effective, while Macdonald et al. [22] showed that the size of the candidate set should approach 5000 documents for ranking Web documents, and for mixed types of information needs it should not consider anchor text. Dang et al. [10] showed that applying proximity to create the candidate set could improve effectiveness. Finally, we note that the candidate set should be created using an identical ranking approach during both offline learning and online ranking - this prevents selection bias, which can occur if relevant documents are artificially inserted into the candidate set used for learning [22, 26].

Transfer learning – the act of transferring knowledge from a *source domain* to a *target domain* – has been investigated within machine learning (e.g. [28] for an overview). Different scenarios exist [29]: *feature transfer* refers to the scenario when there is not full overlap between the features in the source and target domains; on the other hand, when feature sets do overlap, *instance-based transfer* allows training data from the source and target domains to train a learner for the target domain. Techniques (e.g. [9, 15]) in the latter scenario focus on the appropriate selection and combining of training instances from source and target domains to create appropriate models. Instance-based transfer techniques are not naturally applicable to learning-to-rank scenarios. Indeed, the effective learning-to-rank techniques classically encompass a listwise component, and hence selecting at the level of instances (documents) within the candidate sets for a query may hinder accurate calculation of listwise loss functions. For this reason, our study addresses the direct transfer of learning-to-rank models. Later, in Section 4, we describe and use a transfer learning technique that is directly applicable to learning-to-rank. We therefore leave the adaptation of instance-based transfer techniques for future work.

Relatedly, to encourage research within transfer learning for learning to rank, the Yahoo! 2011 Learning to Rank Challenge included a transfer learning task. This tasked participants to examine how different learning to rank techniques could be trained given a large amount of training data on one corpus, and a lesser amount on a different *target* corpus. In particular, the challenge provided two datasets, one from a US sample of the web, and one from an Asian sample with less training data [4]. In contrast, in this work, we examine the extent to which a learned model can be effec-

tively transferred between different samples of the English web, in particular, between smaller and larger corpus subsets, as well as between older and newer Web corpora, when both are represented using identical feature sets. Additionally, the impact on the importance of different types of feature between the corpora are examined. In the next section, we pose two null hypotheses that we address through later experimentation using the ClueWeb09 and ClueWeb12 corpora and 250 queries from the TREC 2009-2013 Web track campaigns.

3. RESEARCH METHODOLOGY & EXPERIMENTAL SETUP

Our experiments are structured around the the general problem of transferability within learning to rank, namely how learned models transfer within different subsets of a corpus, and across corpora. We address these research investigations through experiments with systematic variations of dependent variables, as detailed below. For inferential purposes, the research investigations are formulated into two null hypotheses that follow common practices within the learning to rank community. By showing that these two hypotheses – defined below – can be rejected, we contribute new knowledge and understanding of the deployment of learning to rank.

Firstly, we investigate how learned models can be transferred between training and test corpora, as follows:

NULL HYPOTHESIS 1. *The retrieval effectiveness of a learning to rank technique that is trained on the target corpus will be higher than the retrieval effectiveness of the same technique when it is trained on a corpus other than the target corpus.*

This null hypothesis will allow to determine whether different forms of "other" corpora can provide more effective learned models than can be be obtained from the target corpus itself. In particular, we investigate two types of "other" corpus: (i) a subset of the target Web corpus – which we call *within-corpus* training, and (ii) an older corpora also sampled from the larger Web, which we call *cross-corpus* training.

Moreover, we address the importance of feature sets for an effective learned model, and how this relates to the training and test corpus within a transfer learning scenario, formulated as follows:

NULL HYPOTHESIS 2. *The contribution of different feature sets to the retrieval effectiveness of a learning to rank technique are uniform across corpora.*

In posing this null hypothesis, we argue that the default scenario for a practitioner faced with a new corpus (without training data) would be to consider that the importance of different types of features within a learned model for Web search would be consistent across corpora, and hence they would train only on the old corpus. By empirically investigating this null hypothesis, we can ascertain whether the importance of feature sets change between corpora, and how this affects the effectiveness of the resulting learned models.

In the context of the above null hypotheses, we consider the systematic variation of four factors: (1) training corpus, (2) test (target) corpus, (3) learning to rank technique, and (4) feature set. We apply a *full-factorial* design – i.e. testing all combinations of factors – in order to collect empirical

---

[2]Also known as the sample in [18, 22].

Table 1: Factors and corresponding levels considered in our experiment.

Factors	Levels	Code
Training	ClueWeb09 Cat A	**cw09a**
	ClueWeb09 Cat B	**cw09b**
	ClueWeb12 Cat A	**cw12a**
	ClueWeb12 Cat B	**cw12b**
Test	ClueWeb09 Cat A	**CW09A**
	ClueWeb09 Cat B	**CW09B**
	ClueWeb12 Cat A	**CW12A**
	ClueWeb12 Cat B	**CW12B**
LTR Method	LambdaMART	**LM**
	AFS (linear)	**LIN**
Feature Sets	Weighting Models	**WM**
	Field Models	**FM**
	QI Features	**QI**
	Proximity	**PX**

data as parsimoniously as possible while providing sufficient information to make dependable estimates of the effects of the four factors on retrieval effectiveness. To systematically vary the factors, we assign each factor a discrete set of levels as given in Table 1. The instantiations of these factors are explained in the remainder of this section.

Full factorial designs measure response variables (in our case ERR@20, the official measure for recent TREC Web track campaigns, as per [5]) using every treatment (combination of the factor levels). A full factorial design for n factors with $N_1, ..., N_n$ levels requires $N_1 \times \cdots \times N_n$ experimental runs - one for each treatment. Note that we follow an ablation approach when factoring out the levels of feature sets, in that groups of features are *removed* from a total of 64 commonly applied query dependent and query independent features. For example, NoQI denotes All features minus the query independent features. Therefore, there are 160 combinations of the factor levels in total.

3.1 Corpus and Topics

Our experiments are conducted using open test collections created within the context of the Text REtrieval Conference (TREC). In particular, while various learning to rank datasets exist (such as LETOR, MSLR & Yahoo! Learning to Rank Challenge), we build our own learning-to-rank datasets based upon the TREC test collections for several reasons: the chosen TREC test collections represent identical retrieval tasks upon two different large English Web corpora (and subsets thereof); the features are identically formulated between the different corpora; and finally the features can be explained within the paper[3].

Specifically, we use the ClueWeb09 and ClueWeb12 corpora of Web documents, used by the TREC Web tracks between 2009-2012 [5] and 2013 [6], respectively. In particular, we use two subsets of each corpus: the full category A, which contains all documents identified as being written in English - this is about 500M for ClueWeb09 and 730M for ClueWeb12; and category B, which contains a smaller number of English documents. In particular, the category B subset of ClueWeb09 represents a *controlled* subset of the category A corpus - similar to the first tier index of a com-

mercial Web search engine [32] - in that the 50M selected documents exhibit higher crawl priority. Indeed documents identified earlier within Web crawls are more likely to be relevant because of their higher quality [27]. On the other hand, the category B of ClueWeb12 is built to be a *random* sample, with no higher likelihood of including relevant documents. It is built by selecting every 17th document from the category A corpus, and is ∼7% of the size of category A. As will be seen in Section 4, these contrasting methodologies for the category B subsets impacts upon the results obtained for within-corpus transfer.

For ClueWeb09, there are 200 TREC topics from the 2009-2012 Web tracks with corresponding relevance assessments, graded with labels 1 - 4. Similarly, there are 50 topics from the 2013 Web track with relevance assessments within ClueWeb12. For each topic, relevant documents can be from both the category A or category B subset of each corpus. Moreover, for each corpus, we split the available topics to obtain a fair 5-fold cross validation, with each fold containing 3 parts training, 1 part validation (used by the learning to rank techniques to set parameters such as number of iterations) and 1 part testing topics. Hence, we can conduct 5-fold cross validation separately on each corpus.

Next, we note that this experimental setting allows fair cross-comparisons of the transfer of learned models between older and newer corpora, and between subset of corpora, both within cross-validation setting. For instance, the effectiveness of learned models obtained from the older ClueWeb09 on the newer ClueWeb12 target corpus can be compared with those obtained directly on ClueWeb12 training data. Similarly, the effectiveness of learned models from category B subsets of ClueWeb09 and ClueWeb12 can be contrasted with those obtained directly on the target category A sets.

To explain how these comparisons are achieved and following Table 1, we firstly denote our nomenclature: cw09a and cw09b (cw12a and cw12b) denote learned models trained using the category A and category B subsets of ClueWeb09 (ClueWeb12); in contrast, we denote the corpus used to evaluate/test a learned model in capitals, e.g. CW09A and CW09B. Note that because of a cross-fold validation setting, the testing of a learned model upon the same corpus as it is trained on is clearly possible while maintaining separation of training and testing topics: CW09A(cw09a). Moreover, the converse – CW09B(cw09a) – is also valid, where a learned model is trained on category A, but tested using the feature values and relevance assessments for category B – we call this within-corpus training. In doing so, we can compare the effectiveness of a learned model trained on the same corpus or on a different subset of the corpus. Finally, cross-corpus evaluation can be conducted, e.g. CW12A(cw09a). For such a setting, each test fold, say fold 1, would be evaluated on topics from the test part on the target corpus (CW12A), but using a model learned upon topics from the training and validation parts of the fold 1 of the training corpus, cw09a.

Finally, following past TREC Web tracks [5], we use ERR@20 to measure effectiveness.

3.2 Retrieval System

We conduct experiments using the Terrier IR platform [20], making use of the "fat" framework [23] to efficiently generate document rankings with multiple query dependent features suitable for applying learning to rank. Hence, using Ter-

---

[3]In contrast to the Yahoo! Challenge dataset, where the definitions of the features have not been released.

Table 2: Feature sets applied for both category A and category B.

Code	Features	Total
(Candidate Set)	BM25	1
WM	Weighting models on the whole document [23] (DFRee, DPH [1], PL2 [1], BM25 [31], LM, MQT [22], LGD, DFIC [11, 17], DFIZ [11, 17])	8
FM	Weighting models as above on each field, namely: title, URL, body and anchor text; + PL2F [21]	37
PX	Term-dependence proximity models (MRF [25], pBiL [30])	2
QI	URL (e.g. length) link (e.g. inlink counts, PageRank) & content quality (e.g., fraction of stopwords, table text [2], spam classification [7]) features	16
TOTAL		64

rier v4.0, we index the documents of the CW09A, CW09B, CW12A and CW12B corpora, while considering the body, the title, the URL, and the anchor text from the incoming hyperlinks to be separate fields of each document.

At retrieval time, for each query, we use a light version of Porter's English stemmer, and – following [8] – rank 5000 documents to form the *candidate document set* for each query, which will later be re-ranked by the learned models. We use BM25 [31] to generate the candidate set, as Liu [18] reports this is sufficient for effective retrieval, without considering anchor text, which results in the candidate sets with the highest recall of relevant documents. Indeed, a candidate set size of 5000 documents and use of a representation without anchor text follows from the recommendations in [22].

Upon the candidate document set generated by BM25, we add a further 63 features, which represent common query dependent and query independent features implemented by previous studies [22] and datasets such as LETOR [19] and MSLR. We categorise the features as per Table 1: various effective weighting models (WM) computed on the whole document [23]; field models computed on each field individually (FM) [19, 23]; proximity features (PX), which score highly documents where the query terms occur closely together; and query independent (QI) features to identify high quality documents, based on quality, URL and link evidence. All 64 features are summarised in Table 2.

Finally, we deploy two learning to rank techniques, which differ in the form of their learned model. The first is Automatic Feature Selection (AFS) [24], which greedily selects the next feature that most improves effectiveness upon the training set, and adds it to the currently selected features, with a feature weight selected using simulated annealing [16]. We denote this learning to rank technique as LIN in Table 1, as its learned model takes the form of a linear combination of feature values. For our second technique, we use the state-of-the-art LambdaMART technique (denoted LM in Table 1), which forms a learned model of gradient boosted regression trees [3]. Within such a learned model, the feature values for each document define a path through a decision tree, which produces the outcome value. Many such trees form the final learned model. A LambdaMART implementation won the 2011 Yahoo! Learning to Rank challenge [4]. We use the Jforests implementation[4] of LambdaMART.

---
[4]https://code.google.com/p/jforests/

Table 4: Average ERR@20 scores, factored out w.r.t. training corpus (rows) and test corpus (columns), over 2 learning to rank techniques and 4 feature sets. Values on the diagonal represent Null Hypothesis 1, while † denotes a significant difference from the diagonal result (paired t-test, $p \leq 0.025$).

Training Corpus	Test Corpus				Grand Average
	CW09B	CW12B	CW09A	CW12A	
cw09b	**0.1740**	0.1097	0.1288†	0.1481	0.1401
cw12b	0.1287†	0.1140	0.0987†	**0.1611**	0.1256
cw09a	0.1633†	0.1055	**0.1527**	0.1503	**0.1429**
cw12a	0.1341†	**0.1241†**	0.1108†	0.1595	0.1321
Grand Average	0.1500	0.1113	0.1227	0.1547	0.1352

4. RESULTS

Table 3 reports the ERR@20 effectiveness of the main experiments performed in this paper, including grand averages across test corpora, feature sets, and learning to rank techniques. For example, from the CW09B column (1st column) of Table 3 we observe that training on the same corpus (cw09b) is most effective for all possible combinations of feature sets considered.

Moreover, to aid in the analysis of the various factors in Table 3, Figure 1 summarises the effectiveness as a factor interaction plot. In particular, in the figure, each factor (training corpus, test corpus, learning to rank technique and ablated feature set) varies for each row and column of the plot, with legends on the diagonal. The legends apply to all graphs in the same row. For instance, from the graph in the second column of the first row, we can similarly observe that the effectiveness of learned models tested on CW09A are highest when they are trained on the same corpus (cw09a), over all learning to rank techniques and feature sets. In the remainder of this section, we make use of Table 3 and Figure 1, as well as appropriate summary tables and figures depicting multiple comparison tests, to firstly address Null Hypothesis 1 for within-corpus transfer (Section 4.1) and cross-corpus transfer (Section 4.2), respectively, before addressing Null Hypothesis 2 in Section 4.3.

4.1 Within-Corpus Training

To facilitate the addressing of Null Hypothesis 1, concerning the choice of training corpus, Table 4 shows the *average* ERR@20 scores obtained by factoring out w.r.t. training corpus and test corpus over all learning to rank techniques and feature sets. We firstly note that if Null Hypothesis 1 holds true for within-corpus transfers of learned models, we would expect the highest effectiveness for each test corpus to occur when the corresponding training corpus is used, (e.g. CW09A(cw09A)), which occur on the first diagonal of Table 4. To test whether Null Hypothesis 1 is true, we can perform significance tests comparing the diagonal effectiveness scores with the corresponding scores in the same column listed for the other training corpora.

On analysis of the table, we observe that the highest effectiveness scores (emphasised) occur on the first diagonal for only two test corpora. In particular, for CW09B, training on cw09b provides a significantly more effective learned model than that obtained from cw09a (according to a two-tailed paired t-test with a p-value less than 0.025). Similarly, for CW09A, training on cw09a is significantly more effective

Table 3: Average ERR@20 scores factored out w.r.t. feature set and training corpus (rows) vs. test corpus and learning to rank techniques (columns). Recall that: cw09a, cw09b, etc. denote training corpora; CW09A, CW09B, etc. denote test corpora; ALL, NoWM, etc. are ablated feature sets; and LIN and LM denote the AFS and LambdaMART learning to rank techniques, respectively.

| | | CW09B | | | CW12B | | | CW09A | | | CW12A | | | Grand |
		LIN	LM	Average	LIN	LM	Average	LIN	LM	Average	LIN	LM	Average	Average
ALL	(Average	0.1438	0.1609	0.1523	0.1204	0.1144	0.1174	0.1263	0.1270	0.1267	0.1688	0.1539	0.1614	0.1395
	cw09b	0.1806	0.1800	0.1803	0.1135	0.1023	0.1079	0.1296	0.1375	0.1335	0.1582	0.1405	0.1494	0.1428
	cw12b	0.1198	0.1391	0.1294	0.1158	0.1162	0.1160	0.0912	0.0967	0.0940	0.1719	0.1615	0.1667	0.1265
	cw09a	0.1696	0.1670	0.1683	0.1216	0.1078	0.1147	0.1706	0.1576	0.1641	0.1726	0.1455	0.1591	0.1516
	cw12a	0.1052	0.1575	0.1313	0.1308	0.1314	0.1311	0.1140	0.1163	0.1151	0.1724	0.1680	0.1702	0.1369
NoWM	(Average	0.1607	0.1556	0.1581	0.1143	0.1175	0.1159	0.1286	0.1234	0.1260	0.1620	0.1475	0.1547	0.1387
	cw09b	0.1884	0.1709	0.1796	0.1130	0.1026	0.1078	0.1525	0.1292	0.1409	0.1655	0.1304	0.1480	0.1441
	cw12b	0.1356	0.1307	0.1331	0.1056	0.1229	0.1142	0.0953	0.1050	0.1001	0.1658	0.1558	0.1608	0.1271
	cw09a	0.1794	0.1761	0.1777	0.1089	0.1118	0.1104	0.1575	0.1656	0.1615	0.1564	0.1415	0.1489	0.1496
	cw12a	0.1394	0.1446	0.1420	0.1296	0.1329	0.1313	0.1093	0.0939	0.1016	0.1603	0.1623	0.1613	0.1340
NoFM	(Average	0.1465	0.1603	0.1534	0.1128	0.1003	0.1065	0.1397	0.1318	0.1357	0.1630	0.1465	0.1547	0.1376
	cw09b	0.1811	0.1764	0.1787	0.1093	0.1082	0.1087	0.1319	0.1165	0.1242	0.1629	0.1411	0.1520	0.1409
	cw12b	0.1131	0.1511	0.1321	0.1184	0.1109	0.1146	0.1158	0.1280	0.1219	0.1588	0.1594	0.1591	0.1319
	cw09a	0.1636	0.1626	0.1631	0.1039	0.0813	0.0926	0.1690	0.1563	0.1626	0.1707	0.1375	0.1541	0.1431
	cw12a	0.1281	0.1512	0.1397	0.1198	0.1006	0.1102	0.1422	0.1263	0.1342	0.1595	0.1480	0.1537	0.1345
NoQI	(Average	0.1311	0.1395	0.1353	0.1128	0.1033	0.1081	0.1029	0.1015	0.1022	0.1526	0.1408	0.1467	0.1231
	cw09b	0.1437	0.1562	0.1500	0.1164	0.0897	0.1030	0.1041	0.1097	0.1069	0.1391	0.1280	0.1336	0.1234
	cw12b	0.1094	0.1301	0.1197	0.1044	0.1118	0.1081	0.0826	0.1017	0.0922	0.1598	0.1548	0.1573	0.1193
	cw09a	0.1415	0.1417	0.1416	0.1065	0.0929	0.0997	0.1221	0.1139	0.1180	0.1534	0.1176	0.1355	0.1237
	cw12a	0.1299	0.1300	0.1300	0.1239	0.1189	0.1214	0.1028	0.0806	0.0917	0.1580	0.1628	0.1604	0.1259
NoPX	(Average	0.1463	0.1554	0.1508	0.1213	0.1161	0.1187	0.1229	0.1232	0.1231	0.1652	0.1472	0.1562	0.1372
	cw09b	0.1803	0.1824	0.1813	0.1175	0.1245	0.1210	0.1280	0.1489	0.1384	0.1559	0.1591	0.1575	0.1496
	cw12b	0.1218	0.1359	0.1289	0.1153	0.1191	0.1172	0.0864	0.0843	0.0854	0.1742	0.1490	0.1616	0.1232
	cw09a	0.1620	0.1693	0.1656	0.1240	0.0959	0.1099	0.1626	0.1519	0.1572	0.1659	0.1421	0.1540	0.1467
	cw12a	0.1211	0.1338	0.1275	0.1286	0.1248	0.1267	0.1148	0.1078	0.1113	0.1648	0.1388	0.1518	0.1293
Grand Average		0.1457	0.1543	0.1500	0.1163	0.1103	0.1133	0.1241	0.1214	0.1227	0.1623	0.1472	0.1547	0.1352

than cw09b. Both of these observations can also be made from Figure 1: 1st row, 2nd column.

On the other hand, for ClueWeb12, some different observations arise than from ClueWeb09. In particular, for CW12A, there are no significant differences between the effectiveness of the trained models obtained from cw12a and cw12b. However, for CW12B, training on cw12a results in significantly more effective models - see Table 4.

To explain this surprising observation, which contrasts with that observed for ClueWeb09, recall that ClueWeb12 category B contains randomly sampled documents from the corresponding category A corpus. This being the case, many relevant documents (particularly those with higher relevance grades such as homepages) may be omitted from the smaller corpus. On the other hand, for ClueWeb09, category B contains the higher crawl priority documents within the larger category A. As crawling is inherently a costly process that cannot completely crawl the (infinite) Web, crawl priorities are used to target documents more likely to be relevant [27]. This is true for category B, which contains high crawl priority documents as well as Wikipedia. In contrast, ClueWeb09 category A reportedly contains a higher proportion of spam documents than category B [7].

To explain further the difference between the A and B categories of ClueWeb09 and ClueWeb12, Table 5 shows the number of relevant documents for the different relevance grades (e.g. relevant: ≥ 1; highly relevant: ≥ 2) in both categories of each corpus. From this, for ClueWeb09, it can be seen while category B is only 10% of the size of category A, it contains 58% of the relevant documents (relevance label 1 and above) and 65% of highly relevant documents (label 2 and above), with smaller percentages for document with higher relevance labels, such as perfect (label 4, 67%). In contrast, for ClueWeb12, the category B (which is a 7% random sample of category A) only contains 20% of the relevant documents. While not high compared to ClueWeb09, 20% is higher than the 7% expectation, and can be explained by the fact that there were 9 TREC 2013 category B run submissions that contributed to the assessment pool [6].

Next, Table 5 also reports the statistics of the candidate document sets for each query obtained by BM25, from each of the category A and category B corpora, as well as the statistics of category B documents retrieved within the A candidate sets (denoted $B \in A$). From this, we note that documents from the category B ClueWeb09 corpus form 12% of the retrieved documents in the A candidate sets (126,768 vs. 979,361) - this is in line with the relative proportion of ClueWeb09 category B within the larger category A corpus (10%). Going from the B candidate sets to the A candidate sets increases the number of relevant (labels ≥ 1) documents by 19% (31,995 to 36,101). However, the number of relevant documents retrieved in the A candidate sets that were also retrieved for B are reduced (31,995 to 20,499) - a trend that is mirrored across all relevance grades. Therefore, while more relevant documents are retrieved in ClueWeb09 category A candidate sets, they are less likely to be those from category B, and are also less likely to be perfectly relevant documents (relevance grade 4).

In contrast, for ClueWeb12, category B accounts for a far smaller proportion of the judged and relevant documents (25% and 20%, respectively) – and even sparser for higher relevance grades. This explains why training on cw12a generates better models for CW12B than cw12b does: there are more labelled documents in cw12a, and hence more effective and robust learned models can be obtained.

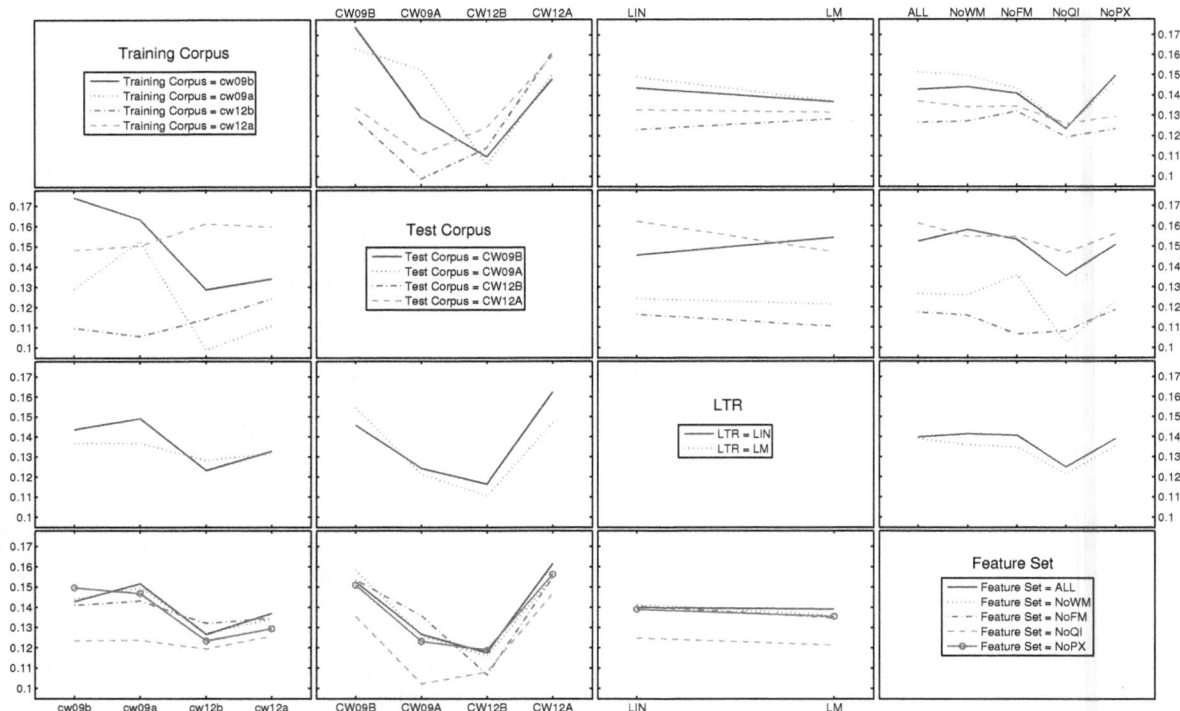

Figure 1: Interactions plot for the four factors (training corpus, test corpus, learning to rank technique and ablated feature set) in our full-factorial experiment.

From these statistics, we draw two conclusions: firstly, that the ClueWeb09 category B reflects an easier corpus, where perfect, highly relevant and relevant documents are easier to identify. This is reflected in the higher number of relevant documents retrieved in the candidate sets, as well as the higher ERR@20 scores obtainable on that corpus; Moreover, this makes cw09a unsuitable as a training corpus for learning effective models for CW09B, as the statistics of features for relevant documents identified on cw09a differ from cw09b; In contrast, for ClueWeb12, as the cw12a candidate document sets are more likely to contain high quality documents, it generates more effective learned models for use on CW12A than does cw12b. In summary, Null Hypothesis 1 cannot be rejected in general for within-corpus training. However, for CW12B there are insufficient labelled, relevant documents in the topics to obtain effective learned models, and hence within-corpus training from cw12a is appropriate.

4.2 Cross-Corpus Training

Similar to Section 4.1, this section also addresses Null Hypothesis 1, but for the cross-corpus transfer of learned models – i.e. from ClueWeb09 to ClueWeb12. For this section, we mostly focus upon the role of ClueWeb09 (cw09a and cw09b) in obtaining effective learned models for the newer ClueWeb12 corpus, c.f. CW12B and CW12A. For this analysis, we return to Table 4. From the table, it can be observed that for CW12A, the effectiveness of the models obtained from cw09a and cw09b are not significantly different from those obtained using cw12a or cw12b. This suggests that ClueWeb09 and ClueWeb12 are statistically indistinguishable as a training corpus for ClueWeb12. In contrast, for CW09A, models obtained from cw12a or cw12b are both

significantly less effective than those obtained from the target corpus itself. From Figure 1 the same observations can be made using the graph within the 1st column of the 2nd row. Within this graph, the lines associated with the ClueWeb12 test corpora are much flatter than those associated with ClueWeb09. This suggests that ClueWeb12 is less sensitive than ClueWeb09 to the change of training corpus, over all learning to rank techniques and feature sets.

Hence based on the significance tests observed in Table 4, Null Hypothesis 1 holds true for ClueWeb09 only, while for ClueWeb12, there is insufficient empirical evidence to reject it, meaning that there appears to be no significant effectiveness disadvantage in simply transferring learned models from ClueWeb09 to ClueWeb12 in general.

For the purpose of such a transfer, instead of using a learned model obtained from a different corpus, it is better to adapt the learned model being transferred to the new target corpus. In the context of the Yahoo! learning to rank challenge transfer task, Geurts and Louppe [12] examined six different methods of achieving transfer learning within learning to rank. Of these six methods, we note that the method that we call *model-feature transfer* was shown to be most effective. In this method, the output of the learned model on the older corpus taken as a new feature on the target corpus before re-learning. More formally, consider the predictions of a learned model $\mathcal{M}$ obtained on a corpus c with features $\mathcal{F}$ is denoted $\mathcal{M}(c, \mathcal{F})$. Then, to predictions using a feature transferred from c_1 to c_2 can be expressed as $\mathcal{M}(c_2, \mathcal{F} + \mathcal{M}(c_1, \mathcal{F}))$.

In Table 6, we report the effectiveness of model-feature transfer learning for CW12A. In particular, for CW12A we report the effectiveness of model-feature transfer, denoted

Table 5: Statistics of ClueWeb09 & ClueWeb12 category A and category B corpora and judgements, as well as corresponding statistics from the BM25 candidate document set. Some of these statistics were previously reported by [32] in the context of ClueWeb09 and the TREC 2009 Web track only. Recall that category B corpora are subset of the corresponding category A (10% for ClueWeb09, 7% for ClueWeb12).

Category	Crawled	Judged	≥ 1	≥ 2	≥ 3	$= 4$
relevance assessments						
CW09A	503,903,810	81,520	18,771	5,675	1,456	858
CW09B	50,220,423 10%	50,593 62%	11,037 58%	3,719 66%	895 61%	580 67%
of which retrieved by BM25						
CW09A	979,361	36,102	10,935	3,412	881	491
CW09B $\in$ CW09A	126,768	20,499	6,177	2,124	493	302
CW09B	972,049	31,995	8,959	3,096	774	498
relevance assessments						
CW12A	732,601,381	14,474	4,150	1,106	186	7
CW12B	52,315,578 7.1%	3,668 25%	829 20%	193 17%	20 11%	0 0%
of which retrieved by BM25						
CW12A	250,000	9,066	3,107	838	114	7
CW12B $\in$ CW12A	17,698	2,008	636	144	11	0
CW12B	250,000	2,647	786	188	20	0

Table 6: Comparison of model-feature transfer learning on ClueWeb12 - the model learned cw09a is used to create a supplemental feature used when training and ranking on cw12a. Significant differences according to the paired t-test compared to the model learned cw09a are denoted by †.

Test Corpus	Feature Set	LIN		LM	
		cw12a	cw09a+ cw12a	cw12a	cw09a+ cw12a
CW12A	ALL	**0.1724**	0.1694	0.1680	**0.1682**
	NoPX	**0.1648**	0.1630	0.1388	**0.1721**†
	NoQI	**0.1580**	0.1574	0.1628	0.1479
	NoFM	0.1595	**0.1663**	0.1480	**0.1544**
	NoWM	**0.1603**	0.1537	0.1623	**0.1672**
	Average	**0.1630**	0.1620	0.1560	**0.1620**

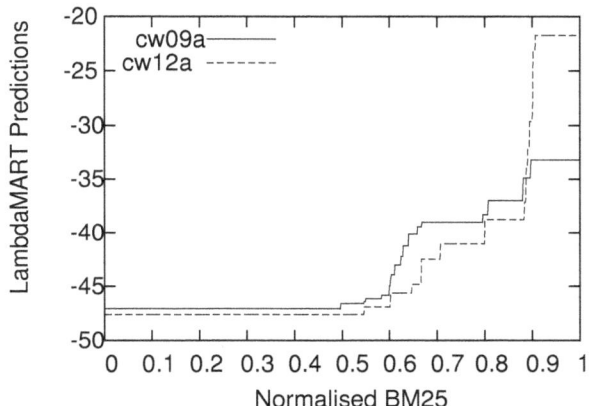

Figure 2: Partial dependence plots showing how predictions from LambdaMART change as a function of BM25, for models trained on cw09a and cw12a.

cw09a + cw12a in contrast to learning on cw12a alone. On analysis of the results in Table 6, we note that model-feature technique benefits the effectiveness of the LambdaMART learning to rank technique on both CW12A. Indeed, while on average AFS is more effective than LambdaMART on CW12A without transfer learning (0.1630 vs. 0.1560), supplementing cw12 with a transfer learning feature from cw09a increases LambdaMART's effectiveness to average 0.1620.

The improvements of LambdaMART is because regression trees need significant training data - particularly to recover linear relationships between a feature value and relevance [13, Chapter 9] such as between BM25 and relevance. By using transfer learning from a corpus with more labelled documents, the linear relationship between (say) BM25 and relevance can be better learned on the older corpus, and the model then fine-tuned on the newer corpus. Indeed, this is illustrated in Figure 2, which shows a partial dependence plot [13] of the LambdaMART predictions for learned models obtained from cw09a and cw12a as BM25 is varied. From the figure, it can be observed that the cw09a model has more decisions points for BM25 within its regression tree than that obtained from learning on cw12a (18 vs. 12).

On the other hand, for AFS, model-feature transfer learning does not benefit effectiveness, as the AFS model is unable to successfully encapsulate the transferred feature. Indeed, on inspection of the learned models obtained for the ALL

feature set, we find that the model trained on cw12a that encapsulates the transferred feature from cw09a actually used more features than the model obtained from cw12a alone. This suggests that AFS is actually trying – unsuccessfully – to 'undo' the work of the AFS model from cw09a to better adapt it to cw12a.

In summary, we find that Null Hypothesis 1 for cross-corpus training holds when targeting ClueWeb09 (see Table 4). However, for ClueWeb12, the available empirical evidence is not as strong as for ClueWeb09, as models trained on ClueWeb12 are not significantly more effective for this corpus than models obtained from ClueWeb09. This means that a learned model from ClueWeb09 can be directly applied for retrieval on ClueWeb12 with statistically comparable effectiveness. On the other hand, cross-corpus training can significantly benefit effectiveness on ClueWeb12 when the training sets from ClueWeb09 and ClueWeb12 are combined using the model-feature transfer learning method defined in [12] (see Table 6).

Table 7: Average ERR@20 scores, factored out w.r.t. test corpora (rows) vs. Feature Set (columns), over all training corpora and learning to rank techniques. † on a score indicates that paired t-test gives significance to the difference between that score and the score the associated method achieved with all features ($p < 0.025$).

Test Corpus	Feature Set					Average
	ALL	NoWM	NoFM	NoQI	NoPX	
CW09B	0.1523	**0.1581**	0.1534	0.1353†	0.1508	0.1500
CW09A	0.1267	0.1260	**0.1357†**	0.1022†	0.1231	0.1227
CW12B	0.1174	0.1159	0.1065†	0.1081	**0.1187**	0.1133
CW12A	**0.1614**	0.1547	0.1547	0.1467	0.1562	0.1547
Average	**0.1395**	0.1387	0.1376	0.1231	0.1372	0.1352

4.3 Feature Sets

Next, we move onto our second null hypothesis, concerning the importance of feature sets. Table 7 reports the observed average ERR@20 scores for the ClueWeb09 and ClueWeb12 test corpora with varying feature sets over all training and learning to rank techniques. This table corresponds to the graph in the 2nd row, 4th column of Figure 1. Recall that as we are performing an ablation study, we analyse the importance of a set of features by observing its impact when removed from the learned model - e.g. NoFM denotes when the FM feature set (field-based weighting models) is removed (ablated) from the ALL feature set.

Multiple comparisons of the possible combinations of the levels of the training corpus, feature set, factors and learning to rank technique under consideration can be made based on the Friedman's test, as shown in Figures 3 & 4 for CW09A and CW12A, respectively. Friedman's test is the nonparametric counterpart of the balanced two-way ANOVA test: it tests for row effect (i.e., runs) after adjusting for possible column effects (i.e., queries). Hence, it is more appropriate for the multiple comparisons of the results of IR experiments than ANOVA and its two-sample Student's t-test counterpart [14]. Within Figures 3 & 4, each group represents a different combination of learning to rank technique, and training corpus, where the feature sets are varied within the groups. Hence, the figures show the pairwise comparisons that are made across all training corpora and feature sets within Table 7.

On analysing Table 7, we note that removing the query independent features (i.e. NoQI) consistently harms the effectiveness obtained on both ClueWeb09 and ClueWeb12. For CW09B and CW09A, this impact is statistically significant relative to the effectiveness obtained using the ALL feature set. Indeed, referring to Figure 3, we observe significant decreases in effectiveness in removing the QI features (as the confidence intervals do not overlap) except when Lambda-MART is trained on cw09b. For CW12B and CW12A - shown in Figure 4, although the loss in effectiveness with respect to the ALL feature set is not statistically significant (possibly due to the fewer topics available for Clue-Web12), removing QI causes more than a 10% decrease in absolute ERR@20 effectiveness. We believe the major difference between ClueWeb09 and ClueWeb12 in this respect is as follows: while ClueWeb09 category A corpus contains many spam documents [7], spam removal was conducted on ClueWeb12[5], which will likely reduce the importance of the query independent features, many of which are intended

---

[5]See http://lemurproject.org/clueweb12/specs.php

to identify low quality documents (e.g. spam classification score). Overall, our QI results suggest that, for the AFS and LambdaMART learning to rank techniques, and for all of the training corpora under consideration, query independent features provide, on average, a major contribution to the effectiveness of the learned models.

In general, as shown in the 4th row, 3rd column of Figure 1, the importance of feature sets is independent of the choice of learning to rank technique, since the lines that correspond to the various feature sets are horizontal over the learning to rank techniques. The difference in the effectiveness of NoQI and the other feature sets again shows us that removing QI features significantly reduces the effectiveness of both learning to rank techniques (see Table 7 & Figure 3).

The case of the field-based weighting models (FM) is different from that of QI, in that removing the query dependent FM features makes a significant gain in the effectiveness of the learned models for CW09A while, in contrast, it causes a significant loss in effectiveness for CW12B (this can also be observed in Figure 1: 2nd row, 4th column, and a marked loss for CW12A. In particular, while the query dependent features in the WM set encapsulate the anchor text, only the FM feature set allows the learner to separately weight the presence of query terms within the anchor text. We believe that these results suggest that the presence of spam within ClueWeb09 (particularly category A) can mislead the learner as to the usefulness of the anchor text - which will vary according to the prevalence of spam in different queries. On the other hand, with the reduced amount of spam in ClueWeb12, the FM feature set is useful for retrieval, and its ablation results in effectiveness degradations, which are significant in the case of CW12B.

In summary, as we have shown that QI and FM feature sets exhibit different effectiveness benefits between the CW09A and CW12B corpora, we conclude that Null Hypothesis 2 can be rejected for these feature sets, meaning that not all the feature sets contribute uniformly to the effectiveness of the learned models across different corpora. This emphasises the importance of appropriate training on the ClueWeb12 corpus, for instance using the model-feature transfer learning method that was investigated in Section 4.2.

5. CONCLUSIONS

This paper studies the generalisation and transferability of learning to rank models using the TREC ClueWeb09 and ClueWeb12 corpora as well as the contrasting the usefulness of different types of features – both within subsets of the same corpus, and across corpora. We formulated these research investigations as two null hypotheses, and conducted a thorough full-factorial experimental design using 250 TREC Web track topics, to derive empirically justified best practices for effective retrieval on the ClueWeb12 corpus. Indeed, our experimental results surprisingly suggest that the transfer of learned models from ClueWeb09 are sufficient for effective retrieval on ClueWeb12. However, the supplemental use of ClueWeb09 training data within the ClueWeb12 learning process can further significantly improve the effectiveness of learned models from the regression-tree based LambdaMART learning to rank technique.

We also found that the category B random subset of the ClueWeb12 corpus has insufficient labelled documents to obtain effective learned models. This contrasts greatly with the category B controlled subset of ClueWeb09, which contains 25% of the relevant documents within category A, despite

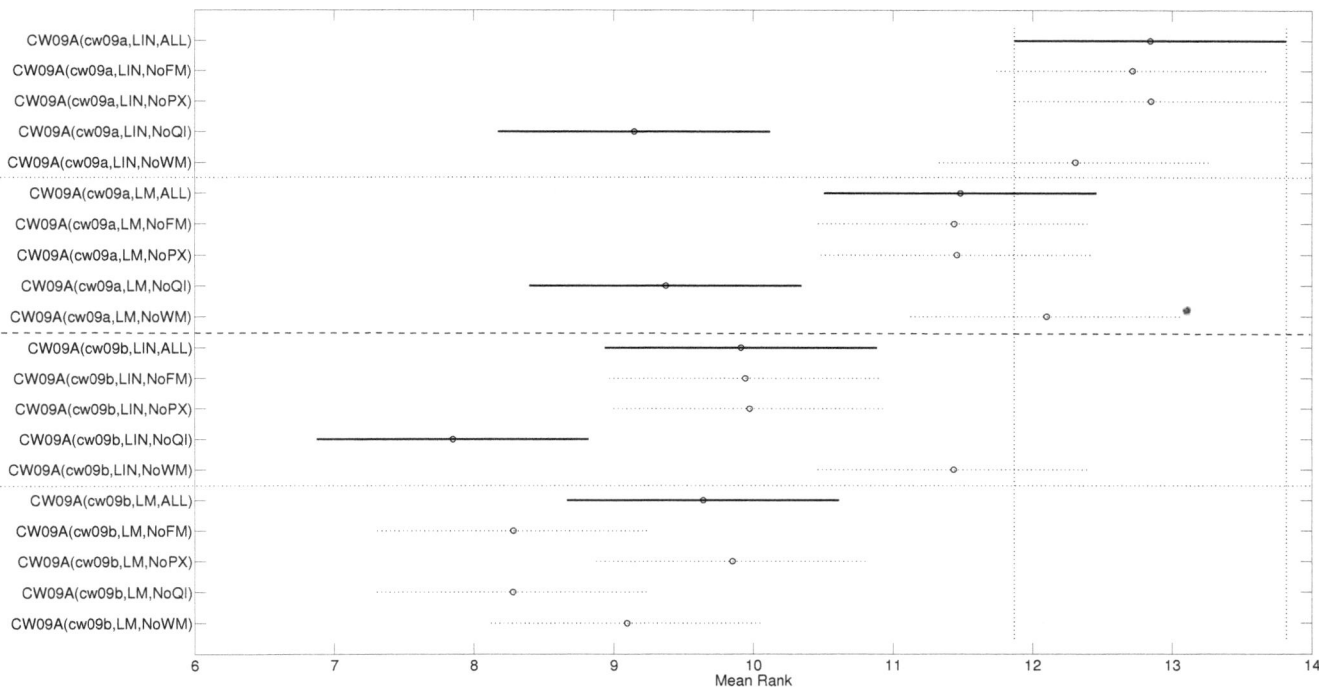

Figure 3: Multiple comparisons for combinations of levels for 3 factors under consideration (training corpus, feature set and learner) for CW09A. The circles show the mean ranks associated with each run in the column and the horizontal lines crossing the circles represent the 95% confidence interval (CI) for the mean ranks. Non-overlapping CIs indicate significant differences.

being only 10% in size. We conclude that the random sampling of ClueWeb12 category B from the larger corpus reduces the experimental value of this corpus, as many queries do not have highly relevant documents within this subset.

Lastly, we empirically showed the value of query independent features, as our results show that – irrespective of the learning to rank technique and the training corpus – every setting of ClueWeb09 requires their presence for effective retrieval. In contrast, the value of query independent features is less strong for ClueWeb12. Moreover, while adding various field-based weighting models as features could add effectiveness for ClueWeb12, their value was less apparent on ClueWeb09 which comparatively has more spam documents than ClueWeb12.

Similar to [4], we believe that the generalisation and transferability of learning to rank models are of significant importance, and hence this paper illustrates how researchers and practitioners must consider any biases present within corpora when conducting transfer learning, and how this may impact upon the usefulness of different types of features. In the future, we aim to adapt existing instance-based transfer learning techniques to the learning to rank scenario, and also investigate how risk-sensitive retrieval can be utilised within a transfer learning setting.

6. REFERENCES

[1] G. Amati, E. Ambrosi, M. Bianchi, C. Gaibisso, and G. Gambosi. FUB, IASI-CNR and University of Tor Vergata at the TREC 2007 Blog track. In *Proceedings of TREC*, 2007.

[2] M. Bendersky, W. B. Croft, and Y. Diao. Quality-biased ranking of Web documents. In *Proceedings of WSDM*, 2011.

[3] C. J. Burges. From RankNet to LambdaRank to LambdaMART: An Overview. Technical Report MSR-TR-2010-82, Microsoft Research, 2010.

[4] O. Chappelle and Y. Chang. Yahoo! learning to rank challenge overview. In *Proceedings of Yahoo! Learning to Rank Challenge*, 2011.

[5] C. L. A. Clarke, N. Craswell, and I. Soboroff. Overview of the TREC 2012 Web track. In *Proceedings of TREC*, 2012.

[6] K. Collins-Thompson, P. Bennett, F. Diaz, C. L. A. Clarke, and E. Voorhees. TREC 2013 Web track overview. In *Proceedings of TREC*, 2013.

[7] G. V. Cormack, M. D. Smucker, and C. L. Clarke. Efficient and effective spam filtering and re-ranking for large web datasets. *Information Retrieval Journal*, 14(5), 2011.

[8] N. Craswell, D. Fetterly, M. Najork, S. Robertson, and E. Yilmaz. Microsoft research at TREC 2009. In *Proceedings of TREC*, 2009.

[9] W. Dai, Q. Yang, G.-R. Xue, and Y. Yu. Boosting for transfer learning. In *Proceedings of ICML*, 2007.

[10] V. Dang, M. Bendersky, and W. B. Croft. Two-stage learning to rank for information retrieval. In *Proceedings of ECIR*, 2013.

[11] B. T. Dinçer, I. Kocabas, and B. Karaoglan. IRRA at TREC 2010: Index term weighting by divergence from independence model. In *Proceedings of TREC*, 2010.

[12] P. Geurts and G. Louppe. Learning to rank with extremely randomized trees. In *Proceedings of Yahoo! Learning to Rank Challenge*, 2011.

[13] T. Hastie, R. Tibshirani, and J. Friedman. *The Elements of Statistical Learning*. Springer, 2001.

[14] D. Hull. Using statistical testing in the evaluation of retrieval experiments. In *Proceedings of SIGIR*, 1993.

[15] T. Kamishima, M. Hamasaki, and S. Akaho. Trbagg: A simple transfer learning method and its application to

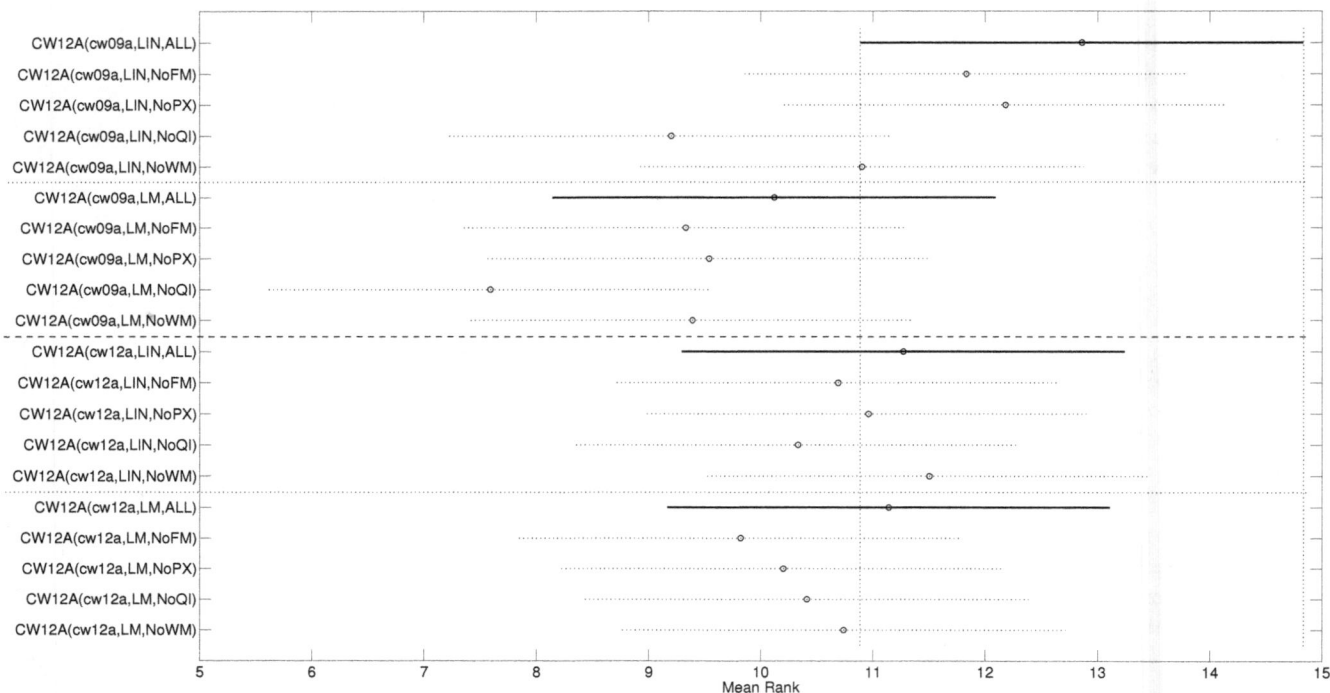

Figure 4: Multiple comparisons for combinations of levels for 3 factors under consideration (training corpus, feature set and learner) for CW12A. The circles show the mean ranks associated with each run in the column and the horizontal lines crossing the circles represent the 95% confidence interval (CI) for the mean ranks. Non-overlapping CIs indicate significant differences.

personalization in collaborative tagging. In *Proceedings of ICDM*, 2009.

[16] S. Kirkpatrick, C. D. Gelatt, and M. P. Vecchi. Optimization by simulated annealing. *Science Jounal*, 220(4598), 1983.

[17] I. Kocabas, B. T. Dinçer, and B. Karaoglan. A nonparametric term weighting method for information retrieval based on measuring the divergence from independence. *Information Retrieval Journal*, 17(2), 2014.

[18] T.-Y. Liu. Learning to rank for information retrieval. *Foundations and Trends in Information Retrieval Journal*, 3(3), 2009.

[19] T.-Y. Liu, T. Qin, J. Xu, W. Xiong, and H. Li. LETOR: Benchmark dataset for research on learning to rank for information retrieval. In *Proceedings of LR4IR at SIGIR*, 2007.

[20] C. Macdonald, R. McCreadie, R. Santos, and I. Ounis. From puppy to maturity: Experiences in developing Terrier. In *Proceedings of OSIR at SIGIR*, 2012.

[21] C. Macdonald, V. Plachouras, B. He, C. Lioma and I. Ounis. University of Glasgow at WebCLEF 2005: Experiments in per-field normalisation and language specific stemming. In *Proceedings of CLEF*, 2005.

[22] C. Macdonald, R. Santos, and I. Ounis. The whens and hows of learning to rank for web search. *Information Retrieval Journal*, 16(5), 2012.

[23] C. Macdonald, R. L. Santos, I. Ounis, and B. He. About learning models with multiple query-dependent features. *Transactions on Information Systems Journal*, 31(3), 2013.

[24] D. Metzler. Automatic feature selection in the markov random field model for information retrieval. In *Proceedings of CIKM*, 2007.

[25] D. Metzler and W. B. Croft. A markov random field model for term dependencies. In *Proceedings of SIGIR*, 2005

[26] T. Minka and S. Robertson. Selection bias in the LETOR datasets. In *Proceedings of LR4IR at SIGIR*, 2008.

[27] M. Najork and J. L. Wiener. Breadth-first crawling yields high-quality pages. In *Proceedings of WWW*, 2001.

[28] S. J. Pan and Q. Yang. A survey on transfer learning. *Transactions on Knowledge and Data Engineering Journal*, 22(10), 2010.

[29] S. J. Pan, Q. Yang, and W. Fan. Tutorial: Transfer learning with applications. In *Proceedings of IJCAI*, 2013.

[30] J. Peng, C. Macdonald, B. He, V. Plachouras, and I. Ounis. Incorporating term dependency in the DFR framework. In *Proceedings of SIGIR*, 2007.

[31] S. E. Robertson, S. Walker, M. Hancock-Beaulieu, A. Gull, and M. Lau. Okapi at TREC. In *Proceedings of TREC*, 1992.

[32] R. L. Santos, C. Macdonald, and I. Ounis. Effectiveness beyond the first crawl tier. In *Proceedings of CIKM*, 2011.

[33] S. Tyree, K. Q. Weinberger, K. Agrawal, and J. Paykin. Parallel boosted regression trees for web search ranking. In *Proceedings of WWW*, 2011.

The Probability Ranking Principle is Not Optimal in Adversarial Retrieval Settings

Ran Ben Basat
Computer Science
Department
Technion
Haifa, Israel
sran@cs.technion.ac.il

Moshe Tennenholtz
Faculty of Industrial
Engineering and Management
Technion
Haifa, Israel
moshet@ie.technion.ac.il

Oren Kurland
Faculty of Industrial
Engineering and Management
Technion
Haifa, Israel
kurland@ie.technion.ac.il

ABSTRACT

The probability ranking principle (PRP) — ranking documents in response to a query by their relevance probabilities — is the theoretical foundation of most ad hoc document retrieval methods. A key observation that motivates our work is that the PRP does not account for potential post-ranking effects, specifically, changes to documents that result from a given ranking. Yet, in adversarial retrieval settings such as the Web, authors may consistently try to promote their documents in rankings by changing them. We prove that, indeed, the PRP can be sub-optimal in adversarial retrieval settings. We do so by presenting a novel game theoretic analysis of the adversarial setting. The analysis is performed for different types of documents (single topic and multi topic) and is based on different assumptions about the writing qualities of documents' authors. We show that in some cases, introducing randomization into the document ranking function yields overall user utility that transcends that of applying the PRP.

Categories and Subject Descriptors: H.3.3 [Information Search and Retrieval]: Retrieval models

Keywords: adversarial retrieval, probability ranking principle

1. INTRODUCTION

The basic ad hoc document retrieval task is ranking documents in a corpus in response to a query by their relevance to the information need the query expresses. Numerous retrieval methods and frameworks have been devised throughout the years; e.g., the vector space model [28], the probabilistic approach, [29], the language modeling framework [23], the divergence from randomness framework [3], and learning-to-rank approaches [21].

The theoretical basis for all probabilistic retrieval methods, and under one interpretation or another, for all retrieval frameworks mentioned above, is the *probability ranking principle* (PRP) [26]. According to the PRP, documents in the corpus should be ranked by the probability that they are rel-

evant to the query, so as to maximize the utility of the user who posted the query; relevance probabilities are assumed to be estimated using all information available to the search system [26][1].

There are two scenarios where the PRP may result in sub-optimal utility. The first is when users have different utility functions (i.e., personalization effects) [26]. The second scenario is when the relevance of one document depends on that of another; i.e., diversification effects [26, 7].

However, there is an additional fundamental aspect of the PRP that has not been accounted for in past work. The PRP, and retrieval methods devised based on the PRP, are based on a static view of the ad hoc retrieval setting. That is, the goal is to optimize user utility for the current query given the current *fixed* snapshot of the corpus[2]. The optimization is performed *regardless* of the incentives of the authors who created the documents, and thus does not account for potential post-retrieval effects — e.g., changes of the corpus, and therefore rankings for future queries, as a result of the ranking induced for the current query. More generally, an underlying implicit premise of the standard approach of designing ranking functions is that optimizing user utility along time can be based on providing the best possible relevance ranking for each query without accounting for future effects. We show in this paper that this static view falls short in dynamic and adversarial settings.

In adversarial retrieval settings such as the Web, documents might be changed by their authors, henceforth *publishers*, so as to have them promoted in rankings induced in response to queries. This practice is often referred to as search engine optimization [15]. Thus, the assumption that the ranking induced for one query will not affect the potential utility attained for future queries is simply wrong; that is, each induced ranking can lead to changes in the corpus upon which future search will be performed. Naturally, these changes can affect the utility attained for future queries. To illustrate this point, consider the following example. Suppose that a Web page is composed of a few sections, some of which contain valuable information which is unique to the page. In terms of page visibility, the publisher of the Web page is mainly concerned about how the page is ranked for queries that match the non-unique sections of the page. Having the page ranked low in response to these queries might

ICTIR '15, September 27-30, 2015, Northampton, MA, USA.
© 2015 ACM. ISBN 978-1-4503-3833-2/15/09$15.00.
DOI: http://dx.doi.org/10.1145/2808194.2809456 .

---

[1] There is also a definition of the PRP for interactive retrieval [13]. Interactive retrieval is outside the scope of this paper.
[2] In some cases, information about previous snapshots of the corpus might also be utilized [11].

lead the publisher to remove some of the unique sections, so as to better emphasize those which should "attract" the queries of concern. Such an action can lead to diminishing the utility of users looking for the unique information.

We present a novel game theoretic analysis of the adversarial ad hoc retrieval setting. The analysis accounts for the following facts (i) document publishers are "players" with *incentives*; namely, having their documents ranked high in response to some queries; (ii) the search engine is a *mediator* which affects the actions of publishers by the rankings it induces in response to queries; and therefore, (iii) the utility attained for the current query can affect that attained for future queries by the virtue of post-retrieval effects on the corpus (i.e., changes to documents). Our analysis assumes that all users have the same utility function (i.e., we do not account for personalization effects), and that the relevance of one document is independent of that of others (i.e., we do not account for the importance of diversifying search results but rather focus on their relevance). In that respect, our analysis is committed to the same conditions under which the PRP was shown to be optimal for a specific query and a static corpus.

A particular advantage of taking a game theoretic approach to modeling the adversarial retrieval setting, is the ability to make insightful statements about the steady state of the dynamics of the setting, namely, an equilibrium. The players — publishers in our case — who act selfishly do not have an incentive to deviate from the equilibrium. Thus, analyzing properties of the equilibrium is important for understanding the implications of a specific (dynamic) game. We note that any change to the actions that the players can take — in our case, the types of documents they can produce — and to the ranking function which serves as the mediator induces a new game with potentially new equilibria.

Inspired by standard practice in work on (algorithmic) game theory, our treatment of the adversarial retrieval setting as a game focuses on the notion of *social welfare*: the sum of utilities provided to users by rankings produced in response to their queries. Indeed, search engines should opt to maximize the social welfare of their users. More specifically, we analyze the worst possible social welfare attained in *any* equilibrium with respect to the best possible social welfare that can be attained. This concept, a.k.a. *price of anarchy* (PoA)[19, 27], is an important tool for analyzing games. In our case, the PoA is a means to contrasting different types of ranking functions in terms of the worst possible social welfare they can lead to in a steady state of the game.

We build up our analysis by starting from the case of having documents that discuss a single topic. We show that applying the PRP in this case, on a per-query basis, results in optimal social welfare if publishers are assumed to have the same writing quality for all topics. Later on we show that if this is not the case — i.e., publishers have differential writing qualities for topics — then applying the PRP is sub-optimal. As it turns out, the PRP is also sub-optimal in the case of having multi-topic documents and publishers with equal writing qualities for all topics. Interestingly, in several cases of our analysis, we show that introducing *randomization* into a ranking function can sometimes lead to social welfare that transcends that of applying the PRP.

The two main contributions of this paper are as follows:

- Presenting a novel game theoretic analysis of the adversarial ad hoc retrieval setting. The analysis accounts for the incentives of document authors to have their documents ranked high in response to queries.

- Showing that the standard practice of inducing a ranking based on the probability ranking principle — i.e., optimizing relevance ranking for a given query and static corpus — can be sub-optimal in terms of the overall utility attained by users of the search engine in the face of changes that the corpus goes through.

We believe that the sub-optimality of the PRP, and more generally, the sub-optimality entailed by the static view taken by current retrieval methods that are based on the PRP, have important implications. For example, our theoretical findings imply that learning ranking functions by optimizing rankings for a train set of queries and a static corpus, as is the current state-of-affairs [21], is a sub-optimal practice. That is, the learning should also account for post-retrieval effects in terms of potential changes applied to documents in the corpus by incentivized document authors.

2. RELATED WORK

The vast majority of published work on adversarial information retrieval has focused on spam classification (mainly content-based and link-based spam), and more generally, on estimating the quality and/or authoritativeness of Web pages (e.g., [12, 15, 4, 30, 20, 18, 8, 5, 9, 1, 2]). There has also been some recent work on estimating for which queries content manipulation of documents is more likely [24] and on estimating global term statistics in adversarial peer-to-peer search systems [25]. Work on adversarial classification treats the classifier and the data generator as two adversaries [10].

In contrast to all this prior work, we present a game theoretic modeling of the adversarial search (i.e., ad hoc retrieval) setting wherein publishers are incentivized to have their documents promoted in rankings. Our analysis does not depend on the nature of actions employed by publishers, namely, whether these are black hat (e.g, spamming), grey hat or white hat search engine optimization efforts [15]. Furthermore, showing that the probability ranking principle is sub-optimal in adversarial settings is a novel contribution of the work presented here.

There has been some (none game theoretic) work on modeling the past versions of a Web page — independently of those of other pages — so as to improve retrieval effectiveness [11]. In contrast, we provide a game theoretic analysis of the effect (specifically, in a steady state) of having multiple publishers change the content of their documents throughout time in response to multiple queries.

There is recent work on devising relevance-based dueling strategies for search engines [16]. Specifically, two search engines compete with each other assuming static publishers and documents. In contrast to our work, analysis of game theoretic aspects (e.g., equilibrium and social welfare) was not presented. Furthermore, our focus is on the competition between dynamic publishers (and documents) given that *some* search engine is used.

3. PRELIMINARIES

Let $[n]$ denote the set $\{1, 2, \ldots, n\}$, and $\Delta(S)$ denote the set of all probability distributions defined over a set S.

Given a distribution $d \in \Delta(S)$, we use $d(i)$ to denote the probability of event i ($\in S$) and $\mathrm{SUP}(d)$ to denote the set of all elements $i \in S$ for which $d(i) > 0$.

3.1 Game theory

We start with a standard definition of a game.

DEFINITION 1. *A strategic form n-player game is a tuple $G = (\{S_i\}_{i \in [n]}, \{U_i\}_{i \in [n]})$. For each player $i \in [n]$, S_i is the set of **actions** of the player. The set $S = S_1 \times S_2 \times \cdots \times S_n$ is called the set of **pure strategy profiles**. For each $i \in [n]$, $U_i : S \to \mathbb{R}$ is the **utility function** of player i.*

In a game, each player tries to maximize the (expected) value of his utility function. Note that the utility of a player depends on actions taken by all players, not only his own. The case of a 2-players game can be represented by a bi-matrix — a matrix in which each cell contains a 2-tuple: the first value is the payoff for the first player, and the second value is the payoff for the second player. Each row in the matrix represents an action of the first player, and each column represents an action of the second player; i.e., the matrix has $|S_1|$ rows and $|S_2|$ columns. For example, consider the following payoff matrix. According to the matrix,

	L	R
U	$(5, 2)$	$(0, 4)$
D	$(3, 6)$	$(1, 1)$

if the players chose actions D and L, the first (row) player payoff will be 3, while the second (column) player payoff will be 6. In a game, each player may choose an action randomly:

DEFINITION 2. *A **mixed strategy** for player i is a distribution $s_i \in \Delta(S_i)$.*

Using this definition, we extend the notion of a strategy profile so that $\Delta S \triangleq \Delta(S_1) \times \ldots \times \Delta(S_n)$ is the set of **mixed strategy profiles**.

We assume that each player i chooses his action according to $\Delta(S_i)$ *independently* of the actions selected by the other players. This allows a straight-forward generalization of the player's utility to the *expected* payoff over the joint distribution. That is, let $s = (s_1, \ldots, s_n) \in \Delta S$ be a mixed strategy profile, then

$$U_i(s) = \sum_{(a_1, \ldots, a_n) \in S} U_i(a_1, \ldots, a_n) \prod_{i=1}^{n} s_i(a_i).$$

We use $s_{-i} = (s_1, \ldots, s_{i-1}, s_{i+1}, \ldots, s_n) \in \Delta S_{-i}$ to denote the strategies played by all players but i. A useful notion is the concept of **best response**. This is the set of actions a player may take to maximize his utility given the actions played by all other players:

DEFINITION 3. *Given a strategy profile s_{-i}, the best response of i is defined as $BR_i(s_{-i}) \triangleq argmax_{a_i \in S_i} U_i(a_i, s_{-i})$.*

Finally, this allows defining a "stable" state of a game: a strategy profile for which no player has an incentive to **deviate**, i.e., change his strategy. This concept is often referred to as the solution of a game.

DEFINITION 4. *A mixed strategy profile $s = (s_1, \ldots, s_n) \in \Delta S$ is a (mixed) **Nash equilibrium**, if for every player $i \in [n] : SUP(s_i) \subseteq BR_i(s_{-i})$. Equivalently, s is an equilibrium if $\forall i \in [n], \forall a_i' \in S_i : U_i(a_i', s_{-i}) \leq U_i(s_i, s_{-i})$. If s is a pure strategy profile, the equilibrium is called **pure**.*

	Football	Opera
Football	$(2, 1)$	$(0, 0)$
Opera	$(0, 0)$	$(1, 2)$

Table 1: Battle of the sexes payoff matrix.

For example, consider the two player game known as "battle of the sexes", where a couple has agreed to go on a date this evening, but forgot to agree on a venue. The husband prefers going to a football match, while the wife wants to see the opera, and they can not communicate. Both would prefer meeting at any place rather than not to meet at all. The game payoffs are given in Table 1. The game has two pure equilibria: jointly watching the match or attending the opera together. This game also has a mixed Nash equilibrium, where the husband goes to the match with probability 2/3 while the wife attends the opera with the same probability. Note that if each were to pick a venue uniformly, they would have met with a higher probability. However, the different preferences of the two incentivize each to try his/hers place of choice with a higher probability. A fundamental result in game theory is Nash Theorem:

THEOREM 1. *[22] Every game with a finite number of players and action sets has a mixed strategies equilibrium.*

A common metric for measuring the "quality" of a given mixed strategy profile is called **social welfare**. The social welfare is defined as the sum of (expected) utilities received by the players playing it; that is, for $s \in \Delta S$ we define $SW(s) \triangleq \sum_{i \in [n]} U_i(s)$.

3.2 Price of anarchy

Given a game, an interesting question is "how inefficient" the system could get in a stable state, due to the selfish behavior of the players. Specifically, an equilibrium of the game is compared with an idealized scenario where all players selflessly collaborate to maximize the profit of the group which is measured by social welfare. A popular measure of this inefficiency is called the **Price of Anarchy** (PoA) [19, 27]. Formally, the price of anarchy is the ratio between the sum of utilities achieved by an optimal strategy profile (i.e., $OPT = \max_{s \in \Delta S} SW(s)$), and the social welfare of the *worst* equilibrium, i.e., the one with the lowest social welfare. Going back to the example from Table 1, when both are going together to either the opera or the football match, we have an optimal social welfare of 3, while the mixed equilibrium only provides a social welfare of 4/3. Thus, the price of anarchy for the game is $\frac{3}{4/3} = 2.25$.

4. ADVERSARIAL AD HOC RETRIEVAL

As already noted, in adversarial retrieval settings such as the Web, the goal of many owners of documents, henceforth referred to as *publishers*, is to have their documents ranked as high as possible in response to queries of interest. Specifically, a ranking induced for a query by a search engine might incentivize publishers of documents that are not highly ranked to change their documents for future rankings. Naturally, this is an on-going process.

We model the dynamics just mentioned as a game. The publishers are players whose actions are document production; i.e., a publisher decides which document to produce at any point in time. The search engine plays the role of a *mediator*. The choice of a ranking function affects the publishers' utilities by the virtue of the induced rankings.

We make the assumption that publishers' utilities and users' utilities are aligned. That is, the payoff a publisher gets for a document with respect to a user query reflects the utility the user attains from reading the document in response to the query. In other words, the premise is that user satisfaction will lead to publisher satisfaction. In that respect, the social welfare of publishers (as players) attained in a game is considered to be the social welfare of the search engine's users. Analysis of more complicated situations, wherein the publishers' and users' utilities are not aligned, is left for future work.

Our goal here is to study the optimality, or lack thereof, of ranking functions that obey the probability ranking principle (PRP) in adversarial retrieval settings; that is, functions that rank documents in response to a query by the relevance (probability) of the documents. To that end, we describe a few games that are defined by the choice of the ranking function and the assumptions about the type of documents the publishers can produce. We assume that in each game the ranking function we want to analyze is fixed. Accounting for changes of the ranking function throughout the game is outside the scope of this paper.

To analyze a ranking function, we examine the equilibria of the game it entails. Specifically, we focus on the price of anarchy of the game (PoA; see Section 3.2), as is common in work on algorithmic game theory. Indeed, this practice allows to reason about the worst case steady state of the game (equilibrium), in terms of the social welfare attained, given the selfish behavior of players — publishers in our case.

4.1 Single-topic documents

Here and after, we assume that each query is about a single topic. We start our analysis in this section with a basic model where every document is also assumed to be about a single topic. The model assumes, in addition, that all publishers have equal writing quality for all topics and that each publisher may write on a topic of his choice. We show that in this model, the probability ranking principle (PRP) is optimal; i.e., using a ranking function that obeys the PRP results in optimal price of anarchy. In Sections 4.2 and 4.3 we extend this model by allowing multi topic documents, and differential writing qualities, respectively, and show that the PRP is no longer optimal in these cases.

4.1.1 Definitions

A **Publishers Game** $PG = (n, m, \mathcal{D}; \mathcal{R})$ is an n **publishers** game over m **topics**. Each publisher selects a topic to write on; i.e., the possible actions are topics. In addition, **queries** are posted, each of which on a specific topic, according to a public query distribution $\mathcal{D} \in \Delta([m])$. Throughout the paper, we assume without loss of generality that $\mathcal{D}(1) \geq \mathcal{D}(2) \geq \ldots \geq \mathcal{D}(m)$. That is, the first topic is always the most frequently queried, then the second, etc.

For the sake of simplifying the analysis, we assume that the user utility with respect to his query is determined solely based on the relevance of the first ranked document. While in practice users examine also documents in lower ranks, it is a well known fact that in the Web setting users pay most of their attention to the most highly ranked documents [17]. In fact, users often prefer to reformulate their queries rather

	1	2	$\ldots$	m
1	$\left(\frac{\mathcal{D}(1)}{2}, \frac{\mathcal{D}(1)}{2}\right)$	$(\mathcal{D}(1), \mathcal{D}(2))$		$(\mathcal{D}(1), \mathcal{D}(m))$
2	$(\mathcal{D}(2), \mathcal{D}(1))$	$\left(\frac{\mathcal{D}(2)}{2}, \frac{\mathcal{D}(2)}{2}\right)$		$(\mathcal{D}(2), \mathcal{D}(m))$
$\vdots$			$\ddots$	
m	$(\mathcal{D}(m), \mathcal{D}(1))$	$(\mathcal{D}(m), \mathcal{D}(2))$		$\left(\frac{\mathcal{D}(m)}{2}, \frac{\mathcal{D}(m)}{2}\right)$

Table 2: Payoff matrix for the game $(2, m, \mathcal{D}; R_{PRP})$.

than spend additional time examining lower ranked documents. Furthermore, it was shown that the precision at rank 1 (i.e., 0 or 1) is highly correlated (with Pearson correlation above 0.5) with average precision at cutoff 1000, which is a standard measure for quantifying the effectiveness of a retrieved list [6]. Thus, we assume that the utility the user attains from the top-most document is highly correlated with the utility the user will attain by examining additional documents further down the ranked list.

Given a query and the set of topics selected by the publishers, the *Ranking Function* $\mathcal{R} : [m] \times [m]^{[n]} \to \Delta([n])$, selects a probability distribution over the documents (i.e., over the players) using which the documents (players) will be ranked; specifically, the probability assigned to a document corresponds to the probability that it will be ranked first. We note that this definition is different than that of standard ranking functions in two respects. First, it does not specify how to rank documents for ranks two and below. Second, the ranking function is allowed to be *probabilistic*, randomizing over the set of documents in the corpus. In contrast, ranking functions used in the information retrieval literature are deterministic. While at first glance randomization may not seem to provide additional value, we show that it could actually result in improved social welfare even if it hurts retrieval effectiveness for a specific query.

As an example of the notation used for ranking functions, consider $\mathcal{R}(1, \langle 1, 1, 2 \rangle) = \langle 0.4, 0.4, 0.2 \rangle$. Given a query on the first topic, if players 1 and 2 wrote on topic 1, and player 3 created a document on topic 2, then each of players 1 and 2 will be ranked first with probability 0.4, while player 3 will be ranked first with probability 0.2. We use $\mathcal{R}_i : [m] \times [m]^{[n]} \to [0, 1]$ to denote the probability assigned to player i for the given input; in our example, $\mathcal{R}_3(1, \langle 1, 1, 2 \rangle) = 0.2$.

We define the payoff for publisher i as 1 for queries he is ranked first on, and 0 for all other queries. His expected payoff is then $U_i(a_i, a_{-i}) = \mathcal{D}(a_i) \cdot \mathcal{R}_i(a_i, (a_i, a_{-i}))$; i.e., the probability that a query on his selected topic arrives times the probability he will be ranked first.

We define the probability ranking principle ranking, **PRP ranking** in short, denoted R_{PRP}, to be the function which always ranks first the document most relevant to a query. Indeed, the PRP [26] states that documents should be ranked by their relevance probabilities, and we care here about the highest ranked document. In this model, the PRP translates to choosing uniformly a document written on the query topic for the first rank. For example, for the two publishers game $(2, m, \mathcal{D}; R_{PRP})$ where the PRP serves for ranking, the payoffs can be expressed by the matrix in Table 2.

4.1.2 Price of anarchy

We focus on the two players game, where a couple of rival publishers compete for the same incoming queries flow, each trying to maximize his payoff by being ranked first. Our goal in this section is showing that in this basic model, the PRP remains optimal. We start with a theorem showing that the PRP ranking yields a game, in which every equilibrium is at most 1.5 times worse than the optimal scenario in terms of social welfare. The optimal scenario is having each of the two publishers write about a different topic among the two most frequently queried topics.

THEOREM 2. *Let $\mathcal{D} \in \Delta([m])$ be a query distribution and let $PG = (2, m, \mathcal{I}; R_{PRP})$ be a two player Publishers Game, then the price of anarchy of PG is at most 1.5.*

The proof, presented in Appendix A, is based on analysis of two cases: when publishers write deterministically on a single topic, and when they choose to randomize over several topics. We show that in any case, the worst equilibrium is reached when both publishers choose a topic only from the two most frequently queried topics.

We complement Theorem 2 by proving that no ranking function is able to achieve price of anarchy smaller than 1.5, for any query distribution. Together, the theorems show that the PRP is optimal in the case where each document (and query) is about a single topic, and all publishers have the same writing quality for all topics. As noted above, optimality refers to the price of anarchy unless otherwise noted.

THEOREM 3. *For any ranking function $\mathcal{R}$, there exists a distribution $\mathcal{D} \in \Delta([m])$, such that the Publishers Game $PG = (2, m, \mathcal{D}; \mathcal{R})$ has a price of anarchy of at least 1.5.*

Intuitively, we show that for the query distribution in which the first topic is queried two-thirds of the time, while the second is queried otherwise, $\mathcal{R}$ can not decrease the price of anarchy below 1.5. The full proof is in Appendix B.

For the case of $m = 2$ topics, we strengthen the result of Theorem 3 by showing that for *any* distribution, one can not improve the social welfare obtained by R_{PRP} using a different ranking function.

THEOREM 4. *For any distribution $\mathcal{D} \in \Delta([2])$ and ranking function $\mathcal{R}$, the social welfare of $(2, 2, \mathcal{D}; \mathcal{R})$ is at most the social welfare of $(2, 2, \mathcal{D}; R_{PRP})$.*

The proof of the theorem is provided in Appendix C. Thus, we get that in the two topics setting, the PRP ranking is optimal in a stronger sense than that considered above (i.e., price of anarchy): there exists *no* query distribution for which an alternative function could achieve higher social welfare than that attained by the PRP.

While we showed that the PRP is optimal in this model, it is not the case in the models considered next. Section 4.2 discusses a setting in which publishers may produce multi-topic documents. Section 4.3 presents a model which accounts for publishers with differential writing qualities.

4.2 Multi-topic documents

We next discuss an extension of the Publishers Game that allows publishers to compose documents about multiple topics. Formally, a **Multiple Topics Publishers Game** $MTPG = (n, m, c, \mathcal{D}; \mathcal{R})$ is similar to Publishers Game, except that publishers may now choose an action

from $[m] \cup \binom{[m]}{2}$; i.e., either writing a document on a single topic or on two topics. We assume that a multiple topics document has equal proportions of the two topics. When a publisher writes on two topics, an additional parameter, $c \in [0, 1]$, is the payoff he receives when ranked first on either of these topics. Assuming that documents are of equal length, the PRP ranking amounts here to determining relevance level (grade) based on the prevalence of relevance information in the document. This graded relevance definition was also applied in work on focused retrieval [14]. Specifically, a document dedicated entirely to the query topic is preferred to any document that discusses two topics. For two documents that discuss two topics, the one which discusses the query topic is preferred to the one which does not; if both documents discuss the query topic, one of the two is randomly selected to be ranked first.

We focus on the special case of two documents and two publishers, showing that even in this restricted scenario, the PRP is not always optimal. We start by showing that if the multi-topic document payoff c is small, then the PRP ranking remains optimal.

THEOREM 5. *Let $c \in [0, 1/2]$. For any distribution $\mathcal{D} \in \Delta([m])$, the Multiple Topics Publishers Game $MTPG = (2, m, c, \mathcal{D}; R_{PRP})$ achieves a price of anarchy of at most 1.5.*

The idea behind the proof, presented in Appendix D, is showing that when multi-topic documents provide just a small benefit, the publishers will never write such documents; in this case, we can use Theorem 3 for the price of anarchy bound.

The next theorem shows that for such small c values, the PRP is indeed optimal as any ranking function will incur a price of anarchy of 1.5 for some query distribution.

THEOREM 6. *Let $c \in [0, 1/2]$. There exists a distribution $\mathcal{D} \in \Delta([m])$, such that for any ranking function $\mathcal{R}$, the Multiple Topics Publishers Game $MTPG = (2, m, c, \mathcal{D}; \mathcal{R})$ has a price of anarchy of at least 1.5.*

Similarly to Theorem 3, we consider a query distribution where the first topic is queried two-thirds of the time, and otherwise the second topic is queried. We show that for this distribution, no ranking function could reduce the price of anarchy when c is small.

Next, when c is sufficiently large, we show an example in which the anarchy entailed by using the PRP ranking could be completely avoided by using an alternative ranking function which does not adhere to the PRP; that is, a social welfare that approaches the optimal can be attained.

EXAMPLE 1. *Consider the distribution $\mathcal{D}(1) = 2/3$, $\mathcal{D}(2) = 1/3$. For any c, the price of anarchy of $MTPG_{PRP} = (2, 2, c, \mathcal{D}; R_{PRP})$ is 1.5, while there exists a ranking function, R_{prob}, such that the price of anarchy of $MTPG_{prob} = (2, 2, c, \mathcal{D}; R_{prob})$ could be arbitrarily close to 1 as $c \to 1$.*

For the example, we propose a non-deterministic, probabilistic, ranking function[3] R_{prob}. The function randomizes the relative ranking of a multi-topic document and a pure

---

[3] As explained in Section 4.1, by probabilistic ranking function, we mean a *non-deterministic* ranking function that applies randomization. This should be differentiated from probabilistic retrieval methods that are deterministic and rank documents by relevance probabilities [29].

document written on the first topic, whenever a query on the first topic is posted. The complete proof is provided in Appendix E.

We conclude this section by showing a large family of games in which the PRP is not optimal, and propose a probabilistic (randomized) ranking function instead. This finding implies that introducing randomness to the *ranking* of documents may result in a more content enriched corpus in the long run, by providing incentives for publishers to diversify the topics they write about.

THEOREM 7. *Let $c \in (1/2, 1]$, $p \in [2/3, \frac{2c}{c+1})$. Consider the distribution $\mathcal{D}(1) = p, \mathcal{D}(2) = 1 - p$. There exists a ranking function R_{prob}, such that the price of anarchy of $(2, 2, c, \mathcal{D}; R_{PRP})$ is strictly larger than that of $(2, 2, c, \mathcal{D}; R_{prob})$.*

The core idea underlying the proof of the theorem, which can be found in Appendix D, is to carefully construct a probabilistic ranking function which occasionally ranks the multi-topic document higher than a document written entirely on the query topic.

4.3 Publishers with differential writing qualities

Heretofore, we assumed that every publisher can write about every topic with the same quality. We now turn to analyze a setting wherein this is not the case. Specifically, we explore an extension of the Publishers Game to a setting where publishers write on a single topic, but have different writing qualities. Formally, a **Different Qualities Publishers Game** $DQPG = (n, m, \mathcal{Q}; \mathcal{R})$ is similar to the Publishers Game, except that publishers now have individual payoff functions representing the utility of the document they create for a queried topic. This setting amounts to assuming, for example, that the utility (for the user, and consequently for the publisher, per our working assumption) attained from the same document produced by two different publishers is different and depends on their writing quality for the topic. Indeed, the less the publisher is authoritative about the topic, the more effort the user will have to put into verifying the content (e.g., by consulting other sources of information), thereby decreasing his utility.

The DQPG game has a **Quality Matrix** parameter, $\mathcal{Q} \in [0, 1]^{[n] \times [m]}$, where $\mathcal{Q}_{i,j}$ is the payoff for publisher i if he is ranked first on topic j. Note that the query distribution parameter has been omitted as we may normalize the Quality Matrix to factor the topic frequencies. For example, if the first topic is queried $2/3$ of the time, and otherwise the second topic is queried, then we multiply the first column of $\mathcal{Q}$ by $2/3$ and the second column by $1/3$. In this setting, we assume that in the PRP ranking, R_{PRP}, the *highest quality* document written on the queried topic is ranked first. In case multiple documents have the same quality, it uniformly selects a top-quality document. That is, originally, the PRP was shown to optimize utility by *implicitly* assuming equal writing qualities of publishers; thus, relevance amounted to utility for a given query. Here, we stick to the original goal of the PRP, optimizing utility, and account for the fact that relevance is not necessarily coupled with utility.

First, we show a tight bound for the price of anarchy achieved by the PRP ranking.

THEOREM 8. *For any Quality Matrix $\mathcal{Q} \in [0, 1]^{[n] \times [m]}$, such that players have distinct writing qualities for any given*

topic, the Different Qualities Publishers Game $DQPG = (n, m, \mathcal{Q}; R_{PRP})$ has a price of anarchy of at most 2.

The essence of the proof, provided in Appendix G, is reducing the problem to finding a matching in the bipartite graph which has the publishers on one partite and the topics on the other. We show that any equilibrium in the game corresponds to a matching which may be generated by the greedy algorithm and that the approximation rate of the algorithm provides a bound on the price of anarchy.

Complementing the theorem, we show that the price of anarchy analysis for R_{PRP} is tight.

THEOREM 9. *For any $\epsilon > 0$, there exists a matrix $\mathcal{Q}^{\epsilon}$, such that the price of anarchy of $(n, m, \mathcal{Q}^{\epsilon}; R_{PRP})$ is $2 - \epsilon$.*

The result is obtained for the simple case where one publisher has writing quality for multiple topics, while another publisher can write mainly on a specific topic. If the first player has even a slight writing quality advantage over the second on that specific topic, he may prefer writing about it, and no publisher would satisfy the information need for the remaining topics. The proof is found in Appendix H.

It is important to note that if a ranking function could act arbitrarily, a search engine could abuse this model to force the optimal strategy, which is the *maximum weight matching* of the complete bipartite graph over $[n] \cup [m]$, where the weight of an edge (i, j) is $\mathcal{Q}_{i,j}$. For example, consider the ranking function which given a query on topic j, ranks first the publisher i, if (i, j) is a part of the maximum weight matching, and i wrote a document on topic j. Otherwise, it places a completely irrelevant document at the top position. In this case, every publisher realizes that the only way users with information need relevant to his page reach his document is by cooperation with the engine, writing on the topic assigned to him in the matching.

In order to avoid ranking functions which dictate for each player the topic to write on, we restrict the discussion to **Fair Ranking Functions**. A Fair Ranking Function is a function which given a query, assigns first-rank probabilities (i.e., probability to be ranked first) to documents written on the topic, without considering the writing qualities of the publishers on *other* topics. More formally, a Fair Ranking Function is a set of functions, $\mathcal{R} = \{\mathcal{R}^k : [0, 1]^{[k]} \to \Delta([k])\}_{k \in [n]}$, such that given a query on a topic that k publishers wrote about, $\mathcal{R}^k$ is applied on the qualities of these publishers to determine the ranking, and the ranker is not allowed to consider the writing qualities of publishers on topics that they did not write on.

Theorem 9 shows that for *any* values of n, m (i.e., number of publishers and number of topics, respectively) the price of anarchy of the PRP is 2. We complement this by showing that for the case of 2-player games, R_{PRP} is not optimal, even when compared only with Fair Ranking Functions.

THEOREM 10. *There exists a Fair Ranking Function R_{uni}, such that for any Quality Matrix $\mathcal{Q} \in [0, 1]^{[2] \times [m]}$, the Different Qualities Publishers Game $DQPG = (2, m, \mathcal{Q}; R_{uni})$ achieves a price of anarchy of at most 1.7.*

To prove the theorem, we consider a probabilistic ranking function R_{uni} which makes a fair coin flip to select the top ranked document, whenever the difference in quality of given documents is "small enough". A more detailed proof sketch for the $n = m = 2$ case appears in Appendix I. The complete proof, and its extension to general number of topics m are omitted due to lack of space.

We conclude the analysis by showing a lower bound on the price of anarchy achievable by *any* Fair Ranking Function.

THEOREM 11. *For any Fair Ranking Function $\mathcal{R}$ and number of topics m, there exists a Quality Matrix $\mathcal{Q} \in [0, 1]^{[2] \times [m]}$, such that the price of anarchy of the Different Qualities Publishers Game $DQPG = (2, m, \mathcal{Q}; R_{uni})$ is at least 1.5.*

In Appendix J, we present a proof which constructs two games with different quality matrices. We show that any ranking function achieves social welfare which is at most two thirds of the optimum, at least for one of the games.

5. CONCLUSIONS

We presented a novel game theoretic analysis of the ad hoc document retrieval task in adversarial settings. The analysis accounts for the incentives of authors to have their documents ranked high in response to queries. Thus, the analysis provides formal grounds for modeling the dynamic nature of the adversarial retrieval setting that results from authors consistently changing their documents so as to promote them in rankings. We performed the analysis for different types of documents (namely, single topic versus multi topic) and by using different assumptions about the writing qualities of authors. One of our most important findings is that the probability ranking principle (PRP), which is the theoretical foundation of most ad hoc retrieval methods, can be sub-optimal in the adversarial setting. Specifically, we showed that in some cases, introducing randomization into the document ranking function can result in user utility higher than that attained by applying the PRP.

Acknowledgements

We thank the reviewers for their comments. This work was supported by and carried out at the Technion-Microsoft Electronic Commerce Research Center.

6. REFERENCES

[1] *AIRWeb — International Workshop on Adversarial Information Retrieval on the Web*, 2005–2009.
[2] *WICOW/AIRWeb Workshop on Web Quality (WebQuality)*, 2012.
[3] G. Amati and C. J. van Rijsbergen. Probabilistic models of information retrieval based on measuring the divergence from randomness. *ACM Transactions on Information Systems*, 20(4):357–389, 2002.
[4] A. A. Benczúr, K. Csalogány, T. Sarlós, and M. Uher. Spamrank – fully automatic link spam detection. In *AIRWeb 2005, First International Workshop on Adversarial Information Retrieval on the Web, co-located with the WWW conference, Chiba, Japan, May 2005*, pages 25–38, 2005.
[5] M. Bendersky, W. B. Croft, and Y. Diao. Quality-biased ranking of web documents. In *Proc. of WSDM*, pages 95–104, 2011.
[6] O. Butman, A. Shtok, O. Kurland, and D. Carmel. Query-performance prediction using minimal relevance feedback. In *Proceedings of ICTIR*, page 7, 2013.
[7] J. G. Carbonell and J. Goldstein. The use of MMR, diversity-based reranking for reordering documents and producing summaries. In *Proc. of SIGIR*, pages 335–336, 1998.
[8] G. V. Cormack. TREC 2007 spam track overview. In *Proc. of TREC*, 2007.
[9] G. V. Cormack, M. D. Smucker, and C. L. A. Clarke. Efficient and effective spam filtering and re-ranking for large web datasets. *Information Retrieval*, 14(5):441–465, 2011.

[10] N. N. Dalvi, P. Domingos, Mausam, S. K. Sanghai, and D. Verma. Adversarial classification. In *Proc. of KDD*, pages 99–108, 2004.
[11] J. L. Elsas and S. T. Dumais. Leveraging temporal dynamics of document content in relevance ranking. In *Proc. of WSDM*, pages 1–10, 2010.
[12] D. Fetterly, M. Manasse, and M. Najork. Spam, damn spam, and statistics: Using statistical analysis to locate spam web pages. In *Proceedings of WebDB*, pages 1–6, 2004.
[13] N. Fuhr. A probability ranking principle for interactive information retrieval. *Information Retrieval*, 11(3):251–265, 2008.
[14] S. Geva, J. Kamps, and R. Schenkel, editors. *Focused Retrieval of Content and Structure, 10th International Workshop of the Initiative for the Evaluation of XML Retrieval, INEX 2011, Saarbrücken, Germany, December 12-14, 2011, Revised Selected Papers*, volume 7424 of *Lecture Notes in Computer Science*. Springer, 2012.
[15] Z. Gyöngyi and H. Garcia-Molina. Web spam taxonomy. In *Proc. of AIRWeb 2005*, pages 39–47, 2005.
[16] P. Izsak, F. Raiber, O. Kurland, and M. Tennenholtz. The search duel: a response to a strong ranker. In S. Geva, A. Trotman, P. Bruza, C. L. A. Clarke, and K. Järvelin, editors, *Proc. of SIGIR*, pages 919–922. ACM, 2014.
[17] T. Joachims, L. A. Granka, B. Pan, H. Hembrooke, and G. Gay. Accurately interpreting clickthrough data as implicit feedback. In R. A. Baeza-Yates, N. Ziviani, G. Marchionini, A. Moffat, and J. Tait, editors, *Proc. of SIGIR*, pages 154–161, 2005.
[18] T. Jones, D. Hawking, and R. Sankaranarayana. A framework for measuring the impact of web spam. In *Proc. of ADCS2007*.
[19] E. Koutsoupias and C. Papadimitriou. Worst-Case Equilibria. In *Proc. of STACS*, 1999.
[20] V. Krishnan and R. Raj. Web spam detection with Anti-Trust rank. In *Proceedings of AIRWeb*, pages 37–40, 2006.
[21] T.-Y. Liu. Learning to rank for information retrieval. *Foundations and Trends in Information Retrieval*, 3(3), 2009.
[22] J. F. Nash. Equilibrium points in n-person games. *Proc. of the National Academy of Sciences of the United States of America*, 36.1:48–49, 1950.
[23] J. M. Ponte and W. B. Croft. A language modeling approach to information retrieval. In *Proc. of SIGIR*, pages 275–281, 1998.
[24] F. Raiber, K. Collins-Thompson, and O. Kurland. Shame to be sham: Addressing content-based grey hat search engine optimization. In *Proc. of SIGIR*, pages 1013–1016, 2013.
[25] S. Richardson and I. J. Cox. Estimating global statistics for unstructured P2P search in the presence of adversarial peers. In *Proc. of SIGIR*, pages 203–212, 2014.
[26] S. E. Robertson. The probability ranking principle in IR. *Journal of Documentation*, pages 294–304, 1977.
[27] T. Roughgarden and E. Tardos. How bad is selfish routing? *Journal of the ACM*, 49(2):236–259, April 2002.
[28] J. Salton, A. Wong, and C. S. Yang. A vector space model for automatic indexing. *Communications of the ACM*, 18(11):613–620, 1975.
[29] K. Sparck Jones, S. Walker, and S. E. Robertson. A probabilistic model of information retrieval: development and comparative experiments - part 1. *Information Processing and Management*, 36(6):779–808, 2000.
[30] B. Wu and B. D. Davison. Identifying link farm spam pages. In *Proc. of WWW*, pages 820–829, 2005.

APPENDIX

A. PROOF OF THEOREM 2

PROOF. The optimal scenario we compare to, is when some publisher writes about topic 1, while the other composes a document on topic 2. The optimal social welfare is therefore $OPT = \mathcal{D}(1) + \mathcal{D}(2) \leq 1$. Next, we examine a few possible equilibria:

1. Each player writes on a different topic.
   When such equilibrium exists, players must write about topics 1 and 2 (or other topics with the same frequency, if such exist). The social welfare of the equilibrium is then $\mathcal{D}(1) + \mathcal{D}(2)$, and the players reach optimal welfare.

2. Both players write about topic 1 with probability 1.
   In this scenario, $\mathcal{D}(1) \geq 2/3$, as the publishers have no incentive to deviate to topic 2. This means the social welfare of the equilibrium is $\mathcal{D}(1)$, and the price of anarchy is at most $\frac{1}{2/3} = 1.5$.

3. The players play a symmetric equilibrium (i.e., both have the same mixed strategy), randomizing their actions over the first two topics.
   As both players have topic 2 in their support, we know that $\mathcal{D}(2) \geq \mathcal{D}(1)/2$. Assume that each player writes about the first topic with probability p. The payoff of writing about topic 1, assuming that the other publishers follows this strategy, is $\mathcal{D}(1)/2$ with probability p (as the ranking function would rank each of the publishers randomly), or $\mathcal{D}(1)$ if the other player chose to write about topic 2, which happens with probability $1 - p$. Therefore the utility is $U(1) = p \cdot \mathcal{D}(1)/2 + (1-p) \cdot \mathcal{D}(1)$. Similarly, the utility of writing about the second topic is $U(2) = p \cdot \mathcal{D}(2) + (1-p) \cdot \mathcal{D}(2)/2$. As both topics are in the support of the players' strategy, the utility of writing on each of them must be equal, i.e. $U(1) = U(2)$. This give us $p = \frac{2\mathcal{D}(1) - \mathcal{D}(2)}{\mathcal{D}(1) + \mathcal{D}(2)}$. Since both publishers play the same mixed strategy, the social welfare of the equilibrium is $P = 2 \cdot U(1) = 2 \cdot U(2) = \frac{3\mathcal{D}(1)\mathcal{D}(2)}{\mathcal{D}(1) + \mathcal{D}(2)}$. Finally, we can express the price of anarchy as

   $$\frac{OPT}{P} = \frac{\mathcal{D}(1) + \mathcal{D}(2)}{\frac{3\mathcal{D}(1)\mathcal{D}(2)}{\mathcal{D}(1) + \mathcal{D}(2)}} = \frac{(\mathcal{D}(1) + \mathcal{D}(2))^2}{3\mathcal{D}(1)\mathcal{D}(2)}.$$

   In the domain $0 \leq \mathcal{D}(1)/2 \leq \mathcal{D}(2) \leq \mathcal{D}(1) \leq 1 - \mathcal{D}(2)$, this function is bounded by $3/2$, which is reached on the line $\mathcal{D}(1) = 2\mathcal{D}(2)$.

4. One of the players does not have the second topic in the support of his strategy.
   Without loss of generality, we assume that player 2 is the one which never writes about topic 2. In this case, since we already covered all equilibria in which players restrict themselves only to the first two topics, the second player must have the third topic in his support (or a different topic with the same query frequency). The first player then must earn at least $\mathcal{D}(2)$, as he would be the only publisher to write on the second topic, should he choose to do so. Player 2 may randomize between the first and third topic, but since he is the only publisher to (occasionally) write on topic 3, his utility is $\mathcal{D}(3)$. Also, since the players can always earn $\mathcal{D}(1)/2$ by writing on the first topic, we get that $\mathcal{D}(2), \mathcal{D}(3) \geq \mathcal{D}(1)/2$. Putting it together, we get a social welfare of $\mathcal{D}(2) + \mathcal{D}(3)$, which means price of anarchy of

   $$\frac{OPT}{P} \leq \frac{\mathcal{D}(1) + \mathcal{D}(2)}{\mathcal{D}(2) + \mathcal{D}(3)} \leq \frac{\mathcal{D}(1) + \mathcal{D}(2)}{\mathcal{D}(2) + \mathcal{D}(1)/2}$$
   $$= \frac{\mathcal{D}(1) + \mathcal{D}(2)}{2\mathcal{D}(2)/3 + \mathcal{D}(2)/3 + \mathcal{D}(1)/2}$$
   $$\leq \frac{\mathcal{D}(1) + \mathcal{D}(2)}{2\mathcal{D}(2)/3 + \mathcal{D}(1)/6 + \mathcal{D}(1)/2} = \frac{3}{2}$$

5. Both players are playing an equilibrium in which the support of each contains topics 1 and 2.
   In this case, we argue that each player must earn at least as much as he did in equilibrium in which both

players only write on the first two topics (case 3). Let $p = \frac{2\mathcal{D}(1) - \mathcal{D}(2)}{\mathcal{D}(1) + \mathcal{D}(2)}$ be the 2-topics symmetric equilibrium probability computed in 3. Notice that for an equilibrium $< s_1, s_2 >$, we get that the utilities received by the players are:

$$U_1 = \mathcal{D}(1)(1 - s_2(1)/2) = \mathcal{D}(2)(1 - s_2(2)/2)$$

$$U_2 = \mathcal{D}(1)(1 - s_1(1)/2) = \mathcal{D}(2)(1 - s_1(2)/2)$$

Now if $\{1, 2\} \subsetneq SUP(s_i)$ then either $s_i(1) < p$ or $s_i(2) < 1 - p$. This means that the profit for the *other* player has to increase. Since the arguments holds for both players, we get that each gains at least $\frac{3\mathcal{D}(1)\mathcal{D}(2)}{2(\mathcal{D}(1) + \mathcal{D}(2))}$ and the bound from 3 give us the required $\frac{3}{2}$ bound on the price of anarchy.

Since we covered all possible equilibria, we established that the price of anarchy is 1.5. $\square$

B. PROOF OF THEOREM 3

PROOF. Consider the simple scenario where queries about the first topic arrive with probability 2/3, while the second topic is queried 1/3 of the time; i.e., $\mathcal{D}(1) = 2/3, \mathcal{D}(2) = 1/3, \forall i \in [m] \setminus \{1, 2\} : \mathcal{D}(i) = 0$. In the PRP-based game, $PG = (2, m, \mathcal{D}; R_{PRP})$, the players' payoffs are given by

$(1/3, 1/3)$	$(2/3, 1/3)$
$(1/3, 2/3)$	$(1/6, 1/6)$

. The ranking function $\mathcal{R}$ is allowed to choose the first-rank probabilities when the players write on different topics; i.e., the probability of ranking a non-relevant document first, rather than one written on the queried topic. This means that $\mathcal{R}$ may modify the game to

$(1/3, 1/3)$	(α, β)
(β, α)	$(1/6, 1/6)$

, for any values of α, β satisfying $0 \leq \alpha \leq 2/3, 0 \leq \beta \leq 1/3$. In the new game, regardless of the values of α and β, there exists an equilibrium in which both players write on topic 1. In this equilibrium, each player payoff is 1/3, while the utility of deviating to the second topic is $\beta \leq 1/3$. This means that the price of anarchy of $\mathcal{R}$ is at least $\frac{1}{2/3} = 1.5$. $\square$

C. PROOF OF THEOREM 4

PROOF. When R_{PRP} is used, the game is a special case of the one presented in Table 2, and is given by the matrix

$\left(\frac{\mathcal{D}(1)}{2}, \frac{\mathcal{D}(1)}{2}\right)$	$(\mathcal{D}(1), \mathcal{D}(2))$
$(\mathcal{D}(2), \mathcal{D}(1))$	$\left(\frac{\mathcal{D}(2)}{2}, \frac{\mathcal{D}(2)}{2}\right)$

. If $\mathcal{D}(1) \geq 2/3$, the game has a unique equilibrium in which both players write about the first topic. This means that the social welfare of the game will be $\mathcal{D}(1)$. When $\mathcal{D}(1) \in [1/2, 2/3)$, the game has an optimal social welfare equilibrium, in which publishers write on different topics. The game also has a mixed strategies equilibrium, in which each writes about the first topic with probability $p = 3\mathcal{D}(1) - 1$. This equilibrium has a social welfare of $3\mathcal{D}(1)\mathcal{D}(2)$. Similarly to Theorem 3, the ranking function $\mathcal{R}$ may rank a document on a different topic before a relevant topic, hence it may modify the game to

$\left(\frac{\mathcal{D}(1)}{2}, \frac{\mathcal{D}(1)}{2}\right)$	(α, β)
(β, α)	$\left(\frac{\mathcal{D}(2)}{2}, \frac{\mathcal{D}(2)}{2}\right)$

for any values of α, β such that $0 \leq \alpha \leq \mathcal{D}(1), 0 \leq \beta \leq \mathcal{D}(2)$. In the case where $\alpha \geq \frac{\mathcal{D}(2)}{2}$ and $\beta \geq \frac{\mathcal{D}(1)}{2}$, this game has a symmetric mixed strategy equilibrium where each player writes about the first topic with probability $p \triangleq \frac{2\alpha + \mathcal{D}(1) - 1}{2\alpha + 2\beta - 1}$. In all other cases, the game has only pure-strategy equilibrium where both surely write about topic 1. The pure strategy equilibrium gives a social welfare of $\mathcal{D}(1)$. This is strictly lower than the $3\mathcal{D}(1)\mathcal{D}(2)$ achieved by R_{PRP} in the $\mathcal{D}(1) \in [1/2, 2/3]$ case, and identical to it when $\mathcal{D}(1) \geq \frac{2}{3}$. The mixed strategies equilibrium gives a social welfare of $\mathcal{D}(1) \cdot p + (\alpha + \beta \cdot (1 - p)) = \frac{4\alpha\beta - \mathcal{D}(1)\mathcal{D}(2)}{2\alpha + 2\beta - 1}$. Fixing $\mathcal{D}(1)$ and $\mathcal{D}(2)$, analysis of the social welfare as a function of α and β reveals that it is maximized at $\alpha = \mathcal{D}(1), \beta = \mathcal{D}(2)$. This shows that in any case, no ranking function outperforms R_{PRP}. $\square$

D. PROOF OF THEOREM 5

PROOF. Although this may sound intuitive, adding an action to players' action sets may actually decrease the social-welfare. We prove that whenever $c < 1/2$, the multi-topic document will never be a part of the support of the players. (The $c = 0.5$ case is technical and omitted due to lack of space.) This is done by showing it is *dominated*, i.e., it is never a part of the players' best-response. Let $s_2 \in \Delta([m])$ be a mixed strategy for the second player and let $j, \ell \in [m]$ be two distinct topics. The first publisher payoffs for writing on the topics are:

$$U(j, s_2) = \mathcal{D}(j) \cdot (1 - s_2(j)/2)$$
$$U(\ell, s_2) = \mathcal{D}(\ell) \cdot (1 - s_2(\ell)/2)$$

Without loss of generality, we assume $U_1(\ell, s_2) \geq U_1(j, s_2)$. The utility of writing the multi topic document is

$$U_1(\{j, \ell\}) = c \cdot (\mathcal{D}(j) \cdot (1 - s_2(j)/2) + \mathcal{D}(\ell) \cdot (1 - s_2(\ell)/2))$$
$$= c \cdot (U_1(j) + U_1(\ell)) < (U_1(j) + U_1(\ell))/2 \leq U_1(\ell).$$

This means that a publisher could always profit more from writing a single-topic document. Thus, publishers will never write on multiple topics in an equilibrium. $\square$

E. PROOF OF EXAMPLE 1

PROOF. The payoff matrix of the $MTPG_{PRP}$ game is

(1/3, 1/3)	(2/3, c/3)	(2/3, 1/3)
(c/3, 2/3)	(c/2, c/2)	(2c/3, 1/3)
(1/3, 2/3)	(1/3, 2c/3)	(1/6, 1/6)

,

where for each player the first action is associated with writing a document on topic 1, the second is writing a multiple topic document and the last action is writing on the second topic. For any value of c, there exists an equilibrium where both players write on topic 1. This equilibrium has a social welfare of $2/3$, while an optimum of 1 is reached if both players write on different topics. This means that for any value of c, the price of anarchy of R_{PRP} is 1.5.

For $c > 1/2$, consider the ranking function R_{prob}, which is identical to R_{PRP}, except for the case where one publisher wrote about topic 1, the other about a multiple topics document, and a query on the first topic was posted. In this case, R_{prob} ranks the multi-topic document first with probability $1 - \frac{3c}{2(1+c)}$. The probabilistic ranking changes the utility of the players which are aiming to maximize their expected payoff, and the resulting payoff matrix is

(1/3, 1/3)	$\left(\frac{c}{1+c}, \frac{c}{1+c}\right)$	(2/3, 1/3)
$\left(\frac{c}{1+c}, \frac{c}{1+c}\right)$	(c/2, c/2)	(2c/3, 1/3)
(1/3, 2/3)	(1/3, 2c/3)	(1/6, 1/6)

.

This game has an optimal pure-strategies equilibria when players write on different documents, and a single mixed strategies equilibrium. In this mixed equilibrium, each player creates a document about the first topic with probability $\frac{3(c-1)}{3c^2 - 7c + 2}$, and a multi topic document otherwise. The resulting social welfare in this case is $\frac{2c(c^2 - 4c + 1)}{(c+1)(3c^2 - 7c + 2)}$, which approaches 1 when c is almost 1. $\square$

F. PROOF OF THEOREM 7

PROOF. In $MTPG_{PRP} = (2, 2, c, \mathcal{D}; R_{PRP})$, there exists a dominant-strategy equilibrium in which both players write on the first topic. Playing it, the publishers earn $U(1) = p/2$, while the utility of writing about multiple topics is $U(\{1, 2\}) = c \cdot (1 - p) \leq 1 - p \leq p/2$, and the utility of writing about the second topic is $U(2) = 1 - p \leq p/2$. This means that the social welfare achieved by R_{PRP} is p. Next, we define R_{prob} as follows:

- Consider a query on the first topic, a document written on the topic, and a multi-topic document. In this case, R_{prob} will rank the multi-topic document first with probability $r \triangleq 1 - \frac{c}{p \cdot (1+c)}$. Notice that since $c \in (1/2, 1]$ and $p \in [2/3, \frac{2c}{c+1})$, we have $r \in [\frac{1}{4}, \frac{1}{2}]$.

- On all other cases, R_{prob} behaves just like R_{PRP}.

The introduction of probabilistic ranking in R_{prob} changes the game payoffs when one player writes on topic 1, while the other on multiple topics. In this case, the utility of writing on topic 1 drops to $U(1, \{1, 2\}) = p(1 - r) = \frac{c}{1+c}$. Similarly, the utility of writing multiple topics rises to $U(\{1, 2\}, 1) = c(1 - p + p \cdot r) = \frac{c}{1+c}$. The game payoff matrix is therefore:

(p/2, p/2)	$\left(\frac{c}{1+c}, \frac{c}{1+c}\right)$	(p, 1-p)
$\left(\frac{c}{1+c}, \frac{c}{1+c}\right)$	(c/2, c/2)	$(c \cdot p, 1-p)$
(1-p, p)	$(1-p, c \cdot p)$	$\left(\frac{1-p}{2}, \frac{1-p}{2}\right)$

First, we notice that the scenario in which both players write on the first topic is no longer an equilibrium, as players are better off deviating to the multi-topic document, earning $\frac{c}{1+c} > p/2$. Next, the strategy of writing on topic 1 still dominates creating a document about the second topic. Finally, we observe that the pure-strategies equilibria $((1, 2)$ or $(2, 1))$ gives a social welfare of $\frac{2c}{1+c} > p$. The only mixed strategies equilibrium in this game is reached when each player writes about topic 1 with probability $x = \frac{c \cdot (c-1)}{c^2 + c \cdot (p-3) + p}$ and otherwise writes a multi-topic document. This gives a social welfare of

$$P = 2U(2) = 2x \cdot \frac{c}{1+c} + (1-x) \cdot c$$
$$= \frac{c}{1+c} \cdot \frac{c^2 p + 2cp - 4c + p}{c^2 + c \cdot (p-3) + p}$$

which, on the domain of $c \in (1/2, 1]$ and $p \in [2/3, \frac{2c}{c+1})$ is strictly larger than p. $\square$

G. PROOF OF THEOREM 8

PROOF. We prove the theorem by showing that any equilibrium is associated with a matching in the bipartite graph which has the publishers on one partite and the topics on the other. Formally, let $G = ([n] \cup [m], [n] \times [m])$ be a full bipartite graph. Let $w : [n] \times [m] \to [0,1]$ be a weight function such that $w(i,j) = Q_{i,j}$. We prove that an equilibrium for the game corresponds to a matching that could be generated by the greedy algorithm for graph matching. The algorithm iteratively expands the matching by simply adding the maximum-weight edge connecting unmatched vertices to the matching. For simplicity, the proof assumes $n \leq m$, although this is not required, as otherwise the utility of $n - m$ players is 0, and they may be removed to obtain a valid matching. We complete the proof by induction over the number of players in the game.

- **Basis:** in a single publisher game, the only equilibrium is when the player writes a document on the topic j maximizing $w(1,j)$, and so does the greedy matching.

- **Induction Step:** Let $i, j \in \text{argmax}\{Q_{i,j}\}$ be a top-quality publisher-topic pair. Since no other player has the same writing quality on topic j, player i writes about j, knowing he will surely be ranked first. The remaining players then know that no gain would come from writing on topic j. Hence, we are left with a game with $n-1$ players and $m-1$ topics. In the graph, this pair represents a maximum weight edge, and therefore may be selected by the greedy algorithm. Using the induction hypothesis, we conclude that the remaining players will also follow the greedy matching algorithm.

We conclude the proof by using the well-known result stating that the greedy algorithm achieves a 2-approximation for the maximum weight matching of the graph. □

H. PROOF OF THEOREM 9

PROOF. Consider the following Quality Matrix

players/topics	1	2	...	m
1	1	$1 - \epsilon/2$		0
2	$1 - \epsilon/2$	0		0
⋮			⋱	
n	0	0		0

All zeros Quality Matrix expect for $(1,1),(1,2),(2,1)$.

Writing a document on topic 1 is a dominating strategy for player 1. Once this is done, the social welfare of the game is 1, regardless of the choice of the remaining players. The price of anarchy is as required, since the optimum is reached when players 1 and 2 write about topics 2 and 1 respectively yielding a social welfare of $2 - \epsilon$. □

I. PROOF SKETCH OF THEOREM 10

PROOF. Since price of anarchy analysis concerns with the *ratio* between the optimal strategy and an equilibrium strategy, it stays the same if $\mathcal{Q}$ is multiplied by a constant. Therefore, we assume that $\mathcal{Q}_{1,1} = 1$, i.e. the first publisher writes about the first topic perfectly. Therefore, a general Quality Matrix can be described using three parameters, $a, b, c \in [0,1]$:

players/topics	1	2
1	1	a
2	b	c

The Quality Matrix $\mathcal{Q}$.

Notice that this notation means that the optimal solution for price of anarchy analysis is $OPT = \max\{1 + c, a + b\}$. We define the ranking function R_{uni} as the function which gives equal probability to all documents written on the topic whose quality is at least $2/3$ times the quality of the best document on the topic. The proof is done by an extensive case analysis over the possible values of a, b and c, and is omitted due to lack of space. □

J. PROOF OF THEOREM 11

PROOF. Intuitively, we show that $\mathcal{R}$ has to be at least 1.5 worse than the optimum in one of two cases. If it prefers a "$\frac{2}{3}$-quality" document over a perfect document with probability larger than third, then both players might write on the topic they are less qualified to write on, thereby incurring a 1.5 anarchy. Alternatively, if $\mathcal{R}$ does not rank the worse document with that probability, players might selfishly write on their topic of choice, and no one would satisfy the information need of the remaining topics.

We denote $p \triangleq \mathcal{R}(2/3, 1)(1)$, i.e. the probability $\mathcal{R}$ ranks a document with quality $2/3$ higher than a document of quality 1. Next, we consider two cases:

- **p ≥ 1/3.** In this case, consider the Quality Matrix:

players/topics	1	2
1	1	2/3
2	2/3	1

This means that the payoff for the players can be represented as:

$(1-p, 2p/3)$	$(1,1)$
$(2/3, 2/3)$	$(2p/3, 1-p)$

. Since $1/3 \leq p \leq 1$, there exists an equilibrium in which player 1 writes about topic 2 while player 2 writes about topic 1. In this equilibrium, the payoff for each player is $2/3$, while the optimum is 2. This means that the price of anarchy of $\mathcal{R}$ is at least $\frac{OPT}{P} = \frac{2}{4/3} = 1.5$.

- **p<1/3.** When $\mathcal{R}$ gives high probability of ranking first the second-best document, it will be far from optimal in the following situation. Consider the Quality Matrix:

players/topics	1	2
1	1	$1-p$
2	2/3	0

The following payoff matrix is then:

$(1-p, 2p/3)$	$(1, 0)$
$(1-p, 2/3)$	$(1-p, 0)^4$

.

Notice that both players writing on the first topic is an equilibrium for the game, while the optimum is reached at 2, 1, thus $\frac{OPT}{P} = \frac{1-p+2/3}{1-p+\frac{2p}{3}} = \frac{5-3p}{3-p} \geq_{(p<1/3)} 1.5$.

□

---

[4]This implicitly assumes that a positive-quality document will be ranked higher than one with quality 0. The theorem holds regardlessly, as the payoff of this scenario is irrelevant.

Dynamic Information Retrieval: Theoretical Framework and Application

Marc Sloan and Jun Wang
Department of Computer Science
University College London
M.Sloan@cs.ucl.ac.uk, J.Wang@cs.ucl.ac.uk

ABSTRACT

Theoretical frameworks like the *Probability Ranking Principle* and its more recent *Interactive Information Retrieval* variant have guided the development of ranking and retrieval algorithms for decades, yet they are not capable of helping us model problems in *Dynamic Information Retrieval* which exhibit the following three properties; an observable user signal, retrieval over multiple stages and an overall search intent. In this paper a new theoretical framework for retrieval in these scenarios is proposed. We derive a general dynamic utility function for optimizing over these types of tasks, that takes into account the utility of each stage and the probability of observing user feedback. We apply our framework to experiments over TREC data in the dynamic multi page search scenario as a practical demonstration of its effectiveness and to frame the discussion of its use, its limitations and to compare it against the existing frameworks.

Categories and Subject Descriptors

H.3.3 [**Information Search and Retrieval**]: Relevance feedback; Retrieval Models; Search process;

Keywords

Dynamic IR, Interactive IR, Ranking and Retrieval Theory

1. INTRODUCTION

The theoretical frameworks that underpin research in Information Retrieval (IR) are based on abstract models of user benefit. For instance, the loss function defined in the classic *Probability Ranking Principle* (*PRP*) [26] leads to justification for the simplest and most powerful ranking rule in IR; ranking documents in decreasing order of their probability of relevance. A recent counterpart is the *Probability Ranking Principle for Interactive Information Retrieval* (*IIR-PRP*) [12], which relaxes the independence assumption in the *PRP*'s model to take into account non-linear decision making. For example, document dependence is a key element in IR diversification that is not handled by the *PRP* [32]. These models deal with traditional ad hoc query ranking and retrieval. Yet search tasks are complex

ICTIR'15, September 27–30, Northampton, MA, USA.
© 2015 ACM. ISBN 978-1-4503-3833-2/15/09 ...$15.00.
DOI: http://dx.doi.org/10.1145/2808194.2809457.

and often exploratory, being comprised of multiple stages of retrieval with information needs specialized or generalized over time [35]. Throughout, a user may broadcast signals of search intent that can help an IR system to improve retrieval. Examples include query reformulation in session search [29] and item ratings in collaborative filtering [15]. The described models are not capable of representing search tasks that operate over multiple stages nor can they incorporate user feedback.

These types of problems belong to the area of IR research known as *Dynamic Information Retrieval* (*DIR*), which we define as exhibiting three characteristics: user feedback, temporal dependency and an overall goal. In this paper we present *DIR* as a natural progression in IR research complexity; where early research concerned *static* problems such as ad hoc retrieval, which gave way to *interactive* tasks such as those incorporating relevance feedback [27], finally leading to *dynamic* systems where tasks such as ranking for session search are optimized [24].

From this progression we mathematically formulate a generalized framework that models the expected benefit to a user of completing a *DIR* task. This benefit is represented as a recursive utility function that is goal oriented and adaptive over time. The components of this utility function represent the three *DIR* features: the likelihood of user feedback, a probability of relevance model conditioned on this feedback and an individual stage utility function. The optimization of this recursive utility leads to an optimal policy of actions dependent on user interactions in the dynamic setting.

This utility is shown to be a form of Bellman equation [3], the framework an instantiation of a *Partially Observable Markov Decision Process* (*POMDP*) [31] and also a generalization over existing research in *DIR* [24, 19]. The components of the utility can also be linked to the cost-benefit parameters of the *IIR-PRP* and the discount-gain functions found in session-based metrics such as *sDCG* [21]. The structure of the utility function and its links to these areas of research give us interesting insights into the behavior of the function in *DIR* problems. These insights, such as how the quality and diversification of rankings vary over multiple stages, are supported by our experiments performed using a specific application of the *DIR* utility function over TREC data. Our experimental setting is the multi-page search scenario of choosing optimal rankings to display over several search pages for a fixed query [22, 19], a simplified *DIR* problem. As well as being a demonstration of the implementation of each of the components that make up the utility, practical aspects such as the computational complexity are also explored.

Thus, through its supporting theory (Section 2) and application (Section 4), we establish our dynamic utility function (Section 3) as a new theoretical framework for the modeling of dynamic information retrieval problems.

2. COMPARISON OF IR FRAMEWORKS

Before setting up our framework for dynamic information retrieval, we consider *DIR* in the context of existing static and interactive theoretical IR frameworks in order to mathematically identify those features that distinguish it.

2.1 Static IR Framework

Definition: A static IR framework is one which models single user interactions, or else multiple *independent* interactions of different search intents. A typical application would be an ad hoc ranking and retrieval system.

The objective of a static system is to choose an **action** a (or sequence of actions $\vec{a} = \langle a_1, a_2, \ldots \rangle$), each of which has an associated **probability of relevance** r (or $\vec{r}$ for a sequence of actions) that maximizes some **static utility function** $U_S(a, r)$. The action represents a choice that can be made by the system and belongs to some action space $\mathcal{A}$. For example, a may be a query suggestion to display to a user, or $\vec{a}$ the ranking order of a set of documents for retrieval. The utility function gives value to the action based on its probability of relevance by modeling the benefit of the action to the user. Utilities such as expected DCG and MAP [33] are examples from document retrieval, rewarding the ranking of relevant documents at high ranking positions.

2.1.1 Probability Ranking Principle (PRP)

The *PRP* defines $U_S(a, r)$ as a loss minimizing function across pairs of documents, which is optimized when ranking documents in decreasing order of probability of relevance (under document independence assumptions) [26]. Nonetheless, in instances where result diversity is important, it can be shown that *PRP* is no longer optimal [32]. We illustrate this with our example in Fig. 1a. Here, we represent a simplified vector space model for ranking and retrieval using a graph over two term axes. In this case, the query is `apple`, an ambiguous term that can describe three subtopic search intents. Those documents within the ranking $\vec{a}_{PRP}$ for the query are retrieved (analogous to ranking under the *PRP*), and as we can see, in this case only two subtopic preferences are captured. Over a population of users, those seeking information on the `apple logo` subtopic would be dissatisfied.

We can capture this probabilistically by supposing that we have two classes of users, `user₁` and `user₂`, where `user₁` has twice as many members as `user₂`. Users in the `user₁` class are satisfied with the `apple logo` and `apple computer` subtopics, but not `apple fruit`, while those in the `user₂` class are only satisfied with the `apple fruit` subtopic. Our action space here is the set of subtopics which we denote $\{a_1 = \texttt{apple logo}, a_2 = \texttt{apple computer}, a_3 = \texttt{apple fruit}\}$ and our goal is to choose the best ranking of subtopics.

If we set $R_{a_k} = 1$ if a_k is relevant, and $r_{a_k} = P(R_{a_k} = 1)$, then we have $r_{a_1} = \frac{2}{3}, r_{a_2} = \frac{2}{3}$ and $r_{a_3} = \frac{1}{3}$. According to the *PRP*, we should rank in decreasing order of the probability of relevance, giving us the ranking sequence $\vec{a}_{PRP} = \langle a_1, a_2, a_3 \rangle$. However, intuitively this is not optimal because users belonging to `user₂` have to reject two subtopics before

reaching their preference [8]. We can explain this mathematically by studying the optimization of the diversity-encouraging metric Expected Search Length. One can also derive the same conclusion analogously using the equivalent Expected Reciprocal Rank or k-call at n measures [5]. In this scenario, $U_S(\vec{a}, \vec{r}) = E[L]_{\vec{a}}$ which is the summation of all possible search lengths L weighted by their respective probabilities, given as

$$E[L]_{\vec{a}} = \sum_i \left((i-1) P(R_1 = 0, \ldots, R_{i-1} = 0, R_i = 1) \right)$$

where R_i is the relevance of the subtopic at rank position i. When assuming subtopics are independent, i.e. $P(R_1 = 0, \ldots, R_i = 1) = P(R_1 = 0) \ldots P(R_{i-1} = 0) P(R_i = 1)$ the expected search length for ranking $\vec{a}_{PRP}$ is

$$
\begin{aligned}
E[L]_{\vec{a}_{PRP}} &= 0 \cdot r_{a_1} + 1 \cdot r_{a_2}(1 - r_{a_1}) + 2 \cdot r_{a_3}(1 - r_{a_2})(1 - r_{a_1}) \\
&= 0 \cdot (2/3) + 1 \cdot (2/3)(1/3) + 2 \cdot (1/3)(1/3)(1/3) = \mathbf{8/27}
\end{aligned}
$$

and for a diversified ranking $\vec{a}_{DIV} = \langle a_1, a_3, a_2 \rangle$ the expected search length is

$$E[L]_{\vec{a}_{DIV}} = 0 \cdot (2/3) + 1 \cdot (1/3)(1/3) + 2 \cdot (2/3)^2 (1/3) = \mathbf{11/27}$$

Thus, in this case the *PRP* ranked documents have a shorter expected search path than the diversified ranking. Here, the *PRP* does lead to the optimal ranking under the independence assumption, but when we remove it this is no longer the case. To see this, we recalculate the expected search length for $\vec{a}_{PRP}$ and $\vec{a}_{DIV}$ but this time without the independence assumption:

$$
\begin{aligned}
E[L]_{\vec{a}_{PRP}} &= 0 \cdot r_{a_1} + 1 \cdot P(R_{a_2} = 1, R_{a_1} = 0)) \\
&\quad + 2 \cdot P(R_{a_3} = 1, R_{a_2} = 0, R_{a_1} = 0) \\
&= 0 \cdot (2/3) + 1 \cdot 0 + 2 \cdot (1/3) = \mathbf{2/3} \\
E[L]_{\vec{a}_{DIV}} &= 0 \cdot (2/3) + 1 \cdot (1/3) + 2 \cdot 0 = \mathbf{1/3}
\end{aligned}
$$

Now we find that the diversified ranking $\vec{a}_{DIV}$ has the shorter expected search length and is thus the optimal ranking, despite the lower probability of relevance for a_3.

2.2 Interactive IR Framework

Definition: An interactive IR framework extends a static framework to cover multiple stages of IR. It is *responsive* to feedback from a previous stage but does not anticipate future feedback.

A **stage** represents an interaction with the search system that is distinct from other interactions but belongs to the same search task, for example a sequence of impressions in session search. Generally, an IR system will operate over $1 \leq t \leq T$ stages with T being potentially infinite.

Further to this, an interactive IR framework incorporates user feedback. Feedback is an **observation** signal o (or a sequence of observations $\vec{o}$) in the space $\mathcal{O}$, that is measurable by the search system. These signals may be *explicit* declarations of the relevance of search items (such as a movie rating), or *implicit* interpretations of user actions (such as document clicks).

The final element of this framework is the **relevance update function** τ where $r_{t+1} = \tau(a_t, r_t, o_t)$. Thus, the objective function for interactive IR at stage $t+1$ can now be represented as $\operatorname{argmax}_{a_{t+1} \in \mathcal{A}} U_S(a_{t+1}, \tau(a_t, r_t, o_t))$. The relevance update function τ introduces temporal dependency into the framework, without it the objective simply devolves to optimization over the static utility $U_S(a, r)$. This is also

Figure 1: An example illustration of document ranking and relevance feedback using the vector space model for query $Q_1 =$ apple. Documents are given as points over two term frequency axes, computer and fruit, and can belong to one of three subtopics apple fruit, apple logo and apple computer. The distance between Q and each document is inversely proportional to its relevance r. The documents ranked for Q_1 or its reformulation Q_2 are contained in each circular shape $\vec{a}$, whose area could be thought of as the static utility $U_S(\vec{a}, \vec{r})$, or U_D the combined area of actions across stages 1 and 2.

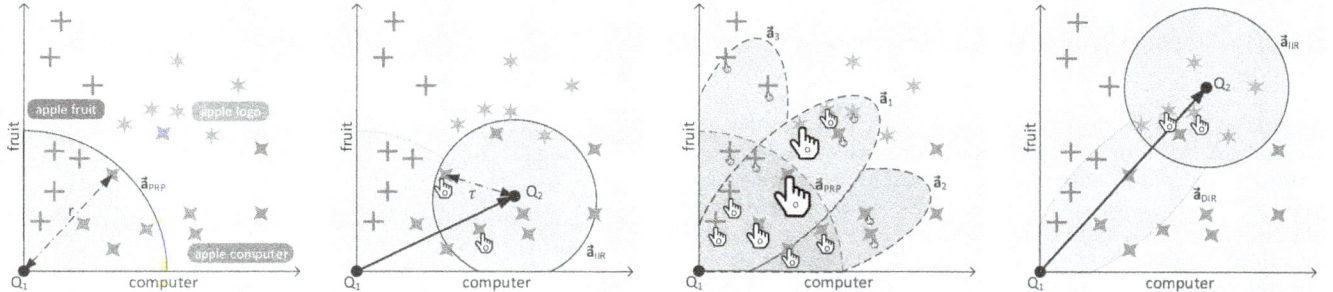

(a) Static IR: Documents within the ranking $\vec{a}_{PRP}$ are shown to the user for query Q_1, but do not cover all subtopics. Optimally ranking using the *PRP* results in choosing those documents with the highest relevance.

(b) Interactive IR: After relevance feedback is observed (the two click observations o) on the static ranking in Fig. 1a, Q_1 is modified to Q_2. Document relevance for Q_2 is now defined by τ and the new interactive ranking given by documents in $\vec{a}_{IIR}$.

(c) Dynamic IR: Four potential rankings $\vec{a}_1$, $\vec{a}_2$, $\vec{a}_3$ and $\vec{a}_{PRP}$ and their observation probabilities (shown as click observations with likelihood relative to size) for Q_1 are explored to find the optimal ranking action for both stages.

(d) Optimal Solution: Action $\vec{a}_1$ is chosen as the optimal stage 1 ranking $\vec{a}_{DIR}$ as it diversely contains documents from all subtopics. As a result, the ranking $\vec{a}_{IIR}$ for Q_2 is more accurately modified after observing interactive feedback.

the case when finding the optimal first stage action a_1 i.e. when there are not yet any observations. In interactive IR, the optimal action is chosen at each stage as a reaction to the feedback observed in the previous stage and there is no consideration for future utility.

With these features in mind, we extend the vector space example to the interactive scenario in Fig. 1b by introducing the Rocchio relevance feedback algorithm [27] for interactively re-ranking documents. Here, clicked documents in the *PRP* ranked first stage are used as implicit signals of relevance to modify the user's original query Q_1 to Q_2. Document re-retrieval occurs using Q_2, returning documents using updated relevance scores given by τ, which is a function of Q_2 and thus the original ranking $\vec{a}_{PRP}$, document relevancies r and observations o. Nonetheless, even in this interactive framework, a user interested in the apple logo subtopic would be dissatisfied with both the $\vec{a}_{PRP}$ and $\vec{a}_{IIR}$ rankings due to a lack of documents for the relevant subtopic.

2.2.1 *Interactive Information Retrieval (IIR)*

For clarification, the area of research traditionally known as *Interactive Information Retrieval (IIR)* has an alternative definition to the interactive IR *framework* discussed in this paper, despite the similarity in name. *IIR* research explores the complex sequence of interactions a user may have with a search ranking within the static framework [28], largely motivated by the contradictory results found from conventional Cranfield style evaluation [7] and observational user studies [14]. With the exception of the *IIR-PRP* framework which we cover in more detail in Section 3.3.1, for the remainder of this paper any reference to interactive IR instead reflects the framework defined in this paper.

3. DYNAMIC IR THEORY

A dynamic system is one which is goal-directed and adaptive to its environment. From this definition we can specify three elements that determine whether an IR system is a dynamic one:

Feedback An observation signal from the user.

Temporal Dependency Operation across multiple stages where each stage depends on the previous stage.

Overall Goal An objective across all stages.

3.1 Dynamic IR Framework

Definition: A dynamic IR framework extends an interactive framework by being responsive to user feedback *and* optimizing for it in advance.

We previously defined systems in the interactive IR framework as exhibiting both feedback and temporal dependency features, but they are only capable of locally optimizing for a single stage at a time. In contrast, the optimization of a dynamic system will find the optimal sequence of actions for all future interactions. A result of this is that the utility of an individual stage may be reduced so that gains can be made in the utility at a future stage.

Unlike the interactive IR framework, the observation o is unknown when evaluating the utility of future stages in the dynamic IR framework. Instead, the *expected* utility can be found by marginalizing the utility function over the space of observations $\mathcal{O}$. When doing this the **observation likelihood function** $P(o|a, r)$ must be specified. This gives the expected utility

$$E[U_S(a, r)] = \sum_{o \in \mathcal{O}} P(o|a, r) U_S(a, r) \qquad (1)$$

The observation likelihood function is represented visually in Fig. 1c. In dynamic IR, the expected utility of potential first stage rankings (given here as $\vec{a}_1$, $\vec{a}_2$, $\vec{a}_3$ and the optimal static ranking $\vec{a}_{PRP}$) are calculated by estimating which documents are likely to receive clicks and the effect this has on the utility of future stages. The *PRP* ranking is simply one among many rank actions that can be considered.

The final component of the *DIR* framework is the **path discount** function $\omega(t)$. When optimizing over a potentially infinite number of future stages, this helps ensure that a solution exists and also gives greater weight to earlier stage utilities.

By bringing together all of the components described so far, we can define the **utility function for dynamic information retrieval** as

$$U_D(r_t, t) = \max_{a_t \in \mathcal{A}} \big[U_S(a_t, r_t) +$$

$$\omega(t) \sum_{o \in \mathcal{O}} P(o|a_t, r_t) U_D(\tau(a_t, r_t, o), t+1) \big] \quad (2)$$

where $U_D(r_T, T) = \max_{a_T \in \mathcal{A}} \big[U_S(a_T, r_T) \big]$ is the static optimization of the final stage. Thus, our objective is to find, through backwards induction, the optimal sequence of actions $\vec{\mathbf{a}}^* = \langle a_1, \ldots, a_T \rangle$ that maximizes the **dynamic utility** U_D given in Eq. (2). To derive this utility we have simply recursively applied the dynamic utility to the expected utility from Eq. (1).

Through the maximization of the dynamic utility, in our example in Fig. 1d we find the optimal action for stage 1, which is to diversify the initial ranking so that it retrieves documents belonging to all three subtopics. While this may harm the immediate retrieval utility score, overall the system improves because it can more accurately re-rank results over the subtopic preferences for all users in the next stage.

We observe that the eight elements of the *DIR* framework: a, r, U_S, t, o, τ, $P(o|a, r)$ and $\omega(t)$, are also the elements that define a *POMDP* [31], and that the dynamic utility function is its corresponding Bellman equation [3]. Intuitively this makes sense, like a *POMDP* the dynamic IR framework finds an optimal Markovian sequence of actions to maximize a reward (here the static utility) subject to discounting (with ω). The state of the system (the underlying document relevance) is unknown but a belief state (the probability of relevance) is updated according to observations. The key difference from a *POMDP* is that for dynamic IR we do not define a transition probability between states as we assume that the hidden relevance of each document does not change throughout the search task.

3.2 Framework Analysis

So far we have described the general framework for dynamic IR but have not addressed the setting of its parameters. Here we analyze each component within the context of dynamic information retrieval.

Relevance. As with any framework in information retrieval, the overall aim is to retrieve relevant information items and present them to the user. The intrinsic 'relevance' of an information item is an unknown quality and the subject of most of the research in IR. In the *DIR* framework any document relevance scoring method can be used. For instance, in our application in the next section we make use of five well established relevance scoring techniques.

The relevance update function τ is more difficult to define as it depends specifically on the action and observation space of the *DIR* task, for instance in Fig. 1b it depends on the distance of the documents from Q_2, which itself depends on Q_1, $\vec{\mathbf{a}}_{\text{PRP}}$ and its clicked documents. This dependence allows τ to adapt to the hidden relevance preferences of the user over the course of the search process.

It may not always be clear how to update the relevance score based on a given observation, the most straightforward setting for τ can simply be to set $r_a = 0$ for actions already chosen by the IR system. Because τ enforces the temporal

dependency, it is the most important aspect in the dynamic utility because without it the utility is static.

Actions. The action space is what distinguishes search tasks from one another and it is the size of this space that dictates the complexity of optimizing over the dynamic utility function. For example, the action space in query suggestion or document ranking is potentially infinite whereas the space of available advertisements in an ad selection problem may be small and finite. In our example the action space is any potential grouping of the documents in the 2D term space (four such groupings are shown in Fig. 1c). Along with τ, the setting of the static utility U_S is important for determining the desirable features of the optimal action sequence $\vec{\mathbf{a}}^*$, such as results diversification.

Observations. The observation space is dependent on the action space, its elements representing the user's response to system actions. Each observation must contain some signal of relevance or search intent, otherwise we would have $\tau(a, r, o) = \tau(a, r)$ and lose the temporal dependency. In some cases the value of the observation likelihood is simply $P(o|a, r) = r$, for instance in search tasks where accurate explicit relevance feedback is guaranteed. Otherwise, in most situations the observations will be click-related and thus the observation probability is the probability of click, as is the case in our example (Fig. 1).

Stages. Typically, the stages in a *DIR* task will represent distinct interactions occurring in a linear time order. In these cases $\omega(t)$ may take a value between 0 and 1 or be set to a monotonically decreasing function that favorably weights the utility scores of immediate stages. Setting $\omega(1) = 1$ and $\omega(t) = 0$ for $t > 1$ gives us the static and interactive scenarios.

Alternatively, a non-linear sequence of interactions (or *search path*) can be modeled as Yang and Lad did with their session-based utility function [37]. For instance in session search, a search path represents a particular sequence of documents examined by the user and the query reformulations made. For our framework, the stage t may instead represent a specific search path, and so $\omega(t)$ could be interpreted as the likelihood of this path rather than an explicit discount, penalizing improbable search paths and rewarding likely ones.

The time horizon T dictates the number of advance stages to optimize for. A large time horizon will lead to explorative action strategies that benefit later stages. In our experiments, we set $T = 2$ so that we only consider exploitative optimizations for the immediate next stage.

Dynamic Utility. Through the recursive evaluation of the utility function we not only learn the optimal sequence of actions to make in the dynamic system, but we also learn the optimal action for each possible observation at each stage. If we were to store these in a lookup table ahead of deployment, then the dynamic system would be immediately responsive to user feedback and able to cater to a population of users. Nonetheless, the construction and storage complexity of such a table may prove intractable. We also note that the static utility U_S may be set as the dynamic utility function U_D of a nested subproblem in the search task. For example, the utility of choosing an optimal *ranking of documents* may be embedded in the utility for determining an optimal *sequence of rankings* for a user in a session, which itself may be defined within the context of modeling a user's *topic preference* from search sessions in their search history.

3.3 Links to Existing Work

Building on our analysis of the *DIR* framework, here we identify links between its components and other related work in *IIR* and session search.

3.3.1 IIR-PRP

The *IIR-PRP* [12] is a framework designed for interactive IR in the traditional sense. The objective function in *IIR-PRP* balances the costs and benefits of choosing actions within a sequence and bears some similarities to our dynamic utility function. Nonetheless, by lacking any form of user feedback or temporal dependency, we do not describe the model as interactive or dynamic, and as already discussed, within the terminology used in this paper this means that it is actually a static method.

By mapping our notation onto the *IIR-PRP* objective function, we get

$$U_{\text{IIR}}(\vec{\mathbf{a}}, \vec{\mathbf{r}}) = \sum_{i=1}^{M} \left[\prod_{j=1}^{i-1}(1 - r_j) \right] \times \left(\omega(i) + r_i \sum_{o \in \vec{\mathbf{o}}} P(o|a_i, r_i) U_S(a_i, r_i) \right) \quad (3)$$

evaluated over a sequence of M actions (usually a ranking of documents). Eq. (3) is a generalization of the formula originally defined, where we recognize that the cost and benefit parameters are simply a utility value, that the probability of whether a user continues searching or not is the observation likelihood, and that the cost of reaching a specific action is the path discount.

Further to this, the *IIR-PRP* defines a simple ranking rule according to this utility model, ranking documents in order of decreasing value of function $\varrho(a, r)$, which balances the costs and benefits of choosing an action as well as its probability of relevance. We can define ϱ in our setting as

$$\varrho(\vec{\mathbf{a}}_{1\dots i}, \vec{\mathbf{r}}_{1\dots i}, \omega) = U_S(\vec{\mathbf{a}}_{1\dots i}, \vec{\mathbf{r}}_{1\dots i}) - \frac{\omega}{r_{a_i}} \prod_{j=1}^{i-1}(1 - r_{a_j}) \quad (4)$$

where the utility of adding an action a_i to an existing sequence is countered by the path discount and the probability of not finding previous actions relevant. We implement this in our algorithm for *IIR-PRP* in Algorithm 2 in the next section.

3.3.2 Session-Based Utility

There have been recent advances in the modeling of user benefit across queries in search sessions. This is in recognition of the fact that ad-hoc retrieval often occurs over multiple queries in a session [35], with one study finding that 32% of search sessions consisted of at least three queries [17]. A simple approach has been to extend discount-gain metrics such as DCG and Average Precision, typically associated with static retrieval, across multiple stages. Using our terminology, a discount-gain function for a single stage has the form $\sum_{i=1}^{M} \omega(i) U_S(a_i, r_i)$. For example, in the DCG metric the setting would be $\omega(i) = \frac{1}{\log_2(i+1)}$ and $U_S(a_i, r_i) = 2^{r_{a_i}} - 1$. For the session-DCG (sDCG) [18] metric, a single

layer of recursion is introduced, where

$$sDCG = \sum_{t=1}^{T} \omega(t) U(\vec{\mathbf{a}}_t, \vec{\mathbf{r}}_t) \quad (5)$$

and the discount and gain functions are set as $\omega(t) = \frac{1}{\log_{2t}(t+1)}$ and

$$U(\vec{\mathbf{a}}_t, \vec{\mathbf{r}}_t) = DCG(\vec{\mathbf{a}}_t, \vec{\mathbf{r}}_t) = \sum_{i=1}^{M} \underbrace{\frac{1}{\log_2(i+1)}}_{\omega(i)} \times \underbrace{(2^{r_{ati}} - 1)}_{U_S(a_{ti}, r_{ti})}$$

Here, the stages operate across a linear sequence of search rankings. In the session-Average Precision (sAP) metric, the path of interaction taken by the user is unknown and so the metric function marginalizes over the space of all such paths to find the expected sAP [21].

4. APPLICATION

So far we have formulated a theoretical framework for dynamic IR and derived the dynamic utility function U_D given in Eq. (2). In this section we apply this framework to the multi page search problem in *DIR*. In doing so we demonstrate functional settings for the elements in the framework and their implementation in a workable algorithm, which gives us useful insight into the practical limitations of optimizing over U_D. We compare our algorithm against *PRP* and *IIR-PRP* based approaches in experiments using TREC data and also investigate static and interactive variants of our objective function. Through this we gain understanding of the effect that dynamic utility optimization has on the quality and diversity of rankings in multi page search.

4.1 Multi Page Search Problem

The *Multi Page Search* (MPS) scenario concerns the ranking of documents over multiple pages of search results [22, 19]. MPS typically models exploratory search queries which are more likely to lead to multi-query sessions and multi-page searches [35] (with one study finding that 27% of all searches occur over multiple pages [16]). In this scenario documents are retrieved for a single query, ranked and then segregated into pages of M documents. On each page, a user may examine and click on documents. We assume that the user will return to the results page and move onto the next page and we define a threshold of T pages which the user will search over. The goal in MPS is to create rankings of relevant documents across T pages. For the pages following the first, document clicks can be used to personalize search rankings, a situation analogous to our example in Fig. 1.

We chose this particular problem to apply our dynamic IR framework to as it exhibits the following beneficial features: 1) it is a *DIR* problem that is familiar and easy to define, 2) it is a simple IR scenario where we only have to consider a single query and a single set of documents, 3) we can use existing ad hoc ranking and retrieval research to find suitable implementations for the *DIR* framework components, 4) we can readily use TREC data collections and relevance judgments to evaluate our algorithms, and 5) it is naturally translatable to the *PRP* and *IIR-PRP* frameworks. A similar analysis of *DIR* in the session search scenario was also conducted by Luo et al. [24]

In this scenario, each page of search represents a stage in our framework, with T the threshold number of pages. We nominally set $T = 2$ although a larger number of pages is feasible and has been studied by Jin et al. [19]. The action sequence $\vec{a}_t = \langle a_{t1}, \ldots, a_{tM} \rangle$ represents the ranking of documents for ranks 1 to M on page t. Before we can fully implement Eq. (2), we must first define each of its functional components in the context of MPS.

4.1.1 Expected DCG

The static utility in multi page search is a measure of the quality of the ranking of documents on each page. As with ad hoc ranking and retrieval, we can evaluate this using a metric such as DCG, MAP or ERR. In the absence of relevance judgments, we can instead find the *expected* metric value which uses probabilities of relevance instead [33]. In our application we set the static utility as the expected DCG function, given by

$$U_S(\vec{a}_t, \vec{r}_t) = \sum_{i=i}^{M} \frac{2^{r_{a_{ti}}} - 1 + 2^{r_{a_{ti}} - 1} \log^2(2) Var[r_{a_{ti}}]}{\log(i+1)} \quad (6)$$

This utility also takes into consideration the variance of the document's probability of relevance.

4.1.2 Examination Hypothesis

In multi page search our observations are document clicks, which we regard as an implicit signal of the relevance of a document to the user. Thus, we can utilize the clicks from previous search pages to update our probability of relevance model and personalize the document rankings for future pages.

For a ranking of M documents, the observation space $\mathcal{O}$ in MPS for a particular page is the combination of binary click events for each document in the ranking. We denote this as the observation vector $\vec{o} = \langle o_1, \ldots, o_M \rangle$ where $o \in \{0, 1\}$. We could naïvely set the observation likelihood to the uniform distribution $P(o|a, r) = \frac{1}{|\mathcal{O}|}$ but eye-tracking studies tell us that this is not the case. Instead, the probability of a click occurring on a ranked document is dependent on not only its probability of relevance but also its rank position, amongst other variables [20]. The probabilistic modeling of user clicks is an extensive area of IR research and in our application we use the simplest model, the *Examination Hypothesis* model [10].

This model supports the eye tracking research by inferring that the probability of a click on a document in a ranked list is equal to the product of its probability of relevance and the bias of its rank position. Thus, the probability of a sequence of clicks is given by

$$P(\vec{o}|\vec{a}_t, \vec{r}_t) = \prod_{i=1}^{M} (b_i r_{a_{ti}})^{o_i} (1 - b_i r_{a_{ti}})^{1 - o_i} \quad (7)$$

where b_i is a rank bias parameter. In our implementation we set Eq. (7) as our observation likelihood function and set $b_i = \frac{1}{\log(i+1)}$ which is the discount value used in our expected DCG utility.

4.1.3 Conditional Multivariate Gaussian Distribution

Once we have a sequence of click observations for a ranking of documents, we can update the probability of relevance distribution for the remaining documents. Here, we achieve this by defining the distribution of all the probabilities of relevance for all documents in the collection as a multivariate

Gaussian distribution $R \sim \mathcal{N}(\vec{r}, \Sigma)$, where R is their collective random variable, $\vec{r}$ the vector of mean relevance scores and Σ the covariance matrix over the documents. $\vec{r}$ may be set as any relevance score and Σ may be set using document similarity or other correlation scores [19]. If $\vec{r}$ represents a probability of relevance, then we can set the distribution as a *truncated* multivariate Gaussian bounded between 0 and 1. If it is not possible to define the distribution of a relevance score, then the distribution of the mean of multiple relevance scoring techniques can be derived, resulting in an approximately Gaussian distribution that incorporates multiple signals of relevance. It is this approach we take in our experiment, where we set $\vec{r}$ and Σ as the means and variances of the retrieval scores from five well known techniques, with the diagonal elements from Σ used as variance values for our utility calculation in Eq. (6).

Modeling the relevance distribution in this way allows us to conditionally update the probabilities of relevance $\vec{r}$ based on our click observations. For a given rank action $\vec{a}_t$ (which includes both clicked and non-clicked documents in the ranking), we denote the remaining non-ranked documents as $\backslash \vec{a}_t$ and partition our distribution parameters as

$$\vec{r} = \begin{bmatrix} \vec{r}_{\backslash \vec{a}_t} \\ \vec{r}_{\vec{a}} \end{bmatrix} \qquad \Sigma = \begin{bmatrix} \Sigma_{\backslash \vec{a}_t \backslash \vec{a}_t} & \Sigma_{\backslash \vec{a}_t \vec{a}_t} \\ \Sigma_{\vec{a}_t \backslash \vec{a}_t} & \Sigma_{\vec{a} \vec{a}} \end{bmatrix}$$

We can then update the mean relevance scores and covariance matrix for non ranked documents using the formulae

$$\vec{r}_{\backslash \vec{a}_t} = \vec{r}_{\backslash \vec{a}_t} + \Sigma_{\backslash \vec{a}_t \vec{a}_t} \Sigma_{\vec{a} \vec{a}}^{-1} (\vec{o} - \vec{r}_{\vec{a}_t}) \quad (8)$$

$$\Sigma_{\backslash \vec{a}_t \backslash \vec{a}_t} = \Sigma_{\backslash \vec{a}_t \backslash \vec{a}_t} - \Sigma_{\backslash \vec{a}_t \vec{a}_t} \Sigma_{\vec{a}_t \vec{a}_t}^{-1} \Sigma_{\vec{a}_t \backslash \vec{a}_t}$$

and observations $\vec{o}$. Thus, for given actions and observations, we can use the functions above to define a new conditional multivariate Gaussian distribution of the probability of relevance of the remaining documents, given as $R_{t+1} \sim \mathcal{N}(\vec{r}_{\backslash \vec{a}_t}, \Sigma_{\backslash \vec{a}_t \backslash \vec{a}_t} | \vec{a}_t, \vec{o})$. For the multi page search setting, we define $\tau(a, r, o)$ as the relevance update function in Eq. (8).

4.1.4 Geometric Discount

The final component required for our application is the discount function $\omega(t)$. In the multi page scenario, we measure the utility of a linear sequence of document rankings rather than the path-based behavior of users. As such, we adopt the simple discount used in a POMDP, setting $\omega = \lambda$ (which is effectively setting it as the geometric discount $\omega(t) = \lambda^{t-1}$ due to the recursion of the dynamic utility).

Here, we can consider $\omega(t)$ as the probability of the user visiting page t. When $\lambda = 0$, we assume only the first page will be visited, and when $\lambda = 1$ all pages are equally likely and given equal weight. The optimal setting for λ will vary depending on the type of searches being performed as well as the corpus and quality of results.

4.2 DIR-MPS

Now that we have defined each of the functional components of the dynamic IR framework for the multi page search scenario, we present the DIR-MPS algorithm in Algorithm 1. This algorithm is a direct implementation of the recursive utility function U_D in Eq. (2) that determines the optimal sequence of document rankings to display for each page.

It is worth noting that Algorithm 1 and the described settings for the *DIR* framework elements are one such instantiation of the framework in the multi page search scenario.

Algorithm 1 The DIR-MPS Algorithm

---

function DIR-MPS$(t, \vec{r}, \mathcal{A})$
  if $t = T + 1$ **then return** $[0, \langle\rangle]$
  end if
  $\vec{a}_t^* = \langle\rangle; \vec{a}_{t+1}^* = \langle\rangle$
  loop $i \leftarrow 1$ to M $\triangleright$ Sequential Ranking Decision
    $\vec{a} = \vec{a}_t^*; u^* = 0$
    for all $a \in \mathcal{A}\backslash\vec{a}$ **do**
      $\vec{a}_t = \langle\vec{a}, a\rangle$
      $u_t = U_S(\vec{a}_t, \vec{r}_t)$ $\triangleright$ Eq. (6)
      for all $\vec{o} \in \mathcal{O}$ **do**
        $\vec{r}_{t+1} = \tau(\vec{a}_t, \vec{r}, o)$ $\triangleright$ Eq. (8)
        $[u_{t+1}, \vec{a}_{t+1}] = $ DIR-MPS$(t + 1, \vec{r}_{t+1}, \mathcal{A}\backslash\vec{a}_t)$
        $u_t = u_t + \lambda \cdot P(\vec{o}|\vec{a}_t, \vec{r}_t) \cdot u_{t+1}$ $\triangleright$ Eq. (7)
      end for
      if $u_t > u^*$ **then**
        $u^* = u_t; \vec{a}_t^* = \vec{a}_t; \vec{a}_{t+1}^* = \vec{a}_{t+1}$
      end if
    end for
  end loop
  return $[u^* \langle\vec{a}_t^*, \vec{a}_{t+1}^*\rangle]$
end function

Our motive in this section is not to develop a state of the art new ranking technique but rather to demonstrate the application of the framework to a *DIR* problem.

4.2.1 Dynamic Utility Approximation

The DIR-MPS algorithm features a number of approximation techniques that increase its computational efficiency as a way to counteract the inherent complexity of the *DIR* framework (discussed further in Section 4.3). Firstly, we reduce the action space of potential rankings by employing a *Sequential Ranking Decision* policy. That is, for each page we find the optimal document to rank at each position one by one. For example, we set $M = 1$ and find the document a^* that maximizes $U_S(a, r_a)$. Then we fix this document, set $M = 2$ and find the next in the sequence that maximizes $U_S(\langle a^*, a\rangle \; \vec{r}_{\langle a^*, a\rangle})$. Continuing in this fashion allows us to find an approximately optimal ranking for a single page, one document at a time, greatly reducing the computational complexity.

A property of the probability distribution given in Eq. (7) also allows us to greatly reduce the observation space. We find that this distribution follows Zipf's law, with a few of the click combinations contributing towards most of the probability mass. In fact, from our experiments we typically found that around 15% of the combinations contributed to 95% of the aggregated probability. As such, in our implementation of DIR-MPS we restrict the observation space to only the most probable click combinations that cumulatively sum to 0.95, trading off the potential 5% inaccuracy for speed.

Finally, it can be shown that when ranking over a single stage, the expected DCG utility function is maximized when documents are ranked according to the *PRP* [33]. We exploit this to increase the efficiency of our algorithm by ranking the threshold page (where we no longer consider a future temporal dependency) according to the *PRP* over the conditionally updated probabilities of relevance.

Algorithm 2 The IIR-PRP-MPS algorithm

---

function IIR-PRP-MPS$(M, T, \lambda, \mathcal{A}, \vec{r})$
  $\vec{a}^* = \langle\rangle$
  loop $i \leftarrow 1$ to $M \times T$
    $a^* = \text{argmax}_{a \in \mathcal{A}\backslash\vec{a}^*} \varrho(\langle\vec{a}^*, a\rangle, \vec{r}, \lambda)$ $\triangleright$ Eq. (4)
    $\vec{a}^* = \langle\vec{a}^*, a^*\rangle$
  end loop
  return $\vec{a}^*$
end function

4.2.2 IIR-PRP-MPS

In our experiments we directly compare DIR-MPS against rankings created from the applied *PRP* and *IIR-PRP* ranking rules. With the *Probability Ranking Principle* we can simply rank documents in decreasing order of the probability of relevance across T pages. However, the *IIR-PRP* has no existing direct application to our scenario. Instead, we use our definition of the ranking function ϱ given in Eq. (4) to create the IIR-PRP-MPS algorithm shown in Algorithm 2.

Here, the sequential ranking rule is also employed to build up an optimal ranking over all pages, one document at a time, by selecting the document that has the highest ϱ value for each rank. Thus, there is some dependency on previously ranked documents, which is not possible in the *PRP*, but like the *PRP* there is no way to take into account user feedback or update the probabilities of relevance.

4.3 Practical Limitations

The general computational complexity of the optimization of U_D can be shown to be PSPACE-Complete (through its connection to *POMDPs*). For small T and observation and action spaces this can be reasonable, but typically these spaces may be impractically large.

For example, an IR task such as information filtering or music recommendation may operate over potentially infinite time steps. In these cases the discount factor and threshold T are important. Further, the observation space may not be as well defined as that in our multi page search scenario where $|\mathcal{O}| = 2^M$, for example, the space of possible reformulations for a query or 2D gaze positions in eyetracking. Finally, the action space can be difficult to optimize over as is the case with DIR-MPS, where the sequential ranking decision reduces the size of the action space from $O(N!/(N - TM)!)$ to $O(TNM - TM^2)$ for a collection of N documents. Our application serves to demonstrate that such approximations may be needed when working with the *DIR* framework, especially given that the optimization of U_D is not guaranteed to be tractable, and an optimal solution may not exist depending on the particular problem settings.

4.4 Experiment

To gain insight into our application of the dynamic IR framework in the multi page search scenario, and to compare with the other theoretical frameworks, we conducted an experiment using the WT10g, AQUAINT and ClueWeb09 datasets, the details of which are included in Table 1. We chose these collections as they were designed for evaluating ranking and retrieval algorithms and were easily extended to the multi page problem. The WT10g dataset allowed us to test the theoretical frameworks in the standard ad hoc ranking and retrieval environment. The Robust data consists of

Table 1: Overview of the three TREC test collections

Name	Task	# Docs	Topics
WT10g	TREC 9 Web Track	1,692,096	451-500
AQUAINT	Robust 2005	1,033,461	50 difficult Robust 2004 topics
ClueWeb09	Diversity Task 2009/10	503,903,810	1-100 (461 subtopics)

difficult to rank ad hoc queries which we hypothesized would be more likely to require several pages of search results. The diversity track data allowed us to test our hypothesis that dynamic optimization leads to increased diversification in ad hoc retrieval. A drawback to using these datasets is that they lack interaction data, which is not needed when optimizing for probable clicks in the *DIR* framework, but important in the interactive setting.

On each collection we retrieved the top 100 documents for each topic scored using each of the TF-IDF, BM25, Jelinek-Mercer, Dirichlet and Two-Stage language model retrieval methods from the Indri[1] search engine. We pooled the documents and subsequently scored them over all the techniques. This gave us an average of 193 ranked documents per topic each with 5 relevance score values. After min-max normalization we averaged each score to give us our probability of relevance vector $\vec{r}$ and covariance matrix Σ. The dependencies in this covariance matrix reflect the level of agreement between the different retrieval methods rather than direct correlations between the documents themselves i.e. similarly ranked documents will be positively correlated with one another. Finally, we selected those documents that had the top 30 mean relevance scores. These were then used by our algorithms to create rankings for two pages of search results with ten documents on each.

We ranked these documents according to the baseline *PRP* approach and also the already described IIR-PRP-MPS and DIR-MPS algorithms. We also investigated an interactive version of DIR-MPS (called IIR-MPS) that ranks the first page of results according to the *PRP* and then optimizes a ranking for the second page of results by marginalizing over potential clicks using Eq. (1). We also created a static version of DIR-MPS (called S-MPS) that removes feedback from U_D entirely to give us the objective function $U_S(\vec{a}_1, \vec{r}) + \lambda U_S(\vec{a}_2, \vec{r})$. We also investigated 'perfect click' variants of the dynamic (DIR-MPS^C) and interactive (IIR-MPS^C) algorithms, where we interpret the hidden relevance labels as clicks on the first page of results, giving us the optimal observation setting and an upper bound on performance for the second page.

To evaluate the quality of the rankings we measured MAP, NDCG and ERR for each page. For the DIR-MPS and IIR-MPS algorithms we actually generate an optimal 2nd page ranking for every click combination in our observation space, giving us different metrics scores for each. In these cases, the reported page two metric scores are averages over the page two scores for all click combination based rankings. This highlights an open area for research; the definition of evaluation metrics for *DIR* that can take into account all of the potential rankings in a dynamic system. We also measure the session-based metrics sDCG (defined in Eq. (5)) and sAP to evaluate performance over both pages, although it

[1] http://www.lemurproject.org/indri.php

Table 3: α-DCG, IA-Precision and ERR-IA scores for page 1 and 2 search results from the diversity track data. The maximum score for each metric on each page is given in boldface. A ^{2} indicates that the result is significantly better than the *IIR-PRP-MPS* baseline score using the Wilcoxon signed-rank test ($p < 0.05$).

Algorithm	Page 1			Page 2		
	α-DCG	IA-Prec	ERR-IA	α-DCG	IA-Prec	ERR-IA
PRP	0.360	**0.083**	0.239	**0.420**	0.085	**0.294**
IIR-PRP-MPS	0.345	0.077	0.230	0.404	0.086	0.269
S-MPS	0.352	0.078	0.233	0.417	**0.089**	0.280
IIR-MPS	0.360	**0.083**	0.239	0.377	0.079	0.243
IIR-MPS^C				0.379	0.080	0.236
DIR-MPS	**0.403^2**	0.082	**0.270**	0.400	0.079	0.264
DIR-MPS^C				0.386	0.077	0.254

is worth noting that these metrics were designed for session search rather than multi page search. Finally, we also measure α−NDCG [6], Intent-Aware Precision (IA-Precision) [1] and Intent-Aware ERR (ERR-IA) [4] for scoring the diversity of rankings in the ClueWeb09 collection.

The results of our experiments are shown in Table 2. For the Web Track and Robust collections, we observe that the 1st page losses of the dynamic techniques (when compared to the *PRP* and *IIR-PRP-MPS* baselines) are made up for by gains in the second page, significantly so on the WT10g dataset. Nonetheless, in these ad hoc ranking scenarios it is clear that the static *PRP* and *IIR-PRP* frameworks are still very effective.

We see different results with the diversity track data. The metric scores for this data in Table 2 were calculated using relevance judgments from all subtopics. We see the opposite relationship between page scores here, with DIR-MPS having higher scores for the 1st page and losses in the second (except for ERR which is significantly improved across both pages). We see further evidence of this with the diversity metric scores in Table 3, where it is clear that diversification is occurring in the first page and less so in the second. This backs up our intuition (in Fig. 1d) that a dynamic technique will initially diversify results to improve future rankings, and also helps explain the losses in performance of the 1st page in the other datasets (which do not have subtopic relevance judgments). The reduced diversity of the 2nd page indicates that it is more tightly focused on the user's subtopic preference.

We observe that the diversity task is more suited as an application of the dynamic IR framework. This is evidenced by the optimal settings for λ in each collection. For the ad hoc ranking task in the WT10g and AQUAINT collections, the setting for λ gives greater weight to the 1st page of results, rewarding immediately effective rankings. Whereas in the diversity task, the utility of the 2nd page has a larger effect on the overall utility, encouraging diversity.

Further to this, the interactive variant scored highly with *session based metrics* on the Robust dataset, but otherwise the static techniques were optimal, even for the diversity task. This may partly be due to the application of a session-based metric to the multi page scenario and also the inability of the metric to take into account the user interaction. Finally, we also see that the 'perfect click' variants generally outperform their counterparts (except over the diversity

Table 2: NDCG, MAP and ERR scores for pages 1 and 2 of the search results and sAP and sDCG over both pages. Static, interactive and dynamic algorithms are grouped. The results shown are those for the optimal value of λ in each collection, found by repeating the experiment for values in the range $[0, 1]$. The maximum score for each metric on each page is given in boldface. A ^{1} or ^{2} indicates that the result is significantly better than the *PRP* or *IIR-PRP-MPS* baseline scores respectively using the Wilcoxon signed-rank test ($p < 0.05$).

Collection	Algorithm	Page 1			Page 2			Both Pages	
		NDCG	MAP	ERR	NDCG	MAP	ERR	sAP	sDCG
Web Track (WT10g) $\lambda = 0.5$	PRP	**0.338**	**0.167**	**0.169**	0.133	0.025	0.053	0.097	1.326
	IIR-PRP-MPS	0.330	0.162	0.162	0.166	0.041	0.078	0.101	1.347
	S-MPS	0.295	0.134	0.130	0.226	**0.070**	0.242^{12}	0.095	1.236
	IIR-MPS				0.125	0.025	0.103^{1}	0.097	1.291
	IIR-MPS^C	**0.338**	**0.167**	**0.169**	0.154	0.040	0.151^{1}	**0.102**	**1.353**
	DIR-MPS				0.212^{1}	0.054^{1}	0.289^{12}	0.069	1.022
	DIR-MPS^C	0.235	0.091	0.092	**0.230^{1}**	0.059	**0.297^{12}**	0.072	1.027
Robust (AQUAINT) $\lambda = 0.5$	PRP	0.624	**0.107**	**0.398**	0.552	0.061	0.294	**0.085**	5.735
	IIR-PRP-MPS	**0.629**	**0.107**	**0.398**	0.514	0.052	0.288	0.083	5.680
	S-MPS	0.608	0.096	0.388	**0.595**	**0.066**	0.887^{12}	0.083	**5.749**
	IIR-MPS				0.519	0.050	0.737^{12}	0.081	5.543
	IIR-MPS^C	0.624	**0.107**	**0.398**	0.554	0.057	0.690^{12}	0.084	5.729
	DIR-MPS				0.575	0.065	0.656^{12}	0.065	4.921
	DIR-MPS^C	0.548	0.063	0.304	0.553	0.058	0.697^{12}	0.062	4.909
Diversity (ClueWeb09) $\lambda = 0.8$	PRP	0.402^{2}	**0.049^{2}**	0.199	**0.476**	0.052	0.265	**0.051^{2}**	**1.883^{2}**
	IIR-PRP-MPS	0.384	0.046	0.193	0.468	0.051	0.257	0.048	1.808
	S-MPS	0.388	0.041	0.193	0.465	**0.054**	0.358^{12}	0.049	1.787
	IIR-MPS				0.431	0.042	0.353^{12}	0.047	1.783
	IIR-MPS^C	0.402^{2}	**0.049^{2}**	0.199	0.436	0.042	0.345^{12}	0.047	1.787
	DIR-MPS				0.445	0.042	**0.373^{12}**	0.046	1.859
	DIR-MPS^C	**0.451^{2}**	0.047	**0.238^{2}**	0.426	0.037	0.356^{12}	0.044	1.839

data), indicating that the 2nd page ranking can be improved when high quality clicks are observed.

In summary, by its nature the *DIR* approach to multi-page search places greater emphasis on different stages of the search task. We find that this may not be suited to all search environments i.e. ad hoc search. In such cases the static approaches can be more effective. Nonetheless, the dynamic IR framework has other desirable properties such as the diversification and personalization of results over time.

5. RELATED WORK

Throughout this paper we have presented the dynamic IR theory within the context of the surrounding literature, so in this section we cover those areas of the related work not already discussed.

For instance, the settings of the components in the *DIR* framework for multi page search cover a wide area of research in IR. Firstly, the examination hypothesis model used is just one of a number of probabilistic click models that could have been employed, including the click-chain model [13] and even a POMDP-based model [34]. Other path-based discount functions have been explored in the literature [36] as well as other multi-stage utilities and metrics such as Time-Based Gain [30]. Related work on using Markov chains to measure the utility of rankings at each time step is a potential method for evaluating *DIR* problems [11]. Further to this, the identification of the dynamic IR framework as a POMDP raises the possibility of using established techniques such as the Witness algorithm [23] to find optimal action policies. Also, the performance of the *PRP* under results diversification is well-reported in the static frameworks quantum-PRP [38] and the portfolio theory of IR [32].

The concept of evaluating for retrieval utility rather than relevance was proposed by Cooper in 1973 [9] and is extended to all the frameworks discussed in this paper, where we aim to maximize some utility function that balances the costs and benefits of an IR system's actions. Other work in this area includes Azzopardi's [2] work on economic models, which is itself an extension of the *IIR-PRP*, and also the work of Mostafa et al. [25] who had a similar motivation to this work, where they defined a framework for running user simulations for information filtering, itself a *DIR* problem.

Other than the *PRP* and *IIR-PRP*, the closest related works to this one are the following: The application of a POMDP to multi page search [19], from which many aspects of our experiments in this paper are derived, including the problem setting and the probability of relevance distribution. This paper extends their formulation to a general one applicable to other *DIR* problems and explores a different setting for the static utility, observation likelihood and discount, while also linking to static and interactive techniques. Our experimental time horizon setting of $T = 2$ is based on the optimal results found in their work. Finally, the work on defining the elements of a POMDP in session search [24] is a close relation to this work, though focusing more on the testing of particular settings of *DIR* components in the session search scenario rather than explicitly gaining an understanding of the framework and components themselves. Nonetheless, their work contains an evaluation of algorithms that fall under the *DIR* framework including one similar to DIR-MPS.

This work differs from the literature in that: 1) ours is the first work to define the characteristics that distinguish dynamic IR from the other theoretical IR frameworks, 2) our utility is the generalization of many existing ranking utilities and incorporates many elements of IR research such as click models, and 3) we confirm the effectiveness of ours and the static frameworks in different scenarios in our experiments.

6. CONCLUSION

In this paper we have established a theoretical framework for *Dynamic Information Retrieval*. By contrasting with *static* and *interactive* frameworks, we found three characteristics that define dynamic IR systems; user feedback, temporal dependency and an overall goal. This motivated the derivation of our dynamic utility function U_D, which has its roots in the POMDP formulation. The components of this utility can be directly implemented using elements from existing research which we apply in the DIR-MPS algorithm, an example instantiation designed for the multi page search problem. Our experiments confirm that in this scenario, one of the effects of optimizing for U_D is the diversification of search results. Otherwise, we also demonstrate that for other scenarios the *PRP* and *IIR-PRP* frameworks are still effective.

Like the *PRP* and *IIR-PRP*, our framework defines certain functional parameters but does not definitively specify how to set them. Instead, this work is a point of reference that can be used for the development of specialized models and algorithms applied to *DIR* problems. Through our application we were able to consider the limitations of the *DIR* framework, a result of which is the approximations used in the DIR-MPS algorithm. Finally, the derivation of a stationary solution to the *DIR* Markovian model is an intended future goal and would be an important result to come from this work.

7. REFERENCES

[1] AGRAWAL, R., GOLLAPUDI, S., HALVERSON, A., AND IEONG, S. Diversifying search results. WSDM '09, ACM, pp. 5–14.

[2] AZZOPARDI, L. Modelling interaction with economic models of search. SIGIR '14, ACM, pp. 3–12.

[3] BELLMAN, R. E. *Dynamic Programming*. Dover Publications, 2003.

[4] CHAPELLE, O., METLZER, D., ZHANG, Y., AND GRINSPAN, P. Expected reciprocal rank for graded relevance. CIKM '09, ACM, pp. 621–630.

[5] CHEN, H., AND KARGER, D. R. Less is more: Probabilistic models for retrieving fewer relevant documents. SIGIR '06, ACM, pp. 429–436.

[6] CLARKE, C. L., KOLLA, M., CORMACK, G. V., VECHTOMOVA, O., ASHKAN, A., BÜTTCHER, S., AND MACKINNON, I. Novelty and diversity in information retrieval evaluation. SIGIR '08, ACM, pp. 659–666.

[7] CLEVERDON, C., AND KEAN, M. Factors determining the performance of indexing systems. Aslib Cranfield Research Project, Cranfield, England, 1968.

[8] COOPER, W. S. The inadequacy of probability of usefulness as a ranking criterion for retrieval system output. *University of California, Berkeley* (1971).

[9] COOPER, W. S. On selecting a measure of retrieval effectiveness. *Journal of the American Society for Information Science 24*, 2 (1973), 87–100.

[10] CRASWELL, N., ZOETER, O., TAYLOR, M., AND RAMSEY, B. An experimental comparison of click position-bias models. WSDM '08, ACM, pp. 87–94.

[11] FERRANTE, M., FERRO, N., AND MAISTRO, M. Injecting user models and time into precision via Markov chains. SIGIR '14, ACM, pp. 597–606.

[12] FUHR, N. A probability ranking principle for interactive information retrieval. *Inf. Retr. 11*, 3 (2008), 251–265.

[13] GUO, F., LIU, C., KANNAN, A., MINKA, T., TAYLOR, M., WANG, Y.-M., AND FALOUTSOS, C. Click chain model in web search. WWW '09, ACM, pp. 11–20.

[14] HERSH, W., TURPIN, A., PRICE, S., CHAN, B., KRAMER, D., SACHEREK, L., AND OLSON, D. Do batch and user evaluations give the same results? SIGIR '00, ACM, pp. 17–24.

[15] JAMBOR, T., WANG, J., AND LATHIA, N. Using control theory for stable and efficient recommender systems. WWW '12, ACM, pp. 11–20.

[16] JANSEN, B. J., AND SPINK, A. How are we searching the world wide web?: A comparison of nine search engine transaction logs. *Inf. Process. Manage. 42*, 1 (2006), 248–263.

[17] JANSEN, B. J., SPINK, A., AND PEDERSEN, J. A temporal comparison of AltaVista web searching: Research articles. *J. Am. Soc. Inf. Sci. Technol. 56*, 6 (2005), 559–570.

[18] JÄRVELIN, K., PRICE, S. L., DELCAMBRE, L. M. L., AND NIELSEN, M. L. Discounted cumulated gain based evaluation of multiple-query IR sessions. ECIR'08, Springer-Verlag, pp. 4–15.

[19] JIN, X., SLOAN, M., AND WANG, J. Interactive exploratory search for multi page search results. In *WWW '13* (2013), pp. 655–666.

[20] JOACHIMS, T., GRANKA, L., PAN, B., HEMBROOKE, H., RADLINSKI, F., AND GAY, G. Evaluating the accuracy of implicit feedback from clicks and query reformulations in web search. *ACM Trans. Inf. Syst. 25*, 2 (2007).

[21] KANOULAS, E., CARTERETTE, B., CLOUGH, P. D., AND SANDERSON, M. Evaluating multi-query sessions. SIGIR '11, ACM, pp. 1053–1062.

[22] KIM, J. Y., CRAMER, M., TEEVAN, J., AND LAGUN, D. Understanding how people interact with web search results that change in real-time using implicit feedback. CIKM '13, ACM, pp. 2321–2326.

[23] LITTMAN, M. L. The witness algorithm: Solving partially observable markov decision processes. Tech. rep., 1994.

[24] LUO, J., ZHANG, S., DONG, X., AND YANG, H. Designing states, actions, and rewards for using POMDP in session search. In *Advances in Information Retrieval*, vol. 9022 of *Lecture Notes in Computer Science*. Springer International Publishing, 2015, pp. 526–537.

[25] MOSTAFA, J., MUKHOPADHYAY, S., AND PALAKAL, M. Simulation studies of different dimensions of users' interests and their impact on user modeling and information filtering. *Information Retrieval 6*, 2 (2003), 199–223.

[26] ROBERTSON, S. E. The Probability Ranking Principle in IR. *Journal of Documentation 33*, 4 (1977), 294–304.

[27] ROCCHIO, J. *Relevance Feedback in Information Retrieval*. 1971, pp. 313–323.

[28] RUTHVEN, I. Interactive information retrieval. *ARIST 42*, 1 (2008), 43–91.

[29] SLOAN, M., YANG, H., AND WANG, J. A term-based methodology for query reformulation understanding. *Information Retrieval Journal 18*, 2 (2015), 145–165.

[30] SMUCKER, M. D., AND CLARKE, C. L. Time-based calibration of effectiveness measures. SIGIR '12, ACM, pp. 95–104.

[31] SONDIK, E. The optimal control of partially observable markov processes over the infinite horizon: Discounted cost. *Operations Research 26*, 2 (1978), 282–304.

[32] WANG, J., AND ZHU, J. Portfolio theory of information retrieval. SIGIR' 09, ACM, pp. 115–122.

[33] WANG, J., AND ZHU, J. On statistical analysis and optimization of information retrieval effectiveness metrics. SIGIR '10, pp. 226–233.

[34] WANG, K., GLOY, N., AND LI, X. Inferring search behaviors using partially observable markov (POM) model. WSDM '10, ACM, pp. 211–220.

[35] WHITE, R., WHITE, R., AND ROTH, R. *Exploratory Search: Beyond the Query-Response Paradigm*. Synthesis Lectures on Information Concepts, Retrieval, and Services Series. Morgan & Claypool, 2009.

[36] WHITE, R. W., RUTHVEN, I., JOSE, J. M., AND RIJSBERGEN, C. J. V. Evaluating implicit feedback models using searcher simulations. *ACM Trans. Inf. Syst. 23*, 3 (2005), 325–361.

[37] YANG, Y., AND LAD, A. Modeling expected utility of multi-session information distillation. In *Advances in Information Retrieval Theory*, vol. 5766 of *Lecture Notes in Computer Science*. Springer Berlin Heidelberg, 2009, pp. 164–175.

[38] ZUCCON, G., AZZOPARDI, L., AND VAN RIJSBERGEN, K. The quantum probability ranking principle for information retrieval. In *Advances in Information Retrieval Theory*, vol. 5766. Springer Berlin Heidelberg, 2009, pp. 232–240.

A Theoretical Analysis of Two-Stage Recommendation for Cold-Start Collaborative Filtering

Xiaoxue Zhao, Jun Wang
Department of Computer Science, University College London
{x.zhao,j.wang}@cs.ucl.ac.uk

ABSTRACT

In this paper, we present a theoretical framework for tackling the cold-start collaborative filtering problem, where unknown targets (items or users) keep coming to the system, and there is a limited number of resources (users or items) that can be allocated and related to them. The solution requires a trade-off between exploitation and exploration since with the limited recommendation opportunities, we need to, on one hand, allocate the most relevant resources right away, but, on the other hand, it is also necessary to allocate resources that are useful for learning the target's properties in order to recommend more relevant ones in the future. In this paper, we study a simple two-stage recommendation combining a sequential and a batch solution together. We first model the problem with the partially observable Markov decision process (POMDP) and provide its exact solution. Then, through an in-depth analysis over the POMDP value iteration solution, we identify that an exact solution can be abstracted as selecting resources that are not only highly relevant to the target according to the initial-stage information, but also highly correlated, either positively or negatively, with other *potential* resources for the next stage. With this finding, we propose an approximate solution to ease the intractability of the exact solution. Our initial results on synthetic data and the MovieLens 100K dataset confirm our theoretical development and analysis.

Keywords

Cold-Start Problem, Collaborative Filtering, Recommender Systems, POMDP

1. INTRODUCTION

For approximately the last two decades, information retrieval has fundamentally transformed the way in which people seek and work with information. Roughly speaking, there are two types of information retrieval (IR) systems [5]. On one hand, we have *ad hoc* information retrieval, e.g., web search [24], which deals with a relatively fixed collection of information items (webpages, documents, images, product descriptions etc.) and dynamically changing users

information requests. On the other hand, there are information filtering systems, such as content recommender systems, to address the situation where user profiles (as information requests) stay relatively static while new information items keep arriving. Nevertheless, in either case the fundamental problem remains the same, which is how to compute and find the *match* between the information items and information requests [23].

A more difficult scenario exists when there is little or no information about the request. For instance, in collaborative filtering (CF), it is hard to initialise recommendations when no past ratings are available. Research has been focused on the user *cold-start* problem [13, 35], such as adopting a questionnaire stage [26, 27, 48], or an interactive procedure [47, 13]. For the item cold-start problem, the main focus has been put on utilising content information [30, 14] or experimental design [2].

In our view, the cold-start problem can be regarded as a resource allocation problem, because in a short period of time, the number of recommendations (for a new item or to a new user) is usually much smaller than the size of the available pool. Thus only a small portion can be selected due to the limited resources. For example, advertisements of a new item can only be sent to a limited number of users, whereas a new user can only rate a limited number of items after joining a web service. Therefore, it is important to utilise the limited recommendation resources wisely.

In this paper, we formulate and analyse a simple yet practical two-stage process to solve the recommendation allocation problem. During the initial stage, we use a portion of recommendation allocations, with which the new item's (user's) model can be updated. After that, during the second stage, we make recommendations using the remaining resources, based on the updated model. We argue that the goal of this process should be to maximise the *total* feedback over two stages, which leads to a trade-off between exploitation and exploration. In other words, with limited resources, we should not separate learning from recommending. Rather, recommendations should be made right from the beginning while also intelligently accommodating the learning requirement. The proposed two-stage recommendation process is depicted in Figure 1. In CF, items and users are usually modeled symmetrically [44, 22], and, as such, we will focus on the item cold-start problem as our working example. However, all the analysis can be easily adapted to a user cold-start scenario.

Dividing the recommendation process into two stages is simple yet powerful as it combines both batch and feedback mechanisms together. The motivations for our analysis on this setting are threefold. First, for the cold-start item, to

ICTIR'15, September 27–30, Northampton, MA, USA.
© 2015 ACM. ISBN 978-1-4503-3833-2/15/09 ...$15.00.
DOI: http://dx.doi.org/10.1145/2808194.2809459.

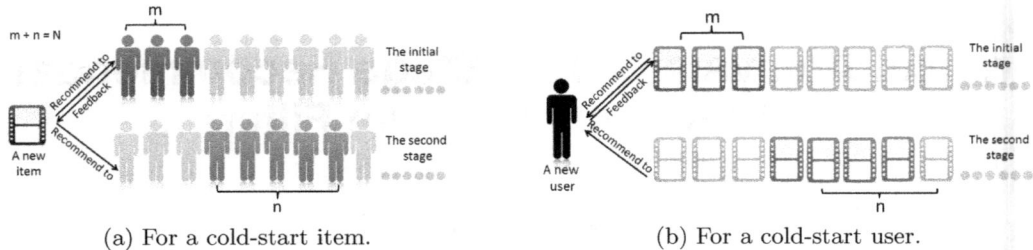

(a) For a cold-start item.

(b) For a cold-start user.

Figure 1: Schematic figures of the two-stage recommendation process for (a) a cold-start item, and (b) a cold-start user. The total N resources are allocated in two stages. In the initial stage, m users (items) are selected, with their feedback used to update the profile of the new item (user). Then another n users (items) are selected in the second stage to exploit the updated profile. The target is to maximise the overall feedback over two stages.

learn its profile over time, one way is to sequentially target the item to one user, observe the feedback, update the item profile model, and find another user with the updated model, in an interactive manner similar to [47]. However, as users differ in their response times, waiting one user's response before targeting to the other is practically infeasible in many cases. Second, it may also be computationally too expensive for the system to update whenever a new rating is registered. A two-stage process, by contrast, enables the system to act economically. Third, statistically analysing the separated two-stage process also enables a clear understanding of the trade-off between exploitation-exploration (EE) embedded in many practical applications.

The two-stage setup also covers a variety of other applications. For example, in IR, when a query is issued, the system shows two subsequent pages to the user such that the second-page results can be refined [36, 19]. And, in online display advertising, for a new campaign, in order to understand which part of users should be targeted, the advertiser can spend some budget to show the ads to different users and collect their feedback (i.e., ad click or conversion), and then after the warming-up stage, leverage the users' feedback and refine the target user groups for higher advertising performance [46].

In this paper, we first formulate the two-stage recommendation with a POMDP framework. We then derive the exact solution for both a correlated-user model (CU) and a matrix factorisation (MF) model, along with a discussion on the link between them. After that, we present our theoretical finding, i.e., the users to choose in the initial stage should be those not only highly relevant according to the initial-stage information, but also able to potentially guide us to find users with high expected values in the next stage with updated information. This ability of guidance can be further abstracted as a strong correlation between the initial-stage users and potential second-stage users, no matter positive or negative. With this finding, we propose an approximation method *guided* exploitation-exploration (GEE). We argue that, as our objective differs from that of an upper confidence bound (UCB) or an active learning (AL) approach, our proposed GEE algorithm is significantly different from them. The effectiveness of the proposed solution is confirmed by our experiments, conducted using both synthetic data and a real dataset.

The rest of this paper is organised as follows. We formulate the problem and present its exact solution in Section 2. In Section 3, we present the proposed approximate solution GEE and afterwards we discuss the related previous work in Section 4. Our experimental results are reported in Section 5, and Section 6 summarises and concludes this paper.

2. THE TWO-STAGE MODEL

In this section, we formulate CF into the POMDP framework. A POMDP models a Markov decision process where the true current state of the system is partially unobservable [20]. In the scenario of the item cold-start recommendation, the true state is each user's genuine (potential) preference as to the new item, which is unknown for the users having not rated it. To model the decision process, we start with the CU model as a probabilistic description of the neighbourhood-based models in CF [17, 10] and formulate it with POMDP. Then, we decompose the user-item rating matrix to gain its formulation in the domain of MF. We provide, for each model, the exact solution on how to select users optimally in order to collect the maximal overall feedback from the users over two stages.

2.1 Correlated-User Model with POMDP

The CU model with POMDP (CU-POMDP) is depicted in Figure 2. Let us denote the available user pool as $\mathcal{I}$. For each new item that joins the system, the recommendation engine should make the following decisions: in the initial stage, choose an initial m users to start with, collect their feedback, and update the system's belief state; and in the second stage, choose another n users to exploit the information gained from the initial stage. $N = m + n$ is the limited number of users that the item can be targeted to. We consider here only one cold-start item, but the scenario is similar if multiple cold-start items are present.

Our goal is to choose an optimal policy to maximise the expected total ratings over two stages. To capture the relations between users' preferences, we model the preferences of all users, denoted by $\boldsymbol{R}$, to follow a multivariate Gaussian distribution

$$p^{(t)}(\boldsymbol{R}) \sim \mathcal{N}(\boldsymbol{\mu}^{(t)}, \boldsymbol{\Sigma}^{(t)}), \ t \in \{1, 2\} \tag{1}$$

with its mean and covariance matrix as $\boldsymbol{\mu}^{(t)}$ and $\boldsymbol{\Sigma}^{(t)}$. The distribution above shows the system's belief over the true state $\boldsymbol{R}$ as a probability distribution at each stage t, referred to as the belief state. By recommending the item to users and receiving their feedback, the belief state evolves from $p^{(1)}(\boldsymbol{R})$ to $p^{(2)}(\boldsymbol{R})$. As the true preferences $\boldsymbol{R}$ are unknown for the new item, but its distribution is modeled as a belief state, the two-stage decision process is a POMDP.

This model is non-trivial because it has utilised all user-user correlations via a multivariate Gaussian model. To obtain the belief state for the initial stage, we can impose an i.i.d. assumption on the users' preferences on different items. As such, $\boldsymbol{\mu}^{(1)}$ can be estimated as the users' mean ratings, and $\boldsymbol{\Sigma}^{(1)}$ can be estimated by the user-user covariances on previously co-rated items. To emphasise the role of user-user

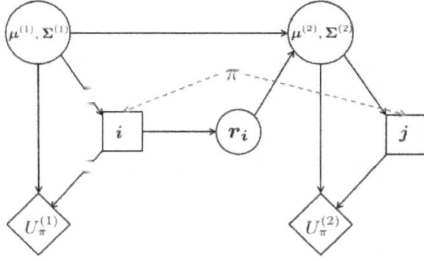

Figure 2: The two-stage CU-POMDP as illustrated by an influence diagram, with respect to the correlated-user model. In the diagram, circular nodes are random variables and square nodes are the recommendation decision, and the rhombus nodes are the utility at each stage.

correlations, in the sequel, we also make use of the following representation

$$\mathbf{\Sigma}^{(1)} = \text{Dg}[\mathbf{\Sigma}^{(1)}]^{1/2} \mathbf{X}^{(1)} \text{Dg}[\mathbf{\Sigma}^{(1)}]^{1/2} \quad (2)$$

$$= \text{diag}[\boldsymbol{\sigma}^{(1)}] \mathbf{X}^{(1)} \text{diag}[\boldsymbol{\sigma}^{(1)}] \quad (3)$$

where $\text{Dg}(\mathbf{\Sigma}^{(1)})$ denotes the matrix of the diagonal elements of $\mathbf{\Sigma}^{(1)}$, $\boldsymbol{\sigma}^{(1)}$ is the vector formed by the users' standard deviations of ratings ($\boldsymbol{\sigma}^{(1)} = \text{diag}[\text{Dg}^{1/2}(\mathbf{\Sigma}^{(1)})])^*$, and $\mathbf{X}^{(1)}$ is the correlation matrix whose element $\rho_{ij}^{(1)}$ is the correlation of ratings between user i and user j.

A policy π is defined to make the decision at each stage on the basis of the available information:

$$\boldsymbol{i} = \pi(\boldsymbol{\mu}^{(1)}, \mathbf{\Sigma}^{(1)}, \mathcal{I}), \text{ and} \quad (4)$$

$$\boldsymbol{j} = \pi(\boldsymbol{\mu}^{(2)}, \mathbf{\Sigma}^{(2)}, \mathcal{I} \backslash \boldsymbol{i}), \quad (5)$$

where we use vectors $\boldsymbol{i}$ and $\boldsymbol{j}$ to denote the user selection decisions for the two stages respectively ($|\boldsymbol{i}| = m$ and $|\boldsymbol{j}| = n$). The total expected ratings collected at each stage is thus the element-wise summation of the expected rating vector of each selection which we refer to as reward $U_\pi^{(t)}$

$$U_\pi^{(1)} = \mathbb{E}^{(1)}[\mathbf{1}^T \boldsymbol{R}_i], \quad (6)$$

$$U_\pi^{(2)} = \mathbb{E}^{(2)}[\mathbf{1}^T \boldsymbol{R}_j], \quad (7)$$

where $\boldsymbol{R}_i$ and $\boldsymbol{R}_j$ are used to denote the correspondent vectors partitioned by the user selections $\boldsymbol{i}$ and $\boldsymbol{j}$ respectively. We will use the same partition rule throughout this paper.

The objective is to find a policy of selecting users such that the expected *total* reward of the two stages are maximised

$$\pi^* = \arg \max_\pi \left(U_\pi^{(1)} + U_\pi^{(2)}\right). \quad (8)$$

2.1.1 Belief Update

Let us consider the problem in a reverse order. Suppose the system has already recommended the item to m users in the initial stage and received feedback $\boldsymbol{r}_i$. Given the feedback, the system can update its belief state on the remaining users $\mathcal{I} \backslash \boldsymbol{i}$ (simplified as $\backslash \boldsymbol{i}$) by the conditional multivariate

---

*Following the convention in mathematical notations we use diag[$\boldsymbol{a}$] to denote the diagonal matrix formed by vector $\boldsymbol{a}$. we also use diag[$\mathbf{A}$] to denote the vector formed by the diagonal elements of $\mathbf{A}$ if $\mathbf{A}$ is a matrix.

Gaussian distribution, conditioned on the observations

$$p^{(2)}(\boldsymbol{R}_{\backslash i}) \sim \mathcal{N}(\boldsymbol{\mu}_{\backslash i}^{(2)}, \mathbf{\Sigma}_{\backslash i, \backslash i}^{(2)}), \text{ where} \quad (9)$$

$$\boldsymbol{\mu}_{\backslash i}^{(2)} = \boldsymbol{\mu}_{\backslash i}^{(1)} + \mathbf{\Sigma}_{\backslash i, i}^{(1)}[\mathbf{\Sigma}_{i,i}^{(1)}]^{-1}(\boldsymbol{r}_i - \boldsymbol{\mu}_i^{(1)}) \quad (10)$$

$$\mathbf{\Sigma}_{\backslash i, \backslash i}^{(2)} = \mathbf{\Sigma}_{\backslash i, \backslash i}^{(1)} - \mathbf{\Sigma}_{\backslash i, i}^{(1)}[\mathbf{\Sigma}_{i,i}^{(1)}]^{-1}\mathbf{\Sigma}_{i, \backslash i}^{(1)}. \quad (11)$$

To gain insight with the view of correlated users, we reformulate the update functions with the correlation matrix $\mathbf{X}^{(1)}$ as follows. According to Eq. (3), we obtain

$$[\mathbf{\Sigma}_{i,i}^{(1)}]^{-1} = \text{diag}[\boldsymbol{\sigma}_i^{(1)}]^{-1}[\mathbf{X}_{i,i}^{(1)}]^{-1}\text{diag}[\boldsymbol{\sigma}_i^{(1)}]^{-1}, \text{ and} \quad (12)$$

$$[\mathbf{\Sigma}_{\backslash i, i}^{(1)}] = \text{diag}[\boldsymbol{\sigma}_{\backslash i}^{(1)}]\mathbf{X}_{\backslash i, i}^{(1)}\text{diag}[\boldsymbol{\sigma}_i^{(1)}]. \quad (13)$$

Substituting Eqs. (13) and (12) into (10) we further get

$$\boldsymbol{\mu}_{\backslash i}^{(2)} = \boldsymbol{\mu}_{\backslash i}^{(1)} + \quad (14)$$

$$\text{diag}[\boldsymbol{\sigma}_{\backslash i}^{(1)}]\mathbf{X}_{\backslash i, i}^{(1)}[\mathbf{X}_{i,i}^{(1)}]^{-1}\text{diag}[\boldsymbol{\sigma}_i^{(1)}]^{-1}(\boldsymbol{r}_i - \boldsymbol{\mu}_i^{(1)})$$

Particularly, if we assume equal rating variance for all users and disregard the correlations among users $\boldsymbol{i}$ such that $\mathbf{X}_{i,i}^{(1)}$ becomes an identity matrix, then Eq. (14) reduces to a weighted summation of the observed ratings centred by their prior expectations $\boldsymbol{r}_i - \boldsymbol{\mu}_i^{(1)}$, with the weights as the correlations between unobserved users and observed users

$$\boldsymbol{\mu}_{\backslash i}^{(2)} = \boldsymbol{\mu}_{\backslash i}^{(1)} + \mathbf{X}_{\backslash i, i}^{(1)}(\boldsymbol{r}_i - \boldsymbol{\mu}_i^{(1)}). \quad (15)$$

Eq. (15) looks very familiar to us because it simulates the popular neighbourhood-based (user-based) CF algorithm, which takes the neighbours' ratings regarding the target item, centres them by the neighbours' mean ratings, and estimates the target user's preference regarding this item as their weighted summation [17], where Pearson correlation is commonly used to calculate the weights [30]. We thus see the user-based recommendation heuristic as an approximation of our CU model.

From the above formula we can see that: (i) by observing users $\boldsymbol{i}$ in the initial stage, the expectations of unobserved users are also updated; (ii) the covariances (correlations) between observed and unobserved users act as the bridge through which feedback from selected users can update our belief regarding other users.

2.1.2 Exact Solution

To obtain the exact solution, consider $V^*(\boldsymbol{\mu}^{(t)}, \mathbf{\Sigma}^{(t)}, T)$ which is the maximally achievable expected total future reward with current information $\boldsymbol{\mu}^{(t)}$, $\mathbf{\Sigma}^{(t)}$ and remaining steps ($T = 1, 2$). With the updated belief according to Eq. (10) and (11) already *given*, the optimal expected reward for the second stage is simply a greedy approach:

$$V_{\text{CU}}^*(\boldsymbol{\mu}^{(2)}, \mathbf{\Sigma}^{(2)}, 1) = \max_\pi U_\pi^{(2)}$$

$$= \max_{j \subset \mathcal{I} \backslash i} \mathbb{E}^{(2)}[\mathbf{1}^T \boldsymbol{R}_j]$$

$$= \max_{j \subset \mathcal{I} \backslash i} \mathbf{1}^T \boldsymbol{\mu}_j^{(2)}. \quad (16)$$

By working backwards the total maximal expected reward for two stages can be obtained as

$$V_{\text{CU}}^*(\boldsymbol{\mu}^{(1)}, \mathbf{\Sigma}^{(1)}, 2) = \max_\pi (U_\pi^{(1)} + U_\pi^{(2)})$$

$$= \max_{i \subset \mathcal{I}} \left(\mathbb{E}^{(1)}[\mathbf{1}^T \boldsymbol{R}_i + V_{\text{CU}}^*(\boldsymbol{\mu}^{(2)}, \mathbf{\Sigma}^{(2)}, 1)]\right) \quad (17)$$

$$= \max_{i \subset \mathcal{I}} \left(\mathbb{E}^{(1)}[\mathbf{1}^T \boldsymbol{R}_i] + \int p^{(1)}(\boldsymbol{R}_i = \boldsymbol{r}_i)V_{\text{CU}}^*(\boldsymbol{\mu}^{(2)}, \mathbf{\Sigma}^{(2)}, 1)d\boldsymbol{r}_i\right).$$

Substituting Eqs. (16) and (10) into (17) we reach the exact solution obtained by value iteration:

$$V_{\text{CU}}^*(\boldsymbol{\mu}^{(1)}, \boldsymbol{\Sigma}^{(1)}, 2) = \max_{i \subset \mathcal{I}} \left\{ \overbrace{\mathbf{1}^T \boldsymbol{\mu}_i^{(1)}}^{\text{exploitation}} + \right. \tag{18}$$

$$\underbrace{\int p^{(1)}(\boldsymbol{R}_i = \boldsymbol{r}_i) \max_{j \subset \mathcal{I} \setminus i} \left[\mathbf{1}^T \left(\boldsymbol{\mu}_j^{(1)} + \boldsymbol{\Sigma}_{j,i}^{(1)} [\boldsymbol{\Sigma}_{i,i}^{(1)}]^{-1} (\boldsymbol{r}_i - \boldsymbol{\mu}_i^{(1)}) \right) \right] d\boldsymbol{r}_i}_{\text{exploration}} \left. \right\}.$$

Eq. (18) suggests that the merit of choosing users i at the initial stage lies in two components:

- **Exploitation**. It is the immediate expected reward, denoted by $\mathbf{1}^T \boldsymbol{\mu}_i^{(1)}$, determined by the prior information on the users.

- **Exploration**. The exploration component shows how the feedback from users i can lead the system to find optimal selections with updated knowledge. Consider that the feedback deviates from the prior information such that $(\boldsymbol{r}_i - \boldsymbol{\mu}_i^{(1)}) \neq \mathbf{0}$, the updated belief state will then lead us to find users which bring "extra" returns via the term $\boldsymbol{\Sigma}_{j,i}^{(1)} [\boldsymbol{\Sigma}_{i,i}^{(1)}]^{-1} (\boldsymbol{r}_i - \boldsymbol{\mu}_i^{(1)})$. No matter the deviation is positive or negative, we can always benefit from it by selecting corresponding optimal users in the second stage. As mentions above, this term relates to correlations between the users of the two stages. The larger the correlations are, the more the system can *gain* from the discrepancy between the observations and the prior information.

2.2 Matrix Factorisation Model with POMDP

To gain insights from the formulation of latent factor models, consider MF with POMDP (MF-POMDP). For this purpose, we use the probabilistic model $\boldsymbol{R} = \mathbf{P}\boldsymbol{q} + \epsilon$ such that $\mathbf{P} = (\boldsymbol{p}_1, \boldsymbol{p}_2, \ldots, \boldsymbol{p}_{|\mathcal{I}|})^T$ is a $|I| \times K$ matrix containing the users' information, $\boldsymbol{q}$ is a K-dimensional item vector, and ϵ is a random variable with zero mean and variance σ_0^2. If we assume fixed user vectors $\mathbf{P}$ and unknown item vector $\boldsymbol{q}$ [47, 37], CU-POMDP is translated to a decision process under the belief state of the unobservable item vector (see Figure 3)

$$p^{(t)}(\boldsymbol{q}) \sim \mathcal{N}(\boldsymbol{\nu}^{(t)}, \boldsymbol{\Omega}^{(t)}), \tag{19}$$

where $\boldsymbol{\nu}^{(1)}$ and $\boldsymbol{\Omega}^{(1)}$ are the mean and covariance matrix on the low-rank representation. The belief state over the item vector then determines our belief over the preferences of users

$$p^{(t)}(\boldsymbol{R}) \sim \mathcal{N}(\mathbf{P}\boldsymbol{\nu}^{(t)}, \mathbf{P}\boldsymbol{\Omega}^{(t)}\mathbf{P}^T + \sigma_0^2 \mathbf{I}). \tag{20}$$

By observing users i with feedback $\boldsymbol{r}_i$ the belief state can be updated according to the Bayes rule

$$p^{(2)}(\boldsymbol{q}) \sim \mathcal{N}(\boldsymbol{\nu}^{(2)}, \boldsymbol{\Omega}^{(2)}), \text{ where} \tag{21}$$

$$\boldsymbol{\nu}^{(2)} = \boldsymbol{\nu}^{(1)} + \boldsymbol{\Omega}^{(1)}\mathbf{P}_i^T(\mathbf{P}_i\boldsymbol{\Omega}^{(1)}\mathbf{P}_i^T + \sigma_0^2 \mathbf{I})^{-1}(\boldsymbol{r}_i - \boldsymbol{\nu}^{(1)}), \tag{22}$$

$$\boldsymbol{\Omega}^{(2)} = [(\boldsymbol{\Omega}^{(1)})^{-1} + \mathbf{P}_i^T\mathbf{P}_i/\sigma_0^2]^{-1}. \tag{23}$$

Thus,

$$\mathbb{E}^{(2)}(\boldsymbol{R}_{\setminus i}|\boldsymbol{r}_i) = \mathbf{P}_{\setminus i}\boldsymbol{\nu}^{(2)} \tag{24}$$

$$= \mathbf{P}_{\setminus i}\boldsymbol{\nu}^{(1)} + \mathbf{P}_{\setminus i}\boldsymbol{\Omega}^{(1)}\mathbf{P}_i^T(\mathbf{P}_i\boldsymbol{\Omega}^{(1)}\mathbf{P}_i^T + \sigma_0^2 \mathbf{I})^{-1}(\boldsymbol{r}_i - \mathbf{P}_i\boldsymbol{\nu}^{(1)}).$$

Comparing Eq. (24) with Eq. (15) we find a nice alignment between the two models. Actually, by dimension reduction the correlation between user i's and user j's ratings

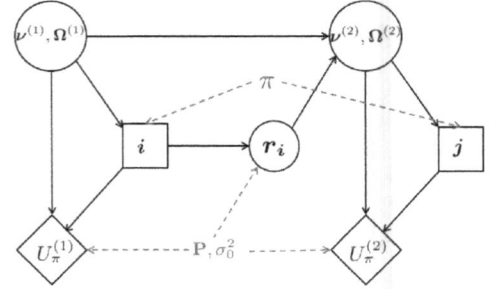

Figure 3: The two-stage MF-POMDP as illustrated by an influence diagram, with respect to the matrix factorisation model.

can be translated as

$$\rho_{i,j}^{(1)} = \boldsymbol{p}_i^T \boldsymbol{\Omega}^{(1)} \boldsymbol{p}_j, \tag{25}$$

when σ_0^2 is very small compared to the covariance between the two users's true preferences ($\sigma_0^2 << \boldsymbol{p}_i^T \boldsymbol{\Omega}^{(1)} \boldsymbol{p}_j$).

By the same token, we write the optimal value function for the MF-POMDP as

$$V_{\text{MF}}^*(\boldsymbol{\nu}^{(1)}, \boldsymbol{\Omega}^{(1)}, 2) = \max_{i \subset \mathcal{I}} \left\{ \mathbf{1}^T \mathbf{P}_i \boldsymbol{\nu}^{(1)} + \right.$$

$$\int p^{(1)}(\boldsymbol{R}_i = \boldsymbol{r}_i) \max_{j \subset \mathcal{I} \setminus i} \left[\mathbf{1}^T \left(\mathbf{P}_j \boldsymbol{\nu}^{(1)} + \right. \right. \tag{26}$$

$$\left. \left. \mathbf{P}_j \boldsymbol{\Omega}^{(1)} \mathbf{P}_i^T [\mathbf{P}_i \boldsymbol{\Omega}^{(1)} \mathbf{P}_i^T + \sigma_0^2 \mathbf{I}]^{-1} (\boldsymbol{r}_i - \mathbf{P}_i \boldsymbol{\nu}^{(1)}) \right) \right] d\boldsymbol{r}_i \right\}.$$

2.3 A Toy Example

Let us look at a simple three-user case and its analytical solution. In this example, one user is selected in each stage to maximise the objective function. We base this example on the CU model so that the effect of user-user correlation can be illustrated more straightforwardly.

Suppose

$$\boldsymbol{\mu}^{(1)} = \begin{pmatrix} \mu_1^{(1)} \\ \mu_2^{(1)} \\ \mu_3^{(1)} \end{pmatrix}, \quad \boldsymbol{\Sigma}^{(1)} = \begin{pmatrix} \Sigma_{1,1}^{(1)} & \Sigma_{1,2}^{(1)} & \Sigma_{1,3}^{(1)} \\ \Sigma_{2,1}^{(1)} & \Sigma_{2,2}^{(1)} & \Sigma_{2,3}^{(1)} \\ \Sigma_{3,1}^{(1)} & \Sigma_{3,2}^{(1)} & \Sigma_{3,3}^{(1)} \end{pmatrix}.$$

Without loss of generality, we assume $\Sigma_{1,3}^{(1)} > \Sigma_{1,2}^{(1)} > \Sigma_{2,3}^{(1)}$ (and ignore the case with equal covariance for now). Supposing user 1 is selected in the initial stage with the observation as r_1, the update for the second and the third users are,

$$\mu_2^{(2)}(r_1) = \mu_2^{(1)} + \Sigma_{2,1}^{(1)}(\Sigma_{1,1}^{(1)})^{-1}(r_1 - \mu_1^{(1)}),$$

$$\mu_3^{(2)}(r_1) = \mu_3^{(1)} + \Sigma_{3,1}^{(1)}(\Sigma_{1,1}^{(1)})^{-1}(r_1 - \mu_1^{(1)}).$$

By introducing $z_1 = (r_1 - \mu_1^{(1)})/\sqrt{\Sigma_{1,1}^{(1)}}$, the above updates become

$$\mu_2^{(2)}(z_1) = \mu_2^{(1)} + \Sigma_{2,1}^{(1)}(\Sigma_{1,1}^{(1)})^{-1/2}z_1,$$

$$\mu_3^{(2)}(z_1) = \mu_3^{(1)} + \Sigma_{3,1}^{(1)}(\Sigma_{1,1}^{(1)})^{-1/2}z_1.$$

We can see that both $\mu_2^{(2)}$ and $\mu_3^{(2)}$ are linear in z_1. The turning point between choosing user 2 or user 3 is obtained when the above two are equal to each other, which is at

$$d_1 = \frac{\mu_2^{(1)} - \mu_3^{(1)}}{\Sigma_{3,1}^{(1)} - \Sigma_{2,1}^{(1)}} \sqrt{\Sigma_{1,1}^{(1)}}.$$

Because $\Sigma_{3,1}^{(1)} > \Sigma_{2,1}^{(1)}$, if $z_1 > d_1$, user 3 should be selected whereas if $z_1 < d_1$ user 2 should be selected in the second stage. Thus, the optimal reward when choosing user 1 at the initial stage is

$$V_{i=1}^*(\mu^{(1)}, \Sigma^{(1)}, 2) =$$

$$\mu_1^{(1)} + \int p^{(1)}(r_1) \cdot \max_{j=2,3} \left(\mu_j^{(1)} + \Sigma_{j,1}^{(1)} (\Sigma_{1,1}^{(1)})^{-1} (r_1 - \mu_1^{(1)}) \right) dr_1$$

$$= \mu_1^{(1)} + \int_{-\infty}^{d_1} p^{(1)}(z_1) \left[\mu_2^{(1)} + \Sigma_{2,1}^{(1)} (\Sigma_{1,1}^{(1)})^{-1/2} z_1 \right] dz_1$$

$$+ \int_{d_1}^{\infty} p^{(1)}(z_1) \left[\mu_3^{(1)} + \Sigma_{3,1}^{(1)} (\Sigma_{1,1}^{(1)})^{-1/2} z_1 \right] dz_1$$

$$= \mu_1^{(1)} + 1/2(\mu_2^{(1)} + \mu_3^{(1)}) + 1/2(\mu_2^{(1)} - \mu_3^{(1)}) \mathbf{erf}(\frac{d_1}{\sqrt{2}})$$

$$- \frac{1}{\sqrt{2\pi}} \frac{\Sigma_{2,1}^{(1)} - \Sigma_{3,1}^{(1)}}{\sqrt{\Sigma_{1,1}^{(1)}}} e^{-\frac{d_1^2}{2}}.$$

Similarly,

$$V_{i=2}^*(\mu^{(1)}, \Sigma^{(1)}, 2) = \mu_2^{(1)} + 1/2(\mu_3^{(1)} + \mu_1^{(1)}) +$$

$$1/2(\mu_3^{(1)} - \mu_1^{(1)}) \mathbf{erf}(\frac{d_2}{\sqrt{2}}) - \frac{1}{\sqrt{2\pi}} \frac{\Sigma_{3,2}^{(1)} - \Sigma_{1,2}^{(1)}}{\sqrt{\Sigma_{2,2}^{(1)}}} e^{-\frac{d_2^2}{2}},$$

$$V_{i=3}^*(\mu^{(1)}, \Sigma^{(1)}, 2) = \mu_3^{(1)} + 1/2(\mu_1^{(1)} + \mu_2^{(1)}) +$$

$$1/2(\mu_2^{(1)} - \mu_1^{(1)}) \mathbf{erf}(\frac{d_3}{\sqrt{2}}) - \frac{1}{\sqrt{2\pi}} \frac{\Sigma_{2,3}^{(1)} - \Sigma_{1,3}^{(1)}}{\sqrt{\Sigma_{3,3}^{(1)}}} e^{-\frac{d_3^2}{2}},$$

where

$$d_2 = \frac{\mu_3^{(1)} - \mu_1^{(1)}}{\Sigma_{1,2}^{(1)} - \Sigma_{3,2}^{(1)}} \sqrt{\Sigma_{2,2}^{(1)}}, \quad d_3 = \frac{\mu_2^{(1)} - \mu_1^{(1)}}{\Sigma_{1,3}^{(1)} - \Sigma_{2,3}^{(1)}} \sqrt{\Sigma_{3,3}^{(1)}}.$$

Note that the above formula are not rotationally symmetric due to the asymmetry caused by $\Sigma_{1,3}^{(1)} > \Sigma_{1,2}^{(1)} > \Sigma_{2,3}^{(1)}$.

To illustrate the results, let us look at a numerical example according to the above solutions. Suppose

$$\mu^{(1)} = \begin{pmatrix} 3.2 \\ 2.5 \\ 3.5 \end{pmatrix}, \quad \Sigma^{(1)} = \begin{pmatrix} 1.6 & 0.25 & 1.6 \\ 0.25 & 3.2 & 0.20 \\ 1.6 & 0.20 & 3.5 \end{pmatrix}.$$

The correlation matrix is thus

$$\mathbf{X}^{(1)} = \begin{pmatrix} 1 & 0.11 & 0.68 \\ 0.11 & 1 & 0.06 \\ 0.68 & 0.06 & 1 \end{pmatrix}.$$

When user 1 is selected at the initial stage:

$$\mu_2^{(2)}(r_1) = \mu_2^{(1)} + \Sigma_{2,1}^{(1)}(\Sigma_{1,1}^{(1)})^{-1}(r_1 - \mu_1^{(1)})$$
$$= 2.5 + 0.25 \times (1.6)^{-1}(r_1 - 3.2),$$
$$\mu_3^{(2)}(r_1) = \mu_3^{(1)} + \Sigma_{3,1}^{(1)}(\Sigma_{1,1}^{(1)})^{-1}(r_1 - \mu_1^{(1)})$$
$$= 3.5 + 1.6 \times (1.6)^{-1}(r_1 - 3.2).$$

Therefore, when $r_1 < 2.01$ we should choose user 2 in the second stage whilst when $r_1 > 2.01$ we should choose user 3 (when $r_1 = 2.01$ choosing either will give the same expected reward in the second stage). The corresponding value function is

$$V_{i=1}^*(\mu^{(1)}, \Sigma^{(1)}, 2)$$
$$= \mu_1^{(1)} + \int p^{(1)}(r_1) \cdot \max_{j=2,3} \left(\mu_j^{(1)} + \Sigma_{j,1}^{(1)}(\Sigma_{1,1}^{(1)})^{-1}(r_1 - \mu_1^{(1)}) \right) dr_1$$
$$= 3.2 + \int_{-\infty}^{2.01} p^{(1)}(r_1)(2.5 + 0.25 \times (1.6)^{-1}(r_1 - 3.2)) dr_1$$
$$+ \int_{2.01}^{+\infty} p^{(1)}(r_1)(3.5 + 1.60 \times (1.6)^{-1}(r_1 - 3.2)) dr_1$$
$$\approx 6.80.$$

Similarly, we can obtain the value functions for choosing user 2 and 3 at the initial stage

$$V_{i=2}^*(\mu^{(1)}, \Sigma^{(1)}, 2) \approx 5.7,$$
$$V_{i=3}^*(\mu^{(1)}, \Sigma^{(1)}, 2) \approx 6.77.$$

And thus obtain the final value function

$$V^*(\mu^{(1)}, \Sigma^{(1)}, 2) = \max(6.80, 5.7, 6.77) = 6.80.$$

It is seen that the value function favours the first user at the first step, even though the prior information about the users favours the third user over the first user. Due to the fact that user 1 is highly correlated to user 3, and is more correlated with user 2 than is user 3, choosing user 1 at the initial stage will enable the system to judge better in the second stage which results in a higher total expected reward over the two stages.

2.4 Computational Complexity

The exact solution of a finite-horizon POMDP has been proven to be PSPACE-complete [25]. In our case, the decision space at the initial stage is $C_m^{|\mathcal{I}|}$. For each decision, the m-dimensional observation space will be divided into $C_n^{|\mathcal{I}|-m}$ regions, each region corresponds to a (possibly) different optimal user combination to choose for the second stage. That is, the exact solution suggested by the value iteration algorithm requires going through all the possible decisions and all possible observations, which is intractable.

3. APPROXIMATION

To approximate the value iteration function, we propose the approximation solution here, named guided exploitation-exploration (GEE). We will detail its form for the CU model and the MF model respectively below.

3.1 Approximation for CU-POMDP

From Section 2.1.2, we have seen that the merit of selecting a group of users lies both in the immediate reward term (the exploitation part of Eq. (18)) and in how it can guide the system to find promising users in the next stage through the system update (the exploration part of Eq. (18)). However, when the decision of the initial stage is made, the system's belief state update is unknown before receiving any observations. To investigate the influence of selecting users i only (before making any observations), let us consider the conditional distribution of unselected users $\backslash i$ over the selection of users i, $p(\boldsymbol{R}_{\backslash i} | i)$. Note that this conditional distribution is different from Eq. (9) because it is the distribution conditioned on the action i instead of the observations, as at the initial-decision stage these observations are still unknown.

Because the observations are not made yet, the expected feedback conditioned on the selection remains unchanged

$$\mathbb{E}[\boldsymbol{R}_{\backslash i} | i] = \boldsymbol{\mu}_{\backslash i}^{(1)}. \quad (27)$$

However, its covariance changes according to the choice of i:

$$\mathrm{Cov}[\boldsymbol{R}_{\backslash i} | i] = \mathrm{Cov}\left[\boldsymbol{\mu}_i^{(1)} + \boldsymbol{\Sigma}_{\backslash i,i}^{(1)}(\boldsymbol{\Sigma}_{i,i}^{(1)})^{-1}(\boldsymbol{R}_i - \boldsymbol{\mu}_i^{(1)}) \right]$$
$$= \boldsymbol{\Sigma}_{\backslash i,i}^{(1)}(\boldsymbol{\Sigma}_{i,i}^{(1)})^{-1}\mathrm{Var}(\boldsymbol{R}_i)(\boldsymbol{\Sigma}_{i,i}^{(1)})^{-1}\boldsymbol{\Sigma}_{i,\backslash i}^{(1)}$$
$$= \boldsymbol{\Sigma}_{\backslash i,i}^{(1)}(\boldsymbol{\Sigma}_{i,i}^{(1)})^{-1}\boldsymbol{\Sigma}_{i,\backslash i}^{(1)}, \quad (28)$$

where the last step is due to $\mathrm{Cov}(\boldsymbol{R}_i) = \boldsymbol{\Sigma}_{i,i}$.

Algorithm 1 CU-GEE by Sampling

Require: Prior mean ratings $\boldsymbol{\mu}^{(1)}$, covariance matrix $\boldsymbol{\Sigma}^{(1)}$,
   GEE parameter λ, available users $\mathcal{I}$
  Initialise $\boldsymbol{i}^* \leftarrow \emptyset$
  for $t = 1 \ldots T$ **do**
    Sample $\boldsymbol{i}_t$ $(|\boldsymbol{i}_t| = m)$ from $\mathcal{I}$
    Calculate $V_{\boldsymbol{i}_t}^{\text{CU-GEE}}$ according to Eq. (30)
    if $V_{\boldsymbol{i}_t}^{\text{CU-GEE}}$ is the largest so far **then**
      Update $\boldsymbol{i}^* \leftarrow \boldsymbol{i}_t$
    end if
  end for

Therefore, with the users at the initial stage selected as $\boldsymbol{i}$, the expected returns at the second stage by choosing users $\boldsymbol{j}$ are bounded by the interval $\Theta_{\boldsymbol{i},\boldsymbol{j}}$:

$$\Theta_{\boldsymbol{i},\boldsymbol{j}} = \left[\mathbf{1}^T \left(\boldsymbol{\mu}_{\boldsymbol{j}}^{(1)} - \lambda \cdot \text{diag} \left[\text{Dg}^{-\frac{1}{2}} \left(\text{Cov}(\boldsymbol{R}_{\boldsymbol{j}}|\boldsymbol{i}) \right) \right] \right), \right.$$
$$\left. \mathbf{1}^T \left(\boldsymbol{\mu}_{\boldsymbol{j}}^{(1)} + \lambda \cdot \text{diag} \left[\text{Dg}^{-\frac{1}{2}} \left(\text{Cov}(\boldsymbol{R}_{\boldsymbol{j}}|\boldsymbol{i}) \right) \right] \right) \right] \quad (29)$$

with the probability at least $(1 - 2e^{-\lambda^2/2})^n$ [42][†].

The GEE algorithm therefore optimistically assumes the highest return could be achieved within this interval [43]. And thus we choose the users $\boldsymbol{i}$ which can achieve the highest total ratings under this assumption

$$\pi_{\text{CU-GEE}}(\boldsymbol{\mu}^{(1)}, \boldsymbol{\Sigma}^{(1)}, \mathcal{I})$$
$$= \arg\max_{\boldsymbol{i} \subset \mathcal{I}} \left\{ \mathbf{1}^T \boldsymbol{\mu}_{\boldsymbol{i}}^{(1)} + \max_{\boldsymbol{j} \subset \mathcal{I} \backslash \boldsymbol{i}} \mathbf{1}^T \left(\boldsymbol{\mu}_{\boldsymbol{j}}^{(1)} + \right. \right.$$
$$\left. \left. \lambda \cdot \text{diag} \left[\text{Dg}^{-\frac{1}{2}} \left(\boldsymbol{\Sigma}_{\boldsymbol{j},\boldsymbol{i}}^{(1)} (\boldsymbol{\Sigma}_{\boldsymbol{i},\boldsymbol{i}}^{(1)})^{-1} \boldsymbol{\Sigma}_{\boldsymbol{i},\boldsymbol{j}}^{(1)} \right) \right] \right) \right\}. \quad (30)$$

This algorithm suggests that, in order to determine the users for stage one, we first calculate the immediate reward based on the prior information. Then we calculate the optimistic reward when acting optimally in the second stage. We call GEE *guided* as the initial-stage decision is optimistically guided by pseudo optimal user selections in the next stage. By inspecting into the next stage, we utilise the correlation between users of the two stages, which will be explained further in Section 3.1.1. To implement this algorithm, we can adopt a sampling-based method depicted in Algorithm 1.

3.1.1 Independent Intra-Stage User Assumption

To align our algorithm with the popular neighbourhood-based CF, we adopt the correlation presentation Eq. (3) and reformulate Eq. (30) as follows:

$$\pi_{\text{CU-GEE}'}(\boldsymbol{\mu}^{(1)}, \boldsymbol{\sigma}^{(1)}, \mathbf{X}^{(1)}, \mathcal{I})$$
$$= \arg\max_{\boldsymbol{i} \subset \mathcal{I}} \left\{ \mathbf{1}^T \boldsymbol{\mu}_{\boldsymbol{i}}^{(1)} + \max_{\boldsymbol{j} \subset \mathcal{I} \backslash \boldsymbol{i}} \mathbf{1}^T \left(\boldsymbol{\mu}_{\boldsymbol{j}}^{(1)} + \right. \right. \quad (31)$$
$$\left. \left. \lambda \cdot \text{diag} \left[\text{Dg}^{-\frac{1}{2}} \left(\text{diag}(\boldsymbol{\sigma}_{\boldsymbol{j}}^{(1)}) \mathbf{X}_{\boldsymbol{j},\boldsymbol{i}}^{(1)} (\mathbf{X}_{\boldsymbol{i},\boldsymbol{i}}^{(1)})^{-1} \mathbf{X}_{\boldsymbol{i},\boldsymbol{j}}^{(1)} \text{diag}(\boldsymbol{\sigma}_{\boldsymbol{j}}^{(1)}) \right) \right] \right) \right\}. $$

If we adopt the intra-stage independent-user assumption, i.e., users in $\boldsymbol{i}$ are independent to each other, and an equal variance assumption, i.e., all the users have the same vari-

---
[†]To be more exact, the conditional vector $\boldsymbol{R}_{\backslash \boldsymbol{i}}|\boldsymbol{i}$ is bounded in an ellipsoid. This form is obtained with an approximation of considering only the diagonal elements of $\text{Cov}(\boldsymbol{R}_{\backslash \boldsymbol{i}}|\boldsymbol{i})$.

Algorithm 2 CU-GEE-I by Sampling

Require: Prior mean ratings $\boldsymbol{\mu}^{(1)}$, correlation matrix $\mathbf{X}^{(1)}$,
   GEE parameter λ', available users $\mathcal{I}$
  Initialise $\boldsymbol{i}^* \leftarrow \emptyset$
  for $t = 1 \ldots T$ **do**
    Sample $\boldsymbol{i}_t$ $(|\boldsymbol{i}_t| = m)$ from $\mathcal{I}$
    Calculate $V_{\boldsymbol{i}_t}^{\text{CU-GEE-I}}$ according to Eq. (32)
    if $V_{\boldsymbol{i}_t}^{\text{CU-GEE-I}}$ is the largest so far **then**
      Update $\boldsymbol{i}^* \leftarrow \boldsymbol{i}_t$
    end if
  end for
---

ance σ^2, Eq. (31) can be further approximated to

$$\pi_{\text{CU-GEE-I}}(\boldsymbol{\mu}^{(1)}, \mathbf{X}^{(1)}, \mathcal{I}) \quad (32)$$
$$= \arg\max_{\boldsymbol{i} \subset \mathcal{I}} \left[\sum_{\alpha=1}^m \mu_{i_\alpha}^{(1)} + \max_{\boldsymbol{j} \subset \mathcal{I} \backslash \boldsymbol{i}} \sum_{\beta=1}^n \left(\mu_{j_\beta}^{(1)} + \lambda' \sqrt{\sum_{\alpha=1}^m (\rho_{i_\alpha, j_\beta}^{(1)})^2} \right) \right],$$

where $\lambda' = \lambda \sigma$. We can see that the effect of inter-stage user-user correlations is shown clearly in the above formula. According to Eq. (32), given the user selection at the initial stage $\boldsymbol{i}$, we can foresee the optimistic return in the next stage through highly expected values (via μ_{j_β}) and also highly correlated users (via the term $\sqrt{\sum_{\alpha=1}^m (\rho_{i_\alpha, j_\beta}^{(1)})^2}$). Identifying these users then guides the system to determine the user selection $\boldsymbol{i}^*$.

The sampling method for this algorithm is illustrated in Algorithm 2.

3.2 Approximation for MF-POMDP

With the MF model, the conditional covariance matrix of $\boldsymbol{R}_{\backslash \boldsymbol{i}}$ given the user selection $\boldsymbol{i}$ is written as

$$\text{Cov}(\boldsymbol{R}_{\backslash \boldsymbol{i}}|\boldsymbol{i}) = \mathbf{P}_{\boldsymbol{i}} \boldsymbol{\Omega}^{(1)} \mathbf{P}_{\boldsymbol{i}}^T (\mathbf{P}_{\boldsymbol{i}} \boldsymbol{\Omega}^{(1)} \mathbf{P}_{\boldsymbol{i}} + \sigma_0^2 \mathbf{I})^{-1} \mathbf{P}_{\boldsymbol{i}} \boldsymbol{\Omega}^{(1)} \mathbf{P}_{\boldsymbol{i}}^T. \quad (33)$$

Following the same reasoning as in Section 3.1, we give the formulation with latent factors obtained by matrix factorisation

$$\pi_{\text{MF-GEE}}(\boldsymbol{\nu}^{(1)}, \boldsymbol{\Omega}^{(1)}, \mathcal{I})$$
$$= \arg\max_{\boldsymbol{i} \subset \mathcal{I}} \left\{ \mathbf{1}^T \mathbf{P}_{\boldsymbol{i}} \boldsymbol{\nu}^{(1)} + \max_{\boldsymbol{j} \subset \mathcal{I} \backslash \boldsymbol{i}} \mathbf{1}^T \left(\mathbf{P}_{\boldsymbol{j}} \boldsymbol{\nu}^{(1)} + \lambda \cdot \right. \right. \quad (34)$$
$$\left. \left. \text{diag} \left[\text{Dg}^{-\frac{1}{2}} \left(\mathbf{P}_{\boldsymbol{j}} \boldsymbol{\Omega}^{(1)} \mathbf{P}_{\boldsymbol{i}}^T (\mathbf{P}_{\boldsymbol{i}} \boldsymbol{\Omega}^{(1)} \mathbf{P}_{\boldsymbol{i}}^T + \sigma_0^2 \mathbf{I})^{-1} \mathbf{P}_{\boldsymbol{i}} \boldsymbol{\Omega}^{(1)} \mathbf{P}_{\boldsymbol{j}}^T \right) \right] \right) \right\} $$

3.2.1 Independent Intra-Stage User Assumption

With the MF model, in addition to the independent intra-stage user assumption which turns $\mathbf{P}_{\boldsymbol{i}} \boldsymbol{\Omega}^{(1)} \mathbf{P}_{\boldsymbol{i}}^T$ into a diagonal matrix, we may also assume independent latent dimensions such that the prior covariance matrix is diagonal: $\boldsymbol{\Omega}^{(1)} = \text{diag}(\boldsymbol{\omega}^{(1)})$. Eq. (34) can be further simplified as:

$$\pi_{\text{MF-GEE-I}}(\boldsymbol{\nu}^{(1)}, \boldsymbol{\omega}^{(1)}, \mathcal{I}) = \arg\max_{\boldsymbol{i} \subset \mathcal{I}} \left\{ \sum_{\alpha=1}^m \boldsymbol{p}_{i_\alpha}^T \boldsymbol{\nu}^{(1)} + \right. \quad (35)$$
$$\left. \max_{\boldsymbol{j} \subset \mathcal{I} \backslash \boldsymbol{i}} \sum_{\beta=1}^n \left(\boldsymbol{p}_{j_\beta}^T \boldsymbol{\nu}^{(1)} + \lambda \sqrt{\sum_{\alpha=1}^m \frac{(\boldsymbol{p}_{j_\beta}^T \text{diag}[\boldsymbol{\omega}^{(1)}] \boldsymbol{p}_{i_\alpha})^2}{\boldsymbol{p}_{i_\alpha}^T \text{diag}[\boldsymbol{\omega}^{(1)}] \boldsymbol{p}_{i_\alpha} + \sigma_0^2}} \right) \right\}.$$

Particularly when assuming $\boldsymbol{\omega}^{(1)} = \omega^{(1)}\mathbf{1}$, i.e., equal prior variance along different dimensions, we gain the form

$$\pi_{\text{MF-GEE-II}}(\boldsymbol{\nu}^{(1)}, \omega^{(1)}, \mathcal{I}) = \arg\max_{i \subset \mathcal{I}} \left\{ \sum_{\alpha=1}^{m} \boldsymbol{p}_{i_\alpha}^T \boldsymbol{\nu}^{(1)} + \right.$$

$$\left. \max_{j \subset \mathcal{I} \setminus i} \sum_{\beta=1}^{n} \left(\boldsymbol{p}_{j_\beta}^T \boldsymbol{\nu}^{(1)} + \lambda \sqrt{\sum_{\alpha=1}^{m} \frac{(\omega^{(1)} \boldsymbol{p}_{j_\beta}^T \boldsymbol{p}_{i_\alpha})^2}{\omega^{(1)} \boldsymbol{p}_{i_\alpha}^T \boldsymbol{p}_{i_\alpha} + \sigma_0^2}} \right) \right\}. \quad (36)$$

Actually, with such a spherical prior variance, Eq. (25) becomes $\rho_{i,j}^{(1)} = \boldsymbol{p}_i^T \boldsymbol{p}_j$, i.e., the simple inner product of their latent factors. This is also the correlation form corresponding to the MF obtained by a regularised linear regression estimation [30].

For the sake of saving space, we omit the algorithms for the MF representation here.

4. RELATED WORK AND DISCUSSION

4.1 Collaborative Filtering

Our work can be considered part of CF research [39]. CF provides efficient and personalised recommendations based on the similarities between users and items. This can be achieved by mainly three approaches [39]: similarity-based approaches such as neighbourhood based CF (user-based and item-based) [17, 10], latent factor models [22, 21, 21, 7], and hybrid methods [9]. We relate our work with the neighbourhood-based CF and latent factor models as follows.

4.1.1 Neighbourhood-Based CF

Neighbourhood based CF provides a straightforward estimation of the target rating as a weighted summation of similar ratings: either the ratings from similar users, or the ratings to similar items, and can therefore provide explainable recommendations [17, 16, 1, 34, 6, 30].

According to our analysis in Section 2.1, neighbourhood-based models can be viewed as an approximate multivariate Gaussian preference model with the following two assumptions: (i) only the correlations between the target user and its neighbours are considered, and the neighbours are assumed to be independent to each other; and (ii) all users have the same variance in their ratings. In some practices, the rating scores are also normalised with their standard deviations [16], which is referred to as the Z-score normalisation. We thus see the Z-score normalisation as a way to alleviate the prediction discrepancy caused by the second assumption. In addition, in practice, only the most-similar users are selected as neighbours, including top-N filtering and threshold filtering strategies, to ease the computational cost [30]. Beside the Pearson correlation, cosine similarity is also used, but it is argued that its performances are not as good as the Pearson correlation similarity measure [8].

4.1.2 Latent Factor Models

Latent factor models first project the user and item onto a latent feature space, and then base the score on the feature vectors of them. The correlations between user pairs are therefore translated as the vector similarity in the latent space (as shown in Section 2.2). Matrix factorisation is probably the most well-known method of latent factor models [22]. Singular value decomposition (SVD) [22], SVD++ [21], pLSA [18] and Latent Dirichlet Allocation [7] are among the more famous ones. Probabilistic matrix factorisation is one of the latent factors which is adopted in this paper [33] with respect its probabilistic property.

4.2 Cold-Start Problems in CF

Cold-start problems [35] remain a major challenge for CF-based recommender systems, as the prediction of ratings purely depends on the previously expressed user-item preferences without the use of any content information, and for a new user or item this information is unavailable.

There is comparatively more literature on the user cold-start problems than the item cold-start problems. For the former, a pre-recommendation "interview" process is usually adopted. In an interview, the user first gives feedback on some questions provided by the system, such as preferences on popular items, highly informative items or a diversified item list [26, 27]. The interview questions can also be designed more intelligently, such as decision trees [26, 48, 12]. AL forms an important branch for designing interview questions, and is most relevant to our approach. We have a thorough comparison in Section 4.4.1.

In addition, many techniques [48, 12, 47] assume an interactive process for sequential query selection, i.e., only one query is chosen at a time for one user. Then after the response is collected, another query will be chosen according to the user response to the previous query. In our case, as well as in many other practical situations, multiple items or users should be recommended in a batch manner to improve efficiency. Therefore, iterative techniques are not applicable.

4.3 Probabilistic Ranking Principle in CF

Originating from information retrieval [29], the probabilistic ranking principle (PRP) has been also related to CF [45]. PRP implies documents to be ranked in descending order by their probabilities of relevance can produce optimal performance under the "independent document" assumption [28]. In the item cold-start problem scenario, supposing the rating is proportional to the relevance probability, the list of users to recommend the item to should be ranked according to the prior information of the users, such as the rank of the user average ratings. On the other hand, in a user cold-start scenario, the rank of recommended items should be the prior average rating information of the items.

We have shown in this paper that PRP is not optimal as the correlations between users play an important role for the system to update, when considered as an interactive process. There are both intra-list correlations between users chosen in the initial stage and inter-list correlations between users in the first and remaining users (Eq. 18). Especially, the inter-list correlations enable the system to update, and finally lead to more accurate predictions.

4.4 Comparisons to Other EE Methods

4.4.1 Comparison to Active Learning

Active learning (AL) methods were adopted to handle the cold-start problems in recommender systems [30, 15, 32, 31], which is also referred to as optimal design by statisticians [40]. AL uses a limited number of items (usually much smaller than the total number of available items) to present to the target user to review, and then learns the user's profile based on the users' feedback on these items. Because the number of items to review is limited, the user model's accuracy largely depends on the training points selected [30, 40]. The objective of AL is usually represented by a statistical measure such as achieving minimal mean squared error in the model estimation (A-optimality criterion) [2] or minimal determinant of resulting covariance matrix of the system (D-optimality criterion) [32]. This objective differs from our objective function, and thus leads to significant differences from our approach.

There are two main differences between AL and our GEE approach. First, AL techniques such as D-Optimal design [32], A-Optimal design [2] and their applications to the cold-start item problem have divided exploration and exploitation into two separate stages. In the exploration stage, a small number of training points are selected for the system to learn, and in the exploitation stage the gained information is fully exploited. However, the returns (or regrets) collected from the exploration stage are not considered. In other words, The objective is imposed onto only the exploitation stage, and thus the trade-off between exploration and exploitation is not modeled [30]. For example, in [2], a budget has been imposed on the number of users to select at the experimental stage, and these users' returns are excluded from the objective function.

Second, the goal of AL is usually measured statistically using a global criterion. The criterion can be, e.g., (to minimise) the mean square error of the estimates [2], or, (to maximise) the differential Shannon information [32]. However, from Eqs. (18) and (26) and from the example, we can see that the exact solution is achieved by prioritising the learning process towards promising users of the next stage. Therefore, it is not necessary to achieve a global optimum. On the contrary, GEE captures this feature and make decisions guided by potential users of the second stage.

4.4.2 Comparison to UCB methods

The EE problem has been intensively studied in the literature of multi-armed bandit problems, where an agent decides dynamically which arm to choose at each step for a total T steps bearing the objective to maximise the total reward collected [3]. Gittins has provided an optimal solution under the condition that only one arm at a time can evolve and arms are independent [11], but this is intractable in practice. UCB seeks a bounded regret instead of optimality and is popularly used to balance the exploitation and exploration in practice [3, 4, 38, 43]. In UCB, usually a decision is made based on both the expectation and uncertainty of the return of individual choices at each step. For example, GP-UCB [38] suggests to make the decision based on the linear combination of the expectation and the standard deviation of the reward of each arm. Recently GP-UCB algorithms have also been applied to solve the user cold-start problems interactively in recommender systems [47, 41].

Our approach differs from UCB approaches in the following ways. First, UCB-based approaches seek to limit the regret within a bound, but they do not model how the specific selection within the bound can influence the outcome. In other words, EE achieved by UCB is not guided by the potential rewarding choices of the following stages, but is rather to limit the regret of the current stage. Second, UCB-based approaches are usually achieved in a long-term and interactive process, and may not be suitable for the two-stage process. Conversely, our algorithm is derived directly from the exact solution of POMDP. It has directly considered the effect that choosing the initial-stage users has on the potential returns from the second stage.

5. EXPERIMENT

In this section, we compare our proposed approximate solutions with several baseline methods. To understand the model further and verify our theoretical analysis, we first present the result comparison between our methods using

Table 1: Total reward compared using synthetic data.

Algorithm	$N = 10$	$N = 20$	$N = 30$	$N = 40$
Greedy	19.084	38.919	52.517	60.55
AL	18.953	37.719	52.655	62.537
UCB	19.568	39.903	54.632	63.959
GEE	21.238	43.151	59.315	69.198
Improvement	8.5%	8.1%	8.6%	8.2%

synthetic data, and then present our performance gains on a real dataset.

5.1 Synthetic Data Experiment

5.1.1 Synthetic Data Generation

First, we define a 5-dimensional latent space and randomly generate a multivariate Gaussian distribution as the prior information of the cold-start item. In detail, each dimension of the multivariate Gaussian mean vector is generated randomly according to $\mathcal{N}(0, 0.1)$, and each dimension's standard deviation is generated according to $\mathcal{N}(0, 1)$. Then we generate 50 cold-start items according to this randomly-generated distribution. Second, we generate 100 users' vectors according to $\mathcal{N}(\mathbf{0}, \mathbf{I})$ as the available user pool for the 50 cold-start items to target to. Their real ratings are then produced according to Eq. (20) with the noise's standard deviation as 0.5. As such, we can obtain a 100×50 rating matrix as the groundtruth. The true prior information is then provided for each compared algorithm to perform recommendations. Finally, the above process is repeated for a total of 30 times, each time with a different prior information of the cold-start items. The results are then averaged over the different trials.

5.1.2 Compared Methods

We compare our proposed GEE algorithm to the following algorithms. (i) **Greedy**. Greedy method chooses the initial-stage users with the highest expected feedback. (ii) **Active learning (AL)**. AL method chooses the users to minimise the uncertainty in the model, so that the users with the highest variances are chosen [15, 30]. (iii) **Upper confidence bound (UCB)**. UCB method chooses the initial-stage users with the highest values calculated as the linear combination of the expected reward and the standard deviation [38]. All the algorithms select the second-stage users greedily after the system's state is updated with observations.

5.1.3 Results

The results are shown in Figure 4, with the evaluation measure as the total reward gained from the two stages. The result of the original GEE algorithm (Eq. (34)) is shown and we emphasise that the result of the GEE algorithm with the intra-stage independence assumption produces similar results.

From this figure, we can make the following observations. (i) For all the algorithms, the performance improves as m increases. This shows that by separating the recommendation process into two stages the performance can be greatly improved over a PRP-like top-N once-for-all batch solution. (ii) For all the algorithms, the total reward increases more sharply than it drops after the performance peak. This phenomenon indicates that a small portion of allocation of users in the initial stage can significantly improve the overall performance. Note that in our synthetic data generation, we have used $K=5$, and the peak is also around $m = 5$. Therefore, the dimension of the latent factor model may be an indicator of the allocation ratio. The best result gained with optimal parameters of each algorithm is shown in Table 1.

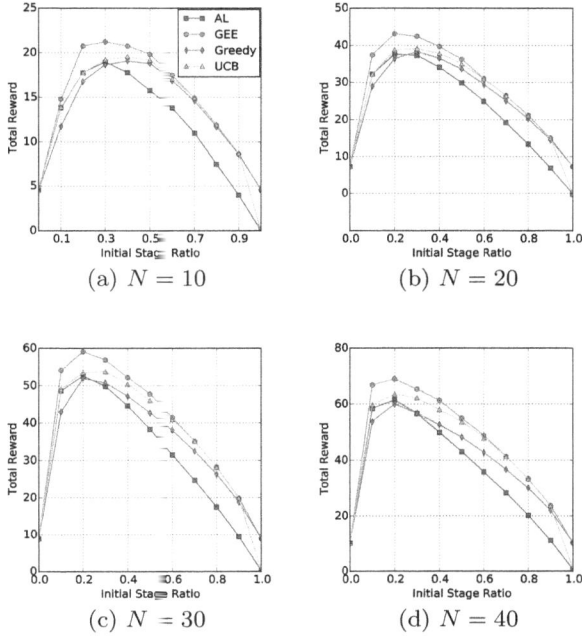

(a) $N = 10$ (b) $N = 20$

(c) $N = 30$ (d) $N = 40$

Figure 4: Total reward compared for the synthetic data experiment. The x-axis is m, the number of users to choose at the initial stage and the y-axis is the total reward of both stages.

5.2 Experiments on the MovieLens Dataset

5.2.1 Experiment setup

As our study is a theoretical one, we use the research-based MovieLens 100K dataset, which is relatively small, containing 943 users and 1,682 movies, with altogether 100,000 ratings ranging from 1 to 5. To conduct the experiment, we first divide the dataset into the training set and test set. For the sake of simulating cold-start item recommendations, we first randomly choose 200 items with sufficient numbers of ratings (at least 50) as the test cold-start items, and use their ratings as the groundtruth in the test dataset. The ratings between users and the remaining items are used to train the model. Similar to the synthetic data experiment, we compare our algorithms with Greedy, AL and UCB. After observing the feedback, the system updates according to the user-based CF model suggested by Eq. (15). The results are evaluated by using both the total reward, and the total hit number – the total number of ratings over the threshold 3 of the two stages. To be consistent with what the user-based CF model suggests, we use the independent intra-user assumption for the GEE algorithm used (CU-GEE-I).

5.2.2 Results

The results are shown in Figure 5, and Tables 2 and 3 with $N = 10, 20, 40$ and 80 respectively. Both the total reward and the total hit number measures are compared. We can see significant improvements over all four cases with the implementation of our algorithm. Similar to the synthetic experiment results, all algorithms show a peaking manner as m increases. From Tables 2 and 3 we can see that the improvements evaluated by using the total reward are even higher than the total hit number, which may be the result of targeting directly to the optimal reward in our objective function.

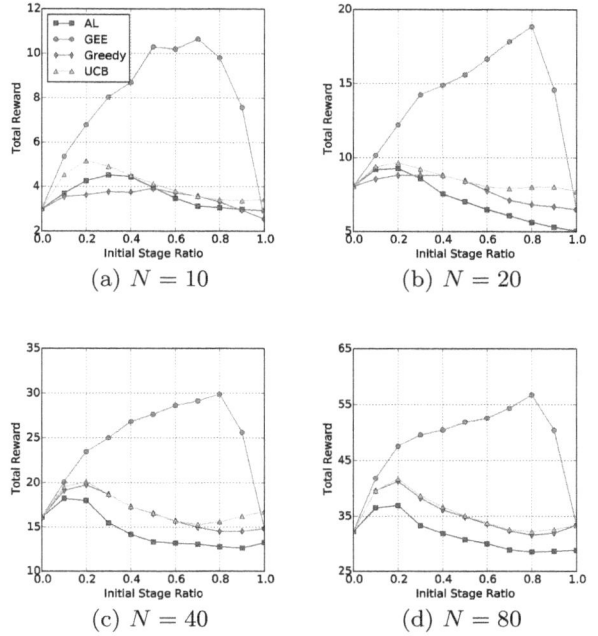

(a) $N = 10$ (b) $N = 20$

(c) $N = 40$ (d) $N = 80$

Figure 5: Total reward compared for the MovieLens 100K data experiment. The x-axis is m, the number of users to choose at the initial stage, and the y-axis is the total reward of both stages.

Table 2: Total reward compared on MovieLens.

Algorithm	$N = 10$	$N = 20$	$N = 40$	$N = 80$
Greedy	4.255	8.95	20.75	45.26
AL	4.705	9.91	21.715	41.665
UCB	5.38	10.2	21.715	45.26
GEE	12.125	19.48	31.05	60.97
Improvement	125.4%	91.0%	43.0%	34.7%

Table 3: Total hit number compared on MovieLens.

Algorithm	$N = 10$	$N = 20$	$N = 40$	$N = 80$
Greedy	0.845	1.745	4.045	8.73
AL	0.875	1.905	4.155	7.815
UCB	1.015	1.955	4.155	8.73
GEE	2.245	3.245	5.325	10.225
Improvement	121.2%	66.0%	28.2%	17.1%

6. CONCLUSION AND FUTURE WORK

In this paper, we presented a novel two-stage recommendation process to address the cold-start problems, with an item cold-start problem as a working example. We formulated the problem using both a correlated-user model and a matrix factorisation model with POMDP. With the exact solution suggested by value iteration, we concluded that the users to choose at the initial stage should be not only of high expected values, but also highly correlated with potential users in the next stage – a property that can guide the system to find promising users in the next stage. With this finding, we proposed the approximate algorithm guided exploitation-exploration (GEE). We conducted initial experiments using GEE and compared the results with several baseline algorithms on both a synthetic and a real dataset, which confirmed the effectiveness of our algorithm.

For future work, we plan to extend the two-stage process to multiple stages and conduct larger scale experiments to study the scalability. We are also interested in obtaining the optimal trade-off parameter λ and the ratio of exploitation-exploration m/n theoretically.

7. REFERENCES

[1] G. Adomavicius and A. Tuzhilin. Toward the next generation of recommender systems: A survey of the state-of-the-art and possible extensions. *TKDE*, 2005.

[2] O. Anava, S. Golan, N. Golbandi, Z. Karnin, R. Lempel, O. Rokhlenko, and O. Somekh. Budget-constrained item cold-start handling in collaborative filtering recommenders via optimal design. In *WWW*, 2015.

[3] P. Auer. Using confidence bounds for exploitation-exploration trade-offs. *JMLR*, 2003.

[4] P. Auer, N. Cesa-Bianchi, and P. Fischer. Finite-time analysis of the multiarmed bandit problem. *Machine learning*, 2002.

[5] N. J. Belkin and W. B. Croft. Information filtering and information retrieval: two sides of the same coin? *Commun ACM*, 1992.

[6] R. M. Bell and Y. Koren. Improved neighborhood-based collaborative filtering. In *SIGKDD Cup Workshop*, 2007.

[7] D. M. Blei, A. Y. Ng, and M. I. Jordan. Latent dirichlet allocation. *JMLR*, 2003.

[8] J. S. Breese, D. Heckerman, and C. Kadie. Empirical analysis of predictive algorithms for collaborative filtering. In *UAI*, 1998.

[9] R. Burke. Hybrid recommender systems: Survey and experiments. *UMUAI*, 2002.

[10] M. Deshpande and G. Karypis. Item-based top-n recommendation algorithms. *TOIS*, 2004.

[11] J. Gittins, K. Glazebrook, and R. Weber. *Multi-armed bandit allocation indices*. John Wiley & Sons, 2011.

[12] N. Golbandi, Y. Koren, and R. Lempel. Adaptive bootstrapping of recommender systems using decision trees. In *WSDM*, 2011.

[13] N. Good, J. B. Schafer, J. A. Konstan, A. Borchers, B. Sarwar, J. Herlocker, and J. Riedl. Combining collaborative filtering with personal agents for better recommendations. In *AAAI/IAAI*, 1999.

[14] A. Gunawardana and C. Meek. Tied boltzmann machines for cold start recommendations. In *RecSys*, 2008.

[15] A. S. Harpale and Y. Yang. Personalized active learning for collaborative filtering. In *SIGIR*, 2008.

[16] J. Herlocker, J. A. Konstan, and J. Riedl. An empirical analysis of design choices in neighborhood-based collaborative filtering algorithms. *Information retrieval*, 2002.

[17] J. L. Herlocker, J. A. Konstan, A. Borchers, and J. Riedl. An algorithmic framework for performing collaborative filtering. In *SIGIR*, 1999.

[18] T. Hofmann. Latent semantic models for collaborative filtering. *TOIS*, 2004.

[19] X. Jin, M. Sloan, and J. Wang. Interactive exploratory search for multi page search results. In *WWW*, 2013.

[20] L. Kaelbling, M. Littman, and A. Cassandra. Planning and acting in partially observable stochastic domains. *Artificial intelligence*, 1998.

[21] Y. Koren. Factorization meets the neighborhood: a multifaceted collaborative filtering model. In *SIGKDD*, 2008.

[22] Y. Koren, R. Bell, and C. Volinsky. Matrix factorization techniques for recommender systems. *Computer*, 2009.

[23] C. D. Manning, P. Raghavan, and H. Schütze. *Introduction to Information Retrieval*. Cambridge University Press, 2008.

[24] L. Page, S. Brin, R. Motwani, and T. Winograd. The pagerank citation ranking: Bringing order to the web. 1999.

[25] C. H. Papadimitriou and J. N. Tsitsiklis. The complexity of markov decision processes. *Mathematics of operations research*, 1987.

[26] A. Rashid, I. Albert, D. Cosley, S. Lam, S. McNee, J. Konstan, and J. Riedl. Getting to know you: learning new user preferences in recommender systems. In *IUI*, 2002.

[27] A. Rashid, G. Karypis, and J. Riedl. Learning preferences of new users in recommender systems: an information theoretic approach. *SIGKDD Explorations Newsletter*, 2008.

[28] C. J. V. Rijsbergen. *Information Retrieval*. Butterworth-Heinemann, 2nd edition, 1979.

[29] S. E. Robertson. The probability ranking principle in ir. *Journal of documentation*, 1977.

[30] N. Rubens, D. Kaplan, and M. Sugiyama. Active learning in recommender systems. In *Recommender systems handbook*, pages 735–767. Springer, 2011.

[31] N. Rubens and M. Sugiyama. Influence-based collaborative active learning. In *RecSys*, 2007.

[32] N. Rubens, R. Tomioka, and M. Sugiyama. Output divergence criterion for active learning in collaborative settings. *IPSJ Online Transactions*, 2009.

[33] R. Salakhutdinov and A. Mnih. Probabilistic matrix factorization. In *NIPS*, 2007.

[34] B. Sarwar, G. Karypis, J. Konstan, and J. Riedl. Item-based collaborative filtering recommendation algorithms. In *WWW*, 2001.

[35] A. I. Schein, A. Popescul, L. H. Ungar, and D. M. Pennock. Methods and metrics for cold-start recommendations. In *SIGIR*, 2002.

[36] X. Shen, B. Tan, and C. Zhai. Implicit user modeling for personalized search. In *CIKM*, 2005.

[37] Y. Shi, X. Zhao, J. Wang, M. Larson, and A. Hanjalic. Adaptive diversification of recommendation results via latent factor portfolio. In *SIGIR*, 2012.

[38] N. Srinivas, A. Krause, S. M. Kakade, and M. Seeger. Gaussian process optimization in the bandit setting: No regret and experimental design. *arXiv preprint arXiv:0912.3995*, 2009.

[39] X. Su and T. M. Khoshgoftaar. A survey of collaborative filtering techniques. *Advances in artificial intelligence*, 2009.

[40] G. Taguchi. *Introduction to quality engineering: designing quality into products and processes*. Asian Productivity Organization, 1986.

[41] H. P. Vanchinathan, I. Nikolic, F. De Bona, and A. Krause. Explore-exploit in top-n recommender systems via gaussian processes. In *RecSys*, 2014.

[42] F. G. Viens. Stein's lemma, malliavin calculus, and tail bounds, with application to polymer fluctuation exponent. *Stochastic Processes and their Applications*, 2009.

[43] T. Walsh, I. Szita, C. Diuk, and M. Littman. Exploring compact reinforcement-learning representations with linear regression. In *UAI*, 2009.

[44] J. Wang, A. P. De Vries, and M. J. Reinders. Unified relevance models for rating prediction in collaborative filtering. *TOIS*, 2008.

[45] J. Wang, S. Robertson, A. P. de Vries, and M. J. Reinders. Probabilistic relevance ranking for collaborative filtering. *Information Retrieval*, 2008.

[46] W. Zhang, S. Yuan, and J. Wang. Optimal real-time bidding for display advertising. In *SIGKDD*, 2014.

[47] X. Zhao, W. Zhang, and J. Wang. Interactive collaborative filtering. In *CIKM*, 2013.

[48] K. Zhou, S. Yang, and H. Zha. Functional matrix factorizations for cold-start recommendation. In *SIGIR*, 2011.

An Analysis of Theories of Search and Search Behavior

Leif Azzopardi
School of Computing Science
University of Glasgow
Glasgow, United Kingdom
Leif.Azzopardi@glasgow.ac.uk

Guido Zuccon
Information Systems School
Queensland University of Technology (QUT)
Brisbane, Australia
g.zuccon@qut.edu.au

ABSTRACT

Theories of search and search behavior can be used to glean insights and generate hypotheses about how people interact with retrieval systems. This paper examines three such theories, the long standing Information Foraging Theory, along with the more recently proposed Search Economic Theory and the Interactive Probability Ranking Principle. Our goal is to develop a model for ad-hoc topic retrieval using each approach, all within a common framework, in order to (1) determine what predictions each approach makes about search behavior, and (2) show the relationships, equivalences and differences between the approaches. While each approach takes a different perspective on modeling searcher interactions, we show that under certain assumptions, they lead to similar hypotheses regarding search behavior. Moreover, we show that the models are complementary to each other, but operate at different levels (i.e., sessions, patches and situations). We further show how the differences between the approaches lead to new insights into the theories and new models. This contribution will not only lead to further theoretical developments, but also enables practitioners to employ one of the three equivalent models depending on the data available.

Categories and Subject Descriptors

H.3.3 [**Information Storage and Retrieval**]: Information Search and Retrieval: Search Process; H.3.4 [**Information Storage and Retrieval**]: Systems and Software: Performance Evaluation

General Terms

Theory, Experimentation, Economics, Human Factors

Keywords

Information Foraging Theory, Search Economic Theory, Interactive Probability Ranking Principle

ICTIR'15, September 27–30, Northampton, MA, USA.
Copyright is held by the owner/author(s). Publication rights licensed to ACM.
ACM 978-1-4503-3833-2/15/09 ...$15.00.
DOI: http://dx.doi.org/10.1145/2808194.2809447

1. INTRODUCTION

The field of Information Seeking and Retrieval (ISR) seeks to understand, predict and explain how people interact with search systems. However, the interaction between a person and search system is non-trivial. It is affected by a host of factors including variables from the person's context (e.g. background, experience, expertise), the interface and the system's configuration [16]. During the course of an ad-hoc topic search session, information seekers pose a number of queries, browse snippets, and assess documents in order to fulfil their information need. This requires them to make many implicit and explicit decisions regarding: what queries to pose, what documents to view, what facets/features to try, whether to continue inspecting snippets for the current query, when to issue a new query, and when to stop searching [32]. Consequently, understanding how information seekers behave and interact with search systems has been a long standing and challenging area of research [8, 17].

While most researchers have focused on cataloguing search behavior based on empirical and observational evidence [19], a number of attempts to formalize the interactions have been proposed [2, 14, 23]. Such formal models use a mathematical framework in which the most salient variables between an information seeker and a system are represented. Given such models, it is possible to describe, predict and crucially explain how and why seekers behave the way they do. Such models also enable the generation of hypotheses regarding search behavior which can be subsequently empirically tested and validated (e.g. [5, 24]). However, these models also have numerous limitations ranging from the low level assumptions engaged by the different models, the variables that they include/exclude and the difficulties arising from the complexities of human behavior. While more sophisticated models are being developed in order to address such limitations (e.g. [3, 4]), our focus is on understanding how the different theories and ensuing models relate to each other. Consequently, in this paper, we will analyze, compare and develop three ISR theories: Information Foraging Theory (IFT) [23], Interactive Probability Ranking Principle (iPRP) [14] and Search Economic Theory (SET) [2]. In this paper, we model the task of ad-hoc topic search using each theory within a common framework. This will enable us to explore how they are similar and different, and what we can learn from each of them. Specifically, we focus on whether these theories make similar predictions about search behavior and how we can develop, refine and extend the different models.

2. BACKGROUND

Numerous models of Information Seeking and Retrieval have been proposed in the literature [6, 7, 8, 9, 13, 16, 17, 18, 20, 36]. Such models fall into two main categories: (1) conceptual and descriptive, and (2) formal and mathematical. Conceptual and descriptive models typically depict the interactions and variables at a high level - they describe the process a searcher takes, and the stages that they may go through. These are particularly useful for understanding the various components involved in the process and which factors are likely to have an influence. Such models are called pre-theoretical in [17] because they provide a picture of the problem domain, which can be used to build more formal models. On the other hand, formal and mathematical models in particular are more precise, enumerating the phenomena as a list of variables and showing how each variable functionally relates to each other[1].

A well known conceptual model of information seeking is the Berry Picker model proposed by Bates [6]. The model draws an analogy between a searcher and a forager (in this case a berry picker). As shown in Figure 1, the berry picker moves from patch to patch collecting the juiciest and ripest berries, before moving onto the next patch. Similarly, the searcher goes from one patch of results to another patch of results selecting the most relevant documents, and moving on to another patch of results. During the course of their search, the searcher's information need evolves and so the type of information they find valuable at any given point also changes (e.g. the berry picker might first collect strawberries, then blueberries, then raspberries, and so on).

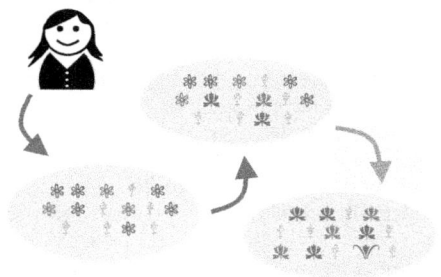

Figure 1: The berry picker foraging patches models a searcher with an evolving information need.

This conceptual model of information seeking is intuitive and most people can easily relate to the idea. However, the model does not provide an indication of how long the searcher will stay in a particular patch or how the time to reach a patch will affect their behavior. Bates suggested that searchers would weigh up the costs and benefits in order to decide what action to take next [7]. Other researchers also considered how searchers are like foragers and initial attempts [27, 29] suggested that Optimal Foraging Theory could be used to model the searching process. Subsequently, this lead to the development of Information Foraging Theory [23] (see subsection below).

The idea of using cost-benefit and decision making tools is not new and a number of other formal models have been developed using such a framework. Indeed, early Information Retrieval (IR) research exploited such tools to examine

IR systems in a number of ways ranging from purchasing decisions [1, 26] to ranking [14, 25, 35] to user behavior [2, 10, 12]. Initial attempts focused on the trade-off between the cost of an IR system and its effectiveness. In [1, 26], Axelrod and Rotheberg compare different mechanized IR systems available during the late 1960s and early 1970s by performing a cost-benefit analysis in order to decide which system to purchase[2]. In [12], Cooper took a more user-oriented perspective. He modeled the trade-off between the amount of time a user should spend searching versus how much time the system should spend searching. In the same period, Robertson [25] examined the problem of ranking in terms of the costs and benefits of ranking one document above another. This led to the formulation of the Probability Ranking Principle (PRP) which essentially applies decision theory to the ranking problem [25]. More recently, Fuhr revised and extended the PRP to consider a series of interactions in the interactive Probability Ranking Principle (iPRP) [14]. This generalized model accounts for the different costs and benefits associated with particular choices when ranking documents (see subsection below).

In [34], Varian outlined three directions in which economics could be useful for search: (1) to obtain better estimates of the probability of relevance, (2) to apply Stigler's theory of Optimal Search Behavior to IR [31], and (3) to examine the economic value of information using consumer theory, "where a consumer is making a choice to maximize expected utility or minimize expected cost" [34]. A number of different works have begun to examine these directions. For example, in [35], Wang and Zhu used Portfolio Theory to obtain better estimates of relevance by accounting for the uncertainty associated with the probability estimates when ranking. While in [10], Birchler and Butler explain how Stigler's theory can be applied to search in order to predict when a user should stop examining results in a ranked list. In a variation on Varian's third suggestion, Azzopardi showed how Production Theory [33] could be used to model the search process [2]. This led to the development of Search Economic Theory (SET) which has been specifically developed to model ad-hoc topic retrieval (see subsection below).

Now that we have provided the context for the different models, we will provide an overview of IFT, iPRP and SET, before developing and comparing the different approaches.

2.1 Information Foraging Theory

Information Foraging Theory is composed of three types of models: *Information Scent model*, *Information Patch model* and *Information Diet model* [23]. Of relevance to this work is the patch model, which describes how long foragers will stay in a patch before moving to a new patch. Under the patch model, the analogy with an information seeker is as follows. Moving between patches is like expressing a new query (and thus incurs a moving/querying cost), while staying within a patch is akin to assessing documents (where each document takes a certain amount of time to process). The Information Patch model predicts how long a forager should stay in a patch before moving on to the next patch.

Under IFT, it is assumed that the forager is rational in that (i) they will visit the patch with the highest yield first, and (ii) they wish to maximize their gain per unit of time. To instantiate the model a gain function parameterized by

---

[1]Note that a formal model need not be mathematical, it could be expressed in some other formal language or construct.

[2]Note the system, while mechanized, also included librarians and technicians as part of the search process.

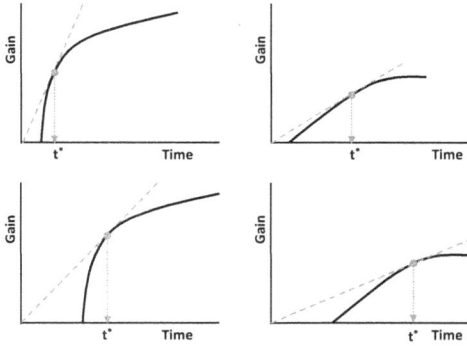

Figure 2: Information Foraging Theory: Top plots are when between-patch times are low, bottom plots are when between-patch times are high. For longer between-patch time. the model predicts foragers will stay longer. For higher yields (left plots), it predicts foragers will move sooner. $t^\star$ indicates optimal time in patch.

time, i.e., $g(t)$ is required. The point where a forager should move to the next patch is when the maximum gain per unit of time is achieved. This depends on the time it takes to get to a patch, the cost of processing documents, and the distribution of relevant information (as specified by the gain function). In Figure 2, the time spent in each patch is shown graphically for patches of different yields. A searcher moves to a patch, they receive no gain for traveling to the patch. They then start to assess and thus extract gain from documents. By drawing a line from the origin to the gain curve, it is possible to determine when the forager should stop, because the tangent is when the forager has achieved the maximum gain per unit of time, and should now switch to a new patch. If the forager stays longer then they will obtain less and less gain (i.e., diminishing returns).

2.2 Interactive PRP

The Interactive Probability Ranking Principle (iPRP) [14] forms an extension to the well known Probability Ranking Principle [25]. However, the iPRP relaxes a number of modeling assumptions made by the PRP: (i) the notion of a fixed information need, and (ii) the relevance of a document is independent of previously seen documents. While these assumptions are reasonable approximations, they have been shown to break down under certain circumstances [15]. The main requirements, when developing the iPRP, were specified as: (i) consider the complete interaction process (i.e., not just document ranking, but other activities), (ii) allow for different costs and benefits of different activities (e.g., a longer document takes longer to process than a shorter document), and (iii) allow for the information need to change through the course of interaction. The motivation of this later point was to incorporate the idea or notion of the Berry Picker model [6] where as the searcher moves from patch to patch their information need changes. Consequently, under the iPRP, when the searcher encounters information, this may change their information need. To instantiate the principle, a number of further assumptions are also made:

1. focus on the function level of interaction (i.e., the different activities a searcher can take and the cost/gain associated with each interaction),

2. decisions form the basis of interaction (i.e., what the searcher does next is based on a decision from the possible set of activities available at that point in time),

3. the searcher evaluates these choices in a linear order (this ordering is either explicit or implicit), and,

4. only decisions which are positive and correct are of benefit to the user.

A key concept in the iPRP is the notion of situations. Each situation essentially represents the current state of the system, and the choices it offers to the user at a particular point during the search. When a user takes a choice, then the system moves to a new state, and the user enters another situation. Note that the system may present entirely new choices, or present the same set of choices during any particular situation. However, the benefit and probability of accepting choices that have been previously presented are likely to change. A situation could contain, for example, the choice to enter a new query, along with a series of choices to examine the documents.

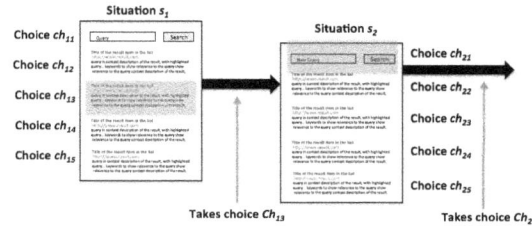

Figure 3: Each choice results in a new situation.

More formally, for a given situation s_i, the user is faced with a number of choices $Ch_i = \{ch_{i1}, \ldots, ch_{in}\}$. For each choice, there is a corresponding probability p_{ij} that the user will accept choice ch_{ij} in situation s_i (see Figure 3). For each situation, it is assumed that the choices are considered in a linear order.

When a user takes a particular choice, ch_{ij}, they will accrue some benefit if they made a good decision (or lose some benefit if they made a bad decision). On average, though, a particular choice ch_{ij}, will result in the average benefit[3], a_{ij}. Under the iPRP, benefit is used to refer to negative costs, and so costs are expressed as negative benefit. This means that the framework uses the same units (such as time) to denote both costs and benefits. This implies that a good decision will result in the user saving time, while a bad decision will result in wasting time. Every choice ch_{ij} also requires a certain amount of effort e_{ij} to be expended, which is also expressed in the same units (i.e., time).

The expected benefit that is accrued from a particular choice can then be formulated as follows:

$$E(ch_{ij}) = e_{ij} + p_{ij}a_{ij}$$

and the expected benefit of taking n choices is:

$$E(ch_{i1}, \ldots, ch_{in}) = \sum_{j=1}^{n} \Big(\prod_{k=1}^{j-1} (1 - p_{ik}) \Big) (e_{ij} + p_{ij}a_{ij})$$

---

[3] $a_{ij} = q_{ij}b_{ij} + (1 - q_{ij})r_{ij}$, where q_{ij} is the probability that the choice was correct and yields b_{ij} benefit. Otherwise the decision incurs a cost r_{ij} with probability $1 - q_{ij}$ to backtrack.

It is shown in [14] that the expected benefit is maximized when the following criterion is met:

$$a_{ij} + \frac{e_{ij}}{p_{ij}} \geq a_{i,j+1} + \frac{e_{i,j+1}}{p_{i,j+1}} \qquad (1)$$

2.3 Search Economic Theory

The initial model proposed in [2] draws upon an analogy with Production Theory [33]. In production theory, a firm produces an *output* (such as goods or services), and to do so requires *inputs* to the process (usually termed, capital and labor) [33]. The firm will utilize some form of *technology* to then produce the output given the inputs. The process of production is similar to the search process. The inputs to the search process are:

Q the number of queries that the user will issue, and,

A the number of documents the user will assess per query.

The output of the search process is a certain amount of utility or gain that the searcher extracts from the relevant documents found during the process. The technology engaged by the user to produce (i.e., find) relevant documents is a retrieval system. This abstraction reduces the search process down to the core variables which directly influence how much utility a user receives through the course of interaction with the system. Consequently, the total amount of gain is proportional to the number of queries and number of documents assessed per query, i.e., the total cumulative gain G is equal to the function $g(Q, A)$. Depending on the particular retrieval system employed, different **technological constraints** are imposed upon the search process such that only certain combinations of inputs will produce a given or specified amount of gain. Under the model a range of different search strategies are potentially possible. For example, for a particular level of gain G, a searcher may pose many queries, and examine a few documents per query, or pose few queries and examine many documents per query. Figure 4 shows an example of a search production function. Each point along the curve represents a combination of inputs that yields the same gain. However, each combination comes at a price. So a cost function $c(Q, A)$ was also defined in [2]. Now, given this model of the search process (i.e., $g()$ and $c()$), a rational searcher would either minimize $c(Q, A)$ in order to obtain a particular level of gain G, or maximize $g(Q, A)$ for a given cost C.

In [4], this model was revised and extended to include a number of other parameters such as the number of snippets examined, the number of result pages viewed, and the probability of examining a document. In this paper, to facilitate the mapping between theories we will focus on building models based on the initial economic model of search and leave such extensions for future work.

3. THEORETICAL DEVELOPMENT

Given the three theories outlined above, the goals of this paper are as follows:

- to develop a model of search based on each theory using the same notion and a common set of assumptions,

- to derive hypotheses about search and search behavior,

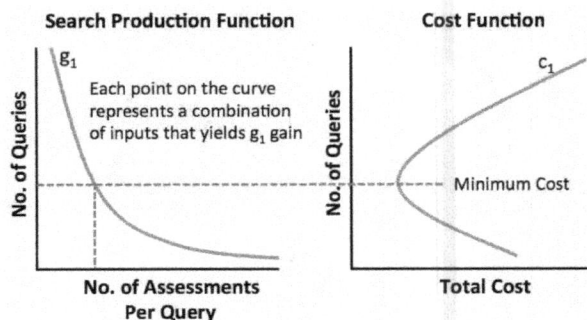

Figure 4: The right plot shows the gain curve that yields g_1 gain, and the left plot shows the corresponding cost function c_1.

- to determine the similarities and differences between the approaches, and,

- to learn how the differences can be used to extend the other models.

We will undertake the theoretical development in the context of ad-hoc topic retrieval where the user would like to find a number of documents relevant to the topic (and have a limited amount of time to perform this task). Gain will be measured as cumulative gain, and the effort / cost will be measured in time (seconds). First, we need to establish a common notation. Let $g()$ denote a cumulative gain function, which can be parameterized either by time or actions. Thus, let $g(t)$ be the cumulative gain at time t, and let $g(Q, A)$ be the cumulative gain given the number of queries Q and the number of assessments per query A. Let G denote a particular level of cumulative gain, and let T denote a particular length in time in seconds, where over a session of length T a searcher receives G cumulative gain. For each action there is an associated cost, which we will represent as time: the time it takes to issue a query t_q and the time it takes to assess a document t_d. Since effort is negative benefit under the iPRP then $e = -c = -t$.

Given this notation, we will first develop the initial SET model proposed in [2], as it already provides a model of search for ad-hoc retrieval over a session. From this model, we will draw a number of hypotheses. We will then develop the other theories to model the same scenario.

4. ECONOMIC MODEL OF SEARCH

As previously mentioned, the basic economic search model [2] is composed of a gain $g()$ and cost $c()$ function, parameterized by Q and A:

$$g(Q, A) = kQ^{\alpha}A^{\beta} \qquad (2)$$

and:

$$c(Q, A) = t_qQ + t_dQA \qquad (3)$$

First, note that we have revised the cost function to be expressed in terms of time, where the total time taken, $(T = c(Q, A))$, is the sum of the amount of time spent querying (t_qQ) and the time spent assessing (t_dQA). The parameters in the gain function represent (and summarize) a number of different elements over the search session. α represents how independent each query is from the next. If

α is set to one, then all queries are independent (i.e., no overlap of the result lists); if α is set to zero, then all the queries return the same result list. While, k and β represent the quality of the result list, where β is typically less than one and suggests that, as the searcher moves down the ranked list, they receive less and less gain (i.e., diminishing returns).

Given these functions, we want to determine the optimal number of queries $Q^\star$ and the optimal number of assessments per query $A^\star$ that maximize the gain for a fixed amount of time T. To solve this, we first create a Lagrangian Multiplier:

$$\Delta = kQ^\alpha A^\beta - \lambda\Big(t_q Q + t_a AQ - T\Big) \qquad (4)$$

Then take the partial derivatives.

$$\begin{aligned}
\frac{\partial \Delta}{\partial A} &= kQ^\alpha \beta A^{\beta-1} - \lambda\Big(t_d Q\Big) \\
\frac{\partial \Delta}{\partial Q} &= k\alpha Q^{\alpha-1} A^\beta - \lambda\Big(t_q + t_d A\Big)
\end{aligned}$$

By setting the partial derivates to zero, we can re-arrange each equation to equal lambda, and then substitute to remove the lambdas, to obtain the optimal number of assessments per query:

$$A^\star = \frac{\beta t_q}{(\alpha - \beta)t_d} \qquad (5)$$

The corresponding number of queries then can be found by substituting $A^\star$ into Equation 2, where we assume that $g(Q, A)$ is equal to G:

$$Q^\star = \left[\frac{G}{k}\right]^{\frac{1}{\alpha}} \left[\frac{(\alpha - \beta)t_d}{\beta t_q}\right]^{\frac{\beta}{\alpha}} \qquad (6)$$

Note that from Equation 5, α must be greater than β because $A^\star$ is required to be zero or greater.

4.1 Search and Search Behavior Hypotheses

Using a method called comparative statics [33], where all variables are held constant, except the one in question, it is possible to generate a number of hypotheses regarding search and search behavior[4]. Assuming that the searcher has a fixed amount of time T, and that they seek to maximize G then the model predicts how the search behavior, characterized by Q and A, would change in response to changes in other variables. For example, according to the model, if k, which relates to the amount of gain in documents, increases, then the model predicts that a user will issue fewer queries. The five hypotheses are summarized below:

k-hypothesis : as k increases, then $Q^\star$ will decrease, but $A^\star$ will stay constant.

α-hypothesis : as α increases, then $A^\star$ will decrease and $Q^\star$ will increase.

β-hypothesis : as β increases, then $A^\star$ will increase and $Q^\star$ will decrease.

t_q-hypothesis : as t_q increases, then $A^\star$ will decrease and $Q^\star$ will increase.

---

[4]Note this simpler economic model of search provides a subset of the hypotheses presented in [4].

t_d-hypothesis : as t_d increases, then $A^\star$ will increase and $Q^\star$ will decrease.

Given this economic model of ad-hoc topic search and the ensuing hypotheses regarding search behavior, an open question is whether the other approaches make similar claims about search behavior. In the following subsections, we will develop models of ad-hoc topic search using IFT and iPRP and determine whether they make similar predictions.

5. IFT MODEL OF SEARCH

In this section we apply IFT to model the ad-hoc search task over a session. Essentially, we wish to determine how many patches will be visited (which corresponds to the number of queries), and how long a forager should stay in a patch (which translates into how many documents they should examine per patch/query) given a fixed amount of time T.

First, we need to formulate IFT in the same terms of SET. To do this, we can take the cost and gain functions from SET (which are expressed in terms of Q and A) and re-express them in terms of gain given time. To simplify this process we shall consider the case when Q is one. By re-arranging Equation 3, the number of documents that are assessed is equal to the total patch time spent t minus the query time t_q, divided by the time per document t_d:

$$A = \frac{t - t_q}{t_d} \qquad (7)$$

We can then substitute A into Equation 2 to arrive at:

$$g(t) = k\left[\frac{t - t_q}{t_d}\right]^\beta \qquad (8)$$

which is the gain given time for one query, where if $t < t_q$ then $g(t) = 0$. To find the optimal time t in a patch, we need to determine when the rate of gain, i.e., $\frac{g(t)}{t}$, is maximized. As shown graphically in Figure 2, this happens to be the tangent to the curve $g(t)$ from the origin. To work this out algebraically, we first need to obtain the slope of the line given the curve. To do this we first take the derivative of the gain function:

$$g'(t) = \frac{k}{t_d}\beta\left[\frac{t - t_q}{t_d}\right]^{\beta-1} \qquad (9)$$

Since we know that the line passes through two points $(0, 0)$ and $(g(t), t)$ and has a gradient given by Equation 9 it is possible to determine the equation for the line. In general, the slope (or gradient) m of a line is given by $m = (y_1 - y_0)/(x_1 - x_0)$; thus equating m to Equation 9 and solving for t, we obtain:

$$\begin{aligned}
\frac{k}{t_d}\beta\left[\frac{t - t_q}{t_d}\right]^{\beta-1} &= \frac{k\left[\frac{t-t_q}{t_d}\right]^\beta - 0}{t - 0} \\
\frac{\beta}{t - t_q} &= \frac{1}{t} \\
\beta t &= t - t_q \\
t^\star &= \frac{t_q}{1 - \beta} \qquad (10)
\end{aligned}$$

By solving the equation above we arrive at the optimal amount of time a forager should spend in a patch, $t^\star$. Sub-

85

stituting $t^\star$ into Equation 7, we arrive at:

$$A^\star = \frac{\beta t_q}{(1 - \beta) t_d} \qquad (11)$$

To obtain a total of G gain then the forager would have to visit a number of patches (by issuing queries). So the number of queries issued would be equal to G divided by the gain obtained per patch. We can determine this as follows.

$$\begin{aligned} Q^\star &= \frac{G}{g(t^\star)} \\ &= \frac{G}{k}\left[\frac{(1 - \beta) t_d}{\beta t_q}\right]^\beta \end{aligned} \qquad (12)$$

In this case, the number of patches visited (i.e. number of queries issued) in a particular period of time T would be equal to $\frac{T}{t^\star}$.

Key Result: The IFT model results in a similar set of equations for $A^\star$ and $Q^\star$ to those of SET. In fact, the formulations are equivalent when $\alpha = 1$, and thus IFT and SET would make the same predictions regarding search behavior (as outlined in subsection 4.1).

α-difference: However, it also shows that there is a clear difference between the models. The IFT model does not immediately cater for the situation that patches (sets of results) may overlap, whereas in SET the α parameter expresses how much overlap there is between the result lists (where $\alpha = 1$ denotes no overlap, and $\alpha = 0$ denotes complete overlap).

Common Assumption: For the equivalence to hold it is assumed that in both IFT and SET the patch/result quality is the same across all patches/result lists. Of course, in practice, result quality varies from query to query. IFT addresses this limitation by employing the following theorem.

5.1 Charnov's Maximum Marginal Theorem

Charvnov's Maximum Marginal Theorem (CMMT) [11] states:

> "that a forager should remain in a patch so long as the slope of the gain function is greater than the average rate of gain in the environment." [23]

The theorem implies that if the forager is within a patch that yields less than the average rate of gain, then the forager should move to another patch, but if they are in a patch that has a higher than average yield, then they should stay in the patch. In Figure 5 the left plot shows the average patch distribution, where the tangent represents the average rate of gain. Let's now assume the forager moves to a patch, such as the one in the right plot, where the patch distribution is lower than the average. Instead of staying until time $t_2^\star$, which would be optimal if all patches were similarly distributed, now the forager would stay only until $t_1^\star$. This is because after this point the rate of gain would be less than the average rate of gain. Note, the theorem assumes that a forager has some idea of the average distribution of yields in patches.

More formally, we can mathematically determine how long an optimal forager would stay in a given patch as follows. Let's assume the forager visits a patch with k_i and β_i and the average patch is k and β. The optimal amount of time to spend in a patch is when the rate of gain in patch i equals the average rate of gain. Consequently, under CMMT, the

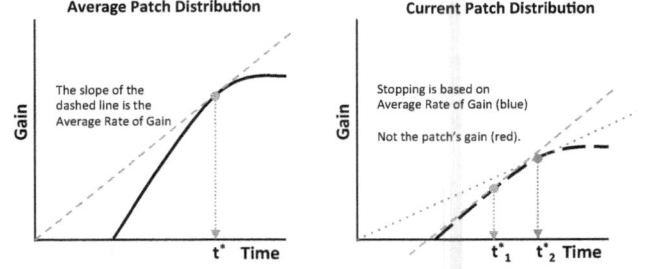

Figure 5: Applying Charnov's Maximum Marginal Theorem. Left plot shows the average patch distribution where the dashed blue line denotes the average rate of gain. The right plot shows that based on the average rate of gain the forager would spend less time in the patch leaving at $t_1^\star$ and not at $t_2^\star$.

model predicts that a forager's behavior changes depending on the patch distribution.

Essentially we would like to know when the rate of gain over time in the average patch (denoted by the slope of the line $(0, 0)$ to $(t^\star, g(t^\star, \beta))$) equals the rate of gain over time in the new patch. Algebraically this becomes:

$$g'(t^\star, \beta) = g'(t_i, \beta_i) \qquad (13)$$

since we know $t^\star$ for the average patch, we can solve for t_i, the total amount of time spent on patch i.

$$\frac{k.\beta}{t_d}\left[\frac{\beta t_q}{(1 - \beta) t_d}\right]^{\beta-1} = \frac{k_i \beta_i}{t_d}\left[\frac{t_i - t_q}{t_d}\right]^{\beta_i-1}$$

$$\left[\frac{k\beta}{k_i\beta_i}\right]^{\frac{1}{\beta_i-1}}\left[\frac{\beta t_q}{(1 - \beta) t_d}\right]^{\frac{\beta-1}{\beta_i-1}} = \frac{t_i - t_q}{t_d}$$

$$t_i = t_q + t_d\left[\frac{k\beta}{k_i\beta_i}\right]^{\frac{1}{\beta_i-1}}\left[\frac{\beta t_q}{(1 - \beta) t_d}\right]^{\frac{\beta-1}{\beta_i-1}} \qquad (14)$$

It is easy to check that if $k = k_i$ and $\beta = \beta_i$ then t_i will equal $t_\star$. If $\beta > \beta_i$ then the amount of time t_i decreases (thus less documents are assessed), and conversely so, if $\beta < \beta_i$. This result is consistent with the β-hypothesis.

k-difference: However, if $k > k_i$ then the amount of time t_i decreases and is less than $t_\star$ (thus less documents are assessed), and conversely so, if $k < k_i$. This result is inconsistent with the k-hypothesis and suggests that k will also influence the time/number of assessments per query. This suggests that the k-hypothesis should be revised, and the SET model should be revised.

6. SET REVISION

Before developing a model of search based on the iPRP, we will first consider how the insights from IFT can be incorporated into the SET model to make it more realistic. From the IFT model, we know that if k_i and β_i in the current patch are different from the average k and/or β then the foragers will change their behavior. However, under the current SET model, changes in k only influence Q because all the patches are assumed to be identically distributed. Below, we remove this limitation from the SET model.

First, assume that the searcher will issue Q queries. For a query q, the gain is characterized by k_q and β_q, and the searcher will examine A_q documents. The total cumulative gain then is the sum over all queries:

$$g(A_1 \ldots A_Q) = \sum_{q=1}^{Q} k_q \alpha(q) A_q^{\beta_q} \qquad (15)$$

and the corresponding cost function is:

$$c(A_1 \ldots A_Q) = Q t_q + \sum_{q=1}^{Q} A_q t_d \qquad (16)$$

where $\alpha(q) = q^{\alpha} - (q-1)^{\alpha}$, i.e., this breaks down the Q^{α} for each query q. Note that if all $k_q = k$, and all $\beta_q = \beta$ then all A_q will equal A, and we return back to the SET model described in Equations 2 and 3.

Now, let us consider the scenario where we have two queries, which have different k values. If we plot the marginal gain curves then we observe that as more documents are assessed the searcher will receive less and less gain (see Figure 6 where the marginal gain curve on the left has a lower k value than the one on the right). According to the CMMT, the depth the searcher ought to go to is when the marginal gain is equal across queries (see the dashed blue line in Figure 6). This shows that for the query with a higher k, an optimal searcher would examine more documents.

To formalize this intuition, lets consider the case where we have the average distribution k and β and the new query q yields k_q and β_q, and $\alpha = 1$; the gain function becomes:

$$g(A, A_q) = k A^{\beta} + k_q A_q^{\beta_q} \qquad (17)$$

and the corresponding cost function is:

$$c(A, A_q) = 2 t_q + t_d A + t_d A_q \qquad (18)$$

Using the Lagrangian Multiplier method, we can solve the equation for A_q to obtain the following:

$$A_q = \left[\frac{k\beta}{k_q \beta_q} \right]^{\frac{1}{\beta_q - 1}} \left[A \right]^{\frac{\beta - 1}{\beta_q - 1}} \qquad (19)$$

The optimal depth to go to when query q yields $k_q = k$ and $\beta_q = \beta$ is $A^{\star}$ (see Equation 5). However, if k_q or β_q decreases, then A_q decreases, while if k_q or β_q increases, then A_q increases. In relation to the IFT model, this revised SET model now makes the same prediction, i.e., if A_q in Equation 19 was expressed as time, then it would equal t_i from Equation 14.

Revised k-hypothesis: Thus, as k_i decreases w.r.t. the average patch distribution k, then A will decrease, and Q will increase. Under the revised SET model, the hypotheses between IFT and SET are now consistent with each other.

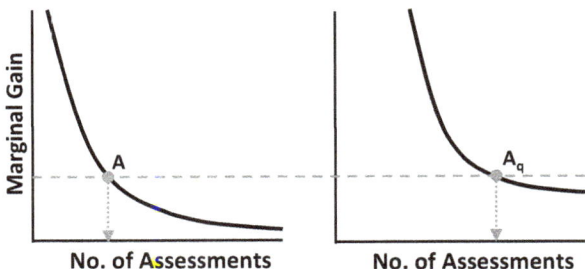

Figure 6: Plot of the Marginal Gain functions.

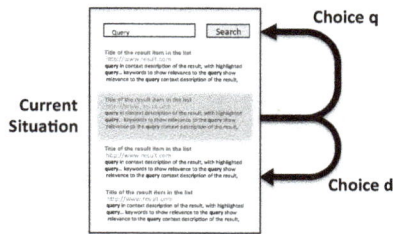

Figure 7: iPRP situations: Choice q: issue a query or choice d: examine the next document.

7. IPRP MODEL OF SEARCH

The iPRP provides a general framework for making low level decisions during the search process. To investigate how the iPRP relates to the other models, we need to frame the problem of ad-hoc topic retrieval in a similar manner. To do this, we consider that at any one point in time during the search process, the user is presented with a decision problem, which comprises of two choices: (i) issue a query or (ii) examine the next document.

More formally, we consider the user being in situation j, where they have just examined document $i - 1$. The user can take one of the following two choices:

Choice d: move to situation $j + 1$ by examining document i, with probability p_d which requires effort e_d; or

Choice q: move to situation $j + 1$ by issuing the query q with probability $p_q = 1 - p_d$ which requires effort e_q.

Since there are only two possibilities then $p_d + p_q = 1$. When the user starts the search they are in situation $j = 0$. As there are no documents to examine then $p_d = 0$ when $j = 0$, and so the only choice they have is to query.

If *choice d* is made, the user acquires a benefit of a_d, i.e. the benefit yielded by document d at rank i; if *choice q* is made, we assume they acquire a benefit of a_q. For the purposes of this analysis, we shall assume that when a user issues a query it also implies that they examine the first document in the ranked list and so the benefit that the user receives comes from the first document in the ranked list[5].

In SET and IFT, querying and assessing efforts are expressed in terms of the time required to form and issue a query, and assess a document. Under iPRP, effort is expressed as negative benefit, so $e_q = -t_q$ and $e_d = -t_d$. The benefit acquired from either of the two choices also needs to be expressed in terms of time. If we assume the same gain function as in SET (and IFT), i.e. $g(A) = k A^{\beta}$, then the gain of a document at rank i is the difference between position i and $i - 1$, i.e., $g(i) - g(i - 1) = k(i^{\beta} - (i - 1)^{\beta})$. To calculate the benefit w.r.t. time, we substitute the gain of a document at rank i into Equation 8 and solve for t, where t equals the benefit a_d. Thus, the benefit of a document (at rank i) is:

$$a_d = t_q + t_d (i^{\beta} - (i-1)^{\beta})^{1/\beta} = t_q + \gamma t_d$$

For simplicity of notation, we have set $\gamma = (i^{\beta} - (i - 1)^{\beta})^{1/\beta}$. Following the assumption that the benefit of a query is provided by the benefit of the first ranked document

---

[5]Note we performed the same derivation but assuming the benefit of the query was zero, and came to similar findings.

87

(i.e., $i = 1$), we have:

$$a_q = t_q + t_d(i^\beta - (i-1)^\beta)^{1/\beta} = t_q + t_d$$

Using these values of efforts and benefits in Inequality 1, we obtain:

$$(t_d + t_q) - \frac{t_q}{1 - p_d} \geq (\gamma t_d + t_q) - \frac{t_d}{p_d}$$

and multiplying each side of the inequality by $p_d(1 - p_d)$:

$$p_d(1-p_d)(t_d+t_q) - p_d t_q \geq p_d(1-p_d)(\gamma t_d + t_q) - (1-p_d)t_d$$

This inequality can be further developed to derive a condition on the relationship between t_q, t_d and the gain γ. Such a condition is expressed as a function of the probability of examining a document, which is informed by a user model (see below). Thus, the above Inequality can be rewritten as:

$$-\frac{t_q}{t_d} \geq p_d(1 - \gamma) + \gamma - \frac{1}{p_d} \qquad (20)$$

When the above condition is satisfied, the iPRP predicts that the user is better off issuing a new query rather than examining the next document.

Differently from SET and IFT, iPRP considers a stochastic user, which assesses a document with probability p_d (or vice versa, issues a query with $p_q = 1 - p_d$). Therefore, we need some way to estimate or model p_d. The user model $\mathcal{U}$ assumed will determine how the user behaves. If empirical data was available it would be possible to estimate the probabilities. For the purposes of this paper, we shall utilize the same user model prescribed by the Rank Biased Precision [22] measure to approximate p_d at each rank.

7.1 RBP User Model Based

A user model that is often used for ad-hoc retrieval is that underlying Rank Biased Precision (RBP) [22], where a user examines the document at rank i with a probability $p_d^{\mathcal{U}_{RBP}}(i) = \rho^{i-1}$. Here, $0.5 < \rho < 1$ is a parameter that indicates the persistence/patience of the user, with $\rho = 1$ representing a persistent user that examines every rank position. Under $\mathcal{U}_{RBP}$, the iPRP predicts assessing is abandoned in favor of querying when the following inequality is satisfied (from Inequality 20):

$$-\frac{t_q}{t_d} \geq \rho^{i-1}(1 - \gamma) + \gamma - \frac{1}{\rho^{i-1}} \qquad (21)$$

Given these Inequalities, the iPRP model can be used to predict the search behavior. To illustrate the Inequalities in action, we have plotted the left (LHS) and right hand side (RHS) in the plots in Figure 8.

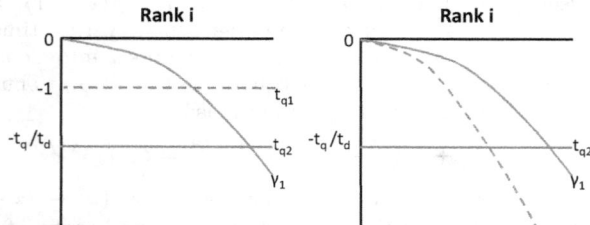

Figure 8: iPRP predicts the user will stop assessing documents and issue the next query when Inequality 21 is satisfied. Graphically, the inequality is satisfied when the red line (LHS) is above the blue line (RHS).

Key Results: First, if t_q increases (see Figure 8, left plot, where $t_{q2} > t_{q1}$), then the LHS becomes more negative, suggesting that a user should examine more documents before issuing a new query. If t_d increases, then the LHS becomes less negative, suggesting that a user would examine less documents before issuing a new query. These predictions are consistent with the t_q and t_d hypotheses.

If the gain increases (either via k or β) then γ increases (see Figure 8, right plot, where $\gamma_1 > \gamma_2$) and the RHS does not curve down as fast, suggesting that a user would examine more documents before issuing a new query. This is also consistent with the k and β hypotheses[6]. These findings mean that the SET, IFT and iPRP models all make similar predictions about search behavior.

p-difference: Differently from the other theories, iPRP models the user as a stochastic agent (rather than fully rational) and thus introduces the probability of accepting choices. In the instantiation presented here this probability is modeled using the user model underneath RBP and thus Inequality 21 is also characterized by the persistence ρ that is attributed to the user. When $\rho = 1$, RHS becomes parallel (and greater) to LHS, meaning that the iPRP predicts the user will keep assessing documents without querying. As ρ becomes smaller, the RHS shape curves down faster and thus meets the LHS earlier. This suggests that as the user becomes more impatient, then they will switching from assessing to querying sooner.

8. EMPIRICAL EXAMPLE

To show the differences between the different models, we have calculated the number of assessments per query for a number of different conditions: (i) when the cost of a query is 30 seconds versus 15 seconds and (ii) when β (quality of result lists) is varied from 0.2 to 0.4. The estimates of k, β, t_q and t_d are based on, and are similar to, the empirically grounded values reported in [4] to provide a realistic set of values for ad-hoc topic retrieval. Table 1 shows the $A^\star$ for the SET model (and through equivalence the IFT model), along with the i value at which the user should switch from assessing to querying for different ρ values for iPRP (thus i and A both represent the number of assessments per query). The first thing to note is that as β increases, A and i increase. Under SET/IFT, the doubling of the query cost, also doubles the depth of assessment A. However, under the iPRP model, the increase in i is much smaller. For the iPRP model, as ρ increases i also increases, where the less patient the searcher the closer they become to the optimal stopping point with respect to the SET/IFT models. Intuitively, though, the predictions regarding the stopping point based on the iPRP seem to be more in line with how actual searchers tend to behave. In terms of the differences, it appears that the user's probability of accepting a choice is more influential in how far down the ranked list they will go than the change in performance (via β) and to a lesser degree the cost of a query (i.e. t_q). These observations motivate a number of lines of future investigation: (1) which model most closely reflects actual behavior, (2) how such a probability can be encoded within the IFT/SET models, and (3) which parameter(s) are the most important or influential in determining search behavior.

---

[6] Note that if we included $\alpha(i)$ into the model, then we could also derive the α hypothesis.

k	β	t_q	t_d	$A^\star$	$i, \rho 0.1$	$i, \rho 0.5$	$i, \rho 0.9$
\multicolumn{8}{l}{When $t_q = t_d$}							
0.25	0.20	15	15	0.25	1.21	1.70	5.57
	0.30			0.43	1.22	1.70	5.57
	0.40			0.67	1.23	1.72	5.59
\multicolumn{8}{l}{When $2t_q = t_d$}							
0.25	0.20	30	15	0.50	1.39	2.28	9.37
	0.30			0.86	1.39	2.28	9.37
	0.40			1.33	1.40	2.29	9.38

Table 1: Stopping points for different conditions. k is held constant across patches. The number of assessments per query is reported for each condition for $A^\star$ and i, ρ. As ρ increases so does the depth, but the change is rather invariant to changes in performance i.e., β increases.

9. DISCUSSION AND CONCLUSION

In this paper, we have taken three theories of Information Seeking and Retrieval and applied them to model ad-hoc topic retrieval. We created models of ad-hoc topic retrieval using the same notation to show how SET, IFT and iPRP are related. We enumerated a list of hypotheses about search behavior stemming from these models, and showed that each model makes similar predictions.

However, our analysis revealed a number of differences between models stemming from three parameters: k (result list quality), α (the result list overlap) and p (probability of accepting a choice).

k-difference: This difference arose because IFT predicted that foragers would stay longer in patches when k_i was increased w.r.t the patch average, whereas SET did not. This is because the original SET model was invariant to k, assuming it was constant across all patches/result lists. In the revised SET model, each result list was parameterized with an individual k_q making the model more realistic and generalizable. As a result, the initial k-hypothesis was revised, such that: as k_i increases w.r.t the average k, then the number of documents assessed (time spent in patch) also increases, thereby reducing the overall number of queries across the session.

α-difference: The α-difference came about because the SET model included an exponent that denotes how related subsequent queries were (essentially how much patch overlap there is). While we did not revise the IFT model, it would be possible to include another parameter in the gain function to denote this when visiting subsequent patches, i.e., the gain at patch q would be $g(t, q) = \alpha(q)g(t)$ where $\alpha(q) = q^\alpha - (q-1)^\alpha$ and q is the qth query issued. Similarly the gain (benefit) from a new query in the iPRP could also be discounted accordingly.

p-difference: The third difference stemmed from the probability of accepting a choice p that is within the iPRP, but not within the other models. The probability of accepting a choice could be incorporated into the other models, where instead of considering the gain and cost functions, they are modified to be expected gain and expected costs. The probability of accepting a choice is essentially the probability of taking an action, and so can be used to compute the expected gain and expected costs. This would mean we could frame the problem in the same way for IFT and SET. For example, the gain function for a single query q would need to be updated such that: $g(A_q) =$

$k_q \sum_i p_i (i^{\beta_q} - (i-1)^{\beta_q})$ where i represents the ith document in the ranked list. Further work will be needed to perform the complete derivation to determine whether the updated gain function results in IFT and SET make predictions similar to iPRP (in terms of direction and magnitude). A key implication of the inclusion of p, under the RBP user model, is that the patience/persistence parameter has a greater influence on the depth a searcher goes to than the performance of the system.

In conclusion, this work represents the first major attempt to compare and integrate the different models/theories - and as such this theory-based paper formally shows under what conditions these models are equivalent, and what we can learn by exploring and developing such theories. This work, therefore, provides a bridge between these theories, paving the way forward for further theoretical developments and innovations in an area that is central to the field of Information Seeking and Retrieval.

This bridge lets us understand the user and system interactions at different levels through the different models, at the session level through SET, the patch level through IFT and the choice level with the iPRP. Thus, testing and validating the predictions of one model will essentially provide evidence to support the others. Also, depending on the specific data available, it is possible to instantiate one (or all) of the models to form common predictions about how changes to the system/interface will affect search behavior. The equivalence means observations and concepts in one model can be transferred to the other models further improving the models and refining the predictions regarding search behavior.

However, there are many future challenges and open questions that remain. Firstly, we need to understand more precisely how the different parameters impact and influence search behavior and search performance. From the examples we have provided we have seen that certain parameters have a greater impact on search behavior and performance than others, e.g., the probability of accepting a choice plays a major role in shaping the searcher's behavior and this appears to dictate interactions more so than a change in performance or cost. Further work is required here to explore a range of user stopping models for p taken from other evaluation metrics (other than RBP) and determine which is the most appropriate/accurate (i.e., which most closely resembles actual user stopping behavior). Secondly, we have only examined one possible gain function, however there are many other possible functions to be explored. Selecting and/or estimating an appropriate and realistic gain function poses a significant challenge. A possible direction here lies in drawing upon estimates/functions used in new measures such as the Time Biased Gain [30] and the U-measure [28] which encode in different ways how searchers extract gain over time from their interaction. This leads to two further points: (i) creating more realistic and accurate models of the gain/cost/interaction, and (ii) the integration between measures and models. Regarding (i) we focused on the most basic model of search, however search is more complex and so more sophisticated models need to be developed in order to better capture how people interact with search systems. Already some work has been done in this area [3, 4] extending the basic model by including interactions with search result page and snippets. The next step is to show how these additional variables and parameters can be added to

IFT and iPRP. Furthermore, we have also seen that through the iPRP model of search, the patience/persistence strongly influences the prediction on how far a searcher will go down in the ranked list. It seems that such model is perhaps more realistic and encoding such probabilities into the models provides a way to relax the rationality assumption. Thus, extending the IFT and SET models in this regard would provide a novel and valuable extension. With respect to (ii) we have shown that the user models employed by evaluation measures can be injected within these models of search. The obvious extension of this work is to explore the range of user models derived from evaluation measures [21], encode them within these models of search, derive the different predictions each one makes, and then empirically explore which user model best fits observed data. Less obvious is that we can look to develop more sophisticated measures of search performance by building these models of search into evaluation measures. Finally, but not exhaustively, is the need to test and validate the predictions and the assumptions given these models of search, and to build a body of evidence to support (or not) these models. Consequently, more empirically based studies that test and examine these hypotheses are required to show when they hold, and in what instances they breakdown. This is a vital step in the model building process as it enables further developments and refinements. The goal of this work was to show how these theories and their corresponding models related, while we have made significant headway in this direction, it is clear that much more research is needed.

Acknowledgments We would like to thank Professor Norbert Fuhr for his help and advice regarding the iPRP.

10. REFERENCES

[1] C. W. Axelrod. The economic evaluation of information storage and retrieval systems. *Information Processing & Management*, 13(2):117–124, 1977.

[2] L. Azzopardi. The economics in interactive information retrieval. In *Proc. of the 34th ACM SIGIR conference*, pages 15–24, 2011.

[3] L. Azzopardi. Economic models of search. In *Proceedings of the 18th Australasian Document Computing Symposium*, ADCS '13, pages 1–1, 2013.

[4] L. Azzopardi. Modelling interaction with economic models of search. In *Proc. of the 37th ACM SIGIR conference*, SIGIR '14, pages 3–12, 2014.

[5] L. Azzopardi, D. Kelly, and K. Brennan. How query cost affects search behavior. In *Proc. of the 36th ACM SIGIR conference*, pages 23–32, 2013.

[6] M. J. Bates. The design of browsing and berrypicking techniques for the online search interface. *Online Information Review*, 13(5):407–424, 1989.

[7] M. J. Bates. Training and education for online. chapter Information search tactics, pages 96–105. Taylor Graham Publishing, London, UK, 1989.

[8] N. J. Belkin. Some(what) grand challenges for information retrieval. *SIGIR Forum*, 42(1):47–54, 2008.

[9] N. J. Belkin, R. N. Oddy, and H. M. Brooks. Ask for information retrieval: part I: background and theory; part II: results of a design study. *Journal of Documentation*, 38(2) 61-71 and 38(3) 145-164, 1982.

[10] U. Birchler and M. Butler. *Information Economics*. Routledge, 1st edition edition, 2007.

[11] E. L. Charnov. Optimal foraging, the marginal value theorem. *Theoretical population biology*, 9(2):129–136, 1976.

[12] M. D. Cooper. A cost model for evaluating information retrieval systems. *Journal of the American Society for Information Science*, pages 306–312, 1972.

[13] S. Erdelez. Information encountering: a conceptual framework for accidental information discovery. In *Proc. of the ISIC conference*, pages 412–421, 1997.

[14] N. Fuhr. A probability ranking principle for interactive information retrieval. *Information Retrieval*, 11(3):251–265, 2008.

[15] M. D. Gordon and P. Lenk. A utility theoretic examination of the probability ranking principle in information retrieval. *JASIS*, 42(10):703–714, 1991.

[16] P. Ingwersen and K. Järvelin. *The Turn: Integration of Information Seeking and Retrieval in Context*. Springer-Verlag New York, Inc., 2005.

[17] K. Järvelin. IR research: systems, interaction, evaluation and theories. *ACM SIGIR Forum*, 45(2):17–31, 2012.

[18] K. Järvelin and T. D. Wilson. On conceptual models for information seeking and retrieval research. *Information Research*, 9(1):9–1, 2003.

[19] D. Kelly and C. Sugimoto. A systematic review of interactive information retrieval evaluation studies, 1967-2006. *Journal of the ASIST*, 64(4):745–770, 2013.

[20] C. C. Kuhlthau. Developing a model of the library search process: Cognitive and affective aspects. *RQ*, pages 232–242, 1988.

[21] A. Moffat, P. Thomas, and F. Scholer. Users versus models: What observation tells us about effectiveness metrics. In *Proc. of the 22nd ACM CIKM conference*, pages 659–668, 2013.

[22] A. Moffat and J. Zobel. Rank-biased precision for measurement of retrieval effectiveness. *ACM Trans. on Information Systems*, 27(1):2:1–2:27, 2008.

[23] P. Pirolli and S. Card. Information foraging. *Psychological Review*, 106:643–675, 1999.

[24] P. Pirolli, P. Schank, M. Hearst, and C. Diehl. Scatter/gather browsing communicates the topic structure of a very large text collection. In *Proceedings of the ACM SIGCHI conference*, pages 213–220, 1996.

[25] S. E. Robertson. The probability ranking principle in ir. *Journal of documentation*, 33(4):294–304, 1977.

[26] D. H. Rothenberg. An efficiency model and a performance function for an information retrieval system. *Information Storage and Retrieval*, 5(3):109 – 122, 1969.

[27] D. M. Russell, M. J. Stefik, P. Pirolli, and S. K. Card. The cost structure of sensemaking. In *Proceedings of the INTERACT/SIGCHI*, pages 269–276, 1993.

[28] T. Sakai and Z. Dou. Summaries, ranked retrieval and sessions: A unified framework for information access evaluation. In *Proc. of the 36th ACM SIGIR conference*, pages 473–482, 2013.

[29] P. E. Sandstrom. An optimal foraging approach to information seeking and use. *The library quarterly*, pages 414–449, 1994.

[30] M. D. Smucker and C. L. Clarke. Time-based calibration of effectiveness measures. In *Proc. of the 35th ACM SIGIR conference*, pages 95–104, 2012.

[31] G. J. Stigler. The economics of information. *The Journal of Political Economy*, 69(3):213–225, 1961.

[32] P. Thomas, A. Moffat, P. Bailey, and F. Scholer. Modeling decision points in user search behavior. In *Proc, of the 5th IIiX conference*, pages 239–242, 2014.

[33] H. R. Varian. *Intermediate microeconomics: A modern approach*. W.W. Norton, New York:, 1987.

[34] H. R. Varian. Economics and search. *SIGIR Forum*, 33(1):1–5, 1999.

[35] J. Wang and J. Zhu. Portfolio theory of information retrieval. In *Proc. of the 32nd ACM SIGIR conference*, pages 115–122, 2009.

[36] T. D. Wilson. Human information behavior. *Informing science*, 3(2):49–56, 2000.

Dynamic Test Collections for Retrieval Evaluation

Ben Carterette
carteret@udel.edu

Ashraf Bah
ashraf@udel.edu

Mustafa Zengin
zengin@udel.edu

Department of Computer and Information Sciences
University of Delaware
Newark, DE USA

ABSTRACT

Batch evaluation with test collections of documents, search topics, and relevance judgments has been the bedrock of IR evaluation since its adoption by Salton for his experiments on vector space systems. Such test collections have limitations: they contain no user interaction data; there is typically only one query per topic; they have limited size due to the cost of constructing them. In the last 15-20 years, it has become evident that having a log of user interactions and a large space of queries is invaluable for building effective retrieval systems, but such data is generally only available to search engine companies. Thus there is a gap between what academics can study using static test collections and what industrial researchers can study using dynamic user data.

In this work we propose *dynamic* test collections to help bridge this gap. Like traditional test collections, a dynamic test collection consists of a set of topics and relevance judgments. But instead of static one-time queries, dynamic test collections generate queries in response to the system. They can generate other actions such as clicks and time spent reading documents. Like static test collections, there is no human in the loop, but since the queries are dynamic they can generate much more data for evaluation than static test collections can. And since they can simulate user interactions across a session, they can be used for evaluating retrieval systems that make use of session history or other user information to try to improve results.

Categories and Subject Descriptors

H.3.4 [**Information Storage and Retrieval**] Performance Evaluation (Efficiency and Effectiveness)

Keywords: information retrieval; evaluation; test collections; sessions; user simulation

1. INTRODUCTION

There are three widely-used models for retrieval evaluation: batch evaluation with reusable test collections, interactive evaluation with users, and log-based evaluation using interleaving and user clicks. Of these, user studies provide the highest fidelity in terms of capturing actual user interactions with actual retrieval systems in a controlled setting that limits the amount of post-hoc interpretation the experimenters must do. Reusable test collections have much lower fidelity, but have been invaluable for rapid development of features and algorithms for indexing and retrieval where user studies might have been prohibitively expensive.

Test collections have almost always been *static*: they are based on a fixed set of topics, each of which has a single fixed query, and static topical relevance judgments. There have been attempts to relax this: the TREC Query track used multiple (unordered) queries for each topic; recent TREC Web tracks have used multi-faceted relevance judgments that allow more detailed evaluation; the TREC Session track provided participants with actual user interactions in a session history. None of these efforts come close to achieving what interactive evaluation with actual users can achieve: that the user's past interaction with the system can affect their future interactions with the same system.

In this work we propose *dynamic* test collections that are capable of responding to a system in a way a user might respond to it: by providing clicks on retrieved documents and reformulations of queries that take into account what the system has retrieved in the past. Dynamic test collections work by *simulating* user interactions. Like static test collections, they consist of a static set of topics and fixed sets of topical relevance judgments. Unlike static test collections, queries are generated procedurally, as are clicks on ranked results. This allows a dynamic test collection to produce new queries in response to system results, and thus model a user that is reformulating queries over a session while attempting to satisfy an information need. In this way they are one step closer to allowing researchers to base their evaluation on user interactivity without having to set up and execute full user studies. The end goal is to be able to experiment on retrieval systems that we cannot experiment on with available test collections—in particular, retrieval systems that try to use the history of user interactions to improve results.

The work we present in this paper is largely a proof-of-concept—we describe a framework for evaluation systems over sessions of interactions (Section 3), and describe simulation methods that we can plug into that framework (Section 4). We present a preliminary evaluation suggesting our approach has merit (Section 5). Before we begin, however, we will place our work in the context of previous work on test collections and session-centric evaluation.

ICTIR'15, September 27–30, Northampton, MA, USA.
ⓒ 2015 ACM. ISBN 978-1-4503-3833-2/15/09 ...$15.00.
DOI: http://dx.doi.org/10.1145/2808194.2809470.

2. PREVIOUS WORK

There has been a great deal of work investigating the use (and abuse) of static test collections for IR evaluation; Sanderson presents a comprehensive overview [25], and Voorhees and Harman give a detailed history of the TREC conferences in which much work on test collections has been done [28]. There is comparatively little work on test collections that model user interactions over sessions, despite widespread acknowledgement (supported by log-based studies and interactive user studies) that reformulating queries is an incredibly important mode of user interaction with search engines. Furthermore, it is clear that retrieval systems that make use of historical interactions derived from user logs in their ranking functions can provide greater effectiveness than systems that do not [23, 26, 17, 24, 2].

Keskustalo et al. were among the first to argue for test collections that include a model of user query reformulation for the purpose of evaluation over sessions [20]. They propose a test collection consisting of multiple query reformulations created by selecting terms from a manually-defined space. Reformulations are generated according to one of four simulation models derived from observing real users' search strategies. They define session success as finding one relevant document, and failure as finding none. With that definition, they could evaluate their simulation models/search strategies in terms of the total time (or cost) required to achieve success. They conclude by arguing that IR test collections should "model processes where the searcher may try out several queries for one topic"; the present work is an answer to that.

In follow-up studies, Baskaya et al. propose a *query modification* simulation strategy to model how words are selected to form an initial simulated query or subsequent queries [6, 4]. They start with a fixed set of terms for each topic, then perform all possible permutations and focus on five strategies that users employ for query modification. For the purpose of simplicity, the model intentionally disregards the fact that users may learn by reading snippets and inspecting documents. Baskaya et al. also model scenarios in which the user involved in a search process based on relevance feedback can make mistakes by providing erroneous feedback [5]. They showed that errors generated under their simulation models can actually provide results as good as correct relevance feedback.

The works cited above, much of which also appears in Baskaya's dissertation [4], have a few common threads: they use a fixed set of terms from which queries can be constructed; they develop query simulation strategies from observing real users; they deploy those strategies deterministically to generate queries from their fixed sets of terms. Our query simulation models, in contrast, are more dynamic: our space of possible terms for constructing queries is larger and updated dynamically based on results retrieved by systems. On the other hand, we eschew (for now) strictly-defined search strategies: our queries are generated by random sampling from a language model over the term space.

There has been some work on test collections to model interactions over sessions that has emerged from TREC and similar evaluation conferences. The TREC Query track [8] provides several different queries for each topic, though they are not constructed as reformulations. The TREC Interactive tracks [14] had users perform tasks with different search system in order to evaluate those systems' efficiency and effectiveness, but the tracks did not produce test collections that could be re-used. The TREC Session track gathered a large amount of user interaction data, but released it in a static form only for use in ranking results for a query that comes after the static historical data [9].

There has been other work on simulating queries and aspects of user behavior. Van Dang and Croft showed that anchor text could be used to generate query reformulations [12]. Jiang et al. propose a model for how users browse results over a session in order to evaluate reformulations [16]. Carterette et al. sample values of parameters in parametrized evaluation measures like RBP to simulate sampling users for an interactive evaluation [10]. In separate works, Yang and Lad [29] and Kanoulas et al. [19] define session evaluation measures based on an expected utility model of user browsing over a session; Järvelin et al. defined a session evaluation measure based on DCG [15].

Almost all of the above work approaches user interactions over sessions from the viewpoint of batch evaluation using test collections and evaluation measures. We have focused on that view because we believe it is valuable and it provides a good starting point for our work. Nevertheless, we would be remiss to not touch on the large amount of work in interactive IR and information science on search over sessions. Some of this work is on cognitive models of search; Bates' "berrypicking" model is a classic example [7]. This model leads to a definition of *task* that lends itself to classification [21, 22] and evaluation [13]. Other work looks at session boundary definition and when tasks change [18] or are interrupted and continue later [1]. We cannot possibly cover the full space of such work here; we mention these works in particular because we believe they touch on aspects of interaction that we may be able to incorporate into our framework in the future.

2.1 Our contributions

This work makes the following novel contributions:

1. a framework for "dynamic test collections" that incorporates simulations of user interactions for the purpose of evaluating retrieval systems that use session history as part of their ranking function (Section 3);

2. methods for simulating clicks, dwell times, and query reformulations within that framework (Section 4);

3. a meta-evaluation methodology for evaluating the use of simulated queries for evaluating retrieval systems that make use of session history (Section 5).

We view our work as sitting on the continuum from fully-automated batch evaluation with test collections to fully-interactive user studies, but closer to the former end of the spectrum. Like existing test collections and much of the work cited above, we use a fixed set of predefined topics—this ensures that the simulation space is tightly constrained, and we needn't worry about identifying session boundaries. Similarly, we use topical relevance—documents are judged based on their relevance to the topic, regardless of where they appear in a ranked list or in a session. The difference is that our method produces what might be thought of as *dynamic* test collections: the queries change in a way that is affected partially by what the system does.

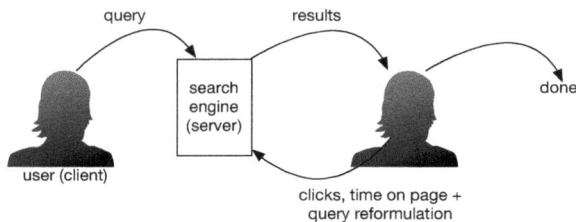

(a) Server-side search engine with which the user interacts from a client machine/web browser.

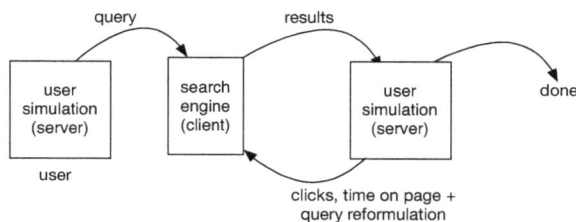

(b) Client-side search engine that pulls interactions from a server running a user simulation.

Figure 1: Illustration of the typical client-server model used in most IR systems (left) versus the client-server architecture we propose for dynamic test collections (right).

2.2 Assumptions and simplifications

Work cited above along with results from the TREC Session track showed that retrieval and ranking functions can make use of even a small amount of session history to improve results over treating a query as an ad hoc independent event [9]. We thus take it for granted that this is something that developers of search systems may want to do, and furthermore that it is worth doing; the main question for them is the availability of data to work with.

We will use TREC Session track data for training models and methods. We therefore assume that Session track sessions are similar enough to real sessions (despite differences in experimental setting) that they are useful for training simulations of user interactions. The best support for this assumption is the work of Raman et al. cited above [24]; they develop a model of interactive search and use it to improve retrieval effectiveness based on proprietary log data as well as TREC Session track data.

We are less concerned with simulating users "realistically". Because evaluation with test collections is already so abstract (in the words of Voorhees, "a ruthless abstraction of the user" [27]), a simulation does not need to model users with high fidelity—it only needs to model them well enough to provide a big enough difference over independent ad hoc queries to be useful for evaluation of retrieval functions using session history

We are also less concerned with causal factors, or *why* users perform certain actions at certain times. There is a wide body of work on cognitive models of retrieval that attempts to address these questions. We use a very simple model: a user decides to reformulate their query or not based on flipping a biased coin. If it comes up tails, they abandon the session; if it comes up heads, they generate a new query from a language model that is continuously updated based on ranked results they have seen over the course of the session. This model does not capture many of the causal factors that researchers are interested in studying apart from a very simple notion of learning on task captured by updating term probabilities in a language model.

At this stage of our work, our focus is on simplicity, keeping the degrees of freedom low just to make it simpler to answer the question of whether it can even work or not. We use popular, well-understood, and above all simple models whenever we can in order to keep focus on that question.

3. A FRAMEWORK FOR DYNAMIC TEST COLLECTIONS

Figure 1a illustrates the typical client-server model that we usually assume in IR. In this model, the user is a "client" (or more accurately using a client machine) that connects to a server running the search engine. The user submits a query to which the server responds with results. The user interacts with the results, with interactions going back to the server, and decides to either continue with a reformulation of their query or abandon the session.

In our framework illustrated in Figure 1b, the search engine is the client. Rather than the client "pushing" queries to the server as in the typical model, in this model the client "pulls" queries from the server, which is simulating queries of the types actual users might use. The client returns ranked results to the server, and in return the server simulates interactions, a decision to abandon or not, and a query reformulation. Since the client is pulling queries, it does not need to wait on actual users to come to the system; it can pull as many queries as it likes.

On the server side, we have selected a fixed set of 30 topics (a sample of the TREC 2014 Session track topics [9]) for which to generate sessions. We will use the TREC term *run*, which typically means the ranked results for every topic in a set, for the ranked results for every query in every session on every topic in the set. The simulation server can run multiple user simulations at the same time to generate M sessions per topic, so a final run will consist of ranked results for each query in each of the M sessions on each of the 30 topics. The number of queries per session will vary depending on the simulation model.

On the client side, researchers/developers working on the search engine run a client script (or connect to a more user-friendly web interface) to begin a run.[1] At that point the server assigns the run a unique ID, which consists of 12 randomly-selected alphanumeric characters. The server then generates a first query for each of the M sessions on each of the 30 topics and returns them to the client in an XML file.

The client-side developers submit these queries to their own retrieval system, generating ranked results for each session on each topic. They send these back to the server (which accepts results in 6-column TREC format consisting of a session number, the string "Q0", a document ID, a score, a rank, and a system ID) using the ID they were previously given.

---

[1]Both the script and the web interface are available at `http://ir.cis.udel.edu/sessions/simulation`.

The server accepts these as the results for the first round of queries, then uses that unique ID along with the fact that it is the first round as a random seed to generate simulated interactions, decisions to stop or continue each session, and query reformulations. These are returned to the client in an XML file to begin the second round of interactions in the sessions. The client submits the reformulations to their retrieval system, which at this point may take advantage of ranked results for the previous query and the provided interactions to generate ranked results for the second query in each session on each topic. These are sent back to the server using the unique ID and the fact that they are the second-round results, and the loop continues until all simulated sessions are complete (or the client-side researchers decide to stop).

Using the ID and the round number as seed ensures that if the researchers later decide to "roll back" to an earlier round of the session, they will get the same simulated interactions when they provide the same results. (Note that simulated interactions could still be different if the submitted results are different.) This helps control some of the variance that is introduced by having more randomness in the queries: since not all runs will be using the same queries, they cannot be compared as directly as standard TREC runs can be.

One simplification we make involves the display of the document ranking. If we were strictly mapping the server-side search engine functionality in Fig. 1a to client-side search engine development in Fig. 1b, we would accept document titles, snippets, and other information from the client. We have decided for now to keep title and snippet generation on the server-side. One reason for this is that not everyone who would like to use our system has the capability to generate snippets; requiring that they do would limit its applicability. Another reason is to ensure that titles and snippets do not confound evaluation of underlying ranking algorithms. We note that accommodating snippets generated on the client-side is something that our framework could support in principle, so if researchers using our service let us know they want it, it can be implemented.

The server-side simulation currently generates the following information:

1. a first query for each session on each topic—with a fixed set of 30 topics, there will always be $30 \cdot M$ queries for the first round of retrieval.

2. after receiving ranked results for queries:
   (a) titles, URLs, and snippets for the top-10 ranked documents for each query (we limit to 10 for now for speed of response);
   (b) clicks and dwell times on ranked documents;
   (c) for each session, a decision to stop the session or continue;
   (d) for each continuing session, a query reformulation.

Thus we need methods for generating this data. We are not restricted to just using one method in each case; the server can support multiple simulations that may be built on very different models. In the present work, however, we focus on a small set of similar methods for each.

4. SIMULATING USER SESSIONS

As suggested in Section 3, our framework is a modular one in which different components can be plugged in; moreover, different methods for the same module can be run simultaneously. In this section we describe a few of the modules we are testing for each component.

All of these modules are based on the ClueWeb12 collection of about 700 million web pages. That collection has been used for a variety of TREC tracks, including the Web track and the Session track.

4.1 Snippet generation

Since we are generating snippets on the simulation server side (see Section 3 for justification), we could use different snippet generation modules. However, in order to ensure there is no variability due to snippets or any other aspect of result display, we just use a single snippet generation module in all simulations: the default `SnippetBuilder` class provided by Indri. Document titles and URLs are extracted directly from our ClueWeb12 index with no modification.

4.2 Simulating clicks

Our main assumption for click simulation is that users base their clicks primarily on features of document titles, URLs, and snippets. Beyond that, we test three different models that offer refinements on this idea:

1. the decision to click on each result is made for each result independently of the others;
2. the decision to click on each result is made in context of other results ranked alongside it;
3. the decision to click on each result is made in context of other results ranked alongside it as well as other clicks the user made on those results.

In each case, we will train a machine-learned model using 0/1 click decisions as the label and a feature vector consisting of features of the result URL/title/snippet (for all three models), other result URLs/titles/snippets (for the second and third models), and other clicks by the same user on these results (for the third model). Note at this point we are not considering results or clicks from earlier in the session; we leave this for future work.

The features we used are derived from those that have been used in the LETOR datasets for learning to rank: retrieval model scores between query and document URL/title/snippet; statistics about query term frequencies (normalized and non-normalized) in document URL/title/snippet; URL length and depth; number of inlinks and outlinks, spam score as computed by Waterloo's model for web spam [11]; and the Alexa ranking for the domain. Most of the textual features can be computed using our Indri index of ClueWeb12; our index also stores spam scores and inlink counts. The Alexa ranking is available through Alexa's API.

4.3 Simulating dwell times

The methods we use for simulating dwell times are similar to those we use for simulating clicks: we start from the assumption that the main basis of dwell time consists of features of the full document the user is looking at, then refine that with other data from ranked results. Our three dwell time models are:

1. the length of time a user stays on a result is based on features of that document;
2. the length of time a user stays on a result is based on features of the document as well as features of URLs/titles/snippets of other ranked results;

topic	length dist	topic	length dist	topic	length dist
2 Dulles airport information		11 infant developmental milestones		48 evaluating employees	
3 benefits o PhD in business		15 selecting internet phone service		60 HIV/malaria charity in Africa	

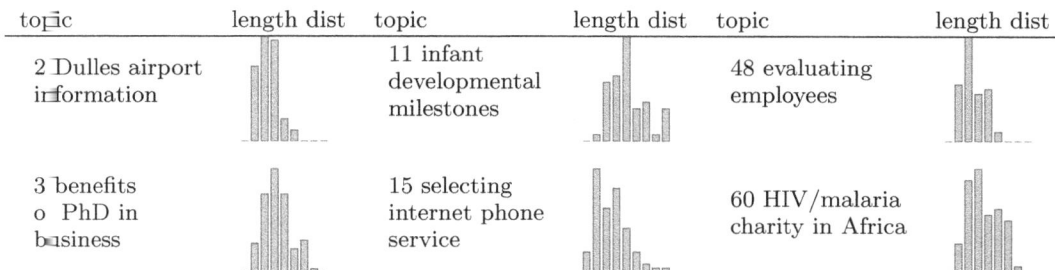

Table 1: Distributions of query lengths for a selection of topics (given as a topic number from the TREC 2014 Session track along with a brief topic description). Each bar plot shows the number of queries of lengths 1 through 10.

3. the length of time a user stays on a result is based on features of the document, features of URLs/titles/snippets of other ranked results, and clicks the user made on those results.

The latter two models augment the first in the same way that the last two click models augment the first, based on the assumption that a user's actions may be influenced by the entire results display.

Since dwell time is (for all intents and purposes) a continuous number, we use a regression model rather than a classification model. The set of features includes all of those used for click simulation, plus features of the full document that we are simulating a user reading. The latter set of features includes a number of different reading level scores such as Flesch-Kincaid, SMOG, Coleman-Liau, and so on.

4.4 Simulating session abandonment

At this stage of the simulation development, we do not model "abandonment" in the sense of a user stopping a session due to success or frustration or any other reason real users might decide to stop. We simply sample a session length from a distribution fit to existing user data.

Let i_{max} be the length of a session (that is, the number of rounds of querying in the session). We will define:

$$P(i_{max}) = \frac{\# \text{ of sessions of length } i_{max}}{\# \text{ of sessions}}$$

To model "abandonment", we simply sample a session length from this distribution, and the session will stop after that many rounds of querying.

4.5 Simulating queries

Simulating queries is the most difficult aspect of simulating users. We use a two-phase process by which we first generate queries by sampling from a language model, then score them based on their discriminative power among topics. The language "model" we use is actually a series of binomial models with parameters $P(w \in Q|T, i, S_{\{1...i-1\}})$, i.e. the probability of a term w being in a query Q given information about a topic T, the current point in the session i (a discrete number from $i-1$ to i_{max}), and the history of the session up to that point $S_{\{1...i-1\}}$.

A key component of our model is that it models query $length$ conditional on topic. Some topics lend themselves more naturally to longer queries. Topic #2, for instance, is looking for information about Dulles International Airport in Washington, DC. $Dulles$ is an extremely important term

for queries on this topic; it appears in almost every real user query. $Airport$ is also an important term appearing in most user queries. Because most queries will contain those two terms by default, queries on this topic should include 3–4 terms to find the specific information requested in the topic description (nearby hotels, parking, shuttles to the airport, buses, etc). For topic #10, on arguments for instituting a tax on "junk food", most queries include the phrase "junk food tax" and therefore have minimum length of 3. Table 1 shows distributions of query lengths for a selection of topics.

Therefore our model starts by marginalizing over query lengths (we suppress the subscript on S for space reasons):

$$P(w \in Q|T, i, S_{\{1...i-1\}}) = \sum_{\ell=1}^{\ell_{max}} P(w \in Q|T, i, S, \ell)P(\ell|T)$$

4.5.1 Topical language model

The basis of our query generation model will be a binomial model for term presence in queries of length ℓ for a topic, that is, $P(w \in Q|T, \ell)$ independent of the session variables. The maximum-likelihood estimate of this probability is simply the number of times the term appears in topic-related queries in the training data divided by the total number of queries in that data.

$$P_{ML}(w \in Q|T, \ell) = \frac{qf_{w,\ell,T}}{qc_{\ell,T}}$$

Here $qf_{w,T}$ is the query frequency, the number of queries of length ℓ term w appears in for topic T, and qc_T is the total number of queries of length ℓ recorded for topic T.

These binomial distributions could only be used to generate queries that recombine terms in previously-seen queries. To make it possible to generate queries using "new" terms (not seen in our source of user queries), we smooth the maximum-likelihood model with additional text data.

For the first query in the session ($i = 1$), we augment using terms in the topic description shown to users before they begin their search. The rationale for this is that empirically, many of the terms users use in their queries also appear in the topic description (this could be because they use the topic description for guidance, or because the topic descriptions tend to include many of the terms users would naturally use—the direction of causality is not clear).

$$P(w \in Q|T, \ell, i = 1) = \frac{qf_{w,\ell,T} + \mu \frac{to_{w,T}}{|T_{desc}|}}{qc_{\ell,T} + \mu}$$

| | | in training data | | sampled |
topic	term	$P(w \in Q)$	$P(w\|Q)$	$P(w \in Q')$
2	dulles	0.95	0.29	1.00
	airport	0.95	0.29	0.99
	hotel	0.13	0.04	0.17
	metro	0.12	0.04	0.19
11	milestone	0.71	0.14	0.87
	culture	0.66	0.12	0.85
	development	0.61	0.11	0.87
	infant	0.44	0.07	0.55
48	evaluate	0.98	0.28	1.00
	employee	0.93	0.27	0.95
	to	0.30	0.09	0.10
	how	0.19	0.06	0.00

Table 2: Top 4 most-frequent terms appearing in queries for three topics with their binomial occurrence model probability $P(w \in Q)$, their multinomial language model probability $P(w|Q)$, and their frequency in queries sampled using the procedure in Section 4.5.2.

where $to_{w,T} = 1$ if term w appears in the topic description of T and $to_{w,T} = 0$ otherwise, and $|T_{desc}|$ is the number of unique terms in the topic description.

For each subsequent query ($i > 1$), we include more information about the session history in the model. In particular, terms from titles and snippets of documents seen by the user in previous results:

$$P(w \in Q|T, \ell, i) = \frac{qf_{w,\ell,T} + \mu \frac{sf_{w,T}}{|S|}}{qc_{\ell,T} + \mu}$$

Here $sf_{w,T} = 1$ if term w appears in the topic description of T, or in the title of any document retrieved by the previous query (the one at $i - 1$), or in the snippet of any document retrieved by the previous query, and $|S|$ is the number of unique terms in titles and snippets retrieved.

Note that this still limits query generation to terms seen in real user queries (which will have high probability) and terms seen in topic descriptions and titles/snippets of retrieved documents (which will have much lower probability distributed uniformly across unique terms).

4.5.2 Sampling queries

First we sample a query length ℓ from a distribution $P(L|T)$ derived from training data. Then we iterate over terms in the language model in order of decreasing probability, flipping a coin to determine whether to add the term or not, until we have a query of length ℓ.

Note that this procedure gives *greater* probability for the highest-frequency terms in real queries to appear in sampled queries. Essentially we boost the probabilities of the most common terms above what they would be otherwise. This is meant to mitigate a problem with language models, that their probabilities tend to underestimate the importance of common terms while overestimating the importance of rare terms. Table 2 shows examples of terms in our topics, their binomial model probabilities, their multinomial language model probabilities, and their frequency of occurrence when sampling using our approach.

At each step i of the session, we generate N candidate queries. One query will be sampled from the set to be returned as the simulated reformulation.

4.5.3 Scoring sampled queries

After generating N candidates, each one is scored according to the probability that each word in the query could generate the *topic* that the query is meant for. This is a way of scoring candidate queries by their ability to discriminate among the topics.

$$P(T|w) = \frac{qtf_{w,T} + stf_{w,T} + \mu\frac{1}{|T|}}{qtf_w + stf_w + \mu}$$

where $qtf_{w,T}$ is the total number of times w appears in queries on topic T, qtf_w is the total number of times w appears in all queries on any topic, and $|T|$ is the total number of unique topics. $stf_{w,T}$ and stf_w are the "session frequencies" of the term (in topic and across topics, respectively), and include the counts of the term in the topic description and in titles and snippets of documents retrieved for previous queries.

Each candidate query Q_j is scored as:

$$P(Q_j|T) = \prod P(w|T) \propto \prod P(T|w)P(w)$$

where $P(w)$ is a prior probability of term w, which for now we treat as uniform.

The scores are then renormalized into a proper probability distribution, i.e.

$$P_{norm}(Q_j|T) = \frac{P(Q_j|T)}{\sum_{k=1}^{N} P(Q_k|T)}$$

and one candidate is sampled from this distribution to be the simulated reformulation.

4.5.4 Summary

We have described a two-stage approach by which queries are first generated from a series of binomial distributions, then scored using a topical discriminator. The first part generates candidates that are practically guaranteed to contain the most important terms and phrases (as observed in real user queries), while the second part ensures that there will still be variety in other terms included in queries.

We use TREC 2013 and 2014 Session track data to fit distributions $P(i_{max})$, $P(\ell|T)$ for each topic T in our set, $P(w \in Q|\ell, T)$ for each query length for each topic T. The full steps are as follows:

1. For each topic T:

   (a) Sample i_{max} and loop from $i = 1$ to i_{max}:

      i. Update $P(w \in Q|\ell, T, i)$ using text in the topic description and results for query $i - 1$

      ii. For $j = 1$ to N:

         A. Sample a query length ℓ

         B. Sample a query Q_j by sampling 1/0 from $P(w \in Q|\ell, T, i)$ until ℓ terms sampled

         C. Score query by $P(T|Q_j)$

      iii. Sample one query Q_{sim} from $P(Q|T)$ to send to client

      iv. Receive retrieval results from the client

   (b) Loop back to step (a) to simulate another session for the same topic

We note that instead of using our two-stage process, we *could* sample queries directly from a traditional multinomial

Method	prec	rec	acc	AUC	ratio
1. independence	0.272	0.070	0.941	0.743	0.258
2. dependence	0.690	0.292	0.961	0.869	0.423
3. dependence+clicks	0.789	0.342	0.966	0.887	0.433

Table 3: Classification evaluation measures for three models of click prediction. The last column is the ratio between number of clicks predicted and actual number of clicks in the test data.

language model. However, the queries such a model generates tend to not look much like real queries: rare terms appear too frequently, terms that frequently appear together in real queries rarely occur together in sampled queries, etc. Some of these problems could be resolved using n-gram models and better smoothing, but our more heuristic approach seems to work well.

5. EXPERIMENTS

Key questions we wish to answer are:

1. How well do our click and dwell time models simulate real users' clicks and dwell times on relevant and nonrelevant documents?
2. To what extent can our simulated queries provide an effective evaluation for systems that make use of session history
3. To what extent do our simulated queries "look like" real user queries? Do sequences of simulated queries resemble sequences of real queries?

5.1 Simulated click evaluation

We evaluate our click simulation models by their effectiveness at predicting actual user clicks, using standard classification evaluation measures like precision, recall, accuracy, and AUC. We also compute the ratio between the number of clicks predicted and the actual number of clicks in the testing data as a measure of how close we are to generating the same overall number of clicks.

We trained and tested random forest models using all sessions from the TREC 2013 and 2014 Session track that used the same 30 topics we use in our simulation. For each ranked result that appears in the Session track data, we have one instance for training/testing: the 0/1 label indicating whether there was a click on that result or not, and the features derived from that result (and possible other results ranked with it depending on the click prediction model we are using). In total there are 39,608 instances in the data, of which 37,513 are no-clicks and 2,095 are clicks. We trained and tested using five-fold cross-validation and report micro-averaged evaluation measures aggregated across all five testing splits.

Table 3 summarizes performance of the three methods. While accuracy is good for all three, this is expected given that 95% of the instances are no-clicks—the low recall suggests that the models are erring on the side of caution by not predicting many clicks, and the last column confirms this, showing that our methods predicted less than half as many clicks as are actually in the testing data. However, note that moving from the result-independence model to a model in which all retrieved results influence the click decision increases recall by 298% and precision by 182%!

Since the 0/1 class distribution is so skewed, we also tried duplicating each instance of a click several times in the training data. Figure 4 shows results: while precision and accu-

Method	prec	rec	acc	AUC	ratio
1* independence	0.209	0.218	0.915	0.742	1.044
2* dependence	0.433	0.422	0.940	0.877	0.974
3* dependence+clicks	0.470	0.445	0.944	0.874	0.946

Table 4: Classification evaluation measures for models of click prediction when "click" instances are duplicated in the training data.

	RMSE	%Δmean	%Δmed
mean	22.51	–	–
median	23.41	–	–
1. independence	23.20	3.00%	-0.89%
2. dependence	22.47	-0.17%	-4.00%
3. dependence+clicks	22.35	-0.71%	-4.50%

Table 5: RMSE of dwell time estimation methods and their performance comparisons to mean and median.

racy drop for all three models, recall increases, and the ratio of predicted clicks to actual clicks is much closer to 1.

5.2 Simulated dwell time evaluation

We evaluate dwell time simulation models by their effectiveness at predicting actual user dwell times, using root mean square error to summarize results. We used the same source for training data, but since only clicked documents have non-zero dwell time, we only have 2,095 possible training and testing instances. Of those, some were clear outliers in which a user stayed on a page for a very long time. In order to not bias towards such outliers, we excluded 39 instances with dwell times greater than 120 seconds.

Table 5 summarizes performance of the three methods along with the RMSE of the mean dwell time of 29.14 seconds and the median dwell time of 22.63 seconds (that is, the RMSE if we just predicted the mean or median for every instance). All three models are close to the mean/median, though unlike the click models, taking into account other ranked results does not help prediction performance.

We also looked at the distribution of dwell times (actual and predicted) grouped by relevance class. For documents with relevance judgments, we binned into three classes: those that were judged non-relevant or spam, those that were judged relevant or highly relevant, and those that were judged "key" or "navigational". Then we plotted the density of dwell times within those classes. Figure 2 shows results for actual dwell times and our second model (the other two produce similar density plots). Our three models all produce distributions with higher peaks and less variation than actual dwell times, but the separation between relevance classes seems (by visual inspection) to be similar. This is interesting considering we did not use relevance as a feature in the model. It also shows that there is value in using our models to produce a distribution of dwell times, even though they do not produce dwell times that are significantly different from the mean or median.

5.3 Simulated query evaluation

Finally we turn to evaluating simulated queries. This is by far the most challenging aspect of evaluation: there is an aspect of human judgment to it (i.e. do the queries look like queries a person would enter?) but it may not be the most important factor. Since we are proposing a method

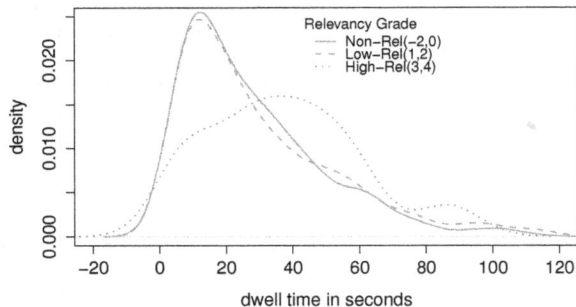

(a) Density of actual dwell times by relevance class.

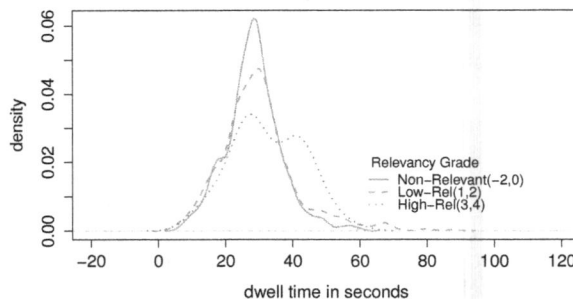

(b) Density of dwell times generated by page/result-dependence model by relevance class.

Figure 2: Dwell time density plots by relevance judgment. (Relevance was not a feature of the model.)

for dynamic test collections, we care most about whether the queries we generate are "good" for evaluating retrieval systems, and in particular, whether they are good for evaluating systems that use features derived from session history.

To that end, in this section we will evaluate simulated queries indirectly by evaluating retrieval systems that take them as input. All of our systems are based on Indri and an index of ClueWeb12 that has been filtered using spam scores from the Waterloo spam classifier [11]. Two of them (LM and MRF) are ad hoc systems that treat each query as an independent event and do not make any use of session history. Four of them (CombCAT-*) fuse different sources of data derived from the session history to server results; these use the CombCAT fusion method that has been successful in the TREC Session track [3]. This method takes strings of text from various sources in the session history, uses those strings as a query, then fuses the results from all strings based on the frequency with which documents occur.

Each of these runs went through the full client-server interaction process described in Section 3. One of the query simulation modules running on the server was providing user queries sampled uniformly from those submitted for the Session track; since they were being sampled randomly they are not based on session history. We refer to this as *non-sim*. Another model was the one described in Section 4.5, which uses terms from previously-ranked documents to generate queries. We refer to this as *sim*.

We evaluate all runs by precision@10 using TREC Session track relevance judgments.

5.3.1 Ad hoc evaluation using simulated queries

We first investigate the suitability of simulated queries for ad hoc evaluation, that is, the extent to which the queries provided in standard static IR test collections could be replaced with simulated queries. Averaged over all runs, sessions, and topics, the average precision@10 for non-simulated queries is 0.134 (± 0.016 confidence interval), while for simulated queries the mean is 0.174 ± 0.020. This difference is statistically significant by an unpaired two-sided t-test ($p \approx 0.002$).

To investigate this more closely, we matched evaluation measures as best we could: for each run, round number within that run, and topic number within that round, we

paired the precision at 10 from the non-simulated case and the precision at 10 from the simulated case if both were available.[2] There is still a difference in P10, but it is much smaller and not statistically significant: 0.144 ± 0.010 for non-simulated queries versus 0.152 ± 0.011 for simulated queries. Among this group, the average percent difference in P10 is about 5%.

From this we conclude that simulated queries are not an unacceptable substitute for real user queries for ad hoc evaluation: the effectiveness measure values they produce are on the same "scale" as those produced by actual queries, though a bit higher on average. We will need to keep this in mind for the next sections, when we compare the ability of the two cases to evaluate systems.

5.3.2 Session evaluation using simulated queries

Next we looked at evaluation over the entirety of the session. Again we compare two cases: one in which sessions consist entirely of real user queries, the other in which sessions consist entirely of simulated queries. This time, our goal is to determine how ad hoc systems that make no use of session history compare to systems that do make use of session history.

There is no widely-accepted evaluation measure for a full session. We will look at mean precision@10 for each run, averaged over sessions, in the non-simulated and simulated cases, for each of the first 6 rounds of the session.

Figure 3 shows the results. We note the following:

- the fact that simulated queries produce higher precision@10 is evident in these two plots;

- the differences between systems are more pronounced with simulated queries than with non-simulated queries;

- the same system is more-or-less consistently at the bottom in both cases: CombCAT-IT, which uses titles of previously-ranked documents as queries, then fuses results for the current round.

- the baseline LM ad hoc system is consistently among the lower-performing systems in both cases;

---

[2]Both would be available only if both runs lasted through the same round number for both the non-simulated and simulated cases, something that is *not* guaranteed due to randomness in when a session is abandoned.

rank	run	non-sim P10	run	sim P10
1	CombCAT-YST	0.1566	CombCAT-Q	0.2345
2	CombCAT-Q	0.1452	CombCAT-YS	0.2003
3	CombCAT-YS	0.1415	MRF	0.1830
4	MRF	0.1082	CombCAT-YST	0.1721
5	LM	0.1001	LM	0.1579
6	CombCAT-T	0.0863	CombCAT-IT	0.1001

Table 6: Overall precision@10 averaged across all sessions and all rounds in each session for each of our six system .

- the top system is not the same: for non-simulated queries, CombCAT-YST appears better, while for simulated queries CombCAT-Q performs better.

Overall, our conclusion is that non-simulated queries and simulated queries provide similar overall session evaluation results.

5.3.3 Ranking systems using simulated queries

Next we look at the ability of simulated queries to *rank* systems by relative effectiveness. An important question about simulated queries is whether they are *necessary*: if simple non-simulated queries can evaluate systems effectively without taking any session history into account (as the previous evaluation suggests), are simulated queries needed at all? Thus our goal is to determine whether simulated queries can distinguish between systems of different effectiveness over the session *more efficiently* than non-simulated queries.

Table 6 presents averages of the precision@10 numbers shown in Figure 3 across all six rounds in the session. The rank correlation between the two is 0.6, mainly because the CombCAT-YST drops from rank 1 with non-simulated queries to rank 4 with simulated queries. It is difficult to say that one ranking is more "correct" than the other, but we note that the differences between systems are larger with simulated queries than with non-simulated queries. This suggests that even if non-simulated and simulated queries agree on the relative ordering of systems, using simulated queries magnifies the differences.

5.3.4 Actual sessions vs simulated sessions

Finally, we return to the question of whether our simulated sessions "look like" real user sessions. Table 7 shows some examples of real user sessions and simulated sessions for a random selection of our 30 topics.

Note that simulated queries often use very similar terms and phrases as actual user queries (though sometimes the ordering of terms in a phrase is lost in the simulated queries). Topic 11 shows an example of a user trying different possible features of a query language such as phrasing with quotes, boolean OR, and looking for a term in the title; none of this can be captured by the simulation as it currently exists.

We do not draw any broad conclusions from this table; we only show it to give a sense of what our simulated queries and sessions look like compared to actual sessions.

6. CONCLUSION

We have presented the idea of *dynamic test collections*, which are test collections that include a simulation component: user interactions such as queries, clicks, dwell times, and reformulations are *simulated* based in part on ranked results from previous queries. In this way the test collection

can respond to the system as a real user would, providing a way for researchers who do not have access to a large user base or user log data to test methods that use interaction history to try to improve results. Similar to how static test collections enabled researchers without built-in user bases to study algorithms for indexing and retrieval, we hope that dynamic test collections can help researchers build effective new algorithms that make use of interaction history.

In addition to the framework, we presented some novel methods for simulating user interactions. Our click and dwell time simulation models assume dependence between ranked results to provide more accurate predictions (and thus, we hope, better simulations) of user clicks and dwell times. Our query reformulation model uses topical language models to generate and filter a space of possible queries, updating language models based on results seen earlier in the session. Note that at this stage we are not attempting to make claims about the relative effectiveness of our methods compared to other published methods. In fact, we intend to adapt and implement other methods into our framework—we do not think there is one "best" method that should be used, but rather there is advantage in providing a variety of different methods. One advantage is that it better models the diversity in real users; another is that it prevents developers from overfitting to the model we have chosen.

We reiterate again that we see this work as a proof of concept. The evaluation is only suggestive at this stage. It will take more work with a larger client base to draw more definitive conclusions about the efficacy of this proposal. We have therefore made the client available to anyone who wishes to use it at `http://ir.cis.udel.edu/sessions/simulation`.

Acknowledgments This work was supported in part by the National Science Foundation (NSF) under grant number IIS-1350799. Any opinions, findings and conclusions or recommendations expressed in this material are the authors' and do not necessarily reflect those of the sponsor.

7. REFERENCES

[1] E. Agichtein, R. White, S. T. Dumais, and P. Bennett. Search, interrupted: understanding and predicting search task continuation. In *Proc. SIGIR*, 2012.

[2] A. H. Awadallah, R. White, P. Pantel, S. T. Dumais, and Y. M. Wang. Supporting complex search tasks. In *Proc. CIKM*, 2014.

[3] A. Bah, K. Sabhnani, M. Zengin, and B. Carterette. University of delaware at TREC 2014. In *Proc. TREC*, 2014.

[4] F. Baskaya. *Simulating Search Sessions in Interactive Information Retrieval Evaluation*. PhD thesis, University of Tampere, 2014.

[5] F. Baskaya, H. Keskustalo, and K. Jarvelin. Simulating simple and fallible relevance feedback. In *Proc. ECIR*, 2011.

[6] F. Baskaya, H. Keskustalo, and K. Jarvelin. Time drives interaction: simulating sessions in diverse searching environments. In *Proc. SIGIR*, 2012.

[7] M. J. Bates. The design of browsing and berrypicking techniques for online search interfaces. *Online review*, 13(5), 1989.

[8] C. Buckley and J. Walz. The TREC-8 Query track. In *Proc. TREC*, 1999.

[9] B. Carterette, E. Kanoulas, P. D. Clough, and M. Hall. Overview of the TREC 2014 Session track. In *Proc. TREC*, 2014.

[10] B. Carterette, E. Kanoulas, and E. Yilmaz. Simulating simple user behavior for system effectiveness evaluation. In *Proc. CIKM*, 2011.

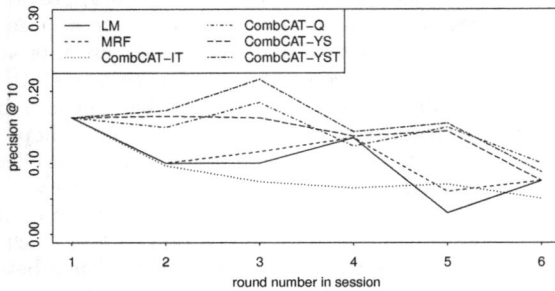

(a) System evaluation with non-simulated queries.

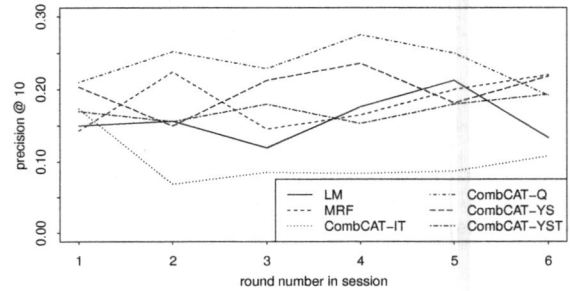

(b) System evaluation with simulated queries.

Figure 3: Comparison of six retrieval systems across six rounds of a session using non-simulated queries (left) and simulated queries (right).

topic	query type	queries
2	non-sim	dulles airport → dulles airport location → dulles hotels
2	sim	airport dulles hotels stop → airport dulles park → airport cheap dulles stop → airport dulles hotels metro → airport dulles metro near → airport dulles hotels metro
3	non-sim	jobs from business phds → business phd
3	sim	benefits business cost master → benefits business phd → business mba phd → business cost master phd → benefits business phd worth → business doctoral phd
11	non-sim	infants development culture → infant development "cultural effects" → infant OR child development intitle:culture → infant OR child development milestones → infant OR child development milestones research
11	sim	culture developmental infant milestones → culture infant milestones → infant milestones → culture developmental infant milestones → culture developmental milestones
15	non-sim	internet phone services → internet phone services review → guide internet phone services → voip providers
15	sim	providers reviews voip → services voip → cheapest internet phone services → providers reviews voip → features voip → providers reviews voip
48	non-sim	employee evaluation → evaluate employees
48	sim	employee evaluation → employee evaluation performance → employee evaluation guide → employee evaluation
60	non-sim	malaria impact on economy africa → malaria economy africa → malaria economy → malaria donations
60	sim	africa aids charity hiv malaria → charity hiv → aids charity → africa aids charity → charity hiv → africa aids charity fight hiv

Table 7: Examples of sequences of queries for six topics in our set. For each topic we show an actual user session of queries and a simulated session.

[11] G. V. Cormack, M. D. Smucker, and C. L. A. Clarke. Efficient and effective spam filtering and re-ranking for large web datasets. *Information Retrieval*, 14(5), 2011.

[12] V. Dang and W. B. Croft. Query reformulation using anchor text. In *Proc. WSDM*, 2010.

[13] A. Hassan, Y. Song, and L. W. He. A task-level metric for measuring web search satisfaction and its application on improving relevance estimation. In *Proc. CIKM*, 2011.

[14] W. Hersh and P. Over. TREC-9 Interactive track report. In *Proc. TREC*, 2000.

[15] K. Jarvelin, S. L. Price, L. M. L. Delcambre, and M. L. Nielsen. Discounted cumulated gain based evaluation of multiple-query IR sessions. In *Proc. ECIR*, 2008.

[16] J. Jiang, D. He, S. Han, Z. Yue, and C. Ni. Conextual evaluation of query reformulations in a search session by user simulation. In *Proc. CIKM*, 2012.

[17] T. Joachims, L. Granka, B. Pan, H. Hembrooke, F. Radlinski, and G. Gay. Evaluating the accuracy of implicit feedback from clicks and query reformulations in web search. *ACM TOIS*, 25(2), 2007.

[18] R. Jones and K. Klinkner. Beyond the session timeout: automatic hierarchical segmentation of search topics in query logs. In *Proc CIKM*, 2008.

[19] E. Kanoulas, B. Carterette, P. D. Clough, and M. Sanderson. Evaluating multi-query sessions. In *Proc. SIGIR*, 2011.

[20] H. Keskustalo, K. Jarvelin, A. Pirkola, T. Sharma, and M. Lykke. Test collection-based ir needs extension towards sessions—a case of extremely short queries. In *Proc. AIRS*, 2009.

[21] J. Liu and N. Belkin. Personalizing information retrieval for multi-session tasks: the roles of task stage and task type. In *Proc. SIGIR*, 2011.

[22] J. Liu, M. J. Cole, C. Liu, R. Bierig, J. Gwizdka, N. J. Belkin, J. Zhang, and X. Zhang. Search behaviors in different task types. In *Proc. JCDL*, 2010.

[23] F. Radlinski and T. Joachims. Query chains: learning to rank from implicit feedback. In *Proc. KDD*, 2005.

[24] K. Raman, P. N. Bennett, and K. Collins-Thompson. Toward whole-session relevance: exploring intrinsic diversity in web search. In *Proc. SIGIR*, 2013.

[25] M. Sanderson. Test collection based evaluation of information retrieval systems. *Foundations and Trends in Information Retrieval*, 4(4), 2010.

[26] A. Singla, R. White, and J. Huang. Studying trailfinding algorithms for enhanced web search. In *Proc. SIGIR*, 2010.

[27] E. M. Voorhees. I come not to bury Cranfield, but to praise it. In *Proc. HCIR*, 2009.

[28] E. M. Voorhees and D. K. Harman, editors. *TREC: Experiment and Evaluation in Information Retrieval*. MIT Press, 2005.

[29] Y. Yang and A. Lad. Modeling expected utility of multi-session information distillation. In *Proc. ICTIR*, 2009.

Development and Evaluation of Search Tasks for IIR Experiments using a Cognitive Complexity Framework

Diane Kelly, Jaime Arguello, Ashlee Edwards and Wan-ching Wu

School of Information and Library Science
University of North Carolina at Chapel Hill
Chapel Hill, NC, USA
[dianek, jarguell, aedwards, wanchinw] @email.unc.edu

ABSTRACT

One of the most challenging aspects of designing interactive information retrieval (IIR) experiments with users is the development of search tasks. We describe an evaluation of 20 search tasks that were designed for use in IIR experiments and developed using a cognitive complexity framework from educational theory. The search tasks represent five levels of cognitive complexity and four topical domains. The tasks were evaluated in the context of a laboratory IIR experiment with 48 participants. Behavioral and self-report data were used to characterize and understand differences among tasks. Results showed more cognitively complex tasks required significantly more search activity from participants (e.g., more queries, clicks, and time to complete). However, participants did not evaluate more cognitively complex tasks as more difficult and were equally satisfied with their performances across tasks. Our work makes four contributions: (1) it adds to what is known about the relationship among task, search behaviors and user experience; (2) it presents a framework for task creation and evaluation; (3) it provides tasks and questionnaires that can be reused by others and (4) it raises questions about findings and assumptions of many recent studies that only use *behavioral signals* from search logs as evidence for task difficulty and searcher satisfaction, as many of our results directly contradict these findings.

Categories and Subject Descriptors

H.3.3 [Information Storage and Retrieval]: Information Search and Retrieval: Search Process

Keywords

Search tasks, user studies, interactive IR, search behavior

1. INTRODUCTION

Search tasks are one of the most important components of information search studies. In most experimental studies, researchers assign search tasks to people in order to study search behavior and evaluate systems. In some cases, search tasks are ancillary to the study purposes but are needed for study participants to exercise systems, while in other cases search tasks act as independent variables. Despite their importance, there is little formal guidance about how to construct and evaluate search

tasks and empirical reports often do not provide thorough descriptions of how search tasks were generated or full descriptions of the tasks, which inhibits reuse. Moreover, the lack of parity in search tasks across studies generates incommensurable results, which ultimately makes it difficult to clearly understand and generalize task and system effects and replicate results.

The development of search tasks can be difficult and time consuming, and often requires specialized knowledge and skills. Search task development is further complicated by the abundance of research demonstrating how variations in search tasks and search task properties can impact searcher behavior [36, 42]. Poor task design can confound results, generate undesirable search behaviors, create additional variables that complicate analysis, and ultimately, result in wasted time and money. Consider a researcher who is interested in evaluating a search interface designed to support exploratory search. Despite a good faith effort to create search tasks that require sustained interaction, the researcher might inadvertently create tasks that can be addressed with a single, easily findable document such as a Wikipedia page. Thus, even the most well designed experiment might be sabotaged by inappropriately designed search tasks.

Task-based search has been identified as a key research direction at several recent meetings, including the Second Strategic Workshop on Information Retrieval (SWIRL) [2]. There have also been long-standing calls for the development of standardized task sets, reference tasks and sharable tasks that can be used in information search studies [23, 36, 41]. At a recent workshop focused on task-based information search systems, the development of simulated search tasks that could be shared among research groups was identified as a major direction [24]. Specifically, the report states that a re-usable set of search tasks and questionnaires would help make user studies more reproducible and allow for future meta-analysis. Similar recommendations regarding sharable materials for IIR studies were made at an earlier NII Shonan Meeting [9], which focused on whole-session evaluation, as well as an earlier workshop on information-seeking support systems [25].

In this paper, we describe an evaluation of 20 search tasks that were designed for use in IIR experiments and developed using a cognitive complexity framework from educational theory. The hope in using this framework was that we would be able to develop a set of search tasks that would induce a range of varied search behaviors in participants. We use Borlund's [10] notion of simulated work tasks, which specifies that tasks be tailored to target participants, who were undergraduate students in this study. This is one of the most common types of participants in IIR experiments and a population that often performs Internet searches. Behavioral and self-report data were collected to understand and characterize differences among tasks, including with respect to difficulty, engagement and satisfaction.

2. BACKGROUND

Several researchers have contributed work that enhances our abilities to discuss, define, create and observe tasks. In one of the first reviews of task-based information seeking research, Vakkari [38] defines a task as an "activity to be performed in order to accomplish a goal" (p. 416). Toms [36] defines a task as having "a defined objective or goal with an intended and potentially unknown outcome or result, and may have known conditional and unconditional requirements" (p. 45). Both Vakkari's and Toms's definitions go beyond an individual search task and focus instead on the larger goals of the user. Byström and Hansen [13] distinguish between a work task and a search task, one or more of which might be conducted to address the work task. Researchers have also articulated definitions for search tasks. Wildemuth, et al. [42] state: "search tasks are goal-directed activities carried out using search systems" (p. 1134). Li and Belkin [27] define an information search task as "a task that users need to accomplish through effective interaction with information systems" (p. 1823). Both of these definitions restrict search tasks to activities done with information systems.

Tasks have been classified according to type (e.g., open, factual, navigational, decision-making) and according to properties (e.g., difficulty, urgency, structure, stage). Toms [36] observes that tasks have been used in two major ways in IR research: (1) as a vehicle for research (citing, for example TREC topics) and (2) as an object of study, where the researcher is interested in how different task types or properties impact search experiences. Li and Belkin [27] unify a variety of task characteristics in a faceted classification of tasks. This classification includes *generic* facets of tasks (e.g., source of task, time, product, process and goal) and *common* facets of tasks including characteristics (e.g., objective task complexity and interdependence) as well as users' perception of task (e.g., salience, urgency, difficulty, subjective task complexity and knowledge of task topic).

Broder's [12] task classification was one of the first in the context of Web search and resulted in three categories of tasks: navigational, informational and transactional. While this classification provided some insight into what people were doing on the Web at the time, its coarseness makes it less useful for designing tasks for IIR studies since so many different types of tasks are grouped together in the informational class. Tasks in this class were also characterized as having single source solutions ("I want a good site on this topic" p. 6). This work launched an interest in navigation and other fact-finding types of tasks, especially since these seemed to be the most common types of tasks people were conducting on the Web. Later, researchers' interests expanded to include more open tasks, such as exploratory tasks. White and Roth [40] provide a discussion of these types of tasks and situate them in the context of other task types.

One of the most common approaches to studying tasks is by separating tasks into types (e.g., fact-finding vs. information gathering; known-item vs. exploratory). For example, Jiang, et al. [22] studied four types of tasks that were created using Li and Belkin's [27] classification: known item, known subject, interpretive and exploratory. They found participants were more active for known subject and interpretive tasks, but issued more queries for known item and exploratory tasks. Toms, et al. [37] examined decision, fact-finding and information gathering tasks, as well as tasks with varying structure: parallel or hierarchical.

Over the years, those creating test collections have also defined and examined a number of different types of tasks, although terminology sometimes differs. TREC has a notion of a topic, which assumes most requests are topical or subject-based [33] and task is used to describe the specific TREC Track focus (e.g., filtering, clinical decision support, microblog). Those studying IIR have used these collections in studies with research participants, although not without some challenges [23]. The TREC Interactive Track also generated and investigated a variety of task types including ad-hoc, filtering, aspectual recall and fact-finding [18]. In 2015, a TREC Track focused on inferring tasks from search behavior[1] has been created.

Another common way that tasks have been characterized in IIR studies is according to difficulty and complexity. Wildemuth, et al. [42] analyze how researchers have conceptually and operationally defined task complexity and task difficulty in a review of over one-hundred IIR studies. They note that despite widespread usage of these concepts, "clear and consistent definitions of these attributes are lacking and there is no consensus on how to distinguish levels of complexity or difficulty within a set of search tasks" (p. 1119). When creating search tasks, each of these attributes needs to be considered separately, and one needs to make a determination about whether one plans to manipulate these attributes or hold them constant. Measurement and manipulation rests on having a solid definition of each construct and a method to consistently measure and observe variations. Wildemuth, et al. go on to note a lack of transparency in how task attributes are measured; task difficulty, in particular, is often conceptualized as a subjective attribute that describes the user's experiences conducting the task and is measured with questionnaires. The content of such questionnaires is often omitted from published reports. Task difficulty is also often measured with a single item; this gross signal lacks precision and likely conflates many different components of difficulty.

One of the more popular conceptualizations of task complexity in the IIR literature comes from the work of Campbell [15], who considered complexity as an objective task characteristic that could be described by four dimensions: (1) the number of potential paths to the desired outcome; (2) the presence of multiple desired outcomes; (3) the presence of conflicting interdependencies between paths; and (4) uncertainty regarding paths. These dimensions are interesting to consider in the context of search task complexity as they suggest that tasks, which have more than one possible solution and allow people to arrive at solutions in many different ways, are more complex. Moreover, the idea of interdependencies between paths suggests that as searchers progress through a task they make a sequence of interconnected decisions that increasingly funnels their focus. Searchers cannot be certain the paths they select will lead to successful solutions until they arrive at the end or may need to shift between paths to resolve these interdependencies.

Another popular conceptualization of task complexity comes from Byström and Järvelin [14] who define task complexity as the *a priori determinability* of tasks, which is the extent to which the searcher can deduce the required task inputs, processes, and outcomes based on the initial task statement. Importantly, this conceptualization was in the context of work tasks, not search tasks. Vakkari [38] described complexity as "the degree of predeterminability of task performance" (p. 826). These conceptualizations are based on subjective task complexity since people make these determinations before conducing a task; Wildemuth, et al. [42] found fewer studies treated search task complexity as a subjective construct, but there is some evidence

---

[1] http://www.cs.ucl.ac.uk/tasks-track-2015/guidelines.html

that objective and subjective complexity are related. For example, Bell and Ruthven [8] used Byström and Järvelin's conceptualization to create artificial search tasks with different levels of task complexity and found that objective task complexity as they had manipulated it, was correlated with users' subjective assessments of complexity.

Wildemuth, et al. [42, p. 1112] identified six ways that task complexity has been defined and operationalized in the IIR literature: (1) number of subtasks or steps required; (2) number of subtopics or facets; (3) number of query terms and operations required; (4) number of sources or items required; (5) the indeterminate nature of the task; and (6) the cognitive complexity of the task. Examples of work using each of these operationalizations can be found in Wildemuth, et al. In general, studies have found that people engage in more search interactions when completing more complex tasks [28, 34]. For example, Li and Belkin [28] found that objective task complexity was related to number of queries issued, mean query length, number of pages viewed, and number of sources consulted.

Jansen et al. [21] used Anderson and Krathwohl's taxonomy of educational objectives [3] to create complex search tasks reflecting six types of cognitive processes: *remember*, *understand*, *apply*, *analyze*, *evaluate* and *create* (see Table 1 for definitions). Jansen et al. observed a number of significant differences in the amount of interaction users exhibited when completing different task types, including session duration, number of queries, and number of pages viewed. However, the distinctions among the tasks were not clear and increases in cognitive complexity did not always result in increased search behavior. Most notably, participants who completed tasks requiring the highest level of cognitive processing only spent about four minutes completing these tasks. Finally, although compelling, it was not obvious how this taxonomy might be used to create new tasks or how one might use Jansen et al.'s general task structure to create new tasks.

Tasks have also been characterized according to difficulty. Wildemuth, et al. [42] noted few studies that examine both task complexity and task difficulty and some confusion in the literature about terminology (e.g., one person's complexity is another person's difficulty). Campbell [15] conceptualized task difficulty as a subjective characteristic that is a result of the person and task interaction. Wildemuth, et al. make the same distinction and extend the definition of difficulty by describing it as a "relationship between the search task and the searcher or between the search task and the corpus being searched that express the amount of effort of skill required and the likelihood of success" (p.1134). Wildemuth, et al. [p. 1129] identified four major approaches to measuring task difficulty in the literature: (1) as a function of searcher performance; (2) the match between terms in the task description and in the target page; (3) the number of relevant documents in the collection; and (4) the searchers' or experts' perceptions of difficulty, which is arguably the most common way to measure task difficulty.

Papers exploring task difficulty have claimed a positive correlation between task difficulty and interaction [19, 26, 29]. For example, Liu, et al. [29] found that when completing more difficult tasks, participants took longer, entered more queries, viewed more pages, and used more sources. In a follow-up study, Liu, et al. [30] asked their participants to describe what made a search task difficult. Many of the reasons given by participants were based on uncertainty at the outset of the task and problems completing the task. For example, participants gave reasons such as uncertainty about how much effort would be involved with

searching for the information, what to do to perform the search, and difficulty formulating queries.

Although not included in Wildemuth, et al.'s [42] review, there are several studies that have used tasks that are insurmountable, or nearly insurmountable; that is, the researchers knew the tasks could not be solved, or solved easily [1, 6]. This is slightly different from selecting tasks based on the number of relevant documents in the collection because both of these studies were done in the context of the Web where the collection was not as defined (most of Wildemuth, et al.'s examples for this approach used TREC test collections). Another interesting case is Smith [36] who used multiple ambiguous terms in the task descriptions to make them difficult. However, all of these cases could still be described by Wildemuth, et al.'s definition of task difficulty.

3. SEARCH TASK DESIGN
To create search tasks, we started from Anderson and Krathwohl's taxonomy of educational objectives [3]. This taxonomy has dimensions to reflect cognitive process and knowledge. Like Jansen et al. [21], we focus on the *cognitive process* dimension (Table 1). There are six types of cognitive processes: *remember*, *understand*, *apply*, *analyze*, *evaluate* and *create*. Each requires increasing amounts of cognitive effort. While this taxonomy is traditionally used to create educational materials such as exercises, we used it as a framework to construct search tasks.

Table 1. Anderson and Krathwohl's Taxonomy of Learning Objectives (Cognitive Process Dimension).

Process	Definition
Remember	Retrieving, recognizing, and recalling relevant knowledge from long-term memory.
Understand	Constructing meaning from oral, written, and graphic messages through interpreting, exemplifying, classifying, summarizing, inferring, comparing, and explaining.
Apply	Carrying out or using a procedure through executing or implementing.
Analyze	Breaking material into constituent parts, determining how the parts relate to one another and to an overall structure or purpose through differentiating, organizing, and attributing.
Evaluate	Making judgments based on criteria and standards through checking and critiquing.
Create	Putting elements together to form a coherent or functional whole; reorganizing elements into a new pattern or structure through generating, planning, or producing.

We selected four domains to use when creating the tasks: health, commerce, entertainment, and science and technology, and following Borlund [10], situated the tasks within scenarios geared toward our target participants, university undergraduates. In many cases, we selected topics that were of regional interest and used informal language when constructing scenarios. We created 20 tasks: one for each cognitive domain and cognitive process, except *apply* because we were unable to create search tasks for this category that were distinct from the other categories. The tasks are available online at http://ils.unc.edu/searchtasksforiir/. Examples from two domains are shown in Table 2.

The tasks differ on two dimensions: the type of information desired (target outcome) and the types of activities that need to be completed. The cognitive processes build on one another as in [3] (see Table 2). *Remember* tasks require a specific fact for their resolution, such as a number or location. These types of tasks require the searcher to identify or recognize the fact as it occurs in an information source. *Understand* tasks require the searcher to provide an exhaustive list of items; for example, health risks. Similar to remember tasks, this type of task primarily requires the searcher to identify a list or factors in an information source and possibly compile the list from multiple sources if a single list cannot be found. *Analyze* tasks require the searcher to find and compile a list of items and to understand and describe their differences. *Evaluate* tasks require the searcher to find and compile a list of items, understand their differences and make a recommendation. The target outcome for *create* tasks is a plan, which requires the searcher to perform the same sets of actions for the evaluate tasks, except instead of a justification the searcher needs to generate something.

Table 2. Cognitive Processes, Target Outcomes, Mental Activities and Example Tasks

Process	Target Outcome	Mental Activities
Remember (R)	Fact	Identify
You recently watched a documentary about people living with HIV in the United States. You thought the disease was nearly eradicated, and are now curious to know more about the prevalence of the disease. Specifically, how many people in the US are currently living with HIV?		
Understand (U)	List (set)	Identify, Compile
Your nephew is considering trying out for a football team. Most of your relatives are supportive of the idea, but you think the sport is dangerous and are worried about the potential health risks. Specifically, what are some long-term health risks faced by football players?		
Analyze (A)	List (prioritized), Description	Identify, Compile, Describe
Having heard some of the recent reports on risks of natural tanning, it seems like a better idea to sport an artificial tan this summer. What are some of the different types of artificial tanning methods? What are the health risks associated with each method?		
Evaluate (E)	Recommendation	Identify, Compile, Describe, Compare, Decide, Justify
One of your siblings got a spur of the moment tattoo and now regrets it. What are the current available methods for tattoo removal, and how effective are they? Which method do you think is best? Why?		
Create (C)	Plan	Identify, Compile, Describe, Compare, Decide, Make
After the NASCAR season opened this year, your niece became really interested in soapbox derby racing. Since her parents are both really busy, you've agreed to help her build a car so that she can enter a local race. The first step is to figure out how to build a car. Identify some basic designs that you might use and create a basic plan for constructing the car.		

These tasks can be related to other conceptualizations of task complexity in the information search literature. Using Campbell's [15] conceptualization of objective task complexity, *Remember* tasks have the fewest solution paths, the fewest number of solutions or outcomes, the least amount of conflicting interdependencies between paths and the least amount of uncertainty regarding paths, while *create* tasks have the greatest numbers. The tasks can also be related to Byström and Järvelin's [14] definition of task complexity in that the expected inputs, processes and outcomes become less certain as one moves from *Remember* to *Create* tasks. Finally, our target outcomes are similar to Li and Belkin's [27] product facet. One of the unique aspects of our framework is that it takes the abstract features described by other researchers and presents them more concretely by providing task descriptions that can be more easily reused, either by using the tasks in their current forms, or by extrapolating

templates with slots that can be filled in with concepts that are tailored to target participants.

Several of the tasks from this study were initially created and used in another research project [5]. The initial development consisted of pilot tests with six participants and then a full user study with 28 participants from the local community with tasks representing the first three levels of cognitive complexity. In this previous study, a significant relationship was found between cognitive complexity and search behaviors: as complexity increased, so did the number of queries issued, URLs visited, search results clicked and time spent conducting the search. The tasks were updated and revised based on the findings from this study and underwent additional critique and analysis. New versions of the tasks were then used in the current study. Preliminary results of this current study have been presented in a poster paper [43]; however, the poster paper described a subset of measures from the first twenty-four participants and for half of the search tasks.

4. METHOD

A laboratory study was conducted to evaluate the search tasks. Each participant completed five search tasks (one representing each cognitive complexity level) from a single domain. Tasks were rotated using a Latin-square. Participants searched the open Web using the search engine of their choice (in all cases, Google) and were asked to create responses to each task by typing answers and/or copying and pasting evidence that helped them arrive at their answers. No task time limits were imposed. Participants were given a monetary honorarium at the end of the study session.

4.1 Pre-Search Questionnaire

Participants completed a pre-search questionnaire before each search with items about interests and knowledge, task complexity and expected task difficulty (Table 3). The scale anchors for the interests and knowledge items can be viewed in Table 6. Unless otherwise specified, all other items were evaluated with a five-point scale, where 1=not at all, 2=slightly, 3=somewhat, 4=moderately and 5=very. Three items were included to measure participants' perceptions of task complexity; these items were based on Byström and Järvelin's [14] definition of task complexity. Although we consider task complexity to be an objective property inherent to tasks we included these items to see how participants would evaluate these attributes.

Expected task difficulty was related to participants' expectations about the potential challenges associated with completing search activities, including results evaluation and determining when they had enough information to stop searching. We use these same items in the Post-Task Questionnaire to measure if and how participants' assessments changed after completing the search tasks. While task complexity relates to the task description, expected difficulty relates to the participant's expected search experience. Thus, in this study, we manipulate cognitive complexity through task design and measure task complexity and task difficulty, via pre- and post-search questionnaires. This allowed us to see how all of these measures were related to each other as well as to search behavior.

Table 3. Pre-Task Questionnaire Items

Interest & Knowledge	How interested are you to learn more about the topic of this task?
	How many times have you searched for information about this task?
	How much do you know about the topic of the task?
Task Complexity	How defined is this task in terms of the types of information needed to complete it?
	How defined is this task in terms of the steps required to complete it?
	How defined is this task in terms of its expected solution?
Expected Task Difficulty	How difficult do you think it will be to *search* for information for this task using a search engine?
	How difficult do you think it will be to *understand* the information the search engine finds?
	How difficult do you think it will be to *decide* if the information the search engine finds is *useful* for completing the task?
	How difficult do you think it will be to *integrate* the information the search engine finds?
	How difficult do you think it will be to determine *when you have enough* information to finish the task?

4.2 Post-Search Questionnaire

The Post-Task Questionnaire was divided into five parts (Table 4). The first part asked participants to describe how they felt while completing the task. The second part asked participants to indicate the extent to which their interests and knowledge changed. The third part consisted of the five difficulty items from the Pre-Search Questionnaire with minor editorial changes to reflect past tense. The fourth and fifth parts elicited summative judgments from participants about difficulty and satisfaction.

Table 4. Post-Task Questionnaire Items

Engagement	How enjoyable was it to do this task?
	How engaging did you find this task?
	How difficult was it to concentrate while you were doing this task?
Interest	How much did your interest in the task increase as you searched?
	How much did your knowledge of the task increase as you searched?
Experienced Task Difficulty	Same five items from Table 3 except items started with, "How difficult was it to …"
Overall Difficulty	Overall, how difficult was this task?
Overall Satisfaction	Overall, how satisfied are you with your solution to this task?
	Overall, how satisfied are you with the search strategy you took to solve this task?

4.3 Exit Questionnaire

The Exit Questionnaire asked participants to rank the tasks according to difficulty and engagement (1=least; 5=most) and to explain their rankings.

4.4 Search Behaviors

Participants' searches were logged using the Lemur Query Toolbar and 11 measures were computed from this log (Table 5). Measures 1-8 were computed at the search session level; these

values were then averaged and are reported according to cognitive complexity level. The last three measures illustrate the extent to which participants who completed a task (complexity-domain combination) deviated from *other* participants who completed the *same* task for queries issued, query-terms used, and URLs visited.

Table 5. Search Behavior Measures

Measure	Definition
Queries	Total number of unique queries submitted by a participant when completing a task.
Query length	Average number of query terms in all unique queries issued for a task.
Unique query terms	Total number of unique query terms used by a participant when completing a task.
SERP clicks	Total number of clicks participants made on SERPs.
URLs visited	Total number of unique URLs visited by participants (includes URLs accessed directly and indirectly via SERP)
Queries w/o SERP clicks	Total number of unique queries where participants did not click on the search engine results page (SERP).
Time to completion	The amount of time (in seconds) participants spent completing search tasks.
SERP dwell time	Average time spent between issuing a new query and clicking on the first search result (in seconds).
Query diversity	Number of queries issued that were not issued by another participant completing the exact same task.
Query term diversity	Number of query terms used that were not used by another participant completing the exact same task.
URL diversity	Number of URLs visited that were not visited by another participant completing the exact same task.

4.5 Participants

Forty-eight undergraduate participants were recruited from our university via mass email solicitation. Thirty-three participants were female and 15 were male. Participants' average age was 20 years old (SD=1.62). The frequency of majors was 10 sciences, 28 social sciences, 3 humanities, 6 professional schools and 1 undecided. Most participants reported conducting information searches daily with an average of 7-9 years of search experience.

4.6 Data Analysis

Unless otherwise specified, repeated-measures ANOVAs were conducted with cognitive complexity level as a within-subject factor. Bonferroni tests were used as the follow-up tests. Alpha was set to 0.01 for all analyses.

5. RESULTS
5.1 Search Behaviors

Figure 1 displays participants' mean search behaviors according to cognitive complexity level, statistical test results (F-tests and follow-up tests) and effect sizes (η^2).[2]

Participants submitted the most queries when completing *create* tasks (M=4.85; SD=4.42) and the fewest when completing *remember* tasks (M=1.68; SD=1.04). Statistical tests showed participants entered significantly fewer queries for *remember* and *understand* tasks than for all other tasks. Significant differences

---

[2] Search interaction data from one participant was not captured because of technical difficulties and the pre-search questionnaires from another participant were not recorded properly, so analyses of search behaviors and pre-search questionnaire responses are based on 47 participants.

were also detected between *analyze* tasks and *create* tasks, and *evaluate* tasks and *create* tasks.

While participants submitted the most queries for *create* tasks, these queries were on average shorter than the queries they submitted for other tasks (M=4.04; SD=1.37). Participants submitted the longest queries for *remember* tasks (M=6.01; SD=2.94). Statistical tests showed participants entered significantly longer queries for the *remember* tasks than for *analyze* and *create* tasks. Queries submitted when completing *understand* and *evaluate* tasks were also significantly longer than those submitted for *create* tasks.

Participants used the greatest number of unique terms in their queries when completing *create* tasks (M=10.68; SD=6.69) and the least for *remember* tasks (M=7.02; SD=3.12). Significant differences were also detected here, with participants submitting significantly more unique query terms when completing *create* tasks than *remember* or *understand* tasks.

Participants made the most SERP clicks when completing *create* tasks (M=5.98; SD=5.02) and the fewest when completing *remember* tasks (M=2.49; SD=1.56). The general trend was that SERP clicks increased as task complexity increased. A statistically significant relationship was detected between task complexity and SERP clicks; follow-up tests detected reliable differences between *remember* and *understand* tasks and *create* tasks. This relationship was even more pronounced for number of URLs visited, with participants viewing an average of 14.43 (SD=12.34) URLs when completing *create* tasks and 3.70 (SD=3.93) when completing *remember* tasks. With respect to URLs viewed, statistical tests showed participants visited significantly more URLs for *create* tasks than any of the other tasks. Participants also visited significantly more URLs for *analyze* and *evaluate* tasks than for *remember* tasks.

As with the previous measures, there was also a general trend for number of queries without clicks to increase with complexity, although *evaluate* tasks had slightly fewer queries without clicks than *analyze* tasks. Statistical tests showed participants issued significantly more queries without clicks for *create* tasks than *remember* or *understand* tasks.

With respect to query diversity, participants submitted the greatest number of unique queries for *create* tasks (M=4.26; SD=3.90) and the fewest for *remember* tasks (M=1.04; SD=1.00). A significant difference was detected with the differences between *remember* and *understand* tasks and *analyze* and *evaluate* tasks being significant, as well as the differences between *analyze* and *evaluate* tasks and *create* tasks.

When we consider query term diversity, we see that the number of unique terms entered by participants was the greatest for *create* tasks (M=2.40; SD=2.79) and the least for *remember* tasks (M=0.77; SD=1.13), indicating much greater overlap in the terms participants used when completing *remember* tasks. Tests show the query terms used for *analyze* and *create* tasks were significantly more diverse than those used for *remember* tasks.

When we consider URL diversity, we see increasing means as we move from *remember* (M=1.43; SD=3.66) to *create* (M=10.43; SD=10.64). Results showed significant differences in the number of unique URLs visited by participants between all pairs of task except *analyze* and *evaluate* tasks.

Our diversity measures considered the *absolute* number of queries, query-terms and URLs that were not observed in another search session for the same task (complexity-domain combination). Given that task complexity had a significant effect on the number of queries and query terms used, and URLs visited, we also computed normalized versions of our diversity measures (not shown in Figure 1). The normalized versions considered the *percentage* of queries, query-terms, and URLs that were not observed in another session for the same task. ANOVAs using these normalized values were also statistically significant.

The time participants spent completing tasks increased with task complexity, with participants spending the most time completing *create* tasks (M=9.868m; SD=5.295m) and least time completing *remember* tasks (M=2.838m; SD=2.453m). Statistical tests showed participants spent significantly more time completing *analyze*, *evaluate* and *create* tasks than *remember* or *understand* tasks, and significantly more time completing *understand* than *remember* tasks. With respect to mean SERP dwell time, there did not appear to be any trend. For most tasks, participants spent around 8 seconds viewing SERPs with the exception being *remember* tasks where they spent about 5.3 seconds; no significant differences were detected.

5.2 Task Knowledge & Interest

Table 6 displays the distribution of responses to the pre-task questionnaire items about prior knowledge. For most tasks (78%) participants indicated they had never searched for information about the task. For about 50% of the tasks, participants indicated they knew nothing. Friedman's test revealed no significant differences in these distributions.

Table 6. Frequency of responses for prior task knowledge.

Times Searched, Knowledge	Never, Nothing	1-2 times, Little	3-4 times, Some	5+ times, Great deal
Remember	81%, 64%	15%, 21%	<1%, 13%	<1%, <1%
Understand	81%, 38%	15%, 44%	<1%, 17%	0%, 0%
Analyze	79%, 43%	19%, 47%	<1%, 1%	0%, <1%
Evaluate	72%, 38%	21%, 34%	1%, 23%	0%, <1%
Create	79%, 60%	1%, 28%	1%, 10%	<1%, <1%

Participants were asked in the post-search questionnaire about the extent to which their knowledge of the tasks increased after searching (Table 7). For most tasks, participants indicated their knowledge increased somewhat. No significant differences were found in participants' responses to this item according to complexity level. Participants' interests in the tasks were elicited in the pre- and post-search questionnaires (Table 7). While there were no significant differences in their pre-search interest ratings, there was a significant difference in post-search ratings [$F(4, 188)=4.09$, $p=0.003$, $\eta^2=0.08$]: participants were significantly more interested in the *evaluate* and *create* tasks than the *remember* tasks. A comparison of the pre- and post-search ratings also shows that interest levels decreased for *remember* and *understand* tasks, but increased for *create* tasks.

Table 7. Mean (SD) Interest and Knowledge Increase. *$p<0.01$

	Remember	Understand	Analyze	Evaluate	Create
Pre-Interest	2.70 (1.25)	2.94 (1.17)	2.70 (1.12)	2.91 (1.30)	2.45 (1.35)
Post-Interest*	2.23 (1.36)	2.54 (1.17)	2.77 (1.15)	2.94 (1.13)	3.02 (1.08)
Knowledge Increase	2.92 (1.18)	3.21 (1.24)	3.15 (1.13)	3.27 (1.14)	3.29 (1.07)

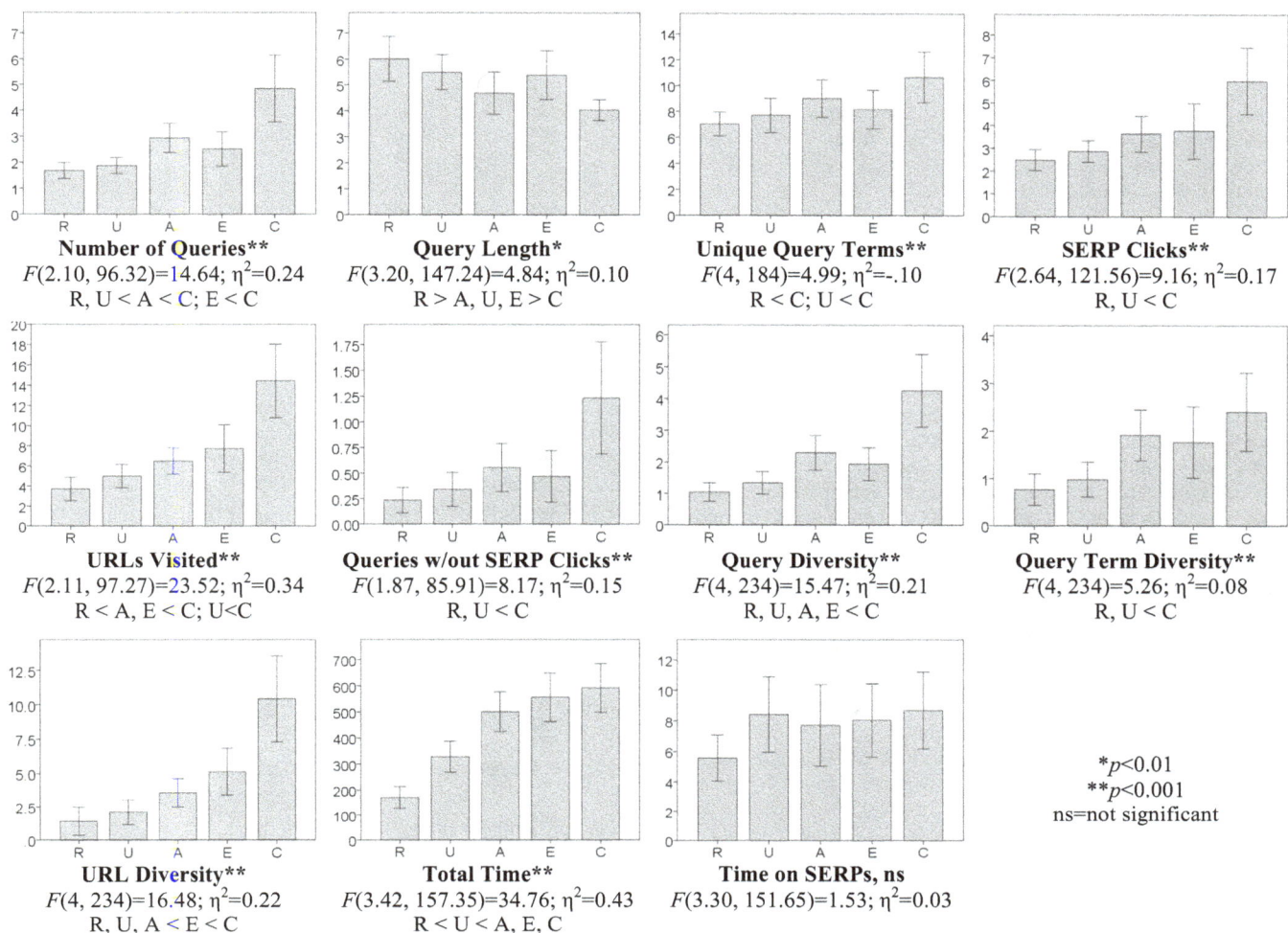

Figure 1. Search behaviors (means, 95% confidence intervals) according to cognitive complexity level. Varying degrees of freedom exist in cases where Mauchly's test of sphericity indicated different variances.

Number of Queries**
$F(2.10, 96.32)=14.64; \eta^2=0.24$
R, U < A < C; E < C

Query Length*
$F(3.20, 147.24)=4.84; \eta^2=0.10$
R > A, U, E > C

Unique Query Terms**
$F(4, 184)=4.99; \eta^2=-.10$
R < C; U < C

SERP Clicks**
$F(2.64, 121.56)=9.16; \eta^2=0.17$
R, U < C

URLs Visited**
$F(2.11, 97.27)=23.52; \eta^2=0.34$
R < A, E < C; U<C

Queries w/out SERP Clicks**
$F(1.87, 85.91)=8.17; \eta^2=0.15$
R, U < C

Query Diversity**
$F(4, 234)=15.47; \eta^2=0.21$
R, U, A, E < C

Query Term Diversity**
$F(4, 234)=5.26; \eta^2=0.08$
R, U < C

URL Diversity**
$F(4, 234)=16.48; \eta^2=0.22$
R, U, A < E < C

Total Time**
$F(3.42, 157.35)=34.76; \eta^2=0.43$
R < U < A, E, C

Time on SERPs, ns
$F(3.30, 151.65)=1.53; \eta^2=0.03$

*p<0.01
**p<0.001
ns=not significant

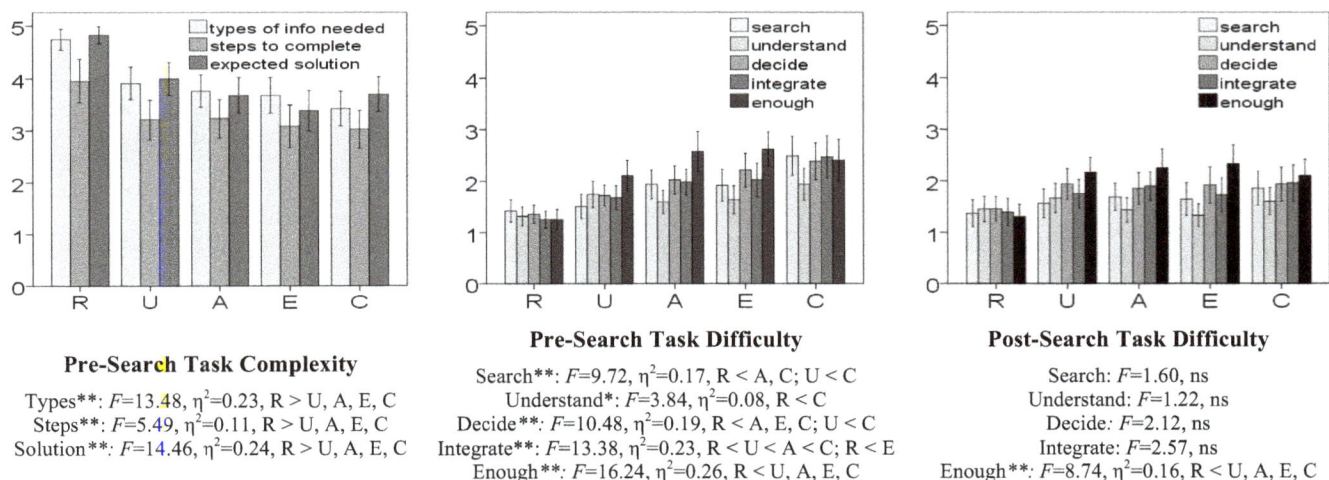

Pre-Search Task Complexity

Types**: $F=13.48, \eta^2=0.23$, R > U, A, E, C
Steps**: $F=5.49, \eta^2=0.11$, R > U, A, E, C
Solution**: $F=14.46, \eta^2=0.24$, R > U, A, E, C

Pre-Search Task Difficulty

Search**: $F=9.72, \eta^2=0.17$, R < A, C; U < C
Understand*: $F=3.84, \eta^2=0.08$, R < C
Decide**: $F=10.48, \eta^2=0.19$, R < A, E, C; U < C
Integrate**: $F=13.38, \eta^2=0.23$, R < U < A < C; R < E
Enough**: $F=16.24, \eta^2=0.26$, R < U, A, E, C

Post-Search Task Difficulty

Search: $F=1.60$, ns
Understand: $F=1.22$, ns
Decide: $F=2.12$, ns
Integrate: $F=2.57$, ns
Enough**: $F=8.74, \eta^2=0.16$, R < U, A, E, C

Figure 2. Task complexity and pre- and post-search difficulty ratings (means, 95% confidence intervals) according to cognitive complexity level. Statistically significant differences are noted with *p<0.01 and **p<0.001, ns=not significant. Degrees of freedom for pre-search items (4, 184) and for post-search items (4, 188).

5.3 Task Complexity

Figure 2 shows participants' mean ratings of the task complexity items. In general, as the cognitive complexity increased, so did participants' ratings of complexity (lower ratings mean more uncertainty). Significant differences were found for all items; follow-up tests showed *remember* tasks were rated as significantly more defined than other tasks.

5.4 Task Difficulty

Overall, participants' pre-search difficulty ratings showed they did not expect tasks to be difficult (Figure 2). *Remember* tasks were uniformly rated as easy across all items. For *understand*, *analyze* and *evaluate* tasks, participants expected that it would be more difficult to determine when to stop searching. In general, as the level of task complexity increased, participants anticipated that tasks would be more difficult. Significant effects for task complexity were found for the five difficulty items; specifically, participants anticipated *remember* tasks would be significantly less difficult than *create* tasks. Participants anticipated *remember* tasks would always be the least difficult and *create* tasks the most difficult. Participants' post-search difficulty ratings (Figure 2) exhibited a similar pattern to those of the pre-search difficulty items, however most ratings were lower. Significant differences were only found for the item about determining if one had enough information to stop; participants' ratings of *remember* tasks were significantly lower than their ratings of other tasks.

We examined the extent to which participants' responses to the pre- and post-search task difficulty items differed. For about 50% of tasks, there were no changes to any of the difficulty items. Participants rated about 15% of tasks as more difficult (+1 point) and 6% as much more difficult (+2 points). Participants rated about 20% of tasks as easier (-1 point) and 10% as much easier (-2 points). Paired-sample t-tests showed participants' experienced less search difficulty than they expected [expected: M=1.86, SD=1.04; experienced: M=1.64, SD=1.10, $t(234)$=2.68, $p<0.01$].

5.5 Enjoyment and Engagement

Overall, participants found all their search tasks somewhat enjoyable (Figure 3). There was a significant difference in participants' engagement ratings [$F(4, 188)$=5.39, $p<0.001$, η^2=0.12]: participants rated the *evaluate* and *create* tasks as significantly more engaging than the *remember* tasks, and the *evaluate* tasks as significantly more engaging than the *understand* tasks. There were no significant differences in participants' abilities to concentrate when completing the different tasks.

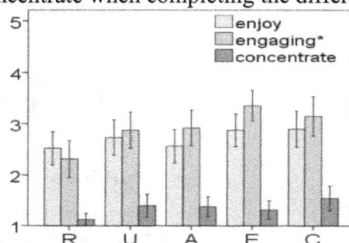

Figure 3. Enjoyment, engagement and concentration. Bars show means and 95% confidence intervals. *$p<0.001$

5.6 Overall Difficulty and Satisfaction

After rating each task according to the difficulty items, participants provided summative evaluations of task difficulty, satisfaction with solution and satisfaction with search strategy (Figure 4). Participants did not find any of the tasks difficult overall and there were no significant differences according to

complexity level. Participants were generally satisfied with their solutions to tasks as well as their strategies.

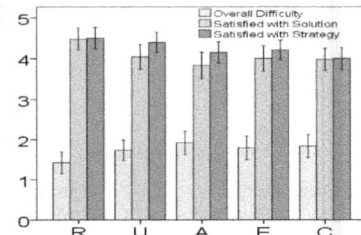

Figure 4. Task difficulty and satisfaction Bars show means and 95% confidence intervals.

5.7 Difficulty and Engagement Rankings

At the end of the study, participants were asked to rank the tasks according to difficulty and engagement (Figure 5). Spearman's Rho showed significant correlations between cognitive complexity and difficulty: ρ=0.413, $p<0.0001$ and engagement: ρ=0.187, p=0.004, but the effect sizes were small.

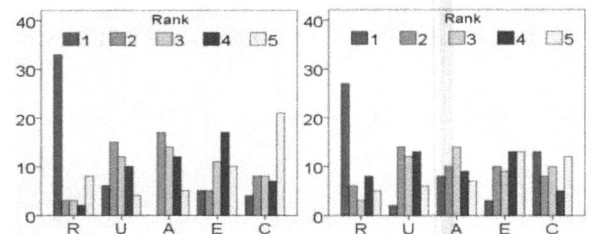

Figure 5. Frequency counts of difficulty (left) and engagement (right) rankings (1=least; 5=most).

The difficulty ranking indicates a fairly clear message about *remember* tasks and while *create* tasks were more often ranked as the most difficult, it is critical to remember that there were no significant differences in participants' ratings of task difficulty. Thus, these rankings should be understood as a relative ordering, which, combined with participants' difficulty ratings, indicate the tasks are clustered in the low area of difficulty. When explaining their difficulty rankings, participants overwhelmingly cited the open-endedness of the task. Many participants described tasks that allowed for more personal input as more engaging. Participants stated that tasks without definite answers were more difficult because this meant they had to make more unique decisions about relevance. While the engagement rankings send a clear message about the *remember* tasks, there was much more variability in the rankings of the other tasks. Participants' explanations of their engagement rankings were overwhelmingly focused on what they found interesting about the task and personal relevance.

6. DISCUSSION & CONCLUSIONS

Results showed when completing tasks of varying levels of cognitive complexity, participants spent significantly different amounts of time and engaged in significantly different amounts of interaction. While there were not always significant differences in search behaviors for tasks of mid-level cognitive complexity (understand, analyze, evaluate), in all cases but one, there were significant differences between the least and most cognitively complex tasks (remember versus create). For most interaction measures, the general trend was for the numbers to increase with cognitively complexity, except for query length, which decreased. An examination of participants' queries for *remember* tasks showed that in many cases participants used most of the information provided in the task description in their queries and sometimes even posed their queries as questions (e.g., What is the deepest point in the ocean?). Given that *remember* tasks were the most specified, these results are not surprising. Participants submitted the fewest queries for these tasks, which suggests their long queries were useful for addressing these tasks.

Participants submitted the most queries for *create* tasks and used significantly more unique query terms for these tasks than for other tasks. These results suggest participants addressed *create* tasks by submitting a greater number of shorter queries and used more unique terms. These results provide some evidence that the most cognitively complex tasks were similar to Campbell's [15] characterization of complex tasks with respect to having multiple interdependent parts that needed to be addressed separately.

With respect to query diversity, query term diversity, and URL diversity we see even stronger results. As a reminder, these diversity measures compare participants' queries and URLs with those of other participants completing the exact same task. The uniqueness measures discussed above only examined a single participant's behaviors. Queries issued by those completing *create* tasks were significantly more diverse than queries issued by those completing any of the other task types. Participants completing *create* tasks used significantly more diverse terms than when completing *remember* or *understand* tasks, and visited significantly more diverse URLs. These findings provide evidence that the task design encouraged participants to engage in more open-ended, self-directed searching by allowing for more unique and varied solutions. This is consistent with Campbell's [15] description of task complexity.

While more cognitively complex tasks required more time to complete and more interaction (e.g., more SERP clicks and URL visits), they were not associated with higher levels of difficulty or lower levels of satisfaction with the outcome. These results are interesting because they show that the relationship between physical effort and self-reported task difficulty are not linear. These findings question recent work that has proposed such relationships [19, 29]. Other studies have proposed that increases in search behavior are related to dissatisfaction and subsequently search engine switching [39] and seeking help from online QA forums [31]. In our study, more cognitively complex tasks were also associated with more queries without SERP clicks. Query abandonment, or queries without clicks, has also been used as a sign of dissatisfaction, or failure [17]. Our results show the relative nature of interaction signals: in some situations a lot of interaction might indicate problems, while in other cases it represents satisfactory progress or positive experiences, which supports recent work on disambiguating interaction data [20].

In the context of task difficulty, these results lead us to speculate that search task difficulty is primarily a function of what a person expects when starting a task. Specifically, we posit that when searchers encounter a search task description, they appraise the task and its requirements in the context of their abilities, desires and other aspects of the search situation (e.g., system familiarity, time limits) and then estimate how much effort they believe is needed to complete the task at their ideal level of performance. A search task, consequently, becomes "difficult" when expended effort exceeds expected effort. Additional research is needed to evaluate this theory. One important aspect of the search situation in IIR experiments is that tasks are typically assigned to participants, which likely impacts how participants evaluate difficulty and the extent to which they engage in search.

We measured both task complexity and task difficulty and maintained distinct definitions of these concepts as recommended by Wildemuth et al. [42]. To measure complexity, we used three

items that reflected Byström and Järvelin's [14] definition and found that overall, participants' rated all the tasks as fairly well-defined (i.e., not complex) and that *remember* tasks were rated as significantly less complex than the other tasks. With respect to measurement of task difficulty, our results also show that difficulty ratings and rankings provide different types of information. While the rankings showed significant differences among the tasks, the ratings did not. These results show none of our tasks were perceived as very difficult, but that participants could still order them relative to one another, and this ordering was likely within the context of the low end of the task difficulty scale. This finding suggests researchers should use caution when asking participants to rank items, since rankings might be misleading. These findings also provoke questions about the range of task complexity and task difficulty that can be observed within laboratory settings.

In this paper, we addressed long-standing calls for the development of shared infrastructure, in particular, search tasks and questionnaires for conducting IIR studies. We presented a set of search tasks, an analytical description of their design (Table 2) and evidence about the types of behaviors these tasks elicit from research participants. We recognize our tasks have some cultural biases built-in; this was necessary in order to create tasks that we thought would appeal to our target participants. We also focused on one type of searcher that is often represented in IIR studies, undergraduate students. Future studies might investigate our tasks with different populations of participants to see if the general relationships hold, especially with regard to search interaction. In our initial work with these tasks, we studied people from our community and found similar results [5]. Since conducting the research reported in this paper, we have used these tasks in other research projects [4, 11, 16]; several of these studies used a crowdsourcing platform and one was done at a public library with members of our local community. The general findings with respect to interaction have been repeated many times, with only slight variations. For example, crowd-sourced participants did not spend as long overall completing the tasks, but the relative differences among cognitive complexity levels remained. Other researchers have also started to use these tasks [7, 32], which demonstrate their potential usefulness for enabling research. We provide our task complexity and task difficulty questionnaires in this paper, which allows for reuse, critique and further development. While we have yet to perform any psychometric analysis of these questionnaire items to establish validity and reliability, we plan to do so in the future.

7. REFERENCES

[1] Ageev, M., Guo, Q, Lagun, D. & Agichtein, E. (2011). Find it if you can: A game for modeling different types of web search success using interaction data. *Proc. of SIGIR*, 345-354.

[2] Allan, J., Croft, B., Moffat, A. & Sanderson, M. (Eds). (2012). Frontiers, challenges and opportunities for Information retrieval: Report from SWIRL 2012. *SIGIR Forum, 46(1)*, 2-32.

[3] Anderson, L. W. & Krathwohl, D. A. (2001). *A taxonomy for learning, teaching and assessing: A revision of Bloom's taxonomy of educational objectives.* New York: Longman.

[4] Arguello, J. (2014). Predicting search task difficulty. *Proc. ECIR*, 88-99.

[5] Arguello, J., Wu, W.C., Kelly, D., & Edwards, A. (2012). Task complexity, vertical display and user interaction in aggregated search. *Proc. of SIGIR*, 435-444.

[6] Aula, A., Khan, R. M. & Guan, Z. (2010). How does search behavior change as search becomes more difficult? *Proc. of SIGCHI Conference*, 35-44.

[7] Bailey, P., Moffat, A., Scholer, F., & Thomas, P. (2015). User Variability and IR System Evaluation. *Proc. of SIGIR*.

[8] Bell, D. J. & Ruthven, I. (2004). Searcher's assessments of task complexity for web searching. *Proc. of ECIR*, 57-71.

[9] Belkin, N. J., Dumais, S. Kando, N. & Sanderson, M. (2012, October). *Whole Session Evaluation of Interactive Information Retrieval Systems*. National Institute of Informatics Shonan Meeting, Shonan Village Center, Japan.

[10] Borlund, P. (2003). The IIR evaluation model: A framework for the evaluation of interactive information retrieval systems. *Information Research, 8*(3), paper 152.

[11] Brennan, K., Kelly, D., & Arguello, J. (2014). The effect of cognitive abilities on information search for tasks of varying levels of complexity. *Proc. of IIiX,* 165-174.

[12] Broder, A. (2002). A taxonomy of web search. *SIGIR Forum, 36*(2), 3-10.

[13] Byström, K. & Hansen, P. (2005). Conceptual framework for tasks in information studies. *JASIST, 56*(10), 1050–1061.

[14] Byström, K. & Järvelin, K. (1995). Task complexity affects information seeking and use. *IP&M, 31*, 191-213.

[15] Campbell, D. J. (1988). Task complexity: A review and analysis. *Academy of Management Review, 13*, 40-52.

[16] Crescenzi, A., Capra, R. & Arguello, J. (2013). Time Pressure, User Satisfaction and Task Difficulty. *Proc. of ASIST Conference*.

[17] Diriye, A., White, R. W., Buscher, G., & Dumais, S. T. (2012). Leaving so soon? Understanding and predicting web search abandonment rationales. *Proc. of CIKM*, 1025-1034.

[18] Dumais, S. T., & Belkin, N. J. (2005). The TREC Interactive Tracks: Putting the user into search. In E. M. Voorhees & D. K. Harman (Eds.) *TREC: Experiment and Evaluation in Information Retrieval* (pp. 123-153), Cambridge, MA: MIT Press.

[19] Gwizdka, J. & Spence, I. (2006). What can searching behavior tell us about the difficulty of information tasks? A study of Web navigation. *Proc. of ASIST*, 1-22.

[20] Hassan, A., White, R. W., Dumais, S. T., & Wang, Y. M. (2014). Struggling or exploring?: Disambiguating long search sessions. *Proc. of WSDM*, 53-62.

[21] Jansen, B. J., Booth, D. & Smith, B. (2009). Using the taxonomy of cognitive learning to model online searching. *IP&M, 45*, 643-663.

[22] Jiang, J., He, D. & Allan, J. (2014). Searching, browsing and clicking in a search session: Changes in user behavior by task and over time. *Proc. of SIGIR*, 607-616.

[23] Kelly, D. (2009). Methods for evaluating interactive information retrieval systems with users. *Foundations and Trends in Information Retrieval, 3(1-2)*.

[24] Kelly, D., Arguello, J., & Capra, R. (2013). NSF workshop on task-based information search systems. *SIGIR Forum, 47*(2).

[25] Kelly, D., Dumais, S., & Pedersen, J. (2009). Evaluation challenges and directions for information seeking support systems. *IEEE Computer, 42*(3), 60-66.

[26] Kim, J. (2006). Task difficulty as a predictor and indicator of web searching interaction. *Proc. of CHI (Extended Abstracts)*, 959-964.

[27] Li, Y. & Belkin, N. J. (2008). A faceted approach to conceptualizing tasks in information seeking. *IP&M, 44*, 1822-1837.

[28] Li, Y. & Belkin, N. J. (2010). An exploration of the relationship between work task and interactive information search behavior. *JASIST, 61*(9), 1771–1789.

[29] Liu, J., Liu, C., Cole, M., Belkin, N. J., & Zhang, X. (2012). Exploring and predicting search task difficulty. *Proc. of CIKM*, 1313-1322.

[30] Liu, J., Kim, C. S. & Creel, C. (2013). Why do users feel search task difficult? *Proc. of ASIST*.

[31] Liu, Q., Agichtein, E., Dror, G., Maarek, Y. & Szpektor, I. (2012). When web search fails, searchers become askers: Understanding the transition. *Proc. of SIGIR*, 801-810.

[32] Moffat, A., Thomas, P., & Scholer, F. (2013). Users versus models: What observation tells us about effectiveness metrics. *Proc. of CIKM*, 659–668.

[33] Robertson, S. (2008). On the history of evaluation in IR. *Journal of Documentation, 34*(4), 439-456.

[34] Singer, G., Norbisrath, U. & Lewandowski, D. (2012). Ordinary search engine users assessing difficulty, effort, and outcome for simple and complex search tasks. *Proc. of IIiX*, 110-119.

[35] Smith, C.L. (2008). Searcher adaptation: A response to topic difficulty. *Proc. of the ASIST Conference*.

[36] Toms, E. (2011). Task-based information searching and retrieval. In Ruthven, I., & Kelly, D. (Eds.) *Interactive Information-seeking, Behaviour and Retrieval* (pp.43-59).

[37] Toms, E., O'Brien, H. L., MacKenzie, T., Jordan, C., Freund, L., Toze, S., Dawe, E., & MacNutt, A. (2007). Task effects on interactive search: The query factor. *Proc. of INEX*, 359-372.

[38] Vakkari, P. (2003). Task-based information searching. *ARIST, 37*, 413–464.

[39] White, R.W. & Dumais, S. T. (2009). Characterizing and predicting search engine switching behavior. *Proc. of CIKM*, 87-96.

[40] White, R. W. & Roth, R.A. (2009). *Exploratory search: Beyond the query-response paradigm*. Morgan & Claypool.

[41] Whittaker, S., Terveen, L., & Nardi, B. (2000). Let's stop pushing the envelope and start addressing it: A reference task agenda for HCI. *Human Computer Interaction, 15*, 75-106.

[42] Wildemuth, B. W., Freund, L. & Toms, E. G. (2014). Untangling search task complexity and difficulty in the context of interactive information retrieval studies. *Journal of Documentation, 70*(6), 1118-1140.

[43] Wu, W.C., Kelly, D., Edwards, A., & Arguello, J. (2012). Grannies, tanning beds, tattoos and NASCAR: Evaluation of search tasks with varying levels of cognitive complexity. *Proc. of IIiX*, 254-257.

Query Expansion with Freebase

Chenyan Xiong
Language Technologies Institute
Carnegie Mellon University
Pittsburgh, PA 15213, USA
cx@cs.cmu.edu

Jamie Callan
Language Technologies Institute
Carnegie Mellon University
Pittsburgh, PA 15213, USA
callan@cs.cmu.edu

ABSTRACT

Large knowledge bases are being developed to describe entities, their attributes, and their relationships to other entities. Prior research mostly focuses on the construction of knowledge bases, while how to use them in information retrieval is still an open problem. This paper presents a simple and effective method of using one such knowledge base, *Freebase*, to improve *query expansion*, a classic and widely studied information retrieval task. It investigates two methods of identifying the entities associated with a query, and two methods of using those entities to perform query expansion. A supervised model combines information derived from Freebase descriptions and categories to select terms that are effective for query expansion. Experiments on the ClueWeb09 dataset with TREC Web Track queries demonstrate that these methods are almost 30% more effective than strong, state-of-the-art query expansion algorithms. In addition to improving average performance, some of these methods have better win/loss ratios than baseline algorithms, with 50% fewer queries damaged.

Keywords

Knowledge Base Query Expansion; Freebase; Pseudo Relevance Feedback

1. INTRODUCTION

During the last decade, large, semi-structured *knowledge bases* or *knowledge graphs* have emerged that are less structured than typical relational databases and semantic web resources but more structured than the texts stored in full-text search engines. The weak semantics used in these semi-structured information resources is sufficient to support interesting applications, but is also able to accommodate contradictions, inconsistencies, and mistakes, which makes them easier to scale to large amounts of information. *Freebase*, which contains 2.9 billion 'facts' (relationships and attributes) about 48 million 'topics' (entities) is one well-known example of this class of resources.

Typically the information in a knowledge base is organized around entities and relations. Knowledge base entities correspond to real-world entities and concepts (e.g., `Carnegie Mellon University`). Most entities have brief text descriptions, attributes, and typed relations to other entities. For example, in *Freebase* the basketball player `Michael Jordan` is represented by an object that is linked to a brief text description, attributes such as his career statistics, categories such as `people` and `athlete`, and related entities such as `Chicago Bulls`.

Although Freebase and other knowledge bases contain information that can improve understanding of a topic, how to use it effectively for information retrieval tasks is still an open problem. An intuitive use is query expansion, which generates expansion terms to enhance the original query and better represent user intent. Most recently, Dalton et al. [13] did query expansion using entity names, aliases and categories with several methods of linking entities to the query. They enumerate all possible expansion queries from combinations of linking methods, expansion fields, and hyper-parameters, and treat every expansion query's ranking scores for documents as features of a learning to rank model. However, the effectiveness on the ClueWeb09 and ClueWeb12 web corpora is mixed when compared with strong, state-of-the-art query expansion baselines. Given their thorough exploration of Freebase information and use of supervision, it seems that expansion using Freebase is a rather complicated and challenging task, in which existing techniques can only provide moderate improvements. How to do query expansion using Freebase in a both simple and effective way, especially on web corpora, remains an open problem.

This paper focuses on query expansion and presents several simple yet effective methods of using Freebase to do query expansion for a web corpus. We decompose the problem into two components. The first component identifies query-specific entities to be used for query expansion. We present implementations that retrieve entities directly, or select entities from retrieved documents. The second component uses information about these entities to select potential query expansion terms. We present implementations that use a tf.idf method to select terms, and category information to select terms. Finally, a supervised model is trained to combine information from multiple sources for better expansion.

Our experiments on the TREC Web Track adhoc task demonstrate that all our methods, when used individually, are about 20% more effective than previous state-of-the-art query expansion methods, including Pseudo Relevance Feedback (PRF) on Wikipedia [27] and supervised query expansion [4]. In addition to these improvements, experimental results show that our methods are more robust and have better *win/loss* ratios than state-of-the-art baseline methods, reducing the number of damaged queries by 50%. This makes query expansion using Freebase more appealing, because it is well-known that most query expansion techniques are 'high risk / high reward' insofar as they often damage as many queries as they improve, which is a huge disadvantage in commercial search systems. The supervised model also successfully combines evidence from multiple methods, leading to 30% gains over the previous state-of-the-art. Besides being the first to improve query expansion this much on the widely used ClueWeb09 web corpus, the methods presented here are also fully automatic.

The next section provides a more in-depth discussion of prior research on query expansion. Section 3 provides a background description of Freebase which is essential to this paper. New methods of using Freebase for query expansion are discussed in Section 4. Experimental methodology and evaluation results are described in Sections 5 and 6 respectively. The last section summarizes the paper's contributions and discusses several interesting open problems suggested by this research.

2. RELATED WORK

Usually queries to web search engines are short and not written carefully, which makes it more difficult to understand the intent behind a query and retrieve relevant documents. A common solution is query expansion, which uses a larger set of related terms to represent the user's intent and improve the document ranking.

Among various query expansion techniques, Pseudo Relevance Feedback (PRF) algorithms are the most successful. PRF assumes that top ranked documents for the original query are relevant and contain good expansion terms. For example, Lavrenko et al.'s RM model selects expansion terms based on their term frequency in top retrieved documents, and weights them by documents' ranking scores:

$$s(t) = \sum_{d \in D} p(t|d) f(q, d)$$

where D is the set of top retrieved documents, $p(t|d)$ is the probability that term t is generated by document d's language model, and $f(q, d)$ is the ranking score of the document provided by the retrieval model [17]. Later, Metzler added inverse document frequency (IDF) to demote very frequent terms:

$$s(t) = \sum_{d \in D} p(t|d) f(q, d) \log \frac{1}{p(t|C)} \quad (1)$$

where $p(t|C)$ is the probability of term t in the corpus language model C [20].

Another famous PRF approach is the Mixture Model by Tao et al. [26]. They assume the terms in top retrieved documents are drawn from a mixture of two language models: query model θ_q and a background model θ_B. The likelihood of a top retrieved document d is defined as:

$$\log p(d|\theta_q, \alpha_d, \theta_B) = \sum_{t \in D} \log(\alpha_d\ p(t|\theta_q) + (1 - \alpha_d)\ p(t|\theta_B)).$$

α_d is a document-specific mixture parameter. Given this equation, the query model θ_q can be learned by maximizing the top retrieved documents' likelihood using EM. The terms that have non-zero probability in θ_q are used for query expansion.

Although these two algorithms have different formulations, they both focus on term frequency information in the top retrieved documents. So do many other query expansion algorithms [11, 18, 22, 28]. For example, Robertson et al.'s BM25 query expansion selects terms based on their appearances in relevant (or pseudo relevant) documents versus in irrelevant documents [24]. Lee et al. cluster PRF documents and pick expansion terms from clusters [18]. Metzler and Croft include multi-term concepts in query expansion and select both single-term concepts and multi-term concepts by a Markov Random Field model [22].

The heavy use of top retrieved documents makes the effectiveness of most expansion methods highly reliant on the quality of the initial retrieval. However, web corpora like ClueWeb09 are often noisy and documents retrieved from them may not generate reasonable expansion terms [3, 14]. Cao et al.'s study shows that top retrieved documents contain as many as 65% harmful terms [4]. They then propose a supervised query expansion model to select good expansion terms. Another way to avoid noisy feedback documents is to use an external high quality dataset. Xu et al. proposed a PRF-like method on top retrieved documents from Wikipedia, whose effectiveness is verified in TREC competitions [14, 27]. Kotov and Zhai demonstrated the potential effectiveness of concepts related to query terms in ConceptNet for query expansion, and developed a supervised method that picks good expansion concepts for difficult queries [15].

Another challenge of query expansion is its 'high risk / high reward' property, that often as many queries are damaged as improved. This makes query expansion risky to use in real online search service because users are more sensitive to failures than successes [8]. Collins-Thompson et al. [11] address this problem by combining the evidences from sampled sub-queries and feedback documents. Collins-Thompson also propose a convex optimization framework to find a robust solution based on previous better-on-average expansion terms [9, 10]. The risk is reduced by improving inner difference between expansion terms, and enforcing several carefully-designed constraints to ensure that expansion terms provide good coverage of query concepts.

The fast development of Freebase has inspired several works that use Freebase in query expansion. Pan et al. use the name of related Freebase objects [23]. The related objects are those whose names exactly or partially match the original query, or have a neighbor whose name matches. Dempster-Shafer theory is used to select expansion terms that have supporting evidence from different objects. More recently, Dalton et al.'s entity query feature expansion (EQFE) method explores many kinds of information in Freebase. [13]. They link query to Freebase objects by query annotation, keyword matching, and annotation of top retrieved documents. The name, alias, Freebase types, and Wikipedia categories of linked entities are considered as possible expansion phrases. The combination of different linking methods, different expansion fields of linked entities, and different values of hyper-parameters are enumerated to generate a vast amount of expansion queries. A document's ranking scores with all expansion queries are treated as fea-

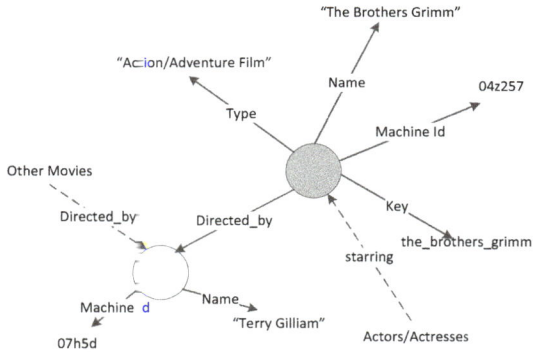

Figure 1: A sub-graph of Freebase.

tures for a learning to rank model. Their methods show great improvements on a cleaner corpus (Robust04), but their effectiveness on noisier web corpora (ClueWeb09 and ClueWeb12) is mixed compared with state-of-the-art expansion baselines. To the best of our knowledge, it remains unclear how to use Freebase for effective query expansion on web corpora.

3. FREEBASE OVERVIEW

Freebase[1] is a large public knowledge base that contains semi-structured information about real world entities and their facts. By July 21st, 2015, Freebase contained 48 million entities and 2.9 billion facts, which makes it the largest among public knowledge bases such as Open Information Extraction [2], NELL [5] and DBPedia [19].

The information in Freebase is organized as a graph, as shown in Figure 1. An entity (object) is expressed as a node in the graph with a unique Machine Id. An edge in the graph links an entity to another entity or its attribute. There are many kinds of edges in Freebase, representing different facts. For example, in Figure 1, **The Brothers Grimm** is connected to **Terry Gilliam** by a **Directed_by** edge, showing that the movie **The Brothers Grimm** is directed by the director **Terry Gilliam**. This research mainly explores some of Freebase's facts, as listed Table 1. For an object's textual fields, such as 'name' and 'description', only the English text is used.

Another resource used in this research is Google's FACC1 [1] annotations, which link Freebase objects to documents in the well-known ClueWeb09 and ClueWeb12 web corpora. The annotation was done automatically by Google. The annotation is of good quality and is tailored to favor Precision over Recall. In a small scale manual examination, the Precision was 80% to 85%; the Recall, although hard to estimate, is believed to be 70% to 85% [1].

4. EXPANSION USING FREEBASE

In this section we introduce our methods of using Freebase for query expansion. We first discuss our unsupervised expansion methods utilizing different information from Freebase. Then we propose a supervised query expansion method to combine evidence from our unsupervised methods.

[1]http://www.freebase.com/

Table 1: Freebase facts used.

Fact	Description
mId	Unique Id
key:en	English Key (if any)
rdfs:label	Object's Name
/common/topic/description	Text Description
rdf:type	Category (if any)

4.1 Unsupervised Expansion Using Freebase

We perform unsupervised query expansion using Freebase in two steps: object linking and term selection. In object linking, we develop implementations that retrieve objects directly, or select them from annotations in top ranked documents. In term selection, we also present two implementations: one uses the tf.idf information from object descriptions; the other uses similarity of query and the term's distributions in Freebase's categories.

Formally, given a query q, and a ranked list of documents from initial retrieval $D = \{d_1, ...d_j..., d_N\}$, the goal of the object linking step is to generate a ranked list of Freebase objects $O = \{o_1, ...o_k..., o_K\}$, with ranking scores $r(O) = \{r(o_1), ...r(o_k)..., r(o_K)\}$. The goal of term selection is to find a set of expansion terms $T = \{t_1, ...t_i..., t_M\}$ and their scores $s(T) = \{s(t_1), ...s(t_i)..., s(t_M)\}$ from linked objects using their descriptions $e(O) = \{e(o_1), ...e(o_k)..., e(o_K)\}$ and Freebase categories $C = \{c_1, ...c_u..., c_U\}$.

4.1.1 Linking Freebase Objects to the Query

Our first linking method retrieves objects directly. The query q is issued to the Google Search API[2] to get its ranking of objects O with ranking scores $r_s(O)$. The ranking score ranges from zero to several thousands, with a typical long tailed distribution. We normalize them so that the ranking scores of each query's retrieved objects sum to one.

Our second approach selects related objects from the FACC1 annotations in top retrieved documents. It is a common assumption that top retrieved documents are a good representation of the original query. Intuitively the objects that appear frequently in them shall convey meaningful information as well. We utilize such information by linking the query to objects that are frequently annotated to top retrieved documents.

Specifically, for a query q's top retrieved documents D, we fetch their FACC1 annotations, and calculate the ranking score for object o_k as:

$$r_f(o_k) = \sum_{d_j \in D} tf(d_j, o_k) \log \frac{|F|}{df(o_k)}. \quad (2)$$

In Equation 2, $tf(d_j, o_k)$ is the frequency of object o_k in document d_j's annotations, and $df(o_k)$ is the total number of documents o_k is annotated to in the whole corpus. $|F|$ is the total number of documents in the corpus that have been annotated in the FACC1 annotation. $\frac{|F|}{df(o_k)}$ in Equation 2 serves as inverse document frequency (IDF) to demote objects that are annotated to too many documents. $r_f(o_k)$

[2]https://developers.google.com/freebase/v1/getting-started

113

is normalized so that ranking scores of each query's objects sum to one.

4.1.2 Selecting Expansion Terms from Linked Objects

We develop two methods to select expansion terms from linked objects.

The first method does tf.idf based Pseudo Relevance Feedback (PRF) on linked objects' descriptions. PRF has been successfully used with Wikipedia articles [3, 14, 27]. It is interesting to see how it works with Freebase.

Given the ranked objects O and $r(O)$, a term's score is calculated by:

$$s_p(t_i) = \sum_{o_k \in O} \frac{tf(e(o_k), t_i)}{|e(o_k)|} \times r(o_k) \times \log \frac{|E|}{df(t_i)} \quad (3)$$

where $tf(e(o_k), t_i)$ is the term frequency of t_i in o's description, $|e(o_k)|$ is the length of the description, $df(t_i)$ is the document frequency of t_i in the entire Freebase's description corpus E. $|E|$ is the total number of entities in Freebase that have a description.

Our second term selection method uses Freebase's entity categories. Freebase provides an ontology tree that describes entities at several levels of abstraction. We use the highest level in the ontology tree, such as /people and /movie, to make sure sufficient instances exist in each category. There are in total $U = 77$ first level categories in Freebase. The descriptions of entities in these categories are training data to learn the language models used to describe these categories.

Our second approach estimates query and terms distributions on categories, and selects terms that have similar category distributions with the query.

The distribution of a term in Freebase categories is estimated using a Naive Bayesian classifier. We first calculate the probability of a term t_i generated by a category c_u via:

$$p(t_i|c_u) = \frac{\sum_{o_k \in c_u} tf(e(o_k), t_i)}{\sum_{o_k \in c_u} |e(o_k)|}$$

where $o_k \in c_u$ refers to objects in category c_u.

Using Bayes' rule, the probability of term t_i belonging to category c_u under uniform priors is:

$$p(c_u|t_i) = \frac{p(t_i|c_u)}{\sum_{c_u \in C} p(t_i|c_u)}.$$

Similarly, the category distribution of a query q is:

$$p(q|c_u) = \prod_{t_i \in q} p(t_i|c_u),$$

$$p(c_u|q) = \frac{p(q|c_u)}{\sum_{c_u \in C} p(q|c_u)}.$$

The similarity between the two distributions $p(c_u|t_i)$ and $p(c_u|q)$ is evaluated by negative Jensen-Shannon divergence:

$$s_c(t_i) = -\frac{1}{2}\mathrm{KL}(p(C|q)||p(C|q,t_i)) - \frac{1}{2}\mathrm{KL}(p(C|t_i)||p(C|q,t_i))$$

where:

$$p(C|q, t_i) = \frac{1}{2}(p(C|q) + p(C|t_i))$$

and $\mathrm{KL}(\cdot||\cdot)$ is the KL divergence between two distributions. $s_c(t_i)$ is the expansion score for a term t_i. We use a min-max normalization to re-range all $s_c(t_i)$ into $[0, 1]$.

Table 2: Unsupervised Query Expansion Methods Using Freebase.

	Link by Search	Link by FACC1
Select by PRF	FbSearchPRF	FbFaccPRF
Select by Category	FbSearchCat	FbFaccCat

As a result, we have two methods that link related Freebase objects to a query, and two methods to select expansion terms from linked objects. They together form four unsupervised expansion methods, as listed in Table 2.

4.2 Supervised Expansion Using Freebase

Different object linking and term selection algorithms have different strengths. Object search links objects that are directly related to the query by keyword matching. FACC1 annotation provides objects that are more related in meanings and does not require exact textual matches. In expansion term selection, PRF picks terms that frequently appear in objects' descriptions. The category similarity method selects terms that have similar distributions with the query in Freebase's categories. They together provide three scores describing the relationship between a query-term pair: tf.idf Pseudo Relevance Feedback score in retrieved objects, tf.idf Pseudo Relevance Feedback score in top retrieved documents' FACC1 annotations, and a negative Jensen-Shannon divergence score between category distributions.

The three scores are used as features for a supervised model that learns how to select better expansion terms. All terms in linked objects' descriptions are used as candidates for query expansion. The ground truth score for a candidate term is generated by its influence on retrieved documents, when used for expansion individually. If a term increases the ranking scores of relevant documents, or decreases the ranking scores of irrelevant documents, it is considered to be a good expansion term, and vice versa.

The influence of a term t_i over retrieved documents is calculated as:

$$y(t_i) = \frac{1}{|R|} \sum_{d_j \in R} (f(q + t_i, d_j) - f(q, d_j))$$

$$- \frac{1}{|\bar{R}|} \sum_{d_j \in \bar{R}} (f(q + t_i, d_j) - f(q, d_j))$$

where R and $\bar{R}$ are the sets of relevant and irrelevant documents in relevance judgments. $f(q, d_j)$ is the ranking score for document d_j and query q in the base retrieval model. $f(q + t_i, d_j)$ is the ranking score for d_j when the query is expanded using expansion term t_i individually. Binary labels are constructed using $y(t)$. Terms with $y(t) > 0$ are treated as good expansion terms and the rest as bad expansion terms.

Our ground truth label generation is a little different than Cao et al.'s [4]. Their labels were generated by a term's influence on documents' ranking positions: if relevant documents are moved up or irrelevant document are moved down by a term, it is considered a good expansion term, otherwise a bad one. In comparison, we use influence on ranking scores which reflect an expansion term's effectiveness more directly. Our preliminary experiments also confirm that both their method and our method work better with our ground truth labels.

We used a linear SVM classifier to learn the mapping from the three features of a term t to its binary label. To get the expansion weights, we used the probabilistic version of SVM in the LibSVM [7] toolkit to predict the probability of a term being a good expansion term. The predicted probabilities are used as terms' expansion scores, and those terms with highest scores are selected for query expansion.

4.3 Ranking with Expansion Terms

We use the selected expansion terms and their scores to re-rank the retrieved documents with the RM model [17]:

$$f^*(d_j, q) = w_q f(q, d_j) + (1 - w_q)(\sum_{t_i \in T} s(t_i) f(t_i, d_j))). \quad (4)$$

In Equation 4, $f^*(q, d_j)$ is the final ranking score to re-rank documents. $f(q, d_j)$ and $f(t_i, d_j)$ are the ranking scores generated by the base retrieval model, e,g, BM25 or query likelihood, for query q and the expansion term t_i respectively. w_q is the weight on the original query. T is the set of selected expansion terms and $s(t_i)$ is the expansion score of the term t_i. Expansion scores are normalized so that the scores of a query's expansion terms sum to one.

5. EXPERIMENTAL METHODOLOGY

In this section we introduce our experimental methodology, including dataset, retrieval model, baselines, hyper-parameters, and evaluation metrics.

Dataset: Our experiments use ClueWeb09, TREC Web Track 2009-2012 adhoc task queries and the relevance judgments provided by TREC annotators. This dataset models a real web search scenario: queries are selected from the search log from Bing, and ClueWeb09 is a widely used web corpus automatically crawled from the internet by Carnegie Mellon University. ClueWeb09 is known to be a hard dataset for query expansion [3, 13, 14], because it is much noisier than carefully edited corpora like the Wall-street Journal, news and government web sets.

We use Category B of ClueWeb09 and index it using the Indri search engine [25]. Typical INQUERY stopwords are removed before indexing. Documents and queries are stemmed using the Krovetz stemmer [16]. Spam filtering is very important for ClueWeb09 and we filter the 70% most spammy documents using the Waterloo spam score [12].

We retrieved Freebase objects, and fetched their descriptions using the Google Freebase API on July 16th, 2014. Entity linking from documents to entities are found in FACC1 annotation [1], which was published in June 2013. Corpus statistics such as term IDF and categories' language models were calculated from the April 13th, 2014 Freebase RDF dump.

Retrieval Model: We use Indri's language model [20] as our base retrieval model. The ranking score of a document is the probability of its language model generating the query. Dirichlet smoothing is applied to avoid zero probability and incorporate corpus statistics:

$$p(q|d_j) = \frac{1}{|q|} \sum_{t_i \in q} \frac{tf(d_j, t_i) + \mu p(t_i|\mathcal{C})}{|d_j| + \mu}, \quad (5)$$

where $p(t_i|\mathcal{C})$ is the probability of seeing term t_i in the whole corpus, and μ is the parameter controlling the smoothing strength, set to the Indri default: 2500.

Baselines: We compare our four unsupervised expansion methods (as listed in Table 2) and the supervised method described in Section 4.2 (**FbSVM**) with several baselines. The first baseline is the Indri language model (**IndriLm**) as in Equation 5. All relative performances and Win/Loss evaluations of other methods are compared with **IndriLm** if without specific reference. Our second baseline is the Sequential Dependency Model (**SDM**) [21], a strong competitor in TREC Web Tracks.

We also include two well-known state-of-the-art query expansion methods as baselines. The first one is Pseudo Relevance Feedback on Wikipedia (**RmWiki**) [3, 14, 27]. We indexed the Oct 1st 2013 Wikipedia dump using same setting we used for ClueWeb09. Standard Indri PRF with the IDF component [14] was performed to select expansion terms.

The other query expansion baseline is the supervised query expansion (**SVMPRF**) [4]. We extracted the 10 features described in their paper, and trained an SVM classifier to select good expansion terms. We used our term level ground truth labels as discussed in Section 4.2, because their model performs better with our labels. Following their paper, the RBF kernel was used, which we also found necessary for that method to be effective.

For clarity and brevity, we do not show comparison with other methods such as RM3 [17], Mixture Model [26], or EQFE [13] because they all perform worse on ClueWeb09 than **RmWiki** and **SDM** in our experiment, previous TREC competitions [14], or in their published papers.

Parameter Setting: Hyper parameters in our experiment, including the number of expansion terms (M), number of objects (K) in Freebase linked for expansion, and number of PRF documents for **RmWiki** and **SVMPRF**, are selected by maximizing the performance on training folds in a five-fold cross validation. The number of expansion terms is selected from $\{1, 3, 5, 10, 15, 20, 30, 40, 50, 60, 70, 80, 90, 100\}$, the number of entities is selected from $\{1, 3, 5, 10, 15, 20, 30, 40, 50\}$ and the number of PRF documents is selected from $\{5, 10, 15, 20, 25, 30\}$.

Parameters of SVM in supervised expansion (**FbSVM** and **SVMPRF**) are selected by another five-fold cross validation. In each of the five folds of the outside cross validation that were used to select expansion parameters, we performed a second level cross validation to select the parameters of SVM. The explored range of cost c of linear kernel and RBF kernel is $\{0.01, 0.1, 1, 10, 100\}$. The range of γ in RBF kernel is $\{0.1, 1, 10, 100, 1000, 10000\}$.

To keep the experiment tractable, other parameters were fixed following conventions in previous work [4, 14, 27]. The weight of the original query w_q is set to 0.5, and the re-rank depth is 1000. We chose re-ranking instead of retrieval again in the whole index because the latter is very expensive with the large set of expansion terms and did not show any significant difference in our experiments. When using FACC1 annotations to link objects, we used the FACC1 annotations in the top 20 retrieved documents provide by **IndriLm**. The candidate terms for **FbSVM** were generated from the top 20 retrieved objects and top 20 linked FACC1 annotations. To reduce noise in object description, we ignored terms that contained less than three characters.

Evaluation Metric. Our methods re-ranked the top retrieved documents, so we mainly focus evaluation on the top 20 documents in the re-ranked list. We chose ERR@20 as

Table 3: Performance of unsupervised expansion using Freebase. Relative gain is calculated using ERR over `IndriLm`. Win/Loss/Tie is the number of queries helped, hurt, and not changed comparing with `IndriLm`. †, ‡, § and ¶ mark the statistic significant improvements ($p < 0.05$) over `IndriLm`, `SDM`, `RmWiki` and `SVMPRF` respectively. The best results in each column are marked **bold**.

Method	MAP@20	NDCG@20	ERR@20	Relative Gain	Win/Loss/Tie
`IndriLm`	0.357	0.147	0.116	NA	NA
`SDM`	$0.387^{\dagger}$	$0.166^{\dagger}$	$0.122^{\dagger}$	5.52%	58/27/115
`RmWiki`	0.362	$0.161^{\dagger}$	0.114	−1.70%	67/72/61
`SVMPRF`	0.367	$0.158^{\dagger}$	0.125	8.00%	63/72/65
`FbSearchPRF`	$\mathbf{0.436}^{\dagger,\ddagger,\S,\P}$	$\mathbf{0.186}^{\dagger,\ddagger,\S,\P}$	$\mathbf{0.152}^{\dagger,\ddagger,\S,\P}$	30.80%	84/30/86
`FbSearchCat`	$0.421^{\dagger,\ddagger,\S,\P}$	$0.182^{\dagger,\ddagger,\S,\P}$	$0.144^{\dagger,\ddagger,\S,\P}$	23.99%	67/43/90
`FbFaccPRF`	$0.428^{\dagger,\ddagger,\S,\P}$	$0.184^{\dagger,\ddagger,\S,\P}$	$0.145^{\dagger,\ddagger,\S,\P}$	24.71%	97/55/48
`FbFaccCat`	$0.400^{\dagger,\S,\P}$	$0.173^{\dagger}$	$0.136^{\dagger,\ddagger,\S}$	17.25%	88/67/45

our main evaluation metric, which is the main metric of the TREC Web Track adhoc task. We also show the evaluation results for MAP@20 and NDCG@20.

6. EVALUATION RESULTS

In this section, we first discuss the average performance of our unsupervised expansion methods using Freebase, comparing with current state-of-the-art baselines. Then we evaluate our supervised expansion method. Besides average performances, we also analysis our methods' robustness at the individual query level. We conclude our analysis with case studies and discussions.

6.1 Performance of Unsupervised Expansion

The average performances on MAP, NDCG and ERR are shown in Table 3. The relative gain and Win/Loss ratio are compared with `IndriLm` on ERR. Statistical significance tests are performed using the Permutation test. Labels †, ‡, § and ¶ indicate statistical significance ($p < 0.05$) over `IndriLm`, `SDM`, `RmWiki` and `SVMPRF` respectively.

Our unsupervised expansion methods outperform all state-of-the-art baselines by large margins for all evaluation metrics. All the gains over `IndriLm` are statistically significant, while `SVMPRF` and `RmWiki` are only significantly better on NDCG. Three of the methods, `FbSearchPRF`, `FbSearchCat` and `FbFaccPRF`, are significantly better than all baselines. `FbFaccCat`'s improvements do not always pass the statistical significance test, even when the relative gains are almost 10%. This reflects the high variance of query expansion methods, which is addressed in Section 6.3.

Comparing the performances of our methods, linking objects by search works better than by FACC1 annotations, and selecting expansion terms by PRF works better than using category similarity. One possible reason is that objects from FACC1 annotation are noisier because they rely on the quality of top retrieved documents. Also the category similarity suffers because suitable categories for query or terms may not exist.

We further compare our unsupervised expansion methods at the query level. The results are shown in Table 4. Each cell shows the comparison between the method in the row and the method in the column. The three numbers are the number of queries in which the row method performs better (win), worse (loss), and equally (tie) with the column method respectively. The results demonstrate that our methods do perform differently. The two most similar

methods are `FbSearchPrf` and `FbSearchCat`, doing the same on 80 queries out of 200. But 36 queries have no returned objects from the Google Search API, on which two methods retreat to `IndriLm`. Otherwise our four unsupervised methods perform the same for at most 49 queries.

These results showed the different strengths of our unsupervised methods. The next experiment investigates whether they can be combined for further improvements by a supervised method.

6.2 Performance of Supervised Expansion

The performance of our supervised method `FbSVM`, which utilized the evidence from our unsupervised methods, is shown in Table 5. To investigate whether the combination of multiple sources of evidence is useful, we conduct statistical significance tests between `FbSVM` with our unsupervised methods. †, ‡, § and ¶ indicates statistical significance in the permutation test over `FbSearchPRF`, `FbSearchCat`, `FbFaccPRF` and `FbFaccCat` correspondingly.

The results demonstrate that evidence from different aspects of Freebase can be combined for further improvements: `FbSVM` outperforms `IndriLm` by as much as 42%. Statistical significance is observed over our unsupervised methods on $NDCG$, but not always on MAP and ERR. We have also run statistical significance tests between `FbSVM` and all other baselines, which are all statistically significant as expected.

`FbSVM` and `SVMPRF` differ in their candidate terms and features. `FbSVM` selects terms from Freebase, while `SVMPRF` selects from web corpus. `FbSVM` uses features from Freebase's linked objects' descriptions and categories, while `FbSVM` uses term distribution and proximity in top retrieved documents from web corpus. Table 6 shows the quality of candidate terms from two sources. Surprisingly, Freebase' candidate terms are slightly weaker in quality (39.4% vs. 41.4%) and there are more of them. However, `FbSVM`'s classification Precision is about 10% relatively better than `SVMPRF`, as shown in Table 7. The Recall of `FbSVM` is lower, but `FbSVM` still picks more good expansion terms given the larger number of good candidate terms in Freebase.

Nevertheless, the marginal gains of `FbSVM` over our best performing unsupervised method `FbSearchPRF` are not as high as expected. Our preliminary analysis shows that one possible reason is the features between query and terms are limited, i.e. only three dimensions. Another possible reason is the way of using the supervised information (document relevance judgments). Document relevance judgments are used to generate labels at the term level using heuristics,

Table 4: The query level Win/Loss/Tie comparison between our methods. Each cell shows the number of queries helped (Win), damaged (Loss) and not changed (Tie) by row method over column method.

	FbSearchPRF	FbSearchCat	FbFaccPRF	FbFaccCat
FbSearchPRF	NA/NA/NA	73/47/80	82/74/44	95/65/40
FbSearchCat	47/73/80	NA/NA/NA	72/86/42	87/72/41
FbFaccPRF	74/82/44	86/72/42	NA/NA/NA	84/67/49
FbFaccCat	65/95/40	72/87/41	67/84/49	NA/NA/NA

Table 5: Performance of supervised expansion using Freebase. Relative gain and Win/Loss/Tie are calculated comparing with IndriLm on ERR. †, ‡, § and ¶ mark the statistically significant improvements over FbSearchPRF, FbSearchCat,FbFaccPRF and FbFaccCat respectively. Best results in each column are marked **bold**.

Method	MAP@20	NDCG@20	ERR@20	Relative Gain	Win/Loss/Tie
FbSearchPRF	0.436	0.186	0.152	30.80%	84/30/86
FbSearchCat	0.421	0.182	0.144	23.99%	67/43/90
FbFaccPRF	0.428	0.184	0.145	24.71%	97/55/48
FbFaccCat	0.400	0.173	0.136	17.25%	88/67/45
FbSVM	**0.444**	**0.199**†,‡,§,¶	**0.165**‡,§,¶	42.42%	96/63/41

while the final document ranking is still computed using unsupervised retrieval models. A more powerful machine learning framework seems necessary to better utilize Freebase information. This would be a good topic for further research.

6.3 Query Level Analysis

A common disadvantage of query expansion methods is their high variances: they often hurt as many queries as helped. To evaluate the robustness of our methods, we compare the query level performance of each method versus IndriLm and record the Win/Loss/Tie numbers. The results are listed in the last columns of Tables 3 and 5. Table 3 shows that SDM, which is widely recognized as effective across many datasets, is reasonably robust and hurts only half as many queries as it helps. It also does not change the performance of 115 queries partly because 53 of them only contain one term on which nothing can be done by SDM. In comparison, RmWiki and SVMPRF hurt more queries than they help, which is consistent with observations in prior work [8].

Our methods have much better Win/Loss ratios than baseline query expansion methods. When selecting terms using PRF from linked objects' descriptions, FbSearchPRF and FbFaccPRF improve almost twice as many queries as they hurt. The variance of term selection by category is higher, but FbSearchCat and FbFaccCat still improve at least 30% more queries than they hurt. Linking by object retrieval has slightly better Win/Loss ratios than by FACC1 annotation, but it also helps a smaller number of queries. One reason is that for some long queries, their is no object retrieved by Google API.

More details of query level performance can be found in Figure 2. The x-axis is the bins of relative performances on ERR compared with IndriLm. The y-axis is the number of queries that fall into corresponding bins. If the performance is the same for a query, we put it into 0 bin. If a query is helped by 0 to 20%, we put it into bin 20%, etc. Figure 2 confirms the robustness of our methods. Especially for FbSearchPRF and FbFaccPRF, more queries are helped, less queries are hurt, and much less queries are extremely damaged.

Table 6: Candidate term quality from top retrieved documents (Web Corpus) and linked objects' descriptions (Freebase). Good and bad refer to the number of terms that have positive and negative influences on ranking accuracy respectively.

Source	Good	Bad	Good Fraction
Web corpus	9,263	13,087	41.4%
Freebase	19,247	29,396	39.6%

Table 7: Classification performance of supervised methods.

Method	Precision	Recall
SVMPRF	0.5154	0.0606
FbSVM	0.5609	0.0400

FbSVM's robustness is average among our expansion methods, and is better than RmWiki and SDM. Fewer queries fall into bin 0, as it is rare that none of our evidence affects a query. However the number of damaged queries is not reduced. One possible reason is that the ground truth we used to train the SVM classifier is the individual performance of each candidate term, and only the average performance is considered in model training/testing. As a result, our model might focus more on improving average performance but not on reducing risk.

6.4 Case Study and Discussion

To further understand the properties of our object linking and term selection methods, Table 8 lists the queries that are most helped or hurt by different combinations of methods. The ↑ row shows the most helped queries and ↓ row shows those most hurt[3]. The comparison is done on ERR compared to IndriLm too.

Table 8 shows the different advantages of linking by object search and FACC1 annotation. For example, the query 'fybromyalgia' is damaged by FbFaccPRF, while improved by FbSearchPRF and FbSearchCat. The FACC1 annotation

---

[3]More details including linked objects and expansion terms are available at http://boston.lti.cs.cmu.edu/appendices/ICTIR2015/.

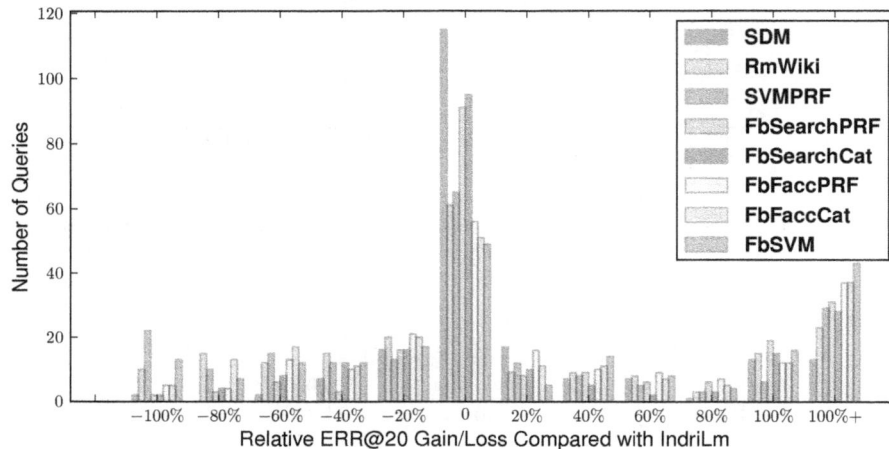

Figure 2: Query level relative performance. X-axis is the bins of relative performance on ERR compared with IndriLm. Y-axis is the number of queries that fall into each bin. Bin 0 refers to queries that were not changed, 20% refers to queries that improved between (0%, 20%], etc. The left-to-right ordering of histograms in each cell corresponds to the top-to-bottom ordering of methods shown in the key.

leads to a set of weakly related objects, like doctors and organizations focused on diseases, which generate overly-general expansion terms. Instead, object search is precise and returns the object about 'fybromyalgia'. Sometimes the generality of FACC1 annotations can help instead. For example, for query 'rock art' whose main topic is about rock painting, object search links to objects about rock music, while FACC1 annotation is more general and links to related objects for both rock painting and rock music.

Our two term selection methods also have different behaviors. An exemplary case is the query 'computer programming', on which FbSearchPRF and FbFaccPRF perform very well, while FbSearchCat and FbFaccCat do not. The linked objects of two methods are both reasonable: object search links to mostly programming languages, and FACC1 annotation brings in programming languages, textbooks and professors. With the good quality of linked objects, PRF selects good expansion terms from their descriptions. However, category similarity picks terms like: 'analysis', 'science', 'application' and 'artificial', which are too general for this query. The granularity of the Freebase ontology's first level is too coarse for some queries, and lower levels are hard to use due to insufficient instances. Nevertheless, when the linked objects are noisy, like for the query 'sore throat', the category information helps pick more disease related terms using the '/medicine' category and provides better performance.

Some queries difficult for all methods. For example, 'wedding budget calculator' contains the entities 'wedding', 'budget' and 'calculator', but actually refers to the concept 'wedding budget' and how to calculate it. Similar cases are 'tangible personal property tax' and 'income tax return online', whose meanings cannot be represented by a single Freebase object.

There are also queries on which Freebase is very powerful. For example, the query 'UNC' asks for the campuses of the University of North Carolina. Freebase contains multiple objects about UNC campuses, and campuses of other related universities, which generate good expansion terms.

Freebase is also very effective for 'Figs', 'Atari', 'Hoboken' and 'Korean Language', whose meanings are described thoroughly by linked Freebase objects.

To sum up, our object linking and term selection methods utilize different parts of Freebase, and thus have different specialties. In object linking, object search is aggressive and can return the exact object for a query, when there are no ambiguities. FACC1 annotation relies on top retrieved documents and usually links to a set of related objects. Thus it is a better choice for queries with ambiguous meanings. In term selection, Pseudo Relevance Feedback via tf.idf directly reflects the quality of linked objects, and is better when the linked objects are reasonable. In contrast, category similarity offers a second chance to pick good expansion terms from noisy linked objects, when proper category definition exists for the query. FbSVM offers a preliminary way to combine the strength from different evidence and does provide additional improvements, however, more sophisticate methods that better use supervision and richer evidence from Freebase are possible for for future research.

Our work and EQFE by Dalton et al. [13] both focus on exploring the effectiveness of Freebase in improving information retrieval. One difference is that EQFE uses the entity's name, alias, and category names as possible expansion phrases, while we select terms from the linked entity's descriptions. Our techniques are also different: EQFE enumerates explored evidence to generate many features, and relies on a learning to rank model to handle them; our methods use classic query expansion techniques like pseudo relevance feedback, distributions of category language models, and term level supervised expansion. We also perform differently in different datasets: EQFE works better on a cleaner corpus (Robust04) while ours works better on a noisier corpus (ClueWeb09). Further study of the differences and strengths of these two approaches may lead to more general methods that can work well under multiple scenarios in future research.

Table 8: The queries most helped and hurt by our methods. ↑ row shows the five most-helped queries for each method, and ↓ shows the most-hurt queries.

	FbSearchPRF	FbSearchCat	FbFaccPRF	FbFaccCat
↑	porterville hobby stores fybromyalgia computer programming figs	unc porterville fybromyalgia bellevue figs	signs of a heartattack computer programming figs idaho state flower hip fractures	porterville idaho state flower bellevue flushing atari
↓	von willebrand disease website design hosting 403b ontario california airport rock art	rock art espn sports ontario california airport computer programming bobcat	wedding budget calculator poem in your pocket day fybromyalgia ontario california airport becoming a paralegal	poem in your pocket day ontario california airport computer programming bobcat blue throated hummingbird

7. CONCLUSION AND FUTURE WORK

In this work, we use Freebase, a large public knowledge base, in query expansion, a classic and widely studied information retrieval task. We present several simple yet effective methods to utilize different Freebase information, including annotation, description and category. We decompose the expansion problem into two components. The first component links Freebase objects to queries using keyword based retrieval, or an object's frequency in FACC1 annotations. The second component uses information about linked objects to select expansion terms. We develop two implementations including a tf.idf based Pseudo Relevance Feedback algorithm, and an algorithm that selects terms whose distributions in Freebase categories are similar with the query's. Finally, a supervised model is trained to combine evidence from multiple expansion methods. Our experiments on the ClueWeb09 dataset and TREC Web Track queries demonstrate that our methods are almost 30% more effective than previous state-of-the-art expansion systems. In addition, some of our methods significantly increases the win/loss ratios by reducing the number of damaged queries by 50%. To the best of our knowledge, our work is the first to show the effectiveness of Freebase for query expansion on the widely used web ClueWeb09 corpus.

This work only focused on a single dataset, albeit a dataset has been difficult for other query expansion methods. Previous query expansion methods have been very successful on cleaner corpora but few of them work well on ClueWeb09. Future research must investigate the generality of our methods on a wider variety of datasets. Analyzing the differences between our methods and previous methods, and perhaps combining them, may lead to a better expansion system.

Entity linking is a widely studied topic, but previous research mostly focused on linking entities to documents, while linking entities to queries is more challenging due to the lower quality of query string. Recently the SIGIR 2014 *Entity Retrieval and Disambiguation Challenge* (*ERD '14*) [6] workshop provided web queries and documents with 'gold standard' Freebase annotations to promote research on identifying Freebase entities in different types of text. It would be beneficial to introduce better query object linking algorithms into our systems.

We have experimented with using a term's tf.idf score and category distribution information to select good expansion terms. One can use additional Freebase resources to derive more features for term selection, for example, relationships,

attributes, and the contexts of FACC1 annotations in web corpus.

Last but not least, when combining evidence from different resources, our model FbSVM only considers average performance and ignores reducing the risk. Fancier models can be developed for better average performance and lower risk at the same time. Extracting more evidence from Freebase about controlling the risk is another potential way to better utilize the rich and complex data in Freebase.

8. ACKNOWLEDGMENTS

We thank the anonymous reviewers for comments that improved the paper. This research was supported by National Science Foundation (NSF) grant IIS-1422676 and a Google Research Award. Any opinions, findings, conclusions, and recommendations expressed in this paper are the authors' and do not necessarily reflect those of the sponsors.

9. REFERENCES

[1] FACC1 Annotation on ClueWeb09. http://lemurproject.org/clueweb09/FACC1/. Accessed: 2014-06-26.

[2] M. Banko, M. J. Cafarella, S. Soderland, M. Broadhead, and O. Etzioni. Open information extraction for the web. In *Processding of the Internaltional Joint Conference on Artifical Intelligence, IJCAI(2007)*, volume 7, pages 2670–2676. IJCAI, 2007.

[3] M. Bendersky, D. Fisher, and W. B. Croft. Umass at Trec 2010 Web Track: Term dependence, spam filtering and quality bias. In *Proceedings of The 19th Text REtrieval Conference, (TREC 2010)*. NIST, 2010.

[4] G. Cao, J.-Y. Nie, J. Gao, and S. Robertson. Selecting good expansion terms for pseudo-relevance feedback. In *Proceedings of the 31st Annual International ACM SIGIR Conference on Research and Development in Information Retrieval, (SIGIR 2008)*, pages 243–250. ACM, 2008.

[5] A. Carlson, J. Betteridge, B. Kisiel, B. Settles, E. R. Hruschka Jr, and T. M. Mitchell. Toward an architecture for never-ending language learning. In *Proceedings of the 24th AAAI Conference on Artificial Intelligence, (AAAI 2010)*, volume 5, page 3. AAAI Press, 2010.

[6] D. Carmel, M.-W. Chang, E. Gabrilovich, B.-J. P. Hsu, and K. Wang. ERD'14: Entity recognition and disambiguation challenge. In *SIGIR '14: Proceedings of the 37th International ACM SIGIR Conference on Research & Development in Information Retrieval*. ACM, 2014.

[7] C.-C. Chang and C.-J. Lin. LIBSVM: A library for support vector machines. *ACM Transactions on Intelligent Systems and Technology*, 2:27:1–27:27, 2011. Software available at http://www.csie.ntu.edu.tw/~cjlin/libsvm.

[8] K. Collins-Thompson. *Robust model estimation methods for information retrieval*. PhD thesis, Carnegie Mellon University, December 2008.

[9] K. Collins-Thompson. Estimating robust query models with convex optimization. In *Proceedings of the 21st Advances in Neural Information Processing Systems, (NIPS 2009)*, pages 329–336. NIPS, 2009.

[10] K. Collins-Thompson. Reducing the risk of query expansion via robust constrained optimization. In *Proceedings of the 18th ACM Conference on Information and Knowledge Management, (CIKM 2009)*, pages 837–846. ACM, 2009.

[11] K. Collins-Thompson and J. Callan. Estimation and use of uncertainty in pseudo-relevance feedback. In *Proceedings of the 30th Annual International ACM SIGIR Conference on Research and Development in Information Retrieval, (SIGIR 2007)*, pages 303–310. ACM, 2007.

[12] G. V. Cormack, M. D. Smucker, and C. L. Clarke. Efficient and effective spam filtering and re-ranking for large web datasets. *Information retrieval*, 14(5):441–465, 2011.

[13] J. Dalton, L. Dietz, and J. Allan. Entity query feature expansion using knowledge base links. In *Proceedings of the 37th Annual International ACM SIGIR Conference on Research and Development in Information Retrieval, (SIGIR 2014)*, pages 365–374. ACM, 2014.

[14] N. Dong and C. Jamie. Combination of evidence for effective web search. In *Proceedings of The 19th Text REtrieval Conference, (TREC 2010)*. NIST, 2010.

[15] A. Kotov and C. Zhai. Tapping into knowledge base for concept feedback: Leveraging ConceptNet to improve search results for difficult queries. In *Proceedings of the Fifth ACM International Conference on Web Search and Data Mining*, pages 403–412. ACM, 2012.

[16] R. Krovetz. Viewing morphology as an inference process. In *Proceedings of the 16th Annual International ACM SIGIR Conference on Research and Development in Information Retrieval, (SIGIR 1993)*, pages 191–202. ACM, 1993.

[17] V. Lavrenko and W. B. Croft. Relevance based language models. In *Proceedings of the 24th Annual International ACM SIGIR Conference on Research and Development in Information Retrieval, (SIGIR 2001)*, pages 120–127. ACM, 2001.

[18] K. S. Lee, W. B. Croft, and J. Allan. A cluster-based resampling method for pseudo-relevance feedback. In *Proceedings of the 31st Annual International ACM SIGIR Conference on Research and Development in Information Retrieval, (SIGIR 2008)*, pages 235–242. ACM, 2008.

[19] J. Lehmann, R. Isele, M. Jakob, A. Jentzsch, D. Kontokostas, P. N. Mendes, S. Hellmann, M. Morsey, P. van Kleef, S. Auer, and C. Bizer. DBpedia - a large-scale, multilingual knowledge base extracted from Wikipedia. *Semantic Web Journal*, 2014.

[20] D. Metzler. *Beyond bags of words: effectively modeling dependence and features in information retrieval*. PhD thesis, University of Massachusetts Amherst, September 2007.

[21] D. Metzler and W. B. Croft. A markov random field model for term dependencies. In *Proceedings of the 28th Annual International ACM SIGIR Conference on Research and Development in Information Retrieval, (SIGIR 2005)*, pages 472–479. ACM, 2005.

[22] D. Metzler and W. B. Croft. Latent concept expansion using markov random fields. In *Proceedings of the 30th Annual International ACM SIGIR Conference on Research and Development in Information Retrieval, (SIGIR 2007)*, pages 311–318. ACM, 2007.

[23] D. Pan, P. Zhang, J. Li, D. Song, J.-R. Wen, Y. Hou, B. Hu, Y. Jia, and A. De Roeck. Using dempster-shafer's evidence theory for query expansion based on freebase knowledge. In *Information Retrieval Technology*, pages 121–132. Springer, 2013.

[24] S. E. Robertson and S. Walker. Okapi/keenbow at TREC-8. In *Proceedings of The 8th Text REtrieval Conference, (TREC 1999)*, pages 151–162. NIST, 1999.

[25] T. Strohman, D. Metzler, H. Turtle, and W. B. Croft. Indri: A language model-based search engine for complex queries. In *Proceedings of the International Conference on Intelligent Analysis*, volume 2, pages 2–6. Citeseer, 2005.

[26] T. Tao and C. Zhai. Regularized estimation of mixture models for robust pseudo-relevance feedback. In *Proceedings of the 29th Annual International ACM SIGIR Conference on Research and Development in Information Retrieval, (SIGIR 2006)*, pages 162–169. ACM, 2006.

[27] Y. Xu, G. J. Jones, and B. Wang. Query dependent pseudo-relevance feedback based on wikipedia. In *Proceedings of the 32nd Annual International ACM SIGIR Conference on Research and Development in Information Retrieval, (SIGIR 2009)*, pages 59–66. ACM, 2009.

[28] C. Zhai and J. Lafferty. Model-based feedback in the language modeling approach to information retrieval. In *Proceedings of the 10th ACM Conference on Information and Knowledge Management, (CIKM 2001)*, pages 403–410. ACM, 2001.

Language-independent Query Representation for IR Model Parameter Estimation on Unlabeled Collections

Parantapa Goswami   Massih-Reza Amini   Eric Gaussier

Université Grenoble Alps,
CNRS-LIG/AMA
Grenoble, France

firstname.lastname@imag.fr

ABSTRACT

We study here the problem of estimating the parameters of standard IR models (as BM25 or language models) on new collections without any relevance judgments, by using collections with already available relevance judgements. We propose different query representations that allow mapping queries (with and without relevance judgments, from different collections potentially in different languages) into a common space. We then introduce a kernel regression approach to learn the parameters of standard IR models individually for each query in the new, unlabeled collection. Our experiments, conducted on standard English and Indian IR collections, show that our approach can be used to efficiently tune, query by query, standard IR models to new collections, potentially written in different languages. In particular, the versions of the standard IR models we obtain not only outperform the versions with default parameters, but can also outperform the versions in which the parameter values have been optimized globally over a set of queries with target relevance judgements.

Categories and Subject Descriptors

H.3 [**Information Storage and Retrieval**]: Information Search and Retrieval - Search process; I.2 [**Artificial Intelligence**]: Learning - Parameter learning

General Terms

Algorithms, Experimentation, Theory

Keywords

IR Theory; Learning IR Parameters; Transfer learning;

1. INTRODUCTION

In many situations, one has to deploy IR models on new collections (on new domains or languages) from scratch. In

ICTIR'15, September 27–30, Northampton, MA, USA.
ⓒ 2015 ACM. ISBN 978-1-4503-3833-2/15/09 ...$15.00.
DOI: http://dx.doi.org/10.1145/2808194.2809451.

such cases, developing relevance judgments so as to adapt the retrieval models to the new collections considered is a costly operation. An alternative is of course to simply rely on default parameters of the IR models, hoping that the results obtained will be reasonable, *i.e.* not too far away from the ones obtained by "adapting" the models (as we will see in Section 4, default results are reasonable on several collections, however not on all of them). This "default" strategy is the one traditionally adopted in IR evaluation campaigns (as TREC or CLEF) when new collections and languages are introduced. In fact, each time a collection changes substantially, *e.g.* through the introduction of new documents, then the IR models that are employed, should be adapted so as to follow the potential evolution of the collection.

Of course, one would like to perform such an adaptation at a minimal cost, and, ideally, without resorting to new, specific relevance judgments, albeit using any relevance judgments available on known, past collections. This is precisely the problem we are investigating in this study, focusing on learning the underlying parameter(s) of standard IR models as BM25 [20], language models (LM) [18] and information-based models (LGD) [7]. Our focus on these particular IR models is motivated by the fact that these models are the most widely used in different IR tasks (as *ad hoc* IR, structured IR or social IR for example) and serve as components of learning to rank models deployed *e.g.* on web collections. Thus, the fundamental problem we address can be formulated as follows: *How to infer the parameter values of standard IR models (BM25, LM, LGD) on collections without any relevance judgments by using past labeled collections?*

We will solve this problem, which relates to different research fields, as model adaptation or transfer learning, by mapping queries from different collections into common vector spaces in which regression functions can be efficiently learned. Two key elements of our approach are: (a) The method proposed allows to obtain parameter values for a single query, so that IR models are optimized per query on the new collection and (b) the representations used are language-independent, and parameter values can be estimated for new collections, in new languages, for any standard IR models.

The remainder of the paper is organized as follows. We first discuss related work in Section 2. We then describe in Section 3 the approach developed for learning the parameter(s) of standard IR models on collections with no relevance judgments, using known collections with relevance judgments. We then illustrate several aspects of the method we propose in Section 4 on several collections, prior to conclude in Section 5.

2. RELATED WORK

IR models are generally defined with free parameters, as the parameters b and k_1, k_3 for BM25 [19], the Dirichlet smoothing coefficient μ for language models with Dirichlet prior [11] and the c parameter for LGD [7]. These parameters are query and collection dependent and hence their tuning is unavoidable to achieve good performance. The necessity of empirical tuning of the parameters of traditional models has been advocated in different studies, as in [26]. In the case where the relevance judgments exist, the optimal values of these free parameters are generally found by testing different parameter values from a predefined set of discrete values for each parameter on a set of queries with associated relevance judgments, and then selecting the parameter values that lead to the best performance with respect to the evaluation measure considered. This greedy search has been found to be competitive compared to simple learning strategies that optimize some differentiable IR measures [23]. This said, creating new test collections, or manually assigning relevance judgments for even a small set of queries, is a tedious task [3].

Other studies directly considered the problem of unsupervised parameter estimation [26, 22]. In [26], an automated *leave-one-out* likelihood method to estimate the Dirichlet prior smoothing parameter μ on unlabeled collection is proposed; the study in [22] does not aim at estimating standard IR model parameters but rather focuses on pseudo-relevance feedback and makes use of a mixture model with a regularized expectation maximization method to estimate the feedback parameter. If these methods have been shown to work well on several collections, they were however developed under the language model framework with a probabilistic view over the generation of words, and cannot be (at least directly) applied to IR models outside the language model family. Some studies also focus on unlabeled collections [21, 25], but with a different, evaluation-oriented goal, namely the one of ranking different IR models. The assumptions and methods used in these studies radically differ from ours.

In between supervised methods, making use of relevance judgements on the collection queried, and unsupervised methods, that do not rely on such relevance judgements, lie methods (often referred to as *transfer* or *cross-domain* learning) that aim at exploiting past relevance judgements, available on some *source* collections, to learn models on unlabeled, *target* collections. Many efforts have indeed already been made to conceive and develop different collections through existing competitions like TREC, and one can wonder whether such annotated collections can be used for unannotated ones.

Several innovative studies have adapted cross-domain approaches to the IR learning to rank framework [5, 4, 8, 9]. While some of them made use of labeled queries in the source and a small set of labeled queries in the target to learn a ranking function [4], the others considered that only the source collection contains labeled information, while queries in the target collection have no associated relevance judgments. In [8, 2], the transfer learning is done by weighting documents in the source collection using unlabeled queries and documents from the target dataset. More precisely, a classifier is first learned aiming at discriminating source and target documents or queries on the basis of standard features similar to the ones used in learning to rank for IR. The score of the classifier on each source (query,document) pair is then used as an indicator of the proximity of this pair to the target collection. A ranking function is then learned on the source collection, with (query,document) pairs weighted according to their proximity to the target collection: the closer a pair is to the target collection, the more importance it will have in the learning process. This approach has been shown to work in the uncommon case where the source and target collections are close to each other. However, when the two collections are far away, then the model learned is not appropriate. To address this problem, [9] proposed a transfer technique approach that relies on relative relevance judgement pairs induced on the target collection from a set of source queries.

Our approach differs from these ones in that we are focusing on learning the parameter values of standard IR models, whereas default values of these models are used in the above studies. Standard IR models are used in many IR tasks and any procedure that can improve their performance on new, unlabeled collections will be beneficial to the IR community. Our approach also differs from the ones proposed in [26] and [22] (discussed above) in that we are proposing a solution that can be used for *any* standard IR model, and not only for the language model family. The representation we are using however bears some similarity with the one used in [26] as they both use query representations based on word frequency distributions over the collections considered (see Section 3). We are however using a richer summary of these distributions through the use of their three first moments. Similar to what is done in [22, 14], we are learning parameter values per query (different target queries may use different parameter values), and are relying, as [14], on a regression framework to do so. If this latter study is close in spirit to ours, it also has some significant differences. In particular, we consider here the standard *ad hoc* IR setting and IR models from different families, whereas [14] focuses on pseudo-relevance feedback for relevance models. Because of this difference, we rely on different features and query representations and, from them, on different regression functions (our query representation calls for kernel regression methods whereas standard regression functions are used in [14]).

3. LEARNING IR MODEL PARAMETERS ON UNLABELED COLLECTIONS

In the remainder, the unlabeled collection queried will be referred to as the *target* collection whereas a collection available with relevance judgements will be referred to as the *source* collection (possibly formed by merging several existing collections). We place ourselves here in a standard *ad hoc* IR setting, only assuming that one has access to standard tools on the target, unlabeled collection (stop-word list and stemming procedure). This corresponds to a standard, general situation, but the methodology we propose can directly be applied if one has access to additional resources and tools on both the source and target collections. Our goal is to learn the parameters of standard IR models on a target, unlabeled collection by transferring relevance information from a source collection, so to improve over the performance obtained with parameters set to their default values. Two questions that directly arise are:

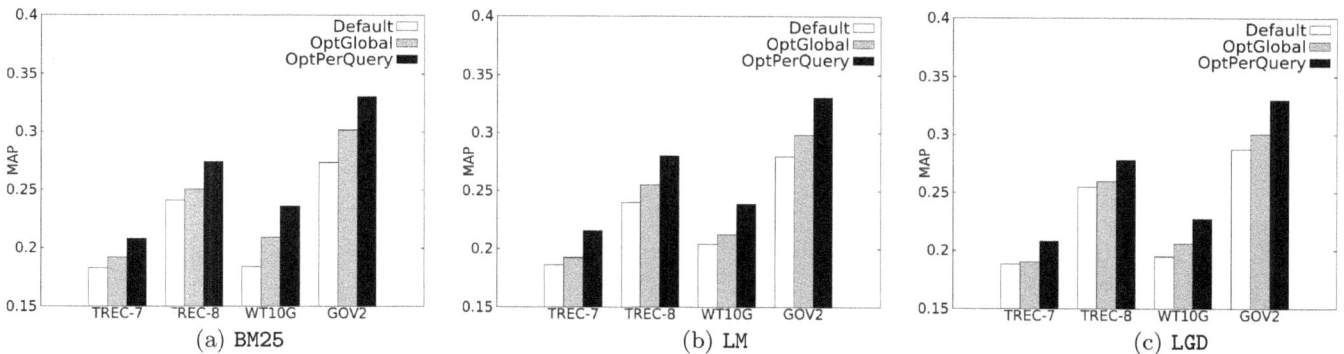

Figure 1: Performance of IR models with default parameter values (□), parameters optimized within the whole collection (▨) and per query basis (■). The results are in terms of MAP on TREC-7,8, WT10G and GOV2 collections for (a) BM25, (b) LM, and (c) LGD IR models.

1. What is the upper bound on the gain one can have over the default strategy corresponding to setting the parameters to their default values? In other words, is it worth trying to improve over this strategy?

2. What are the upper bounds of methods estimating parameter values globally over all queries and of methods estimating those values query per query? In other words, is it worth trying to find parameter estimates individually for each query?

To answer these questions, we computed the mean average precision (MAP) of three standard IR models (BM25, the Dirichlet language model LM and the log-logistic model LGD) on four collections (TREC-7, TREC-8, WT10G and GOV2)[1] with three different settings:

(a) Using the default parameter values of each model;

(b) Selecting, in a given set of values (described in Table 2), the parameter value that provides the highest MAP on all target queries (this makes use of the relevance judgements on the target collection). The associated MAP corresponds to the upper bound of methods aiming at finding the best value globally for all queries;

(c) Selecting, in the same given set of values and for each query, the parameter value that provides the highest average precision for the query (as before, this makes use of the relevance judgements on the target collection). The mean of all the average precisions obtained in this way yields a MAP value that corresponds to the upper bound of methods aiming at finding the best value individually per query.

The results obtained are displayed in Figure 1. As one can note, the difference between default values and optimized ones varies according to the model and the collection considered. This difference is relatively small, in the range [0, 2.5%] for all collections and models, when the optimization is performed globally over all queries. It is more important when the optimization is performed query by query, even though the improvement varies from one collection to another: around 2 to 3% for all models on TREC-7,8, around 5 to 6% for all models on GOV2 and WT10G, the difference being however less marked for LGD. These results show firstly

---
[1]The collections are described in Section 4.

that it may not be possible to obtain significant improvements over default values on all collections, as such values yield results close to the best possible ones, and secondly that higher gains can be expected by estimating the parameters per query.

Estimating parameter values per query is not necessarily a difficult task. Indeed, from a source collection and a given representation of queries, one can learn, using the relevance judgements as in the setting (c) above, a regression function that can then be used to associate parameter values to new queries. However, in order to apply such a regression function on target queries, one needs to rely on a representation of queries common to both the source and target collections.

3.1 Query representation

We consider a source collection $\mathcal{S}$, composed of a set of documents $\mathcal{D}^s$, a set of n queries $\mathcal{Q}^s = \{q_1^s, \ldots, q_n^s\}$ and relevance judgments for each query in $\mathcal{Q}^s$. Furthermore, we consider a target collection $\mathcal{T}$, composed of a set of documents $\mathcal{D}^t$ and a set of u queries $\mathcal{Q}^t = \{q_1^t, \ldots, q_u^t\}$ without any relevance judgments. Each query q, in any collection, is constituted by a set of terms $q = \{w_1^q, \ldots, w_{|q|}^q\}$, corresponding to the standard representation of queries. It is however not possible to rely here on this simple query representation as different collections use different vocabularies, potentially from different languages.

Representation based on the tf distribution

In order to bypass the above problem, we extend the idea of [26], who assumed that the distribution of query words regarding relevant documents does not vary from source to target collections, by considering that two queries are similar if the words they contain have similar idf (inverse document frequency) and tf (term frequency) distributions over their collections. As the tf distributions of source and target words are often high-dimensional and may differ in length (as the collections contain different documents), we rely here on a summary of these distributions obtained through the estimates of their first (mean), second (standard deviation) and third (skewness) moments, respectively denoted by $\mu(q)$, $\sigma(w)$ and $sk(w)$ for a given word w. For a bounded distribution, like the term frequency distribution here, combination of the moments of all orders (from 0 to ∞) uniquely determines the distribution. Thus the first three moments can be considered to define a natural summary of the distribution of the term frequency scores of the word in the collection.

We finally obtain the following representation of a query in which each query word corresponds to a 4-dimensional vector[2]:

$$\begin{cases} q = \{\mathbf{w}_1^q, \ldots, \mathbf{w}_{|q|}^q\} \\ \mathbf{w}^q = (idf(w^q), \mu(w^q), \sigma(w^q), sk(w^q)) \end{cases} \qquad (1)$$

where $idf(w)$ denote the inverse document frequency of the word w.

Learning extended representations with auto-encoders

We further investigate the possibility to enhance the proposed tf and idf based representation (Eq. 1) using an Auto-Encoder (AE). AEs [10] are a family of feed-forward neural networks that are trained to reconstruct the input data by performing two steps. In the first step, an input vector from $\mathbb{R}^d$ is projected to a space $\mathbb{R}^a$, called encoding, using non-linear bijective functions. In the second step, the encoded vector is projected into the original space of dimension d using again non-linear bijective functions. These models have been found effective to extract text or image representations as it has been shown that the neurons of the hidden layer are able to detect generic concepts [13, 12]. The AE model that we developed is trained using stochastic back-propagation algorithm [1] over all the 4-dimensional vector representation of terms ($d = 4$) that are in the source and the target collections[3]. After this step, any query q is then represented as a set of term vectors:

$$\begin{cases} q = \{\mathbf{w}_1^q, \ldots, \mathbf{w}_{|q|}^q\} \\ \mathbf{w}_j^q : \text{ vector found by the auto-encoder} \end{cases} \qquad (2)$$

From these mappings we finally learn the association between query representations and parameter values, as described in the next section.

3.2 Learning the regression function

For each query in the source collection, one can obtain, as mentioned before, the optimal value of the parameter of each of the standard models BM25, LM and LGD. The vector collecting these optimal values for each query in $\mathcal{Q}^s$ will be denoted by $\mathbf{c}_{opt}^s = (c_{q_1^s}, \ldots, c_{q_n^s})^\top$, where $^\top$ corresponds to the transpose operator. Using the association between queries in $\mathcal{Q}^s$ and $\mathbf{c}_{opt}^s$ and relying on a common vector space for queries, one can learn a regression function that maps any query in $\mathcal{Q}^t$ to a parameter value. Figure 2 illustrates this procedure.

In order to use regression methods, one first needs to define a common vector space for queries. We do so by introducing kernels that directly operate on the representations defined above.

Simple PDS kernels

Starting from the representations of queries defined above ($q = \{\mathbf{w}_1^q, \ldots, \mathbf{w}_{|q|}^q\}$, with $\mathbf{w}^q$ obtained either through the idf and tf distribution or from an auto-encoder), we first

---

[2]This corresponds to two additional dimensions wrt the idf and tf measures traditionally considered for query words.
[3]Note that the vectors of terms, as defined in equation 1, do not involve the knowledge of relevance judgments.

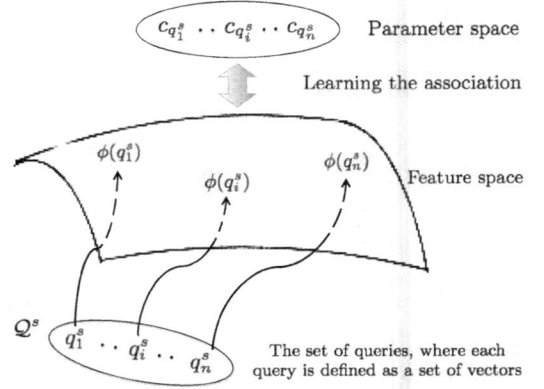

Figure 2: Each target query is mapped in the common vector space and an associated parameter of the IR model is predicted using the learned association model.

consider the following convolution kernel[4]:

$$\kappa_{\text{all}}(q, q') = \frac{1}{|q|}\frac{1}{|q'|}\sum_{i=1}^{|q|}\sum_{j=1}^{|q'|}\left\langle \mathbf{w}_i^q, \mathbf{w}_j^{q'} \right\rangle \qquad (3)$$

Exploiting twice the bi-linearity of the dot product, one has:

$$\begin{aligned} \kappa_{\text{all}}(q, q') &= \frac{1}{|q|}\frac{1}{|q'|}\left(\left\langle \sum_{i=1}^{|q|}\mathbf{w}_i^q, \sum_{j=1}^{|q'|}\mathbf{w}_j^{q'} \right\rangle\right) \\ &= \left\langle \sum_{i=1}^{|q|}\frac{\mathbf{w}_i^q}{|q|}, \sum_{j=1}^{|q'|}\frac{\mathbf{w}_j^{q'}}{|q'|} \right\rangle \end{aligned}$$

The mapping ϕ associated with the above kernel takes the form:

$$\phi(q) = \sum_{i=1}^{|q|}\frac{\mathbf{w}_i^q}{|q|} \qquad (4)$$

ϕ thus corresponds to the average of the vectors of the words present in q and κ_{all} amounts to the dot product between the average word vectors of each query:

$$\kappa_{\text{all}}(q, q') = \langle \phi(q), \phi(q') \rangle \qquad (5)$$

From the form above, one can further define new kernels, by substituting the dot product in equation (5) by any valid PDS kernel. We consider here homogeneous polynomial kernels and Gaussian kernels, widely used in text processing, leading to:

$$\begin{aligned} \kappa_{\text{poly-}\delta}(q, q') &= (\langle \phi(q), \phi(q') \rangle)^\delta \\ \kappa_{\text{gau-}\sigma}(q, q') &= \exp(-\frac{||\phi(q) - \phi(q')||_2^2}{2\sigma^2}) \end{aligned}$$

where δ corresponds to the degree of the polynomial kernel and σ to the standard deviation of the Gaussian kernel.

These different kernels can be used with different kernel regression methods. In this study, we rely on kernel Support Vector Regression (kernel SVR) [24] as this method has been shown to perform well in practice.

---

[4]The subscript "all" in κ_{all} denotes the fact that all pairs of words, from the two queries, are compared.

Kernel regression

Let κ denote any of the above-defined kernels and let $\mathbf{K}$ be the associated Gram (or kernel) matrix ($\mathbf{K}_{i,j} = \kappa(q_i^s, q_j^s)$, $1 \leq i, j \leq n$). From the training set $\{(q_i^s, c_{q_i^s}), 1 \leq i \leq n\}$, the goal of kernel SVR is to learn a regression function in the kernel-induced feature space (potentially of infinite dimension) in order to associate to any new query q^t a parameter value c_{q^t}. The optimization problem for kernel SVR takes the following dual form (see for example [16]):

KSVR-opt:

$$\max_{\boldsymbol{\alpha},\boldsymbol{\alpha}'} -\epsilon(\boldsymbol{\alpha}' + \boldsymbol{\alpha})^{\top}\mathbf{1} + (\boldsymbol{\alpha}' - \boldsymbol{\alpha})^{\top}\mathbf{c}_{opt}^s - \frac{1}{2}(\boldsymbol{\alpha}' - \boldsymbol{\alpha})^{\top}\mathbf{K}(\boldsymbol{\alpha}' - \boldsymbol{\alpha})$$
$$\text{s. t. } 0 \leq \alpha_i, \alpha_i' \leq C (1 \leq i \leq n), \ (\boldsymbol{\alpha}' - \boldsymbol{\alpha})^{\top}\mathbf{1} = 0$$

where $\mathbf{1} \in \mathbb{R}^n$ is a vector containing only 1s and C and ϵ are hyper-parameters usually set through cross-validation (C serves as a regularization parameter and ϵ controls the accuracy with which errors are measured). $\boldsymbol{\alpha}, \boldsymbol{\alpha}' \in \mathbb{R}^n$ are the parameters to be learned and are such that either α_i or α_i' is non null (this happens if q_i^s is a support vector), or they are both null (if q_i^s is not a support vector).

The above optimization problem is a convex quadratic programming problem that can be solved by any convex QP solver. The value predicted for a new query q^t in the target collection is obtained by:

$$c_{q^t} = \sum_{i=1}^{n} (\alpha_i' - \alpha_i)\kappa(q_i^s, q^t) + b_i \quad (6)$$

the offset b_l being defined for any support vector q_l^s by:

$$b_l = \sum_{i=1}^{n} (\alpha_i - \alpha_i')\kappa(q_i^s, q_l^s) + c_{q_l^s} + \epsilon \quad (7)$$

The overall process for predicting the parameter value of standard IR models on new, unlabeled collections can thus be summarized as follows. For each free parameter of the standard IR model under consideration:

1. Training step: Compute $\mathbf{c}_{opt}^s$ in $\mathcal{Q}^s$ and solve the KSVR-opt problem above with any convex QP solver;

2. Prediction: For each query of the target collection q^t, compute c_{q^t} through equations (6) and (7).

4. EXPERIMENTS

We present in this section experiments aimed at evaluating the validity of the approach described before.

4.1 Collections

We perform experiments on nine IR collections: one from CLEF[5], six from TREC[6] and two non-English collections from FIRE[7] containing Hindi and Bengali documents and queries. Basic statistics on these collections are provided in Table 1. We appended TREC-9 and TREC-10 Web tracks to experiment with WT10G, and TREC-2004 and TREC-2005 Terabyte tracks for experimenting with GOV2. Experiments are performed on the Terrier IR platform v3.5 (terrier.org) [17], and as for WEB oriented ad-hoc IR, we only considered the title of queries and dropped their descriptions. The preprocessing

[5] www.clef-campaign.org
[6] trec.nist.gov
[7] www.isical.ac.in/~clia/

Collection	$\mathcal{N}$	l_{avg}	Index size	#queries
GOV2	25,177,217	646	19.6 GB	100
WT10G	1,692,096	398	1.3 GB	100
FIRE-BN	500,122	245	498.6 MB	50
TREC-3	741,856	261	427.7 MB	50
TREC-4	567,529	323	379.0 MB	50
TREC-5	524,929	339	378.0 MB	50
TREC-6,7,8	528,155	296	373.0 MB	50
FIRE-HN	331,599	178	225.5 MB	50
CLEF-3	169,477	301	126.2 MB	60

Table 1: Statistics of various collections used in our experiments, sorted by size.

steps in creating an index include stemming using Porter stemmer and removing stop-words using the stop-word list provided by Terrier. On FIRE collections, we used the stop-word lists available at the corresponding website, but did not use any stemmer.

In most of our experiments, we considered CLEF-3, TREC-3,4,5,6 as source collections, and used TREC-7,8, WT10G and GOV2 for testing. In order to see how the projection in the query space is dependent to the languages of the source and target collections, we also tested our strategy by learning the regression model on English collections WT10G, GOV2 and predicting model parameters on both FIRE collections, as well as the other way around by learning the regression model on FIRE collections and predicting model parameters on WT10G and GOV2. Results are evaluated using the mean average precision, MAP, and precision at 10 documents, P@10 (relevance judgments on the target collections are just used for evaluating the models). As MAP is the measure retained in our experiments to construct c_{opt}^s it is the one we privilege in our discussions (other measures, as P@10 or NDCG could of course be used to construct c_{opt}^s and estimate model parameters) whereas the P@10 is given as a illustrator of the behavior of the methods. A Wilcoxon statistical test, with a p-value of $p = 0.05$, is used to assess whether the difference, in terms of MAP, between two methods is significant or not.

4.2 Experimental setup

We used three different, widely used, IR ranking models, namely BM25, the language model with Dirichlet smoothing (LM), and the log-logistic information-based model LGD from the Divergence from Randomness family, and compared the performance of these models with their default values ($b = 0.75$ for BM25, $\mu = 2500.0$ for LM and $c = 1.0$ for LGD) against the values predicted by the proposed regression approach on target collections. In order to better evaluate the effect of parameter learning on each single free-parameter alone, we just considered the parameter b of BM25 and kept its two other parameters fixed to their default values ($k_1 = 1.2$ and $k_2 = 8.0$) in all of our experiments[8].

Finally, the number of neurons in the hidden layer of the auto-encoder was fixed by cross-validation on the source collections by considering numbers varying from 5 to 20. In all of our experiments, we used a server with an intel Xenon 1.8HGz processor and 16GB of RAM. The training time for learning the representations on this machine, with a maxi-

[8] The codes we used can be found on http://ama.liglab.fr/resourcestools/ir-parameter-learning/

			TREC-7		TREC-8		WT10G		GOV2	
			MAP	P@10	MAP	P@10	MAP	P@10	MAP	P@10
BM25	def		$18.28^{\downarrow}$	*41.80*	$24.09^{\downarrow}$	*47.40*	$18.42^{\downarrow}$	*29.10*	$27.39^{\downarrow}$	*53.84*
	κ_{all}-SVR	★	19.03	*43.01*	**24.95**	*47.20*	**20.52**	*30.90*	**30.31**	*58.79*
		†	**19.05**	*43.20*	24.92	*46.60*	**20.52**	*31.10*	30.09	*58.89*
LM	def		$18.63^{\downarrow}$	*39.20*	$24.01^{\downarrow}$	*43.20*	$20.40^{\downarrow}$	*29.30*	$27.98^{\downarrow}$	*54.45*
	loo [26]		19.06	*43.40*	**25.48**	*45.40*	**21.24**	*30.90*	$28.46^{\downarrow}$	*53.64*
	κ_{all}-SVR	★	19.14	*41.20*	$24.73^{\downarrow}$	*44.80*	21.02	*30.10*	29.44	*55.76*
		†	**19.16**	*41.40*	$24.76^{\downarrow}$	*45.00*	21.06	*30.80*	**29.56**	*54.85*
LGD	def		18.82	*42.80*	25.47	*47.40*	$19.49^{\downarrow}$	*28.70*	$28.76^{\downarrow}$	*54.14*
	κ_{all}-SVR	★	**19.00**	*44.20*	**25.64**	*46.60*	**20.02**	*29.10*	**29.62**	*56.46*
		†	18.99	*43.80*	25.60	*46.40*	19.94	*29.11*	29.49	*56.26*

Table 3: Comparison of IR models with parameters set to their default values (def) against the predicted parameter values obtained with the leave-one-out strategy [26] (loo) for LM, and the proposed κ_{all}-SVR approach for all models in terms of MAP and P@10 (in %). For κ_{all}-SVR, results are presented when terms are coded as in equation 1 (in ★) or equation 2 (in †). The regressor is trained to optimize the average precision of each query on the source collection. For MAP, best results are shown in bold and ↓ indicates that the result is worse than the best one according to a Wilcoxon rank sum test with $p < .05$.

		TREC-7		TREC-8		WT10G		GOV2	
		MAP	P@10	MAP	P@10	MAP	P@10	MAP	P@10
BM25	κ_{all}	**19.03**	*43.01*	**24.95**	*47.20*	20.52	*30.90*	**30.31**	*58.79*
	κ_{poly-2}	18.98	*42.80*	24.89	*46.60*	20.50	*30.80*	29.93	*58.48*
	κ_{poly-3}	18.97	*42.80*	24.89	*46.80*	20.50	*30.80*	29.94	*58.38*
	κ_{poly-4}	18.97	*42.80*	24.90	*46.80*	20.49	*31.00*	29.94	*58.48*
	κ_{gau-10}	19.01	*43.00*	24.91	*47.00*	20.54	*31.10*	29.99	*58.18*
	κ_{gau-50}	19.00	*43.00*	24.91	*46.80*	20.58	*31.20*	29.99	*58.18*
	$\kappa_{gau-100}$	19.00	*43.00*	24.92	*46.80*	**20.59**	*31.20*	29.99	*58.18*

Table 4: Comparison of different kernels in SVR in terms of MAP and P@10 on TREC-7,8, WT10G and GOV2 for BM25. The different kernels used are (a) kernel κ_{all}, (b) polynomial kernels with $\delta = 2$, $\delta = 3$ and $\delta = 4$ ($\kappa_{poly-\delta}$) and (c) Gaussian kernels with $\sigma = 10.0$, $\sigma = 50.0$, $\sigma = 70.0$ and $\sigma = 100.0$ ($\kappa_{gau-\sigma}$).

b (BM25)	$0.1, 0.2, 0.3, 0.4, 0.5, 0.6, 0.7, 0.8, 0.9, 1.0,$ $1.25, 1.5, 1.75, 2.0, 2.25, 2.5, 2.75, 3.0$
μ (LM)	$10, 25, 50, 75, 100, 200, 300, 400, 500, 600,$ $700, 800, 900, 1000, 1500, 2000, 2500, 3000,$ $4000, 5000, 10000$
c (LGD)	$0.1, 0.5, 1.0, 1.5, 2.0, 2.5, 3.0, 3.5, 4.0, 4.5,$ $5.0, 6.0, 7.0, 8.0, 9.0, 10.0, 20.0$

Table 2: Set of values considered to find the optimal parameter values on the source collection of the different IR models.

mum number of iterations fixed to 60 000 000, was less than 10 minutes.

The vectors $\mathbf{c}_{opt}^{s}$ of optimized parameter values on the source collection are constructed by selecting, for each source query and IR model, the value that provides the highest average precision. Table 2 gives the different values considered for each model parameter. As kernel SVR (κ_{all}-SVR), we used the LIBSVM[9] implementation of ϵ-SVR, by fixing ϵ to 0.1, the hyper-parameter C is found by cross-validation on the training set. Each query q here is represented by the vector $\phi(q)$ given in equation (4).

4.3 Experimental results

---

[9] http://www.csie.ntu.edu.tw/~cjlin/libsvm/

In this section, we first assess whether the method we propose improves over the one based on default parameter values. We further compare our approach to the two upper bounds introduced in Section 3, prior to illustrate its use on collections written in different languages. Lastly, we investigate the behavior of the method with respect to the number of queries used for training, and its execution time.

4.3.1 Learned values vs default ones

We first evaluate the proposed transfer approach for parameter tuning by comparing the performance of different IR models (a) with their default parameter values, denoted by def, and (b) with their parameter values estimated by the *leave-one-out* (loo) strategy [26] (for the LM model only), against SVR based on the simple kernel κ_{all} (see Section 3), denoted by κ_{all}-SVR, (for all IR models). For the latter, we considered both term representations based on the *tf* distributions (Eq. 1) and those learned with the auto-encoding model (Eq. 2). Table 3 summarizes these results.

We first note that the performance of IR models with their default values over different collections are in line with those reported in studies which also considered query titles [6, 15]. Further, the proposed method yields MAP results significantly higher according to a Wilcoxon rank sum test with $p < .05$ than the ones obtained with the default values on all models and collections except for LGD on TREC-7,8, for which there is no significant difference between the two. Further, considering the LM model, we see that both κ_{all}-SVR and loo

			FIRE-HN		FIRE-BN		WT10G		GOV2	
			MAP	P@10	MAP	P@10	MAP	P@10	MAP	P@10
BM25	def		$29.46^{\downarrow}$	*45.40*	$14.09^{\downarrow}$	*24.80*	$18.42^{\downarrow}$	*29.10*	$27.39^{\downarrow}$	*53.84*
	κ_{all}-SVR	★	30.29	*47.80*	15.32	*26.80*	**20.75**	*32.50*	**30.17**	*58.08*
		†	**30.33**	*48.20*	**15.35**	*27.20*	**20.75**	*32.50*	30.10	*58.48*
LM	def		$26.82^{\downarrow}$	*46.40*	15.35	*25.20*	$20.40^{\downarrow}$	*29.30*	$27.98^{\downarrow}$	*55.45*
	κ_{all}-SVR	★	**28.39**	*47.40*	**15.76**	*26.40*	**21.05**	*30.60*	**29.33**	*55.15*
		†	28.03	*48.20*	15.75	*26.00*	**21.05**	*30.50*	**29.33**	*54.85*
LGD	def		**30.92**	*46.40*	**15.67**	*28.40*	19.49	*28.70*	$28.76^{\downarrow}$	*54.14*
	κ_{all}-SVR	★	30.78	*48.80*	15.66	*28.20*	**19.85**	*30.40*	**29.05**	*54.55*
		†	30.67	*49.00*	15.64	*27.80*	19.81	*30.30*	28.88	*56.87*
			(a)				**(b)**			

Table 5: MAP and P@10 measures (in %) of IR models with their default parameters (def) and predicted ones using the κ_{all}-SVR strategy on *non-English* FIRE target collections when using WT10G and GOV2 as source collections (a), and on WT10G and GOV2 target collections when using *non-English* FIRE as source collections (b). For κ_{all}-SVR, results are presented when terms are coded as in equation 1 (in ★) or equation 2 (in †). The regressor is trained to optimize the average precision of each query on the source collection. For MAP, best results are shown in bold and a result with ↓ is significantly worse than the best one according to a Wilcoxon rank sum test with $p < .05$.

[26] behave the same across different collections : the performance of LM with parameters found by loo are significantly better on TREC-8 while they are significantly better with parameters found by κ_{all}-SVR on GOV2. As both approaches model the distribution of terms, these results confirm that query terms are distributed likely the same over relevant documents on source and target collections. The difference is however that loo can only be applied to probabilistic IR models using maximum likelihood estimates while the distribution of terms with the κ_{all}-SVR strategy is coded in their vector representations allowing the approach to tune the parameters of more general IR models. Moreover, different term encodings we employed (Eq. 1 and Eq. 2) do not affect the performance of κ_{all}-SVR as the predicted parameters for different IR models with these two settings are slightly the same over different collections. These results suggest that the features space induced by κ_{all}-SVR captures the main information of word distributions by just using the initial word features.

As conjectured in Section 3, the difference between the default values and the approach proposed varies from one collection to the other, and from one model to the other. Indeed, as mentioned before, the difference is not significant for LGD on TREC-7 and TREC-8, which corresponds to two smallest differences between the default values and the upper bounds displayed in Figure 1. There is in this case little room for improvement over the default values.

We also compare the method proposed with the different kernels introduced in Section 3: κ_{all}, $\kappa_{\text{poly}-\delta}$ and $\kappa_{\text{gau}-\sigma}$ with different values for the parameters δ and σ. Table 4 shows those results in terms of MAP and P@10 for BM25[10]. As one can note, the different kernels yield very similar results, without any significant difference between them. This is not really surprising, but still needed experimental confirmation, as the space in which κ_{all} operates is based on (Eq. 1) in which linear kernels are likely to behave well; κ_{all} amounts to a dot product in this space, and the extra dimensions brought by the polynomial and Gaussian kernels are of no

---

[10]For sake of space, we did not report the same kind of results obtained with LM and LGD models.

use here. We thus focus on κ_{all} in the remainder of this study.

4.3.2 Learning from a source dataset of different language than the unlabeled target collection

We investigate here whether κ_{all}-SVR behaves well when the source and target collections considered are written in different languages. To this end, we performed two kind of experiments:

1. We first trained κ_{all}-SVR on WT10G and GOV2 collections and tested it on non-English (Hindi and Bengali) FIRE collections;

2. We then performed the reciprocal experiment by training κ_{all}-SVR on both FIRE collections and testing on WT10G and GOV2 collections.

MAP and P@10 results are respectively reported in Table 5. Except for LGD on FIRE and WT10G collections, one can note that in all other cases, IR models with their predicted free-parameters perform significantly better than with their default values. Furthermore, one can note note that the MAP measures of all IR models for the collections WT10G and GOV2 are similar to the ones reported in Table 3. The representation of queries is based on *tf* moments of query words across a given collection, which allows one to use collections in different languages to learn the regressor, as illustrated in this experiment.

4.3.3 Learned values vs optimized ones

We now compare the results obtained by the method developed in this study and the ones corresponding to two "ideal" cases. The first ideal case corresponds to the scenario in which some target queries (50% in our experiment) are associated with relevance judgements and are used to estimate the parameters of each IR model while the remaining (50%) queries are used for testing. The second ideal case corresponds to the upper bounds already discussed in Section 3 where all the relevance judgements on the target collections are used to optimize the parameters either globally for all queries or query by query.

		TREC-7		TREC-8		WT10G		GOV2	
		MAP	P@10	MAP	P@10	MAP	P@10	MAP	P@10
BM25	10split_{mean}	18.20↓	*41.92*	24.53	*45.52*	19.61↓	*30.94*	**30.54**	*60.18*
	10split_{var}	0.029	*0.053*	0.121	*0.149*	0.046	*0.048*	0.022	*0.041*
	$\kappa_{\mathbf{all}}$-SVR	**19.03**	*43.01*	**24.95**	*47.20*	**20.52**	*30.90*	30.31	*58.79*
LM	10split_{mean}	18.21↓	*42.24*	**25.45**	*45.36*	19.67↓	*30.76*	**30.19**	*56.79*
	10split_{var}	0.035	*0.115*	0.048	*0.059*	0.052	*0.062*	0.019	*0.096*
	$\kappa_{\mathbf{all}}$-SVR	**19.14**	*41.20*	24.73	*44.80*	**21.02**	*30.10*	29.44	*55.76*
LGD	10split_{mean}	18.03↓	*43.04*	**26.08**	*45.84*	19.24↓	*29.08*	**30.26**	*59.01*
	10split_{var}	0.039	*0.167*	0.048	*0.079*	0.053	*0.037*	0.023	*0.088*
	$\kappa_{\mathbf{all}}$-SVR	**19.00**	*44.20*	25.64	*46.60*	**20.02**	*29.10*	29.62	*56.46*

Table 6: Comparison of IR models with optimized parameter values using 10 random splits, against the predicted parameter values using $\kappa_{\mathbf{all}}$-SVR in terms of MAP and P@10 (in %). The regressor is trained to optimize the average precision of each query on the source collection. For MAP, best results are shown in bold and a result with ↓ is significantly worse than the best one according to a Wilcoxon rank sum test with $p < .05$.

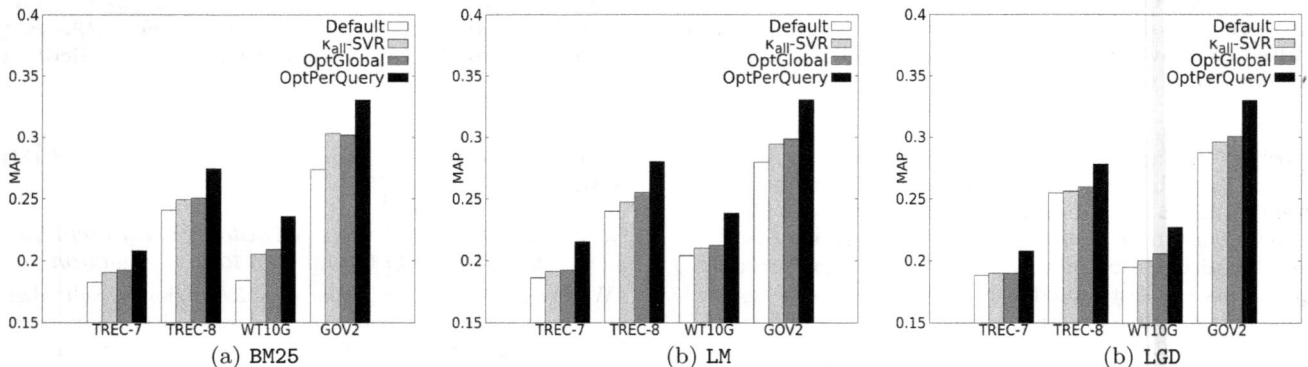

Figure 3: Comparison of IR models with parameters optimized per query basis (■) and optimized within the whole collection (■) against the predicted parameter values using $\kappa_{\mathbf{all}}$-SVR (▨) and default parameter values (□). The results are in terms of MAP on TREC-7,8, WT10G and GOV2 collections for (a) BM25 (b) LM and (c) LGD.

In the first case, we performed 10 random splits of the target queries, using 50% for training and 50% for testing, and report the average and variance obtained over the 10 splits. The training simply consists in selecting the parameter value that yields the best MAP value on the training set. We denote this method 10split. Table 6 displays the results obtained in this setting, together with the ones obtained by our approach. As one can note, the variance is always very small, for all models and collections and for both MAP and P@10, showing that the results remain stable even though the query set considered for training changes. Another interesting fact is that our approach, which does not make use of any relevance judgements on the collection queried, is either better or on a par with the 10split method which uses 25 (for TREC-7,8) or 50 (for WT10G and GOV2) queries with their relevance judgements on each collection.

We finally compare our approach to the ideal situation when the relevance judgements of all target queries are used. Let us recall that this ideal situation provides both an upper bound for the methods selecting a global parameter value for the query set, and an upper bound for the methods selecting a parameter value for each query. Figure 3, which parallels Figure 1 of Section 3, shows the comparison of this ideal situation with respect to our approach and the one relying on default parameters. The first point that one can note is that the results obtained by $\kappa_{\mathbf{all}}$-SVR are very close to the ones of the upper bound of the global optimization

methods (second and third bars on each set of histograms). A Wilcoxon test revealed no significant difference between them, whatever the collection, whatever the model. This shows that our approach is at least as good as any method optimizing IR parameters globally over all queries, whether this method uses relevance judgements or not (the def and 10split strategies are such methods, outperformed, as we have seen before, by our approach).

The second point to notice is that our approach is still 2 to 4% below the upper bound for methods providing optimal parameters per query. This suggests that there is still room for improvement over the approach considered in this study.

Finally, the predicted parameter values for all IR models obtained with $\kappa_{\mathbf{all}}$-SVR are in the ranges of those used to learn the regressor (table 2) with the difference that these predicted real-value parameters are not exactly the same with the latter values.

4.3.4 The effect of the number of queries for training

We also analyze the behavior of the IR models for an increasing number of queries in $\mathcal{Q}^s$ for training the $\kappa_{\mathbf{all}}$-SVR model. Figure 4, illustrates this by showing the evolution of MAP on WT10G and GOV2 with respect to the size of $\mathcal{Q}^s$. To create $\mathcal{Q}^s$, we randomly selected queries from CLEF-3, TREC-3,4,5,6 source collections. As expected all performance curves increase monotonically with respect to the additional training queries, though the increase reaches rapidly

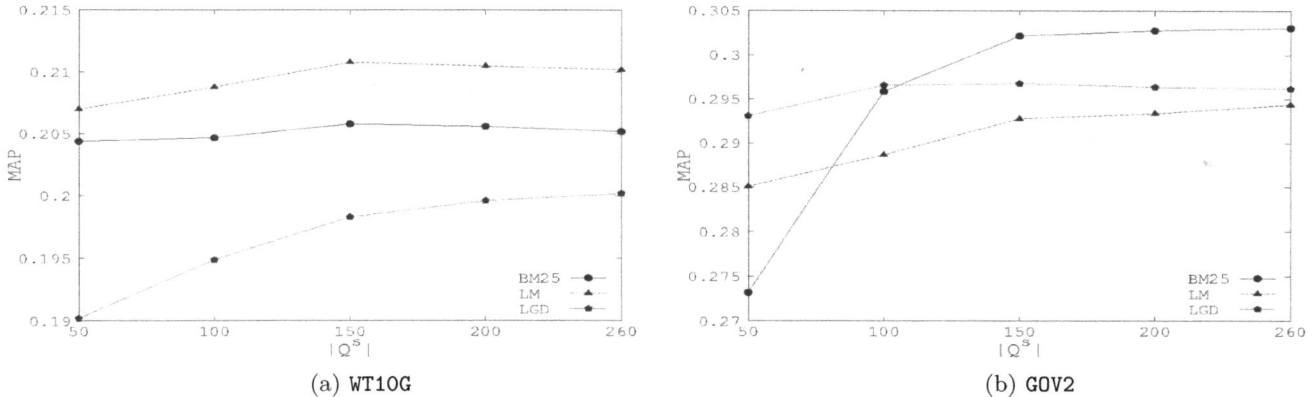

(a) WT10G   (b) GOV2

Figure 4: Evolution of MAP for BM25, LM and LGD on (a) WT10G and (b) GOV2 collections with respect to the size of $\mathcal{Q}^s$. The queries constituting $\mathcal{Q}^s$ are randomly sampled from the collections CLEF-3 and TREC-3,4,5,6.

a plateau and 150 queries seem sufficient on both collections to learn the regressor at the basis of our method. The findings of these results are (a) that a simple linear model is sufficient to learn the association between the mapping of queries in the vector space (Equation 4) and their desired parameter values, and (b) that with a limited amount of source labeled queries, the κ_{all}-SVR model is able to predict accurate parameter values.

4.3.5 Time considerations

As our approach estimates a value for each query, it is important to measure the extra time needed, per query, for this estimation. The word vectors defined by Eq. 1 can be computed offline and stored in the traditional way IDF scores are stored. This means that the query representation defined by Eq. 4 can be computed with (almost) no extra burden. The step that requires additional time with respect to standard IR models is the one corresponding to the application of the regression function on the target query, given by Eq. 6.

As one can note, this step involves the computation of a limited number (at most n, the number of source queries) of dot products between 4-dimensional vectors. One can thus conjecture that the extra time for this step is limited. Here extra time taken for every query is first measured and then the average is calculated for all three models on TREC-7,8, WT10G and GOV2. Table 7 gives this average extra time. As one can note, this extra time is in the range $15 - 30$ milliseconds, and can be easily decreased by parallelizing the different dot products (by e.g. devoting one core to each source query).

	average extra time taken (milisec.)			
	TREC-7	TREC-8	WT10G	GOV2
BM25	31.22	31.03	16.81	16.99
LM	30.89	31.80	17.23	16.94
LGD	31.51	31.41	16.98	17.46

Table 7: Average extra time taken per query (in milliseconds) by κ_{all}-SVR over default parameter value settings.

5. CONCLUSION

We have presented in this paper a new method to predict, on a query by query basis, the values of the param-

eters of standard IR models on new collections for which no relevance judgments are available. To do so, we have first introduced a new representation of queries as a set of 4-dimensional vectors, that we have then extended through the use of auto-encoders. From these representations, we have obtained collection and language independent vector spaces, corresponding to feature spaces of PDS kernels between queries, in which we have learned regression functions.

Our experiments, conducted on standard collections, have revealed several points:

1. The method we propose significantly outperforms, in terms of MAP, the one using default parameter values (def) on the collections and models considered (the MAP is the measure optimized during training); it either significantly outperforms or is on a par with the method that uses half target queries with their relevance judgements to find the best parameter value over all queries (10split). These two methods (def and 10split) are instances of "global methods" which make use of the same parameter value for all queries of a given collection;

2. The number of source queries with relevance judgements required by our method is in the range 150 for all the collections and models we have considered. Furthermore, the source queries used need not be from a collection written in the same language as the one of the collection queried;

3. The extra time required by our method for each query lies in the range 15-30 milliseconds. This extra time corresponds to the application of the regression function on the query representation;

4. Lastly, the method can be easily applied to any IR standard model with few free parameters.

The proposed method, at its current stage, can predict the value of a single parameter. We wish to investigate the extension of the approach to the case where more than one parameter value needs be estimated, for example BM25 (which originally has three free parameters, b, k_1, and k_3). One obvious way is to train separate regressors for each of the parameters, but this works fine as long as there is no dependency between the parameters. Alternatively, this could be done, for example, by relying on a regression function predicting a vector of values so as to take into account the potential dependencies between the parameters considered.

Acknowledgment. This work was supported in part by the project AAP18 FUI Smart Support Center.

6. REFERENCES

[1] L. Bottou. Stochastic gradient tricks. In G. Montavon, G. B. Orr, and K.-R. Müller, editors, *Neural Networks, Tricks of the Trade, Reloaded*, Lecture Notes in Computer Science (LNCS 7700). Springer, 2012.

[2] P. Cai, W. Gao, A. Zhou, and K. Wong. Query weighting for ranking model adaptation. In *Proceedings of the 49th Annual Meeting of the Association for Computational Linguistics (ACL)*, New York, USA, 2011. ACM.

[3] B. Carterette. Robust test collections for retrieval evaluation. In *Proceedings of the 30th Annual International ACM SIGIR Conference on Research and Development in Information Retrieval*. ACM, 2007.

[4] D. Chen, Y. Xiong, J. Yan, G. Xue, G. Wang, and Z. Chen. Knowledge transfer for cross domain learning to rank. *Information Retrieval*, 13(3), June 2010.

[5] D. Chen, J. Yan, G. Wang, Y. Xiong, W. Fan, and Z. Chen. Transrank: A novel algorithm for transfer of rank learning. In *IEEE International Conference on Data Mining Workshops (ICDMW)*. IEEE Xplore, 2008.

[6] S. Clinchant and E. Gaussier. The BNB distribution for text modeling. In *Proceedings of the 30th European Conference on Advances in Information Retrieval (ECIR)*. Springer, 2008.

[7] S. Clinchant and E. Gaussier. Information-based models for ad hoc ir. In *Proceedings of the 33rd Annual International ACM SIGIR Conference on Research and Development in Information Retrieval*, New York, USA, 2010. ACM.

[8] W. Gao, P. Cai, K. Wong, and A. Zhou. Learning to rank only using training data from related domain. In *Proceedings of the 33rd Annual International ACM SIGIR Conference on Research and Development in Information Retrieval*, New York, USA, 2010. ACM.

[9] P. Goswami, M. Amini, and E. Gaussier. Transferring knowledge with source selection to learn ir functions on unlabeled collections. In *Proceedings of the 22nd ACM International Conference on Information & Knowledge Management (CIKM)*. ACM, 2013.

[10] G. E. Hinton and R. R. Salakhutdinov. Reducing the dimensionality of data with neural networks. *Science*, 313(5786):504–507, 2006.

[11] F. Jelinek and R. Mercer. Interpolated estimation of markov source parameters from sparse data. In *Proceedings of the Workshop on Pattern Recognition in Practice*. 1980.

[12] Q. V. Le and T. Mikolov. Distributed representations of sentences and documents. In *Proceedings of the 31th International Conference on Machine Learning*, 2014.

[13] Q. V. Le, M. Ranzato, R. Monga, M. Devin, G. Corrado, K. Chen, J. Dean, and A. Y. Ng. Building high-level features using large scale unsupervised learning. In *Proceedings of the 29th International Conference on Machine Learning*, 2012.

[14] Y. Lv and C. Zhai. Adaptive relevance feedback in information retrieval. In *Proceedings of the 18th ACM Conference on Information and Knowledge Management (CIKM)*, New York, USA, 2009. ACM.

[15] D. Metzler and O. Kurland. Experimental methods for information retrieval. In *Proceedings of the 35th International ACM SIGIR Conference on Research and Development in Information Retrieval*, SIGIR '12, New York, NY, USA, 2012. ACM.

[16] M. Mohri, A. Rostamizadeh, and A. Talwalkar. *Foundations of Machine Learning*. The MIT Press, 2012.

[17] I. Ounis, G. Amati, V. Plachouras, B. He, C. Macdonald, and C. Lioma. Terrier: A high performance and scalable information retrieval platform. In *Proceedings of ACM SIGIR'06 Workshop on Open Source Information Retrieval (OSIR 2006)*, New York, USA, 2006. ACM.

[18] J. Ponte and W. Croft. A language modeling approach to information retrieval. In *Proceedings of the 21st Annual International ACM SIGIR Conference on Research and Development in Information Retrieval*, New York, USA, 1998. ACM.

[19] S. Robertson and S. Walker. Some simple effective approximations to the 2-poisson model for probabilistic weighted retrieval. In *Proceedings of the 17th Annual International ACM SIGIR Conference on Research and Development in Information Retrieval*, New York, USA, 1994. ACM.

[20] S. E. Robertson and H. Zaragoza. The probabilistic relevance framework: Bm25 and beyond. *Foundations and Trends in Information Retrieval*, 3(4), 2009.

[21] I. Soboroff, C. Nicholas, and P. Cahan. Ranking retrieval systems without relevance judgments. In *Proceedings of the 24th Annual International ACM SIGIR Conference on Research and Development in Information Retrieval*, 2001.

[22] T. Tao and C. Zhai. Regularized estimation of mixture models for robust pseudo-relevance feedback. In *Proceedings of the 29th Annual International ACM SIGIR Conference on Research and Development in Information Retrieval*, New York, USA, 2006. ACM.

[23] M. Taylor, H. Zaragoza, N. Craswell, S. Robertson, and C. Burges. Optimisation methods for ranking functions with multiple parameters. In *Proceedings of the 15th ACM International Conference on Information and Knowledge Management*, New York, USA, 2006. ACM.

[24] V. Vapnik. *The Nature of Statistical Learning Theory*. Springer Verlag, 2000.

[25] S. Wu and F. Crestani. Methods for ranking information retrieval systems without relevance judgments. In *Proceedings of the 2003 ACM Symposium on Applied Computing*, 2003.

[26] C. Zhai and J. Lafferty. A study of smoothing methods for language models applied to information retrieval. *ACM Transactions on Information Systems*, 22(2):179–214, 2004.

Terms, Topics & Tasks: Enhanced User Modelling for Better Personalization

Rishabh Mehrotra
Dept of Computer Science
University College London
r.mehrotra@cs.ucl.ac.uk

Emine Yilmaz
Dept of Computer Science
University College London
emine.yilmaz@ucl.ac.uk

ABSTRACT

Given the distinct preferences of different users while using search engines, search personalization has become an important problem in information retrieval. Most approaches to search personalization are based on identifying topics a user may be interested in and personalizing search results based on this information.

While topical interests information of users can be highly valuable in personalizing search results and improving user experience, it ignores the fact that two different users that have similar topical interests may still be interested in achieving very different tasks with respect to this topic (e.g. the type of tasks a broker is likely to perform related to finance is likely to be very different than that of a regular investor). Hence, considering user's topical interests jointly with the type of tasks they are likely to be interested in could result in better personalised experience for users.

We present an approach that uses search task information embedded in search logs to represent users by their actions over a task-space as well as over their topical-interest space. In particular, we describe a tensor based approach that represents each user in terms of (i) user's topical interests and (ii) user's search task behaviours in a coupled fashion and use these representations for personalization. Additionally, we also integrate user's historic search behavior in a coupled matrix-tensor factorization framework to learn user representations. Through extensive evaluation via query recommendations and user cohort analysis, we demonstrate the value of considering topic specific task information while developing user models.

Categories and Subject Descriptors

H.3.3 [**Information Storage And Retrieval**]: Information Search and Retrieval—*User Modelling*

Keywords

Search tasks; User modelling; Tensor Decomposition

ICTIR'15, September 27–30, Northampton, MA, USA.
© 2015 ACM. ISBN 978-1-4503-3833-2/15/09 ...$15.00.
DOI: http://dx.doi.org/10.1145/2808194.2809467.

1. INTRODUCTION

As consumers of the informational content, different users have distinct information seeking preferences; thus accurately understanding their respective information needs and decision preferences is crucial for providing effective support during search interactions. While user behaviours are largely determined by their own goals and preferences, the mined knowledge from log activity data reveals different user intentions and behaviour patterns, which provide unique signals for user centric optimization and personalization.

Web search personalization has recently received a lot of attention by the research community. Personalized search leverages information about an individual to identify the most relevant recommendations for that person. A challenge for personalization is in collecting user profiles that are sufficiently rich to be useful in settings such as result ranking and query recommendations.

Most previous work on personalization has focused on using long term search histories to provide better personalized results. In particular, most recent personalized search systems mainly focus on identifying topics a user might be interested in based on their search history and improving their search experience by identifying and using information from different topics [32, 3].

Even though using topical interest of users can be highly valuable in personalizing search results and improving user experience, it still ignores the fact that two different users that have similar topical interests may still be interested in achieving very different tasks with respect to this topic. For example, a stockbroker and a normal investor while being interested in the same topic (finance), perform quite different set of search tasks and as a result need different kinds and levels of support while tackling these tasks. More generally, while topical interests capture the heterogeneity among users stemming from varied topical interests, such task based approaches would assist in capturing the heterogeneity stemming from differences in user needs and behaviors. Hence, using task information together with topics could result in systems that can provide improved personalized search experience to users.

In this work, we focus on using *search task* information for user modeling, where a search task has been previously defined as an atomic information need that consists of a set of related (sub)tasks [10]. In a recent poster [21], we showed that search tasks can indeed be used for personalization. This work was based on replacing topic models with search tasks for personalization and building task based representations of users for topic modelling. Hence, this work ignores the fact that tasks users are interested in tend to be topic specific: people tend to be interested in achieving certain tasks only for certain topics. In this work, we investigate the idea of task based personalization in detail and develop a model that combines topic based user modelling with task based user models. Additionally, we look at the user's search history that provides information about user's term usage behavior. We integrate user's historical information to the task-topic tensor framework by proposing a coupled matrix-tensor factorization model which jointly learns user representations based on their search history, term usage behavior, topical interest profiles and search task behaviors.

In particular, we show that it is possible to represent the topic specific tasks users are interested in by representing users in terms of a 3-modal $< user - topic - task >$ tensor (multidimensional array). We show that tensor factorization can be used to learn *coupled task-topic based user representations* for each user, thereby incorporating tasks together with topics in representing the user population. The tensor based framework helps in encapsulating the complex interactions between topics and tasks across the entire user population and learns a low dimensional factor model wherein user's interests, preferences and behaviors are determined by an interplay between these latent factors. We further extend the tensor based framework to include user's search history information by proposing a coupled matrix-tensor factorization model wherein the matrix captures user's topical interest and search task information while the matrix captures user's term usage behavior.

Finally, we show that the proposed methods result in better user profiles by evaluating the quality of our approach on a variety of tasks for personalisation including collaborative query recommendation, cluster based recommendation and user cohort analysis.

2. RELATED WORK

There is a growing interest in the information retrieval and machine learning communities in moving beyond context free search experiences, and towards examining how knowledge of a searcher's interests and search context can be used to improve various aspects of search (e.g., ranking, query recommendation, query classification). Even though there is significant amount of prior work on search task identification and personalisation based on topical representations of users, there is no prior work that uses topic based task representations for users. We first summarise the related work on representing users and personalization, and provide a summary of previous work on task identification from search engine query logs, which will be used by the models proposed in this work.

User Representation & Personalization

Irrespective of where the user's data comes from, a model must encode this data. A variety of such models have been used in the past including a vector of weighted terms (e.g. [19]), a set of concepts (e.g. [6]), using topic models (e.g. [7]) or a hierarchical category tree based on ODP and corresponding keywords (e.g. [3]).
Teevan *et al.* [30] constructed user profiles from indexed desktop documents and showed that this information could be used to re-rank search results and improve relevance for individuals. Matthijs and Radlinski [19] constructed user profiles using users' browsing history, and evaluated their approach using an interleaving methodology. Their approach focused on using term based user profiles which often limit the scope of personalization as different users inherently follow different distributions over words. Dou *et al.* [6] investigated a number of heuristics for creating user profiles and generating personalized rankings. Bennett *et al.* [3] made use of hand picked Open Directory Project (ODP) topical categories to construct user profiles. While such topical categories are easily specified, much human effort is required in labelling queries for each topic. ODP categories based methods restricts topic coverage in a major way as search logs offer much richer content both in terms of the number of topics involved as well as the granularity level of each topic. Very recently, Wang *et al* [32] have proposed a generative model which models users as a mixture over latent user groups wherein each group shares a common distribution over queries and a common click preference pattern. Finally, Harvey *et al.* [7] use the topic model based approach to build user profiles from topics obtained and personalize search results based on the learnt user profiles.

Aiming for short-term personalization, Sriram et al. [28] describe a search engine that personalized based on the current user session. A longer term personalization click model can also be used, exploiting clickthrough data collected over a long time period. For example, Speretta and Gauch [27] and Qiu and Cho [25] model users by classifying previously visited web pages into a topic hierarchy, using this model to re-rank future search results. Also, a particularly straightforward yet effective search interaction personalization approach is PClick, proposed by Dou et al. [6]. This method involves promoting URLs previously clicked on by the same user for the same query. The user representation model we present in this work could be easily used in any of these personalization techniques.

Search Task Identification

It was peviously shown that approximately 75% of user search sessions involve multi-tasking [17], which makes task identification an important step towards understanding user goals. People have been shown to pursue a wide range of different *search tasks* online [11, 18] and inferences about task behavior have been shown to have value in areas such as modeling search satisfaction [8]. Information about user's task involvements provides a completely different aspect of user's intents and provide strong contextual cues which could be leveraged by future recommendation and advertising engines to better serve user's needs.

Prior work on identifying search-tasks mainly explores task extraction from search sessions [17], wherein the objective is to segment a search session into disjoint sets of queries where each set represents a different task. Recent work on identifying cross-session tasks has targeted pairs of queries, and made predictions about whether they share the same goal or represent the same task [31, 13]. Unfortunately, pairwise predictions alone cannot generate the partition of tasks, and post-processing is needed to obtain the final task partitions [15].

In addition to extracting task clusters, recent efforts by Mehrotra *et al.* [20] have aimed at extracting hierarchies of search tasks and sub-tasks. Li *et al.* [14] model query temporal patterns using a special class of point process called Hawkes processes, and combine topic model with Hawkes processes for simultaneously identifying and labeling search tasks. While some recent research has considered supporting users in their pursuit of complex search tasks by recommending related tasks from a task graph [9], no explicit user models were proposed in their work.

White *et al.* [33] explore the idea of using task information to personalize search result ranking by finding other users performing similar tasks. In this work, we propose a similar yet different notion of using user's task information and propose techniques for learning user representations which could be used in rather diverse application settings.

To the best of our knowledge, this is the first work to consider user's task behavior information to couple varied user information like topical interests and search histories. We next describe our approach to jointly learn task based as well as topic based coupled user representations.

3. METHODOLOGY

We propose a new direction in learning user representations by modeling user's task behaviors. We posit that topics and tasks capture different set of insights about user's behavior and information needs and can be coupled with their term usage behavior to jointly learn richer user representations, which is the main goal of this work.

To this end, we intend to extract search tasks from a given search log and represent users in terms of these tasks. In the next sub-section, we describe the approach we use to extract search tasks. This is followed by briefly describing our initial efforts in modeling users based on tasks alone ignoring the topical information [21] in section 4. Finally, we present our approach of coupling task and topical information in Section 5 and extend it to include user's language model and term usage behavior in Section 6. We describe the experimental evaluation set up and results in Section 7, while section 8 concludes.

3.1 Notation & Background

We start with defining the notations used throughout the paper. Columns of a matrix are denoted by boldface lower letters with a subscript, e.g., $\mathbf{a_r}$ is the $r-th$ column of matrix $\mathbf{A}$. Entries of a matrix or a tensor are denoted by lowercase letters with subscripts, i.e., i_1 entry. Given two matrices $\mathbf{A} \in \Re^{I \times K}$ and $\mathbf{B} \in \Re^{J \times K}$, their Khatri-Rao product is denoted by $A \odot B$ and defined as column-wise Kronecker product. The result is a matrix of size $(IJ) \times K$ and defined by

$$A \odot B = [a_1 \otimes b_1 a_2 \otimes b_2 \ldots a_K \otimes b_K] \qquad (1)$$

where $\otimes$ denotes Kronecker product. For more details on properties of Kronecker and Khatri-Rao products, the reader is referred to *Kolda et al.* [12].

Table 1 shows a list of symbols used throughout the paper, together with their descriptions.

3.2 Extracting Search Tasks

In order to build task based representaions of users, we first need to identify and extract search tasks users are likely to perform when they use a search engine. Here we describe our approach of extracting these tasks given a search log. Following the approach in Lucchese *et al.* [17], we employ a graph based query-clustering approach based on finding weighted connected components of a graph.

Given a user session ϕ, we build a complete graph $G_\phi = (V, E, w)$, whose nodes V are the queries in ϕ, and whose

Symbol	Description
ALS	Alternating Least Squares
CMTF	Coupled Matrix Tensor Factorization
$\mathbf{A} \odot \mathbf{B}$	Khatri-Rao product
$a \circ b \circ c$	$(a \circ b \circ c)(i,j,k) = a(i)b(j)c(k)$
$\mathbf{A}_1^i$	series of matrices or vectors, indexed by i
$\|A\|_F$	Frobenius norm of $\mathbf{A}$
$\mathbf{T}$	User-Topic-Task tensor
$\mathbf{M}$	User-Term matrix
$\mathbf{U}$	User representation matrix
$\mathbf{S}$	Search Task matrix
$\mathbf{L}$	LDA topics matrix
$\mathbf{W}$	User language model matrix

Table 1: Table of symbols

E edges are weighted by the similarity of the corresponding nodes. The weighting function w is a similarity function $w : E \to R \in [0, 1]$ that can be easily instantiated in terms of the distance functions μ, which we describe a bit later. The graph G_ϕ describes the similarity between any pair of queries in the given session. For evaluating similarity between two queries, we make use of the following two similarity features:

- **Content-based**: Two queries that share some common terms are likely related. Sometimes, such terms may be very similar, but not identical, due to mispelling, or different prefixes/suffixes. To capture content distance between queries, following Lucchese *et al.* [17] we adopt a Jaccard index on tri-grams along with a normalized Levenstein distance which is widely accepted as the best edit-based feature for identifying goal boundaries [17].

- **Semantic-based**: Following Lucchese *et al.* [17], we assume that a Wikipedia article describes a certain concept and that the presence of a term in a given article is an evidence of the correlation between that term and that concept. We represent each term in a high-dimensional concept space, and sum over each query term to obtain a query's concept vectors. The cosine similarity between such concept-vectors of queries provides the semantic similarity between the two queries. The distance between two queries is defined as a (1-weighted average of the two similarities). For further details, users are referred to Lucchese *et al.* [17].

Based on the query pair distances obtained above, weak edges with low similarity are dropped, since the corresponding queries are not related, and clusters are built on the basis of the strong edges, i.e. with high similarity, which identify the related query pairs. The connected components of the pruned query-query graph identify the clusters of related queries and provides us with our set of search tasks. Lucchese *et al.* [17] provide further details on the above mentioned similarity features.

4. LEARNING TASK BASED USER REPRESENTATIONS

We postulate that in a web search setting, search logs contain information about various actions that users perform and profiling users based on search tasks would better capture the heterogeneity in user information and help us in modeling users. In a recent poster [21], we present some preliminary work which describes a purely search task based user representation system (ignoring topical information) as described in this section. We later propose a novel way of combining such task based representations with user's topical interest information to learn a coupled task-topical interest user profile and additionally incorporate user's term histories via a coupled matrix-tensor factorization framework described in Section 6.

User-Task Association Matrix: Based on the extracted search tasks, we construct a user-task association matrix which represents the search tasks users have been involved with. For each user u_i, we consider their search history and create a bag-of-queries representation from the list of queries issued by the user and compare each user with each of the search tasks t_j obtained by the method described in section 3.2. For each user-task $<u_i, t_j>$ pair, we populate the corresponding value in the user-task association matrix (R) with the cosine similarity score (r_{ij}) we obtain for the pair. For tasks in which users do not have any matching queries, we assign a score of 0 to the corresponding pair. The overall motivation behind such a set-up is to capture information about whether or not users have performed such a search task before.

Probabilistic Matrix Factorization for User Representations: We wish to extract task-based user vector representations by jointly mapping users and tasks to a joint latent factor space. Following Salakhutdinov *et al.* [22], we model the user-task association in terms of probabilistic matrix factorization problem and learn latent vector representation for each user from the user-task association matrix by fitting a probabilistic model. Given the user-task association matrix **R**, we find the user feature matrix $\mathbf{U} = [u_i]$ and task feature matrix $\mathbf{T} = [t_j]$. The conditional distribution over the observed user-task associations $R \in \Re^{N \times M}$ is given by:

$$P(R|U, T, \alpha) = \prod_{i=1}^{N} \prod_{j=1}^{M} \left[\mathcal{N}(R_{ij}|U_i^T T_j, \sigma^2) \right]^{I_{ij}} \quad (2)$$

where $\mathcal{N}$ denotes the Gaussian distribution and I_{ij} is the indicator function which is 1 if the user i was involved in search task j. The latent vector representations for the users, the system minimizes the regularized error:

$$min_{u^*, t^* \in \kappa} \sum_{i,j} (r_{ij} - t_j^T u_i)^2 + \lambda(\|u_i\|^2 + \|t_j\|^2) \quad (3)$$

where κ is the set of non-zero r_{ij} values, u_i represents the user and t_j represents a task. The user matrix **U** obtained as a result, contains vector representations of each of the users which is used in further experiments.

So far, we have been able to extract collective search tasks from all users and learnt a user representation based on these search tasks. We show in Section 7 that task based user models indeed result in better performance than basic bag-of-term based or basic topical interest based representation which further motivates us to investigate combining the two different modalities of user information: topical interests and tasks associations. Indeed, the information carried by user's topical interest profiles and their task profile are different and it would make sense to couple both these informations to jointly learn user profiles. In the next section, we further augment our task based user profiles by incorporating user's topical interest profiles and describe our tensor based approach for the joint model.

5. COMBINING SEARCH TASKS WITH TOPICS

Our objective in this section is to build succinct user profiles from the search task information embedded in search logs while at the same time incorporating user's topical interest profiles. Building upon on prior work, we augment our task based user representation model with user's topical information by coupling the topical interest with task based information in the form of a tensor and learning user profiles based on the decomposition of the $< user, topic, task >$ tensor. We first describe the model we use for identifying topical interests of users and further show how we combine this model with task based representation.

5.1 Learning Topical Interest Profiles

Topical interests based methods are quite popular in learning user representations [3, 7]. Given user's history of search queries, we aim to develop a topic interest model which captures user's interest distribution over different topics. We make use of the Latent Dirichlet Allocation (LDA) model to learn the latent set of topics embedded in the search log [7]. It is to be noted that LDA topic model based approaches are standard methods to extract user's topical interest profiles and are widely used across user modelling applications.

We hypothesize that each search query is motivated by choosing a topic of interest first and subsequently a query is issued to describe that search need from the catalogue of words consistent with that particular topic. Based on this intuition, we learn an LDA based topic model and use the learnt model to do topical inference for each user to obtain a topic-distribution for the user over the set of learnt topics. We refer to this distribution as a user's ***topical profile***.

5.2 Coupling Topics & Tasks

Our main intuition behind leveraging both the topical profile as well as the search task profile of users is to better differentiate between users who share similar topical profiles. Topics and tasks capture different information: topical interest information help in capturing the user heterogeneity resulting from varied interests while task information helps in capturing user heterogeneity resulting from different information needs.

We formulate this intuition in our model by coupling task information with topical information on a per-user basis. We construct a 3-mode tensor $< user, topic, task >$ to jointly capture user's topical as well as search task based information. Next, we briefly describe the tensor formulation.

Tensors: a primer
A tensor is a multidimensional array. More formally, a N-way tensor or N-th order tensor is an element of the tensor product of N vector spaces each of which as its own coordinate system. A first-order tensor is a vector, a second-order tensor is a matrix, and tensors of order three or higher are called higher-order tensors. The *order* of a tensor is the number of dimensions, also known as *modes*. A third order tensor can be represented as $T \in \Re^{I_1 \times I_2 \times I_3}$ with each element of the tensor denoted as $t_{i,j,k}$ with $i \in (1, I_1)$,

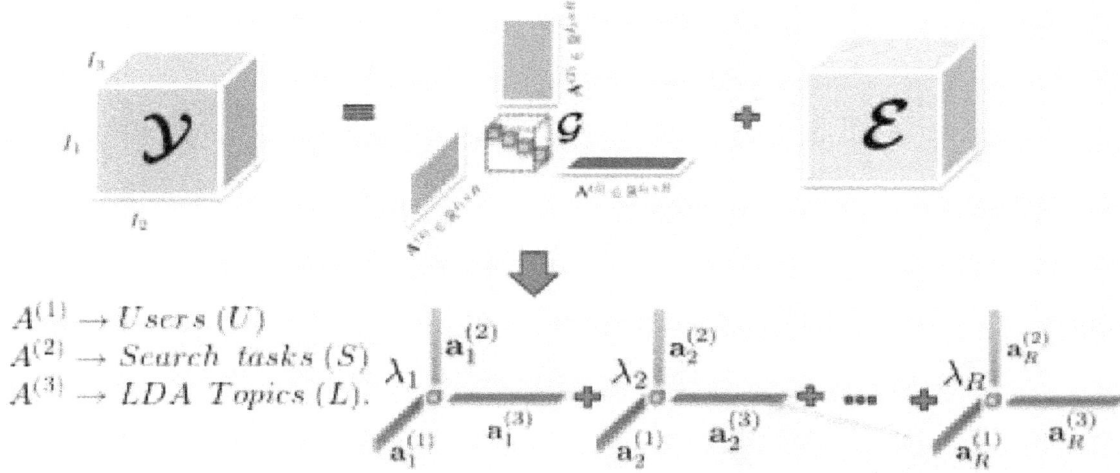

Figure 1: The overview of the user-topic-task tensor constructed by jointly considering user's topical interest profiles alongwith their search task interaction behavior. The tensor decompisiton breaks the tensor into latent factors which encode the complex interactions between the three different modes of the tensor.

$j \in (1, I_2)$ and $k \in (1, I_3)$. The symbol $\circ$ represents the vector outer product.

Constructing $< user, topic, task >$ **Affinity Tensor**

To jointly model the user's topical and task preferences, we construct a 3-mode tensor - users, topics and tasks. Each element of our tensor ($T \in \Re^{I_1 \times I_2 \times I_3}$), $t_{i,j,k}$ defines user i's combined task based and topical preference - a user's participation in a certain task gets weighted by his topical affinity, thereby coupling his task based and topical affinity. More formally, we define each tensor-component value as follows:

$$t_{i,j,k} = U_{i_{topic_j}} \times U_{i_{task_k}} \qquad (4)$$

where $U_{i_{topic_j}}$ is user U_i's topical affinity for topic j obtained from the LDA model learnt before while $U_{i_{task_k}}$ represents the task affinity for user U_i's for search task k obtained in earlier the user-task association phase (Section 4). To obtain user's topical affinity estimates (U_i), we train an LDA topic model on the entire query collection and use user's historical queries to create user's term profile which is then used for estimating the topic proportions using LDA inference techniques. I_1, I_2, I_3 are the different dimensions of the different modes of the tensor - in our case, these represent the number of users, number of topics and the number of search tasks extracted respectively. Thus, for each user we construct his coupled task-topic affinity value and populate the corresponding component in the tensor T.

Tensor Decomposition

Tensor decomposition methods are regarded as higher-order equivalents to matrix decompositions. The PARAFAC tensor decomposition [29] allows us to leverage connections between the different users across different topics and different search tasks. By PARAFAC, the input tensors are transformed into Kruskal tensors, a sum of rank-one-tensors. Formally, the tensor $T \in \Re^{I_1 \times I_2 \times I_3}$ is decomposed into component matrices $U \in \Re^{I_1 \times d}$, $T \in \Re^{I_2 \times d}$ and $S \in \Re^{I_3 \times d}$ and d principal factors λ_i in descending order. Via these, tensor T can be written as a Kruskal tensor by:

$$T \approx \Sigma_{k=1}^{d} \lambda_k \cdot U^k \circ T^k \circ S^k \qquad (5)$$

where λ_k denotes the k-th principal factor. The goal is to compute a decomposition with d-components that best approximates our tensor T, i.e., to find

$$min_{\widetilde{T}} \| T - \widetilde{T} \| \qquad (6)$$

such that

$$\widetilde{T} = \Sigma_{k=1}^{d} \lambda_k \cdot U^k \circ T^k \circ S^k \qquad (7)$$

We make use of the Alternating Least Squares (ALS) approach [12] to solve the above objective - having fixed all but one matrix, the problem reduces to a linear least-squares problem.

Overall, the above formulation helps us to couple user's topical interests with their search task associations and learn a user representation based on this coupled tensor. This tensor decomposition based user modelling approach allows us to use multi-modal user information and leverage insights from each of them while learning user representations.

Similar to other works based on tensors, an important characteristic of the proposed user modelling approach is that this method is generic enough and allows us to plug-in other sources of user information - click models, data from advertisement responses, etc.

6. INCORPORATING HISTORICAL BEHAVIOR

One widely used aspect of user behavior that provides especially strong signals for delivering better personalized services is an individual's history of queries and clicked documents. To construct the profiles necessary for personalization, evidence of a user's interests can be mined from observed past behaviors which can be sourced from their short-term (e.g., the current search session) or the long-term (e.g., across many previous sessions) search histories

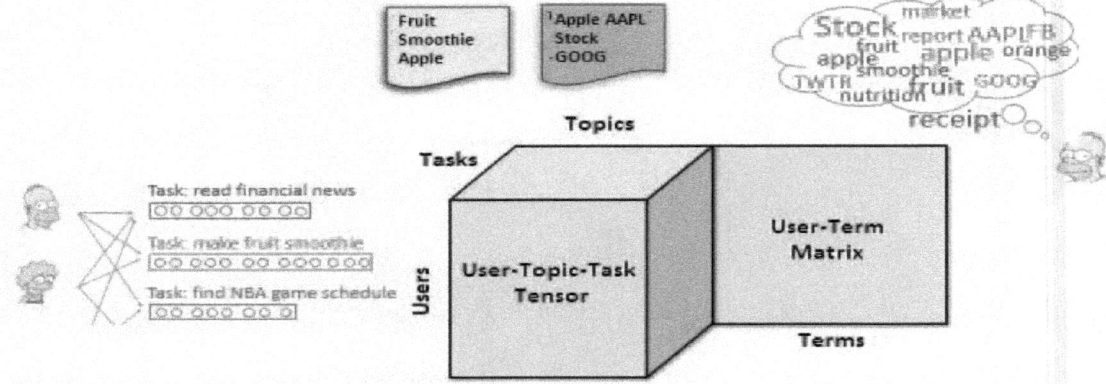

Figure 2: The coupled matrix-tensor obtained by coupling user's term usage behavior matrix with the user-topic-task tensor. The matrix and the tensor share a common mode of 'users'. On the left, we highlight some task related activity of the users and the associated topics obtained and the terms used on the top and right parts of the figure respectively.

[3]. User's term history comprises of the set of terms users used to compose search queries. The tensor based approach described in the previous section looks at utilizing user's topical interest profile along with user's task association information. We hypothesize that additional signals about user's profile could be obtained by jointly modeling user's term usage behavior together with their task and topical interests information.

Overall, our motivation is to combine user's historic term usage behavior with their topical and task based information to learn user representations. We construct a user's term usage behavior over a set of combined vocabulary space. Combining the different users term histories together provides us with a user-term matrix (W), which we intend to jointly factorize while performing tensor factorization of the user-topic-task tensor (T). The idea behind the coupled matrix-tensor decomposition is that we seek to jointly analyze T and M, decomposing them to latent factors who are coupled in the shared user dimension. More specifically, the first mode of T shares the same low rank column subspace as M; this is expressed through the latent factor matrix U which jointly provides a basis for that subspace.

6.1 Coupled Matrix-Tensor Factorization

In the topic-task tensor we described earlier, we have a user by topic by task tensor which encodes user's topical interest profiles and task activities. We also have a semantic matrix which provides additional information for the same sets of users - the user by term matrix. In such cases, we may say that the tensor and the matrix are *coupled* in the *user* mode. We next describe the joint analysis of a matrix (M) and a 3th-order tensor (T) with one mode in common, where the tensor is factorized using the CP model and the matrix is factorized by extracting latent factors using matrix factorization.

Let $T \in \Re^{I_1 \times I_2 \times I_3}$ and $M \in \Re^{I_1 \times I_4}$ have the first mode (user) in common; the objective function for coupled analysis is defined by

$$f(U, S, L, W) = \frac{1}{2}\|T - [U, L, S]\|_F^2 + \frac{1}{2}\|M - UW^T\|_F^2 \quad (8)$$

Our goal is to find the matrices U, L, S, W that minimize this objective. In order to solve this optimization problem, we can compute the gradient and then use any first-order optimization algorithm [23]. Rewriting the equation,

$$f(U, S, L, W) = f_1 + f_2 \quad (9)$$

where $f_1 = \|T - [U, L, S]\|_F^2$ and $f_2 = \|M - UW^T\|_F^2$. The partial derivative of f_1 with respect to the different matrices has been derived in [2] so we just present the results here. Let $Z = [U, L, S]$, then

$$\frac{\partial f_1}{\partial U} = (Z_i - T_i)U^{(-i)} \quad (10)$$

where $U^{(-i)} = U^{(I_1)} \odot \ldots U^{(i+1)} \odot U^{(i-1)} \odot \ldots \odot U^{(1)}$. Similar computations can be made for the other matrices components L and S. The partial derivatives of the second component, f_2, with respect to U, L, S and W can be computed as

$$\frac{\partial f_2}{\partial U} = -MW + UW^T W$$
$$\frac{\partial f_2}{\partial U} = -W^T U + WU^T U \quad (11)$$

Combining the above results, we can compute the partial derivative of f with respect to factor matrix as

$$\frac{\partial f}{\partial U} = \frac{\partial f_1}{\partial U} + \frac{\partial f_2}{\partial U}$$
$$\frac{\partial f}{\partial W} = \frac{\partial f_2}{\partial W} \quad (12)$$

Similar computations can be made for the S and L components. With these gradients, the aforementioned coupled matrix-tensor optimization problem can then be solved using any first-order optimization algorithm [23].

On solving the coupled factorization objective, we obtain latent factor matrices which could be used as latent representations. More specifically, by making use of the latent factor matrix U we're able to learn user representations that jointly express user's topical, task and term profile information.

User Profile Information	TermSim	LDA	Task	TT-Tensor	CMTF
Term History	✓				✓
Topical Interests		✓		✓	✓
Search Task information			✓	✓	✓

Table 2: User profile information encapsulated in each of the compared approaches. We notice that the proposed TT-tensor and CMFT based methods maximally incorporate the different user profile information available.

7. EXPERIMENTAL EVALUATION

In order to evaluate the performance of the proposed user modelling techniques, we use three techniques of evaluation based on collaborative query recommendation, query recommendation based on user groups and user cohort analysis.

7.1 Compared Approaches

We consider the following baselines to evaluate the performance of the proposed tensor based method:

- **TermSim** (TermSim) is a method that only uses bag-of-words based representation for each user where the terms are extracted from user queries and similar users found using cosine similarity between each user's bag-of-word based representations[19].

- **LDA Topic Based** (LDA) is a method of representing users in terms of their topical interests where the topics are extracted via a common Latent Dirichlet Allocation setup [7]. It s important to note that topic based representations are one of the most commonly used representations for personalization.

- **Task Based (section 4):** (Task) The first step towards coupling tasks with topics is representing users just in terms of search tasks. We use the user representations obtained in Section 3 as a result of matrix factorization as another baseline to compare the gain in performance obtained as a result of adding the topical aspect on top of user's search task information [21].

- **TT-Tensor(section 5):** (TT) Topic-Task Tensor (TT-Tensor) based user representation is the proposed technique which combines user's task information with their topical interests.

- **CMTF(section 6):** Coupled Matrix Tensor Factorization (CMTF) based user representation is our second novel contribution which takes into account the user histories in addition to their topical and task based profiles.

Each of the compared approaches work with different user information. In Table 2 we summarize the different modalities of user information used by the different approaches.

7.2 Dataset

We make use of the AOL log dataset which consists of ∼20M web queries collected over three months and use data for a subset of ∼1200 users who have issued more than certain threshold (550) number of queries. We run our Task Discovery algorithm on the set of queries for each of these users which results in a total of ∼0.12M tasks which we cluster to obtain a set of 1521 search tasks. Such a setting for task extraction is in line with the original proposed research

by Lucchese *et al.* [17]. These tasks are then used to create the user-task association matrix, as described in Section 4 and for constructing the coupled matrix-tensor, as described in Section 6. To make fair comparisons between the topical and task based user profiles, we keep the number of latent factors for tasks same as the number of latent topics.

7.3 Collaborative Query Recommendation

A good user profile for query recommendation should capture a user's specific interests and informational needs. Based on this intuition, we evaluate performance of the proposed approach on ***Collaborative Query Recommendation*** [32] where the goal is to recommend queries to a user based on queries issued by similar users. For each user we select the n-most similar users where the similarity is calculated by a cosine similarity score using the user representations learnt. We calculate the weighted frequency of a candidate query for most similar users of the target user u, and select the top-k queries as recommendation.

To evaluate the performance of the above mentioned techniques, we consider the test-set of queries in the target user as relevant, and computed average number of relevant queries matched in the recommendation query set as the performance metric. The training/test set per user is populated based on a 20% split across all user queries. We use the training set for populating the matrix/tensor while the test set of queries per user for evaluating the quality of the recommended queries. We plot precision@10 and precision@20 values based on the average number of query matches between the recommended set of queries (top-10 (left) and top-20 (right)) and user's own test set of (unseen) queries

Discussion

Our results (Figure 3) show that the proposed Topic-Task Tensor based user modelling approach(*TT-Tensor*) and the coupled matrix factorization method (CMTF) performs better than *TermSim* as well as *TaskBased* which demonstrates that combining search task information with user's topical interests thus help us better capture different aspects of user profiles and can serve as potent user modelling tools. Since *TermSim* relies strictly on term matching for measuring user similarities, its coverage is limited: it might not capture insights for the users with too few queries or those who shared the same search interest but issued different queries or performed different tasks. Task based user modelling can help in better differentiating between users which have similar topical interests but perform different tasks.

The proposed tensor based approach combines the best of both the worlds and hence was able to leverage the topical user profile information with the task aspect. Additionally, the CMTF model combines information from all available data modalities and learns a joint user representation. We see that the CMTF model outperforms the other methods which highlights the importance of jointly considering user's term, topic and task information. On analysis of the dataset, we figured out that the overall lower average query recall values can be attributed to the less query overlap between users, i.e., the upper limit of common query among users is indeed low on average.

7.4 Cohort based Query Recommendation

It is well-known that preferences across a user population often decompose into a smaller number of communities of

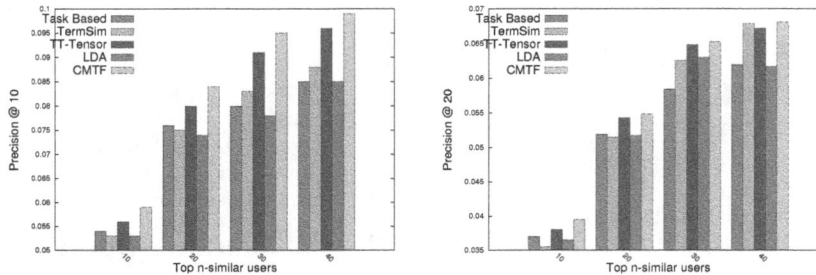

Figure 3: Performance on Collaborative Query Recommendation (left figure: Precision@10 & right figure: Precision@20). Based on the average number of query matches between the recommended set of queries and user's own test set of (unseen) queries, the precision at 10 and precision at 20 values are plotted against the number of similar users considered (n). The results obtained at n=10, 20, 30 (left) and n=10, 20 (right) were statistically significant (p<0.05) based on pairwise tests between the proposed method and the best performing baseline.

nClusters	DB Index					SI Index				
	TermSim	LDA	Task	TT	CMTF	TermSim	LDA	Task	TT	CMTF
10	1.61	1.55	1.98	1.52	**1.46**	0.19	0.20	0.16	0.43	**0.48**
30	1.69	1.66	1.83	**1.48**	1.47	0.23	0.26	0.24	0.36	**0.41**
50	1.58	1.65	1.84	1.52	**1.50**	0.27	**0.28**	**0.28**	0.27	0.27
80	1.71	1.67	1.80	1.58	**1.57**	0.29	0.35	0.28	0.47	**0.51**
100	1.75	1.65	1.76	1.63	**1.59**	0.31	0.57	0.32	0.58	**0.62**

Table 3: Cluster Analysis of User Representations - cluster evaluation metrics performance for the different approaches are shown. *BoT* represents the simple Bag-of-Terms baseline, *LDA* represents the topic model based user representations, *Task* represents user representations learnt via PMF by using task information while *TT* represents the proposed Task-Topic Tensor based user representations.

commonly shared preferences [1, 24]. In this study, we investigate the performance by means of *groupization*: a variant of personalization whereby other users' profiles can be used to personalize current user's experience. As opposed to finding similar users from the entire user population for collaborative query recommendation, we explore the use of user-cohorts obtained above and leverage information from users belonging to the same cluster to aid in query recommendation. A good cluster should contain better similar users - users who are indeed more representative of the current user. Based on this, we evaluate the performance of the proposed approach on Cohort based Query Recommendation where the goal is to recommend queries to a user based on queries issued by users in the same cluster. Following similar set up as before, we present cohort-based query recommendation results (clustering performed with 10 clusters) in Fig. 4.

Discussion

The proposed approach of encapsulating user's historic term usage behavior with their topical and task oriented interests consistently performs better than our baselines in terms of recommending queries from users from the cluster. As can be seen in Fig. 4, the CMTF and coupled task-topic representation performs significantly better right at the start with the difference between the approaches slimming down as we go towards more query recommendations. This is indeed expected since we are measuring precision of queries and eventually not-so-efficient methods will eventually be able to recommend better queries as we increase the number of queries suggested.

Recent research on groupization has focussed on developing different ways of building user cohorts based on topical interests, location, etc [33]. In the present study, we used

simple clustering on user features for building cohorts; in future study we intend to compare cohorts of varying sizes and variants of cohort construction techniques to obtain detailed insights on user cohort behaviors.

In addition to performing cohort based query recommendation, we also investigate the *goodness* of the user cohorts we obtain, which were used for query recommendation as described above. We next describe the experimental set-up to analyze the performance of the compared approaches on the task of user cohort formation.

7.4.1 User Cohort Analysis

We believe that incorporating task behavior of users while learning user representations enables us to better *decompose* users into user cohorts or clusters. In this study, we test the hypothesis that a good user modeling scheme would allow for good cluster formation based on the learnt user representations. We evaluate the user representations learnt in terms of the quality of user clusters formed. Unlike external cluster validation measures, which use external information ("true" cluster membership) not present in our data, internal cluster validation measures only rely on information in the data [16]. In Table 3 and Table 4, we present the cluster validation results on a variety of different metrics, which, to the best of our knowledge, represent a good coverage of the validation measures available in different fields, such as data mining, information retrieval, and machine learning.

The different measures used capture different *goodness* measures of clusters based on inter-cluster and intra-cluster similarities. The Davies-Bouldin index (DB) [5] is calculated as follows. For each cluster C, the similarities between C and all other clusters are computed, and the highest value is assigned to C as its cluster similarity. Then the DB in-

138

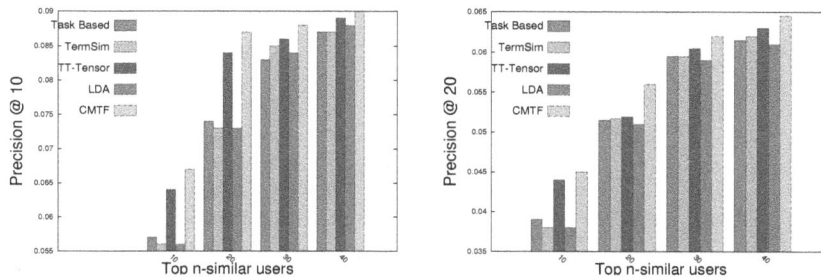

Figure 4: Performance on Cohort Query Recommendation (left figure: Precision@10 & right figure: Precision@20). Based on the average number of query matches between the recommended set of queries and user's own test set of (unseen) queries, the precision at 10 and precision at 20 values are plotted against the number of similar users from user's cluster considered (n). The results obtained between the CMTF and the best performing baseline at n=10, 20 (left) and n=10, 20, 30 (right) were statistically significant (p<0.05) based on pairwise tests between the proposed method and the best performing baseline.

	CH Index				
nClusters	TermSim	LDA	Task	TT	CMTF
10	453	643	352	534	**658**
30	297	353	203	377	**411**
50	213	258	151	285	**299**
80	178	192	116	212	**234**
100	96	165	99	182	**194**

Table 4: Cluster Analysis of User Representations - internal cluster evaluation metric (CH Index) performance for the different approaches are shown. *BoT* represents the simple Bag-of-Terms baseline, *LDA* represents the topic model based user representations, *Task* represents user representations learnt vi PMF by using task information while *TT* represents the proposed Task-Topic Tensor based user representations.

dex can be obtained by averaging all the cluster similarities. The smaller the index is, the better the clustering result is.

The Silhouette index (SI) [26] validates the clustering performance based on the pairwise difference of between and within-cluster distances. The Calinski-Harabasz index (CH) [4] evaluates the cluster validity based on the average between and within cluster sum of squares.

Discussion
As can be seen in Table 3 and table 4, the user clusters obtained from via using topic-task coupled representations indeed perform better than the clusters obtained via just Bag-of-Terms or task baselines. This is in line with our hypothesis that capturing task behaviors across user populations indeed helps us in forming *well-knit* user clusters and thus could help us perform better in "*groupization*". Having good clusters could be useful for many applications, one of them being collaborative query recommendation, as shown above.

8. CONCLUSION

We presented a novel approach to couple user's topical interest information with their search task information and their term usage behavior to learn a joint user representation technique. We demonstrated that coupling user's task information with their topical interests indeed helps us build better user models. We show through extensive experimenta-

tion that our task based method outperforms existing query term based and topical interest based user representation methods. This clearly demonstrates the value of considering *search tasks* rather than just query terms or topics during personalization. Future work involves the development of more sophisticated and generalizable models of task behavior that can model task-relevant activity beyond search engine interactions. The flexibility of the tensor based framework makes our proposed method generic enough to add more data sources and modalities. The user representations learnt can be used for various different applications, something we intend to explore as future work.

9. REFERENCES

[1] E. Abbasnejad, S. Sanner, E. V. Bonilla, and P. Poupart. Learning community-based preferences via dirichlet process mixtures of gaussian processes. In *Proceedings of the Twenty-Third international joint conference on Artificial Intelligence*, pages 1213–1219. AAAI Press, 2013.

[2] E. Acar, D. M. Dunlavy, and T. G. Kolda. A scalable optimization approach for fitting canonical tensor decompositions. *Journal of Chemometrics*, 25(2):67–86, 2011.

[3] P. N. Bennett, R. W. White, W. Chu, S. T. Dumais, P. Bailey, F. Borisyuk, and X. Cui. Modeling the impact of short-and long-term behavior on search personalization. In *ACM SIGIR*, 2012.

[4] T. Caliński and J. Harabasz. A dendrite method for cluster analysis. *Communications in Statistics-theory and Methods*, 3(1):1–27, 1974.

[5] D. L. Davies and D. W. Bouldin. A cluster separation measure. *Pattern Analysis and Machine Intelligence, IEEE Transactions on*, (2):224–227, 1979.

[6] Z. Dou, R. Song, and J.-R. Wen. A large-scale evaluation and analysis of personalized search strategies. In *Proceedings of the 16th international conference on World Wide Web*, pages 581–590. ACM, 2007.

[7] M. Harvey, F. Crestani, and M. J. Carman. Building user profiles from topic models for personalised search. In *Proceedings of the 22nd ACM international conference on Conference on information & knowledge management*, pages 2309–2314. ACM, 2013.

[8] A. Hassan, Y. Song, and L.-w. He. A task level metric for measuring web search satisfaction and its application on improving relevance estimation. In *Proceedings of the 20th ACM international conference on Information and knowledge management*, pages 125–134. ACM, 2011.

[9] A. Hassan Awadallah, R. W. White, P. Pantel, S. T. Dumais, and Y.-M. Wang. Supporting complex search tasks. In *Proceedings of the 23rd ACM International Conference on Conference on Information and Knowledge Management*, pages 829–838. ACM, 2014.

[10] R. Jones and K. L. Klinkner. Beyond the session timeout: automatic hierarchical segmentation of search topics in query logs. In *Proceedings of the 17th ACM Conference on Information and Knowledge Management, CIKM 2008, Napa Valley, California, USA, October 26-30, 2008*, pages 699–708. ACM, 2008.

[11] M. Kellar, C. Watters, and M. Shepherd. A field study characterizing web-based information-seeking tasks. *Journal of the American Society for Information Science and Technology*, 58(7):999–1018, 2007.

[12] T. G. Kolda and B. W. Bader. Tensor decompositions and applications. *SIAM review*, 51(3):455–500, 2009.

[13] A. Kotov, P. N. Bennett, R. W. White, S. T. Dumais, and J. Teevan. Modeling and analysis of cross-session search tasks. In *Proceedings of the 34th international ACM SIGIR conference on Research and development in Information Retrieval*, pages 5–14. ACM, 2011.

[14] L. Li, H. Deng, A. Dong, Y. Chang, and H. Zha. Identifying and labeling search tasks via query-based hawkes processes. In *Proceedings of the 20th ACM SIGKDD international conference on Knowledge discovery and data mining*, pages 731–740. ACM, 2014.

[15] Z. Liao, Y. Song, L.-w. He, and Y. Huang. Evaluating the effectiveness of search task trails. In *Proceedings of the 21st international conference on World Wide Web*, pages 489–498. ACM, 2012.

[16] Y. Liu, Z. Li, H. Xiong, X. Gao, and J. Wu. Understanding of internal clustering validation measures. In *Data Mining (ICDM), 2010 IEEE 10th International Conference on*, pages 911–916. IEEE, 2010.

[17] C. Lucchese, S. Orlando, R. Perego, F. Silvestri, and G. Tolomei. Identifying task-based sessions in search engine query logs. In *WSDM*, 2011.

[18] B. Ma Kay and C. Watters. Exploring multi-session web tasks. In *Proceedings of the SIGCHI Conference on Human Factors in Computing Systems*, pages 1187–1196. ACM, 2008.

[19] N. Matthijs and F. Radlinski. Personalizing web search using long term browsing history. In *Proceedings of the fourth ACM international conference on Web search and data mining*, pages 25–34. ACM, 2011.

[20] R. Mehrotra and E. Yilmaz. Towards hierarchies of search tasks & subtasks. In *Proceedings of the 24th International Conference on World Wide Web Companion*, pages 73–74. International World Wide Web Conferences Steering Committee, 2015.

[21] R. Mehrotra, E. Yilmaz, and M. Verma. Task-based user modelling for personalization via probabilistic matrix factorization. In *Proceedings of the 8th ACM Conference on Recommender Systems (RecSys)*, volume 20, 2014.

[22] A. Mnih and R. Salakhutdinov. Probabilistic matrix factorization. In *NIPS*, 2007.

[23] J. Nocedal and S. J. Wright. *Least-Squares Problems.* Springer, 2006.

[24] A. Postlewaite. Social norms and social assets. *Annu. Rev. Econ.*, 3(1):239–259, 2011.

[25] F. Qiu and J. Cho. Automatic identification of user interest for personalized search. In *Proceedings of the 15th international conference on World Wide Web*, pages 727–736. ACM, 2006.

[26] P. J. Rousseeuw. Silhouettes: a graphical aid to the interpretation and validation of cluster analysis. *Journal of computational and applied mathematics*, 20:53–65, 1987.

[27] M. Speretta and S. Gauch. Personalized search based on user search histories. In *Web Intelligence, 2005. Proceedings. The 2005 IEEE/WIC/ACM International Conference on*, pages 622–628. IEEE, 2005.

[28] S. Sriram, X. Shen, and C. Zhai. A session-based search engine. In *Proceedings of the 27th annual international ACM SIGIR conference on Research and development in information retrieval*, pages 492–493. ACM, 2004.

[29] A. Stegeman and N. D. Sidiropoulos. On kruskalâĂŹs uniqueness condition for the candecomp/parafac decomposition. *Linear Algebra and its applications*, 420(2):540–552, 2007.

[30] J. Teevan, S. T. Dumais, and E. Horvitz. Personalizing search via automated analysis of interests and activities. In *Proceedings of the 28th annual international ACM SIGIR conference on Research and development in information retrieval*, pages 449–456. ACM, 2005.

[31] H. Wang, Y. Song, M.-W. Chang, X. He, R. W. White, and W. Chu. Learning to extract cross-session search tasks. In *Proceedings of the 22nd international conference on World Wide Web*, pages 1353–1364. International World Wide Web Conferences Steering Committee, 2013.

[32] H. Wang, C. Zhai, F. Liang, A. Dong, and Y. Chang. User modeling in search logs via a nonparametric bayesian approach. In *Proceedings of the 7th ACM international conference on Web search and data mining*, pages 203–212. ACM, 2014.

[33] R. W. White, W. Chu, A. Hassan, X. He, Y. Song, and H. Wang. Enhancing personalized search by mining and modeling task behavior. In *Proceedings of the 22nd international conference on World Wide Web*, pages 1411–1420. International World Wide Web Conferences Steering Committee, 2013.

Axiomatic Analysis of Smoothing Methods in Language Models for Pseudo-Relevance Feedback

Hussein Hazimeh
University of Illinois at Urbana-Champaign
Urbana IL, 61801
hazimeh2@illinois.edu

ChengXiang Zhai
University of Illinois at Urbana-Champaign
Urbana IL, 61801
czhai@illinois.edu

ABSTRACT

Pseudo-Relevance Feedback (PRF) is an important general technique for improving retrieval effectiveness without requiring any user effort. Several state-of-the-art PRF models are based on the language modeling approach where a query language model is learned based on feedback documents. In all these models, feedback documents are represented with unigram language models smoothed with a collection language model. While collection language model-based smoothing has proven both effective and necessary in using language models for retrieval, we use axiomatic analysis to show that this smoothing scheme inherently causes the feedback model to favor frequent terms and thus violates the IDF constraint needed to ensure selection of discriminative feedback terms. To address this problem, we propose replacing collection language model-based smoothing in the feedback stage with additive smoothing, which is analytically shown to select more discriminative terms. Empirical evaluation further confirms that additive smoothing indeed significantly outperforms collection-based smoothing methods in multiple language model-based PRF models.

Categories and Subject Descriptors

H.3.3 [**Information Search and Retrieval**]: Relevance Feedback; Retrieval Models

Keywords

Pseudo Relevance Feedback; Smoothing; Divergence Minimization Model; Relevance Model; Geometric Relevance Model

1. INTRODUCTION

Feedback is an essential component in every modern retrieval system as it allows incorporating user preferences. The most reliable type of feedback is relevance feedback where users would label the top documents returned by a retrieval system as relevant or non-relevant. As relevance

feedback is a tedious task that requires labeling large numbers of documents in the collection, pseudo relevance feedback (PRF) is commonly used as an alternative. In PRF, the top documents returned by the retrieval system are assumed to be relevant and are used to expand the query. Although PRF is not as reliable as relevance feedback, empirical studies have shown that it is an effective general technique for improving retrieval accuracy [16, 7, 17, 8, 5]. Since it requires no user effort, the technique can be applied in any retrieval system.

Several types of PRF models exist in the literature (see Section 2 for a detailed review), among which language model (LM) based PRF methods are both theoretically well-grounded and empirically effective [17, 4]. Many PRF models have been proposed, including the divergence minimization model [17], the mixture model [17], the relevance model [7], and the geometric relevance model [15], in addition to many other improved variants [8, 5].

While these models differ in how they are derived, they generally take a set of top-ranked documents from an initial retrieval result as input and attempt to estimate a unigram language model, referred to as the feedback language model, based on these documents to capture their topic. The feedback language model θ_F can then be linearly interpolated with the original query language model θ_Q to form an "expanded" query language model:

$$\theta_Q^{'} = (1 - \alpha)\, \theta_Q + \alpha\, \theta_F$$

where $\alpha \in [0, 1]$ is the interpolation coefficient that determines the weight assigned to the feedback language model. This is similar to how the Rocchio feedback algorithm works in the vector space model [12]. The effectiveness of a PRF method is thus directly determined by the quality of the estimated feedback language model θ_F.

In all the current LM-based PRF models, the estimated feedback LM is based on the aggregation of all the language models of the feedback documents. The aggregation is achieved using an averaging function (such as the arithmetic or geometric mean), and it may also involve weighting each feedback document based on how well it matches the query (i.e., retrieval score of each feedback document in the initial retrieval result), though uniform weighting is also often used. The intuition captured in such an aggregation-based estimate is to favor words that have high probabilities according to all the individual LMs of feedback documents (i.e., occur frequently in all the feedback documents).

Such an aggregation function alone, however, would not consider the occurrences of these terms in the global collec-

ICTIR'15, September 27–30, Northampton, MA, USA.
© 2015 ACM. ISBN 978-1-4503-3833-2/15/09 ...$15.00.
DOI: http://dx.doi.org/10.1145/2808194.2809471.

tion, and indeed it would tend to give high probabilities to many non-informative popular words in the collection that are intuitively not useful for expanding a query. Thus, some of these models further rely on the use of a collection language model to penalize the terms that are too common in the collection. As a result, the terms that have high probabilities in the final estimated feedback LM would be those that occur frequently in all feedback documents, but not very frequently in the entire collection; this is the same effect as what the Rocchio algorithm achieves in the vector space retrieval model when TF-IDF weighting is used.

Formally, let the feedback set be $F = \{D_1, D_2, ..., D_n\}$, where D_i is the ith feedback document. In a language model-based approach to PRF, we consider a unigram language model, θ_i, estimated based on each feedback document D_i, in addition to the collection LM, θ_C, which is estimated based on the entire collection of documents. The goal of a PRF method is to estimate a feedback LM, denoted by θ_F, based on all the document LMs, $\theta_1, ..., \theta_n$, and the collection LM θ_C.

Let w be any feedback word that appears in at least one of the documents in F, then a state-of-the-art PRF method would, in general, assign w a probability $P(w|\theta_F)$ defined as follows:

$$P(w|\theta_F) \propto f\left(A\Big(P(w|\theta_1), ..., P(w|\theta_n)\Big), P(w|\theta_C)\right) \quad (1)$$

where $A : \mathbb{R}^N \to \mathbb{R}$ is an aggregation function that combines the probabilities of words in each of the feedback documents. For example, A can be the arithmetic or geometric mean. $f : \mathbb{R}^2 \to \mathbb{R}$ is an arbitrary function that is increasing in the first argument (so that words that occur frequently in feedback documents would tend to have a higher value of f) and decreasing in the second (so that words that occur frequently in the collection would tend to have a smaller value of f).

This generalized view of the LM-based PRF models is intuitive as we want the final probability of the word to be high for relevant discriminative words, i.e. those that appear in most of the feedback documents and have a low to moderate probability of occurrence in the collection LM.

As in all cases of language model estimation, the feedback documents' LMs (θ_is) have to be smoothed to account for the fact that a document is generally a very small sample for estimating a word distribution over the entire vocabulary. Smoothing is also necessary to avoid assigning zero probabilities to (many) unseen words in documents (an inevitable consequence of the commonly used Maximum Likelihood estimator). The general motivation behind smoothing the feedback documents' language models is that a word may not occur in some of the feedback documents, and not smoothing its probability might overpenalize it. For example, if the PRF model has the function A as the geometric mean and the feedback word occurs in all the feedback documents except one, then the probability assigned to the word will be zero if smoothing is not used.

So far, in virtually all work on LM-based PRF models, smoothing of $P(w|\theta_i)$ has been based on some form of interpolation of the maximum likelihood estimate and the probability of the word according to the collection language model, $P(w|\theta_C)$, which is proportional to the number of occurrences of the word in the whole collection. Dirichlet prior and Jelinek-Mercer are especially popular choices of collection-

based smoothing because of their good performance when used in a retrieval function such as Query Likelihood or Kullback-Leibler (KL) divergence [4]. Indeed, smoothing with a collection language model has not only proven to be effective for retrieval, but also essential for achieving the effect of IDF weighting in a retrieval function [4].

However, in this paper, we show that using collection LM-based smoothing, while effectively avoids the assignment of zero probabilities, is not suitable for LM-based PRF models and can lead to the selection of very frequent and non-informative feedback terms, thus making the PRF model unable to select discriminative feedback terms. Specifically, the problem lies in that when such smoothing is used, the function A will favor words that occur frequently in the collection, and consequently f will assign higher weights to these frequently occurring words. However, PRF models are expected to penalize frequent words (when two words have equal frequencies in the feedback documents, the word with lower frequency in the collection should be favored). While it is still possible to enforce the preference for selecting discriminative words through having $P(w|\theta_C)$ as the second argument in f, our axiomatic analysis of the current PRF models reveals that smoothing based on the collection LM would cause violation of the IDF constraint [5] and introduce an **inherent interference** between smoothing and favoring discriminative words. We show analytically the following dilemma: if we want to avoid favoring common words caused by collection-based smoothing, we must substantially increase the influence of the collection LM, which, however, would result in an extremely skewed word distribution with probability mass mostly concentrated on the matched original query words, restricting the benefit of feedback.

To address this problem, we propose replacing the collection LM-based smoothing strategy with additive smoothing which does not favor frequent words, yet can also dynamically set probabilities for unseen words in adaptation to the document length. We show that using additive smoothing in the current PRF models would ensure that they will not favor common terms anymore, and that some PRF methods will consistently favor discriminative terms thus satisfying the IDF constraint. Empirical evaluation further confirms that additive smoothing indeed significantly outperforms collection-based smoothing methods in multiple LM-based PRF models.

In the rest of the paper, we first review related work in Section 2 and then briefly introduce several representative LM-based PRF methods in Section 3. In Section 4, we present a detailed axiomatic analysis of the collection LM-based smoothing methods with the IDF constraint, and prove theorems to show analytically the inherent interference of smoothing with a collection LM and satisfying the IDF constraint. In Section 5, we then introduce the new strategy of using additive smoothing for PRF and show that it solves the problem of favoring common words in the collection. In section 6, we propose a new measure to empirically assess how discriminative the feedback terms output by a PRF method are. We present our experiment design and results in Sections 7, and summarize our work in Section 8.

2. RELATED WORK

Relevance feedback has been studied first in the vector space model, and the Rocchio feedback algorithm [12], while proposed several decades ago, remains a state-of-the-art feedback method today. Relevance feedback has also been studied in classic probabilistic models and is the basis of the RSJ model [11] and its extensions e.g., [10]. (More discussion on relevance feedback can be found in [6]).

When relevance judgments are available, relevance feedback is generally very effective [11, 14, 2, 13]. While effective, however, relevance feedback requires users to make effort to judge the relevance of the top-ranked documents, which is impractical in many situations. In contrast, pseudo relevance feedback (PRF), also called blind feedback or automatic feedback [3, 16], simply assumes a certain number of top-ranked results from an initial retrieval round to be relevant and performs feedback under this assumption, thus it can be applied to any retrieval system without requiring any effort from the user. PRF leverages the terms in top-ranked documents that have high correlation with the query terms in order to expand the query, and it has proven to be a general effective technique for improving retrieval accuracy, especially for satisfying high-recall information needs.

Most relevance feedback methods can be adapted for pseudo-relevance feedback, but the most effective PRF methods seem to be those based on statistical language models, including, e.g., the relevance model [7], mixture model and divergence minimization [17], and many extensions of these models (e.g., [8, 5, 9]).

Although many LM-based PRF models have been proposed and studied, there seems to be no single winner. [8] compared different LM-based PRF methods and empirically studied the reasons behind the better performance in some of the models. According to this study, the Relevance Model, which uses the arithmetic mean of feedback language models, appears to be slightly advantageous over other models, but a recent work [15] shows that changing the arithmetic mean in the Relevance Model to geometric mean can be beneficial, which implicitly suggests that the divergence minimization model [17] may be also advantageous.

To gain better understanding of relative strengths and weaknesses of different PRF models, [5] performed an axiomatic analysis on several well-known PRF models and studied whether these models satisfy a set of desirable properties. One important property studied by [5] is the IDF effect which states that the PRF model should assign higher probabilities to feedback terms with lower occurrence in the collection. This is an important property to satisfy since when performing feedback we are interested in discriminative words that are usually not so common in the collection. Our work extends this previous work to analyze the relation between smoothing and the IDF effect more accurately and reveals new insights about the interference of smoothing with a collection LM and achieving the IDF effect.

[9] reported that using additive smoothing in the feedback stage in addition to maximizing the entropy in the divergence minimization model led to performance improvements over several datasets. In our analysis, we axiomatically explain the reason behind the improvement in [9]'s new model. We also derive a more general new result: additive smoothing is generally preferred to collection-based smoothing for LM-based PRF methods and this is confirmed in our empirical experiments. Thus, our work directly results in multiple new LM-based PRF models that are potentially more effective than the existing ones and can be used immediately in all retrieval systems.

3. REPRESENTATIVE PRF MODELS

As background, in this section, we give an overview of several representative PRF models that are both efficient and effective.

3.1 Divergence Minimization Model

The Divergence Minimization Model (DMM) estimates $P(w|\theta_F)$ in a way similar to the Rocchio algorithm: θ_F is chosen such that it is close to the centroid of the relevant documents and far away from the collection language model [17]. Formally, the DMM solves the following optimization problem:

$$\theta_F = \arg\min_{\theta} \left(\frac{1}{|F|} \sum_{i=1}^{|F|} D(\theta \,||\, \theta_i) - \lambda D(\theta \,||\, \theta_C) \right)$$

where $D(.||.)$ is the KL divergence and $0 < \lambda < 1$ is a free parameter that determines the extent to which common words in the collection are penalized. Since the objective is a strongly convex function being minimized over a closed convex set (probability simplex), a unique minimizer θ_F exists. Fortunately, the problem has a closed form solution and can be solved using Lagrange multipliers while forcing the constraint $\sum_{w \in V} P(w|\theta_F) = 1$. The solution has the following form:

$$P(w|\theta_F) \propto \frac{\left(\sqrt[|F|]{\prod_{i=1}^{|F|} P(w|\theta_i)} \right)^{\frac{1}{1-\lambda}}}{P(w|\theta_C)^{\frac{\lambda}{1-\lambda}}}$$

where $\propto$ indicates that the probability normalization factor has been omitted. The solution agrees with the intuition of the DMM: the probability of a feedback term is proportional to its occurrence in the feedback set and inversely proportional to that in the collection. Note that the DMM is an instantiation of Equation (1) where A is the geometric mean and $f(x_1, x_2) = \left(\frac{x_1}{x_2} \right)^{\frac{1}{1-\lambda}}$. Although the DMM has a good theoretical justification, several studies have indicated that it suffers in performance. In the next section, we show that the reason behind the poor performance is mainly due to the collection-based smoothing.

3.2 Relevance Model

The Relevance Model (RM) is a well-known LM-based PRF method that has an intuitive probabilistic interpretation and has proven to be effective in several empirical studies. It assumes that each information need (i.e. a topic the user is interested in) has an underlying relevance model R, which is a multinomial distribution over words. Furthermore, it assumes that the query words and the feedback documents' words are randomly sampled from the distribution R, and then tries to estimate R based on simplifying assumptions. Below we present one instantiation of the relevance model:

$$P(w|\theta_F) = \sum_{i=1}^{|F|} P(\theta_i|q)P(w|\theta_i)$$

where q is the query and $P(\theta_i|q)$ can be estimated using the query likelihood (i.e. $P(q|\theta_i)$) assuming a uniform prior on the feedback documents:

$$P(\theta_i|q) = \frac{P(q|\theta_i)P(\theta_i)}{\sum\limits_{i=1}^{|F|} P(q|\theta_i)P(\theta_i)} = \frac{P(q|\theta_i)}{\sum\limits_{i=1}^{|F|} P(q|\theta_i)}$$

When linearly interpolated with the original query, the model we presented above is usually referred to as RM3 [1]. RM3 is an instantiation of Equation (1) where $f = A$ with A being a weighted arithmetic mean.

3.3 Geometric Relevance Model

[15] introduced the Geometric Relevance Model (GRM) which is a refined version of the Relevance Model that uses the normalized geometric mean instead of the weighed arithmetic mean in the aggregation function. The normalized geometric mean has been shown to be a better approximation for the center of mass in the statistical manifold which was the main motivation behind introducing this model [15]. The GRM assigns the following probability to each word in the feedback LM:

$$P(w|\theta_F) \propto \prod_{i=1}^{|F|} P(w|\theta_i)^{P(\theta_i|q)}$$

where $P(\theta_i|q)$ is estimated in the same way as in the RM. The GRM can be viewed as an instantiation of Equation (1) with $f = A$, A being a weighted geometric mean.

4. AXIOMATIC ANALYSIS OF PRF MODELS

In this section, we analyze the effect of collection LM-based smoothing in the feedback stage on the quality of the terms returned by the three models surveyed in Section 3. We do the analysis by inspecting the IDF effect in each model. The IDF effect is a desirable property to have in any PRF model, and it states the following: given two words with the same number of occurrences in the feedback documents, the feedback model should assign a higher probability to the word with higher IDF [5]. For instance, if we observe that the words "the" and "machine" have the *same* number of occurrences in the feedback documents, then we want "machine" to have a higher probability than "the" because the former is more discriminative. This effect is desirable as long as it is not overpenalizing words with low IDF.

Let $c(w, D_i)$ be the count of the word w in the *ith* feedback document. Formally, we define the IDF effect as in [5]:

IDF Effect. Given any two words w_1 and w_2 from the feedback collection F such that $c(w_1, D_i) = c(w_2, D_i)$ $\forall i$ and $P(w_1|\theta_C) < P(w_2|\theta_C)$, a PRF model that outputs a θ_F with $P(w_1|\theta_F) > P(w_2|\theta_F)$ is said to support the IDF effect.

In what follows we assume that document LMs are smoothed using Dirichlet prior smoothing in which the probability of the word w occurring in the *ith* feedback document is smoothed according to:

$$P(w|\theta_i) = \frac{c(w, D_i) + \mu P(w|\theta_C)}{|D_i| + \mu}$$

where $\mu > 0$ is the mean of a Dirichlet distribution and $|D_i|$ is the size of the document D_i. Typically, a high value

of μ such as 1000 is used to smooth document language models in both the retrieval and feedback stages. While the analysis is performed only for Dirichlet prior smoothing, the results still hold for several other collection-based smoothing methods such as Jelinek-Mercer.

4.1 Divergence Minimization Model

Assume w_1 and w_2 are two feedback words as in the definition of the IDF effect . To check if the DMM supports the IDF effect [1], we analyze the sign of $\log P(w_1|\theta_F) - \log P(w_2|\theta_F)$ that should be positive in order to support the effect.

$$\log P(w_1|\theta_F) - \log P(w_2|\theta_F) \propto$$
$$\sum_{i=1}^{|F|} \Big(\log \frac{c(w, D_i) + \mu P(w_1|\theta_C)}{c(w, D_i) + \mu P(w_2|\theta_C)} - \lambda \log \frac{P(w_1|\theta_C)}{P(w_2|\theta_C)} \Big) \quad (2)$$

where $c(w, D_i) = c(w_1, D_i) = c(w_2, D_i)$. Analyzing the sign of (2) directly is a tedious task. In order to facilitate the analysis, we will get an attainable lower bound on (2) and then analyze the sign of the lower bound.

Since (2) is an increasing function in the variable $c(w, D_i)$, the lowest possible value for (2) occurs when w_1 and w_2 appear only once and only in one document in the feedback collection, i.e. when $c(w_1, D_j) = c(w_2, D_j) = 1$ for some j and $c(w_1, D_i) = c(w_2, D_i) = 0$ $\forall D_i \in F$ s.t. $D_i \neq D_j$. This implies that if (2) has a positive sign in the case when w_1 and w_2 appear only once and only in document D_j, then the model will support the IDF effect as this choice of words minimizes (2). Choosing the latter pair of words, we can simplify (2) to:

$$\log \frac{1 + \mu P(w_1|\theta_C)}{1 + \mu P(w_2|\theta_C)} - (|F|\lambda - |F| + 1) \log \frac{P(w_1|\theta_C)}{P(w_2|\theta_C)} \quad (3)$$

Solving for μ that would make (3) positive and assuming $0 < \lambda < 1$, we get an upper bound on μ:

$$\mu \leq \frac{k - 1}{P(w_1|\theta_C) - kP(w_2|\theta_C)} \quad (4)$$

where

$$k = \left(\frac{P(w_1|\theta_C)}{P(w_2|\theta_C)} \right)^{|F|\lambda - |F| + 1}$$

Now that we got an upper bound on μ, we are ready to characterize the IDF behavior of the DMM.

Theorem 1. For $0 < \lambda < \frac{|F|-1}{|F|}$, the DMM cannot support the IDF effect, and for $\frac{|F|-1}{|F|} < \lambda < 1$, $\exists$ $\mu > 0$ such that the DMM supports the IDF effect.

Proof. Any value of μ that satisfies (4) will make the DMM enforce the IDF effect since satisfying (4) will make the lowest possible value of (2) positive. We have two cases to consider:

Case 1: If $0 < \lambda < \frac{|F|-1}{|F|}$ then the right hand side of (4) will be negative since $k > 1$, but μ is the mean of a Dirichlet distribution which cannot be negative. Thus, in this case,

---

[1] The IDF effect for DMM has been already studied in [5], however, we discovered a mistake in their derivation: the inequality under Equation (4) should be $\log(\frac{x}{y}) < \delta \log(\frac{x}{y})$ instead of the other way around, which made them arrive to the wrong conclusion that the DMM always (mildly) supports the IDF effect

the DMM does no support the IDF effect as we identified a choice of w_1 and w_2 for which w_2 will be favored no matter what μ is. It is also important to note that while the DMM does not support the IDF effect in this case, there may be other choices of w_1 and w_2 for which w_1 (the word with higher IDF) will be favored. However, to support the IDF effect, a model should favor w_1 for any choice of w_1 and w_2, and this is not the case here.

Case 2: If $\frac{|F|-1}{|F|} < \lambda < 1$ then the right hand side of (4) will be strictly positive since $k < 1$. Therefore, the DMM supports the IDF effect in this case for a range of μ values (the range can be obtained by choosing w_1 and w_2 that minimize the right-hand side of (4)). $\qquad\square$

One might think that case (2) will lead to performance improvements as the IDF effect is being enforced. However, the condition we got on λ requires it to be close to 1 since the number of feedback documents $|F|$ is usually chosen to be 10 or more.

Theorem 2. If $\lambda \approx 1$, the DMM will assign all the probability mass to exactly one of the feedback terms.

Proof. When λ approaches 1, the DMM will assign one feedback word most of the probability mass, and the other feedback terms will be assigned negligible probabilities. To see why this phenomenon happens, we rewrite $P(w|\theta_F)$ as follows:

$$P(w|\theta_F) \propto \left(\frac{A(w|F)}{P(w|\theta_C)^\lambda} \right)^{\frac{1}{1-\lambda}} \qquad (5)$$

where $A(w|F)$ is the geometric mean of the probabilities of the word w in all the feedback documents. Let w_h be the feedback word with the highest $\frac{A(w|F)}{P(w|\theta_C)}$ ratio among all other feedback words. This word will probably appear a lot in the feedback documents and will have a high IDF. Now, to calculate the final probability assigned by the DMM to the word w_h, we have to normalize by the sum of the probabilities of all other feedback terms. Thus, the final probability of w_h can be written as:

$$P(w_h|\theta_F) = \frac{\left(\frac{A(w_h|F)}{P(w_h|\theta_C)^\lambda} \right)^{\frac{1}{1-\lambda}}}{\left(\frac{A(w_h|F)}{P(w_h|\theta_C)^\lambda} \right)^{\frac{1}{1-\lambda}} + \sum\limits_{w \in F s.t. w \neq w_h} \left(\frac{A(w|F)}{P(w|\theta_C)^\lambda} \right)^{\frac{1}{1-\lambda}}} \qquad (6)$$

Taking the limit as λ tends to 1, we have:

$$\lim_{\lambda \to 1} P(w_h|\theta_F) = 1 \qquad (7)$$

where the limit is equal to 1 since the terms corresponding to w_h in the numerator and denominator have the highest order. In practice, setting λ to any value near 1 will make the word w_h dominate the probability of the feedback language model. Note that in the analysis we assumed that the word with the highest $\frac{A(w|F)}{P(w|\theta_C)}$ ratio is unique. In the unlikely event where more than one word have the highest ratio, the probability mass will be split equally between such words. $\qquad\square$

We conclude that in case (2), when $\frac{|F|-1}{|F|} < \lambda < 1$, one of the feedback terms will essentially get all the probability. Since the original query words usually have the highest occurrence in the feedback set in addition to relatively high IDF, probably one of the query words will be the w_h considered in the analysis above (although there are cases where

a non-query word can have the highest ratio and dominate the feedback LM).

This analysis confirms the empirical studies performed on the divergence minimization model before. [17] noticed that when $|F| = 10$, the DMM's performance severely drops for $\lambda > 0.9$. The reason behind the drop is clear now: $\lambda > 0.9$ falls in case (2) of our analysis where the DMM will assign most of the probability to one term, and consequently the performance will be similar to that of the search engine without feedback. Also, several other studies indicated that the DMM suffers in performance even when its parameter λ is tuned [8, 5]. Such studies found that λ values in the range $(0.1, 0.4)$ give the highest performance which was still below that of other well-known feedback techniques. Small values of λ fall into case (1) in our analysis where the performance drop is due to the lack of support for the IDF effect, and this is in turn due to smoothing using the collection language model in the feedback stage. To conclude, we have clearly identified the problem with the DMM as previous attempts in the literature failed to clearly pinpoint the problem; using a collection LM to smooth the feedback documents will cause the DMM to suffer in performance no matter what the choices of the parameters λ and μ are.

4.2 Relevance Model

Assuming w_1 and w_2 are as in the definition of the IDF effect, we analyze the sign of $P(w_1|\theta_F) - P(w_2|\theta_F)$ when Dirichlet prior smoothing is used:

$$P(w_1|\theta_F) - P(w_2|\theta_F) =$$
$$\sum_{i=1}^{|F|} \left(P(\theta_i|q) \frac{\mu \left(P(w_1|\theta_C) - P(w_2|\theta_C) \right)}{|D_i| + \mu} \right) < 0 \qquad (8)$$

(8) is unconditionally negative for any valid value of μ implying that the currently used RM does not support the IDF effect, and on the contrary, it consistently favors more frequent words in the collection. (8) also shows that the longer the feedback documents are, the lower is the extent to which common words are rewarded. Clearly, this makes the RM's performance dependent on the length of the feedback documents.

4.3 Geometric Relevance Model

Similar to the case of the RM, we analyze the sign of $\log P(w_1|\theta_F) - \log P(w_2|\theta_F)$ where w_1 and w_2 are as in the definition of the IDF effect:

$$\log P(w_1|\theta_F) - \log P(w_2|\theta_F) =$$
$$\sum_{i=1}^{|F|} \left(P(\theta_i|q) \log \frac{c(w, D_i) + \mu P(w_1|\theta_C)}{c(w, D_i) + \mu P(w_2|\theta_C)} \right) < 0 \qquad (9)$$

where $c(w, D_i) = c(w_1, D_i) = c(w_2, D_i)$. Since (9) is negative, the GRM does not support the IDF effect and also suffers from the problem of consistently favoring frequent words in the collection [2]. (9) is an increasing function in $c(w, D_i)$ so a higher $c(w, D_i)$ makes (9) less negative. Therefore, the higher the occurrence of w_1 and w_2 in the feedback documents is, the lower is the extent to which w_2 is favored. This is different from the case of RM where the documents lengths controlled how common words are rewarded.

---

[2] [5] has already pointed this out when using Jelinek-Mercer smoothing

To recap, we have shown that using collection LM-based smoothing at the feedback stage will cause several of the well-known PRF models to penalize discriminative words.

5. ADDITIVE SMOOTHING FOR PRF MODELS

To solve the problem of favoring highly frequent words in LM-based PRF methods, we propose using additive smoothing in the feedback stage, while keeping the collection LM-based smoothing in the retrieval stage in order to preserve the IDF and document length normalization heuristics. In additive smoothing, the probability of each feedback document is adjusted as follows:

$$P(w|\theta_i) = \frac{c(w, D_i) + \gamma}{|D_i| + \gamma|V_F|}$$

where $\gamma > 0$ is the smoothing parameter that can be considered as a pseudo count, and $|V_F|$ is the size of the vocabulary of the feedback documents. Below we study the behavior of the different PRF models under additive smoothing.

5.1 Divergence Minimization Model

Assuming w_1 and w_2 as in the definition of the IDF effect and using additive smoothing we get:

$$\log P(w_1|\theta_F) - \log P(w_2|\theta_F) \propto$$

$$\sum_{i=1}^{|F|} \left(\log \frac{c(w_1, D_i) + \gamma}{c(w_2, D_i) + \gamma} - \lambda \log \frac{P(w_1|\theta_C)}{P(w_2|\theta_C)} \right) =$$

$$- |F|\lambda \log \frac{P(w_1|\theta_C)}{P(w_2|\theta_C)} > 0 \qquad (10)$$

(10) is unconditionally positive for any choice of γ and λ which means that the DMM supports the IDF effect in this case and consequently favors more discriminative words. The extent to which high IDF words are favored can be controlled by the parameter λ. By using additive smoothing, the DMM is now performing what it is intended to do: minimize the divergence from the centroid of the feedback documents' LMs and maximize the divergence from the collection language model. When collection-based smoothing was used, the DMM was not performing the intended objective, while on the contrary, it was favoring frequent words in many cases.

5.2 Relevance Model

Assuming w_1 and w_2 as before while using additive smoothing:

$$P(w_1|\theta_F) - P(w_2|\theta_F) =$$

$$\sum_{i=1}^{|F|} \left(P(\theta_i|q) \frac{c(w_1, D_i) + \gamma - c(w_2, D_i) - \gamma}{|D_i| + \gamma|V_f|} \right) = 0 \quad (11)$$

(11) shows that when we use additive smoothing for the RM, the model will not favor common words and will treat all words equally, i.e. irrespective of how they occurred in the collection. Since $P(w_1|\theta_F) = P(w_2|\theta_F)$, strictly speaking, the IDF effect is still not supported as it requires $P(w_2|\theta_F) > P(w_1|\theta_F)$. Although the IDF effect is not supported, the performance is expected to improve since the model no longer favors common terms as was the case with collection-based smoothing.

5.3 Geometric Relevance Model

Assuming w_1 and w_2 as before while using additive smoothing:

$$\log P(w_1|\theta_F) - \log P(w_2|\theta_F) \propto$$

$$\sum_{i=1}^{|F|} \left(P(\theta_i|q) \log \frac{c(w_1, D_i) + \gamma}{c(w_2, D_i) + \gamma} \right) = 0 \qquad (12)$$

When additive smoothing is used, the GRM will also treat words irrespective of their frequency of occurrence in the collection, in contrast to the case of collection-based smoothing where common terms are always favored. We should note that this behavior is expected since the RM and GRM are not designed to penalize common words.

6. MEASURING PRF METHOD DISCRIMINATION

Although the IDF effect is an interesting property to analyze, it cannot provide direct insight on the extent to which the terms output by a certain PRF method are discriminative. Therefore, we need a good empirical measure that can indicate how discriminative the feedback terms are. Previous attempts in the literature have used the average of the IDF of the top terms output by the PRF method to quantify the method's discrimination. For example, [5] used Average_IDF $= \frac{1}{|Q|} \sum_{q \in Q} \sum_{w \in F} \frac{\log_{10} \frac{N}{N_w}}{t}$ where Q is the set of queries, N is the total number of documents in the collection, N_w is the frequency of the word in the collection C, and t is the number of feedback terms considered. However, such approaches do not take into account the probabilities assigned to the terms which might be problematic. For instance, consider a PRF method that consistently outputs many discriminative terms, in addition to a few common terms that get all the probability mass. In such a case, the average of the IDF values of all the top terms will be high, however the method is assigning most of the probability to the common terms so it is practically updating the query with common terms. Thus, using the average of the IDF might not be a good measure. A more suitable measure should assess the extent to which discriminative terms will *change* the query.

We propose a simple measure called the Discrimination Measure (DM) for quantifying the discriminative power of a PRF method. The measure takes into account both the IDF **and** the probabilities of the top terms and captures the idea that the higher the probability assigned to discriminative terms, the higher is the discrimination of the PRF method. Let $Q = \{q_1, q_2, ..., q_m\}$ be a set of queries associated with a probability distribution θ_Q, and $\theta_F(q)$ be the feedback language model output by the PRF method for the query q. Given a PRF method, we define the Discrimination Measure as:

$$DM = \frac{\mathbb{E}_{\theta_C}[\theta_C]}{\mathbb{E}_{\theta_Q}\mathbb{E}_{\theta_F(q)}[\theta_C]} \approx \frac{\sum_{w \in C} P(w|\theta_C)^2}{\frac{1}{|Q|} \sum_{q \in Q} \sum_{w \in F(q)} P(w|\theta_{F(q)}) P(w|\theta_C)}$$

where a uniform prior over the queries is assumed to get the right-hand side. The denominator can be viewed as the expected value of the DF (Document Frequency) of the feedback terms under the PRF method's distribution. The numerator is a normalization factor that makes the measure's values more meaningful. Consider a hypothetical PRF method that consistently outputs a feedback LM whose distribution is the same as that of the collection LM (i.e. $\theta_F = \theta_C$), the DM of this method is equal to 1. If a PRF method puts more probability mass on common terms compared to the hypothetical method, then $DM < 1$. On the other hand, if a PRF method assigns higher probabilities to discriminative terms compared to the hypothetical method, then $DM > 1$. In general, the more probability the PRF method assigns to discriminative terms, the lower is the expected DF of the feedback terms, and consequently the higher is the DM.

7. EMPIRICAL EVALUATION

To validate the results of the axiomatic analysis and gain more insight on the performance of LM-based PRF methods, we ran several experiments to empirically examine the validity of our analytical results and the main hypothesis that additive smoothing performs better than collection-based smoothing for PRF.

7.1 Datasets and Parameter Setting

We used four TREC collections in the experiments: AP (Associated Press 88-89, TREC Disks 1 & 2), WSJ (Wall Street Journal 87-92, TREC Disks 1 & 2), Robust (Robust 2004, TREC Disks 4 & 5 minus Congressional Record), and WT10g (TREC Web Corpus). A summary of the datasets' statistics is shown in Table 1. The queries were extracted from the title field of each topic. We carried out the experiments using MeTA toolkit[3] where we preprocessed all the collections using MeTA's default stopword list and performed stemming using the Porter2 English stemming algorithm. The KL divergence retrieval function was used along with Dirichlet prior smoothing with the smoothing coefficient μ set to 1000. The additive smoothing parameter γ was also fixed to 1 in all the experiments, except for the experiment in Section 7.2.3 which involves sweeping this parameter.

In all the experiments, we split each dataset's topics into training and testing subsets as shown in Table 1. The training topics are used to learn the model parameters that optimize the MAP (Mean Average Precision), and the testing topics are used to report the MAP which is evaluated for the top 1000 retrieved documents, in addition to the P10 (Precision at 10 documents) and the DM (Discrimination Measure). In the training phase we sweep the number of feedback documents $|F|$ between {10, 25, 50, 75, 100}, the number of feedback terms between {10, 25, 50, 75, 100}, and the interpolation coefficient α between {0.1, 0.2,..., 0.9}. Additionally, for the DMM with collection-based smoothing, we sweep the parameter λ in the range {0.1, 0.3, 0.5, 0.7, 0.9}, whereas for the additive smoothing variant of the DMM we sweep the parameter λ in the range {0.01, 0.03, 0.05, 0.07, 0.09} (the DMM requires larger values of λ to suppress the common terms and reach its optimal performance in case of collection-based smoothing).

---
[3]https://meta-toolkit.org/

Collection	AP	WSJ	Robust	WT10g
#Docs	164k	173k	528k	1692k
#Queries (w. qrels)	99	100	249	100
Training Queries	51-100	51-100	301-450	451-500
Testing Queries	101-150	101-150	601-700	501-550

Table 1: Datasets' Statistics

7.2 Experimental Results

We now present both qualitative and quantitative results from our experiments to examine the analytical results and hypotheses.

7.2.1 Interference of Collection-based Smoothing with IDF Effect

We first examine the empirical behavior of the PRF methods when using collection-based smoothing vs. additive smoothing with specific consideration of the IDF effect. Specifically, we ran multiple queries and manually inspected the top feedback terms extracted by the three PRF methods using both Dirichlet prior smoothing and additive smoothing for different parameters.

In Table 2, we show the top 10 feedback terms for the query "Computer" extracted by the DMM and GRM using the AP collection (i.e. the words are shown before interpolation). Although we could not include the top feedback terms of the RM due to space constraints, it extracted words similar to the other two models. We should also note that the results obtained using this query are very representative of the other queries we examined in terms of the quality of the extracted terms.

When using DMM with Dirichlet prior smoothing and $\lambda = 0.1$ (Table 2 (a)), most of the top feedback terms are very common and not informative, and this is a direct consequence of the lack of support for the IDF effect as demonstrated in Theorem 1. Changing to $\lambda = 0.95$ (Table 2 (b)) while keeping the Dirichlet prior smoothing actually extracted high quality terms, and this is explained by the support for the IDF effect since $\lambda > \frac{|F|-1}{|F|}$ ($|F|$ is set to 10 for the results in Table 2). However, almost all the probability mass is being assigned to the original query word, and this validates the result we got in Theorem 2 where we showed that the DMM will assign the majority of the probability to one word when λ becomes close to 1. When we switched to additive smoothing (Table 2 (c)), most of the terms became discriminative and the original query word got only 21% of the total probability mass.

Similarly, the GRM had very common terms when using Dirichlet prior smoothing (Table 2 (d)). When we switched to additive smoothing (Table 2 (e)), more discriminative terms got introduced. This confirms the results of the axiomatic analysis where we showed that the GRM and RM will no longer favor common terms when additive smoothing is used.

7.2.2 Additive vs. Collection-based Smoothing

Next, we want to examine the expected empirical benefit of additive smoothing over collection-based smoothing. Thus, we compared the MAP, precision at 10 documents, and the Discrimination Measure of the three methods for both Dirichlet prior smoothing and additive smoothing over the four collections. The results are reported in Table 3. Note that we optimized the parameters ($|F|$, number of feed-

w	$P(w|\theta_F)$	w	$P(w|\theta_F)$	w	$P(w|\theta_F)$	w	$P(w|\theta_F)$	w	$P(w|\theta_F)$
comput	0.2213	comput	0.9999	comput	0.2099	comput	0.1561	comput	0.1962
time	0.0296	arpanet	3.8e-07	virus	0.0342	state	0.0326	virus	0.0334
state	0.0293	virus	1.6e-15	system	0.0294	time	0.0310	system	0.0302
new	0.0280	bug	6.2e-19	univers	0.0265	new	0.0309	univers	0.0282
nation	0.0253	hacker	3.0e-20	network	0.0258	percent	0.0279	network	0.0254
percent	0.0250	network	8.3e-21	program	0.0239	nation	0.0279	program	0.0251
two	0.0229	adv-research	2.2e-21	research	0.0231	say	0.0254	research	0.0238
say	0.0228	mellon	3.9e-22	time	0.0227	two	0.0254	time	0.0235
system	0.0228	thecomput	1.6e-22	arpanet	0.0187	report	0.0247	nation	0.0194
report	0.0223	data	9.8e-23	data	0.0182	year	0.0242	center	0.0182
(a) DMM - Dirichlet Smoothing $\lambda = 0.1$		(b) DMM - Dirichlet Smoothing $\lambda = 0.95$		(c) DMM - **Additive Smoothing** $\lambda = 0.03$		(d) GRM - Dirichlet Smoothing		(e) GRM - **Additive Smoothing**	

Table 2: Top 10 Feedback Terms for the Query "Computer" for different smoothing strategies and parameters. Tables (a), (b), and (d) refer to the traditional Collection LM-based smoothing method used in the literature. Tables (c) and (e) show how using additive smoothing can lead to the selection of more discriminative terms.

Dataset	Measure	DMM		RM		GRM	
		Collection	Additive	Collection	Additive	Collection	Additive
AP	MAP	0.261	0.301*	0.291	0.303*	0.258	0.286*
	P10	0.4	0.44	0.412	0.434	0.416	0.426
	DM	0.524	1.94	0.648	1.69	0.527	1.75
WSJ	MAP	0.254	0.268*	0.253	0.267*	0.239	0.258*
	P10	0.426	0.458	0.46	0.494	0.42	0.46
	DM	0.75	2.67	0.84	2.36	0.686	2.45
Robust	MAP	0.287	0.299*	0.312	0.324*	0.298	0.322*
	P10	0.44	0.442	0.447	0.466	0.445	0.47
	DM	1.72	9.47	1.89	6.51	1.54	11.1
WT10g	MAP	0.196	0.215	0.205	0.214*	0.198	0.213*
	P10	0.324	0.349	0.339	0.351	0.337	0.355
	DM	0.812	10.6	1.16	6.56	0.808	8.57

Table 3: Comparison of retrieval performance between collection-based and additive smoothing for the DMM, RM, and GRM. All additive smoothing MAP values with an asterisk are statistically significant from their collection-based smoothing counterparts based on a paired two-tailed t-test with significance level = 0.05.

back terms, and α) only for collection-based smoothing and used the learned parameters for additive smoothing, which might give collection-based smoothing an advantage in some of the reported values.

As shown in Table 3, additive smoothing improved the MAP and precision at 10 documents for all the methods and datasets. The improvement in MAP is statistically significant for almost all the values which confirms our hypothesis that additive smoothing can enhance the performance of PRF methods by preventing them from rewarding common terms. The average improvement in MAP for the DMM, RM, and GRM over all the datasets are 8.7%, 4.5%, and 8.6%, respectively. The average improvement in precision at 10 for the DMM, RM, and GRM over all the datasets are 6.4%, 5.1%, and 5.7%, respectively. The DMM and GRM seem to benefit more from additive smoothing compared to RM, and this can be attributed to the reliance of the RM on the arithmetic mean which is less sensitive to the smoothing method used. Another observation is that the difference in performance between the three methods becomes significantly smaller when using additive smoothing.

The Discrimination Measure is low for all the collection-based smoothing variants and has values below 1 for three out of the four datasets, meaning that the traditional PRF methods were assigning more probability mass to the com-

mon words compared to the probability assignments of the collection LM θ_C. After switching to additive smoothing, all the methods got a several-fold increase in the DM implying that the expected value of the document frequency of the extracted terms got a several-fold decrease. The results show that the DMM generally has the highest DM when using additive smoothing, and this can be explained by the fact that the DMM supports the IDF effect, whereas the other two models do not discriminate based on the document frequency of the terms (the Robust collection is an exception where GRM had the highest DM and this due to the small λ (=0.01) that optimized the MAP in this case).

We also swept the number of feedback documents and the number of feedback terms over a range of values to study the robustness of the models under each smoothing scheme. The results on the AP data set are shown in Figure 1 (the other three data sets have shown similar patterns). The sensitivity of the different PRF methods under additive smoothing is very similar to that under collection-based smoothing, implying that additive smoothing does not affect the robustness of the different models. The performance of the models with additive smoothing is consistently higher than the collection-based smoothing counterparts for any value of |F| and any number of feedback terms. We should also note that when the number of feedback documents increases, the

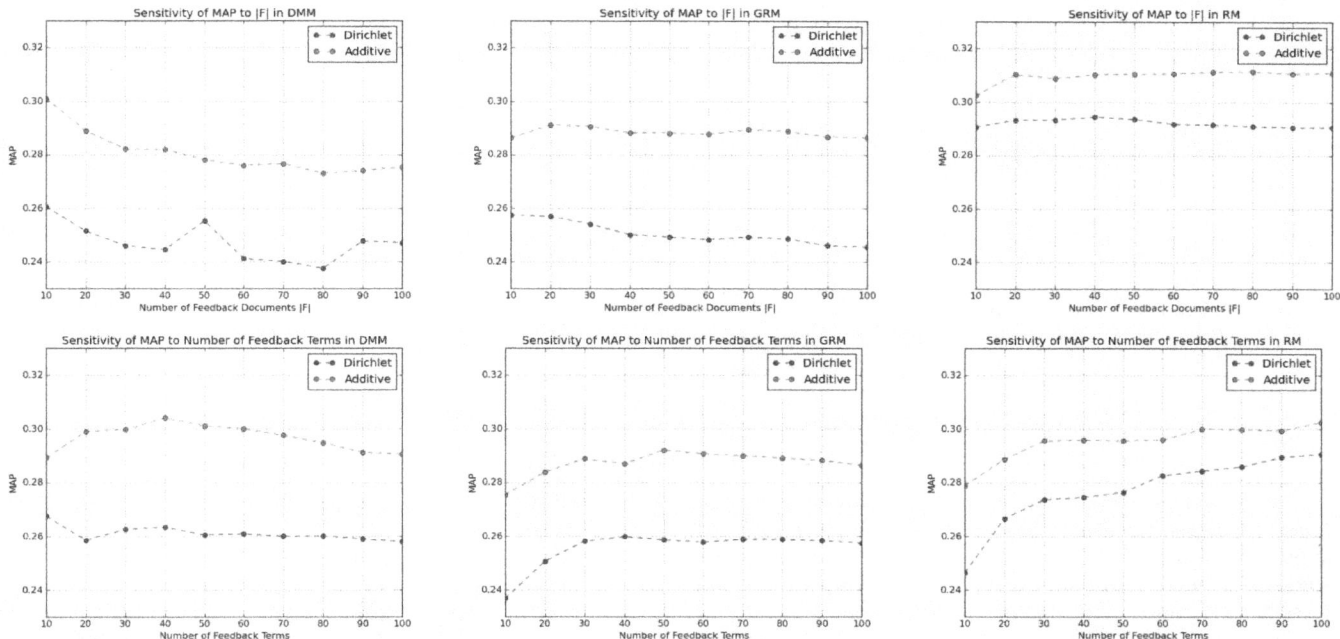

Figure 1: Sensitivity of the MAP to the number of feedback documents $|F|$ and the number of feedback terms for the DMM, GRM, and RM using Dirichlet prior Smoothing and Additive Smoothing. Additive smoothing significantly outperforms Dirichlet prior smoothing in all the models and for all values of the parameters.

RM and GRM appear to be more stable than the DMM, and this can be attributed to the fact that the DMM treats all documents equally whereas the RM and GRM assign each document a weight equal to its probability of relevance (i.e. lower ranked documents would have less effect on the extracted feedback terms).

7.2.3 Additive Smoothing Parameter

The results above show a clear advantage of additive smoothing over collection-based smoothing for PRF. We now turn to the question about how to optimize additive smoothing for PRF, particularly how to optimize its parameter γ. To this end, we swept the additive smoothing parameter γ by decades between 10^{-5} and 1 to study its effect on performance. As shown in Figure 2, the RM maintains very stable performance as the additive smoothing parameter changes. In fact, we tried running the RM without any smoothing (i.e. $\gamma = 0$), and its performance remained the same (not using smoothing at the feedback stage will stop rewarding the common terms when compared to the collection-based smoothing, thus giving the same effect as additive smoothing). The MAP and precision at 10 of the DMM and GRM increase as γ increases (with one minor outlier), and the performance is maximized by $\gamma = 1$ which corresponds to the conventional add-one smoothing. Although the graphs shown were generated using AP collection, the same results discussed in this section are also valid for the three other collections.

7.3 Summary of Main Findings

Our experimental results have confirmed the predictions of our axiomatic analysis of the smoothing methods for LM-based PRF models, showing that the traditionally used collection-based smoothing indeed forces LM-based PRF models to re-

ward common words, and additive smoothing solves the issue by focusing the probability mass on more discriminative terms thus increasing the retrieval performance significantly.

Our results also show that the additive smoothing parameter $\gamma = 1$ maximized the performance of the DMM and GRM over all the collections. The RM's performance is not affected by the smoothing parameter, and running it without any smoothing (i.e. $\gamma = 0$) gives the same performance as additive smoothing. Overall, these results, along with our theoretical analysis, suggest that additive smoothing, instead of collection-based smoothing, should be used in all the LM-based PRF methods.

8. CONCLUSION AND FUTURE WORK

Language model-based pseudo relevance feedback methods have proven effective in enhancing retrieval and can be applied to any retrieval system without requiring extra effort from users. Smoothing of language models for the feedback documents is necessary in these methods to address the issue of data sparsity and has been achieved using a collection language model-based smoothing strategy in virtually all the work so far. Although collection-based smoothing has been shown to be necessary and effective in the retrieval stage, we have axiomatically shown that collection-based smoothing in the feedback stage is non-optimal and inherently interferes with the desired preference for discriminative terms for feedback since it forces pseudo-relevance feedback methods to favor very frequent and non-informative words. We proposed replacing collection-based smoothing at the feedback stage with additive smoothing, which is analytically proven to ensure that the learned feedback model favors discriminative terms and empirically shown to achieve better retrieval accuracy when compared to collection-based smoothing.

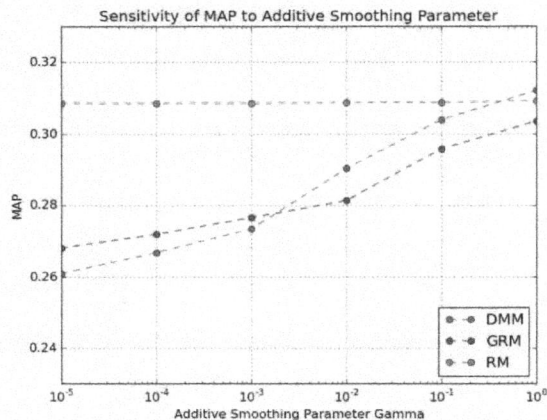

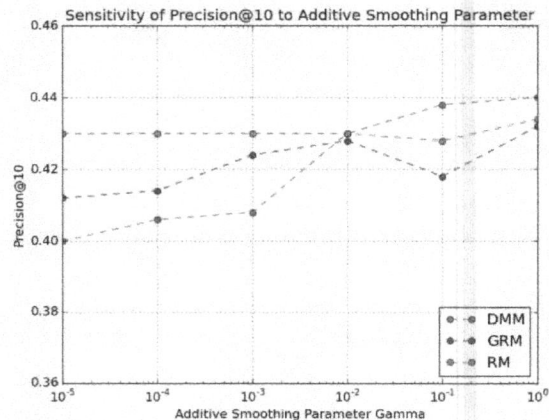

Figure 2: Sensitivity of the MAP and precision at 10 to the additive smoothing parameter γ.

The experiments show that the three models perform similarly when using additive smoothing, although the DMM supports the IDF effect whereas the RM and GRM treat feedback terms irrespective of their occurrence in the collection. This motivates an interesting question about the significance of the IDF effect. It has been established that by not rewarding common terms, the PRF method can attain good performance, however, does favoring discriminative terms through supporting the IDF lead to significant performance improvement? Our analysis also reveals a connection between a parameter in the divergence minimization model and the number of feedback documents; this is an interesting direction worth further exploration in the future. Yet another question motivated by our study is how to analytically bound the parameter of additive smoothing when used for PRF. The empirical results show that setting $\gamma = 1$ seems to work well in the experiments we have done, but could it be possible to derive analytical bounds for this parameter?

9. REFERENCES

[1] N. Abdul-Jaleel, J. Allan, W. B. Croft, F. Diaz, L. Larkey, X. Li, M. D. Smucker, and C. Wade. Umass at trec 2004: Novelty and hard. Technical report, DTIC Document, 2004.

[2] J. Allan. Relevance feedback with too much data. In *Proceedings of ACM SIGIR 1995*, pages 337–343, 1995.

[3] C. Buckley, G. Salton, J. Allan, and A. Singhal. Automatic query expansion using smart: Trec 3. *NIST special publication sp*, pages 69–69, 1995.

[4] Cheng. Statistical language models for information retrieval a critical review. *Found. Trends Inf. Retr.*, 2(3):137–213, Mar. 2008.

[5] S. Clinchant and E. Gaussier. A theoretical analysis of pseudo-relevance feedback models. In *Proceedings of the 2013 Conference on the Theory of Information Retrieval*, ICTIR '13, pages 6:6–6:13, New York, NY, USA, 2013. ACM.

[6] H. Fang and C. Zhai. Web search relevance feedback. In *Encyclopedia of Database Systems*, pages 3493–3497, 2009.

[7] V. Lavrenko and W. B. Croft. Relevance based language models. In *Proceedings of ACM SIGIR 2001*, SIGIR '01, pages 120–127, New York, NY, USA, 2001. ACM.

[8] Y. Lv and C. Zhai. A comparative study of methods for estimating query language models with pseudo feedback. In *Proceedings of ACM CIKM 2009*, CIKM '09, pages 1895–1898, New York, NY, USA, 2009. ACM.

[9] Y. Lv and C. Zhai. Revisiting the divergence minimization feedback model. In *Proceedings of the 23rd ACM International Conference on Conference on Information and Knowledge Management*, CIKM '14, pages 1863–1866, New York, NY, USA, 2014. ACM.

[10] C. J. V. Rijsbergen. *Information Retrieval*. Butterworth-Heinemann, Newton, MA, USA, 2nd edition, 1979.

[11] S. E. Robertson and K. S. Jones. Relevance weighting of search terms. *Journal of the American Society for Information science*, 27(3):129–146, 1976.

[12] J. Rocchio. Relevance feedback in information retrieval. *SMART Retrieval System Experiments in Automatic Document Processing*, 1971.

[13] I. Ruthven and M. Lalmas. A survey on the use of relevance feedback for information access systems. *Knowl. Eng. Rev.*, 18(2):95–145, June 2003.

[14] G. Salton and C. Buckley. Improving retrieval performance by relevance feedback. *Journal of the American Society for Information Science*, 41(4):288–297, 1990.

[15] J. Seo and W. B. Croft. Geometric representations for multiple documents. In *Proceedings of ACM SIGIR 2010*, SIGIR '10, pages 251–258, New York, NY, USA, 2010. ACM.

[16] J. Xu and W. B. Croft. Query expansion using local and global document analysis. In *SIGIR '96: Proceedings of the 19th annual international ACM SIGIR conference on Research and development in information retrieval*, pages 4–11, New York, NY, USA, 1996. ACM.

[17] C. Zhai and J. Lafferty. Model-based feedback in the language modeling approach to information retrieval. In *Proceedings of ACM CIKM 2001*, CIKM '01, pages 403–410, New York, NY, USA, 2001. ACM.

On Divergence Measures and Static Index Pruning

Ruey-Cheng Chen[†][*]   Chia-Jung Lee   W. Bruce Croft

[†]RMIT University, GPO Box 2476, Melbourne VIC 3001, Australia
University of Massachusetts, 140 Governors Drive, Amherst, MA 01003-9264
ruey-cheng.chen@rmit.edu.au, {cjlee, croft}@cs.umass.edu

ABSTRACT

We study the problem of static index pruning in a renowned divergence minimization framework, using a range of divergence measures such as f-divergence and Rényi divergence as the objective. We show that many well-known divergence measures are convex in pruning decisions, and therefore can be exactly minimized using an efficient algorithm. Our approach allows postings be prioritized according to the amount of information they contribute to the index, and through specifying a different divergence measure the contribution is modeled on a different returns curve. In our experiment on GOV2 data, Rényi divergence of order infinity appears the most effective. This divergence measure significantly outperforms many standard methods and achieves identical retrieval effectiveness as full data using only 50% of the postings. When top-k precision is of the only concern, 10% of the data is sufficient to achieve the accuracy that one would usually expect from a full index.

Categories and Subject Descriptors

H.3.3 [**Information Storage and Retrieval**]: Information Search and Retrieval

Keywords

Static index pruning; f-divergence; Rényi divergence

1. INTRODUCTION

The study on inducing succinct data representation has a long history in the domain of information retrieval. Inspired by the need of offering search on handheld devices with limited storage space, Carmel et al. [9] motivated a technique, called *static index pruning*, that aims at creating a condensed version of an inverted index such that there is little difference from the user perspective in the top k returned results. Since an inverted index is essentially a

---

[*]Part of the work was done at National Taiwan University.

warehouse of links between terms and documents, it makes sense to see this as a problem of choosing the most useful links, i.e., signals or features that best distinguish a relevant document from non-relevant ones, allowing the creation of an effective condensed or summarized index. Many early efforts took this perspective and have succeeded in applying relevance measures and heuristics common in information retrieval to this problem [4, 7, 9]. Some later developments used a log-based approach, exploiting session logs to uncover regularity in user queries and locate information that is likely to be reused [2, 25]. Due to this success, the notion of static index pruning as a *cache problem* has become prevalent. Although some progress has been made in exploring more sophisticated abstractions [5, 26], a dedicated theory for this task has not been described.

The problem of static index pruning appeals to theoreticians for it being a related process to relevance estimation. Instead of asking how one estimates the degree of relevance in a posting, it asks if the postings can be ordered in a way such that the least informative part can be thrown away as necessary. This perspective is valuable since it outlines an important task that people recently have started to look at, which is to create highly succinct summaries about large data in an unsupervised fashion.

In a recent paper by Chen and Lee [10], it has been shown that static index pruning has a connection to probabilistic inference, a well-motivated problem solved usually by minimizing relative entropy [17]. Their work outlined a mathematical foundation for static index pruning, but it also came with some caveats that makes exact inference difficult and hinders further implications. Several interesting research questions were left unsettled due to this difficulty. For instance, can the optimization framework generalize over a broader family of divergences, such as f-divergence or the famous Rényi divergence? Can the analysis be extended to model multiple-term queries? Does removing term posting lists entirely from the index lead to decreased performance? None of these questions can be easily answered without us first being able to develop new mathematical tools.

In this paper, we introduce a new mathematical analysis to address these issues. We built on top of the existing divergence minimization framework for static index pruning, but used a different way to describe the optimization problem. We show that both f-divergence and Rényi divergence can be exactly minimized under this formulation, and the exact solution can be efficiently computed in time complexity $O(|\mathcal{D}|L \log L)$, where $|\mathcal{D}|$ is the total number of documents and L the maximum document length in the index. The same analysis can also be extended to model multiple-term queries. We show that, with suitable assumptions (bag-of-words), the entire Rényi divergence family can be exactly solved for up to infinite terms. This problem is readily solvable even in the presence of billions of variables, allowing us to avoid a numerical solution impractical for a problem of this scale. We also seek comparison with other strong results in the application domain. Our empirical results on the GOV2 data shows that Rényi divergence helps preserving top-k precision and document ranking. Our approach outperforms many standard methods of the task and compares well to the strong baseline in top-k precision.

The rest of paper is structured as follows. Section 2 covers some backgrounds of static index pruning. In Section 3, we develop a convex analysis that has eventually led to an exact algorithm for minimizing all the divergence measures mentioned in this work. Section 4 covers the experimental results. Our findings are discussed in Section 5 and we give out concluding remarks in Section 6.

2. BACKGROUND

Static index pruning first appeared as a theoretical problem in Carmel et al. [9] and later found application in web search [7, 14]. It is a technique that removes less important postings permanently from an index. Initially developed to mitigate efficiency issues caused by operating a large index, static index pruning later has grown into a wide range of studies that focus on reducing the seemingly inevitable performance loss. To date, many successful approaches have relied on posting importance measures, including impact [7, 9] or odds ratio in the probability ranking principle [5]. Some later efforts have based this measurement on more sophisticated techniques, such as statistical hypothesis testing [26], query-view methods [2], or information theory [10, 11].

Our approach most closely resembles the work of Chen and Lee [10] in the way the pruning problem is framed. While we use relative entropy minimization (i.e., Kullback's principle of minimum cross-entropy) much the same way as in the previous work to infer truncated models, we rely on a different generative process that eventually leads to document-centric pruning strategies. This departure helps to avoid many modeling issues previously associated with term-centric formulations. Our pruning problems are sufficiently simple and can be solved exactly using analytic techniques alone. Our approach is free of approximations such as surrogates or assumptions about uniform priors and probability renormalization, and can be easily extended to model multiple-term queries. These improvements in modeling make our results less restrictive and more practical.

3. DIVERGENCE-BASED METHOD

We start this analysis by treating inverted indexes in the context of language modeling [23]. We will view an inverted index as a joint probability measure over query terms $Q = \langle T_1, T_2, \ldots, T_n \rangle$ and document D. By saying an index is a joint probability measure, we mean that an index has the ability to produce a probability value $p(Q, D)$ for any given pair of Q and D that allows for document ranking. Here, n is said to be the *cardinality* of query.

A typical language modeling approach would suggest the following generative structure: One first chooses a document D and then makes n independent draws $T_1, T_2, \ldots, T_n$

from the discrete distribution θ_D that represents the language model for document D.

$$D \sim \text{Uniform}(1, |\mathcal{D}|),$$
$$T_k \sim \text{Discrete}(\theta_D) \quad \text{for } k = 1 \ldots n.$$

An inverted index represented this way can also be seen as a mixture of document language models. It is then straightforward to rank documents based on the joint likelihood. More advanced variants also exist that take document priors, term dependency, or proximity into account. See Zhai and Lafferty [28] for a complete treatment.

Ideally, the support of this mixture would cover the set of all possible queries and all documents. But practically this would break down to just all the postings in the index, each of the form (t, d). So if we are asked to induce a concise version of this mixture, it would be reasonable to just find a subset of given size from these postings.

Let us write the original index as a measure p, and say a fraction ρ of the postings needs to be removed from p in order to produce the concise version q. Then we define the domain of q as $\mathcal{Q}(\rho)$, the set of all probability measures to which only part of the original postings (as indicated by fraction $1 - \rho$) are made available. We make the usual generative assumption that a joint model has a document prior and a likelihood component, e.g., $p(t, d) = p(d)p(t|d)$ and $q(t, d) = q(d)q(t|d)$. The document prior $p(d)$ does not need to be uniform, though it has to be unique, i.e., $p(d) = q(d)$.

With this definition, it is straightforward to describe static index pruning as a search problem in the probability space. One standard approach to find the best measure is through relative entropy minimization [17]:

$$
\begin{aligned}
\text{minimize} \quad & D(q||p) \\
\text{subject to} \quad & \mathbb{I}_{t,d} \in \{0, 1\} \text{ for all } (t, d) \\
& \sum_{t,d} \mathbb{I}_{t,d} = (1 - \rho)N \\
& q \in \mathcal{Q}(\rho)
\end{aligned}
\tag{1}
$$

with the last line expands into the following:

$$
q \in \mathcal{Q}(\rho) \Leftrightarrow q(t_{1:n}|d) = \frac{p(t_{1:n}|d) \prod_j \mathbb{I}_{t_j,d}}{\sum_{t'_{1:n}} p(t'_{1:n}|d) \prod_j \mathbb{I}_{t'_j,d}}.
\tag{2}
$$

The objective $D(q||p)$ is the Kullback-Leibler (KL) divergence from q, the probability measure to be induced, to p, the original. This divergence can be replaced by other divergence measures, as we shall briefly show. Each indicator $\mathbb{I}_{t,d}$ represents a binary choice of whether posting (t, d) will be included in q or not. For any given fraction ρ, exactly $(1 - \rho)N$ such indicators have to be "turned on" (N is the total number of postings.) The binary choices $\langle \mathbb{I}_{t,d} | \forall t, d \rangle$ as a whole should create a *truncated* probability measure q out of the measure p by limiting access to part of the support. Technically, the support still covers all postings, but those not selected to enter the new index, i.e., $\mathbb{I}_{t,d} = 0$, would receive zero probability in measure q.[1] After truncation, the measure q needs to be renormalized as in (2) as its total probability mass may no longer sum to one. The denominator in (2) will hereafter be denoted as Z_d for brevity.

To sum up, comparing this formulation with that of Chen and Lee [10], it is less restrictive and free of approximation. Further exploration on divergence measures and query cardinality is thus made feasible.

---

[1] We disregard smoothing at the modeling stage as it would make the problem complicated.

3.1 *f*-Divergence and Rényi Divergence

For many decades, researchers in information theory have sought interesting ways to generalize KL divergence [13, 18, 20, 24]. Many well-known measures, such as Hellinger's distance or variational distance, are found related and can be used in place of ordinary Kullback-Leibler divergence in inference problems such as (1). In this paper, one of the focus will be on applying these results to our problem. For the choice of divergence measures, we will mainly look at two families: *f*-divergence and Rényi divergence of order α.

The *f*-divergence is independently rediscovered many times in the past for generalizing KL divergence [13, 20]. In our notation, it is written as:

$$\mathrm{D}_f(q||p) = \sum_{t_{1:n},d} p(t_{1:n},d) f\left(\frac{q(t_{1:n},d)}{p(t_{1:n},d)}\right), \qquad (3)$$

where f is a convex function such that $f(1) = 0$. A broad range of divergence measures can be modeled this way via different definitions of f. Some of its special cases, such as χ^2-divergence, Hellinger's distance, and variational distance (or *total variation*), are given as follows [18].

Kullback-Leibler divergence	$f(x) = x \log x$
Variational distance	$f(x) = |1 - x|$
Hellinger's distance	$f(x) = (\sqrt{x} - 1)^2$
χ^2-divergence	$f(x) = (x - 1)^2$

Rényi divergence of order α comes from another independent attempt to generalize the KL divergence. This family is parametrized via a positive real number α. It was introduced in Alfred Rényi's seminal work [24], in the following form:

$$\mathrm{D}_\alpha(q||p) = \frac{1}{\alpha - 1} \log \left(\sum_{t_{1:n},d} q(t_{1:n},d)^\alpha p(t_{1:n},d)^{1-\alpha} \right). \quad (4)$$

Rényi divergence is equivalent to KL divergence when $\alpha \to 1$. Setting $\alpha = 2$ would lead to the logarithm of the χ^2-divergence. It is worth noting that one can actually take α to infinity, and by doing that we will get a special closed form for Rényi divergence of order infinity [27]:

$$\mathrm{D}_\infty(q||p) = \log \sup_{t_{1:n},d} \frac{q(t_{1:n},d)}{p(t_{1:n},d)}. \qquad (5)$$

3.2 Analysis

The problem described in (1) is overwhelmingly large because the number of variables can easily exceed billions on any web retrieval system. A problem of this scale is infeasible, so further work is needed to simplify the objective. In this analysis, we basically look at two things: convexity and relations between divergence measures. We first check whether the objective in (1) is convex. The objective can be exactly minimized if it is convex [16], or otherwise efficient inference would not seem feasible. Once the convexity is established, we check if the measure is analytically related to some other measures that we have analyzed. As we shall cover later, some divergence measures are related to themselves in lower cardinality. This interesting property allows us to solve high-cardinality problems using solutions to low-cardinality ones.

Divergence	Analytic Form
KL$^{(1)}$	$-\sum_d p(d) \log \left(\sum_{t'} \mathbb{I}_{t',d} p(t'|d) \right)$
VD$^{(1)}$	$-\sum_d p(d) \left(\sum_{t'} \mathbb{I}_{t',d} p(t'|d) \right)$
Hellinger$^{(1)}$	$-\sum_d p(d) \left(\sum_{t'} \mathbb{I}_{t',d} p(t'|d) \right)^{1/2}$
χ^2-div$^{(1)}$	$\sum_d p(d) \left(\sum_{t'} \mathbb{I}_{t',d} p(t'|d) \right)^{-1}$
Rényi$_\alpha^{(1)}$ $(1 < \alpha < \infty)$	$\sum_d p(d) \left(\sum_{t'} \mathbb{I}_{t',d} p(t'|d) \right)^{1-\alpha}$
Rényi$_\infty^{(1)}$	$\sup_d \left(\sum_{t'} \mathbb{I}_{t',d} p(t'|d) \right)^{-1}$

Table 1: Analytic forms for cardinality $n = 1$.

Convexity for Cardinality $n = 1$. It is known that *f*-divergence and Rényi divergence are convex in probability measures p and q, but in pruning decisions $\langle \mathbb{I}_{t,d} | \forall t, d \rangle$ the convexity is not yet established.

Let us start with the simplest case where query cardinality n equals 1. In this case, (3), (4), and (5) become:

$$\mathrm{D}_f(q||p) = \sum_{t,d} p(t,d) f\left(\frac{\mathbb{I}_{t,d}}{Z_d}\right),$$

$$\mathrm{D}_\alpha(q||p) = \frac{1}{\alpha - 1} \log \sum_{t,d} p(t,d) \left(\frac{\mathbb{I}_{t,d}}{Z_d}\right)^\alpha, \qquad (6)$$

$$\mathrm{D}_\infty(q||p) = \log \sup_{t,d} \frac{\mathbb{I}_{t,d}}{Z_d}.$$

Note that Z_d also falls back to a simpler form: $\sum_{t'} p(t'|d)\mathbb{I}_{t',d}$.

We shall now establish that, with the following two lemmas, that (1) is a convex programming problem under *f*-divergence and Rényi divergence for $n = 1$. In the first lemma, we will directly prove that *f*-divergence is jointly convex in pruning decisions, while in the second we will not be able to do so due to the presence of a logarithm function. Instead, we show that minimizing Rényi divergence has an equivalent surrogate that is convex. In other words, we get the same exact solution by minimizing the inside of logarithm.

LEMMA 1 (CONVEXITY). *Given $Z_d > 0$ for all d, $\mathrm{D}_f(q||p)$ defined in (6) is jointly convex in pruning decisions $\langle \mathbb{I}_{t,d} | \forall t, d \rangle$ for any convex function f with $f(1) = 0$.*

LEMMA 2 (SURROGATE CONVEXITY). *Given $Z_d > 0$ for all d, minimizing $\mathrm{D}_\alpha(q||p)$ in (6) has an equivalent surrogate that is jointly convex in $\langle \mathbb{I}_{t,d} | \forall t, d \rangle$ for $\alpha > 1$.*

Proofs for these two lemmas are given in the appendix. Now, with a bit of algebra, we are able to write out a simplified form for each of these divergence measures. These equations are given in Table 1. Sharp-eyed reader may notice the similarities between these equations. We shall discuss how this can be exploited to develop a general algorithmic solution in a later subsection regarding finding optimal allocation.

Convexity for Cardinality $n > 1$. When query cardinality n is greater than 1, term dependency can make the problem very hard to solve. Generally, when $n > 1$, minimizing (1) under both divergence families leads to a sophisticated geometric programming problem, for which we are not aware of any efficient solution in the billion-variable scale.

This problem can however be alleviated with the term independence ("bag-of-words") assumption, which is to let

Divergence	Analytic Form for $n > 1$
$\text{KL}^{(n)}$	$\text{KL}^{(1)}$
$\text{VD}^{(n)}$	Not convex
$\text{Hellinger}^{(n)}$	$\text{VD}^{(1)}$ for $n = 2$; Not convex otherwise
$\chi^2\text{-div}^{(n)}$	$\text{Rényi}^{(1)}_{n+1}$
$\text{Rényi}^{(n)}_\alpha$	$\text{Rényi}^{(1)}_{n\alpha-n+1}$ for $1 < \alpha < \infty$
$\text{Rényi}^{(n)}_\infty$	$\sup_d \left(\sum_{t'} \mathbb{I}_{t',d} p(t'|d) \right)^{-n}$

Table 2: Relations between divergences of different cardinalities. KL divergence and Rényi divergence can both be solved for arbitrarily high cardinalities.

$p(t_{1:n}|d) = \prod_j p(t_j|d)$. We repeated the convex analysis as in $n = 1$ under this assumption, and found each measure for $n > 1$ fits into one of the following classes: (i) The measure is convex and can reduce to itself or other measures in cardinality 1, with examples including Kullback-Leibler divergence, Rényi divergence, and χ^2-divergence. Divergence measures in this class can be solved for arbitrary cardinality and therefore provide the greatest flexibility in modeling user queries; (ii) The measure is not convex on high cardinality, e.g., both variational distance for $n \geq 2$ and Hellinger's distance for $n > 2$ are not convex. In this case, the exact solution cannot be efficiently computed.

More detailed analyses are given in the appendix. Our full result is summarized in Table 2. Among all these measures, we find that Kullback-Leibler divergence, Rényi divergence, and χ^2-divergence the most interesting since they can be solved for arbitrary cardinality and therefore can be used to model arbitrary-length queries properly. Variational distance and Hellinger's distance fall short on this flexibility. In later section, we shall see how this theoretical limit is reflected on practical performance.

3.3 Optimal Allocation

Having established the convexity, we now turn to develop algorithmic solutions for the divergence measures. A common pattern that we observed in Table 1 is all these measures (except Rényi divergence of order infinity) are of the following format:

$$\sum_d p(d)\, G\left(\sum_t \mathbb{I}_{t,d} p(t|d) \right), \qquad (7)$$

where $G(x)$ is some convex function. We call this G a *gain function*. Figure 1 (left) summarizes this for all the divergences in discussion. For divergence measures in the f-family, this function is simply $G(x) = (1-x)f(0) + xf(1/x)$, for $x > 0$. For the Rényi family, we have $G(x) = x^{1-\alpha} - 1$ for $x > 0$, $\alpha > 1$. Note that for f-divergence the gain function has a property that $G(1) = 0$; we make this consistent with Rényi divergence by adding a trailing -1.

We found that minimizing the objective (7) under the constraint (2) is equivalent to solving a multiple-resource allocation problem on convex returns [16]. It turns out that, in this problem, our objective is to minimize a mixture of document-level pay-offs, which is directly connected to the gain function $G(\cdot)$. Figure 1 (right) has a summary plot in which we print all these gain functions in different line patterns and those associated with Rényi divergence in different colors. From the plot, one can easily tell that all these measures appear to be convex, non-increasing monotone on

$(0, 1]$ ("diminishing returns"). To minimize a single pay-off on any document d, it suffices to order the postings in descending order of probability $p(t|d)$ and have them enter the index consecutively until the budget runs out. The same idea also applies to a mixture of pay-offs.

General Solution. Let us denote a term t in some document d as $t_{[j]}$ by its rank j in descending order of $p(t|d)$. For any posting $(t_{[k]}, d)$ to enter the index, postings in document d with higher probabilities $(t_{[1]}, d), (t_{[2]}, d), \ldots, (t_{[k-1]}, d)$ have to be included first. Now by allowing posting $(t_{[k]}, d)$ to enter the final index, we *gain* this much in the overall objective:

$$p(d) \left[G\left(\sum_{i=1}^{k} p(t_{[i]}|d) \right) - G\left(\sum_{i=1}^{k-1} p(t_{[i]}|d) \right) \right] \qquad (8)$$

Note that this value is negative. To minimize the overall gain, it suffices to go from some steady state and distribute the remaining budget to documents in a iterative fashion using the following greedy algorithm.

---

input: threshold ϵ
1   **for** $d \in \mathcal{D}$ **do**
2   Sort terms in descending order of $p(t|d)$
3   **for** $k = 1, \ldots, n$ **do**
4   Compute $\Delta(t_{[k]}, d)$ according to (8)
5   Remove posting $(t_{[k]}, d)$ if $|\Delta(t_{[k]}, d)| < \epsilon$

Algorithm 1: The general algorithm for computing optimal allocation under f-divergence and Rényi divergence.

Algorithm 1 computes the optimal allocation of $(1 - \rho)N$ index entries that minimizes the divergence between the pruned and the full indexes. This algorithm has a time complexity of $O(|\mathcal{D}|L \log L)$ where $|\mathcal{D}|$ is the total number of documents in the collection and L is the maximum document length. This algorithm has a linear-time variants for variational distance, as given in Algorithm 2. These algorithms can all be linked to the result in Fox [15] by establishing the mapping between G and the function ϕ_j. Interested readers are referred to Ibaraki and Katoh [16] for more details.

---

input: threshold ϵ
1   **for** $d \in \mathcal{D}$ **do**
2   **for** $t \in \text{posting}(d)$ **do**
3   Remove posting (t, d) if $p(d)p(t|d) < \epsilon$

Algorithm 2: Linear-time variant for variational distance.

Rényi Divergence of Order Infinity. To compute the allocation for Rényi divergence of order infinity on arbitrary cardinality n, replace (8) in Algorithm 1 with the following:

$$\left(\sum_{i=1}^{k} p(t_{[i]}|d) \right)^{-n}. \qquad (9)$$

Note that, since $p(d)$ is not involved in this equation, setting document priors would have no effect to this divergence measure. Given this condition, one can easily show that (9) is actually rank invariant for all $n > 0$. This means that Rényi divergence of order infinity can be solved for an arbitrarily high cardinality and the solution would still be the same as that of cardinality 1.

Divergence	Gain $G(x)$
f-divergence	$(1-x)f(0) + xf(1/x)$
KL divergence	$-\log x$
Variational distance	$1-x$
Hellinger's distance	$1-x^{1/2}$
χ^2-divergence	$x^{-1}-1$
Rényi divergence ($1 < \alpha < \infty$)	$x^{1-\alpha}-1$

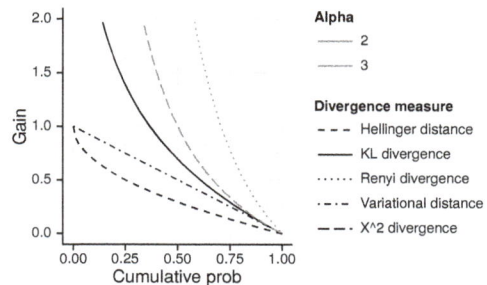

Figure 1: Gain functions (left) and plots (right) for many well-known divergence measures.

Title queries	50%			70%			90%		
	MAP	P20	J20	MAP	P20	J20	MAP	P20	J20
Full index	0.253	0.464	—	0.253	0.464	—	0.253	0.464	—
KL	0.234	<u>0.465</u>	**0.826**	0.210	0.461	0.664	0.143	0.357	0.360
Hellinger	0.208	0.453	0.800	0.162	0.418	0.586	0.074	0.238	0.237
Variational	0.117	0.382	0.565	0.059	0.301	0.275	0.015	0.129	0.078
χ^2-divergence	0.245	<u>0.474</u>	0.799	0.232	<u>0.467</u>	0.668	0.181	0.437	**0.373**
Renyi, $\alpha = 50$	0.252	<u>0.476</u>	0.743	0.244	**<u>0.485</u>**	0.603	**0.198**	<u>0.467</u>	0.325
Renyi, $\alpha \to \infty$	**<u>0.253</u>**	**<u>0.478</u>**	0.741	**0.245**	**<u>0.485</u>**	0.598	**0.198**	**<u>0.468</u>**	0.323

Table 3: Retrieval performance of experimental runs on Terabyte '06 title queries, measured at prune ratios 50%, 70%, and 90%. Runs that outperform full index are underlined and best results printed in boldface.

4. EXPERIMENTS

Totally two sets of pruning experiments were conducted in this study. Our experiments were carried out on the GOV2 collection [12] using TREC 2006 Terabyte track data [8]. The GOV2 collection is a standard collection for various web-related retrieval tasks. It has 25.2 million documents and is roughly 426GB in size. We used the Indri toolkit[2] to create indexes and develop pruning algorithms. Standard preprocessing steps such as stemming and stopword removal were applied using the InQuery stoplist and porter stemmer.

We used both ad-hoc and efficiency topics as it is interesting to see how pruning algorithms respond to different types of queries. Ad-hoc topics in the Terabyte track are carefully selected questions with proper annotation, so this set is suitable for testing general retrieval performance. Efficiency topics are unannotated queries collected from session logs. Since these are real queries submitted by users, testing on top of this set gives us a better idea how pruning algorithms work "in the wild." For ad-hoc task we use all annotated topics 701-850, and for efficiency task we used the first 1,000, which are topics 1-1000. We used only title queries for both tasks.

For comparison, we chose five reference methods: term-based pruning [9], uniform pruning [9,10], document-centric pruning [7], popularity-based pruning [2,21], and two-sample two proportion (2N2P) test [26].[3] These methods implement different ideas in static index pruning and their performance have been extensively studied. Some of them such as term-based pruning and popularity-based pruning are known as standard methods of the task.

We use BM25 wherever applicable in post-pruning retrieval and in pruning (with the 2N2P test being the only exception) [1] to strengthen the baseline performance. Default parameters in the Indri toolkit are used: $k_1 = 1.25$ and $b = 0.75$. For term-based pruning, we used the top-k version and set $k = 10$. For document-centric pruning, we used Method 2 and set $\lambda = 1 - \rho$. To set up popularity-based pruning, we used term frequencies from the AOL query log [22] to compute term popularities. For the 2N2P test, we used only the Z-score version without implementing power analysis and also updated collection term frequencies. All other details were implemented based on standard settings.

We used a uniform prior $p(d)$ in our experiment. To estimate $p(t|d)$, we tested various retrieval methods, including BM25 and language modeling with both Dirichlet and Jelinek-Mercer smoothing. As BM25 is in general more effective, to prevent clutter we will not discuss the results for language modeling in this paper. Note that, since the BM25 scores are not valid probabilities, we use a softmax function to convert these scores as if they were coming out from a multinomial logistic regression model [3, p. 198]:

$$\frac{\exp\left(\mathrm{BM25}(t,d)\right)}{\sum_{t' \in d} \exp\left(\mathrm{BM25}(t',d)\right)}. \tag{10}$$

This estimate is not ideal since the "posterior" produced has little to do with the generative process. It is nevertheless a convenient way to incorporate non-probabilistic methods into our framework; further justification on its validity is beyond the scope of this paper.

Retrieval performance is measured at three prune ratios, 50%, 70%, and 90%. In all the experimental runs, prune ratio is controlled by using sample quantile [10] with reservoir sampling to find the right threshold ϵ. This estimation error was empirically bounded to within 0.005%. Given the same original index to start with, a pruning method is deemed

---

[2]http://www.lemurproject.org/indri.php

[3]We also tested two other methods, probability-ranking principle [5] and information preservation [11], but due to space limit these results are not included in this paper.

Title queries	50%				70%				90%			
	MAP	P20	J20	T (s)	MAP	P20	J20	T (s)	MAP	P20	J20	T (s)
Full index	0.253	0.464	—	101.7	0.253	0.464	—	101.7	0.253	0.464	—	101.7
2N2P test	0.239	0.467	0.714	40.3	0.203	0.434	0.535	18.3	0.076	0.248	0.198	2.2
Popularity-based	0.223	0.417	0.780	89.4	0.189	0.365	0.574	65.4	0.077	0.161	0.199	16.3
Uniform	0.231	0.445	0.760	**33.5**	0.187	0.376	0.566	**14.4**	0.110	0.241	0.273	**1.8**
Term-based, $k = 10$	0.218	0.457	**0.853**	67.9	0.187	0.441	**0.675**	46.8	0.109	0.311	0.350	14.7
Document-centric	**0.253**	0.478	0.743	54.7	0.244	0.485	0.602	38.8	**0.198**	0.465	0.325	16.1
KL	0.234	0.465	0.826	64.9	0.210	0.461	0.664	41.7	0.143	0.357	0.360	10.6
χ^2-divergence	0.245	0.474	0.799	59.9	0.232	0.467	0.668	38.2	0.181	0.437	**0.373**	13.2
Renyi, $\alpha = 50$	0.252	0.476	0.743	54.4	0.244	0.485	0.603	37.4	**0.198**	0.467	0.325	15.5
Renyi, $\alpha \rightarrow \infty$	**0.253**	0.478	0.741	54.9	**0.245**	0.485	0.598	37.0	**0.198**	0.468	0.323	15.6

SD queries	50%				70%				90%			
	MAP	P20	J20	T (s)	MAP	P20	J20	T (s)	MAP	P20	J20	T (s)
Full index	0.264	0.491	—	516.9	0.264	0.491	—	516.9	0.264	0.491	—	516.9
2N2P test	0.242	0.481	0.722	190.7	0.204	0.442	0.537	81.3	0.076	0.249	0.188	7.6
Popularity-based	0.232	0.439	0.781	389.6	0.198	0.375	0.581	277.4	0.080	0.170	0.194	56.0
Uniform	0.238	0.461	0.755	**141.3**	0.192	0.389	0.576	**50.4**	0.111	0.246	0.262	**3.5**
Term-based, $k = 10$	0.223	0.474	**0.852**	330.3	0.188	0.451	0.664	212.9	0.107	0.312	0.320	61.7
Document-centric	**0.259**	0.499	0.743	269.3	0.248	0.507	0.588	192.2	**0.200**	0.472	0.306	73.2
KL	0.240	0.476	0.842	313.1	0.211	0.470	**0.678**	181.2	0.137	0.340	0.337	39.3
χ^2-divergence	0.252	0.487	0.824	296.9	0.234	0.481	0.677	177.5	0.180	0.441	**0.354**	51.9
Renyi, $\alpha = 50$	0.258	0.498	0.750	269.1	0.248	0.506	0.592	183.4	**0.200**	0.472	0.306	71.3
Renyi, $\alpha \rightarrow \infty$	**0.259**	0.498	0.740	264.9	**0.249**	0.508	0.584	182.2	**0.200**	**0.474**	0.303	71.9

Table 4: **Overall comparison with reference methods on Terabyte '06 title queries (top) and SD queries (bottom). Performance is measured at prune ratios 50%, 70%, and 90% where query execution is also timed. Runs do better than or equally well to full index are underlined; boldface indicates the best result.**

better if the produced index delivers better result. To evaluate retrieval performance, we used the following measures: mean average-precision (MAP), precision-at-20 (P20) and top-20 Jaccard coefficient (J20). MAP and P20 measure how well one algorithm does in preserving postings that are relevant. J20 measures the degree of overlap in top 20 documents between retrieval results before and after pruning, commonly used as a proxy of precision-based measures when relevance judgments are not available. Note that other rank coefficient measures such as Kendall's tau may also be used in place of J20. These measures were selected mainly for consistency with the existing work.

4.1 Ad-Hoc Task

In the first task, we used 150 ad-hoc topics in the test. Besides title queries, we also managed to perform pruning experiments on sequential dependence (SD) queries [19]. Our purpose is to see how pruning algorithms respond to the change in term dependencies. In our case, the change is from full independence to sequential dependence. Although setting up SD queries on top of BM25 is unusual, it did achieve better performance as we had expected.

The result for our experimental runs on title queries is given in Table 3. Two variants of Rényi divergence are reported here: $\alpha = 50$ and $\alpha \rightarrow \infty$ (order infinity). Among all the experimental runs, we found that Rényi divergence generally does the best, χ^2-divergence the second, and KL divergence the third. This seems to suggest that, for Rényi divergence, larger α tends to provide a better returns curve.

An overall comparison with reference methods is summarized in Table 4 with title queries on the top and SD queries on the bottom. Hellinger's distance and variational

distance were not included in this comparison as the performance is below standard. Among the reference methods we tested, document-centric pruning does the best on MAP and P20. It outperforms all other reference runs by a large margin. The runner-up is term-based pruning, followed by 2N2P test, uniform pruning, and popularity-based pruning. The 2N2P test performed well on MAP at low prune ratio. In our test, the performance of uniform pruning is on par with term-based pruning on MAP, which is consistent with the previous results [10]. Popularity-based pruning also appeared comparable, but at high prune ratio its performance is just disappointing. Our result suggests that popularity-based method has no advantage in the ad-hoc task, although its parameters was trained on a very sizable source.

From Table 4, all four proposed methods do fairly well with precision-based measures. Rényi divergence of order infinity outperforms all the baseline methods on MAP and P20; the other three measures also achieve good performance but do not appear to surpass the strong baseline. On J20, KL divergence and χ^2-divergence both appear comparable to term-based method. We found that, in the Rényi family, the ones with small alpha (KL divergence and χ^2-divergence) tend to do better on J20 and the ones with large alpha ($\alpha = 50$ and $\alpha \rightarrow \infty$) do better on MAP and P20. Among all the proposed methods, only Rényi divergence managed to achieve comparable performance on MAP and P20 to the strong baseline. For testing statistical significance, we ran a 4-way ANOVA upfront followed by a Tukey's HSD test, whose result is given in Table 5. All effects in ANOVA come back significant for $p < 0.001$. The Tukey's test suggests that Rényi divergence and document-centric pruning significantly outperform all the other meth-

	Effect	DF	F	η_p^2
MAP	Query Type	1	15.1	.0015
	Method	8	96.6	.0693
	Prune Ratio	3	1262.0	.2673
	Topic	147	306.9	.8129
P20	Query Type	1	30.8	.0030
	Method	8	82.2	.0596
	Prune Ratio	3	355.4	.0931
	Topic	147	197.9	.7371

MAP	Mean	Grp	P20	Mean	Grp
Rényi, $\alpha \to \infty$	.2419	a....	Rényi, $\alpha \to \infty$	.4865	a...
Document-centric	.2416	a....	Document-centric	.4858	a...
Rényi, $\alpha = 50$	.2415	a....	Rényi, $\alpha = 50$	.4853	a...
χ^2-divergence	.2318	.b...	χ^2-divergence	.4709	a...
KL	.2130	..c..	KL	.4434	.b..
Popularity-based	.2073	..cd.	Term-based	.4278	.bc.
Uniform	.2034	...de	2N2P test	.4123	..cd
2N2P test	.1959	....e	Uniform	.3991	...d
Term-based	.1949	....e	Popularity-based	.3940	...d

Table 5: 4-way ANOVA (left) and Tukey's HSD result (right).

Efficiency queries	50%		70%		90%		Index Status at 90%		
	J20	T (s)	J20	T (s)	J20	T (s)	PruneT (s)	PL Kept (%)	Avg Size
Full index	—	990.49	—	990.49	—	990.49	—	100.0%	128.6
2N2P test	0.605	365.94	0.426	148.29	0.128	15.07	2858.09	100.0%	12.9
Popularity-based	**0.772**	815.23	0.515	643.52	0.182	209.14	**2382.56**	0.6%	2126.4
Uniform	0.646	**272.07**	0.450	**106.51**	0.178	**6.12**	3188.70	55.4%	23.2
Term-based	0.753	639.65	**0.563**	419.35	**0.296**	138.49	2694.58	100.0%	12.7
Document-centric	0.639	548.52	0.487	311.22	0.235	128.71	6987.10	40.9%	31.8
KL	0.730	545.84	0.538	324.64	0.235	85.96	6541.08	36.0%	35.8
χ^2-divergence	0.707	622.85	0.546	317.95	0.251	102.88	6767.16	37.9%	34.0
Renyi, $\alpha = 50$	0.642	511.48	0.490	306.96	0.236	128.26	8240.08	40.4%	31.9
Renyi, $\alpha \to \infty$	0.637	551.26	0.484	347.12	0.233	130.40	6830.29	40.6%	31.7

Table 6: Overall comparison with reference methods on 1,000 Terabyte '06 efficiency queries. Retrieval performance is evaluated using J20 as the sole indicator since relevance judgments are not available; pruning (PruneT) and query execution (T) are both timed and reported. Runs do better than or equally well to full index are underlined; boldface indicates the best result. Note that pruning time for popularity-based method does not include the time needed to preprocess query logs and is only indicative.

ods both on MAP and P20 (on P20 χ^2-divergence is also in the leading group). Rényi divergence appears to have a slight advantage over document-centric pruning, but the improvement is not significant.

The performance of document-centric pruning has raised some concerns. We believe that its effectiveness has been previously overlooked, since many studies either compared with the version with the KLD score function, which is inferior to our implementation, or did not replicate the result at all. According to our experiments, which cover many recent approaches, document-centric pruning may currently be the best pruning strategy for preserving top-k precision.

Based on all these findings, we conclude that the proposed divergence-based methods are effective in producing quality pruned indexes, and their performance is among the best on the GOV2 data. One thing worth noting is that on title queries with Rényi divergence, we delivered better P20 scores than on the full index at all prune ratios up to 90%. On SD queries the same method delivered better P20 results for prune ratios up to 70%.

4.2 Efficiency Task

We conducted the second experiment on the efficiency task data. This is to see how pruning algorithms react to more realistic query topics. In the experiment, we tested each pruning method against the first 1,000 efficiency topics. As relevance judgments are not available, we had to rely on J20 as the sole performance indicator. Note that one caveat with this experimental setting is that J20 can be optimistic and does not reliably reflect true retrieval performance, as can

be seen in the result of our first experiment. Nevertheless, without relevance judgments it is perhaps the best proxy measure to the true performance.

We also conducted timing experiments on a dedicated server with a 3.30 GHz Intel Core i5-2500 CPU (4 cores) and 16GB RAM. We report time needed to produce the pruned index (PruneT), and query execution time (T) over the entire set of 1,000 topics. Note that PruneT is only indicative because it was an one-off measurement; we did not make a second timing pass because pruning is very costly. Query execution time is however properly measured in a two-pass timing procedure to isolate possible caching effects.

The result is given in Table 6. We only report PruneT for 90% prune ratio for simplicity. On J20, popularity-based method works the best at 50% prune ratio, but as prune ratio increases term-based pruning tends to deliver better performance. Other reference methods are not effective on J20. Among the experimental runs, J20 favors more towards KL divergence but at high prune ratio Rényi divergence also does equally well. Overall, term-based pruning delivers the best performance on J20.

The timing result on PruneT (pruning time, in seconds) confirms that term-centric methods, e.g., the 2N2P test, popularity-based, uniform, and term-based, are more efficient to run. Among all these methods, Rényi divergence (the one of finite order) would be the most expensive, since its gain function has a power component that takes more time to compute. The others in the document-centric camp appear roughly comparable on pruning time. On query execution time T (in seconds), uniform pruning is the fastest in most cases, although in our previous experiment this speed gain did not translate into precision. The 2N2P test is also fast and performs better than uniform pruning at low prune ratio. Divergence measures and document-centric pruning are not known to be fast; in our test, they all seem equally slow. Nevertheless popularity-based and term-based took even more time to evaluate queries. Although these methods are known to produce more matching against user input, the result is still surprising. Also, we noticed something unusual that, on 90% prune ratio, uniform pruning ran through 1,000 query topics in only 6.12 seconds. These anomalies suggest that the final index produced by these methods may have been seriously degraded.

4.3 Distribution of Posting List Size

To investigate why some reference algorithms had been acting strangely in the timing test, we came back to the indexes on 90% prune ratio and did more analysis. We started by looking at two indicators, which are percentage of non-empty posting lists (PL Kept), and average posting list size (Avg Size), both included in Table 6. We also find it informative to look at the frequency distribution of posting list size, which is covered in Figure 2. Table 6 shows that divergence-based methods and document-centric pruning keep only 36–40% of the posting lists and maintained an average size of posting list at 31–36 postings. The frequency distributions (Figure 2) also look fairly smooth and normal, suggesting that these pruning algorithms are well-behaved.

While uniform pruning and the 2N2P test both have very similar frequency distributions and are more or less comparable in retrieval performance, on PL Kept and Avg Size it is term-based pruning that agrees more with the 2N2P test. Uniform pruning does nothing unusual as well; it did not make large changes to long/short posting lists nor eliminate more postings than the others do. From the distribution plot, it appears to fit the original distribution fairly well. The number of posting lists in the index (55.4%) can be a little bit more, but this should not be an issue because it takes *less* time processing queries. The real problem with uniform pruning, we suspect, is that meaningless contents such as HTML fragments or overlong words found their way into the index. BM25 incorrectly assigned high scores to these strings, producing a large set of high-probability garbage that uniform pruning provides no safe-guard mechanism against. Evaluating queries on the index would result in far less execution time because the underlying index contains many useless terms and nothing is left in there to match.

Popularity-based pruning is found to overfit the query log data in an amusing way. Table 6 shows that it threw away more than 99% of term posting lists and kept only 0.6% in the final index. In Figure 2, we can see there is a noticeable gap between the size distribution and the original, a sign that indicates *under-fitting*. This extreme strategy would not have succeeded unless carried out in an environment where the majority of query topics are covered in the training data. This explains why popularity-based pruning is more successful in log-based experiments and why it was not working as expected on Terabyte '06 ad-hoc topics.

5. DISCUSSIONS

We have gone through a series of analyses in light of answering the research questions we raised in Section 1. Our

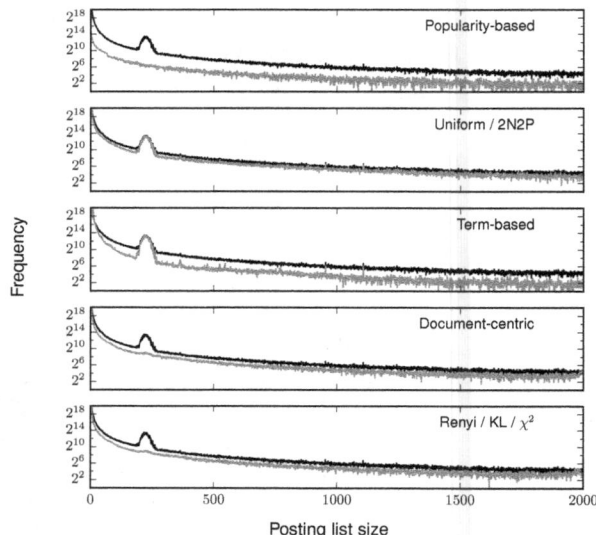

Figure 2: Semi-log plots on posting list size and frequency. Each plot has a black curve for the full index and a red curve for the 90% pruned index using the named method(s).

first finding is that generalizing the divergence measure in problem (1) is not only feasible but advantageous. Through experimentation, we show that using Rényi divergence of order infinity in place of ordinary KL divergence gives the best result. This is in line with our theoretical analysis in Section 3.2 which states that Rényi divergence has the greatest flexibility in modeling multiple-term queries.

We also found that modeling multiple-term queries does not make optimization any harder. Many divergence measures that we considered can be solved for arbitrarily high cardinality, and therefore the solutions can be empirically achieved and tested.[4]

Term-based pruning is known for retaining top k postings for each term, effectively keeping all posting lists active in the final index [9]. In our study, we found that Rényi divergence shares this interesting trait that it retains at least one posting on each document, ensuring access to every document is possible. This is due to the nature of its document pay-offs. As the gain functions for Rényi-compatible measures are unbounded at the point where the cumulative probability is zero, by allowing the first posting in each document to enter the index we would gain minus infinity in the objective value. This "keeping everything accessible" strategy is actually a side effect of the returns curves.

Our experiments also showed that the J20 measure does not align well with precision, and methods with a strong presence in J20 can be weak on both precision and recall, which is evidenced by low MAP values at higher prune ratios. Optimizing top-k similarity in web search to produce quality data summary may now seem like an unfounded idea.

---

[4]For measures that are not convex at higher cardinality, their actual performance remains unknown because the true solutions cannot be computed using our algorithm.

6. CONCLUSIONS

In this paper, we provide a thorough study on a wide range of divergence measures and their use on static index pruning. We developed a set of theoretical analyses on the improved divergence minimization framework. Our work has paved the way for practical implementation of optimal pruning strategies for large-scale nonparametric models such as inverted indexes. We have also uncovered interesting effects that different divergence measures and cardinality settings may have on the solution quality. The analysis of cardinality suggests that using Rényi divergence of order infinity in static index pruning delivers the best performance across different query cardinality settings, which is confirmed empirically with extensive experiments.

For future work, one possible direction would be to use the returns curves of divergence measures to assign term weights. This technique may be directly applied to other problems such reranking or summarization. As static index pruning relies heavily on term weighting schemes (i.e., score functions) to estimate posting importance, it is worthwhile to explore the relationship between the two.

7. ACKNOWLEDGMENTS

This work was supported in part by ARC Discovery Grant DP140102655, in part by the Center for Intelligent Information Retrieval, and in part by NSF IIS-1160894. Any opinions, findings, and conclusions or recommendations expressed in this material are those of the authors and do not necessarily reflect those of the sponsors.

8. REFERENCES

[1] I. S. Altingovde, R. Ozcan, and O. Ulusoy. A practitioner's guide for static index pruning. In *Proceedings of ECIR '09*, pages 675–679. Springer Berlin / Heidelberg, 2009.

[2] I. S. Altingovde, R. Ozcan, and O. Ulusoy. Static index pruning in web search engines: Combining term and document popularities with query views. *ACM Trans. Inf. Syst.*, 30(1), Mar. 2012.

[3] C. M. Bishop. *Pattern Recognition and Machine Learning*. Springer-Verlag New York, Inc., 2006.

[4] R. Blanco and A. Barreiro. Static pruning of terms in inverted files. In *Proceedings of ECIR '07*, pages 64–75. Springer Berlin Heidelberg, 2007.

[5] R. Blanco and A. Barreiro. Probabilistic static pruning of inverted files. *ACM Trans. Inf. Syst.*, 28(1), Jan. 2010.

[6] S. Boyd and L. Vandenberghe. *Convex Optimization*. Cambridge university press, 2004.

[7] S. Büttcher and C. L. A. Clarke. A document-centric approach to static index pruning in text retrieval systems. In *Proceedings of CIKM '06*, pages 182–189. ACM, 2006.

[8] S. Büttcher, C. L. A. Clarke, and I. Soboroff. The TREC 2006 terabyte track. In *TREC*, volume 6, page 39, 2006.

[9] D. Carmel, D. Cohen, R. Fagin, E. Farchi, M. Herscovici, Y. S. Maarek, and A. Soffer. Static index pruning for information retrieval systems. In *Proceedings of SIGIR '01*, pages 43–50. ACM, 2001.

[10] R.-C. Chen and C.-J. Lee. An information-theoretic account of static index pruning. In *Proceedings of SIGIR '13*, pages 163–172. ACM, 2013.

[11] R.-C. Chen, C.-J. Lee, C.-M. Tsai, and J. Hsiang. Information preservation in static index pruning. In *Proceedings of CIKM '12*, pages 2487–2490. ACM, 2012.

[12] C. Clarke, N. Craswell, and I. Soboroff. Overview of the TREC-2004 terabyte track. In *Proceedings of TREC-2004*, 2004.

[13] I. Csiszár and P. C. Shields. Information theory and statistics: A tutorial. *Foundations and Trends® in Communications and Information Theory*, 1(4):417–528, 2004.

[14] E. S. de Moura, C. F. dos Santos, D. R. Fernandes, A. S. Silva, P. Calado, and M. A. Nascimento. Improving web search efficiency via a locality based static pruning method. In *Proceedings of WWW '05*, pages 235–244. ACM, 2005.

[15] B. Fox. Discrete optimization via marginal analysis. *Management science*, 13(3):210–216, 1966.

[16] T. Ibaraki and N. Katoh. *Resource Allocation Problems: Algorithmic Approaches*. MIT Press, 1988.

[17] S. Kullback. *Information Theory and Statistics*. Wiley, 1959.

[18] F. Liese and I. Vajda. On divergences and informations in statistics and information theory. *IEEE Trans. Inf. Th.*, 52(10):4394–4412, Oct. 2006.

[19] D. Metzler and W. B. Croft. A Markov random field model for term dependencies. In *Proceedings of SIGIR '05*, pages 472–479. ACM, 2005.

[20] T. Morimoto. Markov processes and the H-Theorem. *Journal of the Physical Society of Japan*, 18(3):328–331, Mar. 1963.

[21] A. Ntoulas and J. Cho. Pruning policies for two-tiered inverted index with correctness guarantee. In *Proceedings of SIGIR '07*, pages 191–198. ACM, 2007.

[22] G. Pass, A. Chowdhury, and C. Torgeson. A picture of search. In *Proceedings of the 1st international conference on Scalable information systems*, page 1. ACM, 2006.

[23] J. M. Ponte and W. B. Croft. A language modeling approach to information retrieval. In *Proceedings of SIGIR '98*, pages 275–281. ACM, 1998.

[24] A. Rényi. On measures of entropy and information. *Proceedings of the Fourth Berkeley Symposium on Mathematical Statistics and Probability, Volume 1: Contributions to the Theory of Statistics*, pages 547–561, 1961.

[25] G. Skobeltsyn, F. Junqueira, V. Plachouras, and R. B. Yates. ResIn: a combination of results caching and index pruning for high-performance web search engines. In *Proceedings of SIGIR '08*, pages 131–138. ACM, 2008.

[26] S. Thota and B. Carterette. Within-document term-based index pruning with statistical hypothesis testing. In *Proceedings of ECIR '11*, pages 543–554. Springer Berlin Heidelberg, 2011.

[27] T. van Erven and P. Harremoes. Rényi divergence and Kullback-Leibler divergence. *IEEE Trans. Inf. Th.*, 60(7):3797–3820, July 2014.

[28] C. Zhai and J. Lafferty. A study of smoothing methods for language models applied to information retrieval. *ACM Trans. Inf. Syst.*, 22(2):179–214, Apr. 2004.

APPENDIX

Convexity

In this section, we outline the proofs of Lemma 1 on convexity of f-divergence and Lemma 2 on convexity of a surrogate of Rényi divergence.

LEMMA 1 (CONVEXITY). *Given $Z_d > 0$ for all d, $D_f(q\|p)$ defined in (6) is jointly convex in pruning decisions $\langle \mathbb{I}_{t,d} | \forall t, d \rangle$ for any convex function f with $f(1) = 0$.*

PROOF. Let us split the support of the summation and organize. We have:

$$
\begin{aligned}
D_f(q\|p) &= \sum_{t,d} p(t,d)\left[(1 - \mathbb{I}_{t,d})f(0) + \mathbb{I}_{t,d}f(1/Z_d)\right] \\
&= \sum_d p(d)\left[(1 - Z_d)f(0) + Z_d f(1/Z_d)\right].
\end{aligned}
\tag{11}
$$

The term $Z_d f(1/Z_d)$ is convex in Z_d because it is a special type of perspective function [6]. Since Z_d is affine in pruning decisions, this proof follows. □

LEMMA 2 (SURROGATE CONVEXITY). *Given $Z_d > 0$ for all d, minimizing $D_\alpha(q\|p)$ in (6) has an equivalent surrogate that is jointly convex in $\langle \mathbb{I}_{t,d} | \forall t, d \rangle$ for $\alpha > 1$.*

PROOF. Since logarithm function is monotone, when $\alpha > 1$, minimizing $D_\alpha(q\|p)$ as in (6) is equivalent to minimizing

$$
\sum_{t,d} p(t,d)\left(\frac{\mathbb{I}_{t,d}}{Z_d}\right)^\alpha = \sum_d p(d) Z_d^{1-\alpha},
\tag{12}
$$

which is jointly convex in pruning decisions $\langle \mathbb{I}_{t,d} | \forall t, d \rangle$. □

Analysis for Cardinality $n > 1$

In the following paragraphs, we describe how to simplify and analyze each divergence measures discussed in the paper.

Kullback-Leibler Divergence. It can be shown that minimizing KL divergence for cardinality $n > 1$ is equivalent to minimizing for $n = 1$. The key idea is to split

$$
\log[q(t_{1:n}, d)/p(t_{1:n}, d)]
$$

into a summation $\sum_j \log[q(t_j|d)/p(t_j|d)]$. Then we have

$$
\begin{aligned}
&\arg\min n \left(\sum_d p(d) \sum_t q(t|d) \log \frac{\mathbb{I}_{t,d}}{Z_d}\right) \\
&= \arg\min -\sum_d p(d) \log Z_d.
\end{aligned}
\tag{13}
$$

Variational Distance. This divergence measure is not convex even under the bag-of-words assumption. To see how, we first write out the definition and split support:

$$
\begin{aligned}
&\sum_{t_{1:n},d} p(t_{1:n},d)\left|1 - \prod_j \frac{\mathbb{I}_{t_j,d}}{Z_d}\right| \\
&= \sum_{t_{1:n},d} p(t_{1:n},d)\left(\prod_j \mathbb{I}_{t_j,d}(Z_d^{-n} - 1) + (1 - \prod_j \mathbb{I}_{t_j,d}).\right)
\end{aligned}
\tag{14}
$$

Then this would lead to $2(1 - \sum_d p(d) Z_d^n)$, which is not convex for all integer $n > 1$.

Hellinger's Distance. When $n = 2$ Hellinger's distance has the same analytic form as variational distance with cardinality 1. For $n > 2$, the divergence no longer remains convex. At some point in the derivation, we have Hellinger's distance in the following form:

$$
\begin{aligned}
&2\left(1 - \sum_{t_{1:n},d} p(d) Z_d^{-n/2} \prod_j p(t_j|d)\mathbb{I}_{t_j,d}\right) \\
&= 2\left(1 - \sum_d p(d) Z_d^{n/2}\right).
\end{aligned}
\tag{15}
$$

This would fall back to variational distance with cardinality 1 (cf. Table 2) when $n = 2$.

χ^2-Divergence. There is a one-one mapping between χ^2-divergence of cardinality n to Rényi divergence of cardinality 1 with $\alpha = n + 1$. Let us start by plugging the bag-of-words assumption into the definition and replace all the $q(t_j|d)/p(t_j|d)$ with $\mathbb{I}_{t_j,d}/Z_d$. Organize a bit, the divergence is written as follows:

$$
-1 + \sum_d p(d)\left(\sum_t p(t|d)\frac{\mathbb{I}_{t,d}}{Z_d^2}\right)^n = -1 + \sum_d p(d) Z_d^{-n}.
\tag{16}
$$

This has the same analytic form as Rényi divergence. Therefore, minimizing χ^2-divergence for arbitrary cardinality n is equivalent to minimizing Rényi divergence of $\alpha = n + 1$ in cardinality 1.

Rényi Divergence of Order α. It turns out Rényi divergence has an interesting property that, under the term independence assumption, minimizing Rényi divergence of order α in cardinality n is equivalent to doing Rényi divergence of order $n\alpha - n + 1$ in cardinality 1. Following the same maneuver, we have:

$$
\begin{aligned}
&\frac{1}{\alpha - 1} \log \sum_d p(d)\left(\sum_t p(t,d)\mathbb{I}_{t,d} Z_d^{-\alpha}\right)^n \\
&= \frac{1}{\alpha - 1} \log \sum_d p(d) Z_d^{n(1-\alpha)}.
\end{aligned}
\tag{17}
$$

It is clear that since $n(1 - \alpha) = 1 - (n\alpha - n + 1)$, this is equivalent to minimizing a cardinality-1 Rényi divergence. This is a bijection as $\alpha > 1 \Leftrightarrow n\alpha - n + 1 > 1$ for all integer $n \geq 0$.

Rényi Divergence of Order Infinity. This measure is perhaps the most curious one in the study. Despite being a special case of Rényi divergence of order α, when evaluated in high cardinality n the divergence does *not* automatically fall back to itself in cardinality 1. Nevertheless, this divergence is actually rank invariant for all cardinalities $n > 0$ (cf. Section 3.3). Its analytic form can be derived as follows:

$$
\log \sup_{t_{1:n},d} Z_d^{-n} \prod_j \mathbb{I}_{t_j,d} = \log \sup_d Z_d^{-n}.
\tag{18}
$$

Partially Labeled Supervised Topic Models for Retrieving Similar Questions in CQA Forums

Debasis Ganguly
ADAPT Centre, School of Computing
Dublin City University
Dublin 9, Ireland
dganguly@computing.dcu.ie

Gareth J.F. Jones
ADAPT Centre, School of Computing
Dublin City University
Dublin 9, Ireland
gjones@computing.dcu.ie

ABSTRACT

Manual annotations, e.g. tags and links, of user generated content in community question answering forums and social media play an important role in making the content searchable. During the active phase of a new question entered into a CQA forum, a moderator or an answerer often has to make a significant effort to manually search for related question threads (which we refer to as documents), that he may consider linking to the current question. This manual effort can be greatly reduced by an automated search process to suggest a list of candidate documents to be linked to the new document. We described our investigation of link recommendation for this task. We approach the problem as an ad-hoc information retrieval (IR) task in which a new document (question) acts as the query and the intention is to retrieve a list of potentially relevant documents (previously asked questions in the forum), which could then be linked (manually) to the new one. In contrast to standard ad-hoc search, two pieces of human annotated additional information, namely the tags of the documents and the known links between existing document pairs, can potentially be used to improve the search quality for new questions. To utilize this additional information, we propose a generative model of tagged documents which jointly estimates the distribution of topics corresponding to each tag of a document along with the likelihood of a document being linked to another one. The model predictions are then incorporated in the query likelihood estimate of a standard language model (LM) of IR. Experiments conducted on three months of a crawled StackOverflow dataset show that utilizing the tag specific topic distributions results in a significant improvement in retrieval of the candidate set of related documents.

Categories and Subject Descriptors

H.3.3 [**INFORMATION STORAGE AND RETRIEVAL**]: Information Search and Retrieval—*Retrieval models, Relevance Feedback, Query formulation*

General Terms

Theory, Experimentation

Keywords

Supervised Partially Labeled Topic Model, StackOverflow Linked Question Retrieval

1. INTRODUCTION

The amount of user generated content on the web, ranging from status updates and comments on social media to questions and their corresponding answers on community question answering (CQA) forums, has grown at a rapid rate in recent years. This ever increasing growth of user generated content is necessitating the development of new technologies to manage these materials. The design principle of these systems is to allow users to not only easily manage their newly created content, but also to allow them to search for content created by other users.

One useful content management feature is the ability of a user to label or tag[1] his content. An example of this is the hashtags of tweets[2], or the tags associated to the questions in StackOverflow[3] (a programming related CQA website), e.g. "Java", "Lucene" etc.

The second useful interactive content management feature, particularly in the context of CQA forums, is the facility to manually insert links to related documents. For example in StackOverflow, a user may insert a hyperlink within the text of a question, answer or a comment to another StackOverflow question that may be related to the current question. Figure 1 illustrates the use of tags and linked questions in the StackOverflow website.

At the time of writing, the number of questions in Stack-Overflow is over 8 million, the number of answers over 13 million, and the number of users over 3 million. Such large numbers suggest that it is of the utmost importance to quality control the user generated content of the forum so that newly created content is easily accessible to other users [10]. As a part of the quality control process, during the active phase of a StackOverflow question, a moderator or an answerer often needs to spend a significant effort to manually locate related documents that he may consider linking to the current one. To do this, a user may have to manually

---

[1] Throughout the rest of the paper we use the terms "label" and "tag" interchangeably.

[2] https://twitter.com/

[3] http://stackoverflow.com/

Figure 1: Tags and "Linked Questions" on Stack-Overflow.

formulate search queries by extracting keywords from different parts (e.g. title, body, etc.) of the current question in order to identify a candidate list of related questions. It should be noted that although the search process for finding related questions in a CQA forum itself is automatic (since questions in a CQA forum are indexed so that they can be retrieved with the help of keyword based queries), the query formulation process is manual and often time consuming.

Generally speaking, for any large content-base, this manual effort can be greatly reduced by incorporating an automated process to suggest a list of candidate documents that a user may consider linking to the new document. A document from this set to which a user may eventually link the new document can be considered as *relevant* for this new document. Clearly, an automated search method will be more useful if it is able to suggest more relevant questions (i.e. those on which links should be inserted due to their relatedness with the new question) at top ranks. In standard information retrieval (IR) terminology, the new document acts as a pseudo-query[4] and the manually linked documents correspond to the relevant documents for this query.

In this paper, we investigate retrieval of a set of questions (documents) which are most likely to be related to a newly created question (document), and hence it is likely for a moderator to link these previous questions to the new one. We view the problem as an IR task where the intention is to retrieve a list of relevant documents in response to a new document implicitly acting as the query.

An important observation with respect to this work is that the user interfaces to the popular user generated content management systems have contributed to the availability of a massive amount of human annotated additional information within the documents, e.g. the tags associated with a StackOverflow question and the links between them. However, the potential benefits of making use of this additional information to improve the search effectiveness over such content has not yet been investigated.The main aim of our work is to develop a retrieval model which in a principled approach can make use of this additional information to improve retrieval effectiveness. In particular, we aim to reduce the manual effort involved in linking questions on CQA forums, e.g. StackOverflow, by suggesting a list of relevant related questions to the users at top ranks.

---

[4]Simply referred to as "query" throughout the rest of this paper.

Previous research in IR has demonstrated the usefulness of topic smoothing by extending the query likelihood language model (LM) with latent Dirichlet allocation (LDA) probabilities [17]. While such unsupervised topic smoothing is useful for standard IR document collections, such as news and web text, retrieval of user generated content provides the scope to explore the use of additional annotation information, e.g. tags and links. This necessitates firstly the development of generative models of text which take into account the tags of and links between documents, and secondly integrating such a model within the framework of a standard IR model. While partially supervised generative models of text have been developed to take into account the tags as observed variables in documents, so as to estimate tag specific topic distributions [16], such models have not been integrated within the framework of IR.

For our experimental investigation, we use a three months subset of the entire StackOverflow dump. With reference to the StackOverflow dataset, a query-document (or a pseudo-query) in our case refers to the title and body of a new StackOverflow question. The document collection used for retrieval is a set of previously asked questions (comprising of the title and body) on StackOverflow. The research challenge is to devise an appropriate indexing and retrieval scoring mechanism which, in addition to the document content, also takes into account the topics within the documents. We use a tag specific topic distribution because such a distribution is likely to be more fine-grained than a global topic distribution which ignores tags. We also make use of the existing links within the documents (StackOverflow questions) to estimate a latent relationship between the tag specific topics and the links. The hypothesis is that some topics are more likely to generate linked content than others.

Research Questions. Our work seeks to develop a tag specific topic model which in addition to the tags also takes into account the likelihood of documents to be linked to the other ones. In particular, we focus on the following research questions:

1. How can a tag specific topic model be used within the framework of IR to improve retrieval effectiveness of "linked" documents?

2. How can such a model be trained with existing link information and can these topics be estimated with previously seen links to improve retrieval effectiveness for new documents?

The rest of the paper is organized as follows. Section 2 describes the related work. Section 3 presents our proposed model. Section 4 gives a detailed account of the experimental settings including the dataset description and the parameter settings. This is followed by Section 5, where we present and analyze the results. Finally, Section 6 concludes the paper with directions for future work.

2. RELATED WORK

Finding related questions in CQA forums. Finding similar questions on CQA forums has attracted significant research interest of late. For example, [7] investigates the effect of relative importance of fields, such as the title, body and the answers to the questions on retrieval quality, and observes that the best retrieval performance is achieved when all the fields are combined. Moreover, the authors also apply

IBM word alignment model to learn concept pairs in order to improve recall. Experiments in [7] were conducted on a Korean CQA forum. The work in [14] involves applying probabilistic latent semantic analysis (PLSA) for retrieval of similar questions for Yahoo! Answers.

Tag Suggestion. Somewhat similar to the task of suggesting questions to link from a newly created question in a CQA forum, is the challenge of suggesting tags to best describe a new question. There has been considerable research interest in automatic question annotation for CQA services. For example, [9] proposes a collaborative tagging system by combining information from content related tags and user profile tags. [11] attempts to construct a hyper-graph in the question space by integrating multiple facets including CQA content analytics, tag-sharing information and user connections, and selects the most descriptive tags from the tag candidates by considering measures such as informativeness and stability. The work in [3] investigates the use of topical entropy and reputation features of users for retrieving best answers in various StackExchange forums. These features respectively refer to the distribution of a user's posts across different tags (treated as topics) and their reputation with respect to a particular tag. The use of user supplied tag names as topics has been shown to perform well in [3].

Link Analysis and Prediction. Somewhat similar to the problem of related questions suggestion is the problem of predicting links between a collection of documents. The work in [4] proposes the relational topic model (RTM), a supervised LDA approach [1] extended to take into account document pairs instead of a single document. Training the RTM involves estimating topics that best explain the observed annotated links between document pairs. For new document pairs, a new topic model is inferred from the estimated model. The response is predicted with a linear regression model. The main disadvantage of RTM is its scalability. Since RTM can only make predictions for a document pair, this means that the task of suggesting related questions for a newly created one would involve computing pairwise RTM responses between every existing question in the collection and the query. Moreover, the RTM does not take into account the tags of the documents while inferring the topics. A recent study involves a joint estimation of the tags, topics and user expertise of StackOverflow questions within a generative modeling framework [19]. This framework is then used for retrieving the linked questions in StackOverflow. In the model proposed in [19], generation of both the tags and the words depends on the topics, which has the implication that tags are treated as special types of words. Contrastingly, in our model we estimate a tag specific topic distribution instead of topic specific word and tag distributions. Moreover, a major difference between [19] and our work is that the former does not seek to incorporate the topic model weights into an IR model. Instead, the authors simply use the JS divergence of the topic distributions computed with the help of the proposed model to rank related questions by pairwise similarity values between every document pair. Since the experiments were conducted on a small corpus of 1,173 questions there was no need to employ an IR system. It is thus difficult to see how such an approach would scale for much larger-sized question collections.

Tag specific topics. There are a number of approaches which simultaneously model the relationship between tags and topics. Labeled LDA (LLDA) [15] is a generative model of labeled (tagged) documents which assumes that each label (tag) in a document is responsible for generating the words in the documents from the per-tag distribution over terms. A limitation of LLDA is that it only estimates the distribution of the documents over their observed labels and that of the labels over the words, instead of modeling any latent topics (neither global nor within a label). This limitation was overcome by the partially labeled LDA (PLDA), which is a generalization of LLDA in the sense that it models latent topics per label [16].

Differences between our work and previous research. Our proposed model is mainly inspired from the PLDA model. While the PLDA model is essentially an unsupervised model, our model is a supervised one which estimates the per label distribution of topics that best predicts the likelihood of a document to be linked to another. This likelihood is treated as an output variable in our model, similar to the working principle of supervised LDA (SLDA) [1] and the RTM [4].

The (semi-)supervised variants of LDA [2] proposed in [15, 16, 1] have not yet been explored in IR. The only topic modeling approach that has been investigated for IR is the LDA [17], where the LDA term-topic and document-topic distributions were used to smooth the query likelihood language model [12, 6]. While the LDA smoothing works well for ad-hoc IR on news articles, the retrieval task which we focus on here is very different. Consequently, we propose making use of the tags and the link information between documents to first estimate a more expressive topic model than LDA and then use the topic distribution weights learned from our model to smooth the LM query likelihood.

The work in [20] investigates the use of LDA based topic modeling and relevance model [8] for query expansion. In this paper, we do not conduct any experiments on pseudo-relevance feedback and query expansion. Instead, we aim to improve the initial retrieval effectiveness.

3. PARTIALLY LABELED SUPERVISED LDA

We start this section with a description of our proposed supervised model for joint estimation of tag specific topics and the document linkage likelihoods. We then discuss approximate inferencing of the model with the help of Gibbs sampling. This is followed by a discussion on how our proposed model can be applied to the task of linked question retrieval.

3.1 Model Description

Before formally presenting our partially labeled supervised topic model, we first introduce the notations. Let $\mathbb{D}$ be a collection of documents. A document d in this collection comprises of words w_n, where $n = 1 \ldots N_d$, N_d being the number of words in d. Let $\mathbb{V}$ be the vocabulary from which the content words are drawn. Let $\mathbb{L}$ be the set of global labels from which the individual document labels are drawn from. Let Λ_d (shown as Λ in the plate diagram of Figure 2 for simplicity) be a document specific subset of available label classes, represented as a sparse binary vector ($\in \mathbb{R}^L$) generated from a sparse binary vector. It should be noted that since each document's label-set Λ_d is observed, its sparse vector prior is unused and hence is not shown in Figure 2. Each label $l \in L$ is mapped to a set of K_l topics chosen from a total of K topics, where $\sum_l K_l = K$. Every topic of a document d is drawn from a label specific topic

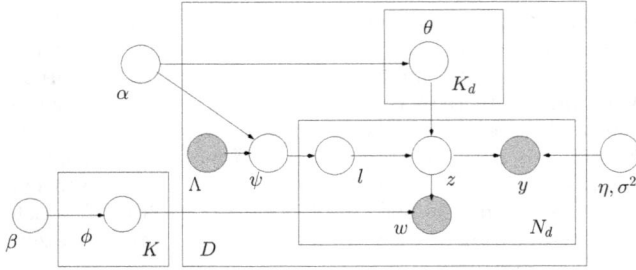

Figure 2: SPLDA Plate Diagram

distribution θ_l, where $\theta_l \in \mathbb{R}^{K_l}$. K_d represents the number of labels a document d has, i.e., the number in the sparse binary vector Λ_d. The words in d are then chosen from these latent topic assignments. This part of the modeling process is identical to the PLDA model proposed in [16].

Additionally, a response variable y_d (shown as y in Figure 2 for simplification) is associated with every document d in the collection. The value of this variable for a document is dependent on the latent topic assignments which in turn depend on the labels of the document. Due to the added response variable which depends on the latent topic assignments, our proposed model becomes supervised, and hence we call our model supervised PLDA (SPLDA). The generative process for SPLDA is formally presented as follows.

1. For document d, draw a set of labels $\Lambda_d | \alpha \sim Dir(\alpha)$
2. A document specific mixture of observed labels ψ_d is drawn as a multinomial of size Λ_d from the Dirichlet prior α.
3. For each label l drawn from ψ_d, draw label specific topic proportions $\theta_l | \alpha \sim Dir(\alpha)$
4. For each word $w_{d,n} \in d$, $n = 1 \ldots N_d$
   (a) Draw label specific topic assignments $z_n | \theta_l \sim Mult(\theta_l)$
   (b) Draw word $w_n | z_n, \phi_{l_{1:K_l}} \sim Mult(\phi_{l_{z_n}})$, where $Mult(\phi_{l_{z_n}})$ is drawn from a Dirichlet prior β.
5. Draw response variable $y_d | z_{d,1:N_d}, \eta, \sigma \sim \mathcal{N}(\eta^T \overline{z_d}, \sigma)$

Intuitively speaking, the SPLDA generative process ensures that a word $w_{d,n}$ in a document d is drawn in proportion with how much this document prefers the label l, how much that label prefers the topic $z_{d,n}$, and how much that topic prefers the word $w_{d,n}$. The response variable of a document depends on the topic distribution $\overline{z_d} = \sum_{n=1}^{N_d} z_{d,n}$ which in turn depends on its observed labels. The hyper parameters of the response variable y_d come from a normal linear model with regression coefficient η and variance of σ similar to [1].

3.2 Gibbs Sampling Estimation of SPLDA

In this section, we describe how the model is estimated. Note that in the SPLDA model shown in Figure 2, the values of the labels are never explicitly used. The role which an observed label variable plays is simply to index into a label (tag) specific topic distribution.

First, we introduce the notation $n_{d,j,k,t}$ to refer to the number of occurrences of label $j \in \Lambda_d$ assigned to topic $k \in 1 \ldots K_j$ on term t in document d. A dot (.) in the subscript of this notation defines a summation over all possible values from its corresponding type, e.g. $n_{d,j,k,.}$ denotes a total

count of all terms in document d that are assigned the label j and topic k, whereas $n_{.,j,k,t}$ denotes the total number of times the term t is assigned a label j and topic k computed over all documents in the collection and so on. The superscript $(\neg d, n)$ denotes a count of label-topics for the nth word in document d that excludes the current label and topic assignments used in the sampling process.

The topics that can be assigned to a label j are indexed from $1 \ldots K_j$, where K_j denotes the number of topics assigned to label j. Mapping these local topic indices on to a global index of K ($K = \sum_j K_j$) topics is implementation specific.

With this notation, the joint distribution of the label and topic assignments for the nth word in document d, denoted by $l_{d,n}$ and $z_{d,n}$, respectively, is approximately inferred by the Gibbs sampling update formula shown in Equation 1. Details on the derivation of Equation 1 can be found in [16].

$$P(l_{d,n} = j, z_{d,n} = k | l_{\neg d,n}, z_{\neg d,n}, w_{d,n} = t; \alpha, \beta)$$
$$\propto \mathbb{I}[j \in \Lambda_d \wedge k \in 1 \ldots K_j]\left(\frac{n_{.,j,k,t}^{(\neg d,n)} + \beta}{n_{.,j,k,.}^{(\neg d,n)} + V\beta}\right)(n_{d,j,k,.}^{\neg d,n} + \alpha) \tag{1}$$

For supervised topic models, given a document d and a response y_d, the posterior distribution of the topic assignments can be found by variational expectation maximization as in [1]. Instead, we apply Gibbs sampling for estimating the posterior as in [4]. The Gibbs sampling updates for the response variable y_d are shown in Equation 2.

$$P(l_{d,n} = j, z_{d,n} = k | \alpha, \beta, w, y, \eta, \sigma, z_{\neg d,n})$$
$$\propto \mathbb{I}[j \in \Lambda_d \wedge k \in 1 \ldots K_j]\left(\frac{n_{.,j,k,t}^{(\neg d,n)} + \beta}{n_{.,j,k,.}^{(\neg d,n)} + V\beta}\right) \tag{2}$$
$$(n_{d,j,k,.}^{\neg d,n} + \alpha)\exp(-(y_d - \eta^T \overline{z_d} - \sigma)^2)$$

For derivation of Equation 2, refer to the derivation of Gibbs sampling equation for SLDA in the appendix chapter of [4]. The maximum likelihood estimates for the regression parameters are shown in Equations 3 and 4. A is a $D \times K$ matrix the rows of which are $\overline{z_d}^T$ and Y is the $D \times 1$ matrix of document response variables. The values of $\hat{\eta}$ are $\hat{\sigma}$ are updated after sampling each document during each iteration of Gibbs sampling.

$$\hat{\eta} = (A^T A)^{-1} A^T Y \tag{3}$$
$$\hat{\sigma} = \frac{1}{D}((Y^T Y) - Y^T A(A^T A)^{-1} A^T Y) \tag{4}$$

Following the derivation of [5], the posterior estimates for the label specific document-topic distribution $\hat{\theta}_d$ are computed according to Equation 5. The estimates for the term-topic distributions are shown in Equation 6.

$$\hat{\theta}_{d,j,k} = \sum_{j \in \Lambda_d} \sum_{k \in 1 \ldots K_j} \frac{n_{(d,j,k,.)} + \alpha}{n_{(d,.,.,.)} + K_j\alpha} \tag{5}$$

$$\hat{\phi}_{j,k,t} = \sum_{j \in \Lambda} \sum_{k \in K} \frac{n_{(.,j,k,t)} + \beta}{n_{(.,.,.,t)} + V\beta} \tag{6}$$

3.3 Applying SPLDA on StackOverflow Data

In the context of our research problem of linked question retrieval, the labels in SPLDA correspond to the annotated tags of StackOverflow questions. With the help of the model, we intend to estimate the topic distributions corresponding to each tag of a StackOverflow question. We hypothesize that the per tag topic distributions may potentially improve retrieval effectiveness. This is because the manually annotated tags are likely to guide the topic assignment process better than the purely unsupervised LDA model. In fact, previous research has shown that LM smoothing in IR with manually constructed topic models outperforms the automatically constructed ones [18].

However, a purely manual construction of topic models is intractable in practice for large volumes of data. SPLDA provides a tractable solution by using the tags as an initial guiding step for the topic assignments. In fact, the model is potentially able to discover more fine-grained topics corresponding to each coarse level topic manifested in a tag, e.g. SPLDA may discover that encapsulated within the tag "jquery" are the more fine-grained topics representing "look-n-feel" and "user interaction".

In the case of StackOverflow, the output variables for each document in SPLDA correspond to the linkage likelihood. More formally, if a document d is linked to $n(d)$ other documents, then the value of the output response variable y_d is set to $n(d)/D$ during the training phase.

3.4 SPLDA Smoothing on LM

Language Modeling in IR is a generative model of query likelihood with the assumption that the terms in a query q are generated independently from a document d. The generative process that is commonly used takes into account two possible events: i) generating a term w from the document d, denoted by $P_{MLE}(w, d)$; or ii) generating the term w from the collection, denoted by $P(w)$ [12, 6]. This is shown in Equation 7, where λ is the probability of choosing a term by the maximum likelihood estimate from document d and $(1 - \lambda)$ is that of choosing the term from the collection. The latter is usually referred to as smoothing. The notations $tf(t, d)$ and $cf(t)$ represent the term frequency of term t in document d and the collection frequency of term t respectively.

$$P(q|d) \propto \prod_w P(w|d) = \prod_w \lambda P_{MLE}(w|d) + (1 - \lambda)P(w)$$
$$= \prod_w \lambda \frac{tf(w, d)}{\sum_{t \in d} tf(t, d)} + (1 - \lambda)\frac{cf(w)}{\sum_t cf(t)} \quad (7)$$

The query likelihood generative process can be extended by inserting one additional event with say probability $P_{TM}(w|d)$ in the generative process, that is of choosing a term from the latent topics estimated with the help of a topic model [17]; this is shown in Equation 8.

$$P(w|d) \propto \lambda P_{MLE}(w|d) + \mu P_{TM}(w|d) + (1 - \lambda - \mu)P(w) \quad (8)$$

Note that for SPLDA in particular, the probability of generating a word w from document d is given by the estimated label specific posterior document-topic $\hat{\theta}_{d,j,k}$ (see Equation 5) and topic-term $\hat{\phi}_{j,k,t}$ distributions (see Equation 6) marginalized over the set of all observed labels in d; this is shown in Equation 9. Substituting the value of $P_{TM}(w|d)$ from Equation 9 into Equation 8 gives an SPLDA smoothed query LM for IR.

$$P_{TM}(w|d) = \sum_{j \Lambda_d} \sum_{k \in [1, K_j]} P(w|j, k; \hat{\phi}_{j,k,w})P(j, k|d; \hat{\theta}_{d,j,k}) \quad (9)$$

Since SPLDA is essentially a supervised model, it requires a training set of documents with observed labels from which it can estimate the per label topic distributions of documents that best explain the observed labels. When given a new set of documents (the test set), the model infers the topic distribution of and also predicts the response for these new documents. For the StackOverflow linked question retrieval problem, we do not make use of the responses predicted for documents in the test set. For the topic modeling smoothed LM retrieval, we only make use of the topic distributions inferred on the test set of documents, which in turn are predicted from the information on the tags and link likelihoods of the training set documents.

At this point, we would like to emphasize that the reason we do not use the link information in the test documents is because, in practice, such information is not immediately available for new documents. However, the intention is to see how the link information of previously asked questions might be used to effectively retrieve a list of related questions for a new question, i.e. the query.

4. EXPERIMENTAL SETTINGS

In this section, we first describe the dataset used for our experiments. This is followed by details of the experimental setup and the parameter settings.

4.1 Dataset

Our experimental investigations were conducted on three months of crawled StackOverflow data. First, we crawled all StackOverflow questions, along with the associated answers and comments, which were asked during the period of January to March 2013. Crawling was carried out using the StackOverflow API[5]. Questions from January and February 2013 were used as the training set for the SPLDA model, while those from March 2013 served as the test set.

Each question in the crawled dataset may have links to other questions. The link information was obtained from the StackOverflow database dump[6]. While crawling, we ensured that the "linked" questions were added to our dataset as well. Since the links in StackOverflow are undirected it is possible during crawling to encounter a question, asked on or after 1st March 2013, to be linked to a question in the training set. Consequently, before adding a linked question to our dataset we checked its creation time-stamp and ensured that only those questions which were asked on or before 28th February 2013 were added to the training dataset in order to ensure that the SPLDA training is only restricted to previously existing content.

Table 1 provides an overview of the dataset characteristics. Some of the tags in StackOverflow are synonymous. We used the list of $2,782$ synonym pairs provided by StackOverflow[7] to normalize the tag names to a single member from each synset, e.g. ".java" is normalized to "java".

The text extracted from the question along with its answers and comments were pre-processed by applying stopword removal and stemming. Specifically, we employed the

---

[5] https://api.stackexchange.com/docs/questions
[6] https://archive.org/download/stackexchange/ stackoverflow.com-PostLinks.7z
[7] http://stackoverflow.com/tags/synonyms

Table 1: Document collection statistics

Dataset	Period	#Docs				#Tags	#Vocab
		Linked	Unlinked	Total	Avg. #Links		
Train	Jan-Feb '13	42850	149350	192200	0.3006	980	314958
Test	Mar '13	23751	83149	106900	0.3021	979	207141

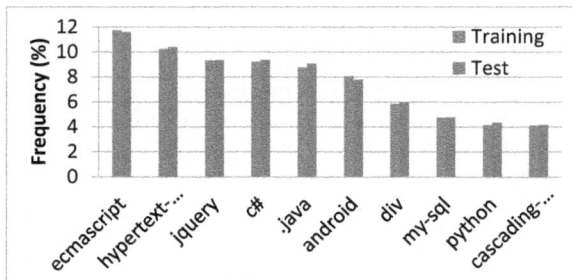

Figure 3: Top 10 most frequent tags.

Table 2: Types of queries experimented with.

#Queries	Avg. #rel	Query type	Avg. #terms
100	8.77	Tags only	2.9
		Title + Body	58.64
		Title + Body + Tags	61.55
		Title + Body + Answers	435.46
		Title + Body + Answers + Tags	438.37

SMART stopword list[8] of 571 words and applied Porter stemming [13]. The vocabulary size reported in Table 1 was computed after stopword removal and stemming.

It can be seen that although the creation times of the training and test set questions were different, there is noticeable similarity in the vocabulary sizes of the words and the tags, as shown in Table 1. It can also be seen that the ratios of the number of linked documents and the total number of documents in the two sets are very close.

Intuitively speaking, for the SPLDA inference to work reasonably well, the tag-sets (and hence the tag specific topic sets) of the training and the test sets should overlap sufficiently. To see if this is the case in our dataset, we computed the relative frequencies of the tags for both the datasets. Figure 3 shows the results for the top 10 most frequent tags for each dataset. It can be seen that the frequency distribution of the top most frequent tags is also very close, the general implication of which is that the new questions on StackOverflow follow roughly the same tag (and hence tag-topic) distribution.

4.2 Retrieval Setup

In this section, we describe the baselines, the implementation tools and the parameter settings for our experiments.

4.2.1 Baselines

In order to measure the relative performance of SPLDA in comparison to other existing models, we incorporate the topic model smoothing from other models into the LM query likelihood as baselines. Note that LDA-like models (including LDA itself) output two distributions, namely the document-topic ($\hat{\theta}$) and the topic-term ($\hat{\phi}$) distributions. Different values of these estimates can then be plugged into Equation 9 giving rise to different similarity functions for LM (see Equation 8).

As baseline approaches, we conduct experiments with LDA [2], SLDA [1] and PLDA [16]. Since LDA and SLDA models do not use the tags of documents, Equation 9 computes the outer summation over a single "global" label only. Of

the baseline approaches, LDA and PLDA are unsupervised, whereas SLDA is supervised. Since the unsupervised approaches cannot handle document responses, the training set for these models was only useful in estimating the topics, which were then used to infer the test set documents. In contrast, the supervised models, namely SLDA and SPLDA, do make use of the additional document link likelihoods estimated from the training set of documents.

4.2.2 Indexing and Retrieval

We used Lucene[9] for our retrieval experiments. The document collection consisted of the 106900 test set documents. To make use of the tags as query terms, the tags themselves were indexed in a separate field. The topic modeling weights values, $P_{TM}(w|d)$ (see Equation 9), obtained after executing topic modeling inference with Gibbs sampling on the test set documents, were stored as payloads in the inverted list entries corresponding to term w and document d. Consequently, these values could then be efficiently used for similarity computation during retrieval time. Our proposed model SPLDA is implemented as an open source Java application[10]. To ensure a fair comparison, all the other baseline models were also implemented as parts of the same Java application.

Out of the 23,751 linked questions in the test set (see Table 1), a random sample of 100 StackOverflow posts were used as queries (see Table 2). The task of the retrieval method is to retrieve a ranked list of candidate documents from the indexed collection of 106900 documents. The intention of the experiment is to retrieve the known linked questions at top ranks. The set of known linked questions thus acts as the set of manually assessed relevance judgments for each query.

A collection of 106,900 documents may seem somewhat small compared to the collection sizes used for most current IR research. However, we should emphasize that the retrieval problem is itself far more challenging than IR on standard document collections. The main reason being the absence of a manually constructed query which is representative of some information need. In fact, previous research on the StackOverflow linked question retrieval problem has shown that the results obtained in previous work are far

---

[8]http://www.lextek.com/manuals/onix/stopwords2.html

[9]http://lucene.apache.org/

[10]https://github.com/gdebasis/splda

Table 3: Parameter Settings on LM Baseline

Query type	Evaluation Metrics		
	MAP	MRR	Recall
Tags only	0.0055	0.0317	0.0846
Title + Body	0.0158	0.0601	0.1311
Title + Body + Tags	0.0160	0.0615	0.1322
Title + Body + Answers	0.0192	0.0752	0.1630
Title + Body + Answers + Tags	**0.0193**	**0.0788**	**0.1644**

from satisfactory [19]. Even with a very small collection size of 1,173 StackOverflow questions, coupled with a pairwise similarity computation between a query with each document in the collection, the best MRR (mean reciprocal rank, i.e. the average rank at which the first relevant document is retrieved) obtained was a very low value of only 0.0713. Hence, by comparison to previous work, the collection size that we use is reasonably large and definitely requires an IR approach instead of a pairwise similarity computation for each document in the collection.

4.2.3 Parameter Settings

The hyper-parameters of the LDA based models, namely α and β, were set to 0.1 and 0.01 respectively, as in [5, 16]. The number of Gibbs sampling iterations that we use to estimate the topic models is 1000.

A parameter of the SPLDA is the number of topics to be preassigned to each label. Although it is possible to specify a variable number of topics to be assigned to different labels based on some heuristics, in order to simplify the experimental procedure we assign an identical number of topics to each tag. Let this number be denoted by k (not to be confused with K which is the total number of topics), i.e. $K_j = k, \forall j \in \mathbb{L}$. Note that if $k = 1$, a label simply acts as a single topic. Since it is practically infeasible to run all sets of experiments with different values of k, we first set this value to 2 in our initial sets of experiments reported in Table 4. Later on, we took the best performing approach and varied this parameter to see how it affects retrieval quality.

An initial retrieval baseline for the related question retrieval problem is the standard LM approach (see Equation 7). We performed initial empirical investigations on this baseline approach in order to obtain the optimal parameter settings, which were then used in the subsequent experiments reported in Section 5.

First, we explored optimal ways of constituting search queries from the StackOverflow questions. More specifically, we investigated a) whether tags from the queries should be used as search terms; b) should terms from only the question title and body be used in the query or should answers and comments be also included; and c) should all or only a selected number of terms be used to formulate the query.

Table 2 lists the different query types used in our investigation. It can be seen that the queries constituted only from the title and the body of StackOverflow questions are significantly smaller than those which in addition use the answers and the comments.

Table 3 shows the retrieval results obtained with the different query types. Firstly, it can be seen that the use of tags alone as search terms do not prove effective. However, it can also be observed that inclusion of of the tags in the query improves the search results, indicating that the combination of tags with the content words can potentially improve retrieval effectiveness. The search result improvements obtained by appending the tags as search terms are small. This is because the average number of tags found in a StackOverflow question is about 3, and hence this small number of additional query terms does not play a significant role in retrieval.

Secondly, the combination of all the text fields in a question, i.e. question title and body along with the answers and comments, produces better queries for retrieval in comparison to the question title and body. This can be explained as follows. Although it is the questions which are shown linked in StackOverflow, the endpoints of some links could in fact be comments or answers. This happens when a user puts a link to an answer to a related question from an answer to the current question. Consequently, terms extracted from the answers and comments can play a crucial role in retrieval as well. It is thus the combination of all fields which performs the best.

The best result obtained with the baseline LM approach is an MRR value of 0.0788. Although this baseline result seems to be rather low, we would remind readers that this baseline result is in fact slightly stronger than the results obtained with topic modeling on a smaller collection of StackOverflow questions [19]. Hence, it is reasonable to conclude that this LM baseline result is at least competitive with existing work.

5. RESULTS

In this section, we first report the retrieval effectiveness of SPLDA in comparison to other topic model baselines. We then investigate the effect of the number of topics on SPLDA's performance. This is followed by a study on query formulation with selective terms using SPLDA term weights and a per query analysis of the SPLDA retrieval results.

5.1 Comparison of SPLDA with baselines

In this section, we report the retrieval performance of SPLDA relative to the baselines described in Section 4.2.1. The parameter λ for maximum likelihood document model in LM query likelihood was set to 0.7 as prescribed in [17].

The topic model smoothing parameter μ (see Equation 8) was set to 0.2. The retrieval results obtained with various topic model smoothing are presented in Table 4. We retrieved a ranked list of 1000 documents for each query. The same number of topics were used for all the topic model smoothing approaches. The PLDA and SPLDA results were obtained by using a small number of topics (specifically set to 2) per label. Later, in Section 7, we vary the number of topics and show that the performance of SPLDA is relatively insensitive to the number of topics per tag. To achieve a fair and meaningful comparison between the global topic modeling and the per-tag topic modeling approaches, the number of topics in LDA and SLDA were set to the total number of topics used in PLDA and SPLDA. Thus, in the case of LDA and SLDA, the number of topics was set to 1960 (i.e. 980×2).

It can be seen from Table 4 that the use of LDA significantly improves the results. The results conform to the observations of [17], where it was reported that LDA smoothing improves ad-hoc IR effectiveness by about 22% on news documents. The improvements obtained are even higher in magnitude in the case of StackOverflow questions. The use of SLDA smoothing has not been investigated in the litera-

Table 4: StackOveflow "linked questions" retrieval with different models.

IR Model	Metrics		
	MRR	MAP	Recall
LM	0.0788	0.0193	0.1644
LDA	0.1443	0.0396	0.2041
SLDA	0.1211	0.0339	0.2006
PLDA	0.1621	0.0432	0.2063
SPLDA	**0.2311**	**0.0696**	**0.2246**

ture before. It can be seen that the results decrease slightly in comparison to LDA. A possible reason for this is that the topic distribution of a flat topic model, such as SLDA, may be too coarse to satisfactorily estimate which topics favour the link likelihoods and which topics do not.

The next important observation is that PLDA improves results significantly[11] in comparison to LDA. In contrast to LDA, PLDA is able to utilize additional information from the observed tags of the documents. Thus, while the topic estimations of PLDA are more fine-grained due to the guidance of the top level topics represented by the tags, the distribution learnt by LDA is essentially a coarse one.

Table 5 illustrates this difference in granularity of the topics with an example. From the LDA model, we show the topics which contain the word "Java" as one of its top 5 terms (as measured by the $\hat{\phi}_{k,t}$ values). Similarly, we also show the top 5 terms corresponding to the two topics pertaining to the label "Java". The topics represented via LDA are somewhat coarse, e.g. the topics pertaining to the database connectivity and I/O. Some are even hard to describe manually due to the presence of unrelated words, e.g. the presence of the words "perl" and "part" in the last row of the LDA topics. By comparison, the topics learned with the help of PLDA are more meaningful and fine-grained due to the additional tag information used in constituting the topics.

Finally, the results are further improved significantly by using the supervised version of PLDA. This in fact confirms our hypothesis that it is beneficial to discover topics that are likely to be relevant. In our particular problem of linked question retrieval, these are the topics that are principally responsible for link creation. Table 5 shows that SPLDA is able to discover the topic about "runtime errors". It is more likely that the questions in StackOverflow discuss errors in general and that the questions on common error types tend to be linked together. The SPLDA model is able to discover this latent factor in the linkage pattern, which PLDA being an unsupervised model, is not able to. SPLDA thus leverages the additional information about the previously existing links between questions and is able to retrieve more relevant linked questions for new query questions.

Table 6 shows a few additional examples of per-label topic distributions estimated with the help of SPLDA on the StackOverflow test data. The latent aspects corresponding to each label are fairly evident in most cases, e.g. the first topic corresponding to "Python" is about array and string functions, whereas the second topic is about handling JSON data files. Another example is seen in the topics corresponding to the

---

[11]Measured by Wilcoxon statistical significance test with 95% confidence.

Table 6: Top 5 terms for topics in each label estimated with SPLDA (#topics for each label is 2).

Label	Word stems				
database	databas	store	tabl	oracl	updat
	databas	tabl	item	record	combobox
jquery	jqueri	ui	click	div	code
	form	jqueri	button	code	page
c#	code	call	string	applic	properti
	method	class	type	object	inherit
java	java	class	method	object	inherit
	code	error	except	file	run
swing	button	gui	swing	click	text
	move	drag	layer	mous	ball
python	function	string	arrai	data	error
	json	code	data	file	arrai
html	page	html	div	css	imag
	tabl	html	width	element	code
lucene	jar	test	server	code	java
	field	lucen	search	queri	index

Table 7: The effect of the number of topics per tag for SPLDA estimation on retrieval quality.

#Topics per tag	Evaluation Metrics			
	MRR	MAP	Recall	P@5
1	0.2276	0.0678	0.2223	**0.1460**
2	**0.2311**	**0.0696**	**0.2246**	0.1420
5	0.2297	0.0690	**0.2246**	0.1420

"Lucene" tag where the first topic is about Lucene installation whereas the second is about indexing and retrieval.

5.2 Number of Topics Per Tag

Selecting the optimal number of topics is important for topic modeling. However, in the case of IR, previous research has reported that the retrieval effectiveness obtained with LDA smoothing on LM is not overly sensitive to the number of topics used in LDA. Moreover, due to a large number of documents in IR collections it is intractable to optimize this parameter for all sets of experiments reported in Table 4. Thus, in this section we only explore the effect of the number of topics on the best performing model, i.e. SPLDA (see Table 4).

The parameter to vary in the case of SPLDA is the number of topics that are assigned to a tag. We assign an identical number of topics to each tag. Table 7 shows the results. It can be seen that the retrieval results are relatively insensitive to the number of topics used in the SPLDA smoothing. The best results are achieved when 2 topics are used for each tag. Even a parsimonious setting of using just a single topic for each tag, i.e. essentially treating each tag as a topic, yields statistically indistinguishable results in comparison to using 5 topics per tag.

5.3 Term Selection for Query Formulation

The number of terms used as queries for retrieving documents against each StackOverflow question is fairly large, the average number of terms being about 438 (see Table 2). The presence of a large number of terms in the queries may not be desirable from an efficiency point of view. In this sec-

Table 5: Topics related to "Java" as learnt by the different topic models.

Topic Model	Top terms					Manual Description
LDA	java	eclips	jdk	version	jvm	Dev environment
	java	oracl	javas	refer	gener	Database connectivity
	java	read	write	post	easi	I/O
	java	perl	def	part	add	Unclear
PLDA	method	class	code	java	object	Classes and objects
	java	jre	code	run	applic	Running application
SPLDA	java	class	method	object	inherit	Classes and objects
	code	error	except	java	run	Runtime Errors

Table 8: Query term selection for SPLDA.

λ	μ	MRR
0.2	0.2	0.1503
	0.4	0.1515
	0.6	**0.1527**
	0.8	0.1078
0.4	0.2	0.1516
	0.4	0.1515
	0.6	0.1078
0.6	0.2	0.1516
	0.4	0.1078

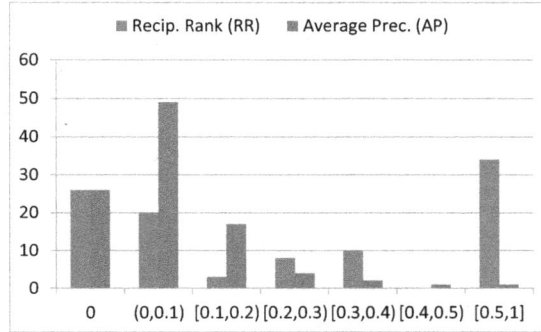

Figure 4: Per Query Results on StackOverflow linked question retrieval (Total #Queries: 100).

tion, we investigate whether this can be reduced to improve efficiency without impacting on retrieval effectiveness.

Each term w in the query can be scored by its LM term score, which is the probability of generating it from the container document or from the collection (see Equation 7). The terms with high $P(w|d)$ values can often act as the representative terms of a document [12]. In our current retrieval task, we may use the topic model smoothed values of $P(w|d)$, as shown in Equation 8. The intention is to see whether the additional information from the tag-specific topics help in choosing suitable representative terms from a query.

We experimented with a fixed number of terms, namely 20, selected from the queries. The parameters to be varied were λ and μ, which are the contributions from the term frequency based maximum likelihood and the SPLDA topic likelihoods respectively (see Equation 8).

The results are shown in Table 8. Note that the shaded cells represent degenerate cases where $(1 - \lambda - \mu)$, i.e. the probability of generating a term from the collection becomes zero. The complete absence of collection statistics produces poor results. The important observation is that best results are obtained with a high value of μ (and a low value of λ) which suggests that the topic model probabilities play a pivotal role in determining term importance. This is indicative of the fact that the topics themselves are good.

5.4 Per Query Analysis

Generally speaking, the StackOverflow "linked question" retrieval problem is hard, as indicated by the low MAP and recall values. An interesting question is to see if the performance for all queries is consistently poor or whether there is a subset of queries which perform particularly badly and more importantly, if so then why. Consequently, we measured the per query metrics of average precision (AP) and reciprocal rank (RR) for each of the 100 queries in our test set. The per query results values were then grouped in fixed length intervals as shown in Figure 4. The frequencies for each range, i.e. how many queries produce results within each individual range is then shown in Figure 4.

Figure 4 shows that a significant proportion (about one-third) of the queries register an RR value between 0.5 and 1, or in other words for these queries the first relevant document is found within the top two positions in the ranked list of retrieved results.

However, in Figure 4 we can also observe that about a quarter of the queries fail to retrieve any relevant documents. One example of such a StackOverflow question is the question shown in Table 9. For the sake of comparison, some of the representative terms (representative according to our judgment) are underlined in the text. It can be seen that there is practically no overlap in the representative terms. This is also true at the level of topics, e.g. the words "modified" and "closure" are not expected to belong to the same topic as "thread", "spawn" and "processing". Due to this low semantic similarity between the current question and the questions linked from it, it is difficult to retrieve these two questions.

6. CONCLUSIONS AND FUTURE WORK

In this paper, we investigated the problem of StackOverflow "linked questions" retrieval. In contrast to standard ad-hoc IR, the content in user generated forums is often tagged and interlinked manually. Our aim was to see if this additional information can be used in a principled approach to improve retrieval effectiveness of such content. We proposed a supervised partially labeled topic model (SPLDA) to estimate the per tag topic distributions. The topics learned by the model were guided firstly by the tags of the documents in the sense that each tag gives rise to its own set of more fine-grained topics; and secondly by the linkage likelihoods of the documents in the sense that the estimated topics of a document best explain the its likelihood of being linked.

Table 9: A sample question along with two linked questions (original text shown without corrections). No relevant documents were retrieved for this query.

Query: **multithreading re-entrancy issue**
I'm trying to spawn different threads for some processing. I use the for loop index for some logic inside each thread. How can I get the different threads to print 1,2,3,4, 5 in the code,below? Each time I run this, I get different numbers as output -,3,3,3,4,6,6 & 2,2,3,5,5,6 etc. I tried using the lock object, but it stil wasn't doing it correctly., Can anyone help me achive this. I just want to make sure each,thread/task gets the right index. Note that each task has been forced to,run on a separate thread.
Linked Question 1: **Access to Modified Closure**
The above seems to work fine though ReSharper complains that this is "access to modified closure". Can any one shed light on this? (this topic continued here)
Linked Question: 2 **Access to Modified Closure (2)**
This is an extension of question from Access to Modified Closure. I just want to verify if the following is actually safe enough for production use. I only run through the above once per startup. For now it seems to work alright. As Jon has mentioned about counterintuitive result in some case. So what do I need to watch out here? Will it be ok if the list is run through more than once?

The model was trained on a collection of about 200K StackOverflow questions. An IR collection of about 100K documents was constructed out of which 100 documents were chosen as queries, the pre-existing links of which served as the relevance judgments. Our experiments show that SPLDA was able to significantly improve retrieval effectiveness as compared to the simple baseline approach of standard LM query likelihood and other topic model smoothed extensions of LM including LDA, SLDA and PLDA.

The reasons for the improvement can be attributed to the additional human annotated information prevalent in these documents, namely the tags and the links. Firstly, the per tag fine-grained topics are more "meaningful" than purely automatically inferred topics such as those obtained in (S)LDA. Secondly, usage of the cross-link information between the documents during training such a per-tag based topic model results in a better topic model, the topics of which are able to capture the latent relationship with the links.

As a part of future work, we plan to investigate other human annotation information of user generated content, e.g. the votes of questions, answers or comments in StackOverflow, or the profile information of users to help improve search quality. Automatically detecting the exact points of links is a more general and harder problem than the retrieval of linked questions, and we would like to focus on this problem as well in future.

7. ACKNOWLEDGEMENTS

This research is supported by Science Foundation Ireland through the CNGL Programme (Grant 12/CE/I2267) in the ADAPT Centre (www.adaptcentre.ie) at Dublin City University.

8. REFERENCES

[1] D. M. Blei and J. D. McAuliffe. Supervised topic models. In *Proceedings of NIPS '07*, 2007.

[2] D. M. Blei, A. Y. Ng, and M. I. Jordan. Latent Dirichlet allocation. *J. Mach. Learn. Res.*, 3:993–1022, 2003.

[3] G. Burel, Y. He, and H. Alani. Automatic Identification of Best Answers in Online Enquiry Communities. In *Proceedings of ESWC'12*, pages 514–529, 2012.

[4] J. Chang. *Uncovering understanding and predicting links*. PhD thesis, Princeton University, 2011.

[5] T. L. Griffiths and M. Steyvers. Finding scientific topics. *PNAS*, 101:5228–5235, 2004.

[6] D. Hiemstra. *Using Language Models for Information Retrieval*. PhD thesis, CTIT, AE Enschede, 2000.

[7] J. Jeon, W. B. Croft, and J. H. Lee. Finding similar questions in large question and answer archives. In *Proceedings of CIKM '05*, pages 84–90. ACM, 2005.

[8] V. Lavrenko and B. W. Croft. Relevance based language models. In *Proceedings of SIGIR'01*, pages 120–127. ACM, 2001.

[9] M. Lipczak and E. Milios. Learning in efficient tag recommendation. In *Proceedings of the Fourth ACM Conference on Recommender Systems*, RecSys '10, pages 167–174. ACM, 2010.

[10] L. Mamykina, B. Manoim, M. Mittal, G. Hripcsak, and B. Hartmann. Design Lessons from the Fastest Q&A Site in the West. In *Proceedings of the CHI '11*, pages 2857–2866.

[11] L. Nie, Y.-L. Zhao, X. Wang, J. Shen, and T.-S. Chua. Learning to recommend descriptive tags for questions in social forums. *ACM Trans. Inf. Syst.*, 32(1):5:1–5:23, Jan. 2014.

[12] J. M. Ponte. *A language modeling approach to information retrieval*. PhD thesis, University of Massachusetts, 1998.

[13] M. F. Porter. An algorithm for suffix stripping. *Program*, 14(3):130–137, 1980.

[14] M. Qu, G. Qiu, X. He, C. Zhang, H. Wu, J. Bu, and C. Chen. Probabilistic question recommendation for question answering communities. In *Proceedings of the WWW '09*, pages 1229–1230. ACM, 2009.

[15] D. Ramage, D. Hall, R. Nallapati, and C. D. Manning. Labeled lda: A supervised topic model for credit attribution in multi-labeled corpora. In *Proceedings of EMNLP '09*, pages 248–256, 2009.

[16] D. Ramage, C. D. Manning, and S. Dumais. Partially labeled topic models for interpretable text mining. In *Proceedings of the 17th ACM SIGKDD*, KDD '11, pages 457–465. ACM, 2011.

[17] X. Wei and W. B. Croft. LDA-based document models for ad-hoc retrieval. In *Proceedings of SIGIR '06*, pages 178–185. ACM, 2006.

[18] X. Wei and W. B. Croft. Investigating retrieval performance with manually-built topic models. In *Proceedings of RIAO '07*, 2007.

[19] L. Yang, M. Qiu, S. Gottipati, F. Zhu, J. Jiang, H. Sun, and Z. Chen. CQArank: Jointly Model Topics and Expertise in Community Question Answering. In *Proc. of CIKM '13*, pages 99–108, 2013.

[20] X. Yi and J. Allan. A comparative study of utilizing topic models for information retrieval. In *Proceedings of ECIR '09*, pages 29–41. Springer-Verlag, 2009.

Entity Linking in Queries: Tasks and Evaluation

Faegheh Hasibi
Norwegian University of
Science and Technology
faegheh.hasibi@idi.ntnu.no

Krisztian Balog
University of Stavanger
krisztian.balog@uis.no

Svein Erik Bratsberg
Norwegian University of
Science and Technology
sveinbra@idi.ntnu.no

ABSTRACT

Annotating queries with entities is one of the core problem areas in query understanding. While seeming similar, the task of entity linking in queries is different from entity linking in documents and requires a methodological departure due to the inherent ambiguity of queries. We differentiate between two specific tasks, semantic mapping and interpretation finding, discuss current evaluation methodology, and propose refinements. We examine publicly available datasets for these tasks and introduce a new manually curated dataset for interpretation finding. To further deepen the understanding of task differences, we present a set of approaches for effectively addressing these tasks and report on experimental results.

Categories and Subject Descriptors

H.3 [**Information Storage and Retrieval**]: H.3.1 Content Analysis and Indexing; H.3.3 Information Search and Retrieval

Keywords

Entity linking; semantic mapping; interpretation finding; query understanding

1. INTRODUCTION

Query understanding has been a longstanding area of research in information retrieval [13, 38]. One way of capturing what queries are about is to annotate them with entities from a knowledge base. This general problem has been studied in many different forms and using a variety of techniques over the recent years [6, 8, 10, 12, 15, 27]. Approaches have been inspired by methods that recognize and disambiguate entities appearing in full-text documents by mapping them to the corresponding entries in a knowledge base, a process known as *entity linking* [29] (or *wikification* [31]). Successful approaches to entity linking incorporate context-based features in a machine learning framework to disambiguate between entities that share the same surface form [16, 30–32]. While the same techniques can be applied directly to short, noisy texts, such as microblogs or search queries, there is experimental evidence showing that the same methods perform substantially worse on short texts (tweets) than on longer documents (news) [11, 37]. One problem

is the lack of proper spelling and grammar, even of the most basic sort, like capitalization and punctuation. Therefore, approaches that incorporate richer linguistic analysis of text cannot be applied.

There is, however, an even more fundamental difference concerning entity annotations in documents vs. queries that has not received due attention in the literature. When evaluating entity linking techniques for documents, it is implicitly assumed that the text provides enough context for each entity mention to be resolved unambiguously. Search queries, on the other hand, typically consist of only a few terms, providing limited context. Specifically, we focus on a setting where there is no context, such as previous queries or clicked results within a search session, available for queries. In this setting, it may be impossible to select a single most appropriate entity for a given query segment. Consider, as an illustrative example, the query "new york pizza manhattan." It could be annotated, among others, as "[NEW YORK CITY] pizza [MANHATTAN]" or as "[NEW YORK-STYLE PIZZA][MANHATTAN]," and both would be correct (linked entities are in brackets).

A cardinal question, then, is how should the inherent ambiguity of entity annotations in queries be handled? One line of prior work has dealt with this problem by adopting a retrieval-based approach: returning a ranked list of entities that are semantically related to the query [6, 27]. We refer to it as *semantic mapping*. The Entity Recognition and Disambiguation (ERD) Challenge [8] represents a different perspective by addressing the issue of ambiguity head-on: search queries can legitimately have more than a single interpretation. An interpretation is a set of entities, with non-overlapping mentions, that are semantically compatible with the query text [8]. We term this task *interpretation finding*. Both approaches have their place, but there is an important distinction to be made as they are designed to accomplish different tasks. Semantic mapping is a tool for aiding users with suggestions that could be beneficial for enhancing navigation or for contextualization. Interpretation finding is a means to machine-understanding of queries, which, in our opinion, is the ultimate goal of entity linking in queries.

Once these differences are established and the tasks are defined, our next research question concerns the evaluation methodology and metrics. The current practice of rank-based evaluation is appropriate for the semantic mapping task. As for interpretation finding, interpretations are considered as atomic units, i.e., an interpretation is correct only if it contains the exact same entities as the ground truth; partial matches are not rewarded [8]. This is a rather crude method of evaluation. We present a relaxed alternative that considers both the correctness of interpretations, as atomic units, and the set of entities, recognized in the query.

As with any problem in information retrieval, the availability of public datasets is of key importance. The recently released Yahoo! Webscope Search Query Log to Entities (YSQLE) dataset [1], is suitable for semantic mapping, but not for interpretation finding.

The ERD Challenge platform [8] is fitting for interpretation finding, however, only the development set (91 queries) is publicly available, which is not large enough for training purposes. We therefore, introduce and make publicly available a new dataset based on YSQLE, called Y-ERD. It contains interpretations for 2398 queries and is accompanied by a clear set of annotation guidelines.

In addition, we present simple, yet effective methods for addressing the semantic mapping and interpretation finding tasks. We introduce a pipeline architecture for both and identify shared components. Finally, we evaluate our approaches on the different datasets, which offer further insights into these tasks.

In summary, the main theoretical contribution of this work is the methodological distinction between two tasks within the problem area of entity linking in queries: semantic mapping and interpretation finding. Technical contributions include (i) the development of a dataset and evaluation methodology for interpretation finding, (ii) solid and easy-to-implement approaches for both tasks, and (iii) experimental results and insights. All resources developed within this paper are made publicly available at `http://bit.ly/ictir2015-elq`.

2. RELATED WORK

In this section we review related work on entity linking and on query understanding, and finally on the intersection of these two.

2.1 Entity linking

Recognizing entity mentions in text and linking them to the corresponding entries in a knowledge base provides means for understanding documents (and queries). The reference knowledge base is most commonly Wikipedia. The Wikify! system [31], one of the earliest approaches, performs concept detection by extracting all n-grams that match Wikipedia concepts and then filters them. Their most effective filtering approach utilizes link probabilities obtained from Wikipedia articles. For the entity disambiguation step, they use a combination of knowledge-based and feature-based learning approaches. In another early work, Cucerzan [14] employs contextual and category information extracted from Wikipedia and calculates the similarity between the document and candidate entities' pages. Later, Milne and Witten [32] employed a machine learning approach, using commonness and relatedness as main features. Their work gained substantial improvements over prior approaches. DBpedia Spotlight [30] is another entity linking system, which uses the Vector Space Model to disambiguate named entities.

2.2 Query understanding

Query understanding refers to process of "identifying the underlying intent of the queries, based on a particular representation" [13]. One main branch of approaches focuses on determining the "aboutness" of queries by performing a topical classification of the query contents [7, 22, 25, 39]. Segmentation represents another approach to understanding queries, where the query is divided into phrases, such that each phrase can be considered as an individual concept [4, 21, 40]. Although query segmentation is not directly related to our task, some ideas can be borrowed for grouping named entities and forming interpretation sets. For instance, Hagen et al. [21] used n-gram frequencies and Wikipedia to efficiently segment queries. They incorporated the length of each segment as a weight factor; this is done to favor long segments with low frequency to short ones with high frequency.

Recognizing named entities in queries was first addressed by Guo et al. [18]; their goal was to detect named entities in a given query and classify them into a set of predefined classes such as "movie" or "music." The proposed approach employs probabilistic methods together with a weakly supervised learning algorithm

(WD-LDA). Alasiry et al. [2] proposed a processing pipeline for entity detection in queries, which involves the following steps: query pre-processing (e.g., spell checking), grammar annotation (POS and ORTH tagging), segmentation, and entity recognition (based on a small set of manually constructed rules). Importantly, these works are limited to detecting mentions of entities and do not perform disambiguation or linking; that follows in the next subsection.

2.3 Entity linking in queries

Entity linking for short texts, such as queries and tweets, has gained considerable attention recently. The TAGME system [16] extends the approach of Milne and Witten [32] by incorporating a voting schema for the relatedness feature and by discarding unrelated anchors. Meij et al. [28] proposed a two step approach for linking tweets to Wikipedia articles. In the first step, they extract candidate Wikipedia concepts for each n-gram. Next, a supervised learning algorithm with an excessive set of features is used to classify relevant concepts. Their strategy is to first obtain high recall and then improve precision by employing machine learning. Guo et al. [19] also studied microblog texts and employed a structural SVM algorithm in a single end-to-end task for mention detection and entity disambiguation.

Unlike these works, which revolve around ranking entities for query spans, the Entity Recognition and Disambiguation (ERD) Challenge [8] viewed entity linking in queries as the problem of finding multiple query interpretations. The task advances the conventional entity linking task (as it is known for long texts) and finds set(s) of (semantically related) linked entities, where each set reflects a possible meaning (interpretation) of the query. Even though it was one of the main considerations behind the ERD Challenge to capture multiple query interpretations, only a handful of systems actually attempted to address that; out of these, [15] performed best and was the third best performing system in overall. In this paper, we discuss why entity linking in queries should be addressed as an interpretation finding task and how the other tasks studied in the literature are different from it.

3. TASKS AND EVALUATION

In this section we first discuss the entity linking task for documents in Section 3.1. Next, in Section 3.2, we identify some principal differences when the same task is to be performed for queries and point out why the same evaluation methodology cannot be used. In Section 3.3 we look at the semantic mapping task and show that albeit the current practice of rank-based evaluation is appropriate, the task itself is easier than entity linking and resembles more of a *related entity finding* problem. Finally, in Section 3.4 we present the interpretation finding task, which deals with the inherent ambiguity of search queries. We introduce existing evaluation metrics and also propose refinements to the evaluation metrics used in [8] that can give credit for partial correctness.

3.1 Entity linking for documents

Entity linking is the task of recognizing entity mentions in text and linking (disambiguating) them each to the most appropriate entry in a reference knowledge base. This task implicitly assumes that the input text (document) provides enough context so that all entity occurrences can be resolved unambiguously.

Evaluation is performed against a gold-standard data set that consists of manual annotations. These annotations comprise of the specific entity mentions (offsets in the text) and the corresponding links to the knowledge base. Effectiveness is measured in terms of precision and recall, where precision is defined as the number of correctly linked mentions divided by the total number of links established by the system, and recall is defined as the number of

	Entity Linking[†]	Semantic Mapping	Interpretation Finding
Result	set	ranked list	sets of sets
Entities explicitly mentioned	Yes	No	Yes
Mentions can overlap	No	Yes	No[‡]
Evaluation criteria	mentioned entities found	relevant entities found	interpretations found
Evaluation metrics	set-based	rank-based	set-based
Examples			
"obama mother"	{BARACK OBAMA}	ANN DUNHAM BARACK OBAMA	{{BARACK OBAMA}}
"new york pizza manhattan"	{NEW YORK CITY, MANHATTAN}[*]	NEW YORK CITY NEW YORK-STYLE PIZZA MANHATTAN MANHATTAN PIZZA . . .	{{NEW YORK CITY, MANHATTAN}, {NEW YORK-STYLE PIZZA, MANHATTAN}}
"the music man"	{THE MUSIC MAN}[*]	THE MUSIC MAN THE MUSIC MAN (1962 FILM) THE MUSIC MAN (2003 FILM) . . .	{{THE MUSIC MAN} {THE MUSIC MAN (1962 FILM)}, {THE MUSIC MAN (2003 FILM)}}

[†] This refers to traditional entity linking (for documents) applied to queries. We argue in this paper that entity linking in this form should be avoided.

[‡] Not within the same interpretation.

[*] A single interpretation is selected arbitrarily; there are multiple options.

Table 1: Entity linking tasks.

correctly linked mentions divided by the total number of links in the gold-standard annotations [31]. For overall system evaluation the F-measure is used. Both micro- and macro-averaging can be employed [11]. Since mention segmentation is often ambiguous, and the main focus is on the disambiguation of entities, the correctness of entity mention boundaries is often relaxed [8]. On the other hand, evaluation is rather strict in that credit is only given for a given mention if the linked entity (unique entity identifier) perfectly matches the gold standard. Overlapping entity mentions in the annotations are not allowed, i.e., any given segment of the document may be linked to at most a single entity.

3.2 Entity linking for queries

Existing entity linking approaches can be used out-of-the-box to annotate queries with entities, analogously to how it is done for documents; after all, the input is text, which is the same as before, just shorter and less grammatical (the quality of the resulting annotations is another matter). The fundamental difference between documents and queries is that queries offer very limited context. A search query, therefore, "can legitimately have more than one interpretation," where each interpretation consists of a set of "non-overlapping linked entity mentions that are semantically compatible with the query text" [8]. Formally, let q be a query and $\hat{I}$ be the set of interpretations for this query (according to the ground truth), $\hat{I} = \{\hat{E}_1, \ldots, \hat{E}_n\}$, where n is the number of interpretations, $\hat{E}_i$ is a query interpretation, $\hat{E}_i = \{(m_1, e_1), \ldots, (m_k, e_k)\}$, and (m, e) is a mention-entity pair. For simplicity, the specific offsets of entity mentions are not considered, however, the corresponding entity mentions in $\hat{E}_i$ must not overlap. It is important to point out that the query might not have any interpretations ($\hat{I} = \emptyset$).

If the traditional evaluation methodology were to be adopted (as in Section 3.1, with the simplification of ignoring the offsets of mentions), the ground truth would need to consist of a single set of entities; we denote this set as $\hat{E}$. As long as the query has a single interpretation it is straightforward; entities in that interpretation will amount to the ground truth set. Having no valid interpretation is also painless, we set $\hat{E} = \emptyset$. For entities with multiple interpretations, there are two natural ways of setting $\hat{E}$.

Collapsing interpretations The first option is to collapse all interpretations into a single set: $\hat{E} = \bigcup_{i \in [1..n]} \hat{E}_i$. (This is similar in spirit to the approach that is followed in the semantic mapping task, see later in Section 3.3.) With this solution, however, the requirements that the linked entities within an interpretation must be semantically related and their mentions must not overlap are violated. It also ignores the element of multiple interpretations altogether.

Selecting a single interpretation The second option is to pick a single interpretation $\hat{E} = \hat{E}_j$, where $j \in [1..n]$. Given that all interpretations are of equal importance, selecting j in an arbitrary way would be unfair, as it would randomly favor certain systems over others. A better alternative would be to choose j individually for each system such that it maximizes the system's performance on a given evaluation metric, e.g., F1-score. Essentially, the system's output would be scored based on the closest matching interpretation. While the latter variant appears to be a viable solution, it still disregards the fundamental aspects of finding multiple interpretations for queries.

In summary, the entity linking task cannot be performed the same way for queries as it is done for documents, because of the element of multiple interpretations. In the remainder of this section we discuss two alternatives used in the literature and make suggestions for further methodological refinements.

3.3 Semantic mapping

Semantic mappings are primarily intended to support users in their search and browsing activities by returning entities that can help them to acquire contextual information or valuable navigational suggestions [27]. For semantic mapping, all entities from all interpretations are relevant. Beyond those, entities that are not explicitly mentioned, but referred to, may also be considered relevant; we elaborate further on this in Section 7. See Table 1 for illustrative examples. The goal, therefore, is quite different from that of finding interpretation(s) of the query for machine understanding. The requirements on the linked entities are relaxed: (i) the mentions can be overlapping, (ii) they do not need to form semantically compatible sets, (iii) they do not even need to be explicitly mentioned, as long as they are semantically related to the query.

Formally, let $\hat{E}$ denote the set of relevant entities for the semantic mapping task. This set is formed from entities across all interpretations, plus, optionally, additional entities (E^*) that are indirectly referenced from the query: $\hat{E} = \bigcup_{i \in [1..n]} \hat{E}_i \cup E^*$. Semantic mapping returns a ranked list of entities $\vec{E} = \langle e_1, \ldots, e_m \rangle$, which is compared against $\hat{E}$ using standard rank-based metrics, such as mean average precision (MAP) or mean reciprocal rank (MRR). Importantly, if $\hat{E} = \emptyset$ then the given query is ignored in the evaluation, meaning, that there is no difference made between system A that does not return anything and system B that returns meaningless or nonsense suggestions. This is undesired behavior; it also stands in contrast to standard entity linking, where false positives decrease system performance.

It is our opinion that above relaxations make semantic mapping a substantially easier task (that of finding "related entities") than what entity linking for queries entails in its entirety. Therefore, we believe that the terminological distinction is important and useful.

3.4 Interpretation finding

The inherent presence of multiple query interpretations is addressed head-on by the setup introduced at the Entity Recognition and Disambiguation (ERD) Challenge [8], where "interpretations of non-overlapping linked entity mentions" [8] are to be returned. We argue that this formulation is the proper way to go about entity linking in queries.

We write $\hat{I} = \{\hat{E}_1, \ldots, \hat{E}_m\}$ to denote the query interpretation according to the ground truth, and $I = \{E_1, \ldots, E_n\}$ is the interpretation returned by the system. Precision and recall, for a given query, are defined at the ERD Challenge as follows:

$$P = \frac{|I \cap \hat{I}|}{|I|}, \qquad R = \frac{|I \cap \hat{I}|}{|\hat{I}|}. \qquad (1)$$

Note that according to this definition, if the query does not have any interpretations in the ground truth ($\hat{I} = \emptyset$) then precision is undefined; similarly, if the system does not return any interpretations ($I = \emptyset$), then recall is undefined. We correct for this behavior by defining precision and recall for interpretation-based evaluation:

$$P_{\text{int}} = \begin{cases} |I \cap \hat{I}|/|I|, & I \neq \emptyset \\ 1, & I = \emptyset, \hat{I} = \emptyset \\ 0, & I = \emptyset, \hat{I} \neq \emptyset. \end{cases} \qquad (2)$$

$$R_{\text{int}} = \begin{cases} |I \cap \hat{I}|/|\hat{I}|, & \hat{I} \neq \emptyset \\ 1, & \hat{I} = \emptyset, I = \emptyset \\ 0, & \hat{I} = \emptyset, I \neq \emptyset. \end{cases} \qquad (3)$$

This evaluation is methodologically correct, it captures the extent to which the interpretations of the query are identified. It does so, however, in a rather strict manner: partial matches are not given any credit. This strictness is also pointed out in [8]. Their alternative solution, albeit purely for analysis purposes, was to measure micro-averaged precision, recall, and F1-score on the entity level. That metric, on its own, is inappropriate as "entities belonging to different interpretations were mixed together" [8]. Further, by micro-averaging, the query borders are also collapsed. We propose an alternative "lean" evaluation for interpretation finding that rewards partial matches while respecting query boundaries.

Lean evaluation. Our proposal is to combine interpretation-based evaluations (cf. Equations 2 and 3) with the conventional entity linking evaluation, referred to as entity-based evaluation, from now on. Formally, entity-based evaluation is defined as follows:

$$P_{\text{ent}} = \begin{cases} |E \cap \hat{E}|/|E|, & E \neq \emptyset \\ 1, & E = \emptyset, \hat{E} = \emptyset \\ 0, & E = \emptyset, \hat{E} \neq \emptyset. \end{cases} \qquad (4)$$

$$R_{\text{ent}} = \begin{cases} |E \cap \hat{E}|/|\hat{E}|, & \hat{E} \neq \emptyset \\ 1, & \hat{E} = \emptyset, E = \emptyset \\ 0, & \hat{E} = \emptyset, E \neq \emptyset. \end{cases} \qquad (5)$$

We write $\hat{E}$ to denote the set of all entities from all interpretations in the ground truth, $\hat{E} = \bigcup_{j \in [1..m]} \hat{E}_j$, and E is a set of all entities from all interpretations returned by the entity linking system, $E = \bigcup_{i \in [1..n]} E_i$.

Finally, we define precision and recall as a linear combination of interpretation-based and entity-based precision and recall:

$$P = \frac{P_{\text{int}} + P_{\text{ent}}}{2}, \qquad R = \frac{R_{\text{int}} + R_{\text{ent}}}{2}. \qquad (6)$$

For simplicity, we consider them with equal weight, but it could easily be controlled by adding a weight parameter. In all cases, the F-measure is computed according to:

$$F = \frac{2 \cdot P \cdot R}{P + R}. \qquad (7)$$

For computing precision, recall, and the F-measure on the whole evaluation set, an unweighed average over all queries are taken (i.e., macro-averaging is used). This provides an intuitive, easy-to-implement, and methodologically correct solution. A reference implementation is made publicly available.

4. TEST COLLECTIONS

We present two publicly available test collections for the semantic mapping and interpretation finding tasks, and introduce a new dataset for interpretation finding.

4.1 YSQLE

The Yahoo Search Query Log to Entities (YSQLE) dataset [1] comprises a selection of queries that are manually annotated with Wikipedia entities. Annotations are performed within the context of search sessions. Each annotation is aligned with the specific mention ("span") of the query. In addition, the linked entities may be labelled as *main*, to specify the intent or target of the user's query, regardless of whether the entity is mentioned explicitly in the query. For example, the query "france 1998 final" is annotated with three entities, FRANCE NATIONAL FOOTBALL TEAM, FRANCE, and 1998 FIFA WORLD CUP FINAL, of which only the last one is considered as the main annotation. Out of 2635 queries in the YSQLE dataset, 2583 are annotated with Wikipedia entities.

YSQLE is claimed to be designed for training and testing entity linking systems for queries. However, there is a number of issues. First and foremost, the dataset does not provide query interpretations, which is an essential part of entity linking in queries as we discussed in Section 3. Moreover, it is not possible to automatically form interpretation sets from the annotations. An example is the query "france world cup 1998", linked to the entities 1998 FIFA WORLD CUP, FRANCE NATIONAL FOOTBALL TEAM, and FRANCE. This query has two valid interpretations {1998 FIFA WORLD CUP, FRANCE NATIONAL FOOTBALL TEAM} and {1998 FIFA WORLD CUP, FRANCE}. One could assume that the main annotations would serve as interpretations, but it does not hold, as there exist queries with multiple or overlapping main annotations.

For example, the query "yahoo! finance," has two main annotations, linking the mention "yahoo!" to YAHOO! and the mention "yahoo! finance" to YAHOO! FINANCE. Second, the linked entities are not necessarily mentioned explicitly in the query, but sometimes are only being referred to. For example , the query "obama's mother" is linked to BARACK OBAMA and ANN DUNHAM, where the latter is specified as the main annotation. Another example is "charlie sheen lohan," which is linked to ANGER MANAGEMENT (TV SERIES) and to the two actors CHARLIE SHEEN and LINDSAY LOHAN. While this, in a way, is just a matter of how the annotation guidelines are defined, it nevertheless is non-standard behavior; entity linking should only be performed on explicit mentions, reference resolution is not part of the task. Carmel et al. [8] brings the query "Kobe Bryant's wife" as an example, which should be annotated as "[KOBE BRYANT]'s wife." Accordingly, the "obama's mother" query should have a single interpretation, BARACK OBAMA. Further, annotations are created by considering other queries from the session; this represents a different setting from what is discussed in Section 3.4. Lastly, the annotations in YSQLE are not always complete, meaning that some query spans that should be linked to entities are ignored. For instance the query "louisville courier journal" is annotated with THE COURIER JOURNAL, whereas the link for the mention [louisville] (to LOUISVILLE, KENTUCKY) is missing.

In summary, even though the YSQLE dataset is intended for the purpose of entity linking in queries, in practice it is mostly suitable for the semantic mapping task. Nevertheless, it offers a great starting point; we show in Section 4.3 that with some manual effort, YSQLE can be adjusted to suit interpretation finding evaluation.

4.2 ERD

The Entity Recognition and Disambiguation (ERD) Challenge [8] introduced the first query entity linking evaluation platform that properly considers query interpretations. For each query, it contains all possible interpretations (from the pool of all participating systems). Human annotations are created in accordance with the following three rules [8]: (i) the longest mention is used for entities; (ii) only proper noun entities should be linked; (iii) overlapping mentions are not allowed within a single interpretation. A training set, consisting of 91 queries, is publicly available.[1] The ERD Challenge runs evaluation as a service; entity linking systems are evaluated upon sending a request to the evaluation server (hosted by the challenge organizers). Therefore, the test set, comprising of 500 queries, is unavailable for traditional offline evaluation. In order to make a distinction between the two query sets provided by the ERD Challenge, we refer to the former one (91 queries) as ERD-dev and to the latter one (500 queries) as ERD-test.

The ERD-dev dataset includes a small number of queries, of which only half (45 queries) are linked to entities; see Table 2. Therefore, the dataset cannot be used for training purposes and the need for a large entity linking test collection for queries still remains. In the following, we describe our new test collection, which aims to provide just that.

4.3 Y-ERD

To overcome the limitations of the YSQLE and ERD datasets, we set out to develop a test collection for interpretation finding based on YSQLE. Taking YSQLE as our starting point, we manually (re)annotated all queries following a set of guidelines (Section 4.3.2), which are based on the ERD Challenge. The application context is general web search. The resulting dataset, referred to as *Y-ERD*, contains 2398 queries in total; see the statistics in Table 2.

[1] http://web-ngram.research.microsoft.com/
erd2014/Datasets.aspx.

Query types	Y-ERD	ERD-dev
No entity	1142	46
Single entity	1133	34
Single set; >1 entity	114	7
Multiple sets	9	4
Total	2398	91

Table 2: Statistics of the interpretation finding test collections.

We further note that there is a small overlap between ERD-dev /test and Y-ERD (18 queries, to be precise). We removed those queries from Y-ERD for our experiments, so that it is possible to train systems using Y-ERD and evaluate them using ERD-dev/test.

4.3.1 From YSQLE to Y-ERD

Taking the YSQLE dataset as our input, we proceeded as follows. First, we filtered out duplicate queries. Recall that YSQLE queries are annotated within the context of search sessions and there are queries that appear in multiple sessions. We annotate queries on their own, regardless of search sessions, just like it was done at the ERD Challenge. Next, we created candidate interpretations using the following rules: (i) if the mentions are not overlapping, the linked entities form a single interpretation; (ii) if the entity mentions are identical, then each entity is considered as a separate interpretation (a set with a single element); (iii) queries that have been linked to a single entity, a single-element interpretation is created. Then, we asked three human annotators to judge these candidate query interpretations (including both finding interpretations and aligning the linked entities with the specific mention) following a set of annotation guidelines.

4.3.2 Annotation guidelines

These guidelines are based on those of the ERD Challenge [8], complemented by some additional rules:

R1 The annotated entities should be proper noun entities rather than general concepts [8]. E.g., the query "SUNY albany hospital location" is only linked to UNIVERSITY AT ALBANY, SUNY and the entity LOCATION (GEOGRAPHY) is ignored.

R2 The query should be linked to an entity via its longest mention [8]. E.g., in the query "penticton bc weather," the longest mention for the entity PENTICTON is "penticton bc." This implies that the term "bc" is not to be linked to BRITISH COLUMBIA.

R3 Terms that are meant to restrict the search to a certain site (such as Facebook or IMDB) should not be linked. E.g., the entity FACEBOOK is not linked in the query "facebook obama slur," while is it a valid annotation for the query "how to reactivate facebook."

R4 Linked entities must be explicitly mentioned in the query. One example is the query "charlie sheen lohan" that we already discussed for YSQLE in Section 4.1. For us, only CHARLIE SHEEN and LINDSAY LOHAN are valid annotations. Another example is "Kurosawa's wife," which should be linked solely to the entity AKIRA KUROSAWA, and not to YŌKO YAGUCHI.

R5 It could be argued either way whether misspelled mentions should be linked to entities or not. In our definition, misspellings that are recorded as name variants in DBpedia are not considered as spelling errors. We believe that annotating misspelled mentions would introduce noise into the training data. Therefore, we do not perform spell correction and not consider misspelled mentions in our ground truth in the experiments reported in this paper. Nevertheless, we also made a spell-corrected version of Y-ERD publicly available.

Based on the above rules, the assessors were instructed to: (i) identify mentions, (ii) drop invalid linked entities, (iii) change linked entities to different ones if they are a better match, (iv) complement existing interpretations with more entities. Note that by the last rule, we restrict annotators to not adding new entities to those originally identified in YSQLE, except for the case of erroneous interpretation sets. Recall that our application domain is general web search; we trust that the annotations in YSQLE include all entities that are "meaningful" in this context. One might argue that annotations are dominated by popular entities; while this may be the case, it is no different from how annotations for the ERD Challenge were performed.

4.3.3 Resolving disagreements

Regarding the interpretations (i.e., the sets of linked entities) all three annotators agreed on 84% of the queries, two agreed on 5%, and they all disagreed on the remaining 11%. For the entities linked by at least 2 assessors, the agreement on the mentions was 94%.

Disagreements were resolved through discussion, where the conflicting cases were categorized into *medium* and *hard* classes (unanimously agreed queries are regarded as *easy*). The former could be resolved through little discussion, while the latter was challenging to find agreements on. The difficulty levels are also recorded and released with the dataset.

5. METHODS

This section presents approaches for tackling the two tasks we have introduced in Section 3: semantic mapping (SM) and interpretation finding (IF). Recall that SM is the task of returning a ranked list of entities that are related to the query. IF is about finding (possibly multiple) interpretations, where an interpretation is a set of semantically related entities that are each mentioned in the query. We address both tasks in a pipeline architecture, shown in Figure 1. This pipeline is motivated by the canonical entity linking approach for documents; our components (mention detection, entity ranking, and interpretation finding) roughly correspond to the *extractor*, *searcher*, and *disambiguator* steps in traditional entity linking [20]. While this is a reasonable choice, it is certainly not the only one. We leave the exploration of alternative architectures to the future work. Notice that the first two components of the pipeline (discussed in Sections 5.1 and 5.2) are shared by the SM and IF tasks. For IF, there is an additional interpretation finding step to be performed (Section 5.3).

Before we continue, let us clarify the terminology. The term *span* refers to a query substring (n-gram). By *entity surface forms* (or *aliases*) we mean the names that are used to make reference to a particular entity. When we want to focus on a span that refers to (i.e., may be linked to) an entity, we use the term *mention*. A mention, therefore, is a pair, (m, e), where m is a span matching one of the surface forms of entity e.

5.1 Mention detection

The objective of the *mention detection* step is to identify query spans that can be linked to the entities. We view this as a recall-oriented task, as we do not want to miss any of the entities that are part of the query's interpretation(s). To identify entities mentioned in the query, we perform lexical matching for all possible n-grams in the query against known entity surface forms. (Given that web queries are typically short, this is manageable.) Surface forms are

gathered from two sources: from a manually curated *knowledge base* and from machine-annotated *web corpora*.

Knowledge base. We consider known surface forms from DBpedia that are recorded under the `<rdfs:label>` and `<foaf:name>` predicates. The names of redirected entities are also included. We write A_e to denote the set of aliases for entity e. Let M_{kb} be the set of entity mentions in the query:

$$M_{kb} = \{(m, e) | \exists a \in A_e : a = m, m \in q\}, \qquad (8)$$

where $m \in q$ is a query span (can be the entire query) that matches one of the aliases (a) of entity e. Because DBpedia is a high-quality resource, we do not perform any additional filtering or cleansing step on this set.

Web corpora. We make use of web-scale document collections in which entity mentions have been automatically linked to the Freebase knowledge base. Google, Inc. has recently created and made available this resource, referred to as Freebase Annotations of the ClueWeb Corpora (FACC), for the ClueWeb09 and ClueWeb12 datasets [17]. We create a dictionary of surface forms that contains the linked Freebase IDs along with frequencies and link entities to DBpedia via `<sameAs>` relations. Note that we aggregate data from both ClueWeb collections (hence the usage of "corpora").

Considering all entities that match a given surface form might leave us with a huge set of candidates; for example, "new york" matches over two thousand different entities. Therefore, we filter the set of matching candidate entities based on *commonness*. Commonness measures the overall popularity of entities as link targets [26]. Essentially, commonness is the maximum-likelihood probability that entity e is the link target of mention m:

$$\text{commonness}(m, e) = P(e|m) = \frac{n(m, e)}{\sum_{e'} n(m, e')}, \qquad (9)$$

where $n(m, e)$ is the total number of times mention m is linked to entity e according to the FACC annotations. M_w refers to the set of mentions with a certain minimum commonness score:

$$M_w = \{(m, e) | m \in q, \text{commonness}(m, e) > c\}, \qquad (10)$$

where the commonness threshold c is set empirically (or set to 0 if no pruning is to be performed). Using FACC as a source of entity surface forms and for a more reliable estimation of commonness scores is a novel approach; as we show later, it can warrant over 90% recall.

Combining sources. The final set of mentions is created by combining the entities identified using the knowledge base and the web annotations: $M = M_{kb} \cup M_w$.

5.2 Candidate entity ranking

We now turn to the second component of our pipeline, which ranks the entities identified by the mention detection step. Formally, this step takes a list of mention-entity pairs (m, e) as input and associates each with a relevance score. For the SM task, this ranking will constitute the final output. We note that (i) our methods are limited to returning entities explicitly mentioned in the query; this is not unreasonable (the same limitation is present, e.g., in [6]); (ii) for each entity we only consider its highest scoring mention. For IF, the resulting ranking provides input for the subsequent interpretation finding step (cf. Figure 1). As the entity relevance scores will be utilized in a later component, it is essential that they are comparable across queries. (This requirement is not unique to our approach; it would also be the case if one were to use supervised learning, for example.)

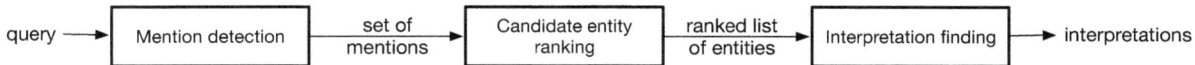

Figure 1: Pipeline for semantic mapping (first two steps) and interpretation finding (all steps).

5.2.1 Commonness

Commonness is shown to be a powerful baseline for the semantic mapping task [6, 28]. We follow the heuristic of looking for the longest matching mentions and ranking the corresponding entities according to their commonness score. Specifically, let l denote the length of the longest matching mention; if there are no entities mentioned in the query ($M = \emptyset$) then l is set to 0. If $l > 0$, then the matching entities are scored according to Eq. 11, otherwise no entities are returned.

$$score(e) = \max\{commonness(m, e) : |m| = l\}. \quad (11)$$

5.2.2 Mixture of Language Models

The predominant approach to ranking structured entity representations (typically described as a set of RDF triples) is to employ fielded extensions of standard document retrieval models, such as BM25F [5] or the Mixture of Language Models (MLM) [3, 33]. The MLM approach [36] combines language models estimated for different document fields. The model can readily be applied to ranking (document-based representations) of entities by considering different predicates as fields [23, 33]. The probability of a term t given the language model of an entity e is estimated as follows:

$$P(t|\theta_e) = \sum_{f \in F} \mu_f P(t|\theta_{e_f}), \quad (12)$$

where F is the set of possible fields, f is a specific field, μ_f is the field weight (such that $\mu_f \in [0..1]$ and $\sum_{f \in F} \mu_f = 1$), and θ_{e_f} is the field language model, which is a maximum-likelihood estimate smoothed by a field-specific background model:

$$P(t|\theta_{e_f}) = (1 - \lambda_f) \frac{n(t, e_f)}{|e_f|} + \lambda_f P(t|C_f). \quad (13)$$

Here, $n(t, e_f)$ denotes the number of occurrences of term t in field f of entity e and $|e_f|$ is the length of the field. To keep things simple, we use a single smoothing parameter for all fields: $\lambda_f = 0.1$, based on the recommendations given in [41] for title queries.

The most common approach in language modeling is to rank items (here: entities) based on query likelihood:

$$P(e|q) = \frac{P(q|e)P(e)}{P(q)} \propto P(e)P(q|\theta_e) \quad (14)$$

$$= P(e) \prod_{t \in q} P(t|\theta_e)^{n(t,q)}, \quad (15)$$

where θ_e is the entity language model (defined in Eq. 12) and $n(t, q)$ denotes the number of times term t is present in query q. When a single query is considered, dropping the query probability $P(q)$ in Eq. 14 can be done conveniently. For us, however, scores (probabilities) need to be comparable across different queries, as they are utilized in the subsequent interpretation finding step (cf. Section 5.3). Therefore, the denominator, which depends on the query, should not be dropped. We perform normalization as suggested in [24] (length normalized query likelihood ratio):

$$P(e|q) = P(e) \frac{\prod_{t \in q} P(t|\theta_e)^{P(t|q)}}{\prod_{t \in q} P(t|C)^{P(t|q)}}, \quad (16)$$

where $P(t|q) = n(t, q)/|q|$ is the relative frequency of t in q. Therefore, the normalized MLM score is obtained by computing

$P(t|\theta_e)$ based on Eq. 12 and $P(t|C)$ is taken to be a linear combination of collection language models $\sum_{f \in F} \mu_f P(t|C_f)$.

The specific instantiation of the model (fields and weights) is discussed in Section 6.1.

5.2.3 Combining MLM and commonness

Let us point out that MLM ranks entities, mentioned in the query, based on their relevance to the query. This is done irrespective of the specific surface form that is referenced in the query. There is useful prior information associated with surface forms, which is captured in commonness (Eq. 9). The commonness-based ranking method (Eq. 11), on the other hand, does not consider the query itself, which might provide additional contextual clues. It, therefore, makes good sense to combine MLM and commonness. We propose two ways of doing this.

MLMc. The first method, MLMc, simply filters the set of entities that are considered for ranking based on commonness, by applying a threshold c in Eq. 10. The setting of c is discussed in Section 6.1.

MLMcg. The second method, MLMcg, also performs filtering, exactly as MLMc does. But, in addition to that, it also integrates the commonness scores in a generative model. It ranks entities based on the highest scoring mention, i.e., ranking is dependent not only on the query but on the specific mention as well:

$$P(e|q) \propto \arg\max_{m \in q} P(e|m)P(q|e), \quad (17)$$

where $P(q|e)$ is estimated using MLM (Eq. 15) and $P(m|e)$ is the same as commonness (cf. Eq. 9). We show later experimentally that this novel method provides solid results and is more effective than MLM and MLMc.

5.3 Interpretation finding

The aim of this phase is to find the interpretations of a query, where an interpretation is a set of non-overlapping and semantically compatible entities that are mentioned in the query. Given a ranked list of mention-entity pairs from the previous step, our goal (and, as we argued, this should be the ultimate goal of entity linking in queries) is to identify all interpretations of the query.

We present an algorithm, named *Greedy Interpretation Finding* (GIF), that can detect multiple interpretations of a query; see Algorithm 1. It takes as input a list of mention-entity pairs (m, e), each associated with a relevance score. Consider an example query "jacksonville fl," for which the input for the algorithm would be {("jacksonville fl', JACKSONVILLE FLORIDA): 0.9, ("jacksonville", JACKSONVILLE,FLORIDA): 0.8, ("jacksonville fl", NAVAL AIR STATION JACKSONVILLE): 0.2}. In the first step (line 1), GIF prunes entities based on absolute scores, controlled by the threshold parameter s. E.g., with a threshold of 0.3, ("jacksonville fl", NAVAL AIR STATION JACKSONVILLE) would be filtered out here. We note that s is a global parameter, therefore ranking scores must be comparable across queries. (As mentioned in the previous section, our query length normalized ranking scores enable this.) In the next step (line 2), containment mentions are also filtered out, based on their retrieval scores. E.g., out of the two containment mentions "jacksonville fl" and "jacksonville", only the pair ("jacksonville fl", JACKSONVILLE FLORIDA) with the score of 0.9 is

177

Algorithm 1 Greedy Interpretation Finding (GIF)

Input: Ranked list of mention-entity pairs M; score threshold s
Output: Interpretations $I = \{E_1, ..., E_m\}$

begin
  1: $M' \leftarrow \text{Prune}(M, s)$
  2: $M' \leftarrow \text{PruneContainmentMentions}(M')$
  3: $I \leftarrow \text{CreateInterpretations}(M')$
  4: **return** I
end
  1: **function** CREATEINTERPRETATIONS(M)
  2:   $I \leftarrow \{\emptyset\}$
  3:   **for** (m, e) in M **do**
  4:     $h \leftarrow 0$
  5:     **for** E in I **do**
  6:       **if** $\neg$ hasOverlap$(E, (m, e))$ **then**
  7:         $E.\text{add}((m, e))$
  8:         $h \leftarrow 1$
  9:       **end if**
 10:     **end for**
 11:     **if** $h == 0$ **then**
 12:       $I.\text{add}(\{(m, e)\})$
 13:     **end if**
 14:   **end for**
 15:   **return** I
 16: **end function**

---

kept. Then (in line 3), query interpretations are created in an iterative manner: adding an entity-mention pair to an existing interpretation E, such that it does not overlap with the mentions already present in E. In case it overlaps with all existing interpretations, the mention-entity pair constitutes a new interpretation; this will result in multiple interpretations for a query. The implementation of GIF is made publicly available.

6. EXPERIMENTS

In this section we present results for the semantic mapping and interpretation finding tasks, using the test collections introduced in Section 4 and the methods presented in Section 5.

6.1 Experimental setup

Knowledge base. We consider entities present in both DBpedia and Freebase as our reference knowledge base. This choice is made for pragmatic reasons: (i) existing test collections provide annotations (or ground truth) either for one or the other, (ii) Freebase-annotated ClueWeb collections (FACC) [17] are leveraged for mention detection and (reliable) commonness estimation, (iii) entity descriptions in DBpedia provide a solid basis for entity ranking.

Entity ranking. For ranking entities using MLM, we followed Neumayer et al. [34] and used an index with two fields, name and content, with a weight of 0.2 and 0.8, respectively. The *name* field holds the primary names of the entity (`<rdfs:label>`, `<foaf:name>`) and name variants extracted from redirected entities. The *content* field includes the content of the top 1000 most frequent predicates across the whole DBpedia collection. All URIs in the content fields are resolved, i.e., replaced with the name of the entity or title of the page they point to. The index is confined to the entities having a name and a short abstract (i.e., `<rdfs:label>` and `<rdfs:comment>`).

Semantic mapping. The SM task is evaluated on the YSQLE test collection. We compare commonness (CMNS), MLM, MLMc,

	YSQLE	Y-ERD	ERD
KB	0.7489	0.7976	0.8556
Web	0.9127	0.9716	0.9956
KB+Web	**0.9163**	**0.9724**	**1.0000**

Table 3: Recall of different sources for mention detection.

	MAP	S@1	MRR
CMNS	0.6334	0.5751	0.6442
MLM	0.4582	0.3601	0.4638
MLMc	0.6228	0.5413	0.6312
MLMcg	**0.7078**	**0.6403**	**0.7151**
TAGME[†]	0.6230	0.6016	0.6385

[†]TAGME is an entity linking system and should not be evaluated on the semantic mapping task using rank-based metrics.

Table 4: Semantic mapping results on the YSQLE dataset.

and MLMcg from Section 5.2 and also include results for the TAGME system [16]. The commonness threshold c for MLMc and MLMcg (Eq. 10) is set to 0.1 by performing a sweep using cross-validation. For CMNS, we use FACC to compute commonness.

Interpretation finding. For the IF task, we report our results on the Y-ERD and ERD-dev test collections. In this case, our reference knowledge base is confined to the entities present in the knowledge base snapshot used at the ERD Challenge [8]. This snapshot contains 2,351,157 entities; taking its intersection with DBpedia resulted in the removal of 39,517 entities.

The GIF method (see Section 5.3) is applied on top of the four candidate entity ranking systems. We use cross-validation (5-fold for Y-ERD and leave-one-out for ERD-dev) for setting the score threshold of GIF, by performing a sweep for the parameter s. In addition, we report on two baselines. The first, called *TopRanked*, uses the best performing entity ranking approach (MLMcg) and forms a single interpretation set from the top ranked entity. The second baseline is TAGME.

TAGME. We report on TAGME [16], a state-of-the-art entity linking system for short texts. Even though TAGME is available through an API, we used our own implementation, given that our reference knowledge base is different. Specifically, we used a Wikipedia dump from June 16, 2015 to extract commonness and link probability and followed [9] in implementing semantic relatedness [32].

6.2 Mention detection

The mention detection component is shared by both the semantic mapping and interpretation finding tasks, therefore we evaluate it on its own account. Specifically, we compare three options based on the source(s) of surface forms, as described in Section 5.1: (i) DBpedia (KB), (ii) web corpora (Web), and (iii) the combination of both (KB+Web). As this step is recall oriented, (i.e., all entity matches should be retrieved), we only report on recall.

Table 3 presents the results. We find that the machine-annotated web corpora provides a rich source of entity surface forms for this task and is a better source than DBpedia alone. Not surprisingly, the combination of the two sources yields the highest recall, albeit the improvement over Web is marginal. We also note that while recall is nearly perfect on the interpretation finding datasets (Y-ERD and ERD), it is a bit lower for YSQLE. Recall that YSQLE is created for evaluating the semantic mapping task, where implicit entity mentions are also considered as relevant; these are not captured by our dictionary-based mention detection approach and would need to be identified by different means.

Method	Strict eval.			Lean eval.		
	P	R	F	P	R	F
TopRanked	0.4554	0.4542	0.4545	0.4771	0.465	0.4689
TAGME	0.6647	0.6642	0.6643	0.6821	0.6853	0.6815
GIF-CMNS	0.6927	0.6938	0.6929	0.7093	0.7072	0.7062
GIF-MLM	0.5259	0.5254	0.5255	0.5363	0.5387	0.5361
GIF-MLMc	0.6351	0.6354	0.6348	0.6422	0.642	0.6409
GIF-MLMcg	**0.7191**	**0.7213**	**0.7195**	**0.7305**	**0.7308**	**0.7288**

Table 5: Interpretation finding on the Y-ERD dataset.

Method	Strict eval.			Lean eval.		
	P	R	F	P	R	F
TopRanked	0.3846	0.3645	0.3700	0.4231	0.3837	0.3956
TAGME	0.7143	0.7015	0.7051	**0.7418**	**0.7372**	**0.7333**
GIF-CMNS	0.5824	0.5824	0.5824	0.6071	0.5962	0.5998
GIF-MLM	0.5824	0.5608	0.5659	0.5934	0.5718	0.5760
GIF-MLMc	0.7253	0.7037	0.7088	0.7445	0.7174	0.7234
GIF-MLMcg	**0.7143**	**0.7125**	**0.7114**	0.7335	0.7262	0.7260

Table 6: Interpretation finding on the ERD-dev dataset.

6.3 Semantic mapping

Table 4 presents the results for semantic mapping. Given that this is a ranking task, we report on mean average precision (MAP), success at position 1 (S@1), and mean reciprocal rank (MRR). Though we include results for TAGME, we note that this comparison, despite having been done in prior work (e.g., in [6]), is an unfair one. TAGME is an entity linking system that should not be evaluated using rank-based metrics. The very reason we include TAGME is to illustrate that one can easily achieve improvements over a state-of-the-art entity linking system on the semantic mapping task, but those claims would be false and misleading. We find that MLMcg is the most effective method; it shows that incorporating commonness in a generative model (MLMcg) is better than using commonness alone (CMNS) or as a filter before ranking entities (MLMc).

6.4 Interpretation finding

Tables 5 and 6 present the results for interpretation finding on the Y-ERD and ERD-dev datasets, respectively. Two sets of evaluation metrics are used: (i) strict (which is the same as in [8]) and (ii) lean (Section 3.4). We notice at first glance that the TopRanked baseline is considerably worse than the other approaches. This shows that, even though there are many queries containing a single entity in our data sets (cf. Table 2), forming sets of entities is a crucial aspect of the interpretation finding task. The GIF algorithm in combination with MLMcg delivers solid performance and is the best performing of all approaches in all but one setting. In comparison with TAGME, GIF performs substantially better on the Y-ERD dataset, while being in par with TAGME on ERD-dev. While our focus was not on efficiency, we also note that GIF has a considerably lower response time than TAGME. GIF utilizes the retrieval scores of the mentioned entities and involves virtually no computation. Additionally, it is able to generate multiple query interpretations. This makes it the preferred alternative over TAGME for entity linking in queries. Comparing the two evaluation metrics, lean evaluation gives higher results for all systems. This is in line with our expectations based on the theoretical definitions of the metrics (Section 5.3); when an interpretation is incomplete, yet contains relevant entities, the strict evaluation does not give any credit for returning correct entities, whereas the lean one does. We note that for the Y-ERD experiments, we also tried to use the spell-corrected queries (with the corresponding qrels), but no considerable differences were observed.

7. DISCUSSION

We now answer our research questions, and subsequent sub-questions, based on the results presented in Section 6.

How should the inherent ambiguity of entity annotations in queries be handled? Entity linking in queries should ultimately be addressed as an *interpretation finding* task, where an interpretation is a set of non-overlapping entities that are semantically re-lated to each other. If the query is ambiguous, with little or no context, there exist multiple interpretations, all of which should be found. Otherwise, a single interpretation should be detected, which is similar to the traditional entity linking task for documents. Determining when the query has no interpretations (in terms of entity annotations) is also a crucial part of the problem that should be addressed (and considered in the evaluation). The *semantic mapping* task (Section 3.3), which ranks entities based on their relevance to the query, serves a different purpose and should be considered as an entity linking task, even for the simplified scenario of finding a single interpretation. This is because relevant entities can be overlapping and are not required to be semantically related to each other. Furthermore, entity disambiguation is an essential part of entity linking, an aspect that is completely ignored in semantic mapping. A number of earlier studies refer to entity linking, while what they do in fact is semantic mapping [6, 27, 28, 35]. Comparing semantic mapping to results generated by traditional entity linking methods is inappropriate (cf. Section 6.3).

What are the similarities and differences between semantic mapping and interpretation finding in terms of approaches? The semantic mapping and interpretation finding tasks can be addressed by using a similar pipeline architecture (see Section 5). Both tasks share the first component, mention detection, which can effectively be addressed by combining surface forms stored in knowledge bases and extracted from a large machine-annotated web corpora (cf. Section 6.2). The second component, which generates a ranked list of the mentioned entities based on their relevance to the query, can also be shared. One issue that requires special attention is the question of implicit mentions, that is, entities that are referred to but not explicitly mentioned in the query (e.g., "Obama's mother"). These are not identified by the mention detection step and consequently not considered for ranking either. One interesting research challenge in semantic mapping is finding these referred entities. For interpretation finding, the third component is responsible for forming (possibly multiple) sets of entities. This is a highly nontrivial subtask that makes interpretation finding substantially more difficult than semantic mapping.

What are appropriate evaluation methodology and metrics? For interpretation finding, similar to the traditional entity linking task [16, 31, 32], evaluation uses set-based metrics (precision, recall and F-measure). However, since the output is a set of interpretations (and not entities) the evaluation methodology is different. The method presented in [8] considers the exact match between the retrieved sets and the ground truth, which is rather strict. The lean evaluation method (Section 5.3), on the other hand, combines interpretation-based and entity-based evaluations. For semantic mapping, standard rank-based metrics (MAP, MRR, S@1) can be employed.

As most queries have a single interpretation, how much effort should be expedited to find multiple interpretations? Although having multiple interpretations is an intrinsic feature of entity linking in queries, most of the queries in our test collections (both ERD and Y-ERD) have a single interpretation (see Table 2). This implies that a system can achieve high overall score by focusing on returning a single interpretation. This is also evidenced by the ERD Challenge results, where the top two performing systems [10, 12] return a single interpretation. We note that returning multiple interpretations, without hurting queries with single a interpretation, is an open research question.

8. CONCLUSIONS

In this paper we have addressed fundamental questions in the problem area of entity linking in queries. We have differentiated between two tasks, semantic mapping and interpretation finding. The former ranks entities that are related to (but not necessarily explicitly mentioned in) the query, while the latter aims to identify sets of semantically related entities that are mentioned in the query, and is able to return more than one of such sets if the query has multiple interpretations. We have discussed evaluation methodology and carefully examined publicly available test collections for both tasks, and introduced a large, manually curated test collection for interpretation finding. Technical contributions of this study include methods for effectively addressing these tasks, accompanied by a set of results. One obvious direction for further work is to evaluate the retrieval impact of entity-annotated queries.

References

[1] Yahoo! Webscope L24 dataset - Yahoo! search query log to entities, v1.0. URL http://webscope.sandbox.yahoo.com/.
[2] A. Alasiry, M. Levene, and A. Poulovassilis. Detecting candidate named entities in search queries. In *Proc. of SIGIR '12*, pages 1049–1050, 2012.
[3] K. Balog and R. Neumayer. A test collection for entity search in DBpedia. In *Proc. of SIGIR '13*, pages 737–740, 2013.
[4] S. Bergsma and Q. I. Wang. Learning noun phrase query segmentation. In *Proc. of EMNLP-CoNLL '07*, pages 819–826, 2007.
[5] R. Blanco, P. Mika, and S. Vigna. Effective and efficient entity search in RDF data. In *Proc. of ISWC '11*, pages 83–97, 2011.
[6] R. Blanco, G. Ottaviano, and E. Meij. Fast and space-efficient entity linking for queries. In *Proc. of WSDM '15*, pages 179–188, 2015.
[7] H. Cao, D. H. Hu, D. Shen, D. Jiang, J.-T. Sun, E. Chen, and Q. Yang. Context-aware query classification. In *Proc. of SIGIR '09*, pages 3–10, 2009.
[8] D. Carmel, M.-W. Chang, E. Gabrilovich, B.-J. P. Hsu, and K. Wang. ERD'14: Entity recognition and disambiguation challenge. *SIGIR Forum*, 48(2):63–77, 2014.
[9] D. Ceccarelli, C. Lucchese, S. Orlando, R. Perego, and S. Trani. Learning relatedness measures for entity linking. In *Proc. of CIKM'13*, pages 139–148, 2013.
[10] Y.-P. Chiu, Y.-S. Shih, Y.-Y. Lee, C.-C. Shao, M.-L. Cai, S.-L. Wei, and H.-H. Chen. NTUNLP approaches to recognizing and disambiguating entities in long and short text at the ERD challenge 2014. In *Proc. of Entity Recognition & Disambiguation Workshop*, pages 3–12, 2014.
[11] M. Cornolti, P. Ferragina, and M. Ciaramita. A framework for benchmarking entity-annotation systems. In *Proc. of WWW '13*, pages 249–260, 2013.
[12] M. Cornolti, P. Ferragina, M. Ciaramita, H. Schütze, and S. Rüd. The SMAPH system for query entity recognition and disambiguation. In *Proc. of Entity Recognition & Disambiguation Workshop*, pages 25–30, 2014.
[13] W. B. Croft, M. Bendersky, H. Li, and G. Xu. Query representation and understanding workshop. *SIGIR Forum*, 44(2):48–53, 2011.
[14] S. Cucerzan. Large-scale named entity disambiguation based on Wikipedia data. In *Proc. of EMNLP-CoNLL '07*, pages 708–716, 2007.
[15] A. Eckhardt, J. Hreško, J. Procházka, and O. Smrž. Entity linking based on the co-occurrence graph and entity probability. In *Proc. of Entity Recognition & Disambiguation Workshop*, pages 37–44, 2014.
[16] P. Ferragina and U. Scaiella. TAGME: On-the-fly annotation of short text fragments (by Wikipedia entities). In *Proc. of CIKM '10*, pages 1625–1628, 2010.
[17] E. Gabrilovich, M. Ringgaard, and A. Subramanya. FACC1: Freebase annotation of ClueWeb corpora, Version 1 (Release date 2013-06-26, Format version 1, Correction level 0), 2013. URL http://lemurproject.org/clueweb12/.
[18] J. Guo, G. Xu, X. Cheng, and H. Li. Named entity recognition in query. In *Proc. of SIGIR '09*, pages 267–274, 2009.
[19] S. Guo, M.-W. Chang, and E. Kiciman. To link or not to link? a study on end-to-end tweet entity linking. In *Proc. of HLT-NAACL*, pages 1020–1030, 2013.
[20] B. Hachey, W. Radford, J. Nothman, M. Honnibal, and J. R. Curran. Evaluating entity linking with Wikipedia. *Artif. Intell.*, 194:130–150, 2013.
[21] M. Hagen, M. Potthast, B. Stein, and C. Bräutigam. Query segmentation revisited. In *Proc. of WWW '11*, pages 97–106, 2011.
[22] J. Hu, G. Wang, F. Lochovsky, J.-t. Sun, and Z. Chen. Understanding user's query intent with Wikipedia. In *Proc. of WWW '09*, pages 471–480, 2009.
[23] J. Kim, X. Xue, and W. B. Croft. A probabilistic retrieval model for semistructured data. In *Proc. of ECIR '09*, pages 228–239, 2009.
[24] W. Kraaij and M. Spitters. Language models for topic tracking. In *Language Modeling for Information Retrieval*, pages 95–123, 2003.
[25] X. Li, Y.-Y. Wang, and A. Acero. Learning query intent from regularized click graphs. In *Proc. of SIGIR '08*, pages 339–346, 2008.
[26] O. Medelyan, I. H. Witten, and D. Milne. Topic indexing with Wikipedia. In *Proc. of the AAAI WikiAI workshop*, pages 19–24, 2008.
[27] E. Meij, M. Bron, L. Hollink, B. Huurnink, and M. de Rijke. Mapping queries to the Linking Open Data cloud: A case study using DBpedia. *Web Semant.*, 9(4):418–433, 2011.
[28] E. Meij, W. Weerkamp, and M. de Rijke. Adding semantics to microblog posts. In *Proc. of WSDM '12*, pages 563–572, 2012.
[29] E. Meij, K. Balog, and D. Odijk. Entity linking and retrieval for semantic search. In *Proc. of WSDM '14*, pages 683–684, 2014.
[30] P. N. Mendes, M. Jakob, A. García-Silva, and C. Bizer. DBpedia spotlight: Shedding light on the web of documents. In *Proc. of I-Semantics '11*, pages 1–8, 2011.
[31] R. Mihalcea and A. Csomai. Wikify!: Linking documents to encyclopedic knowledge. In *Proc. of CIKM '07*, pages 233–242, 2007.
[32] D. Milne and I. H. Witten. Learning to link with Wikipedia. In *Proc. of CIKM '08*, pages 509–518, 2008.
[33] R. Neumayer, K. Balog, and K. Nørvåg. On the modeling of entities for ad-hoc entity search in the web of data. In *Proc. of ECIR '12*, pages 133–145, 2012.
[34] R. Neumayer, K. Balog, and K. Nørvåg. When simple is (more than) good enough: Effective semantic search with (almost) no semantics. In *Proc. of ECIR '12*, pages 540–543, 2012.
[35] D. Odijk, E. Meij, and M. de Rijke. Feeding the second screen: Semantic linking based on subtitles. In *Proc. of OAIR '13*, pages 9–16, 2013.
[36] P. Ogilvie and J. Callan. Combining document representations for known-item search. In *Proc. of SIGIR '03*, pages 143–150, 2003.
[37] G. Rizzo, M. van Erp, and R. Troncy. Benchmarking the extraction and disambiguation of named entities on the semantic web. In *Proc. of LREC '14*, 2014.
[38] D. E. Rose and D. Levinson. Understanding user goals in web search. In *Proc. of WWW '04*, pages 13–19, 2004.
[39] D. Shen, J.-T. Sun, Q. Yang, and Z. Chen. Building bridges for web query classification. In *Proc. of SIGIR '06*, pages 131–138, 2006.
[40] B. Tan and F. Peng. Unsupervised query segmentation using generative language models and Wikipedia. In *Proc. of WWW '08*, pages 347–356, 2008.
[41] C. Zhai and J. Lafferty. A study of smoothing methods for language models applied to information retrieval. *ACM Trans. Inf. Syst.*, 22(2): 179–214, 2004.

Random Walks on the Reputation Graph

Sabir Ribas
CS Dept, UFMG
Belo Horizonte, Brazil
sabir@dcc.ufmg.br

Berthier Ribeiro-Neto
CS Dept, UFMG & Google Inc
Belo Horizonte, Brazil
berthier@dcc.ufmg.br

Rodrygo L. T. Santos
CS Dept, UFMG
Belo Horizonte, Brazil
rodrygo@dcc.ufmg.br

Edmundo de Souza e Silva
COPPE, UFRJ
Rio de Janeiro, Brazil
edmundo@land.ufrj.br

Alberto Ueda
CS Dept, UFMG
Belo Horizonte, Brazil
ueda@dcc.ufmg.br

Nivio Ziviani
CS Dept, UFMG & Zunnit Tech
Belo Horizonte, Brazil
nivio@dcc.ufmg.br

ABSTRACT

The identification of reputable entities is an important task in business, education, and many other fields. On the other hand, as an arguably subjective, multi-faceted concept, quantifying reputation is challenging. In this paper, instead of relying on a single, precise definition of reputation, we propose to exploit the *transference* of reputation among entities in order to identify the most reputable ones. To this end, we propose a novel random walk model to infer the reputation of a target set of entities with respect to suitable sources of reputation. We instantiate our model in an academic search setting, by modeling research groups as reputation sources and publication venues as reputation targets. By relying on publishing behavior as a reputation signal, we demonstrate the effectiveness of our model in contrast to standard citation-based approaches for identifying reputable venues as well as researchers in the broad area of computer science. In addition, we demonstrate the robustness of our model to perturbations in the selection of reputation sources. Finally, we show that effective reputation sources can be chosen via the proposed model itself in a semi-automatic fashion.

Categories and Subject Descriptors

G.3 [**Probability and Statistics**]: *Stochastic processes*; H.3.3 [**Information Storage and Retrieval**]: Information Search and Retrieval—*Retrieval models*

Keywords

Reputation flows; random walks; academic search

1. INTRODUCTION

Reputation is a widespread notion in society, albeit an arguably ill-defined one. In general, the reputation of an entity reflects the public perception about this entity developed over time. This public perception may be either

good or bad, and touches a variety of aspects that may impact the identity of the entity before the public, such as its competence, integrity, and trustworthiness. Moreover, the reputation of an entity can change rapidly following an event in which the entity is involved, by means of word-of-mouth dissemination—whether traditional or electronic. As a result, reputation has been subject of professional management by public relations departments as well as of collective management by members of online communities, such as question-answering forums and online marketplaces [12].

The identification of reputable entities is an important task in many fields. Indeed, more reputable entities are presumably a better fit for most purposes. However, the subjective nature of reputation makes its quantification—and hence the identification of reputable entities—challenging. As a result, existing attempts to quantify the reputation of an entity rely on either manual assessments or on a restrictive definition of reputation, e.g., in terms of authority [16, 28], influence [2], or expertise [3]. In contrast, in this paper, we take an agnostic view of reputation. In particular, instead of relying on a single, precise definition of reputation, we propose to exploit the *transference* of reputation among entities in order to identify the most reputable ones.

In this paper, we propose a novel random walk model for ranking a target set of entities with respect to suitable sources of reputation. To this end, we model reputation sources and reputation targets as nodes in a heterogeneous graph, with edges connecting any pair of nodes whenever there is a reputation transfer between them. To validate our proposed model, we instantiate this so-called *reputation graph* in an academic search setting. In particular, we model research groups as reputation sources and publication venues as reputation targets, with edges running from a source to a target and back again to indicate the transference of reputation through one or more publications. Through a series of experiments, we empirically demonstrate the effectiveness of our model in contrast to standard citation-based approaches for identifying reputable venues as well as individual researchers in the broad area of computer science. In addition, we demonstrate the robustness of our model to random perturbations in the selection of reputation sources, and the suitability of semi-automatically choosing effective reputation sources using the model itself.

In summary, our main contributions are:

1. A novel random walk model for ranking entities according to the reputation collectively transferred to them by other entities in a reputation graph.

2. An empirical validation of the effectiveness and robustness of our proposed model for two academic search tasks, namely, venue and researcher ranking.

3. A preliminary investigation of the suitability of automatically choosing effective reputation sources.

In the remainder of this paper, Section 2 presents related work on ranking based on random walks as well as in ranking in an academic setting. Section 3 introduces our proposed random walk model for reputation-oriented ranking, whereas Section 4 describes its instantiation in an academic search setting. Sections 5 and 6 describe the setup and the results of the empirical evaluation of our model. Lastly, Section 7 provides our concluding remarks.

2. RELATED WORK

In this section, we review the related literature on ranking based on random walks, as well as approaches devoted to generating rankings in an academic search setting.

2.1 Ranking with Random Walks

Page and Brin [28] designed the PageRank algorithm to calculate the importance of pages on the Web. PageRank simulates a web surfer's behavior. In particular, with probability $p < 1$, the surfer randomly chooses one of the hyperlinks of the current page and jumps to the page it links to; otherwise, with probability $1 - p$, the user jumps to a web page chosen uniformly at random from the collection. This defines a Markov chain on the web graph, where each probability of the stationary distribution corresponds to the rank of a web page, referred to as its *pagerank*.

Kleinberg [16] divided the notion of "importance" of a web page into two related attributes: *hub*, measured by the authority score of other pages that the page links to, and *authority*, measured by the hub score of the pages that link to the page. These attributes are calculated in his Hyperlinked-Induced Topic Search (HITS) algorithm. Both algorithms, PageRank and HITS, have been successfully applied to rank the importance of different web pages through analyzing the link structure of the web graph.

Extensions of the random walk model were also studied for scoring several types of objects—e.g., products, people and organizations—in different applications. For instance, Nie et al. [27] presented PopRank, a domain-independent object-level link analysis model to rank objects within a specific domain, by assigning a popularity propagation factor to each type of object relationship. Different popularity propagation factors for these heterogeneous relationships were assessed with respect to their impact on the global popularity ranking. Xi et al. [37] proposed a unified link analysis framework, called Link Fusion, which considers two different categories of links: intra-type links, which represent the relationship of data objects of a homogeneous data type (e.g., web pages), and inter-type links, which represent the relationship of data objects of different data types (e.g., between users and web pages). Regarding the recommendation of generic types of object, Jamali and Ester [13] proposed TrustWalker, a random walk method that combines trust-based and item-based recommendation, considering not only ratings of the target item, but also those of similar items.

Under the context of social networking systems, social friendship and random walks have been shown to be beneficial for collaborative filtering-based recommendation systems. These works argue that social friends—for instance, in Facebook or Twitter—tend to share common interests and thus their relationships should be considered in the process of collaborative filtering [40]. In this context, a random walk sees a social network as a graph with probabilistically weighted links that represent social relations and thus is able to accurately predict users' preferences to items and their social influence with respect to other users. Backstrom and Leskovec [1] proposed an algorithm based on supervised random walks that combines the information from the network structure with node and edge level attributes, using these attributes to guide the random walk on the graph. Konstas et al. [17] showed that extra knowledge provided by the users' social activity can improve the performance of a recommendation system using random walk with restarts. Weng et al. [35] proposed TwitterRank to measure the influence of users in Twitter, considering both the topical similarity between users and the link structure of the social network.

2.2 Ranking in Academic Search

Ranking has traditionally played an important role in academic search, particularly for tasks related to assessing the scientific productivity of academic entities. In particular, one of the earliest metrics proposed to quantify academic impact was Garfield's Impact Factor [8]. Despite its wide usage since it was proposed in 1955, it has been largely criticized [32]. As a result, many alternatives have been proposed in the literature, such as other citation-based metrics like the H-Index [11], download-based metrics [4], and PageRank-like metrics [39]. However, as argued by Leydesdorff [20], each metric has its own bias and there are both advantages and disadvantages associated with each one.

Citation-based metrics have been applied to rank computer and information science journals [15, 25]. Also, several citation-based metrics have been proposed to measure the quality of a small set of conferences and journals in the database field [30], and to rank documents retrieved from a digital library [19]. Mann et al. [22] introduced topic modeling to further complement the citation-based bibliometric indicators, producing more fine-grained impact measures. Yan and Lee [39] proposed two measures for ranking the impact of academic venues which aim at efficiency and at mimicking the results of the widely accepted Impact Factor. An alternative method was presented by Zhuang et al. [42], who proposed a set of heuristics to automatically discover prestigious and low-quality conferences by mining the characteristics of program committee members.

Piwowar [29] recently claimed that citation-based metrics are useful, but not sufficient to evaluate research. In particular, he observed that metrics like the H-Index are slow. Indeed, the first citation of a scientific article can take years. As a result, he argued for the development of alternative metrics to complement citation analysis. In a similar vein, Lima et al. [21] argued that productivity indices should account for the singularities of the publication patterns of different research areas, in order to produce an unbiased assessment of the impact of academic output. Accordingly, they proposed to assess a researcher's productivity by aggregating his or her impact indicators across multiple areas. Finally, Gonçalves et al. [10] investigated the importance of various academic features to scholar popularity and concluded that only two features are needed to explain all the variation in popularity across different scholars: (i) the number of publications and (ii) the average quality of the scholar's publication venues. In this paper, we validate our proposed approach by exploiting exactly these these two features to rank different venues and different researchers.

The idea of reputation, instead of citations, was discussed by Nelakuditi et al. [24]. In particular, they proposed a metric called peers' reputation, which measures the selectivity of a publication venue based upon the reputation of its authors' institutions. The proposed metric was shown to be a better indicator of selectivity than the acceptance ratio. In addition, the authors observed that many conferences have similar or better peers' reputation than journals. Another approach related to ours was proposed by Cormode et al. [6], who attempted to rank authors according to their similarity with respect to a reference author. To allow the identification of comparable people in similar research areas, they first represented a researcher as a sequence of her publication records, based on research topic similarity and venue quality, and estimated the distance between any two researchers using sequence matching. As we will discuss in Section 3, our approach also explores the notion of a reference source of reputation. However, in contrast to the aforementioned approaches, we allow for multiple entities—as opposed to a single one—to serve as a source of reputation. More importantly, instead of identifying similar entities from whom to propagate reputation, we explore the notion of reputation sources as part of a stochastic Markov process. As a result, our approach is able to produce a global reputation-oriented ranking of multiple interconnected entities.

2.3   Random Walks in Academic Search

Earlier works have studied the application of random walks for ranking authors, papers and venues in an academic setting. For instance, Sun and Giles [33] proposed a popularity weighted ranking algorithm for academic digital libraries that uses the popularity factor of a publication venue. Their approach overcomes some limitations of the Impact Factor and performs better than PageRank, citation counting and HITS. Relatedly, Zhou et al. [41] proposed a method for co-ranking authors and their publications using several networks. Similarly, Yan et al. [38] presented a new informetric indicator, P-Rank, for measuring prestige in heterogeneous scholarly networks containing articles, authors and journals. P-Rank differentiates the weight of each citation based on its citing papers, citing journals and citing authors.

In a narrower perspective, random walks have also been used for the task of expert finding in academic search collections. For instance, Deng et al. [7] proposed a joint regularization framework to enhance expertise retrieval in academia by modeling heterogeneous networks as regularization constraints on top of a document-centric model [3]. Relatedly, Wu et al. [36] proposed to model authors and publications as nodes of a publication network, with additional edges representing co-authorship information (author-author edges). In a similar vein, Tang et al. [34] proposed a probabilistic topic modeling approach to enrich a heterogeneous graph comprising multiple academic entities as nodes, including authors, papers, and publication venues, with directed edges representing a variety of relationships such as "written by" and "published in". The stationary distribution computed after a random walk on this graph was then used to rank these entities with respect to an input query. A very similar approach was proposed by Gollapalli et al. [9], by assigning

topics to nodes and then computing the unique stationary distribution of the associated Markov chain.

In contrast to the aforementioned works, we use random walks to model the *transference* of reputation from *multiple* reference sources to selected targets in a reputation graph, as discussed in Section 3. In order to validate our model, we instantiate it in an academic search setting by using research groups as reputation sources and publication venues as reputation targets. Moreover, while previous approaches have exploited multiple ranking signals, we demonstrate the power of the notion of reputation transfer by relying on publishing behavior as the only reputation signal.

3.   REPUTATION FLOWS

Identifying reputable entities is an important task in many domains. While quantifying the reputation of a given entity is a challenging task, we argue that the flow of reputation among entities can be accurately modeled as a stochastic process. To this end, in this section, we propose a conceptual framework for ranking entities that interact with (and hence convey reputation to) one another in some manner. To formalize our approach, in Section 3.1, we introduce the reputation graph, a data structure that models the flow of reputation from selected sources to multiple targets. In Section 3.2, we formalize a stochastic process to estimate the amount of reputation transferred to target entities. Lastly, in Section 3.3, we discuss a simple mechanism to rank entities according to their inferred reputation.

3.1   The Reputation Graph

We define a *reputation graph* as a graph with three node types: reputation sources, reputation targets, and reputation collaterals, as illustrated in Figure 1. The reputation graph models the transference of reputation from a reference set of reputation sources to reputation targets, and then to reputation collaterals. To refer to the reputation graph, we adopt the following notation: S is the set of reputation sources, T is the set of reputation targets, and C is the set of reputation collaterals.

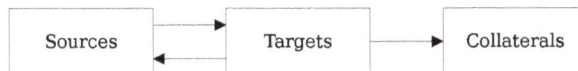

Figure 1: Structure of the reputation graph.

The reputation of source nodes influences the reputation of target nodes as much as the reputation of target nodes influences the reputation of source nodes. Note that the reputation of target nodes also influences the reputation of collaterals, but the reputation of collaterals has no impact in the reputation of sources and targets. The use of collaterals allows us to isolate the impact of a set of arbitrary nodes on the reputation graph, fixing reputation sources as the only set of nodes providing reputation. While this design choice aimed primarily at effectiveness, it also contributes to the efficiency of our approach, as a random walk is only performed on the selected source and target nodes. This way, the overall cost of our approach remains the same even for large sets of collateral nodes. To illustrate, in Section 4, we apply these concepts to model reputation flows in academia. Specifically, we instantiate research groups as reputation sources, publication venues as reputation targets, and individual researchers as collaterals.

Given that the reputation of collaterals has no effect on the reputation of nodes of other types, we can split the model in two phases. In the first phase, we propagate the reputation of the sources to the targets. In the second phase, we propagate the reputation of the targets to the collaterals. These phases are discussed in the following sections.

3.2 Reputation Flows

The interaction between reputation sources and reputation targets is inspired by the notion of *eigenvalue centrality* in complex networks [26], which also provides the foundation to PageRank [18, 5]. In the reputation graph, if we consider only sources and targets, it is easy to identify reputation flows from sources to sources, from sources to targets, from targets to sources, and from targets to targets. These reputation flows can be modeled as a stochastic process as we now discuss. In particular, let $\mathbf{P}$ be a *right stochastic* matrix of size $(|S| + |T|) \times (|S| + |T|)$ with the following structure:

$$\mathbf{P} = \left[\begin{array}{c|c} (d^{\langle S \rangle}).\mathbf{P}^{\langle SS \rangle} & (1 - d^{\langle S \rangle}).\mathbf{P}^{\langle ST \rangle} \\ \hline (1 - d^{\langle T \rangle}).\mathbf{P}^{\langle TS \rangle} & (d^{\langle T \rangle}).\mathbf{P}^{\langle TT \rangle} \end{array} \right], \quad (1)$$

where each quadrant represents a distinct type of reputation flow. Matrix $\mathbf{P}$ depends on the following matrices:

$\mathbf{P}^{\langle SS \rangle}$: right stochastic matrix of size $|S| \times |S|$ representing the transition probabilities between reputation sources;

$\mathbf{P}^{\langle ST \rangle}$: matrix of size $|S| \times |T|$ representing the transition probabilities from reputation sources to targets;

$\mathbf{P}^{\langle TS \rangle}$: matrix of size $|T| \times |S|$ representing the transition probabilities from reputation targets to sources;

$\mathbf{P}^{\langle TT \rangle}$: right stochastic matrix of size $|T| \times |T|$ representing the transition probabilities between reputation targets.

The parameters $d^{\langle S \rangle}$ and $d^{\langle T \rangle}$ control the relative importance of the reputation sources and targets, which are modeled in the four matrices above. Specifically, $d^{\langle S \rangle}$ is the fraction of reputation one wants to transfer between source nodes and $d^{\langle T \rangle}$ is the fraction of reputation one wants to transfer between target nodes. These are useful parameters and the ability to set them is important to calibrate the impact of different reputation flows in the final score. If we do not want to consider reputation flows between nodes of the same type, it is sufficient to set both parameters to zero. If, instead, we want to consider reputation flows between nodes of the same type, we may increase these parameters according to the desired relative importance. Note that, as (*i*) the sub-matrices $\mathbf{P}^{\langle SS \rangle}$ and $\mathbf{P}^{\langle TT \rangle}$ are *right stochastic*, (*ii*) each of the rows of matrices $\mathbf{P}^{\langle ST \rangle}$ and $\mathbf{P}^{\langle TS \rangle}$ sums to 1, and (*iii*) the parameters $d^{\langle S \rangle}$ and $d^{\langle T \rangle}$ are both in the range $[0,1)$, then $\mathbf{P}$ defines a Markov chain. Assuming that the transition matrix $\mathbf{P}$ is ergodic, we can compute the steady state probability of each node and use it as a reputation score. Specifically, we can obtain values for ranking the set of nodes by solving:

$$\boldsymbol{\gamma} = \boldsymbol{\gamma} \mathbf{P}, \quad (2)$$

where $\boldsymbol{\gamma}$ is a row matrix with $|S| + |T|$ elements, where each one represents the probability of a node in the set $S \cup T$. This system of linear equations can be easily solved by standard Markov chain techniques. Then, from Equation (2), we obtain the steady state probabilities of all nodes in $S \cup T$, a.k.a. reputation sources and reputation targets.

3.2.1 Flow Equations

We recursively define the reputation of sources in terms of the reputation of targets, and the reputation of targets in terms of the reputation of sources. Specifically, the reputation γ_s of a source s is defined as:

$$\gamma_s = \sum_{t \in T} (1 - d^{\langle T \rangle}).\mathbf{P}_{ts}{}^{\langle TS \rangle} \gamma_t + \sum_{s' \in S} (d^{\langle S \rangle}).\mathbf{P}_{s's}{}^{\langle SS \rangle} \gamma_{s'}. \quad (3)$$

In the summation, $\mathbf{P}_{ts}{}^{\langle TS \rangle}$ is the transition probability from t to s, given by $\mathbf{P}_{ts}{}^{\langle TS \rangle} = n_{ts}/n_t$, where n_{ts} is the number of edges running from t to s and n_t is the total number of edges running from t. Finally, γ_t is the reputation of target t, defined recursively as:

$$\gamma_t = \sum_{s \in S} (1 - d^{\langle S \rangle}).\mathbf{P}_{st}{}^{\langle ST \rangle} \gamma_s + \sum_{t' \in T} (d^{\langle T \rangle}).\mathbf{P}_{t't}{}^{\langle TT \rangle} \gamma_{t'}. \quad (4)$$

Similarly, in the summation, $\mathbf{P}_{st}{}^{\langle ST \rangle}$ is the transition probability from s to t, given by $\mathbf{P}_{st}{}^{\langle ST \rangle} = n_{st}/n_s$, where n_{st} is the number of edges running from s to t and n_s is the total number of edges running from s. Recall that γ_s is the reputation of source s, defined according to Equation (3).

3.2.2 Bipartite Reputation Graph

Some scenarios can be represented as a bipartite reputation graph. In these cases, the transition matrix $\mathbf{P}$ is reduced to a periodic Markov chain with the following structure:

$$\mathbf{P} = \left[\begin{array}{c|c} \mathbf{0} & \mathbf{P}^{\langle ST \rangle} \\ \hline \mathbf{P}^{\langle TS \rangle} & \mathbf{0} \end{array} \right]. \quad (5)$$

From decomposition theory [23], we can obtain values for ranking the set of reputation *sources* by solving:

$$\boldsymbol{\gamma}^{\langle S \rangle} = \boldsymbol{\gamma}^{\langle S \rangle} \mathbf{P}', \quad (6)$$

where $\mathbf{P}' = \mathbf{P}^{\langle ST \rangle} \times \mathbf{P}^{\langle TS \rangle}$ is a stochastic matrix and $\boldsymbol{\gamma}^{\langle S \rangle}$ is a row matrix with $|S|$ elements, where each one represents the probability of a node in the set S of reputation sources.

Note that matrix $\mathbf{P}'$ has dimension $|S| \times |S|$ only and can be easily solved by standard Markov chain techniques. Then, from Equation (7), we obtain the reputation of all reputation *targets* linked by the reputation sources:

$$\boldsymbol{\gamma}^{\langle T \rangle} = \boldsymbol{\gamma}^{\langle S \rangle} \times \mathbf{P}^{\langle ST \rangle}. \quad (7)$$

By modeling a scenario as a bipartite reputation graph instead of a general reputation graph, we reduce the network from a graph of size $(|S| + |T|) \times (|S| + |T|)$ to a graph of size $|S| \times |S|$, which allows us to compute the steady state probabilities much more efficiently. However, by using a bipartite graph, we are certainly losing some information, which may be critical for some applications. It is important to consider this trade-off when instantiating our framework.

3.3 Reputation-based Ranking

The steady state probability of a node can be interpreted as its relative reputation, as transferred from other nodes in the reputation graph. Thus, we can directly use the value of this probability to rank reputation sources or reputation targets. Additionally, this probability can be further propagated to nodes we want to compare, which are in the collateral set. This propagation depends on a matrix $\mathbf{P}^{\langle TC \rangle}$ of size $|T| \times |C|$ representing the transitions from reputation targets to collateral nodes. More generally, we can define the reputation score of an entity e according to:

$$\text{P-score}(e) = \begin{cases} \sum_{t \in T} \mathbf{P}_{te}^{\langle TC \rangle} \gamma_t & \text{if } e \in C, \\ \gamma_e & \text{otherwise,} \end{cases} \quad (8)$$

where $\mathbf{P}_{te}^{\langle TC \rangle}$ is the transition weight from a target node t to a collateral node $e \in C$. The P-score of all candidate entities (targets or collaterals) can then be used to produce an overall reputation-oriented ranking of these entities.

4. REPUTATION FLOWS IN ACADEMIA

In this section, we discuss the instantiation of our conceptual framework of *reputation flows* in the academic context to model the transference of reputation between authors, papers, research groups and publication venues. The relations between these scientific entities may be captured through distinct metrics and, as far as we know, the most important ones (including citation-based metrics) fit well in our conceptual framework. In particular, let us start by defining the relations between authors and papers. It is easy to identify *reputation flows* from authors to authors, from authors to papers, from papers to authors, and from papers to papers. Each one of these *reputation flows* is associated with a specific quadrant of an Author-Paper × Author-Paper relation matrix, as illustrated in Figure 2.

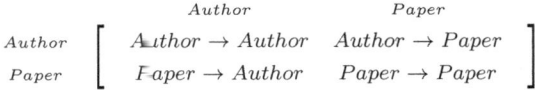

$$\begin{array}{cc} & \begin{array}{cc} Author & Paper \end{array} \\ \begin{array}{c} Author \\ Paper \end{array} & \left[\begin{array}{cc} Author \to Author & Author \to Paper \\ Paper \to Author & Paper \to Paper \end{array} \right] \end{array}$$

Figure 2: Reputation flows between authors and papers.

In the first quadrant, the framework represents the reputation flow from authors to authors, which can be expressed in terms of co-authorship relations or citations from an author to another. In the second and third quadrants, the framework represents author-paper and paper-author relations, respectively. An author who publishes a paper somehow transfers its own reputation to that paper or the converse, a paper may transfer its reputation or acceptance by the community to the authors who published it. In the fourth quadrant, the framework represents the reputation flow between papers. When a paper cites another, it is somehow transferring part of its reputation to the cited paper. This last quadrant is the focus of much more attention than the other ones by the academic community. The raw number of citations among papers, as well as well known citation-based metrics such as H-Index and Impact Factor can be represented in this quadrant. Additionally, there are further indicators such as the number of downloads of a paper. It is an indicator intrinsically related to the papers and has nothing to do with the reputation flow from authors to papers. In other words, the number of downloads is a reputation flow from the audience of paper readers to the papers. These external indicators can be expressed as bias variables.

The idea of reputation flows is broad and encompasses a large amount of indicators. Here, we define a more specific concept called *publication flows* to refer to the study of reputation flows where the transference of reputation is made by using only publication volume and without using citation data. In our experiments, we study how the reputation of a reference set of research groups is propagated to the venues they publish in and to other individual researchers by ap-

plying the concept of publication flows. In this conceptual framework, publication venues are aggregations of papers and research groups are aggregations of authors, as shown in Figure 3. These aggregations are sufficient to establish core relations that allow ranking these entities.

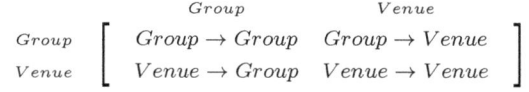

$$\begin{array}{cc} & \begin{array}{cc} Group & Venue \end{array} \\ \begin{array}{c} Group \\ Venue \end{array} & \left[\begin{array}{cc} Group \to Group & Group \to Venue \\ Venue \to Group & Venue \to Venue \end{array} \right] \end{array}$$

Figure 3: Reputation flows between groups and venues.

4.1 Overview and Assumptions

The basic idea of the P-score metric is to associate a reputation with publication venues based on the publication patterns of a *reference set* of research groups in a given area or sub-area of knowledge. Given a pre-selected set of reference research groups, P-score associates weights with the publication venues the researchers in the reference groups publish in. Further, these weights can be used to rank other research groups or authors.

The reputation of a research group is strongly influenced by the reputation of its members, which is largely dependent on their publication records. We assume that:

1. A research group conveys reputation to a publication venue proportionally to its own reputation.

2. A publication venue conveys reputation to a research group proportionally to its own reputation.

Once a reference group is selected, the reputation of its members is transferred to the venues. Recursively, since the reputation of research groups is correlated with the reputation of the venues in which they published, the venues transfer reputation to the groups. A score for venues can then be computed by solving a system of linear equations relating publication venues and research groups in the reputation graph, as exemplified next.

4.2 A Small Example

Figure 4 shows an example with two research groups used as reputation sources, Group 1 and Group 2, and three venues used as reputation targets, venues v_1, v_2 and v_3.

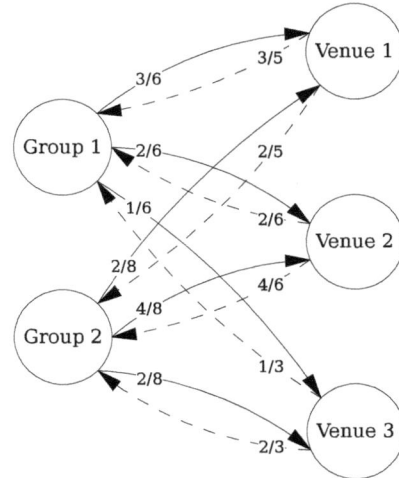

Figure 4: Markov chain for an example with 2 research groups and 3 publication venues.

185

From Figure 4, Group 1 published 3 papers in venue v_1, 2 papers in venue v_2, and 1 paper in venue v_3. The number of publications of Group 1 is 6. Venue v_1 receives 3 papers of Group 1, and 2 papers of Group 2. The fractions of publications from groups to venues and from venues to groups are the edge weights. We have:

$$\mathbf{P} = \left[\begin{array}{cc|ccc} 0 & 0 & 3/6 & 2/6 & 1/6 \\ 0 & 0 & 2/8 & 4/8 & 2/8 \\ \hline 3/5 & 2/5 & 0 & 0 & 0 \\ 2/6 & 4/6 & 0 & 0 & 0 \\ 1/3 & 2/3 & 0 & 0 & 0 \end{array} \right].$$

This stochastic matrix corresponds to the Markov chain displayed in Figure 4, which can be immediately aggregated to a two-state Markov chain, yielding:

$$\mathbf{P}' = \left[\begin{array}{cc} 0.467 & 0.533 \\ 0.400 & 0.600 \end{array} \right],$$

which is the stochastic matrix we use in the solution of Equation (6). (Recall that the dimension of $\mathbf{P}'$ is $T \times T$ and, as such, much smaller than that of $\mathbf{P}$ for real size problems.) Solving Equation (6) and applying Equation (7), we obtain the ranking for the three venues:

$$\boldsymbol{\nu} = \langle 0.36, 0.43, 0.21 \rangle. \qquad (9)$$

Venue v_2 has the highest rank, followed by v_1, and then by v_3. We remark that the individual values give the *relative reputation* of each publication venue.

5. EXPERIMENTAL SETUP

In this section, we describe the setup that supports the empirical evaluation of our proposed model for reputation-oriented ranking, as described in Section 3. In particular, we aim to answer the following research questions:

Q1. How effective is our proposed random walk model for reputation-oriented ranking?

Q2. How robust is our model with respect to perturbations in the chosen reputation sources?

Q3. Can we alleviate the cost of manually selecting effective reputation sources within our model?

In order to evaluate our model, we consider its instantiation in an academic search setting, as described in Section 4. In the remainder of this section, we describe the academic search dataset built for our experiments, our evaluation procedure, and the baselines used in our investigation.

5.1 Academic Search Dataset

In order to evaluate our proposed model for reputation-oriented ranking, we built a test collection for two distinct academic search tasks. To this end, we focused on the tasks of ranking publication venues and individual researchers in the broad area of computer science, for which we could obtain appropriate ground-truths, as described next.

5.1.1 Ground-Truths

For the venue ranking task, we considered as ground-truth the set of venues classified by the Qualis system maintained by CAPES, a government agency linked to the Brazilian

Ministry of Education. CAPES[1] assigns a committee of experts to each area of knowledge and these experts are responsible for evaluating all information acquired about the venues and produce a classification. This classification is updated annually and follows a set of criteria, such as: the number of publications in each venue, the number of repositories in which it is indexed, the amount of institutions publishing in it, citation information whenever available, among others. According to the Qualis system, the venues in each area of knowledge are classified (in decreasing order of importance) as A1, A2, B1, B2, B3, B4, B5 or C.

For the researcher ranking task, we considered as ground-truth the set of researchers with an active (as of 2014) productivity grant awarded by CNPq,[2] the Brazilian National Council for Scientific and Technological Development, as a means to stimulate excellence in research. In order to apply for a productivity grant, researchers working in Brazil must submit detailed information about their academic career to CNPq, including a research project to be conducted over the coming years. To award the grants, CNPq evaluates a set of productivity indicators including academic output, contribution to the formation of human resources, academic leadership, among others, and classifies researchers in five different levels of productivity in descending order of prestige: 1A, 1B, 1C, 1D, and 2. The starting point for any newly awarded researcher is the productivity level 2.

5.1.2 Reputation Sources, Targets, and Collaterals

In order to instantiate the reputation graph in our evaluation, as a starting point, we chose as candidate reputation sources the top 126 US computer science graduate programs (which represent research groups in our instantiation) evaluated in the 2011 assessment conducted by the US National Research Council (NRC).[3] In particular, for each of these groups, we retrieved the list of group members, which were then manually reconciled against the DBLP repository.[4]

As reputation targets, we considered all publication venues in DBLP with at least one publication by any of the aforementioned 126 candidate reputation sources and with at least one citation in Google Scholar,[5] as required by the baselines described in Section 5.3. Of these, we retained a total of 704 publication venues included in the venue ground-truth presented in Section 5.1.1, which comprise the venues to be ranked by our model and the baselines. For the researcher ranking task, we modeled individual researchers as reputation collaterals, so as to assess the quality of their ranking as induced by the selected reputation targets. To this end, we considered all computer science researchers with at least one publication in any of the previously selected publication venues and at least one citation in Google Scholar. Of these, we retained a total of 274 researchers included in the researcher ground-truth described in Section 5.1.1.

Table 1 summarizes salient statistics about our produced dataset, including the total number of reputation sources, targets, and collaterals. In addition, we describe the number of reputation targets and collaterals in each of the classes defined by our ground-truths. Table 2 shows the number of edges running across these nodes in the reputation graph.

---

[1] http://www.capes.gov.br/
[2] http://www.cnpq.br/
[3] http://www.nap.edu/rdp/
[4] http://dblp.uni-trier.de/
[5] http://scholar.google.com/

Table 1: Salient statistics about the academic search dataset used in our experimental evaluation.

	Total	Nodes per relevance level							
		8	7	6	5	4	3	2	1
Sources	126								
Targets	704	102	115	186	110	86	91	14	0
Collaterals	274				15	17	22	52	168

Table 2: Total number of edges running across the different node types in the reputation graph.

	Sources	Collaterals
Targets	203415	15596

5.2 Evaluation Procedure

To compare the rankings produced by P-score and the baselines described in Section 5.3 for the venue and researcher ranking tasks, we use the discounted cumulative gain (DCG) metric [14]. DCG adopts a non-binary notion of relevance, by assessing a given ranking based upon a graded scale, from less relevant to more relevant. This metric also uses a log-based discount factor that reduces the impact of the gain as we move lower in the ranking. Let l_i be the non-binary relevance level associated with the item ranked at the i-th position. The DCG at a rank position k is defined as:

$$DCG@k = \sum_{i=1}^{k} \frac{2^{l_i} - 1}{\log_2(i+1)}. \qquad (10)$$

To bind the results within the interval [0,1], we use the normalized version of DCG, denoted nDCG, which is obtained by dividing the DCG@k value by the maximum possible value at the same ranking cutoff k. As relevance levels, we consider a linear mapping from the classes defined by each of our ground-truths, as described in Table 3.

Table 3: Mapping from Qualis and CNPq classes (discussed in Section 5.1.1) to the relevance levels used by nDCG.

nDCG level	8	7	6	5	4	3	2	1
Qualis class	A1	A2	B1	B2	B3	B4	B5	C
CNPq class				1A	1B	1C	1D	2

5.3 Ranking Baselines

We compare P-score with two citation-based baselines, namely, a raw citation count and the well known H-Index. Our choice of these baselines is motivated by the wide adoption of citation–based metrics for assessing productivity in academia. Indeed, nowadays citation counts and H-Index are both considered standard indicators to compare publication venues or individual researchers. As discussed in Section 5.1, we collected all citation data from Google Scholar.

6. EXPERIMENTAL RESULTS

In this section, we discuss the results of the empirical validation of our random walk model for reputation-based ranking. In the following, Sections 6.1, 6.2, and 6.3 address the three research questions stated in the previous section, regarding the effectiveness and robustness of our model, as well as the selection of suitable reputation sources.

6.1 Ranking Effectiveness

In order to address research question Q1, we assess the effectiveness of P-score in contrast to existing citation-based metrics used as baselines, as discussed in Section 5.3. To this end, we analyze rankings of publication venues and individual researchers in terms of nDCG at multiple ranking cutoffs. To instantiate P-score, we consider two simple alternatives for selecting reputation sources. The first alternative (denoted P-score 10) considers only the top 10 research groups ranked by the NRC whereas the second (denoted P-score 126) considers all 126 ranked groups as reputation sources, as described in Section 5.1.2. A further alternative for semi-automatically choosing an effective reference set of reputation sources is later investigated in Section 6.3.

6.1.1 Ranking Publication Venues

To assess the effectiveness of P-score, we first consider its application for the task of ranking publication venues, which represent reputation targets in the instantiation of our model. In particular, Figure 5 shows the effectiveness of the two aforementioned P-score variants and the H-Index baseline[6] in terms of nDCG at multiple ranking cutoffs k up to the number of venues to be ranked, namely, 578.

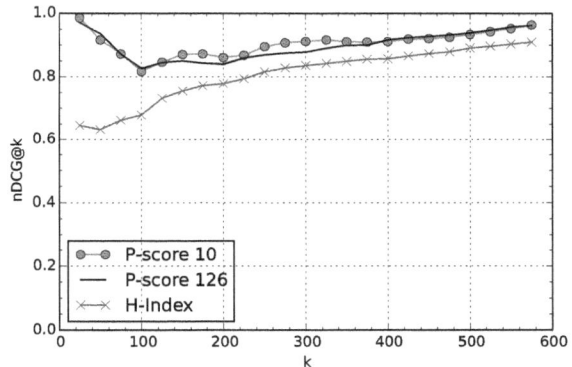

Figure 5: Venue ranking effectiveness.

From Figure 5, we first observe that the two variants of P-score, using either the top 10 or top 126 NRC groups as reputation sources, perform similarly across the entire range of nDCG@k values. This suggests that a few highly reputable sources are enough to transfer reputation to the target set of publication venues. More importantly, both variants of P-score consistently and substantially outperform the H-Index baseline for all ranking cutoffs. This is a remarkable result, given that citation information is a core element of manual academic assessments, such as the ones conducted to produce the ground-truth used in this investigation, as discussed in Section 5.1.1. In contrast, the current instantiation of our model, which solely exploits publishing behavior as a reputation signal, delivers the best ranking performance.

6.1.2 Ranking Individual Researchers

The results in Section 6.1.1 demonstrated the effectiveness of P-score for ranking reputation targets, represented by publication venues. In this section, we further assess the

---

[6]The citations baseline could not be assessed since raw venue citation information is not available from Google Scholar.

effectiveness of our model at transferring reputation from target nodes to collateral nodes, represented by individual researchers.[7] This evaluation is motivated by the possibility of reusing the immediate results of the random walk performed on the reputation graph to rank entities outside the initial set of reputation targets. To this end, Figure 6 contrasts the effectiveness of P-score with the Citations and H-Index baselines for the task of ranking researchers. Once again, effectiveness figures are given in terms of nDCG at multiple ranking cutoffs k, up to the total number of researchers to be ranked, namely, 274.

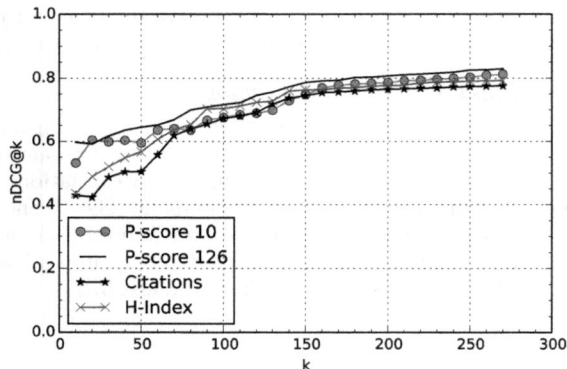

Figure 6: Researcher ranking effectiveness.

From Figure 6, we first note that P-score 10 once again outperforms both the Citations as well as the H-Index baselines in terms of nDCG@k for ranking cutoffs up to $k = 70$. In addition, P-score 126 is consistently the most effective of all tested approaches throughout the full range of nDCG@k values. Recalling research question Q1, the results in this and the previous section attest the effectiveness of P-score as a ranking approach for two different academic search tasks. Moreover, they show that the model can successfully transfer reputation from selected sources to both immediate targets as well as to collateral nodes in a post-hoc fashion. Lastly, the relative effectiveness between P-score 10 and P-score 126 raises an interesting observation. In particular, while a few reputation sources may perform effectively (as was the case with the results in Figure 5 for the ranking of publication venues), these sources must be carefully selected. In the next section, we will further assess the robustness of our model to perturbations in the selected reputation sources.

6.2 Ranking Robustness

The results in Section 6.1 attested the effectiveness of our proposed model for ranking publication venues and individual researchers when a careful selection of research groups are used as reputation sources. Nevertheless, this selection may eventually include noisy reputation sources, making it sub-optimal. To address research question Q2, we assess the robustness of the rankings produced by P-score with respect to random perturbations in the selected reputation sources. Figure 7 shows the results of this investigation for venue rankings. In particular, the x-axis denotes the amount of noise randomly injected into a reference set of reputation sources—in our case, the top k research groups ranked by

the NRC, for $k \in \{5, 10, 20\}$. For instance, $x = 0.2$ indicates that 20% of the reputation sources are replaced by research groups randomly chosen from outside the reference set. Accordingly, $x = 0.0$ indicates no noise (i.e., the untouched top k NRC groups), whereas $x = 1.0$ indicates maximum noise (i.e., a random set of k research groups). On the y-axis, we show mean nDCG@100 figures averaged across 30 repetitions of this perturbation process, with shaded areas denoting the observed standard deviation from the mean. An additional curve including all 126 NRC groups as reputation sources is shown as a reference for comparison.

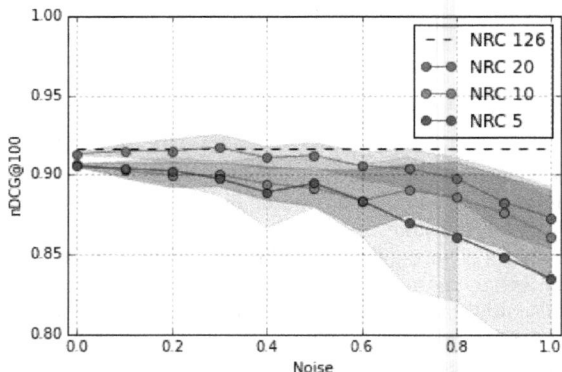

Figure 7: Venue ranking robustness with respect to random perturbations of the selected reputation sources.

From Figure 7, we observe that larger sets of reputation sources are generally more robust to noise, as demonstrated by the green curve (NRC 20). Indeed, this setting delivers nearly the same ranking effectiveness as the one achieved when using all 126 NRC groups as reputation sources. More importantly, all venue rankings produced by our model are relatively stable up to a noise level around 0.3 (i.e., when 30% of the reputation sources are randomly chosen). Recalling question Q2, these results attest the robustness of the rankings produced by our model with respect to random perturbations in the selected reputation sources. Moreover, they open up an interesting direction towards automatically identifying a robust set of reputation sources.

6.3 Selecting Reputation Sources

The results in the previous sections demonstrated the effectiveness of our model and its robustness to random perturbations in the reference set of reputation sources. For both experiments, as discussed in Section 5.1.2, a careful selection of manually chosen reference reputation sources—the top 126 research groups ranked by the NRC—was used. Note that our reputation-based method provides good rankings of venues in comparison with h-index even when we choose reputation sources at random (see Figures 5 and 7). Our intuition for this fact is that the NRC ranking for CS is composed by reliable research groups. This way, even on maximum noise we are basing our method in good references. In practice, such a manual selection of reputation sources can be costly. While a completely automatic alternative is beyond the scope of our current investigation, we performed an experiment to demonstrate the feasibility of semi-automatically choosing suitable reputation sources.

---

[7]A preliminary version of the experiment discussed in Section 6.1.2 appeared as a short workshop paper [31].

To address question Q3, we experiment with our proposed model itself as a means to identify effective reputation sources. Specifically, starting with all 126 groups evaluated by the NRC, we randomly choose a subset of 10 groups to use as reputation sources, with the remaining 116 groups used as reputation collaterals. After convergence, we choose the top 10 ranked collateral nodes as the new set of reputation sources. We repeat this procedure until the set of top 10 groups no longer changes. We applied this procedure 100 times to the aforementioned set of 126 groups. At each run, we repeated the selection of a new reference set of reputation sources (starting from a random selection) until the set of top 10 groups stabilized. Table 4 lists the 12 groups that appeared among the top 10 at least once in a given run, after the process stabilized. Moreover, the first 8 listed groups appeared among the top 10 at every single run.

Table 4: Research groups that appeared at least once among the top 10 selected reputation sources after 100 selections that started from a random choice.

1	Carnegie Mellon University
2	Georgia Institute of Technology
3	Massachusetts Institute of Technology
4	Stanford University
5	University of California-Berkeley
6	University of California-Los Angeles
7	University of California-San Diego
8	University of Illinois at Urbana-Champaign
9	University of Maryland College Park
10	University of Southern California
11	University of Michigan-Ann Arbor
12	Cornell University

From Table 4, we observe that all 12 listed groups are among the top 5th percentile in the official ranking produced by the NRC. Moreover, when used as reference reputation sources for ranking publication venues and individual researchers, these semi-automatically selected groups yield a comparable retrieval effectiveness to the ones attained when using the top 10 groups ranked by the NRC itself as reputation sources, as previously shown in Sections 6.1.1 and 6.1.2. Recalling question Q3, these results show that it is possible to alleviate the manual effort incurred by the selection of reputation sources through a semi-automatic procedure with no penalty in effectiveness. Moreover, these results provide encouragement for further investigating fully automatic mechanisms to identify effective reputation sources.

7. CONCLUSIONS

In this paper, we have proposed a novel random walk model to identify the most reputable entities of a domain, based on a conceptual framework of reputation flows. Our model overcomes the challenges of quantifying reputation (arguably, a subjective and multi-faceted concept) by instead focusing on the transference of reputation among different entities. We instantiated our model in an academic search setting and empirically validated its effectiveness and robustness for two academic search tasks in the broad area of computer science namely, publication venue and individual researcher ranking. Specifically, we demonstrated the effectiveness of our model in contrast to standard citation-based approaches for identifying reputable venues and researchers as well as its robustness to perturbations in the selection

of reputation sources. Furthermore, we showed that effective reputation sources can be chosen in a semi-automatic fashion using our proposed random walk model itself.

Both the conceptual framework and its instantiation in an academic context open opportunities for future work. At the model level, we intend to further verify the generality of the concept of reputation flows when applied to other domains, such as enterprise search. At the instantiation level, we intend to further explore fully automatic mechanisms for identifying suitable reputation sources for academic search. In addition, we plan to test our model for academic search tasks in areas other than computer science.

ACKNOWLEDGEMENTS

This work was partially sponsored by the Brazilian National Institute of Science and Technology for the Web (MCT/CNPq 573871/2008-6) and the authors' individual grants and scholarships from CNPq, FAPEMIG and FAPERJ.

8. REFERENCES

[1] L. Backstrom and J. Leskovec. Supervised random walks: Predicting and recommending links in social networks. In *Proc. of WSDM*, pages 635–644, 2011.

[2] E. Bakshy, I. Rosenn, C. Marlow, and L. Adamic. The role of social networks in information diffusion. In *Proc. of WWW*, pages 519–528, 2012.

[3] K. Balog. Expertise retrieval. *Found. Trends Inf. Retr.*, 6(2-3):127–256, 2012.

[4] J. Bollen, H. van de Sompel, J. Smith, and R. Luce. Toward alternative metrics of journal impact: A comparison of download and citation data. *Information Processing & Management*, 41(6):1419–1440, 2005.

[5] S. Brin and L. Page. The anatomy of a large-scale hypertextual web search engine. *Comput. Netw.*, 30(1-7):107–117, 1998.

[6] G. Cormode, S. Muthukrishnan, and J. Yan. People like us: mining scholarly data for comparable researchers. In *Proc. of WWW*, pages 1227–1232, 2014.

[7] H. Deng, J. Han, M. R. Lyu, and I. King. Modeling and exploiting heterogeneous bibliographic networks for expertise ranking. In *Proc. of JCDL*, pages 71–80, 2012.

[8] E. Garfield. Citation indexes for science. *Science*, 122(3159):108–111, 1955.

[9] S. D. Gollapalli, P. Mitra, and C. L. Giles. Ranking authors in digital libraries. In *Proc. of JCDL*, pages 251–254, 2011.

[10] G. D. Gonçalves, F. Figueiredo, J. M. Almeida, and M. A. Gonçalves. Characterizing scholar popularity: A case study in the computer science research community. In *Proc. of JCDL*, pages 57–66, 2014.

[11] J. Hirsch. An index to quantify an individual's scientific research output. *Proc. Nat. Acad. Sciences*, pages 16569–16572, 2005.

[12] J. G. Hutton, M. B. Goodman, J. B. Alexander, and C. M. Genest. Reputation management: the new face of corporate public relations? *Pub. Rel. Rev.*, 27(3):247–261, 2001.

[13] M. Jamali and M. Ester. Trustwalker: A random walk model for combining trust-based and item-based

recommendation. In *Proc. of SIGKDD*, pages 397–406, 2009.

[14] K. Järvelin and J. Kekäläinen. Cumulated gain-based evaluation of IR techniques. *ACM Trans. Inf. Syst.*, 20(4):422–446, 2002.

[15] P. Katerattanakul, B. Han, and S. Hong. Objective quality rankings of computing journals. *Commun. ACM*, 45, 2003.

[16] J. M. Kleinberg. Authoritative sources in a hyperlinked environment. *J. ACM*, 46(5):604–632, 1999.

[17] I. Konstas, V. Stathopoulos, and J. M. Jose. On social networks and collaborative recommendation. In *Proc. of SIGIR*, pages 195–202, 2009.

[18] A. LangVille and C. Meyer. *Google's PageRank and Beyond: The Science of Search Engine Rankings*. Princeton University Press, 2006.

[19] B. Larsen and P. Ingwersen. Using citations for ranking in digital libraries. In *Proc. of JCDL*, pages 370–370, 2006.

[20] L. Leydesdorff. How are new citation-based journal indicators adding to the bibliometric toolbox? *J. Am. Soc. Inf. Sci. Technol.*, 60(7):1327–1336, 2009.

[21] H. Lima, T. H. P. Silva, M. M. Moro, R. L. T. Santos, W. M. Jr., and A. H. F. Laender. Aggregating productivity indices for ranking researchers across multiple areas. In *Proc. of JCDL*, pages 97–106, 2013.

[22] G. Mann, D. Mimno, and A. McCallum. Bibliometric impact measures leveraging topic analysis. In *Proc. of JCDL*, pages 65–74, 2006.

[23] C. Meyer. Stochastic complementation, uncoupling Markov chains, and the theory of nearly reducible systems. *SIAM Review*, 31(2):240–272, 1989.

[24] S. Nelakuditi, C. Gray, and R. R. Choudhury. Snap judgement of publication quality: how to convince a dean that you are a good researcher. *Mobile Computing and Commun. Review*, 15(2):20–23, 2011.

[25] S. Nerur, R. Sikora, G. Mangalaraj, and V. Balijepally. Assessing the relative influence of journals in a citation network. *Commun. ACM*, 48(11):71–74, 2005.

[26] M. Newman. *Networks: An Introduction*. Oxford University Press, 2010.

[27] Z. Nie, Y. Zhang, J.-R. Wen, and W.-Y. Ma. Object-level ranking: Bringing order to web objects. In *Proc. of WWW*, pages 567–574, 2005.

[28] L. Page, S. Brin, R. Motwani, and T. Winograd. The pagerank citation ranking: Bringing order to the web. In *Proc. of WWW*, pages 161–172, 1998.

[29] H. Piwowar. Altmetrics: Value all research products. *Nature*, 493(7431):159–159, 2013.

[30] E. Rahm and A. Thor. Citation analysis of database publications. *ACM Sigmod Record*, 34(4):48–53, 2005.

[31] S. Ribas, B. Ribeiro-Neto, E. de Souza e Silva, A. H. Ueda, and N. Ziviani. Using reference groups to assess academic productivity in computer science. In *Proc. of WWW*, pages 603–608, 2015.

[32] S. Saha, S. Saint, and D. Christakis. Impact factor: a valid measure of journal quality? *J. Med. Lib. Assoc.*, 91(1):42–46, 2003.

[33] Y. Sun and C. L. Giles. *Popularity weighted ranking for academic digital libraries*. Springer, 2007.

[34] J. Tang, R. Jin, and J. Zhang. A topic modeling approach and its integration into the random walk framework for academic search. In *Proc. of ICDM*, pages 1055–1060, 2008.

[35] J. Weng, E.-P. Lim, J. Jiang, and Q. He. Twitterrank: Finding topic-sensitive influential twitterers. In *Proc. of WSDM*, pages 261–270, 2010.

[36] H. Wu, Y. Pei, and J. Yu. Detecting academic experts by topic-sensitive link analysis. *Front. Comp. Science in China*, 3(4):445–456, 2009.

[37] W. Xi, B. Zhang, Z. Chen, Y. Lu, S. Yan, W.-Y. Ma, and E. A. Fox. Link fusion: A unified link analysis framework for multi-type interrelated data objects. In *Proc. of WWW*, pages 319–327, 2004.

[38] E. Yan, Y. Ding, and C. R. Sugimoto. P-rank: An indicator measuring prestige in heterogeneous scholarly networks. *J. Am. Soc. Inf. Sci. Technol.*, 62(3):467–477, 2011.

[39] S. Yan and D. Lee. Toward alternative measures for ranking venues: a case of database research community. In *Proc. of JCDL*, pages 235–244, 2007.

[40] M. Ye, P. Yin, W.-C. Lee, and D.-L. Lee. Exploiting geographical influence for collaborative point-of-interest recommendation. In *Proc. of SIGIR*, pages 325–334, 2011.

[41] D. Zhou, S. A. Orshanskiy, H. Zha, and C. L. Giles. Co-ranking authors and documents in a heterogeneous network. In *Proc. of ICDM*, pages 739–744, 2007.

[42] Z. Zhuang, E. Elmacioglu, D. Lee, and C. Giles. Measuring conference quality by mining program committee characteristics. In *Proc. of JCDL*, pages 225–234, 2007.

Entropy and Graph Based Modelling of Document Coherence using Discourse Entities: An Application to IR

Casper Petersen
Department of Computer Science
University of Copenhagen, Denmark
cazz@di.ku.dk

Jakob Grue Simonsen
Department of Computer Science
University of Copenhagen, Denmark
simonsen@di.ku.dk

Christina Lioma
Department of Computer Science
University of Copenhagen, Denmark
c.lioma@di.ku.dk

Birger Larsen
Department of Communication
Aalborg University Copenhagen, Denmark
birger@hum.aau.dk

ABSTRACT

We present two novel models of document coherence and their application to information retrieval (IR). Both models approximate document coherence using discourse entities, e.g. the subject or object of a sentence. Our first model views text as a Markov process generating sequences of discourse entities (entity n-grams); we use the entropy of these entity n-grams to approximate the rate at which new information appears in text, reasoning that as more new words appear, the topic increasingly drifts and text coherence decreases. Our second model extends the work of Guinaudeau & Strube [28] that represents text as a graph of discourse entities, linked by different relations, such as their distance or adjacency in text. We use several graph topology metrics to approximate different aspects of the discourse flow that can indicate coherence, such as the average clustering or betweenness of discourse entities in text. Experiments with several instantiations of these models show that: (i) our models perform on a par with two other well-known models of text coherence even without any parameter tuning, and (ii) reranking retrieval results according to their coherence scores gives notable performance gains, confirming a relation between document coherence and relevance. This work contributes two novel models of document coherence, the application of which to IR complements recent work in the integration of document cohesiveness or comprehensibility to ranking [5, 55].

Categories and Subject Descriptors

H.3.3 [Information Search and Retrieval]

General Terms

Theory, Experimentation

ICTIR '15, Septembe 27-30, 2015, Northampton, MA, USA
© 2015 ACM. ISBN 978-1-4503-3833-2/15/09 ...$15.00.
DOI: http://dx.doi.org/10.1145/2808194.2809458.

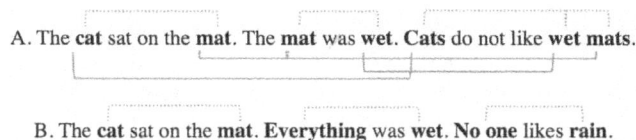

A. The **cat** sat on the **mat**. The **mat** was **wet**. **Cats** do not like **wet mats**.

B. The **cat** sat on the **mat**. **Everything** was **wet**. **No one** likes **rain**.

Figure 1: Example of more (A) and less (B) coherent text. Discourse entities are in bold. Dotted lines mark *within-sentence relations* of discourse entities. Solid lines mark *between-sentence relations*, which newly introduced entities do not have, decreasing coherence.

1. INTRODUCTION

The extent to which text makes sense by introducing, explaining and linking its concepts and ideas through a sequence of semantically and logically related units of discourse is called *coherence*. Several models of text coherence exist. On a high level, these models capture text regularities or patterns predicted by a theory or otherwise hypothesised to indicate coherence. For instance, according to early discourse theories [26], three core factors of text coherence are (i) the discourse purpose (*intentional structure*), (ii) the specific discourse items discussed (*attentional structure*), and (iii) the organisation of the *discourse segments*. Of these factors, coherence models have been presented for both intentional structure [44], and discourse segments [4, 23], but attentional structure has received the most attention and is the basis for most existing models of text coherence. One approach to attentional structure that has been used extensively in coherence models is *Centering Theory* [25, 31] (CT), which posits that a reader's attention is centered on a few salient entities in text, and that these exhibit patterns signalling the reader to switch or retain attention. A widely used application of CT is the *entity grid* model [3], which assumes that coherence can be measured from sequences of repeated discourse entities, such as the subject and object of a sentence. In this work, we use the entity grid as our basis to propose two novel classes of models for document coherence.

Our first class of models calculates coherence using the information *entropy* [52] of the salient discourse entities in the entity grid. The information entropy rate of a document can be thought of as the rate at which new information appears as one reads the document. The main idea is that, as more new information appears, the document becomes less focussed on a single topic, so its coherence decreases. This assumption, which is already verified in the literature [5], is illustrated in Figure 1, which juxtaposes the discourse flow between three entities (cat(s), mat(s), wet) and six entities (cat, mat, everything, wet, no one, rain) in texts A and B respectively. As entities are linked between sentences, i.e. repeated, text becomes more topically focussed and hence more coherent. However, when many new entities are introduced, since they are by definition not linked to previous discourse, the topic of the text becomes less clear and overall coherence decreases. To the best of our knowledge, discourse entropy has not been used for text coherence estimation before (there is however work on *lexical entropy* for text readability, which we discuss in Section 2).

Our second class of document coherence models maps the entity grid to **graphs** following Guinaudeau & Strube [28], where entities are vertices, linked by various relations between them, e.g. distance or adjacency. The topologies of these graphs model the flow of discourse. We investigate whether graph properties, such as the clustering coefficient, or iterative graph ranking algorithms, such as PageRank, can approximate document coherence. This class of models extends work by Guinaudeau & Strube that used only a single such metric, namely outdegree, to calculate text coherence.

We present several instantiations of the above two classes of coherence models and we evaluate their effectiveness, first as coherence models per se, and second when integrated to information retrieval (IR). In the first case, we evaluate our coherence models in the standard *sentence reordering* task. We find that our models are more accurate than two well known baselines in coherence modelling (one of them being the entity grid [3] that we extend), even without any parameter tuning or training. In the second case, we investigate whether factoring coherence in the IR process improves retrieval precision, on the basis that coherence should be a reasonable predictor of relevance. Experiments with standard TREC Web track data show that reranking retrieval results according to their coherence scores improves retrieval precision, especially for the top 20 retrieved results.

In the rest of the paper, Section 2 overviews related work; Sections 3 & 4 present our entropy and graph based coherence models respectively; Section 5 discusses the experimental evaluation of these models, and Section 6 their limitations and future extensions. Sections 7 summarises our conclusions.

2. RELATED WORK

We overview the Natural Language Processing (NLP) literature on models of text coherence (Section 2.1), focussing in particular on those using discourse entities (Section 2.2). We also discuss related work on applying text coherence to improve NLP tasks and IR (Section 2.3).

2.1 Local and global coherence

A text can be coherent at a *local* and *global* level [20]. *Local* coherence is measured by examining the similarity between neighbouring text spans, e.g., the well-connectedness of adjacent sentences through lexical cohesion [29], or entity repetition [27]. *Global* coherence, on the other hand, is measured through discourse-level relations connecting re-

mote text spans across a whole text, e.g. sentences [35, 45].

There is extensive work on local coherence that uses different approaches, including bag of words methods at sentence level [22], sequences of content words (of length ≥ 3) at paragraph level [53], local lexical cohesion information [2], local syntactic cues [17], and combining local lexical and syntactic features, e.g., term co-occurrence [38, 55]. Overall, various aspects of CT have long been used to model local coherence [37, 51], including the well-known entity approaches that rank the repetition and syntactic realisation of entities in adjacent sentences [3, 17].

There is also work on *global* coherence, focussing on the structure of a document as a whole [4, 13, 17, 23]. However, not many coherence models represent both local and global coherence, even though those two are connected: local coherence is a prerequisite for global coherence [3], and there is psychological evidence that coherence on both local and global levels is manifested in text comprehension [57, 59]. Among the few models that capture both local and global text coherence is the sentence ordering model of Zhang [59]: on a local level, sentences are represented as concept vectors where concepts are equivalent to content words; on a global level, sentences are represented as vertices, and sentence relations as edges in a document graph.

Our work captures both local and global coherence as explained in Sections 3 & 4, which practically means that it can model document coherence both in the simple case of capturing adjacent discourse transitions like those illustrated in Figure 1, but also in the more complex (yet more realistic) case of capturing non-adjacent discourse transitions like those illustrated in Figure 3.

2.2 Entity based coherence models

The basis of our two coherence models is the entity grid [3], which represents a document by its salient discourse entities and their syntactic roles, see Table 1 for example. The entity grid indicates the location of each discourse entity in a document, which is important for coherence modelling because mentions of an entity tend to appear in clusters of neighbouring sentences in coherent documents. This last assumption is adapted from CT where consecutive utterances are regarded as more coherent if they keep mentioning the same entities [27, 51]. There are several extensions and variations of the entity grid, including adaptations for German [21], coupled with extensions integrating high level sentence structure [14]; extensions integrating writing quality features (e.g. word variety and style indicators) [9]; extensions of the original entity grid (which captures sentence-to-sentence entity transitions) to capture term occurrences in sentence-to-sentence relation sequences [41]; extensions focussing on syntactic regularities [44]; a *topical entity grid* that considers topical information instead of only discourse entities [18]; and extensions incorporating modifiers and named entity types into the entity grid to distinguish important from less important entities [19]. A recent extension [28] maps the entity grid into a graph where coherence is calculated as the average outdegree of the nodes in the graph. While this model is only presented as a local coherence model, it does represent both local and global coherence: entities are represented as nodes in a graph representing the document, allowing to connect entities occurring in non-adjacent sentences, hence spanning globally in the document. The coherence models we present in this paper employ the entity grid of [3], but use several novel computations based on this grid: first entropy, and second an extension of the work of Guinaudeau & Strube [28] with several more complex graph metrics than outdegree.

2.3 Applications of text coherence

Apart from being an interesting problem in itself, coherence models and hence coherence prediction are important to a variety of NLP tasks and applications, such as summarisation [2, 4, 11, 40, 59], machine translation [40, 58], separating conversational threads [18], text fluency/reading difficulty detection [7, 48, 50], grammars for natural language generation [1, 36, 37], genre classification [3], sentence insertion [12] and sentence ordering [3, 33, 34]. In IR in particular, the document coherence scores produced by our models can be seen as similar to several document quality measures that have been used in the past to improve retrieval. Examples of document quality include, for instance, document complexity, which Mikk [47] predicts using a corrected term frequency measure based on word commonness. In the context of web search in particular, document quality has been studied extensively. For instance, Bendersky et al. [5] estimate the quality of web documents by features indicating readability, layout and ease-of-navigation, such as: the number of terms that are rendered visible by a web browser; the number of terms in the title; the average number of characters of visible terms on the page (used also as an estimate of readability by [3]); the fraction of anchor text on the page (used also as discriminative of content by [49]); the fraction of text that is rendered visible by a web browser, compared to the full source of the page (also known as information-to-noise ratio and used as feature of document quality in [60]); the stopword/non-stopword ratio of the page; and the lexical entropy of the page, computed over the terms occurring in the document. In fact, Bendersky et al. use this type of lexical entropy as an estimate of document cohesiveness, reasoning that documents with lower entropy will tend to be more cohesive and more focussed on a single topic. This inversely proportional relation between text entropy and its cohesiveness is also used in our model; the difference is that we compute the discourse entropy (entropy of discourse entity n-grams), whereas Bendersky et al. compute the lexical entropy (entropy of individual words).

Tan et al. [56] also present a model of text comprehensibility using lexical features, such as bag of words, word length and sentence length, to approximate semantic and syntactic complexity. They build a classifier that uses these features to assign a comprehensibility score to each document, and then rerank retrieved documents according to this comprehensibility score. We also rerank results using our coherence scores, and like [56], find this to be effective. The difference of our work to that of Tan et al. is that (i) our coherence scores are not produced by a classifier but they are computed either as entropy or graph centrality approximations without tuning parameters; and (ii) we do not use lexical frequency statistics, but solely discourse entities, e.g. subject, object, which we consider better approximations of semantic complexity than lexical frequency features.

3. MODEL I: DISCOURSE ENTROPY FOR DOCUMENT COHERENCE

Our first coherence model uses information entropy. En-

Table 1: Entity grid example. Discourse entities: subject (s), object (o). 1-5 are sentence numbers.

SAMPLE TEXT
1 "One", the old man said; his hope and his confidence had never gone.
2 "Two", the boy said.
3 "Two", the old man agreed; "you didn't steal them?"
4 "I would", the boy said, "but I bought these.".
5 "Thank you", the old man said.

ENTITY GRID							
	MAN	HOPE	CONFIDENCE	BOY	YOU	THEM	I	THESE
1	s	s	s	—	—	—	—	—
2	—	—	—	s	—	—	—	—
3	s	—	—	s	o	—	—	—
4	—	—	—	s	—	—	s	o
5	s	—	—	—	o	—	—	—

tropy has been used in various areas e.g., lossless data compression [30], or cryptography [10]. See Berger et al. [6] for an older but comprehensive introduction to entropy for NLP.

Information entropy is the expected value of the information content of a random variable. If a document is seen as a sequence of N i.i.d. events $a_1 a_2 \cdots a_N$, the entropy is, roughly, a measure of the average "surprise" of observing an event a_i. For example, if all events occur with equal probability, the entropy is *high*; however if a single event occurs much more frequently than others, the entropy is *low* (the average surprise is low as a single event will occur very often, as expected).

For a positive integer n, we may consider the probability $p(a_i | a_{i-1} \cdots a_{i-n})$ of observing event a_i given the preceding n events. In this case, the entropy, roughly, measures the average surprise of seeing event a_i given the history of n-preceding events (a so-called n-gram). In particular, if the events are *discourse entities*, low entropy will occur if only a few distinct discourse entities can occur, on average, after each n-gram of other discourse entities. In contrast, if new discourse entities are being introduced throughout the text independently of the preceding entities, e.g., recall the example in Figure 1, high entropy will occur. Based on these observations, we compute a document coherence score as the reciprocal entropy of a random variable constructed from the probability of discourse entities in the document. We next describe how we compute this probability of discourse entities (Section 3.1) and the final coherence score per document (Section 3.2).

3.1 Discourse entities and their probabilities

We build an entity grid as per Barzilay and Lapata [3]: the rows correspond to the sentences of a document d, in order, and each column corresponds to a salient entity occurring in the sentence, in order of their occurrence in d. The entry in each row and column of the grid is the syntactic role of the corresponding salient entity. We use the syntactic roles of **subject** (**s**) and **object** (**o**) because they are the most important discourse items [3], denoting respectively the *actor* and the *entity that is acted upon*. Table 1 displays an example of the entity grid built from an excerpt of Hemmingway's "The Old Man and the Sea". For instance, MAN is a discourse entity occurring as a subject in sentences 1, 3, and 5.

We propose to measure coherence using entropy in the following way. From the entity grid, we extract n-grams of entities in the order they occur in the text, i.e. per row in the grid. We then compute the probability of each entity n-gram using the standard maximum likelihood language modelling frequency approximations (more elaborate approximations are also possible, see for instance [46], but we choose this for simplicity in this preliminary work). That is, for an 1-gram, we compute the probability $p(e_i)$ of a discourse entity e_i in document d as:

$$p(e_i) = \frac{f(e_i)}{|E|} \quad (1)$$

where $f(e_i)$ is the frequency of e_i in d, and $|E|$ is the total frequency of all discourse entities in d. Similarly, for a 2-gram, we compute the probability $p(e_i|e_{i-1})$ of entity e_i following entity e_{i-1} as:

$$p(e_i|e_{i-1}) = \frac{f(e_{i-1}, e_i)}{f(e_i)} \quad (2)$$

where $f(e_{i-1}, e_i)$ is the number of times that entity e_i occurs as the first entity after entity e_{i-1} in d. The resulting probability distributions may be smoothed by standard methods (e.g., Dirichlet or Good-Turing). For simplicity we do not do so in this basic model. We use these probabilities to compute entropy as explained next.

3.2 Entropy and coherence scores

Formally, the entropy, $H(X)$, of a discrete random variable X with sample space Ω is:

$$H(X) = -\sum_{x \in \Omega} p(x) \log_2 p(x) \quad (3)$$

where $p(x) = \Pr(X = x)$ for all $x \in \Omega$. We model each document as a Markov process generating discourse entities. For a k-order Markov process, the probability of generating a discourse entity e_i depends solely on the preceding n-gram of discourse entities. Using Equation 3 it is straightforward to obtain explicit expressions for the entropy of the probability distribution generating events. For instance, for $k = 0, 1$, the resulting expressions are, respectively:

$$H_0(E) = -\sum_{e_i \in \Omega} p(e_i) \log_2 p(e_i) \quad (4)$$

$$H_1(E) = -\sum_{e_i \in \Omega} p(e_i) \sum_{e_{i-1} \in \Omega} p(e|e_{i-1}) \log_2 p(e|e_{i-1}) \quad (5)$$

where Ω is the set of all discourse entities E in the document, $p(e_i)$ is computed using Equation 1, and $p(e_i|e_{i-1})$ is computed using Equation 2. Subscripts $_{0,1}$ denote the order of the entropy model, which increases as the value n of the n-gram increases.

Our document coherence score is then the reciprocal of this entropy value:

$$C = \frac{1}{H_k(E)} \quad (6)$$

to boost low entropy scoring documents according to our assumption that coherence and entropy are inversely related. The value of C is always non-negative, but has no upper bound. So we normalise it as follows:

$$COH(H_k(E)) = \frac{C}{C_{max}} \quad (7)$$

where C_{max} is the maximum value of C across all documents in the collection for a k-order model. The division by C_{max} is a simple normalisation of the coherence scores of the documents in the collection. Other normalisation approaches can also be used, which, if parameterised, can result in better performing models than the ones we report. In this preliminary work, we use this basic normalisation. In addition, different values of k give different orders of the Markov process, hence different coherence model instantiations, and hence distinct coherence scores. In this work, we experiment with 0-order, 1-order and 2-order models, as explained in Section 5.

Our entropy coherence model captures only local coherence through entity transitions occurring within sentences. We next present a family of models that capture both local and global coherence through entity transitions between both adjacent and non-adjacent sentences in a document.

4. MODEL II: DISCOURSE GRAPH METRICS FOR DOCUMENT COHERENCE

We represent a document d as a directed bipartite graph where each node in the first partition is a sentence, and each node in the second partition is a discourse entity. There is an edge from a sentence-node to an entity-node iff the sentence contains the entity. This representation was first suggested by Guinaudeau & Strube [28]. Using this directed bipartite graph, we can build an undirected graph whose nodes are sentences and where there is an edge between two distinct nodes iff they share at least one common entity. This undirected graph can be unweighted or weighted; if weighted, the weight can reflect salient properties of the document and sentences, e.g. the distance of the sentences in the text. An example of a bipartite graph and its corresponding undirected graph is shown in Figure 2.

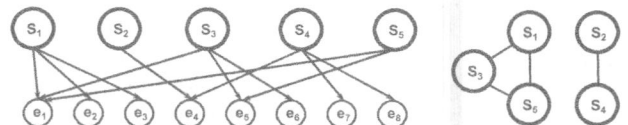

Figure 2: Bipartite graph of the entity grid in Table 1 (left) and the corresponding (unweighted) undirected graph (right). S marks sentence nodes and e entities extracted from the entity grid.

The intuition is that as these graphs model relationships between sentences and entities, properties of the graphs will reflect the coherence of a document, as in coherent text, sentences occurring close to each other should have closely related entities. Guinaudeau and Strube [28] use only the outdegree of such graphs constructed from discourse entities to calculate a coherence score. Note that while Guinaudeau and Strube write that their model only takes *local* coherence into account, the bipartite graph can also be used to reason about *global* coherence, as it models connections between non-adjacent sentences. We extend the approach of Guinaudeau and Strube by experimenting with a number of other graph metrics that capture various aspects of the topology of the graphs (and accordingly, we conjecture, the narrative flow of the text). Our methodology consists of two main steps: (i) we build, for each d, a discourse entity graph (Section 4.1), and (ii) we compute our proposed graph topology measures and use these as coherence scores for each document d (Section 4.2). We next describe these steps in detail.

4.1 Building discourse entity graphs

For a document d containing N sentences $s = \{s_i, \ldots, s_N\}$: $i = 1, \ldots, N-1$ we denote by $\hat{G}_d = (V, U, E)$ the labelled directed bipartite graph with $V = |N|$ and U nodes where $v \in V$, $u \in U$, $V \cap U = \emptyset$. $E = \{(v, u) : V \times U\}$ consists of ordered pairs of nodes from $V \times U$. A node $v \in V$ denotes a sentence and $u \in U$ an entity found in the entity grid that can be shared by multiple nodes in V. $\hat{G}_d$ is called the *bipartite graph* of d. The labelling of the nodes is used to retain the *order* in which the sentences represented by nodes occur in d.

We denote by $G_d = (V, E)$ the undirected graph with V nodes and E edges where $v, u \in V$ are nodes in V and $(v, u) \in E$ is an edge between pairs of nodes $v, u \in V$ with a non-zero real-valued weight. A node $v \in V$ denotes a sentence in d and an edge $(v, u) \in E$ between nodes $v, u \in V$ corresponds to an entity shared by v and u. G_d is called the *projection graph* of d.

4.2 Using graph metrics for coherence scores

We use several graph metrics applied to the graphs $\hat{G}_d$ and G_d associated to document d. Each metric produces a separate coherence score for d. We present these next.

4.2.1 PageRank

PageRank [8] is a vertex ranking metric that gives higher scores to the best connected vertices in a graph. The PageRank score of a node in a graph depends on its indegree and the PageRank scores of those nodes linking to it (the latter being considered as recommendation). Formally, the PageRank of G_d is given by:

$$PR = c \sum_{v \to u} \frac{1}{d_v} PR(u) + (1 - c) \tag{8}$$

where $PR(u)$ is the PageRank of u, d_v is the number of edges incident on node v, and c is a damping factor (typically $c = 0.85$). We hypothesise that a lower median PageRank score is indicative of a more coherent document: as G_d becomes more connected, the relative importance of each node or sentence decreases in the PageRank score. We use the median rather than the average because the average PageRank score does not distinguish between star-graphs (where all but one node are connected to the single remaining node, and no other edges occur) and path graphs (where the nodes occur in sequence); however, path graphs intuitively correspond to coherent discourse flow whereas star graphs do not.

So we propose that the final coherence score of d is the *median* PageRank of nodes of G_d:

$$COH_{PR} = \text{median}_{u \in V} \left(c \sum_{v \to u} \frac{1}{d_v} PR(u) + (1 - c) \right) \tag{9}$$

4.2.2 Clustering Coefficient

The clustering coefficient (CC) measures the extent to which the neighbours of a node in G_d are connected to each other. We hypothesise that a lower clustering coefficient score is indicative of a more coherent document: the fact that the neighbours of any given node in G_d are themselves connected suggests that this node's importance to the overall discourse is very low; if no neighbours are connected, all nodes are equally important for coherence.

We compute the coherence score of d as the global clustering coefficient of G_d:

$$COH_{CC} = \frac{1}{|V|} \sum_{u \in V} \frac{\delta(u)}{\tau(u)} \tag{10}$$

where $\delta(u)$ is the number of closed triplets containing u, and $\tau(u)$ is the total number of open and closed triplets containing u (a *triplet* is a subset of V containing exactly three nodes. A triplet is *open* if exactly two of its three nodes are connected, and *closed* if all three nodes are connected).

4.2.3 Betweenness

The betweenness of a node u measures the fraction of shortest paths in G_d that contain u. We hypothesise that a higher average betweenness score for the nodes of G_d is indicative of a more coherent document: a coherent document d in our context should resemble a path graph where a sentence is connected only to the preceding and next sentence.

We compute the coherence score of d as the average of all betweenness scores in G_d:

$$COH_{BW} = \frac{1}{|V|} \sum_{\forall u \in V} \sum_{s \in V} \sum_{t \in V \setminus s} \frac{\beta_{s,t}(u)}{\beta_{s,t}} \tag{11}$$

where $\beta_{s,t}(u)$ is the number of shortest paths between s and t in V containing u, and $\beta_{s,t}$ is the total number of shortest paths between s and t.

4.2.4 Entity distance

The entity distance between two sentences u and v is the smallest number of words occurring between u and v that do not contain an entity shared by u and v. We reason that a short entity distance implies that shared entities between u and v aid the flow of the text, whereas a high distance means that many other entities are mentioned in between u and v, implying topic drift, and hence lower coherence.

We compute the coherence score of d as the inverse of the average entity distance over all entities shared by two or more sentences:

$$COH_{ED} = \left(\frac{1}{|S|} \sum_{\forall e \in \mathcal{E}} \sum_{i=1} \sum_{j=i+1} l_j(e) - l_i(e) \right)^{-1} \tag{12}$$

where $|S|$ is the number of sentences in d, $\mathcal{E}$ is the set of entities of d occurring in at least two distinct sentences, and $l_i(e)$ and $l_j(e)$ are the locations of entity e in the document. For example, for sentence s_i, the location of entity e could be the 20th term in d, and for s_{i+1}, e could be the 30th term in d.

4.2.5 Adjacent Topic Flow (ATF)

We propose an adjacent topic flow (ATF) metric, which is, roughly, the average of the reciprocal number of shared entities between adjacent sentences. In a coherent document, consecutive sentences should share common entities between them to relate current discourse to past discourse: the fewer shared entities (minimum one) between adjacent sentences, the more focused the discourse and the more coherent the text. We compute the coherence score of d as the average reciprocal of the union of entities between adjacent sentences:

$$COH_{ATF} = \frac{1}{N-1} \sum_{(s_i, s_{i+1})} \frac{1}{\sigma(s_i, s_{i+1})} \qquad (13)$$

where $s_1, \ldots, s_N$ are the sentences in the document and $\sigma(s_i, s_{i+1})$ is the union of entities from sentences s_i and s_{i+1}. The intuition is that adjacent sentences should share entities, but if the union of their entity sets is large this strains the focus of the reader as these entities need not be necessarily linked to previous discourse.

4.2.6 Adjacent Weighted Topic Flow (AWTF)

The ATF metric determines if a pair of adjacent sentences share a single entity irrespective of whether several entities are shared. Thus, a text with two (or more) main topics (e.g. security and heartbleed) mentioned in adjacent sentences would not be detected. For coherence, more shared entities can be seen as more salient words aiding the reader to retain focus as more links exist between current and past discourse. We present a version of ATF called Adjacent Weighted Topic Flow (AWTF) where we *weigh* a document according to the number of entities shared by adjacent sentences. The resulting coherence score is:

$$COH_{AWTF} = \frac{1}{N-1} \sum_{(s_i, s_{i+1})} \omega(s_i, s_{i+1}) \qquad (14)$$

where $\omega(s_i, s_{i+1})$ is the number of shared entities.

4.2.7 Non adjacent Topic Flow Metrics

ATF and AWTF rely on *local* coherence between adjacent sentences to capture global coherence. However, a coherent text may contain discourse gaps where several topics are treated locally, then abandoned, yet later on picked up again. For example, consider a document with three paragraphs of which two are on the same topic as illustrated in Figure 3. Figure 3(B) shows that the application of an

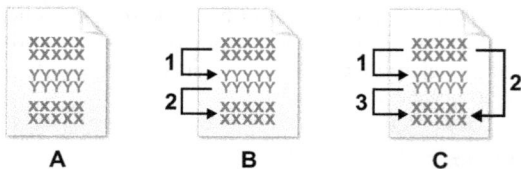

Figure 3: (A) Document with three paragraphs where two are on the same topic. X and Y indicate topics. (B) Application of an adjacent topic flow metric. (C) Application of an non adjacent topic flow metric. Numbers indicate order of comparison.

adjacent-based topic flow metric would find no coherence between the first two and last two sentences. Conversely, Figure 1(C) shows that a *non*-adjacent topic flow metric would find some coherence between the first and last sentence in the second comparison (indicated by the number 2) as they are on the same topic.

We define two coherence models (i) *non-adjacent topic flow (nATF)* and (ii) on *non-adjacent weighted topic flow (nAWTF)*, with corresponding coherence scores:

$$COH_{nATF} = \frac{1}{\hat{E}} \sum_{s_i} \sum_{s_j} \frac{1}{\sigma(s_i, s_j)} \qquad (15)$$

and

$$COH_{nAWTF} = \frac{1}{\hat{E}} \sum_{s_i} \sum_{s_j} \begin{cases} 1 & : \hat{e} \in s_i \wedge s_j \\ 0 & : \text{otherwise} \end{cases} \qquad (16)$$

where $\hat{E}$ is the number of all entities in d shared between at least two sentences. If $\hat{E} = 0$, we set $COH_{nAWTF} = 0$ reflecting that there is no coherence in the document.

Strictly speaking, Equations 13–16 are not graph centrality metrics but as our bipartite graph is a labelled graph all are invariant under graph isomorphism.

We next evaluate the above graph-based models, as well as the entropy models of document coherence presented in Section 3.

5. EVALUATION

First we evaluate the accuracy of our coherence models in Section 5.1, and then retrieval precision when reranking documents according to their coherence scores in Section 5.2.

5.1 Experiment 1: Coherence Model Accuracy

5.1.1 Experimental Setup

We evaluate our coherence models in the *sentence reordering* task, which is standard for coherence evaluation. The main idea is that we scramble the order of the sentences in each document, and subsequently then determine the number of times the original document is deemed more coherent than its permutations. Specifically, for each original document d_o in a dataset, we reorder its sentences 20 times, producing 20 permutations $d_i : i \in [1, \ldots, 20]$. We assume that the more sentences are reordered, the less coherent d_i becomes on average; this assumption has been validated with human assessments [41]. We run our coherence model on all (d_o, d_i) pairs, and measure accuracy by considering as *true positive* each case where d_o gets a higher coherence score than its d_i permutation.

We use the earthquakes and accidents dataset[1], which has been used in previous work on coherence prediction [3], so that we can directly compare our coherence model to the state of the art. This dataset contains relatively clean, curated articles about earthquakes from the North American News Corpus and narratives from the National Transportation Safety Board, of relatively short length and not much variation in document length (statistics in Table 2). We identify entities in documents using the Stanford parser[2]. Due to the steep increase in parsing time as sentence length increases, we only consider sentences of 60 terms or less, which is approximately 3 times the average length of a sentence in English [54]. If a sentence is longer than 60 terms, we do not exclude it, but rather cut it at length 60, to speed up processing.

---

[1] http://people.csail.mit.edu/regina/coherence/
[2] http://nlp.stanford.edu/software/lex-parser.shtml

Table 2: Statistics of the earthquakes and accidents dataset. Average document length is measured in terms; MAD denotes mean absolute deviation.

	Earthquakes	Accidents
# documents	100	100
average doc. length	257.3	223.5
MAD doc. length	101.8	31.9

Our baselines are (i) Barzilay and Lapata's original entity grid model [3], and (ii) Barzilay and Lee's well-known HMM-based model [4]. We do not use Guidnaudeau and Strube's indegree model [28] as they use a different dataset. For the remaining baselines, we compare the *tuned* scores reported in [3] with *untuned* scores of our models.

5.1.2 Sentence Reordering Findings

Table 3 presents the accuracy and statistical significance of the sentence reordering experiments. Our models are overall comparable to the baselines. Our 0-order entropy model outperforms both baselines for both datasets. As its order increases, its performance decreases (but still outperforms both baselines for the accidents dataset). This happens because as the order of our model grows, we expect to find fewer higher-frequency n-grams because our model will rely on increasingly longer sequences of entities. This results in overall higher entropy scores. For example, a 2-gram and 3-gram coherence model of the example entity grid in Table 1 would result in these respective entropy scores $H(2) = 3.2776$ and $H(3) = 3.3219$, which grow as the value of n in the n-gram increases.

Looking at cases where our entropy model errs, we see that there is a potentially negative bias of our model against shorter documents. As our entropy model scores document coherence using the frequency of entity transitions that occur in a document, short documents are at a disadvantage. For example, a very short document of only one sentence where all n-grams occur exactly once will receive a very high entropy score (hence very low coherence score). The minimum number of sentences found in documents in our data were 2 and 3 for the earthquakes and accidents datasets respectively. Our entropy model will very likely deem these documents as incoherent, even if they are not.

Regarding our graph coherence metrics, the PageRank, betweenness, entity distance, ATF, nATF and nAWTF variants also outperform the baselines at all times. Entity distance and betweenness are overall best, outperforming our entropy model too. Both entity distance and betweenness measure the same feature, that is distance between discourse entities, but in different ways: betweenness in terms of shortest path in the graph; entity distance in terms of absolute number of terms separating the entities. It seems that this distance, measured in either way, is more discriminative of coherence than e.g. any clustering or recommendation of discourse entities captured by the clustering coefficient or PageRank respectively.

Overall, manual inspection of the documents where most of our models failed reveals two main reasons for this: (I) These documents contain sentences of very large length, exceeding the 60 term limit we have defined. As we artificially cut these sentences at 60 terms, the discourse flow of the text is disturbed. Moreover, several very long sentences tend to

Table 3: Coherence accuracy in the sentence reordering task. $\pm\%$ is the difference from the strongest baseline and bold means $\geq$ strongest baseline. * marks statistical significance at the 0.05 interval using the paired t-test and ‡ means best overall.

	Method	Earthquakes Acc.	$\pm\%$	Accidents Acc.	$\pm\%$
BASELINES	Entity grid model [3]	69.7%*	–	67.0*	–
	HMM-based model [4]	60.3*	–	31.7*	–
ENTROPY	Entropy-0 order	**75.0**	+7.6%	**73.0***	+9.0%
	Entropy-1 order	64.0	−8.2%	**70.0***	+4.5%
	Entropy-2 order	64.0	−8.2%	**70.0***	+4.5%
GRAPH	PageRank	**75.0**	+7.6%	**73.0***	+9.0%
	Clustering Coef.	67.0	−3.9%	66.0*	−1.5%
	Betweenness	**73.0***	+4.7%	**‡77.0***	+14.9%
	Entity Distance	**‡76.0**	+9.0%	**75.0***	+11.9%
	Adj. Topic Flow	**70.0***	+0.4%	**74.0***	+10.4%
	Adj. W. Topic Flow	61.0*	−12.5%	66.0*	−1.5%
	nAdj. Topic Flow	**70.0**	+0.4%	**70.0**	+4.5%
	nAdj. W. Topic Flow	**70.0**	+0.4%	**70.0***	+4.5%

introduce a large number of new entities into the discourse, which may be topically relevant but not necessarily identical, e.g. *... accommodation with a bed, table, cupboard, attached washroom, television, broadband Internet facility, telephone, small kitchen with facilities to prepare tea, coffee, etc.* (II) The versions of our models that concentrate on entities shared by adjacent sentences risk underperforming, because about 50% of the sentences in English are estimated not to share any entities and 60% of them to be related by weak discourse relations [43]. E.g., for journalistic texts like the earthquake dataset, the spatial proximity of sentences does not necessarily correlate with their semantic relatedness, as related sentences can be placed at the beginning and the end for emphasis [59]. Indeed in Table 3 our two adjacent topic flow metrics ATF and AWTF have lower accuracy in the earthquakes than accident dataset, and also compared to their non-adjacent versions (nATF and nAWTF). Note that this spatial proximity limitation is a major disadvantage of *all* models of local text coherence, not only ours. We discuss this point in Section 6.

Overall, our *untuned* models perform on par with the *tuned* baselines, occasionally outperforming them. Motivated by the good performance of our coherence models, we next study their potential usefulness to retrieval.

5.2 Experiment 2: Retrieval with Coherence

5.2.1 Experimental Setup

We now test whether our document coherence scores can be useful to retrieval. Our assumption is that more coherent documents are likely to be more relevant. To test this we rerank the top 1000 documents retrieved by a baseline model according to their coherence scores. Our baseline ranking model is a unigram, query likelihood, Dirichlet-smoothed, language model. Let RSV be the baseline retrieval status value of a document, and COH be the coherence score of a document computed as per any of our coherence models (Equations 7–16). For our entropy coherence model we use only the 0-order variant, as this performed best in the sentence reranking task. We use a simple *linear* combination [16] to compute the reranked RSV of each document, denoted $\widehat{RSV}$:

$$\widehat{RSV} = RSV \times \alpha + COH \times (1 - \alpha) \qquad (17)$$

where $0 \leq \alpha \leq 1$ is a smoothing parameter controlling the effect of RSV over COH.

We use Indri 5.8[3] for indexing and retrieval without stemming or stopword removal. We use the ClueWeb09 cat.B[4] test collection with queries 150-200 from the Web AdHoc track of TREC 2012. ClueWeb09 contains free text crawled from the web, likely to be more noisy and containing documents that are overall longer and with more variation in document length than in the earthquakes and accidents dataset. We remove spam from ClueWeb09 using the spam rankings of Cormack et al. [15] with a percentile-score < 90 indicating spam. This threshold is stricter than the one recommended in [15], practically meaning that we remove many more documents assumed to be spam. This reduces the number of documents from ca. 50 million to ca. 16 million. We apply such strict spam filtering for the following reason: as we hypothesise that a lower entropy scoring document will be more coherent, documents containing the same repeated entities will be judged more coherent. For example, a document containing only the sentence **free domains, free domains, free domains** would receive an entropy score of 0 (i.e., highest coherence) but is, arguably, not very coherent. While this problem does not occur in the earthquakes and accidents dataset, spam documents are plentiful in ClueWeb09 [15] which is why apply such a strict threshold when removing spam from this collection. We evaluate retrieval with Mean Reciprocal Rank (MRR) of the first relevant result, Precision at 10 (P@10), Mean Average Precision (MAP) of the top 1000 results, and Expected Reciprocal Rank at 20 (ERR@20).

The baseline and our reranking method include parameters μ and α that we tune using 5-fold cross-validation. We report the average of the five test folds. We vary the ranking baseline's $\mu \in \{100, 500, 800, 1000, 2000, 3000, 4000, 5000, 8000, 10000\}$; and the reranking parameter $\alpha \in \{0.5..1\}$ in steps of 0.05.

5.2.2 Retrieval Findings

Table 4 displays the retrieval results. We see that reranking documents by their coherence score overall outperforms the baseline in terms of retrieval precision, with few exceptions. Specifically, the MRR gains vary between +66.2% and +170.9%, which practically translates to a boosting of the first relevant document by moving it approximately one position higher in the ranking on average. The P@10 gains vary between +13.1% and +83.8%, which practically translates to an increase of the portion of relevant documents found in the top 10 from less than 2 in the baseline to over 3 documents on average, except once (for entity distance). This gaining trend also applies to the top 20 retrieved results, as can be seen by the improvements in ERR@20. However, looking at MAP for the top 1000 retrieved documents we see only marginal gains and twice drops in performance (for entropy and entity distance). This means that coherence improves mainly early precision, i.e. has the potential to refine the very top of the ranked list, but not alter it significantly at more depth.

Interestingly, while entity distance was among the best performing models in the sentence reranking task (Table 3), it is the weakest performing model when integrated to retrieval. This complements previous findings in the litera-

[3]http://www.lemurproject.org
[4]http://www.lemurproject.org/clueweb09.php/

Table 4: Retrieval precision without and with coherence. ±% is the difference from the strongest baseline and bold means ≥ strongest baseline.

	Method	MRR	±%	P@10	±%
	Baseline	20.57		19.80	
COHERENCE	Entropy-0 order	**49.50**	+140.6%	**33.00**	+66.7%
	PageRank	**49.85**	+142.3%	**34.40**	+73.7%
	Clustering Coef.	**51.82**	+151.9%	**34.60**	+74.7%
	Betweeness	**49.74**	+141.8%	**36.40**	+83.8%
	Entity Distance	**34.18**	+66.2%	**22.40**	+13.1%
	Adj. Topic Flow	**55.73**	+170.9%	**34.20**	+72.7%
	Adj. W. Topic Flow	**51.60**	+150.8%	**34.20**	+72.7%
	nAdj. Topic Flow	**50.62**	+146.1%	**34.40**	+73.7%
	nAdj. W. Topic Flow	**50.79**	+146.9%	**34.60**	+74.7%

	Method	MAP	±%	ERR@20	±%
	Baseline	10.07		11.78	
COHERENCE	Entropy-0 order	09.79	−2.8%	**20.18**	+71.3%
	PageRank	**10.12**	+0.5%	**21.15**	+79.5%
	Clustering Coef.	**10.20**	+1.3%	**21.19**	+79.9%
	Betweeness	**10.08**	+0.1%	**21.98**	+85.6%
	Entity Distance	07.22	−28.3%	**15.86**	+34.6%
	Adj. Topic Flow	**10.12**	+0.5%	**21.87**	+85.6%
	Adj. W. Topic Flow	**10.12**	+0.5%	**22.65**	+92.3%
	nAdj. Topic Flow	**10.13**	+0.6%	**21.16**	+79.6%
	nAdj. W. Topic Flow	**10.13**	+0.6%	**21.15**	+79.5%

ture showing that, when using an NLP component in IR, higher NLP accuracy does not necessarily result in higher retrieval performance [24]. The reason why entity distance underperforms when integrated to retrieval compared to sentence reranking could be the different dataset characteristics: earthquakes and accidents include relatively short documents (roughly 240 terms long on average) that are fairly uniform (on average 65 terms of mean absolute deviation), see Table 2. ClueWeb09 on the other hand includes documents that are longer (1461 terms long on average) and more heterogeneous in style and size. In fact, quite a few of the ClueWeb09 documents are Wikipedia articles, which are fairly long and organised in thematic subsections, meaning that salient entities might be introduced, then dropped for a while, and later on picked up again in different subsections. This is likely to affect negatively entity distance, much more than our other coherence metrics, as it is the only metric that measures the actual distance in words between occurrences of the same entity in different sentences. So, for those documents where this distance varies wildly, reaching both very low and very high numbers, the entity distance will produce notably different coherence scores for different documents, rendering a comparison between documents on the basis of these scores difficult.

Finally, note that the baseline scores in Table 4 are not directly comparable to the ones reported in the literature when using no spam filter or another spam filter threshold, because the stricter the spam filtering, the smaller the final dataset used for retrieval and the higher the risk of removing relevant documents. Indeed, it has been reported that for ClueWeb09 cat.B, removing spam results in overall lower precision [5, 42]. We also anecdotally report that several documents among the ones we removed as spam were assessed as relevant in the TREC relevance judgements.

Overall we conclude that the improvements in Table 4 show that coherence can be a discriminative feature of relevance.

6. DISCUSSION AND FUTURE WORK

We now discuss interesting caveats of our coherence models and potential solutions.

One weakness of our coherence models, and of the entity grid in fact, is in capturing the contribution of newly introduced entities to discourse: it is long assumed that repeated mentions of the same entities contribute to coherence; however, related-yet-not-identical entities also contribute to text coherence. To our knowledge, this is something that occurs frequently in text but that is not yet captured by automatic models of coherence prediction. Doing so would require a richer set of metrics and representations, involving for instance methods long used in IR for detecting near-synonyms, such as WordNet-type ontologies, or term associations extracted from large scale query logs or other relevant corpora. This is an interesting research direction that we intend to follow in the future.

A further limitation of our coherence models is the selection of salient discourse entities: following [3], we consider all subjects and objects as salient discourse entities. This assumption implies that (a) all subjects and objects are equally salient in text, and (b) all subjects and objects are topical (as opposed to having a modifying or periphrastic role in the discourse). However, neither of these assumptions is true. Assumption (a) could be removed by including some salience weighting component in the selection of entities. In the past, this has been attempted through the use of linguistic features, such as modifiers and named entity types [19]. It will be interesting to see if we can also use statistical approximations to this end, looking into the rich IR literature in term weighting. Assumption (b) could be removed by including a similar topical weighting component, such as in [18]. In the case where coherence scores are used for IR, it makes sense to align this topical detection to the query topic, so that, for instance, coherence is computed only for documents whose topic is relevant to the query topic. Such a tight integration of coherence modelling to ranking would be an interesting direction to explore in future work.

7. CONCLUSIONS

Modelling text coherence is an area that has received a lot of interest, with a surge of automatic methods in the last decade. We presented two novel classes of models of document coherence which extend the well-known *entity grid* representation [3]. Our first model approximates coherence as the inverse of the discourse entropy in text, based on the assumption that repeated entities in text, which have low entropy, indicate higher coherence. Our second class of coherence models map the entity grid of a document into a graph, as proposed by Guinaudeau & Strube [28], and then approximate document coherence using different metrics of graph topology and their variations. The assumption is that the discourse flow of a document can be reflected in the topology of its entity graph, hence any regularities of the former may be measured from the latter.

We report two experiments. In the first, we find that our coherence models are comparable to two well-known text coherence models. Given that our models are completely untuned, their performance may be further improved through smoothing. In the second experiment, we find that using our coherence scores to rerank retrieved documents improves retrieval precision, especially for the top 1-20 results.

Overall, this work contributes two novel classes of document coherence models that approximate coherence from discourse entity n-grams. Their application to retrieval complements recent work in IR showing a positive relation between relevance and document cohesiveness or comprehensibility [5, 56] (albeit computed differently than we do). This is a promising research direction for IR that we intend to pursue in the future.

Acknowledgments.

Partially funded by the second author's *FREJA research excellence* fellowship (grant no. 790095).

8. REFERENCES

[1] E. Banik. Extending a surface realizer to generate coherent discourse. In *ACL/IJCNLP (Short Papers)*, pages 305–308. ACL, 2009.

[2] R. Barzilay, N. Elhadad, and K. McKeown. Inferring strategies for sentence ordering in multidocument news summarization. *J. Artif. Intell. Res. (JAIR)*, 17:35–55, 2002.

[3] R. Barzilay and M. Lapata. Modeling local coherence: An entity-based approach. *ACL*, 34(1):1–34, 2008.

[4] R. Barzilay and L. Lee. Catching the drift: Probabilistic content models, with applications to generation and summarization. In *HLT-NAACL*, pages 113–120, 2004.

[5] M. Bendersky, W. B. Croft, and Y. Diao. Quality-biased ranking of web documents. In *WSDM*, pages 95–104, 2011.

[6] A. L. Berger, V. J. D. Pietra, and S. A. D. Pietra. A maximum entropy approach to natural language processing. *ACL*, 1996.

[7] K. Bicknell and R. Levy. A model of local coherence effects in human sentence processing as consequences of updates from bottom-up prior to posterior beliefs. In *NAACL*, pages 665–673, 2009.

[8] S. Brin and L. Page. The anatomy of a large-scale hypertextual web search engine. *CN & ISDN*, pages 107–117, 1998.

[9] J. Burstein, J. Tetreault, and S. Andreyev. Using entity-based features to model coherence in student essays. In *NAACL*, pages 681–684, 2010.

[10] C. Cachin. *Entropy measures and unconditional security in cryptography.* Hartung-Gorre Konstanz, 1997.

[11] A. Çelikyilmaz and D. Hakkani-Tür. Discovery of topically coherent sentences for extractive summarization. In Lin et al. [39], pages 491–499.

[12] E. Chen, B. Snyder, and R. Barzilay. Incremental text structuring with online hierarchical ranking. In *EMNLP-CoNLL*, pages 83–91. ACL, 2007.

[13] H. Chen, S. R. K. Branavan, R. Barzilay, and D. R. Karger. Global models of document structure using latent permutations. In *HLT-NAACL*, pages 371–379. ACL, 2009.

[14] J. C. K. Cheung and G. Penn. Entity-based local coherence modelling using topological fields. In *ACL*, pages 186–195, 2010.

[15] G. V. Cormack, M. D. Smucker, and C. L. Clarke. Efficient and effective spam filtering and re-ranking for large web datasets. *IR*, 14(5):441–465, 2011.

[16] N. Craswell, S. Robertson, H. Zaragoza, and M. Taylor. Relevance weighting for query independent evidence. In *SIGIR*, pages 416–423, 2005.

[17] M. Elsner and E. Charniak. Coreference-inspired coherence modeling. In *ACL (Short Papers)*, pages 41–44. ACL, 2008.

[18] M. Elsner and E. Charniak. Disentangling chat with local coherence models. In Lin et al. [39], pages 1179–1189.

[19] M. Elsner and E. Charniak. Extending the entity grid with entity-specific features. In *AMACL*, pages 125–129, 2011.

[20] T. Enos. *Encyclopedia of rhetoric and composition: Communication from ancient times to the information*

age, volume 1389. 1996.

[21] K. Filippova and M. Strube. The german vorfeld and local coherence. *Journal of Logic, Language and Information*, 16(4):465–485, 2007.

[22] P. Foltz, W. Kintsch, and T. Landauer. The measurement of textual coherence with latent semantic analysis. *Discourse Processes*, 25(2&3):285–307, 1998.

[23] P. Fung and G. Ngai. One story, one flow: Hidden markov story models for multilingual multidocument summarization. *TSLP*, 3(2):1–16, 2006.

[24] W. Gao, C. Niu, J. Nie, M. Zhou, K. Wong, and H. Hon. Exploiting query logs for cross-lingual query suggestions. *ACM Trans. Inf. Syst.*, 28(2), 2010.

[25] B. J. Grosz, A. K. Joshi, and S. Weinstein. Providing a unified account of definite noun phrases in discourse. In *AMACL*, pages 44–50, 1983.

[26] B. J. Grosz and C. L. Sidner. Attention, intentions, and the structure of discourse. *ACL*, pages 175–204, 1986.

[27] B. J. Grosz, S. Weinstein, and A. K. Joshi. Centering: A framework for modeling the local coherence of discourse. *ACL*, pages 203–225, 1995.

[28] C. Guinaudeau and M. Strube. Graph-based local coherence modeling. In *ACL*, pages 93–103, 2013.

[29] M. K. Halliday and R. Hasan. *Cohesion in English*. Longman, London, 1976.

[30] D. A. Huffman. A method for the construction of minimum-redundancy codes. *IRE*, 40(9):1098–1101, 1952.

[31] A. K. Joshi and S. Weinstein. Control of inference: Role of some aspects of discourse structure-centering. In *IJCAI*, pages 385–387, 1981.

[32] T. Kanungo and D. Orr. Predicting the readability of short web summaries. In *WSDM*, pages 202–211, 2009.

[33] N. Karamanis. Evaluating centering for sentence ordering in two new domains. In *NAACL*, pages 65–68, 2006.

[34] N. Karamanis, C. Mellish, M. Poesio, and J. Oberlander. Evaluating centering for information ordering using corpora. *ACL*, 35(1):29–46, 2009.

[35] A. Kehler. *Coherence, Reference and the Theory of Grammar*. CSLI Publications, California, 2002.

[36] R. Kibble. A reformulation of rule 2 of centering theor. *ACL*, 27(4):579–587, 2001.

[37] R. Kibble and R. Power. Optimizing referential coherence in text generation. *ACL*, 30(4):401–416, 2004.

[38] M. Lapata. Probabilistic text structuring: Experiments with sentence ordering. In *ACL*, pages 545–552, 2003.

[39] D. Lin, Y. Matsumoto, and R. Mihalcea, editors. *ACL 2011*. ACL, 2011.

[40] Z. Lin, C. Liu, H. T. Ng, and M.-Y. Kan. Combining coherence models and machine translation evaluation metrics for summarization evaluation. In *ACL (1)*, pages 1006–1014. ACL, 2012.

[41] Z. Lin, H. T. Ng, and M.-Y. Kan. Automatically evaluating text coherence using discourse relations. In Lin et al. [39], pages 997–1006.

[42] C. Lioma, B. Larsen, and W. Lu. Rhetorical relations for information retrieval. In *SIGIR*, pages 931–940, 2012.

[43] A. Louis and A. Nenkova. Creating local coherence: An empirical assessment. In *NAACL*, pages 313–316, 2010.

[44] A. Louis and A. Nenkova. A coherence model based on syntactic patterns. In *EMNLP-CoNLL*, pages 1157–1168. ACL, 2012.

[45] W. C. Mann and S. A. Thompson. Rhetorical structure theory: Toward a functional theory of text organization. pages 243–281, 1998.

[46] C. D. Manning and H. Schütze. *Foundations of statistical natural language processing*. MIT Press, 2001.

[47] J. Mikk. Prior knowledge of text content and values of text characteristics. *Journal of Quantitative Linguistics*, 8(1):67–80, 2001.

[48] E. Miltsakaki and K. Kukich. Evaluation of text coherence for electronic essay scoring systems. *Natural Language Engineering*, 10(1):25–55, 2004.

[49] A. Ntoulas, M. Najork, M. Manasse, and D. Fetterly. Detecting spam web pages through content analysis. In L. Carr, D. D. Roure, A. Iyengar, C. A. Goble, and M. Dahlin, editors, *WWW*, pages 83–92. ACM, 2006.

[50] E. Pitler and A. Nenkova. Revisiting readability: A unified framework for predicting text quality. In *EMNLP*, pages 186–195. ACL, 2008.

[51] M. Poesio, R. Stevenson, B. D. Eugenio, and J. Hitzeman. Centering: A parametric theory and its instantiations. *ACL*, 30(3):309–363, 2004.

[52] C. E. Shannon. A mathematical theory of communication. *Bell System Technical Journal*, 3(27):379–423, 1948.

[53] H. Shin and J. F. Stach. Using long runs as predictors of semantic coherence in a partial document retrieval system. In *NAACL-ANLP*, pages 6–13, 2000.

[54] B. Sigurd, M. Eeg-Olofsson, and J. Van Weijer. Word length, sentence length and frequency–zipf revisited. *Studia Linguistica*, 58(1):37–52, 2004.

[55] R. Soricut and D. Marcu. Discourse generation using utility-trained coherence models. In N. Calzolari, C. Cardie, and P. Isabelle, editors, *ACL*. ACL, 2006.

[56] C. Tan, E. Gabrilovich, and B. Pang. To each his own: personalized content selection based on text comprehensibility. In *WSDM*, pages 233–242, 2012.

[57] I. Tapiero. *Situation Models and Levels of Coherence: Towards a Definition of Comprehension*. Lawrence Erlbaum Associates, Manwah, New Jersey, 2007.

[58] D. Xiong, Y. Ding, M. Zhang, and C. L. Tan. Lexical chain based cohesion models for document-level statistical machine translation. In *EMNLP*, pages 1563–1573, 2013.

[59] R. Zhang. Sentence ordering driven by local and global coherence for summary generation. In *ACL*, pages 6–11, 2011.

[60] Y. Zhou and W. B. Croft. Document quality models for web ad hoc retrieval. In *CIKM*, pages 331–332, 2005.

Improving Patent Search by Search Result Diversification

Youngho Kim
yhkim@cs.umass.edu

W. Bruce Croft
croft@cs.umass.edu

Center for Intelligent Information Retrieval, College of Information and Computer Sciences
University of Massachusetts Amherst, MA 01003, USA

ABSTRACT

Patent retrieval has some unique features relative to web search. One major task in this domain is finding existing patents that may invalidate new patents, known as prior-art or invalidity search, where search queries can be formulated from query patents (i.e., new patents). Since a patent document generally contains long and complex descriptions, generating effective search queries can be complex and difficult. Typically, these queries must cover diverse aspects of the new patent application in order to retrieve relevant documents that cover the full scope of the patent. Given this context, search diversification techniques can potentially improve the retrieval performance of patent search by introducing diversity into the document ranking. In this paper, we examine the effectiveness for patent search of a recent term-based diversification framework. Using this framework involves developing methods to identify effective phrases related to the topics mentioned in the query patent. In our experiments, we evaluate our diversification approach using standard measures of retrieval effectiveness and diversity, and show significant improvements relative to state-of-the-art baselines.

Categories and Subject Descriptors

H.3.3 [**Information Storage and Retrieval**]: Information Search and Retrieval – retrieval models

General Terms

Algorithms, Experimentation.

Keywords

Search result diversification; prior-art search; patent retrieval;

1. INTRODUCTION

Patent Information Retrieval (Patent IR) is unique and very different from general web search. One major task in this domain is finding existing patents that may invalidate new patents, known as prior-art search or invalidity search [15][30][35]. In this task, users typically input a query document (the new patent), and the search system returns the set of "relevant" patents. Since the whole document is input as an initial query, query processing techniques (e.g., automatic query generation) need to be employed. Henceforth, we refer to this type of prior-art search as "patent search" or "patent retrieval".

Since a patent document generally contains long and complex descriptions of its invention, formulating effective queries is a very difficult task [2][22]. To reduce the burden for users, an automatic

Query Patent
Title: Method and apparatus for providing content on a computer system based on usage profile.
Abstract A method and apparatus for determining a *computer system usage profile* … A *basic input output system (BIOS) module* and/or an *operating system module* obtain computer system usage profile information by tracking events such as the *frequency of reboots*, the *time* required to *boot up* and *shutdown* the operating system … data is collected and communicated to a *profile server*…

Search Query Automatically Generated by [42]
usage, *profile*, *reboot*, *time*, *os*, bootstrap, *boot*, memory, manage, processor, video, firmware, *network*, database, ~

List of Relevant Documents

No.	Title	Topic
R1	Extended *BIOS* adapted to establish remote communication for diagnostics and repair	*BIOS*
R2	*BIOS* emulation of a hard file image as a diskette	
R3	*Operating system* architecture with reserved memory space resident program code identified in file system name space	*operating system*
R4	Method for loading an *operating system* through a network	
R5	Method and apparatus for *controlling network* and workstation access	*profile server*
…	…	…

Figure 1: Query Patent Example

query generation has been researched (e.g., [16][33][42]). Since the generation is based on the whole query patent, generated queries could potentially contain hundreds of terms. Note that in this paper, we assume that users only provide a query patent, and search queries are automatically generated based on the input query patents. Typically, search queries must cover diverse aspects of the new patent application in order to retrieve relevant documents that cover the full scope of the patent. Figure 1 shows an example query patent. In this example, the patent application includes several components such as "usage profile", "BIOS", and "operating system". Accordingly, the queries automatically generated for this patent contain the terms to describe each component (e.g., {"reboot", "time", "boot"} for "usage profile information"). In other words, multiple aspects (or topics) are covered in a patent query, and it is important to diversify any retrieval result by covering as many of these aspects as possible. We discuss this example again later in this section.

In the literature, one important task for patent search is automatically generating effective queries. Given a query patent, several methods (e.g., [33][42]) focus on ranking the terms from the query patent, and selecting the top *n* terms to form a query. Similarly, sentence ranking, i.e., selecting the top ranked sentences from the patent to use as a query, has also been proposed [16]. In addition, query expansion techniques have been applied to this task of generating effective queries (e.g., [17][32]). Other research on patent retrieval has developed effective retrieval frameworks (e.g., [29][34]). None of this research has studied the problem of search result diversification for patent search.

Search result diversification is the process of re-ordering an initial retrieval result so that the final ranked list can include more diverse topics associated with the query [10][39] (henceforth, "query aspect" is referred to as "query topic" [8][12]). In web search, this technique is adopted for clarifying vague information needs, e.g., a web query "slate" can represent one of a broad range of topics. However, in this paper, we exploit diversification techniques for improving the retrieval performance of patent search by covering more of the topics described in a query patent.

In general, a patent document contains approximately 3,900 words on average [20] and includes complex structure [2][14] (e.g., title, abstract, claim, background and summary sections). In that structure, diverse claims are specified, and background patents related to the application are described. In addition, patent applications can describe multiple components. Thus, we can find a range of topics in a query patent, and the relevant documents can relate to some or all of these topics. Returning to the example in Figure 1, the patent application describes several important topics such as *BIOS*, *operating system,* etc. We can group similar relevant documents pertaining to each topic. For example, R1 and R2 are related to a topic *BIOS*, whereas R3 and R4 refers to *operating system*. In addition, R5 describes a method for controlling network, which relate to another query topic (i.e., *profile server*). Based on these topics, the retrieval result can be diversified, meaning that the ranked documents can be optimized to cover the range of topics. Although a long search query can contain diverse query terms (as shown in Figure 1), the diversity of its retrieval result is not optimized unless a result-level diversification technique is applied. Since relevant documents are related to diverse query topics, diversification techniques (e.g., [1][39]) could also improve overall retrieval effectiveness. For example, the diversification framework proposed in [11] has been shown to improve the ranking of relevant documents in TREC collections, not only in terms of diversity but also in terms of general effectiveness measures (see [11]).

Given this motivation, we explore the problem of *patent search result diversification*. In this diversification process, query topics are first identified, and then re-ranking algorithms (e.g., [10][39]) are applied with the identified topics. Most early research on diversification for web search relied on manually identified topics for a query. In recent research, automatic identification of the topics related to a query has been shown to be effective (e.g., [12][13][18]), but the topics are derived from other resources (e.g., web corpora, web anchor text, and query logs [12][13][36]) that are limited to provide clear information about query topics. On the other hand, in patent search we can potentially identify query topics via the detailed descriptions contained in query patents. Thus, we propose a method to automatically identify query topics based on query documents as follows. Note that we use the terms "query document" and "query patent" interchangeably to refer to a new patent document being validated by prior-art search.

Given a query patent, we extract phrase-level topic vocabulary as the basis for query topics. However, we do not adopt any additional topic structures or grouping of phrases because recognizing such structure is expensive and typically does not lead to significant

improvements on diversification performance [11]. Instead, we rank candidate phrases (extracted from a query patent) by combining information such as topicality [27], predictiveness [28], query performance predictors (e.g., query clarity [9]), relevance to query patents, cohesiveness, etc. Then, we consider the top k phrases as topic phrases used for diversification. Following [11], we also use topicality and predictiveness for finding topic phrases. In addition to this, we assume that query performance predictors (e.g., query scope [19]), relevance to query patents (e.g., relevance model [26]) and cohesiveness of phrase terms will also help to identify topic phrases. In order to combine these features, we adopt a learning-to-rank framework that places phrases important to more relevant topics (i.e., topics of relevant documents) at higher ranks. After generating topic phrases, we apply a state-of-the-art diversification algorithm and diverse ranked results are produced.

To summarize, the main contribution of our work is a study of *patent search result diversification* with the aim of improving patent search performance. Our work is the first attempt to exploit result-level diversification techniques for patent search. In addition, through experiments, we investigate the effectiveness of diversification techniques in patent search environments. The primary difference of our work to existing diversification research (e.g., [11][13]) is that we directly derive phrase-level topics from query documents that provide more information than web queries. In addition, we investigate multiple features (e.g., relevance and cohesiveness) to identify query topics. These are reflected in our topic phrase identification method (in Section 3.3). We evaluate our method by comparing it with DSPApprox, a state-of-the-art topic term identification method [11].

The rest of this paper is organized as follows. Section 2 describes related work. In Section 3, we formulate the problem of patent search result diversification, and present our diversification framework. Section 4 describes experimental settings, and Section 5 provides results. Finally, Section 6 concludes this paper.

2. RELATED WORK

2.1 Patent Search

The research related to improving patent search can be classified into two categories: 1) automatic query generation (e.g., [16][33][42]), and 2) developing retrieval models (e.g., [34][43]). There is other research related to patent retrieval (e.g., patent query translation), but this is less relevant for our work.

Automatic query generation: To generate effective queries, previous studies have used the full text of patent applications. They rank the terms in query patents, and select the top n terms for the query. Xue and Croft [42] extracted query terms from the "brief summary" section of query patents by TFIDF scoring. Mahdabi et al. [33] used Kullback-Leibler divergence between query models and collection models for term ranking. To improve single term queries, they extracted key phrases by TFIDF and Mutual Information-based scoring, and expand the initial term queries by the key phrases. Similar to this approach, Ganguly et al. [16] selected the top sentences ranked by similarity to pseudo-relevant documents for query patents. Another approach to generating effective queries exploits query expansion techniques (e.g., [17][32]). Some of this research used external resources for the expansion, e.g., Wikipedia [29] and WordNet [32]. Also, [23] used decision trees to generate effective terms from pseudo-relevant documents. Among these approaches, we applied several methods (i.e., [16][33][42]) in our experiments and used the best one to generate the initial retrieval results for diversification. The most recent and related approach for generating queries is proposed in

[25]. Similar to our work, they also propose to retrieve diverse relevant documents. However, given a query patent, they generate n diverse queries, and accordingly n different retrieval results are returned (i.e., query-side diversification), which may delay completing a search task. On the other hand, we propose a result-diversification framework, and a single retrieval result is generated for each query patent.

Retrieval models: In early research, existing retrieval models for adhoc retrieval were studied in the context of patent search (e.g., [20]). Through several evaluation competitions for patent retrieval (e.g., NTCIR [15], TREC [30], and CLEF-IP [35]), various refinements to the retrieval methods have been proposed. In experiments, we run an initial retrieval for diversification by using one of the best approaches in these competitions (i.e., [29]).

2.2 Search Result Diversification

Search result diversification is the task of generating a ranked list of documents that covers a range of query topics (or aspects). Previous work on this task can be categorized as: 1) implicit or 2) explicit [39]. We provide a brief summary for each category.

Implicit diversification: The implicit approach does not assume any explicit representation of query topics. MMR [3] and its probabilistic variants [45] can be included in this approach. For diversification, these methods assume that each document in the initial retrieval results represents its own topic and iteratively selects the documents that are dissimilar to previously chosen documents. To measure the dissimilarity, MMR used content-based similarity functions, but probabilistic distance in the language modeling framework has also been used in [45]. In addition, the correlation between documents is adopted as a similarity measure [37][41], and the diversification problem is viewed as minimizing the correlation.

Explicit diversification: In contrast to the implicit method, this approach requires some representation of query topics (e.g., [1][10] [39]). There are two different approaches to implementing explicit diversification: *redundancy* and *proportionality*. The redundancy approach is used in many existing methods (e.g., IA-Select [1], xQuAD [39]). These aim to provide less redundant information in the diversified results, i.e., documents are promoted if they include *novel* content that has not appeared in early ranks. On the other hand, the proportionality-based algorithms (e.g., PM-2 [10]) choose the documents with respect to the "popularity" of their topics in the initial ranking, i.e., ranking the documents is proportional to the popularity of each query topic. Both of these approaches have been successful with test collections that contain manually created query topics (e.g., from TREC descriptions [10][39] and taxonomies [1]).

To provide a more realistic context, methods for automatically generating query topics have been studied (e.g., [11][12][36]). As an example, query topics have been generated by clustering similar queries from query logs [36] or anchor texts from the web [12]. More recently, term-level diversification [11] has showed the effectiveness of automatic topic generation based on identifying important vocabulary terms. In this approach, query topics are described by some set of terms, and instead of generating the topics directly, only the important words and phrases associated with the topics are automatically identified, e.g., the words "pain", "joint", "woodwork", and "type" are identified for the latent topics of "joint pain" and "woodwork joint type". After identifying the important vocabulary, the diversification framework (e.g., xQuAD or PM-2) is applied using the identified topic terms (the frameworks consider each term as a topic). The effectiveness of these automatically-

found topic terms has been shown to be similar to the manually generated topics, and significantly better than other approaches to automatic topic identification. Our diversification framework for patents uses this approach, and we focus on identifying topic phrases (e.g., "file system" and "system service") and diversifying with respect to these phrases.

2.3 Automatic Topic Term Identification

As reported in [11], automatically identifying topic terms helps to improve diversification. In [11], a set of terms to represent initial retrieval results is generated for an initial ranked list of documents. This is similar to the goal of multi-document summarization (e.g., [27][28][38]). Thus, DSPApprox, a hierarchical summarization algorithm proposed in [28], has been used for identifying topic terms in [11]. This algorithm iteratively selects the terms which maximize *predictiveness* and *topicality*. We describe this algorithm in Section 3.3. In addition to predictiveness and topicality, in this paper we explore additional features to identify topic phrases, i.e., relevance, cohesiveness, and query performance predictors (see Section 3.3.2). Moreover, we examine the effectiveness of these features in the context of diversification.

3. PATENT SEARCH DIVERSIFICATION

3.1 Problem Formulation

Diversification in patent search is designed to improve the retrieval effectiveness of initial ranked results. As discussed in Section 1, we assume that diverse topics are involved in a query patent, and that diversification of initial search results based on those topics will improve retrieval performance.

Given a query patent Q, let $T = \{t_1, t_2, ..., t_n\}$ be a topic set for Q and for each topic t_i, some weight $w(t_i)$ is defined. Note that this weight is used as the importance [39] or popularity [10] by the diversification algorithm applied. In addition, an initial document list for Q is given, $D = \{d_1, d_2, ..., d_m\}$, and each d_i's relevance to t_i can be estimated, $\Pr(d_i|t_i)$. Using $\langle T, w(t_i), \Pr(d_i|t_i) \rangle$, diversification algorithms (e.g., [10][39]) typically generate a subset of D which forms a diverse rank result S where S contains a target number of documents. However, recent work [11] found that explicitly specified topic structures (i.e., T) (e.g., grouping topic terms to represent topics such as $t_1 = \{$"user", "data"$\}$ and $t_2 = \{$"share", "security"$\}$) are less beneficial for improving search performance. Instead, only identifying topic terms (e.g., "data", "security", "share", "user") and directly using such terms without the more complex step of topic identification can be effective. Based on this observation, we apply a term-level diversification method to patent search. Instead of using unigram terms, we use phrases to express patent topics because patent documents frequently contain longer technical terms (e.g., "file system"). In addition, phrasal concepts can be effective to retrieve more relevant documents [24][33]. Thus, we identify a set of topic phrases for T, and apply diversification frameworks using these phrases. The formal definition of this diversification method is given as follows.

Let us assume that a topic $t \in T$ can be represented by an arbitrary set of phrases, i.e., $t = \{p_1, p_2, ..., p_{\#(t)}\}$ where p_i is a topic phrase for Q and $\#(t)$ is the number of phrases to form t. Then, T can be rephrased as:

$$T' = \left\{ \left\{ p_1^{t_1}, p_2^{t_1}, ..., p_{\#(t_1)}^{t_1} \right\}, ..., \left\{ p_1^{t_n}, p_2^{t_n}, ..., p_{\#(t_n)}^{t_n} \right\} \right\}$$

We define a set of phrases that can contain all phrases in T', i.e., $P' = \{p | \forall p \in T'\}$, and the phrase-level diversification is defined as generating a diverse ranked list $S \subset D$ using P'. In effect, each phrase is treated as a topic in the diversification model (see Section

3.2). As a result of diversification, S covers more topic phrases and contains more diverse relevant documents. Next, we describe the diversification framework we use.

3.2 Diversification Framework

Explicit diversification methods (e.g., PM-2 [10] and xQuAD [39]) assume that some set of query topics (or aspects) is specified, and generate diverse ranked results based on these topics. Among many algorithms, we select to use the proportionality-based approach (PM-2) [10] for our diversification task, which is the most recently proposed state-of-the-art technique. The proportionality-based approach focuses on generating a proportional representation of query topics in the final retrieval result, i.e., the documents related to an "important" (i.e., large-portion) query topic are promoted. So, more relevant documents for such an important topic would be found in the diversified result. On the other hand, redundancy-based approaches (e.g., xQuAD) attempt to have as many diverse topics as possible in the final result by demoting the documents related to the query topics already considered in the diversification process. Thus, relevant documents related to some important query topics could be missed by diversification.

The proportionality-based approach exploits the Sainte-Laguë method, allocating seats in proportional representation, for assigning the portions of topics in S such that the number of each topic's documents in S is *proportional* to the weight of the topic, i.e., w_i. Specifically, PM-2 requires a set of topics T, an initial document retrieval list D, and an empty list S. In each iteration, the quotient qt_i of each topic t_i is computed as:

$$qt_i = \frac{w_i}{2s_i + 1} \qquad (1)$$

where s_i is the current portion of t_i in S.

Using this, PM-2 selects the most proportional topic t_i^* with the largest qt_i, and places the document $d^* \in D$ into S such that d^* is mostly relevant to t_i^* as well as other topics:

$$d^* \leftarrow \underset{d \in D}{\mathrm{argmax}}\ \lambda \cdot qt_i^* \cdot \Pr(d|t_i^*) + (1 - \lambda) \sum_{i \neq i^*} qt_i \cdot \Pr(d|t_i) \quad (2)$$

where $p(d|t_i)$ is an estimated relevance of d to t_i.

Although Eq. (2) is effective for diversifying web search results, this looks somewhat limited to work for patent search. In PM-2, Eq. (2) only considers the relevance of a document to each topic, not directly to the whole query patent. This setting could work for web search results because the diversification aims to clarify ambiguous web queries. On the other hand, patent search is recall-oriented, i.e., not missing relevant documents in a relatively long retrieval result is more important than placing them at top ranks. So, keeping the documents "relevant" to Q (by some estimation) in S is important. To do this, we combine Eq. (2) with the relevance score of d for Q.

$$d^* \leftarrow \underset{d \in D}{\mathrm{argmax}}\ \mu \cdot \mathrm{relevance}(d) + (1 - \mu) \cdot \mathrm{diversity}(d) \quad (3)$$

where $\mathrm{relevance}(d)$ is an estimated relevance score of d for Q and $\mathrm{diversity}(d)$ is the diversity score calculated by Eq. (2).

By Eq. (3), we can choose the document not only related to the appropriate topic but also highly relevant to the query patent. In other words, we basically keep as many relevant documents as possible in S, and would promote the relevant documents related to important topics by the diversity term (i.e., Eq. (2)). In experiments, we use the retrieval score obtained by the baseline retrieval model

as the estimation of $\mathrm{relevance}(d)$. After selecting d^*, the algorithm updates the portion of each topic in S (i.e., s_i) by its normalized relevance to d^*:

$$s_i = s_i + \frac{\Pr(d^*|t_i)}{\sum_j \Pr(d^*|t_j)} \qquad (4)$$

Then, this process is repeated with the updated s_i, and stops after S contains a target number of documents (e.g., top 100 documents in a retrieval result). Besides, the final ranking of a document is determined by the order in which the document is included in S.

As described in Section 3.1., we use phrase-level diversification for patent search, and thus the set of topic phrases (interpreted as topics) is the input to this diversification model. In the next section, we present our method to generate topic phrases, which is important for diversification performance.

3.3 Automatic Topic Phrase Identification

The goal of identifying topic phrases is generating a list of effective phrases for diversification. As discussed in Section 3.1, we need to generate P' which contains all possible phrases to represent query topics. This is an important task because the diversification model (in Section 3.2) assigns the documents in S primarily based on the input phrases. To identify topic phrases, we assume that each query patent includes sufficient terms to represent its topics.

Given a query patent Q, we extract a set of candidate noun phrases, $P = \{p_1, p_2, ...\}$ syntactically recognized[1] in Q, and some subset of P would be an effective set of topic phrases, i.e., P'. To obtain P', previous work [11] has used DSPApprox, the multi-document summarization technique proposed in [27][28]. Since this algorithm can generate a set of terms to efficiently summarize target documents, it is also useful to find a diverse set of topic terms (i.e., phrases) for Q (as shown in [11]). Thus, we can also use DSPApprox for generating P' as follows.

Given an initial document list for Q, we define a set of vocabulary as the terms that appear in at least two documents and are not numbers. For each candidate phrase, we define *topicality* as the extent of how informative the phrase is to describe Q, and *predictiveness* as its ability to predict the occurrences of other vocabulary terms. Note that these terms are also defined in [27][28]. To measure topicality, a relevance model [26] for Q is generated and the clarity score [9] of each phrase is computed using the relevance model. To estimate predictiveness, the conditional probability of a phrase for a vocabulary term can be used (as done in [27]). Specifically, the affinity of a phrase to each vocabulary term is estimated by the conditional probability, and highly predictive phrases are more likely to appear with more vocabulary terms. Based on these definitions, DSPApprox iteratively selects topic phrases by maximizing their topicality and predictiveness. The details of this approach are described in [11].

Since DSPApprox is a simple greedy algorithm only considering topicality and predictiveness, to improve the identification process we propose a learning-to-rank framework that combines these two features with other features. In experiments, we compare the diversification results obtained by both DSPApprox and the learning-to-rank method.

3.3.1 Learning-to-rank Topic Identification

In order to identify effective topic phrases, we rank the candidate phrases extracted from the query patent, i.e., P, and use the top k phrases as topic phrases. For this, our ranking model produces a

---

[1] The open NLP tool (http://opennlp.apache.org/) is used.

ranked list of the phrases in descending order of their (predicted) effectiveness to derive more query topics. This is formally defined as follows.

Given a query patent Q, let $P = \{p_1, p_2, \ldots, p_l\}$ be a set of candidate phrases extracted from Q where l denotes the number of extracted phrases. Suppose that $Y = \{y_1, y_2, \ldots, y_l\}$ is a set of ranks, and the order of the ranks is given as: $y_1 > y_2 > \cdots > y_l$ where $>$ indicates the preference between two ranks. For each phrase $p_j \in P$, some corresponding rank, y_{p_j}, is assigned. To learn a ranking function, we need to generate training examples, i.e., a ground-truth rank list of P. However, labeling the ground-truth rank of each phrase is too complex because determining its effectiveness for diversification is very difficult (running diversification with every possible ranking of the phrases is intractable). To alleviate this, we exploit DSPApprox to obtain the ground-truth rank list.

Let $R = \{r_1, r_2, \ldots\}$ be the set of relevant patents for Q and we generate the rank of each phrase by DSPApprox using R. We first define a vocabulary set as the terms appeared in R. Then, we calculate the topicality and predictiveness of each phrase based on R, and run DSPApprox using these, which gives a list of ranked phrases as: $\hat{Y} = \{\widehat{y_{p_1}}, \widehat{y_{p_2}}, \widehat{y_{p_3}}, \ldots\}$ where p_1 is the first selection of DSPApprox, p_2 is the second, p_3 is the third, and so on. The topicality (i.e., query clarity [9]) based R is calculated as:

$$\text{Topic}_R(p) = \Pr(p|R) \cdot \log_2\{\Pr(p|R)/\Pr_c(p)\} \quad (5)$$

where $\Pr(p|R)$ is the probability of a phrase p by the smoothed language model [44] derived from R and $\Pr_c(p)$ is the collection probability.

In addition, the predictiveness [27] using R is also computed as:

$$\text{Predict}_R(p) = \frac{1}{Z} \cdot \sum_{v \in CX_p^R} \Pr_w(p|v) \quad (6)$$

where CX_p^R is the set of vocabulary terms that co-occur with p within the windows recognized in R, w is the size of each window, which is empirically set as 20, $\Pr_w(p|v)$ indicates such co-occurrence probability using w, and Z is the normalization factor, which is set as the size of vocabulary (see [27] for more detail).

Based on these, the phrases more topically represent R and can cover more terms in R are highly ranked in the ground-truth list, and we assume that such phrases are effective to find diverse "relevant" documents in the diversification process. Note that the topic term identification described in [11] uses DSPApprox without relevance judgments (i.e., unsupervised approach for ranking topic terms), but in our work, we use the supervised learning-to-rank framework with relevant documents and DSPApprox is used for generating training examples by R (thus, the relevant documents are not necessary in testing). In the training phase, a set of query patents, $\mathbb{Q} = \{Q_1, Q_2, \ldots\}$, are given, and a feature vector $x_{ij} = f(Q_i, p_{ij}) \in X_i$ is generated for the pair of a query patent and its candidate phrase. Then, $\langle X_i, \hat{Y}_i \rangle$ is used for learning a ranking function. In experiments, we use Ranking SVM [21] as a learning algorithm, and select various numbers of phrases as topic phrases.

3.3.2 Features

To compose a feature vector in our ranking model, we use four types of features: 1) relevance, 2) importance, 3) predictiveness, and 4) cohesiveness. We describe each type as follows.

Relevance: *Relevance* estimates some probabilistic relevance of each phrase to the query patent. Typically a patent document consists of four sections (i.e., title, abstract, claim, and description), and previous work (e.g., [43]) has used section information for retrieving relevant documents by finding a weight on each section. Similar to this, we generate three different section language models: (1) title and abstract, (2) claim, and (3) description, and define a relevance feature based on each language model. For example, given a phrase p, the relevance based on the claims in the query document Q is estimated as:

$$\text{Rel}_{Q(\text{claim})}(p) = \prod_{t \in p} \frac{tf_{t,Q(\text{claim})} + \mu \cdot \Pr_c(t)}{|Q| + \mu} \quad (7)$$

where t is a unigram in a phrase p, $Q(\text{claim})$ is the claim text of Q, $tf_{t,Q(\text{claim})}$ is the frequency of t in $Q(\text{claim})$, μ is the Dirichlet smoothing parameter [44].

In addition, we also generate another three section language models by using pseudo-relevant documents (i.e., the top N patents ranked in the initial retrieval result), and define three more relevance features based on these models. Overall, the six relevance features would help to identify the phrases more likely to be associated with the section language models, and our learning algorithm could find an optimal weight for each section model.

Importance: *Importance* indicates retrieval effectiveness related to finding relevant documents. To measure this, we leverage the features for predicting query performance (e.g., [9][19]). Given a phrase, we calculate its query clarity score [9] based on the query model directly derived from the query patent or the relevance model of the query patent. Note that the contribution of the topicality feature used in DSPApprox is the same as that of the query clarity feature we use. In addition, we use query scope [19], inverse document frequency, inverse collection term frequency, and word count, which are generally used for measuring pre-retrieval effectiveness. Since the diversification algorithm (described in Section 3.2) mainly uses the topic phrases for diversification, identifying highly effective phrases for retrieving relevant documents is important to increase the retrieval effectiveness of the final retrieval result.

Predictiveness: *Predictiveness* [28] measures the extent to which a term predicts the occurrences of other terms in a query vocabulary. We use two different types of query vocabulary: 1) all terms in the query patent and not numbers, and 2) the terms that appeared in at least two pseudo-relevant documents and not numbers. Note that stop-words and section terms (e.g., background and summary) are ignored. For each query vocabulary, we measure the predictiveness of an instance (i.e., phrase): $\text{Predict}_Q(p)$ and $\text{Predict}_{PR}(p)$ where PR is the pseudo-relevant documents of Q. As used in DSPApprox, these predictiveness features are effective for extracting diverse phrases that can represent the terms in each topic vocabulary.

Cohesiveness: *Cohesiveness* quantifies the coherence of the terms in a phrase. We assume that the terms more co-occurring in query contexts can be keywords. As an example, for the patent of "Method and apparatus for proving content on a computer system based on usage profile" the terms "usage" and "profile" would frequently co-occur, and it is probable that these also appear in relevant documents. Note that predictiveness measures the conditional probability of a phrase to a query vocabulary, but cohesiveness estimates the lexical affinity of each word to the other in a phrase. To capture this, we generate every possible pair of words in a phrase, and calculate the average of Point-wise Mutual Information (PMI) values for all pairs by using Q as follows.

$$\text{CHSV}_Q(p) = \frac{1}{\binom{n}{2}} \cdot \sum_{w_i, w_j \in p, i \neq j} \text{PMI}_Q(w_i, w_j) \quad (8)$$

Table 1. Four Types of Ranking Features

Type	Features
Relevance	Query Relevance (QR) by Title and Abstract, QR by Claim, QR by Description, Pseudo Relevance (PR) by Title and Abstract, PR by Claim, PR by Description
Importance	Inverse Collection Term Frequency, Inverse Document Frequency, Word Count, Query Clarity [9], Query Scope [19]
Predictiveness	Query Document-based ($Predict_Q$), Pseudo-Relevant-based ($Predict_{PR}$)
Cohesiveness	Query Document-based ($CHSV_Q$), Pseudo-Relevant-based ($CHSV_{PR}$)

where $PMI_Q(w_i, w_j) = \left(f(w_i, w_j) \times n\right) / \left(f(w_i) \cdot f(w_j)\right)$, $f(w)$ is the number of windows containing w in Q, n is the number of all windows in Q and the size of each window is set as 20.

If p is a unigram ($n = 1$), instead of using Eq. (8), we define cohesiveness as the portion of the windows containing p to all windows, i.e., $f(w)/n$. Besides, we also define this cohesiveness feature based the pseudo-relevant documents, i.e., $CHSV_{PR}(p)$.

Table 1 summarizes these feature types, and we analyze the effectiveness of each feature type in experiments.

4. EXPERIMENTAL SETUP

To evaluate our approach, we conduct the experiments as follows. For each query document, we generate a baseline query and employ a baseline retrieval model to produce an initial retrieval result. Then, we apply the diversification framework (see Section 3.2) with topic phrases. To generate the topic phrases, we use either DSPApprox or the learning-to-rank method (see Section 3.3).

4.1 Test Collections

We use two different document collections. The first one contains USPTO (United States Patent and Trademark Office) patents provided by NTCIR-6 [15]. This collection contains 981,948 patents published from 1993 to 2000. To develop query patents (new patents), we randomly select 150 patents published in 2000, ensuring that their citations list more than 20 patents, and at least 90% of them are included in the collection. As done in [15], we consider patents cited in each query patent as "relevant", and 22.64 relevant documents are found on average. We call this collection USPTO. The other collection we use is the CLEF-IP 2010 [35] corpus which contains 2.6 million EPO (European Patent Office) patents. We randomly select 300 query patents from the query patent pool they provide. Although the query documents are described in the three official EPO languages (English, German, French), we only work with English documents. Relevance assessments are provided, which also use the citations listed in each query patent (see [35] for more details). The average number of relevant documents is 28.87, and we call this collection EPO. Queries and documents are stemmed using the Krovetz stemmer and standard stop-words are removed.

4.2 Evaluation Metrics

Since we attempt to diversify patent search results, we use conventional IR evaluation metrics to measure retrieval effectiveness as well as diversity metrics which measure "diversity" on retrieval results. For measuring relevance, we utilize MAP, NDCG, and Recall, which are typically used for adhoc retrieval tasks. In addition, PRES [31] is adopted, which is particularly designed for recall-oriented search tasks. This metric reflects the normalized recall incorporated with the quality of ranks of relevant documents observed within the maximum numbers of documents that the user examines (see [31] for details).

As diversity metrics, NRBP [7], α-NDCG [8], ERR-IA (a variant of ERR [5]), MAP-IA [1], and subtopic recall (S-Recall) are used. These metrics penalize redundancy in retrieval results, i.e., how much of the information in each retrieved relevant document the user has already obtained in earlier ranks. Note that these have been used as standard metrics for diversity tasks in TREC [6]. Since patent examiners (i.e., the search users) typically examine 100 patents on average in the invalidity search processes [22], we assume that the top 100 ranked documents are used to calculate the value of each metric.

4.3 Topic Relevance Judgment

Although we develop the list of relevant documents for each query patent, the diversity metrics require the identification of query aspects for the relevant documents. In other words, for each query patent, we need to group relevant documents if they belong to the same topic. The manual judgments required for this would be too laborious, and patent experts are essential because they can fully understand patent topics. To alleviate this, we devise a semi-automatic method. Each patent document contains a list of IPC (International Patent Classification) [2] codes that classify the document into a hierarchical taxonomy. As an example, the IPC code "H01S 3/14" indicates the patents related to "lasers characterized by the material used as the active medium". So, we exploit these codes to generate the topics of each query patent as follows.

Given a query patent, we first extract all IPC codes from its relevant documents. We sort the codes in descending order of the number of corresponding relevant documents, i.e., $c_a \succ c_b$ if #rel(c_a) > #rel(c_b) where #rel(c) indicates the number of relevant documents containing the code c. Then, we scan from the top and remove the code if it covers all relevant documents (i.e., #rel(c) = $|R|$) because such a code is too general and does not help to measure true diversity. After this, we assume that each remaining code can represent a topic for the query patent, and map relevant documents to their corresponding topics. In our experiments, the queries in USPTO and EPO include 4.94 and 8.66 topics, respectively.

Since patent documents generally contain IPC codes, it could be argued that diversification can be performed using IPC codes that appear in initial retrieval results. That is, the topic set for each query patent is directly estimated by the IPC codes, i.e., $T = \{t_1 = c_a, t_2 = c_b, ...\}$. However, the topics of IPC codes are very abstract and general, e.g., "H01F 1/01" means "magnets or magnetic bodies of inorganic materials". Thus, many documents in the initial retrieval result are related to the same IPC topics, and the diversification algorithm may not perform effectively. Instead, we assume that true topics in a query patent are more specific and concrete. So, we generate sufficient topic phrases for representing detailed topics (as described in Section 3.3). In addition, we consider IPC codes as a crude estimation for true topics, and use them for only evaluating diversity in retrieval results. In the future, we are able to evaluate the IPC-based diversification approach if manually judged query aspects are provided.

---

[2] http://www.wipo.int/classifications/en/

Table 2: Retrieval Results using Relevance Metrics. The baseline retrieval results for USPTO are generated by the query generation method described in [33], and the baseline for EPO uses the retrieval model proposed in [29]. DSP and LTR denote DSPApprox [11] and our learning-to-rank topic identification method (Section 3.3), respectively. In each column, a significant improvement over each method is marked by the first letter of the method, e.g., B indicates improvement over Baseline, and the paired t-test is performed with $p < 0.05$. The best performance is marked by bold. Each retrieval result is truncated at rank 100.

Collection	Method	MAP	PRES	NDCG	Recall@20	Recall
USPTO	Baseline	0.1221 (0.0%)	0.3441 (0.0%)	0.3112 (0.0%)	0.1849 (0.0%)	0.4261 (0.0%)
	DSP	0.1473 [B] (+20.64%)	0.3643 [B] (+5.86%)	0.3483 [B] (+11.92%)	0.2109 [B] (+14.06%)	0.4282 (+0.49%)
	LTR	**0.1568** [BD] (+28.42%)	**0.3789** [BD] (+10.10%)	**0.3596** [BD] (+15.55%)	**0.2216** [BD] (+19.85%)	**0.4441** [BD] (+4.22%)
EPO	Baseline	0.2414 (0.0%)	0.5030 (0.0%)	0.4328 (0.0%)	0.2369 (0.0%)	0.5159 (0.0%)
	DSP	0.2481 [B] (+2.78%)	0.5070 (+0.79%)	0.4416 [B] (+2.03%)	0.2447 [B] (+3.29%)	0.5166 (+0.14%)
	LTR	**0.2585** [BD] (+7.08%)	**0.5109** (+1.57%)	**0.4546** [BD] (+5.04%)	**0.2543** [BD] (+7.34%)	**0.5189** (+0.58%)

Table 3: Diversification Results. Base indicates the method to generate initial retrieval results for each collection ([33] is used for USPTO, and [29] is employed for EPO). DSP and LTR denote DSPApprox [27] and our learning-to-rank topic identification method (Section 3.3), respectively. In each column, a significant improvement over each method is marked by the first letter of the method, e.g., B indicates improvement over Baseline, and the paired t-test is performed with $p < 0.05$. Also, the best performance is marked by bold. Each retrieval result is truncated at rank 100.

Collection	Method	NRBP	α-NDCG	ERR-IA	MAP-IA	S-Recall
USPTO	Baseline	0.1662 (0.0%)	0.4158 (0.0%)	0.2015 (0.0%)	0.0832 (0.0%)	0.7074 (0.0%)
	DSP	0.2299 [B] (+38.35%)	0.4850 [B] (+16.64%)	0.2607 [B] (+3.55%)	0.1007 [B] (+7.24%)	0.7088 (+0.19%)
	LTR	**0.2370** [BD] (+42.63%)	**0.4914** [B] (+18.18%)	**0.2686** [BD] (+13. 10%)	**0.1057** [B] (+22.10%)	**0.7186** [B] (+1.58%)
EPO	Baseline	0.1312 (0.0%)	0.4345 (0.0%)	0.1650 (0.0%)	0.1289 (0.0%)	0.6256 (0.0%)
	DSP	0.1433 [B] (+9.22%)	0.4493 [B] (+3.41%)	0.1766 [B] (+7.03%)	0.1314 [B] (+1.94%)	0.6257 (+0.02%)
	LTR	**0.1446** [B] (+10.21%)	**0.4522** [B] (+4.07%)	**0.1778** [B] (+7.76%)	**0.1325** [B] (+2.79%)	**0.6296** (+0.64%)

4.4 Baseline Retrieval Generation

To generate initial retrieval results, automatic patent query generation methods were employed. Three query generation methods (i.e., [16][33][42]) were tested, and EX-RM [33] was chosen as a baseline method because it significantly outperformed the others in our initial experiment using the USPTO collection. Following previous work [33], we first generate unigram queries by ranking the single terms in query documents; we derive unigram language models based on query documents, and use Kullback-Leibler divergence between query models and collection models for the ranking. Then, the original queries are expanded by relevance models derived from the same IPC documents (i.e., the documents containing at least one common IPC code of the query patent). This expanded query is called EX-RM. In addition to this, noun phrases from query documents are selectively appended to the EX-RM query (EX-RM-NP) because in the experiments of [33] some queries are degraded by added phrases. In our work, we only use EX-RM as a baseline query since selection of effective noun phrases requires more complex statistical learning, and EX-RM-NP could not significantly outperform EX-RM over all queries (see

[33]). For retrieval, we use the Indri language model framework [40].

To develop baseline retrieval results for EPO, we use the method described in [29], which performed effectively on the same corpus in CLEF-IP 2010 [35]. Briefly, each query patent was processed by lemmatization and key-phrase extraction, and lemmas and extracted phrases were indexed separately. Then, Okapi BM25 and Indri were used for producing multiple retrieval results, and a SVM regression was employed to merge the different retrieval results (see [29] for more details).

4.5 Parameter Settings

The diversification algorithm described in Section 3.2 is applied to the top 200 documents in initial retrieval results. For web search tasks, the PM-2 performed better with top 50 documents [10], but prior-art search requires the examination of more documents (e.g., top 100 documents [22]). Thus, we empirically use top 200 documents, and consequently, the topic phrase identification techniques (i.e., DSPApprox and the learning-to-rank method) are also performed with these top 200 documents. In addition, we need

Table 4: Feature Analysis using USPTO. In each column, a * indicates a significant difference from {All}, and the paired *t*-test is performed with $p < 0.05$. Each metric is measured by the top 100 documents of retrieval results.

Features	MAP	NRBP
{All}	0.1568 (0.0%)	0.2370 (0.0%)
{All} − {Cohesiveness}	0.1534 (−2.17%)	0.2291 (−3.33%)
{All} − {Relevance}	0.1465* (−6.57%)	0.2223* (−6.20%)
{All} − {Importance}	0.1407* (−10.27%)	0.2171* (−8.40%)
{All} − {Predictiveness}	0.1355* (−13.58%)	0.2084* (−12.07%)

to tune two free parameters for this algorithm, i.e., λ and μ (see Eq. (2) and Eq. (3)). For this, we consider each value in the range of [0.1,1.0] with an increment of 0.1. Also, the topic phrase identification techniques require the free parameter, i.e., k, which indicates the number of topic phrases to be extracted from the candidate pool. We consider k = {5, 10, 20, 40, 60, 80, 100}. For fair comparison, tuning for these parameters is performed under 10-fold cross-validation with random partitioning; we randomly divide all queries into 10 partitions, and conduct 10 different tests in which each case tests with 1-partition queries by training with the other 9-partition queries. The learning-to-rank topic identification is also performed using the same 10-fold cross-validation. Note that the average number of phrases in the pool is 487.17 and 313.89 over USPTO and EPO query patents, respectively.

5. RESULTS

5.1 Retrieval Effectiveness

We first verify the retrieval effectiveness of the ranked results obtained by each method. Table 2 shows the evaluation results using both USPTO and EPO. In that, DSP and LTR denote diversification using DSPApprox and the learning-to-rank topic identification, respectively. Each retrieval result is truncated at rank 100. For each retrieval result, its retrieval effectiveness is measured by the relevance metrics (i.e., MAP, NDCG, PRES, and recall), and we report an average value of each metric over the query patents in each corpus.

First, our diversification framework can significantly improve baseline retrieval results on most metrics, while recall (at 100) is only improved by LTR using the USPTO collection. That is, the diversification keeps the relevant documents appearing in the initial rank results, and effectively promotes their ranks. This is what we intended by Eq. (3) (in Section 3.2) and the promoted relevant documents would be related to more topic phrases since the diversification algorithm can place the documents for salient topics at higher ranks. In addition, this result is important because, using the diversification, patent examiners are more likely to find relevant patents in early ranks. To highlight this, we measure early recall (recall@20) that can identify the extent of the relevant documents promoted from relatively lower ranks (i.e., below the top 20). From this, we observe that the diversification can retrieve significantly more relevant documents at rank 20. Moreover, the MAP and NDCG scores increase if we use either LTR or DSP for the topic phrase identification, which also supports the same result. Second, LTR looks more effective than DSP in terms of relevance metrics. In USPTO, LTR significantly outperforms DSP in all cases. In

particular, recall (at 100) is significantly improved by LTR, which means that the topics identified by LTR can help to promote the relevant documents initially ranked below the top 100 and patent examiners can find more relevant documents by LTR. However, in EPO LTR is significantly better in terms of MAP, NDCG, and early recall while PRES and recall scores are not significantly improved. This is because in EPO LTR is not helpful to promote the relevant documents initially ranked below the top 100 and PRES is significantly affected by recall performance (Note that PRES reflects the normalized recall). Comparing to EPO, the baseline retrieval of USPTO poorly performs (e.g., 0.4261 vs 0.5159 in recall), and LTR may have more chances to promote the relevant documents initially ranked below the top 100 in USPTO.

5.2 Diversification Performance

Next, we evaluate the "diversity" of retrieval results obtained by each method. Specifically, we measure the values of NRBP, α-NDCG, ERR-IA, MAP-IA, S-Recall at overall ranks. Table 3 presents the diversity-based evaluation results. First, for both collections, our diversification approach is effective for generating significantly more diversified results. The diversity performance in USPTO is especially improved, e.g., +42.63% is achieved in terms of NRBP. This result indicates that the diversification can increase the ranks of relevant documents related to diverse topics, and enabling the user to recognize the diverse aspects of query patents. Second, the sub-topic recall is less improved by the diversification. We believe the cause of this result is that within rank 100, the baseline has already found sufficient amounts of each topic from retrieved relevant documents. Thus, the diversification may not find new topics not covered by the initial retrieval results. Third, the diversification performance in USPTO looks better than that in EPO whereas the retrieval effectiveness measured in EPO is much better than that measured in USPTO (see Table 2). This is because the relevant documents in EPO includes more topics, i.e., the (average) number of topics in relevant documents of USPTO and EPO is 4.94 and 8.66, respectively. Thus, the retrieval results for USPTO easily contain relatively more topics, i.e., the ratio of found topics to the whole topics. Lastly, different from the relevance results (Table 2), LTR is significantly better than DSP in terms of only NRBP and ERR-IA when using the USPTO collection. As discussed in the relevance results, the ranks of the overall relevant documents in USPTO are largely promoted by LTR (see Table 2), and such improvements may influence on the NRBP and ERR-IA measures.

Although we use the diversity measures for the evaluation, prior-art search primarily focuses on retrieving more relevant documents and improving retrieval effectiveness is more significant. However, more diversified results can be useful as the users can recognize diverse aspects of the query patent. Furthermore, our diversification approach does not miss the relevant documents in initial retrieval results, and improved retrieval effectiveness is promising because more relevant documents are found at early ranks.

5.3 Feature Analysis

We now provide an analysis of features used in the learning-to-rank topic identification (LTR) described in Section 3.3. As summarized in Table 1, we use four different types of features for LTR, and conduct another experiment to examine the influence of each feature type for diversification. Since calculating the effects of some features on the topic phrase identification is very difficult, we indirectly measure their effectiveness by performing diversification using the topic phrases generated by the target features. We first extract topic phrases by LTR using all features with 10-fold cross-validation, and diversify initial retrieval results. Then, following

Table 5: Examples of the top 5 topic phrases for a sample query patent. AvePrec denotes Average Precision, and each metric is measured by the top 100 documents in the retrieval result of each method. The baseline retrieval result is generated by [33]. DSP and LTR indicate DSPApprox [27] and our learning-to-rank method (Section 3.3) to generate topic phrases, respectively.

Query Patent
Title: Method and apparatus for providing content on a computer system based on usage profile.
Abstract
A method and apparatus for determining a *computer system usage profile* . . A *basic input output system (BIOS) module* and/or an *operating system module* obtain computer system usage profile information by tracking events such as the frequency of re-boots, the time required to boot-up and shut-down the operating system … data is collected and communicated to a *profile server*…

Baseline	
AvePrec	0.1288
NRBP	0.2366

Diversification		
	DSP	**LTR**
AvePrec	0.1544	0.2183
NRBP	0.2948	0.3594
Top 5 Identified Topic Phrases	1. computer device 2. event 3. execution 4. OS 5. microprocessor	1. user profile data 2. BIOS module 3. boot process 4. disk drive 5. boot time

the same partitions, we identify topic phrases by all features except for one feature type, and run the diversification with the identified phrases. After this , we observe the final performance change by the feature drop, i.e., how much the topic phrase identification depends on the dropped feature type. Note that the parameters for this experiment are the same as used previously.

Table 4 shows the feature analysis using the USPTO collection where LTR is notably effective. In that, we use MAP and NRBP (by top 100 documents) for the analysis. First, all the features we used seem to have positive effects on diversification. Whenever a feature is dropped, the value of every metric decreases. Second, the cohesiveness features look less influential than the others since these features may not cause a significant decrease in both MAP and NRBP metrics. One possible reason for this is that the PMI values to represent "cohesiveness" of topic phrases (see Section 3.3.2) might be less effective to find "relevant" phrases (i.e., useful for retrieving relevant documents). However, we additionally identify other significant features, i.e., relevance and importance that represent the relevance of phrases to each section of query patents and their predicted effectiveness to retrieve relevant documents (i.e., query performance predictors).

5.4 Qualitative Analysis

In this section, we provide a qualitative analysis of our topic phrase identification using an example. Table 5 shows the top 5 topic phrases generated for an example query patent (which is in the same as Figure 1 in Section 1). The application in this patent provides profiled information about computer system usage, and several modules such a Basic Input Output System (BIOS), Operating

System (OS), and Profile Server make up the whole system. For this query patent, the baseline performs reasonably well (its average precision score is slightly higher than MAP over all queries (see Table 2)), and diversification is effective for improving the initial retrieval result.

One observation is that DSPApprox can identify phrases that describe other query terms, i.e., phrases with high predictiveness. For example, "computer device" appears to be highly representative for the peripheral devices used for BIOS, e.g., printer and keyboard, and "event" stands for the actions recorded in the usage profile, e.g., re-boot and shut-down. On the other hand, our learning-to-rank method (LTR) can recognize key phrases that describe significant topics in the query patent and that are more effective for retrieving relevant documents. As an example, "user profile data" and "BIOS module" are important components for the application, and as discussed in Section 1 (using Figure 1), we assume that such components may form query topics. In addition, these phrases are related to several relevant documents for this query patent (see Figure 1). Moreover, the other phrases, e.g., "boot process" and "boot time" are also effective for retrieving relevant documents such as "Reducing operating system start-up/boot time through disk block relocation" (the title of a relevant document for this query patent).

Another interesting observation is that DSPApprox favors unigram phrases. Although we use the same phrase pool for both methods, unigram phrases are more highly ranked by DSPApprox. This bias can be caused by the high predictiveness scores of one-word phrases since they tend to co-occur with more terms than multi-word phrases. The LTR method uses a supervised learning framework, and the weight on the predictiveness feature can be effectively controlled.

6. CONCLUSION

In this paper, we addressed the problem of diversifying patent search results based on query patents. To solve this, we propose a phrase-level diversification approach. Given an initial retrieval result of each query patent, we identify topic phrases to represent underlying query topics, and diversify based on the identified phrases. Through experiments, we showed that this phrase-level diversification can improve patent search results in terms of retrieval effectiveness and diversity. In addition, we devise a learning-to-rank method to identify topic phrases, and verify its effectiveness in comparison to the state-of-the-art topic term identification algorithm. One advantage of our approach is that laborious human effort to generate training examples or relevance judgments is not required, and this can help to reproduce the proposed work. However, evaluation with manually-judged relevance and diversity topics could help to verify the practical effectiveness of our method. This is left for future work. In addition, we plan to apply our approach to other domains (e.g., legal search), and verify its generalizability.

7. ACKNOWLEDGMENTS

This work was supported in part by the Center for Intelligent Information Retrieval. Any opinions, findings and conclusions or recommendations expressed in this material are those of the authors and do not necessarily reflect those of the sponsor.

8. REFERENCES

[1] Agrawal, R., Gollapudi, S., Halverson, A., and Leong, S. (2009). Diversifying search results. *WSDM*, 5-14.

[2] Bashir, S. and Rauber, A. (2010). Improving retrievability of patents in prior-art search. *ECIR*, 457-470.

[3] Carbonell, J., and Goldstein, J. (1998). The use of MMR, diversity-based reranking for reordering documents and producing summaries. *SIGIR*, 335-336.

[4] Carterette, B. and Chandar, P. (2009). Probabilistic models of ranking novel documents for faceted topic retrieval. *CIKM*, 1287-1296.

[5] Chapelle, O., Metlzer, D., Zhang, Y., and Grinspan, P. (2009). Expected reciprocal rank for graded relevance. *CIKM*, 621-630.

[6] Clarke, C. L. A., Craswell, N., Soboroff, I., and Cormack, G. V. (2010). Overview of the TREC 2010 web track. *TREC*.

[7] Clarke, C. L. A., Kolla, M., and Vechtomova, O. (2009). An effectiveness measure for ambiguous and underspecified queries. *ICTIR*, 188-199.

[8] Clarke, C. L. A., Kolla, M., Cormack, G. V., Vechtomova, O., Ashkan, A., Buttcher, S., and MacKinnon, I. (2008). Novelty and diversity in information retrieval evaluation. *SIGIR*, 659-666.

[9] Cronen-Townsend, S., Zhou, Y., and Croft, W. B. (2002). Predicting query performance. *SIGIR*, 299-306.

[10] Dang, V., and Croft, W. B. (2012). Diversity by proportionality: an election-based approach to search result diversification. *SIGIR*, 65-74.

[11] Dang, V. and Croft, W. B. (2013). Term level search result diversification. *SIGIR*, 603-612.

[12] Dang, V., Xue, X., and Croft, W. B. (2011). Inferring query aspects from reformulations using clustering. *CIKM*, 2117-2120.

[13] Dou, Z., Hu, S., Chen, K., Song, R., and Wen, J.-R. (2011). Multi-dimensional search result diversification. *WSDM*, 475-484.

[14] Fall, C. J., Torcsvari, A., Benzineb, K., and Karetka, G. (2003). Automated categorization in the international patent classification. *ACM SIGIR Forum*, 37(1): 10–25.

[15] Fujii, A., Iwayama, M., and Kando, N. (2007). Overview of the patent retrieval task at the NTCIR-6 workshop. *NTCIR-6*.

[16] Ganguly, D., Leveling, J., Magdy, W., and Jones, G. J. F. (2011). Patent query reduction using pseudo-relevance feedback. *CIKM*, 1953-1956.

[17] Ganguly, D., Leveling, J., Magdy, W., and Jones, G. (2011). United we fall, divided we stand: a study of query segmentation and PRF for patent prior art search. *PaIR*.

[18] He, J., Hollink, V., and de Vries, A. (2012). Combining implicit and explicit topic representations for result diversification. *SIGIR*, 851-860.

[19] He, B., and Ounis, I. (2006). Query performance prediction. *Information System*, 31(7): 585-594.

[20] Iwayama, M., Fujii, A., Kando, N., and Marukawa, Y. (2003). An empirical study on retrieval models for different document genres: patents and newspaper articles. *SIGIR*, 251-258.

[21] Joachims, T. (2006). Training linear SVMs in linear time. *KDD*, 217-226.

[22] Joho, H., Azzopardi, L., and Vanderbauwhede, W. (2010). A survey of patent users: an analysis of tasks, behavior, search functionality and system requirement. *IIiX*, 13-22.

[23] Kim, Y., Seo, J., and Croft, W. B. (2011). Automatic Boolean query suggestion for Professional Search. *SIGIR*, 825-834.

[24] Kim, Y., Seo, J., Croft, W. B., and Smith, D. A. (2014). Automatic suggestion of phrasal-concept queries for literature search. *Information Processing & Management*, 50(4): 568-583.

[25] Kim, Y. and Croft, W. B. (2014). Diversifying query suggestions based on query documents. *SIGIR*, 891-894.

[26] Lavrenko, V. and Croft, W. B. (2001). Relevance-based language model. *SIGIR*, 120-127.

[27] Lawrie, D. (2003). Language models for hierarchical summarization. *PhD Thesis*, University of Massachusetts.

[28] Lawrie, D., Croft, W. B., and Rosenberg, A. (2001). Finding topic words for hierarchical summarization. *SIGIR*, 349-357.

[29] Lopez, P., and Romary, L. (2010). Experiments with citation mining and key-term extraction for prior-art search. *CLEF*.

[30] Lupu, M., Piroi, F., Huang, X., Zhu,, J., and Tait, J. (2009). Overview of the TREC 2009 chemical IR track. *TREC-18*.

[31] Magdy, W. and Jones, G. J. F. (2010). PRES: a score metric for evaluating recall-oriented information retrieval applications. *SIGIR*, 611-618.

[32] Magdy, W. and Jones, G. J. F. (2011). A study on query expansion methods for patent retrieval. *PaIR*, 19-24.

[33] Mahdabi, P., Andersson, L., Keikha, M., and Crestani, F. (2012). Automatic refinement of patent queries using concept importance predictors. *SIGIR*, 505-514.

[34] Mase, H., Matsubayashi, T., Ogawa, Y., Iwayama, M., and Oshio, T. (2005). Proposal of two-stage patent retrieval method considering the claim structure. *ACM Transactions on Asian Language Information Processing*, 4: 190-206.

[35] Piroi, F., and Tait, J. (2010). CLEF-IP 2010: Retrieval experiments in the intellectual property domain. *IRF Technical Report*.

[36] Radlinski, F., Szummer, M., and Craswell, N. (2010). Inferring query intent from reformulations and clicks. *WWW*, 1171-1172.

[37] Rafiei, D., Bharat, K., and Shukla, A. (2010). Diversifying web search results. *WWW*, 781-790.

[38] Sanderson, M. and Croft, W. B. (1999). Deriving concept hierarchies from text. *SIGIR*, 206-213

[39] Santos, R. L. T., Macdonald, C., and Ounis, I. (2010). Exploiting query reformulations for web search result diversification. *WWW*, 881-890.

[40] Strohman, T., Metzler, D., Turtle, H., and Croft, W. B. (2005). Indri: a language-model based search engine for complex queries (extended version). *UMASS CIIR Technical Report*.

[41] Wang, J. and Zhu, J. (2009). Portfolio theory of information retrieval. *SIGIR*, 115-122.

[42] Xue, X. and Croft, W. B. (2009). Transforming patents into prior-art queries. *SIGIR*, 808-809.

[43] Xue, X. and Croft, W. B. (2009). Automatic query generation for patent search. *Proc. SIGIR*, 2037-2040.

[44] Zhai, C. and Lafferty, J. (2001). A study of smoothing methods for language models applied to ad hoc information retrieval. *SIGIR*, 334-342.

[45] Zhai, C., Cohen, W. W., and Lafferty, J. (2003). Beyond independent relevance: methods and evaluation metrics for subtopic retrieval. *SIGIR*, 10-17.

On Microblog Dimensionality and Informativeness

Exploiting microblogs' structure and dimensions for ad-hoc retrieval

Jesus Alberto Rodriguez Perez
School of Computing Science
University of Glasgow
Glasgow
Jesus.RodriguezPerez@glasgow.ac.uk

Joemon M. Jose
School of Computing Science
University of Glasgow
Glasgow
Joemon.Jose@glasgow.ac.uk

ABSTRACT

In recent years, microblog services such as Twitter have gained increasing popularity, leading to active research on how to effectively exploit its content. Microblog documents such as tweets differ in morphology with respect to more traditional documents such as web pages. Particularly, tweets are considerably shorter (140 characters) than web documents and contain contextual tags regarding the topic (hashtags), intended audience (mentions) of the document as well as links to external content(URLs).

Traditional and state of the art retrieval models perform rather poorly in capturing the relevance of tweets, since they have been designed under very different conditions. In this work, we define a microblog document as a high-dimensional entity and study the structural differences between those documents deemed relevant and those non-relevant. Secondly we experiment with enhancing the behaviour of the best observed performing retrieval model by means of a re-ranking approach that accounts for the relative differences in these dimensions amongst tweets. Additionally we study the interactions between the different dimensions in terms of their order within the documents by modelling relevant and non-relevant tweets as state machines. These state machines are then utilised to produce scores which in turn are used for re-ranking.

Our evaluation results show statistically significant improvements over the baseline in terms of precision at different cut-off points for both approaches. These results confirm that the relative presence of the different dimensions within a document and their ordering are connected with the relevance of microblogs.

Categories and Subject Descriptors

H.3.3 [**Information Storage and Retrieval**]: Information Search and Retrieval

ICTIR'15, September 27–30, Northampton, MA, USA.
© 2015 ACM. ISBN 978-1-4503-3833-2/15/09 ...$15.00.
DOI: http://dx.doi.org/10.1145/2808194.2809466.

Keywords

Ad-hoc Retrieval, Ranking, Microblog, Dimensions, State Machine, Modelling

1. INTRODUCTION

Microblogs have grown in popularity in recent years, gradually transforming the way we find out about the latest events and communicate. Twitter is the most prominent service [1], as it is used by millions, posting over 340 million tweets every day[2]. Microblog services are used for various purposes including: (i) self promotion, (ii) advertising, (iii) real-time news broadcasting, (iv) social discussions etc. The most important aspect of Twitter is that it provides unique insight into real-time events, such as first hand reports of events as they are developing, along with the opinion of those discussing them. This information makes Twitter a uniquely valuable media source, which led to obtaining much attention by research and industrial communities.

Ad-hoc retrieval is one of the most widely investigated tasks in Information Retrieval (IR) where the goal is to return documents that are relevant to an immediate information need. Recently ad-hoc retrieval has been actively studied in the context of microblogs, particularly during the microblog tracks at TREC 2011, 2012 and 2013 [18].

Searching Twitter can be extremely challenging because of document morphology. Their content is limited as messages posted to Twitter (known as *Tweets*) are limited to 140 characters in length. Furthermore they are generally of a varied linguistic quality [27] due to colloquialisms and users attempting to fit the content within the message limitations. More specifically tweets pose new constraints for which state of the art retrieval models were not designed for[3]. To the best of our knowledge, nobody has properly assessed the effect that these new characteristics or dimensions have on the current relevance assumptions in which retrieval models are based.

Whilst few recent works have identified some features as possibly being detrimental in microblog ad-hoc retrieval [25,

---

[1] https://twitter.com/
[2] http://blog.twitter.com/2012/03/twitter-turns-six.html
[3] Models such as: Okapi BM25 [21]; Divergence From Randomness (DFR) [3]; Hiemstra's Language Model (HLM) [9]; and Dirichlet Language Model (DLM) [29]

16], no study has been carried out to determine their behaviour with respect to state of the art retrieval models. The main objective of this work is not the improvement over the very best scores achieved for each of the microblog collections. Instead we investigate the connection of the structure of microblog documents with their relevance during an ad-hoc search task.

Firstly we observe the performance of state of the art retrieval models in the context of Twitter corpora selecting the best retrieval model as a baseline. Then we study the behaviour of the different features and characteristics that make up microblog documents and finally evaluate their suitability for enhancing the behaviour of state of the art retrieval models by combining them. Moreover, a number of experiments are performed to demonstrate which features are most indicative of the relevance of microblogs by demonstrating statistically significantly improved retrieval performance for ad-hoc search.

Finally, we extend our analysis by considering the ordering of the different component that make up microblog documents. In order to do so, we encode structure of observed relevant and non-relevant documents in state machines, which in turn are used to produce scores for re-ranking. We utilise the 2013 microblog collection to construct such the state machines, and test our approach on the 2011 and 2012 microblog collections combined. Our results show statistically significantly improved results over the selected baseline, demonstrating the connection of microblog structure with their relevance.

With the objective of studying microblog document's structures, we set the focus of this work in the context of these research questions:

- **RQ1.** Does document length have any connection with the relevance of microblog documents?

- **RQ2.** Are there structural differences between relevant and non-relevant microblog documents? Can we exploit them for ad-hoc retrieval?

- **RQ3.** Can microblog features be exploited to help retrieval models better capture relevance when ranking documents?

- **RQ4.** Is the order of the different elements in a microblog document connected with relevance? Can it be utilised for ad-hoc retrieval?

The rest of the chapter is organised as follows. First, we cover some of the relevant literature regarding microblog searches and introduce the concepts utilised throughout this work (Section 2). Section 3 sets the evaluation environment in which our investigation is carried out, giving way to our main analysis (Section 4). Finally Section 5 concludes the work and indicates future research directions.

2. BACKGROUND

In this Section we will introduce some concepts needed to understand the paper as well as related work.

Table 1: TREC Tracks results in terms of precision@30

	2011		2012		2013
Best	Median	Best	Median	Best	Median
0.502	0.298	0.470	0.362	0.560	0.370

Probability of Relevance Framework. For years researchers have tried to define what is relevance, thus many works have led to many definitions. A product from that research is the Probability of Relevance Framework (PRF) [22] which is based on the probability of relevance $P(r|\hat{d}, q)$, where r refers to relevance, q a given query and $\hat{d}$ represents a document as a vector of features $\hat{d} = (f_1, ...f_n)$. Note that vector features can be any imaginable data.

Document length normalization [25] has been employed by retrieval models to counterbalance the effects of longer documents, which may not necessarily add any new information to a topic, but are prone to contain higher term frequencies. In line with this effort, the design of BM25 by [21] involved the study of document characteristics, resulting in the definition of the **scope** and **verbosity** hypotheses. The **verbosity** hypotheses supports that some authors are more verbose than others, thus applying length normalization by dividing by the length of the document is beneficial to better capture relevance, as repetition of terms is superfluous. On the other hand, the **scope** hypotheses states that some authors simply have more to say, thus adding more relevant information to the topic and occupying more space. BM25 applies a soft normalisation that takes into account both cases.

Microblog retrieval tracks were organized by TREC over three consecutive years 2011, 2012 and 2013. The collections sampled documents from a Twitter stream over a period of time. The total number of available topics is 170, where 50 topics belong to the 2011 collection, and 120 split evenly between the 2012 and 2013 collections. The summary results for each of the tracks are presented in Table 1 for reference. Amongst the top performing participants we can find [2, 12, 14] for microblog 2011 and [11, 1, 8] for 2012, which mostly employed query and document expansion techniques as well as learning to rank (L2R) approaches. Additionally, the 2013 track followed a similar trend producing works in the same categories L2R [24, 7], query expansion [20, 19] and document expansion [10].

Moreover, the work by [5] produced a comprehensive summary of the features used by different approaches, and demonstrated how to successfully combine them using naive bayes as an L2R approach combining a number of features including hashtags, mentions, url presence, recency, etc.

Work by [28] studied the effects that preprocessing had on retrieval performance. Their findings showed that the best performance was achieved when applying all preprocessing steps, which include (i) language detection, (ii) Emotion removal, (iii) Lexical normalization, (iv) Mention Removal and (v) Link Removal. Moreover, works by [6, 16] have identified that problems affecting retrieval models in microblogs are related to *term frequency* and *document length normalization*.

Making Sense Of Microposts. The MSM workshop [4] presented participants with a challenge. The objective was to build systems able to identify and extract concepts from microblog documents, in a semi-supervised manner. The participant systems were to categorise concepts as belonging to the categories person **PER**, organisation **ORG**, location **LOC** and miscellaneous **MISC**. A similar task is that of microblog summarisation [23] in that tweets have to be processed and made sense of in order to produce a richer representation.

Amongst the works submitted to this workshop, we can highlight the work by Tao, Ke et al. [26]. In their work they perform an in depth analysis of both topic dependent and independent features for the MSM task. Some of the topic independent features consider the presence of hashtags, urls and the length of the documents to be in connection with the relevance of documents. In our work, we pay attention to the same features, but from a different angle, by looking how much space relative to the total characters in the document is dedicated to each of the microblogs elements.

Other Microblog retrieval features. Work by [13] explored the use of other features to improve ad-hoc retrieval. These features include emoticons, hyperlinks, shouting, capitalization, retweets and followers. Work by [15] extended the study concerning the use of social features such as the number of followers and followees to enhance ad-hoc retrieval performance. While all these works attempt to exploit some microblog features or augment them with external resources, they do not try to explain how these features relate to the relevance of microblog documents. In our work, we consider features based purely on microblog characteristics, explain their relationship with relevance, and finally use those features that seem beneficial to improve the behaviour of a state of the art retrieval model.

3. EXPERIMENTAL SETTING

Datasets. In this evaluation we have used the three collections from the TREC Microblog track. The 2011 and 2012 collections share the same corpus but have different topics and relevance assessments. On the other hand the 2013 corpus is an order of magnitude bigger than previous collections. However, its relevance assessments are comparable in size to the 2012 track. Moreover, the ratio of documents $\frac{relevant}{non-relevant}$ is much higher for the 2013, which can result in generally better retrieval performance than previous tracks by default. In total there are 170 topics with query lengths ranging from 2 to 3 tokens, in line with the literature [27]. Refer to Table 2 for an extended overview of these collections.

Evaluation measures. We pay attention to precision at different ranks, with a maximum cut-off point at rank 100. Future evidence is accepted only at the collection statistics

Table 2: Descriptive statistics for the collections being used in this study

TREC Microblog track collection year	2011	2012	2013
Number of topics	50	60	60
# documents	16M	16M	260M
# assessed documents	40855	73073	71279
# assessed non-relevant documents	38124	66893	62268
# assessed relevant documents	2731	6180	9011
Ratio $\frac{Relevant\ Docs}{Non-Relevant\ Docs}$	0.07	0.09	0.14
Avg. relevant documents per topic	58.45	106.54	150.18

level as agreed by TREC organisers disregarding any documents after the query issuing time when computing evaluation measures [4].

Baseline selection. Table 3 contains evaluation results for the considered state of the art retrieval models when applied to Twitter corpora from the 2011, 2012 and 2013 Trec microblog collections. The models considered in this evaluation are TF-IDF (IDF)[5], BM25, DFRee (DFR), Dirichlet's LM (DLM) and Hiemstra's LM (HLM) [6]. Since DFR is generally the best performing model we will be using it as our baseline.

4. ANALYSIS AND DISCUSSION

In this Section we first study the structure of microblog documents in order to define a hypotheses that captures their relevance. Subsequently, we test our hypotheses through the implementation of a number of approaches that capture microblogs' structure and their evaluation with respect to our DFR baseline. Additionally, we evaluate the relation of the order of the different dimensions within the microblogs, and determine how to utilise this evidence for ad-hoc retrieval.

4.1 Informativeness of Microblogs

For web and similar documents, relevance is modelled by the inclusion of statistical measures extracted both from the collection as a whole, and the documents themselves. Most retrieval models take into consideration document based statistics, such as document length and term frequency, in an attempt to capture the relevance of the documents according to the scope and verbosity hypotheses (or similar assumptions). For the purposes of this work, we can think of each retrieval model as a delicate relationship "$\boxed{?}$" between document length $|D|$ and term frequency $P(q \cap D|Q)$ amongst other components. We pay attention to those components as they are most likely affected by the structure of microblogs.

$$P(I|Q, D) = |D| \boxed{?} P(q \cap D|Q) \qquad (1)$$

---

[4]https://github.com/lintool/twitter-tools/wiki/TREC-2013-Track-Guidelines

[5]*Where* $TF = 1$. Results worsen considerably if we do not set TF to a constant.

[6]We use the Terrier IR platform [17] implementation and settings for all models.

Table 3: Evaluation results for the state of the art models considered. (Bold denotes the best performing system)

	(a) 2011 collection					(b) 2012 Collection					(c) 2013 collection				
	Precision					Precision					Precision				
	@5	*@10*	*@15*	*@20*	*@30*	*@5*	*@10*	*@15*	*@20*	*@30*	*@5*	*@10*	*@15*	*@20*	*@30*
BM25	0.51	0.46	0.44	0.42	0.38	0.40	0.37	0.35	0.35	0.31	0.54	0.50	0.45	0.42	0.38
DFR	0.60	**0.57**	**0.52**	0.48	0.42	**0.45**	0.42	0.39	**0.37**	**0.35**	**0.64**	**0.59**	**0.54**	**0.51**	**0.45**
DLM	0.59	0.55	**0.52**	**0.49**	0.43	0.44	**0.43**	**0.40**	**0.37**	0.35	0.47	0.41	0.39	0.37	0.34
HLM	0.57	0.51	0.47	0.44	0.41	0.42	0.38	0.37	0.35	0.33	0.44	0.41	0.38	0.35	0.33
IDF	**0.62**	0.54	0.50	0.47	**0.44**	0.42	0.38	0.36	0.35	0.33	0.63	0.58	0.53	0.50	**0.45**

Microblog documents are however very short as they have a fixed maximum size. Additionally, authors tend to optimise their content to fit within the character limits and constraints set by the platform, leading to a more or less constant document length (~ 15 terms in the case of Twitter). Moreover, due to these limitations, the value of non-stop term frequencies revolve around $\sim 1, 2$ thus not offering much information.

Both the **scope** and **verbosity** hypotheses are defined within the assumption that authors may write as much as they desire. As a result, it is logical to assume that, if this condition is broken, unexpected behaviour and rankings may arise for retrieval models relying on such hypotheses. Fortunately, microblog documents are highly dimensional since different information is encoded in the same message following an organic community-agreed vocabulary. In our work we draw inspiration from the ideas behind the scope and verbosity hypotheses and describe a new hypotheses tailored to microblog retrieval, which highlights characteristics of microblog documents' structure.

Firstly, we assume that microblog documents (**D**) are 4-dimensional entities comprised of **Text** $T(D)$; a **URL** $U(D)$ (Linking to an external resource); **Hashtags** $\#(D)$ (Terms preceded by $\#$) indicating a topical context and **Mentions** $@(D)$ (Terms preceded by $@$) indicating an intended audience. We believe that the amount of space in a microblog document dedicated to each of the dimensions may have a connection with how likely it is to be relevant to the searcher. Having these characteristics in mind, we define (**H1**) **Microblog Informativeness** (MI) as the probability for a Microblog document D being informative given a query $P(MI|Q, D)$, which depends on an optimal unobserved combination "$\boxed{?}$" of the aforementioned dimensions:

$$P(MI|Q, D) = T(D) \boxed{?} U(D) \boxed{?} \#(D) \boxed{?} @(D) \boxed{?} P(q \cap D|Q) \quad (2)$$

where $T(D)$, $U(D)$, $\#(D)$ and $@(D)$ are the ratios in terms of number of characters spent in the document for each of the dimensions considered [7]. For example, the ratio for the text dimension $T(D)$ is given by:

---

[7]URL's are automatically shortened by Twitter, thus their length is constant.

$$T(D) = \frac{\#ofCharsforTextDimension}{Total\#ofChars}, \quad (3)$$

In order to test our hypotheses and learn about what are the most prominent characteristics that make up relevant microblog documents, we analyse retrieval runs produced by the state of the art baseline DFR because it is the best performing model as shown in Table 3. We use the documents in the runs instead of all documents in the relevance judgements in order to analyse the documents that are most likely to contain query terms and find differences amongst those documents. We take into consideration the TREC Microblog topics 1 to 110 so that we can confirm our findings through an evaluation on the newer 111 to 170 topics which belong to TREC's 2013 iteration of the microblog search task.

Tables 4(a...e) introduce the mean ratios for each of the dimensions for all documents at the cut-offs @10, @20, @30, @50 and @100 respectively. The asterisk indicates statistically significant differences between relevant and non-relevant documents for that dimension. The last row on each table on the other hand, indicates the average document length in number of characters for both relevant and non-relevant documents.

First we look at "DocLength". As we can observe in Tables 4(a...e), the differences between relevant and non-relevant documents are not significant. Furthermore, we can see how relevant documents tend to be shorter than non-relevant documents for cut-offs @10 and @20, whereas then they become longer than non-relevant documents for any cut-off after @20. It is evident that the behaviour of this feature is unstable, and the differences between both groups of documents change wildly depending on the cut-off point, contradicting each other.

Based on this observation we can conclude that the document length feature, popular amongst retrieval models, is ineffective in estimating the relevance of a microblog document. Therefore, this helps us to confirm that the scope and verbosity hypothesis do not hold for microblog documents, as differences should have followed a more clear trend if the hypotheses were true. (i.e. One relevance group should have remained higher than the other for all cut-off cases.). Therefore we can confirm that in the case of microblog documents,

Table 4: Ratio of each dimension for relevant (Rel) and non-relevant (Non-Rel) documents at different cutoffs.

(a) Cutoff @ 10

	Rel	Non-Rel
Hash	1.960	1.619
Ment	2.750	2.444
Urls	17.32	14.16 *
Text	77.95	81.77 *
DocLength	97.47	100.2

(b) Cutoff @ 20

	Rel	Non-Rel
Hash	2.626	1.861 *
Ment	2.453	2.402
Urls	17.54	13.54 *
Text	77.37	82.18 *
DocLength	96.50	97.38

(c) Cutoff @ 30

	Rel	Non-Rel
Hash	2.514	1.999
Ment	3.061	2.671
Urls	17.13	14.28 *
Text	77.29	81.04 *
DocLength	96.21	95.76

(d) Cutoff @ 50

	Rel	Non-Rel
Hash	2.820	2.518
Ment	2.968	3.136
Urls	17.19	14.32 *
Text	77.01	80.01 *
DocLength	95.90	94.45

(e) Cutoff @ 100

	Rel	Non-Rel
Hash	2.638	2.514
Ment	2.893	3.315 *
Urls	17.69	14.13 *
Text	76.77	80.03 *
DocLength	93.96	92.56

longer (or shorter) does not have a connection with a document being relevant.

Secondly, we look at the **Urls** and **Text** dimensions of microblog documents in Figure 1. In the case of **Urls**, this dimension tends to be significantly larger on relevant documents than in their non-relevant counterparts. This is in line with previous works suggesting that the presence of URL's increases the likelihood for a document to be relevant [13]. Figure 1a shows the changes in space dedicated to the URL dimension as we go down the result list. An interesting behaviour that can be observed is that, relevant documents behave in exactly the opposite way to non-relevant documents. As we traverse the result list the space for the URL's in relevant documents increases whereas, it slowly decreases for non-relevant documents.

The **Text** dimension on the other hand, is significantly smaller for relevant documents, across all cut-offs. However, as observed in Figure 1b, the behaviour as we traverse the list towards lower cut-off points is similar for both relevant and non-relevant documents. Thus the differences in characters dedicated to this dimension remain stable between relevant and non-relevant documents.

The stability in the differences of both the **Urls** and **Text** dimensions make them especially interesting feature candidates to be studied, and possibly employed to improve the behaviour of retrieval systems.

Figure 3 shows the behaviour for the Hash and Mention dimensions. In terms of the **Hash** dimension, differences are only significant when looking at the @20 cut-off. Additionally, relevant documents seem to have a higher portion of the content dedicated to this dimension than non-relevant documents. This behaviour can be observed in Figure 3a, as relevant documents seem to dedicate more space for hashtags regardless of the cut-off chosen. Another observation

that can be made, is that as we traverse the result list, the presence of hashtags become more pronounced for both relevant and non-relevant documents, thus the increased (or decreased) presence of hashtags does not serve as a discriminative factor in microblog ranking.

Finally, we observe the behaviour of the **Mention** dimension in Figure 3b. For the three first cut-offs @10; @20 and @30, relevant documents seem to spend more space in defining an audience than non-relevant documents. After the @30 cut-off the roles are swapped and non-relevant documents spend more space in referring to the target users than relevant documents. This makes sense if we assume that many non-relevant documents may be conversational in nature, instead of introducing facts interesting to a wider audience. In fact the differences in terms of the space dedicated to the **Mentions** dimension is only significant once we are much lower in the ranking at the @100 cut-off.

One could argue that our conclusions may be biased since the result lists are produced with respect to the retrieval model inherent features (e.g. document length). However, we can see that the differences in the observations between relevant and non-relevant documents for the good dimensions (Urls, Text and Hash) are relatively constant, thus independent from the rank for our purposes.

4.2 Modelling Microblog Informativeness

In the previous section we observed that relevant Microblog documents present different characteristics to those non-relevant in terms of the aforementioned dimensions (Figure 2). More specifically, relevant documents tend to use less space for text, and more space to contain the URLs, and hashtag dimensions than non-relevant documents. An important note is that we cannot assume that the less space dedicated to text the more relevant the document will be,

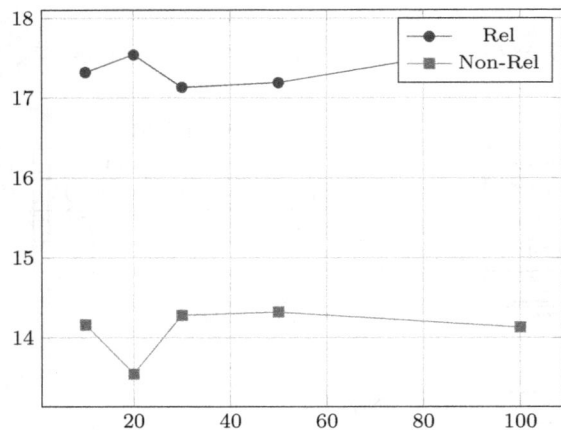 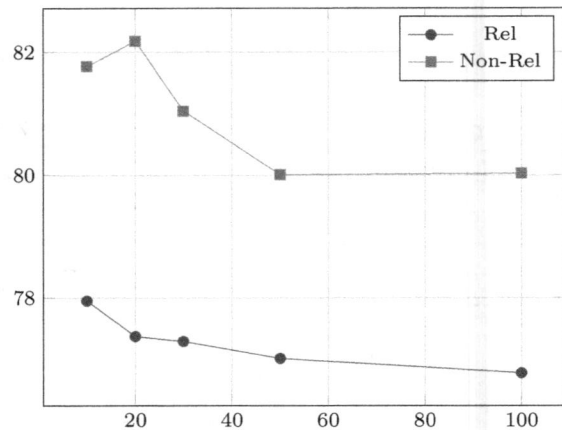

(a) Urls   (b) Text

Figure 1: Rate (%) of space dedicated to Urls and Text in Relevant and Non-Relevant documents at different cut-off points.

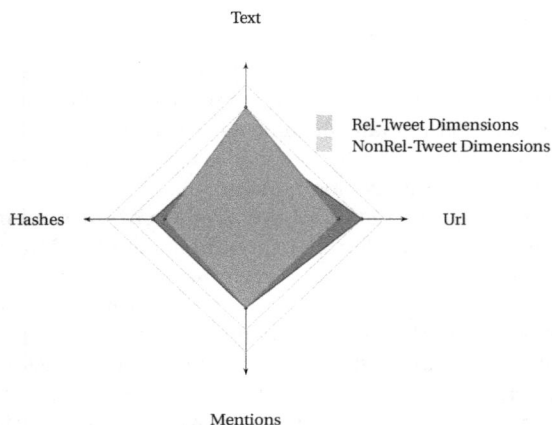

Figure 2: Dimensional differences between relevant and non-relevant documents. Statistically significant differences are exaggerated for easier visualization.

as that would make a text-less document the one with the highest likelihood of being relevant.

Therefore, we estimate that a relevant document has an optimal amount of space dedicated to the text dimension which ranges from 76% to 78% as observed in Figure 1b. Thus we model informativeness in terms of the retrieval model score $P(q \cap D|Q)$ for document D given query Q and its Text dimension as:

$$P(MI|D,Q) = P(q \cap D|Q) + \lambda[1 - |T(D) - 0.76|], \quad (4)$$

where we give a lower score to those documents diverging from the optimal text dimension rate 0.76[8]. We test this formulation using DFR to produce the $P(q \cap D|Q)$ score over the microblog 2013 collection, which was **not** used in producing the analysis results in the previous section. We retrieve the first 500 documents using DFR and re-rank them using our first model (Equation 4) with λ set to 1. The results are shown in the RR-text[9] row within Table 5. As we can observe, the performance of DFR is enhanced by taking into account the textual dimension of the microblog documents, being statistically significantly better in terms of P@20.

Similarly, we combine the URL dimension expressed as a rate with the score of the retrieval model as follows:

$$P(MI|D,Q) = P(q \cap D|Q) + \omega U(D), \quad (5)$$

where we set the free parameter ω to 1. The results obtained for the experiments with this model are shown in Table 5 in row RR-Url. The use of the URL dimension on its own also improves the performance over the DFR itself, most significantly for P@10 and P@20. Furthermore, it produces slightly better results than the RR-Text approach. Additionally we combined both models to produce:

$$P(MI|D,Q) = P(q \cap D|Q) + \lambda[1 - |T(D) - 0.76|] + \omega U(D), \quad (6)$$

---

[8]The optimal 76% rate of presence for the text dimension specified above, which we normalise between 0 and 1.
[9]"RR-" stands for "Re Ranking", and precedes the features utilised in the operation

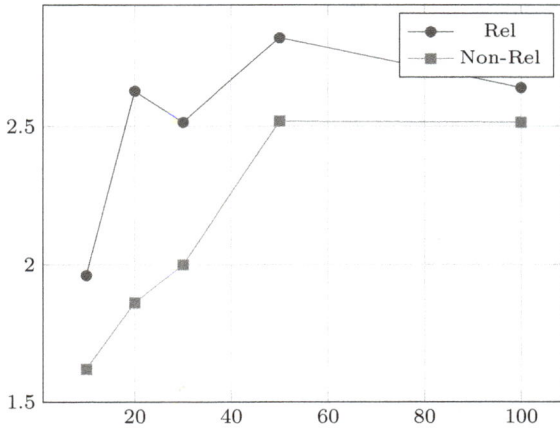

(a) Hashtags

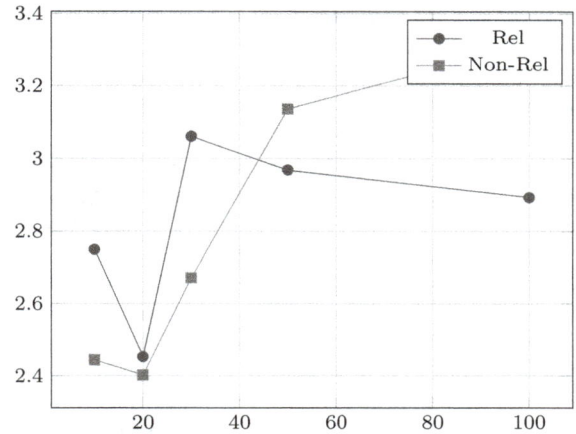

(b) Mentions

Figure 3: Rate (%) of space dedicated to HashTags and Mentions in Relevant and Non-Relevant documents at different cut-off points.

The results for this combination are shown in Table 5 as row RR-text-url. Further improvements with respect to previous approaches are introduced at all cut-offs except P@10, where RR-url performs slightly better than the combined approach. Finally we also added components to account for the hash and mention dimensions, producing the following two models:

$$P(MI|D,Q) = P(q \cap D|Q) + \lambda[1 - |T(D) - 0.76|] \\ + \omega U(D) + \gamma\#(D), \quad (7)$$

$$P(MI|D,Q) = P(q \cap D|Q) + \lambda[1 - |T(D) - 0.76|] \\ + \omega U(D) + \gamma\#(D) + \delta@(D), \quad (8)$$

where the free parameters are set to 1^{10} . The results for both models 7 and 8 are shown in Table 5 as RR-text-url-hash and RR-text-url-hash-ment respectively. The performance achieved by adding the hash component over the previous models is further increased specially for P@10, whereas it performs slightly worse than RR-text-url in terms of P@30. The addition of the mentions component in RR-text-url-hash-ment reduces retrieval performance across P@10, P@15 and P@20 with respect to the last model.

If we consider Figures 1a, 1b, 3a and 3b and Table 5 we can see how the dimensions that showed constant differences across all cut-offs are the features enhancing the performance of the baseline. The only feature which results in poorer retrieval performance is the mentions dimension, which as observed in Figure3b follows an erratic behaviour

---

[10]Parameter optimisation would be beneficial in the future, although it was not considered for the purposes of this work

Table 5: Results when experimenting with the different dimensions over the 2013 TREC Microblog collection (*$p < 0.05$ over the DFR).

Model	P@5	P@10	P@15	P@20	P@30
DFR	0.65	0.59	0.54	0.51	0.45
text	0.65	0.59	0.54	0.52*	0.45
url	0.65	0.61*	0.54	0.52*	0.46
text-url	0.66*	0.61*	0.55*	0.52*	**0.47**
text-url-hash	**0.66***	**0.62***	**0.56***	**0.53***	0.46
text-url-hash-ment	0.66*	0.61*	0.55	0.52*	0.46

(For earlier cut-offs more space is dedicated to the mentions in relevant documents, and then after the cut-off 40 is the opposite case).

Based on our experimental results, we can assert that there are structural differences between relevant and non-relevant documents in terms of the dimensions defined in this work. More specifically, we have come up with a possible instantiation which captures Microblog characteristics in the shape of a model given by Equation 7. The implications of these findings and experiments are that users produce Microblog documents in different ways, with certain formats more likely to satisfy the information need of a searcher. In the following subsection, we expand our analysis by taking into consideration the order of the dimensions.

4.3 Dimensions Interaction.

To further our analysis in the structure of microblog documents we studied how the different dimensions interact with each other. Apart from the presence of the dimensions above discussed, we believe that the order in which they appear, and the interactions between them are also important. In fact, there are several documents on the web [11] which are meant to assist in writing the perfect tweet to grab the attention of readers.

To properly model such interactions is no simple task. In our study we utilised all documents in the relevance judgements from the Tweets 2013 collection as our training set. Each tweet is tokenised, and each token is categorised as representing each of the "text", "hashtag", "mention" and "url" dimensions, with the help of simple regular expressions matching. Moreover we quantify the frequency that a dimension is followed by another one. For example, we count the number of times when text leads to a hashtag, or a mention leads to a url. The frequencies of each dimensions leading to another dimension of the microblog documents are then utilised to build a simple state machine (or automata). Figure 4 shows an example, denoting how state 1, can transition to other states, such as state 2, with the probabilities stated above the arrows [12].

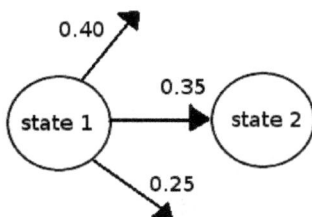

Figure 4: State machine example.

Figures 5a and 5b show state machines for both relevant and non relevant documents respectively. Both these figures contain a node to represent each of the dimensions studied in previous sections. Additionally they contain a "start" and "end" nodes, to denote the beginning and ending of the microblog document. Consequently, every existing tweet can be characterised by a particular path from the **start** to the **end**.

While both figures look very similar, there are some differences that are worth noting. Firstly, looking at the transition from mentions to the end of the document, we can see that the probability for relevant documents is more than double (+21%) than that for non-relevant documents. This means that relevant documents are more likely to finish mention than non-relevant microblogs.

Likewise the probability of ending a relevant document with a token of text is 12% less than for non-relevant documents. Moreover the chance of transitioning from a text token to a url token is 13% higher for relevant documents compared to non-relevant microblogs. Finally the chances to start a document with a mention is half (6% less) for relevant documents with respect to non-relevant ones.

---

[11] http://blog.hubspot.com/marketing/tweet-formulas-to-get-you-started-on-twitter
[12] Notice that all transition probabilities for a node add up to 1.

Table 6: Experimental results for the State retrieval method on the 2011 and 2012 collections. (* $p < 0.05$ and † $p < 0.01$)

	P@5	P@10	P@15	P@20	P@30	MAP
Baseline	0.458	0.432	0.399	0.382	0.362	0.109
State_0.02	0.451	0.434	0.408	0.396*	0.358	0.108
State_0.03	0.475	0.452†	0.414*	0.395*	0.362	0.108
State_0.05	0.478	**0.469†**	**0.428†**	0.395*	**0.369**	**0.110**
State_0.07	**0.481**	0.454	0.416	**0.398***	0.361	0.107
State_0.10	0.458	0.424	0.397	0.377	0.349	0.103

In order to test whether we can use this evidence for producing better rankings, we devised our **"State"** approach. The State approach is a re-ranking method that linearly combines the score given by any retrieval method with the aggregation of probabilities from start to end nodes w.r.t a microblog's structure.

As an example, consider the following tweet: *"Astronomers discover ancient system with five small planets. Details: http://go.nasa.gov/1wCpkJn @NASAKepler"*. Following the approach described above, we can infer the following structure: *"[start]− > [text]− > [url]− > [mention]− > [end]"*. If we take the automata for relevant documents (Figure 5a) as the source of probabilities it would produce the score: $0.89 + 0.60 + 0.01 + 0.37 = 1.87$.

The "State" score therefore is given by the following equation:

$$
\begin{aligned}
State(D, Q) = (1 - \alpha)P(q \subset D|Q) \\
+ \alpha * (R\_Score(D) - NR\_Score(D)),
\end{aligned}
\tag{9}
$$

where $R\_Score(D)$ and $NR\_Score(D)$ are the scores computed by traversing the automatas in Figures 5a and 5b respectively and α is a weighting factor which balances the linear combination. Notice the subtraction of the score given by the automata based on non-relevant documents with respect to the score based on relevant documents. The intuition is that, we want documents that agree with the structure observed for relevant documents, whilst diverging from that of non-relevant documents.

Table 6 shows the retrieval results for our re-ranking approach over the 2011 and 2012 collections. P@5 to P@30 represents Precision at the different cut-off points, whereas MAP denotes Mean Average Precision at cut-off 30. The first column contains the model being evaluated. Baseline represents a simple retrieval run using DFR only for ranking, whereas "State_n" contain the results for our "State" approach with different values of α.

As we can observe, retrieval effectiveness is improved significantly for a number of measures. Specifically the "State_0.05" configuration achieved a p value below 0.01 for both P@10 and P@15. We can see how the most prominent improvements are achieved at the top cut-off points. This result suggests that taking into consideration the structure of documents, helps in bringing more relevant documents to the very first few documents, which is a highly desirable

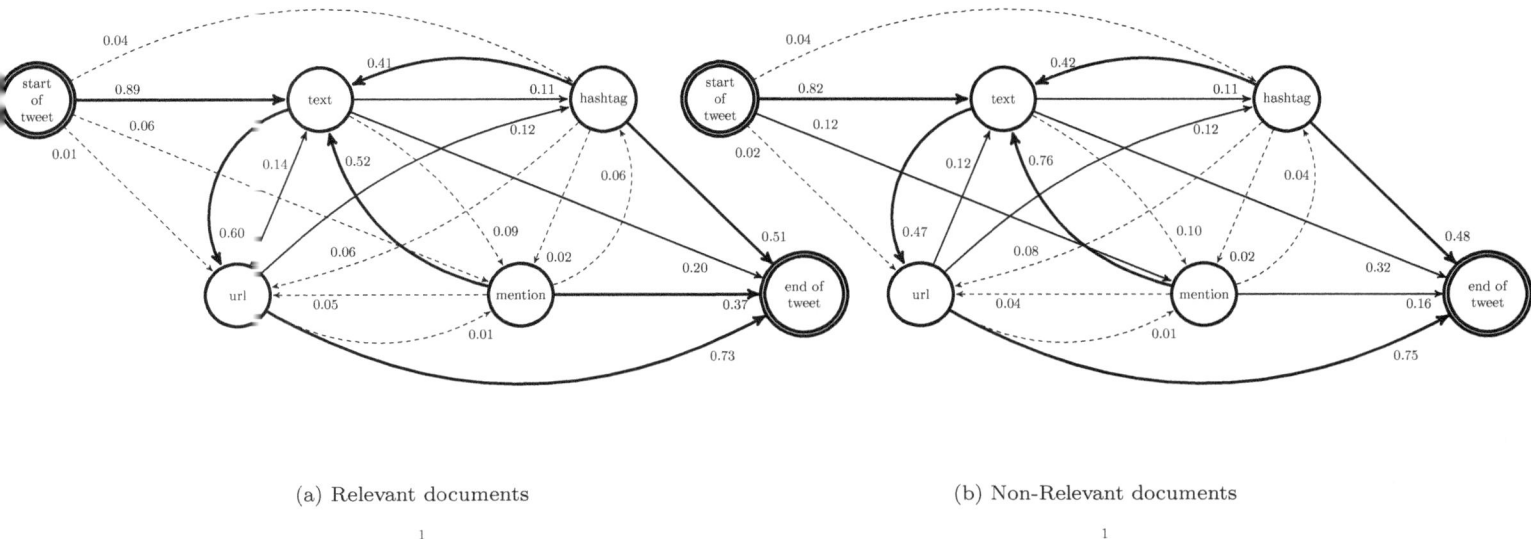

(a) Relevant documents

(b) Non-Relevant documents

Figure 5: Tweet automatas for the 2013 collection

product due to the fast-paced environment that is microblog search.

We can conclude from these experiments that the structure of tweets can be extracted and leveraged to produce better rankings. We can confirm that not only it is the relative space in terms of characters dedicated to each dimension that links to relevance, but also how these dimensions relate to each other within the document.

4.4 Additional notes

The simplicity of the state modelling allows for it to be conveniently stored and re-used in real-time. The states are stored as a set of precomputed heuristics which include the dimensions in the transition and its associated probability based on the observed data. The model itself should be updated from time to time to accommodate any shifting in the structuring and style of micro-bloggers.

5. CONCLUSIONS

In this work, we verified whether the scope and verbosity hypotheses still hold for microblog document retrieval. We hypothesise that, since microblog documents have a fixed maximum size, the scope and verbosity hypotheses do not hold, as they assume the author of the document is able to produce documents of any length. Furthermore we showed that there are no statistical differences in document length between relevant and non-relevant documents, therefore supporting our hypotheses.

This finding highlights the need for alternative ways to capture relevance in microblog documents. Firstly we rede-

fine a microblog document as a 4-dimensional entity. In the case of Tweets, the document contains 4 distinct dimensions namely, Text; Url; Mentions and Hashtags. Moreover, we proposed the notion of "Informativeness", which states that a microblog document's relevance or interestingness with respect to a user's information need expressed as a query, has a strong relationship with the structure of the document in terms of how much space is dedicated to each dimension.

Secondly, we propose a technique which re-weights the retrieval score of microblog documents based on how much the space dedicated to each dimension diverges from the optimal. By doing so, we were able to significantly improve the behaviour of a state of the art retrieval model in the context of microblog retrieval.

Finally, we extend our analysis to account for the different variations in the ordering of microblog dimensions. We devised state machines to model the structure of known relevant and non-relevant documents. Then we developed an approach that makes use of the probabilities provided by such state machines to produce scores which reflect on the structure of the documents. Our experimentation, shows with statistical significance that it is possible to utilise the structure of tweets to improve their ranking in an ad-hoc retrieval scenario.

Future work will further expose the relations between these dimensions as well as finding further applications of the features described in this paper for other purposes, such as Automatic Query Expansion.

6. REFERENCES

[1] Y. Aboulnaga, C. L. A. Clarke, and D. R. Cheriton. Frequent itemset mining for query expansion in microblog ad-hoc search.

[2] G. Amati, G. Amodeo, M. Bianchi, G. Marcone, F. U. Bordoni, C. Gaibisso, G. Gambosi, A. Celi, C. Di Nicola, and M. Flammini. Fub, iasi-cnr, univaq at trec 2011 microblog track. In *TREC*, 2011.

[3] G. Amati, C. Joost, and V. Rijsbergen. Probabilistic models for information retrieval based on divergence from randomness. 2003.

[4] A. E. C. Basave, A. Varga, M. Rowe, M. Stankovic, and A.-S. Dadzie. Making sense of microposts (# msm2013) concept extraction challenge. In *# MSM*, pages 1–15, 2013.

[5] F. Damak, K. Pinel-Sauvagnat, M. Boughanem, and G. Cabanac. Effectiveness of state-of-the-art features for microblog search. In *Proceedings of the 28th Annual ACM Symposium on Applied Computing*, SAC '13, pages 914–919, New York, NY, USA, 2013. ACM.

[6] P. Ferguson, N. O'Hare, J. Lanagan, O. Phelan, and K. McCarthy. An investigation of term weighting approaches for microblog retrieval. In *Advances in Information Retrieval*, pages 552–555. Springer, 2012.

[7] J. Gao, G. Cui, S. Liu, Y. Liu, and X. Cheng. Ictnet at microblog track in trec 2013.

[8] Z. Han, X. Li, M. Yang, H. Qi, S. Li, and T. Zhao. Hit at trec 2012 microblog track. *TREC Microblog 2012*, 2012.

[9] D. Hiemstra. Using language models for information retrieval. 2001.

[10] L. B. Jabeur, F. Damak, L. Tamine, G. Cabanac, K. Pinel-Sauvagnat, and M. Boughanem. Irit at trec microblog track 2013.

[11] Y. Kim, R. Yeniterzi, and J. Callan. Overcoming vocabulary limitations in twitter microblogs. *TREC Microblog 2012*, 2012.

[12] Y. Li, Z. Zhang, W. Lv, Q. Xie, Y. Lin, R. Xu, W. Xu, G. Chen, and J. Guo. Pris at trec 2011 microblog track. In *TREC*, 2011.

[13] K. Massoudi, M. Tsagkias, M. de Rijke, and W. Weerkamp. Incorporating query expansion and quality indicators in searching microblog posts. In *Advances in Information Retrieval*, pages 362–367. Springer, 2011.

[14] D. Metzler and C. Cai. Usc/isi at trec 2011: Microblog track. In *Proceedings of the Text REtrieval Conference (TREC 2011)*, 2011.

[15] R. Nagmoti, A. Teredesai, and M. De Cock. Ranking approaches for microblog search. In *Web Intelligence and Intelligent Agent Technology (WI-IAT), 2010 IEEE/WIC/ACM International Conference on*, volume 1, pages 153–157. IEEE, 2010.

[16] N. Naveed, T. Gottron, J. Kunegis, and A. C. Alhadi. Searching microblogs: coping with sparsity and document quality. In *Proceedings of the 20th ACM international conference on Information and knowledge management*, pages 183–188. ACM, 2011.

[17] I. Ounis, G. Amati, V. Plachouras, B. He, C. Macdonald, and D. Johnson. Terrier information retrieval platform. In *Advances in Information Retrieval*, pages 517–519. Springer, 2005.

[18] I. Ounis, C. Macdonald, J. Lin, and I. Soboroff. Overview of the trec-2011 microblog track. In *Proceeddings of the 20th Text REtrieval Conference*, 2011.

[19] J. A. R. Perez, A. J. McMinn, and J. M. Jose. University of glasgow (uog_twteam) at trec microblog.

[20] B. Pre-Processing. Bjut at trec 2013 microblog track.

[21] S. Robertson and H. Zaragoza. *The probabilistic relevance framework: BM25 and beyond*. Now Publishers Inc, 2009.

[22] T. Roelleke. Information retrieval models: Foundations and relationships. *Synthesis Lectures on Information Concepts, Retrieval, and Services*, 5(3):1–163, 2013.

[23] B. Sharifi, M.-A. Hutton, and J. Kalita. Experiments in microblog summarization. In *Social Computing (SocialCom), 2010 IEEE Second International Conference on*, pages 49–56, Aug 2010.

[24] Y. Y. H. W. G. C. Siming Zhu, Zhe Gao. Pris at 2013 microblog track.

[25] A. Singhal, C. Buckley, and M. Mitra. Pivoted document length normalization. In *Proceedings of the 19th annual international ACM SIGIR conference on Research and development in information retrieval*, pages 21–29. ACM, 1996.

[26] K. Tao, F. Abel, C. Hauff, and G.-J. Houben. What makes a tweet relevant for a topic? *Making Sense of Microposts (# MSM2012)*, pages 49–56, 2012.

[27] J. Teevan, D. Ramage, and M. Morris. # twittersearch: a comparison of microblog search and web search. In *Proceedings of the fourth ACM international conference on Web search and data mining*, pages 35–44. ACM, 2011.

[28] S. K. J. Y. P. Thomas. Searching and filtering tweets: Csiro at the trec 2012 microblog track.

[29] C. Zhai and J. Lafferty. A study of smoothing methods for language models applied to ad hoc information retrieval. In *Proceedings of the 24th annual international ACM SIGIR conference on Research and development in information retrieval*, pages 334–342. ACM, 2001.

Online News Tracking for Ad-Hoc Information Needs

Jeroen B. P. Vuurens
The Hague University of Applied Science
Delft University of Technology, The Netherlands
j.b.p.vuurens@tudelft.nl

Arjen P. de Vries
CWI
Delft University of Technology, The Netherlands
arjen@acm.org

Roi Blanco
Yahoo Labs, London, England UK
roi@yahoo-inc.com

Peter Mika
Yahoo Labs, London, England UK
pmika@yahoo-inc.com

ABSTRACT

Following online news about a specific event can be a difficult task as new information is often scattered across web pages. In such cases, an up-to-date summary of the event would help to inform users and allow them to navigate to articles that are likely to contain relevant and novel details. We propose a three-step approach to online news tracking for ad-hoc information needs. First, we continuously cluster the titles of all incoming news articles. Then, we select the clusters that best fit a user's ad-hoc information need and identify salient sentences. Finally, we select sentences for the summary based on novelty and relevance to the information seen, without requiring an a-priori model of events of interest. We evaluate this approach using the 2013 TREC Temporal Summarization test set and show that compared to existing systems our approach retrieves news facts with significantly higher F-measure and Latency-Discounted Expected Gain.

Categories and Subject Descriptors

H.3.3 [**Information Search and Retrieval**]: Information Filtering

General Terms

Clustering, Multi-document summarization

1. INTRODUCTION

Internet users are turning more frequently to online news as a replacement for traditional media sources such as newspapers or television shows. Still, discovering news events online and following them as they develop can be a difficult task. Although the Web offers a seemingly large and diverse set of information sources ranging from highly curated professional content to social media, in practice most sources base their stories on previously published works and add a much more limited set of new information. Thus users often end up spending significant amount of effort re-reading the same parts of a story before finding relevant and novel information. Most recently, the TREC Temporal Summarization track[1]

---

[1] http://www.trec-ts.org/

have taken up this challenge, promoting research in the area of *online* news summarization, i.e. focusing on developing news, as opposed to archival news. Online summarization is a crucial aspect of real-world products such as online live streams for natural disasters, product launches, financial or political events, breaking news notifications on mobile devices and topical daily news summaries like Yahoo! news digest[2].

In this study, we propose a novel approach for the temporal summarization of news. Our approach works in an online fashion and provides previously unseen information related to a predefined ad-hoc information need, expressed as a user query. Contributions of this work are the use of a specifically designed clustering approach to detect news that is supported by multiple online providers, and the online selection of the best sentences according to a specifically tailored relevance model over recently seen information, that allows the retrieval of unanticipated information by adapting to information recently seen instead of requiring an a-priori model of events of interest, and requires no manual intervention and contains a small number of parameters that can be tuned in straightforward fashion.

We evaluate our approach using the 2013 TREC Temporal Summarization test set. In these experiments, our approach significantly outperformed the top performing systems on both F-measure and latency-discounted expected gain. To facilitate further research in this area, we also publish our implementation of the described model, the results of empirical experiments and the annotated ground truth[3].

The remainder of this paper is structured as follows: Section 2 discusses related work in the area of temporal summarization of online news information and the necessary prerequisites. In Section 3, we present our approach to extract sentences containing news facts from an online stream of news articles. In Section 4, we describe the implementation, test set used for the empirical evaluation, and how the data in the collection was processed. In Section 5, we present the results of the empirical evaluation, and analyze parameter sensitivity. The conclusions are presented in Section 6.

2. RELATED WORK

2.1 News tracking and summarization

The task of detecting events can be automated using information about the events published online. For this purpose, the Topic Detection and Tracking (TDT) program was initiated to discuss applications and techniques for detecting and tracking events that occur in real-time and the infrastructure to support common evaluations

---

[2] https://mobile.yahoo.com/newsdigest
[3] http://newstrackerpaper.github.io/

of component technologies. The *tracking of news* involves the on-line identification of stories that discuss a targeted event, which needs to begin as soon as a only a few training documents have become available to model a real world setting. For this, Allan et al. present an information filtering approach, in which a tf-idf vector made from training documents is used as a query to match only documents that exceed a similarity threshold. In one experiment, "surprising" (previously rarely seen) words were used for tracking events, but they found that these words do not provide a broad enough coverage to capture all stories on the event and that many of these "surprising" words are useless for retrieval. They also found that a query based on initial training documents does not allow to track stories when the discussion of an event changes over time. For some queries at least, results were improved by using a tracking model that adapts the query based on new information seen, similar to the notion of pseudo-relevance feedback [5].

The temporal summary of news stories can help a person monitor changes in the coverage of news stories over time, which are typically very redundant and increase the effort required to identify genuinely new information [13]. The core technique of temporal summarization is to summarize multiple texts by extracting salient sentences. Regarding measures of salience that can be used to choose the best sentences for news summarization, the literature provides no clear consensus. Two general criteria to select the best candidates sentences are the most *useful* and *novel* sentences, i.e., related to the topic and non-redundant. Techniques that use these criteria for instance consider the words in the sentences, look for cue words and phrases, consider features such as sentence length and the case of words, or compare patterns of relationships between sentences. Often, these approaches use statistics from the corpus itself to decide on the importance of sentences, and some leverage existing training sets of summaries to learn the properties of a summary [3]. Candidate sentences can subsequently be ranked based on estimated importance, e.g. [11, 18, 21]. Some work has focused more specifically on the summarization of news in an online setting. Radev et al. presented a news delivery and summarization system "News In Essence", that supported retrieval of news related to a document that the user provided [19]. Gabrilovich et al. present a methodology for filtering news stories based on novelty, by selecting the articles that are most different to those already read [13]. This work also focuses on summarization in an online setting.

The salience of sentences is more easy to determine in retrospect than for online systems [23]. In retrospect, there is more information to compare possible solutions based on size and the coverage of the possible relevant facts over the stream of redundant information. Erkan et al. argue that sentences that are similar to many of the other sentences in a cluster are more central (or salient) to the topic, and propose an algorithm with resemblances the HITS algorithm that uses similarity edges instead of hyperlinks to estimate the salience of sentences [11]. Yu et al. present an approach to detect opinions in contrast to factual information with very high precision and recall, by using a fairly straightforward Bayesian classifier [24]. In recent work, Tran et al. used this classification approach in reverse to select headlines containing factual news. They further refined their detection of salient headlines by assuming that a higher *spread* indicates more important news, and that the relatedness to subsequent events indicates *influential* news, but it appears their approach is more specific for summarization in retrospect [21].

The clustering of information that discusses the same topic can be useful for several purposes related to temporal summarization. Some studies use the heuristic that the most similar sentences tend to be salient, which can be detected using clustering [12, 11, 14].

Clustering has also been used to extract concise information from redundant sources [4, 18]. Allan et al. experimented with different variants and obtained better results using single linkage clustering with cosine similarity [4]. In single linkage clustering, every data points is assigned to its nearest neighbor, in accordance to the k-Nearest Neighbor (kNN) decision rule described by Cover and Hart for classification [10]. They show that for the classification of n-samples there exists no $k \neq 1$ with a lower probability of error than $k = 1$ against all distributions. A known problem for finding nearest neighbors in large datasets is that the required number of computations increases quadratically [17].

The main contribution of this work is a novel approach to select the most salient sentences in a news stream, by leveraging the redundancy that is typical between news articles that discuss the same event. We introduce a variant of kNN clustering called 3-NN, which differs from existing work by forming clusters around a minimum of three sentences that are in each others' $k = 3$ sets of nearest neighbors and published by different news agents. For the online summarization of these salient sentences, we use an adaptive approach that resembles that of [5], but rather based on recently seen salient sentences to limit the selection of sentences to the most relevant according to the most recent news. The complete system we used to evaluate these efforts can be viewed as a hybrid combination of techniques for query based online news tracking and summarization, adapted from [5, 3]. Our approach differs by a stronger emphasis on novelty of information emitted (like [13]). Hereto, we estimate the amount of previously unseen information to use only sentences that are likely to contain novel information.

2.2 TREC Temporal Summarization

In recent years, TREC stimulated research on online summarization of news related to a specific topic or query, by initiating the Temporal Summarization track. The PRIS team participated with a manual system in the 2013 edition of the TS track and obtained the highest Expected Gain. They use hierarchical Latent Dirichlet Allocation on documents describing similar events as the topic to mine ten subtopic descriptions per TREC topic. From the generated topic descriptions they manually selected the keywords that describe each topic best. The sentences that are most similar to the selected keywords of a topic are selected as output [25]. In the same track edition, ICTNET obtained the highest F-measure of all participants. A list of relevant words is learned from training documents, which are then matched to the sentences of documents that contain all query terms in the title. A matching sentence is then compared to previously emitted sentences, and removed if the similarity exceeds a threshold [15]. These participants provided the best performing runs, out of 27 submitted for this task, and we will compare our results to the results of these systems in the evaluation. These query based approaches dominantly make use of a model crafted over similar events, e.g. other earthquakes or train crashes documented on Wikipedia. These approaches are optimized for retrieving the same, often reported types of information about common types of events, but may fail when the type of the event is not known or the type of information is not typical for the type of event. The proposed method uses only a single query to represent the event and does not require further training data.

3. DESIGN

News facts can be obtained from several sources on the Web, e.g. online news sites, blogs, social media, Wikipedia. One advantage over traditional broadcast news is that online news facilitates easy access to additional information. However, manually tracking relevant and novel news facts online is rendered inefficient by the high redundancy between multiple sources that discuss more or less the same information. This research focuses therefore on the automated extraction of relevant and novel news facts for ad-hoc information needs, allowing to push newly published facts to a user the instant they are published; or, alternatively, to present the user a summary of the most important news facts over a timeline. Additionally, presenting the most important news facts on a timeline may also be useful to help keep update knowledge bases up-to-date, such as Wikipedia or the knowledge graphs used by search engine companies. From an end-user perspective, we consider it important that a high percentage of results is on-topic, and therefore this study uses news articles as the sole source. We expect their content to be mostly factually correct, timely, and presented in an accessible form [19]. Events that are of interest to many people are naturally reported in different news articles, from different sources [5, 9]. In our approach, we leverage the redundancy between news articles, clustering sentences that are likely to discuss the same news facts to select salient sentences and to avoid biased information [14]. Eventually, our work may serve as a baseline to evaluate approaches that also consider alternative sources like social media.

In this Section, we describe a new approach to extract sentences from an online stream of published news articles that are related to a user's ad-hoc query. We operate in a strict online setting, processing the articles one at a time as they arrive. The remainder of this Section first discusses observed characteristics for factual news. We outline the process that is proposed to extract sentences containing news facts from a stream of online news articles, followed by a detailed discussion of each step in this process.

3.1 News extraction process

We first outline the proposed method for the online tracking of ad-hoc user needs in a stream of news articles, which consists of three steps: *route*, *identify salient sentences* and *summarize*. The key method underpinning our approach is a clustering method that takes care of both the routing and the identification of salient sentences. In the first step, a single graph is maintained in which all news articles are clustered, and 'query matching clusters' are *routed* to a query specific module to identify salient sentences. In this second step, per query that is being tracked, we cluster the contents of clusters that match that query to *identify* the most central sentences, which we consider the most salient ones. In the third step, per query that is being tracked we *summarize* the salient information by qualifying only the most novel and useful sentences from the current document.

3.1.1 Routing

The first step of the outlined process identifies clusters of news articles by several news agents that share information, and route 'query matching clusters' to the designated identification and summarization process that is executed per query. Here, we define *query matching clusters* as the clusters that contain at least one news article that matches that query; in this study, an article matches a query when all query terms appear in its title. This section first gives a rationale for the features used to assign a document's nearest neighbors, and then describes the clustering method in detail.

To estimate which news articles are likely to discuss the same event, we use the similarity of the titles and the proximity of the publication times. The use of titles is motivated by the observation of Tran et al., that news article titles are often short sentence abstracts of the news contained, to allow readers to gain a quick overview of the news based on titles and to invite them to read the full article if it is of interest to them [21]. Additionally, titles contain less words than entire documents, and so the collection of

news article titles can be fitted into the memory of a single computer, allowing to process the data without the need to partition it. The latter is primarily a practical argument when developing an online news summarization approach. The use of proximity in publication times is motivated by the observation that stories about the same event often occur in proximate time, most particularly for unexpected events where the news media exhibit strong interest in a story [5, 23].

We introduce a *3-NN* streaming variant of k-Nearest Neighbor clustering, that assigns directed edges to each article's three nearest neighbors while not allowing nearest neighbor links within the same web domain. We use an online algorithm to detect newly formed clusters as 2-cores, according to the theory of k-degenerate graphs [16]. These 2-cores identify the most central information based on similarity in content, proximity in publication time and support by multiple news agents. The selected news is therefore is more likely to be factual, correct and important.

In 3-NN, a new 2-core is formed only when the arriving node is part of a bi-directional loop of nodes that is currently not clustered. Multiple bi-directional loops that are connected by a single bi-directional edge are considered to be separate clusters. Nodes that are not part of a 2-core are still assigned to a cluster if their majority of nearest neighbors is a member of the same cluster. Figure 1 illustrates the online process that takes place upon the arrival of new articles (that correspond to nodes in the graph), when clusters are formed, expanded or disbanded. Edges in the graph point to one of a node's k-nearest neighbors, labeled with the similarity between the nodes. Dashed arrows indicate the similarity between new arriving nodes and existing nodes.

Considering the example of Figure 1a in more detail, nodes A and B are not clustered because there is no evidence that the majority of both nodes nearest neighbors must belong to the same cluster (C and D could belong to different clusters). When a new node F arrives (Figure 1b), it is compared to the existing nodes, to assign its three nearest neighbors. Since F is more similar to B than B's currently weakest nearest neighbor E, an edge from B to F will replace the edge from B to E. After F has been added (Figure 1c), nodes A, B and F form a bi-directional loop. For this particular situation, we can deduce that A, B and F must have their majority of nearest neighbors in the same cluster, and therefore they form a cluster. We will refer to the nodes that form a bidirectional loop to establish a cluster as its *core nodes*. In Figure 1d, E is added to the cluster consisting of A, B, F, because its majority of nearest neighbors connect to that cluster. In Figure 1e, when a new node G arrives that is more similar to A than its weakest of nearest neighbors F is, the edge from A to F will be replaced by an edge from A to G. With this change, the bi-directional loop from which we deduced the existence of a cluster A, B, F, is now gone. Therefore, in Figure 1f, there is no more cluster.

The nearest neighbors of a given title or sentence are found by computing the similarity to all other titles or sentences. The similarity between two sentences s_i and s_j is scored using Equation 1, which combines the cosine similarity between the binary vector representation of the two sentences with the difference in publication time, in accordance to the observations by [23]. Equation 2 estimates the temporal proximity of two publications, $\tau \in [0,1]$, as the absolute time between the publication times of $s_i.t$ and $s_j.t$, truncated by a constant maximum period T. Equation 3, δ is a function that guarantees that assigned nearest neighbors are published within a time span with duration T, and originate from a different source domain ($s_i.d \neq s_j.d$).

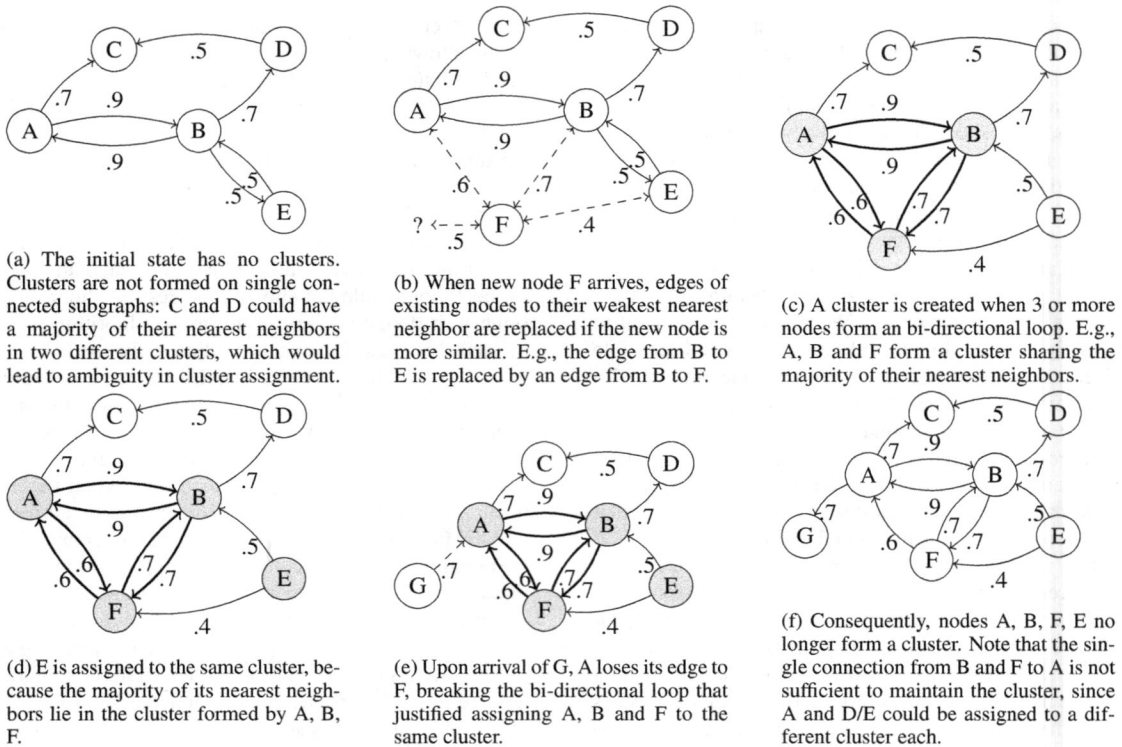

(a) The initial state has no clusters. Clusters are not formed on single connected subgraphs: C and D could have a majority of their nearest neighbors in two different clusters, which would lead to ambiguity in cluster assignment.

(b) When new node F arrives, edges of existing nodes to their weakest nearest neighbor are replaced if the new node is more similar. E.g., the edge from B to E is replaced by an edge from B to F.

(c) A cluster is created when 3 or more nodes form an bi-directional loop. E.g., A, B and F form a cluster sharing the majority of their nearest neighbors.

(d) E is assigned to the same cluster, because the majority of its nearest neighbors lie in the cluster formed by A, B, F.

(e) Upon arrival of G, A loses its edge to F, breaking the bi-directional loop that justified assigning A, B and F to the same cluster.

(f) Consequently, nodes A, B, F, E no longer form a cluster. Note that the single connection from B and F to A is not sufficient to maintain the cluster, since A and D/E could be assigned to a different cluster each.

Figure 1: Explaining when clusters are created and broken using the nearest neighbor heuristic, $K = 3$, with the requirement that nodes are only clustered when they are members of a 2-degenerate core or when their majority of nearest neighbors is a member the same cluster.

$$sim(s_i, s_j) = cos\left(s_i, s_j\right) \cdot \tau\left(s_i, s_j\right) \cdot \delta\left(s_i, s_j\right) \quad (1)$$

$$\tau(s_i, s_j) = 1 - \frac{|s_i.t - s_j.t|}{T} \quad (2)$$

$$\delta(s_i, s_j) = \begin{cases} 0, & \text{if } |s_i.t - s_j.t| > T \text{ or } s_i.d = s_j.d \\ 1, & \text{otherwise} \end{cases} \quad (3)$$

3.1.2 Identification of salient sentences

For each tracked query, we identify salient sentences in a separate graph. The routing will result in forwarding the clusters that match a query to the corresponding 'sentence graph', to which a node is added for every sentence in the query matching clusters. For sentences we follow an analogous rationale as for titles; salient sentences are likely to be published in proximate time and share information and are thus likely to be clustered together, and we therefore cluster the sentences according to the same 3-NN heuristics as described above. Within the clusters of such a 'sentence graph', the core nodes are the most central sentences and thus in this study regarded as the most salient. Operating in an online setting, we only consider sentences from the current document as *candidate sentences* for the news summary. However, if candidate sentences are clustered, their entire cluster will be passed to the summarization step, since the cluster provides part of the context needed to qualify (future) candidate sentences.

3.1.3 Summarization

In general, for an optimal summary of news we should select sentences that are the most useful and novel, i.e. related to the topic and non-redundant with other sentences in the summary [3]. In this step, we qualify which candidate sentence(s) are added to the news summary. Obviously, this is easier to optimize in retrospect than in an online setting, since we must decide whether or not to use a sentence without knowledge of what is yet to come. Operating in an online setting, we only consider sentences from the current document to use in the summary. Once the decision has been made to add a sentence to the summary, this cannot be reversed if the original sentence is removed from the cluster when a new sentence arrives. For the qualification we formulate a set of heuristics to select useful and novel sentences.

Erkan et al. hypothesize that sentences that are similar to many other sentences in the cluster are more salient to the topic [11]. In our 3-NN clustering, the core nodes are thus likely to be the most salient sentences. Initially, we expand clusters by adding non-core nodes that have a majority of nearest neighbors in one cluster. However, nodes can be assigned to a non-related cluster in the absence of closely related content. A directed path from a core node to another cluster member is likely to identify closely related content. To reduce the risk of using off-topic sentences, we apply a variant of graph peeling [1] by removing nodes to which there exists no directed path from a core node. In the remainder of this section when we refer to cluster members we only consider the cluster members for which a directed path exists from a core node.

In our approach, a redundant stream of news articles is aggregated into a concise summary by selecting only sentences that are most relevant to the most recent developments for the topic. Without the use of training documents, we obtain a model of the most important information from the news stream, however, what information is important for a topic can change over time [5]. Yang et al. observed that a time gap between bursts of topically similar stories is often an indication of different events, suggesting a need for monitoring cluster evolution over time and a possible benefit from using a time window for event scoping [23]. If significant shifts in vocabulary indicate stories that report a novel event, this motivates the use of an adaptive model that allows to identify novel events. Analogous to [8], we propose an unsupervised 'berry-picking' approach that estimates relevance at some point in time based on the information seen in a window over the prior h hours, and compares the estimated relevance of the candidate sentences to sentences already summarized, to selectively qualify only candidate sentences that rank among the top-r sentences. The rationale for this berry-picking approach is that news topics tend to evolve over several subtopics; consider for example a crime happening, the police investigation, a suspect being arrested, etc. Some subtopics are repeatedly reported over a longer period, while others are mentioned only briefly. We construct a relevance model per news topic (a current 'event profile'), which is initially seeded with the user's query terms. The model is continuously expanded with the core node sentences from all query matching clusters to limit the risk of adding off-topic information. An adaptive relevance model is obtained at time t by removing sentences that were published before $t - h$ hours, allowing to shift the notion of relevance to recently seen information. In the event the relevance model contains no sentences published after $t - h$, the relevance model returns to the original query terms. For ranking, we express the relevance at a given a point in time as a word vector, where the frequency of each word is the number of sentences it appeared in over the last h hours. The candidate sentences of the latest arriving document are then ranked among the sentences currently in the summary, using the cosine similarity between each sentence and the relevance vector. Candidate sentences ranked outside the top-r are disqualified for use in the summary.

New sentences that share no words with information already seen can disorient the reader, being possibly off-topic as well. To reduce topical drift and improve readability of the timeline created, we require qualified sentences to contain at least one of the query terms and two words that appear jointly in either the query or in a sentence already used in the summary. Formally, in Equation 4, we define $WC(s)$ as the collection of all combinations of words (w_1, w_2) that appear in sentence s, and $QWC(s,q)$ as the subset of $WC(s)$ in which at least one of the words appears in the query q. In Equation 6, we define K as the collection of all word combinations containing at least one query term that was previously seen in either the query q or one of the sentences in the summary S. Finally, in Equation 7 is the constraint that at least on of the word combinations in the candidate sentence c must be in $K(S,Q)$. This simple requirement effectively filters out the (unrelated) sentences that still form clusters, such as navigational elements or links to other news stories.

$$WC(s) = \{(w_1, w_2) \mid w_1 \in s \land w_2 \in s \land w_1 < w_2\} \quad (4)$$

$$QWC(s,q) = \{(w_1, w_2) \in WC(s) \mid w_1 \in q \lor w_2 \in q\} \quad (5)$$

$$K(S,q) = \cup_{s \in S} QWC(s,q) \cup WC(q) \quad (6)$$

$$K(S,q) \cap WC(c) \neq \emptyset \quad (7)$$

Additionally, qualified sentences must add information that is not previously seen and is supported by another source. Previously unseen information could be simply measured by the number of previously unseen unigrams. Alternatively, the amount of information shared by sentences can be estimated by the number of two-word combinations that appear jointly in both sentences, which is possibly less affected by noise and will be used unless stated otherwise. Formally, in Equation 8, we define the set of possible sentences that can provide support for word combinations $SUP(CL,c)$, as the sentences s in cluster CL that are published on a news site $s.d$ that is different from the news site of the candidate sentence $c.d$. In Equation 9, we define the information gain G as the number of two-word combinations that appear in both the candidate sentence c and a sentence on a different news site, but not in one of the sentences that was used in summary S. In Equation 10, we set a threshold based on the number of possible word combinations that contains at least one non-query term. We use a parameter $g \in [0,1]$ to control the fraction of two-term combinations that must be gained to qualify a sentence to use in the summary.

$$SUP(CL,c) = \{s \in CL \mid s.d \neq c.d\} \quad (8)$$

$$G(c,CL,S) = |\cup_{s \in SUP(CL,c)} WC(s) \cap WC(c) - \cup_{s \in S} WC(s)| \quad (9)$$

$$G(c,CL,S) >= (|c - q|) \cdot (|c| - 1) \cdot g \quad (10)$$

4. EXPERIMENT

4.1 Feasibility of online KNN Clustering

Clustering all news articles using the nearest neighbor heuristic, requires the computation of similarity of each news article against all others. For incremental online clustering, the number of required comparisons can be reduced by using a criterion to remove nodes and clusters that are outdated, by Aggerwal et al. referred to as 'cluster death' [2]. Since in this approach a zero score is assigned between sentences with a publication time more than T away (see Equation 3), we can do so with a high probability of not affecting clustering results. Since the news sentences of such a limited period of time fits into memory, we do not require an approximation such as Latent Semantic Hashing to partition the data. Additionally, we use in-memory posting lists on the words that appear in sentences, so that we do not compare sentences that have no word in common. In practice, this results in an algorithm of order $n \cdot log(n)$. Figure 2 shows the clustering efficiency over a stream of news articles in the KBA corpus, from 2011-11-06 until 2011-11-27, that was clustered on a standard laptop, in approx. 100 seconds. On the left-hand side of the graph, we observe that the clustering speed slows down slightly when more articles are in memory. The vertical drops in the graph are the result of removing 'expired' articles as discussed above. This graph shows online processing of all published news titles is feasible using the proposed clustering approach.

In the proposed 3-NN clustering method, nodes that do not have 2 nearest neighbors in the same cluster correspond to the outliers of Aggarwal and Philip [2] and remain un-clustered. In our experiments using sentences of news articles, on average 20% is unclustered at any given time.

In theory, a chain of nearest neighbors could span a period greater than T, and, although unlikely, cluster assignment could be affected over a larger time span. To allow for such anomalies, at the end of each day we prune sentences older than $T + 1$ days, except for clustered sentences which are not pruned until all its members are older than $T + 1$ days. For the 2013 KBA Streaming corpus, we compared the clustering results of a pruned run to a run that does not prune the articles from memory, and confirm that the clustering is not affected by removing 'expired' items.

4.2 Evaluation

To evaluate our approach, we used the test collection from the Sequential Update Summarization task at the 2013 TREC Temporal Summarization track, and compare effectiveness against the two best performing systems. For this track, the 2013 KBA Streaming

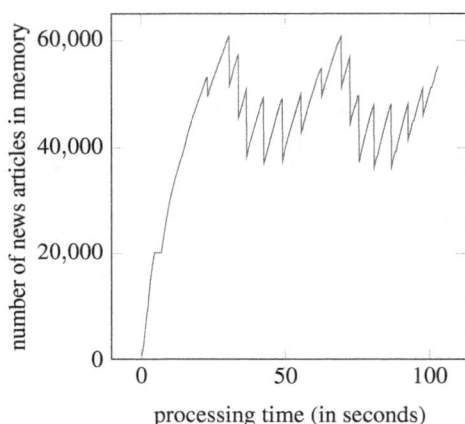

Figure 2: during the clustering of a stream of 3 weeks, the number of news articles in memory over time

corpus was used, in which the documents are already parsed into sentences by the organizers, and the sentence numbers are being referred to from the existing ground truth set. The task is to retrieve a list of timestamped extracted sentences (referred to as *updates*), for a set of 9 topics that contain a query referring to a news event. The effectiveness of a system is measured using a set of gold standard updates (referred to as *nuggets*), that were extracted from Wikipedia event pages and timestamped according to the revision history of the page. The TREC participants submitted a list of updates, from which a pool of 3,268 updates was manually compared to the 1275 identified nuggets for 9 topics, resulting in 2,416 matches between updates and nuggets and 2,142 updates that do not match a nugget (one update can match multiple nuggets).

Of the sentences returned in our experiments we found that an insufficient number has been annotated by TREC to obtain reliable metrics (see Section 5.4 for the empirical data and discussion). As a resolution, we manually annotated all missing sentences *against the existing nuggets*. During the annotation, to the best of our ability we retrieved similar results that were scored by TREC annotators to score our results consistently. Occasionally, we encountered updates that seemed very relevant but could not be matched to any nugget. Since we assume that no nuggets were added in the process of scoring the updates for participating TREC systems, we did not add any nuggets to the ground truth. Adding the updates to the pool without a matching nugget is equivalent to scoring these as irrelevant.

4.3 Data processing and cleaning

In an exploratory phase we used a crawl of online news articles over the first part of 2014 for construction and training of the system. For this crawl, we extracted a list of domains that are referenced on the Wikipedia Current Event Portal between January 1st 2013 and September 1st 2014, from the WikiTimes portal [20]. We removed all domains from Asia, Africa, non-English and non-news domains, resulting in 141 domains. For the evaluation on the KBA Streaming corpus, we use the same system and consider only news articles from the described domains.

The KBA Streaming corpus contains the original HTML source of the documents and sentences that were extracted by the organizers. This extraction was done using rudimentary heuristics, which in the absence of periods occasionally produced sentences of several hundreds of words that for instance include entire paragraphs, tables or navigational labels. Since our approach specifically de-

pends on the quality of title clusters, we extracted the actual document titles from within the HTML title tags, stripped non-news elements (e.g. categories and news paper names) using a manually constructed list of general and domain specific regular expressions (e.g. truncating titles after the a dash and removing the word TIME if this was the last word in a title from the `time.com` domain). These actual titles are used for clustering the articles. For a fair comparison of the proposed model to the best TREC participants, we performed a *no titles* run that emits only sentences as extracted by the TREC organizers and thus is conform to the TREC guidelines. In Section 5.1, we will compare the performance to a run that does allow *HTML titles* to be emitted.

For processing, all sentences were tokenized by separating tokens on non-alphanumeric characters, the tokens were lowercased, and stop words were removed, however, we did not use any stemming.

4.4 Parameter settings

The approach proposed in this paper contains several parameters: k as the number of nearest neighbors used for kNN clustering, T as a time period used to discount the difference in publication time in the similarity function (Equation 2), r for the rank to be obtained to qualify a sentence to use in the summary (Section 3.1.3), l for the maximum length allowed for sentences used (Equation 3.1.3), h for the time in hours used for the relevance model (Section 3.1.3), and g to control the minimum amount of new information an qualified sentence must have (Equation 10). In the exploration phase of this research we analyzed the effect of these parameters on seven topics that were annotated using the guidelines of the TREC TS track, and on online news that is tracked in a live demo [22].

For the number of nearest neighbors, we used a fixed setting $k = 3$. By using an odd number of nearest neighbors there is no need to resolve ties. A value of $k > 1$ increases the likelihood to cluster around information that is supported by several news domains, while compared to high settings for k a low setting for k is likely to retrieve news faster and may improve recall. We leave the comparison of different values of k for future work, noting that this may be especially useful in more redundant domains like social media. For T, we have used a fixed setting $T = 3$ days throughout our study, based on the observation that it is not uncommon for news providers to post news that is more than a day old and allowing these articles to be clustered with the same content brought more promptly by other providers. Each of the remaining parameters was added to restrain the model in some respect. We observe that clustering results may vary largely dependent on parameter settings, which is possibly due to the high redundancy that is typical for news collections. The necessity of new manual annotation for each clustering outcome renders parameter training practically infeasible. Despite the variation in clustering results, the overall system performance is largely unaffected by changes in parameters. Therefore, we use a set of default settings $r = 5$, $l = 20$, $h = 1$ and $g = 0.3$, and will show in Section 5.2 that the model performance is insensitive to parameter sweeps.

5. RESULTS

5.1 Comparison of temporal summarization

For evaluation of the proposed method, we follow the guidelines of the Sequential Update Summarization task of the 2013 TREC Temporal Summarization track [6]. The effectiveness is measured using *Mean Expected Gain*, and *Mean Comprehensiveness*, which are similar to the traditional notions of respectively precision and recall in information retrieval systems, and we additionally use the

Mean Latency Discounted Expected Gain in which the gain is discounted based on the difference between the time of the first update that matches a nugget and the time the corresponding fact was added to Wikipedia. Formally, in Equation 11, the gain G of an update u in a set of updates S is based on a gain function g on the nuggets n for which u is the earliest matching update as returned by the function M^{-1}. In Equation 13, the Mean Expected Gain MEG_v for a system is the average gain over a set of events ε, for each of which the system produced sets of updates S^e (emitted sentences), for g (Equation 11) a binary function is used that returns 1 if an update matches a nugget, and the total gain is normalized by the verbosity of the updates $V(u)$ (Equation 12), which discounts by the number of words in u that are not part of an earliest matching string for a nugget divided by the average number of words in the strings of nuggets $|words_n|$. In Equation 14, the Comprehensiveness C for a set of updates S for a specific event is number of matched nuggets G divided by the number of available nuggets for the event $|N|$. In Equation 15, the Mean Comprehensiveness MC is computed over all events ε. The Latency-Discounted Expected Gain is a variant of Equation 13 by using a modified function g (Equation 11) in which the binary relevance of matched nuggets is discounted by a monotonically decreasing function over the difference between the time of the earliest matching update en the time it was put on Wikipedia. For more details regarding these metrics, we refer to [6]. We also report the variant of the *F-measure* that summarizes the Expected Gain and Comprehensiveness in one metric and was used as the primary metric of the 2014 Temporal Summarization track.

$$G(u,S) = \sum_{n \in M^{-1}(u,S)} g(u,n) \tag{11}$$

$$V(u) = 1 + \frac{|all\_words_u| - |nugget\_matching\_words_u|}{avg|words_n|} \tag{12}$$

$$MEG_v = \frac{1}{|\varepsilon|} \sum_{e \in \varepsilon} \left(\frac{1}{\sum_{u \in S^e} V(u)} \sum_{u \in S^e} G(u,S^e) \right) \tag{13}$$

$$C(S) = \frac{1}{|N|} \sum_{u \in S} G(u,S) \tag{14}$$

$$MC = \frac{1}{|\varepsilon|} \sum_{e \in \varepsilon} C(S^e) \tag{15}$$

In Table 1, we compare four variants of our approach with the top participants of the Temporal Summarization Track. The "no titles" variant only uses the extracted HTML titles for clustering, but never uses these in the summary, therefore the results of this run are conform the track guidelines and comparable to other TREC participants. For the "HTML title" variant, we additionally allowed emission of the actual HTML titles which was not an option for TREC participants, the "unigram" variant is the same as "HTML titles" except that it measures new and previously seen information using unigrams instead of two-word combinations, and the "IDF weighted" variant uses the inverse document frequency obtained from Wikipedia on January 2012 (which predates the test collection) to compute the cosine similarity between sentences.

The results show that the "no titles" variant is significantly more effective than the top TREC in both F-measure and Latency-Discounted Expected Gain. Statistical significance was tested using a paired Student t-Test, 2-tailed, $p < 0.05$. Given the low number of topics, we also tested significance using Wilcoxon Signed-Rank test, 2-tailed, $p < 0.05$, which confirmed the significant improvements for all but the improvement in F-Measure of the "unigram" variant over ICTNET. At the topic level, our approach was outperformed by PRIS on topic 5 "Hurricane Isaac", and by ICTNET on topic

Table 1: Comparison of performance using the 2013 TREC TS track against the top participants. † significant improvements over PRIS, ‡ significant improvement over ICTNET, using paired Student t-Test, 2-tailed, $p < 0.05$

System	Expected Gain	Latency DEG	Comprehension	F
PRIS-cluster5	0.1491	0.1364	0.0994	0.060
ICTNET-run2	0.1024	0.1270	0.1921	0.067
no titles	0.2607 ‡	0.3067 †‡	0.1778	0.106 †
HTML titles	0.2449 ‡	0.3019 †‡	0.1901	0.107 †‡
unigram	0.2474 ‡	0.2934 †‡	0.1700	0.101 †‡
IDF weighted	0.2100 ‡	0.2763 †‡	0.1664	0.093 †

6 "Hurricane Sandy", using approaches that target words typically seen on the Wikipedia pages of hurricanes such as wind speeds, casualties and damage.

Compared to the "no titles" variant, the "HTML titles" variant obtains higher Comprehensiveness and a relatively higher Latence-Discounted Expected Gain. Possibly, some facts are only used in titles and some facts are introduced in titles before they are used in sentences. In Section 5.3, we look into the differences observed between these variants in more detail.

5.2 Parameter sensitivity

To study sensitivity of the effectiveness to variation of parameters, we performed parameter sweeps for the "HTML titles" variant, and plotted the results in Figure 3. During each sweep we changed only one parameter, using the default settings described in Section 4.4 for the remaining parameters.

Interestingly, we observe that the efficiency is insensitive to the size h of the time window used to estimate a relevance model of recently seen information. Possibly, if news is important it is mostly reported by different agents within half an hour, explaining why the effectiveness is comparable for a window of that size. For the rank r a sentence must obtain to qualify, we expected an increase in Comprehensiveness when increasing the size, but this effect is only observed for $r < 5$. For g, which controls the minimum amount of new information a qualified sentence must add to the summary, a low g will more greedily use sentences with a relative small amount of new information, resulting in a classic trade-off of recall for precision. In these experiments, setting $g > 0.5$ hurts performance, possibly because sentences that contain novel information often include previously seen information.

On this particular test collection, sentence extraction by the TREC organizers occasionally resulted in large parts of content being mistaken for a sentence, to which our model is particularly sensitive. When our approach is used on a stream of correctly parsed news sentences, the maximum sentence length l could become obsolete, since the results show a higher setting of l results in slightly higher comprehensiveness and F-measure. However, these metrics do not take into account that shorter sentences improve readability, which may be preferable on mobile platforms.

In our evaluation, the difference in performance for alternate parameter settings is marginal when compared to the difference with competing systems. Therefore our default parameter settings are not likely to overfit the model to the data.

5.3 Model variants

In Figure 4, we compare the performance between the four variants of the proposed model in more detail, by changing the mini-

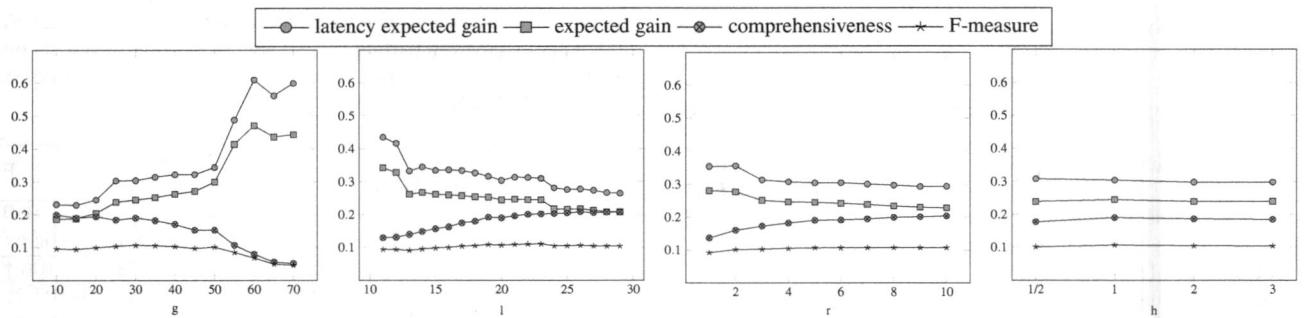

Figure 3: Impact of parameter values in the model performance, g=percentage of new word-pairs, not yet in the summary and co-occurring in the cluster, l=the maximum number of unique non stop words in a sentence, r=the minimum relevance rank amongst output sentences, h=number of (past) hours used to estimate the relevance model

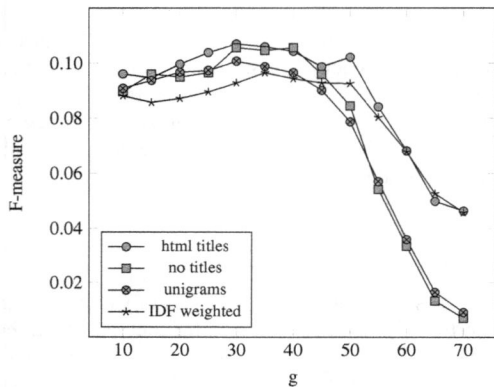

Figure 4: Comparison of the F-measure of model variants over different minimal information gains (g), a variant that is allowed to emit html titles, a variant that does not emit titles, a variant that estimates information gain using unigrams instead of word combinations, and a variant that uses IDF to estimate the cosine similarity for clustering sentences.

mum amount of new information g required to qualify sentences. For $g < .5$, the "no titles" variant obtains results that are very close to the "HTML titles" variant, indicating that most nuggets are also found in non-title sentences of the redundant news stream. The described approach does not use term weighting, except for the variant named "IDF weighted". Our experiments show that using IDF for the estimation of similarity between news sentences hurts effectiveness. One observation is that relevant news sentences often contain numbers, however especially low numbers have relatively low IDF weights in most collections. Lastly, measuring the amount of previously unseen information using unigrams is less effective than using 2-word combinations.

The analysis of different variants shows that all variants outperform the existing systems for $g < 0.5$, indicating that using 3-NN clustering of sentences combined with the qualification of sentences against a relevance model over recently seen information does improve over current state-of-the-art approaches.

5.4 Groundtruth

According to the TREC definition, for the computation of Expected Gain, non-annotated sentences are ignored. For this study, only 5 of the 529 sentences in our main run had been annotated, which is clearly insufficient for a reliable estimation for both Ex-

Table 2: Comparison of the performance of our HTML titles run, over the official TREC ground truth, the Waterloo extended set and a fully annotated set.

Ground truth set	Expected Gain	Latency DEG	Compre-hension	F
TREC official	0.3224	0.4337	0.0149	0.014
Waterloo extended	0.2741	0.3640	0.0356	0.032
Fully annotated	0.2449	0.3019	0.1901	0.107

pected Gain and Comprehensiveness, as can be seen in Table 2. Baruah et al. found that duplicate sentences in the KBA corpus have not been added to the official TREC ground truth [7]. Therefore, for a system that returned a sentence that was annotated, results were different than for a system that returned an un-annotated duplicate of that same sentence. They extended the official ground truth with duplicate sentences in the collection, which we labeled the "Waterloo extended" set in Table 1. This extended ground truth set contains 38 of the sentences we returned. However, the results show an overestimation of Expected Gain, presumably because between systems there is more likely an overlap in relevant sentences than there is in non-relevant sentences. According to our observation, neither the official TREC ground truth nor the Waterloo extended set suffice for the evaluation of an external system; sentences missing in the existing ground truth would have to be annotated.

5.5 Example of cluster in action

In Figure 5, we show a real example how a news article from the KBA corpus was processed for topic 4 "sikh temple shooting", from an article from which 2 sentences qualify for emission using the default ranking requirement $r = 5$. At 6:28pm a new article arrives, for which a node is added to the the title clustering. The nearest neighbors for the nodes are updated, and the new node forms a bi-directional loop with two of its nearest neighbors, thus a new cluster is formed. At least one of the cluster members contains all query terms in its title, therefore all articles in the 'query matching cluster' are routed to the sentence clustering graph for that query. To this graph, all sentences in the articles of the 'query matching cluster' are added, but only the article of the current document (6:28pm) are candidates to be added to the summary. Two candidate sentences become a member of a sentence cluster and therefore these are checked if they qualify. First, the Relevance model is updated by removing outdated sentences and adding the core node sentences that are not a candidate sentence. Then the candidate sentences are ranked in a list with the sentences already in the summary using to the relevance model. In this example, both sentences satisfy the requirements for novelty, old information and rank in the top-5. The qualified sentences are added to the summary and the candidate sentences are added to the Relevance Model.

6. CONCLUSION

In this study, we propose an approach for online temporal summarization of new related to ad-hoc information needs, expressed as a user query. In this approach, sentences are clustered based on cosine similarity, proximity in publication time and being supported by different news providers. The news extraction proceeds in three phases, first the titles of all incoming news articles are clustered, then we select the clusters in which the query terms appear and cluster the sentences contained in the clustered articles, and finally qualify a sentence as output when it contains sufficient new information and is more relevant than the top sentences already in the summary. Our approach requires no a-priori model that separates news containing sentences from other content for an event type or in general and can therefore be used to extract relevant news facts without knowledge about the type of the news event, and requires no manual intervention and contains a small number of parameters that can be tuned in straightforward fashion.

We evaluated the performance against the best systems using the 2013 TREC Temporal Summarization track test set. Our approach significantly improved results over the existing systems in F-measure and Latency-Discounted Expected Gain. Results indicate that news on average is reported before it was added to Wikipedia. Since in the crawled collection the publication time was estimated to be the crawl time, it is reasonable to expect further improvement in latency for a system that monitors news sites in real-time for new publications.

We explain the effectiveness of the approach by our focus on information that is support by several news providers and has a strong relatedness to the original query. However, as described, this approach is also likely to have limitations regarding the recall that can be obtained. Specifically, the requirement that a cluster contains a sentence that contains all words in the query makes the method more suitable to minimal queries than for elaborate queries or when the topic is likely to described using synonyms. An interesting direction for future work is to study how these constraints may be alleviated to improve recall.

References

[1] J. Abello and F. Queyroi. Fixed points of graph peeling. In *Advances in Social Networks Analysis and Mining (ASONAM), 2013 IEEE/ACM International Conference on*, pages 256–263. IEEE, 2013.

[2] C. C. Aggarwal and S. Y. Philip. On clustering massive text and categorical data streams. *Knowledge and information systems*, 24(2):171–196, 2010.

[3] J. Allan, R. Gupta, and V. Khandelwal. Temporal summaries of new topics. In *Proceedings of the 24th annual international ACM SIGIR conference on Research and development in information retrieval*, pages 10–18. ACM, 2001.

[4] J. Allan, V. Lavrenko, D. Malin, and R. Swan. Detections, bounds, and timelines: Umass and TDT-3. In *Proceedings of Topic Detection and Tracking Workshop (TDT-3)*, pages 167–174. Vienna, VA, 2000.

[5] J. Allan, R. Papka, and V. Lavrenko. On-line new event detection and tracking. In *Proceedings of the 21st annual international ACM SIGIR conference on Research and development in information retrieval*, pages 37–45. ACM, 1998.

[6] J. Aslam, M. Ekstrand-Abueg, V. Pavlu, F. Diaz, and T. Sakai. TREC 2013 Temporal Summarization. In *Proceedings of the 22nd Text Retrieval Conference (TREC), November*, 2013.

[7] G. Baruah, A. Roegiest, and M. D. Smucker. The Effect of Expanding Relevance Judgements with Duplicates. In *Proceedings of the 37th international ACM SIGIR conference on Research & development in information retrieval*. ACM, 2014.

[8] M. J. Bates. The design of browsing and berrypicking techniques for the online search interface. *Online review*, 13(5):407–424, 1989.

[9] H. L. Chieu and Y. K. Lee. Query based event extraction along a timeline. In *Proceedings of the 27th annual international ACM SIGIR conference on Research and development in information retrieval*, pages 425–432. ACM, 2004.

[10] T. Cover and P. Hart. Nearest neighbor pattern classification. *Information Theory, IEEE Transactions on*, 13(1):21–27, 1967.

[11] G. Erkan and D. R. Radev. LexRank: Graph-based lexical centrality as salience in text summarization. *J. Artif. Intell. Res.(JAIR)*, 22(1):457–479, 2004.

[12] J. G. Fiscus and G. R. Doddington. Topic detection and tracking evaluation overview. In *Topic detection and tracking*, pages 17–31. Springer, 2002.

[13] E. Gabrilovich, S. Dumais, and E. Horvitz. Newsjunkie: providing personalized newsfeeds via analysis of information novelty. In *Proceedings of the 13th international conference on World Wide Web*, pages 482–490. ACM, 2004.

[14] G. Leban, B. Fortuna, J. Brank, and M. Grobelnik. Event registry: learning about world events from news. In *Proceedings of the companion publication of the 23rd international conference on World wide web companion*, pages 107–110. International World Wide Web Conferences Steering Committee, 2014.

[15] Q. Liu, Y. Liu, D. Wu, and X. Cheng. ICTNET at temporal summarization track trec 2013. In *Proceedings of the The Twenty-Second Text REtrieval Conference*, 2013.

[16] P. Meladianos, G. Nikolentzos, F. Rousseau, Y. Stavrakas, and M. Vazirgiannis. Degeneracy-based real-time sub-event detection in twitter stream. In *Ninth International AAAI Conference on Web and Social Media*, 2015.

[17] S. Petrović, M. Osborne, and V. Lavrenko. Streaming first story detection with application to twitter. In *Human Language Technologies: The 2010 Annual Conference of the North American Chapter of the Association for Computational Linguistics*, pages 181–189. Association for Computational Linguistics, 2010.

[18] D. Radev, T. Allison, S. Blair-Goldensohn, J. Blitzer, A. Celebi, S. Dimitrov, E. Drabek, A. Hakim, W. Lam, D. Liu, et al. MEAD-a platform for multidocument multilingual text summarization. In *Proceedings of the 4th International Conference on Language Resources and Evaluation (LREC 2004)*, 2004.

Routing: query matching cluster of titles

Identifying salient sentences for "Sikh temple shooting"

6:10pm At least seven killed in shooting at Sikh temple in Wisconsin

6:28pm At least seven killed in shooting at Sikh temple in Wisconsin

0.99

6:09pm Seven killed, including suspect, in Wisconsin Sikh temple shooting

0.85

0.86

sentence 0 — **6:28pm** At least seven killed in shooting at Sikh temple in Wisconsin

6:10pm At least seven killed in shooting at Sikh temple in Wisconsin — 0.99

sentence 1 — 6:28pm (Reuters) - A shooting at a Sikh temple outside Milwaukee left at least seven people dead on Sunday, police said.

0.85 — **6:09pm** Seven killed, including suspect, in Wisconsin Sikh temple shooting — 0.86

sentence 2 — **6:28pm** Four people were shot inside the Sikh Temple of Wisconsin and three outside, including a gunman killed by police, Greenfield Police Chief Bradley Wendtlandt told reporters.

0.99 — **6:10pm** Four people were shot inside the Sikh Temple of Wisconsin and three outside, including a gunman killed by police, Greenfield Police Chief Bradley Wendtlandt told reporters.

sentence 3 — 6:28pm Police were still uncertain if there were other shooters in the temple .

0.48

0.46 — **6:15pm** Police were called to respond to the shooting at the Sikh Temple of Wisconsin in the suburb of Oak Creek on Sunday morning, when witnesses said several dozen people were gathering for a service. Greenfield Police Chief Bradley Wentlandt said four people were found dead inside the temple, while three, including the suspected shooter, were found dead outside.

sentence 5 — 6:28pm Thomson Reuters journalists are subject to an Editorial Handbook which requires fair presentation and disclosure of relevant interests.

Summarizing: qualifying candidate sentences

term	frequency	term	frequency	term	frequency
sikh	17	hospital	6	5	4
temple	17	milwaukee	6	shot	3
shooting	17	treating	6	condition	3
wisconsin	9	3	5	killed	3
oak	7	2012	4	critical	3
creek	7	victims	4	seven	3

rank	score	sentence
1	0.085	Milwaukee Hospital Treating 3 Shot at Sikh Temple MILWAUKEE August 5, 2012 (AP) A Milwaukee hospital is treating three victims of a shooting at a Sikh temple south of the city, all in critical condition.
2	0.066	August 5, 2012 (AP) A police dispatcher in Wisconsin says there has been a shooting at a Sikh temple outside of Milwaukee .
3	0.062	US 'shooting' at Sikh temple in Oak Creek, Wisconsin
4	**0.060**	**At least seven killed in shooting at Sikh temple in Wisconsin**
5	**0.054**	**Four people were shot inside the Sikh Temple of Wisconsin and three outside, including a gunman killed by police, Greenfield Police Chief Bradley Wendtlandt told reporters.**

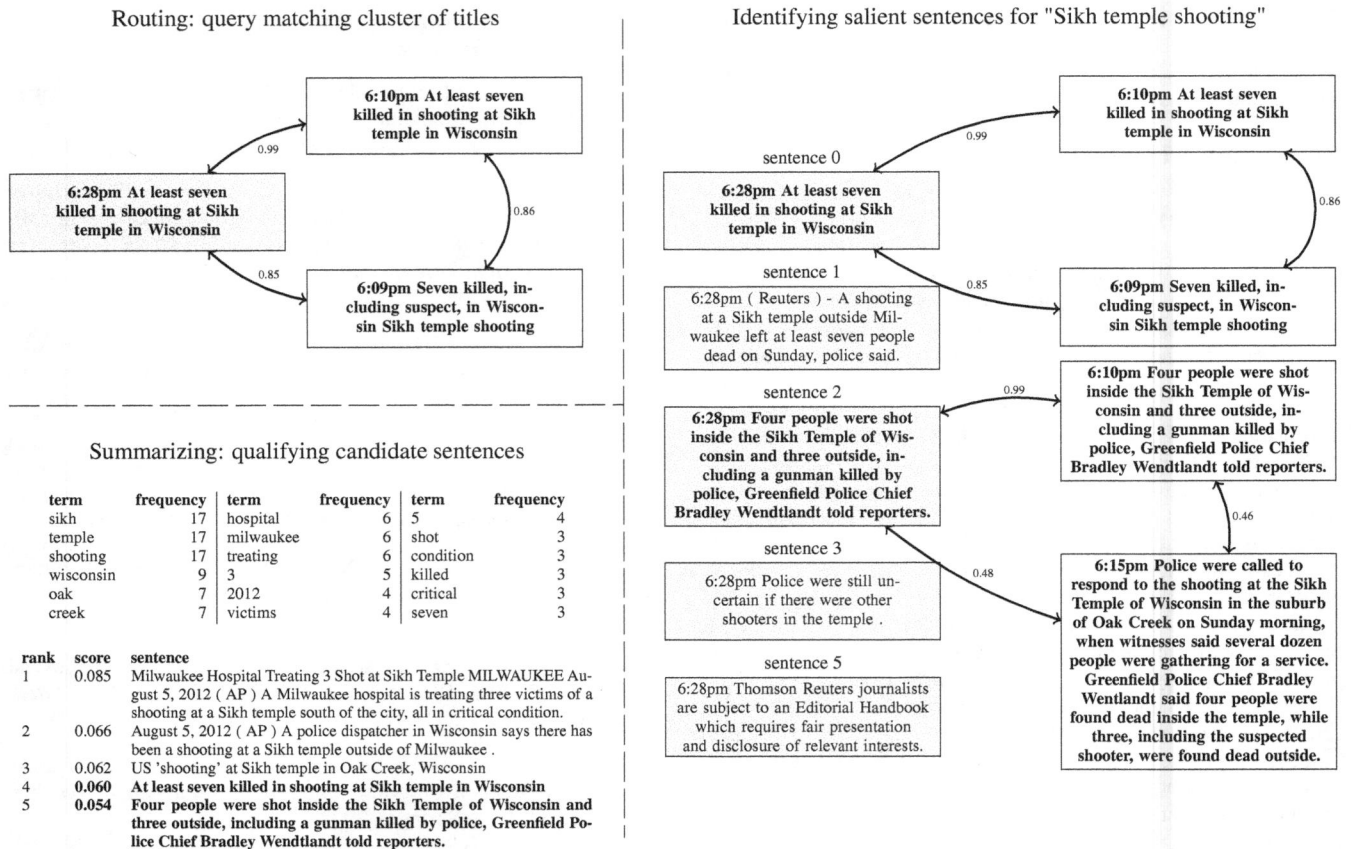

Figure 5: A concrete example to illustrate data processing. Routing. A new article arrives at 6:28pm, and its title is added to a nearest neighbor graph of all existing titles. After assigning its nearest neighbors, it is part of a query matching (title) cluster, and therefore is routed to identify salient sentences. Identification. All sentences in the query matching cluster are added to the query's sentence clustering graph, the sentences from the current document being candidate sentences for the summarization. Two candidate sentences are clustered in sentence clusters that match the query and thus forwarded to the summarization of news for that query. Summarize. The core node sentences from the query matching sentences are added to the Relevance Model. The candidate sentences are ranked with the sentences that were already used in the summary. Both candidate sentences qualify because they are comprehensible (limited length and containing old information), contain a sufficient amount of new information and rank in the top-5. The two qualified sentences are added to the summary and the candidate sentences are added to the Relevance Model.

[19] D. Radev, J. Otterbacher, A. Winkel, and S. Blair-Goldensohn. NewsInEssence: summarizing online news topics. *Communications of the ACM*, 48(10):95–98, 2005.

[20] G. B. Tran and M. Alrifai. Indexing and analyzing Wikipedia's current events portal, the daily news summaries by the crowd. In *Proceedings of the companion publication of the 23rd international conference on World wide web companion*, pages 511–516. International World Wide Web Conferences Steering Committee, 2014.

[21] G. B. Tran, M. Alrifai, and E. Herder. Timeline summarization from relevant headlines. In *Proceedings of the IR research, 37th European conference on Advances in information retrieval*, 2015.

[22] J. B. P. Vuurens, A. P. de Vries, R. Blanco, and P. Mika. Online news tracking for ad-hoc queries. In *SIGIR Demo*. ACM, 2015.

[23] Y. Yang, T. Pierce, and J. Carbonell. A study of retrospective and on-line event detection. In *Proceedings of the 21st annual international ACM SIGIR conference on Research and development in information retrieval*, pages 28–36. ACM, 1998.

[24] H. Yu and V. Hatzivassiloglou. Towards answering opinion questions: Separating facts from opinions and identifying the polarity of opinion sentences. In *Proceedings of the 2003 conference on Empirical methods in natural language processing*, pages 129–136. Association for Computational Linguistics, 2003.

[25] C. Zhang, W. Xu, F. Meng, H. li, T. Wong, and L. Xu. The Information Extraction systems of PRIS at Temporal Summarization Track. In *Proceedings of the The Twenty-Second Text REtrieval Conference*, 2013.

IR meets NLP: On the Semantic Similarity between Subject-Verb-Object Phrases

Dmitrijs Milajevs, Mehrnoosh Sadrzadeh and Thomas Roelleke
School of Electronic Engineering and Computer Science, Queen Mary University of London
London, UK
d.milajevs@qmul.ac.uk, m.sadrzadeh@qmul.ac.uk, t.roelleke@qmul.ac.uk

ABSTRACT

Measuring the semantic similarity between phrases and sentences is an important task in natural language processing (NLP) and information retrieval (IR). We compare the quality of the distributional semantic NLP models against phrase-based semantic IR. The evaluation is based on the correlation between human judgements and model scores on a distributional phrase similarity task. We experiment with four NLP and two IR model variants. On the NLP side, models vary over normalization schemes and composition operators. On the IR side, models vary with respect to estimation of the probability of a term being in a document, namely $P(t|d)$ where only term co-occurrence information is used and $P(t|d, \text{sim})$ which incorporates term distributional similarity. A mixture of the two methods is presented and evaluated. For both methods, word meanings are derived from large corpora of data: the BNC and ukWaC. One of the main findings is that grammatical distributional models give better scores than the IR models. This suggests that an IR model enriched with distributional linguistic information performs better in the long standing problem in IR of document retrieval where there is no direct symbolic relationship between query and document concepts.

Categories and Subject Descriptors

I.2.7 [**Artificial Intelligence**]: Natural Language Processing; H.3.3 [**Information Search and Retrieval**]: Retrieval Models

General Terms

Algorithms; Theory

Keywords

NLP; Distributional Semantics; Semantic IR; Subject-Verb-Object (SVO) Phrases.

1. INTRODUCTION

Traditional information retrieval (IR) deals with document retrieval where a similarity measure is applied to rank documents with re-spect to a query, and the measure is usually based on *word* frequencies (within-document frequencies and collection-wide frequencies) and involves frequency and length normalisations. Natural language processing (NLP) is concerned about preserving and utilising the *meaning* of words and sentences where words representations are composed using grammatical relations to form sentence representations. We compare in this paper the methods of semantic phrase-based IR and distributional vector-based NLP and investigate the integration of their techniques. We focus on "subject verb object" phrases (in NLP terminology: simple transitive sentences) and measure and utilise their semantic similarities

The first challenge is finding an appropriate answer to the question: what is the semantic similarity between

"agent sells property" and "family buys home"?

These are two subject-verb-object phrases and they contain different words, with regard to traditional IR, there is a "term mismatch" problem. Even though there is no syntactic word match, the phrases are semantically related. In this case, this is because if an agent sells a property, then this potentially implies that a family buys a home. Also, from an ontology point of view, a "home" is a "property", and this makes the objects to be related. Finally, despite the fact that there is no obvious relationship between "agent" and "family", the verbs "buys" and "sells" are strongly semantically related. Consequently, one has to provide an answer to the sequel question: how one can quantify similarity between two phrases?

To illustrate different levels of similarity, consider two phrases that deem to be semantically more similar than the phrases above:

"woman drinks water" and "wife pours tea".

The phrases are more related than the phrases of the first example, because there is also a strong semantic relationship between the subjects, which is not present in the first example.

The research questions motivating this work are: how do NLP models compare to IR models? Under which conditions each approach works best? And how can one combine them? We experiment with a variety of semantic phrase-based IR and distributional vector-based NLP models and address these.

1.1 Structure and Contributions

The remainder of this paper is structured as follows. Section 2 provides the background on the distributional vector-based NLP models and their compositionality, IR models and phrase-based semantic IR. Section 3 explains the task and methodologies for solving it. Section 4 compares the DS and IR models and presents an integrated model. Section 5 goes over the evaluation methodology and experiment set up. Section 6 presents results and offers an analysis. Finally, Section 7 concludes the work.

The main contributions of this paper are the comparison of DS-based and IR-based techniques. Another contribution is the investigation of the performance of an integrated DS+IR model.

2. BACKGROUND

2.1 Vector-based Distributional NLP

NLP models reason about meanings of words and phrases of language (we follow the IR terminology and throughout the paper use "phrase" to refer to a sequence of words, including sentences). They can be classified into two broad categories: statistical and rule-based. The former represents meanings of words based on the likelihood of their occurrence in text; examples herein are Markov-based models, distributional semantics, and neural embeddings. The latter offer a logical analysis of the structures of phrases and sentences based on the grammatical rules of language. Examples thereof are Montague semantics, type-logical grammars, and context-free grammars. For the purpose of this paper, we work with distributional semantics shorthanded to DS (see [33] for an overview). These have been shown to lend themselves to both word and phrase level analysis and constitute an active field of research. Distributional semantics is based on the idea of Firth [10] that the meaning of a word depends on the contexts in which it often occurs. Hence, words that often occur close to same features have similar meanings. For example, 'boat' and 'ship' have similar meanings, since they both occur close to 'ocean' and 'sail'. Their meaning is not similar to that of 'cat' and 'dog', since the latter often occur close to 'pet' and 'furry'.

These models are formalized in the form of a vector space whose basis vectors are a fixed set of features [23]. The meaning of a words of interest, referred to as a *target* word, is a vector in this vector space. Each such vector is built after fixing a corpus of text (a large collection of documents), a set of features, and a neighboring window of k words (e.g. 5). For a target word t and a feature f, raw frequencies are counted by summing the number of times t occurred k-words on either side of f, divided by the number of times t got counted (i.e. the size of the window). Dividing this by the total number of times t occurred in the corpus (e.g. L), provides a probabilistic measure of the raw counts:

$$\text{freq}_k(t) = \frac{\sum_f N(f, t)}{k} \qquad P_k(t) = \frac{\text{freq}_k(t)}{L}$$

Distributional models have been applied to different language tasks, for example, in [31] they were applied to reason about word synonymy, in [21] they were used for induction and knowledge acquisition, in [32] and [22] they were used for modelling word sense discrimination and clustering. Many of these applications rely on the presence of quantitative measures in the vector space to represent the similarity in meaning using the distance between the vectors. In a study by Bullinaria and Levy [4], it was shown that the geometric distance based on the cosine of the angle between the vectors performed best in semantic word similarity tasks $\text{sim}(w, w') = \cos(\vec{w}, \vec{w}')$. In this paper we focus on the cosine and do not extend on other measures such as Jaccard, Dice, and Tversky indexes; the latter are moreover set-based and not sufficient for the vector-based setting of this paper.

Note that for two words to have a similar meaning it is not necessary that they often occur close to each other, but necessary that they have occur close to (or have) same features. For example, it is not very common that 'ship' and 'boat' occur in the vicinity of 5-words of each other, but it is indeed the case that they both often occur 5 words close to same verb, such as 'sail' and same noun modifiers, such as 'ocean'. As a result, vectors of 'ship' and 'boat'

have a small geometric distance (and a high cosine value). The more same features two words w, w' have in common, the higher the corresponding coordinate on that feature will be. This will increase the inner product of word vectors $\vec{w}$ and $\vec{w}'$ and their *cosine* similarity, the latter being based on inner product.

Whereas traditional distributional models focus on meaning representations for words (and perhaps sometimes for short two-word phrases such as adj-noun), compositional versions of them are able to represent meanings of phrases and sentences by combining the vectors of the words therein. The most general such approaches are heavily based on the grammatical structure of a string of words, expressed in a typed categorial syntax such as pregroup grammars, syntactic calculus [6, 5], or Combinatorial Categorical Grammar (CCG) [24, 20]. From an abstract perspective, the vector representation of a sequence of words $w_1, \ldots, w_n$ is obtained by the following composition of functions

$$f((g(w_1), \ldots, g(w_n)), (x_1, \ldots, x_n)) \qquad (1)$$

where, the meaning of a word w_i with a basic grammatical type x_i is represented by a vector in an atomic space X with a fixed basis:

$$g(w_i) = \vec{w_i} \in X$$

The meaning of a word w_j with a grammatical functional type $((x \to y) \to \cdots) \to z$ is represented by induction as a linear map $((X \to Y) \to \cdots) \to Z$, or equivalently (using the map-state duality) a matrix in the tensor space $((X \otimes Y) \otimes \cdots) \otimes Z$. We use a simplified notation and denote these by vector signs as well:

$$g(w_i) = \vec{w_i} \in ((X \otimes Y) \otimes \cdots) \otimes Z$$

Most generally, the composition function f could be the multilinear algebraic operation of tensor-contraction. In the context of this paper, we work with svo-phrases "subj verb obj". Here, basic words "subj" and "obj" are nouns with type n; their meanings are vectors in a fixed-basis atomic feature space N. Function words are transitive verbs with type $(n \to n) \to s$; this means that they input two noun phrases and output a phrase of type sentence s. The verb meanings are linear maps $(N \to N) \to S$, equivalently tensors in the space $(N \otimes N) \otimes S$. Here, f becomes matrix multiplication. The meaning of the svo-phrase "subj-verb-obj" is a vector in the sentence space S, computed by the following general formula:

$$f((\vec{w}_1, \vec{w}_2, \vec{w}_3), (\text{subj}, \text{verb}, \text{obj})) = (\vec{w}_2 \times \vec{w}_3) \times \vec{w}_1 \quad (2)$$

We shorthand the right hand side of the above as follows, identifying the notation for words with that of their grammatical types:

$$(\overrightarrow{\text{verb}} \times \overrightarrow{\text{obj}}) \times \overrightarrow{\text{subj}} \qquad (3)$$

Once again, one can use the cosine similarity, this time between the phrase vectors, to measure their degree of similarity.

2.2 IR Models and Phrase-based Semantic IR

Whereas traditional IR relies on the "so-called" bag-of-words retrieval models, semantic IR deals with entities and relationships. The following queries illustrate the difference between word-only IR and semantic IR.

```
1   # Retrieve Documents in which the words
2   # peter, friend, and mary occur.
3   ?— D[ peter & friend & mary ];

5   # Retrieve Documents in which the proposition
6   # ``peter is a friend of mary" occurs.
7   ?— D[ peter . friendOf(mary) ];
```

The first query will retrieve documents in which the respective words occur. Whether there is a conjunctive or disjunctive interpretation is for the moment of secondary priority. Regarding the score contribution of the different words, all retrieval models will give more impact to rare words, and a document scores high if it has many occurrences of the query words.

The second query will retrieve all documents in which the respective *proposition* is true. The syntax applied in the examples has been introduced in [29, 11]. The probabilistic object-oriented logic (POOL) is a high-level abstraction to describe semantic retrieval and to represent knowledge. POOL is related to description logic [25] and frame-based logics [19].

The main challenge is to define a retrieval status value (RSV) that takes into account the semantic meaning of the proposition. The most naive approach would be to consider the proposition as an atomic symbol, and simply introduce something like a Proposition-Frequency and the IDF of a proposition. With this approach, a proposition is treated as a phrase (compound, sequence of words). Obviously, such an approach will be too specific in the sense that we wish to retrieve documents that contain propositions that are similar to query proposition.

Therefore, in semantic retrieval we apply a compositional approach which in essence retrieves documents for the entities and relationships of a proposition. [2, 1] introduce techniques to process and classify semantic queries. The main approach is to score documents with respect to an aggregated score that is composed of a score representing the match wrt to the subject, relationship name (or attribute name), and object (or attribute value).

To illustrate the composition of the aggregated score, consider first the simple, only word-based (term-based) TF-IDF model, where $\mathrm{TF}(t, d)$ is the *term frequency*, and $\mathrm{IDF}(t)$ is the inverse document frequency. The retrieval status values (RSV) is commonly defined as follows:

$$\mathrm{RSV}_{\text{TF-IDF}}(d, q) := \sum_{t \in q} \mathrm{score}(t, d, q)$$

$$\mathrm{score}(t, d, q) := \mathrm{TF}(t, d) \cdot \mathrm{IDF}(t)$$

The generalisation is a formulation for phrases rather than terms (words):

$$\mathrm{RSV}_{\text{semantic-TF-IDF}}(d, q) := \sum_{\text{phrase} \in q} \mathrm{score}(\text{phrase}, d, q)$$

$$\mathrm{score}(\text{phrase}, d, q) := \text{# see section 3.2}$$

We refer to this approach as a *macro* score, since the aggregation is over scores that originate from a score for the respective phrase. The score of a phrase is composed of scores for the phrase components (subjects, relationships, objects, attribute names, and attribute values). Section 3.2 will expand on the approach chosen for this paper.

The following examples illustrate the difference between relationship and attributes. The phrase peter.friendOf(mary) and peter.worksFor(ibm) are subject.relship(object) propositions, whereas ibm.business_area("IT") and mary.job_title("Lecturer") are object.attrName(attrValue) propositions. For the context of the work reported in this paper, there is an additional type of proposition, namely

subject.verb(object)

where for the dataset considered, subject and object are to be understood as object types (e.g. agent, mother, land, house) rather than concrete objects. The indexing process builds indexes for subjects, relationship names, objects, attribute names, and attribute values. The retrieval process interprets a query such as

"D[peter.friendOf(mary)]" and ranks the documents with a score that is based on the composition of sub-scores as described above. Though we utilise in this paper only the semantic variant of TF-IDF score, it is evident that this approach applies for any retrieval model [2].

This approach to semantic IR is powerful but poses major challenges. Firstly, the parser (for IR, usually a simple tokeniser) needs to recognise propositions, and build a space of propositions. Secondly, the query processing requires to match similar propositions (similar components), i.e. it is not sufficient to simply apply a syntactic match.

This is precisely where results of DS research contribute to solve one of the major short-comings of semantic retrieval, namely the mismatch problem between semantic propositions.

3. SIMILARITY IN NLP AND IR

Considering a subject-verb-object phrases as a source (query), in IR the task is to rank other phrases (targets) such that the ranking reflects that the target phrase is considered "relevant" with respect to the source phrase.

From a retrieval point of view, we retrieve documents that contain target phrases that are implied by the source phrase. The following example illustrates the scenario:

```
1   # 1. The case of word—based IR:
2   ?— D[ vehicle ];
3   # d123[ boat ]
4   # ontology: boat is a sub—concept of vehicle, in other
          words, boat—>vehicle.
5   # Since boat implies vehicle, retrieve doc123.

7   # 2. The case of knowledge—based (semantic) IR:
8   ?— D[ person.spends(money) ];
9   # doc456[ lecturer .buys(boat) ]
10  # Since the sentence lecturer .buys(boat) implies person.
          spends(money), retrieve doc123.
11  # Note that lecturer implies person (semantic relationship
          between subjects), but
12  # boat does not semantically imply money (no semantic
          relationship between objects).
```

The DS approach would rank documents that contain phrases similar to the query higher than documents that do not have similar phrases. Distributional similarity is an appealing concept because although being symmetric [33], it is shown to correlate with human judgements [4]. In principle, one expects that it should be able to capture both ontological and semantic relationships in feature spaces: "woman" and "mother" will appear in similar context (thus share many features), and all the things that are capable of buying will co-occur with "buy" in a corpus (thus share a feature).

Whereas similarity measures are symmetric, document retrieval scores for a query are not symmetric. For example, if the query is about vehicles, then documents about both cars and bicycles are relevant. However, for a query about bicycles, not all documents about all different kinds of vehicles (e.g. cars) are relevant. Thus, similarity can also be defined through entailment, two entities (words or phrases) are similar if entailment holds in both directions.

The DS notion of similarity is defined as follows:

DEFINITION 1 (SENTENCE SIMILARITY). *The degree of similarity between two sentences s and t is a function r of their semantic representations* $[\![s]\!]$ *and* $[\![t]\!]$, *respectively obtained from the composition f of the semantic representations* $[\![v_1]\!], \ldots, [\![v_m]\!]$ *and* $[\![w_1]\!], \ldots, [\![w_n]\!]$ *of the words therein and their corresponding* *grammatical roles $x_1, \ldots, x_m$ and $y_1, \ldots, y_n$. Formally, we have:*

$$\text{sim}(s, t) := r([\![s]\!], [\![t]\!])$$
$$:= r(f(([\![v_1]\!], \ldots, [\![v_m]\!]), (x_1, \ldots, x_m)),$$
$$f(([\![w_1]\!], \ldots, [\![w_n]\!]), (y_1, \ldots, y_n)))$$

In both IR and DS, the semantic representations of words and sentences are their vector representations. In DS r is the cosine of the angle and f is the composition function as defined in Equation 1. In IR, r is summation and f is the TF-IDF quantification. For both cases, in this paper we have $m = n = 3$.

The vector-based instantiation of our notion of similarity falls under the category "statistical similarity", relates to the LSA model reviewed in [15], and is an area of research studied by SemEval (a series of workshops for evaluation of computational semantic analysis systems). Traditional LSA is word-based and is more recently extended to sentences by set-based methods such as addition and multiplication. Our notion is grammar-based and leads to composition operators such as tensor contraction. SemEval datasets consider a wide variety of sentences, wheres our dataset was designed for svo phrases in order to keep the task clean and avoid the noise caused by, e.g. articles and individual entities. Further challenge would be to generalise our notion to any type of phrase.

Sentence similarity in DS is a difficult task to design and to decide. Occurrence frequencies within a corpus and semantic word hierarchies from lexical databases such as `WordNet` are used to design such tasks and human annotators are used to decide them.

When building similarity datasets, instructions are given to humans to reflect the symmetry of similarity. A participant is asked to provide a Boolean answer (yes if sentences are similar and no if sentences are not similar) or a number from a scale e.g. from 1 to 7 (1 for dissimilar and 7 for similar). To come up with similarity scores shown in Figure 1 one can compute the percentage of positive answers for Boolean answers or take the average of responses if they are on a scale or count. The number of judgements per sentence pair plays an important role in deciding the final score. For Boolean answers, that are easy to answer, one would want to collect more responses than for the scale based answers. The number of sentence pairs also plays an important role. Is it better to have judgements for more pairs, but a few Boolean answers; or for less pairs, but a lot of scale based responses?

IR evaluation datasets tend to prefer more pairs to be evaluated, despite the evaluation thoroughness, while DS datasets [27, 16, 17] tend to prefer more elaborated responses for fewer items.

	Sentence 1			Sentence 2		Average
Subject	Verb	Object	Subject	Verb	Object	Similarity
woman	drink	water	wife	pour	tea	2.696
			doctor	use	test	1.125
			system	use	method	1.083
agent	sell	property	delegate	buy	land	3.360
			family	buy	home	3.125
			group	hold	meeting	1.167

Figure 1: Examples of average human annotations for svo-phrase similarity scores. Averages are over 20 judgements per sentence pair.

3.1 Vector-based Distributional Similarity

Distributional semantic models are varied over three sets of parameters: the normalisation method, the underlying corpus of text, and the composition operators. The latter differ over size and the sparsity of the information they provide about meanings of words: the larger they are, the less sparse information they contain.

The normalisation methods provide different weighting schemes for the co-occurrence counts (previously denoted by $N(f, t)$) of the word vectors. To be more explicit, the raw counts in a window of size 5 are denoted by $N5(f, t)$, the most basic normalisation method is a conditional probability, the *likelihood ratio* version of which has been shown to perform well in semantic tasks [4]. The logarithmic non-negative version of likelihood ratio, referred to by *positive point-wise mutual information* (PPMI), has been shown to perform better than *likelihood ratio* in semantic tasks [18]. These methods are summarised below:[1]

1. Raw Counts: $N5(f, t)$,
2. Conditional Probability: $P5(f|t) = \frac{P(f,t)}{P(t)}$,
3. Likelihood Ratio: $LR5(f, t) = \frac{P(f|t)}{P(f)} = \frac{P(f,t)}{P(f)P(t)}$,
4. Positive PMI: $PPMI5(f, t) = \max(0, \log(\frac{P(f|t)}{P(f)}))$.

EXAMPLE 1 (WORD LEVEL MEANING REPRESENTATION).
Given a feature (vector) space that consists of 1,000 words. Let "ocean", "sailing", "animal", "pet" be the first four words.
Note that the feature words are independent of the source and target words. This is the main difference to the IR approach where the association between source and target is assumed to be quantified. The target vectors for "ship", "boat", "cat", and "dolphin" could be as follows:

$$\overrightarrow{ship} = (4, 3, 0, 0, \ldots) \qquad \overrightarrow{boat} = (2, 3, 0, 0, \ldots)$$
$$\overrightarrow{cat} = (0, 0, 4, 3, \ldots) \qquad \overrightarrow{dolphin} = (2, 1, 1, 0, \ldots)$$

These express that the target word "ship" occurs four times in the neighborhood of "ocean" (the feature before or after the target word) and three times in the neighborhood of 'sailing', but 0 times in the neighborhoods of "animal" and "pet". Whereas, "cat" occurs 0 times in the neighborhoods of "ocean" and "sailing and 4 and 3 times in the neighborhoods of "animal" and "pet".
For the purpose of demonstration suppose that all the other coordinates of these ship and boat are zero, hence the lengths of their vectors become $\sqrt{25}$ and $\sqrt{13}$, and we obtain $\cos(\overrightarrow{ship}, \overrightarrow{boat}) = 0.943$; this is despite the fact that ship (as target) and boat (as source) have occurred together or not.
Let the word ship occur 20 times, and ocean and sailing occur 100 and 10 times, respectively, in the corpus the co-occurrence matrix is based upon. Then, for $P(ocean) = 100/1000$ and $P(sailing) = 10/1000$, we obtain:

$$N5(ocean, ship) = 4 \qquad N5(sailing, ship) = 3$$
$$P5(ocean|ship) = {}^4/_{20} \qquad P5(sailing|ship) = {}^3/_{20}$$
$$LR5(ocean, ship) = 2 \qquad LR5(sailing, ship) = 15$$
$$PPMI5(ocean, ship) = 0.301 \qquad PPMI5(sailing, ship) = 1.176$$

A point-wise application of the above schemes to each coordinate of a target vector provides vectors for each scheme. The vectors of "ship" in each scheme is as follows:

$$N5 = (4, 3, 0, 0, \ldots)$$
$$P5 = ({}^4/_{20}, {}^3/_{20}, 0, 0, \ldots)$$
$$LR5 = (2, 15, 0, 0, \ldots)$$
$$PPMI5 = (0.301, 1.176, 0, 0, \ldots)$$

---

[1] We show the parameters for the window size 5. Any window can be chosen: 2, 5 and 10 are most common in DS.

For an svo-phrase, the most general composition operator is matrix multiplication. In this case, the distributional hypothesis over a feature space only provides us with vectors for atomic words. Hence, a crucial challenge is how to concretely build a cube (tensor of rank 3) for the verb. This area constitutes an active recent trend in DS. The most costly models thereof, generalise the original approach of [3] and use multi-step linear regression to combine feature vectors of "verb-obj" and "subj-verb" phrases [12]. A slightly more simplified approach argues for the use of matrices rather than cubes and combines the verb matrices built by linear regression from "verb-obj" and "subj-verb" phrases [28]. Less costly approaches, however, argue against the use of vector support machines at all and work with combinations of feature vectors of subjects and objects of the verb [13]. A much cheaper model which has outperformed quite a few of the above is taking the Kronecker product of the feature vector of the verb with itself [14]. Finally, the most simple setting (which has also performed a par with other models) is to work with the feature vector of the verb, where composition reduces to point-wise multiplication or addition of vectors [27]. For the purpose of this paper, we work with these and the Kronecker as our models.

1. Addition: $\vec{s} = \overrightarrow{\text{subject}} + \overrightarrow{\text{verb}} + \overrightarrow{\text{object}}$

2. Point-wise multiplication: $\vec{s} = \overrightarrow{\text{subject}} \odot \overrightarrow{\text{verb}} \odot \overrightarrow{\text{object}}$

3. Kronecker: $\vec{s} = \overrightarrow{\text{verb}} \odot (\overrightarrow{\text{subject}} \otimes \overrightarrow{\text{object}})$

The additive model is disjunctive over the information of the terms of the phrase. Its resulting vector contains all the features of subject, verb, and object, hence a bit noisy. The multiplicative model is conjunctive and consists of features that are shared between the phrases; hence too refined. The Kronecker method doubles the information of the verb into a tensor, one copy interacts with the subject, one with the object, and the results are merged, allowing the subject and object interact with each other through the verb features. This becomes evident by observing:

$$\overrightarrow{\text{verb}} \odot (\overrightarrow{\text{subject}} \otimes \overrightarrow{\text{object}}) = (\overrightarrow{\text{verb}} \odot \overrightarrow{\text{subject}}) \otimes (\overrightarrow{\text{verb}} \odot \overrightarrow{\text{object}})$$

The first $\odot$ intersects the features of verb and subject, the second one does so with the features of verb and object, the $\otimes$ puts this two together in a matrix. This lessens the noise and is not as refined.

EXAMPLE 2 (COMPOSITION). *Consider the N5 model, the sentence "dolphins follow boats", and the verb vector therein* $\overrightarrow{follow} = (1, 1, 2, 1, \ldots)$. *The additive and multiplicative vectors and the Kronecker tensor are as follows:*

$$\overrightarrow{dolphins} + \overrightarrow{follow} + \overrightarrow{boats} = (5, 5, 3, 1, \ldots)$$
$$\overrightarrow{dolphins} \odot \overrightarrow{follow} \odot \overrightarrow{boats} = (4, 3, 0, 0, \ldots)$$

$$\overrightarrow{follow} \odot (\overrightarrow{dolphins} \otimes \overrightarrow{boats}) = \begin{pmatrix} 4 & 6 & 0 & 0 & \cdots \\ 2 & 3 & 0 & 0 & \cdots \\ 4 & 6 & 0 & 0 & \cdots \\ 0 & 0 & 0 & 0 & \cdots \\ \cdots & \cdots & \cdots & \cdots & \cdots \end{pmatrix}$$

$$= \begin{pmatrix} 1 & 1 & 2 & 1 & \cdots \\ 1 & 1 & 2 & 1 & \cdots \\ 2 & 2 & 4 & 2 & \cdots \\ 1 & 1 & 2 & 1 & \cdots \\ \cdots & \cdots & \cdots & \cdots & \cdots \end{pmatrix} \odot \begin{pmatrix} 4 & 6 & 0 & 0 & \cdots \\ 2 & 3 & 0 & 0 & \cdots \\ 2 & 3 & 0 & 0 & \cdots \\ 0 & 0 & 0 & 0 & \cdots \\ \cdots & \cdots & \cdots & \cdots & \cdots \end{pmatrix}$$

The additive vector has non-zero coordinates on "ocean", "sailing", and "animal", i.e. the features of "dolphins", "follow", and "boats". The multiplicative only has non-zero features on "ocean" and "sailing". The Kronecker has pairs of features of all the terms, thus relating their non-zero coordinates, e.g. "(animal, ocean)" relates features of "dolphin" to that of "boat", whereas "boat" had originally a zero coordinate on "animal", making the two interact with each other through the non-zero "animal" feature of "follow".

3.2 Phrase-based Semantic IR

The main strands of IR models (TF-IDF, BM25, LM) can be related to the measuring the dependence between document (source) and query (target). The document-query independence (DQI) measure is as follows [30]:

$$\text{DQI}(d, q) := \log \frac{P(d, q)}{P(d) \cdot P(q)} \qquad (4)$$

This component occurs for a distribution of documents and queries in the formulation of the mutual information $\text{MI}(D, Q)$, and is also referred to as point-wise mutual information ($\text{DQI}(d, q) = \text{pmi}(d, q)$).

Depending on the decomposition of the participating probabilities, one can derive TF-IDF or LM. TF-IDF for $P(d|q)/P(d)$ and LM for $P(q|d)/P(q)$. For the purpose of this paper, we focus on the TF-IDF-side of retrieval, and we choose the disjunctive decomposition of $P(q|d)$ over a space of disjoint terms.

For $P(q)$ being constant when ranking documents, one obtains:

$$P(q|d) = \sum_t P(q|t) \cdot P(t|d)$$

Herein, $P(q|t)$ can be represented by the IDF ($P(q|t)$ high for rare terms), and $P(t|d)$ is proportional to the TF quantification. This leads to the TF-IDF score:

$$\text{RSV}_{\text{TF-IDF}}(d, q) = \sum_{t \in q} \text{IDF}(t) \cdot \text{TF}(t, d)$$

BM25 (without relevance information) is basically TF-IDF where the TF quantification becomes $\text{tf}_d/(\text{tf}_d + 1)$ for a document of average length (omitting BM25-TF parameters such as k_1 and b).

In the following, this probabilistic derivation and formulation of TF-IDF is extended with respect to:

1. Generalised TF-IDF score for matching subject-verb-object phrases.

2. Relate query concept (e.g. subject) to document concept since the concepts may be different (no symbolic match).

Let svo_d and svo_q be subject-verb-object phrases, where d is the source, and q is the target. The source phrase is denoted as $\text{svo}_d = s_d, v_d, o_d$, and the target phrase is $\text{svo}_q = s_q, v_q, o_q$.

For the IR-based models, we require a notion of TF, i.e. the degree to which a query subject, relationship/verb and object represents a virtual document. For example, for the query "sailor enjoys trip", we want to retrieve documents that contain "dolphins follow boat". For each component of the query phrase, we need an estimate of $P(t_q|d)$, where t_q is the component of the query phrase, and d is a virtual document that contains the target phrase.

Such estimate can be obtained via a sampling (voting). Then, the sampling over a space of disjoint concepts is:

$$P(t_q|d) = \sum_{t \in T} P(t_q|t) \cdot P(t|d)$$

Here, T is a space of concepts and the concepts are assumed to be disjoint events. The probability $P(t_q|t)$ is estimated based on co-occurrence information. For example:

$$P(t_q|t) = P(s_q|s_d) = P(\text{sailor}|\text{dolphins}) = \frac{\text{N5}(\text{sailor}, \text{dolphins})}{\sum_x \text{N5}(x, \text{dolphins})}$$

With regard to logical and probabilistic retrieval, we are utilising this information into a model based on the probability that the source document implies the target query.

$$P(d \rightarrow q) = P(\text{dolphins, follow, boat} \rightarrow \text{sailor, enjoys, trip})$$

Target w_t	Source w_s	N5	$P5(w_t|w_s)$
sailor	dolphins	100	100/1,000
dolphins	sailor	100	100/2,000
trip	boat	500	500/3,000
boat	trip	500	500/4,000
follow	enjoy	800	800/8,000
enjoy	follow	800	800/10,000

In addition, for each word there are the usual statistics such as the number of times the word occurs. This may include the number of locations $N_{\text{Locations}}(w)$, the number of documents $N_{\text{Documents}}(w)$, the number of sentences, the number of document titles, etc. For the purpose of this work, it is sufficient to consider the main two counts, number of locations and number of documents.

For example, sailor occurs $2,000$ times over $1,000$ documents ($\text{avgtf}(\text{sailor}) = 2$) and dolphins occurs $1,000$ times over 800 documents ($\text{avgtf}(\text{dolphins}) = 1.25$). For illustrating the score computation, assume the following statistics:

word w	$N_{\text{Locations}}(w)$	$N_{\text{Documents}}(w)$
dolphins	1,000	800
sailor	2,000	1,000
boat	3,000	1,500
trip	4,000	2,000
enjoy	8,000	3,000
follow	10,000	4,000

Let there be 10^6 documents in total.

EXAMPLE 3 (SCORE COMPUTATION). *Let d and q be svo-phrases. Then, the probability of the implication is estimated via the conditional probability, which is estimated via the total probability theorem.*

$$P(d \rightarrow q) = P(q|d) = \sum_{x \in \{subject, verb, object\}} P(q|d, x) \cdot P(x)$$

Here, x is the type of the component, i.e. subject, verb or object. The sample over a space of word types breaks up the phrase into its components, and applies type-specific probabilities. For example, for the subject:

$$P(q|d, subject) = P(sailor|d, subject)$$

The implication dolphin $\rightarrow$ sailor can be viewed as a translation task. A term t_q is assigned to a document d if the term is similar to many terms that occur in d. This estimate is based on the total probability:

$$P(t_q|d) = \sum_{t'} P(t_q|t') \cdot P(t'|d)$$

Since the virtual document d contains exactly one phrase, $P(t'|d) = 1$. This would be more general for a real retrieval task where q and d are sets of phrases.

For the query example "sailor enjoys trip", where the document contains "dolphins follow boat", for the subject, the following expression show-cases the estimation of $P(t_q|d, subject)$.

$$P(sailor|d, subject) = P(sailor|dolphins) \cdot P(dolphins|d, subject)$$

For the subject-subject, verb-verb, and object-object probabilities, we have:

$$P(sailor|dolphins) = 100/2,000 = 0.05$$
$$P(enjoys|follow) = 800/8,000 = 0.1$$
$$P(trip|boat) = 500/4,000 = 0.125$$

This leads to the following score reflecting the inference between the two svo-phrases:

$$
\begin{aligned}
score(d, q) &= \\
&= P(s_q|d) \cdot IDF(s_q) + P(v_q|d) \cdot IDF(v_q) + P(o_q|d) \cdot IDF(o_q) \\
&= 0.05 \cdot \log \frac{10^6}{1,000} + 0.1 \cdot \log \frac{10^6}{3,000} + 0.125 \cdot \log \frac{10^6}{2,000}
\end{aligned}
$$

The example illustrates clearly that the score is not symmetric; this is evident because $P(t_q|d)$ is different from $P(t_d|q)$. Also, the IDF component is applied to the query components.

The score is high if the components of the query phrases are related (modelled by $P(t_q|d)$) and the query component is rare (modelling by $IDF(t_q)$).

Note that in this approach we consider subject, verb and object as *disjoint* events. A more general approach could consider the relationship between subject-verb and verb-object and subject-object. Moreover, the IDF could be specific with respect to the component type, i.e. the IDF of a subject is different from the IDF of a verb. This issue becomes evident for words that are both, noun and verb, such as "help", "need" and "demand".

Depending on the co-occurrence information chosen, that is 1) N5, 2) P5, 3) LR5, and 4) PPMI5, the estimate of $P(t_q|d)$ is different, and this leads to four different candidate models.

In the evaluation we measure the performance of different instantiations of this semantic TF-IDF model where we vary the way the IDF is defined, and, more importantly, we vary the way the TF component is derived from the co-occurrence information.

The main questions we investigate are:

1. How does the score described for the compositional TF-IDF compare to the DS approach computing phrase similarity via distributional (co-occurrence) representations?

2. How sensitive are the approaches with respect to the data feed? The quality of the co-occurrence information between symbols is essential for IR, whereas DS relies on the indirect measure.

4. NLP MEETS IR

The DS approach uses a high-dimensional feature term space to measure the similarity between terms. The primary events of this space are the target and features terms. The meaning of a term in this space is represented by a vector of its features and the meaning of a document is a sequence of its terms. This is different from conventional IR approaches [8] that are based on a co-occurrence quantification such as the number of documents both terms occur in, or approaches in LM that measure the probability that two terms are related. In these approaches, the primary events are the document and the query and the meaning of a term is just an atomic symbolic entity. The model does not represent the meaning of a term in any form and it is only concerned about whether it occurs with another symbol or inside a document. The correspondence between the IR and DS approaches is summarized in the Table 1.

The combination of the two approaches enables us to put together the symbolic meanings of terms in a foreground IR model (both in a query and in a document) with vector representations coming

	Distributional Semantics	Information Retrieval
Co-occurrence	Co-occurrence between the semantic symbol (target word) and feature words.	Co-occurrence between the semantic symbols (words) themselves.
Representation of words	Distributional.	Symbolic.
Single vs set	Similarity between two *single phrases*.	Relationship (implication, entailment) between two *sets of phrases*.
Relationship symmetry	Similarity is a symmetric function.	Relationship between sets is not symmetric; moreover, the phrase-based score is not necessarily symmetric.
Similar/relevant	Phrase t_i is similar to phrase t_j.	Document d (source) is relevant with respect to query q (target).
Scores	The similarity score is estimated based on the distance/angle between distributional vectors.	The relevance score is estimated based on the retrieval model that computes the implication between the set of document and the set of query propositions.
Probabilistic semantics	(In)dependence between a target word and a feature word: $\frac{P(w_t, w_f)}{P(w_t) \cdot P(w_f)}$.	(In)dependence between a document and a query: $\frac{P(d,q)}{P(d) \cdot P(q)}$.

In this work: virtual query has exactly one proposition; virtual document has exactly one proposition; therefore, the similarity score $\text{sim}(phrase1, phrase2)$ *can be compared to the retrieval score* $\text{RSV}(document: set\ of\ phrases, query: set\ of\ phrases)$.

Table 1: Distributional semantics and IR side by side. DS focuses on the similarity between two target words and phrases; IR focuses on the similarity between a source document and a query document.

from a background DS model. A main consequence of the internal representations of DS is that these models are able to utilise an intermediate representation, namely the co-occurrence quantification of term over a space of feature terms, whereas the conventional IR approach relies on the explicit relationship between terms. One could embed the intermediate representation into the IR model by forming a λ-mixture model: keep λ percent of the co-occurrence quantification from the IR model $P_{fg}(s_q \mid s_d)$ and substitute the other $1 - \lambda$ percent with a quantification over the degree of similarity between the DS model $P_{bg}(s_q \mid s_d)$:

$$P_{\lambda\text{mix}}(s_q \mid s_d, \text{fg}) = \lambda P_{\text{fg}}(s_q \mid s_d) + (1 - \lambda)P_{\text{bg}}(s_q \mid s_d) \quad (5)$$

We refer to this variant by DS-based IR or Symb&Distr.
To illustrate, instantiate $\lambda = 0.5$. Consider two sentences "men love yachts" and "women love porsches" with data as follows (usual probabilities for the IR model and the cosine distance for the DS model):

$$P_{\text{IR}}(\text{men}|\text{women}) = 0.2 \qquad P_{\text{IR}}(\text{yachts}|\text{porsches}) = 0.1$$
$$P_{\text{DS}}(\text{men}, \text{women}) = 0.72 \qquad P_{\text{DS}}(\text{yachts}, \text{porsches}) = 0.80$$

where "yachts" occurred a total of 1,016 times in the corpus, "porsches" 259 times, "love" 22,348 times, "men" 37,007 times (data from BNC). The weights of the DS-based IR model will be:

$$P_{\lambda\text{mix}}(\text{men}|\text{women}, \text{sim}) = \frac{0.2}{2} + \frac{0.72}{2}$$

$$P_{\lambda\text{mix}}(\text{yachts}|\text{porsches}, \text{sim}) = \frac{0.1}{2} + \frac{0.80}{2}$$

In the absence of number of documents from the data corpora of DS, we work with the number of times a term occurred in the whole corpus (taking this assumption in an IR setting means we are assuming that the term occurred one time in each document). Hence, $P(t_q \mid d)$ becomes the total number of terms in the corpus (in this example 1^8) divided by the number of times t occurred in the corpus. The IR score between the sentences is now computed as follows:

$$\left(\frac{0.2}{2} + \frac{0.72}{2}\right) \cdot \log\frac{10^8}{37,007} + 1 \cdot \log\frac{10^8}{22,348} + \left(\frac{0.1}{2} + \frac{0.80}{2}\right) \cdot \log\frac{10^8}{1,016}$$

The mixture model yields a higher score than the IR-only model. This is because the similarity based background DS model has higher values (e.g. 0.72) than the IR model direct occurrence (e.g. 0.2). The IR model however performs surprisingly well on its own.

From an IR/LM perspective, there is only a relationship between yachts and porsches if the words (symbols) occur together in some context. From a DS perspective, the relationship is established over the co-occurrence with feature terms, e.g. "expensive" and "run". Since boats and cars occur in the context of the same feature terms, a semantic relationship is established.

Furthermore, DS is phrase-oriented, whereas in IR, the bag-of-words approach is still dominant. The standard IR models are formulated for words, there is no agreed standard for semantic and/or compositional models.

5. EVALUATION

We evaluate models by the correlation between model score and reference score. For DS models this is similarity based, for IR models, we have a simulation where a query contains exactly one phrase and a document also contains only one phrase.

We evaluate models described in Section 3 on a document scoring task. Concretely, given a query and several candidate documents, a model has to assign scores to candidates. The average score correlation per query is measured.

5.1 Evaluation Dataset

The transitive sentence similarity dataset[2] described in [17, 16] is used. It consists of 108 subject-verb-object subject-verb-object phrase pairs, some of them are shown on Figure 1. There are 2,603 reference similarity scores (scale 1-7, 1 for least similar, 7 for most similar). These correspond to 20-25 reference scores per pair. To have a unique score per pair, we use the average of human judgements as the gold standard. Hereby, the reference score distribution is based on the dataset where each test phrase is paired with three other which represent a relatively similar, a medium similar, and a least similar candidates.

---
[2] http://www.cs.ox.ac.uk/activities/compdistmeaning/emnlp2013_turk.txt

Hyper Parameters		DS Models						IR Models			
Corpus	Quantification	Addition	Verb		Multiplication		Kronecker		Symbolic		Symb&Distr	
BNC	N5	0.372	0.380	+0.023	0.107	-0.712†	0.159	-0.572*	0.559	+0.505*	0.593	+0.596†
	P5	0.555	0.380	-0.316*	0.107	-0.808‡	0.159	-0.714‡	0.573	+0.033	0.637	+0.148
	PPMI5	0.704	0.412	-0.415‡	0.701	-0.004	0.680	-0.034	0.674	-0.043	0.725	+0.029
	LR5	0.660	0.648	-0.018	0.773	+0.171	0.826	+0.251‡	0.699	+0.059	0.724	+0.097
ukWaC	N5	0.495	0.425	-0.142	0.212	-0.572‡	0.167	-0.663‡	0.649	+0.311*	0.698	+0.411†
	P5	0.632	0.425	-0.329†	0.212	-0.665‡	0.167	-0.736‡	0.639	+0.010	0.769	+0.216†
	PPMI5	0.741	0.496	-0.331‡	0.770	+0.038	0.766	+0.033	0.742	+0.001	0.779	+0.051
	LR5	0.724	0.561	-0.226*	**0.841**	**+0.161***	**0.861**	**+0.189†**	0.767	+0.058	0.785	+0.083

Figure 2: Average score (Pearson) correlation per query. Signed numbers show a relative improvement with respect to the baseline (Addition). Average relative increase from Symbolic IR models to Mixed IR models is 0.068 for BNC and 0.063 for ukWaC. *statistically significant under $p < 0.1$. †s.s. under $p < 0.05$, ‡s.s. under $p < 0.01$. T-test of two independent samples.

We assume that in the retrieval scenario similarity scores can be converted to retrieval score rankings, in other words, for each query phrase its most similar counterpart is the most relevant document, the somewhat similar counterpart is the second relevant document, and, finally, the dissimilar sentence is the least relevant document.

5.2 Model Hyper Parameters

Two corpora are used to obtain co-occurrence counts for the DS feature vector spaces and the IR term relatedness scores. The British National Corpus (BNC)[3] [7] contains both written and spoken language and consists of 200 million words. Currently, BNC is considered to be a small resource to build distributional vector space models. Instead, ukWaC[4] [9], a 2 billion word collection of `dot-uk` web-pages, is used. In our experiments we used PukWac (a dependency parsed version of ukWaC). Source corpus is one of the model hyper parameters that can influence model performance. In general it is expected that the larger is the corpus the more reliable are the model results.

During the co-occurrence matrix construction lemmatized versions of words were gathered[5]. Both target words and feature words were part of speech tagged, so there were different vectors for the verb "help" and the noun "help". 2000 most frequent nouns, verbs, adjectives and adverbs in a corresponding corpus formed the features. In all our experiments we used a symmetric window of 5 words.

The second hyper parameter is the quantification of the co-occurrence counts. We start off with the simplest quantification of target-feature relatedness which is the raw co-occurrence count (referred as N5). The P5 quantification is the conditional probability of feature given target.

We have two models that express feature-target (in)dependence, namely PPMI5, which is the PPMI score, and LR5, which is the likelihood ratio (refer to Section 3 for more details). Research performed on the original sentence similarity task [17, 16] reports results of more elaborated vector spaces (such as neural word embeddings and spaces based on dimensionality reduction) that are comparable to the numbers we observed for PPMI5 and LR5 [26]; that is why in this paper we only use these models.

We evaluate 8 hyper parameter combinations based on 2 corpora (BNC and ukWaC) and 4 quantification methods (N5, P5, PPMI5 and LR5).

---

[3] http://www.natcorp.ox.ac.uk/
[4] http://wacky.sslmit.unibo.it/
[5] For PukWaC lemmas were additionally lower-cased, as we noticed quite a lot of nouns that start with a capital latter, for example "University" when it is a part of university's name.

5.3 Candidate Models

Based on the hyper parameters and the aim to compare DS versus IR models we test 4 DS models and 2 IR models. On the DS side we experiment with models based on various compositional methods, on the IR side we contrast symbolic estimate $P(t_q|d)$ (see Section 3.2) with a mixture of symbolic and distributional evidence $P_{0.5\text{mix}}(t_q \mid d, \text{sim})$ (see Section 4, Equation 5).

We treat DS Addition as the baseline in the experiments as it is the most straightforward model. To control whether composition is done competitively, we introduce model Verb that does not do any composition and considers only the verb component of an svo-phrase. The argument here is that a verb contains a significant part of the phrase meaning and a good compositional method should not distract this signal when composing with the subject and object. Overall, we test 4 DS models (Addition, Verb, Multiplication, Kronecker) and 2 IR models (Symbolic and DS-based).

6. RESULTS AND ANALYSIS

The results are presented in Table 2 and are depicted in Figure 3. Regarding the DS models, the Kronecker model with an LR5 vector performed best in both BNC and ukWaC. In IR, the Dist&Symb model with LR5 did slightly better than the Symbolic IR with LR5. The non-compositional verb-only model was not very low, although it was below the additive baseline. The LR5 model of all of the other compositional DS and IR models increased the LR5 of the additive baseline.

In general, LR5 worked better than the N5 and P5 in both DS and IR models. This is because the LR5 is a non-logarithmic version of the *independence* measure discussed in Equation 4, hence it is a measure aware of the independence between the target and source terms and the vector components provided thereof have a better quality. Both N5 and P5 lack the explicit independence-aware expression. In the same lines, the P5 weighting measure of IR does not work so well on its own, as it is lacking independence

All models got a boost by moving from N5 and P5 to LR5 and PPMI5. This boost was particularly high in the DS multiplication model, since the introduction of likelihood ratios and logarithms decrease the eliminating effect of close-to-zero raw coordinates and probabilities. For the same reason, the amount of increase was not as much in the additive and verb-only models. This might be overcome by multiplying it with an explicit IDF component. A further observation is that despite the previous word-level DS predictions [18] PPMI5 did not do as well as LR5. This could be caused by the effect of using cosines together with composition operators, a combination seemingly less sensitive to logarithmic manipulations.

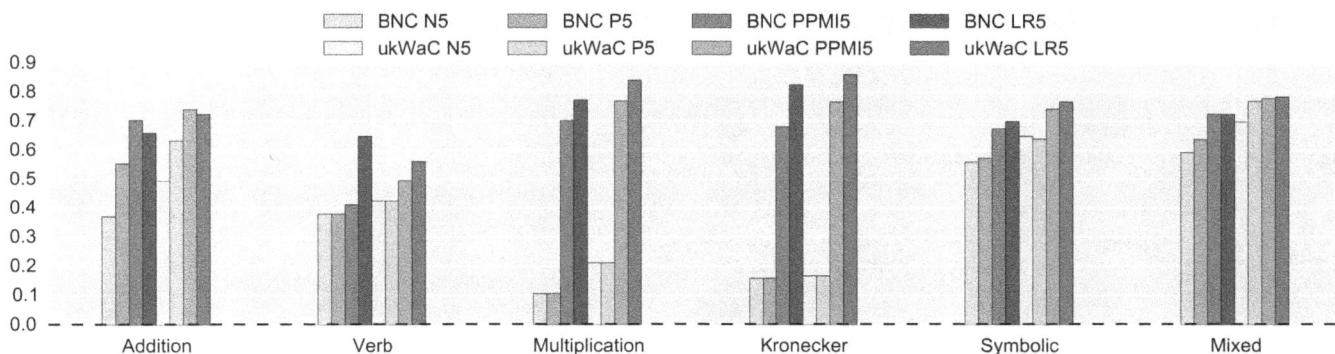

Figure 3: Graphical representation of Average score (Pearson) correlation per query. All models got a boost by using a larger corpus and the LR5 weighting. The symbolic IR model got an extra improvement when mixed with background NLP data. For each model hyper parameters are (listed from left to right): BNC N5, BNC P5, BNC PPMI5, BNC LR5, ukWaC N5, ukWaC P5, ukWaC PPMI5, ukWaC LR5.

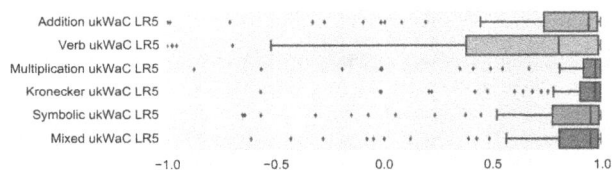

Figure 4: Distribution boxplot of query score correlations for each model. It shows distributions of query score correlations for each model, based on LR5 quantification and ukWaC corpus. All models (except Verb) got a distribution with lower standard deviation than Addition.

The best DS model was closely followed by multiplication. Figure 4 shows a more detailed analysis of this situation. We observe that the inter-quartile range of Multiplication is less than that of Kronecker. This means that Multiplication is a less conservative composition operator: it gives higher results than Kronecker on its good queries, but makes more severe mistakes on the more complex ones. The average lower performance of Multiplication is depicted by the larger number of its extreme outliers.

Somewhat unexpectedly, the original averages of the IR model (in comparison to the Symb&Distr IR) are already quite high. The involvement of explicit cosine similarities from the background DS model to the foreground IR model had a relatively small increase of 0.068 for BNC and 0.063 for ukWaC. The stability of the amount of this increase across the two corpora (despite their huge size difference) shows that a bigger corpus does not fully solve the sparsity problem of Symbolic IR. The added cosine terms, nonetheless, caused dramatic increases in particular individuals where the correlations were low (even negative). The best example herein is "case require attention", which was given a negative correlation of -0.14 by the Symbolic IR model, whereas the Symb&Distr IR model increased that by 70% to 0.56. Even more so, Symbolic IR ranked "member attend conference" as the highest match, whereas the correct option was "patient need treatment", correctly ranked so by the integrated model. Understanding which kinds of individuals lend themselves to such improvements is a direction for future work.

7. SUMMARY AND CONCLUSIONS

In this paper, we have presented the comparison of two principle methodologies to measure the similarity between semantic phrases. In particular, subj-verb-object phrases were presented, though the methodologies are not restricted to this special case.

The methodologies differ in word meaning representation and come from the fields of NLP and IR: in the DS domain of NLP, words are represented as vectors in a space of feature terms where each vector component reflects a co-occurrence quantification; in phrase-based IR, there is no internal representation of terms other than their mutual degree of co-occurrence.

The match between phrases is based on compositional models. For DS, a composition of subject, verb and object vectors represents the phrase, and the similarity between phrases is measured by cosine. For phrase-based IR, we showed a methodology to compute a score that reflects the degree to which a source phrase implies a target phrase. A source phrase corresponds to a proposition that occurs in the query, and a target phrase corresponds to a proposition that occurs in the document.

This paper tackles the term mismatch problem in information retrieval with regards to documents without direct occurrences of query terms in them. We present how this problem can be solved by using symbolic co-occurrence information. In addition, we experiment with how mixing the symbolic model with the similarity model improves the result. One of the major findings is that the DS+IR model's improvement over the IR model is less than expected, which means that the IR model score computation utilises the symbolic model to its maximum. On the other hand, the result of the NLP grammatical approach shows that there is a potential improvement if the IR models were more grammar aware.

In IR, the relevance of the source with respect to the target is based on the availability of information about the direct co-occurrence of source components (e.g. subject) and target components. The score reflecting the relevance should therefore be sensitive to the amount and quality of semantic information available. Our investigation shows that this improvement was small in average but substantial for individual cases. The impact for NLP is the finding that the more grammatically oriented composition operators, in our case the Kronecker model, provides better scores. This offers another impact to IR, which has a more set-based view on the components of phrases and should be studied in more details in the future. On the NLP side, the future work would be to look into similarity between sets of phrases, namely documents, and explore component-wise relevance measures between phrase terms. Looking at real data for the original phrase comparisons of the introduction supports this point. Namely, "agent sells property" is ranked the closest to "delegate buys land" and second closest to "family buys home". This is because "agent" is more similar to "delegate" than to "family", and "property" is more similar to "land" than to "home".

The work of this paper suggests that the NLP-based signal about the word co-occurrence is essential to perform semantic IR tasks. It also shows that the IR retrieval score, which is not a similarity measure by itself, correlates reasonably well with similarity reference scores. To show the effectiveness of the proposed approach, the method should be evaluated on a standard IR benchmark. Analytical investigation into dualities between the vector-based NLP approach to represent semantics and probabilistic IR models, including TF-IDF, Language Modelling and BM25 is another direction of extending this work. Concluding, NLP methodologies are highly beneficial for semantic IR tasks.

8. ACKNOWLEDGEMENTS

We thank the anonymous reviewers for their comments. Support from EPSRC grant EP/F042728/1 is gratefully acknowledged.

9. REFERENCES

[1] Hany Azzam and Thomas Roelleke. SQR: a semantic query rating scheme. In *Proceedings of the third workshop on Exploiting semantic annotations in information retrieval*, ESAIR '10, pages 21–22, New York, NY, USA, 2010. ACM.

[2] Hany Azzam, Sirvan Yahyaei, Marco Bonzanini, and Thomas Roelleke. A schema-driven approach for knowledge-oriented retrieval and query formulation. In *Proceedings of the Third International Workshop on Keyword Search on Structured Data*, KEYS '12, pages 39–46, New York, NY, USA, 2012. ACM.

[3] Marco Baroni and Roberto Zamparelli. Nouns are vectors, adjectives are matrices: Representing adjective-noun constructions in semantic space. In *Proceedings of the 2010 Conference on Empirical Methods in Natural Language Processing*, EMNLP '10, pages 1183–1193, Stroudsburg, PA, USA, 2010. ACL.

[4] John A. Bullinaria and Joseph P. Levy. Extracting semantic representations from word co-occurrence statistics: A computational study. *Behavior Research Methods*, pages 510–526, 2007.

[5] Bob Coecke, Edward Grefenstette, and Mehrnoosh Sadrzadeh. Lambek vs. lambek: Functorial vector space semantics and string diagrams for lambek calculus. *Ann. Pure Appl. Logic*, 164(11):1079–1100, 2013.

[6] Bob Coecke, Mehrnoosh Sadrzadeh, and Stephen Clark. Mathematical foundations for a compositional distributional model of meaning. *CoRR*, abs/1003.4394, 2010.

[7] Steve Crowdy. The BNC spoken corpus. *Leech et al*, pages 224–235, 1995.

[8] Susan T. Dumais, George W. Furnas, Thomas K. Landauer, Scott Deerwester, and Richard Harshman. Using latent semantic analysis to improve access to textual information. In *In Proceedings of Computer Human Interaction '88*, pages 281–285. ACM Press, 1988.

[9] Adriano Ferraresi, Eros Zanchetta, Marco Baroni, and Silvia Bernardini. Introducing and evaluating ukWaC, a very large web-derived corpus of English. In *Proceedings of the 4th Web as Corpus Workshop (WAC-4) Can we beat Google*, pages 47–54, 2008.

[10] John R. Firth. A Synopsis of Linguistic Theory, 1930-1955. *Studies in Linguistic Analysis*, pages 1–32, 1957.

[11] N. Fuhr, N. Gövert, and Th. Roelleke. Dolores: A system for logic-based retrieval of multimedia objects. In W. Bruce Croft, Alistair Moffat, C. J. van Rijsbergen, Ross Wilkinson, and Justin Zobel, editors, *Proceedings of the 21st Annual International ACM SIGIR Conference on Research and Development in Information Retrieval*, pages 257–265, New York, 1998. ACM.

[12] Edward Grefenstette, Georgiana Dinu, Yao-Zhong Zhang, Mehrnoosh Sadrzadeh, and Marco Baroni. Multi-step regression learning for compositional distributional semantics. *Proceedings of the 10th International Conference on Computational Semantics (IWCS 2013)*, 2013.

[13] Edward Grefenstette and Mehrnoosh Sadrzadeh. Experimental support for a categorical compositional distributional model of meaning. In *Proceedings of the Conference on Empirical Methods in Natural Language Processing*, pages 1394–1404. ACL, 2011.

[14] Edward Grefenstette and Mehrnoosh Sadrzadeh. Experimenting with transitive verbs in a DisCoCat. In *Proceedings of the GEMS 2011 Workshop on GEometrical Models of Natural Language Semantics*, pages 62–66, Edinburgh, UK, July 2011. ACL.

[15] Montmain J. Harispe S., Ranwez S. Janaqi S. Semantic similarity from natural language and ontology analysis. *Synthesis Lectures on Human Language Technologies*, 8(1):1–254, 2015.

[16] Dimitri Kartsaklis and Mehrnoosh Sadrzadeh. Prior disambiguation of word tensors for constructing sentence vectors. In *Proceedings of the 2013 Conference on Empirical Methods in Natural Language Processing (EMNL)*, Seattle, USA, October 2013. ACL.

[17] Dimitri Kartsaklis and Mehrnoosh Sadrzadeh. A study of entanglement in a categorical framework of natural language. In *Proceedings of the 11th Workshop on Quantum Physics and Logic (QPL)*, Kyoto, Japan, June 2014.

[18] Douwe Kiela and Stephen Clark. A systematic study of semantic vector space model parameters. In *Proceedings of the 2nd Workshop on Continuous Vector Space Models and their Compositionality (CVSC)*, pages 21–30, Gothenburg, Sweden, April 2014. ACL.

[19] F. Kifer and G. Lausen. F-logic: A higher-order language for reasoning about objects, inheritance, and scheme. In *Proceedings of the ACM SIGMOD International Conference on the Management of Data*, pages 134–146, New York, 1989.

[20] Jayant Krishnamurthy and Tom Mitchell. *Proceedings of the Workshop on Continuous Vector Space Models and their Compositionality*, chapter Vector Space Semantic Parsing: A Framework for Compositional Vector Space Models. ACL, 2013.

[21] T. Landauer and S. Dumais. A Solution to Plato's Problem: The Latent Semantic Analysis Theory of Acquision, Induction, and Representation of Knowledge. *Psychological Review*, 1997.

[22] D. Lin. Automatic retrieval and clustering of similar words. In *Proceedings of the 17th international conference on Computational linguistics-Volume 2*, pages 768–774. ACL, 1998.

[23] K. Lund and C. Burgess. Producing high-dimensional semantic spaces from lexical co-occurrence. *Behavior Research Methods Instruments and Computers*, 28(2):203–208, 1996.

[24] Jean Maillard, Stephen Clark, and Edward Grefenstette. A type-driven tensor-based semantics for ccg. *EACL 2014 Type Theory and Natural Language Semantics Workshop*, 2014.

[25] C. Meghini, F. Sebastiani, U. Straccia, and C. Thanos. A model of information retrieval based on a terminological logic. In R. Korfhage, E. Rasmussen, and P. Willett, editors, *Proceedings of the Sixteenth Annual International ACM SIGIR Conference on Research and Development in Information Retrieval*, pages 298–308, New York, 1993. ACM.

[26] Dmitrijs Milajevs, Dimitri Kartsaklis, Mehrnoosh Sadrzadeh, and Matthew Purver. Evaluating neural word representations in tensor-based compositional settings. In *Proceedings of the 2014 Conference on Empirical Methods in Natural Language Processing (EMNLP)*, pages 708–719, Doha, Qatar, October 2014. ACL.

[27] Jeff Mitchell and Mirella Lapata. Composition in distributional models of semantics. *Cognitive Science*, 34(8):1388–1439, 2010.

[28] Denis Paperno, The Nghia Pham, and Marco Baroni. A practical and linguistically-motivated approach to compositional distributional semantics. In *Proceedings of the 52nd Annual Meeting of the Association for Computational Linguistics (Volume 1: Long Papers)*, pages 90–99. Association for Computational Linguistics, 2014.

[29] T. Roelleke and N. Fuhr. Retrieval of complex objects using a four-valued logic. In H.-P. Frei, D. Harmann, P. Schäuble, and R. Wilkinson, editors, *Proceedings of the 19th International ACM SIGIR Conference on Research and Development in Information Retrieval*, pages 206–214, New York, 1996. ACM.

[30] Thomas Roelleke and Jun Wang. Tf-idf undercovered: A study of theories and probabilities. In *SIGIR*, 2008.

[31] H. Rubenstein and J.B. Goodenough. Contextual Correlates of Synonymy. *Communications of the ACM*, 8(10):627–633, 1965.

[32] H. Schütze. Automatic word sense discrimination. *Computational Linguistics*, 24(1):97–123, 1998.

[33] Peter D Turney, Patrick Pantel, et al. From frequency to meaning: Vector space models of semantics. *Journal of artificial intelligence research*, 37(1):141–188, 2010.

A Theoretical Analysis of Cross-lingual Semantic Relatedness in Vector Space Models

Lei Zhang
Karlsruhe Institute of
Technology (KIT)
76128 Karlsruhe, Germany
l.zhang@kit.edu

Thanh Tran
San Jose State University
One Washington Square, San
Jose, CA 95192-0249, USA
ducthanh.tran@sjsu.edu

Achim Rettinger
Karlsruhe Institute of
Technology (KIT)
76128 Karlsruhe, Germany
rettinger@kit.edu

ABSTRACT

Semantic relatedness is essential for different text processing tasks, especially in the cross-lingual setting due to the vocabulary mismatch problem. Many concept-based solutions to semantic relatedness have been proposed, which vary in the notions of concept and document representation. In our contribution, we provide a unified model that generalizes over the existing approaches to cross-lingual semantic relatedness. It shows that the main existing solutions represent different ways for constructing the concept space, which result in different document representations and implications for semantic relatedness computation. In particular, it allows us to provide theoretical justifications of existing solutions. Through the experimental evaluation, we show that the results support our theoretical findings.

Categories and Subject Descriptors

H.3.3 [**Information Storage and Retrieval**]: Information Search and Retrieval

General Terms

Theory, Languages

Keywords

Semantic Relatedness, Cross-lingual, Vector Space Models

1. INTRODUCTION

Semantic relatedness has been used in many fields of natural language processing (NLP), including word sense disambiguation, text summarization and annotation, information extraction and retrieval. In this regard, understanding semantic relatedness is crucial for processing natural language texts, especially when they are composed in different languages. Cross-lingual semantic relatedness measures the strength of semantic connection between documents (or other textual units such as words, sentences and paragraphs) in different languages.

ICTIR'15, September 27–30, Northampton, MA, USA.
© 2015 ACM. ISBN 978-1-4503-3833-2/15/09 ...$15.00.
DOI: http://dx.doi.org/10.1145/2808194.2809450.

Approaches to semantic relatedness can be classified according to the type of used resources: (1) *dictionary-based* approaches, where entries in dictionaries can be exploited to define semantic relatedness between terms; (2) *thesaurus-based* approaches, where terms are grouped together based on different kind of relations, such as synonymy and hyponymy; (3) *corpus-based* approaches, where co-occurrences of terms are often interpreted as an estimation of semantic relatedness. While dictionary-based and thesaurus-based approaches can measure semantic relatedness in a more precise way, the advantage of corpus-based approaches lies in the large amount of available data. In this work, we focus on the corpus-based solutions [4, 9, 2, 19, 13, 6] for computing semantic relatedness.

For cross-lingual semantic relatedness, a straight-forward way is to first translate the documents into the same language using statistical machine translation (SMT) systems and then apply the monolingual semantic relatedness methods. However, the drawbacks of applying SMT systems to translate the documents on the fly is the potentially longer execution time and the requirement of parallel training corpora, which are still missing for many language pairs. Several cross-lingual extensions [5, 11, 14, 18, 12] of the corpus-based approaches to semantic relatedness have been proposed. These approaches can rely on either a parallel corpus or an aligned comparable corpus[1], which is much easier to obtain, e.g., it can be derived from Wikipedia. However, these solutions as well as existing studies comparing them (see [21, 10, 3]) do not provide a theoretical understanding of and justification for differences among existing methods.

In this work, we provide *a generalized model for cross-lingual semantic relatedness* based on the notions of (1) interlingual concept space, (2) document representation and (3) semantic relatedness measure. In our *theoretical study,* we show that the main existing solutions can be conceived as instantiations that can be mapped to components of this generalized model. In particular, they represent different ways for constructing the concept space, which result in different document representations and implications for computation of the cross-lingual semantic relatedness measure. Through the *experimental evaluation,* we then show that these differences among existing solutions translates to different performance achievements in a cross-lingual search and retrieval scenario.

The remainder of the paper is structured as follows: in Sec. 2, we provide an overview of the main approaches stud-

---

[1]Parallel corpus consists of translated equivalents of each document, while aligned comparable corpus contains aligned documents in different languages that address the same topics but may differ in length, detail and style.

ied in this paper and the related work. Then, we present a generalized model for computing cross-lingual semantic relatedness in Sec. 3, which is later instantiated by different approaches. Based on the generalized model, we analyze different approaches and provide theoretical justifications for these solutions in Sec. 4. Experimental results are presented in Sec. 5, followed by conclusions in Sec. 6.

2. OVERVIEW AND RELATED WORK

The vector space models (VSM) [16, 15] have been widely used for representing documents as term vectors. Using terms from the documents alone to compute their similarity, however, suffers from the *vocabulary mismatch problem*: the similarity score is small when they have few terms in common, even though they are semantically very related. This problem is more serious in the cross-lingual setting because documents in different languages rarely share common terms.

Solutions to semantic relatedness aim to address this problem. Essentially, they can be conceived as different ways of (1) mapping terms to vectors in a semantic vector space spanned by concepts (2) to produce concept-based document representations, based on which (3) documents can be compared using standard similarity measures. In the cross-lingual setting, an *interlingual concept space* is needed, which is constructed using a parallel corpus or an aligned comparable corpus. Existing solutions vary in the notions of concept and document representation. In this work, we will study the following three main models in detail.

Clustering Model. Cluster analysis is a common technique for statistical data analysis in many fields. One specific application of clustering is to derive features or concepts from documents. If such concepts need to be valid for different languages, clustering has to be performed on a language-aligned document collection. As a common used method, K-means clustering [8] is employed in this paper to group the concatenated bilingual documents into clusters, which act as concepts.

Latent Model. Various latent approaches have been proposed to identify latent dimensions or concepts inherent in the background corpus. Among these approaches, we investigate Latent Semantic Indexing (LSI) [4] in particular, which is a well-known method based on Singular Value Decomposition (SVD). LSI was originally employed for dimensionality reduction on the term-document matrix of a corpus. The reduced dimensions correspond to latent concepts. By using a parallel corpus or an aligned comparable corpus, it can be applied to cross-lingual contexts [5].

Explicit Model. Recently, explicit approaches have been proposed as alternative to latent approaches based on externally defined knowledge (e.g. Wikipedia), which is exploited to define concepts. One prominent instantiation by now is Explicit Semantic Analysis (ESA) [6]. To adopt ESA for the cross-lingual setting, cross-language links in Wikipedia has been used [14, 18]. In this work, besides Wikipedia we also use the parallel corpus to extend ESA and the experiments show its good performance.

There are some studies that compare different solutions to cross-lingual information retrieval (CLIR), which consists of providing a query in one language and searching documents in one or more different languages. In this context, the work in [21] has reported a thorough evaluation of multiple methods for CLIR, which fall into two categories: machine translation (MT) based approaches, where dictionary-based and

corpus-based MT systems have been studied, and statistical information retrieval (IR) approaches including General Vector Space Model (GVSM) [20] and LSI. The comparative study shows that corpus-based MT approaches clearly surpass general-purpose dictionary-based MT approaches and the performance of LSI proves comparable to that of other corpus-based approaches including the MT ones. The work in [10] has reported a series of experiments comparing the performance of GVSM and LSI on monolingual and translingual retrieval tasks. The results show that LSI performs better but have a larger preprocessing cost. In [3], latent models of concepts, namely LSI and Latent Dirichlet Allocation (LDA) [2], have been compared to ESA on a mate retrieval task and it claimed that ESA outperforms LSI/LDA unless the latter are trained and tested on the same dataset instead of Wikipedia as the training data. However, these studies do not provide theoretical understanding of and justification for differences among existing solutions.

In this paper, we focus on three representative instantiations of the above models, namely K-means clustering, LSI and ESA. Most other approaches in each category are just variations and incremental improvements of these three approaches. For example, LDA is a probabilistic extension of LSI [9, 2] and it has shown that ESA is very close to GVSM in the recent studies [1, 7]. Different from the existing studies, we provide both theoretical justifications and empirical comparisons of these approaches.

3. GENERALIZED MODEL

In this section, we present a unified model for cross-lingual semantic relatedness. This model generalizes over the existing approaches and we will show how different approaches can be expressed as instantiations and mapped to components of this model. Firstly, we discuss the model components and their roles w.r.t. cross-lingual semantic relatedness, where documents are represented as semantic vectors in a certain interlingual concept space, which abstracts from the background parallel or aligned comparable corpus and builds on the standard cosine similarity measure to access cross-lingual semantic relatedness.

Consider two documents x and y in languages X and Y, the vocabulary sizes of which are p and q, respectively. Based on VSM, we have

$$\mathbf{x} = (x_1, x_2, \ldots, x_p)^T \quad (1)$$

$$\mathbf{y} = (y_1, y_2, \ldots, y_q)^T \quad (2)$$

where $\mathbf{x}$ and $\mathbf{y}$ are term vectors of x and y, x_i and y_i are the weights of terms i and j. Different weighting functions can be used, such as binary, TF and TF-IDF models. In the traditional VSM, two documents in the same language can be compared based on their term vectors using the standard similarity measure. However, in the cross-lingual setting, we cannot compare the documents directly due to the vocabulary mismatch problem. As discussed, a class of concept-based approaches have been suggested to exploit the interlingual concept space. Based on a mapping function, term vectors of documents in different languages can be mapped to concept vectors in the interlingual concept space, where they can be compared using the standard similarity measure.

We first introduce some notations to facilitate the following discussion. Let $B = \binom{B'}{B''}$ be the term-document matrix of the parallel or aligned comparable corpus containing m bilingual documents, where $B' = (b'_{ij})_{p \times m}$ and

$B'' = (b''_{ij})_{q \times m}$ are matrices for documents in languages X and Y with vocabulary size p and q respectively, and each pair of the vector $\mathbf{b}'_i$ in B' and the aligned vector $\mathbf{b}''_i$ in B'' form the vector of the concatenated bilingual document $\mathbf{b}_i = \binom{\mathbf{b}'_i}{\mathbf{b}''_i}$ in B.

Interlingual Concept Space. The construction of the interlingual concept space relies on the background corpus. Given its matrix B, we apply different approaches to obtain two sets of aligned vectors of concepts for X and Y

$$U = (\mathbf{u}_1, \mathbf{u}_2, \ldots, \mathbf{u}_n) \tag{3}$$

$$V = (\mathbf{v}_1, \mathbf{v}_2, \ldots, \mathbf{v}_n) \tag{4}$$

where each pair of aligned vectors $\mathbf{u}_i$ and $\mathbf{v}_i$ represent the same concept. The vectors $\mathbf{u}_i$ and $\mathbf{v}_i$ can be represented as

$$\mathbf{u}_i = (u_{1i}, u_{2i}, \ldots, u_{pi})^T \tag{5}$$

$$\mathbf{v}_i = (v_{1i}, v_{2i}, \ldots, v_{qi})^T \tag{6}$$

where the entries u_{ji} in $\mathbf{u}_i$ and v_{ki} in $\mathbf{v}_i$ corresponding to terms j and k are considered as importance indicators of terms j and k in the concept. An interlingual concept space A can be formed using U and V where each dimension corresponds to a pair of aligned vectors in U and V.

Document Representation. To produce the concept-based representation, each document in languages X and Y can be mapped to a concept vector in A

$$U(\mathbf{x}) = U^T \cdot \mathbf{x} = (\langle \mathbf{u}_1, \mathbf{x} \rangle, \ldots, \langle \mathbf{u}_n, \mathbf{x} \rangle)^T \tag{7}$$

$$V(\mathbf{y}) = V^T \cdot \mathbf{y} = (\langle \mathbf{v}_1, \mathbf{y} \rangle, \ldots, \langle \mathbf{v}_n, \mathbf{y} \rangle)^T \tag{8}$$

where each entry is the inner product of term vectors of the document and the corresponding concept representing the association strength between them.

Semantic Relatedness Measure. The semantic relatedness between x and y can be calculated using cosine similarity between $U(\mathbf{x})$ and $V(\mathbf{y})$ as

$$
\begin{aligned}
sim(x, y) &= cos(U(\mathbf{x}), V(\mathbf{y})) = \frac{\langle U(\mathbf{x}), V(\mathbf{y}) \rangle}{|U(\mathbf{x})| \cdot |V(\mathbf{y})|} \\
&= \frac{(\mathbf{x}^T \cdot U) \cdot (V^T \cdot \mathbf{y})}{\sqrt{(\mathbf{x}^T \cdot U) \cdot (U^T \cdot \mathbf{x})} \cdot \sqrt{(\mathbf{y}^T \cdot V) \cdot (V^T \cdot \mathbf{y})}} \\
&= \frac{\sum_{j=1}^{p} \sum_{k=1}^{q} x_j \cdot y_k \cdot g_{jk}}{\sqrt{\sum_{j=1}^{p} \sum_{k=1}^{p} x_j \cdot x_k \cdot g'_{jk}} \cdot \sqrt{\sum_{j=1}^{q} \sum_{k=1}^{q} y_j \cdot y_k \cdot g''_{jk}}}
\end{aligned}
\tag{9}
$$

where $g_{jk} = \sum_{i=1}^{n} u_{ji} \cdot v_{ki}$ denotes the correlation between term j from document x and term k from document y, $g'_{jk} = \sum_{i=1}^{n} u_{ji} \cdot u_{ki}$ ($g''_{jk} = \sum_{i=1}^{n} v_{ji} \cdot v_{ki}$) captures the term correlation between j and k from x (y). Essentially, the term correlation between j and k is based on their associations with each concept i.

In contrast to the standard VSM, computing semantic relatedness in the concept space introduces some new factors. In the numerator of Eq. 9, we observe that the semantic relatedness between documents x and y is *proportional* to the sum of values of $x_j \cdot y_k \cdot g_{jk}$ for each pair of terms j from x and k from y. The component g_{jk}, called *term relatedness*, captures the term correlation between j and k from different documents. Obviously, when two documents have more correlated term pairs yielding more non-zero components $x_j \cdot y_k \cdot g_{jk}$, and these term pairs appear more frequently in

the respective documents and have closer correlation yielding larger values of $x_j \cdot y_k \cdot g_{jk}$, the score of semantic relatedness is higher. The term relatedness factor is used to incorporate this effect.

Regarding the denominator of Eq. 9, the semantic relatedness between x and y is *inversely proportional* to the square root of the sum of values of $x_j \cdot x_k \cdot g'_{jk}$ ($y_j \cdot y_k \cdot g''_{jk}$), called normalization factor, which has two effects. Firstly, the components $x_j \cdot x_k$ and $y_j \cdot y_k$ have the effect of *document length normalization*, which is similar to that in the standard VSM. Clearly, long documents usually use the same terms repeatedly and also contain numerous different terms resulting in higher term frequencies and more terms, and thus the components $x_j \cdot y_k$ in the numerator of Eq. 9 are larger for long documents. This increases the semantic relatedness score between long documents and others. Document length normalization is used to remove the advantage of long documents over short ones. Higher term frequencies and more terms in x (y) increase the values of $x_j \cdot x_k$ ($y_j \cdot y_k$), yielding a larger normalization factor and penalizing the documents in accordance with their lengths [17].

In addition, the components g'_{jk} and g''_{jk}, called *term dependency* of documents, discard the effect of term correlation within documents on semantic relatedness. Consider documents consisting of terms that are highly dependent, in other words, many terms in them are semantically correlated. This might increase the number of correlated term pairs, thus yielding larger semantic relatedness, with other documents. The *term dependency normalization* is used to compensate for this effect. High term dependency of x and y increases the values of g'_{jk} and g''_{jk} and thus results in a larger normalization factor, thus removing the advantage of documents with high term dependency.

Although term relatedness component g_{jk} and term dependency components g'_{jk}, g''_{jk} play different roles in the computation of semantic relatedness, they all capture the term correlation between j and k. The only difference is that the terms j and k are from different documents in different languages for g_{jk}, but from the same document (thus in the same language) for g'_{jk} and g''_{jk}. We will focus our analysis on *term relatedness g_{ij}* across documents.

4. THEORETICAL ANALYSIS

We have presented the model components and discussed the effects of specific factors on the semantic relatedness measure. Based on this, we now provide a theoretical analysis of the existing approaches, namely K-means clustering, LSI and ESA. We show how they can be mapped to the model components and in this way, make clear their differences in the semantic relatedness computation.

While all approaches exploit the *term co-occurrence* in the background corpus, the main difference between them lies in the *interlingual concept space* construction. As shown in Fig. 1, the aligned vectors of concepts $\mathbf{u}_i$ and $\mathbf{v}_i$ spanning the interlingual concept space are derived differently in these approaches. This results in different ways of computing the *cross-lingual semantic relatedness*, in particular, the term relatedness g_{jk} that can be calculated as

$$g_{jk} = \sum_{i=1}^{n} u_{ji} \cdot v_{ki} \tag{10}$$

4.1 K-means Clustering based Approach

K-means clustering groups the m bilingual documents in the background corpus into n clusters and each cluster w_i corresponds to a concept, so as to minimize the within-

(a) K-means clustering based approach

(b) LSI based approach

(c) ESA based approach

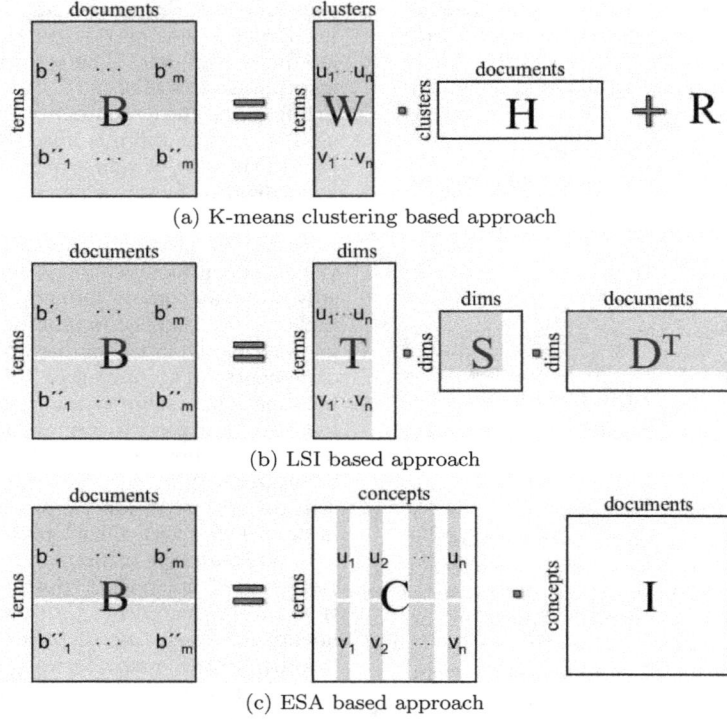

Figure 1: Matrix representations of interlingual concept space construction

cluster sum of squared differences $\sum_{i=1}^{n} \sum_{b_j \in w_i} \|\mathbf{b}_j - \mathbf{w}_i\|^2$, where $\mathbf{b}_j$ is the term vector of the concatenated bilingual document b_j and the vector $\mathbf{w}_i$ corresponds to the centroid of cluster w_i. The K-means clustering based approach to interlingual concept space construction can be represented as the following matrix factorization

$$B = W \cdot H + R, \quad W = \binom{U}{V} \quad (11)$$

After the clustering performed on B, we obtain the matrix of concepts W, where the sub-matrices U and V contain the aligned vectors of concepts for languages X and Y, respectively. Each column $\mathbf{w}_i = \binom{\mathbf{u}_i}{\mathbf{v}_i}$ in W contains the term weights of a cluster centroid, which is the average of term weights for all bilingual documents in this cluster. Each column in H contains many "0"s but only one "1" indicating the membership of the document in a cluster. That means each bilingual document can only belong to one cluster. For instance, if the i-th entry h_{ij} in the column $\mathbf{h}_j$ is 1, we have $b_j \in w_i$, i.e. document b_j belongs to cluster w_i.

Given $b_j \in w_i$, the column $\mathbf{r}_j = \mathbf{b}_j - \mathbf{w}_i$ in R can be considered as noise introduced by clustering into the concept $\mathbf{w}_i$. Thus the smaller $\|\mathbf{b}_j - \mathbf{w}_i\|^2$ is, the more precisely b_j is assigned to w_i. The matrix R is called residual matrix such that clustering minimizes sum of squares of all its columns. Note that the number of clusters n is predefined and each document must belong to one of these clusters. Considering that the background corpus covers a wide range of concepts/topics, some documents might be assigned to the concepts incorrectly resulting in larger $\|\mathbf{b}_j - \mathbf{w}_i\|^2$, i.e., the concepts might contain noise.

To facilitate the following discussion, we firstly introduce some concepts about *term co-occurrence*.

PROPOSITION 1. *Given a term-document matrix $M = (b_{ji})_{m \times n}$ with each entry b_{ji} reflecting the term frequency of term j in document i, $Z = M \cdot M^T$ is its term co-occurrence matrix. For each pair of terms j and k, the entry z_{jk} in Z represents the term co-occurrence frequency of j and k.*

PROOF. Based on different weighting functions, the term frequency b_{ji} in M has different meanings. For instance, it is the raw term frequency in TF model but the normalized frequency in TF-IDF model by taking the importance of terms into account. Each entry in Z can be calculated as $z_{jk} = \sum_{i=1}^{n} b_{ji} \cdot b_{ki}$ and it reflects the term co-occurrence frequency w.r.t. all the documents in M. □

In order to derive the conclusions of the value of g_{jk} in the K-means clustering based approach, we model the *term co-occurrence* matrix $Z^{K-means}$ as

$$Z^{K-means} = (B - R) \cdot (B - R)^T$$
$$= \underbrace{B \cdot B^T}_{Z_B} \underbrace{- B \cdot R^T - R \cdot B^T + R \cdot R^T}_{N} \quad (12)$$

where Z_B represents the term co-occurrence matrix of the background corpus and N stands for the noise introduced by clustering. In this regard, each entry z_{jk} in $Z^{K-means}$ captures the co-occurrence frequency of terms j and k in the background corpus with added noise.

LEMMA 1. *Given the matrix of concepts $W = \binom{U}{V}$, each entry z_{jk} in $Z^{K-means}$ for terms j and k in different languages can be calculated as*

$$z_{jk} = \sum_{i=1}^{n} |w_i| \cdot u_{ji} \cdot v_{ki} \quad (13)$$

PROOF. According to Eq. 11, we have $B - R = W \cdot H$ and $Z^{K-means} = (W \cdot H) \cdot (W \cdot H)^T = W \cdot H \cdot H^T \cdot W^T =$

$W \cdot \Sigma \cdot W^T$, where W contains the vectors $\mathbf{w}_i = \binom{\mathbf{u}_i}{\mathbf{v}_i}$ and $\Sigma = H \cdot H^T$ is a diagonal matrix with $\sigma_i = |w_i|$ on the diagonal. $\square$

THEOREM 2. *The term relatedness g_{jk} in the K-means clustering based approach has a* positive correlation *with the term co-occurrence frequency z_{jk} in the background corpus with additional noise yielded by clustering, i.e., when $z_{jk} > 0$, we have $g_{jk} > 0$ and $\frac{z_{jk}}{\max_{1 \le i \le n}(|w_i|)} \le g_{jk} \le \frac{z_{jk}}{\min_{1 \le i \le n}(|w_i|)}$; otherwise $g_{jk} = 0$.*

PROOF. Following Lemma 1, when $z_{jk} > 0$, there is at least one cluster with $u_{ji} \cdot v_{ki} > 0$ such that $g_{jk} > 0$. Since $\max_{1 \le i \le n}(|w_i|) \cdot g_{jk} = \sum_{i=1}^{n} \max_{1 \le i \le n}(|w_i|) \cdot u_{ji} \cdot v_{ki} \ge \sum_{i=1}^{n} |w_i| \cdot u_{ji} \cdot v_{ki} = z_{jk}$ and $\min_{1 \le i \le n}(|w_i|) \cdot g_{jk} = \sum_{i=1}^{n} \min_{1 \le i \le n}(|w_i|) \cdot u_{ji} \cdot v_{ki} \le \sum_{i=1}^{n} |w_i| \cdot u_{ji} \cdot v_{ki} = z_{jk}$, we have $\frac{z_j}{\max_{1 \le i \le n}(|w_i|)} \le g_{jk} \le \frac{z_{jk}}{\min_{1 \le i \le n}(|w_i|)}$. $\square$

4.2 LSI based Approach

Given the matrix B of the background corpus, LSI [4] finds an optimal approximation X of B with low-rank at most n based on Singular Value Decomposition (SVD), so as to minimize the Frobenius norm of the matrix difference $\|B - X\|_F = \sqrt{\sum_{i=1}^{p+q} \sum_{j=1}^{m} (b_{ij} - x_{ij})}$. After SVD performed on matrix B, we obtain a loss-free factorization of the form $B = T \cdot S \cdot D^T$, where T and D, called left and right singular vectors, are two orthogonal matrices and S is a diagonal matrix with non-negative values on the diagonal usually in descending order, known as singular values of B. It is conventional to represent S as an $r \times r$ matrix, where r is the rank of B. Accordingly, T and D^T are represented as two $(p + q) \times r$ and $r \times m$ matrices, respectively. Each column $\mathbf{t}_i$ in T represents a semantic dimension corresponding to the concept t, which is a linear combination of vectors in B and each entry indicates how strongly a term is related to the semantic dimension. Each of singular value of B in S measures the importance of the corresponding semantic dimension. Each entry in D^T indicates how strongly a document is related to the concept represented by the semantic dimension.

Based on SVD, LSI reduces the dimensions of the matrix B by grouping the related terms to form the semantic dimensions. Nevertheless, the number of dimensions, equal to the rank of the matrix B, might be still large. In addition, the semantic dimensions with small singular values are not important such that they can be eliminated. Based on that, LSI aims to find a low-rank approximation of the matrix B by retaining only the n largest singular values. Thus, we have the matrix representation as follows

$$B_n = T_n \cdot S_n \cdot D_n^T, \quad T_n = \binom{U}{V} \tag{14}$$

where $S_n = diag(s_1, \ldots, s_n)$ contains the n largest singular values, $T_n = (\mathbf{t}_1, \ldots, \mathbf{t}_n)$ and $D_n = (\mathbf{d}_1, \ldots, \mathbf{d}_n)$ contain the corresponding first n vectors in T and D. The vectors in T_n will be used to span the interlingual concept space. The Eckart-Young theorem provides the fact that omitting the smallest $r - n$ singular values and their corresponding singular vectors yields the optimal approximation of matrix B with the lowest Frobenius error, namely $\min_{\text{rank}(X)=n} \|B - X\|_F = \|B - B_n\|_F = \sqrt{\sum_{i=n+1}^{r} s_i^2}$. Such an approximation has the effect of preserving the important information while reducing noise in the background corpus.

In order to provide a better understanding of g_{jk} in the LSI based approach, we firstly investigate the term co-occurrence matrix $Z^{LSI} = B_n \cdot B_n^T$ and then discuss its relation to the l-th order term co-occurrence in the background corpus.

LEMMA 2. *Given the term co-occurrence matrix $Z_B = B \cdot B^T$ of the background corpus, the term co-occurrence matrix $Z^{LSI} = B_n \cdot B_n^T$ of the optimal low-rank approximation of B is a linear combination of the powers of Z_B. That is*

$$Z^{LSI} = B_n \cdot B_n^T = \sum_{l=1}^{r} \alpha_l \cdot Z_B^l \tag{15}$$

where r is the rank of B, α_l are constants depending on singular values of B.

PROOF. According to the factorization of $B = T \cdot S \cdot D^T$ using SVD, where T and D are orthogonal matrices and S is a diagonal matrix, we have $Z_B = (T \cdot S \cdot D^T) \cdot (T \cdot S \cdot D^T)^T = T \cdot S \cdot D^T \cdot D \cdot S \cdot T^T = T \cdot S^2 \cdot T^T$. Then, we can derive $Z_B^l = (T \cdot S^2 \cdot T^T)^l = T \cdot S^2 \cdot T^T \cdot T \cdot S^2 \cdot T^T \cdots T \cdot S^2 \cdot T^T = T \cdot S^{2l} \cdot T^T$ and each entry $z_{jk}^l = \sum_{i=1}^{r} t_{ji} \cdot t_{ki} \cdot s_i^{2l}$. With different $l \le r$, we get a linear system $A\mathbf{x} = \mathbf{b}$ with $A = \begin{bmatrix} s_1^2 & \cdots & s_r^2 \\ \vdots & \ddots & \vdots \\ s_1^{2r} & \cdots & s_r^{2r} \end{bmatrix}$, $\mathbf{x} = \begin{bmatrix} t_{j1} \cdot t_{k1} \\ \vdots \\ t_{jr} \cdot t_{kr} \end{bmatrix}$, $\mathbf{b} = \begin{bmatrix} z_{jk}^1 \\ \vdots \\ z_{jk}^r \end{bmatrix}$. The matrix A is commonly referred to as a Vandermonde matrix and its determinant is given as $det(A) = \prod_{1 \le j \le r}(s_j^2) \prod_{1 \le i < j \le r}(s_i^2 - s_j^2)$. Assume that the singular values s_i of B are mutually distinct[2], which is always the case in practice, we have $s_i^2 - s_j^2 \ne 0$ when $i \ne j$ and thus $det(A) \ne 0$, such that the linear system has a unique solution. Using the Cramer's rule, we have $x_i = t_{ji} \cdot t_{ki} = \frac{det(A_i)}{det(A)}$, where A_i is the matrix formed by replacing the i-th column of A by the vector $\mathbf{b}$ and $det(A_i) = \sum_{l=1}^{r} z_{jk}^l \cdot (-1)^{i+l} \cdot M_{il}$ based on the Laplace expansion, where M_{il} is the (l, i) minor of A_i, i.e. the determinant of the submatrix of A_i formed by deleting the l-th row and i-th column. Then we have $x_i = \sum_{l=1}^{r} \frac{(-1)^{i+l} \cdot M_{il}}{det(A)} \cdot z_{jk}^l$, where $det(A)$ and M_{il} are constants, which only depend on the singular values s_i of B. We conclude that $Z^{LSI} = (T_n \cdot S_n \cdot D_n^T) \cdot (T_n \cdot S_n \cdot D_n^T)^T = T_n \cdot S_n \cdot D_n^T \cdot D_n \cdot S_n \cdot T_n^T = T_n \cdot S_n^2 \cdot T_n^T$ and each entry $z_{jk} = \sum_{i=1}^{n} t_{ji} \cdot t_{ki} \cdot s_i^2 = \sum_{i=1}^{n} (\sum_{l=1}^{r} \frac{(-1)^{i+l} \cdot M_{il}}{det(A)} \cdot z_{jk}^l) \cdot s_i^2 = \sum_{l=1}^{r} (\sum_{i=1}^{n} \frac{(-1)^{i+l} \cdot M_{il}}{det(A)} \cdot s_i^2) \cdot z_{jk}^l = \sum_{l=1}^{r} \alpha_l \cdot z_{jk}^l$, where $\alpha_l = \sum_{i=1}^{n} \frac{(-1)^{i+l} \cdot M_{il}}{det(A)} \cdot s_i^2$ is a constant. Therefore, we have $Z^{LSI} = \sum_{l=1}^{r} \alpha_l \cdot Z_B^l$. $\square$

DEFINITION 1. *Given the background corpus, its* term co-occurrence graph *is an undirected graph $G = (N, E)$, with each node $n_j \in N$ standing for term j and each edge $e(n_j, n_k) \in E$ capturing the co-occurrence of terms j and k in the background documents, where the weight of $e(n_j, n_k)$ is the co-occurrence frequency of j and k. The l-th order co-occurrence relation between terms j and k exists, if there is a path of length l from n_j to n_k in G, with the path weight as the product of weights of edges along the path. The l-th order term co-occurrence frequency of j and k is the sum of the weights of all paths from n_j to n_k in G.*

---

[2]When two or more singular values s_i of B are equal, one may use a generalization called confluent Vandermonde matrix, which is out of the scope of this work.

PROPOSITION 3. *Given the term co-occurrence matrix* $Z_B = B \cdot B^T$ *of the background corpus, the entry* z_{jk}^l *in* Z_B^l *for terms* j *and* k, *which is the l-th power of* Z_B, *is nonzero if the l-th order co-occurrence relation between* j *and* k *exists and the value of* z_{jk}^l *is the l-th order term co-occurrence frequency of* j *and* k.

PROOF. Let $Z_B = B \cdot B^T = (z_{jk})_{(p+q) \times (p+q)}$, where $B = \binom{B'}{B''}$ with $B' = (b'_{ij})_{p \times m}$ and $B'' = (b''_{ij})_{q \times m}$. Each entry z_{jk}^l in Z_B^l is calculated as $z_{jk}^l = \sum_{i_1=1}^{p+q} \sum_{i_2=1}^{p+q} \cdots \sum_{i_{l-1}=1}^{p+q} z_{ji_1} \cdot z_{i_1 i_2} \ldots z_{i_{l-2} i_{l-1}} \cdot z_{i_{l-1} k}$, where $i_1, i_2, \ldots, i_{l-2}, i_{l-1}$ represent different terms and $z_{ji_1}, z_{i_1 i_2}, \ldots, z_{i_{l-2} i_{l-1}}, z_{i_{l-1} k}$ denote the term co-occurrence frequencies in B. If there is a path $p = \langle e(n_j, n_{i_1}), e(n_{i_1}, n_{i_2}), \ldots, e(n_{i_{l-2}}, n_{i_{l-1}}), e(n_{i_{l-1}}, n_k) \rangle$ in the co-occurrence graph G, we have $z_{ji_1} \neq 0, z_{i_1 i_2} \neq 0, \ldots, z_{i_{l-1} k} \neq 0$. The weight of path p can be computed as $w_p = z_{ji_1} \cdot z_{i_1 i_2} \ldots z_{i_{l-1} k} \neq 0$ and thus $z_{jk}^l \neq 0$. Given the set P of all paths with length l from n_j to n_k, we have $z_{jk}^l = \sum_{p \in P} w_p$. □

LEMMA 3. *Given the matrix of concepts* $T_n = \binom{U}{V}$ *obtained by LSI, each entry* z_{jk} *in* Z^{LSI} *for terms* j *and* k *in different languages can be calculated as*

$$z_{jk} = \sum_{i=1}^n s_i^2 \cdot u_{ji} \cdot v_{ki} \qquad (16)$$

PROOF. According to Eq. 14, we have $Z^{LSI} = (T_n \cdot S_n \cdot D_n^T) \cdot (T_n \cdot S_n \cdot D_n^T)^T = T_n \cdot S_n \cdot D_n^T \cdot D_n \cdot S_n \cdot T_n^T = T_n \cdot \Sigma \cdot T_n^T$, where T_n contains the vectors $\mathbf{t}_i = \binom{\mathbf{u}_i}{\mathbf{v}_i}$ and $\Sigma = S_n^2$ is a diagonal matrix with $\sigma_i = s_i^2$ on the diagonal. □

THEOREM 4. *The term relatedness* g_{jk} *between* j *and* k *computed in the LSI based approach has a positive correlation with the term co-occurrence frequency in the optimal low-rank approximation of the background corpus, i.e.* z_{jk} *in* Z^{LSI}, *which can be represented as a linear combination of the l-th order co-occurrence frequency for terms* k *and* j *in the background corpus. When* $z_{jk} > 0$, *then* $g_{jk} > 0$ *and* $\frac{z_{jk}}{\max_{1 \le i \le n}(s_i^2)} \le g_{jk} \le \frac{z_{jk}}{\min_{1 \le i \le n}(s_i^2)}$; *otherwise* $g_{jk} = 0$.

For the sake of space, we omit the proof of Theorem 4, which is similar to the proof of Theorem 2.

4.3 ESA based Approach

Recent work [1] has reported that instead of Wikipedia, documents in other corpora can be employed to construct the concepts in ESA and achieve good performance. In this work, besides Wikipedia we also use the parallel corpus to extend ESA. Since ESA [6] simply uses the documents in the background corpus as concepts, we have the matrix representation $B = C \cdot I$, where I is an identity matrix such that the matrix of the concepts C is same as B. Given two documents x and y in different languages, ESA maps them into concept vectors in a high dimensional concept space constructed by the bilingual documents, where the entries in the concept vector represent the association strength between the input documents and the corresponding concepts.

Without dimension reduction in ESA, the number of concepts is equal to the number of bilingual documents in the background corpus. In order to speed up processing and yield more compact vectors, ESA considers only the top-k concepts with the highest relevance scores w.r.t. each input document to construct the interlingual concept space [18]. Given a pair of input documents x and y in languages X and Y, we first generate two top-k concept sets $S_x = \{b_s | b'_s \in$

$kNN(x)\}$ and $S_y = \{b_s | b''_s \in kNN(y)\}$, where $kNN(x)$ $(kNN(y))$ is the set of k nearest neighbors (most highly-ranked concepts) retrieved using x (y) based on the inner product $\langle \mathbf{x}, \mathbf{b}'_s \rangle$ $(\langle \mathbf{y}, \mathbf{b}''_s \rangle)$.

Clearly, the entries in the concept vector of x (y) corresponding to the concepts which are not contained in S_x (S_y) will be zero. Therefore, given the documents x and y, only the concepts contained in $S_x \cap S_y$ will play a role in the semantic relatedness computation. In this sense, x and y are transformed into vectors in a concept space constructed by such concepts in $S_x \cap S_y$, which forms the matrix $C_{xy} = (\mathbf{c}_1, \ldots, \mathbf{c}_n)$. Then we have

$$C_{xy} = C_{[S_x \cap S_y]}, \quad C_{xy} = \binom{U}{V} \qquad (17)$$

where $C_{[S_x \cap S_y]}$ represents the sub-matrix defined as the columns of C corresponding to the concepts listed in $S_x \cap S_y$. The dimensionality n of the concept space is the size of $S_x \cap S_y$. In contrast to K-means clustering and LSI based approaches, n varies for different input documents and also depends on the background corpus, which will be shown in the experiments.

In the following, we model the *term co-occurrence* matrix Z^{ESA} and discuss the correlation between g_{jk} and z_{jk} in Z^{ESA}. Firstly, we define Z^{ESA} as

$$Z^{ESA} = C_{xy} \cdot C_{xy}^T \qquad (18)$$

Each entry z_{jk} in Z^{ESA} captures the co-occurrence frequency of terms j and k in the top-k background documents retrieved for both input documents x and y.

LEMMA 4. *Given the matrix of concepts* $C_{xy} = \binom{U}{V}$ *yielded by ESA, each entry* z_{jk} *in* Z^{ESA} *for terms* j *and* k *in different languages can be calculated as*

$$z_{jk} = \sum_{i=1}^n u_{ji} \cdot v_{ki} \qquad (19)$$

According to Eq. 18, the proof of Lemma 4 is obvious. Following Lemma 4, it is straightforward to derive the following Theorem based on Eq. 10 and Eq. 19.

THEOREM 5. *The term relatedness* g_{jk} *computed in the ESA based approach is equal to* the *term co-occurrence frequency in the* most relevant part of the background corpus w.r.t. the input documents, *i.e.* z_{jk} *in* Z^{ESA}.

4.4 Summary

In this section, we summarize the different approaches w.r.t. *interlingual concept space construction* and the resulting ways of *cross-lingual semantic relatedness computation*. A summary of these approaches is shown in Table 1.

Interlingual Concept Space Construction. The concepts generated by the K-means clustering based approach are *clusters of bilingual documents* from the *entire background corpus*, where the documents are folded into these clusters and their centroids act as concepts. The number of clusters n is *predefined* and each document can only belong to a *single cluster*. When grouping the similar documents into clusters, K-means clustering might introduce *noise* (captured by the residual matrix H) into the concepts.

The LSI based approach reduces the dimensions of the term document matrix B by bringing the related terms together to form *semantic dimensions*. It uses the n most important semantic dimensions that yield the *optimal low-rank approximation* of B as concepts. Different from the K-means clustering based approach, each document could

	K-means clustering	LSI	ESA
Interlingual Concept Space Construction	$B = W \cdot H + R$ $W = \binom{U}{V}$	$B = T \cdot S \cdot D^T$ $B_n = T_n \cdot S_n \cdot D_n^T$ $T_n = \binom{U}{V}$	$B = C \cdot I$ $C_{xy} = C_{[S_x \cap S_y]}$ $C_{xy} = \binom{U}{V}$
Concept Representation	clusters of bilingual documents	semantic dimensions of related terms in different languages	bilingual documents
	based on the entire background corpus	based on the optimal approximation of the background corpus	based on the most relevant part of the background corpus w.r.t. inputs
Dimensionality	static and low	static and low	dynamic and high
Cross-lingual Semantic Relatedness Computation	$sim(x,y) = \dfrac{\sum_{j=1}^p \sum_{k=1}^q x_j \cdot y_k \cdot g_{jk}}{\sqrt{\sum_{j=1}^p \sum_{k=1}^p x_j \cdot x_k \cdot g'_{jk}} \cdot \sqrt{\sum_{j=1}^q \sum_{k=1}^q y_j \cdot y_k \cdot g''_{jk}}}$		
	$g_{jk} = \sum_{i=1}^n u_{ji} \cdot v_{ki}$	$g_{jk} = \sum_{i=1}^n u_{ji} \cdot v_{ki}$	$g_{jk} = \sum_{i=1}^n u_{ji} \cdot v_{ki}$
	$u_{ji} = W[j,i] \in \mathbf{w}_i$ $v_{ki} = W[k,i] \in \mathbf{w}_i$	$u_{ji} = T_n[j,i] \in \mathbf{t}_i$ $v_{ki} = T_n[k,i] \in \mathbf{t}_i$	$u_{ji} = C_{xy}[j,i] \in \mathbf{c}_i$ $v_{ki} = C_{xy}[k,i] \in \mathbf{c}_i$
Term Co-occurrence Matrix and Implication of its Entry ($Z_B = B \cdot B^T$)	$Z^{K-means} = Z_B + N$	$Z^{LSI} = \sum_{l=0}^r \alpha_l \cdot Z_B^l$	$Z^{ESA} = C_{xy} \cdot C_{xy}^T$
	$z_{jk} = \sum_{i=1}^n |w_i| \cdot u_{ji} \cdot v_{ki}$	$z_{jk} = \sum_{i=1}^n s_i^2 \cdot u_{ji} \cdot v_{ki}$	$z_{jk} = \sum_{i=1}^n u_{ji} \cdot v_{ki}$
	term co-occurrence frequency in the background corpus with added noise	a linear combination of the high-order term co-occurr frequency in the background corpus	term co-occurrence frequency in the most relevant part of the background corpus
Correlation of g_{jk} with z_{jk}	g_{jk} has a positive correlation with z_{jk}	g_{jk} has a positive correlation with z_{jk}	g_{jk} is equal to z_{jk}

Table 1: Concept-based approaches to cross-lingual semantic relatedness

be folded into *more than one semantic dimension* and the weight of a document on a semantic dimension reflects its fractional membership, which can be viewed as a soft clustering *without noise* generated.

In contrast to K-means clustering and LSI based approaches, ESA based approach considers the *bilingual documents* in the background corpus as concepts. For each pair of input documents, it constructs the interlingual concept space dynamically using the intersection of two sets of top-k background documents that are *most relevant* to the respective input documents. Instead of a *fixed and relatively low* dimensionality n of the concept space in K-means clustering and LSI based approaches, n in ESA based approach is determined *dynamically*.

Cross-lingual Semantic Relatedness Computation. While all these approaches are based on term co-occurrence derived from the background corpus, the difference of interlingual concept space construction between these approaches results in different ways of computing cross-lingual semantic relatedness and term relatedness g_{jk} in particular.

In the K-means clustering based approach, g_{jk} is *coarse-grained* due to the term co-occurrence captured at *cluster* level ($u_{ji}, v_{ki} \in \mathbf{w}_i$) and *sensitive to the noise* yielded by K-means clustering. This results in a *positive correlation* of g_{jk} with the term co-occurrence frequency z_{jk} in the background corpus with added *noise*.

In the LSI based approach, g_{jk} is also *coarse-grained* due to the term co-occurrence captured at *semantic dimension* level ($u_{ji}, v_{ki} \in \mathbf{t}_i$), but *not sensitive to any noise*. This leads to a *positive correlation* of g_{jk} with the term co-occurrence frequency z_{jk} in the *optimal low-rank approximation* of the background corpus, which has been proved to be a linear combination of the *high-order term co-occurrence frequency* in the background corpus.

In the ESA based approach, g_{jk} is *fine-grained* due to the term co-occurrence captured at *document* level ($u_{ji}, v_{ki} \in \mathbf{c}_i$) and *sensitive to the dimensionality* n of the interlingual concept space constructed dynamically. And g_{jk} is equal to the term co-occurrence frequency z_{jk} in the *most relevant part* of the background corpus w.r.t. the input documents.

	English	German	Spanish
#Wikipedia articles	4,014,643	1,438,325	896,691

(a) Number of Wikipedia articles

	English-German	English-Spanish	German-Spanish
#Cross-language links ($\rightarrow$)	721,878	568,210	295,415
#Cross-language links ($\leftarrow$)	718,401	581,978	302,502
#Cross-language links (merged)	722,069	593,571	307,130

(b) Number of cross-language links

Table 2: Statistics about Wikipedia dataset used in our experiments

5. EVALUATION

In order to investigate the performance of different approaches to cross-lingual semantic relatedness, we carried out the experiments, similar to [3], in a cross-lingual search and retrieval scenario using a standard mate retrieval setup for different language pairs covering English, German and Spanish.

5.1 Data and Methodology

To provide the background corpus, we extracted large collections from the parallel corpus JRC-Acquis[3] and the aligned comparable corpus Wikipedia[4] (henceforth also denoted by JRC and Wiki). The JRC-Acquis corpus comprises of approximately 23,000 legislative documents from European Union in each of 22 European languages. We used a random sample of 90% of parallel documents in English, German and Spanish from JRC-Acquis corpus as the background corpus and the remaining 10% parallel documents in these languages for testing. For constructing the aligned Wikipedia comparable corpus as the additional background corpus, we analyzed cross-language links between Wikipedia articles for each pair of supported languages in both directions and keep articles for which aligned versions exist at least in one direction. For instance, we extracted 721,878 cross-language links from English Wikipedia to German Wikipedia, and 718,401 cross-language links from German to English. By merging them, we obtain 722,069 cross-language links, which are used to construct the aligned Wikipedia comparable corpus of the English-German language pair. Table 2 shows some statistics of the Wikipedia dataset used in our experiments.

For mate retrieval evaluation, we take the document in one language as query and retrieve the relevant documents in another language. We assumed that only the translated version (mate) is considered as relevant to the query document. In this experimental setup, we are concerned about whether the translation can appear on top of the ranked result list and the observed position of the mate is also used as a comparison factor. Based on such observation, we consider recall at cutoff rank k (R@k) and Mean Reciprocal Rank (MRR) as quality criteria. Recall defines the number of relevant documents that are retrieved in relation to the total number of relevant documents. R@k is defined by only considering the top-k results. In the mate retrieval setting, R@k defines the number of queries for which the mate document was found in the top-k results. MRR measures the average reciprocal ranks of the mate documents. Different from R@k, MRR also takes into account the position of the

mate document, resulting in higher value when the position of the mate in the ranked result list is higher.

5.2 Results

In the experiments, we observed that the performance of all these approaches varied with the parameters, namely the number n of the concepts used by K-means clustering and LSI based approaches and the number k of the most highly-ranked concepts under consideration for each input document in ESA based approach. Figs. 2(a-b) show the MRR results of three approaches using JRC-Acquis and Wikipedia as the background corpora averaged on different language pairs (i.e. English-German, English-Spanish and German-Spanish).

As shown in Fig. 2(a), the performance of K-means clustering and LSI based approaches tends to increase from 100 to 500[5] concepts using both JRC-Acquis and Wikipedia as the background corpora. For K-means clustering, the reason is that less noise will be introduced during clustering when n increases because the background documents can be assigned to more concepts, especially for Wikipedia which covers a wide range of topics. This explains why the performance of K-means clustering using Wikipedia as the background corpus improves significantly when n increases. For LSI with larger n, more semantic dimensions are involved to capture the term co-occurrence for semantic relatedness computation.

In ESA based approach, the dimensionality n of the interlingual concept space changes dynamically for specific input documents and it also depends on the top-k concepts under consideration for each input document. As shown in Fig. 2(b), ESA reaches its peak performance at $k = 10,000$ when using JRC-Acquis as the background corpus and the performance tends to slightly increase after $k > 10,000$ using Wikipedia as the background corpus. In general, ESA needs a minimum number of concepts to perform reasonably, but also reaches a point where further concepts will not help and may start introducing noise. After the top-10,000 concepts for each input document are considered, the number of the overlapped concepts for both input documents, i.e. the dimensionality n of the concept space, is large enough to capture the term co-occurrence when using JRC-Acquis as the background corpus, while there is still room to increase n when using Wikipedia as the background corpus. We will discuss this issue later.

It is observed that JRC-Acquis as the background corpus leads to much better results than Wikipedia for all approaches. That is due to the large vocabulary overlap be-

---

[3]http://langtech.jrc.it/JRC-Acquis.html
[4]http://dumps.wikimedia.org

[5]The exploration of the concept space in the K-means clustering and LSI based approaches ends with 500 dimensions due to computational limitations of our servers.

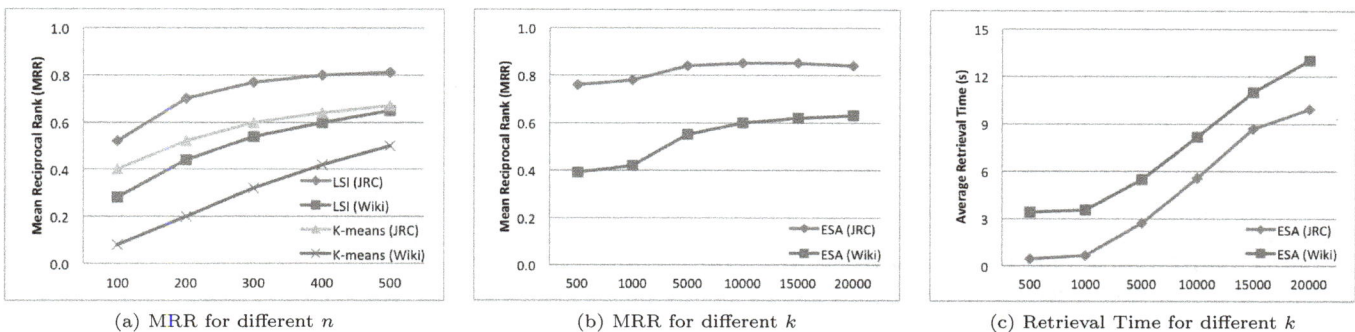

(a) MRR for different n (b) MRR for different k (c) Retrieval Time for different k

Figure 2: Evaluation results for different parameters

Method	R@1	R@10	R@100	MRR	R@1	R@10	R@100	MRR	R@1	R@10	R@100	MRR
	English-German				English-Spanish				German-Spanish			
K-means (JRC)	0.49	0.84	0.98	0.61	0.70	0.94	0.99	0.78	0.50	0.85	0.98	0.61
LSI (JRC)	0.67	0.93	**1.00**	0.77	0.83	0.97	**1.00**	0.89	0.68	**0.94**	**1.00**	0.77
ESA (JRC)	**0.75**	**0.94**	**1.00**	**0.82**	**0.86**	**0.98**	**1.00**	**0.91**	**0.76**	**0.94**	**1.00**	**0.82**
K-means (Wiki)	0.32	0.61	0.85	0.42	0.57	0.82	0.94	0.66	0.34	0.62	0.85	0.43
LSI (Wiki)	0.52	0.81	**0.98**	**0.62**	**0.66**	**0.90**	**0.99**	**0.74**	**0.49**	**0.81**	**0.98**	**0.60**
ESA (Wiki)	**0.53**	**0.82**	0.96	0.59	0.60	0.86	**0.99**	0.67	0.47	0.76	0.95	0.55

Table 3: Evaluation results using the optimal settings

Language Pair	Min. dim.	Max. dim.	Avg. dim.	Min. dim.	Max. dim.	Avg. dim.	Fixed dim.
	ESA(JRC)			ESA(Wiki)			K-means/LSI
English-German	1,678	8,569	4,499	23	5,749	929	500
English-Spanish	1,550	8,830	4,519	10	6,407	1,131	500
German-Spanish	1,643	8,373	4,502	93	5,660	1,299	500
Average	1,624	8,591	4,489	42	5,939	1,120	500

Table 4: Dimensionality of the interlingual concept space

tween the test collection and the background corpus since the semantic relatedness computed in these approaches are all based on term co-occurrence derived from the background corpus. Moreover, in contrast to a parallel corpus, Wikipedia is a comparable corpus where the aligned articles may vary in size, quality and vocabulary. In other words, the term co-occurrence frequency in JRC-Acquis reflects more reliable term relatedness than that in Wikipedia.

In K-means clustering and LSI based approaches, each query document can be processed in less than 1 second on average. This is because the time complexity of both approaches only depends on the dimensionality n of the concept space, which is relatively small ($n \leq 500$) in both approaches. For the sake of space, we omit the results because individual times exhibit only minor differences.

Fig. 2(c) shows the average retrieval time of ESA based approach for each query document. We observe that ESA takes significantly more time than the other two approaches, because it has to compare each candidate document to retrieve with the background documents to yield the top-k concepts. This results in a much higher time complexity depending on m, which is the total number of all background documents. In practice, the inverted index and top-k query processing techniques can be employed such that the time complexity is much smaller than the worst case. However, compared with K-means clustering and LSI based approaches, the computation in ESA based approach is still more expensive, especially when k is large.

While K-means clustering and LSI are more efficient than ESA for online retrieval process, ESA does not require comprehensive computation for offline preprocessing, which is needed for K-means clustering and LSI. In our experiments, the preprocessing of ESA can be performed within 1 hour for any desired number of concepts. In contrast, the preprocessing of K-means clustering and LSI takes from several hours to several days with the increasing dimensionality.

For the reported evaluation results, we used these settings ($n = 500$ for K-means clustering and LSI based approaches and $k = 10,000$ for ESA based approach) to achieve the trade-off between the effectiveness (MRR) and the efficiency (retrieval time). Table 3 shows the R@k and MRR results of all three approaches using JRC-Acquis and Wikipedia as the background corpora for different language pairs, where the best results are formatted in bold.

LSI and ESA outperform K-means clustering in all the cases. With the previous theoretical analysis, we can explain this with the differences in the semantic relatedness computation: the term relatedness in K-means clustering is related to the term co-occurrence frequency in the background corpus with *noise* yielded by clustering, which leads to distortion of the computed term relatedness.

ESA outperforms LSI in most cases using JRC-Acquis as the background corpus. This is because the term relatedness captured in ESA is *fine-grained*, i.e. at the *bilingual document* level, while LSI captures a relatively *coarse-grained* term relatedness at the *semantic dimension* level. In addition, ESA calculates the term relatedness based on the term co-occurrence frequency in the *most relevant part* of the background corpus w.r.t. the input documents, which reduces the noise, i.e. the irrelevant background documents, while the term relatedness computed in LSI is related to a linear combination of the high-order term co-occurrence frequency in the background corpus without considering the input documents.

Interestingly, when using Wikipedia as the background corpus, LSI achieves slightly better results than ESA. The reason is that the term relatedness in ESA is sensitive to the dimensionality n, which is determined dynamically based on the input documents and the background corpus. As shown in Table 4, we investigate the values of n yielding the results in Table 3. While K-means clustering and LSI have a fixed n, it varies significantly in ESA when the background corpus changes from JRC-Acquis to Wikipedia. This is due to the large size and wide range of covered topics of Wikipedia, such that the overlap between the top-k concepts for the input documents and thus the dimensionality n is much smaller compared with the case when using JRC-Acquis as the background corpus. Since ESA needs a large number of concepts spanning the concept space to perform reasonably, we can generate more top-k concepts from Wikipedia for each input document to increase n. However, this will also result in more retrieval time as shown in Fig. 2(c).

6. CONCLUSIONS

In this paper, we study the foundation of cross-lingual semantic relatedness in vector space models. We investigate three fundamental solutions: the clustering model instantiated by K-means clustering, the latent model instantiated by LSI and the explicit model instantiated by ESA. Most approaches proposed earlier or later are variations and incremental improvements of these three approaches. As the main contribution, we establish a generalized model, which subsumes and helps to analyze the differences among the three existing approaches. In particular, we elaborate on differences in interlingual concept space construction and cross-lingual semantic relatedness computation based on concepts. We perform a theoretical analysis of these approaches and validate them in the experiments in a cross-lingual search and retrieval scenario.

The merit of our work is twofold. Firstly, it helps to obtain a better understanding of existing approaches; while the work is carried out in the more general cross-lingual context, the results are transferable to semantic relatedness in the monolingual case. Secondly, it can be used as a guide to choose among existing approaches and to design future semantic relatedness solutions for the particular type of data and tasks at hand.

7. ACKNOWLEDGMENTS

The research leading to these results has received funding from the European Union Seventh Framework Programme (FP7/2007-2013) under grant agreement no. 611346.

8. REFERENCES

[1] M. Anderka and B. Stein. The esa retrieval model revisited. In *SIGIR*, pages 670–671, 2009.

[2] D. M. Blei, A. Y. Ng, M. I. Jordan, and J. Lafferty. Latent dirichlet allocation. *Journal of Machine Learning Research*, 3:993–1022, 2003.

[3] P. Cimiano, A. Schultz, S. Sizov, P. Sorg, and S. Staab. Explicit versus latent concept models for cross-language information retrieval. In *IJCAI*, pages 1513–1518, 2009.

[4] S. C. Deerwester, S. T. Dumais, T. K. Landauer, G. W. Furnas, and R. A. Harshman. Indexing by latent semantic analysis. *JASIS*, 41(6):391–407, 1990.

[5] S. Dumais, T. Letsche, M. Littman, and T. Landauer. Automatic cross-language retrieval using latent semantic indexing. In *AAAI Symposium on Cross-Language Text and Speech Retrieval*, 1997.

[6] E. Gabrilovich and S. Markovitch. Computing semantic relatedness using wikipedia-based explicit semantic analysis. In *IJCAI*, pages 1606–1611, 2007.

[7] T. Gottron, M. Anderka, and B. Stein. Insights into explicit semantic analysis. In *CIKM*, pages 1961–1964, 2011.

[8] J. Hartigan. *Clustering algorithms*. Wiley series in probability and mathematical statistics: Applied probability and statistics. Wiley, 1975.

[9] T. Hofmann. Probabilistic latent semantic indexing. In *SIGIR*, pages 50–57, 1999.

[10] M. Littman and F. Jiang. A comparison of two corpus-based methods for translingual information retrieval. Technical report, 1998.

[11] D. Mimno, H. M. Wallach, J. Naradowsky, D. A. Smith, and A. McCallum. Polylingual topic models. In *EMNLP*, pages 880–889, 2009.

[12] C. Müller and I. Gurevych. Using wikipedia and wiktionary in domain-specific information retrieval. In *Working Notes of the Annual CLEF Meeting*, 2008.

[13] C. Müller, I. Gurevych, and M. Mühlhäuser. Integrating semantic knowledge into text similarity and information retrieval. In *ICSC*, pages 257–264, 2007.

[14] M. Potthast, B. Stein, and M. Anderka. A wikipedia-based multilingual retrieval model. In *ECIR*, pages 522–530, 2008.

[15] G. Salton and M. J. McGill. *Introduction to Modern Information Retrieval*. McGraw-Hill, Inc., New York, NY, USA, 1986.

[16] G. Salton, A. Wong, and C. S. Yang. A vector space model for automatic indexing. *Commun. ACM*, 18(11):613–620, 1975.

[17] A. Singhal, C. Buckley, and M. Mitra. Pivoted document length normalization. In *SIGIR*, pages 21–29, 1996.

[18] P. Sorg and P. Cimiano. Cross-lingual information retrieval with explicit semantic analysis. In *Working Notes of the Annual CLEF Meeting*, 2008.

[19] M. Strube and S. P. Ponzetto. Wikirelate! computing semantic relatedness using wikipedia. In *AAAI*, pages 1419–1424, 2006.

[20] S. K. M. Wong, W. Ziarko, and P. C. N. Wong. Generalized vector space model in information retrieval. In *SIGIR*, pages 18–25, 1985.

[21] Y. Yang, J. G. Carbonell, R. D. Brown, and R. E. Frederking. Translingual information retrieval: Learning from bilingual corpora. *Artif. Intell.*, 103(1-2):323–345, 1998.

Context Retrieval for Web Tables

Hong Wang*, Anqi Liu*, Jing Wang*, Brian D. Ziebart*, Clement T. Yu*, Warren Shen†

*Department of Computer Science
University of Illinois at Chicago
Chicago, IL 60607
{hwang207, aliu33, jwang69, bziebart, cyu}@uic.edu

†Cohesity
451 El Camino Real
Santa Clara, CA 95050
warren@cohesity.com

ABSTRACT

Many modern knowledge bases are built by extracting information from millions of web pages. Though existing extraction methods primarily focus on web pages' main text, a huge amount of information is embedded within other web structures, such as web tables. Previous studies have shown that linking web page tables and textual context is beneficial for extracting more information from web pages. However, using the text surrounding each table without carefully assessing its relevance introduces noise in the extracted information, degrading its accuracy. To the best of our knowledge, we provide the first systematic study of the problem of table-related context retrieval: given a table and the sentences within the same web page, determine for each sentence whether it is relevant to the table. We define the concept of relevance and introduce a Table-Related Context Retrieval system (TRCR) in this paper. We experiment with different machine learning algorithms, including a recently developed algorithm that is robust to biases in the training data, and show that our system retrieves table-related context with F1=0.735.[1]

Categories and Subject Descriptors

H.3.3 [**Information Storage and Retrieval**]: Information Search and Retrieval

Keywords

Web tables; context retrieval; covariate shift

1. INTRODUCTION

The construction of modern knowledge bases (KBs) has gained popularity in recent years. Most KBs [29, 7, 2, 21, 27, 37, 32] are built by extracting information from millions

---

[1]Part of this work was done during the first author took his summer internship with Google Inc., under the supervision of the last author in year 2013.

ICTIR'15, September 27–30, Northampton, MA, USA.
ⓒ 2015 ACM. ISBN 978-1-4503-3833-2/15/09 ...$15.00.
DOI: http://dx.doi.org/10.1145/2808194.2809453.

of texts. In addition to web text resources, there is also a huge amount of information embedded within other web structures, such as web tables.

Several studies [4, 5, 6] have been conducted to extract information in web tables. Dong et al. [9] extract the entities and relations (defined in a fixed ontology) from text and tables separately. Govindaraju et al. [11] claim that there are many cues buried in the surrounding text that enable us to understand the table. Compared with modeling the text and table separately, jointly modeling both of them extracts more relations. However, Limaye et al. [19] show that simply relating surrounding context with the table also introduces unrelated information to table information extraction. Gupta et al. [12] mention that 41% of errors in their algorithm for recovering web tables' semantics are caused by unrelated information in the text surrounding tables, and they suggest using table-related text instead.

Motivated by these previous observations, and Knowledge-based applications, such as Semantic Search and Question Answering (QA) (Section 2), we develop a Table-Related Context Retrieval system (TRCR) for identifying texts that are relevant to a table. Our approach differs from related work (Section 3) in problem formulation and the supervised machine learning approach we employ. We define the concept of "relevance" between web table and sentences within the same page in Section 4 and our method for identifying the relevant sentences in Section 5. This includes a description of the features we engineered for the task and machine learning methods that address the situation that annotated training data may not represent the test data well. We believe this latter concern—source sample bias—is an important but overlooked issue for data that is annotated at the document level, producing many training examples for a small number of documents. We introduce our data sets and demonstrate the benefits of our approach in Section 6. We conclude by discussing future work in Section 7.

2. MOTIVATION AND CONTRIBUTIONS

In this section, we use two examples to demonstrate the motivations that lead to our study. The first example demonstrates that retrieving table-related context improves the coverage of QA. Consider sending the following question to Google:

Q1: "How many episodes did Constance Zimmer act in Boston Legal?".

From the returned snippet shown in Figure 1, we find no certain answer. Entering the first retrieved web page http://en.wikipedia.org/wiki/Constance_Zimmer, by in-

How many episodes did Constance Zimmer act in Boston Legal?

Constance Zimmer - Wikipedia, the free encyclopedia
en.wikipedia.org/wiki/**Constance_Zimmer** ▾ Wikipedia ▾
Constance Zimmer 11th Annual Inspiration Awards (cropped).jpg ... as Claire Simms
on the critically acclaimed ABC legal comedy-drama **Boston Legal** .... In early 2006,
Zimmer was cast as Brianna, the competitive **law** undergrad, in the ... Zimmer is an
involved AIDS activist and attends **many** celebrity benefits for charity.

Figure 1: Snippets from Google for "How many episodes did Constance Zimmer act in Boston Legal?"

specting text only, we find the most related sentence to $Q1$:

S1: "She joined the cast of Boston Legal, where she played associate attorney Claire Simms on..."

where the triples:

(she, joined the cast of, Boston Legal) and

(she, played, associate attorney Claire Simms),

can be extracted by Open Information Extraction (Open IE) tools, like ReVerb [10]. By utilizing coreference resolvers (e.g. Stanford Deterministic Coreference Resolution System [25, 18]), *"she"* is replaced with *"Constance Zimmer"*. Unfortunately, this information is still not sufficient to answer the question.

By inspecting the table (Figure 2) in the same page alone, we find a row that contains the words *"Boston Legal"* and *"Claire Simms"*. However without matching *"Constance Zimmer"* with *"Claire Simms"*, even though *"23 episodes"* in the last cell of the row is the correct answer, the question is still not answerable.

2006–2007	Boston Legal		Claire Simms	23 episodes

Figure 2: Table from Wikipedia page "Constance Zimmer".

By realizing $S1$ is related to the table, the following information can be linked together. The QA system can then utilize such linked information to infer the answer for $Q1$.

(Constance Zimmer, joined the cast of, Boston Legal)
(Constance Zimmer, played, associate attorney Claire Simms)
(Boston Legal, Claire Simms, 23 episodes)

This example shows that using text information jointly with a table can provide information beyond that of the sentence alone and that of the table alone.

The second example shows that retrieving only table-related context can avoid irrelevant information and improve the QA accuracy. Consider the following the question:

Q2: "Which mines were closed in Yellowknife?"

Google again returns snippets instead of any certain answer (see Figure 3). Notice that the 4th returned snippet *"The Diavik Diamond Mine"* is actually incorrect since this mine is still operating, even it appears in the corresponding Wikipedia page http://en.wikipedia.org/wiki/Yellowknife:

S2: "A second mine, Diavik Diamond Mine, began production in 2003."

S3: "The following is a list of the major mines, all of which are now closed."

$S2$ is irrelevant to the table on the same page (Figure 4), since the table is about the mines are now closed. On the contrary, $S3$ is not only relevant to that table, but also matches $Q2$. From this demonstration, we see that by com-

Which mines were closed in Yellowknife?

Giant Mine - Wikipedia, the free encyclopedia
en.wikipedia.org/wiki/Giant **Mine** ▾ Wikipedia ▾
Closed **Yellowknife - Wikipedia, the free encyclopedia**
greenst en.wikipedia.org/wiki/**Yellowknife** ▾ Wikipedia ▾
when a
Jump t **List of mines in the Northwest Territories - Wikiped**
centre en.wikipedia.org/.../List of **mines** in the Northwest Territor...
... by **The Diavik Diamond Mine** - Home page
opera www.diavik.ca/ ▾ Diavik Diamond Mine ▾
includ Rio Tinto is a world leader in finding, **mining** and processing
Ptar Diavik, **Yellowknife** Community Foundation congratulate sch

Figure 3: Snippets from Google for "Which mines were closed in Yellowknife?" *(tailored to fit in the page)*

bining the table with related context (e.g. $S3$), while eliminating irrelevant information (e.g. $S2$), it is possible to obtain highly accurate answers to the questions.

Mine ◆	Years of Operation ◆	Minerals Mined ◆
Con Mine (includes Rycon)	1938–2003	gold
Giant Mine	1948–2004	gold

Figure 4: Table from Wikipedia page "Yellowknife".

In this paper, we provide an in-depth study of the table-related context retrieval problem: given a table and the sentences within the same web page, determine for each sentence whether it is relevant to the table. The contributions of this paper are fourfold:

1) To the best of our knowledge, we are the first to define and systematically study the problem of retrieving table-related context on web pages. We exploit six types of relatedness between the sentence and the table to define the notion of relevance.

2) We propose the Table-Related Context Retrieval system (TRCR) that solves the table-related sentence retrieval problem. Our approach employs 61 features to characterize text-table relationships, including page structure, token matching, and semantic analysis.

3) We provide a new set of data, where each instance is a table-sentence pair. Each pair is labeled as RELEVANT or IRRELEVANT by different annotators with stable agreement. It provides a gold standard that other researchers can perform experiments on[2].

4) We experiment with different machine learning algorithms, including a recently developed algorithm that is robust to biases in the training data, and show that our system retrieves table-related context with F1=0.735.

3. RELATED WORK

Google's WebTables [4, 5, 6] pioneered the study of extracting and leveraging web tables that contain billions of instances of high-quality relational information. Their current work mostly focuses on extracting relational data from HTML tables, without connecting tables with their related context.

Knowledge Vault [9] extracts the entities and relations (defined in a fixed ontology) from texts and tables sepa-

---

[2]Code and data can be found at https://code.google.com/p/uic-cs-dbis/.

rately. Due to the limited textual content in the tables, the relations between columns in tables cannot be captured by standard schema matching methods [30], and only a small amount of information is extracted from the tables.

A recent study [11] has found that the surrounding text of a table can help improve human recall capability by more than 60% for humans trying to understand table content. Motivated by this, their model for relation extraction from tables achieves an F1 score twice as high as the performance of either pure-table or pure-text systems. However in that work, the entire document text is considered to be context related to the table and is used to extract relations.

Limaye et al. [19] use probabilistic graphical models to annotate web table columns, cells, and pairs of columns with types, entities (persons, organizations, locations, etc.), and binary relations from the YAGO catalog [29] respectively. The table content (headers and data rows), and also some amount of textual context around table are used in matching. However, the authors of that work only mention that they "capture some amount of textual context around tables" and point out that those textual contexts contain irrelevant information; neither a detailed algorithm nor a measurement of relevance between the captured surrounding sentence and the table is given.

Biperpedia is an ontology built by Google [12]. It is used to improve the performance of recovering the semantics of web tables by mapping columns to Biperpedia attributes. Because web tables have no schema, the surrounding text is particularly important in the mapping algorithm. Similar to the work using probabilistic graphical models [19], the authors also indicate that the surrounding text often also contains irrelevant information, and the most frequent cause of error in their algorithm is due to this irrelevant information.

System WWT [23] takes a query with a set of column keywords, extracts relevant columns from KB of web tables, consolidates them, and returns a single structured table. Headers, data cells and the surrounding context of the table are used to match query keywords in WWT. It considers "any text node x that is a sibling of a node on the path from T to the root of d" as the related context, where T is the node in DOM tree d of the web page that contains the table. However, in that paper, relatedness is not explicitly given, and their approach seems[3] to extract context by structure only. Microsoft's InfoGather [34] measures the relatedness between a table and its surrounding text by tf-idf cosine similarity functions. In contrast to their work, our system utilizes structural, content, and semantic features.

Despite the common agreement across multiple studies that related text is useful for understanding the table and extracting relations, no systematic study on web table related context retrieval has been performed to our knowledge.

4. DEFINITION OF RELEVANCE

In this work, we study the problem of retrieving table-related context from HTML web pages. The context is relevant to a table if it is related to the contents of the table and it could provide information beyond that of the sentence alone and that of the table alone. Given a web table as input, our proposed Table-Related Context Retrieval system (TRCR) retrieves the context on the same web page that is

relevant to the table. Similar to a previous study [31], we limit our consideration to horizontal HTML tables (i.e., table headers are aligned in the first row(s)). Since a sentence is a grammatical unit of one or more words that expresses an independent statement, question, request, command, exclamation[4], and most existing Open IE systems like TextRunner [3] and ReVerb [10] extract relations from English sentences, we define the concept of "context" as sentences in the same HTML page as the table of interest. Based on our observation, six types of relatedness between the sentence and the table are exploited to define the notion of relevance as follows. We provide example from Wikipedia of each type. Note that in this study, we focus on using this six types of relatedness to help us define the relevance, rather than differentiating these six types, which is left as one of our future works.

1) Table summary
A sentence that summarizes the table's content and/or what the table is about. As we demonstrated in the second example in Section 2, $S3$ is in such relevance. By combining the sentence and table, the irrelevant information (i.e. $S2$) could be filtered out like we showed in that example.

2) Header description
A sentence that describes what a header of a table column is, and/or any attribute that the header has. For example, the sentence *"Model organisms are in vivo models and are widely used to research human disease when..."* in page `http://en.wikipedia.org/wiki/Model_organism`, describes an attribute of the first column header (i.e. "Organism") of the following table (Figure 5).

Organism	Genome Sequenced
Prokaryote	
Escherichia coli	Yes
Eukaryote, unicellular	
Dictyostelium discoideum	Yes
Saccharomyces cerevisiae	Yes

Figure 5: Table from Wikipedia page "Model organism".

3) Header relation
A sentence that expresses a relation involving at least two column headers of the table. For example, in `http://en.wikipedia.org/wiki/List_of_Eurovision_Song_Contest_winners`, the sentence *"The country awarded the most points is declared the winner"* expresses a relation between two headers: "winner" and "points" in the table in Figure 6.

Year ⬦	Date	Host City ⬦		Winner	⬦	Song	⬦
Performer ⬦		Writers	Points	Margin	Runner-up		

Figure 6: Table from Wikipedia page "List of Eurovision Song Contest winners".

4) Data relation
A sentence that expresses a relation among two or more data cells (usually in one table row, but not necessarily so)

---
[3]No precise algorithm is given in that paper.

[4]"Sentence" - Definitions from Dictionary.com (`http://dictionary.reference.com/browse/sentence`)

in web table. For example, in `http://en.wikipedia.org/wiki/Erdos-Bacon_number`, the sentence *"Astronomer Carl Sagan has an Erdős number of no more than 4 and a Bacon number of 2, for a total of 6"* expresses a relation involving all four data cells within a row in the table in Figure 7.

Name	♦ Erdős number ♦	Bacon number ♦	Erdős–Bacon number ♦
Carl Sagan	4[6]	2[b][5]	6

Figure 7: Table from Wikipedia page "Erdős-Bacon number".

5) Header-data relation
A sentence that expresses a relation among two or more columns of the web table, including at least one column header, and one data cell. For example, for the same page and table as the example above (Figure 7), the sentence *"Notable scientists with defined Erdős-Bacon numbers include popular astronomer Carl Sagan"* expresses a relation between the header "Erdős-Bacon numbers" and the data cell "Carl Sagan".

6) Page subject-data relation
There's another type of relevance where the whole web page talks about someone or something (we call it the subject of the page), while the content of the web table in that page is all about aspects of that subject. A sentence talks about the page subject's certain attributes which are also expressed in the table. For example, as we already seen in the first example in Section 2, the subject of the web page is "Constance Zimmer", and the sentence *S1* is related to the table in this type of relevance. With the combination of the sentence and the table, we could infer the information as we demonstrated.

5. TABLE-RELATED CONTEXT RETRIEVAL SYSTEM (TRCR)

5.1 Overview

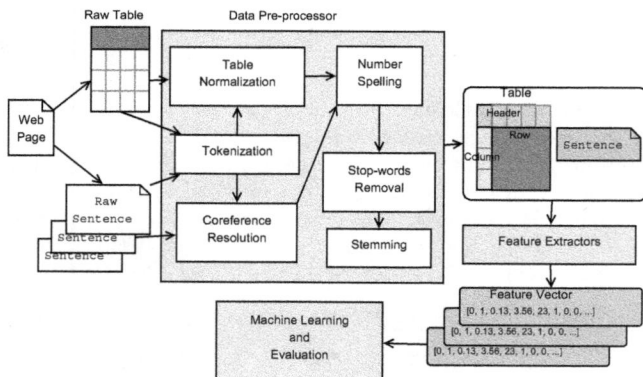

Figure 8: Architecture of TRCR.

Our proposed TRCR system consists of three main components (see Figure 8):
- Data pre-processor: all the sentences are read from our labeled data set, together with table content. Text from sentences and tables is processed using standard IR techniques, which we will discuss in detail in the following section.

- Feature extractors: from the pre-processed data, we extract 61 features, 33 of them are boolean-valued, the rest are numerical features.
- Machine learning algorithms and evaluators: extracted features from previous component are sent to different machine learning algorithms. Models are trained on a training data set, and evaluated on a test data set.

In the following sections, we first introduce our data pre-processing methods. Next, we provide a detailed description of the features we engineer for this task. Finally, we introduce several algorithms, together with the motivation and the merit of considering source data sample bias.

5.2 Data pre-processing

Tokenization, stop words removal, stemming
Like other standard Information Retrieval systems, we first tokenize sentences and table content. We use Apache Lucene [13] in our TRCR. Stop words are removed from tokens. Tokens are then stemmed using the Porter Stemmer algorithm [24]. Numbers are also normalized during tokenization, e.g. "12,000,000" becomes "12000000". Diacritics are removed from non-English letters, e.g. "Yves Allégret" becomes "Yves Allegret".

Number spelling
Tables often contain numeric tokens, but a relevant sentence contains the spelled forms, or vice versa. So for each numeric token, we spell it out in English using ICU4J[5]. For example, on page `http://en.wikipedia.org/wiki/World_Series_of_Poker`, the sentence *"Gold pocketed US$12 million for his victory"* has a numeric token *"12"*, which is spelled out as *"twelve"*; while in the table there's a data cell *"12000000"* that is also spelled out in English as *"twelve million"*. The spelled out English tokens are added as synonyms of the original numeric token for further text matching. In addition, "2" and "3" are also added and spelled as synonyms of "twice", and "thrice" respectively, since they are very common replacements of "two times" and "three times."

Coreference resolution
We also use a coreference resolver [25, 18] on each entire web page to resolve the coreferences of third-person pronouns in sentences. For example, on the page `http://en.wikipedia.org/wiki/Rani_Mukerji`, *"she"* and *"her"* in the sentence *"At the age of fourteen, she was cast by her father for a supporting role in his Bengali film Biyer Phool (1992)"* are replaced by *"Rani Mukerji"* through coreference resolution. Because the models of the coreference resolver available online are for the CoNLL-2011 shared task, which is different from our Wikipedia data set, its accuracy is far from perfect[6]. We employ some modifications based on the original resolution results to accommodate our data set and increase its accuracy. The input of our modified coreference resolution algorithm are: token t; sentence S which token t belongs to; coreferences C of token t that are resolved by the original resolver; the most representative mention $r \in C$ that the original resolver selected; heading h of the section that sentence S belongs to; and page title p. The algorithm's outputs are tokens R that are considered as replacements of token t. It resolves only third person pronouns, and processes in

---

[5] International Components for Unicode, http://site.icu-project.org/

[6] http://nlp.stanford.edu/software/dcoref.shtml

steps. The algorithm first checks the most representative mention but with an additional constraint that requires this representative mention to appear in the current sentence or to have already appeared in an earlier sentence. If these conditions are both satisfied, representative mention is returned as the replacement of input token t. If not, our algorithm selects the longest coreference that appears in either page title or sentence section heading as the replacement. If there's still no replacement found (i.e., each coreference $c \in C$ is neither recognized as representative by the original resolver that appears in/before sentence S, nor appears in the title or sentence section heading), the algorithm checks three sentences ahead together with the current sentence. The closest coreference to token t that has all tokens with their initial letters capitalized is considered as the replacement. Details of this modified coreference resolution algorithm in TRCR are listed in Algorithm 1. Its accuracy on our training data set is 82.33%.

Algorithm 1 Coreferences Resolution
INPUT: t, S, C, r, h, p; **OUTPUT**: R

```
1:  // 3rd person pronouns
2:  3PRP ← {"he", "him", "his", "she", "her", "hers", "it", "its",
       "they", "them", "their", "theirs"};
3:  // 1st and 2nd person pronouns
4:  12PRP ← {"i", "me", "my", "mine", "we", "us", "our", "ours",
       "you", "your", "yours"};
5:  if C = Φ || t ∉ 3PRP then return Φ;
6:  R ← Φ;
7:  S_ ← any_sentence_before(S);
8:  for all c ∈ C do
9:      if t ∉ 3PRP && t ∉ 2PRP && c = r
10:        && (c ∈ S || c ∈ S_) then
11:          R ← R + c;
12: if R = Φ // no replacement retrieved yet then
13:      // longest coreference first
14:      sort_in_descending_order_of_length(C);
15:      for all c ∈ C do
16:          if t ∉ 3PRP && t ∉ 2PRP
17:              && (c ∈ p || c ∈ p) then
18:                  R ← R + c; break;
19: if R = Φ // no replacement retrieved yet then
20:      // closest coreference first
21:      sort_in_descending_order_of_distance_to_t(C);
22:      S_{-1-2-3} ← at_most_3_sentences_away_before(S);
23:      for all c ∈ C do
24:          if t ∉ 3PRP && t ∉ 2PRP
25:              && has_all_tokens_initial_capitalized(c)
26:              &&(c ∈ S || c ∈ S_{-1-2-3}) then
27:                  R ← R + c; break;
28: return R;
```

Web table normalization

Some table columns may contain "yes" or "no" terms only, like the table shown in Figure 5. We replace "yes" with the column header ("Genome Sequenced" in this example). Each "no" is ignored since cells with "no" in them are supposed to be irrelevant to the header.

A table may also contain "year" columns in which consecutive years are represented in the pattern "$xxxx - yyyy$", where "$xxxx$" is the start year, and "$yyyy$" is the end year, like those shown in Figure 4. We check if the header of the table contains the token "year" or "years". If the header contains any of them, we check each data cell content in that column to see if it contains text in the pattern "$xxxx-yyyy$" (white-spaces within this pattern are optional), and "$xxxx$", "$yyyy$" are numeric tokens where $xxxx < yyyy$. If it does, we consider the cell to contain consecutive years, and "refill" the cell data by adding all years between $xxxx$ and $yyyy$ into it.

For example, "*1941-1943, 1947-1949*" becomes "*1941, 1942, 1943, 1947 1948, 1949.*"

After pre-processing, each sentence in the web page is stored and indexed by its section number, paragraph number and sentence number with respect to its position in the original web page (a section is considered a sequence of paragraphs led by a heading, except the first section). The web table is stored separately from the page's textual content, and is indexed by its section number.

5.3 Feature engineering

We have 61 features in two categories. One is from the sentence alone. The others are extracted from both the sentence and the table. In the rest of this section, we describe the features of each category and an intuition for their usefulness in detail.

Sentence features (18 features)

Sentence position. We use nine boolean features to capture the position information about each sentence, i.e., whether the sentence is the first sentence, the last sentence, or neither first nor last of: the entire page, a section, or a paragraph. We observe the phenomena that the first sentence in a web page often provides a summarization of the topic of the page; the first sentence in same section as the table often summarizes the content of the table, etc.

Sentence-title overlapping. The title of the web page can be considered the subject of the page, and may have some degree of relevance to the table. So we extract two features to check whether or not any or all of the tokens in the page title exist in the sentence.

Sentence-title semantic overlapping. In a sentence, there are some tokens that are more semantically indicative than others. In order to extract such tokens, we integrate ReVerb [10] to find semantic binary relationships. Each relationship is in the format of a triple (argument1, relation, argument2), where each component of the triple is a phrase that is extracted from the given sentence. We use a boolean feature for each component to indicate if it overlaps with the title.

"Table" or "list". For "table summary" relevance, we observe that the sentence usually contains the term "table" or "list", like the sentence "The following table presents..." So we create a boolean feature to check whether the sentence contains "table" or "list."

Sentence sentiment. We observe that the distributions of sentiment polarity (i.e., positive, negative, neutral) are different between RELEVANT and IRRELEVANT sentences. Positive or negative sentences are more likely to be RELEVANT when compared with neutral sentences; whereas neutral sentences have the highest chance of being IRRELEVANT. In this work, we integrate the Recursive Neural Tensor Networks (RNTN) method [28] to analyze the sentiment for each sentence. We use three boolean features to represent the possible polarities.

Table-sentence features (43 features)

Table-sentence distance. Intuitively, when a sentence is closer to the table, it is more likely to be relevant. We use a boolean feature to indicate whether the sentence and the table are in the same section. Across different sections, we observe that a sentence before the table has a higher chance of being relevant than a sentence after the table. In order to capture this insight, we create two additional numeric features to measure the section-distance in the following way:

suppose the total number of sections in the web page is N, the sentence is in section i, the table is in section j, then:

$$SD\%^- = \begin{cases} (j-i)/N & \text{if } i <= j \\ 0 & \text{otherwise,} \end{cases} \quad SD\%^+ = \begin{cases} (i-j)/N & \text{if } i >= j \\ 0 & \text{otherwise,} \end{cases}$$

where $SD\%^-$ represents the relative section-distance that the sentence and the table are apart, if the sentence is located before the table. Similarly, $SD\%^+$ represents the relative section-distance if the sentence is located after the table.

Header description. Sentences may use an equals sign ("=") to explain a table header's meaning, especially for abbreviations or acronyms, like "HR = Home runs". Also, sentences that follow the pattern "*<header> <be>*" (where "<be>" is a conjugation of the verb "to be", e.g., "is", "are", "was", "were") are likely to be a description of the header. We use boolean features to indicate whether the sentence contains such patterns.

Structure-indicative numbers. If a sentence talks about the table's topic, it is possible that the sentence provides a count of some data in the table. For example, in the sentence "Major stock exchanges (top 20 by market capitalization)..." from `http://en.wikipedia.org/wiki/List_of_stock_exchanges`, the number "20" is exactly the number of rows in the corresponding table. So, in order to capture such patterns, we create a boolean feature to check whether any number in the sentence matches the total number of data rows. Furthermore, a relevant sentence may count the number of occurrences of some data cell's content. Consider the sentence "The country with the highest number of wins is Ireland, with seven" in the page `http://en.wikipedia.org/wiki/List_of_Eurovision_Song_Contest_winners`. Information expressed by it can be found from the "winner" column of the table, within which "Ireland" occurs exactly seven times. One boolean feature is built to capture such cases.

Sentence-header overlapping. A header is considered as an important clue of the information in the table column. If the sentence shares common tokens with the header, it is likely to be of header-related relevance. Suppose the web table has C columns, each header of column is h_j, s is the sentence. We define five features as follows:

$$\#H_{any} = \sum_{j=1}^{C} I_{any}(h_j, s), \qquad \#H_{all} = \sum_{j=1}^{C} I_{all}(h_j, s),$$

$$H_{any}\% = \frac{\#H_{any}}{C}, \qquad H_{all}\% = \frac{\#H_{all}}{C},$$

$$SH\% = \frac{|s \bigcap_{j=1}^{C} h_j|}{|s|},$$

where $|s \bigcap_{j=1}^{C} h_j|$ is the number of common tokens in both sentence s and header h_j, $|s|$ is the number of tokens in sentence s, and:

$$I_{any}(h_j, s) = \begin{cases} 1 & \text{if any token in } h_j \text{ exists in s} \\ 0 & \text{otherwise,} \end{cases}$$

$$I_{all}(h_j, s) = \begin{cases} 1 & \text{if all tokens in } h_j \text{ exist in s} \\ 0 & \text{otherwise.} \end{cases}$$

Sentence-table overlapping. We use a set of features to measure the overlap between the sentence and the table row or column. In addition to a count of the common tokens, the alphabetic and numeric tokens are also analyzed separately. We describe some of them formally as follows: assume R is the total number of rows in a table, C is the number of columns, and c_{ij} represents the content of the data cell in row i and column j:

$$CR_{any} = \max_{i=1...R} \sum_{j=1}^{C} I_{any}(c_{ij}, s), \qquad CR_{all} = \max_{i=1...R} \sum_{j=1}^{C} I_{all}(c_{ij}, s),$$

$$CC_{any} = \max_{j=1...C} \sum_{i=1}^{R} I_{any}(c_{ij}, s), \qquad CC_{all} = \max_{j=1...C} \sum_{i=1}^{R} I_{all}(c_{ij}, s),$$

$$CR_{any}\% = \frac{CR_{any}}{C}, \qquad CR_{all}\% = \frac{CR_{all}}{C},$$

$$SR\% = \max_{i=1...R} \frac{|s \bigcap_{j=1}^{C} c_{ij}|}{|s|}.$$

Sentence-header/table semantic overlapping. Similarly, we use ReVerb to extract relational triples from the sentence. Then, header tokens and table cell tokens are checked against each component of them to determine whether they share any or all of the tokens in common, generating six boolean features.

Sentence-heading overlapping. Usually, a table section's heading, as well as the table caption (if it exists), summarize the table content. When the sentence shares tokens with them, it has a higher probability of being relevant to the table. Hence, boolean features are built to indicate whether the overlaps exist.

5.4 Machine learning algorithms

We construct the TRCR system using supervised machine learning methods to estimate the probability of a sentence being relevant to a table given the features characterizing the sentence-table relationships. We denote this estimated distribution as $\hat{P}(y|x)$. The vast majority of supervised machine learning methods assume that data available for training the method is representative of (i.e., drawn from the same distribution as) data that the method will encounter at "test time." When data labels are provided in units of entire documents, and annotation is relatively expensive, a disproportionate amount of training data is produced from a small set of documents, creating non-representative training data sets. In addition to evaluating the performance of prevalent machine learning algorithms that ignore possible non-representative training data, including Decision Trees, k-Nearest Neighbors, Naïve Bayes, Support Vector Machine (SVM), and Logistic Regression, we evaluate two methods that take training set bias into account. These methods consider the special case of covariate shift [26] sample selection bias in which the conditional sentence relevance given input features is shared between training and test data sets, but the distribution of the input features differs between data sets: $P_{\text{train}}(x)P(y|x) \neq P_{\text{test}}(x)P(y|x)$.

5.4.1 Sample reweighted method

We consider a traditional approach for learning under covariate shift that uses importance weighting of the empirical loss function for the training distribution to approximate the expected loss for the test data distribution [36, 14, 8]. We call this the Sample Reweighted method (SR) in this paper. From the transfer learning perspective, the sample reweighted approach is a case of transductive transfer learning [22] and has been used in tasks including name entity recognition [1, 15], text categorization, and sentiment classification [33] in natural language processing. Model parameters θ using this method are chosen by:

$$\min_\theta \mathbb{E}_{\tilde{P}_{\text{train}}(x)P(y|x)} \left[\frac{P_{\text{test}}(X)}{P_{\text{train}}(X)} \text{loss}(\hat{P}_\theta(Y|X), Y) \right].$$

Conceptually, this produces parameter estimates that minimize predictive loss on sample data from $\tilde{P}_{\text{train}}(x)$ that is more representative of the test data set. Note that labels from the test data set are not required by this method; only the input features are needed.

5.4.2 Robust Bias-Aware method

The second approach we consider is the Robust Bias-Aware (RBA) classifier [20], a recently developed approach that tries to be robust to the worst-case uncertainty created by covariate shift, rather than trying to remove it. The conditional label distribution is obtained by solving a convex optimization problem. The solution has a parametric form with Lagrange multiplier θ:

$$\hat{P}_\theta(y|x) = \frac{e^{\frac{P_{\text{train}}(x)}{P_{\text{test}}(x)} \theta \cdot \mathbf{f}(x,y)}}{\sum_{y' \in \mathcal{Y}} e^{\frac{P_{\text{train}}(x)}{P_{\text{test}}(x)} \theta \cdot \mathbf{f}(x,y')}}.$$

The density ratio, $P_{\text{train}}(x)/P_{\text{test}}(x)$, adjusts the model to be more certain when a test data point is similar to the training data and less certain when it is not as similar. We employ a previously developed method, RuLSIF [35], to estimate the density ratio for both covariate shift approaches.

6. EXPERIMENTS

6.1 Data sets

To the best of our knowledge, we are the first to address this table-related context retrieval problem and know of no existing annotated data sets suitable for this task. We limited our study in this paper on Wikipedia pages and collected data from it. We randomly picked 36 pages that contain horizontal HTML tables with headers from Wikipedia dump[7]. We also selected 27 pages from Wiki_Manual data set which was used in previous studies [19]. Nine of the original 36 pages in Wiki_Manual were dropped because they are not suitable for our problem, e.g. the "Ian Fleming" page contains no table, the "List of newspapers in New York" page contains HTML lists rather than tables. In total there are 63 HTML web pages in our data set.

If one web page contains more than one table, we keep the largest table, which we assume contains more information. We note that in practice, since a web page may contain more than one table, instead of retrieving the relevant sentences for each table, we may want to determine for each sentence which table(s) is/are relevant. Our system can be easily adapted to this setting, because all models used in TRCR can produce probabilistic predictions. We can feed all tables in a web page to TRCR one by one. TRCR will return the probability of how likely each table-sentence pair is relevant. Then sentences can be ranked according to the probability of the relevance of each table-sentence pair, hence the most related table(s) can be found from the final ranked list. The data is annotated by two experts independently, both of whom annotate all of the instances. Each table-sentence pair is labeled as RELEVANT or IRRELEVANT, according to the definition of relevance described in Section

[7] http://dumps.wikimedia.org/enwiki/, April 4, 2013

4. The inter-annotator agreement κ was calculated by Cohen's kappa coefficient, which adjusts for chance, ranging from [0,1], where 1 indicates perfect agreement, and 0 indicates agreement by chance. The total κ for the data set is 0.8998. In interpreting κ, Landis and Koch [17] suggest that values above 0.61 indicate substantial strength of agreement, and therefore, we believe our annotation result is consistent enough to support our conclusions. A consensus on the final labeling is made by all the annotators.

We split our data into two data sets, one for feature engineering and training, and the other strictly for testing purposes. The statistics of our data sets are shown in Table 1. Notice that our data sets are highly imbalanced, i.e., only a small portion of pairs are labeled as RELEVANT.

Data set	Training	Test
# table-sentence pairs	2633	1962
# RELEVANT pairs	415	163
# IRRELEVANT pairs	2218	1799

Table 1: Statistics of data sets.

6.2 Baselines

As one baseline, we blindly consider all of the sentences in the same section with the web table as RELEVANT. We call this baseline as the Surround Text (ST) method. We also consider applying our definitions of relevance naïvely as another baseline: Naïve Definition (ND). The algorithm of ND is listed in Algorithm 2, where input S is the sentence, T is the table, and p is the web page.

Algorithm 2 Naïve Definition
INPUT: S, T, p
OUTPUT: S and T are RELEVANT or IRRELEVANT

```
1: boolean b1 ← "table" ∈ S || "list" ∈ S;
2: boolean b2 ← any_header_token(T) ∈ S
3:          || any_cell_token(T) ∈ S;
4: boolean b3 ← any_section_heading_token(T) ∈ S;
5: boolean b4 ← any_title_token(p) ∈ S;
6: boolean b5 ← section_number(T) = section_number(S);
7:
8: if b1 || b2 || ((b3 || b4) && b5) then
9:     return RELEVANT;
10: else
11:     return IRRELEVANT;
```

Since both ST and DT are not machine learning algorithms, we check their performances on both training and test data sets, and list them in Table 2. Also because we have highly imbalanced data (i.e. the number of IRRELEVANT pairs are far larger than the number of RELEVANT pairs), we care more about the performance of RELEVANT predictions in practice. Therefore, we do not report the performance on predicting the IRRELEVANT pairs.

Baseline	Data set	F1	Precision	Recall
ST	Training	0.245	0.486	0.164
	Test	0.186	0.581	0.110
ND	Training	0.336	0.202	1.000
	Test	0.227	0.128	1.000

Table 2: Baseline performances.

From the results, we can see that although nearly half of the surrounding sentences are relevant to the table, the recall is very low. This is because the number of sentences (both RELEVANT and IRRELEVANT) in same section with the table is very small. In the training data set, only 140 sentences out of 2633 were in the same section as the table (68 of them are actually RELEVANT). In the test data set, only 31 sentence out of 1962 were in the same section as the table (18 of them are RELEVANT). So blindly using surrounding text would ignore a large amount of relevant information and bring nearly the same amount of noise as relevant information. This also serves as evidence of sample selection bias between training and test data sets, even though no bias was intentionally created.

We note that the recall of ND on both data sets are 1, which means to be relevant, the table and sentence pair must have some common tokens. On the other hand, low precision means that just using the token matching based on the definition of relevance without any sophisticated understanding technique is far from sufficient.

6.3 Experiments and evaluations

We evaluate the performance of Decision Trees (DT), k-Nearest Neighbors (k-NN, where k=10), Naïve Bayes (NB), SVM (linear kernel), Logistic Regression with ℓ_1 regularization (LR), Sample Reweighted (SR) logistic regression, and the Robust Bias-Aware (RBA) classifier on our data sets. Each model is trained from training data, and tuned using 10-fold cross-validation. Then we evaluate the learned models on a withheld test data set. Again, we skip the reports of performance of IRRELEVANT pairs. The performance of each algorithm on test data set is listed in Table 3.

Algorithm	F1	Precision	Recall
DT	0.489	0.447	0.540
k-NN	0.448	0.644	0.344
NB	0.484	0.369	0.706
SVM	0.685	0.696	0.675
LR	0.703	0.658	**0.755**
SR	0.674	0.617	0.742
RBA	**0.735**	**0.722**	0.748

Table 3: ML algorithm performances on test data set.

As we can see from the results in Table 3, all the Machine Learning algorithms perform better than baselines. The Decision Tree does not work particularly well with respect to both precision and recall. The k-Nearest Neighbor model has a precision of 0.644 but very low recall. On the contrary, the Naïve Bayes model has a recall of 0.706 while its precision is the lowest among all the models we learned. Using Logistic Regression, we can reach F1=0.703, which is the best model that doesn't consider sample selection bias. SVM has better precision than LR, but a lower recall, resulting in a lower F1. The consideration of sample selection bias in training data doesn't gain Sample Reweighted logistic regression any advantage over normal logistic regression model. The RBA classifier provides the second highest recall, and achieves higher precision than LR, achieving the best F1 of 0.735.

To find out the most useful features for RELEVANT prediction, we list them in descending order according to their weights of RELEVANT prediction in the learned RBA model (due to lack of space, we don't show the list here). 35 features have positive weights, which means with them an instance has a higher likelihood to be RELEVANT. However,

note that using only the top features is not good enough for reaching the best performance. We experiment with models that using only top 10, 20, 30 and 35 top features, the F1's are 0.418, 0.518, 0.650, and 0.675, respectively. Comparing with F1=0.735 when using all the features, we can see that the negative-weighted features are also useful in the RELEVANT prediction.

In the feature list, the top one is the "<header> <be>" pattern that has a much more heavier weight than the others, since it directly captures the "header description" relatedness. Most of the rest top features measure tokens overlapping, either plain sentence or semantics (arguments or relation of the triple extracted by ReVerb). For instance, among the top 10 features, 8 of them indicate commonalities, either explicitly or implicitly. An explicit commonality is that there are common tokens overlapping between the sentence and the table (which is also indicated by the baseline ND, i.e. recall=1, that to be relevant there should be a certain degree of commonalities). An implicit commonality is that the sentence contains some tokens in the title of the page or the heading of the table section. As we mentioned in Section 5.3, the former captures the subject of the web page, the later captures the subject of the table, and such subject-relevances implicitly indicate the relatedness between the sentence and the table. The boolean feature that checks whether any number in the sentence matches the total number of data rows is ranked 10th, which suggests such pattern is common in summarizing the information within the web table. The feature that checks whether the sentence and the table are in the same section has a negative weight and is ranked 57th. Since the negative-weighted feature contributes IRRELEVANT prediction, it implies that a sentence can still have a large chance of being IRRELEVANT to the table even they are in the same section. It provides a support to the authors of [12]'s claim that the surrounding text often contains irrelevant information.

Commonality is important in our model, however, most of the errors are also due to it. For example, mis-classifying the IRRELEVANT sentence *"It is sometimes reported that Erdős himself has an Erdős-Bacon number of three."* as RELEVANT is mainly because it contains tokens *"Erdős"*, *"Bacon"* and *"3"* which appear in the table (see Figure 7) that actually doesn't contain the instance about the person *"Erdős"*. Solving such problem requires a much more deeper understanding of both the sentence and the table content, which we will explore in the future.

6.4 Advantages of RBA model

As we see in Table 3, RBA performs best among all the learning algorithms. In order to prove that the increase in performance from taking training data bias into account is significant, we conduct a series of experiments to compare RBA with LR. Each provides the best F1 of the models assuming sample selection bias, and no sample selection bias respectively. So as to make each pair of training and test data sets different from others while still keeping enough data points in each data set, we randomly split our training data ($TRAIN$) into 10 folds ($TRAIN_1, TRAIN_2, ..., TRAIN_{10}$). Then we conduct 10 experiments, each time using 9 folds of the training data ($TRAIN - TRAIN_i$, where i = 1, 2, ..., 10) to train both LR and RBA models, and then test each model on the test data. We find that in the 10 experiments, the recall measures are almost the same on

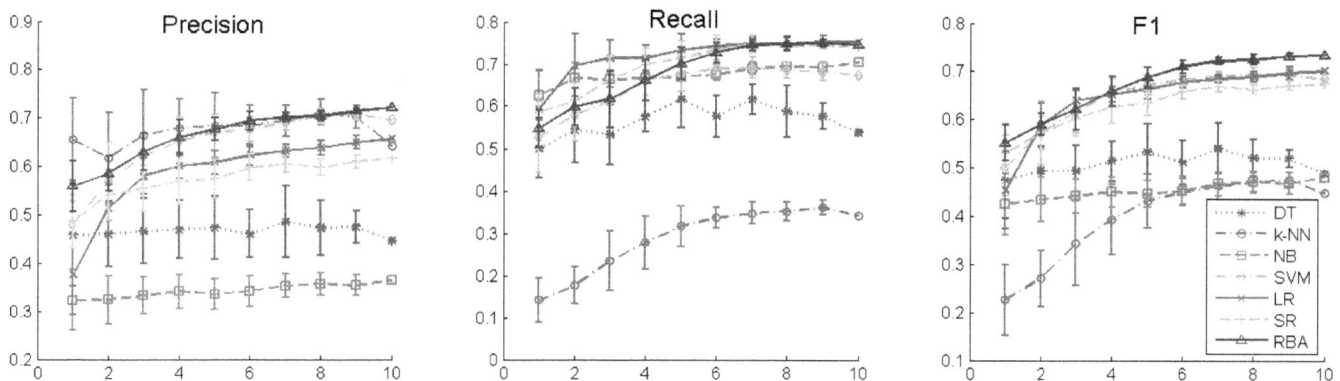

Figure 9: Performances of algorithms on size-accumulated experiments (the x-axis is the number of folds of training data).

both models, but RBA is always better on precision than the LR model, and hence achieves the better F1 scores. Both of the performance improvements of precision and F1 from RBA over LR are statistically significant, with p-values at 10^{-9} and 10^{-7} respectively.

RBA also requires less training data to reach a good performance. In order to examine the influence of training data size on the performance of each algorithm, we conduct another series of experiments. We randomly shuffle the training data 10 times. The experiments conducted each time form an experiment group $i \in [1, 10]$. We split the shuffled training data set from group i into 10 equal size folds ($TRAIN_{i1}, TRAIN_{i2}, ..., TRAIN_{i10}$). For each experiment $j \in [1, 10]$, $\bigcup_{k=1}^{j} TRAIN_{ik}$ folds are used as training data (i.e. starting with one fold of data, during each experiment, we accumulatively add one more fold into the training data). Then each learned model is tested on the whole test data set. We show the measures of performance of each algorithm in Figure 9. Those measures are averaged among the 10 experiment groups, the vertical bars at each data point indicates the corresponding standard deviation (note that under our experiment setting, we always have the whole training data set (i.e. $\bigcup_{k=1}^{10} TRAIN_{ik}$) in the last experiment in each group, hence the last standard deviations are zero). From the results, we can observe that for the same size of training data, RBA has consistent performance, and outperforms all other algorithms (its averaged F1 score is significantly better than any other algorithm's with the p-value of at most 10^{-3}). Furthermore, we can find that RBA reaches the second best F1 score (from LR) at x-axis point around 5 in the Figure. This indicates that using just half of the amount of training data, RBA can reach a better F1 score than any other experimented algorithm that uses the whole training data. In other words, in practice, with the help of RBA, we need to only label half the size of the original labeled training data to reach the same level of performance. Hence, the labeling burden for the model learning can be reduced remarkably.

7. CONCLUSION AND FUTURE WORK

In this paper, we systematically study the problem of table-related context retrieval: given a web table and the sentences within the same web page, determine for each sentence whether it is relevant to the table, where six types of relatedness are exploited to define the notion of rele-

vance. We propose a Table-Related Context Retrieval system (TRCR) that retrieves table-related sentences. We provide the detailed description of the features we engineer for this system. Using a set of different machine learning algorithms, including a recently developed algorithm (RBA) that is robust to biases in the training data, we show that our system achieves the best F1=0.735, when RBA is used to retrieve table-related context. We also demonstrate that using RBA, a decent performance can be achieved with a smaller size of labeled training data than using traditional supervised algorithms.

There are many open avenues for further study. First, we intend to build another system that utilizes TRCR's retrieved relevant sentences of a web table as the input. The system will extract and link relations from both the table and the related sentences, and eventually discover more information and augment a knowledge base. Second, the study could be furthered by distinguishing different types of relevance. In this way, we will locate the exact part of the table that is relevant to the sentence. Third, like POS tagging and named entity recognition in the NLP research area, the structure information among sentences can be utilized, together with probabilistic graphical models (e.g. conditional random fields [16]), to improve the performance of TRCR.

8. REFERENCES

[1] A. Arnold, R. Nallapati, and W. W. Cohen. A comparative study of methods for transductive transfer learning. In *Data Mining Workshops, 2007. ICDM Workshops 2007. Seventh IEEE International Conference on*, pages 77–82. IEEE, 2007.

[2] S. Auer, C. Bizer, G. Kobilarov, J. Lehmann, R. Cyganiak, and Z. Ives. *Dbpedia: A nucleus for a web of open data*. Springer, 2007.

[3] M. Banko, M. J. Cafarella, S. Soderland, M. Broadhead, and O. Etzioni. Open information extraction for the web. In *IJCAI*, volume 7, pages 2670–2676, 2007.

[4] M. J. Cafarella, A. Halevy, and N. Khoussainova. Data integration for the relational web. *Proceedings of the VLDB Endowment*, 2(1):1090–1101, 2009.

[5] M. J. Cafarella, A. Halevy, D. Z. Wang, E. Wu, and Y. Zhang. Uncovering the relational web.

[6] M. J. Cafarella, A. Halevy, D. Z. Wang, E. Wu, and Y. Zhang. Webtables: exploring the power of tables on

the web. *Proceedings of the VLDB Endowment*, 1(1):538–549, 2008.

[7] A. Carlson, J. Betteridge, B. Kisiel, B. Settles, E. R. Hruschka Jr, and T. M. Mitchell. Toward an architecture for never-ending language learning. In *AAAI*, volume 5, page 3, 2010.

[8] C. Cortes, Y. Mansour, and M. Mohri. Learning bounds for importance weighting. In *Advances in neural information processing systems*, pages 442–450, 2010.

[9] X. L. Dong, K. Murphy, E. Gabrilovich, G. Heitz, W. Horn, N. Lao, T. Strohmann, S. Sun, and W. Zhang. Knowledge vault: A web-scale approach to probabilistic knowledge fusion, 2014.

[10] A. Fader, S. Soderland, and O. Etzioni. Identifying relations for open information extraction. In *Proceedings of the Conference on Empirical Methods in Natural Language Processing*, pages 1535–1545. Association for Computational Linguistics, 2011.

[11] V. Govindaraju, C. Zhang, and C. Ré. Understanding tables in context using standard nlp toolkits. In *ACL (2)*, pages 658–664, 2013.

[12] R. Gupta, A. Halevy, X. Wang, S. E. Whang, and F. Wu. Biperpedia: An ontology for search applications. *Proceedings of the VLDB Endowment*, 7(7), 2014.

[13] E. Hatcher, O. Gospodnetic, and M. McCandless. Lucene in action, 2004.

[14] J. Huang, A. Gretton, K. M. Borgwardt, B. Schölkopf, and A. J. Smola. Correcting sample selection bias by unlabeled data. In *Advances in neural information processing systems*, pages 601–608, 2006.

[15] J. Jiang and C. Zhai. Instance weighting for domain adaptation in nlp. In *ACL*, volume 7, pages 264–271. Citeseer, 2007.

[16] J. Lafferty, A. McCallum, and F. C. Pereira. Conditional random fields: Probabilistic models for segmenting and labeling sequence data. 2001.

[17] J. R. Landis and G. G. Koch. The measurement of observer agreement for categorical data. *biometrics*, pages 159–174, 1977.

[18] H. Lee, Y. Peirsman, A. Chang, N. Chambers, M. Surdeanu, and D. Jurafsky. Stanford's multi-pass sieve coreference resolution system at the conll-2011 shared task. In *Proceedings of the Fifteenth Conference on Computational Natural Language Learning: Shared Task*, pages 28–34. ACL, 2011.

[19] G. Limaye, S. Sarawagi, and S. Chakrabarti. Annotating and searching web tables using entities, types and relationships. *Proceedings of the VLDB Endowment*, 3(1-2):1338–1347, 2010.

[20] A. Liu and B. Ziebart. Robust classification under sample selection bias. In *Advances in Neural Information Processing Systems*, pages 37–45, 2014.

[21] F. Niu, C. Zhang, C. Ré, and J. Shavlik. Elementary: Large-scale knowledge-base construction via machine learning and statistical inference. *International Journal on Semantic Web and Information Systems (IJSWIS)*, 8(3):42–73, 2012.

[22] S. J. Pan and Q. Yang. A survey on transfer learning. *Knowledge and Data Engineering, IEEE Transactions on*, 22(10):1345–1359, 2010.

[23] R. Pimplikar and S. Sarawagi. Answering table queries on the web using column keywords. *Proceedings of the VLDB Endowment*, 5(10):908–919, 2012.

[24] M. F. Porter. An algorithm for suffix stripping. *Program: electronic library and information systems*, 14(3):130–137, 1980.

[25] K. Raghunathan, H. Lee, S. Rangarajan, N. Chambers, M. Surdeanu, D. Jurafsky, and C. Manning. A multi-pass sieve for coreference resolution. In *Proceedings of the 2010 Conference on Empirical Methods in Natural Language Processing*, pages 492–501. ACL, 2010.

[26] H. Shimodaira. Improving predictive inference under covariate shift by weighting the log-likelihood function. *Journal of statistical planning and inference*, 90(2):227–244, 2000.

[27] A. Singhal. Introducing the knowledge graph: things, not strings. *Official Google Blog, May*, 2012.

[28] R. Socher, A. Perelygin, J. Y. Wu, J. Chuang, C. D. Manning, A. Y. Ng, and C. Potts. Recursive deep models for semantic compositionality over a sentiment treebank. In *Proceedings of the Conference on Empirical Methods in Natural Language Processing (EMNLP)*, pages 1631–1642. Citeseer, 2013.

[29] F. M. Suchanek, G. Kasneci, and G. Weikum. Yago: a core of semantic knowledge. In *Proceedings of the 16th WWW*, pages 697–706. ACM, 2007.

[30] P. Venetis, A. Halevy, J. Madhavan, M. Paşca, W. Shen, F. Wu, G. Miao, and C. Wu. Recovering semantics of tables on the web. *Proceedings of the VLDB Endowment*, 4(9):528–538, 2011.

[31] J. Wang, H. Wang, Z. Wang, and K. Q. Zhu. Understanding tables on the web. In *Conceptual Modeling*, pages 141–155. Springer, 2012.

[32] W. Wu, H. Li, H. Wang, and K. Q. Zhu. Probase: A probabilistic taxonomy for text understanding. In *Proceedings of the 2012 ACM SIGMOD*, pages 481–492. ACM, 2012.

[33] R. Xia, J. Yu, F. Xu, and S. Wang. Instance-based domain adaptation in nlp via in-target-domain logistic approximation. In *Proceedings of the Twenty-Eighth AAAI*, 2014.

[34] M. Yakout, K. Ganjam, K. Chakrabarti, and S. Chaudhuri. Infogather: entity augmentation and attribute discovery by holistic matching with web tables. In *Proceedings of the 2012 ACM SIGMOD*, pages 97–108. ACM, 2012.

[35] M. Yamada, T. Suzuki, T. Kanamori, H. Hachiya, and M. Sugiyama. Relative density-ratio estimation for robust distribution comparison. In *Advances in neural information processing systems*, pages 594–602, 2011.

[36] B. Zadrozny. Learning and evaluating classifiers under sample selection bias. In *Proceedings of the twenty-first international conference on Machine learning*, page 114. ACM, 2004.

[37] J. Zhu, Z. Nie, X. Liu, B. Zhang, and J.-R. Wen. Statsnowball: a statistical approach to extracting entity relationships. In *Proceedings of the 18th WWW*, pages 101–110. ACM, 2009.

Session Search by Direct Policy Learning

Jiyun Luo, Xuchu Dong, Hui Yang
Department of Computer Science, Georgetown University
{jl1749,xd47}@georgetown.edu, huiyang@cs.georgetown.edu

ABSTRACT

This paper proposes a novel retrieval model for session search. Through gradient descent, the model finds optimal policies for the best search engine actions from what is observed in the user and search engine interactions. The proposed framework applies direct policy learning to session search such that it greatly reduce the model complexity than prior work. It is also a flexible design, which includes a wide range of features describing the rich interactions in session search. The framework is shown to be highly effective evaluated on the recent TREC Session Tracks. As part of the efforts to bring reinforcement learning to information retrieval, this paper makes a novel contribution in theoretical modeling for session search.

Categories and Subject Descriptors

H.3.3 [**Information Systems**]: Information Storage and Retrieval—*Information Search and Retrieval*

Keywords

Dynamic Information Retrieval; Policy Learning; Session Search

1. INTRODUCTION

Session search is a complex information retrieval (IR) task. It is the information retrieval task that aims to find relevant documents for a session of multiple queries. Session search often happens when a user searches for an information need containing multiple aspects. For instance, in the Text REtrieval Conference (TREC) 2013 Session Track (Table 1 session 2), the information need is about *purchasing scooters*, which composes of five sub information needs on *brands, store names, price information, quality* and *reliability*; the user issued 8 queries to accomplish the search task. Session search also happens when an information need is vague or exploratory in nature. For example, in Table 1 session 87, the information need is *planning a trip to the United*

Table 1: Examples in TREC Session Tracks

TREC'13 session 2, Information need:
You want to buy a scooter. So you're interested in learning more facts about scooters including: what brands of scooters are out there? What brands of scooters are reliable? Which scooters are cheap? Which stores sell scooters? which stores sell the best scooters?

query1: scooter brands	**query2:** scooter brands reliable
query3: scooter	**query4:** scooter cheap
query5: scooter review	**query6:** scooter price
query7: scooter stores	**query8:** where to buy scooters

TREC'13 session 87, Information need:
Suppose you're planning a trip to the United States. You will be there for a month and able to travel within a 150-mile radius of your destination. With that constraint, what are the best cities to consider as possible destinations?

query1: best us destinations	**query2:** distance new york boston
query3: maps.bing.com	**query8:** hartford visitors
query9: hartford connecticut tourism ...	
query19: philadelphia nyc travel	**query20:** philadelphia nyc train
query21: philadelphia nyc bus	

TREC'14 session 1011, Information need:
...You would like to provide your friend with relevant information about: different ways to quit smoking, programs available to help quit smoking, benefits of quitting smoking, second effects ...

query 1: quit smoking	**query 2:** quit smoking hypnosis
query 3: side effects quit smoking	

States for a month and able to travel within 150-mile radius of the destinations. The user issued 21 queries in the session with various search attempts, such as checking the map and searching for the distances between two cities.

Session search is different from classic ad-hoc retrieval. Ad-hoc retrieval focuses on finding relevant documents for a single query. Session search aims to retrieve relevant documents for the entire session. Not surprisingly, in a session, ad-hoc retrieval, even with a relevant feedback scheme, would treat each query independently. On the contrary, session search takes the challenge to handle the dependency between queries and the dependency between documents retrieved at different iterations. Their differences also lie in that session search aims to optimize a long term reward, which is an expectation over the overall rewards in the whole session, while ad-hoc retrieval doesn't have to do that.

In a typical search session, search happens in episodes, which we term "search iterations." Each search iteration is a complete cycle of ad-hoc retrieval. A user issues a series of queries $q_1, q_2, \ldots, q_n$, and the search engine retrieves a series of document lists, $D_1, D_2, \ldots, D_n$, for the corresponding queries. The user skims a document list and clicks on some documents, which yields clicks and other implicit feedback, such as the time spent on reading the documents (also known as *dwell time*). The clicks also form a sequence, $C_1, C_2, \ldots, C_n$, for the corresponding retrievals. Between the neighboring queries, the user performs query reformations to re-write the earlier query or search along a different path. All these signals, including queries, retrieved documents, clicks, viewed documents, dwell time, and query reformulations, intertwine together and jointly impact on the session. Given the high complexity of the task, session search demands novel retrieval algorithms which are able to capture the characteristics of search sessions and able to enhance session search effectiveness.

In a session, users often search in a *trial-and-error* fashion: repeatedly trying different search paths via writing various queries, until succeeding in finding relevant documents to satisfy the information need. The search engine receives immediate, instant feedback from the user at each search iteration and hopes to return documents that are relevant for a long term search goal. Such characteristics of session search make it fit well with the family of Reinforcement Learning (RL) algorithms [28].

Recent development in session search algorithms ([9], [22]) show that using RL for session search is a promising new direction. However, existing approaches often trade model complexity off for efficiency. Reducing the number of states and actions is often a must-do to achieve real-time interactions between the user and the search engine. For instance, only four decision-making states are modeled in [22]. In the pursuit of efficiency, an obvious drawback of the prior work is that the details of the rich user-search-engine interactions could get lost.

In this paper, we propose a novel retrieval model for session search. We aim to create a framework that is able to incorporate a variety of features to adequately represent the complex interactions in a session. Our approach is based on partially observable Markov decision processes (POMDPs). It is a direct policy learning algorithm that skips the trouble of calculating beliefs for states, but directly learns the optimal policies from observations obtained easily in the user and search engine interactions. During every search iteration, the search engine maximizes the long-term reward towards the ultimate information need, instead of finding a local maximum for the current query. The framework learns a mappings via gradient descent from observations to actions, and sequentially handles a search iteration in three phases, including a browse, a query, and a rank phase. By learning over a history of actions and observations, our algorithm is able to efficiently learn policies with less model complexity than prior work. Experiments with the TREC 2012-2014 Session Tracks demonstrate that our algorithm exhibits a statistically significant improvement over several state-of-the-art session search systems. To our knowledge, this paper is the first to study direct policy learning for session search.

The rest of the paper is organized as follows. Section 2 presents related work. Section 3 describes the optimization framework. Section 4 presents the formulation of history and the three phases. Section 5 details the proposed direct policy learning algorithm. Section 6 evaluates the approach and Section 7 concludes the paper.

2. RELATED WORK

As a challenging IR task, session search has received increasing attention from both academia and industry in a number of IR fields, such as user and task modeling [19, 20, 29], retrieval models [24], interactive search [1, 17], query log analysis [7], and evaluation [8, 10]. The TExt Retrieval Conference (TREC) has encouraged a good deal of research in session search by organizing the Session Track since 2010 [13, 15]. Efforts from industry also have promoted the broadening of research in session search through the recent WSCD (Web Search Click Data) workshops.[1]

Many session search methods are based on large query logs. [3] derived a query-flow graph, a graph representation of user behavior, from query logs. The approach detected query chains in the graph and recommended queries based on maximum weights, random walk, or the previous query. [24] employed sub-modular optimization for document ranking for a specific type of sessions – sessions showing multiple subtopics (which they termed as having "intrinsic diversity"). [21] broke the session into partitions that correspond to subtasks. Other mining approaches [3, 27] identify the importance of query change in sessions; however, they require the luxury of large query logs. In the top TREC systems, for instance, the best TREC 2012 system [13] employs an adaptive browsing model by manipulating past retrieved documents; however, it did not demonstrate how to adapt to changing user intent, which sometimes requires relevant documents and sometimes requires novel documents. In the WSCD 2014 workshop, the best submitted system took a learning-to-rank approach [23]. The features being used included document ranks in the original ranking, query statistics, clicks, missed clicks, snippet quality, user click habits, and workweek and weekend seasonality. They claimed that there were session-level features, too; in the paper, they were not clearly listed. However, this supervised learning method assumed the batch relevance feedback were available, which is not true for the online learning setting in session search.

In this paper, we propose a novel session search framework based on a partially observable Markov decision process, which belongs to the family of reinforcement learning (RL). In RL, agents take inputs from the environment and output actions. The actions in turn influence the states of the environment. An RL algorithm often performs optimization over actions and policies, based on long-term benefits for solving problems with uncertainty, and satisfying the Markov property. The environment in reinforcement learning is usually formalized as a Markov Decision Process (MDP) [28], which is able to support modeling temporal dynamics in tasks like session search. Basic RL algorithms include model-based algorithms, such as value iteration and policy iteration, and model-free methods, such as Q-learning and TD-learning [14]. Reinforcement Learning has been successfully applied to robotics and artificial intelligence in general [14] such as

---

[1]https://www.kaggle.com/c/yandex-personalized-web-search-challenge

natural language grounding [5]. However, RL algorithms can be computationally demanding. Therefore, for problems with a large state space or action space, generalization is often used to reduce the state-value or state-action mappings [25]. Policy gradient descent [2] is a popular direct policy search approach. It optimizes the parameters via gradient descent, and its parameterized function can be learned through Monte-Carlo sampling, by simulating the interactions between agents and the environment. In this paper, we adopt policy gradient descent as a key technique in the proposed framework.

Researchers have just started to explore RL in IR. There are only a few existing approaches that use RL to study IR problems. The related approaches include using MDP [9], POMDP [22], exploratory online learning [11] and decision theories [26], to study interactive search. Although not all of them are based on RL, they all share the idea of using states, actions, and rewards. Among them, [22] is the most similar to our work. The authors formulated session search into classic POMDPs with hidden decision making states, actions, observations and observation functions. Their formulation was complex. Our work differs from theirs in that we learn direct mapping from observations to actions, which greatly simplifies the learning process. Moreover, our model is not limited to use states to capture the dynamic changes in session search as what [22] did. Instead, our framework is flexible enough to add a wide range of features that describe the session search process with richer details.

3. FRAMEWORK

Our framework is built on top of the Partially Observable Markov Decision Process (POMDP) [14]. A POMDP is represented by a tuple, $<S, G, A, O, B, T, R>$, which indicates states, agents, actions, observations, and beliefs over the states, transitions, and rewards. The states S (actions A) are a finite set of discrete states (actions). Observations O is a finite set of discrete symbols that an agent observes about the states. In a POMDP, hidden information can be modeled as states, while visible signals can be modeled as observations or actions. Reward $r = R(s_t = s, a_t = a, s_{t+1} = s')$ is the immediate reward when transitioning from state s to s' by taking action a at time t. The agents take inputs from the environment by making observations and output actions, which in turn influence the environment. In session search, there are in fact two agents, the user and the search engine [9]. However, since they do not appear as the main actor at the same time in a session, we merge them into one agent and skips the complexity of handling two.

Here our states are search iterations. Actions include browsing documents, such as reading and clicking documents, writing queries, and retrieving documents. Every state and action pair receives an immediate reward at the state transitions. The POMDP aims to optimize the long term overall rewards for the entire process.

To solve an RL problem is to find the best policy for it. This is called "policy learning." In a POMDP, a policy π describes the general rules of which actions for each agent to perform at each time step, given a history of state and action pairs since time 0. The goal of policy learning is to find a policy that optimizes the expected discounted long-term cumulative reward – i.e., the value function

$$V_\theta(s_0) = E\Big(\sum_{t=0}^{\infty} \gamma^t r(t) | s_0\Big) \qquad (1)$$

where γ is discounts the expected future or past rewards, since they could be inflated now. $r(t)$ is the immediate reward at time t. s_0 is the starting state.

If we denote by H the set of all possible history of search behavior sequences h and $r(t, h)$ the tth reward in the history h, the value function in Eq. 1 can be written as:

$$V_\theta(s_0) = \sum_{t=0}^{\infty} \gamma^t \sum_{h \in H} P(h|\theta) r(t, h) \qquad (2)$$

where $P(h|\theta)$ is the probability distribution over all possible histories given the parameter vector θ. $r(t, h)$ is the reward obtained at time step t. γ is the discount factor and t indexes the search iterations.

The best policy π^* can be induced from optimization of $V_\theta(s_0)$, which is equivalent to learning the best parameter vector θ. The value function can optimized by solving the Bellman equation if the model is known [9]. When the model is not known, there is no close form solution to it and we need to use gradient descent to find the optimal solution.

Two challenges of our framework are 1) defining the history and calculating $P(h|\theta)$, and 2) optimizing the value function via gradient descent. The former is addressed in Section 4 and the latter in Section 5.

4. HISTORY AND THREE PHASES

Given that many factors in session search, such as a set of continuous queries, documents, and clicks, it is non-trivial to clearly describe the dynamics in it. To tackle this, we propose to decompose a search history into two layers. The first is to break the history into search iterations, indexed by t. Further, an iteration is decomposed into three phases: the browse, the query, and the rank phases. The first two phases are led by the user and the last by the search engine. With such a decomposition, we are able to perform further study to model the search at a more fine-grained level.

4.1 History

We define a history to be the record of a session from search iteration 0 to the current search iteration t.[2] A history keeps track of the dynamic changes of states, observations, actions, and rewards during session search. It is a chain of events happening in a session. Every search iteration in the history consists of clicks C, dwell time T, query q, query changes Δq, and retrieved documents D. The history at time t can be written as:

$$h_t = [h_{t-1}, C_t, T_t, q_t, \Delta q_t, D_t]$$

where h_{t-1} is a prefix history in h_t.

Figure 1 illustrates a history gathered for TREC 2014 session 1011. The information need is s *You would like to provide your friend with relevant information about: different ways to quit smoking, programs available to help quit smoking, benefits of quitting smoking, second effects.* The session started with the first query (q_1) *quit smoking*. The history up to the end of the first iteration is h_1, which contains q_1 and a set of documents D_1 returned by the search engine. We assume a dummy starting query q_0. Therefore, the new added terms are just q_1 and the removed terms are none.

The second search iteration started when the user browsed the previously returned document set D_1. The user clicked

---

[2]We use 'iteration' and 'time step' interchangeably to refer to search iteration t.

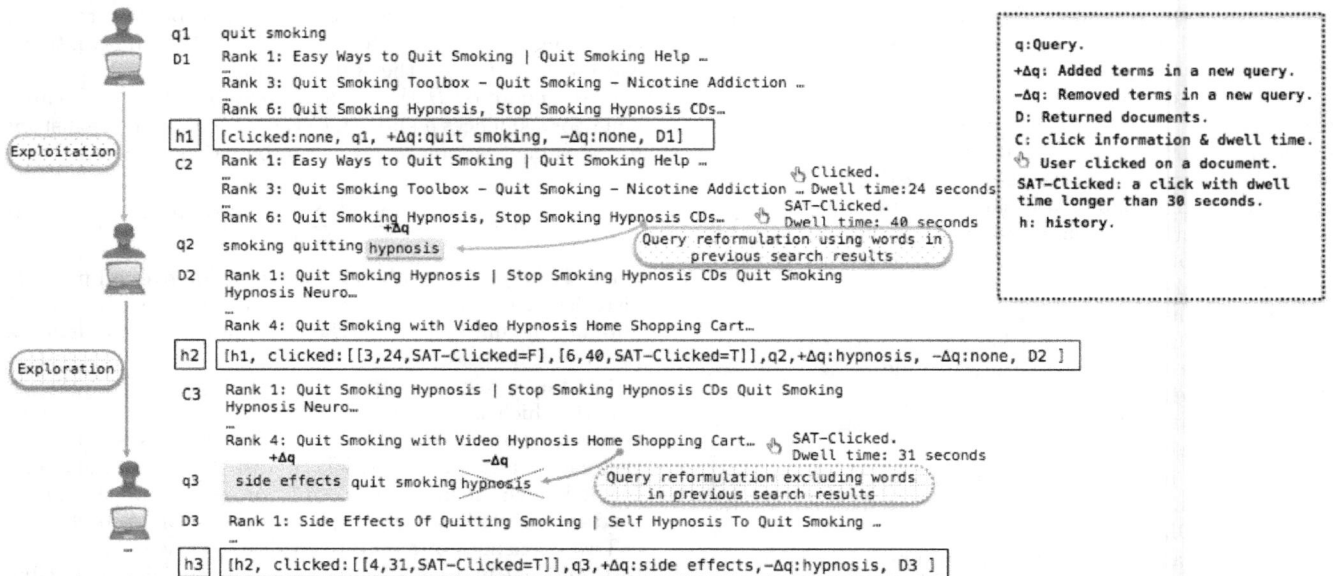

Figure 1: Example History in Session Search (TREC 2014 Session 1011).

documents ranked at positions 3 and 6. On the 3rd document d_3, a dwell time of 24 seconds was spent and on the 6th, 40 seconds. d_6 is considered as a satisfactory click (SAT-Click) since its dwell time is longer than 30 seconds, which is a simple rule that we use to identify SAT-Clicks [6]. The user then entered the next query, q_2 (*quit smoking hypnosis*).

The changes between the new query q_2 and the previous query q_1, termed as *query changes*, which suggest the users' judgment on document relevance and their degrees of desire to explore. Adopting the definitions in [9], we define the query changes as the syntactic editing changes between two consecutive queries.[3] They include positive query change ($+\Delta q$), i.e., the added terms in the new query, and negative query change ($-\Delta q$), i.e., the removed terms from the old query. Here we obtain $+\Delta q_2$ as *hypnosis* and $-\Delta q_2$ as none.

We also notice that the added query terms (in this case *hypnosis*) can be found in the SAT-Clicked document d_6; which suggests that the user could be inspired by reading the documents retrieved at the previous iteration and issued a new query to find more about it. Since the query reformulation used words in the previously retrieved documents, the transition from the first to the second iteration is identified as an "exploitation" – the user stays at the same subtopic. The search engine then returned documents D_2 for q_2. The history up to iteration 2 is h_2, which includes the earlier history h_1 and the new updates in this iteration.

At the third search iteration, the history h_3 also records the earlier histories, clicked documents (the 4th ranked document is SAT-Clicked), the new query q_3 (*side effects quit smoking*), the query changes (added terms $+\Delta q_3$=*"side effects"* and removed terms $-\Delta q_3$=*"hypnosis"*), and the new documents being returned D_3. The positive query changes from q_3 to q_2 are not found in the SAT-Clicked document; instead, the term *"hypnosis"*, which is from the previously

returned documents, is removed from q_3. Because the query reformulation excludes words from the previous search results, we consider this transition as an "exploration" – the user would like to shift to a new subtopic.

4.2 Three phases

Within a search iteration, we can see that the complexity for session search is still high – there involve queries, documents, clicks and query changes, among which many dependencies exist. However, we also notice that clicks, query, and retrieval in fact happen at different phases. Finer decomposition of the history beyond search iterations is thus possible. Based on such a decomposition, we can obtain a generative model which represents how a session is produced by both the user and the search engine. It will be greatly helpful to explore the interactions between the two agents. In this section, we present a influence diagram which describes a generative model with further decomposition of the history.

Figure 2 depicts the influence diagram of the observations, actions, and states in session search. The left most and the right most parts of the graph exhibit the states and their transitions, where the states are search iterations and indexed by t. Within an iteration, there are three phases: *browse* phase, *query* phase, and *rank* phase. They are separated by vertical lines in the figure. The upper part of the figure shows the phases that involves the user, and the lower part the search engine. At each phase, an agent performs the action and after that, an observation is made by the other agent. For instance, a_{rank} at time t (the search engine's ranking algorithm) yields o_{rank} at time $t+1$ (the document retrieved by the ranking algorithm). The observations will be used at later phases to make decisions for action selection, for instance, o_{rank} influences how a_{browse} should be selected. The observation in the current phase and earlier phases could be stored in an internal states n, which is not a real state that transitions, but a unit to memorize the observations and actions so far. Here n_1, n_2, n_3 are internal

---

[3]This definition of query reformulation patterns omit fine-grained classifications. However, it works effectively in session search, as reported by [9].

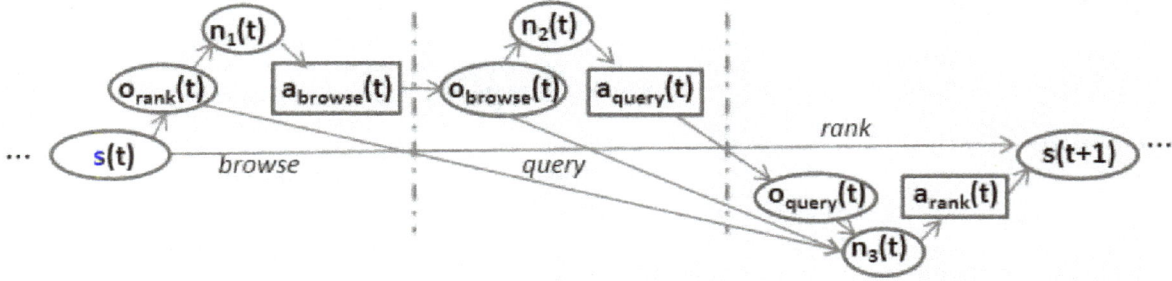

Figure 2: Influence Diagram for Session Search.

states, where 1 indicates browse, 2 query, and 3 rank.

Below are details about the three phases we propose here.

- *Phase 1: Browse.* The main actor in this phase is the user. The browse phase is after the search results are shown to the user and before the user starts to write the next query. The *browse* phase records how the user perceives and examines the (previously retrieved) search results. From a search engine's perspective, the emphasis is on getting users' feedback on these search results. Most feedback in this phase is implicit, including dwell time T and clicks C. These feedbacks and the derived feedback, such as SAT Clicks [18], are quite reliable relevance judgments from the user and hence can be used to calculate the reward function $r(t, h)$.

  Symbols that are used later in this paper and related to the browse phase are:

    - $o_{rank}(t)$ They are the observations of what the search engine's actions yield. For the previously returned documents at time $t-1$, we denote them as D_{t-1}. If the current iteration t is the only search iteration in context, we omit t from now on, for most symbols.
    - a_{browse} are the actions that the user takes to browse D_{t-1}. The actions include clicking and reading documents. The selection of the browsing actions depends on query q_t and retrieved documents D_{t-1}.
    - n_1 is an internal state at the user side. It memorizes o_{rank}.

- *Phase 2: Query.* The main actor in this phase is still the user.

  The phase happens when the user writes a new query. We assume that the query is created based on what has been seen in the browse phase, i.e., the previously retrieved documents, and the user's information need about the entire session. The new query triggers another iteration of document retrieval.

  Symbols related to the query phase are:

    - o_{browse} is the observations about how the user behaves in the browse phase. It includes the click information C_t and dwell time T_t for the previously retrieved documents. Note they are for D_{t-1} the documents retrieved at the previous iteration.
    - a_{query} is q_t, the query that the user writes at the current iteration t.

    - n_2 is another internal state at the user side. It records o_{browse} and helps the user obtain hints from documents being clicked or documents being read for a long time to write the new query q_t.

- *Phase 3: Rank.* The main actor in this phase is the search engine. The rank phase happens after the query is entered and before the search results are returned. The search engine delivers a ranked list of documents based on the current query and other earlier signals being collected. It is the search engine's ranking algorithm and the focus of this paper. The retrieved documents will be examined at the beginning – i.e., the browse phase – of the next iteration. The loop continues until the search stopped by the user. In the first iteration, there is no browse phase.

  Symbols related to the rank phase are:

    - o_{query} is what the search engine observes from what the user wrote as a query. It includes the query q_t and the query changes from q_t to q_{t-1}. The query changes contain two parts, the added terms $+\Delta q_t$ and the removed terms $-\Delta q_t$.
    - a_{rank} is the search engine action to retrieve a ranked list of documents. We define it as the action to put a document d at the top of a ranked list. It depends on a combination of query change Δq_t, previously retrieved documents D_{t-1}, and user clicks C_t and dwell time T_t for D_{t-1}.
    - n_3 is an internal state at the search engine side. It memorizes o_{rank}, o_{browse} and o_{query}, to allow the search engine generates optimal actions based on all three types of observations.

The three-phase design of the search history help produce a generative model of how the user and the search engine work together in a session. It has great potentials to study the interactions between the user and the search engine. However, in this paper, we focus on creating better search algorithms, therefore only utilizing the search engine part of the generative model.

5. SESSION SEARCH POLICY LEARNING

In this section, we describe how to learn a policy from the history, formed by observations and actions, by gradient descent.

According to the influence diagram in Figure 2, we write

the history distribution as

$$P(h|\theta) = \prod_{t=1}^{len(h)} P(o_{rank}(t), a_{browse}(t),$$

$$o_{browse}(t), a_{query}(t), o_{query}(t), a_{rank}(t)|h_{t-1}, \theta) \quad (3)$$

where $len(h)$ is the length of history h and t indexes the search iterations.

By the chain rule, each factor in the history can be further factorized. In addition, by applying the Markov property and dropping the constants, $P(h|\theta)$ can be reduced into three factors:

$$P(h|\theta) \propto \prod_{t=1}^{len(h)} P(a_{browse}(t)|o_{rank}(t), \theta_1)$$

$$\times P(a_{query}(t)|o_{browse}(t), \theta_2) \quad (4)$$

$$\times P(a_{rank}(t)|o_{browse}(t), o_{query}(t), o_{rank}(t), \theta_3)$$

After simplifying Eq. 4 with index i to indicate the phases (1 indicates the browse phase, 2 for query, and 3 for rank):

$$P(h|\theta) \propto \prod_{t=1}^{len(h)} \prod_{i \in \{1,2,3\}} P(a^i(t)|n_i(t), \theta_i) \quad (5)$$

where θ_1, θ_2 and θ_3 are sub-vectors of θ at each phase. n_1, n_2, n_3 are internal states in the POMDP that memorize the observations and actions so far at time t. n_1 stores o_{rank}, n_2 stores o_{browse}, and n_3 stores o_{rank}, o_{browse}, and o_{query}.

The actions of an agent will be selected from a range of options. The best actions are expected to be discovered through optimization. To force gradient descent to obey the simplex constraints, we assume that the actions follow the Softmax function [28]. Specifically, for an action in the ith phase in a search iteration, we define the action selection distribution as

$$P(a^i|n_i, \theta_i) = \frac{e^{\theta_i \cdot \phi(a^i, n_i)}}{\sum_{a'i} e^{\theta_i \cdot \phi(a'^i, n_i)}} \quad (6)$$

where ϕ is the feature vector and θ is the parameter vector. Section 5.2 shows feature examples used in this work.

To find the optimal action, that is to obtain the optimal model parameters for θ_1, θ_2 and θ_3, we apply gradient descent [4] on the long term reward function, i.e., the value function. If we take the gradient on the value function, we get:

$$\frac{\partial V_\theta(s_0)}{\partial \theta_k} = \sum_{t=1}^{\infty} \gamma^t \sum_{h \in H} r(t, h) \frac{\partial P(h|\theta)}{\partial \theta_k}$$

$$= \sum_{t=1}^{\infty} \gamma^t \sum_{h \in H} r(t, h) P(h|\theta)$$

$$\times \sum_{i=0}^{t} \frac{\partial ln[P(a_{browse}|n_1, \theta_1) P(a_{query}|n_2, \theta_2) P(a_{rank}|n_3, \theta_3)]}{\partial \theta_k} \quad (7)$$

where H is the set of all the possible histories and for phase i, the gradient is:

$$\frac{\partial ln P(a^i|n_i, \theta_i)}{\partial \theta_i} = \phi(a^i, n_i) - \sum_{a'} \phi(a'^i, n_i) P(a'^i|n_i, \theta_i) \quad (8)$$

Actions at different phases in a search iteration can all be modeled in a form similar to Eq. 6. In this paper, we focus on finding the optimal actions for the search engine. In the rank phase, the search engine agent needs abundant information from the history. The history information, including o_{rank}, o_{query}, and o_{browse}, is stored in n_3. The ranking actions a_{rank} are selected based on:

$$P(a_{rank}|n_3, \theta_3) = \frac{e^{\theta_3 \cdot \phi(a_{rank}, n_3)}}{\sum_{a'_{rank}} e^{\theta_3 \cdot \phi(a'_{rank}, n_3)}} \quad (9)$$

where θ_3 is a vector of parameters relating to the policy at the rank phase.

Specifically, for the rank phase, the gradient is:

$$\frac{\partial ln P(a_{rank}|n_3, \theta_3)}{\partial \theta_3} = \phi(a_{rank}, n_3) -$$

$$\sum_{a'_{rank}} [\phi(a'_{rank}, n_3) \ P(a'_{rank}|n_3, \theta_3)] \quad (10)$$

By solving the gradient, we obtain a formula to update θ_3 at each step:

$$\Delta \theta_3 = \sum_{h \in H} \sum_{t=1}^{len(h)} \gamma^t r(t, h) \times \sum_{i=1}^{t} [\phi(a_{rank}, n_3) -$$

$$\sum_{a'_{rank}} \phi(a'_{rank}, n_3) \ P(a'_{rank}|n_3, \theta_3)] \quad (11)$$

where H is a set of histories.

The remaining of this section explains the gradient descent policy learning algorithm, features, document ranking function, and the reward function $r(t, h)$.

5.1 Algorithm

Algorithm 1 outlines the direct policy learning algorithm for session search.

The algorithm takes inputs from a set of histories H and a limiting threshold ϵ for gradient descent. The model parameter θ_3 is randomly initialized between 0 and 1.

The algorithm then enters a loop to examine all the histories and to learn the model parameter θ_3. Inside the loop, a history h is sampled from the set. We then examine each search iteration in h and obtain values for the observations o_{rank} and o_{browse}, which are about the previously retrieved documents D_{t-1}, and clicks and dwell time for it at time t, C_t and T_t. It also calculates the query changes Δq_t between the queries and stores it in observation o_{query}.

The search engine then calculates a document ranking score, which is $P(a_{rank}|n_3, \theta_3)$, for all the documents based on the current model parameter θ_3, and the features. A new ranking of the documents are produced based on $P(a_{rank}|n_3, \theta_3)$, which is calculated by Eq. 9. The new rankings are used to calculate the gradient updates $\Delta \theta_3$.

The loop stops when the gradient update $\Delta \theta_3$ stops changing much or we have examined all the training data.

5.2 Features

The features used in our algorithm are $\phi(a_{rank}, n_3)$. They are descriptors of observations o_{browse}, o_{query}, and o_{rank}, to show the interactions among the queries, documents, query changes, and clicks. We use 112 features in this work.

Algorithm 1 Direct Policy Learning for Session Search.

```
 1: procedure DPL(H, ε)
 2:      ▷ H is the training history set. ε is a threshold.
 3:      θ₃ ← random(0, 1)
 4:
 5:      repeat
 6:          Sample history h from H:
 7:          q₀, D₀, C₀, T₀ ← ∅, r(1, h) ← 0, Δθ₃ ← 0
 8:
 9:          for t = 1 to len(h) do
10:              o_rank ← D_{t-1}, n₁ ← o_rank
11:
12:              ▷ a_browse is performed by the user
13:              o_browse ← (C_t, T_t), n₂ ← o_browse
14:
15:              r(t, h) ← CalculateReward(D'_t, o_browse, h)
16:
17:              ▷ a_query is performed by the user
18:              o_query ← GetQueryChange(q_t, q_{t-1})
19:              n₃ ← (o_rank, o_browse, o_query)
20:
21:              Sample a search engine action a_rank
22:                  ∼ P(a_rank|n₃, θ₃)
23:              D'_t ← DocRanking(a_rank)
24:
25:              Δθ₃ ← UpdateGradient(r(t, h), D'_t, n₃, θ₃)
26:              θ₃ ← θ₃ + Δθ₃
27:          end for
28:      until Δθ₃ < ε or H is running out
```

Table 2: Example Features.

Notations
w is a term
t is the current search iteration
q_t is the current query
q_{t-1} is the previous query
$+\Delta q_t$ is the added terms in q_t, comparing to q_{t-1}
$-\Delta q_t$ is the removed terms in q_t, comparing to q_{t-1}
D_{t-1} is the previously retrieved documents/snippets
Query Features
Test if search term $w \in q_t$ and $w \in q_{t-1}$
# of times that a term w occurs in $q_1, q_2, \ldots, q_t$
Document Features
the length of the content of a document
the length of the snippet of a document
Query-Document Features
Test if a search term $w \in +\Delta q_t$ and $w \in D_{t-1}$
Test if a document d contains a term $w \in -\Delta q_t$
$tfidf$ score of a document d to q_t
Click Features
Test if there are SAT-Clicks in D_{t-1}
# of times a document being clicked in the current session
# of seconds a document being viewed and reviewed in the current session
Query-Document-Click Features
Test if q_i leads to SAT-Clicks in D_i, where $i = 0 \ldots t - 1$
Session Features
the length of the current session
position at the current session

The features can be classified into a few groups. Query features, document features, and session features are descriptors of the queries, the documents and the session, respectively. Query-document features are statistics about the interaction of the query terms and the previously retrieved documents. Click features are about the clicking information and the dwell time. The most exciting ones are the query-document-click features. They are about the interactions of all three elements. Table 2 lists some example features. It is worthy noting that out framework is able to take into account as many features as possible.

5.3 Document Ranking

It is worthy noting that $P(a_{rank}|n_3, \theta_3)$ is the scoring function for a document d. We use $a_{rank} = d$ to denote that the search engine will take an action to generate a document list with document d at the top.

$P(a_{rank}|n_3, \theta_3)$ originally presents the probability of selecting a particular action. In the context of session search, we use it to present the probability $P(a_{rank} = d|n_3, \theta_3)$ that selecting d to be put at the top of a ranked list under n_3 and θ_3 at the tth search iteration. A ranked list of document is generated by sorting through the probabilities.

5.4 Calculating the Reward

The reward function $r(t, h)$ is to estimate the benefits from an action, specifically a_{rank}. A reward function can guide the search engine throughout the entire dynamic process of session search.

Since session search is a document retrieval task, it's natural that *the reward function is about document relevance*. Our reward function $r(t, h)$ uses the a weighted average of

clicks and SAT Clicks as the reward. First, we define a strong SAT-Click as a click with dwell time longer than 30 seconds, and a weak SAT-Click as a click with dwell time between 10 and 30 seconds. We calculate the reward as

$$r(t, h) = \sum_{d_i \in D_t} \frac{\text{normalized } gain(d_i, t, h)}{log_2(rank_{d_i} + 1)} \quad (12)$$

where $rank_{d_i}$ is document d_i's rank position in D_t, and $gain$ is what a document contributes up to time t in history h:

$$gain(d, t, h) = a \times Count(\text{Strong SAT-Click}) + b \times Count(\text{Weak SAT-Click}) \quad (13)$$

where $Count()$ counts the occurrences of the types of clicks in h_t. The weights are normalized by the sum of such clicks in h. Experimentally we set $a = 1$ and $b = 0.5$. This reward function encourages to rank the strong SAT-Clicked documents high in a document list.

Rewards can also be directly generated from user's relevance assessments when the assessments are available [9, 22]. For instance, the reward function can be nDCG [12] with ground truth. However, in real time interactions, we will not have the ground truth before hand and therefore could not use this reward. In the experiments, we used it as an ideal reward to produce upper bound runs.

6. EXPERIMENTS

We evaluate the proposed approach on the recent TREC Session Tracks. The TREC Session Track [15, 16] has run since 2010. It is an annual evaluation for session search systems conducted at the National Institute of Standards and Technology (NIST). The task of TREC Session Tracks is to

Table 3: TREC Session Dataset Statistics.

	TREC'12	TREC'13	TREC'14
#Sessions	98	87	1021
#Queries	297	442	4226
Avg. session length	3.03	5.08	4.14
Max session length	11	21	16
#Sessions w/ length <4	75	38	466
#Sessions w/ length 4~10	22	42	543
#Sessions w/ length >10	1	7	12

retrieve a list of 2,000 documents for the last query in a session to satisfy the information need for the entire session. For each session, queries, the top 10 retrieved documents for each query, and interaction information in the current session are provided. The participating systems are not allowed to use the search topics – i.e., the search engine does not know the information need ahead of time.

We evaluate our algorithm on the TREC Session 2012, 2013 and 2014 data. TREC 2010 and TREC 2011 are earlier years for this Track and the tasks are less relevant. Note that for TREC 2013, many relevant documents are not included by pooling from very few submitted runs. Hence, the ground truth data is not complete. The tasks in our experiments are equivalent to TREC 2012 RL4, TREC 2013 RL2, and TREC 2014 RL2.

6.1 Dataset

The document collection used in this evaluation is ClueWeb. For TREC 2012 Session, we use ClueWeb09 CatB, which contains 50 million English webpages crawled in 2009. For TREC 2013 and 2014 Session, we use ClueWeb12 CatB, which contains 50 million English webpages crawled in 2012. The spam documents and duplicated documents are removed. We use the TREC 2012 data for training when testing on 2013 and 2014 data, and use the 2014 data for training when testing on 2012 data.

The sessions and queries were provided to the participating systems in a query log. When the log was created, users were given search topics containing a complex information need. The information need usually contains multiple subtopics. For examples, Table 1 lists three examples TREC sessions. The user then wrote a set of queries and interacted with a search engine to find relevant documents for the search topic. All user interactions and clicking information, urls, snippets, and returned document identification numbers for each query, were recorded in the log.

TREC 2012 has 98 sessions with an average session length of 4 queries. TREC 2013 has 87 sessions with an average length of 5. TREC 2014 has 1021 sessions with an average length of 4. Table 3 lists the dataset statistics.

6.2 Evaluation Metrics

The main evaluation criterion in our experiments is the whole-session search accuracy, which is the official TREC evaluation metric. It evaluates the nDCG@10 [12] for the retrieval results for the last query but the ground truth was created based on document relevance to the entire session. The relevance judgments consists of six relevance grades: -2 for spams, 0 for non-relevant, 1 for relevant, 2 for highly relevant, 3 for key pages, and 4 for navigational pages (a homepage that exactly matches the search topic) [15].

Table 4: Whole-Session Search Accuracy on TREC 2012 Session († indicates a stat. significant improvement over the baseline (p<0.05, t-test, one-sided))

	nDCG@10	σ^2	MAP	σ^2
TREC median	0.2314	0.0575	0.1221	0.0152
TREC best(baseline)	0.3153	0.0844	0.1588	0.0191
lemur	0.2622	0.0800	0.1342	0.0160
winwin-short	0.2658	0.0785	0.1552	0.0195
qcm	$0.3368^\dagger$	0.0948	0.1536	0.0196
dpl	$0.3382^\dagger$	0.0932	0.1544	0.0193
winwin-long	$0.3631^\dagger$	0.0847	0.1651	0.0198
dpl-upper	$0.3643^\dagger$	0.0944	0.1609	0.0197

Table 5: Whole-Session Search Accuracy on TREC 2013 Session († indicates a stat. significant improvement over the baseline (p<0.05, t-test, one-sided))

	nDCG@10	σ^2	MAP	σ^2
TREC median	0.1504	0.0245	0.0506	0.0029
TREC best(baseline)	0.1706	0.0401	0.1008	0.0096
lemur	0.1043	0.0184	0.0398	0.0023
winwin-short	0.1253	0.0299	0.0334	0.0023
qcm	0.1555	0.0305	0.0568	0.0037
dpl	0.1604	0.0319	0.0600	0.0039
dpl-upper	$0.2093^\dagger$	0.0467	0.0734	0.0071
winwin-long	$0.2137^\dagger$	0.0396	0.0632	0.0037

6.3 Systems to Compare

We compare the following session search systems in the experiments. 1) **lemur**, which is the state-of-the-art academic search engine created by UMass and CMU. We use Lemur's multinomial language modeling and Dirichlet smoothing with the smoothing parameter μ set to 5000. The last query of each session is fed to Lemur to start the search. 2) 2) **qcm**, the query change mode, which is a state-of-the-art session search system proposed by Guan et. al. [9]. It is developed based on Markov Decision Processes and focuses on adjusting term weights based on user query reformulation patterns in a session. The term re-weighting parameters used here are theme terms $\alpha = 2.2$, added old terms $\beta = 1.8$, added new terns $\epsilon = 0.07$, and removed terms $\theta = 0.4$ (please see [9] for parameter meanings). 3) **winwin**, a session search framework proposed by Luo et. al. in [22]. This system models session search as POMDPs with four hidden decision-making states. It is like a meta-search-engine with an action space consisting many alternative retrieval algorithms, including language model, BM25, pseudo-relevance feedback, query expansion, and qcm. We implemented two version of winwin, **winwin-short** and **winwin-long**. Winwin-short uses immediate feedback, i.e. the user clicks, as a short-term feedback. Winwin-long uses an ideal reward function generated from the ground truth, which gives an upper bound for winwin. 5) **dpl**, the direct policy learning framework proposed here. 6) **dpl+upper**, the proposed framework using ground truth as the reward function (the same as in winwin-long), which gives us an upper bound performance of the algorithm.

6.4 Results

In this experiment, we conduct the official evaluation in TREC Session Tracks. We report the nDCG@10, which is

Table 6: Whole-Session Search Accuracy on TREC 2014 Session Track († indicates a stat. significant improvement over the baseline (p<0.05, t-test, one-sided))

	nDCG@10	σ^2	MAP	σ^2
TREC median	0.1876	0.0383	0.3750	0.1125
TREC best(baseline)	0.2482	0.0471	0.4270	0.1266
lemur	0.2169	0.0470	0.3860	0.1162
winwin-short	0.2241	0.0420	0.3540	0.0875
qcm	0.2422	0.0451	0.4140	0.1236
dpl	$0.2608^\dagger$	0.0435	0.4390	0.1182
winwin-long	$0.3076^\dagger$	0.0549	$0.4800^\dagger$	0.1158
dpl-upper	$0.3266^\dagger$	0.0606	0.4320	0.1208

Table 7: Efficiency on TREC 2012 Session Track.

Approach	TREC 2012		
	Wall Clock	CPU Cycle	Speed Up
winwin-long	2.5×10^4s	6.8×10^{13}	1.00
winwin-short	2.5×10^4s	6.8×10^{13}	1.00
qcm	5.6×10^3s	1.5×10^{13}	4.46
dpl-upper	3.2×10^3s	8.7×10^{12}	7.81
dpl	3.1×10^3s	8.4×10^{12}	8.06
lemur	2.6×10^3s	7.0×10^{12}	9.62

Table 8: Efficiency on TREC 2013 Session Track.

Approach	TREC 2013		
	Wall Clock	CPU Cycle	Speed Up
winwin-long	9.4×10^3s	2.5×10^{13}	1.00
winwin-short	8.4×10^3s	2.3×10^{13}	1.12
dpl	2.3×10^3s	6.2×10^{12}	4.09
qcm	1.5×10^3s	3.9×10^{12}	6.27
dpl-upper	1.4×10^3s	3.8×10^{12}	6.71
lemur	3.3×10^2s	9.0×10^{11}	28.48

Table 9: Efficiency on TREC 2014 Session Track.

Approach	TREC 2014		
	Wall Clock	CPU Cycle	Speed Up
winwin-short	6.0×10^3s	1.6×10^{13}	1.00
winwin-long	5.3×10^3s	1.4×10^{13}	1.13
qcm	1.2×10^3s	3.4×10^{12}	5.00
dpl	6.4×10^2s	1.7×10^{12}	9.38
dpl-upper	6.2×10^2s	1.7×10^{12}	9.68
lemur	2.0×10^2s	5.4×10^{11}	30.00

the official TREC Session evaluation metric, as well as MAP averaged over all the sessions and their standard derivations.

Tables 4, 5 and 6 report the whole-session search accuracy. Here we also report the results from the TREC median and TREC best runs. We use TREC best as a strong baseline here. They are the best performing system actually submitted to the evaluation. All the statistical significance tests are performed against this baseline.

From Tables 4, 5 and 6, we are happy to see that dpl shows the highest nDCG@10 score among the systems that use clicks as the reward function. In TREC 2012, dpl achieves a 7.3% improvement of nDCG@10 over the TREC best and in TREC 2014, a 5% improvement of nDCG@10 over the TREC best. Both improvements are statistically significant ($p < 0.05$, one-sided t-test). Moreover, dpl shows a 2.8% MAP improvement over the TREC best. More exciting, dpl is 7.6% statistically significant better than the state-of-the-art session search system qcm in nDCG@10 in TREC 2014.

Sometimes a run that has high nDCG@10 score may have a low MAP score, for instance winwin-short in TREC 2014. It is because that some models focus on achieving high precision in the top 10 retrieval documents, while their MAP over all 2000 returned documents could be low.

We observe that winwin-long and dpl-upper produce impressive results. It is not surprising because that they both use an ideal reward function nDCG@10 calculated using the ground truth data – winwin-long uses this idea reward function to pick the best retrieval algorithms from the action space, while dpl-upper uses the true document relevance grades as a feature to pick the most relevant documents from all retrieved ones. These two runs are supposed to outperform all the rest runs since it uses ground truth as the rewards, to pick an optimal action from the action sets. Note that during the process of session search, a search engine won't be able to know the ground truth data. We therefore

use them to inform us an upper bound of winwin and dpl, respectively.

6.5 Efficiency

One motivation of this paper is to design a more efficient session search algorithm. We therefore conduct the efficiency tests for the algorithms under evaluation.

Tables 7, 8 and 9 compare the algorithms' retrieval efficiency over TREC datasets. We report the actual wall clock running time to finish the entire set of experiments in that year, cpu cycles, the speed up to (how many times faster than) winwin-long in the tables. The systems are sorted by wall clock time in decreasing order in the tables. The shorter the time, the faster the system. A hardware support of 4 CPU cores (2.70GHz), 32GB Memory and 22 TB NAS are used in this set of experiments.

Among the approaches being evaluated, winwin-short and winwin-long are the slowest. Qcm, dpl and dpl-upper are 5 ~ 10 times faster than the winwin approaches. dpl and dpl-upper only take as half time as qcm on TREC 2012 and TREC 2014. They are pretty fast. Lemur appears to use the least amount of time, however it is not a session search algorithm but actually an ad-hoc approach, which only deals with the current (last) query. We can conclude that dpl is a much more efficient session search algorithm.

7. CONCLUSION

This paper presents a novel document retrieval algorithm for session search. From a new perspective based on reinforcement learning, we produce a long term optimized ranking function for documents. The direct policy learning reduces model complexity and enable us to achieve a more efficient and less complex model. In addition, we are able to flexibly incorporate a wide range of features to describe the rich interactions in session search. Due to the limitation of the setting of the TREC Session Tracks, where a real user and search engine interaction is missing, we could not actually fully apply our modeling to handle both the user side and the search engine side, however, the modeling is general enough to allow future practice of it in experiments with real time interactions. Nonetheless, the framework is shown to be highly effective by evaluations conducted on three years of TREC Session Tracks. It statistically significantly outperforms the TREC best runs in 2012 and 2014.

Due to its trial-and-error nature, session search is an excellent application for reinforcement learning (RL). As part of the efforts to bring RL to IR, this paper makes a contribution in studying direct policy learning for session search. We hope this paper encourages more future work in dynamic search for high complexity tasks.

8. ACKNOWLEDGMENT

The research is supported by DARPA FA8750-14-2-0226, NSF IIS-1453721, and NSF CNS-1223825. Any opinions, findings, conclusions, or recommendations expressed in this paper are of the authors, and do not necessarily reflect those of the sponsor.

References

[1] M. Ageev, Q. Guo, D. Lagun, and E. Agichtein. Find it if you can: A game for modeling different types of web search success using interaction data. In *SIGIR '11*.

[2] L. Baird and A. Moore. Gradient descent for general reinforcement learning. In *Advances in neural information processing systems 11*. 1999.

[3] P. Boldi, F. Bonchi, C. Castillo, D. Donato, A. Gionis, and S. Vigna. The query-flow graph: Model and applications. In *CIKM '08*.

[4] S. Boyd and L. Vandenberghe. *Convex Optimization*. Cambridge University Press, 2004.

[5] S. R. K. Branavan, H. Chen, L. S. Zettlemoyer, and R. Barzilay. Reinforcement learning for mapping instructions to actions. In *ACL '09*.

[6] K. Collins-Thompson, P. N. Bennett, R. W. White, S. de la Chica, and D. Sontag. Personalizing web search results by reading level. In *CIKM '11*.

[7] C. Eickhoff, J. Teevan, R. White, and S. Dumais. Lessons from the journey: A query log analysis of within-session learning. In *WSDM '14*.

[8] S. Fox, K. Karnawat, M. Mydland, S. Dumais, and T. White. Evaluating implicit measures to improve web search. *ACM Trans. Inf. Syst.*, 23(2):147–168, 2005.

[9] D. Guan, S. Zhang, and H. Yang. Utilizing query change for session search. In *SIGIR '13*.

[10] A. Hassan, R. Jones, and K. L. Klinkner. Beyond dcg: User behavior as a predictor of a successful search. In *WSDM '10*.

[11] K. Hofmann, S. Whiteson, and M. de Rijke. Balancing exploration and exploitation in learning to rank online. In *ECIR'11*.

[12] K. Järvelin and J. Kekäläinen. Cumulated gain-based evaluation of ir techniques. *ACM Trans. Inf. Syst.*, 20(4):422–446, 2002.

[13] J. Jiang, D. He, and S. Han. Pitt at trec 2012 session track. In *TREC '12*.

[14] L. P. Kaelbling, M. L. Littman, and A. W. Moore. Reinforcement learning: A survey. *J Artificial Intelligence Res.*, 4:237–285, 1996.

[15] E. Kanoulas, B. Carterette, M. Hall, P. Clough, and M. Sanderson. Overview of the trec 2013 session track. In *TREC'13*.

[16] E. Kanoulas, B. Carterette, M. Hall, P. Clough, and M. Sanderson. Overview of the trec 2014 session track. In *TREC'14*.

[17] J. Y. Kim, M. Cramer, J. Teevan, and D. Lagun. Understanding how people interact with web search results that change in real-time using implicit feedback. In *CIKM '13*.

[18] Y. Kim, A. Hassan, R. W. White, and I. Zitouni. Modeling dwell time to predict click-level satisfaction. In *WSDM '14*.

[19] A. Kotov, P. N. Bennett, R. W. White, S. T. Dumais, and J. Teevan. Modeling and analysis of cross-session search tasks. In *SIGIR '11*.

[20] J. Liu and N. J. Belkin. Personalizing information retrieval for multi-session tasks: The roles of task stage and task type. In *SIGIR '10*.

[21] C. Lucchese, S. Orlando, R. Perego, F. Silvestri, and G. Tolomei. Identifying task-based sessions in search engine query logs. In *WSDM '11*.

[22] J. Luo, S. Zhang, and H. Yang. Win-win search: Dual-agent stochastic game in session search. In *SIGIR '14*.

[23] P. Masurel and K. Lefevre-Hasegawa. Dataiku's solution to yandex's personalized web search challenge. In *WSCD '14*.

[24] K. Raman, P. N. Bennett, and K. Collins-Thompson. Toward whole-session relevance: Exploring intrinsic diversity in web search. In *SIGIR '13*.

[25] J. Schmidhuber. Sequential decision making based on direct search. In R. Sun and C. L. Giles, editors, *Sequence Learning: Paradigms, Algorithms, and Applications*. Springer, 2001.

[26] X. Shen, B. Tan, and C. Zhai. Implicit user modeling for personalized search. In *CIKM '05*.

[27] Y. Song and L.-w. He. Optimal rare query suggestion with implicit user feedback. In *WWW '10*.

[28] R. S. Sutton and A. G. Barto. *Reinforcement Learning: An Introduction*. MIT Press, 1998.

[29] R. W. White, I. Ruthven, J. M. Jose, and C. J. V. Rijsbergen. Evaluating implicit feedback models using searcher simulations. *ACM Trans. Inf. Syst.*, 23(3):325–361, 2005.

Learning to Reinforce Search Effectiveness

Jiyun Luo, Xuchu Dong, Hui Yang
Department of Computer Science
Georgetown University
37th and O Street, NW, Washington, DC, 20057
{jl1749,xd47}@georgetown.edu, huiyang@cs.georgetown.edu

ABSTRACT

Session search is an Information Retrieval (IR) task which handles a series of queries issued for a search task. In this paper, we propose a novel reinforcement learning style information retrieval framework and develop a new feedback learning algorithm to model user feedback, including clicks and query reformulations, as reinforcement signals and to generate rewards in the RL framework. From a new perspective, we view session search as a cooperative game played between two agents, the user and the search engine. We study the communications between the two agents; they always exchange opinions on "whether the current stage of search is relevant" and "whether we should explore now." The algorithm infers user feedback models by an EM algorithm from the query logs. We compare to several state-of-the-art session search algorithms and evaluate our algorithm on the most recent TREC 2012 to 2014 Session Tracks. The experimental results demonstrates that our approach is highly effective for improving session search accuracy.

Categories and Subject Descriptors

H.3.3 [**Information Systems**]: Information Storage and Retrieval—*Information Search and Retrieval*

Keywords

Dynamic Information Retrieval Modeling; Reinforcement Learning; Stochastic Game; Session Search

1. INTRODUCTION

Session search is an Information Retrieval (IR) task which extends classic ad-hoc retrieval by handling more than one queries in a retrieval task. This form of search happens everyday when people search online using a series of queries for a complex information need, such as planning a trip to Paris or purchasing a new home. The process of submitting multiple queries in a session to accomplish a complex information need is called *session search*.

ICTIR'15, September 27–30, 2015, Northampton, MA, USA.
© 2015 ACM. ISBN 978-1-4503-3833-2/15/09 ...$15.00.
DOI: http://dx.doi.org/10.1145/2808194.2809468.

A session usually starts with the user issuing a query to the search engine. The user then receives a list of ranked documents that are ordered by the decreasing relevance to the query. The user then goes through the list and skims the snippets, clicks on some interesting ones and spends a fair amount of time reading them. This is a complete cycle of an ad-hoc retrieval process. Here in session search, we call one such information retrieval cycle a "search iteration" and it repeats in the session. In the next search iteration, the user either reformulates the previous query or writes a new one to start another search. The loop stops when the user's information need is satisfied or the user abandons the search [8]. As a result, there are a series of search iterations in a session – which include a series of queries $q_1, ..., q_n$, a series of returned documents $D_1, ..., D_n$, and a series of clicks $C_1, ..., C_n$, some of which are examined by the user for a long time and thus potentially highly relevant documents (They are called SAT-clicks, or *satisfactory clicked documents* [10]).

Session search has obtained increasing attentions in the IR community, for instance, in the recent dynamic information retrieval modeling approaches [34, 35] and in the TExt Retrieval Conference (TREC) 2010-2014 Session Tracks [19, 20]. The current approaches include (1) extending existing IR techniques, such as learning to rank and using large scale query logs, from ad-hoc retrieval for one-shot query to session search, and (2) emerging efforts in applying reinforcement learning (RL) to session search. For instance, [27] proposed a Partially Observable Markov Decision Process (POMDP) approach for session search, where they attributed document retrieval to a decision-making process, where term-weight adjustments are modeled as the actions that a search engine could take.

Our paper belongs to the RL-style session search algorithms, with its focus on modeling the two-way communication between the user and the search engine.

There are rich user and search engine interactions occurred during session search. We believe that they are valuable resources and we should take advantage of them to improve search results effectiveness. For instance, Figure 1 illustrates the interactions and the messaging between the two agents (the user and the search engine) in a session. The example is taken from TREC 2014 Session 52, which searches for *the efficiency, technology, and environment effect of hydropower*. At iteration 1 ($t = 1$), the user enters the first query "hydropower efficiency."[1] The search engine sends out its ranked documents D_1 as its message. At iteration 2 ($t = 2$), the user sends out the browsing information, includ-

---

[1] There has yet been clicking nor browsing at iteration 1.

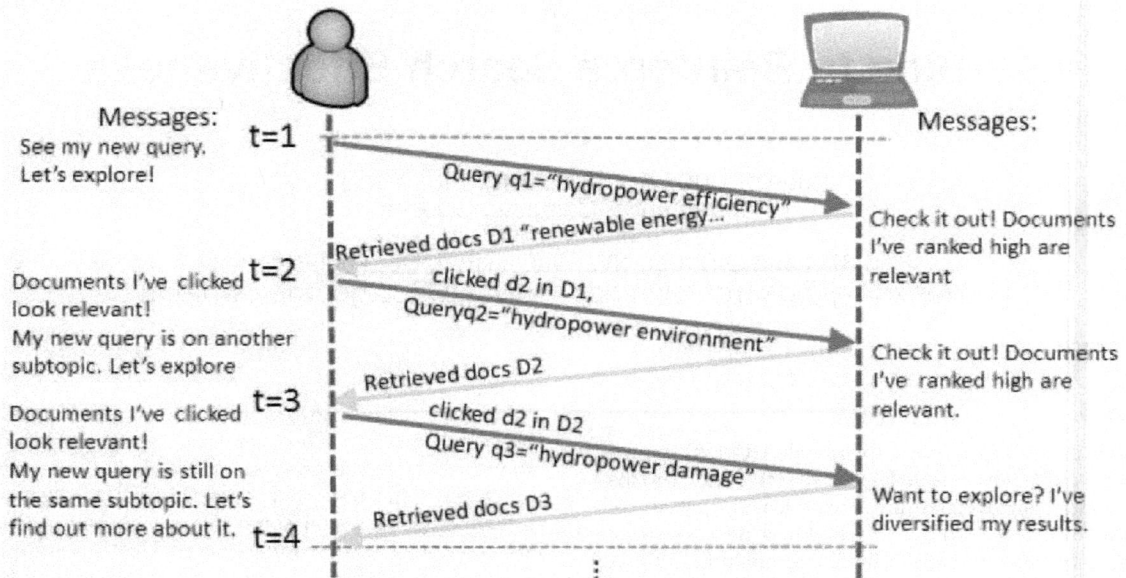

Figure 1: Interactions in Session Search. (Example is from TREC'14 Session 52. d_n is the nth document in a ranked list D at iteration t.)

ing clicked documents (some of them are SAT-clicked[2]) and time spent on those documents, and then sends out a reformulated query q_2. Both the browsing information and the query reformulations are messages (feedback) that the user sends to the search engine. The search engine then sends out a new set of documents D_2 for this iteration. At $t = 3$, the user again sends out the browsing information and the reformulated query q_3, and the search engine replies with D_3. The loop continues until the search is done.

In this paper, we propose to look at the interactions in session search from a new perspective: we view session search as a cooperative game played between the user and the search engine. In our point of view, the interactions between the two agents show the following characteristics:

Common goal. The two parties (agents) in session search, the user and the search engine, share a common goal, which is to find documents that can satisfy the ultimate information need. Throughout the process, the two agents cooperate and explore together, seeking a better understanding of the information need and how to satisfy it by finding relevant documents.

Exploration in the unknown information space. The user and the search engine interact in a complex search system to realize a goal: satisfying a ultimate information need. The search process is guided by a hidden, complex, sometimes vague information need, which is always in the user's mind, and may evolve and become clearer as the search develops. The user and the search engine work together step by step, exploring an unknown information space, to find the relevant documents to satisfy the information need. Within the process, a search iteration could be generalization, specification, slight change, or completely change to the previous query. All these search attempts from the user, accumulate knowledge and information that allows the user to better

understand the ultimate search goal, and the change and dynamics presented in the search process.

Equal partners. We view both the user and the search engine as autonomous agents who are *equal partners* in their cooperation. Our view is different from prior work on interactive search where the users are the only main target in the study. Hence, the roles of the user and the search engine are not that one is teaching and another is learning. Instead, in a joint exploration, neither of them may have a clear picture of how to approach the information need. Sometimes neither of them knows how to describe the information need. For instance, the user may have difficulty articulating a query that precisely describes the information need, especially when the search task is complex. Therefore, we would like to point out that both parties are equal, and that they take turns in exploring the environment and communicating with each other to reach the goal.

Cooperative exploration. Both the user and the search engine can make decisions on relevance, as well as on when and where to explore the information space. A user can issue a new query from one subtopic to another. This drift drives the search process into a new direction. Similarly, the search engine can also drive the search process into new paths, by introducing diversity in the search results that it recommends. In our opinion, both agents are not only able to tell each other what documents they find to be relevant from their own points of views, but are also able to suggest to each other new directions for exploration.

In this paper we propose a new concept, *universal messages*, which are exchanged in a session between the two agents. Both the user and the search engine communicate and act using these messages. Basically, the two agents use *documents* and other actions, such as queries, to express their opinions on two things: (1) which documents are *relevant*, and (2) whether they would like to inform the other party to *explore* other subtopics as a team. The is to say,

---

[2]In this work, we consider a document with dwell time longer than 30 seconds are satisfactory clicks (SAT-Clicks).

Table 1: Message Interpretations.

Messages	"These are Relevant!"	"Let's Explore!"
User:	"Hey, after reading the documents, those documents that I have clicked or SAT-clicked are potentially relevant. Please pay attention to those documents that I have clicked"	"I have written a query that *shifts* to new topics. I would like us to explore some new topics together."
Search Engine:	"Hello, the documents that I've ranked high for you are supposed to be relevant. The more relevant I think they are, the higher that I rank them. Please take a look."	I have a method to recommend novel documents to you as well. When I do it, I introduce some documents on new topics to increase *diversity*. Please take a look at those documents that I bring to the top positions in the ranking list but may seem not directly related to your current query; they are what I recommend on new topics and hope we both to explore on them."

there is a two-way feedback mechanism in which the user and the search engine talk to each other every time when they communicate – *whether an agent judges the previously retrieved/recommended documents by the other agent are relevant* and *whether an agent would like to lead both of them to explore and move to the next sub information need.*

Table 1 shows our interpretations of their messages. We use this intuition to model the two-way feedback between the user and the search engine.

In this work, we propose an RL framework based on direct policy learning in partially observable stochastic game (POSG) to model the feedback among the two agents, aiming to improve the search effectiveness in sessions. We first propose a contextual bandit formulation of the two way communication between the two agents along two dimensions – relevance and novelty. We then use an Expectation Maximization algorithm [7] to learn the reward function. Through learning a probabilistic reward function for each agent, we model the interactions between two equal partners in a uniform framework. We apply our algorithm to the TREC Session Tracks [19, 20]. TREC Session track is an evaluation for session search systems which has been organized by NIST annually from 2010 to 2014. The experiment results show that our approach are highly effective and outperforms the state-of-the-art session search systems.

The remainder of this paper are organized as follows. Section 2 presents the related work. Section 3 describes the problem setting of our framework in the reinforcement learning context. Section 4 models the interactions between the agents. Section 5 presents the EM algorithm. Section 6 evaluates the approach. Section 7 fosters a discussion and Section 8 concludes the paper.

2. RELATED WORK

In this paper, we propose a novel session search framework based on a partially observable stochastic game (POSG), which belongs to the family of reinforcement learning (RL). Reinforcement Learning has been successfully applied to robotics [23, 28] and artificial intelligence in general [17], resource-bounded information extraction [18], and natural language grounding [1, 3, 5, 6, 9, 12, 21, 24, 33].

RL algorithms can be classified into model-based and model free. The two basic model-based algorithms for RLs are value iteration [2] and policy iteration [14]. Model-free algorithms for solving problems modeled by Markov Deci-

sion Processes (MDPs) are more popular [31]. Temporal-difference learning and Q-learning are two elementary approaches falling in this category.

When applying reinforcement learning to session search problems, there usually exist unobservable information, such as user information needs, to be modeled. Commonly used RL techniques, such as value iteration, policy iteration, and Q-learning, can be adapted to RL problems with hidden states [? ? ? ? ?].

Among various models in the RL family, Partially Observable Markov Decision Processes (POMDP) [17] has been applied recently on IR problems including session search [27] and document re-ranking [?]. In a POMDP, hidden information can be modeled as hidden states, while visible signals in the process can be modeled as observations or actions.

RL algorithms can be computationally demanding. Therefore, for problems with a large state space or action space, generalization is often used to reduce the state-value or state-action mappings [30]. Branavan et al. proposed a Monte-Carlo search algorithm utilizing non-linear value function approximation for very large decision-making problems provided with external textual sources, such as game manuals[4]. They employ a four-layer neural network as a non-linear approximation to the state-action value function.

Our work is closely related to multiple-agent cooperative reinforcement learning [22, 25, 32]. Most multi-agent RL algorithms are proposed for deterministic environments, such as minmax-Q to learn an optimal policy in a zero-sum Markov game [25] and projecting central Q-table for distributed Q-learning [22]. Through experiments in the simulated prey/hunter game tasks, Tan found that cooperative agents can learn faster and better than independent agents, especially in joint tasks. Tan studied three types of cooperations among multiple agents, sharing instantaneous information, sharing historical episodes, and sharing learned policies [32]. Georgila et al. proposed an approach to learn the system policy and the simulated user policy concurrently in dialogue policies [11]. They used multi-agent RL techniques [11]. The two multi-agent RL algorithms, PHC (Policy Hill-climbing) and PHC-WoLF (Win or Learn Fast Policy Hill Climbing), showed better performance than the single-agent algorithm of Q-learning in experiments on a resource allocation negotiation scenario.

We are inspired by [29]. In their work, Peskin et al. proposed a gradient descent method to find optimal policies in a

273

partially observable multiple agent stochastic game. Their method used a finite state controller to construct policies with memory. In their model for a cooperative multi-agent environment, all the agents are treated identically, which means that the actions of different agents could happen in parallel. That is not suitable for session search, where there is a strict order of turns of the user's actions and the search engine's actions.

The work most similar to ours is [26], which introduced two Bayesian policy learning algorithms to learn human trainer's feedback strategies. One algorithm assumes a fixed universal feedback strategies for all human trainers, and the other infers trainer strategies from the training history. In their methods, human feedback was classified into three categories: explicit positive feedback, explicit negative feedback, and lack of feedback. Our approach differs from them by focusing on implicit positive and negative feedback. Because modern search engines rarely ask users to input explicit feedback. Another difference is that we study the user feedback from the perspectives of relevance and novelty rather than the perspectives of reward and punishment.

3. PROBLEM SETTING

Our framework is built on top of Partially Observable Stochastic Games (POSGs) [29], which is the multi-agent version of the Partially Observable Markov Decision Process (POMDP) [17]. A POSG is represented by a tuple, $<S, G, T, R>$, which indicates states, agents, transitions from state to state, and rewards. G is a set of agents, each represented by a tuple, $<A, O, B>$, indicating an agent's actions, observations, and beliefs over the states. The agents take inputs from the environment by making observations and output actions, which in turn influence the environment.

In a POMDP, hidden information can be modeled as hidden states, while visible signals can be modeled as observations or actions. In particular, states S is a (finite) set of discrete states. Actions A is a (finite) set of discrete actions. Observations O is a (finite) set of discrete symbols that an agent observes about the states. Reward $r = R(s_t = s, a_t = a, s_{t+1} = s')$ is the immediate reward when transitioning from state s to s' by taking action a at time t. In session search, the relationships between the two agents are cooperative. However, they are not identical; they differ in the actual actions and reward functions. We therefore do not use identical payoff models.

Observations We consider the received messages by the search engine agent as its observations to the user's behavior. The search-engine-side observations include *user clicks* and *user's query changes*, where query changes [13] are the syntactic editing changes between two adjacent queries q_{i-1} and q_i. They include positive query change ($+\Delta q$), that is the added terms in the new query q_i, and negative query change ($-\Delta q$), that is the deleted terms from the old query q_{i-1}. The user-side observations are retrieved documents D_t by the search engine at time step t.

Actions and Observation-Action Pairs We consider the action of the search engine agent as to generating a ranked document list. The search engine agent's action leads to *a ranked list of documents and their snippets*. (o_t, a_t) is a set of observation-action pairs. In this paper, o_t indicates at time t that we can observe how the user has browsed the previously retrieved search results, clicked the documents, and reformulated the query at the current search iteration.

a_t indicates that, at time t, the search engine selects among its search algorithm options, executes the search algorithms, and provides a ranked list of search results.

History We define a *history* to keep track of the dynamic changes of states, observations, actions, and rewards during a session. In this work, we treat the states as unknown, hence the history only records a series of observations, actions and rewards generated at each step from search iteration 1 to the current iteration t. In this paper, we use 'iteration' and 'time step' interchangeably to refer to search iteration t. The *history* up to time t is

$$h_t = (o_1, a_1, r_1, o_2, a_2, r_2, \ldots, o_t, a_t, r_t).$$

Optimization To solve an RL problem is to learn its best policy. In a POMDP, a policy π is a function used to decide which actions for the agent to take at each time step, given a history of state and action pairs since time 0. By taking the selected action, the goal is to maximum a reward function, which, in the most widely used infinite horizon discounted model, is defined as the expected discounted long-term cumulative reward:

$$V_\theta(s_0) = E\Big(\sum_{t=0}^{\infty} \gamma^t r_t | s_0\Big)$$

which is also known as the *value function*, with γ as a discount factor that discounts the expected future rewards, since they have not been realized yet and could be inflated now. In this paper, we directly learn the policy from observation to actions

$$\pi : O \to A$$

and skip defining the states and beliefs.

4. MODELING THE TWO-WAY FEEDBACK

We are fascinated by the complexity of how users generate feedback to the search engine. We also would like to take the challenge to model the search engine as an autonomous agent who behaves as an equal partner to the user; and we model its feedback to the user as well. The two-way feedback is modeled as a contextual bandit for the proposed framework.

In the introduction section, we have discussed the concept of "universal messaging". Here we illustrate more about it. The user's query can be considered as a piece of short text that attempts to describe the information need. Documents or ranked document list returned by search engine can be considered as a 'big chunk' of text that the search engine used to illustrate what in its mind to describe the information need or what are relevant to the information need.

By showing the retrieved documents to the user, which is like showing search engine's understanding of the information need, the search engine completes its turn of driving the exploration process. The user can also show his or her feedback via clicking documents or spending a certain amount of time to examine the snippets, title or documents. These explicit or implicit feedback from the user can be captured by the search engine. It is the user's way of expression for what he or she believes that can describes the information need and relevant to the information need.

As shown in Table 1, the messages are about two dimensions: 1) "relevant dimension" – whether an agent thinks the returned documents by the other agent are relevant, and 2) "exploration dimension" – whether an agent would like to drive both agents to explore another subtopic.

To model the various forms of feedback in session search, we define a decision-making distribution $\mathcal{J}$, which is a distribution over the agents' decision-making states. We assume that an agent judges a set of ranked retrieved documents as relevant with probability

$$P(relevant) = 1 - \varepsilon$$

and, the agent judges that it would like to explore with probability

$$P(explore) = \mu$$

At time step , given the observations o, action a, and target policy π^*, the decision-making distribution $\mathcal{J}$ is defined as:

$$p(\mathcal{J} = RE|o, a, \pi^*) = (1 - \varepsilon)\mu \tag{1}$$

$$p(\mathcal{J} = NRE|o, a, \pi^*) = \varepsilon\mu \tag{2}$$

$$p(\mathcal{J} = RNE|o, a, \pi^*) = (1 - \varepsilon)(1 - \mu) \tag{3}$$

$$p(\mathcal{J} = NRNE|o, a, \pi^*) = \varepsilon(1 - \mu) \tag{4}$$

Here, $\mathcal{J}$ can take four values: 'RE' means 'relevant' and 'explore'; 'NRE' means 'non-relevant' and 'explore'; 'RNE' means 'relevant' and 'non-exploratory'; 'NRNE' means 'non-relevant' and 'non-exploratory.' These correspond to the four decision-making states proposed in [27].

Note that the best policy π^* would take an action a_t, s.t. $\pi^*(o_t) = a_t$. The four formulas sum to one, and the highest value among the four indicates the most likely decision-making state. The corresponding value will be used to compose the immediate reward function to guide the reinforcement learning framework.

4.1 Feedback from the User

In our opinion, user feedback is presented in two forms in session search: clicks to indicate relevance, and query change to indicate both relevance and the user's desire to explore.

Here we use time step t to index the search iterations. For query q_t at the tth search iteration, the set of retrieved documents for t is denoted as D_t. The set of documents that are previously retrieved for the previous query at the $(t - 1)^{th}$ search iteration is called the previously retrieved documents and denoted as D_{t-1}. It is believed that the previously retrieved documents are very influential in the current run of search, too [13]. They probably influence how the user will write the current query since the user have read some of the documents in D_{t-1} or at least have skimmed the snippets in the list.

The first dimension of judgment is related to *document relevance*.

At search iteration t, if the set of previously returned documents, D_{t-1}, leads to one or more SAT clicks, the current state is likely to be relevant; otherwise it is non-relevant. The intuition is that if while examining D_{t-1}, if the user clicks some documents, it is a good indicator that the user considers the set of the documents that were retrieved by the search engine is relevant at this moment, i.e., at time t. Here we model the user clicks as feedback to the previous iteration of search results.

Table 2: TREC 2014 Session 1011

Information need:

You would like to provide your friend with relevant information about: different ways to quit smoking, programs available to help quit smoking, benefits of quitting smoking, second effects ...

query 1: quit smoking
query 2: quit smoking hypnosis
query 3: side effects quit smoking

Hence, we model the user's underlying judgment on relevance as:

$$\varepsilon = 1 - \frac{\# \text{ of SAT-Clicked documents} \in D_{t-1}}{\# \text{ of returned documents} \in D_{t-1}} \tag{5}$$

where $P(non\text{-}relevant) = \varepsilon$ represents the probability of "non-relevant" cases in the previously retrieved documents D_{t-1}. $P(relevant) = 1 - \varepsilon$ represents the probability of finding any "relevant" documents in D_{t-1}.

Another dimension of judgment is related to *exploitation vs. exploration*. It is an indicator of how much the user desires to explore.

Here we study the changes between every consecutive queries as "query change" and denote it as Δq. For the changes between the current query q_t to the previous query q_{t-1}, their query changes at time t is denoted as Δq_t. It is the syntactic difference between the two queries, not the semantic differences. We use it for its simplicity and efficiency for the use in an online setting.

Moreover, the query changes can be grouped into a few categories. They are added terms to the current query, removed query terms from the old query (not in the new query any more), and kept terms in both the current and the old query. We are especially interested in the added terms and the removed terms, because they somehow suggest the user's query intent. We denote them as positive query change $+\Delta q_t$ or negative query change $-\Delta q_t$.

Continue on the idea of the second dimension of judgment. The idea is that given that previously retrieved documents D_{t-1} is the message from the search engine and the current query change Δq_t is the message from the user, if an added query term $+\Delta q_t$ appeared in D_{t-1}, it is very likely that the user will stay with the same subtopic from iteration $t - 1$ to t. It is a state that we call 'exploitation.'

On the other hand, if the added term $+\Delta q_t$ did not appear in D_{t-1}, it is quite likely that the user has moved to the next subtopic from iteration $t - 1$ to t. It is a state that we call 'exploration.'

We model the user's underlying judgment on "exploitation vs. exploration" as:

$$\mu = 1 - \frac{\# \text{ query changes} \in D_{t-1}}{\# \text{ of permutations of query terms} \in q_t} \tag{6}$$

where $P(exploration) = \mu$ represents the probability of "exploratory" cases at time t, and $P(exploitation) = 1 - \mu$ represents the probability of "exploitation" at time t.

Use an example to show our formulations. In the second iteration of Session 1011 in Table 2, there are 3 terms in the query "quit smoking hypnosis". The only added term is "hypnosis". It appears in "clueweb12-0010wb-76-01490", a SAT-clicked document in the previously set of retrieved documents.

In addition, there are 10 documents displayed to the user in the first 10 search results (SERP). Only one out of the 10 receives a SAT-click.

Therefore, for this iteration, we have $\epsilon = 1 - \frac{1}{10} = 0.1$ and $\mu = 1 - \frac{1}{3!} = 0.83$.

4.2 Feedback from the Search Engine

Likewise, the search engine's feedback is also presented in two forms: One to indicate what the search engine thinks are *relevant*, and anther to indicate what the search engine desires to explore in the process.

For the first dimension, we consider that the search engine uses the top-scored or top-ranked documents ranked by itself, to indicate relevance.

It means that we can use the similarity scores that the search engine assigns to each retrieval result to indicate the search engine's judgment on relevance. The assumption is that across different queries, query length normalization is taken care of, and the search engine is able to measure query-to-document similarity in a relatively consistent manner. However, in the datasets that we experiments on, such similarity scores are not available. Therefore, instead of using the actual ranking scores, we use the Maximum Likelihood Estimation (MLE) of relevant documents among the top ranked documents to present search engine's judgment on this dimension.

At the tth search iteration, we model the search engine's underlying judgment on relevance by leveraging the probability that a top returned document is indeed relevant, which means the document appears in the ground truth is a relevant document.

The estimation of ε for search engine is

$$\varepsilon = 1 - \frac{\text{\# of relevant documents in the top } n \text{ retrieved}}{n} \tag{7}$$

Here, $P(NR) = \varepsilon$ represents the overall probability of "non-relevant" cases at time t. $P(R) = 1 - \varepsilon$ represents the probability of finding any "relevant" documents at time t in the top n returned documents. n is empirically set to 5 in our experiments.

The second dimension is about *exploration*. Here we consider that the search engine introduces diversity in the retrieval results, to indicate the search engine's desire to explore.

To express its feedback/opinion on whether to *exploit or explore*, the search engine shows different degrees of diversity in its returned results. The idea is that the search engine can return diversified results – i.e. multiple topical clusters in its results – to promote "exploration." We can detect this by observing the word distribution and indirectly measure the diversity in the top returned snippets. According to the Zipf's law, assuming that the top returned documents or snippets are on a single topic, it is expected that the slope of the word distribution will be steeper. On the other hand, if the documents are diversified, it is expected that the slope of the word distribution will be flatter.

We therefore model the search engine's underlying message on exploration as

$$\mu = 1 - \frac{\text{total \# of the top } m \text{ frequent non-stop-words in } D_t}{\text{total \# of non-stop-words in } D_t} \tag{8}$$

Here, $P(exploration) = \mu$ represents the overall probability of how "exploratory" the results are by measuring the percentage of top m occurring words in all words returned in the search results. Here we only examine the first 10 snippets since they are the content that the search engine would like to use to influence the user at the first sight. They are what the search engine presents in front of the user, and would like to use them to influence the user the most to do a cooperative exploration together. We empirically set m to 5 words.

We use an example to show the details. In the second iteration of Session 1011, 8 out of the top 10 documents retrieved by the search engine are highly relevant, as provided in the ground truth. Therefore, $\epsilon = 1 - \frac{4}{5} = 0.2$.

Moreover, there are 428 non-stop-words totally in the top 10 snippets, and the most frequent 5 words are:

"smoke"(59), *"quit"*(34), *"hypnosis"*(30), *"stop"*(19), *"button"*(7)

The total counts of these 5 most frequent non-stop-words {"smoke", "quit", "hypnosis", "stop", "button"} is 123. Therefore, $\mu = \frac{123}{428} = 0.29$.

Based on the estimation for the two dimensions, the maximum judgment distribution value is 0.568 which means "relevant and exploitation" for this iteration, which is correct based on our manual evaluation.

In future work, we will learn n and m through supervised learning for better prediction accuracy.

5. AN EM ALGORITHM FOR FEEDBACK LEARNING

We propose to use Expectation Maximization [7] to compute the maximum likelihood estimation (MLE) of the decision-making distribution.

Algorithm 1 outlines the EM algorithm. The EM algorithm starts with a random/initial estimation of the two hidden parameters, ϵ and μ, and an initial random policy, which generates random actions for both agents given an observation. For the history up to the tth search iteration, we are able to go into the history and go through iteration by iteration to update the policy.

In the Expectation step, we compute the decision-making distribution based on Equations (1) to (4). The most likely joint decision by both dimensions are indexed by j. The reward function $r(t, h)$ is calculated by the decision-making distribution. A new policy is estimated by finding the best policy at step t given the current estimates of ϵ and μ, at line 13. At line 14, an action is selected based on the new estimate of the policy, and at line 15, the corresponding agents, either the user or the search engine, will perform the action to the documents. If it is the search engine's turn, it will retrieve documents. If it is a user's turn, the user will click or browse the documents.

In the Maximization step, we re-compute ε and μ at time t based on the new estimate of π' and the new actions yielded from π', by using the formulas (5) to (8).

The loop repeats until the history is running out or reaching convergence. The algorithm then outputs the final learned policy π^*.

Algorithm 1 Feedback Learning by EM.

1: **procedure** FEEDBACKLEARNING(π, h)
2:    $\pi \leftarrow randomPolicy()$
3:    $\varepsilon \leftarrow random(0,1)$, $\mu \leftarrow random(0,1)$
4:    **while** the search session has not finished **do**
5:       $o_t \leftarrow observe()$
6:       $a_t \leftarrow \pi(o_t)$
7:       $h_t \leftarrow [h_{t-1}, (o_t, a_t)]$
8:       **repeat**
9:          **E Step:**
10:          compute $P(\mathcal{J}|o_t, a_t, \pi)$ by Eq. (2) to (5)
11:          $j = \arg\max_{j' \in ['RE', 'NRE', 'RNE', 'NRNE']} P(J = j'|o_t, a_t, \pi)$
12:          $r(t, h) = P(\mathcal{J} = j|o_t, a_t, \pi)$
13:          $\pi' \leftarrow \arg\max_\pi \int_0^1 \int_0^1 p(\varepsilon, \mu|h, \pi)\ln p(h, \varepsilon, \mu|\pi)d\varepsilon d\mu$
14:          $a'_t = \pi'(o_t)$
15:          performAction(agent, a'_t)
16:          **M-Step:**
17:          compute ε' and μ'
18:       **until** $\varepsilon = \varepsilon'$ and $\mu = \mu'$
19:       $t \leftarrow t + 1$
20:    **end while**
21:    $\pi^* = \pi$
22:    **output** π^*

---

6. EXPERIMENTS

We apply our model to the recent TREC Session Tracks. The TREC Session Track [19, 20] has has been running since 2010 to 2014. I is an annual evaluation for session search systems conducted at the National Institute of Standards and Technology (NIST). For each session, queries, top 10 retrieved documents and interaction information in the current session is given in a query log. The last query that the user issues does not have interaction data.

The query log provided to the participants was created by the following process. Users are provided search topics containing the information need for a session. The information need usually contains multiple sub-topics. Table 2 lists an example of sessions from TREC Session Tracks. In order to find relevant documents for the search topic, users formulate a series of queries, examine the returned snippets, and click some urls to read the full documents if the snippets seem worthy to read more. It also records every user's query formulations, click operations and dwell time on documents into the log file. The search task is to retrieve a ranked list of 2,000 documents for the last query that users' trigger in each search session. The interactions are recored in the log.

The task of TREC Session Tracks is to retrieve a list of 2,000 documents for the last query in a session to satisfy the information need for the entire session. The document collection used to build the index is ClueWeb. In TREC 2012, the corpus is ClueWeb09 CatB with 50 million English web pages crawled in 2009. In 2013 and 2014, the corpus is ClueWeb12 CatB with also 50 million English web pages crawled in 2012. The participating systems are supposed to retrieve documents for the last query. The participating systems are not allowed to use the topics when performing retrieval. In our implementation, the spam documents are removed if their Waterloo spam scores are less than 70.

We evaluate our algorithm on the TREC Session 2012, 2013 and 2014 data for their recency and the completeness of the ground truth data. In the earlier years of TREC Session Tracks, such as TREC 2010 and 2011, the tasks and how the sessions were created were different from the recent years; we therefore did not experiment on them. The tasks in this set of experiments are equivalent to TREC 2012 RL4, TREC 2013 RL2 and TREC 2014 RL2.

6.1 Evaluation Metrics

One of the most attractive features of session search algorithms is that they have the potential to perform early retrieval for documents relevant to later queries or to the entire session, even if the document may not seem relevant to the current query. Using the relevance judgment for the whole session, we can evaluate at earlier iterations how well a search engine can predict and produce relevant documents for future queries. We therefore measure the search accuracy at each search iteration and term this accuracy as "immediate search accuracy". We evaluate it on TREC 2012, TREC 2013, and TREC 2014 Session Tracks using nDCG@10 [16]. The six grades of relevance relevance judgments are provided by NIST. There are -2 for spams; 0 for non-relevant, 1 for relevant documents, 2 for highly relevant documents, 3 for key web pages, and 4 for navigational pages, for instance that the homepage to a site that exactly matches the entire session is retrieved.

6.2 Systems to Compare

We compare the following session search systems in the experiments.

- **lemur**, which is a state-of-the-art ad-hoc search engine.[3] We use Lemur's multinomial language modeling and Dirichlet smoothing with the smoothing parameter $\mu = 5000$. The last query of each session is used as a query and sent to Lemur.

- **lemur+all.** Lemur with all queries in a session combined as a single query, feeding into it. For instance, TREC 2014 session 1011 yields a combined query *quit smoking quit smoking hypnosis side effects quit smoking*. Repeated terms are kept as they are.

- **qcm**, the query change retrieval mode, which is a state-of-the-art session search system. It is proposed by Guan et. al. [13].

- **winwin-short**, the win-win search session search framework proposed by Luo et. al. in [27]. This system models session search as POMDPs and works like a meta-search algorithm. Winwin-short only use the user clicks as a short-term feedback, to guide the session search.

- **winwin-long** is another version of winwin. Different from winwin-short, it uses an ideal reward function nDCG@10, which is generated by using the ground truth documents. Here we use winwin-long as an upper bound.

- **fl**, the **feedback learning** framework proposed here.

---

[3]lemurproject.org.

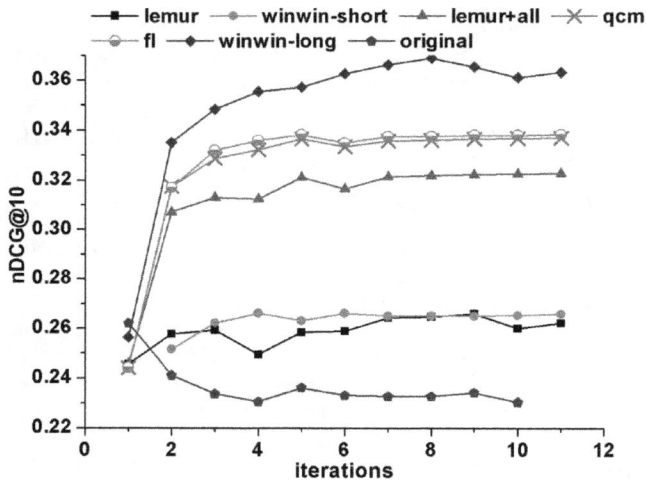

Figure 2: Immediate Search Accuracy (TREC 2012).

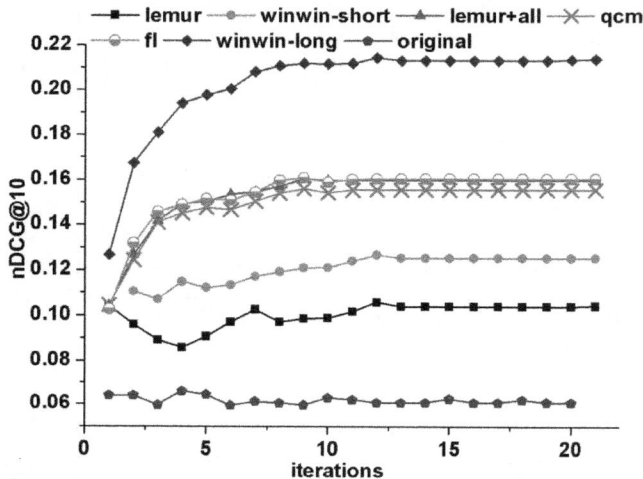

Figure 3: Immediate Search Accuracy (TREC 2013).

6.3 Immediate Search Accuracy

In order to compare the average immediate retrieval accuracy over all sessions, we first obtain the max lengths t_{max} of the sessions in a dataset. For TREC 2012, the maximum session length is 11. For TREC 2013, the maximum session length is 21. For the top 100 sessions in TREC 2014, the maximum session length is 8.

We compare the proposed algorithm *fl* with the *original* run, which is the retrieval results of the search engine used by the organizers to generate the sessions. We also compare our models to *lemur, lemur+all, qcm, winwin-short,* and *winwin-long* in this experiment. Among them, *qcm* and *winwin* are both RL-style session search systems, without using feedback learning.

Figures 2, 3 and 4 show the comparison result of above algorithms' immediate retrieval accuracy over TREC 2012, 2013 and 2014 datasets. Note that for the original run, it has one less iteration than the other runs, because the log file doesn't record retrieval results for the current/last query,

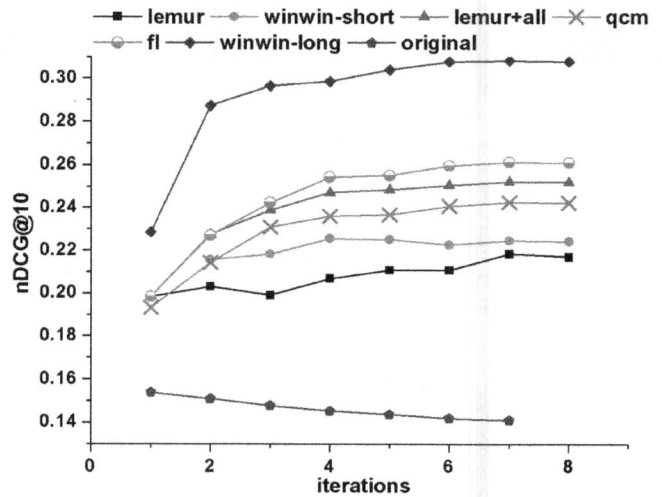

Figure 4: Immediate Search Accuracy (TREC 2014).

which means a session with n steps only has $n - 1$ steps in the original run. For the winwin-short run, we don't plot the point of the first iteration, because winwin-short uses user clicks in the current session as reward signal, but at the first iteration there is no user clicks available yet.

We are happy to see that the proposed algorithm, fl, performs the best besides the upper bound algorithm (winwin). It is a strong indicator that our algorithm is very effective for session search. Our algorithm leads the immediate search accuracy since the second search iteration, and the advantage becomes larger as the number of iterations increases while the session develops.

Moreover, for all three TREC datasets, the immediate accuracy of lemur+all, qcm, winwin-long and fl all climb up, when the session continues and feedbacks are continually collected. We observe a boost of search accuracy around the second search iteration for lemur+all, qcm, winwin-long and fl in TREC 2012. And we observe the same phenomenon for them in both TREC 2013 and TREC 2014. The gains from the later queries are marginal, which suggests that the first few queries may be more representative for the whole session than the later ones.

In addition, we observe a consistent retrieval accuracy order of above algorithms over all three TREC datasets. Since iteration 2, the retrieval accuracy order is winwin-long $\geq$ fl, qcm and lemur+all $\geq$ winwin-short $\geq$ lemur $\geq$ original. Here winwin, fl, qcm and lemur+all utilize every queries in the current session. Winwin-short shows a better retrieval accuracy than lemur, however it is the lowest nDCG@10 score among all RL-style algorithms. It suggests that pure click models which use clicks as the reward function is not adequate. More complex modeling, such as what we proposed here, including the query reformulations, previously retrieved documents and clicks, as a whole to produce the reward function is more promising.

Finally, we observe that most runs reach their convergence after 5 or 6 search iterations. It suggests that in a long session, feedbacks received after step 5 or 6 provide less benefits to the search algorithm than feedbacks from the earlier iterations. It suggests from another angle that the proposed session search algorithm is able to reach a pretty good whole-session search accuracy at an early stage, which will greatly save the user's search efforts in real-time interactive search.

We set qcm as the baseline system and performed a one-tailed t-test for proposed algorithms against the baseline. Note that qcm is a strong baseline. Nonetheless, the experiments show that fl could achieve a 3% and a 5% absolute nDCG@10 improvement over qcm for the 2nd and 3rd iterations on the TREC 2013 dataset. The improvements are statistically significant, with p-value 0.05. fl also achieves a 2%~7% absolute nDCG@10 improvement over qcm for all iterations on the TREC 2014 dataset, which is statistically significant with p-value 0.05.

7. DISCUSSION

Our solution to the feedback-learning framework adopts multiple-agent reinforcement learning. EM algorithms can often be guaranteed to converge to local minimum points. When there are two (or more) agents in the process, in theory, they are able to jointly reach the local optima for a common solution, which is known as the Nash equilibrium [15] in game theory.

To reach Nash equilibrium, it is assumed that all agents are rational and try their best to reach own local optima. This assumes that the user is rational and always produces good queries to show the search intent. However, the assumption is often not true. We see many non-optimal user actions, which impact negatively on the retrieval.

For instance, TREC 2014 Sessions 232 and 89 are two session sharing the same information need – "*You are writing a summary article about the Pocono Mountains region. Find as many relevant articles as you can describing the region, things to ee and do there ...*" In Session 232, the user submitted three queries: "pocono mountains," "mountains," and "mountains." We can see that the second and the last query are not very informative. It turns out that the number of relevant documents retrieved in the top 10 results drops from 6 to 4 when transitioning from the first query to the rest. It shows that when a user did not work hard enough to produce reasonable and cooperative queries, it is not surprising to see a negative impact on retrieval results. This suggests that it is important for both parties to commit to cooperative activities in session search. In the future, our research could potentially be used to detect user behaviors that could be explained by rational models and develop new user models from there.

On the contrary, in Session 89, the user submitted "Pocono Mountains", "Pocono Mountain parks", "Pocono Mountain things to do", "Pocono Mountain community", "Pocono Mountain community". Among the 6 relevant search results from the first query, the user clicked and examined "clueweb12-0304wb-75-0303" for 23.77 seconds. The document talks about "... *State National Parks Forests ... The Camelbeach Mountain Waterpark has hours of family-friendly activities for you. ... Hickory Run State Park and Boulder Field has acres of land sure to break in the toughest of hiking footwear* ...." The word "park" appears multiple times and probably inspired the user to create the second query "Pocono Mountain parks." The matching between the query change and the previously retrieved documents is interpreted as "exploitation" in our model, which generates positive reward for $r(t, h)$ as if the user performs optimally. As a result, in this run of search, the number of relevant documents in

top 10 boosts from 6 to 8. It suggests that when the user behaviors align well with our models, i.e., the user acts optimally, the cooperation between the user and the search engine functions well and yields good retrieval results. It leaves opportunities for future work in query suggestion.

8. CONCLUSION

In this paper, we study the interactions in session search from a new perspective. We model the user and the search engine as two equal partners who collaborate and explore together to achieve a common goal – satisfying the information need. Based on this assumption, we are the first to recognize the two-way feedback messages from both the search engine and the user, such as documents retrieved, user clicks and query formulations, as rewarding signals to guide session search in a reinforcement learning framework.

By modeling the two-way feedback from both the relevance and the exploration perspectives, we successfully integrate the rich forms of feedbacks in sessions, both explicit and implicit, and use them as rewards to enhance search accuracy in session search. The proposed EM algorithm provides an initial attempt to formalize the research along this direction. In the experiment, we compare our approaches' immediate search accuracy with the state-of-the-art session search algorithms over three years of TREC Session Track data. The results show that our approach greatly improves the immediate search accuracy by effectively utilizing the abundant feedback.

9. ACKNOWLEDGMENT

The research is supported by DARPA FA8750-14-2-0226, NSF IIS-1453721, and NSF CNS-1223825. Any opinions, findings, conclusions, or recommendations expressed in this paper are of the authors, and do not necessarily reflect those of the sponsor.

References

[1] Y. Artzi and L. Zettlemoyer. Bootstrapping semantic parsers from conversations. In *EMNLP '11*.

[2] D. P. Bertsekas. *Dynamic Programming: Deterministic and Stochastic Models*. Prentice-Hall, 1987.

[3] S. R. K. Branavan, H. Chen, L. S. Zettlemoyer, and R. Barzilay. Reinforcement learning for mapping instructions to actions. In *ACL '09*.

[4] S. R. K. Branavan, D. Silver, and R. Barzilay. Non-linear monte-carlo search in civilization ii. In *IJCAI'11*.

[5] S. R. K. Branavan, L. S. Zettlemoyer, and R. Barzilay. Reading between the lines: learning to map high-level instructions to commands. In *ACL '10*.

[6] D. L. Chen and R. J. Mooney. Learning to sportscast: A test of grounded language acquisition. In *ICML '08*.

[7] A. P. Dempster, N. M. Laird, and D. B. Rubin. Maximum Likelihood from Incomplete Data via the EM Algorithm. *J. Roy. Statist. Soc. Ser. B*, 39(1):1–38, 1977.

[8] A. Diriye, R. White, G. Buscher, and S. Dumais. Leaving so soon?: Understanding and predicting web search abandonment rationales. In *CIKM '12*, pages 1025–1034, 2012.

[9] J. Eisenstein, J. Clarke, D. Goldwasser, and D. Roth. Reading to learn: constructing features from semantic abstracts. In *EMNLP '09*.

[10] S. Fox, K. Karnawat, M. Mydland, S. Dumais, and T. White. Evaluating implicit measures to improve web search. *ACM Trans. Inf. Syst.*, 23(2), Apr. 2005.

[11] K. Georgila, C. Nelson, and D. Traum. Single-agent vs. multi-agent techniques for concurrent reinforcement learning of negotiation dialogue policies. In *ACL '14*.

[12] D. Goldwasser, R. Reichart, J. Clarke, and D. Roth. Confidence driven unsupervised semantic parsing. In *HLT '11*.

[13] D. Guan, S. Zhang, and H. Yang. Utilizing query change for session search. In *SIGIR '13*.

[14] R. Howard. *Dynamic Programming and Markov Process*. MIT Press, 1960.

[15] J. Hu and M. P. Wellman. Multiagent reinforcement learning: Theoretical framework and an algorithm. In *ICML '98*.

[16] K. Järvelin and J. Kekäläinen. Cumulated gain-based evaluation of ir techniques. *ACM Trans. Inf. Syst.*, 20(4):422–446, 2002.

[17] L. P. Kaelbling, M. L. Littman, and A. W. Moore. Reinforcement learning: A survey. *J Artificial Intelligence Res.*, 4:237–285, 1996.

[18] P. Kanani, A. McCallum, and S. Hu. Resource-bounded information extraction: Acquiring missing feature values on demand. In *Advances in Knowledge Discovery and Data Mining*, 2010.

[19] E. Kanoulas, B. Carterette, M. Hall, P. Clough, and M. Sanderson. Overview of the trec 2013 session track. In *TREC'13*.

[20] E. Kanoulas, B. Carterette, M. Hall, P. Clough, and M. Sanderson. Overview of the trec 2014 session track. In *TREC'14*.

[21] R. J. Kate and R. J. Mooney. Learning language semantics from ambiguous supervision. In *AAAI '07*.

[22] M. Lauer and M. A. Riedmiller. An algorithm for distributed reinforcement learning in cooperative multi-agent systems. In *ICML '00*.

[23] V. Lesser, B. Horling, F. Klassner, A. Raja, T. Wagner, and S. Zhang. BIG: An Agent for Resource-Bounded Information Gathering and Decision Making. *Artificial Intelligence Journal, Special Issue on Internet Information Agents*, 118(1-2):197–244, 2000.

[24] P. Liang, M. I. Jordan, and D. Klein. Learning semantic correspondences with less supervision. In *ACL '09*.

[25] M. L. Littman. markov games as a framework for multi-agent reinforcement learning. In *ICML '94*.

[26] R. T. Loftin, J. MacGlashan, B. Peng, M. E. Taylor, M. L. Littman, J. Huang, and D. L. Roberts. A strategy-aware technique for learning behaviors from discrete human feedback. In *AAAI '14*.

[27] J. Luo, S. Zhang, and H. Yang. Win-win search: Dual-agent stochastic game in session search. In *SIGIR '14*.

[28] D. Meger, P.-E. Forssén, K. Lai, S. Helmer, S. McCann, T. Southey, M. Baumann, J. J. Little, and D. G. Lowe. Curious george: An attentive semantic robot. *Robot. Auton. Syst.*, 56(6):503–511, 2008.

[29] L. Peshkin, K.-E. Kim, N. Meuleau, and L. P. Kaelbling. Learning to cooperate via policy search. In *UAI '00*.

[30] J. Schmidhuber. Sequential decision making based on direct search. In R. Sun and C. L. Giles, editors, *Sequence Learning: Paradigms, Algorithms, and Applications*. Springer, 2001.

[31] R. S. Sutton and A. G. Barto. *Reinforcement Learning: An Introduction*. MIT Press, 1998.

[32] M. Tan. Multi-agent reinforcement learning: Independent vs. cooperative agents. In *ICML '93*.

[33] A. Vogel and D. Jurafsky. Learning to follow navigational directions. In *ACL '10*.

[34] H. Yang, M. Sloan, and J. Wang. Tutorial on dynamic information retrieval modeling. In *SIGIR '14*.

[35] H. Yang, M. Sloan, and J. Wang. Tutorial on dynamic information retrieval modeling. In *WSDM '15*.

[36] C. Zhang, S. Abdallah, and V. Lesser. Efficient multi-agent reinforcement learning through automated supervision. In *AAAS '08*.

Learning Asymmetric Co-Relevance

Fiana Raiber
Technion, Israel
fiana@tx.technion.ac.il

Oren Kurland
Technion, Israel
kurland@ie.technion.ac.il

Filip Radlinski
Microsoft Cambridge, UK
filiprad@microsoft.com

Milad Shokouhi
Microsoft Cambridge, UK
milads@microsoft.com

ABSTRACT

Several applications in information retrieval rely on asymmetric co-relevance estimation; that is, estimating the relevance of a document to a query under the assumption that another document is relevant. We present a supervised model for learning an asymmetric co-relevance estimate. The model uses different types of similarities with the assumed relevant document and the query, as well as document-quality measures. Empirical evaluation demonstrates the merits of using the co-relevance estimate in various applications, including cluster-based and graph-based document retrieval. Specifically, the resultant performance transcends that of using a wide variety of alternative estimates, mostly symmetric inter-document similarity measures that dominate past work.

Categories and Subject Descriptors: H.3.3 [Information Search and Retrieval]: Retrieval models

Keywords: asymmetric co-relevance

1. INTRODUCTION

The cluster hypothesis states that *closely associated documents tend to be relevant to the same requests* [13, 38]. One operational interpretation of the hypothesis is that inter-document similarities can serve as *symmetric co-relevance* estimates. That is, given two highly similar documents, they will either both be relevant, or not, to any given query. Many cluster-based (e.g., [13, 40, 18, 26, 28, 16, 17, 33]) and some graph-based [49, 7, 20] retrieval methods implicitly assume the correctness of this hypothesis.

However, a number of retrieval methods and applications rely, by design, on estimating *asymmetric co-relevance* [40, 11, 7, 16, 29, 20, 33], namely the relevance of a document to a query given another document assumed to be relevant. For example, nearest-neighbor clustering of top-retrieved documents is used in many cluster-based document retrieval methods, where each cluster consists of a document and its nearest neighbors in the similarity space [28, 16, 33]. These

ICTIR'15, September 27–30, Northampton, MA, USA.
Copyright is held by the owner/author(s). Publication rights licensed to ACM.
ACM 978-1-4503-3833-2/15/09 ...$15.00.
DOI: http://dx.doi.org/10.1145/2808194.2809454 .

similarities presumably reflect asymmetric co-relevance. Voorhees' nearest-neighbor cluster hypothesis test is another example [40]: a relevant document is fixed and its co-relevant documents are sought. Yet another example is graph-based re-ranking methods, where the weight of a *directed* edge connecting two documents should reflect the probability that the target document is relevant assuming that the source document is relevant [20]. Despite all these applications, there has been very little work on devising asymmetric co-relevance estimates [49, 20]. Often, symmetric inter-document similarities are simply used instead [11, 28, 29].

We propose a novel model to learn an asymmetric co-relevance estimate. Most retrieval methods that rely on co-relevance estimates operate on a result list of the documents most highly ranked by initial search [16, 29, 20, 33]. Hence, our model is applied to documents in *some* initial result list.

The proposed model estimates co-relevance to a given document in the result list by utilizing rankings of documents in the list. The rankings are produced using a variety of functions. Some of the functions are based on the similarity with the query, the given document, or both. Several functions utilize passage-based document representations. Others utilize query-independent document-quality measures. We then train a supervised model that produces a co-relevance estimate by fusing the induced rankings. Given the ranking functions used, the learned estimate is inherently asymmetric.

Our experimental results show that the proposed estimate substantially outperforms numerous previously proposed co-relevance estimates in a variety of applications, including several state-of-the-art cluster-based and graph-based document retrieval methods.

Our main contributions can be summarized as follows.

- Presenting a novel supervised model for learning an asymmetric co-relevance estimate.

- Showing that using the proposed estimate in several state-of-the-art retrieval methods yields significant performance improvements over a wide variety of alternative estimates.

2. RELATED WORK

Numerous symmetric query-independent inter-document similarity measures were proposed for estimating co-relevance, including [2, 7, 20, 45]. Since documents co-relevant to one query are not necessarily co-relevant to another query [12], symmetric query-biased inter-document similarities have also been proposed [37, 30]. Our asymmetric co-relevance estimation approach integrates both query-biased and query-independent inter-document similarity measures, and leads to better performance in several retrieval methods and applications compared to using these measures separately.

The assumption underlying the optimum clustering framework is that documents should be deemed similar if they are co-relevant to many queries [10]. In contrast, one of the assumptions on which our method relies is that documents should be deemed co-relevant if they are similar given many ranking functions. We show that our method outperforms an inter-document similarity measure instantiated from the optimum clustering framework in various applications.

Beyond the document level, several inter-document similarity measures utilize query-independent passage-based similarities [41, 42, 32]. Inter-passage similarities were also used for document retrieval [15]. We also include several such methods in our supervised model [32], thereby benefiting from passage-level similarities when estimating co-relevance.

Asymmetric similarity measures have been used in the vector space model [49] and the language modeling framework [20] for asymmetric co-relevance estimation. The merits of one such language model estimate [48] were demonstrated with respect to other (e.g., symmetric) language-model-based estimates [20] and (e.g., asymmetric) vector-space-based measures [49]. This estimate is integrated in, and outperformed by, our method.

Models utilizing true or pseudo-relevance feedback [23] could also be viewed as addressing a general asymmetric co-relevance estimation task. These models aim to estimate the relevance of a document given that a *few* other documents are (or are assumed to be) relevant. Such models leverage the commonalities between the given documents (e.g., shared terms). In our settings such commonalities cannot be used as a *single* document is fixed, and co-relevance is estimated with respect to this document. However, we also modify a technique developed for (pseudo-) relevance feedback, term clipping[1] [1], to produce a query-biased model of the input document here. Using the cross entropy between document models results in an asymmetric co-relevance estimate that is, to the best of our knowledge, another contribution of our work. Furthermore, this estimate often outperforms other estimates that are used for reference comparisons, although the performance is in most cases worse than that attained by using our method.

Finally, we note that in contrast to previous work on co-relevance estimation, ours is the first that applies a learning-to-rank approach and uses query-independent document-quality measures.

3. ASYMMETRIC CO-RELEVANCE

The core task addressed by probabilistic retrieval methods is to estimate the probability that a given document d is relevant to a given query q [36]. There are retrieval settings where the goal is to estimate *co-relevance*; that is, the probability that documents d and d' are both relevant to q. For example, many cluster-based document retrieval methods rank document clusters by their presumed relevance to the query [27, 16, 29, 33]. Estimating cluster relevance amounts to estimating co-relevance of documents in the cluster.

The focus of much work on probabilistic retrieval methods is estimating the relevance likelihood of a single document [36, 21]. Similarly, our starting point is estimating the likelihood of *symmetric* co-relevance:

$$p(d, d'|R = 1, q), \qquad (1)$$

where R ($\in \{0, 1\}$) is a binary-relevance random variable. That is, the goal is to estimate the likelihood that d and d' are an unordered pair of documents relevant to q. Such estimation can rely, for example, not only on the similarity of each document to the query, but also on the similarity between the two documents. Equation 1 can be written

$$p(d'|d, R = 1, q)p(d|R = 1, q). \qquad (2)$$

Now, suppose that we fix document d and set as a goal to rank documents d' by the resultant symmetric co-relevance likelihood of pairing them with d. In that case, following Equation 2, the goal becomes estimating the relevance likelihood of d' assuming that d is relevant:

$$p(d'|d, R = 1, q). \qquad (3)$$

We refer to the resulting estimation task, which is our focus in this paper, as *asymmetric* co-relevance estimation. As already noted, quite a few retrieval methods and applications rely on such estimation (e.g., [40, 11, 7, 16, 29, 20]). For example, nearest-neighbor clustering which is often applied in cluster-based document retrieval [28, 16, 29, 33]; graph-based re-ranking methods [49, 7, 20]; and, Voorhees' nearest-neighbor cluster hypothesis test [40]. These applications are used in Section 5.2 for empirical evaluation of the estimate we devise and the reference comparisons.

4. LEARNING CO-RELEVANCE

Many methods that rely on asymmetric co-relevance estimation operate on top-retrieved documents returned by a retrieval method so as to re-rank them [28, 16, 29, 20, 33]. Therefore, we design our experimental setup to follow similar constraints, and apply our estimations only to documents in $\mathcal{D}_{\text{init}}$: an initial result list of documents from corpus $\mathcal{D}$ that are the most highly ranked in response to query q by a retrieval method; $sim_{\text{init}}(q, d)$ is the initial retrieval score assigned to document d in $\mathcal{D}_{\text{init}}$. As we show next, this allows us to view asymmetric co-relevance estimation as fusion of document rankings.

To estimate the co-relevance of documents in $\mathcal{D}_{\text{init}}$ to a fixed document d in $\mathcal{D}_{\text{init}}$ (Equation 3), we use a set of permutations (rankings) of $\mathcal{D}_{\text{init}}$, denoted $\Pi(\mathcal{D}_{\text{init}})$. A permutation π is induced using a document ranking function that assigns document d' ($\in \mathcal{D}_{\text{init}}$) the score: $score_\pi(d'; q, d)$. The ranking function can be based on (i) the similarity between d' and q; (ii) the similarity between d' and d which can be computed in a query dependent or independent fashion; and, (iii) the estimated quality of d' which serves for a relevance prior. We then define the co-relevance estimate of document d' with respect to d as

$$CoRel(d'; d, q) \stackrel{def}{=} \sum_{\pi \in \Pi(\mathcal{D}_{\text{init}})} f_\pi(d'; q, d)w(\pi); \qquad (4)$$

$f_\pi(d'; q, d)$ is the feature value of d' generated from the permutation π, and $w(\pi)$ is the permutation importance

---

[1]Namely, representing a document using a small set of terms which are assigned the highest probability by a language model induced from the document.

weight.[2] We note that Equation 4 represents a linear fusion of permutations [39].

Having framed co-relevance estimation as a linear function of features generated from the permutations, we next describe the ranking functions that serve to induce these permutations. Then, in Section 4.3 we describe the feature values and the approach employed for learning importance weights of permutations.

4.1 Permutations

Query-based permutation. As it was created in response to q, we use $\mathcal{D}_{\text{init}}$'s ranking as one of the permutations, π_Q, with the score of d' being its initial score in $\mathcal{D}_{\text{init}}$:

$$score_Q(d'; q, d) \overset{def}{=} sim_{\text{init}}(q, d').$$

Document-based permutations. The next set of permutations are created using an inter-textual similarity estimate $sim(\cdot, \cdot)$, using a bag-of-terms representation. Section 4.2 provides the details regarding the three estimates used in our experiments. Permutation π_D is created by ranking documents by their similarity with d:

$$score_D(d'; q, d) \overset{def}{=} sim(d, d'). \quad (5)$$

Documents can be long and topically heterogeneous. Thus, inter-document similarities, as well as document-query similarities, estimated using bag-of-terms, might not reflect aspects in specific zones (passages) in the documents. This observation has motivated much work on passage-based document retrieval (e.g., [25, 15]). Thus, the following permutations are induced by utilizing passage-based information. We write $g \in d$ to indicate that passage g belongs to document d.

Permutations π_{MaxP} and π_{AvgP} are based on the maximum and average similarity between passages in d' and d:

$$score_{\text{MaxP}}(d'; q, d) \overset{def}{=} \max_{g \in d, g' \in d'} sim(g, g');$$

$$score_{\text{AvgP}}(d'; q, d) \overset{def}{=} \underset{g \in d, g' \in d'}{\text{average}} sim(g, g').$$

Using passage-based representations for short or topically coherent documents has potential drawbacks [5]. Hence, we also use the permutations π_{MaxDP}, π_{AvgDP}, π_{MaxPD} and π_{AvgPD}. These are induced using the similarity between passages in d' and d as a whole, and vice versa. Specifically,

$$score_{\text{MaxDP}}(d'; q, d) \overset{def}{=} \max_{g' \in d'} sim(d, g');$$

$$score_{\text{AvgDP}}(d'; q, d) \overset{def}{=} \underset{g' \in d'}{\text{average}} sim(d, g');$$

$$score_{\text{MaxPD}}(d'; q, d) \overset{def}{=} \max_{g \in d} sim(g, d');$$

$$score_{\text{AvgPD}}(d'; q, d) \overset{def}{=} \underset{g \in d}{\text{average}} sim(g, d').$$

Query-document-based permutations. The ranking functions we define next compare d and d' in a query-dependent manner. Let $g_{q;x}$ be the passage most similar to q in document x: $g_{q;x} \overset{def}{=} \arg\max_{g \in x} sim(q, g)$. Then,

$$score_{\text{QPP}}(d'; q, d) \overset{def}{=} sim(g_{q;d}, g_{q;d'});$$

$$score_{\text{QDP}}(d'; q, d) \overset{def}{=} sim(d, g_{q;d'});$$

$$score_{\text{QPD}}(d'; q, d) \overset{def}{=} sim(g_{q;d}, d').$$

Document-quality-based permutations. Inspired by work on Web retrieval [4], we also use several query-independent document-quality measures to create permutations. These measures serve as estimates for the document prior relevance likelihood.

The first two measures are based on the assumption that a document containing many occurrences of highly frequent terms in the corpus (e.g., stopwords) adheres to the typical use of general language. Therefore, such a document is presumably of high quality [31, 4]. Considering a stopword as any term among the 100 most frequent alphanumeric terms in the corpus [31, 4], we define: (i) $score_{\text{SW1}}(d'; q, d)$: the ratio between the number of stopwords and non-stopwords in d'; and, (ii) $score_{\text{SW2}}(d'; q, d)$: the fraction of stopwords on a stopwords list that appear in d'.

The next two measures are based on the assumption that low content repetition in a document implies to the use of rich language [31, 4], and therefore to high document quality. Accordingly, we use the inverse compression ratio of a document: $score_{\text{ICR}}(d'; q, d)$ is the ratio between the compressed (using gzip) and uncompressed document size [31]. The second quality measure is the entropy of the term distribution in a document [4]. Formally, let $p_{d'}^{Dir[0]}(w)$ be the maximum-likelihood estimate of term w with respect to document d'. (Technical details are provided in Section 4.2.) Then,

$$score_{\text{ENT}}(d'; q, d) \overset{def}{=} - \sum_{w \in d'} p_{d'}^{Dir[0]}(w) \log p_{d'}^{Dir[0]}(w).$$

4.2 Inter-textual similarity measures

Some of the permutations used by our approach are created using an inter-textual similarity measure, $sim(\cdot, \cdot)$. We use three permutations in such cases, each instantiated using one of the three similarity measures described next.

The **LM** measure utilizes language models [22]:

$$sim_{\text{LM}}(x, y) \overset{def}{=} \exp\left(-CE\left(p_x^{Dir[0]}(\cdot) \,\middle\|\, p_y^{Dir[\mu]}(\cdot)\right)\right); \quad (6)$$

CE is the cross entropy measure; $p_z^{Dir[\mu]}(\cdot)$ is the Dirichlet-smoothed unigram language model induced from z with a smoothing parameter μ; here and after we set $\mu = 1000$ [22]; $p_x^{Dir[0]}(w)$ is the maximum likelihood estimate of term w with respect to x. This standard language-model measure was used in work on cluster-based and passage-based document retrieval [16, 17, 15, 20, 33].

The **Cos** measure [35], $sim_{\text{Cos}}(x, y)$, is the cosine between the tf.idf vectors representing x and y. Raw tf values are used. Herein, the idf value of term w is defined in all measures as: $idf_w \overset{def}{=} \log \frac{|\mathcal{D}| - df_w + 0.5}{df_w + 0.5}$; $|\mathcal{D}|$ is the number of documents in the corpus, and df_w is w's document frequency.

The **BM25** estimate [34], $sim_{\text{BM25}}(x, y)$, which was shown to be effective for estimating inter-document similarities [44], is the Okapi BM25 score assigned to y treating x as a query.

---

[2]The co-relevance estimates for documents d' ($\in \mathcal{D}_{\text{init}}$) do not constitute a probability distribution over $\mathcal{D}_{\text{init}}$, although they can be sum-normalized to that end. This normalization does not affect the ranking of documents with respect to d. We also note that the co-relevance estimate in Equation 4 is assumed to be correlated with the co-relevance probability defined in Equation 3 by the virtue of the way it is devised.

4.3 Asymmetric co-relevance estimation

To instantiate a specific co-relevance estimate using Equation 4 and the permutations described in Section 4.1, we have to define the feature value of a document per permutation and permutation importance weights.

As feature values generated from the permutations, we use $f_\pi(d'; q, d) \stackrel{def}{=} |\mathcal{D}_{\text{init}}| - rank(d', \pi) + 1$, where $|\mathcal{D}_{\text{init}}|$ is the number of documents in $\mathcal{D}_{\text{init}}$ and $rank(d', \pi)$ is the rank of document d' in permutation π; the rank of the highest ranked document is 1. This is motivated by work on the Borda fusion method [3], suggesting that such rank-to-score transformation is effective when combining the scores of different ranking functions.

The importance weights $w(\pi)$ can be learned using any learning-to-rank method [24]. As detailed in Section 5.3, we use SVM^{rank} [14] in our experiments. Thus, in the spirit of past work on fusing result lists (e.g., [39, 3]), we assume that the importance of a permutation created by a ranking function can be estimated based on the importance of permutations created for other (train) queries using the same function.

Given the above, the co-relevance estimate derived from Equation 4 is essentially a Weighted Borda fusion score [3]. Thus, in what follows we use **WBorda** to refer to our proposed co-relevance estimation method.[3]

Finally, we note that non-linear (in features) ranking functions could be used as an alternative to the linear function defined in Equation 4. We also experimented with using a gradient boosted regression trees method for learning permutation importance weights [9]. However, for all the applications considered for evaluation in Section 5, the resultant performance was inferior to that of using a linear method trained with SVM^{rank}. (Actual performance numbers are omitted as they convey no additional insight.)

5. EVALUATION

We study the performance of several applications when using our WBorda method to estimate asymmetric co-relevance. We compare WBorda with a large number of reference comparison estimates. Table 1 summarizes the estimates and applications. One application relies by design on a symmetric co-relevance estimate. Thus, to symmetrize WBorda and the asymmetric reference comparisons in this case, we use:

$$\frac{CoRel(d'; d, q) + CoRel(d; d', q)}{2}. \qquad (7)$$

5.1 Reference comparison estimates

There has been very little prior work on asymmetric co-relevance estimation [49, 20]. Thus, many of the reference comparisons are symmetric inter-document similarity measures. Most of the reference comparisons are query-independent; a few use passage-based information. In comparison, the WBorda method integrates query-dependent and query-independent information, as well as passage-based.

Basic estimates. Using each of LM, Cos and BM25 (described in Section 4.2) to measure inter-document similarities constitutes a reference comparison. The resultant methods are also used in WBorda to create the three π_D permutations (see Equation 5). LM and BM25 are asymmetric while Cos is symmetric. Some work [20] demonstrated the merits of LM as an asymmetric co-relevance estimate with respect to other asymmetric and symmetric estimates [49, 20]. A symmetric BM25 estimate, **OK**, was specifically designed for estimating inter-document similarities [45].

Information theoretic estimate. The information theoretic estimate, **IT**, is a symmetric parameter-free inter-document similarity measure. It is defined as the ratio between the amount of information shared by two documents and the amount of information contained in each [2].

Query sensitive estimates. Query sensitive similarity estimates (QSSM) are symmetric query-biased inter-document similarities [37]. These estimates use a vector representation of the terms shared by two documents, d' and d. The cosine between this vector and that of the query is used to scale $sim_{\text{Cos}}(d', d)$ in the **QSSM(M1)** measure, and is linearly interpolated with $sim_{\text{Cos}}(d', d)$, using a free-parameter α, in the **QSSM(M3)** measure.

Probabilistic estimate. The odds-based co-relevance estimate, **ProbCoR**, is a language-model-based asymmetric query-biased inter-document similarity measure proposed for symmetric co-relevance estimation [30]. The estimate is based on a linear interpolation of the similarity between d and d' and the similarity of each to the query; an interpolation parameter α is used.[4]

Optimum clustering framework estimates. The assumption of the optimum clustering framework, **OCF**, is that documents should be deemed similar if they are relevant to the same queries [10]. A symmetric inter-document similarity estimate instantiated from OCF is:

$$sim_{\text{OCF}}(d', d) \stackrel{def}{=} \sum_{w \in d' \cup d} sim(w, d') sim(w, d),$$

where each term w ($\in d' \cup d$) that occurs in at least one of the two documents represents a query.[5] We use here the three estimates, LM, Cos and BM25, for $sim(\cdot, \cdot)$, which results in three OCF instantiations: OCF(LM), OCF(Cos) and OCF(BM25).

Passage-based estimates. The asymmetric **AvgMaxP** estimate [32], proposed for agglomerative clustering, uses whole-document-based and passage-based inter-document similar-

---

[3] If we apply min-max normalization to $score_\pi(d'; q, d)$ and use the normalized score for $f_\pi(d'; q, d)$, then the co-relevance estimate amounts to a weighted CombSUM fusion score [8, 39]. The resulting performance in the applications we consider is inferior to that of using Borda's score. (Performance numbers are omitted as they convey no additional insight).

[4] $sim_{\text{ProbCoR}}(d', d) \stackrel{def}{=} (1 - \alpha) sim_{\text{LM1}}(d', d) + \alpha sim_{\text{LM1}}(q, d)$ $+ sim_{\text{LM1}}(q, d')$, where $sim_{\text{LM1}}(x, y) \stackrel{def}{=} \log \left(\frac{\mu}{\sum_{w'} tf_{w', y} + \mu} \right)$ $+ \sum_w p_x^{Dir[0]}(w) \log \left(\frac{tf_{w, y}}{\mu p_{\mathcal{D}}^{Dir[0]}(w)} + 1 \right)$; $tf_{w, x}$ is the number of times w appears in x; $\mu = 1000$.

[5] For the large corpora we use, having each term in the vocabulary represent a query, as originally proposed [10], is computationally expensive. Therefore, we only consider terms that occur in at least one of the two documents.

ities as is the case for WBorda:

$$sim_{\text{AvgMaxP}}(d', d) \stackrel{def}{=} (1 - \alpha)sim(d', d) +$$

$$\frac{\alpha}{|\{g' : g' \in d'\}|} \sum_{g' \in d'} \max_{g \in d} sim(g', g);$$

$|\{g' : g' \in d'\}|$ is the number of passages in d'. While Avg-MaxP was originally instantiated using Cos [32], here we also use LM and BM25 which results in three measures: AvgMaxP(LM), AvgMaxP(Cos) and AvgMaxP(BM25).[6]

Relevance-model-based estimate. We study an additional asymmetric co-relevance estimate, **RM3**, that utilizes relevance models [23, 1]. To the best of our knowledge, this estimate has not been utilized in the various applications that we use for evaluation. (See Section 5.2.) The co-relevance of d' to d is estimated by the similarity of d' with a query-biased representation of the terms most "dominant" in d:

$$sim_{\text{RM3}}(d', d) \stackrel{def}{=} \exp\left(-CE\left(p_{R(d,q)}(\cdot) \,\Big|\Big|\, p_{d'}^{Dir[\mu]}(\cdot)\right)\right);$$

$R(d, q)$ is relevance model #3 [1] which uses a parameter α:

$$p_{R(d,q)}(w) \stackrel{def}{=} (1 - \alpha)p_q^{Dir[0]}(w) + \alpha p_{d^{clip}}^{Dir[\mu]}(w);$$

$p_{d^{clip}}^{Dir[\mu]}(\cdot)$ is a clipped language model of d attained by setting to zero the probabilities of all but the β terms (β is a free parameter) to which the Dirichlet-smoothed language model induced from d assigns the highest probability; sum-normalization is applied to the probabilities of these terms to yield a valid language model.[7]

Unweighted Borda estimate. To study the merits of using a supervised learning model to set the permutation importance weights in WBorda, we also use an unsupervised model that utilizes the same permutations but with uniform importance weights. The resultant Unweighted Borda fusion method, **UBorda**, sets

$$CoRel(d'; d, q) \stackrel{def}{=} \sum_{\pi \in \Pi(\mathcal{D}_{\text{init}})} f_\pi(d'; q, d). \text{ (See Equation 4.)}$$

5.2 Applications

We next describe the applications in which WBorda, and the reference comparisons, are used. All applications, except for one (Regularization), rely by design on an asymmetric co-relevance estimate. Yet, in past work, symmetric inter-document similarities were also used in these applications. Table 1 provides a summary of the applications.

The nearest-neighbor cluster hypothesis test. Voorhees' nearest-neighbor (NN) test [40] is the most commonly used test for the cluster hypothesis. The test is also often used to compare inter-document similarities [37, 30, 45].

For each *relevant* document $d \in \mathcal{D}_{\text{init}}$, a ranking of all the documents $d' \in \mathcal{D}_{\text{init}} \setminus \{d\}$ is created using a co-relevance estimate. This is a natural asymmetric co-relevance estimation task. Ranking effectiveness is measured using precision at top ranks or average precision. The final NN test score is the average over all queries in a test set of the average ranking effectiveness for the relevant documents.

---

[6]To avoid using negative values in the estimates, min-max normalization was applied to the similarity values of BM25, OK, ProbCoR, OCF(BM25) and AvgMaxP(BM25).

[7]Using RM3 in our WBorda method to produce a permutation did not result in consistent, or substantial, performance improvements in the applications we consider.

Table 1: Summary of the reference comparison estimates and applications considered.

Reference Comparisons		Applications	
Asymmetric	Symmetric	Asymmetric	Symmetric
LM	Cos	NN test	Regularization
BM25	OK	Interpf	
ProbCoR	IT	ClustMRF	
AvgMaxP	QSSM	ClustRanker	
RM3	OCF	RWI	

We note that the NN cluster hypothesis test is essentially a relevance-feedback-based retrieval task. That is, a single relevant document, $d \in \mathcal{D}_{\text{init}}$, is provided, and the task is to re-rank $\mathcal{D}_{\text{init}}$ using this relevance feedback.

Cluster-based document retrieval. There are various document re-ranking methods that utilize information induced from clusters of documents in an initially retrieved list [46, 26, 19, 28, 27, 47, 16, 29, 17, 33]. Most of these methods were applied using nearest-neighbor (NN) clustering which was shown to be highly effective with respect to other clustering schemes [17, 33].

A cluster is created for each document $d \in \mathcal{D}_{\text{init}}$ by ranking the documents $d' \in \mathcal{D}_{\text{init}} \setminus \{d\}$ with respect to d; often, inter-document similarities are used. A cluster then comprises d and the $k - 1$ most highly ranked documents, i.e., d's $k - 1$ nearest neighbors. Thus, $|\mathcal{D}_{\text{init}}|$ (overlapping) clusters are created, each contains k documents. Because the documents in $\mathcal{D}_{\text{init}}$ are ranked with respect to a fixed d, in a query context (i.e., $\mathcal{D}_{\text{init}}$), the task of creating a nearest-neighbor cluster amounts to estimating asymmetric co-relevance as was the case for the nearest-neighbor cluster hypothesis test. Indeed, using the precision-at-top-ranks evaluation metric in the nearest-neighbor test corresponds to measuring the percentage of relevant documents in a nearest-neighbor cluster constructed from a relevant document.

The cluster-based re-ranking methods that we use apply various approaches of utilizing cluster-based information. Thus, to ameliorate metric divergence effects [24], we evaluate the quality of a co-relevance estimate used to create the clusters with respect to re-ranking effectiveness.

The interpolation-f [17] method, **Interpf**, interpolates the (normalized) initial retrieval score of a document, $sim_{\text{init}}(q, d)$, with its (normalized) cluster-based score; λ is a free interpolation parameter. Interpf could be viewed as a generalized version of methods that apply cluster-based [26] and topic-based [43] document language model smoothing.

Interpf ranks documents directly using cluster-based information. Some other cluster-based methods apply a two-steps procedure. First, document clusters are ranked based on their presumed relevance to the information need underlying the query. Then, the cluster ranking is transformed to document ranking by replacing each cluster with its documents while omitting repeats; the order of documents in a cluster is determined by their initial retrieval scores. The two state-of-the-art cluster-based methods that we consider differ in the way by which clusters are ranked with respect to the query, i.e., the rankings produced in the first step.

The **ClustMRF** method ranks a cluster based on integrating, using a learning-to-rank approach, different information types that presumably attest to the cluster relevance [33]. Some of these information types, the stopwords-based measures, SW1, SW2, the inverse compression ratio

ICR, and the entropy of the term distribution ENT, are also used by WBorda to create permutations. We use WBorda, and the reference comparisons, not only to create the clusters, but also to induce the inter-document similarities used for measuring cluster cohesion in ClustMRF.

The **ClustRanker** method [16] ranks clusters using cluster-query, document-query, inter-document and inter-cluster similarities. We use WBorda, and the reference comparisons, in ClustRanker not only to induce clusters, but also to compute inter-document similarities for inducing document centrality. A free parameter λ controls the balance between using whole-cluster-based and document-based information.

In all the cluster-based retrieval methods described above, query-cluster, document-cluster and inter-cluster similarities are induced using the LM estimate from Equation 6.[8]

Graph-based document retrieval. The graph-based reranking methods that we consider use a co-relevance estimate to determine the nearest neighbors of a document and to set edge weights in a weighted nearest-neighbor graph. We evaluate the quality of the co-relevance estimate used with respect to the resultant re-ranking effectiveness.

The recursive weighted influx method (**RWI**) [20] induces document centrality over a nearest-neighbor graph composed of the documents in $\mathcal{D}_{init}$; the PageRank algorithm is used with a dumping factor γ. Documents in $\mathcal{D}_{init}$ are re-ranked by scaling their initial retrieval score, $sim_{init}(q, d)$, with their centrality value. The weight of a directed edge connecting document d with one of its nearest neighbors d' reflects the likelihood that d' is relevant assuming that d is relevant. Thus, to determine the nearest neighbors of a document, and to set edge weights, asymmetric co-relevance estimates are used. Originally, an asymmetric language model inter-document similarity measure was used.[9]

Following the cluster hypothesis, the **Regularization** reranking method is based on the premise that similar documents in $\mathcal{D}_{init}$ should be assigned with similar retrieval scores [7]. The method uses a nearest-neighbor graph to regularize (with a parameter γ) the initial retrieval score of document d, $sim_{init}(q, d)$, using the scores of its nearest neighbors. A *symmetric* co-relevance estimate is used to determine nearest neighbors and to set edge weights. Originally, the multinomial diffusion kernel, **MDK**, which relies on a free-parameter t, was used.

5.3 Experimental setup

Data & evaluation metrics. We conducted our experiments on several TREC datasets specified in Table 2. AP and ROBUST are small collections, composed mainly of news articles. WT10G is a small Web collection and GOV2 is a crawl of the .gov domain. CW09B is the Category B of the ClueWeb09 Web collection and CW12B is the Category B of ClueWeb12. Two additional Web settings, CW09BF and CW12BF, were created by filtering out from the initial rankings of CW09B and CW12B, respectively, documents

[8]A cluster is represented by the big document that results from concatenating its constituent documents [28, 16, 29, 17]. The order of concatenation has no effect since unigram language models are used.

[9]The measure [20] is closely connected to the LM measure (Equation 6) in that it uses the exponent of the negative KL divergence between the documents' language models.

Table 2: Data used for experiments.

corpus	# of documents	data	queries
AP	242,918	Disks 1-3	51-150
ROBUST	528,155	Disks 4-5 (-CR)	301-450,600-700
WT10G	1,692,096	WT10g	451-550
GOV2	25,205,179	GOV2	701-850
CW09B CW09BF	50,220,423	ClueWeb09 Category B	1-200
CW12B CW12BF	52,343,021	ClueWeb12 Category B	201-250

assigned with a score below 50 by Waterloo's spam classifier [6]. The residual corpus rankings were used to create the initial result lists, which presumably contain fewer spam documents than those for CW09B and CW12B.

Topic titles served as queries. We applied Krovetz stemming to queries and documents, and removed stopwords from queries using the INQUERY list. The Indri toolkit[10] was used for experiments.

All the applications described in Section 5.2 operate on an initial result list, $\mathcal{D}_{init}$. The list contains the $|\mathcal{D}_{init}| = 50$ documents d in the corpus that yield the highest $sim_{init}(q, d) \stackrel{def}{=} sim_{LM}(q, d)$; i.e., a standard language-model-based initial ranking is used. Such a short (often, language-model-based) initial result list was also used in the original reports on the applications we use here [40, 7, 16, 17, 33].

The mean average precision of the 50 documents in $\mathcal{D}_{init}$ (**MAP**) and the precision of the top-5 documents (**p@5**) serve for retrieval evaluation metrics. Statistically significant differences of performance are determined using the two-tailed paired t-test with a 95% confidence level.

Training parameters. The permutation importance weights used in WBorda were learned using SVM^{rank} [14] applied with a linear kernel and default free-parameter values. In the learning phase, each document d ($\in \mathcal{D}_{init}$) which is relevant to q served as a "pseudo query" for which all other documents d' ($\in \mathcal{D}_{init} \setminus \{d\}$) are either relevant or not according to TREC's binary relevance judgements for q.[11]

The permutation weights, the free-parameter values of the reference comparison estimates, and those of the retrieval methods that serve as applications, were set using ten-fold cross validation; folds were created based on query IDs. Unless stated otherwise, MAP served as the optimization criterion in the learning phase. For WBorda, the same training set was used to learn the permutation weights and to set the passage size. We used half-overlapping fixed-size windows of terms for passages as these were shown to be highly effective for passage-based retrieval [25, 15]. The window size used for WBorda and AvgMaxP was selected from $\{100, 150, 200, 250, 300\}$.

The values of the parameters α (QSSM(M3), ProbCoR, AvgMaxP and RM3) and λ (Interpf, ClustRanker and ClustMRF) were selected from $\{0, 0.1, \ldots, 1\}$. The number of nearest neighbors, k, used in RWI and Regularization, is in $\{5, 10, 25, 50\}$. The size, k, of the nearest-neighbor clusters used, specifically, in Interpf, ClustRanker and ClustMRF, was set to 5 following the original reports [16, 17, 33]. The values of t^{-1} (Regularization) and γ (RWI and Regulariza-

[10]www.lemurproject.org/indri

[11]Learning the weights by ranking documents with respect to both relevant and non-relevant documents resulted in less effective performance.

Table 3: Voorhees' nearest-neighbor cluster hypothesis test. '*b*' marks statistically significant difference with WBorda. The best result in a column is boldfaced.

	AP		ROBUST		WT10G		GOV2		CW09B		CW09BF		CW12B		CW12BF	
	MAP	p@4	MAP	p@4	MAP	p@4	MAP	p@4	MAP	p@4	MAP	p@4	MAP	p@4	MAP	p@4
LM	12.8	77.0	21.6_b	68.5_b	13.5_b	62.5_b	14.2_b	81.3_b	23.2_b	72.5_b	23.6_b	71.9_b	24.5_b	51.4_b	20.9_b	47.6_b
Cos	11.4_b	70.4_b	19.6_b	62.2_b	13.6_b	62.4_b	14.2_b	80.1_b	22.7_b	69.1_b	23.4_b	70.6_b	25.3_b	54.8_b	21.6_b	51.8_b
BM25	12.8	77.1	22.0_b	68.8_b	14.3_b	63.1_b	14.6_b	83.2_b	23.0_b	71.4_b	23.5_b	71.3_b	24.6_b	53.1_b	21.2_b	48.5_b
IT	12.8	77.0	21.8_b	68.9_b	14.2_b	64.4_b	14.5_b	81.8_b	23.5	73.0	23.8_b	71.1_b	26.0_b	54.7	22.6	53.7
OK	12.8	**78.1**	22.1_b	69.8_b	14.4_b	64.0_b	14.7_b	83.6_b	23.0_b	71.0_b	23.7_b	71.1_b	25.1_b	53.9_b	21.4_b	48.2_b
QSSM(M1)	11.6_b	66.8_b	20.1_b	59.0_b	13.0_b	58.4_b	13.5_b	76.2_b	20.8_b	58.9_b	22.6_b	66.9_b	23.0_b	49.7_b	19.4_b	44.1_b
QSSM(M3)	11.8_b	70.6_b	20.7_b	64.9_b	13.8_b	63.5_b	14.2_b	80.1_b	22.7_b	69.1_b	23.4_b	70.3_b	25.2_b	53.9_b	21.4_b	51.8_b
ProbCoR	**13.0**	77.9	23.5	73.6	14.2_b	64.2_b	14.4_b	82.9_b	23.3_b	72.2_b	24.3_b	74.3_b	25.3_b	54.2	22.0	50.2_b
OCF(LM)	10.6_b	60.0_b	16.1_b	42.8_b	11.2_b	52.7_b	13.2_b	71.3_b	19.7_b	47.2_b	21.6_b	60.7_b	23.8_b	53.0_b	20.3_b	47.9_b
OCF(Cos)	11.4_b	70.4_b	19.6_b	62.2_b	13.6_b	62.4_b	14.2_b	80.1_b	22.7_b	69.1_b	23.4_b	70.6_b	25.3_b	54.8_b	21.6_b	51.8_b
OCF(BM25)	12.8	77.7	22.5_b	70.5_b	14.3_b	63.6_b	14.6_b	83.4_b	22.9_b	70.7_b	23.7_b	72.3_b	25.0_b	51.3_b	21.5	48.9_b
AvgMaxP(LM)	12.9	77.6	22.6_b	70.5_b	14.7_b	65.3_b	14.6_b	81.8_b	23.3_b	72.4_b	23.8_b	71.5_b	25.9_b	55.9	22.1	48.4_b
AvgMaxP(Cos)	11.4_b	70.7_b	19.7_b	62.1_b	13.9_b	64.3_b	14.3_b	80.5_b	23.0_b	71.0_b	23.6_b	71.7_b	26.4	58.8	22.0	51.7_b
AvgMaxP(BM25)	12.8	77.2	22.0_b	69.1_b	14.2_b	63.8_b	14.7_b	83.3_b	22.9_b	70.8_b	23.6_b	72.3_b	25.4_b	53.3_b	21.3_b	48.9_b
RM3	12.9	77.0	23.4_b	73.2_b	14.6_b	67.5_b	14.7_b	82.9_b	**23.7**	73.4	24.5	73.8_b	26.5	56.4	23.2	52.8_b
UBorda	12.7	76.6	22.8_b	71.3_b	**15.5**	69.7	14.8_b	82.6_b	23.6	72.4_b	24.2_b	72.3_b	26.9	57.2	23.2	55.1
WBorda	12.9	76.9	**23.7**	**74.4**	15.4	**71.0**	**15.1**	**85.1**	**23.7**	**74.8**	**24.7**	**76.9**	**28.3**	**62.4**	**24.6**	**62.2**

tion) were selected from $\{0.1, 0.2, \dots, 0.9\}$. The number of terms, β, used in RM3 was set to a value in $\{25, 50, 75, 100\}$. The free parameters of Okapi BM25, k_1 and b, are set as follows. When using the BM25 inter-textual estimate in our WBorda method, and in the OCF(BM25) and AvgMaxP(BM25) reference comparisons, default parameter values are used: $k_1 = 1.2$ and $b = 0.75$. When using BM25 as a stand-alone reference comparison, or in the highly effective recently proposed OK estimate that serves as a reference comparison [45], k_1 and b are set to values in $\{1.2, 2, 4, 8, 12\}$, and $\{0.25, 0.5, 0.75, 1\}$, respectively.

5.4 Experimental results

In this section, we compare the effectiveness of WBorda with that of the various reference comparison estimates in the different applications (summarized in Section 5.2).

The nearest-neighbor cluster hypothesis test. The results of the nearest-neighbor (NN) cluster hypothesis test, applied with the various co-relevance estimates, are presented in Table 3. To evaluate the effectiveness of the rankings created with respect to each relevant document, we used MAP, computed for the 49 documents in $\mathcal{D}_{init} \setminus \{d\}$, and p@4, computed for the 4 most highly ranked documents.[12] The free-parameter values were set to optimize MAP and p@4 separately (on the train query set), as each of the two metrics is a somewhat different quantification of the extent to which the cluster hypothesis holds according to the test.

Our main observation based on Table 3 is that in the vast majority of the cases the cluster hypothesis, as measured by the NN test, holds to the largest extent when the WBorda estimate is used. Although WBorda is outperformed in some cases by some reference comparisons for AP and by UBorda for WT10G, the differences are not statistically significant.

In a pairwise comparison of RM3 with each of the other estimates, we see that in most relevant comparisons (8 experimental settings × 2 evaluation metrics) the test performance attained for RM3 is better; we note that many of these differences are also statistically significant. (To avoid

---

[12] We use p@4 since using four nearest neighbors of a document conceptually corresponds to using nearest-neighbor clusters of five documents as is the case for the cluster-based retrieval methods we evaluate below.

Table 4: Top four permutations. The inter-textual similarity estimates used to instantiate the permutations are specified in parentheses.

	1	2	3	4
AP	D(BM25)	Q	AvgDP(LM)	AvgP(LM)
ROBUST	Q	ICR	MaxDP(LM)	MaxPD(BM25)
WT10G	SW2	QPP(Cos)	ICR	MaxP(BM25)
GOV2	AvgPD(Cos)	Q	AvgP(LM)	ICR
CW09B	SW1	Q	MaxDP(Cos)	AvgDP(BM25)
CW09BF	Q	AvgPD(Cos)	SW2	AvgPD(BM25)
CW12B	AvgPD(Cos)	SW1	AvgP(Cos)	ENT
CW12BF	Q	AvgPD(Cos)	ENT	SW1

cluttering the table, we do not mark the significance of differences between the reference comparison estimates.) Recall that using RM3 as a co-relevance estimate for the NN cluster hypothesis test, as well as for the retrieval methods we consider below, is novel to this study. Nevertheless, the test performance for RM3 is almost always lower — often to a statistically significant degree — than that for WBorda. The only case in which RM3 outperforms WBorda is p@4 for AP, yet the difference is not statistically significant.

Comparing the weighted WBorda estimate with its unweighted version UBorda, we see that the test performance for UBorda is better than that for WBorda only in a single case of MAP for WT10G, but the difference is not statistically significant. This finding attests to the merits of using a supervised model to set the permutation weights in WBorda.

Permutation analysis. We next turn to study the relative importance of the (35) permutations used by WBorda. The permutation weights are learned in an application-independent manner. That is, a relevant document is fixed and all other documents are ranked with respect to this document and the query. (Refer to Section 5.3 for details.) The passage size used by WBorda is learned per application. Thus, to analyze permutation importance in an application-independent way, we averaged over folds and passage sizes the weights assigned to the permutations by SVM^{rank} in the learning phase. Table 4 presents for each experimental setting the four permutations assigned with the highest averaged weights.

We can see that all four types of permutations (query-based, document-based, query-document-based and document-quality-based) have at least one representative in Table 4.

Table 5: Using Interpf, ClustMRF and ClustRanker to re-rank the initial list. 'i' and 'b' mark statistically significant differences with the initial ranking (Init) and WBorda, respectively. The best result in a column for a cluster-based method is boldfaced.

	AP		ROBUST		WT10G		GOV2		CW09B		CW09BF		CW12B		CW12BF	
	MAP	p@5	MAP	p@5	MAP	p@5	MAP	p@5	MAP	p@5	MAP	p@5	MAP	p@5	MAP	p@5
Init	9.0	43.6	18.8	48.7	13.8	33.4	11.4	55.5	9.9	22.7	12.7	34.7	14.2	23.6	14.0	22.8
							Interpf									
LM	9.1	46.1	19.4^i	48.8_b	13.4	32.6_b	12.0_b^i	56.4_b	12.2_b^i	32.7_b^i	13.5_b^i	38.0_b	14.2	23.6	13.6	22.8
Cos	8.8_b	43.4	19.2	49.2	13.8	35.7	11.9_b^i	55.0_b	11.8_b^i	29.4_b^i	13.5_b^i	37.5_b	14.2	23.6	13.3	21.2
BM25	9.1	**48.3**	19.4^i	48.4_b	13.7	33.8_b	12.0_b^i	57.2_b	12.1_b^i	31.4_b^i	13.3_b^i	37.0_b	14.0	22.8	**14.3**	22.4
IT	9.2	46.9	$\mathbf{19.7}^i$	49.2	**13.9**	35.5	12.0_b^i	56.1_b	12.3_b^i	31.7_b^i	13.6_b^i	37.0_b	14.2	23.6	13.7	23.6
RM3	9.2	46.1	19.5^i	49.9	12.9	34.4	12.1_b^i	58.2	12.6^i	35.1^i	13.9^i	38.4_b^i	14.2	20.8	13.8	22.0
UBorda	9.2	46.9	19.4^i	49.0_b	13.0	35.3	12.0_b^i	56.4_b	12.0_b^i	31.2_b^i	13.4_b^i	36.4_b	14.2	23.6	13.6	20.8
WBorda	**9.3**	47.7	19.4^i	**50.4**	13.3	**36.5**	$\mathbf{12.6}^i$	$\mathbf{61.5}^i$	$\mathbf{12.8}^i$	$\mathbf{36.4}^i$	$\mathbf{14.4}^i$	$\mathbf{41.1}^i$	**16.7**	**25.2**	13.9	**24.0**
							ClustMRF									
LM	9.3	42.2	19.4	48.6_b	14.3	36.7	$\mathbf{12.7}_b^i$	$\mathbf{66.1}^i$	13.7^i	$\mathbf{40.3}^i$	$\mathbf{14.8}^i$	41.4^i	20.9^i	32.0^i	18.5^i	33.2^i
Cos	8.4_b^i	40.2	18.4_b	48.6_b	14.8	37.7	12.4^i	62.8^i	13.6^i	37.5^i	14.2^i	39.9^i	21.1_b^i	35.2^i	19.5^i	30.8^i
BM25	9.1	**43.8**	19.3	51.1	13.8	37.9	12.2_b^i	64.1^i	13.3_b^i	38.4^i	14.7^i	42.6^i	18.7^i	32.0^i	16.9	29.2
OCF(BM25)	9.5	42.8	$\mathbf{19.6}^i$	50.9	13.9	39.0	12.0_b^i	61.8^i	12.8_b^i	37.5^i	14.4^i	$\mathbf{43.4}^i$	21.2^i	31.2	$\mathbf{21.7}^i$	32.0^i
AvgMaxP(LM)	9.0_b	42.0	19.5^i	50.8	14.7	38.1	12.6^i	63.0^i	13.7^i	38.1^i	14.6^i	41.6^i	$\mathbf{21.9}^i$	32.0^i	18.4^i	30.0
UBorda	9.2_b	**43.8**	$\mathbf{19.6}^i$	50.8	$\mathbf{15.8}^i$	$\mathbf{40.6}^i$	12.4^i	63.0^i	13.2^i	39.1^i	14.5^i	41.2^i	21.4^i	$\mathbf{35.6}^i$	20.3^i	34.4^i
WBorda	**9.6**	43.6	$\mathbf{19.6}^i$	$\mathbf{52.1}^i$	14.9	37.9	$\mathbf{12.7}^i$	65.7^i	$\mathbf{14.0}^i$	40.2^i	14.6^i	42.8^i	19.0^i	34.8^i	20.5^i	$\mathbf{35.2}^i$
							ClustRanker									
LM	9.3	47.5	19.2	46.2_b	13.2	29.9	12.1_b^i	58.0_b	12.2_b^i	32.2_b	12.8_b	32.3_b	13.1	20.8_b	10.2_b^i	13.2_b^i
Cos	8.7	41.8	17.9_b^i	42.8_b^i	12.4_b	28.9	11.6_b	53.8_b	11.5_b^i	28.6_b	12.9_b	32.0_b	12.6_b	17.6_b^i	13.0_b	21.6_b
BM25	9.0	45.9	**19.3**	47.4_b	12.7	30.3	12.3^i	59.9_b	11.9_b	29.9_b	13.0	35.7_b	16.4	23.2	12.8_b	16.8_b
ProbCoR	**9.4**	**47.7**	19.1	45.9_b	13.3	32.8	11.8_b	53.5_b	12.6^i	33.4_b^i	13.1_b	35.6_b	14.0	22.4	12.5_b	21.2_b
RM3	8.9	45.7	18.3_b	43.8_b^i	13.0	29.7	12.2^i	58.5_b	12.4_b^i	32.7_b^i	$\mathbf{14.1}^i$	39.8^i	$\mathbf{18.5}^i$	$\mathbf{31.6}^i$	12.9_b	23.6_b
UBorda	8.5_b	40.4_b	19.1	48.7	13.7	**33.2**	12.4^i	61.8^i	11.6_b^i	29.4_b	$\mathbf{14.1}^i$	39.4^i	14.2	20.8_b	14.5	24.8_b
WBorda	9.0	45.7	19.1	**50.4**	**13.8**	32.2	$\mathbf{12.6}^i$	$\mathbf{65.1}^i$	$\mathbf{13.1}^i$	$\mathbf{38.6}^i$	14.0^i	$\mathbf{40.5}^i$	15.9	29.6	$\mathbf{19.3}^i$	$\mathbf{34.4}^i$

The query-based permutation π_Q is almost always among the top four permutations[13], which attests to the merits of using the query for estimating asymmetric co-relevance. One of the document-based permutations that uses passages, i.e., π_{MaxP}, π_{AvgP}, π_{MaxDP}, or π_{AvgPD} is always among the top four. This finding attests to the merit in using passage-based information to estimate asymmetric co-relevance. The query-document-based permutations have a single occurrence in Table 4 (QPP(Cos)); however, they are always among the top nine permutations. The AP setting is the only one for which a document-quality-based permutation, π_{SW1}, π_{SW2}, π_{ICR} or π_{ENT}, is not among the top four permutations. It is also the only setting for which WBorda was outperformed when using a reference comparison estimate (excluding UBorda) for the nearest-neighbor cluster hypothesis test reported in Table 3.

Comparing the results in Table 3 and Table 4, we see that when used alone for estimating the extent to which the cluster hypothesis holds, the performance attained for Cos is often lower than that attained for LM and BM25. Conversely, permutations instantiated using Cos have more representatives in the top four permutations than those instantiated using BM25 and LM.

Retrieval performance. In what follows, we study the effectiveness of the retrieval methods discussed in Section 5.2 when using the co-relevance estimates. The estimates are used to determine the nearest neighbors of a document in the graph-based methods and set the edge weights, create the NN clusters in the cluster-based methods, and induce some of the other features used by the methods. As reference comparisons to WBorda, we use the LM, Cos and BM25 estimates which it integrates. For each retrieval method we present the performance of two additional reference comparison estimates which led to the best performance in most relevant comparisons compared to the other reference comparisons. We also present the performance of the unweighted UBorda estimate. We note that some of the performance numbers reported here are not comparable with those reported in past literature for the following reasons: (i) we use larger sets of queries than those used in past work addressing the same datasets (e.g., [4, 33]); and (ii) we report MAP@50, as our focus is on re-ranking an initial list of 50 documents, rather than MAP@1000 (e.g., [7, 4]).[14]

Cluster-based methods. Table 5 presents the results for the cluster-based re-ranking methods. We can see that using WBorda yields the best performance in most relevant comparisons (8 experimental settings × 2 evaluation metrics) for Interpf and ClustRanker. For both methods, WBorda outperforms any reference comparison in a vast majority of the relevant comparisons with many of the improvements being statistically significant. In the few cases where WBorda is outperformed by a reference comparison, the performance differences are statistically indistinguishable.

We can also see that WBorda outperforms any reference comparison in a vast majority of the relevant comparisons for ClustMRF; many of the improvements are statistically significant. In addition, WBorda is statistically significantly outperformed only in a single case for the CW12B setting.

The findings presented above attest to the clear merits of using WBorda to induce nearest-neighbor clusters that are used by highly effective cluster-based retrieval methods.

---

[13] For WT10G π_Q is among the top six permutations and for CW12B it is among the top five.

[14] The p@5 performance for cluster-based retrieval methods might be somewhat lower than that reported in past literature as the optimization metric here was MAP.

Table 6: Using the graph-based RWI and Regularization methods to re-rank the initial list. 'i' and 'b' mark statistically significant differences with the initial ranking (Init) and WBorda, respectively. The best result in a column per a graph-based method is boldfaced.

	AP		ROBUST		WT10G		GOV2		CW09B		CW09BF		CW12B		CW12BF	
	MAP	p@5	MAP	p@5	MAP	p@5	MAP	p@5	MAP	p@5	MAP	p@5	MAP	p@5	MAP	p@5
Init	9.0	43.6	18.8	48.7	13.8	33.4	11.4	55.5	9.9	22.7	12.7	34.7	14.2	23.6	14.0	22.8
RWI																
LM	8.9_b	46.1	19.2_b	49.9_b	12.8_b	35.1_b	12.0^i_b	60.5^i_b	12.2^i_b	33.1^i_b	13.2_b	38.0_b	14.3_b	23.6_b	16.2_b	25.2_b
Cos	9.0	44.2_b	18.9_b	48.8_b	13.8	37.1^i_b	12.0^i_b	60.8^i_b	11.6^i_b	31.6^i_b	13.6^i_b	37.4_b	15.3_b	24.4_b	14.7_b	25.2_b
BM25	9.0	47.9	18.9_b	49.4_b	13.8	35.5_b	12.7^i_b	63.1^i	11.6^i_b	30.8^i_b	13.5^i_b	39.8^i_b	14.2_b	22.0_b	13.9_b	24.8_b
IT	8.9_b	46.1_b	19.0_b	49.2_b	13.1_b	35.9_b	12.6^i_b	61.6^i_b	12.5^i_b	34.8^i_b	14.1^i	38.9_b	14.6_b	24.8_b	16.4_b	25.2_b
RM3	8.9_b	44.8_b	19.3	48.7_b	13.8	36.5_b	12.7^i_b	62.0^i_b	12.5^i_b	33.7^i_b	14.0^i	40.3^i_b	14.8_b	27.6	15.6_b	28.4_b
UBorda	9.0	46.7	19.1_b	50.0_b	14.2	37.5_b	12.8^i_b	64.2^i	12.2^i_b	32.4^i_b	14.2^i	41.2^i_b	14.9_b	25.6_b	15.5_b	27.6^i_b
WBorda	**9.3**	**49.1**^{i}	**19.7**^{i}	**52.5**^{i}	**14.2**	**40.4**^{i}	**13.1**^{i}	**65.9**^{i}	**13.1**^{i}	**39.5**^{i}	**14.6**^{i}	**43.8**^{i}	**18.4**^{i}	**33.2**^{i}	**18.7**^{i}	**34.0**^{i}
Regularization																
MDK	9.0	44.2_b	19.7^i_b	50.1_b	13.9	35.5	12.2^i_b	59.1^i_b	12.3^i	32.7^i	13.4^i_b	37.3_b	13.9_b	24.0_b	14.3_b	24.0_b
Cos	8.8_b	44.2_b	19.2^i_b	48.8_b	13.6_b	37.1	11.9^i_b	58.8_b	11.6^i_b	28.7^i_b	13.6^i_b	39.2^i	13.8_b	24.0_b	14.8_b	26.4^i
BM25	9.1	46.5	20.2^i	51.0^i	14.3	36.5	12.1^i_b	58.1_b	12.4^i	34.8^i	13.7^i_b	38.2_b	13.0_b	20.8_b	15.9	21.6_b
OCF(BM25)	9.2	46.1	20.1^i	50.2_b	14.3^i	35.3_b	12.3^i_b	58.5_b	**12.7**^{i}	34.6^i	13.8^i	39.3^i	13.8_b	23.2_b	15.7	21.6_b
RM3	9.0_b	45.1_b	19.7^i_b	49.9_b	**15.1**	38.8^i	12.6^i_b	61.2^i	12.0^i	30.1_b	14.4^i	41.1^i	15.5_b	26.4_b	14.9	27.6
UBorda	**9.3**^{i}	46.9	20.2^i	51.7^i	14.9	40.4^i	12.6^i_b	62.6^i	11.8^i_b	31.4^i_b	13.9^i_b	39.8^i	15.1_b	24.4_b	14.1_b	24.4_b
WBorda	**9.3**^{i}	**48.1**^{i}	**20.3**^{i}	**52.4**^{i}	14.8	39.8^i	**12.9**^{i}	**64.3**^{i}	12.2^i	33.2^i	14.3^i	41.6^i	**18.4**^{i}	**30.4**^{i}	**17.3**^{i}	**28.8**^{i}

Graph-based methods. Table 6 presents the results for the graph-based RWI and Regularization methods. We see that for both RWI and Regularization the best performance is almost always attained when WBorda is used. Most of the improvements over the reference comparisons are substantial and statistically significant. Furthermore, in the few cases where WBorda is outperformed by one of the reference comparisons, the performance differences are not statistically significant.

We make the following additional observations. The RWI method relies on an asymmetric co-relevance estimate. Our asymmetric WBorda estimate leads to better performance of RWI than all symmetric and asymmetric reference comparisons, including the originally proposed asymmetric LM estimate [20]. On the other hand, Regularization relies on a symmetric co-relevance estimate. The symmetric version of WBorda used in Regularization yields better performance than all the symmetric reference comparisons, namely MDK (which is the originally proposed measure for Regularization [7]), Cos and OCF(BM25) and all the symmetric versions of the asymmetric reference comparison estimates: BM25, RM3 and UBorda.

Finally, we note that for both the cluster-based and graph-based re-ranking methods, WBorda outperforms UBorda in a vast majority of the relevant comparisons with quite a few of the improvements being statistically significant. This finding, which is in line with those reported above for the cluster hypothesis test, attests to the merits of learning permutation weights rather than using uniform weights.

Symmetric vs. asymmetric co-relevance estimation. Table 7 presents the comparison of the originally proposed asymmetric WBorda estimate with its symmetric version (see Equation 7). For the Regularization method, which relies on a symmetric co-relevance estimate, we present the results only for the symmetric version. We see that, with the exception of ClustMRF, the percentages for the asymmetric estimate are higher than those for its symmetric version. In addition, asymmetric WBorda is statistically significantly outperformed by the symmetric WBorda only in a few cases for ClustMRF. Furthermore, while both versions

Table 7: Comparing asymmetric with symmetric WBorda. The percentage of the 16 cases (8 experimental settings × 2 evaluation metrics) in which asymmetric (symmetric) WBorda outperforms (statistically significantly outperforms) symmetric (asymmetric) WBorda. And, the percentage of the 240 cases (8 experimental settings × 2 evaluation metrics × 15 reference comparisons excluding UBorda) in which WBorda outperforms (statistically significantly outperforms) the reference comparisons. In the first column percentages might not sum to 100 due to ties and rounding.

		Asymmetric/Symmetric WBorda		Reference Comparisons	
		Better	Sig. Better	Better	Sig. Better
NN test	Asymmetric	100.0	50.0	94.6	83.8
	Symmetric	0.0	0.0	86.7	77.1
Interpf	Asymmetric	87.5	18.8	85.0	43.3
	Symmetric	12.5	0.0	62.1	18.3
ClustMRF	Asymmetric	43.8	6.3	84.2	25.0
	Symmetric	43.8	12.5	85.8	27.9
ClustRanker	Asymmetric	68.8	31.3	88.3	59.2
	Symmetric	25.0	0.0	83.3	44.2
RWI	Asymmetric	50.0	31.3	99.6	83.8
	Symmetric	37.5	0.0	91.3	67.5
Regularization	Symmetric	–	–	92.9	66.3

of WBorda outperform the reference comparisons in most cases, the asymmetric version does so (to a statistically significant degree) in a vast majority of the relevant comparisons. These findings attest to the merits of (i) integrating the measures used in WBorda to induce (either a symmetric or an asymmetric) co-relevance estimate; and (ii) using the originally proposed asymmetric WBorda in applications which call for asymmetric co-relevance estimation (namely, all those considered except Regularization).

6. CONCLUSIONS

We presented a method of estimating asymmetric co-relevance: the relevance of a document given another document assumed to be relevant. The co-relevance estimate is based on a learning-to-rank method that integrates various types of similarities with the query and the assumed relevant document, as well as query-independent document-quality measures. We showed that using our proposed estimate in three applications yields much better performance than that of using previously proposed co-relevance estimates. Studying how asymmetric co-relevance estimates can be used for results diversification is an interesting future venue.

Acknowledgments We thank the reviewers for their comments and Kripabandhu Ghosh for initial discussions. This work has been supported by and carried out at the Technion-Microsoft Electronic Commerce Research Center. This work has also been supported in part by Microsoft Research through its Ph.D. Scholarship Program.

7. REFERENCES

[1] N. Abdul-Jaleel, J. Allan, W. B. Croft, F. Diaz, L. Larkey, X. Li, M. D., and C. Wade. UMASS at TREC 2004 — novelty and hard. In *Proc. of TREC*, 2004.

[2] J. A. Aslam and M. Frost. An information-theoretic measure for document similarity. In *Proc. of SIGIR*, pages 449–450, 2003.

[3] J. A. Aslam and M. Montague. Models for metasearch. In *Proc. of SIGIR*, pages 276–284, 2001.

[4] M. Bendersky, W. B. Croft, and Y. Diao. Quality-biased ranking of web documents. In *Proc. of WSDM*, pages 95–104, 2011.

[5] M. Bendersky and O. Kurland. Utilizing passage-based language models for ad hoc document retrieval. *Information Retrieval*, 13(2):157–187, 2010.

[6] G. V. Cormack, M. D. Smucker, and C. L. A. Clarke. Efficient and effective spam filtering and re-ranking for large web datasets. *Information Retrieval*, 14(5):441–465, 2011.

[7] F. Diaz. Regularizing query-based retrieval scores. *Information Retrieval*, 10(6):531–562, 2007.

[8] E. A. Fox and J. A. Shaw. Combination of multiple searches. In *Proc. of TREC*, 1994.

[9] J. H. Friedman. Greedy function approximation: A gradient boosting machine. *The Annals of Statistics*, 28(5):1379–1389, 2001.

[10] N. Fuhr, M. Lechtenfeld, B. Stein, and T. Gollub. The optimum clustering framework: implementing the cluster hypothesis. *Information Retrieval*, 15(2):93–115, 2012.

[11] A. Griffiths, H. C. Luckhurst, and P. Willett. Using interdocument similarity information in document retrieval systems. *Journal of the American Society for Information Science*, 37(1):3–11, 1986.

[12] M. A. Hearst and J. O. Pedersen. Reexamining the cluster hypothesis: Scatter/Gather on retrieval results. In *Proc. of SIGIR*, pages 76–84, 1996.

[13] N. Jardine and C. J. van Rijsbergen. The use of hierarchic clustering in information retrieval. *Information Storage and Retrieval*, 7(5):217–240, 1971.

[14] T. Joachims. Training linear SVMs in linear time. In *Proc. of KDD*, pages 217–226, 2006.

[15] E. Krikon, O. Kurland, and M. Bendersky. Utilizing inter-passage and inter-document similarities for re-ranking search results. *ACM Transactions on Information Systems*, 29(1), 2010.

[16] O. Kurland. The opposite of smoothing: A language model approach to ranking query-specific document clusters. In *Proc. of SIGIR*, pages 171–178, 2008.

[17] O. Kurland. Re-ranking search results using language models of query-specific clusters. *Journal of Information Retrieval*, 12(4):437–460, 2009.

[18] O. Kurland and L. Lee. Corpus structure, language models, and ad hoc information retrieval. In *Proc. of SIGIR*, pages 194–201, 2004.

[19] O. Kurland and L. Lee. Respect my authority! HITS without hyperlinks utilizing cluster-based language models. In *Proc. of SIGIR*, pages 83–90, 2006.

[20] O. Kurland and L. Lee. PageRank without hyperlinks: Structural reranking using links induced by language models. *ACM Transactions on information systems*, 28(4):18, 2010.

[21] J. Lafferty and C. Zhai. Probabilistic relevance models based on document and query generation. In *Language Modeling and Information Retrieval*, pages 1–10. Kluwer Academic Publishers, 2003.

[22] J. D. Lafferty and C. Zhai. Document language models, query models, and risk minimization for information retrieval. In *Proc. of SIGIR*, pages 111–119, 2001.

[23] V. Lavrenko and W. B. Croft. Relevance-based language models. In *Proc. of SIGIR*, pages 120–127, 2001.

[24] T.-Y. Liu. Learning to rank for information retrieval. *Foundations and Trends in Information Retrieval*, 3(3), 2009.

[25] X. Liu and W. B. Croft. Passage retrieval based on language models. In *Proc. of CIKM*, pages 375–382, 2002.

[26] X. Liu and W. B. Croft. Cluster-based retrieval using language models. In *Proc. of SIGIR*, pages 186–193, 2004.

[27] X. Liu and W. B. Croft. Experiments on retrieval of optimal clusters. Technical Report IR-478, Center for Intelligent Information Retrieval, University of Massachusetts, 2006.

[28] X. Liu and W. B. Croft. Representing clusters for retrieval. In *Proc. of SIGIR*, pages 671–672, 2006.

[29] X. Liu and W. B. Croft. Evaluating text representations for retrieval of the best group of documents. In *Proc. of ECIR*, pages 454–462, 2008.

[30] S.-H. Na. Probabilistic co-relevance for query-sensitive similarity measurement in information retrieval. *Information Processing and Management*, 49(2):558–575, 2013.

[31] A. Ntoulas, M. Najork, M. Manasse, and D. Fetterly. Detecting spam web pages through content analysis. In *Proc. of WWW*, pages 83–92, 2006.

[32] S. Paliwal and V. Pudi. Investigating usage of text segmentation and inter-passage similarities to improve text document clustering. In *Proc. of MLDM*, pages 555–565, 2012.

[33] F. Raiber and O. Kurland. Ranking document clusters using markov random fields. In *Proc. of SIGIR*, pages 333–342, 2013.

[34] S. E. Robertson, S. Walker, S. Jones, M. Hancock-Beaulieu, and M. Gatford. Okapi at TREC-3. In *Proc. of TREC*, 1994.

[35] G. Salton. *Automatic Text Processing: The Transformation, Analysis, and Retrieval of Information by Computer*. Addison-Wesley, 1989.

[36] K. Sparck Jones, S. Walker, and S. E. Robertson. A probabilistic model of information retrieval: development and comparative experiments - part 1. *Information Processing and Management*, 36(6):779–808, 2000.

[37] A. Tombros and C. J. van Rijsbergen. Query-sensitive similarity measures for information retrieval. *Knowledge and Information Systems*, 6(5):617–642, 2004.

[38] C. J. van Rijsbergen. *Information Retrieval*. Butterworths, 1979.

[39] C. C. Vogt and G. W. Cottrell. Fusion via a linear combination of scores. *Information Retrieval*, 1(3):151–173, 1999.

[40] E. M. Voorhees. The cluster hypothesis revisited. In *Proc. of SIGIR*, pages 188–196, 1985.

[41] X. Wan. A novel document similarity measure based on earth mover's distance. *Information Sciences*, 177(18):3718–3730, 2007.

[42] X. Wan. Beyond topical similarity: a structural similarity measure for retrieving highly similar documents. *Knowledge and Information Systems*, 15(1):55–73, 2008.

[43] X. Wei and W. B. Croft. LDA-based document models for ad-hoc retrieval. In *Proc. of SIGIR*, pages 178–185, 2006.

[44] J. S. Whissell and C. L. A. Clarke. Improving document clustering using Okapi BM25 feature weighting. *Information Retrieval*, 14(5):466–487, 2011.

[45] J. S. Whissell and C. L. A. Clarke. Effective measures for inter-document similarity. In *Proc. of CIKM*, pages 1361–1370, 2013.

[46] P. Willett. Query specific automatic document classification. *International Forum on Information and Documentation*, 10(2):28–32, 1985.

[47] L. Yang, D. Ji, G. Zhou, Y. Nie, and G. Xiao. Document re-ranking using cluster validation and label propagation. In *Proc. of CIKM*, pages 690–697, 2006.

[48] C. Zhai and J. D. Lafferty. A study of smoothing methods for language models applied to ad hoc information retrieval. In *Proc. of SIGIR*, pages 334–342, 2001.

[49] B. Zhang, H. Li, Y. Liu, L. Ji, W. Xi, W. Fan, Z. Chen, and W.-Y. Ma. Improving web search results using affinity graph. In *Proc. of SIGIR*, pages 504–511, 2005.

Implicit Preference Labels for Learning Highly Selective Personalized Rankers

Paul N. Bennett
Microsoft
pauben@microsoft.com

Milad Shokouhi
Microsoft
milads@microsoft.com

Rich Caruana
Microsoft
rcaruana@microsoft.com

ABSTRACT

Interaction data such as clicks and dwells provide valuable signals for learning and evaluating personalized models. However, while models of personalization typically distinguish between clicked and non-clicked results, no preference distinctions within the non-clicked results are made and all are treated as equally non-relevant.

In this paper, we demonstrate that failing to enforce a prior on preferences among non-clicked results leads to learning models that often personalize with no measurable gain at the *risk* that the personalized ranking is worse than the non-personalized ranking. To address this, we develop an implicit preference-based framework that enables learning highly selective rankers that yield large reductions in risk such as the percentage of queries personalized. We demonstrate theoretically how our framework can be derived from a small number of basic axioms that give rise to well-founded target rankings which combine a weight on prior preferences with the implicit preferences inferred from behavioral data.

Additionally, we conduct an empirical analysis to demonstrate that models learned with this approach yield comparable gains on click-based performance measures to standard methods with far fewer queries personalized. On three real-world commercial search engine logs, the method leads to substantial reductions in the number of queries re-ranked (2×-7× fewer queries re-ranked) while maintaining 85-95% of the total gain achieved by the standard approach.

Categories and Subject Descriptors

H.3.3 [**Information Retrieval**]: Retrieval Models

Keywords

Personalization risk, robust algorithms, re-ranking

1. INTRODUCTION

Personalizing search results based on context has been consistently reported to improve retrieval effectiveness [3, 27, 31, 34, 35]. However, personalization cannot help all queries and knowing when to *selectively* apply personalization is one of the key challenges of personalization [33]. In particular, when personalization is not necessary, personalizing the ranking runs the *risk* of decreasing performance relative to the non-personalized ranker. In order to per-

ICTIR'15, September 27–30, Northampton, MA, USA.
© 2015 ACM. ISBN 978-1-4503-3833-2/15/09 ...$15.00.
DOI: http://dx.doi.org/10.1145/2808194.2809464.

sonalize appropriately, we need an indication of the user's personal preferences as a target for learning.

Ideally one would obtain explicit judgments from each person for each personalized query, but that is not feasible at scale. A common alternative is to use "satisfied"[1] or long-dwell clicks to infer an implicit relevance judgment. In particular, the literature suggests that clicks indicate a relative preference over non-clicks but should not be interpreted as absolute relevance [1, 2, 22, 24]. As a result, a number of personalization studies have been conducted where the goal is to see a relative change in how high clicked results are ranked in the personalized versus non-personalized rankings [3, 4]. For example, an increase in the mean average precision of satisfied-clicked results (relevant) vs. the remaining results (non-relevant) over the non-personalized baseline indicates that, on average, the personalized ranker lists results users prefer higher in the rankings.

While technically correct, the lack of a prior on the many *unclicked* documents leads to models that often re-rank even when there are no demonstrable gains. This leads to a risk of personalization failure [37] not captured by click-based measures of risk. Furthermore, spuriously re-ranking when there is no need increases variance in the rankings. This variance masks the signal of performance improvements when any new improvement is tested – increasing the cost of interleaving [25] and A/B testing by requiring longer experiments and slowing development cycles. Ultimately, this occurs because click-based behavioral measures of relevance treat any ranking of the unclicked results as equivalent. We alleviate this by introducing a method which uses the non-personalized ranking to inform the target ranking of unclicked results in the absence of other information.

Table 1 presents an illustrative example of the problem of interpreting interactions as implicit relevance judgments. Here the user has been presented with a set of search results in response to the query [acl] in the ranked order of the first column (*Rank*) and clicked and dwelled on the sixth result for the "Association for Computational Linguistics" homepage. The table presents two hypothetical rankings, *A* and *B*, which both place the satisfied clicked item first but differ greatly in how the non-clicked results are ranked.

Ranking *A* leaves all of the remaining results in their original order; for both learning and evaluation this is highly conservative—if personalization is not appropriate, a set of users for whom the original non-personalized order was appropriate would find a desired result at most one position lower. Likewise, the variance from the original ranking or across people who may experience different personalized rankings is minimal at this conservative point. In contrast, after the satisfied clicked result is placed first, ranking *B* then inverts the order of the original first five results and then gives the last four results in their original order. Intuitively, if we believe the original

---

[1] We use the common definition of a "satisfied" click as a click with dwell of $\geq 30s$ or one that terminates the search session [7, 17].

Table 1: Given ranked documents presented to a user with a click interaction given in "Satisfied Click", we show two possible re-rankings which order the documents as: A = $[6, 1, 2, 3, 4, 5, 7, 8, 9, 10]$ and B = $[6, 5, 4, 3, 2, 1, 7, 8, 9, 10]$. Both rankings have the same average precision (AP) when treating clicks as relevance judgments, but A is much more conservative in reordering the non-personalized ranking while B is much riskier. The columns on the right show two sets of gains derived according to the method in Section 2.1 that would both give rise to ranking A as the ideal ranking, but the column on the left places more weight on the original non-personalized ranking when computing the gains. See Section 2.1 for details.

Rank	Title and URL	Satisfied Click	Proposed Re-rankings		Target Gain (α, β)	
			A	B	(1,0.5)	(1,0.05)
1	Anterior cruciate ligament - Wikipedia, the free encyclopedia en.wikipedia.org/wiki/Anterior_cruciate_ligament	No	2'	6'	4.0	0.40
2	Austin City Limits Music Festival - Official Site www.aclfestival.com	No	3'	5'	3.5	0.35
3	ACL compliance, audit, governance & risk software www.acl.com	No	4'	4'	3.0	0.30
4	Anterior Cruciate Ligament (ACL) Injuries-Topic Overview www.webmd.com/a-to-z-guides/anterior-cruciate-ligament-acl-injuries-topic-overview	No	5'	3'	2.5	0.25
5	Access control list - Wikipedia, the free encyclopedia en.wikipedia.org/wiki/Access_control_list	No	6'	2'	2.0	0.20
6	Association for Computational Linguistics | ACL Homepage www.aclweb.org/	Yes	1'	1'	9.0	9.0
7	Association of Christian Librarians: Welcome www.acl.org/	No	7'	7'	1.5	0.15
8	About ACL - Administration for Community Living www.acl.gov/About_ACL/Index.aspx	No	8'	8'	1.0	0.10
9	ACL Cargo www.aclcargo.com	No	9'	9'	0.50	0.05
10	ACL Live, Austin, Texas acl-live.com	No	10'	10'	0	0

ranking is tuned for the overall population, ranking *B* is riskier since a high penalty is paid when the original non-personalized ranking is the correct intent. Even when correct, it introduces variance that can lengthen experiment time to determine statistical significance. Click-based measures of risk cannot capture distinctions among the order of the unclicked items, but other measures can – such as the percentage of queries re-ranked (personalized) and the correlation of the personalized rankings with the non-personalized rankings.

We seek to formally capture these intuitions about how to combine interaction data with the original ordering. We continue in the next section by establishing two simple axioms for deriving preference strengths from clicks. We demonstrate that when preference is defined according to these axioms, the pairwise preferences give rise to a target ranking with desirable properties.

2. PROBLEM APPROACH

We propose our model – referred to as *Weight-Initial-Pref* hereafter – based on a set of axioms which determine how we assign the strength of preferences between results based on their original presented position[2] and click-derived relevance. We demonstrate that when preferences are assigned in accordance with these axioms, the target ranking of results that can be derived from the preferences is constrained in terms of how far it can deviate from the non-personalized ranking. We then respect these constraints during training personalized rankers by using the target ranking derived from the preferences to learn a more conservative model.

In order to balance the search engine's non-personalized ranking and user interaction, we take a simple approach which encodes the strength of preferences between two search results as a function of the ranking and interaction. These pairwise strengths are then

accumulated to each result to indicate the overall utility or gain that the result has. When sorted from greatest to least gain this yields a desired or *target* ranking with associated gains to use in learning a ranking. We demonstrate how starting from basic principles in designing the pairwise preference function, the final target ranking has several desirable properties.

2.1 Axioms for Stable, Personalized Ranking

As illustrated in Table 1, using whether a result received a satisfied click as a relevance label[3] does not distinguish between results in the same relevance class. It is this lack of a default order that ultimately gives rise to the variance in rankings when learning from clicks. An intuitive order to use as a default prior is the ordering given by the non-personalized ranking. We thus desire a way to incorporate this default order with the relevance signal from interaction and a way to increase or decrease the weight on the prior. In this section, we demonstrate a simple approach to achieving these goals.

More formally, we assume we have a set of results $\mathcal{D}$ that have been returned to the user in response to a particular query. Further, we assume an initial complete ordering Π over the results; that is, Π yields a consistent, transitive set of pairwise orderings of any two results $d_i, d_j \in \mathcal{D}$ which we indicate by $d_i \succ_\pi d_j$, to signify d_i is preferred to d_j. In our setting Π is the ranking of results that a user was presented with and d_i being ranked "above" or "higher" than d_j is indicated by $d_i \succ_\pi d_j$.[4]

We assume a setting where given the presented ranking Π and a set of interactions, we would like to define a function, $\text{pref}(d_i \succ d_j)$, that indicates the strength of updated beliefs given the interactions consistent with the following two axioms:

---

[2]We typically refer to the non-personalized ranking as determining presentation order but the model easily applies to the case where the user interacted with a personalized ranker, and these interactions will be used to learn a new, updated personalized model.

[3]When we reach the empirical evaluation, those results with a satisfied click will be deemed to be in the relevant class while the remaining will be deemed to be non-relevant.

[4]Note that if i and j correspond to the ranks of the results in Π then $d_i \succ_\pi d_j$ if and only if $i < j$.

1. The strength of preference for a relevant result over a non-relevant result should be stronger than any other preference.

2. For any labeled result from the same relevance class (relevant, non-relevant), the preference should reflect the preference of the presented ranking, Π.

The first of these axioms is commonly accepted in the literature. However, the second axiom is novel and essentially introduces the notion that: absent of any deciding behavioral signal from the user, the default preference should conservatively break ties by preferring the non-personalized ranking – which has benefited from being optimized over a large set of non-personalized relevance judgments.

In this paper, we assume the interactions partition the results into two sets, the satisfied clicks or relevant results, $\mathcal{R}$, and the non-satisfied clicks or non-relevant results, $\mathcal{I}$. We assume two user-defined parameters α, β such that $\alpha, \beta > 0$ where α indicates the preference for a relevant result over an irrelevant result and β indicates the preference for maintaining the prior ranking for results in the same relevance class. We break the definition into two parts:

When $d_i \in \mathcal{R}$:
$$\text{pref}(d_i \succ d_j) = \begin{cases} \beta & d_j \in \mathcal{R}, d_i \succ_\pi d_j \\ 0 & d_j \in \mathcal{R}, d_i \prec_\pi d_j \\ \alpha & d_j \in \mathcal{I} \end{cases}$$

When $d_i \in \mathcal{I}$:
$$\text{pref}(d_i \succ d_j) = \begin{cases} 0 & d_j \in \mathcal{R} \\ \beta & d_j \in \mathcal{I}, d_i \succ_\pi d_j \\ 0 & d_j \in \mathcal{I}, d_i \prec_\pi d_j \end{cases}$$

The gain for a result d_i is then defined to be:

$$G(d_i) = \sum_{d_j \in \mathcal{D}, d_i \neq d_j} \text{pref}(d_i \succ d_j) \qquad (1)$$

where a higher gain is considered to be more highly relevant. That is, the gain for a result is simply the sum of the strength of preferences across all pairs of documents in the result set for this query.

In our approach we will maximize the normalized discounted cumulative gain (NDCG) [20] using these gains. We choose to do this since NDCG encourages placing the results with the highest gains high in the rankings, but one could also use the gains to optimize a measure that does not weight according to position in the ranking if desired. The ranking derived from sorting the results according to these gains can be considered to be the target ranking as far as a learning algorithm is considered.

Properties of the Target Ranking. To provide guidance in setting α, β, we now consider what properties the target rankings *that are used for learning* have when the parameters take values satisfying $\alpha > \beta > 0$. This is important for demonstrating that the goal of optimization is sensible and meets our overall goals of improving personalized relevance while being conservative. We sketch the proofs of these statements briefly below.

First, we can prove that in the target ranking all results in the relevant set are above any from the non-relevant set (see Theorem 1 and Corollary 1). Additionally, we can prove that the target ranking is conservative in that when there are multiple results in the relevant set, the original non-personalized ranking is preserved among the relevant set in the target ranking (see Theorem 2 and Corollary 2). Finally, we can prove that the target ranking is conservative in that when there are multiple results in the non-relevant set, the original non-personalized ranking is preserved among the non-relevant set in the target ranking (see Theorem 3 and Corollary 3).

If $\beta > \alpha$ is allowed, target rankings can result where an irrelevant result has a higher gain than a relevant result. As β increases, these violations of the first axiom occur more frequently in target

rankings in the training set. We omit this from the experimental section but performance degrades almost immediately when $\beta > \alpha$, demonstrating the desirability of the first axiom.

Proof Sketches. We remind the reader of the assumption of an initial complete ordering Π over the documents whose ordering of two documents $d_i, d_j \in \mathcal{D}$ is indicated by, $d_i \succ_\pi d_j$, to signify d_i is preferred to d_j. In our setting Π is the non-personalized ranking that a user was presented with and d_i being ranked "above" or "higher" than d_j indicates $d_i \succ_\pi d_j$.

THM. 1. *If* $\alpha > \beta > 0$, $d_i \in \mathcal{I}$, *and* $d_j \in \mathcal{R}$ *then* $G(d_i) < G(d_j)$.

$$G(d_i) = \text{pref}(d_i \succ d_j) + \sum_{d_k \in \mathcal{D}, d_k \neq d_i, d_j} \text{pref}(d_i \succ d_k) \qquad (2)$$

Since $d_i \in \mathcal{I}, d_j \in \mathcal{R}$, and $\alpha > \beta > 0$, then $\forall d_k \, \text{pref}(d_i \succ d_k) \leq \text{pref}(d_j \succ d_k)$, and

$$\leq \text{pref}(d_i \succ d_j) + \sum_{d_k \in \mathcal{D}, d_k \neq d_i, d_j} \text{pref}(d_j \succ d_k) \qquad (3)$$

Since $d_i \in \mathcal{I}$ and $d_j \in \mathcal{R}$, then we have $\text{pref}(d_i \succ d_j) < \text{pref}(d_j \succ d_i)$, yielding

$$< \text{pref}(d_j \succ d_i) + \sum_{d_k \in \mathcal{D}, d_k \neq d_i, d_j} \text{pref}(d_j \succ d_k) \qquad (4)$$

$$= G(d_j). \qquad \square$$

COROLLARY 1. *In the target ranking, all relevant documents are above all non-relevant documents. Proof: Follows trivially from Theorem 1 and sorting in descending order by gain.* $\square$

THM. 2. *If* $\alpha, \beta > 0$, $d_i \in \mathcal{R}$, $d_j \in \mathcal{R}$, *and* $d_i \succ_\pi d_j$, *then* $G(d_i) > G(d_j)$.

$$G(d_i) = \text{pref}(d_i \succ d_j) + \sum_{d_k \in \mathcal{D}, d_k \neq d_i, d_j} \text{pref}(d_i \succ d_k) \qquad (5)$$

$$= \text{pref}(d_i \succ d_j) + \sum_{d_k \in \mathcal{R}, d_k \neq d_i, d_j} \text{pref}(d_i \succ d_k)$$

$$+ \sum_{d_k \in \mathcal{I}, d_k \neq d_i, d_j} \text{pref}(d_i \succ d_k) \qquad (6)$$

Note we have $\forall d_k \in \mathcal{R}$ s.t. $d_k \succ_\pi d_j$, $\text{pref}(d_j \succ d_k) = 0$ and $\forall d_k \in \mathcal{R}$ s.t. $d_j \succ_\pi d_k$, $d_i \succ_\pi d_k$ since $d_i \succ_\pi d_j$ and Π is a complete ranking. Therefore $\forall d_k$, $\text{pref}(d_i \succ d_k) \geq \text{pref}(d_j \succ d_k)$ yielding

$$\geq \text{pref}(d_i \succ d_j) + \sum_{d_k \in \mathcal{D}, d_k \neq d_i, d_j} \text{pref}(d_j \succ d_k) \qquad (7)$$

Finally since $d_i, d_j \in \mathcal{R}$ and $d_i \succ_\pi d_j$, $\text{pref}(d_i \succ d_j) > \text{pref}(d_j \succ d_i)$ yielding

$$> \text{pref}(d_j \succ d_i) + \sum_{d_k \in \mathcal{D}, d_k \neq d_i, d_j} \text{pref}(d_j \succ d_k) \qquad (8)$$

$$= G(d_j). \qquad \square$$

COROLLARY 2. *In the target ranking, all relevant documents have the same order as in the initial ranking, Π. Proof: Follows trivially from Theorem 2 and sorting in descending order by gain.* $\square$

THM. 3. *If* $\beta > 0$, $d_i \in \mathcal{I}$, $d_j \in \mathcal{I}$, *and* $d_i \succ_\pi d_j$, *then* $G(d_i) > G(d_j)$. *(The proof of this theorem follows the same basic approach as Theorem 2 and is omitted.)*

COROLLARY 3. *In the target ranking, all non-relevant documents have the same order as in the initial ranking, Π. Proof: Follows trivially from Theorem 3 and sorting in descending order by gain.* □

Implications of Choices for α and β. To provide further guidance in how a user can control risk via the parameters, we consider the interpretation of the values of α and β. As β increases relative to α, an increasing amount of cumulative gain across all results comes from enforcing the preference for the non-personalized ranking. Therefore, increasing β can be viewed as being increasingly risk averse since a higher percentage of the cumulative gain can be increasingly achieved by returning the non-personalized ranking. This is illustrated in Table 1 by the two gain columns – each of which would give rise to the target ranking A in the table. When the ratio of β to α is $0.5 : 1 = 1 : 2$ the non-personalized ranking achieves 0.80 NDCG@10 relative to the optimal ranking A. When we decrease β relative to α to $0.05 : 1 = 1 : 20$ the non-personalized ranking only achieves 0.20 NDCG@10 relative to the optimal. Thus, fixing α and varying β from 0 to α is a smooth way of creating increasingly risk-averse models. In the empirical section, we demonstrate this holds empirically as well.

2.2 Extension to Unexamined Results

Next, we consider the results that were not examined by the user and therefore not clicked due to lack of examination rather than lack of relevance. That is, we may want to treat unexamined results differently than results examined and intentionally not clicked (skips). In particular we may desire to weaken the constraint of the second axiom and not require the order of the *unexamined* results to be maintained in the target ranking.

To this end, we adapt earlier work to our setting. In particular, Radlinski & Joachims [24] used implicit preferences to learn preference-based models and achieved the best results by treating a clicked result as more relevant than both the unclicked results above it as well as the immediately next result when unclicked. Their findings gave rise to the cascade-model [11] of user interaction where a user scans from top to bottom and the results below the lowest click are not examined. As Radlinski & Joachims noted, however, if unexamined results are simply omitted when learning a personalized model, a machine learning model overfits the data by learning to "flip the ranking" since a click is nearly always the lowest (or second to lowest) result in the ranking. To correct this, they introduce a positivity weight constraint strictly greater than zero on the weight of a feature derived from the non-personalized ranking. Increasing the weight constraint in their model corresponded to placing more emphasis on the non-personalized ranking. We generalize their approach to be usable in situations where the learning algorithm cannot easily deal with weight-based constraints by limiting the results for each query in the training set to only those results from one position beyond the lowest click and above. Then, using the weighting model of Section 2.1 with $\beta > 0$ is highly similar to Radlinski & Joachims' introduction of a constraint and increasing β is like increasing their weight constraint. Note that because there are almost no irrelevant results low in the rankings (which boost the gain of irrelevant results above them), β can slightly exceed α for a small amount before target rankings end up with an irrelevant result with higher gain than a relevant result. Because empirically a larger range is permissible, in the empirical section we allow a greater range of exploration of the β parameter for this method.

3. EMPIRICAL METHODOLOGY

We compare our approach (Weight-Initial-Pref) against several baselines from the literature on three large-scale datasets from commercial search engine logs. As in other works that attempt to reduce the risk of a retrieval method, the goal here is not to further increase relevance but to reduce re-ranking percentage and risk and yield a better tradeoff [9, 10, 37].

We implement our approach of using both the interaction data together with the weighted initial preferences within the LambdaMART framework [6]. Specifically, we aggregate the preferences according to Eq. 1 to determine gains using the definition of the strength of preference function, "pref" defined in Section 2.1. We then simply optimize NDCG using this definition of gain. Because it is primarily the ratio of α to β which controls the emphasis placed on the original ranking, we fix $\alpha = 1$ and vary $\beta \in \{0.01, 0.02, \ldots, 0.09, 0.1, 0.2, \ldots, 1\}$. We select a particular model by selecting the value of β that yielded the largest area under the gain vs. re-ranking percentage curve over validation data.

3.1 Performance Measures

We examine two primary measures of effectiveness which have been used by many others, mean average precision (MAP) and normalized discounted cumulative gain (NDCG) [20] where satisfied clicks are relevant and the remaining are non-relevant. Although such an approach is imperfect, we use it because changing both the optimization and evaluation methods together could lead to bias that favors the method we introduce. We use MAP as a measure of effectiveness in our first two datasets that only distinguish two degrees of relevance (non-relevant, relevant). We use NDCG in the WSCD '14 dataset, because the dataset publishers set that as the standard for that dataset. The dataset publishers have defined relevance labels of irrelevant, relevant, and highly relevant according to how long the user dwelled on a document. We describe MAP and the measures derived from MAP in detail and omit the details of NDCG whose derived measures are analogous.

MAP and Δ MAP. To remind the reader, the average precision (AP) of a ranking for a particular query is the average of the precision@k at each position k where a relevant document is ranked. Because the average is taken only with respect to where relevant documents occur, it encourages ranking relevant documents higher in the ranking. AP consequently has a value of 1 when all relevant documents are ranked above non-relevant documents. Note that in the results section we scale all measures in the $[0, 1]$ interval to $[0, 100]$ for ease of readability. The mean average precision (MAP) is the mean of the average precision across all queries.

We may also consider the mean change in average precision for a system S relative to the non-personalized ranker baseline (BASE):

$$\Delta \text{MAP} = \frac{1}{N} \sum_q [\text{AP}_S(q) - \text{AP}_{\text{BASE}}(q)] \qquad (9)$$

where N is the total number of queries in the test set. This change is equivalent to the MAP of a system with the baseline's performance removed – meaning it is positive when personalization increases performance relative to the non-personalized ranker and negative otherwise. We focus on Δ MAP as our primary gain measure since it follows the same trends as MAP and proprietary reasons prevent releasing absolute MAP numbers on one dataset.

Combining Effectiveness and Reranking. In addition to mean average precision and NDCG, we will also use other measures that provide a more accurate view of the tradeoff between relevance and risk. In particular, we examine gain per query re-ranked, mean correlation with the non-personalized ranking, and the mean correlation per query re-ranked.

Each re-ranked query implies a risk of performance degradation. To normalize for the number of re-rankings, we can divide by the total number of queries for which a system generated a re-ranking different than the non-personalized ranker, R_S. When penalizing the difference in MAP this way, we refer to it as Δ MAP/R.

Risk, Reward, and Gain. Wang et al. [37] took an approach to risk by separating the differences in performance from a baseline ranker (*e.g.*, Eq. 9) into the queries where performance is improved Q_+ and the queries where performance is decreased Q_-. The overall gain can then be rewritten as a difference of the reward, which for MAP is $\frac{1}{N} \sum_{q \in Q_+} [\mathrm{AP}_S(q) - \mathrm{AP}_{\mathrm{BASE}}(q)]$, and the risk, $\frac{1}{N} \sum_{q \in Q_-} [\mathrm{AP}_{\mathrm{BASE}}(q) - \mathrm{AP}_S(q)]$. When we use the term "risk" in the empirical section we mean this specific click-based measure of risk – not the broader notions of risk discussed earlier in the paper. As in their work, the maximal risk, reward, and gain are achieved by simply maximizing gain. For ease of interpretation, we normalize changes in risk and gain by dividing by performance of the model with maximal gain (which also has maximal risk). We give the result as a percentage. While this performance-based definition of risk has become more common in the last several years (*e.g.*, as one of the key measures for the TREC Web Track [10]), there is a difference between using it for personalization and using it for standard ad-hoc relevance. This is because, in personalization, there are pseudo-nonrelevant judgments, but in the TREC Web Track setting, there are actual relevance judgments. In the same work, Wang et al. also looked at several other measures that implied risk even when relevance judgments and clicks were not available – namely the percentage of queries re-ranked and the mean Kendall's τ ranking correlation with the non-personalized ranking. We display both of these as well as the mean Kendall's τ over just those queries that are re-ranked ("% Re-ranked", K-τ, and K-τ|R, respectively), but we focus on the percentage of queries that are re-ranked as a better reflection of a more general notion of risk.

3.2 Baselines

Standard Gain. First, we compare to optimizing ranking performance as has been usually done (e.g. [3]) – treating all satisfied clicks as relevant and the rest as non-relevant. We do this using LambdaMART which is an application of the LambdaRank approach [5] to gradient-boosted decision trees. Gradient-boosted decision trees have been very successful in a number of information retrieval tasks (*e.g.*, the Yahoo! Learning To Rank challenge Track 1 where LambdaMART was a key component [6]). We set the key parameters for LambdaMART to default settings appropriate for learning problems with similar amounts of data: we set number of leaves = 10, minimum documents per leaf = 2000, number of trees = 500, learning rate = 0.25, and used the validation set for pruning. Since all of the models are integrated to work with LambdaMART, to aid comparability we do not change these parameter settings. We refer to this as the *Standard Gain* approach.

Naïve. We can reduce the gain, risk, and re-ranking of a personalized model in a naïve way that gives up an amount of gain proportional to the amount of risk/re-ranking reduced. Namely, take the personalized *Standard Gain* model and apply it on a per-query basis by flipping a biased coin with probability p and use the personalized *Standard Gain* model when the coin comes up "heads" and the non-personalized ranker for "tails". By selecting an appropriate $p \in [0, 1]$ any point on the line between the *Standard Gain* and the non-personalized ranker can be attained.

Lowest Click Plus One. To see the impact on re-ranking when the likely unexamined results were not included to stabilize the ranking, we implemented the method of Section 2.2. Again this was integrated into LambdaMART using the aggregated gains of Eq. 1 and the strength of preference function of 2.1. We again fix $\alpha = 1$ and vary $\beta \in \{0.1, 0.2, \ldots, 2\}$. To show this method in the best light, we chose to perform model selection for this approach by maximal gain over the validation set.

Risk-sensitive Optimization. As mentioned throughout the paper, we also could use the risk-sensitive optimization introduced by Wang et al. [37]. In particular, they decompose the change of gain relative to a baseline into risk and reward and introduce a parameter $\alpha_{risk} \geq 0$ such that increasing α_{risk} makes the learning algorithm learn increasingly low risk models. We implement this in our setting by optimizing over the training set of queries, Q, the reward minus the weighted risk:

$$\mathrm{RS}(Q, \alpha_{risk}) = \frac{1}{N} \cdot [\sum_{q \in Q_+} [\mathrm{AP}_S(q) - \mathrm{AP}_{\mathrm{BASE}}(q)]] \quad (10)$$

$$-(\alpha_{risk} + 1)[\sum_{q \in Q_-} [\mathrm{AP}_{\mathrm{BASE}}(q) - \mathrm{AP}_S(q)]].$$

Here $\alpha_{risk} = 0$ is equivalent to the *Standard Gain* model. Since Wang et al. demonstrated both a reduction in the number of queries re-ranked and an increase in correlation with the non-personalized ranking with increasing α_{risk} (at a cost to a less than proportional reduction in gain), this method makes a natural baseline. On the validation set we explore $\alpha_{risk} \in \{0, 0.1, 0.2, \ldots, 0.9, 1, 2, 3, \ldots 10\}$. We select a particular model by selecting the value of α_{risk} that yielded the largest area under the gain vs. re-ranking percentage curve over validation data. We also consider how re-ranking would compare if we compared a risk-sensitive model at the same gain achieved as the *Weight-Initial-Pref* model. We do this and present the results for this as *RS (Min Risk, Gain Parity)*. Likewise, we could use the risk-sensitive model that has the same re-ranking as the *Weight-Initial-Pref* model and observe the difference in gain. We present results for this as *RS (Max Gain, near Rerank)*.

4. DATA & FEATURES

We evaluate the methods on three datasets. The first is a proprietary dataset from Bing, Microsoft's search engine. The second and third are anonymized public datasets from the Yandex search engine first released to participants of the Relevance Prediction Challenge[5] which was part of the WSDM 2012 WSCD workshop and for the Personalized Web Search Challenge[6] organized in conjunction with the WSDM 2014 WSCD workshop. We refer to these testbeds, respectively, as the *WSCD '12* and *WSCD '14* datasets.

The Bing dataset consists of queries sampled between 25 October 2013 and 14 November 2013 (three weeks). We use the first week of data for training and the last two respectively for validation and testing. The training/validation/test sets contain 449K/444K/443K queries respectively. Because we have full access to this dataset we are able to compute a variety of short- and long-term features for personalization studied elsewhere in the literature. In particular, we implemented the features studied by others for long-term personal navigation in [34], location features in [4], and short- and long-term topical and navigation features as in [3]. Since our focus is not on features we refer the reader to those articles for details; it is only important to us that the *Standard Gain* model represent

---

[5] http://imat-relpred.yandex.ru/en
[6] https://www.kaggle.com/c/yandex-personalized-web-search-challenge

a competitive and realistic baseline for personalization from the literature. In particular, in order to have non-trivial relationships between gain and risk at the model level, the feature set should contain a rich set of features with the potential for the trade-off to be exploited.

To complement the analysis over the Bing data, the WSCD '12 and WSCD '14 datasets give two publicly available datasets to reproduce a similar style of experiment where the amount of personalization is limited by the types of features that are available. In particular in the WSCD '12 dataset only short-term (session) identifiers for users are available while the WSCD '14 dataset has both short- and long-term information via a consistent user ID across sessions. In both datasets, query text and URLs have been replaced with numerical IDs and topic and location information are not available. Thus, some well-studied personalization features in the literature dependent on location and topic cannot be computed. However, we can compute proxies for many studied features and have implemented the proxies for short-term refinding, personal navigation, and query similarity features described in [30] for the WSCD '12 dataset and both short- and long-term proxies of the same for the WSCD '14 dataset. We note that, on all datasets, we have the original position and score of documents under the ranking presented to the user as both a re-ranking feature and to compute our preference models.

For the WSCD '12 dataset, we split the data according to the SessionID metadata in the logs. Sampled sessions with SessionID smaller than $3E + 07$ were used for training and validation, and the remainder were used for testing. In total, the sampled train/validation/test sets contain 593K/591K/592K queries respectively. We performed a similar partitioning by user ID over the published training set for WSCD '14 and downsampled to obtain train/validation/test sets of 1.31M/654K/654K queries, respectively.

5. RESULTS AND DISCUSSION

Performance Summary. We start by discussing results on the Bing dataset in Table 2 (top) . First, we note that all of the personalization models selected achieve significant gains in Δ MAP over the non-personalized baseline. Furthermore, the baseline *Standard Gain* model demonstrates similar performance to reported models in the literature that use both short- and long-term features [3]; However, it also re-ranks quite often (41.19%), and when the change in MAP is penalized by dividing by the number of queries re-ranked the credit drops to a difference of 2.58 (Δ MAP/R). This re-ranking can also be seen by Kendall's τ where the average overall (K-τ) is lower than all of the other models except the *Lowest-Click-Plus-One* model even though the average Kendall's τ over only those queries re-ranked (K-τ|R) for the *Standard Gain* model is comparable to those other models: this indicates when the model does change the ranking, the number of pairwise swaps relative to the non-personalized ranking is about the same. However, it changes the rankings far more often with no measurable gain. Both our method, *Weight-Initial-Pref* and the *Risk Sensitive* models improve the tradeoff of gain to percentage of queries re-ranked, but *Weight-Initial-Pref* is able to reduce the percentage of queries far more while maintaining gain. In the following discussion section, we describe more details about the differences in these methods.

When examining the *Lowest-Click-Plus-One* model, large gains relative to the non-personalized ranking are achieved, but a large number of queries are re-ranked (62.02%), and when changed, they are reordered on average the most of any method (K-τ|R=86.68). As a result, a favorable tradeoff relative to the *Standard Gain* model is never attained. One possibility is that this model is simply increasing the variance among the unexamined documents; however, this exploration comes at a noticeable cost to measurable relevance.

Summarizing the results on WSCD '12 and WSCD '14 (respectively middle and bottom sections in Table 2), we note the same trends generally hold up although they are less pronounced in these datasets where less rich personalization features are available. Once again the personalized *Standard Gain* model produces gains over the non-personalized baseline ranking presented to the user. We suspect that the absence of many personalization signals (due to the anonymized nature of the release) is why none of the models reach as high of a level of effectiveness for low re-ranking as observed in the Bing data. Comparing between models, in the WSCD '12 dataset the *Weight-Initial-Pref* model again demonstrates a substantially higher re-ranking penalized change in MAP (Δ MAP/R = 2.48) while maintaining 84.60% of the gain. This is while reducing re-ranking by a 2× factor from the *Standard Gain* model of 98.14% and a 1.33× factor from the most comparable gain *Risk Sensitive* model of 65.35%. Results trend similarly on WSCD '14.

Discussion. The trade-offs between gains and percentage of queries reranked are illustrated in Figures 1 - 3 respectively for Bing, WSCD '12 and WSCD '14 datasets. In all these figures, the x-axis represents the percentage of re-ranked queries while the y-axis shows the performance of different methods in terms of *normalized gain*. The left plots in each figure are generated based on models *selected* for each approach while the right plots depict the gain vs. reranking trade-offs across all parameter values. Next we describe our selection criterion for picking these models.

Examining the left figures for *Naïve* baseline, as $p \to 1$, the resulting mixed model has a performance that moves to the top right and as $p \to 0$, the mixed model is increasingly the non-personalized ranking that has no relative improvements. The *Naïve* baseline represents the achievable performance by fixing p to some value in $[0, 1]$. Therefore, only improvements above and to the left of the *Naïve* line represent useful tradeoffs not dominated by some *Naïve* model's performance with appropriately chosen p. More generally, for any two models, the tradeoffs along the line between them can be achieved in the same fashion. This means that increasing the convex hull[7] is better, and in particular, having a set of models whose area under the curve is maximized.

On the Bing dataset (Figure 1) we see that both the *Weight-Initial-Pref* models and *Risk Sensitive* models achieve improved tradeoffs of gain and percentage of queries re-ranked relative to the *Naïve* method. However, relative to all of the risk sensitive models, the *Weight-Initial-Pref* model offers substantial improvements, maintaining 95.28% of the total gain while only re-ranking 5.92% of the queries (See Table 2 for details). This is a 7× reduction in number of queries re-ranked relative to the *Standard Gain* model while keeping nearly all of the gain. As can be seen from the impact on queries where the SAT clicked results changed position, this was achieved by learning a model where the changed queries have a larger average gain than the *Standard Gain* model, and when penalized for re-ranking, the amount of improvement per query re-ranked (Δ MAP/R = 17.08) is much better than the other methods.

In comparing the *Weight-Initial-Pref* model to various risk sensitive tradeoffs, we see that if we try to choose a risk sensitive model with a similar gain but minimum risk, *RS (Min Risk, Gain Parity)*, we re-rank 3.5× more often (5.92% vs. 20.77%). This is the horizontal space between the black diamond and orange plus in Figure 1 *(left)*. If we try to choose a risk sensitive model with a similar amount of re-ranking but maximal gain, *RS (Max Gain, near Rerank)*, we never reach as little re-ranking before gain starts dropping precipitously for 81.54% gain at 8.43% of re-ranking for the risk model vs.

---

[7]The outer edge not below a line connecting any other two points.

Table 2: Results on Bing (*top*), WSCD '12 (*middle*), and WSCD '14 (*bottom*). There are 443k, 592K, and 654K queries in the test sets, respectively. Statistically significant ($p \leq 0.05$ two-tailed paired t-test) gains relative to the non-personalized ranker are underlined.

Method	Param.	Δ MAP	Δ MAP/R	% Re-ranked	% Risk	% Gain	K-τ	K-τ|R
Standard Gain	$\alpha_{risk}=0$	1.06	2.58	41.19	100.00	100.00	95.43	88.90
Weight-Initial-Pref	$\beta=0.2$	1.01	17.08	5.92	59.27	95.28	99.39	89.70
Risk Sensitive	$\alpha_{risk}=5$	0.95	9.46	10.04	37.87	89.39	99.02	90.23
RS (Min Risk, Gain Parity)	$\alpha_{risk}=1.6$	1.01	4.87	20.77	57.95	95.21	97.83	89.55
RS (Max Gain, near Rerank)	$\alpha_{risk}=10$	0.87	10.27	8.43	26.99	81.54	99.24	90.98
Lowest-Click-Plus-One	$\beta=1.2$	0.93	1.50	62.02	50.46	87.53	91.74	86.68

Method	Param.	MAP	Δ MAP	Δ MAP/R	% Reranked	% Risk	% Gain	K-τ	K-τ|R
Standard Gain	$\alpha_{risk}=0$	68.12	1.43	1.46	98.14	100.00	100.00	80.82	80.46
Weight-Initial-Pref	$\beta=0.4$	67.90	1.21	2.48	49.01	55.34	84.60	96.18	92.21
Risk Sensitive	$\alpha_{risk}=1.7$	67.90	1.22	1.87	65.35	43.37	85.19	92.60	88.68
RS (Min Risk, Gain Parity)	$\alpha_{risk}=1.7$	67.90	1.22	1.87	65.35	43.37	85.19	92.60	88.68
RS (Max Gain, near Rerank)	$\alpha_{risk}=3$	67.66	0.97	1.92	50.82	25.24	67.93	95.39	90.93
Lowest-Click-Plus-One	$\beta=0.9$	67.02	0.34	0.34	99.87	28.15	23.72	74.87	74.84

Method	Param.	NDCG@10	Δ NDCG@10	Δ NDCG@10/R	% Re-ranked	% Risk	% Gain	K-τ	K-τ|R
Standard Gain	$\alpha_{risk}=0$	80.54	0.8255	0.88	93.99	100.00	100.00	88.38	87.64
Weight-Initial-Pref	$\beta=0.01$	80.45	0.7324	4.24	17.27	55.20	88.72	97.74	86.91
Risk Sensitive	$\alpha_{risk}=3$	80.41	0.6949	4.21	16.50	32.37	84.18	98.07	88.30
RS (Min Risk, Gain Parity)	$\alpha_{risk}=2$	80.45	0.7317	3.39	21.58	40.39	88.64	97.54	88.60
RS (Max Gain, near Rerank)	$\alpha_{risk}=3$	80.41	0.6949	4.21	16.50	32.37	84.18	98.07	88.30
Lowest-Click-Plus-One	$\beta=1$	80.13	0.4162	0.42	99.98	45.45	50.42	79.7	79.70

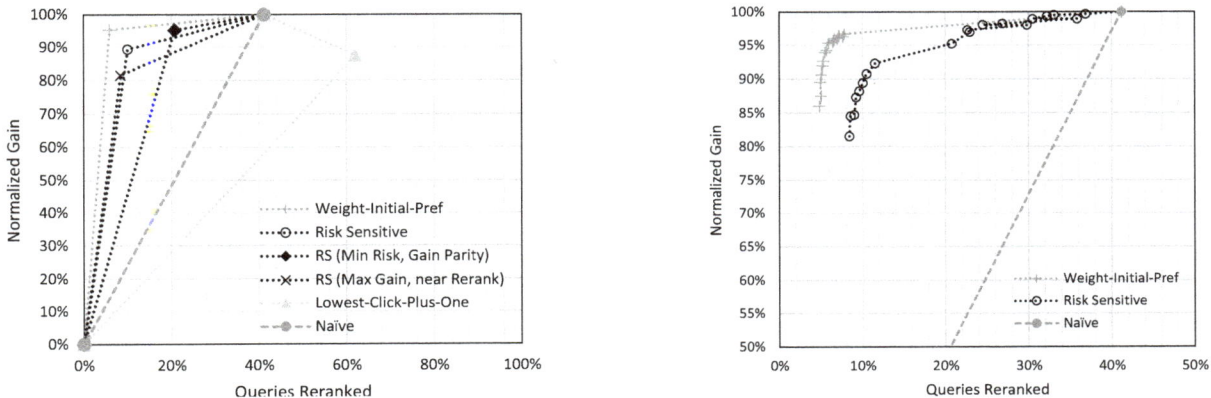

Figure 1: In the Bing dataset, trade-off between gain (normalized to max of standard model) and queries re-ranked for selected models (*Left*) and at all parameter values for the Risk-Sensitive and Weight-Initial-Pref approaches (*Right*).

95.28% gain at 5.92% re-ranking for the *Weight-Initial-Pref* model (vertical distance between the black 'x' and orange '+' in Figure 1). If we select the risk sensitive model to maximize the area for gain vs. re-ranked, both gain and re-ranking suffer; the risk model has 89.39% gain with 10.04% re-ranking vs. 95.28% gain at 5.92% re-ranking for the *Weight-Initial-Pref* model (diagonal distance between the black 'o' and orange '+' in Figure 1). In addition, while the *Weight-Initial-Pref* model is slightly worse in measurable risk than the *Risk Sensitive* model (59.27% to 57.95%) the comparable gain indicates that there has been an increase in measurable reward. Thus, for a slight increase in click-based risk there is a corresponding increase in click-based reward and a major reduction in re-ranking. Furthermore, we see in Figure 1 across the whole range of gain vs. re-ranking tradeoffs that the *Weight-Initial-Pref* models perform at least as well as the risk models and substantially outperform them in the low re-ranking, high gain corner (the optimal top left corner).

On the WSCD datasets, the *Weight-Initial-Pref* models also achieve better gain for comparable re-ranking across the full range in Figure 2 (*right*). In the WSCD '14, the impact is the lowest, here the edge of gain to re-ranking percentage is the least but still visible in Figure

3. In comparison to the risk-sensitive model that attains the same gain, *RS (Min Risk, Gain Parity)*, there is still a 20% reduction in re-ranking and a 5× reduction relative to the *Standard Gain* model. We believe improvements on this dataset could be increased by generalizing our method to preserve order between degrees of relevance – this is the only dataset with multiple degrees of relevance.

In summary, on all datasets the *Weight-Initial-Pref* models show large decreases in the amount of re-ranking relative to the baseline personalized *Standard Gain* models while reducing measurable gain slightly. It also provides moderate to large reductions in re-ranking relative to the risk-sensitive and *Lowest-Click-Plus-One* models while providing as much to substantially more gain than them.

6. RELATED WORK

Our work is related to prior research in personalization, learning to rank, axiomatic IR, click modeling, and online learning. We briefly review the most relevant work in each of these areas next.

Search Personalization. Personalizing search results based on context has been consistently reported to improve retrieval effective-

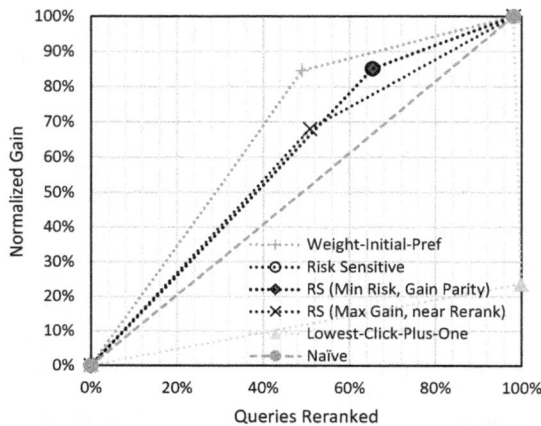

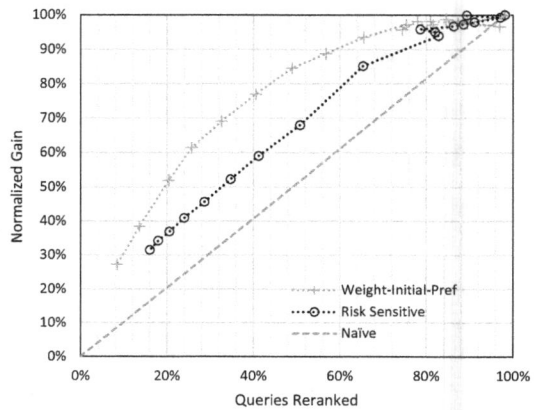

Figure 2: In the WSCD '12 dataset, trade-off between gain (normalized to max of standard model) and queries re-ranked for selected models (*Left*) and at all parameter values for the Risk-Sensitive and Weight-Initial-Pref approaches (*Right*).

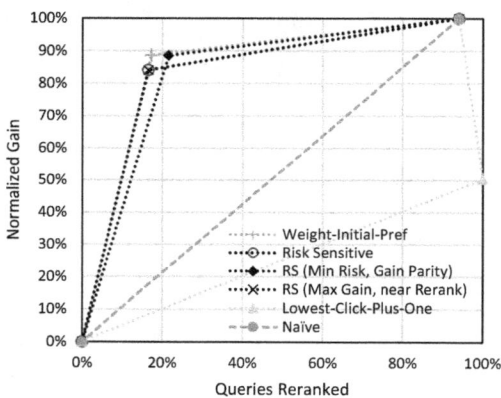

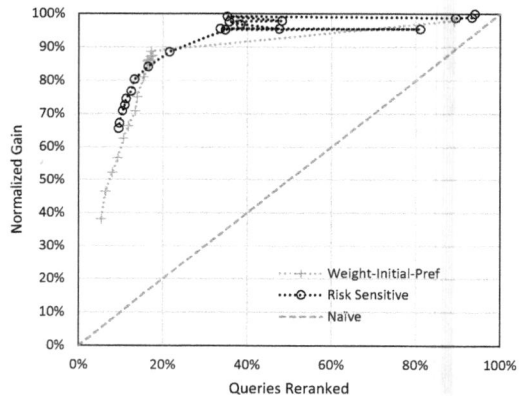

Figure 3: In the WSCD '14 dataset, trade-off between gain (normalized to max of standard model) and queries re-ranked for selected models (*Left*) and at all parameter values for the Risk-Sensitive and Weight-Initial-Pref approaches (*Right*).

ness [3, 27, 31, 34, 35]. Typically, *context* refers to anything that can distinguish the user from the rest – or most – of the population. The most widely used contextual features are users' previous queries and clicks [3, 30, 34, 39], but other contextual features based on a user's browsing history [35], user-specific topical profiles [3, 31], location [4] or demographics [29] have also been demonstrated to be effective for personalizing search results.

In the majority of these studies, the original results returned by a context-independent ranker are passed to a *re-ranker* trained for personalization. Like those works, we assume throughout that personalization will be conducted by learning a single model which re-ranks the results from a non-personalized ranker [3, 34, 35], but our technique is equally applicable for learning a single re-ranking model per user or constructing a target ranking for evaluation by other personalization frameworks. Such re-rankers are typically trained by sampling sessions from search logs and consider *satisfied* clicks in those sessions as ground-truth relevance.

What has often been overlooked by these techniques is the potential pairwise preferences between non-SAT or non-clicked documents. By treating all such documents as equally non-relevant, the personalized re-ranking models ignore the underlying pairwise preferences between such documents that could be inferred by respecting the positions in the original non-personalized ranking. In this paper, we demonstrate how integrating preferences based on the

original ordering and click modeling can significantly reduce the risk of wrong re-rankings in personalization.

Multi-objective Learning to Rank. Learning to rank [23] covers a large body of supervised and semi-supervised techniques in which the goal is to *learn* a ranking function over available retrieval features. The labels for training are usually collected manually for a set of documents, or as stated earlier, are inferred based on collected clicks. The common objective among ranking models is to optimize for relevance. However, in many ranking scenarios, there might be more than one measure for optimization. For instance, Dong et al. [13] demoted outdated labels in their training data and developed a ranker that can be optimized for freshness and relevance. In a similar vein, Svore et al. [32] used historical clicks to break the ties in training when a pair of documents share the same relevance label.

Our work is related to these *multi-objective* scenarios, as we are interested in maximizing the personalization gain while minimizing the risk of diverging from the original preferences. The closest study to our work, which we also use as one of our experimental baselines, is the risk-sensitive optimization framework of Wang et al. [37] that is trained to maximize the difference between the total improvement in ranking relative to a baseline and the weighted total decrease in performance. Increasing the weight penalizes failures more heavily to learn more risk-averse models. Quite recently Dinçer et al. [12] extended this framework to a query-specific risk-weighting where the weight was derived from the significance of deviation in risk relative to the overall risk distribution. In experimentation, we demonstrate that only optimizing a click-based measure of risk in personalization using the uniform weighting of queries as in [37] yields an inferior overall solution viewed according to several other measures of risk – such as percentage of queries re-ranked. Furthermore, although we do not pursue it here, our approach could be combined with either the optimization of the uniform query-weighting of risk or the query-specific weighting by using the implicit preferences to infer a target ranking and the optimization framework to optimize the risk-objective relative to the inferred target ranking.

Axiomatic Information Retrieval. Our work is related to other axiomatic approaches in information retrieval. For example, Fang and Zhai [15] proposed a set of constraints for weighting terms in documents based on document length and term statistics. The same authors later generalized term weighting models to incorporate the semantic similarity of terms [16]. Gollapudi and Sharma [18] discussed a set of axioms for balancing novelty and relevance in diversification and showed that no diversity function can satisfy them all. We develop an axiomatic approach for *personalization* where interaction feedback is combined with non-personalized relevance.

Click Modeling. Clicks capture a user's implicit feedback about documents and have been shown to provide effective ranking features [1] and large-scale pseudo-relevance labels [22]. Consequently, much attention has been devoted to click modeling and interpreting clicks in search logs. Joachims [21] pioneered the application of clicks as labels for optimizing rankers. In a follow up study, Joachims et al. [22] showed that clicks are subject to various presentation biases and proposed a set of rules for inferring pairwise preferences based on clicks. In another work, Agichtein et al. [2] reported similar biases and showed accounting for these biases can significantly improve retrieval effectiveness. Agichtein et al. [1] incorporated features based on click data in training rankers and proposed a set of features for predicting relevance preferences from clicks. We leverage these earlier insights to establish axioms for constraining the *strength* a preference should have; by comparing to an adaptation of the constrained preference ranking of Radlinski and Joachims [24], we demonstrate that which preferences are included for learning are key in controlling the risk of personalization.

Several studies have attempted to model user search behavior for better interpretation of clicks and separating out the relevance aspect from position bias [11, 14, 19]. In one of the earliest work in this area, Craswell et al. [11] suggested a *cascade* model in which users browse results from top to bottom and leave as soon as they find a document that satisfies their intent. The dynamic Bayesian network model (DBN) of Chapelle and Zhang [7] explains the clicks on documents based on their *perceived* and actual relevance. The former factor is determined according to the probability of click based on the URL, while the latter measures the probability of satisfaction given that the document is clicked. A recent work by Chuklin et al. [8] presents a comparative analysis over several state-of-the-art click models. When learning from clicks, Ustinovskiy and Serdyukov [35] investigate a simple fusion method of the scores of the personalized and non-personalized ranker to avoid over-personalizing. This is like our naïve baseline (see Section 3.2) although their method is targeted at increasing the correlation of the personalized ranking with the non-personalized ranking and not at optimizing the trade-off between the percentage of queries personalized and total gain. We demonstrate both increased correlation and a reduction in the percentage of queries personalized. Very recently, Ustinovskiy et al. [36] learned the weights to give to URLs during training by using

interaction signals only available at training time. However, they do not demonstrate a reduction in risk and show a very marginal gain in relevance. Whether their method of using training time signals to learn weights can be incorporated with our approach is an interesting avenue for future work. In contrast to previous click modeling work, our focus is not only on predicting what will be clicked by the user, but we also enforce constraints during learning that ensure relevant documents are at the top while documents deemed non-relevant remain in their most conservative order.

Online Learning. Several recent approaches to online learning from interaction data are also related. In particular, Shivaswamy and Joachims [28] present and Raman et al. [26] later extend a coactive learning method for personalizing rankings from implicit feedback by using online learning to incrementally update a trained model from user click data. In their approach, the user feedback is in the form of clicks that are used to perform an online update to the model in order to improve the search results for the following searches. Perhaps the main limitation of the coactive learning method is the dependence on a linear weight vector over features; often complex non-linear models such as boosting [38] perform substantially better than linear models, and it is not clear how to extend the Coactive learning method to non-linear models that do not depend on linear weight vectors. In contrast, our method can be used by a variety of learning algorithms including gradient-boosted decision trees. Also, in order to make coactive learning robust to imperfect feedback, the rankings presented to users must be slightly perturbed to promote unbiased exploration [26]. In contrast, the method we propose in this paper avoids the problem of oscillation by learning personalized rankings that are consistent with the original pre-personalized ranking over all the data instead of in an online fashion — thus preventing the large changes in ranking that can occur with coactive learning in the presence of noisy user feedback.

In contrast to previous work, we demonstrate that click-based approaches to evaluating personalization do not capture all aspects of the risk of decreasing relevance by personalizing results when not appropriate. In particular, we focus on what axioms must be satisfied in determining the strengths of preferences to provide both a personalized signal of relevance while maintaining an overall conservative approach. We develop a framework that can be flexibly used to set gains for learning personalized models with a wide variety of learning methods including both linear models and gradient-boosted decision tree approaches. Empirically, we demonstrate that risk can be managed in personalization by incorporating information from the non-personalized ranking *while still maintaining* the constraint that clicked or satisfied clicked results are ranked highest.

7. FUTURE WORK & CONCLUSIONS

This work has many potential future extensions of interest. In particular, the strength of preference functions we give here are only one way to satisfy the axioms. There are other ways that would yield a weight on the non-personalized ranker preference (β) less than (α). This includes but is not limited to making (β) query-specific where the number of past impressions might differentially weight updates to head or tail queries, dealing with query result churn by using the number of times a pair is displayed rather than the query, and using a Bayesian approach that models the strength as a probability and performs a Bayesian update depending on other factors (*e.g.*, eye and or cursor tracking). Likewise, considering how to integrate explicit preference judgments or multiple grades of relevance from either the user or an annotator are interesting extensions and might be used as the basis of considering other weightings on the unexamined results after the lowest click. These extensions result directly from casting the problem as a preference assignment problem – while directly defining the target ranking given interaction feedback may be hard, it is both more principled and easier to define how to update pairwise preferences based on those interactions and how to aggregate the preferences to define a target ranking.

In summary, we identified a problem previously unappreciated in the literature. Namely, treating implicit data as relevance judgments leads to often re-ranking queries when there is no demonstrable gain. After identifying this problem, we formulated two simple axioms that lead to global constraints on a target ranking which has the relevant results always on top and then orders results within type consistent with the original ranking results after that. In three real-word commercial search engine logs, learning using this target ranking leads to a substantial reduction in the number of queries re-ranked of 2×-7× fewer queries re-ranked while maintaining 85-95% of the total gain achieved by the standard approach.

References

[1] E. Agichtein, E. Brill, and S. Dumais. Improving web search ranking by incorporating user behavior information. In *Proc. SIGIR*, 2006.

[2] E. Agichtein, E. Brill, S. Dumais, and R. Ragno. Learning user interaction models for predicting web search result preferences. In *Proc. SIGIR*, 2006.

[3] P. Bennett et al. Modeling the impact of short- and long-term behavior on search personalization. In *Proc. SIGIR*, 2012.

[4] P. N. Bennett, F. Radlinski, R. W. White, and E. Yilmaz. Inferring and using location metadata to personalize web search. In *Proc. SIGIR*, 2011.

[5] C. Burges, R. Ragno, and Q. Le. Learning to rank with non-smooth cost functions. In *Proc. NIPS*, 2006.

[6] C. J. C. Burges, K. M. Svore, P. N. Bennett, A. Pastusiak, and Q. Wu. Learning to rank using an ensemble of lambda-gradient models. *JMLR*, 14, 2011.

[7] O. Chapelle and Y. Zhang. A dynamic bayesian network click model for web search ranking. In *Proc. WWW*, 2009.

[8] A. Chuklin, P. Serdyukov, and M. de Rijke. Click model-based information retrieval metrics. In *Proc. SIGIR*, 2013.

[9] K. Collins-Thompson. Reducing the risk of query expansion via robust constrained optimization. In *Proc. CIKM*, 2009.

[10] K. Collins-Thompson, P. N. Bennett, F. Diaz, C. Clarke, and E. M. Voorhees. Trec 2013 web track overview. In *TREC '13*, 2013.

[11] N. Craswell, O. Zoeter, M. Taylor, and B. Ramsey. An experimental comparison of click position-bias models. In *Proc. WSDM*, 2008.

[12] B. T. Dinçer, C. Macdonald, and I. Ounis. Hypothesis testing for the risk-sensitive evaluation of retrieval systems. In *Proc. SIGIR*, 2014.

[13] A. Dong et al. Time is of the essence: Improving recency ranking using twitter data. In *Proc. WWW*, 2010.

[14] G. E. Dupret and B. Piwowarski. A user browsing model to predict search engine click data from past observations. In *Proc. SIGIR*, 2008.

[15] H. Fang and C. Zhai. An exploration of axiomatic approaches to information retrieval. In *Proc. SIGIR*, 2005.

[16] H. Fang and C. Zhai. Semantic term matching in axiomatic approaches to information retrieval. In *Proc. SIGIR*, 2006.

[17] S. Fox et al. Evaluating implicit measures to improve web search. *ACM Trans. Inf. Syst.*, 23(2), Apr. 2005.

[18] S. Gollapudi and A. Sharma. An axiomatic approach for result diversification. In *Proc. WWW*, 2009.

[19] F. Guo, C. Liu, A. Kannan, T. Minka, M. Taylor, Y.-M. Wang, and C. Faloutsos. Click chain model in web search. In *Proc. WWW*, 2009.

[20] K. Järvelin and J. Kekäläinen. Cumulated gain-based evaluation of ir techniques. *ACM Trans. Inf. Syst.*, 20(4), Oct. 2002.

[21] T. Joachims. Optimizing search engines using clickthrough data. In *Proc. SIGKDD*, 2002.

[22] T. Joachims, L. Granka, B. Pan, H. Hembrooke, F. Radlinski, and G. Gay. Evaluating the accuracy of implicit feedback from clicks and query reformulations in web search. *ACM Trans. Inf. Syst.*, 25(2), Apr. 2007.

[23] T.-Y. Liu. Learning to rank for information retrieval. *Foundations and Trends in Information Retrieval*, 3(3), 2009.

[24] F. Radlinski and T. Joachims. Query chains: Learning to rank from implicit feedback. In *Proc. SIGKDD*, 2005.

[25] F. Radlinski, M. Kurup, and T. Joachims. How does clickthrough data reflect retrieval quality. In *CIKM '08*, 2008.

[26] K. Raman, T. Joachims, P. Shivaswamy, and T. Shnabel. Stable coactive learning via perturbation. In *Proc. ICML*, 2013.

[27] X. Shen, B. Tan, and C. Zhai. Context-sensitive information retrieval using implicit feedback. In *Proc. SIGIR*, 2005.

[28] P. Shivaswamy and T. Joachims. Online structured prediction via coactive learning. In *Proc. ICML*, 2012.

[29] M. Shokouhi. Learning to personalize query auto-completion. In *Proc. SIGIR*, 2013.

[30] M. Shokouhi, R. W. White, P. Bennett, and F. Radlinski. Fighting search engine amnesia: Reranking repeated results. In *Proc. SIGIR*, 2013.

[31] A. Sieg, B. Mobasher, and R. Burke. Web search personalization with ontological user profiles. In *Proc. CIKM*, 2007.

[32] K. M. Svore, M. N. Volkovs, and C. J. Burges. Learning to rank with multiple objective functions. In *Proc. WWW*, 2011.

[33] J. Teevan, S. T. Dumais, and D. J. Liebling. To personalize or not to personalize: modeling queries with variation in user intent. In *Proc. SIGIR*, 2008.

[34] J. Teevan, D. J. Liebling, and G. Ravichandran Geetha. Understanding and predicting personal navigation. In *Proc. WSDM*, 2011.

[35] Y. Ustinovskiy and P. Serdyukov. Personalization of web-search using short-term browsing context. In *Proc. CIKM*, 2013.

[36] Y. Ustinovskiy, G. Gusev, and P. Serdyukov. An optimization framework for weighting implicit relevance labels for personalized web search. In *Proc. WWW*, 2015.

[37] L. Wang, P. N. Bennett, and K. Collins-Thompson. Robust ranking models via risk-sensitive optimization. In *Proc. SIGIR*, 2012.

[38] Q. Wu, C. Burges, K. Svore, and J. Gao. Adapting boosting for information retrieval measures. *Journal of Information Retrieval*, 2009.

[39] B. Xiang, D. Jiang, J. Pei, X. Sun, E. Chen, and H. Li. Context-aware ranking in web search. In *Proc. SIGIR*, 2010.

Anytime Ranking for Impact-Ordered Indexes

Jimmy Lin[1] and Andrew Trotman[2]

[1] David R. Cheriton School of Computer Science
University of Waterloo

[2] eBay Inc.

ABSTRACT

The ability for a ranking function to control its own execution time is useful for managing load, reigning in outliers, and adapting to different types of queries. We propose a simple yet effective anytime algorithm for impact-ordered indexes that builds on a score-at-a-time query evaluation strategy. In our approach, postings segments are processed in decreasing order of their impact scores, and the algorithm early terminates when a specified number of postings have been processed. With a simple linear model and a few training topics, we can determine this threshold given a time budget in milliseconds. Experiments on two web test collections show that our approach can accurately control query evaluation latency and that aggressive limits on execution time lead to minimal decreases in effectiveness.

Categories and Subject Descriptors: H.3.4 [Information Storage and Retrieval]: Systems and Software

Keywords: score-at-a-time query evaluation; impact scores

1. INTRODUCTION

Anytime algorithms are algorithms where the quality of results improves as the computation time increases [21]. Typically, such algorithms return a valid solution even if interrupted before they naturally complete. This idea was introduced in the mid-1980s by Dean and Boddy [9] in the context of time-dependent planning. Applied to information retrieval, an anytime ranking function is able to provide a document ranking in response to a user's query, given an arbitrary time constraint. We would, of course, expect the output quality to rise as the time budget increases.

This idea is relevant to search because managing query latency is an important aspect of modern information retrieval, particularly in a web search context. Users are impatient and latency has measurable costs: for example, Brutlag [5] reports for Google search that artificially injecting delays ranging 100 to 400 ms reduces the daily number

of searches per user by 0.2% to 0.6%. Query latencies are typically managed by partitioning the document collection across many (in the case of the web, thousands) of servers such that the latency at each individual server is small. However, this is often not enough. We see at least three compelling applications for anytime ranking functions:

First, they can be applied for load shedding. During periods of unexpectedly large query loads (e.g., flash mobs) it would make sense to restrict the running time of the ranking algorithm. Although this may come at some cost in effectiveness, degrading quality slightly for *everyone* is often preferable to long latencies (or even timeouts) for *some*.

Second, they can be applied to control variance in execution times, particularly outliers called "tail latencies" [8]. Partitioned systems are particularly vulnerable to this phenomenon, since overall latency is dictated by the latency of the slowest component. An anytime ranking function can be configured to "reign in" these tail latencies without affecting the majority of the queries.

Third, anytime ranking functions can be used in conjunction with effectiveness prediction techniques [11] to treat "easy" and "hard" queries differently (e.g., spend less time on easy queries). In a multi-stage retrieval architecture where the initial ranking serves as input to machine-learned ranking models [4], this might yield the same level of effectiveness with less overall computational effort.

We present a novel anytime ranking algorithm on impact-ordered indexes in main memory. Building on a score-at-a-time query evaluation strategy, which processes postings segments in decreasing order of impact scores, we add an early termination check to stop when a specified number of postings ρ has been processed. A simple linear model with a few training topics allows us to work backwards from a time budget (in milliseconds) to the proper setting of ρ. Experiments on two web test collections show that our approach is both simple and effective: we can accurately control query evaluation latency and we find that aggressive limits on execution time leads to minimal decreases in effectiveness.

2. BACKGROUND AND RELATED WORK

Following the standard formulation of ranked retrieval, we assume that the score of a document d with respect to a query q can be computed as an inner product: $S_{d,q} = \sum_{t \in d \cap q} w_{d,t} \cdot w_{q,t}$, where $w_{d,t}$ is the weight of term t in document t and $w_{q,t}$ represents the weight of term t in the query. The goal of top k retrieval is to return the top k documents ordered by S. Typically, w's are a function of term frequency, document frequency, and the like. This formulation captures traditional vector-space models, probabilistic models such as BM25, as well as language modeling and divergence from randomness approaches.

Nearly all modern search engines depend on an inverted index for top k retrieval. As is common today, we assume that the entire index and all associated data structures reside in main memory. The literature describes a few ways in which inverted indexes can be organized: In *document-ordered* indexes, postings lists are sorted by document ids in increasing order. Term frequencies are stored separately. In *frequency-ordered* indexes, document ids are grouped by their term frequencies; within each grouping, document ids are sorted in increasing order, but the groupings are arranged in decreasing order of term frequency. In *impact-ordered* indexes, the focus of this work, the actual score contributions of each term (i.e., the $w_{d,t}$'s) are pre-computed and quantized into what are known as *impact scores*. We refer to a block of document ids that share the same impact score as a postings segment. Within each segment, document ids are arranged in increasing order, but the segments themselves are arranged by decreasing impact score. Regardless of the index organization, the postings are usually compressed with integer coding techniques. There has been plenty of work on index compression, which is beyond the scope of this work, but see a recent study for details [17].

Different query evaluation techniques exhibit affinities for different index organizations. Document-at-a-time (DAAT) techniques, which are the most popular today, work well with document-ordered indexes and term-at-a-time (TAAT) techniques work well with frequency-ordered indexes. Similarly, score-at-a-time (SAAT) strategies take advantage of impact-ordered indexes. A review of query evaluation techniques is beyond the scope of this short paper, but we refer readers to a survey by Zobel and Moffat [22].

The idea of anytime ranking is not entirely new. In the context of learning to *efficiently* rank, Wang et al. [20, 19] proposed machine-learned ranking models that can control their own execution costs. Along the same lines, Cambazoglu et al. [6] introduced early-exit optimizations for ensembles of machine-learned rankers. In a DAAT query evaluation strategy, Macdonald et al. [14] incorporate query performance prediction to facilitate query scheduling. Although Zobel and Moffat [22] allude in passing to an approach along the lines of what we propose, we are not aware of any work that has detailed a concrete implementation with appropriate performance evaluations.

3. ANYTIME RANKING

We take as a starting point the standard inner-product formulation of ranked retrieval described above. In impact-ordered indexes, the $w_{d,t}$'s are pre-computed and quantized into b bits (called its impact score). Here, we use BM25 term weighting. The literature discusses a number of techniques for quantizing the term weights, but in this work we adopt the *uniform* quantization method of Anh et al. [1]:

$$i_{d,t} = \left\lfloor \frac{w_{d,t} - \min(w_{d,t})}{\max(w_{d,t}) - \min(w_{d,t})} \times 2^b \right\rfloor \quad (1)$$

which is an index-wide linear scaling of the term weights and b is the number of bits used to store the impact. In our implementation we set $b = 8$. Crane et al. [7] showed that this setting achieves effectiveness that is indistinguishable from using exact term weights.

3.1 Index Organization

Our indexes are organized as follows: The dictionary provides the entry point to each postings list; each term points to a list of tuples containing (score, start, end, count). Each tuple, which we refer to as a header, corresponds to a postings segment with a particular impact score; start and end are pointers to the beginning and end of the segment data, and count stores the number of documents in that segment. Segments for each term are ordered in decreasing impact score and within each segment, documents are ordered by increasing document id.

Document ids are compressed with QMX [17], which can be thought of as an extension of the Simple family [3] that takes advantage of SSE (Streaming SIMD Extensions) instructions in the x86 architecture. Experiments [17] have shown QMX to be more efficient to decode than SIMD-BP128 [13] (previously the most decoding efficient overall) and competitive with all SIMD and non-SIMD techniques in terms of size.

Following convention, postings code differences between document ids (called *d*-gaps) instead of the document ids directly. In our case, we compute gaps with respect to the document id four positions earlier, i.e., the fifth integer encodes the difference relative to the first, the sixth relative to the second, etc. This approach takes advantage of a SIMD instruction to decode four gaps in one instruction.

3.2 Query Evaluation

Our anytime ranking algorithm builds on a score-at-a-time (SAAT) query evaluation strategy. The algorithm begins by fetching the headers of all postings lists that correspond to the query terms and sorting the headers by decreasing impact score. The postings segments are then processed in this order. For each document id in a segment, the impact score is added to the accumulator, and thus the final result is an unsorted list of accumulators. To avoid sorting this list, a heap of the top k can be maintained during processing. That is, after adding the current impact score to the accumulator, we check to see if its score is greater than the smallest score in the heap; if so, the pointer to the accumulator is added to the heap. The heap keeps at most k elements, and we break ties arbitrarily based on document id.

With SAAT query evaluation, several approaches to accumulator management have been proposed [15, 1, 2, 12]. In this work, we implement the approach of Jia et al. [12]. Since the impact scores are 8 bits, and queries are generally short, it suffices to allocate an array of 16-bit integers, one per document indexed by the document id; modern hardware has ample memory to keep the accumulators in memory. This approach is much simpler than other accumulator management strategies focused on accumulator pruning (e.g., [15, 2]), which made sense when memory was scarce.

Since we are processing postings segments in decreasing impact order, we can terminate at any time. By definition, the segments are processed in decreasing importance: larger score contributions will be added earlier such that the ranking is gradually refined as query evaluation progresses. Early termination to satisfy a time budget is controlled by a parameter ρ, the maximum number of postings to process. Translating a time budget (in milliseconds) into ρ is accomplished using a simple linear model, described later.

The query evaluation algorithm keeps a cumulative count of the number of postings it has processed. Before process-

Name	# Docs	TREC Topics
ClueWeb09b	50,220,423	51-200 ('10-'12)
ClueWeb12-B13	52,343,021	201-300 ('13-'14)

Table 1: Summary of TREC collections and topics used in our experiments.

ing the next postings segment, it checks if processing this particular segment will exceed ρ; if so, we break out of the processing loop. At this point, all that remains is to extract the top k results from the heap (which has a constant cost). This means that our algorithm is also *interruptible*, in that the algorithm does not need to know in advance the time budget; we can demand the termination of the algorithm at any time with an external signal.

One might wonder why it is necessary to build a query efficiency prediction model: why not simply check the query latency after processing each segment? This would not be feasible because the system calls for time measurement are costly operations (relative to processing postings). Even if one wanted to use such measurements to more carefully control query evaluation latency, it still makes sense to use a prediction model to guide the timing of the system calls.

4. EXPERIMENTAL SETUP

Our anytime ranking algorithm is implemented in C++ (compiled with gcc version 4.9.1) and part of an open-source retrieval engine called JASS.[1] Instead of implementing a complete search engine, we use inverted indexes built by the ATIRE system [18],[2] which saved us from having to write a separate indexer. Our system reads indexes generated by ATIRE and rewrites data into an internal format.

Experiments used two standard TREC web test collections: ClueWeb09 (category B), CW09 for short, and ClueWeb12-B13 (i.e., "category B"), CW12 for short. Details for these collections are provided in Table 1, showing the sizes of each and the corresponding topics used to evaluate effectiveness. For simplicity, we kept collection processing to a minimum: for each document, all invalid UTF-8 characters were converted into spaces, alphabetical characters were separated from numerical characters; stemming was applied but no additional document cleaning was performed other than markup tag removal. All experiments were conducted on a server with dual Intel Xeon E5-2680 v3 2.5GHz (12 cores) with 768 GB RAM, running Red Hat Enterprise Linux (RHEL) 7. All experiments were conducted on a single thread on an otherwise idle machine.

For each of the two test collections, the first ten topics were used for training and the remaining topics were used for testing. Our efficiency metric is query latency, the time it takes for our query evaluation engine to produce the top k ranking, measured with the **chrono** library. Measurements exclude file I/O costs, i.e., we keep track of the time it takes to materialize the top k documents in main memory, but do not include the time taken to write the output files for evaluation. We also exclude one-time startup costs such as loading dictionaries, postings, etc. into main memory. We used NDCG@10 as the effectiveness metric, and thus our experiments retrieved only the top 10 results.

---

[1] https://github.com/lintool/JASS

[2] http://atire.org/

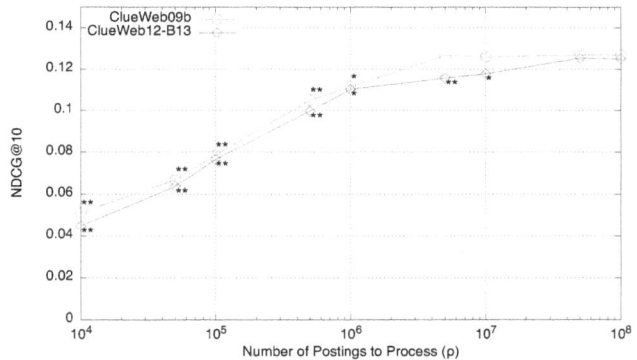

Figure 1: Effectiveness for different ρ settings.

5. RESULTS

Our first set of experiments was designed to highlight the relationship between ρ (number of postings to process) and effectiveness. We accomplished this by a parameter sweep across a wide range of ρ values (10k, 50k..., 100m) and measuring the effect on NDCG@10; these results, across all topics in both collections, are shown in Figure 1. Significance testing with respect to exhaustive evaluation (of all postings) was conducted using Fisher's two-sided, paired randomization test [16]; following convention, * denotes $p < 0.05$ and ** denotes $p < 0.01$. The rightmost setting of ρ yields identical results to exhaustive evaluation. Note that we do not correct for repeated hypothesis testing, so our tests are conservative. These results show that we can reduce the number of postings processed quite a bit without significantly hurting effectiveness. From this figure, we suggest that setting ρ to 10% of the collection size achieves a reasonable balance between effectiveness and efficiency.

The next step was to train a model for predicting ρ (number of postings to process) given a time budget (in milliseconds). We used the first ten topics of each test collection for training and conducted the same parameter sweep as above, recording per-query latency and the number of postings processed; this procedure was repeated for three trials. Given the 10% heuristic above, we retained only data points where the number of postings processed was less than 10% of the collection, since this is the operating region we wish to focus on. For both CW09 and CW12, the data fit a linear regression well, which corresponds to a model that includes a constant overhead plus a cost per posting processed. For space considerations, we are unable to include the scatter plot of the performance model, but the best fit line for CW09 has a slope of 2×10^{-5} with an intercept of 11.741 (R^2 of 0.944); the best fit line for CW12 has a slope of 3×10^{-5} with an intercept of 18.404 (R^2 of 0.982). In our final model of ρ, we rounded the intercept values up to 12 and 19 for CW09 and CW12, respectively.

Finally, we evaluated our anytime algorithm with time budgets of {25, 50, 100, 150, 200} milliseconds. For each time budget, we used the linear model above to determine the appropriate setting of ρ. Results are shown in Table 2, averaged over three trials. Each row shows a particular time budget; relative effectiveness differences are computed with respect to exhaustive processing (final row denoted "max"). Note that NDCG@10 is computed over *all* topics to facilitate comparison with published results, but the remaining columns are with respect to the *test* topics only (140 for

target	ClueWeb09b						ClueWeb12-B13					
	NDCG@10	time	ET	miss	mean	max	NDCG@10	time	ET	miss	mean	max
25ms	0.1076 (−15%) **	22.3	112	45	0.79	2.3	0.0798 (−36%) **	25.4	87	76	0.64	1.2
50ms	0.1159 (−8.7%) *	37.2	97	3	0.77	1.5	0.1102 (−12%) *	47.5	74	49	1.3	3.2
100ms	0.1244 (−2.0%)	59.5	77	0	-	-	0.1118 (−11%) **	80.1	63	9	1.7	3.8
150ms	0.1280 (+0.9%)	75.6	71	0	-	-	0.1172 (−6.2%) *	104	55	0	-	-
200ms	0.1264 (−0.4%)	87.8	62	0	-	-	0.1149 (−8.1%) **	122	49	0	-	-
max	0.1269	160	0	-	-	-	0.1250	291	0	-	-	-

Table 2: Evaluation of our anytime algorithm for various time budgets and exhaustive processing ("max"). Times are measured in milliseconds; NDCG@10 is computed over all topics, but other columns are with respect to the test topics only (see text for explanation).

CW09 and 90 for CW12): The column "time" shows the mean latency for that condition. The column "ET" shows the number of topics that terminated early. The column "miss" shows the number of topics that missed the time budget on average across the three trials. For these topics, "mean" shows the average deficit (i.e., how far past the allotted time) in milliseconds, and "max" is the maximum. For example, in the 25ms condition, 45 out of 140 queries in CW09 exceeded the time budget, by an average of 0.79ms and a maximum of 2.3ms. For reference, exhaustively processing all postings averaged 160ms for CW09 (max 1.51s); 291ms for CW12 (max 1.21ms).

Overall, we are able to quite precisely control the execution time of our anytime ranking function. In the cases where the time budget is violated, the delays are minor, and it would be simple to add a constant "safety factor" if we desired a more stringent observance of the time budget. Our algorithm becomes more conservative as the time budget increases, since segments with lower impact scores tend to be longer and we never partially process a postings segment. Note that exhaustively processing all postings takes much longer on CW12 than CW09, which means that the same time budget leads to more effectiveness compromises; thus, we see significant losses in NDCG@10 for CW12.

Finally, these experiments highlight the ability of our anytime algorithm to control tail latencies. For example, consider the 200ms case with CW09: the mean latency across all topics is only 87.8ms and $140 - 62 = 78$ topics (the "ET" column) in fact finish processing all postings within the time budget. The ρ cutoff in effect aborts queries that are taking too long, without significantly compromising effectiveness.

6. CONCLUSION

Our SAAT strategy represents a very different approach to query evaluation than DAAT algorithms that are popular today [10]. Although we see a few different ways that a DAAT strategy can be modified into an anytime algorithm, they all seem much more complex than our SAAT approach. However, the interesting question is: for a given time budget, can we achieve higher effectiveness with the SAAT approach here or a yet-to-be-developed DAAT anytime algorithm? This remains an open question deserving future investigation.

7. ACKNOWLEDGMENTS

This work was supported by NSF awards IIS-1218043 and CNS-1405688 while the first author was at the University of Maryland. Any opinions, findings, conclusions, or recommendations expressed are the authors' and do not necessarily reflect the views of the sponsor.

8. REFERENCES

[1] V. N. Anh, O. de Kretser, and A. Moffat. Vector-space ranking with effective early termination. *SIGIR*, 2001.

[2] V. N. Anh and A. Moffat. Pruned query evaluation using pre-computed impacts. *SIGIR*, 2006.

[3] V. N. Anh and A. Moffat. Inverted index compression using word-aligned binary codes. *Software: Practice and Experience*, 40(2):131–147, 2010.

[4] N. Asadi and J. Lin. Effectiveness/efficiency tradeoffs for candidate generation in multi-stage retrieval architectures. *SIGIR*, 2013.

[5] J. Brutlag. Speed matters for Google web search. Technical report, Google, 2009.

[6] B. B. Cambazoglu, H. Zaragoza, O. Chapelle, J. Chen, C. Liao, Z. Zheng, and J. Degenhardt. Early exit optimizations for additive machine learned ranking systems. *WSDM*, 2010.

[7] M. Crane, A. Trotman, and R. O'Keefe. Maintaining discriminatory power in quantized indexes. *CIKM*, 2013.

[8] J. Dean and L. A. Barroso. The tail at scale. *CACM*, 56(2):74–80, 2013.

[9] T. Dean and M. Boddy. Time-dependent planning. *AAAI*, 1988.

[10] S. Ding and T. Suel. Faster top-k document retrieval using block-max indexes. *SIGIR*, 2011.

[11] C. Hauff, V. Murdock, and R. Baeza-Yates. Improved query difficulty prediction for the web. *CIKM*, 2008.

[12] X.-F. Jia, A. Trotman, and R. O'Keefe. Efficient accumulator initialisation. *ADCS*, 2010.

[13] D. Lemire and L. Boytsov. Decoding billions of integers per second through vectorization. *Software: Practice and Experience*, 45(1):1–29, 2015.

[14] C. Macdonald, N. Tonellotto, and I. Ounis. Learning to predict response times for online query scheduling. *SIGIR*, 2012.

[15] A. Moffat and J. Zobel. Self-indexing inverted files for fast text retrieval. *TOIS*, 14(4):349–379, 1996.

[16] M. D. Smucker, J. Allan, and B. Carterette. A comparison of statistical significance tests for information retrieval evaluation. *CIKM*, 2007.

[17] A. Trotman. Compression, SIMD, and postings lists. *ADCS*, 2014.

[18] A. Trotman, X.-F. Jia, and M. Crane. Towards an efficient and effective search engine. *Workshop on Open Source Information Retrieval*, 2012.

[19] L. Wang, J. Lin, and D. Metzler. A cascade ranking model for efficient ranked retrieval. *SIGIR*, 2011.

[20] L. Wang, D. Metzler, and J. Lin. Ranking under temporal constraints. *CIKM*, 2010.

[21] S. Zilberstein. Using anytime algorithms in intelligent systems. *AI Magazine*, 17(3):73–83, 1996.

[22] J. Zobel and A. Moffat. Inverted files for text search engines. *ACM Computing Surveys*, 38(6):1–56, 2006.

Balancing Aspects in Retrieved Search Results

David Wemhoener
Center for Intelligent Information Retrieval
College of Information and Computer Sciences
University of Massachusetts
Amherst, Massachusetts
wem@cs.umass.edu

James Allan
Center for Intelligent Information Retrieval
College of Information and Computer Sciences
University of Massachusetts
Amherst, Massachusetts
allan@cs.umass.edu

ABSTRACT

Many queries contain explicit aspects which must be balanced in any retrieved result in order to meet a user's information need: if aspects of the query are missing or disproportionately represented in documents, the results will be of lower quality than desired. This balancing thus needs to occur both within the retrieved documents individually and across the entire set. We introduce the concept of query-aspect balance and describe a new evaluation measure, β-NDCG, that allows the evaluation of query-aspect balance on multivalued query-aspect judgments. We apply β-NDCG to a small test collection and explore its utility. We show that β-NDCG captures problems of query aspect balance within and across documents in the ranked list.

Categories and Subject Descriptors

H.3.3 [**Information Storage and Retrieval**]: Information Search and Retrieval—*Retrieval Models*

Keywords

effectiveness; models; aspects

1. INTRODUCTION

In many retrieval tasks, it is important to ensure that the entirety of a query is covered by the search results. The different information needs, or aspects, presented in a query are not independent of each other and documents in which they co-occur are more likely to be valuable to the user. If a user requests documents relating to "sports on the beach", it stands to reason that the system should not only return a set of documents that are as a whole evenly balanced between information about "sports" and "beaches" but also each individual document should be well-balanced between these two aspects of the query. The user did not likely intend to get a set which is half documents about sports and half documents about beaches, rather they were seeking documents in which the two information needs occurred together. We

address that issue, proposing a new way of evaluating retrieved results based on this notion of query-aspect balance. The measure that we propose, based on the family of NDCG measures, is called β-NDCG.

2. RELATED WORK

There is an extensive line of research into identifying and quantifying query components under the banner of subtopics, also referred to as nuggets, categories or instances. Early work on the problem by Carbonell and Goldstein [2] proposed the maximal marginal relevance method for selecting novel documents while also maintaining relevance to the original query. Clarke et al. [5] codified a framework which distinguished between novelty and diversity and proposed α-NDCG as a measure for comparing ranked lists on the basis of those two factors in the case of subtopic retrieval. Chapelle et al. [3] proposed expected reciprocal rank (ERR)as a means of addressing short comings in traditional relevance measures. Although ERR does not measure diversity, it does capture the notion that the shape of the density of the information retrieved matters. Craswell et al. [6] proposed a cascade model for measuring ranked lists. Argawal et al. [1] propose a series of intent-aware versions of classical retrieval measures. Clarke et al. [4] compared intent-aware and cascade models.

All of those methods and measures are intended to ensure that the ranked list somewhat evenly represents the subtopics within the retrieved set. The aspects of the query itself are not considered except to the extent that documents covering all aspects seem more likely to be relevant and these methods operate on the start of a ranked list. In contrast, this study explicitly incorporates the query's aspects into an evaluation measure and "rewards" ranking methods that correctly balance them.

3. ASPECT COVERAGE

An aspect is an explicit idea expressed within a query. For example, in the query "sports on the beach" there is a "sports" aspect and a "beach" aspect. Intuitively, a relevant document will include both of those aspects. More generally, a document will have a higher degree of relevance the more query aspects it includes. Moreover, a document that balances those aspects, not unduly covering one sub-topic at the expense of others, should be preferred because it evenly "covers" the query. For that reason, we assume that document relevance judgments for aspects are non-binary, supporting a range of possible degrees of relevance. A perfectly balanced ranked list of documents $d_1...d_n$ for a query q with aspects $a_1...a_i$ is one in which the relevance of the documents to the aspects is evenly distributed both within each document and within the entire list.

Based on that idea, a measure for aspect coverage should have the following properties:

- *Relevance:* All other properties being identical, it should reward documents that maximize total relevance to the query aspects.

- *Internal Balance:* It should reward documents that have equal coverage of aspects, minimizing the variance across aspects mentioned. For example, a document that covers all aspects equally has perfect balance, whereas one that covers one aspect well and others poorly will have high variance so poor balance. We note that documents retrieved in response to a query will usually have *some* coverage of each query aspect, but they may not be well-balanced.

- *List Balance:* It should reward documents that cover aspects under-represented in the previously seen documents. Note that internal balance is still important when selecting documents to improve list balance.

- *Multi-valued:* It should function on aspect judgments with multiple levels of relevance so that it is possible to recognize disproportionate over- or under-representation of aspects.

We assume the classic ad-hoc retrieval setting, where the user is issuing a query for which there is not an exact answer, but rather is looking for a range of material on the subject. For example, a user might be looking for a survey of information related to the use of support vector machines in classifying the authorship of scanned documents and enter the query "SVM for scanned document authorship classification." Although some documents are more relevant to this query than others, it is not posed or intended as a question that can be completely answered by any single document.

4. POSSIBLE MEASURES

There are several commonly-used measures that initially appear to be appropriate for this evaluation task. We contend that although they consider similar issues, they have significant weaknesses that make them inappropriate for the task of measuring aspect coverage.

The first measure we consider is α-NDCG [5]. In its original form, we have the following gain G at rank k:

$$G_k = \sum_{i=1}^{m} J(d_k, i)(1-\alpha)^{r_{i,k-1}}$$

where $J(d_k, i)$ represents the judgment of the document at rank k for topic i and $r_{i,k-1}$ is the number of documents from ranks 1 to $k-1$ in which topic i occurs. When judgments are binary as they are assumed to be in α-NDCG, then the only way to increase the gain in a document is to cover more topics. Thus a document can only be high scoring if it covers many topics. However, because we desire the *multi-valued* property, we must incorporate non-binary judgments. In that case, by α-NDCG, a document can be high scoring because it heavily represents a single topic which violates the *internal balance* property: we want documents that have multiple aspects, and would rather see a balanced document

that talks a little about an under-discussed topic then an unbalanced document that talks only about an undiscussed topic. To adapt α-NDCG to handle multi-valued judgments, we change $r_{i,k-1}$ to $s_{i,k-1}$, the sum of the judgments for aspect i on all documents up to rank $k-1$. Unfortunately, the result is that $(1-\alpha)^{r_{i,k-1}}$, regardless of the value of α, rapidly becomes so small that the gain at any rank after the topmost is very small as well. We further note that α-NDCG does not explicitly honor the *internal balance* property because it considers topics independently.

These observations are not surprising: α-NDCG was designed to evaluate the diversity and novelty of a ranked list relative to a set of binary-valued topic judgments [5], where novelty is "the need to avoid redundancy" and diversity is "the need to resolve ambiguity." There are two key differences between our task and the one envisioned for α-NDCG [5], and these inform the differences between the two measures. The first is that aspects, unlike topics, are explicit in the query. Thus we are concerned with the aforementioned issue of balance as opposed to diversity, as we are not trying to resolve ambiguity in the query. The second difference is that we do not assume that our aspects are given binary judgments. For aspects, unlike topics, binary judgments would be fairly uninformative, as most results will likely be at least relevant on some minor level to most aspects since they are explicitly in the query and most retrieval systems will retrieve results that reference all of the terms in the query. The issue is that there is a big difference between a document about beaches that mentions volleyball once and a document about beach volleyball even though it would be perfectly reasonable to argue that both documents would be relevant on a binary scale to both beaches and sports.

The cascade model [6] assumes that the quality of prior documents is important to the value of the current document, however it is predicated on the notion that the user's information need is finite and thus attempts to calculate the rank at which the user is satisfied. It also does not support any notion of query aspects. Thus measures such as ERR that are based on the cascade model could not be used.

Intent-Aware NDCG (NDCG-IA) [1] calculates a separate NDCG score for each category and then aggregates them with the score for each category weighted in proportion to the distribution of the categories for that query. Since each aspect's score is calculated independently of the others it neither rewards documents that cover aspects under-represented in the previously seen documents (i.e., that satisfy the *list balance* goal) nor does it reward documents that minimize aspect variance (i.e., satisfy the *internal balance* property). Since all intent-aware measures likewise calculate the score for each category independently, they cannot serve as the basis for our measure.

5. β-NDCG

As our score should be calculated on multi-valued judgments, the widely-used NDCG family of measures is a logical starting point for designing a measure capable of integrating query-aspect balance. These measures have a cumulative gain function that is discounted as the ranked list is traversed and provide a score normalization against an ideal ranking.

The document gain functions in the original NDCG and its α-NDCG variant do not support our desired objectives, so we will replace them with a new function. Based on our previously specified requirements, the gain for a document should include three components. The first is a positive function of the combined value of the judgment scores for the aspects. The second is a penalty for having unequal coverage of aspects. The third is a penalty for covering aspects that are over-represented in previously seen documents. All of these components should function on multi-valued relevance judgments, not just of documents (as does NDCG) but on aspects (unlike α-NDCG). We start with a skeleton in which the gain for a document is the sum of its aspect judgments, down-weighted by two functions: f_1 is a function of the aspect's relative magnitude and α, which is a parameter indicating our preference for internal aspect balance; and f_2 which is a function of the variance of the aspects in the document and β, which is an indicator of our preference for list aspect balance.

$$G_k = \sum_{i=1}^{m} J(d_k, i) f_1(i, \alpha) f_2(\sigma_{d_k}, \beta) \qquad (1)$$

Since we want f_1 to be negatively correlated with the *proportion* of the previously seen aspects accounted for by aspect i, we set it to be equal to:

$$f_1 = 1 - \alpha \frac{\sum_{h=1}^{k-1} J(d_h, i)}{\sum_{h=1}^{k-1} J(d_h)} \qquad (2)$$

where $J(d_h)$ is the sum of the judgment scores for the aspects of the document at rank h. The penalty will thus increase as the proportion increases with the penalty being zero if we have never seen this aspect before and one if this aspect accounts for the entirety of the previously seen aspects.

Since we want f_2 to be negatively correlated with the variance of the document aspects, we set it to:

$$f_2 = \frac{1}{1 + \beta \sigma_k} \qquad (3)$$

A document with perfectly even balance will have a variance of zero and thus no penalty, while there is a growing penalty as variance increases. Inserting these two equations into equation (1) gives us

$$G_k = \sum_{i=1}^{m} J(d_k, i) \left(1 - \alpha \frac{\sum_{h=1}^{k-1} J(d_h, i)}{\sum_{h=1}^{k-1} J(d_h)} \right) \frac{1}{1 + \beta \sigma_k} \qquad (4)$$

For both α and β, setting the parameter to zero will completely remove any penalty from their respective functions. Setting both to zero gives us NDCG with the gain from each document being simply the sum of its aspect judgments.

We call this measure β-NDCG to reflect its purpose of evaluating the "balance" of aspects within and across documents in a ranked list.

6. EXPERIMENTS

We applied β-NDCG to a set of 21 queries from the TREC Web Track years 2009, 2010 and 2011. The queries were randomly selected from the 50 longest queries in those three years. For each of these queries we created judgments for manually selected aspects. 25 queries were initially selected, however four of the queries were not judged as there were no identifiable aspects. Queries not used included "to be or not to be that is the question" and "all men are created equal." Judgments were assigned on a zero to three scale, where zero was "not relevant" and three was "extremely relevant." The results were generated using the query-likelihood model as implemented in the Galago search engine.

Table 1: "TREC Web Track Queries β-NDCG@10"

Query	$\alpha=0, \beta=0$	$\alpha=0, \beta=1$	$\alpha=1, \beta=0$	$\alpha=1, \beta=1$
2	0.807	0.794	0.765	0.764
16	0.537	0.504	0.528	0.494
18	0.893	0.762	0.912	0.796
44	0.939	0.852	0.946	0.877
53	0.827	0.671	0.427	0.345
105	0.564	0.564	0.667	0.667
106	0.660	0.652	1.000	1.000
109	0.725	0.598	0.698	0.569
112	0.893	0.893	0.667	0.667
116	0.937	0.936	0.947	0.932
117	0.606	0.606	0.609	0.609
119	0.728	0.728	0.333	0.333
122	0.948	0.872	0.866	0.750
123	0.963	0.905	0.934	0.812
125	0.965	0.882	0.962	0.901
129	0.938	0.859	0.929	0.870
136	0.392	0.338	0.520	0.437
139	0.881	0.665	0.879	0.630
143	0.929	0.745	0.569	0.373
146	0.897	0.912	0.930	0.883
148	0.740	0.492	0.579	0.369
149	0.933	1.000	0.908	0.977
MEAN	0.805	0.738	0.753	0.684

We applied β-NDCG using several different parameter settings. Applying β-NDCG with α and β set to zero is equivalent to NDCG with the document relevance scores being equal to the sum of the aspect scores. β set to zero while varying α rewards list balance without rewarding internal balance. α set to zero while varying β rewards list balance but not internal balance. Although internal balance may appear to imply list balance and a set of perfectly internally balanced documents would give a perfectly balanced list, if the list contains documents that are imbalanced, then the internal balance penalty will not distinguish between a set of unbalanced documents which together are balanced and a set of unbalanced documents which are together unbalanced. The decrease in performance of the set when measured with α or β greater than zero indicates that the measure does capture list characteristics which are distinct from the combined weight of the aspects.

The performance of query 139 "rocky mountain news" illustrates the effects of α and β. Query 139's two aspects are "rocky mountain" and "news." When the parameters are both set to zero, query 139 has a score of 0.881. Setting

Table 2: "Query 139 Aspect Relevance Judgments"

Aspect/Rank	1	2	3	4	5	6	7	8	9	10
Rocky Mountain	3	1	1	1	1	2	2	2	2	2
News		1	3	3	3	3	3	3	3	3

$\alpha = 1$ imposes a slight penalty, indicating that the ranked list is slightly list-imbalanced towards one of the two topics (in this case "news"). Increasing β to one, however, imposes a much larger penalty, indicating that although the list is as a whole fairly balanced relative to the idealized cumulative gain list, the documents selected are internally unbalanced. An examination of the result list in Table 2 reveals that none of the documents are internally balanced. "Rocky Mountains" is over represented at rank 1 and "News" is over-represented in the lower ranks. Since the first document over-represents an aspect that is under-represented in the other ranks, the list as whole is relatively balanced which is the cause of the small list balance penalty.

Table 3: "Query 139 Ideal Ranked List $\alpha=0,\beta=1$ "

Aspect/Rank	1	2	3	4	5	6	7	8	9	10
Rocky Mountain	2	2	2	2	2	2	2	2	2	2
News	2	2	2	2	3	3	3	3	3	3

Table 4: "Query 139 Ideal Ranked List $\alpha=1,\beta=0$ "

Aspect/Rank	1	2	3	4	5	6	7	8	9	10
Rocky Mountain	2	2	2	2	2	2	2	2	2	3
News	3	3	3	3	3	3	3	3	3	1

Tables 3 and 4 depict the ideal ranked lists for the maximum settings for α and β, respectively. Maximizing β draws balanced documents to the top of the list, however no list balancing occurs once the internally balanced documents have been exhausted. Maximizing α creates a list that attempts to maintain balance without regard to the internal balance of the documents selected.

It is important to note that the normalized scores reflect the best possible list given the available documents. If there are not balanced documents available, then a list would score highly even if it were in-balanced. A higher score for one query over another does thus not indicate that that query is more balanced in an absolute sense.

7. CONCLUSIONS

We introduced a new perspective on retrieval evaluation, query-aspect balancing, and a new measure, β-NDCG, that addresses it. We demonstrated on a small set of queries that the evaluation measure successfully identifies unbalanced result sets. We also illustrated how variations of β-NDCG can be used to understand the impact of internal balance issues (captured by α) and list balance issues (captured by β).

We have shown that β-NDCG captures a previously unconsidered evaluation issue that is a factor for some complex queries. The challenge of using this measure, however, is that it requires a new type of relevance judgment that has not been collected in the past: a division of a query into aspects and document-level judgments of the relevance of the document to each query aspect.

Future work includes expanding β-NDCG to subtopic balance, striving for balance among subtopics (with multi-level relevance judgments) in the retrieved set. In order to do so, the principles underlying this measure would have to be adjusted to accommodate the notion of ambiguity that is used by subtopic oriented measures. β-NDCG applied to subtopics could be compared to α-NDCG.

8. ACKNOWLEDGEMENTS

This work was supported in part by the Center for Intelligent Information Retrieval and in part by NSF grant IIS-0910884. Any opinions, findings and conclusions or recommendations expressed in this material are those of the authors and do not necessarily reflect those of the sponsor.

9. REFERENCES

[1] R. Agrawal, S. Gollapudi, A. Halverson, and S. Ieong. Diversifying search results. In *Proceedings of the Second ACM International Conference on Web Search and Data Mining*, WSDM '09, pages 5–14, New York, NY, USA, 2009. ACM.

[2] J. Carbonell and J. Goldstein. The use of mmr, diversity-based reranking for reordering documents and producing summaries. In *Proceedings of the 21st Annual International ACM SIGIR Conference on Research and Development in Information Retrieval*, SIGIR '98, pages 335–336, New York, NY, USA, 1998. ACM.

[3] O. Chapelle, D. Metlzer, Y. Zhang, and P. Grinspan. Expected reciprocal rank for graded relevance. In *Proceedings of the 18th ACM Conference on Information and Knowledge Management*, CIKM '09, pages 621–630, New York, NY, USA, 2009. ACM.

[4] C. L. Clarke, N. Craswell, I. Soboroff, and A. Ashkan. A comparative analysis of cascade measures for novelty and diversity. In *Proceedings of the Fourth ACM International Conference on Web Search and Data Mining*, WSDM '11, pages 75–84, New York, NY, USA, 2011. ACM.

[5] C. L. Clarke, M. Kolla, G. V. Cormack, O. Vechtomova, A. Ashkan, S. Büttcher, and I. MacKinnon. Novelty and diversity in information retrieval evaluation. In *Proceedings of the 31st Annual International ACM SIGIR Conference on Research and Development in Information Retrieval*, SIGIR '08, pages 659–666, New York, NY, USA, 2008. ACM.

[6] N. Craswell, O. Zoeter, M. Taylor, and B. Ramsey. An experimental comparison of click position-bias models. In *Proceedings of the 2008 International Conference on Web Search and Data Mining*, WSDM '08, pages 87–94, New York, NY, USA, 2008. ACM.

Building a Self-Contained Search Engine in the Browser

Jimmy Lin

David R. Cheriton School of Computer Science
University of Waterloo
jimmylin@uwaterloo.ca

ABSTRACT

JavaScript engines inside modern web browsers are capable of running sophisticated multi-player games, rendering impressive 3D scenes, and supporting complex, interactive visualizations. Can this processing power be harnessed for information retrieval? This paper explores the feasibility of building a JavaScript search engine that runs completely self-contained on the client side within the browser—this includes building the inverted index, gathering terms statistics for scoring, and performing query evaluation. The design takes advantage of the IndexDB API, which is implemented by the LevelDB key–value store inside Google's Chrome browser. Experiments show that although the performance of the JavaScript prototype falls far short of the open-source Lucene search engine, it is sufficiently responsive for interactive applications. This feasibility demonstration opens the door to interesting applications and architectures.

Categories and Subject Descriptors: H.3.4 [Information Storage and Retrieval]: Systems and Software

Keywords: JavaScript; LevelDB; IndexedDB

1. INTRODUCTION

In nearly all deployments, search engines handle the vast bulk of processing (e.g., document analysis, indexing, query evaluation) on the server; the client is mostly relegated to results rendering. This approach vastly under-utilizes the processing capabilities of clients: web browsers today embed powerful JavaScript engines capable of running real-time collaborative tools [5], powering online multi-player games [3], rendering impressive 3D scenes, supporting complex, interactive visualizations,[1] enabling offline applications [6], and even running first-person shooters.[2] These applications take advantage of HTML5 standards such as WebGL, WebSocket, and IndexedDB, and therefore do not require additional plug-ins (unlike with Flash).

---

[1] d3js.org
[2] www.quakejs.com

Can we apply this processing power for information retrieval in interesting new ways? This paper explores the feasibility of building a JavaScript search engine that runs completely self-contained in the browser—this includes parsing documents, building the inverted index, gathering terms statistics for scoring, and performing query evaluation.

Is such a design merely a curiosity, or does it offer advantages over traditional client–server architectures? Even as a curiosity, this work explores how far browser technologies have advanced in the previous decade or so, where they have emerged as a viable platform for delivering rich user experiences. However, browser-based search engines provide interesting opportunities for information retrieval, both from the perspective of enabling novel applications and opening up the design space of search architectures.

In addition to discussing the implications of a browser-based search engine, this paper—which is a shorter version of a previous report [7]—describes the design and implementation of JScene (pronounced "jay-seen", rhymes with Lucene), an open-source proof of concept that illustrates the feasibility of these ideas. JScene takes advantage of the IndexedDB API, which is supported by a few modern web browsers and implemented using LevelDB in Google's Chrome browser. The result is a completely self-contained search engine that executes entirely on the client side without any external dependencies. As a reference, JScene is compared against the popular open-source Java search engine Lucene; it should not be a surprise that JScene falls short of Lucene in performance, but results nevertheless demonstrate that a pure JavaScript implementation is sufficiently responsive to support interactive search capabilities.

2. DESIGN IMPLICATIONS

Suppose it were possible to build an in-browser JavaScript search engine that is fully self-contained and delivers reasonable performance: so what? More than a technical curiosity, such a design promises to open up many interesting possibilities, detailed below (see more discussion in [7]).

Offline access. One obvious advantage of this design is that the user doesn't need to be connected to the internet, so documents are available for searching offline. One can imagine a background process that continuously ingests web pages that the user has visited in the recent past and updates an index of these documents—search capabilities would then be available even if the computer were disconnected from the network. Previous studies have shown that a significant fraction of users' search behavior on the web consists of "refinding" [9], or searching for pages they had encountered before. Thus, a reasonably-sized local index might achieve good coverage of many user queries.

Private search. Another advantage of a search engine that resides completely self-contained within the browser is that there is no third party logging queries, clicks, and other interactions. This is particularly useful when a user has a collection of documents she wishes to search privately—for example, when researching a medical condition, some stigmatized activity, or other sensitive topics. This scenario would be operationalized by coupling the in-browser search engine with a focused crawler: the user would, for example, direct the crawler at a collection of interest (e.g., a website with medical information), and the search engine would then ingest documents according to crawl settings.

Load shedding. From the perspective of a commercial search engine company, which needs to continuously invest billions in building datacenters, in-browser search capabilities are appealing from the perspective of reducing server load. However, "dispatching" queries for local execution on the client's machine may eliminate the opportunity to generate revenue (i.e., via ad targeting), but this is an optimization problem that search engine companies can solve. Although the coverage of a local index would be miniscule compared to the centralized index of a commercial search engine, for particular classes of queries (such as the "refinding" queries discussed above), the local collection might be adequate (and it is possible that refinding queries provide fewer ad targeting opportunities anyway).

Split execution. Instead of purely server-side or client-slide query execution, there are possibilities for split execution where query evaluation is performed cooperatively. One possibility is search personalization, where generic search results are tailored to a user's interests on the client side.

Distributed search marketplace. Synthesizing the ideas discussed above, one possible future scenario is the emergence of a marketplace for hybrid models of centralized and distributed search where optimization decisions are arrived at jointly by rational economic actors driven by incentives.

For example, a commercial search engine company might offer an incentive for a user to execute all or part of a search locally, in the form of a micropayment or the promise of privacy (e.g., not storing the queries and interactions). From the search engine company perspective, the value of the incentive can be computed from the costs of datacenters, revenue opportunities from ad targeting, etc. Commercial search engine companies have a clear sense of which searches are "money-makers" (rich ad targeting opportunities) and which aren't. Yet, all searches currently cost the companies money. From the users' perspective, they can control in a fine-grained manner their preferences for privacy and resource usage. The marketplace determines when the incentives on both ends align. To the extent that "money-losing" queries overlap with the types of queries that can be handled locally, such transactions are mutually beneficial.

3. FEASIBILITY STUDY

Having discussed the interesting applications and architectural possibilities of self-contained, in-browser search engines, it is now time to address the practical question: Is such a design actually feasible? Note that the goal of JScene, the proof of concept described in this paper, is to show that it is possible to build a pure JavaScript in-browser search

engine with *reasonable* performance—within users' latency tolerance for interactive search. Of course, the performance of the system will not come close to a custom-built search engine (e.g., Lucene), but that's not the point; a feasibility demonstration confirms that this general concept warrants further exploration. To facilitate follow-on work, the JScene prototype is released under an open-source license and available to anyone interested.[3]

At the storage layer, JScene depends on LevelDB, an on-disk key–value store built on the same basic design as the Bigtable tablet stack [2]. It is implemented in C++ and was open-sourced by Google in 2011. The key–value store provides the Chrome implementation of the Indexed Database (IndexedDB) API, which is formally a W3C Recommendation.[4] LevelDB supports basic put, get, and delete operations on collections called "stores". Keys are maintained in sorted order, and the API supports forward and backward iteration over keys (i.e., to support range queries). Data are automatically compressed using the Snappy compression library, which is optimized for speed as opposed to maximum compression. The upshot is that inside every Chrome browser, there is a modern key–value store accessible via JavaScript. The JScene prototype takes advantage of LevelDB, as exposed via the IndexedDB API, to store all index structures.

3.1 Index Construction

The biggest challenge of building JScene is implementing an inverted index using the provided APIs. The IndexedDB API is built around key–value pairs, where values can be complex JavaScript objects and keys can be JavaScript primitives, a field inside the value object, or auto generated. In JScene, the postings are held in a store called `postings`, where the key is a concatenation of the term and the docid containing the term, and the value is the term frequency. For example, if the term "hadoop" were found twice in document 2842, the key would be "hadoop+2842" (with "+" as the delimiter) with a value of 2. In the tweet search demo application (see below), tweet ids can be used directly as docids, but in the general case, docids can be sequentially assigned as documents are ingested. A postings list corresponds to a range of keys in the `postings` store, and thus query evaluation can be translated into range scans, which are supported by IndexDB.

A few alternative designs were considered, but then rejected (at least for this prototype): it seemed more natural to map each individual posting onto a key–value pair as opposed to accumulating a list as the value of a single key (the term), since in that case the indexer would need to rewrite the value every time a term was encountered. Of course, it is possible to batch data and perform term–document inversion in memory, but this adds complexity that is perhaps not necessary for a proof of concept. In many retrieval engines, terms are mapped to unique integer ids, which allows the postings to be more compactly encoded. Since IndexDB keys are strings, this doesn't seem like much help.

Given this design, the indexer operation is straightforward. Each input document is represented as a JSON object and the entire collection is stored in an array. The indexer processes each document in turn and generates key–value pair insertions corresponding to the inverted index design

---

[3] jscene.io
[4] www.w3.org/TR/IndexedDB/

described above. All transactions in IndexDB are asynchronous, where the caller supplies an `onsuccess` callback function which is executed once the transaction completes. Thus, a naïve indexer implementation based on a for loop that iterates over the documents would simply queue potentially millions of transactions, completely overwhelming the underlying store. Instead, the indexer is implemented using a chained callback pattern—the `onsuccess` callback function of a transaction to insert a key–value pair initiates the next insertion, iterating through all tokens in a document and then proceeding to the next document, until the entire collection has been processed. This style of programming, although foreign in languages such as C/C++ or Java, is common in JavaScript.

Separately, the index also needs to store document frequencies for scoring purposes. These statistics are held in a separate store, aptly named `df`. The document frequencies are first computed by iterating over the entire collection and keeping track of term statistics in a JavaScript object (i.e., used essentially as a hash map). Once all documents have been processed, all entries in the object are inserted into the store, with the term as the key and the document frequency as the value. Once again, the chained callback pattern described above is used for these operations.

3.2 Query Evaluation

With an inverted index, query evaluation algorithms traverse postings in response to user queries to generate a top k ranking of results. Query evaluation for keyword search, of course, is a topic that has been extensively studied (see [10] for a survey). In the context of this work, the goal is to explore the feasibility of in-browser query evaluation using JavaScript, not raw performance per se. Thus, experiments in this paper used a simple approach based on $tf\text{-}idf$ scoring that requires the first query term to be present in any result document. There are several reasons for this choice: First, previous work has shown that this scoring model works reasonably well in practice [1]. Second, terms in a user's query are often (implicitly) sorted by importance, and so it makes sense to treat the first query term in a distinguished manner. Third, this approach serves as a nice middle ground between pure conjunctive (AND) and pure disjunctive (OR) query evaluation. Finally, this approach lends itself to a very natural implementation in JavaScript described below.

The prototype query evaluation algorithm uses a very simple hash-based approach in which a JavaScript object is used as the accumulator to store current document scores, with the document id as the property and the score as the value (essentially, a hash map). In the initialization step, the document frequencies of all query terms are first fetched from the `df` store. Next, a range query corresponding to the first query term is executed, and all postings are scanned. The accumulator hash map is initialized with scores of all documents that contain the term. After the first query term is processed, the query evaluation algorithm proceeds to the next query term, which results in another range scan; for each posting, the accumulator structure is probed, and if the key (document) is found, the value (document score) is updated. All query terms are processed in this manner. At the end, the contents of the accumulator are sorted by value to arrive at the top k.

Two details are worth discussing. First, this query evaluation algorithm bears resemblance to the so-called SvS al-

gorithm for postings intersection (i.e., AND-ing of all query terms) that cyclically intersects the next postings list with the current partial results [4]. However, the standard implementation takes advantage of binary search, skip lists, and other techniques—given the limitations of the LevelDB API, it is not entirely clear how such optimizations can be implemented in JavaScript. Second, the design of the IndexedDB API makes the JScene query evaluation code somewhat convoluted. A range scan begins by acquiring a cursor, which is an asynchronous operation with an associated `onsuccess` callback. An object passed into the callback provides a method that advances the cursor. Thus, the entire query evaluation algorithm is implemented (somewhat awkwardly) as chained callbacks: when the sequence of callbacks corresponding to the processing of the first query term completes, it triggers the range query for the second term and the series of callbacks associated with that, and so on. As with indexing, this style of programming is foreign to developers used to building systems in C/C++ or Java.

4. EXPERIMENTS

Experiments were conducted on a 2012-generation Macbook Pro, with a quad-core Intel Core i7 processor running at 2.7 GHz with 16 GB RAM and a 750 GB SSD. The machine ran Mac OS X 10.9.2 with Google Chrome version 33.0.1750.146. Experiments used the Tweets2011 collection from the TREC 2011 Microblog track [8], which consists of 16 million tweets. Initial trials indicated that JScene would not be able to index the entire Tweets2011 collection within a reasonable amount of time. Thus, a smaller collection comprising 1.12m tweets was created by random sampling. In total, the documents contain 13.9m tokens with 1.74m unique terms, occupying 140 MB on disk uncompressed.

For evaluation, JScene was compared to the Lucene search engine (version 4.7.0). To provide a fair comparison, the Lucene queries were formulated to specify the same constraints as in JScene. To ensure that both systems were processing the same content, for JScene the collection was first tokenized with the Lucene tools provided as a reference implementation in the TREC Microblog evaluations[5] and the resulting tokens were then re-materialized as strings to create the JSON documents used by JScene.

Evaluations used 109 queries from the Microblog tracks at TREC 2011 and 2012 (ignoring the query timestamps). The relevant metrics in these experiments are indexing and query evaluation speed. No effectiveness evaluation was conducted, which is saved for future work.

It took JScene 644 minutes (~10.7 hours) to build the inverted index for 1.12m tweets and another 152 minutes (~2.5 hours) to construct the document frequency table (both averaged over two trials). While building the inverted index, the Mac OS X Activity Monitor showed CPU usage oscillating roughly between 15% and 25%, where the peaks correspond to LevelDB compaction events. These utilization levels suggest that the process is IO bound (even though the machine is equipped with an SSD). The LevelDB data for the postings occupy approximately 1.6 GiB on disk, and the document frequency table another 0.2 GiB.

Indexing results translate into a sustained write throughput of around 360 postings per second. However, these figures are not directly comparable with other performance

---

[5] `twittertools.cc`

System	mean	median	P90	max
JScene	146	106	311	1058
Lucene	1.4	0.8	2.8	9.8

Table 1: Query evaluation performance comparing JScene and Lucene; all values in milliseconds.

evaluations of LevelDB because of at least two reasons: first, it is unclear how much overhead JavaScript and the IndexDB API introduce, and second, our chained callback implementation means that the insertions were performed sequentially (i.e., synchronously), which is known to be much slower than the standard asynchronous write mode.[6]

For reference, Lucene took 27 minutes to index the same collection on a single thread (averaged over two trials). The on-disk index size is just 154 MiB. It is quite clear that JScene indexing throughput falls far short of Lucene, and that Snappy compression is far less effective than special-purpose compression schemes designed specifically for search. This should not be surprising.

Table 1 compares query latency of JScene and Lucene for the 109 queries from TREC 2011 and 2012: figures show mean, median, 90th-percentile, and max values (averaged over three trials). Results for both are with a warm cache and Lucene ran in a single thread. In terms of the mean latency, JScene is roughly two orders of magnitude slower than Lucene; the performance gap is about the same based on the other metrics. This is of course not surprising since Lucene uses specialized data structures and has received much attention from the open-source community. However, JScene is reasonably responsive, with query latencies within the range that users would expect for interactive systems.

To further explore the performance of JScene, a set of terms were randomly sampled from the `df` store and treated as single-term queries. The performance of these queries are shown as solid squares in Figure 1. The figure focuses on terms with *df* less than 1000, but the linear relationship extends to all sampled terms. The solid squares give a sense of the lower bound on query latency, since any document-at-a-time query evaluation algorithm will need to scan all postings for the single query term. For comparison, the TREC queries are plotted as circles based on the *df* of their first query term. This plot illustrates two points: First, there remains much room for improvement in JScene. Second, even in the limit, query evaluation with IndexedDB (via LevelDB), at least with the current storage layout, will still be measured in tens of milliseconds.

5. FUTURE WORK AND CONCLUSION

What can we conclude from these experiments? Results suggest that although a self-contained, in-browser JavaScript search engine is much slower than a custom native application (big surprise), the JavaScript implementation is sufficiently responsive for interactive querying. The current prototype is sufficiently performant to be deployed for searching (most) users' timelines, i.e., *all* tweets that a user has ever read. From this perspective, the design is most definitely feasible and worthy of further exploration.

These experimental results, however, reflect only a first attempt at realizing the general concept. The prototype reflects a straightforward (i.e., dumb) technical implementation, without applying any of the standard efficiency tricks

---
[6]`leveldb.googlecode.com/svn/trunk/doc/benchmark.html`

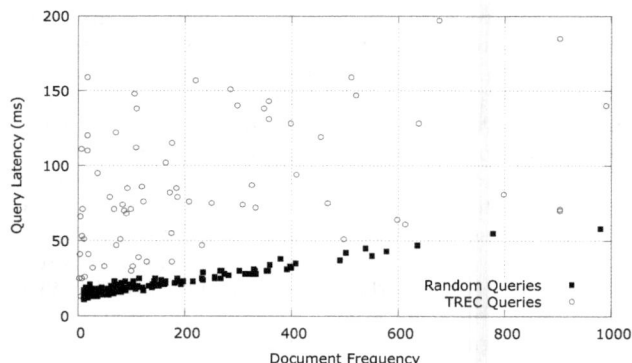

Figure 1: Latency vs. document frequency of query term for randomly-generated and TREC queries.

that are available in every researcher's toolbox. These include various types of compression, alternative schemas and storage layouts, optimizing data access patterns for better locality, etc. These techniques, coupled with future improvements in the IndexedDB implementation, will narrow the gap between in-browser and native search applications.

Given this feasibility demonstration, it would not be premature to start exploring some of the applications and architectures discussed in Section 2. Performance and scalability will continue to improve and become less and less of an issue: in the limit, local indexes have an inherent performance advantage in eliminating network latencies.

6. ACKNOWLEDGMENTS

This research was supported by NSF awards IIS-1218043 and CNS-1405688 while the author was at the University of Maryland. Any opinions, findings, conclusions, or recommendations expressed are the author's and do not necessarily reflect the views of the sponsor.

7. REFERENCES

[1] N. Asadi and J. Lin. Fast candidate generation for real-time tweet search with Bloom filter chains. *ACM TOIS*, 31, 2013.

[2] F. Chang, J. Dean, S. Ghemawat, W. Hsieh, D. Wallach, M. Burrows, T. Chandra, A. Fikes, and R. Gruber. Bigtable: A distributed storage system for structured data. *OSDI*, 2006.

[3] B. Chen and Z. Xu. A framework for browser-based multiplayer online games using WebGL and WebSocket. *ICMT*, 2011.

[4] J. Culpepper and A. Moffat. Efficient set intersection for inverted indexing. *ACM TOIS*, 29(1), 2010.

[5] C. Gutwin, M. Lippold, and T. Graham. Real-time groupware in the browser: Testing the performance of web-based networking. *CSCW*, 2011.

[6] R. Leblon. Building advanced, offline web applications with HTML 5. Master's thesis, Universiteit Gent, 2010.

[7] J. Lin. On the feasibility and implications of self-contained search engines in the browser. *arXiv:1410.4500*, 2014.

[8] I. Ounis, C. Macdonald, J. Lin, and I. Soboroff. Overview of the TREC-2011 Microblog Track. *TREC*, 2011.

[9] S. K. Tyler and J. Teevan. Large scale query log analysis of re-finding. *WSDM*, 2010.

[10] J. Zobel and A. Moffat. Inverted files for text search engines. *ACM Computing Surveys*, 38(6):1–56, 2006.

Condensed List Relevance Models

Fernando Diaz
Microsoft
fdiaz@microsoft.com

ABSTRACT

Pseudo-relevance feedback has traditionally been implemented as an expensive re-retrieval of documents from the target corpus. In this work, we demonstrate that, for high precision metrics, re-ranking the original feedback set provides nearly identical performance to re-retrieval with significantly lower latency.

1. INTRODUCTION

Pseudo-relevance feedback refers to the use of an initial retrieval to find effective query expansion terms or phrases [1, 5]. The expanded query is often substantially longer than the original query and, as a result, incurs higher latency due to more posting lists being evaluated. This problem is exacerbated by retrieval systems which have been aggressively optimized (both in terms of efficiency and effectiveness) for short, web-like queries. That said, pseudo-relevance feedback consistently improves retrieval effectiveness in many domains [7, 10, 2].

In this paper, we exploit the high overlap between the first and second retrievals in pseudo-relevance feedback in order significantly improve efficiency. This overlap allows fast score computation of those documents already fetched as part of the first stage of the pseudo-relevance feedback process. In order to demonstrate this phenomenon, we computed the overlap between the top ten documents retrieved after pseudo-relevance feedback and those retrieved in the initial retrieval (Table 1). The results show that, with extremely high probability, the top ranked documents after pseudo-relevance feedback have already been fetched. Although this probability falls with the rank of the document in the final retrieval, many retrieval metrics emphasize the top of the ranked list.

We propose the following simple modification to pseudo-relevance feedback: re-rank the initial retrieval instead of re-retrieving. Our experiments test two hypotheses. First, re-ranking the original retrieval set performs as well as re-retrieving. Second, re-ranking the original retrieval is much

Table 1: Top n locality of pseudo-relevance feedback. We computed the probability of the highest ranked documents *after* pseudo-relevance feedback occurring in the top 1000 documents of the initial retrieval. Probabilities are computed from 1000 random parameter settings for an RM3 model.

rank	trec12	robust	web
1	1	0.999	0.998
2	0.996	0.996	0.995
3	0.994	0.993	0.996
4	0.996	0.989	0.993
5	0.992	0.987	0.991
⋮	⋮	⋮	⋮
996	0.374	0.416	0.389
997	0.383	0.385	0.388
998	0.368	0.363	0.359
999	0.377	0.385	0.383
1000	0.395	0.387	0.402

more efficient than re-retrieving. The evidence from our experiments supports both of these hypotheses.

2. RELATED WORK

Although there has been a great deal of work on improving the effectiveness and robustness of pseudo-relevance feedback techniques, there has been very little work on improving the efficiency of pseudo-relevance feedback.

Cartright *et al.* present several corpus pre-processing methods for improving the efficiency of relevance model-based feedback [4]. The techniques operate under the assumption of massive query expansion where the size of the expanded query is as large as the vocabulary. This allows systems to construct an corpus-level inter-document similarity matrix *a priori* and then exploit this data structure to quickly compute relevance model scores. Although this work is technically exciting, the assumption of a fixed expansion size is problematic. Wu and Fang present a method for incrementally performing pseudo-relevance feedback [12]. This method is similar to ours insofar as the authors reuse computation from the initial retrieval. However, our method seems to be a missing baseline for their experiments.[1] Furthermore, the experiments in Wu and Fang explore very small

---

[1] Our method is discussed and dismissed as probably leading to poor performance.

numbers of feedback terms (5-20) which limits the generalizability to more realistic, larger expanded queries.[2]

Re-ranking an initial retrieval is not novel. Broder *et al.* present a two-pass method for efficiently scoring documents for standard retrieval [3]. MacDonald *et al.* present a staged ranking method applying fast retrieval methods to establish a candidate set and then applying a slower learning to rank approach on this candidate set [9]. In the context of image retrieval Lin *et al.* proposing re-ranking images using pseudo-relevance information [8]. Finally, Diaz presents a graph-based re-ranking technique which is mathematically related to pseudo-relevance feedback [6].

To the best of our knowledge, we are the first to examine this method for pseudo-relevance feedback on standard text document retrieval.

3. ALGORITHMS

Pseudo-relevance feedback techniques often take three parameters: the number of feedback documents (k), the number of feedback terms (m), and the interpolation weight with the original query (λ). Another, often overlooked, parameter is the number of final documents retrieved for evaluation (n). Standard TREC-style runs often set this value to a default of 1000.

3.1 Relevance Model

Relevance modeling refers to pseudo-relevance feedback in the language modeling retrieval framework. Given a query q, the maximum likelihood query language model is defined as,

$$p(w|\theta_q) = \frac{\#(w, q)}{\sum_{w' \in q} \#(w', q)} \quad (1)$$

The initial retrieval scores documents according to Kullback-Leibler divergence between the query language model and the document model,

$$D(\theta_q \| \theta_d) = \sum_{w \in q} p(w|\theta_q) \log \frac{p(w|\theta_q)}{p(w|\theta_d)} \quad (2)$$

where θ_d is the language model for document d. The top k documents for pseudo-relevance feedback are retrieved here.

The expanded query or relevance model (RM) is defined as,

$$p(w|\theta_{RM1}) = \sum_{i=1}^{k} \frac{p(q|\theta_d)}{\mathcal{Z}} p(w|\theta_d) \quad (3)$$

where $p(q|\theta_d)$, known as the query likelihood, is a simple transformation $D(\theta_q \| \theta_d)$; and $\mathcal{Z} = \sum_{i=1}^{k} p(q|\theta_d)$. As a heuristic, a system often clips $p(w|\theta_{RM1})$ to only include the m terms with the largest probabilities. The probability of other terms is set to 0 and the probability of the top m are renormalized.

In practice, linearly interpolating with the original query model (Equation 1) improves performance. This model, RM3, is defined as,

$$p(w|\theta_{RM3}) = \lambda p(w|\theta_q) + (1 - \lambda) p(w|\theta_{RM1}) \quad (4)$$

where $p(w|\theta_{RM1})$ is the clipped relevance model. In the second retrieval, documents are again ranked by Equation 2, but this time with $p(w|\theta_{RM3})$ instead of $p(w|\theta_q)$. At this point, the top n documents are retrieved for evaluation.

3.2 Condensed List Relevance Model

We propose the following small change to relevance model retrieval. Instead of retrieving k in our initial retrieval, we retrieve n. We still estimate the relevance model with the smaller set of k documents (Equation 3). However, our final ranking of n documents is a re-ranking of the initial retrieval. We refer to this method as the *condensed list relevance model* (CLRM) because we remove unscored documents in the same way condensed list evaluation metrics remove unjudged documents [11]. In practice, we use the interpolated relevance model (Equation 4) and refer to our algorithm as CLRM3.

4. METHODS

We evaluate our method on three *ad hoc* datasets: trec12 consists of topics 51-200 associated with the Tipster 1 and 2 disks; robust consists of topics 301-450 and 601-700 associated with the Tipster 4 and 5 disks; web consists of topics 1-200 associated with Clue Web 2009 Category B. We removed documents from web with a Waterloo spam score less than 70.[3] We indexed corpora using Indri with the SMART stopword list and with Krovetz stemming. We ran our experiments on a cluster of nine machines, each with 24 Intel Xeon 2.27GHz CPUs and 24 GB of RAM. All indexes were built and accessed locally with one IndriRunQuery process per query.

We use the Indri implementation of RM3 and implemented our algorithm by adding roughly fifteen lines of code to `IndriRunQuery.cpp`. This patch will be available on acceptance.

We performed ten-fold cross-validation to tune the k, m, and λ parameters. The Dirichlet μ was fixed at 2500, the Indri default, and n was fixed at 1000, as is customary in TREC evaluations. We ran one cross-validation for each of the presented metrics so the results reflect the performance of an algorithm whose parameters are cross-validated for that metric. We compare methods by concatenating the ten testing folds and then performing a paired Student's t-test on queries.

5. RESULTS

We present effectiveness results in Table 2 broken down by precision and recall oriented metrics. Because Table 1 suggests that most of the top documents will be preserved with CLRM3, we expect performance for high precision metrics to be comparable to RM3. Indeed, the results in Table 2 confirm this suspicion. Across all conditions, we find that CLRM3 performs as well as RM3; in one case, it outperforms RM3. This provides evidence supporting our first hypothesis. The recall-oriented metrics describe the performance farther down the ranked list. In particular, the recall metric suggests that RM3 is more effective at retrieving more relevant documents, although the effect may not be noticeable at the top of the ranked list.

We inspected the effectiveness of individual query and parameter settings in our sweep. We found almost identical

---

[2]Previous results demonstrate that optimal parameters for relevance models lie in the 75-100 range for number of terms [6, Table 3].

[3]https://plg.uwaterloo.ca/ gvcormac/clueweb09spam/

Table 2: Effectiveness results for precision and recall oriented metrics. Numbers in bold indicates statistically significant improvement over the alternative for that metric using a Student's paired t-test ($p < 0.05$).

(a) Precision-oriented metrics

	RR	NDCG5	NDCG10
trec12			
RM3	0.7343	0.6047	0.5629
CLRM3	**0.7599**	0.6091	0.5661
robust			
RM3	0.7100	0.4810	0.4767
CLRM3	0.7100	0.4808	0.4757
cw09b			
RM3	0.4907	0.2161	0.2032
CLRM3	0.4907	0.2161	0.2032

(b) Recall-oriented metrics

	MAP	Rprec	recall
trec12			
RM3	**0.3164**	**0.3532**	**0.6834**
CLRM3	0.2921	0.3410	0.5939
robust			
RM3	**0.2892**	0.3140	**0.7625**
CLRM3	0.2767	0.3140	0.6914
cw09b			
RM3	0.1613	0.2108	**0.4712**
CLRM3	0.1606	0.2108	0.4644

Table 3: Fraction of runs with equal metric values for RM3 and CLRM3 during a parameter sweep. For a random setting of parameters in our sweep, this is the probability that RM3 and CLRM3 will perform identically.

	RR	NDCG5	NDCG10	MAP	Rprec	recall
trec12	0.958	0.989	0.976	0.087	0.699	0.129
robust	0.968	0.995	0.985	0.297	0.901	0.397
cw09b	0.894	0.998	0.992	0.403	0.947	0.562

performance between RM3 and CLRM3 for high precision metrics (Table 3). This similarity in performance disappears for recall-oriented metrics. In Figure 1, we present scatterplots for those query-parameter samples where performance differed. We notice that recall-oriented metrics exhibit a horizontal banding effect for those queries whose performance can improve when in the RM3 condition but are constrained by the original retrieval for the CLRM3 condition.

In terms of efficiency, CLRM3 is substantially faster than RM3, operating at 5.68% (trec12), 5.03% (robust), and 10.1% (web) of RM3 at optimal parameter settings. In order to address the concern that this improvement was an artifact of our single machine infrastructure, we distributed the web index across our nine servers and reproduced our experiments. The efficiency improvements were identical to those on the single machine architecture. These experiments support our second hypothesis.

The latency incurred by these approaches can be affected by our pseudo-relevance feedback parameters. Here, we define latency as the per-query algorithm runtime above a baseline without feedback (i.e. query likelihood). We present this analysis in Figure 2. In general, we find that changing the number of feedback documents (k) does not affect performance for either algorithm. The interpolation weight (λ) improves the runtime for RM3. This is most

likely a result of term weights becoming more skewed, allowing more aggressive pruning of candidate documents by the retrieval system. Because CLRM3 scores a fixed set of documents, we do not see this effect for the new algorithm. The number of feedback terms (m) significantly affects runtime. A naïve linear model predicts each additional term adding $\sim$ 8000 milliseconds to the retrieval for RM3 and $\sim$ 100 milliseconds for CLRM3.

6. CONCLUSION

We found our results as impressive as the algorithm was simple. We believe that researchers and practitioners should strongly consider condensed list pseudo-relevance feedback when there are efficiency concerns with two-pass pseudo-relevance feedback.

7. REFERENCES

[1] R. Attar and A. S. Fraenkel. Local feedback in full-text retrieval systems. *J. ACM*, 24(3):397–417, July 1977.
[2] M. Bendersky, D. Metzler, and W. B. Croft. Effective query formulation with multiple information sources. In *WSDM*, 2012.
[3] A. Z. Broder, D. Carmel, M. Herscovici, A. Soffer, and J. Zien. Efficient query evaluation using a two-level retrieval process. In *CIKM*, 2003.
[4] M.-A. Cartright, J. Allan, V. Lavrenko, and A. McGregor. Fast query expansion using approximations of relevance models. In *CIKM*, 2010.
[5] W. B. Croft and D. J. Harper. Using probabilistic models of document retrieval without relevance information. *Journal of Documentation*, 35(4):285–295, 1979.
[6] F. Diaz. Regularizing query-based retrieval scores. *Information Retrieval*, 10(6):531–562, December 2007.
[7] V. Lavrenko. *A Generative Theory of Relevance*. PhD thesis, University of Massachusetts, 2004.
[8] W.-H. Lin, R. Jin, and A. Hauptmann. Web image retrieval re-ranking with relevance model. In *Web Intelligence*, 2003.
[9] C. Macdonald, N. Tonellotto, and I. Ounis. Effect of dynamic pruning safety on learning to rank effectiveness. In *SIGIR*, 2012.
[10] D. Metzler and W. B. Croft. Latent concept expansion using markov random fields. In *SIGIR*, 2007.
[11] T. Sakai. Alternatives to bpref. In *SIGIR*, 2007.
[12] H. Wu and H. Fang. An incremental approach to efficient pseudo-relevance feedback. In *SIGIR*, 2013.

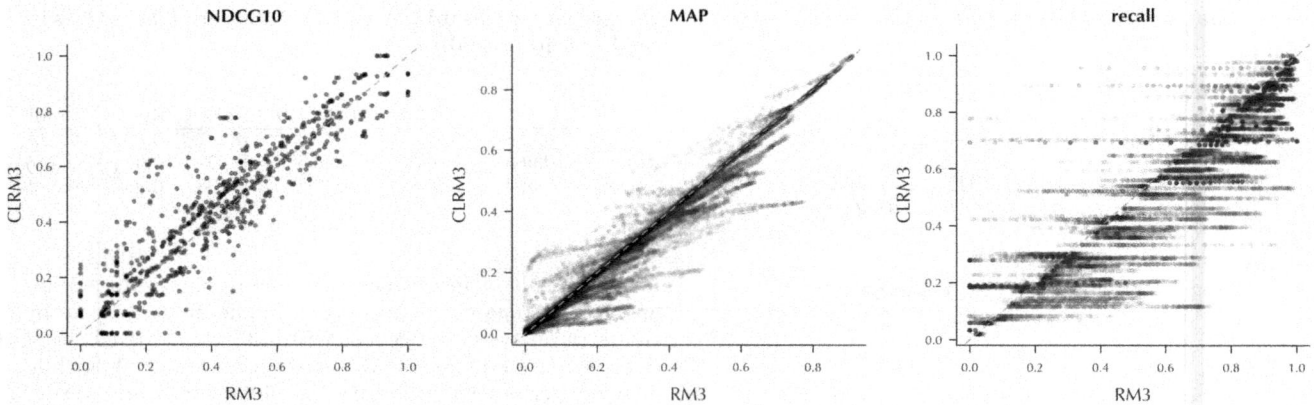

Figure 1: Correlation between RM3 and CLRM3 for metrics with different recall orientation on the web dataset. Each point represents the performance of each algorithm for a unique query-parameter setting. We have omitted points lying *exactly* on the diagonal (see Table 3). Horizontal banding reflects queries whose performance can increase by retrieving new documents from a second retrieval.

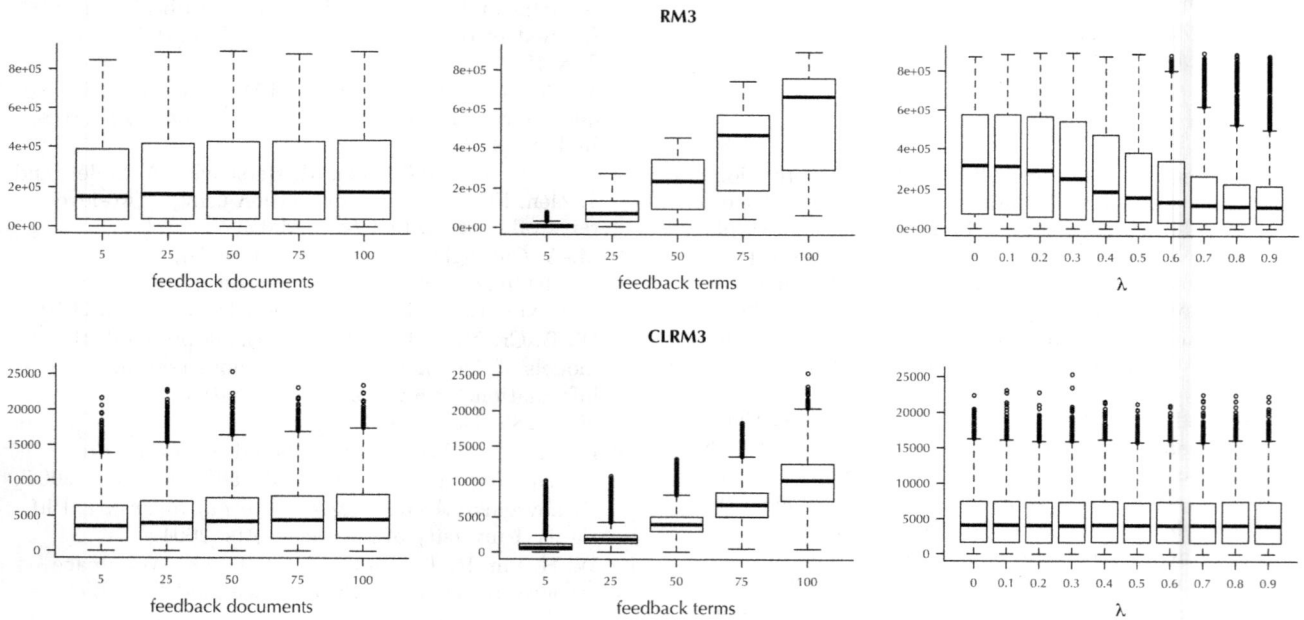

Figure 2: Distribution of latency (ms) incurred from relevance modeling as a function of relevance model parameters. Note that while the vertical axes are comparable for a given algorithm, the axes for CLRM3 are *significantly* different from those of RM3. Runtime is measured on the full set of parameters in the sweep for all queries in web.

Estimating the Uncertainty of Average F1 Scores

Dell Zhang
DCSIS
Birkbeck, University of London
Malet Street
London WC1E 7HX, UK
dell.z@ieee.org

Jun Wang
Dept of Computing Science
University College London
Gower Street
London WC1E 6BT, UK
j.wang@cs.ucl.ac.uk

Xiaoxue Zhao
Dept of Computing Science
University College London
Gower Street
London WC1E 6BT, UK
x.zhao@cs.ucl.ac.uk

ABSTRACT

In multi-class text classification, the performance (effectiveness) of a classifier is usually measured by micro-averaged and macro-averaged F_1 scores. However, the scores themselves do not tell us how reliable they are in terms of forecasting the classifier's future performance on unseen data. In this paper, we propose a novel approach to explicitly modelling the uncertainty of average F_1 scores through Bayesian reasoning.

Categories and Subject Descriptors

H.3.4 [**Information Storage and Retrieval**]: Systems and Software—*performance evaluation (efficiency and effectiveness)*; I.5.2 [**Pattern Recognition**]: Design Methodology—*classifier design and evaluation*

General Terms

Experimentation, Measurement, Performance

Keywords

Text Classification; Performance Evaluation; Bayesian Inference

1. INTRODUCTION

Automatic text classification [7] is a fundamental technique in information retrieval (IR) [4]. It has many important applications, including topic categorisation, spam filtering, sentiment analysis, message routing, language identification, genre detection, authorship attribution, and so on. In fact, most modern IR systems for search, recommendation, or advertising contain multiple components that use some form of text classification.

The most widely used performance measure for text classification is the F_1 score [8] which is defined as the harmonic mean of precision and recall. It is known to be more informative and more useful than classification accuracy etc. due

ICTIR'15, September 27–30, Northampton, MA, USA.
© 2015 ACM. ISBN 978-1-4503-3833-2/15/09 ...$15.00.
DOI: http://dx.doi.org/10.1145/2808194.2809488.

to the prevalent phenomenon of class imbalance in text classification. When multiple classes exist in the document collection (such as Reuters-21578 with its 118 classes), we often want to compute a single aggregate measure that combines the F_1 scores for individual classes. There are two methods to do this: micro-averaging and macro-averaging [4]. The former pools per-document decisions across classes, and then computes the overall F_1 score on the pooled contingency table. The latter just computes a simple average of the F_1 scores over classes. The differences between these two averaging methods can be large: micro-averaging gives equal weight to each per-document classification decision and therefore is dominated by large classes, whereas macro-averaging gives equal weight to each class. It is nowadays a common practice for IR researchers to evaluate a multi-class text classifier using both the micro-averaged F_1 score (denoted as $\text{mi}F_1$) and the macro-averaged F_1 score (denoted as $\text{ma}F_1$), since their introduction by Yang and Liu's seminal SIGIR-1999 paper [9].

However, the average F_1 scores themselves only reflect a text classifier's performance on the given test data. How can we be sure that it will work well on unseen data? Given any finite amount of test results, we can never be guaranteed that one classifier's performance will definitely achieve a certain acceptable level (say 0.80) in practice. For example, suppose that a classifier got $\text{mi}F_1$ 0.81 on 100 test documents. Due to the small number of test documents, we probably do not have much confidence in pronouncing that its future performance will definitely be above 0.80. If instead the classifier got $\text{mi}F_1$ 0.81 on 100,000 test documents, we can be more confident than in the previous case. Nevertheless, there will always be some degree of uncertainty. The central question here is how to assess the uncertainty of a classifier's performance as measured by $\text{mi}F_1$ and $\text{ma}F_1$, given a set of test results.

In this paper, we address this problem by appealing to Bayesian reasoning [3], and demonstrate that our approach provides rich information about a multi-class text classifiers' performance.

2. OUR APPROACH

2.1 Model

Let us consider a multi-class classifier which has been tested on a collection of N labelled test documents, $\mathcal{D}$. Here we focus on the setting of multi-class single-label (aka "one-of") classification where one document belongs to one and only one class [4, 7]. For each document $\boldsymbol{x}_i$ ($i = 1, \ldots, N$),

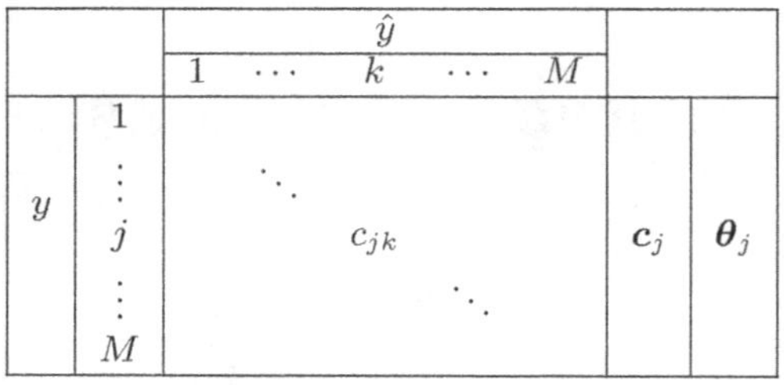

Figure 1: A schematic diagram of confusion matrix.

we have its true class label y_i as well as its predicted class label $\hat{y}_i$. Given that there are M different classes, the classification results could be fully summarised into an $M \times M$ confusion matrix $\boldsymbol{C}$ where the element c_{jk} at the j-th row and the k-th column represents the number of documents with true class label j but predicted class label k, as shown in Figure 1.

The performance measures miF_1 and maF_1 can be calculated straightforwardly based on such a confusion matrix. However, as we have explained earlier, we are not satisfied with knowing only a single score value of the performance measure, but instead would like to treat the performance measure (either miF_1 or maF_1) as a random variable ψ and estimate its uncertainty by examining its posterior probability distribution.

The test documents can be considered as "independent trials", i.e., their true class labels y_i are independent and identically distributed (i.i.d.). For each test document, we use $\boldsymbol{\mu} = (\mu_1, \dots, \mu_M)$ to represent the probabilities that it truly belongs to each class: $\mu_j = \Pr[y_i = j]$ $(j = 1, \dots, M)$, $\sum_{j=1}^{M} \mu_j = 1$. This means that the class sizes $\boldsymbol{n} = (n_1, \dots, n_M)$ would follow a Multinomial distribution with parameter N and $\boldsymbol{\mu}$: $\boldsymbol{n} \sim \text{Mult}(N, \boldsymbol{\mu})$, i.e.,

$$
\begin{aligned}
\Pr[\boldsymbol{n}|N, \boldsymbol{\mu}] &= \frac{N!}{n_1! \dots n_M!} \prod_{j=1}^{M} \mu_j^{n_j} \\
&= \frac{\Gamma\left(\sum_{j=1}^{M}(n_j + 1)\right)}{\prod_{j=1}^{M}\Gamma(n_j + 1)} \prod_{j=1}^{M} \mu_j^{n_j} \ .
\end{aligned}
$$

It would then be convenient to use the Dirichlet distribution (which is conjugate to the Multinomial distribution) as the prior distribution of parameter $\boldsymbol{\mu}$. More specifically, $\boldsymbol{\mu} \sim \text{Dir}(\boldsymbol{\beta})$, i.e.,

$$
\Pr[\boldsymbol{\mu}] = \frac{\Gamma\left(\sum_{j=1}^{M} \beta_j\right)}{\prod_{j=1}^{M}\Gamma(\beta_j)} \prod_{j=1}^{M} \mu_j^{\beta_j - 1} \ ,
$$

where the hyper-parameter $\boldsymbol{\beta} = (\beta_1, \dots, \beta_M)$ encodes our prior belief about each class's proportion in the test document collection. If we do not have any prior knowledge, we can simply set $\boldsymbol{\beta} = (1, \dots, 1)$ that yields a uniform distribution, as we did in our experiments.

Furthermore, let $\boldsymbol{c}_j = (c_{j1}, \dots, c_{jM})$ denote the j-th row of the confusion matrix. In other words, $\boldsymbol{c}_j$ shows how those documents belonging to class j are classified. For each test document from that class j, we use $\boldsymbol{\theta}_j = (\theta_{j1}, \dots, \theta_{jM})$ to represent the probabilities that it is classified into different classes: $\theta_{jk} = \Pr[\hat{y}_i = k | y_i = j]$ $(k = 1, \dots, M)$, $\sum_{k=1}^{M} \theta_{jk} = 1$. This means that for each class j, the corresponding vector $\boldsymbol{c}_j$ would follow a Multinomial distribution with parameter

n_j and $\boldsymbol{\theta}_j$: $\boldsymbol{c}_j \sim \text{Mult}(n_j, \boldsymbol{\theta}_j)$, i.e.,

$$
\begin{aligned}
\Pr[\boldsymbol{c}_j|n_j, \boldsymbol{\theta}_j] &= \frac{n_j!}{c_{j1}! \dots c_{jM}!} \prod_{k=1}^{M} \theta_{jk}^{c_{jk}} \\
&= \frac{\Gamma\left(\sum_{k=1}^{M}(c_{jk} + 1)\right)}{\prod_{k=1}^{M}\Gamma(c_{jk} + 1)} \prod_{k=1}^{M} \theta_{jk}^{c_{jk}} \ .
\end{aligned}
$$

It would then be convenient to use the Dirichlet distribution (which is conjugate to the Multinomial distribution) as the prior distribution of parameter $\boldsymbol{\theta}_j$. More specifically, $\boldsymbol{\theta}_j \sim \text{Dir}(\boldsymbol{\alpha}_j)$, i.e.,

$$
\Pr[\boldsymbol{\theta}_j] = \frac{\Gamma\left(\sum_{k=1}^{M} \alpha_{jk}\right)}{\prod_{k=1}^{M}\Gamma(\alpha_{jk})} \prod_{k=1}^{M} \theta_{jk}^{\alpha_{jk} - 1} \ ,
$$

where the hyper-parameter $\boldsymbol{\alpha}_j = (\alpha_{j1}, \dots, \alpha_{jM})$ encodes our prior belief about a classifier's prediction accuracy for class j. If we do not have any prior knowledge, we can simply set for each class $\boldsymbol{\alpha}_j = (1, \dots, 1)$ that yields a uniform distribution, as we did in our experiments.

Once the parameters $\boldsymbol{\mu}$ and $\boldsymbol{\theta}_j$ $(j = 1, \dots, M)$ have been estimated, it will be easy to calculate, for each class, the contingency table of "expected" prediction results: true positive (tp), false positive (fp), true negative (tn), and false negative (fn). For example, the anticipated number of true positive predictions, for class j, should be the number of test documents belonging to that class $N\mu_j$ times the rate of being predicted by the classifier into that class as well θ_{jj}. The equations to calculate the contingency table for each class j are listed as follows.

$$
\begin{aligned}
tp_j &= N\mu_j\theta_{jj} & fp_j &= \sum_{u \neq j} N\mu_u\theta_{uj} \\
fn_j &= \sum_{v \neq j} N\mu_j\theta_{jv} & tn_j &= \sum_{u \neq j}\sum_{v \neq j} N\mu_u\theta_{uv}
\end{aligned}
$$

In *micro-averaging*, we pool the per-document predictions across classes, and then use the pooled contingency table to compute the micro-averaged precision P, micro-averaged recall R, and finally their harmonic mean miF_1 as follows.

$$
\begin{aligned}
P &= \frac{\sum_{j=1}^{M} tp_j}{\sum_{j=1}^{M}(tp_j + fp_j)} = \sum_{j=1}^{M} \mu_j\theta_{jj} \\
R &= \frac{\sum_{j=1}^{M} tp_j}{\sum_{j=1}^{M}(tp_j + fn_j)} = \sum_{j=1}^{M} \mu_j\theta_{jj} \\
miF_1 &= \frac{2PR}{P + R} = \sum_{j=1}^{M} \mu_j\theta_{jj}
\end{aligned}
$$

It is a well-known fact that in multi-class single-label (aka "one-of") classification, $miF_1 = P = R$ which is actually identical to the overall accuracy of classification [4].

In *macro-averaging*, we use the contingency table of each individual class j to compute that particular class's precision P_j as well as recall R_j, and finally compute a simple average of the F_1 scores over classes to get maF_1 as follows.

$$
\begin{aligned}
P_j &= \frac{tp_j}{tp_j + fp_j} = \frac{\mu_j\theta_{jj}}{\sum_{u=1}^{M} \mu_u\theta_{uj}} \\
R_j &= \frac{tp_j}{tp_j + fn_j} = \theta_{jj}
\end{aligned}
$$

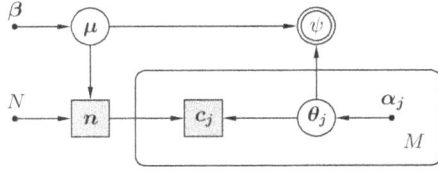

Figure 2: The probabilistic graphical model for estimating the uncertainty of average F_1 scores.

$$\mathrm{ma}F_1 = \left(\sum_{j=1}^{M} \frac{2P_j R_j}{P_j + R_j} \right) / M$$

In the above calculation of $\mathrm{mi}F_1$ and $\mathrm{ma}F_1$, N has been cancelled out so it does not appear in the final formulae. Therefore the deterministic variable ψ for the performance measure of interest (either $\mathrm{mi}F_1$ or $\mathrm{ma}F_1$) is a function that depends on μ and $\theta_1, \ldots, \theta_M$ only:

$$\psi = f(\mu, \theta_1, \ldots, \theta_M) .$$

The above model describes the generative mechanism of a multi-class classifier's test results (i.e., confusion matrix). It is summarised as follows, and also depicted in Figure 2 as a probabilistic graphical model (PGM) [2] using common notations.

$$\begin{aligned}
\mu &\sim \mathrm{Dir}(\beta) \\
n &\sim \mathrm{Mult}(N, \mu) \\
\theta_j &\sim \mathrm{Dir}(\alpha_j) \qquad \text{for } j = 1, \ldots, M \\
c_j &\sim \mathrm{Mult}(n_j, \theta_j) \text{ for } j = 1, \ldots, M \\
\psi &= f(\mu, \theta_1, \ldots, \theta_M)
\end{aligned}$$

Our model can be considered as a generalisation of the two-class F_1 score model proposed by Goutte and Gaussier [1] to multiple classes. More importantly, it opens up many possibilities for adaptation or extension.

2.2 Implementation

The purpose of building the above model for classification results is to assess the Bayesian posterior probability of ψ that represents either $\mathrm{mi}F_1$ or $\mathrm{ma}F_1$. An approximate estimation of ψ can be obtained by sampling from its posterior probability distribution via Markov Chain Monte Carlo (MCMC) [3] techniques.

We have implemented our model with an MCMC method *Metropolis-Hastings sampling* [3]. The default configuration is to generate 50,000 samples, with no "burn-in", "lag", or "multiple-chains". The program is written in Python utilising the module PyMC3[1] [5] for MCMC based Bayesian model fitting. The source code will be made open to the research community on the first author's homepage.

3. EXPERIMENTS

In order to demonstrate the usage of our model for estimating the uncertainty of average F_1 scores, we have conducted experiments on the confusion matrix given by the test results from a multi-class classifier on a real-world text dataset. The confusion matrix provides all the data that

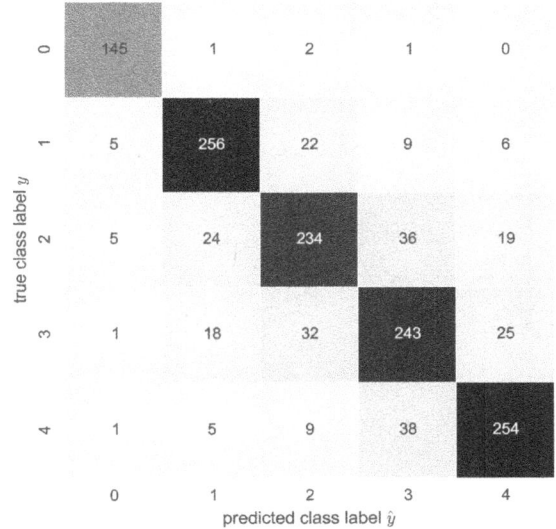

---

[1]http://pymc-devs.github.io/pymc3/

Figure 3: The confusion matrix used for our experiments.

our model requires. It is shown in Figure 3 to ensure the reproducibility of experiments.

Our proposed Bayesian estimation approach offers rich information about the given classifier's average F_1 scores, as shown in Table 1. In addition to the original performance score ($\mathrm{mi}F_1$ or $\mathrm{ma}F_1$), we have shown its posterior mean, standard deviation (std), Monte Carlo error (MC error), the percentage lower or greater than the reference performance score 0.8 (LG pct), and the 95% Highest Density Interval (HDI). In particular, the 95% HDI is a useful summary of where the bulk of the most credible values of ψ falls: by definition, every value inside the HDI has higher probability density than any value outside the HDI, and the total mass of points inside the 95% HDI is 95% of the distribution [3].

The Bayesian estimations of $\mathrm{mi}F_1$ and $\mathrm{ma}F_1$ are visualised in Figure 4 and 5 respectively. The left component in each figure plots the posterior probability distribution of the performance measure variable ψ, while the right component plots the corresponding MCMC trace which proves the convergence of sampling.

4. CONCLUSIONS

The main contribution of this paper is a Bayesian estimation approach to assessing the uncertainty of average F_1 scores in the context of multi-class text classification. Obviously the more general F_β measure ($\beta \geq 0$) [4, 8] can be dealt with in the same way.

Our model for estimating the uncertainty of average F_1 scores has been described in the multi-class single-label (aka "one-of") classification setting, but it is readily extensible to the multi-class multi-label (aka "any-of") classification setting [4, 7]. In that case, the Dirichlet/Multinomial distributions should simply be replaced by multiple Beta/Binomial distributions each of which corresponds to one specific target class, because a multi-class multi-label classifier is nothing more than a composition of independent binary classifiers.

By modelling the full posterior probability distribution of $\mathrm{mi}F_1$ or $\mathrm{ma}F_1$, we are able to make meaningful *interval estimation* (e.g., the 95% HDI) instead of simplistic *point*

Table 1: Bayesian estimation of the average F_1 scores.

	score	mean	std	MC error	LG pct	HDI
miF_1	0.814	0.803	0.011	0.000	39.6%<0.8<60.4%	$[0.782, 0.823]$
maF_1	0.828	0.815	0.010	0.000	6.1%<0.8<93.9%	$[0.796, 0.835]$

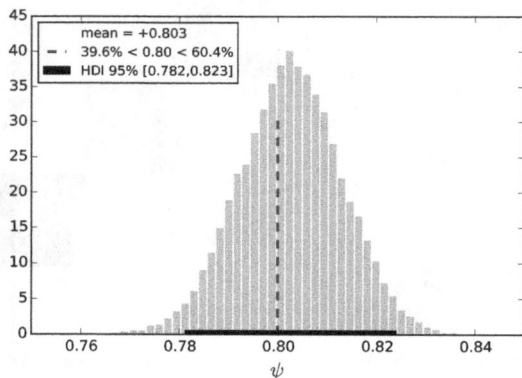

(a) posterior plot

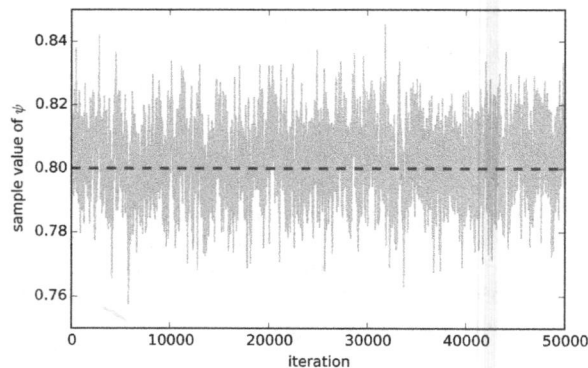

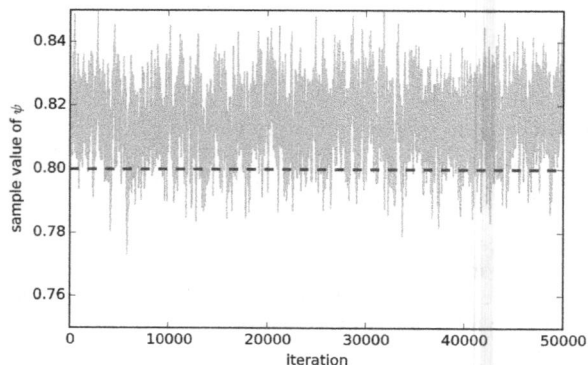

(b) trace plot

Figure 4: Bayesian estimation of miF_1.

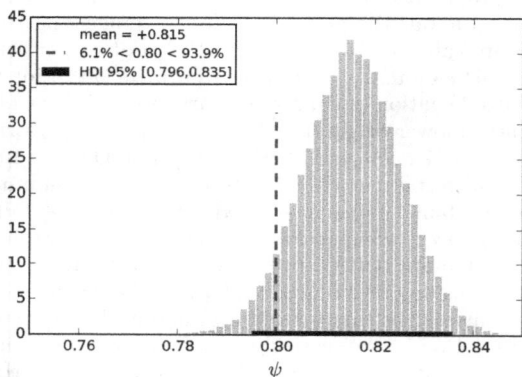

(a) posterior plot

(b) trace plot

Figure 5: Bayesian estimation of maF_1.

estimation of a text classifier's future performance on unseen data. The rich information provided by our model will allow us to make comprehensive performance comparisons between text classifiers, by taking the uncertainty of average F_1 scores into account. It would be interesting to conduct more extensive experiments to verify whether the proposed Bayesian approach has advantages over traditional hypothesis testing [6, 9].

5. REFERENCES

[1] C. Goutte and E. Gaussier. A probabilistic interpretation of precision, recall and *F*-score, with implication for evaluation. In *Proceedings of the 27th European Conference on IR Research (ECIR)*, pages 345–359, Santiago de Compostela, Spain, 2005.

[2] D. Koller and N. Friedman. *Probabilistic Graphical Models - Principles and Techniques.* MIT Press, 2009.

[3] J. K. Kruschke. *Doing Bayesian Data Analysis: A Tutorial with R, JAGS, and Stan.* Academic Press, 2nd edition, 2014.

[4] C. D. Manning, P. Raghavan, and H. Schütze. *Introduction to Information Retrieval.* Cambridge University Press, 2008.

[5] A. Patil, D. Huard, and C. J. Fonnesbeck. PyMC: Bayesian stochastic modelling in Python. *Journal of Statistical Software*, 35(4):1–81, 2010.

[6] T. Sakai. Evaluating evaluation metrics based on the bootstrap. In *Proceedings of the 29th Annual International ACM SIGIR Conference on Research and Development in Information Retrieval (SIGIR)*, pages 525–532, Seattle, WA, USA, 2006.

[7] F. Sebastiani. Machine learning in automated text categorization. *ACM Computing Surveys (CSUR)*, 34(1):1–47, 2002.

[8] C. J. van Rijsbergen. *Information Retrieval.* Butterworths, London, UK, 2nd edition, 1979.

[9] Y. Yang and X. Liu. A re-examination of text categorization methods. In *Proceedings of the 22nd Annual International ACM SIGIR Conference on Research and Development in Information Retrieval (SIGIR)*, pages 42–49, Berkeley, CA, USA, 1999.

The Feasibility of Brute Force Scans for Real-Time Tweet Search

Yulu Wang[1] and Jimmy Lin[2]

[1] Department of Computer Science, University of Maryland
[2] David R. Cheriton School of Computer Science, University of Waterloo

ylwang@umd.edu, jimmylin@uwaterloo.ca

ABSTRACT

The real-time search problem requires making ingested documents immediately searchable, which presents architectural challenges for systems built around inverted indexing. In this paper, we explore a radical proposition: What if we abandon document inversion and instead adopt an architecture based on brute force scans of document representations? In such a design, "indexing" simply involves appending the parsed representation of an ingested document to an existing buffer, which is simple and fast. Quite surprisingly, experiments with TREC Microblog test collections show that query evaluation with brute force scans is feasible and performance compares favorably to a traditional search architecture based on an inverted index, especially if we take advantage of vectorized SIMD instructions and multiple cores in modern processor architectures. We believe that such a novel design is worth further exploration by IR researchers and practitioners.

Categories and Subject Descriptors: H.3.4 [Information Storage and Retrieval]: Systems and Software—Performance evaluation

Keywords: search architectures; multi-core processors

1. INTRODUCTION

Real-time tweet search exemplifies a class of retrieval problems that requires dealing with a host of architectural challenges compared to "traditional" web search. Many of these were identified by Busch et al. [5], including the need for rapid data ingestion of high velocity data streams and ensuring that documents are immediately searchable. As they discussed, one major performance bottleneck is the construction of the inverted index in an incremental fashion. For performance considerations, indexes and related data structures must be kept completely in main memory (which is a standard assumption today). Nevertheless, inverted indexing requires non-regular data structures and data access patterns that are at odds with modern processor architectures. This

paper explores the following question: What if we abandoned document inversion? Can we envision a retrieval architecture that addresses the architectural challenges of real-time tweet search in a completely different way?

We explore the feasibility of a simple retrieval architecture based on brute force scans of document representations. The sketch of the approach is as follows: whenever we encounter a new document (tweet), we convert it into arrays of integers. "Indexing" simply means appending this representation to an existing in-memory buffer. For retrieval, we perform a *brute force scan* of these representations and compute query–document scores according to a scoring model. We can build on this simple idea by exploiting vector SIMD instructions and modern multi-core processors to further increase performance. Note that although this approach may seem reminiscent of bit signatures [9], the critical difference is that we work with *exact* document representations since there is no hashing involved.

Surprisingly, the retrieval performance of such an architecture is quite reasonable compared to a search engine built on a standard inverted index. We experimentally verified our techniques on data from the TREC Microblog evaluations from 2011 and 2012. Compared to the open-source search engine Lucene (a variant of which Twitter deploys for real-time search in production), we achieve query latencies that are within 30% when exploiting SIMD instructions and intra-query parallelism to its fullest.

2. BACKGROUND AND RELATED WORK

Initially, query evaluation based on brute force scans seems impractical, perhaps even outlandish. Nevertheless, we argue that this approach is worth considering for a couple of reasons. One challenge in designing software for modern architectures is the so-called "memory wall" [3]: increases in processor speeds have far outpaced improvements in memory latency. Today, memory latencies are hidden by hierarchical caches, but cache misses remain expensive. Another salient property of modern CPUs is pipelining, where instruction execution is split between many stages. Modern *superscalar* CPUs add the ability to dispatch multiple instructions per clock cycle. Pipelining suffers from two dangers or "hazards": *Data hazards* occur when one instruction requires the result of another, such as when manipulating pointers. Subsequent instructions cannot proceed until we first compute the memory location and the processor stalls. *Control hazards* are instruction dependencies introduced by branches. Such hazards are alleviated, but not completely eliminated, by branch prediction techniques.

document pool	1	2	3	4	5	6	7	3	8

tfs		2	1	1	1	1	1	1	1	1

uniq		5	4

docids		1	2

Figure 1: Document representations for two tweets.

The upshot is that branches and irregular memory accesses such as pointer chasing significantly reduce a processor's maximum performance. Unfortunately, inverted indexing and query evaluation algorithms are rife with exactly these inefficiencies. In contrast, brute force scans yield predictable memory accesses and code with minimal branching, yielding higher instructions-per-clock-cycle throughput. We wonder: has the latter caught up with the former?

The case for brute force scans is further bolstered by vector instructions that are common in today's processors. Advanced Vector Extensions (AVX) are extensions to the x86 instruction set architecture that support SIMD (single instruction multiple data) processing. AVX provides a number of instructions for operating on special 128-bit registers and 256-bit registers; AVX2 expands most vector integer AVX instructions to operate on 256-bit registers. The simplicity of the brute force scan approach allows us to exploit these instructions to achieve high instruction throughput.

3. SYSTEM DESIGN

3.1 Document Representations

We begin with a dictionary that provides a mapping from terms to 32-bit integer term ids. For simplicity, newly-encountered terms are assigned the next available term id. Whenever a new document (i.e., tweet) is encountered, it is first converted into an array of unique term ids, which is then appended to the end of a large array called the document pool. A parallel array of 8-bit integers stores corresponding term frequencies (tfs). We keep track of the number of unique terms in each document in a third array of 8-bit integers (uniq), which provides pointers into the otherwise unsegmented document pool. A final array keeps track of document ids. Figure 1 illustrates these data structures for two tweets: "BBC News: The BBC cuts budget" and "Just watched The Rite" (tokenized to "bbc new the bbc cut budget" and "just watch the rite"). To work with AVX2 instructions, we pad the document pool and the tf array to the nearest multiple of eight to align document boundaries with SIMD instructions. Thus, we have unpadded and padded variants of the data structures. To facilitate the computation of document scores, we also need to store document lengths and collection frequencies (but these data structures are not specific to our approach).

One aspect of our design is worth discussing: we decided *not* to compress the document pool for two reasons. First, our approach to assign term ids incrementally means that, on the whole, the ids are relatively large, and hence the document pool does not compress well. In an initial experiment, we tried compression using SIMD-BP128 [6], which yielded slower performance at only a modest saving in memory; we decided the tradeoff was not worthwhile. Although it is possible to assign term ids to facilitate compression (e.g., ordering terms based on frequency), this would complicate

---

Algorithm 1 Scan1

```
 1: procedure SCAN1(Q, pool, tfs, uniq, docids)
 2:     b ← 0
 3:     for i ← 1 to N do
 4:         s ← 0
 5:         for j ← 1 to uniq[i] do
 6:             for k ← 1 to |Q| do
 7:                 if Q[k] = pool[b + j] then
 8:                     s ← s + S(·)
 9:                 end if
10:             end for
11:         end for
12:         if s > 0 then
13:             heap.add(docids[i], s)
14:         end if
15:         b ← b + uniq[i]
16:     end for
17: end procedure
```

dictionary construction in a real-time scenario. Second, leaving the document pool uncompressed makes it straightforward to exploit SIMD instructions (more later); compression would significantly complicate matters.

3.2 Query Evaluation

We explored a number of query evaluation approaches based on a brute force scan of the document representations to compute query-document scores (query-likelihood in our case). The top k are retained in a heap and returned after all documents are processed. Four different implementations are described below:

Scan1. Our first approach (Algorithm 1) operates on the unpadded document pool and is a straightforward implementation consisting of three nested loops: over all documents, over all unique terms in each document, and over all query terms. The notation $S(·)$ is shorthand for computing the score contribution of the current query term.

Scan2. In our second approach, which also uses the unpadded document pool, we unroll the innermost loop of the first approach (i.e., lines 6–10). This is accomplished by creating a separate query evaluation function for every query length (a relatively small number); such a design allows us to hard code the number of query terms and avoid branch mispredicts in the innermost loop.

AVXScan1. This approach replaces the two inner loops of Algorithm 1 with SIMD instructions. The key is an AVX2 instruction that performs element-wise comparison of two vectors of eight 32-bit integers concurrently (in 256-bit registers); the result is a mask indicating which of the integers match. Our approach is as follows: for each query term, we replicate its term id eight times in a 256-bit register, and then apply the AVX2 vectorized comparison to eight integers at a time from the document pool. Based on reading the result mask, if there is a match, we then compute the query term score contribution and add it to the current score. Thus, we scan eight unique term ids within a document at a time. As with the Scan2 algorithm, we implement different query evaluation functions for queries of different lengths to reduce branching when scanning the document pool (however, branches involved in checking the mask are unavoidable). Note that this technique requires padding the document pool and tf array with zeros to the nearest multiple of eight so that the AVX2 instructions do not cross document boundaries. We lack the space to provide detailed pseudo-code, but we welcome the reader to examine our open-source code for more details.

AVXScan2. In this approach, we build on the previous algorithm by partially unrolling the outer loop that iterates over the documents. Instead of considering one document at a time, we consider six documents at a time, and use the vectorized comparison operation described in the AVXScan1 approach to score each document. Partial scores are held in a six-document array, and once all query-document scores have been computed, we examine each element in the array and insert non-zero scores into the heap; this is accomplished in a fully-unrolled loop to avoid branches.

The intuition behind this approach is to reduce loop overhead, and is similar to vectorized processing in databases [4]. The number of documents to process at once requires balancing two factors: a value too small does not significantly reduce loop overhead, while a value too large might cause cache churn. In our application, the value of six was heuristically determined. As with before, we lack sufficient space to provide the pseudo-code for this approach, but our source code is available online.

3.3 Exploiting Parallelism

Modern processors contain multiple cores, so it makes sense to explore how we can exploit parallelism in our brute force scan approach. The two obvious strategies are inter-query parallelism and intra-query parallelism.

With inter-query parallelism, we simply run our query evaluation algorithm on multiple threads, each of which operates on one query independently. In this approach, as the number of threads grows, query throughput increases up to a certain point, after which performance no longer increases (or may suffer) due to resource contention.

With intra-query parallelism, we split the collection into equal portions and scan the document pool in parallel on multiple threads; each thread maintains its own heap. There is a synchronization point in waiting for the threads to finish, and then to merge all the heaps to produce a final top k ranking. With this approach, we still evaluate one query at a time, but parallelism decreases latency. However, we eventually run into diminishing returns: beyond a certain point, the costs of synchronization outweigh the benefits of increased parallelism.

4. EXPERIMENTAL SETUP

We implemented our system in C and compared against the open-source search engine Lucene (version 4.3.1). All code used in our experiments is released under an open-source license.[1] The use of Lucene, which is written in Java, might strike some as an odd baseline, but we provide the following rationale: Lucene has been proven to be "industrial strength", with numerous deployments in production settings. Twitter itself runs a variant of Lucene for real-time search, and numerous other companies including LinkedIn and Bloomberg rely on Lucene in production. Thus, it is substantially more mature than research systems that may be implemented in C/C++. More importantly, though, Lucene has two features lacking in many research systems: First, near-real-time indexing, where ingested documents are available for search within a short amount of time. This is a key feature of our brute force scan approach

and it would be unfair to compare our techniques against a system that does not have this feature. Second, Lucene has robust support for multi-threaded retrieval, which provides a point of comparison to parallel versions of our brute force scan approach. To provide a fair comparison, all Lucene indexes were loaded into main memory at startup. For both Lucene and brute force scan, we retrieved the top 1000 hits, per usual practice in IR research.

Experiments were conducted on a machine with two Intel Xeon E5-2680 v3 processors at 2.5 GHz. Each processor has 12 cores, with a total of 24 physical cores capable of supporting 48 virtual cores via hyperthreading. Our machine has 768 GB of RAM, although our experiments used only a small fraction of the total. The machine runs RedHat Enterprise Linux (release 6.6) and we used gcc version 4.9.1. All reported results represent the average of three trials.

We used test collections from the recent Microblog tracks at TREC [7, 8]. The 2011 and 2012 evaluations used the Tweets2011 collection (16 million tweets). We first verified with the TREC topics that our system generates exactly the same document scores and ranking as Lucene; subsequent experiments focused exclusively on efficiency. For these experiments, we took the first 1000 queries from the TREC 2005 terabyte track efficiency queries (we needed more queries for reliable measurements). The TREC Microblog queries are associated with timestamps, which are missing from these efficiency queries; thus, we searched over the entire collection (without any early termination).

5. RESULTS

After processing, the size of the document pool was 162 million; all data structures (but not the vocabulary) occupy 1026 MB memory. For the padded AVX2 representations, the document pool expanded to 225 million, or an increase of 39%. The padded data structures occupy 1341 MB memory in total. For reference, the Lucene index occupies 4.8 GB (although it stores positions and other metadata).

5.1 Single-Threaded Experiments

Results for the single-threaded experiments are shown in the first row of Table 1. We report average query latency (in milliseconds) of Lucene and our brute force scan approaches (with 95% confidence intervals). We see that the Scan1 approach is approximately 4.3× slower than Lucene, but each successive improvement to the basic brute force scan approach improves query latency. We get a big gain from unrolling the inner loop over query terms and writing a query evaluation function for queries of different lengths (Scan2). Applying SIMD instructions in the inner loop (AVXScan1) yields small improvements, but processing six documents at a time (AVXScan2) makes a noticeable contribution. Bottom line: the best brute force scan approach is within a factor of two of the performance of Lucene.

5.2 Multi-Threaded Experiments

Multi-threaded performance exploiting intra-query parallelism is shown in the rest of Table 1. We report query latency (in milliseconds) of Lucene versus the four brute force scan approaches (with 95% confidence intervals).

The results show that Lucene achieves maximum performance with 24 threads, which equals the number of physical cores in our machine—in other words, hyperthreading doesn't help. On the other hand, we get a small gain in

[1] https://github.com/lintool/c-bfscan

Threads	Lucene	Scan1	Scan2	AVXScan1	AVXScan2
1	178±25	769±4	417±11	408±13	361±3
2	109±37	610±23	358±56	297±16	261±15
4	86±38	456±24	270±6	228±7	189±1
8	76±13	297±7	168±7	141±5	135±1
12	73±8	217±3	126±5	107±8	109±7
24	62±1	156±3	92±1	87±3	88±7
48	81±1	134±2	89±2	81±2	84±3

Table 1: Latency (in milliseconds) with 95% confidence intervals of Lucene versus brute force scan, exploiting intra-query parallelism.

going from 24 to 48 threads with our brute force scan approaches. Interestingly, we noticed a different relative performance ordering of the brute force scan approaches compared to the single-threaded results. Even though AVX-Scan2 achieves the fastest single-threaded performance, it is (slightly) slower than AVXScan1 beyond 12 threads. Overall, the maximum performance we achieve with brute force scan (AVXScan1 with 48 threads) is about the same speed as Lucene under the same parallelism setting, but still a bit slower than the absolute best Lucene results (24 threads). Bottom line: the best brute force scan approach is only 30% slower than the best Lucene performance.

Multi-threaded performance exploiting inter-query parallelism is shown in Table 2. We report the throughput of Lucene versus the four different brute force scan approaches (with 95% confidence intervals). We see that maximum throughput with Lucene is achieved with 24 threads. This suggests that the benefits of additional parallelism are outweighed by resource contention that reduces overall throughput. Unfortunately, none of our brute force scan approaches are able to achieve anywhere close to the throughput of Lucene. Interestingly, however, just as in the intra-query parallelism case, we noticed a different relative performance ordering of the brute force scan approaches compared to the single threaded results. The Scan2 approach achieves the highest throughput with maximum parallelism, even though it has significantly lower performance on a single thread. Bottom line: inter-query parallelism does not appear to be the best way to exploit multiple cores using brute force scan techniques in today's processors.

6. FUTURE WORK AND CONCLUSION

What do we make of these results? Although none of the brute force scan approaches beat Lucene in terms of performance, we were surprised that the results are even this close. To recap: on a single thread, retrieval using the best brute force scan approach is within a factor of two of using an inverted index, and when exploiting intra-query parallelism to the fullest extent, the performance gap drops to 30%. We believe that we are a couple more optimizations away from achieving performance parity, and invite other researchers to help us get there.

The obvious advantage of our approach is that it eliminates the complexities of document inversion, which we do not show with indexing experiments here. In real-time search, there is another important advantage: users most often care only about the latest results. With an inverted index, it is desirable to traverse postings lists "backwards" (from most recent) and early exit when enough results have been accumulated [2]. Most systems are not designed this way, which foregoes optimization opportunities; adapting traditional query evaluation algorithms to operate in this

Threads	Lucene	Scan1	Scan2	AVXScan1	AVXScan2
1	7.5 ±0.1	1.3±0.1	2.5±0.3	2.5±0.1	2.9±0.3
2	20.7 ±1.5	2.6±0.1	4.8±0.6	5.1±0.2	5.9±0.1
4	38.2 ±0.7	5.0±0.1	9.4±0.7	9.6±0.3	11.0±0.1
8	52.6±12.0	9.3±0.2	17.1±1.3	17.0±0.3	19.2±0.5
12	104.0 ±4.6	13.5±0.3	24.5±2.2	23.8±1.2	25.8±1.5
24	188.7±21.0	25.3±1.2	41.6±5.1	38.3±1.9	40.0±0.1
48	164.4±10.3	30.3±0.5	53.1±2.7	49.3±2.5	48.4±4.2

Table 2: Throughput (query per second) with 95% confidence intervals of Lucene versus brute force scan, exploiting inter-query parallelism.

manner is non-trivial. In contrast, with an approach based on brute force scans, it is easy to factor in temporal constraints: since the documents are arranged chronologically, we simply stop scanning once we've reached the proper time.

We see an additional advantage beyond optimizations for real-time search: many web search engines today adopt a multi-stage architecture [1] that begins with a simple ranker (e.g., BM25) followed by one or more complex (machine-learned) rankers. Later stages typically access document-level features (e.g., static priors) that are not stored in the inverted index, thus requiring a separate "document store" from which those feature vectors are fetched or computed. This requires storing two separate structures (in essence, both a forward and an inverted index). With the brute force scan approach, the document store is no longer necessary, as document-level features can be directly stored in the document pool (suitably encoded). This yields a simpler and potentially more efficient end-to-end architecture.

To conclude: we show that the simplest possible approach to document retrieval—one based on simply scanning all documents in the collection—is surprisingly feasible given today's hardware. We hope to inspire future work that further explores this novel line of inquiry.

7. ACKNOWLEDGMENTS

This work was supported by the U.S. National Science Foundation under IIS-1218043 and CNS-1405688. Any opinions, findings, conclusions, or recommendations expressed are those of the authors and do not necessarily reflect the views of the sponsor.

8. REFERENCES

[1] N. Asadi and J. Lin. Effectiveness/efficiency tradeoffs for candidate generation in multi-stage retrieval architectures. *SIGIR*, 2013.

[2] N. Asadi, J. Lin, and M. Busch. Dynamic memory allocation policies for postings in real-time Twitter search. *KDD*, 2013.

[3] P. Boncz, M. Kersten, and S. Manegold. Breaking the memory wall in MonetDB. *CACM*, 51(12):77–85, 2008.

[4] P. Boncz, M. Zukowski, and N. Nes. MonetDB/X100: Hyper-pipelining query execution. *CIDR*, 2005.

[5] M. Busch, K. Gade, B. Larson, P. Lok, S. Luckenbill, and J. Lin. Earlybird: Real-time search at Twitter. *ICDE*, 2012.

[6] D. Lemire and L. Boytsov. Decoding billions of integers per second through vectorization. *Software: Practice and Experience*, 45(1):1–29, 2015.

[7] I. Ounis, C. Macdonald, J. Lin, and I. Soboroff. Overview of the TREC-2011 Microblog Track. *TREC*, 2011.

[8] I. Soboroff, I. Ounis, C. Macdonald, and J. Lin. Overview of the TREC-2012 Microblog Track. *TREC*, 2012.

[9] J. Zobel, A. Moffat, and K. Ramamohanarao. Inverted files versus signature files for text indexing. *ACM Transactions on Database Systems*, 23(4):453–490, 1998.

Improving Pseudo Relevance Feedback in the Divergence from Randomness Model

Dipasree Pal
Indian Statistical Institute
203, B.T. Road
Kolkata - 700108, India
dipasree.pal@gmail.com

Mandar Mitra
Indian Statistical Institute
203, B.T. Road
Kolkata - 700108, India
mandar@isical.ac.in

Samar Bhattacharya
Jadavpur University
188, Raja S.C. Mallick Rd
Kolkata - 700032, India
samar_bhattacharya@ee.jdvu.ac.in

ABSTRACT

In an earlier analysis of Pseudo Relevance Feedback (PRF) models by Clinchant and Gaussier (2013), five desirable properties that PRF models should satisfy were formalised. Also, modifications to two PRF models were proposed in order to improve compliance with the desirable properties. These resulted in improved retrieval effectiveness. In this study, we introduce a sixth property that we believe PRF models should satisfy. We also extend the earlier exercise to Bo1, a standard PRF model. Experimental results on the ROBUST, WT10G and GOV2 datasets show that the proposed modifications yield improvements in effectiveness.

Categories and Subject Descriptors

H.3.3 [**Information Storage and Retrieval**]: Information Search and Retrieval—*Relevance feedback, Retrieval models*

General Terms

Theory, Experimentation

Keywords

Pseudo relevance feedback, Divergence from randomness

1. INTRODUCTION

At ICTIR 2013, Clinchant and Gaussier [3] presented a theoretical analysis of several well-established and relatively recent Pseudo Relevance Feedback (PRF) models. As a part of this study, they formalised five desirable properties that PRF models should satisfy, and analysed various PRF models with respect to these properties. The authors also proposed modifications to two PRF models: the mixture model [9, 5] and the geometric relevance model [7]. The modified models are more compliant with the five desiderata listed by them. Experimental results show that these modifications also result in performance improvements.

Our goal in this study is two-fold: (i) to introduce a sixth property that we believe PRF models should satisfy; and

ICTIR'15, September 27–30, 2015, Northampton, MA, USA.
© 2015 ACM. ISBN 978-1-4503-3833-2/15/09 ...$15.00.
DOI: http://dx.doi.org/10.1145/2808194.2809494.

(ii) to extend Clinchant and Gaussier's exercise to Bo1, a standard PRF model used within the Divergence From Randomness framework [1]. This model was also analysed in [3], and found wanting with respect to the five desired properties. However, no modifications were proposed for Bo1.

In the next section, we review the five conditions listed in [3], and introduce a sixth condition. In Section 3, we review the Bo1 expansion method, and propose a simplified version of the Bo1 formula. Next, we suggest a set of modifications to both the original and the simplified forms of the Bo1 formula. These changes are intended to improve compliance with the criteria that PRF methods should fulfil. Experimental results on the TREC ROBUST, WT10G and GOV2 datasets are presented and discussed in Section 4. As expected, the modified version (called *Bo1new* in this paper) yields significantly better retrieval effectiveness than the original Bo1.

2. DESIDERATA FOR PRF METHODS

We adopt the following notation from [3].

q, d	Original query, document
$c(w, d)$	# of occurrences of w in d
l_d	Length of d
l_{avg}	Average document length in collection
N	# of docs. in collection
N_w	# of docs. in collection containing w
$IDF(w)$	IDF of w (i.e., $\log(N/N_w)$)
$t(w, d)$	Normalised # of occurrences of w in d (i.e., $\frac{c(w,d)}{l_d}$)
$\mathbf{F}$	set of documents used for PRF
$TF(w)$	Total term-frequency of w in $\mathbf{F}$
$DF(w)$	# docs. in $\mathbf{F}$ containing w
$FW(w, \mathbf{F})$	Feedback weight for expansion term w from $\mathbf{F}$
n	# of docs in $\mathbf{F}$
t	# of expansion terms added to q

Table 1: Notation

A PRF method / model should have the following desirable properties (also adopted from [3]).

TF effect FW should increase with $c(w, d)$, i.e.

$$\frac{\partial FW(w, \mathbf{F})}{\partial c(w, d)} > 0.$$

Concavity effect The above increase should be less marked as $c(w,d)$ increases, i.e.

$$\forall d \in F, \quad \frac{\partial^2 FW(w, \mathbf{F})}{\partial c(w,d)^2} < 0.$$

IDF effect Let w_a and w_b be two words such that $IDF(w_b) > IDF(w_a)$ and $\forall d \in \mathbf{F}, \ t(w_a, d) = t(w_b, d)$. Then

$$FW(w_b, \mathbf{F}) > FW(w_a, \mathbf{F}).$$

Document length effect The feedback weight for w should decrease as the length of any PRF document it occurs in increases.

$$\forall d \in \mathbf{F} \text{ s.t. } d \text{ contains } w, \quad \frac{\partial FW(w, \mathbf{F})}{\partial l_d} < 0.$$

DF effect If w_a and w_b are two feedback terms with the same IDF and $TF(w)$, but $DF(w_b) > DF(w_a)$, then

$$FW(w_a, \mathbf{F}) < FW(w_b, \mathbf{F}).$$

In addition to the above properties listed in [3], we propose the following additional property, in order to formalise the intuition that the information obtained from a more relevant document is more likely to be useful. This idea has been discussed in [8], where a regularized estimation method for estimating the importance of each PRF document has been proposed.

Relevance effect If a term w occurs in two documents $d_1, d_2 \in \mathbf{F}$, and d_1 is more relevant than d_2, then

$$FW(w, \mathbf{F} \setminus \{d_1\}) < FW(w, \mathbf{F} \setminus \{d_2\}).$$

Since true relevance information is not available, we make use of the obvious extension of the intuition underlying PRF: the similarity score of a document with respect to the query is assumed to be indicative of its relevance.

This property has the following additional effect. The DF effect penalises terms occurring in only a few documents; the Relevance effect avoids over-penalising candidate terms if they occur in a few highly ranked documents.

3. MODIFICATIONS TO BO1

Amati [1] (Section 2.4) models documents as bins or urns, and the words as (indistinguishable) balls. If there are T occurrences of w in a given collection of N documents, and these are distributed across the N documents, then the probability that an arbitrary d contains exactly k occurrences of term w is

$$P[c(w,d) = k] = \frac{\binom{N-T-k-2}{T-k}}{\binom{N+T-1}{T}}. \quad (1)$$

Assuming that $N \gg k$, Equation 1 can be simplified to

$$P[c(w,d) = k] \sim \frac{1}{1 + T/N} \cdot \left(\frac{T/N}{1 + T/N}\right)^k. \quad (2)$$

In a PRF setting, the PRF documents are regarded as a single bin $\mathbf{F}$ containing $TF(w)$ occurrences of w. Equation 2 then reduces to

$$P[TF(w) = k] \sim \frac{1}{1 + T/N} \cdot \left(\frac{T/N}{1 + T/N}\right)^k. \quad (2a)$$

The weight of an expansion term is given by its information content, i.e., $-\log_2(P)$. Thus,

$$FW(w) = TF(w) \times \log_2\left(\frac{N}{T} + 1\right) + \log_2\left(1 + \frac{T}{N}\right). \quad (3)$$

The compliance of Bo1 with the five conditions listed in Section 2 is summarised in Table 2. Our goal is to modify

	TF	Concave	IDF	Doc Len	DF
Bo1	YES	NO	NOT SYSTEMATICALLY	NO	NO

Table 2: Compliance of Bo1 with the five conditions given in Section 2 (taken from [3])

the Bo1 formula so that all / most of the entries in Table 2 can be marked YES.

3.1 Simplifying the Bo1 formula

As the first step towards this goal, we consider Equation 3. The first term is made up of ingredients that enforce the TF effect and the IDF effect. If Equation 3 is considered in isolation, the second term does not have such a straightforward interpretation. In fact, because of the presence of this second term, there is "no guarantee that this model is compliant with the IDF condition" [3]. However, for terms that are not too common, we expect $T/N \ll 1$, and thus $\log_2(1 + T/N) \sim 0$. Table 3 compares the values of the two terms in Equation 3 for some words (these are candidate expansion words for Query 453 of the TREC WT10G collection). While the first two are useful expansion words, the third is a high-IDF word that is not useful, while the last word is a low-IDF word that is also not useful.

Given these observations (both analytical and empirical), we simplify Equation 3 by dropping the 2nd term. Under this scheme, referred to as *Bo1(s)*, the feedback weight of a term is given by

$$FW(w) = TF(w) \times \log_2\left(\frac{N}{T} + 1\right). \quad (4)$$

This form is simpler to understand and analyse. In particular, for Bo1(s), the IDF column in Table 2 can be marked YES. Further, results in Section 4 show that this simplification does not adversely impact retrieval effectiveness.

3.2 Modifying the Bo1 and Bo1(s) formulae

Document length, concavity effect. Recall that $TF(w) = \sum_{d \in \mathbf{F}} c(w,d)$ in Equations 3 and 4. In order to introduce the document length effect, we simply divide $c(w,d)$ by the normalised length of document d. For the document length, we adopt a form suggested by the BM25 term weighting formula [6]. Thus,

$$TF_l(w) = \sum_{d \in \mathbf{F}} \frac{c(w,d)}{l_d^{(n)}}, \quad (5)$$

where

$$l_d^{(n)} = (1 - b) + b \times \frac{l_d}{l_{\text{avg}}}.$$

Word	$TF(w) \times \log_2\left(\frac{N}{T} + 1\right)$	$\log_2(1 + T/N)$
poverti	137.19	0.02
relief	45.02	0.03
victoria	19.41	0.05
internet	4.61	0.61

Table 3: Magnitude of the two terms in Equation 3 for TREC query 453 ("hunger")

Based on preliminary experiments, we set $b = 0.25$.

In addition, to satisfy the concavity property, we use the widely-used log function.

$$T_{lc}(w) = \sum_{d \in \mathbf{F}} \log_2 \left(1 + \frac{c(w,d)}{l_d^{(n)}} \right) \quad (6)$$

DF, relevance effect. The DF effect suggests that, all other things being the same, we should prefer an expansion term that occurs in a larger number of pseudo relevant documents (PRDs). However, it is questionable whether a term that occurs in say 6 relatively poorly ranked PRDs is actually preferable to a term that occurs in 3 highly ranked PRDs. Therefore, we introduce the following multiplicative factor in Equations 3 and 4, instead of simply using the raw DF information:

$$DF_r(w) = \sum_{d \in \mathbf{F} \wedge w \in d} \log_2(n - rank(d)). \quad (7)$$

The final modified forms corresponding to Equations 3 and 4 are given in Figure 1. We use the names Bo1new and Bo1(s)new to refer to these formulae.

4. EXPERIMENTAL RESULTS

Table 4 lists the test collections used in our experiments. At the time of indexing, stopwords are removed and Porter's stemmer is used as preprocessing. All documents and queries are indexed using single terms, no phrases are used. Only the title field of each query was indexed. We used the Terrier[1] retrieval system for our experiments. Baseline MAP values were obtained by using the original unexpanded queries with the IFB2 weighting scheme from the Divergence From Randomness model [2]. For query expansion, unless otherwise specified, we use the default parameter settings $n = 3$ documents and $t = 10$ terms recommended in [1].

Query Id.	# of Queries	Documents
ROBnew 601–700	100	TREC disks 4, 5 - CR
TREC9D 451–550	100	WT10G
Gov2 700–850	150	Gov2

Table 4: Test collections

4.1 Simplifying the Bo1 formula

We first test the simplification proposed in Equation 4. Table 5 confirms that the change does not adversely impact retrieval effectiveness. Most queries remain unaffected; the AP values for the remaining queries do not change much.

4.2 Comparing Bo1 and Bo1new

Table 6 shows the MAP and Robustness Index (RI)[2] [4] values obtained using the original queries, and expanded queries weighted using the standard Bo1 formula as well as Bo1new (Eq 8). On all collections, Bo1new outperforms Bo1, with the differences on WT10G and Gov2 being significant (paired t-test, 1% level of significance).

[1] http://terrier.org/

[2] When computing RI, a difference of 5% or less is ignored.

Dataset	Diff. in MAP	Bo1 > Bo1(s) (# queries,	Bo1 < Bo1(s) MAX diff. in AP)
ROBnew	0.0002	18, 0.0122	5, 0.0002
WT10G	0.0000	7, 0.0025	4, 0.0065
Gov2	0.0000	15, 0.0073	10, 0.0030

Table 5: Comparing Bo1 (Eq 3) and Bo1(s) (Eq 4)

Dataset	Measure	Baseline	Bo1	Bo1new
ROBnew	MAP	0.278	0.324 (16.7)	0.331 (19.1)
	RI	0	0.222	0.444
WT10G	MAP	0.195	0.209 (7.2)	0.222* (13.9)
	RI	0	0.061	0.255
Gov2	MAP	0.272	0.290 (6.5)	0.301* (10.6)
	RI	0	0.114	0.141

Table 6: Comparing Bo1 and Bo1new. Figures in parentheses denote % improvement over the baseline. Significant improvements are marked by a *.

4.3 Parameter settings

As mentioned above, the results in Section 4.2 were obtained using $n = 3$ documents and $t = 10$ terms. Next, we compared Bo1new with Bo1 across a range of parameter values on all collections. Figure 2 shows the results for WT10G. Similar results are obtained for the other collections, with Bo1new consistently outperforming Bo1 across the range of values that we studied.

A closer look at the MAP values shows that, for Bo1 and Bo1new, the parameters (n, t) should be set to $(3, 60)$ and $(5, 40)$ respectively, for "optimal" performance across collections. Table 7 compares Bo1 and Bo1new at these settings, i.e., when Bo1 and Bo1new are each at their individual "best".

Dataset	Measure	Baseline	Bo1 $n=3, t=60$	Bo1new $n=5, t=40$
ROBnew	MAP	0.278	0.336 (20.9)	0.340 (22.5)
	RI	0	0.313	0.475
WT10G	MAP	0.195	0.208 (6.5)	0.234* (19.7)
	RI	0	0.143	0.327
Gov2	MAP	0.272	0.296 (8.7)	0.318* (16.9)
	RI	0	0.121	0.342

Table 7: Comparing Bo1 and Bo1new for $n = 3, t = 60$ and $n = 5, t = 40$.

4.4 Analysing Bo1new and Bo1(s)new

Recall that the formulae for Bo1new and Bo1(s)new were obtained via a sequence of changes that were intended to progressively increase compliance with the desiderata listed in Section 2. In this section, we study the individual effect of each change. For these experiments, we used $n = 5, t = 40$.

The column headings in Table 8 denote the following.

$$FW(w) = TF_{lc}(w) \cdot DF_r(w) \cdot \log_2\left(\frac{N}{T} + 1\right) + \log_2\left(1 + \frac{T}{N}\right). \quad (8)$$

$$FW(w) = TF_{lc}(w) \cdot DF_r(w) \cdot \log_2\left(\frac{N}{T} + 1\right). \quad (9)$$

Figure 1: Modified Bo1 and Bo1(s) formulae

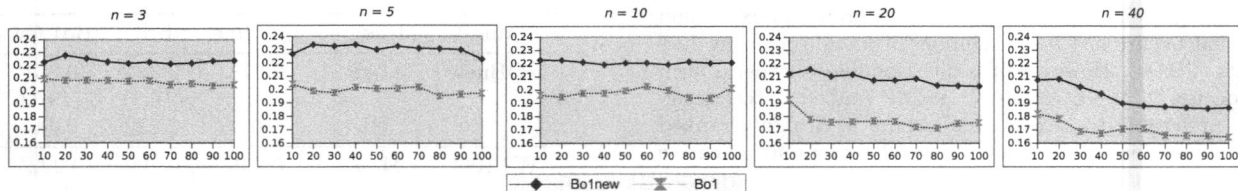

Figure 2: Comparison of Bo1 and Bo1new on WT10G across a range of parameters. The X and Y axes correspond to the number of expansion terms (t) and MAP respectively.

Dataset	Measure	Baseline	Bo1	Bo1+dl	Bo1+log	Bo1+df	Bo1new
ROBnew	MAP	0.278	0.331 (19.0)	0.332 (19.4)	0.335 (20.4)	0.337 (21.3)	0.340 (22.5)
	RI	0	0.212	0.283	0.323	0.465	0.475
WT10G	MAP	0.195	0.202 (3.3)	0.199 (1.9)	0.205 (5.2)	0.221 (12.9)	0.234 (19.7)
	RI	0	0.082	0.061	0	0.306	0.327
Gov2	MAP	0.272	0.293 (7.8)	0.302 (10.9)	0.294 (8.3)	0.314 (15.5)	0.318 (16.9)
	RI	0	0.141	0.148	0.094	0.349	0.342

Table 8: Effect of individual modifications suggested in Section 3.2.

- Bo1+dl: In Equation 3, $TF(w)$ is replaced by $TF_l(w)$ (given by Equation 5).
- Bo1+log: In Equation 3, $TF(w)$ is replaced by $TF_{lc}(w)$ (given by Equation 6).
- Bo1+df: $TF(w)$ is used (as in the original Bo1 formula), but the DF effect is introduced via $DF_r(w)$ (given by Equation 7). This may also be viewed as a modified version of Equation 8, in which $TF(w)$ is used instead of $TF_{lc}(w)$.

Each individual change yields marginal improvements. Indeed, it is not clear whether incorporating the Document length and Concavity effects consistently improves effectiveness across collections. The DF and Relevance effects seem more reliable in this respect. It is encouraging to note that these changes, in combination, yield improvements that are generally significant. They also seem to positively affect the robustness of a Bo1-based query expansion scheme. We repeated a similar analysis for Bo1(s)new, and obtained almost identical results.

In future work, we hope to more systematically explore

- other functions to incorporate the Document length, Concavity, DF, and Relevance effects;
- the Relevance effect in the context of the PRF methods already studied in [3] (e.g., the mixture model and the geometric relevance model);
- comparing Bo1new with other state-of-the-art PRF methods.

Acknowledgments. We thank the anonymous reviewers for their comments. The first author was supported by the CLIA project, DIT, Govt. of India.

5. REFERENCES

[1] G. Amati. *Probability odels for Information Retrieval Based on Divergence from Randomness.* U. Glasgow, 2003.

[2] G. Amati and C. Van Rijsbergen. Probabilistic models of information retrieval based on measuring the divergence from randomness. *AC TOIS*, 20:357–389, 2002.

[3] S. Clinchant and É. Gaussier. A theoretical analysis of pseudo-relevance feedback models. In *ICTIR '13*, pages 6–13, 2013.

[4] K. Collins-Thompson and J. Callan. Estimation and use of uncertainty in pseudo-relevance feedback. In *SIGIR '07*, pages 303–310. ACM, 2007.

[5] Y. Lv and C. Zhai. A comparative study of methods for estimating query language models with pseudo feedback. In *CIK '09*, pages 1895–1898. ACM, 2009.

[6] S. Robertson and H. Zaragoza. *The probabilistic relevance framework: B 25 and beyond.* Now Publishers Inc, 2009.

[7] J. Seo and W. B. Croft. Geometric representations for multiple documents. In *SIGIR '10*, pages 251–258. ACM, 2010.

[8] T. Tao and C. Zhai. Regularized estimation of mixture models for robust pseudo-relevance feedback. In *SIGIR '06*, pages 162–169. ACM, 2006.

[9] C. Zhai and J. Lafferty. Model-based feedback in the language modeling approach to information retrieval. In *CIK '01*, pages 403–410. ACM, 2001.

An Initial Analytical Exploration of Retrievability

Aldo Lipani[1]   Mihai Lupu[2]   Akiko Aizawa[1]   Allan Hanbury[2]

[1]National Institute of Informatics
2-1-2 Hitotsubashi, Chiyoda-ku
Tokyo, Japan
{surname}@nii.ac.jp

[2]Inst. of Software Technology & Interactive Systems
Vienna University of Technology
Vienna, Austria
{surname}@ifs.tuwien.ac.at

ABSTRACT

We approach the problem of retrievability from an analytical perspective, starting with modeling conjunctive and disjunctive queries in a boolean model. We show that this represents an upper bound on retrievability for all other best match algorithms. We follow this with an observation of imbalance in the distribution of retrievability, using the Gini coefficient. Simulation-based experiments show the behavior of the Gini coefficient for retrievability under different types and lengths of queries, as well as different assumptions about the document length distribution in a collection.

Categories and Subject Descriptors

H.3.4 [**Information Storage and Retrieval**]: Systems and Software—*Performance evaluation*

Keywords

accessibility, retrievability, boolean model, Gini coefficient

1. INTRODUCTION

In the recent years a number of works have proposed and advocated to evaluate Information Retrieval (IR) models not just from the point of view of their efficacy but also from the accessibility that the model gives to the documents [1]. All these studies are fundamentally empirical, and no theoretical analysis has been done yet.

Accessibility plays a particularly important role in recall oriented domains. For example, patent experts are concerned about the fact that certain IR systems are biased towards particular patents rather than others. Also in the medical domain, medical researchers, while doing systematic reviews, to avoid such a bias include in their protocol the use of different search engines.

In essence, a retrievability study consists in automatically generating a number of queries, issuing them to an IR system, then counting how many times a document has been

ICTIR'15, September 27 - 30, 2015, Northampton, MA, USA.
Copyright is held by the owner/author(s). Publication rights licensed to ACM.
ACM 978-1-4503-3833-2/15/09 ...$15.00.
DOI: http://dx.doi.org/10.1145/2808194.2809495 .

retrieved. Each step of the process has different parameters useful to characterize the IR system: the likelihood that a query, the parameters of the IR model, and at which rank a document is considered retrievable.

The idea of this paper comes from the recent experimental discoveries in which it has been pointed out that given an IR model, the length of the document influences its accessibility [5]. In the present study we therefore explore, under some assumptions, to which degree this happens. We do so analytically and through simulations. We start with the analysis of the perfect match models (boolean models), never conducted in previous retrievability studies. We then bridge the discoveries to the best match models, thanks to a small theoretical result that states their relationship.

The remainder of the paper is structured as follows: Section 2 provides the intuition of our method and introduces the required concepts. And we plot and briefly discuss the results in Section 3.

2. ANALYSIS

The retrievability concept is summarized by a measure [2] that defines how likely it is that a document is retrieved. Formally, the retrievability r of a document d with respect to a set of queries Q filed on a particular IR system, is defined as:

$$r(d) = \sum_{q \in Q} o_q f(d, q, c) \qquad (1)$$

where o_q is the opportunity of the query being chosen, q a query, and f a utility function that measures how retrievable the document d is for a query q given the rank cut-off c. It is common to use as utility function f a function that gives 1 if the document is retrieved with rank above or equal to the cut-off c, and 0 if below.

For this initial study we focus however on the boolean search model. In this context, the outcome of the system is not a ranked list of documents but rather a set.

In previous retrievability studies, the queries Q have been generated following one of two strategies: a) starting from the indexed terms, for single term queries, all the terms that appear in the collection at least 5 times; for bi-terms queries, each bi-gram in the collection [2] b) starting from the documents, extracting all the bi-grams from the collection, and selecting those that appear more than 20 times [3, 4]. In both cases, the adopted procedure is an approximation of the entire set of possible queries.

The study of boolean models does not require the generation of all the possible queries. We only need some assumption the class of query used. There are only a few characteristics of a query: it is length in terms, whether it is a unigram or n-gram, and whether it is conjunctive or disjunctive. Therefore, given the type of queries, we set off to analytically calculate the expected $r(d)$ for each document that has a specific number of unique terms.

2.1 Retrievability

Before going further, we introduce the notation used: T_d refers to the set of unique terms in the document d, T_q is the set of unique terms in the query q, T_c is the set of unique terms in the collection (i.e. the dictionary of the collection), and N_c the number of documents in the collection. $\sigma(d, q) : D \times Q \rightarrow \mathbb{R}$ is a scoring function assigning higher scores to more relevant documents, and

$$rank(d,q) = \begin{cases} |\{x \in D, \sigma(x,q) > \sigma(d,q)\}|, & \text{if } \sigma(d,q) > 0. \\ \infty, & \text{otherwise.} \end{cases} \quad (2)$$

a ranking function.

A Boolean model (also referred to sometimes as a perfect match model) is defined in the usual way: it considers relevant (and returns) a document matching the (sub)set of terms in the query. A best match model is essentially a ranking model applied on top of a Boolean model. Therefore, in this study we do not consider those ranking models which bypass individual terms and do their similarity computation in an abstract semantic space (e.g. Latent Semantic Indexing and Latent Dirichlet Allocation). In other words, a best match model here is any model where the implementation can be done using an inverted list and a weighting method.

2.1.1 The Conjunctive Case

For conjunctive queries all the query terms are required in order to retrieve a specific document. Given n, the size of the query, we can calculate $r(d)$ by interpreting the components of Eq. 1. The opportunity to use query q, o_q, is generally defined as Eq. 1 in Azzopardi's and colleagues' work [2, 6]. In this case, we can focus on the function f. We shall come back to o_q shortly.

The utility function f is essentially an indicator function with codomain in $\{0, 1\}$ if its parameter is false or true. For a Boolean model, the utility function is therefore $f_B(d, q, c) = I(T_q \subseteq T_d)$, while for a best match (ranking) model, it is $f_R(d, q, c) = I(rank(d, q) < c)$.

For a random document d and query q, in the case of the Boolean model, the expectation of the utility function is the probability $P(T_q \subseteq T_d)$, which can be calculated by considering all possible sets of n terms ($|T_q| = n$) from the collection dictionary:

$$P(T_q \subseteq T_d) = \binom{|T_d|}{n}\binom{|T_c|}{n}^{-1}$$

Therefore, in the case of $o_q = 1$:

$$r(d) = \sum_{q \in Q_n} \binom{|T_d|}{n}\binom{|T_c|}{n}^{-1}$$

Given that $|Q_n| = \binom{|T_c|}{n}$, we finally have:

$$r(d) = \binom{|T_d|}{n} \quad (3)$$

However, if o_q was considered 1 for practical reasons in simulations, in this theoretical exercise where we already assumed that the vocabulary is limited by the collection vocabulary, we can estimate the probability of a query of length n as $\binom{|T_c|}{n}^{-1}$. Feeding that in the equation above, we obtain:

$$r(d) = \sum_{q \in Q_n} \binom{|T_c|}{n}^{-1}\binom{|T_d|}{n}\binom{|T_c|}{n}^{-1}$$

and following the same motivation as above:

$$r(d) = \binom{|T_d|}{n}\binom{|T_c|}{n}^{-1} \quad (4)$$

This is closer to a probabilistic perspective of retrievability, but in what follows we shall continue to use the form of Eq. 3 because, on one hand, it is simpler, and on the other hand, it is closer to what related empirical studies have been working with.

Now, let us consider all possible query sizes, that is with n that goes from 1 to $|T_c|$ the size of the test collection. The retrievability of a document d in case of using any combinations of n terms as conjunctive queries, is zero if $n > |T_d|$. Otherwise:

$$r(d) = \sum_{n=1}^{|T_c|} \binom{|T_d|}{n} = \sum_{n=1}^{|T_d|} \binom{|T_d|}{n} = 2^{|T_d|} - 1$$

2.1.2 The Disjunctive Case

When the queries are filed in disjunction, this means that at least one query term is required to retrieve a document. Given n, the size of query, we can calculate $r(d)$ similarly to the conjunctive case above. In this case, the utility function is $f_B(d, q, c) = I(T_q \cap T_d \neq \emptyset)$. Again, the expectation of this function is given by the probability

$$P(T_q \cap T_d \neq \emptyset) = \sum_{i=1}^{min(|T_q|,|T_d|)} P(|T_q \cap T_d| = i)$$

and consequently for any query of length $n \leq min(|T_q|, |T_d|)$, we have:

$$r(d) = \sum_{i=1}^{n} \binom{|T_d|}{i} \quad (5)$$

When considering queries of different lengths:

$$r(d) = \sum_{n \in N} \sum_{i=1}^{n} \binom{|T_d|}{i} \quad (6)$$

And, when considering all possible query lengths we have:

$$r(d) = \sum_{n=1}^{|T_d|} \sum_{i=1}^{n} \binom{|T_d|}{i}$$

2.1.3 Best-match models

Now, moving on to best match models, it becomes difficult to analytically consider their retrievability. However, a first observation is given in the theorem and corollary below.

THEOREM 1. *The retrievability of a document under a Boolean retrieval model B is an upper bound for the retrievability of the same document and the same query types, under any ranking system R.*

PROOF. $r_R(d) \leq r_B(d) \Leftrightarrow$
$\sum_{q \in Q} o_q f_R(d, q, c) \leq \sum_{q \in Q} o_q f_B(d, q, c) \Leftrightarrow$
$f_R(d, q, c) \leq f_B(d, q, c)$

For the conjunctive case, we have that the above is equivalent to $I(rank(d, q) < c) \leq I(T_q \subseteq T_d)$

Now, assume the contrary, $I(rank(d, q) < c) > I(T_q \subseteq T_d)$.

$\Leftrightarrow I(rank(d, q) < c) = 1$ and $I(T_q \subseteq T_d) = 0$.

similarly, for the disjunctive case we would have

$\Leftrightarrow I(rank(d, q) < c) = 1$ and $I(T_q \cap T_d \neq \emptyset) = 0$.

Both contradict our definition of the ranking function in Eq. 2 $\square$

COROLLARY 1. *When there is no cutoff ($c = |N_c|$), the retrievability of a document in any of the best match models is equal to its retrievability in the Boolean model.*

2.1.4 N-Grams

In the analysis so far we have only considered queries of various sizes, but not with multi-word terms (n-grams). However, since n-grams are essentially terms in themselves, the only thing that would change is the scale of the calculation, rather than the observations about the nature of retrievability itself. We would agree that a more in-depth study into retrievability with n-grams is desirable, if only to prove our statement above, but we do make this simplification for this particular study.

2.2 Gini Coefficient

The purpose of this section is to observe the distribution of retrievability not over documents but rather over document lengths, counted in unique terms. This is because we want to observe the effect of the latter on the former, but also because in the current analytical view, two documents with the same number of unique terms are indistinguishable. To assess the bias of an IR model it is possible to observe the Lorenz curve, which visualizes the inequality among documents within a collection. The Lorenz curve has already been introduced in retrievability studies as the cumulative distribution of $r(d)$ ordered in non-decreasing order with varying of d. The Gini coefficient was proposed as a way to summarize with a single value the amount shown by the Lorenz curve [2, 6]. It is defined as:

$$G = \frac{n+1}{n} - \frac{2 \sum_{i=1}^{n} (n+1-i) y_i}{n \sum_{i=1}^{n} y_i} \qquad (7)$$

where y_i is the population indexed in non-decreasing order ($y_i \leq y_{i+1}$), and n is the size of the population.

As we have observed in the previous analysis, $r(d)$ for a perfect match model is a function of the number of unique terms in the document. It can be in fact shown that $r(d)$ is monotonically increasing with $|T_d|$. Therefore, given a distribution of document lengths (based on unique terms) in a collection of documents, with probability mass function $u(s) = P(S = s)$, where S is the length of a document counted in unique terms, and $n = N_c$, the numerator in Eq. 7 is:

$$\sum_{i=1}^{N_c} (N_c+1-i) r(d_i) = \sum_{i=1}^{\infty} \sum_{j=1}^{\phi(i)} \left[N_c+1 - \left(j + \sum_{s=1}^{i-1} \phi(s) \right) \right] r(d_{\phi(i)})$$

where $\phi(i) = \lfloor N_c u(i) + 1/2 \rfloor$ is the expected number of documents of length i, and $d_{\phi(i)}$ is a document of length i. The denominator is substituted by:

$$\sum_{i=1}^{N_c} r(d_i) = \sum_{i=1}^{\infty} \sum_{j=1}^{\phi(i)} r(d_{\phi(i)})$$

Simplifying, we obtain:

$$G = \frac{N_c + 1}{N_c} - \frac{2 \sum_{i=1}^{\infty} [N_c + \frac{1}{2} - (\sum_{s=1}^{i-1} \phi(s) + \frac{\phi(i)}{2})] \phi(i) r(d_{\phi(i)})}{N_c \sum_{i=1}^{\infty} \phi(i) r(d_{\phi(i)})}$$

3. DISCUSSION AND CONCLUSION

With this definition of the Gini coefficient (G), we can now observe the effects of the query length and type (via $r(d)$) and of the distribution of document lengths in the collection (via $u(s)$). We do this in Fig. 1. We observe that the inequality always increases with the query length, the slope depends on the distribution of document lengths, and that the query type has a negligible effect. This last observation is potentially surprising. We explore this in Fig. 2. Here, the left-most element shows that the results become more skewed in different ways: in the conjunctive case a majority of documents get $r(d)$ equals to zero, while in the disjunctive case, a majority obtain high scores, when varying the length of the document. The other two plots show $r(d)$ for various query lengths n. In the case of single term queries, retrievability is essentially document length (again, counted as number of unique terms).

We have shown that retrievability for the Boolean model can be approached analytically. While in this study we considered different probability distributions for document lengths, the method can also be used in the presence of an actual test collection to calculate accessibility without the need for generating large sets of synthetic queries. Furthermore, the relationship between document length and retrievability, even in this particular retrieval model, may provide insights into new normalization factors for best match models.

4. REFERENCES

[1] L. Azzopardi and V. Vinay. *Accessibility in Information Retrieval*, volume 4956. Springer, 2008.

[2] L. Azzopardi and V. Vinay. Retrievability: An evaluation measure for higher order information access tasks. In *Proc. of CIKM*. ACM, 2008.

[3] S. Bashir and A. Rauber. Improving retrievability of patents with cluster-based pseudo-relevance feedback documents selection. In *Proc. of CIKM*, New York, NY, USA, 2009. ACM.

[4] S. Bashir and A. Rauber. *Improving Retrievability of Patents in Prior-Art Search*, volume 5993. Springer, 2010.

[5] C. Wilkie and L. Azzopardi. Relating retrievability, performance and length. In *Proc. of SIGIR*. ACM, 2013.

[6] C. Wilkie and L. Azzopardi. *Retrievability and Retrieval Bias: A Comparison of Inequality Measures*, volume 9022. Springer, 2015.

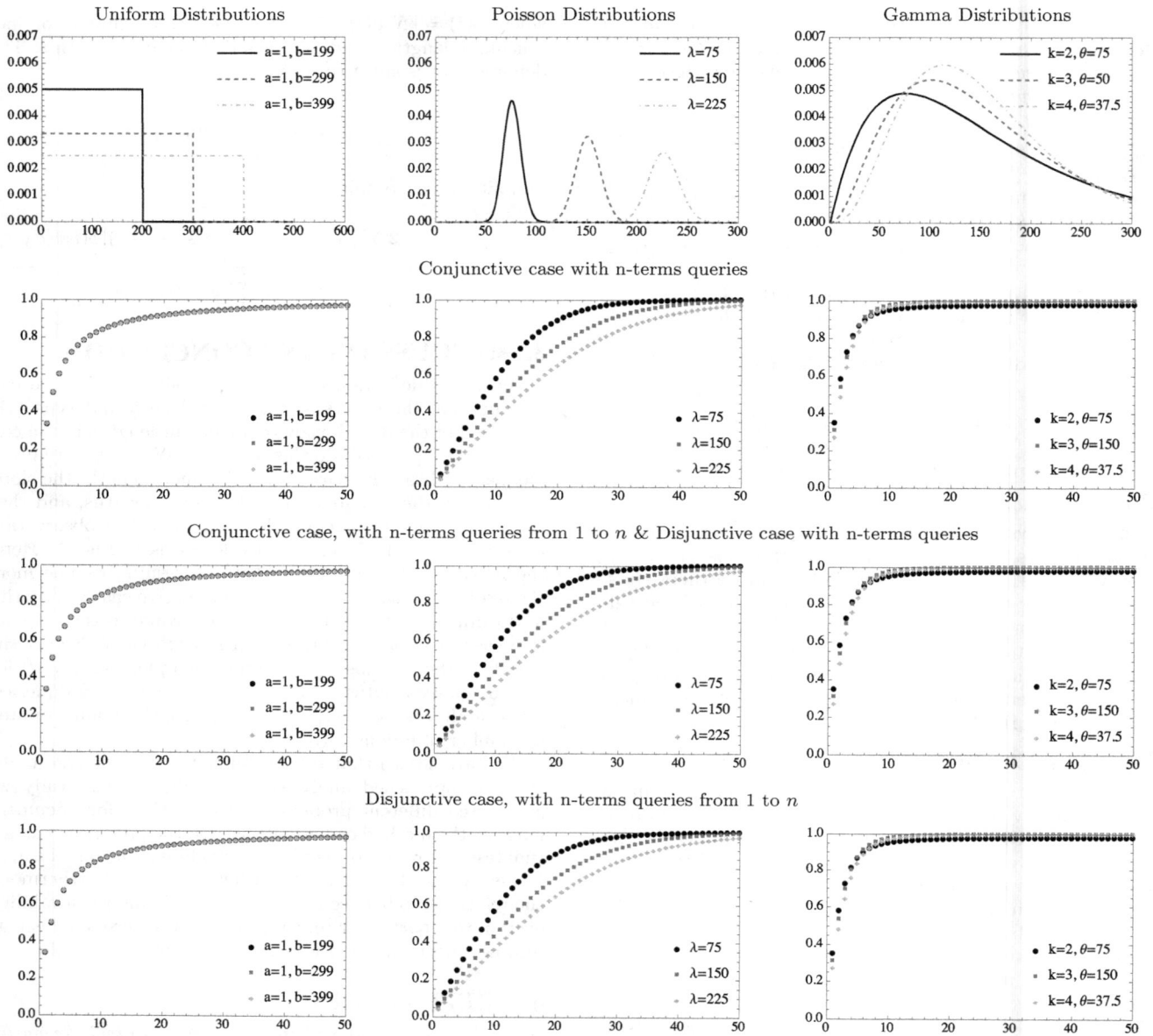

Figure 1: Gini coefficient, given a document length distribution of a collection of documents vs different cases with varying of n of n-term queries. The middle row shows the two cases, conjunctive case, with n-terms queries from 1 to n and disjunctive case with n-terms queries, based on the observation that Eq. 5 models them both.

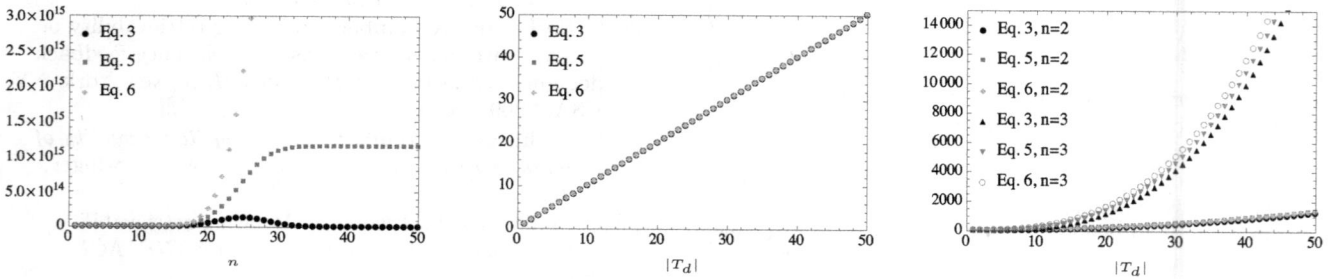

Figure 2: Retrievability $r(d)$ in the three cases: conjunctive with varying of n (Eq. 3), conjunctive with varying of n from 1 to n & disjunctive with varying of n (Eq. 5) and disjunctive from with varying of n from 1 to n (Eq. 6). The first plot to the left shows how the retrievability varies for a document of $|T_d| = 50$ with varying of n query terms; The second plot shows how the retrievability varies with varying of $|T_d|$ for single term queries; The third plot is similar to the second plot but with n equal to 2 and 3.

On the Behavior of PRES Using Incomplete Judgment Sets

Ellen M. Voorhees
National Institute of Standards and Technology
ellen.voorhees@nist.gov

ABSTRACT

PRES, the Patent Retrieval Evaluation Score, is a family of retrieval evaluation measures that combines recall and user effort to reflect the quality of a retrieval run with respect to recall-oriented search tasks. Previous analysis of the measure was done using the test collection for the CLEF-IP 2009 track, a collection that contains a limited range of number of relevant documents, making it difficult to assess the behavior of PRES for varying recall contexts. This paper examines the effect of incomplete judgments on PRES scores using the well-studied TREC-8 ad hoc test collection, a collection with a much more varied number-of-relevants profile. Experiments with small judgment sets created through a typical collection-building process show the PRES measures are resilient to incomplete judgment sets.

Categories and Subject Descriptors

H.3.4 [**Information Storage and Retrieval**]: Systems and Software—Performance Evaluation

Keywords

PRES measure; Test collections; Incomplete judgments

1. INTRODUCTION

Magdy and Jones [2, 3] introduced the 'Patent Retrieval Evaluation Score' (PRES) as a family of measures for recall-oriented search tasks. A particular instance of the family is defined based on a rank threshold N_{max}:

$$PRES_{N_{max}} = 1 - \frac{\frac{\sum r_i}{R} - \frac{R+1}{2}}{N_{max}}$$

where r_i is the rank at which the ith relevant document is retrieved and R is the total number of relevant documents. PRES, inspired by the normalized recall measure, measures the effectiveness of a ranking of at most N_{max} documents with respect to both the best and worst possible rankings. In comparison to the two other measures frequently used to evaluate recall-oriented search, PRES emphasizes the total number of relevant documents found in the top N_{max} ranks more than average precision while emphasizing the ranks at which those relevant were found more than recall.

Magdy and Jones analyzed the PRES measures using data from CLEF-IP 2009. While the prior art search task of CLEF-IP is a recall-oriented task, the test collection is atypical for a high-recall task. The document set consists of ap-

proximately one million patents and the systems' task was to automatically retrieve all the patents found in the collection that were cited by a source patent (the topic). The original citations as created by the patent applicants or the patent office are used as the relevance judgments. The variant of the collection that Magdy and Jones used in their studies consisted of 400 topics that had a mean of six relevant documents per topic, with a minimum of three relevant and a maximum of 42 relevant [2]. The distribution of relevant documents per topics is highly skewed toward fewer relevant: more than 100 topics (one quarter of the topics) have exactly three relevant documents, and fewer than 100 topics have more than ten relevant documents.

Most retrieval evaluation measures are inherently unstable (small changes in a ranked list can lead to large changes in the score) with so few relevant. This in turn leads to average scores being unstable because the averages become dominated by whichever topics happen to get relatively large scores in that instance. While Magdy and Jones report small levels of agreement between rankings of systems as ordered by mean average precision (MAP) using the original relevance judgments or incomplete relevance judgments [2], the effect they observed can equally likely be a manifestation of instability rather than incompleteness, especially since an incomplete judgment set has even smaller numbers of relevant documents.

A second concern with analyzing PRES using a collection with a limited range of number of relevant documents is the impossibility of observing the behavior of PRES as the relative size of N_{max} and the number of relevant varies. Magdy and Jones suggest that PRES is best-behaved when $N_{max} > R$ [3]. But how does mean PRES behave when N_{max} is larger than R for some topics only? And do characteristics of test collection creation, such as pool depth, affect the values of N_{max} that can subsequently be used with collection?

This paper examines the effect of incomplete judgments on PRES scores when topics have a widely-varying number of relevant documents. Incomplete judgments give rise to two concerns: that certain kinds of runs are penalized because the type of relevant documents they retrieve are not represented in the judgment sets, and that too few judgments could be performed with available judging resources during collection construction to allow stable evaluation overall. The paper investigates both issues using a workflow that is typical for building collections in community evaluations such as TREC or CLEF. The next section examines the first issue by testing whether runs that did not contribute to the judgment set can be fairly evaluated using PRES. The following section examines the behavior of the measures when many fewer documents, between 30–45% of the known relevant set, are retained as relevant documents. Both sets of

This paper is authored by an employee of the United States Government and is in the public domain. Non-exclusive copying or redistribution is allowed, provided that the article citation is given and the authors and agency are clearly identified as its source.

ICTIR '15 September 27–30, 2015, Northampton, MA, USA

ACM 978-1-4503-3833-2/15/09

DOI:http://dx.doi.org/10.1145/2808194.2809484

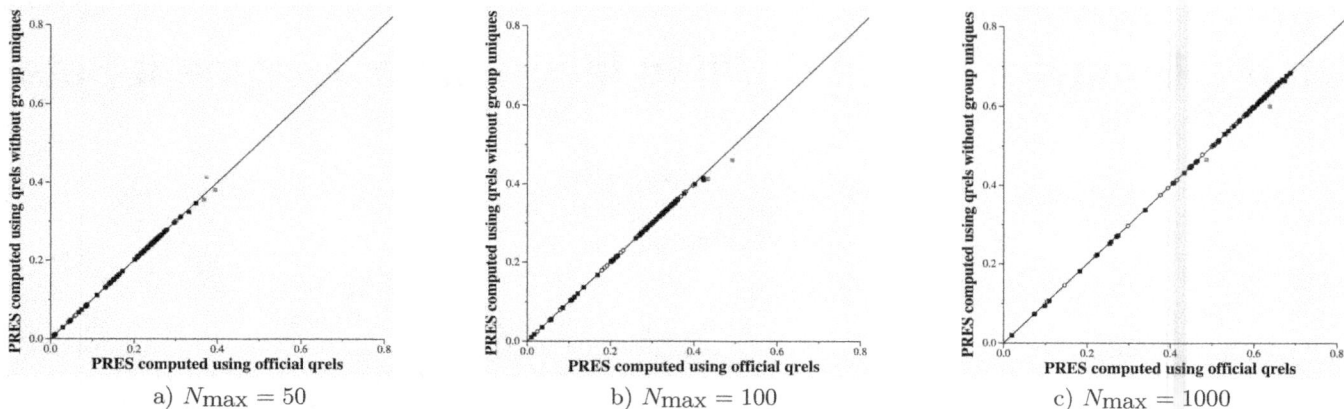

a) $N_{max} = 50$ b) $N_{max} = 100$ c) $N_{max} = 1000$

Figure 1: Leave-out-uniques test results for PRES scores with different N_{max} thresholds. Pool runs are plotted with filled boxes and other runs are plotted with open circles. Points that fall below the diagonal are runs that would score worse had that team not participated in the collection building process. The two red boxes are `READWARE` runs that clearly demonstrate the effect of N_{max} on the PRES measure (see text).

Table 1: Number of topics with a given number of relevant documents (R)

Range of R	# topics
$R \le 10$	1
$10 < R \le 50$	18
$50 < R \le 100$	11
$100 < R \le 200$	15
$R > 200$	5

experiments show that PRES is resilient to these changes in the relevant set.

2. LOU TEST

All of the experiments in this paper use the TREC-8 ad hoc test collection. This collection contains about 528,000 mostly newswire documents and 50 topics. Binary relevance judgments were created through pooling. The pools were formed from the top 100 documents from each of 71 judged runs (out of the 129 runs that were submitted to the track) as well as some documents contributed by runs submitted to other TREC-8 tracks. Among the runs that contributed to the pools were several effective manual runs. The collection was chosen for this study because of its extensive relevance judgments and because it has a wide range of number of relevant for different topics: a mean of 95, with a minimum of 6 and a maximum of 347. Table 1 summarizes the distribution of the number of relevant per topic for the collection.

One test of the sensitivity of a measure to incomplete relevant documents is the 'leave-out-uniques' (LOU) test [1]. For pool-built test collections, relevant documents that were contributed to the pools by runs from a single team are called *unique* relevant documents. If that team had not participated in the collection-building process, those documents would have remained unjudged and would thus be treated as not relevant. The change in the score when a run is evaluated first using the full set of relevance judgments and then using the set of relevance judgments created when the team's unique relevant documents are removed reflects the sensitivity of the measure to missing relevant documents.

Figure 1 shows the results of the LOU test for PRES[1] using three different N_{max} thresholds. Call the set of relevance judgments used to evaluate a retrieval run a *qrels*. Each point in a graph represents a TREC-8 run where the x-axis is the run's mean PRES score as computed using the original qrels and the y-axis is the run's mean PRES score as computed using the the qrels that has the run's team's unique relevant documents removed. Runs that did not contribute to the original pools are plotted with open circles and runs that did contribute to the pools (*pool runs*) are plotted with filled boxes. The leftmost graph in the figure plots $PRES_{50}$ scores, the center graph plots $PRES_{100}$ scores, and the rightmost graph plots $PRES_{1000}$ scores.

TREC-8 had several effective manual runs that contributed to the pools, and these runs contain relatively many unique relevant documents [5]. Two of these manual runs, `READWARE` and `READWARE2`, are plotted in red in Figure 1. In Figure 1(a), these runs are the most effective runs and lie just beneath the diagonal line that represents equal mean PRES scores from both qrels. Points below the diagonal are runs whose mean PRES scores degrade when their unique relevant documents are treated as nonrelevant. The vast majority of the runs lie right on the diagonal line for each of the different N_{max} thresholds, and those few runs that do degrade are only minimally affected. These results demonstrate that PRES is robust against small changes in the judgment sets caused by changing participants in the collection building exercise.

Figure 1 also shows how the mean PRES scores vary with changing threshold. Not surprisingly, scores increase as the threshold increases (there is a greater chance to find relevant documents in larger ranked lists). The behavior that PRES was designed to reward is also evident in the plots. The manual `READWARE` runs include many fewer than the 1000 documents per topic that TREC allows as a maximum. `READWARE2` is the most effective run as measured by $PRES_{50}$ and $PRES_{100}$, and it is also the most effective run as measured by MAP (evaluated through rank 1000). However,

---

[1]PRES scores in this paper were computed using the PRESeval script available at http://alt.qcri.org/~wmagdy/PRES.htm.

Table 2: Size and number of relevant documents per qrels. Entries are means over ten trials, except for the Full Set, 100% sampling rate entry that gives the statistics for the original qrels.

	Full Set		Half Set	
%	Size	# Rels	Size	# Rels
10	10,963.0	1,813.9	7,127.5	1,430.9
25	12,302.5	1,914.2	8,017.4	1,519.9
50	14,556.1	2,089.2	9,510.8	1,673.6
100	86,830	4,728	12,478.9	1,979.9

it is not in the top ten runs as measured by $PRES_{1000}$ because its total of relevant documents retrieved out of 1000 is smaller than the other runs.

3. INCOMPLETE JUDGMENT SETS

The LOU test results show that PRES is insensitive to a few missing relevant documents from an otherwise extensive judgment set. But test collections with nearly complete judgment sets are very expensive to build and thus are very rare. More often, test collections are built using sampling techniques that require many fewer judgments than deep pools. This section explores how PRES fares using collections known to have significantly incomplete judgments. We create reduced qrels sets from the TREC-8 data by using a sampling strategy that supports the computation of extended inferred measures [6], a common method for building new test collections. We then create a ranking of the TREC-8 runs ordered by PRES score using the reduced qrels, and compute the Kendall τ correlation between that ranking and the ranking induced by the original qrels.

We can create reduced qrels by sampling fewer documents from all pool runs or by having fewer runs contribute to the judgment sets. We use both strategies, calling qrels created from all pool runs 'Full Set' qrels and qrels created from fewer runs 'Half Set' qrels. For Half Set qrels, we randomly select half of the participating teams and use those teams' pool runs as the set of runs that contribute to the judgment sets. We use ten different random splits of teams into contributor and non-contributor sets. Since TREC-8 teams submitted different numbers of runs, different splits produce slightly different numbers of contributing runs.

Given a set of contributing runs, we produce reduced qrels by using a '2strata' sampling strategy [4]. Specifically, qrels are built by selecting the top ten documents from all contributing runs plus an X% sample of the documents found in ranks 11–100 of the contributing runs, for X=10, 25, 50, or 100. The sampling process is repeated 10 times, with each time called a trial[2].

Table 2 shows the size of resulting qrels (i.e., number of documents requiring judgments) and the number of relevant documents within the qrels for the original qrels and the various reduced qrels. The Full Set, 100% sampling rate entry gives the statistics for the original qrels. These counts are larger than a true 100% sample of all pool runs would give because other TREC-8 tracks also contributed runs to the pools. All other entries are means over ten trials, and the trial values are themselves means over ten different contributor splits for sampling rates less than 100% and Half Set

---

[2]The set of qrels files resulting from this process is available from `https://ir.nist.gov/ictir2015/PRESjudgments.tar.gz`.

Table 3: Kendall τ correlation between rankings of runs induced by the original qrels and the reduced qrels. Reported values are are means over ten trials.

	10%	25%	50%	100%
infAP	.9243	.9345	.9339	—
$PRES_{50}$	.8996	.9082	.9188	—
$PRES_{100}$	.8937	.9032	.9161	—
$PRES_{1000}$	.8838	.8932	.9050	—

a) Full Set qrels

	10%	25%	50%	100%
infAP	.8959	.9057	.9095	.9136
$PRES_{50}$	.8607	.8694	.8824	.9017
$PRES_{100}$	.8515	.8616	.8761	.8984
$PRES_{1000}$	.8624	.8707	.8819	.8989

b) Half Set qrels

qrels. The number of judgments required for all reduced qrels is no more than 15% of the judgments within the original qrels. The number of relevant documents is reduced as well, ranging from 30–45% of the known relevant documents.

Table 3 gives the mean Kendall τ correlation between induced rankings for PRES scores as well as for extended inferred average precision (infAP) scores vs. original MAP scores for reference. The values reported are means over the ten trials, and, for Half Set qrels built from sampling rates less than 100%, individual trial values are means over ten contributor splits.

As expected, correlations are greater for larger sampling rates (and thus larger qrels). Correlations are also greater using a more diverse contributor set (Full Set vs. Half Set): while Full Set qrels are always larger than the same sampling rate Half Set qrels, the Half Set qrels sampled at 100% is the same size as the Full Set qrels sampled at 25% and the Full Set correlations are greater than the Half Set correlations except for $PRES_{1000}$. Correlations using infAP are greater than the correlations using PRES, but all correlations are generally good, with all observed individual correlations over contributor splits, trials, and thresholds greater than 0.8 (minimum of 0.8088).

A more detailed look at how reduced qrels affects PRES scores is given in Figure 2. The figure contains scatter plots of TREC-8 runs where the x-axis is the original qrels score and the y-axis is the reduced qrels score. The scatter plots show scores computed for Half Set qrels for one selected contributor split (split 2) and the first trial. Full Set qrels results are not shown because they are less variable than Half Set qrels results. This particular contributor split was selected because it is one of the splits that does not contain the **READWARE2** run as a contributor so it represents a more challenging case. All runs from contributor teams are plotted with an open box and all runs from non-contributor teams are plotted with filled circles. There are nine separate scatter plots, one each for the cross-product of three sampling rates (10%, 50%, 100%) and three N_{max} thresholds (50, 100, 1000).

Most scores lie above the diagonal demonstrating that PRES computed on reduced qrels overestimates the PRES score of the full qrels. But it is relative scores between runs that is important, not fidelity to the original score, so the ideal case is any straight-line of scores. None of the scatter plots contain perfectly aligned scores, but only a few runs— largely the highly effective manual runs that contributed

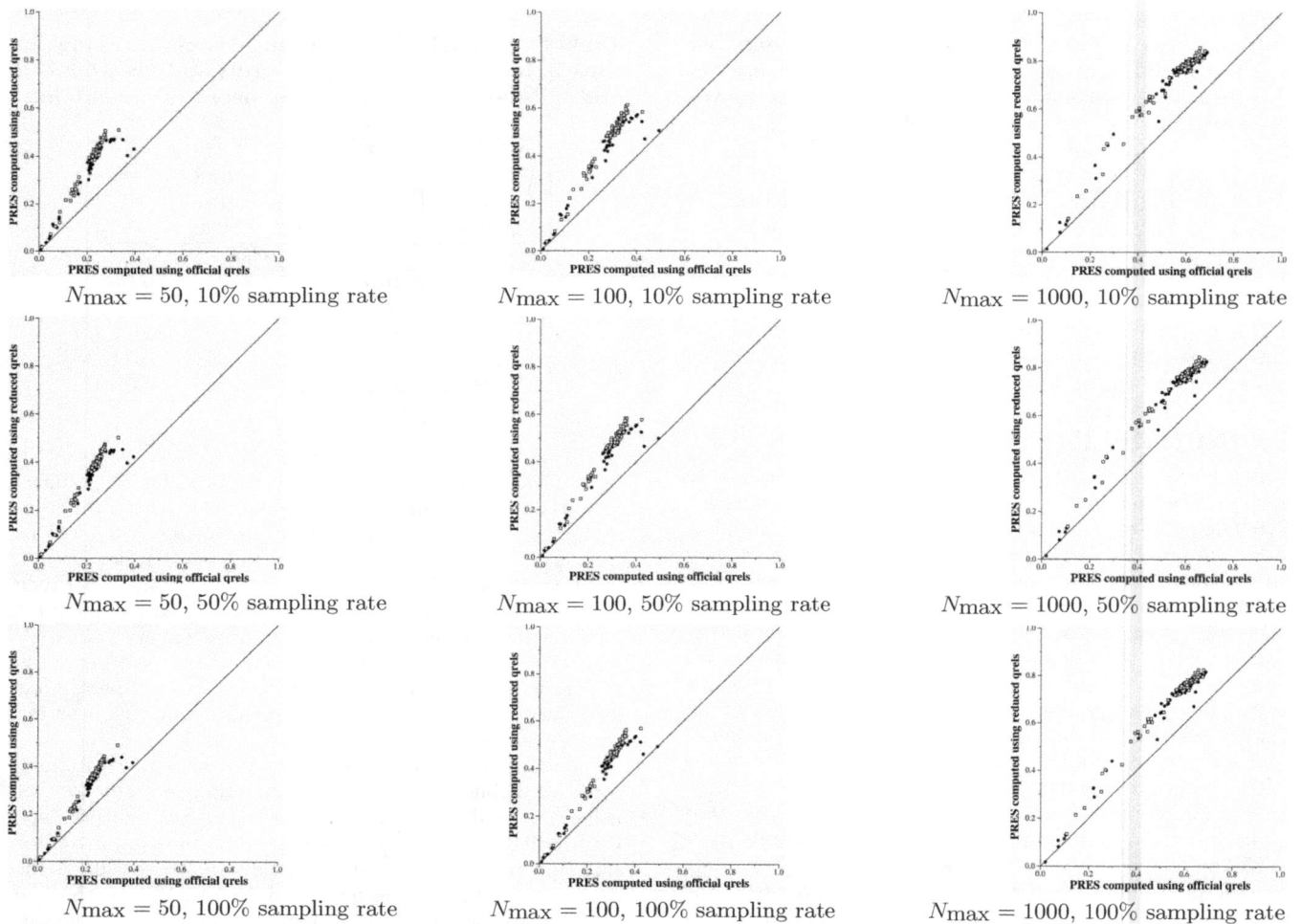

Figure 2: PRES evaluation scores as qrels size and N_{max} threshold vary for one selected contributor split and the first trial. The selected contributor split did not contain the `READWARE2` run, and thus the plots show worse-than-average behavior. All runs submitted by contributor teams are plotted with open boxes; non-contributor teams' runs are plotted with filled circles.

relatively many unique relevant documents to the original qrels—are noticeably misaligned.

4. CONCLUSION

Using a collection with a wide range of relevant documents per topic, we created qrels sets containing 30–45% of the known relevant documents using a typical collection-building workflow and showed that mean PRES scores are resilient in the face of such incompleteness. We also confirmed that mean PRES scores do indeed reflect an emphasis on recall as compared to average precision at this scale.

While the TREC-8 collection used here has a much wider range of relevant documents per topic than the CLEF-IP 2009 collection used in earlier experiments, its maximum number of relevant is 347 which is still smaller than the relevant sets for some high-recall tasks, and smaller than the largest N_{max} threshold used. Additional studies will need to be performed to assess the behavior of PRES when a sensible N_{max} threshold (representing the total number of documents a user will examine) is much smaller than the relevant set size.

5. REFERENCES

[1] C. Buckley, D. Dimmick, I. Soboroff, and E. M. Voorhees. Bias and the limits of pooling for large collections. *Information Retrieval*, 10:491–508, 2007.

[2] W. Magdy and G. J. Jones. Examining the robustness of evaluation metrics for patent retrieval with incomplete relevance judgments. In *Proceedings of CLEF 2010, LNCS 6360*, pages 82–93, 2010.

[3] W. Magdy and G. J. Jones. PRES: A score metric for evaluating recall-oriented information retrieval applications. In *Proceedings of SIGIR 2010*, pages 611–618, 2010.

[4] E. M. Voorhees. The effect of sampling strategy on inferred measures. In *Proceedings of SIGIR 2014*, pages 1119–1122, 2014.

[5] E. M. Voorhees and D. Harman. Overview of the eighth Text REtrieval Conference (TREC-8). In *Proceedings of TREC-8*, pages 1–24, 1999.

[6] E. Yilmaz, E. Kanoulas, and J. A. Aslam. A simple and efficient sampling method for estimating AP and NDCG. In *Proceedings of SIGIR 2008*, pages 603–610, 2008.

Optimal Packing in Simple-Family Codecs

Andrew Trotman
eBay Inc.
San Jose, USA

Michael Albert
Department of Computer Science
University of Otago
Dunedin, New Zealand

Blake Burgess
Department of Computer Science
University of Otago
Dunedin, New Zealand

ABSTRACT

The Simple family of codecs is popular for encoding postings lists for a search engine because they are both space effective and time efficient at decoding. These algorithms pack as many integers into a codeword as possible before moving on to the next codeword. This technique is known as left-greedy. This contribution proves that left-greedy is not optimal and then goes on to introduce a dynamic programming solution to find the optimal packing. Experiments on .gov2 and INEX Wikipedia 2009 show that although this is an interesting theoretical result, left-greedy is empirically near optimal in effectiveness and efficiency.

Categories and Subject Descriptors

H.3.1 [**Information Storage and Retrieval**]: Content Analysis and Indexing - *Indexing methods*

General Terms

Algorithms, Performance.

Keywords

Inverted Files, Compression, Procrastination.

1. INTRODUCTION

The typical index seen in a search engine is known as an inverted file. An inverted file stores a vocabulary of all unique terms seen in the collection along with a postings list for each term. These postings lists are usually represented as an ordered list of $<d, tf>$ tuples, where d is a document identifier and tf is the term frequency (more accurately, the number of times the term occurs in the document). As indexing can be performed in a single linear pass over the document collection, the document identifiers form a strictly monotonically increasing sequence but the term frequencies do not.

In a term-frequency ordered index [9] the $<d, tf>$ tuples are sorted first on decreasing tf, then on increasing d. The index is thus represented $<tf_1: d_{1,1}, d_{1,2}, ... d_{1,n}>...<tf_m: d_{m,1}, d_{m,2}, d_{m,n}>$ where tf scores decrease as m increases and d scores increase as n increases. The sequences of document identifiers continue to form monotonically increasing sequences; however such a representation is smaller than a document-ordered index as fewer integers are stored overall.

In a process known as *impact ordering* [2], the ranking function is partially computed at indexing time and the result is quantized into a fixed sized value (typically a single-byte or smaller). In this

case the $<tf_m: d_{m,1}, d_{m,2}, d_{m,n}>$ sequences in the term-frequency ordered index are replaced with $<q_m: d_{m,1}, d_{m,2}, d_{m,n}>$ sequences, where q_m is the quantized impact of the term with respect to the document. Such an impact score might be computed from a ranking function such as BM25 [10]. Regardless of how it is computed, the document identifiers continue to form strictly monotonically increasing sequences. An impact ordered index is typically larger than a term-frequency ordered index, but faster to process.

Postings lists are normally compressed in order to reduce their size and to increase throughput. A substantial amount of prior work exists on this topic.

First a monotonic sequence is converted into a series of d-gaps [8] (also known as deltas, or differences). There are two popular approaches. In the first, known as D1 and used herein, each d-gap, g_n, is computed by subtracting the previous integer, d_{n-1} from the current integer, d_n: $g_n = d_n - d_{n-1}$. For example, the sequence $<3, 5, 8, 21, 23, 24, 26, 28>$ becomes $<3, 2, 3, 13, 2, 1, 2, 2>$. These d-gap sequences further compress more effectively than when d-gaps are not used because each g_n can be no larger than d_n.

In the second approach, known as D4, four such interleaved d-gap sequences are constructed; $(g_n, g_{n+1}, g_{n+2}, g_{n+3}) = (d_n, d_{n+1}, d_{n+2}, d_{n+3}) - (d_{n-4}, d_{n-3}, d_{n-2}, d_{n-1})$. In this way the sequence $<3, 5, 8, 21, 23, 24, 26, 28>$ becomes $<3, 5, 8, 21, 20, 19, 18, 7>$. This second approach is seen with schemes that use SIMD instructions to decode [8].

There are four approaches to compressing these d-gaps. The first, bit-aligned codes, is typified by schemes such as Elias gamma [5] and Golomb [6] encoding. The second, byte aligned codes, is typified by Variable Byte Encoding [11] and Group Varint [4]. The third, word-aligned codes (also known as the Simple family), is typified by Simple-9 [1], Simple-16 [15], Simple-8b [3], and variants such as PForDelta [16] and VSEncoding [12]. The fourth are SIMD schemes such as SIMD-BP128 [7] and QMX [13].

Common to the third and fourth approaches is the task of packing integers into machine words. This is typically implemented in a left-greedy fashion, packing as many integers as possible into the current codeword before moving on to the next. We ask:

Is left-greedy packing optimal?

And show by counter example that it is not.

We then present a graph-based model of the optimal packing, and a dynamic programming solution to find it.

We apply it to three members of the Simple family resulting in *Simple-9 packed*, *Simple-16 packed*, and *Simple-8b packed*.

Experiments on two standard collections show a small but negligible difference in both space effectiveness and decoding efficiency. Despite the elegance of being optimal, empirically we find that: *left-greedy packing is near optimal in space and decoding time.*

2. SIMPLE ENCODING

This section provides an overview of three Simple family codecs and discusses left-greedy packing.

2.1 Simple-9

In Simple-9 [1] a 32-bit codeword is broken into two parts, (called snips), a *selector* and a *payload*. The payload carries as many fixed-width integers as possible, while the selector gives the number of integers in the payload (and hence their width in bits). For Simple-9 the selector is 4 bits wide and the payload is 28 bits wide.

Table 1: Simple-9 integer packings

Selector	0	1	2	3	4	5	6	7	8
Integers	1	2	3	4	5	7	9	14	28
Width	28	14	9	7	5	4	3	2	1

Table 1 lists the 9 possible ways to pack fixed-width integers into a 28-bit payload. The first row lists the selectors, the second lists the number of integers, while the third row lists the width of each integer. For example, encoding the sequence <260, 270, 240> using Simple-9 requires 9 bits per integer, and hence the sequence would become (in binary): <0010><100000100, 100001110, 011110000>.

2.2 Simple-16

Simple-16 [15] adds two space savings to Simple-9. First, it is observed that only 9 of the possible 16 selectors are used; in Simple-16 the remaining 7 are used to store asymmetric combinations. The second saving is that some Simple-9 combinations result in wasted bits; for example, storing five 5-bit integers leaves three unused bit. Simple-16 alters these selectors to make them asymmetric and in doing so is no worse than the Simple-9 original.

Table 2 lists the way the selectors are used in Simple-16. The first column gives the selector value, the second gives the number of integers that are being stored, while the third gives the usage of the 28-bits (the remaining columns are discussed in Section 2.3). For example, the selector value 6 represents one 3-bit integer followed by four 4-bit integers followed by three 3-bit integers.

The first space saving is seen in a selector such as 2, which stores 21 integers in a combination not possible in Simple-9. The second space saving is seen in selectors such as 10 and 11 which store combinations of 5-bit and 6-bit integers without wastage whereas Simple 9 stores five 5-bit integers with 3 bits wasted.

2.3 Simple-8b

Both Simple-9 and Simple-16 store codewords in 32-bit integers made up of selectors and payloads. Simple-8b [3] extends the size of the codeword to 64-bits, but retains the 4-bit selector. Doing so results in a space saving because fewer selectors are stored per encoded bit (4 per 60 encoded bits rather than 4 per 28 encoded bits).

Table 2 additionally lists the Simple-8b selectors and their meanings. The first column gives the selector value, the fourth column the number of integers being stored and the fifth gives the width in bits. For example, selector 6 indicates that the payload stores twelve 5-bit integers.

The space saving comes when a long sequence of similar sized integers must be stored, for example twelve 5-bit integers can be stored in one 64-bit codeword with Simple-8b whereas it would take three 32-bit codewords using Simple-9. A second space saving comes due to the addition of selectors 0 and 1 which encode long sequences of 0s.

When decoded on a 64-bit architecture Simple-8b is more efficient than Simple-9 because 64-bit instructions can be used to perform shifts during decoding.

Table 2: Simple-16 and Simple-8b integer packings

Selector	Simple-16		Simple-8b	
	Integers	Integers × Width	Integers	Width
0	28	28×1	240	0
1	21	7×2, 14×1	120	0
2	21	7×1, 7×2, 7×1	60	1
3	21	14×1, 7×2	30	2
4	14	14×2	20	3
5	9	1×4, 8×3	15	4
6	8	1×3, 4×4, 3×3	12	5
7	7	7×4	10	6
8	6	4×5, 2×4	8	7
9	6	2×4, 4×5	7	8
10	5	3×6, 2×5	6	10
11	5	2×5, 3×6	5	12
12	4	4×7	4	15
13	3	1×10, 2×9	3	20
14	2	2×14	2	30
15	1	1×28	1	60

2.4 Encoding

Encoding integers using the Simple family is straightforward. Compute the number of bits necessary to store the first integer in the sequence. If storing that number of bits fills a codeword then move on to the next codeword. If not then examine the next integer, and so on until a codeword is full, and then move on to the next codeword.

This packing approach is left-greedy. As many integers as possible are packed into the current codeword before moving on to the next.

3. PACKING

This section shows that left-greedy is not optimal and then introduces the optimal packing algorithm.

3.1 Non-optimal Left-greedy Packing

Left-greedy can be shown to be non-optimal by using a proof by counter example using Simple-9

Take the thirty-two integer sequence <260, 260, 1, 1, 1, 1, 1, 1, 1, 1, 1, 1, 1, 1, 1, 1, 1, 1, 1, 1, 1, 1, 1, 1, 1, 1, 1, 1, 1, 1, 260, 260>, that is, two 9-bit integers followed by twenty-eight 1-bit integers, followed by two 9-bit integers. Such a sequence might be the d-gaps for a single term in the inverted index.

Packing left-greedy, three 9-bit integers <260, 260, 1> are packed, then fourteen 2-bit integers <1, 1, 1, 1, 1, 1, 1, 1, 1, 1, 1, 1, 1, 1>, then seven 4-bit integers <1, 1, 1, 1, 1, 1, 1> then five 5-bit integers <1, 1, 1, 1, 1> then three 9-bit integers <1, 260, 260> for a total of 5 codewords.

A smaller packing stores two 14-bit integers <260, 260> then twenty-eight 1-bit integers <1, 1, 1, 1, 1, 1, 1, 1, 1, 1, 1, 1, 1, 1, 1,

1, 1, 1, 1, 1, 1, 1, 1, 1, 1, 1, 1, 1> then two 14-bit integers <260, 260> for a total of 3 codewords.

Hence, by counter example, left-packing is not space-optimal for all sequences.

3.2 Optimal Packing

In Simple-9 there are at most 9 possible ways any one integer might be packed (see Table 1). As such, an integer sequence can be thought of as a 9-way branching tree with each vertex representing the start of the next codeword and each edge labeled with the number of integers to pack to get to that codeword. The optimal packing is the shortest valid path through this tree, the path that touches the minimum number of nodes (ignoring edge weights). A similar construction exists for Simple-16, Simple-8b, and similar codecs. Without loss of generality, the solution to Simple-9 is presented.

For long integer sequences, such as long postings lists, it is prohibitively expensive to build and exhaustively search the tree. The optimal path can, however, be built using dynamic programming. Doing so requires starting at the final integer to be encoded, the right hand end of the sequence, and working backwards. At each step the optimal solution *up to that point* is computed.

The first integer can be optimally packed into one codeword, so store a 1 for this integer (in extra storage). Moving back one integer, there are at most two ways the integer might be packed: on its own, or with the next integer. Compute all valid packings and store for this integer: the minimum number of codewords necessary to store this integer and the tail of the sequence, and which branch in the tree to take to get that packing. Move to the previous integer, which might be packed in three ways, and repeat the process. By the tenth integer there are at most nine combinations to check – one of which is optimal if the sequence started there; so store the optimal number of codewords, and the branch to take. Repeat the process until the start of the list is reached.

At each point the extra storage holds the optimal number of codewords necessary to store that integer and the tail of the sequence, along with the optimal branch to take if starting at that point. At most 9 branches need be followed for each integer – and hence the computation is linear time in the length of the sequence to be compressed, O(n).

Given the extra storage it is possible to now move forward and pack. Start at the left-hand end of the extra storage. Repeatedly follow the tree-branch and packing accordingly. As each branch is optimal starting at that point, so to must be the result. The packing process is also linear time, O(n).

As stated at the start of this section, this approach is optimal. At all times the optimal packing of the tail of the list is known, and the optimal way to add one integer to the start is computed.

4. EXPERIMENTS

Two experiments were conducted, one measuring the effect, per integer, on the index, the other measuring the effect *in situ* in the search engine.

4.1 Effect Per Integer

The two packing approaches discussed in Section 3 (left-greedy and optimal packing) were implemented for the 3 Simple family schemes discussed in Section 2 giving a total of 6 schemes. Implementation was in the ATIRE search engine [14].

For the experiments the left-greedy algorithms are known as S9, S16, S8b for Simple-9, Simple-16 and Simple-8b. The optimally packed versions are suffixed with a 'p' (e.g. S9p).

Experiments were conducted on two collections. First, the TREC .gov2 collection of 25,205,179 web pages crawled from the .gov domain in 2004. Second, the INEX 2009 Wikipedia collection of 2,666,190 documents, a dump taken in 2008 annotated using YAGO and converted into XML. A single core of a 64-core AMD Opteron 6276 at 2.3GHz with 512 GB RAM was used throughout.

A term-frequency ordered index was built for each collection and the mean number of bits per integer used to store the document identifiers was recorded. The term-frequency index was preferred because it is smaller than a document-ordered or impact-ordered index of the same collection. The time taken to decode each postings list was measured 10 times using the CPUID RDTSC combination and the minimum was recorded. The minimum of 10 was preferred because it reduces the effect of outliers.

Table 3 presents the size and time required to store and decode each document identifier in the postings lists (7,688,185,119 for .gov2 and 813,998,392 for Wikipedia). The first column gives the name of the codec, the second column the average size of an integer in bits per integer (bpi), the third column the mean time to decompress in cycles per integer (cpi). The table shows that, as expected, a Simple-8b index is smaller than a Simple-16 index, which is smaller than a Simple-9 index. It also shows virtually no difference between the left-greedy and optimal versions of each codec – suggesting that left-greedy is near-optimal.

Table 3: bits per integer (bpi) and cycles per integer (cpi) averaged over the entire index

	.gov2		Wikipedia	
	bpi	cpi	bpi	cpi
S9	11.09	6.87	11.85	9.29
S9p	11.08	6.87	11.84	9.31
S16	10.73	6.71	11.49	9.01
S16p	10.73	6.72	11.49	9.02
S8b	10.00	4.56	11.01	6.79
S8bp	9.99	4.55	11.00	6.77

4.2 Effect *In Situ*

A search engine index contains many short postings list, which are unlikely to appear in queries; it also contains many long lists also unlikely to appear in queries. This section measures the index size, and time effect on the search engine by using queries.

The size of the six indexes (in gigabytes) is presented in Figure 1. Top shows .gov2 and bottom shows Wikipedia. ATIRE produces only a single index file containing postings, vocab, external docids, and so on; so these figures show the true size of the entire index not just the postings size. The figure also shows that there is little effect due to optimal-packing.

To measure the throughput effect on the Wikipedia collection, the titles of all the assessed topics available for it (2009 & 2010, 120 topics in total) were used. For .gov2, the titles of the TREC *ad hoc* topics 701-850 were used. The search process was annotated to measure the time to fully decompress the postings lists before being processed. The experiment was repeated 95 times (overnight). The mean time to decode all lists is presented as it is reasonably resembles the expected time, however variation was very small, with standard deviations always less than 1% of the mean.

Figure 2 presents the sum of times required to decode the lists. For example, it took approximately 2 seconds to decode all the postings lists for the 150 topics for .gov2. The figure shows virtually no difference between Simple-9 and Simple-16, but Simple-8b is more efficient. The variation between the left-greedy and optimal packing is negligible, varying from 2% worse to 2% better; simple-8b, however, took 36% less time than Simple-9. The improvement due to switching schemes is vastly greater than due to the packing strategy – again suggesting that left-greedy is near optimal.

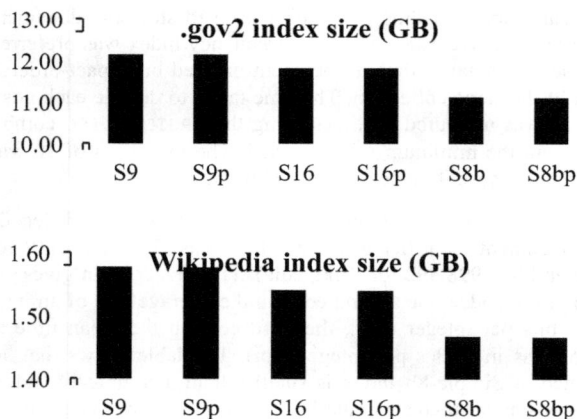

Figure 1: Index size in GB

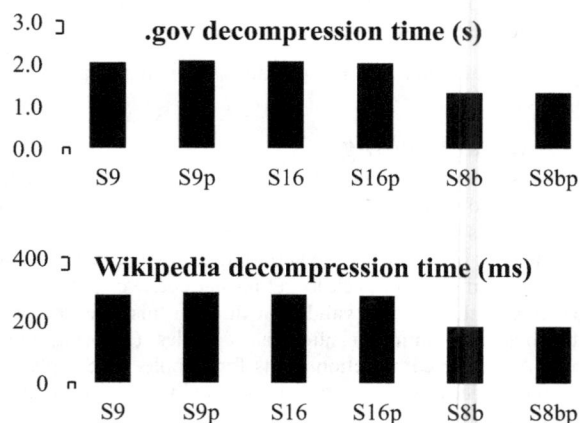

Figure 2: Mean time to decompress

5. CONCLUSIONS

In an inverted file based search engine the postings lists are typically compressed using d-gaps and then further compressed using a scheme such as Simple-9, Simple-16, or Simple-8b.

Compression is used for two reasons. First it can reduce the size of the index and second it can increase throughput. If the index is stored in memory, as is often the case, then the space saving makes it possible to store the index of a larger number of documents in the same amount of space. If the index is stored on disk then the reduction in size decreases the time necessary to read a postings list from disk. Regardless of where the index is stored, touching fewer memory cells to achieve the same goal can decrease processing time in a system that is memory bandwidth limited (such as a modern PC). The Simple family of compression algorithms has proven popular because schemes such as Simple-9 are both space efficient and fast to decode whereas previous schemes such as Elias gamma and Golomb were space efficient but costly to decode.

This investigation proved by counter example that the left-greedy approach to packing integers into codewords typically seen in implementations of the Simple family is not optimal. The optimal packing is given as the shortest path through the tree representing all possible packings. A linear time dynamic programming algorithm is given for computing this.

Experiments conducted on .gov2 and the INEX Wikipedia 2009 collections compared left-greedy with optimal and show negligible difference between the two. This suggests that the prior use of left-greedy has been effective and should be continued. Despite not being optimal, left-greedy is straightforward to implement and requires less work to compute.

REFERENCES

[1] Anh, V.N., A. Moffat, Inverted Index Compression Using Word-Aligned Binary Codes. *Information Retrieval*, 8(1):151-166, 2005.

[2] Anh, V.N., A. Moffat, Simplified Similarity Scoring Using Term Ranks. In *SIGIR 2005*, pp. 226-233

[3] Anh, V.N., A. Moffat, Index Compression Using 64-bit words. *Software Practice & Experience*, 40(2):131-147, 2010.

[4] Dean, J. Challenges in Building Large-Scale Information Retrieval Systems. In *WSDM 2009*

[5] Elias, P., Universal Codeword Sets and the Representation of the Integers. *IEEE Transactions on Information Theory*, 21(2):194-203, 1975.

[6] Golomb, S.W., Run-length Encodings. *IEEE Transactions on Information Theory*, 12(3):399-401, 1966.

[7] Lemire, D., L. Boytsov, Decoding Billions of Integers per Second Through Vectorization. *Software: Practice & Experience*, To Appear.

[8] Lemire, D., L. Boytsov, N. Kurz, SIMD Compression and the Intersection of Sorted Integers. *CoRR abs/1401.6399*, 2014.

[9] Persin, M., J. Zobel, R. Sacks-Davis, Filtered Document retrieval with Frequency-Sorted Indexes. *J. Am. Soc. Inf. Sci.*, 47(10):749-764, 1996.

[10] Robertson, S.E., S. Walker, S. Jones, M.M. Beaulieu, M. Gatford. Okapi at TREC-3. In *TREC-3*, pp. 109-126, 1994.

[11] Scholer, F., H.E. Williams, J. Yiannis, J. Zobel. Compression of Inverted Indexes for Fast Query Evaluation. In *SIGIR 2002*, pp. 222-229

[12] Silvestri, F., R. Venturini, VSEncoding: Efficient Coding and Fast Decoding of Integer Lists via Dynamic Programming, In *CIKM 2010*, 1219-1228.

[13] Trotman, A., Compression, SIMD, and Postings Lists, In *ADCS 2014*, pp. 50-57.

[14] Trotman, A., X. Jia, M. Crane, Towards an Efficient and Effective Search Engine, In *SIGIR 2012 Workshop on Open Source Information Retrieval*. pp. 40-47.

[15] Zhang, J., X. Long, T. Suel, Performance of Compressed Inverted List Caching in Search Engines, In *WWW 2008*, pp. 387-396.

[16] Zukowski, M., S. Heman, P. Nes, P. Boncz, Super-Scalar RAM-CPU Cache Compression, In *ICDE 2006*.

Pooling for User-Oriented Evaluation Measures

Gaurav Baruah
Computer Science
University of Waterloo
gbaruah@uwaterloo.ca

Adam Roegiest
Computer Science
University of Waterloo
aroegies@uwaterloo.ca

Mark D. Smucker
Management Sciences
University of Waterloo
mark.smucker@uwaterloo.ca

ABSTRACT

Traditional TREC-style pooling methodology relies on using predicted relevance by systems to select documents for judgment. This coincides with typical search behaviour (e.g., web search). In the case of temporally ordered streams of documents, the order that users encounter documents is in this temporal order and not some predetermined rank order. We investigate a user oriented pooling methodology focusing on the documents that simulated users would likely read in such temporally ordered streams. Under this user model, many of the relevant documents found in the TREC 2013 Temporal Summarization Track's pooling effort would never be read. Not only does our pooling strategy focus on pooling documents that will be read by (simulated) users, the resultant pools are different from the standard TREC pools.

Categories and Subject Descriptors

H.3.4 [**Systems and Software Performance evaluation**]: Efficiency and Effectiveness

Keywords

Evaluation; Pooling; User models;

1. INTRODUCTION

Traditionally, pooling mechanisms select documents based upon predicted relevance by individual systems. This coincides with the fact that almost all search systems present their results in a Search Engine Result Page (SERP), wherein a list of documents ranked by their likelihood of relevance, is presented to the user. SERPs correspond to the Probability Ranking Principle, which states that results should be ordered by their likelihood of being relevant for optimal retrieval. Recent research has given impetus to generating user models for effective evaluation of systems [6], although most research still focuses on a ranked list over which a model of user behavior is inferred.

The continued growth of real-time information access platforms (e.g, Facebook, Twitter and other social media), has resulted in the need for retrieving information from large dynamic streams of documents. Increasing effort is being made to design and evaluate such systems. Primarily such efforts have focused on filtering relevant information from temporally ordered streams of documents. In particular, the TREC Temporal Summarization [2] track (retrieving sentences) and the Microblog [12] track (retrieving microblog posts), have investigated the evaluation of such filtering systems. While the Microblog track has typically used standard IR evaluation measures, the Temporal Summarization track (TST) introduces evaluation measures that incorporate notions of latency, length, as well as relevance of returned updates (sentences). Both tracks have used score-based pooling, a standard TREC practice [14, 2], where documents from each system are ordered by a system assigned score and the top-k documents (or updates) are taken from each run and evaluated by assessors, where k is the pool depth.

For many retrieval and filtering tasks standard score-based pooling techniques are effective and (generally) robust evaluation mechanisms. Score-based pooling also coincides with how users will typically use such systems. For example, a user performing a search using Google would typically expect the most likely to be relevant documents to be near the top of the result page.

A different user model may be more suitable for temporally ordered information. A user that is browsing Twitter will likely expect the posts to be ordered in roughly reverse chronological order. In fact, there was a large outcry when Facebook changed the default ranking of updates to be their own internal scoring mechanism rather than a temporal ordering [9]. Accordingly, we posit that score-based pooling is likely an unsuitable mechanism for the creation of evaluation pools for filtering tasks involving temporally ordered documents.

We employ a user model for streaming information access [3] and identify which updates were read by simulated users for the runs submitted to TST 2013. We observe that a large proportion of these simulated users may not read all the relevant updates (Figure 1). Additionally, the pool may have been too shallow as McCreadie et al. [11] found that there was little overlap between the Temporal Summarization pool and their proposed system, causing them to procure additional assessments.

We believe that it may be better to focus on those updates that can be identified as most likely to be read by (simulated) users. In this work, we present a method of pooling that selects updates by computing the probabilities of an update being read based upon an underlying user model. It is our hypothesis that our method will allow pools to be created that consist of documents that have a higher probability of being read by (simulated) users and are more reflective of actual user experience and expectation. Accordingly, we create pools by selecting top-k updates based on their probability of being read. Furthermore, we show that the overlap between our top-k probability-based pool and the top-k score-based pool of the 2013 Temporal Summarization track, is quite low; only 60% of the relevant updates are found in the probability-based pools even when the 1000 most likely to be read updates are selected from each system. Indicating that the TST evaluation may be representative of what is being read by (simulated) users. We also show that, depending on how the probability mass is distributed over the updates, the number of judgments required to construct a test collection differs considerably (Section 4).

This investigation lays the groundwork for further exploration of pooling methods that utilize user models. Test collections based on such user-oriented pooling may benefit user-model oriented evaluation measures and move beyond the simple rank based evaluation for complex retrieval tasks.

2. USER MODELS AND POOLING

Historically, TREC has investigated retrieval as well as evaluation methods for filtering tasks [10], Topic Detection and Tracking [1] and more recently for Temporal Summarization [2]. The evaluation measures used for these tasks assume a simplified user model and use set-based (similar to Precision and Recall) evaluation criteria. They do acknowledge that criteria, like recency and novelty [2, 1] as well as verbosity [2], should be considered for evaluation of systems filtering information from a stream. Evaluation measures have attempted to subsume these evaluation criteria into a precision/recall analogous scoring system.

The Temporal Summarization Track [2] (TST) in particular, requires that the participating runs return updates (sentences) that are likely relevant to given news topics, from a time-ordered document stream. These updates are returned at any instant within a specified time period of interest (typically 10 days) for the topic. The updates have associated timestamps noting when the system released the updates. An end user presumably reads the complete stream of updates returned for a topic. The track defines measures, Expected Latency Gain and Latency Comprehensiveness (analogous to precision and recall respectively), that evaluate results from a system at the end of the interest period.

In recent work, Modeled Stream Utility [3] (MSU) is proposed as measure for evaluating information retrieval over a streaming corpus. MSU is a user focused evaluation that incorporates a model of a user browsing the results of a system producing a stream of updates. In effect, for MSU, a simulated user alternates between spending some time reading results and some time away from the system, for as long as the user is interested in the topic. A more interested user spends more time on reading and less time away from the system and vice-versa.

For each simulated user, MSU identifies the updates read, and increments gain when a relevant update is read by the user. Thus, across all simulated users, there could be some updates that have a higher likelihood of being read than others. This has interesting ramifications for pooling. For

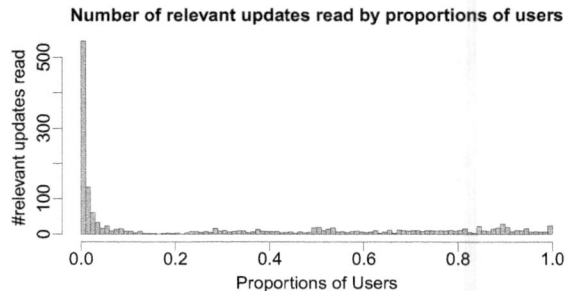

Number of relevant updates read by proportions of users

Figure 1: The number of relevant updates read by proportions of simulated users, for topic 10 from the Temporal Summarization track, at TREC 2013.

a fairer evaluation of systems, considering most frequently read updates as part of the test collection may result in a more meaningful evaluation. Figure 1 shows that for topic 10 of TST 2013, relevant updates are not necessarily the most often read updates; all other topics of TST 2013 have similar proportions. After simulating 10,000 users, only 5 relevant updates, across all runs, were read by all users (with 25 updates read by 99% of the users). It is worthy of note that 546 relevant updates (out of a total 1616 returned across all runs) were read by less than 1% of the simulated users.

The MSU user model forms the core of our methodology. Accordingly, we use the "reasonable" parameters [3], such that a user population spends on average 2 minutes (std.dev. 1 minute), every 3 hours (std.dev. 1.5 hours), for reading updates produced by a system. Users sampled from this population may spend different durations of time for reading sessions and times spent away than the population mean. The reading speed of a user helps to determine which updates are read at each user session. We sample reading speeds from a reading speed distribution described in Clarke and Smucker [7]. By simulating 10,000 users with this user model, we construct a probability distribution over the updates indicating their likelihood of being read.

3. GENERATING UPDATE PROBABILITIES

We present two possible methods of computing the probability of an update being read. Consider a set $U = \{u_i | 1 \leq i \leq m\}$ of m simulated users, a set $D = \{d_j | 1 \leq j \leq n\}$ of n updates submitted by a given system for a particular topic, and let $read_{ij} = \{0, 1\}$ indicate if the update d_j was read by user u_i. Then $P(d_j)$, the probability of an update d_j being read can be computed as:

1. A *balanced* notion of probability: average the probabilities for d_j across all simulated users.

$$P(d_j) = \frac{1}{|U|} \sum_i \frac{1}{\sum_q read_{iq}}, (1 \leq q \leq n) \qquad (1)$$

2. An *unbalanced* notion of probability: the ratio of the number of users that have read d_j, over, the total number of documents read by all simulated users.

$$P(d_j) = \frac{\sum_i read_{ij}}{\sum_i \sum_q read_{iq}}, (1 \leq q \leq n) \qquad (2)$$

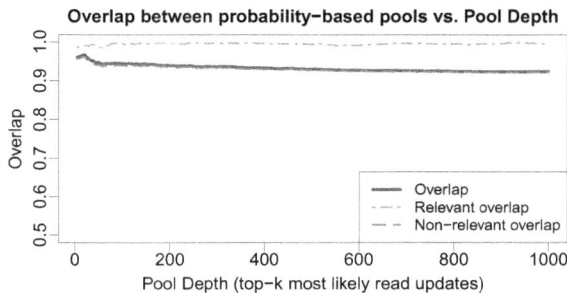

Figure 2: Overlap between the top-k probability-based pools created with balanced and unbalanced probabilities.

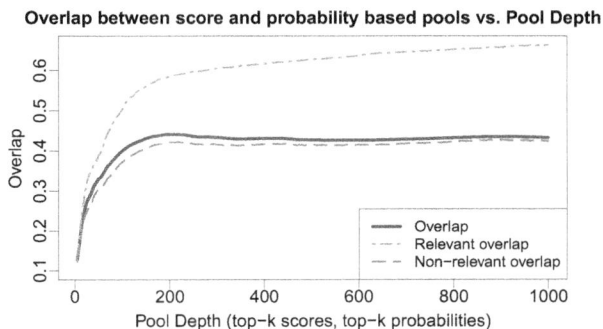

Figure 3: Overlap between the top-k score-based and top-k unbalanced probability-based pools.

Simulated users who read more are weighted more heavily in the *unbalanced* computation, whereas all simulated users are weighted equally in the *balanced* computation.

Figure 2 depicts the overlap between the two probability generation methods when depth pooling is used. Due to the high overlap between the two methods, it is likely the case that while absolute probabilities may differ, many updates are shared.

Due to the similarity between the balanced and unbalanced probability-based pools, we expect that there is little meaningful difference between them. Accordingly, the remainder of this work uses the unbalanced probability generation method due to the simplicity of the underlying theory and its implementation.

3.1 Score-based vs Probability-based Pools

Figure 3 clearly illustrates that top-k score-based pooling and top-k probability-based pooling do not produce identical pools at same depths. In general, overlap between the probability-based pool and the TREC style score-based pool, does not exceed 45%. For relevant updates, the overlap does not exceed 70%, even for extremely large k (depths).

This indicates that a non-trivial portion of the probability-based pool is different from the score-based pool. In conjunction with the proportions from Figure 1, it is clearly seen that these pools are different enough to warrant further investigation into probability-based pooling. This lack of overlap lends further credence to our hypothesis that score-based pooling does not accurately reflect user experience.

4. GLOBAL AND LOCAL PROBABILITIES

The MSU user-model induces a probability of being read on every update. Top-k probability-based pooling using balanced (or unbalanced) probabilities is one method to pool using these probabilities. Since we have probability distributions for each run, another method to construct a pool would be to select the most likely to be read updates until a specified level of probability mass over the updates is covered for each run. We call this method of pooling "local probability pooling," since the probabilities are "local" to each run. This ensures that each run has the same amount of probability mass covered. This is in contrast to depth (top-k) pooling, where, the systems may be disproportionately represented in the pool if each system returned a different number of updates. In fact, the number of updates returned by TST 2013 runs varies from 110 to 2.8 million updates per run.

An alternate method would be to average these "local" probabilities into a "global" probability distribution, such that the probability of an update not present in a run is assumed to have a local probability of 0. Pooling proceeds by ordering updates by their global probability and selecting documents in descending order until a desired probability mass is achieved. The goal of global pooling is to focus assessment effort on those updates which are most likely to be read across all runs.

As illustrated by Figure 4, the overlap between global and local pooling techniques grows in an approximately linear fashion as more probability mass is covered. The high levels of overlap likely correspond to the fact that the local pooling technique produces a much larger pool than global pooling (Figure 5). The larger pool size is likely due to the fact that runs that returned thousands of updates have a much lower local probability mass per update (requiring more updates to cover a specified local probability mass). Whereas the global probability mass per update tends to be concentrated in the updates that are most likely to be read in all runs. Figure 6, shows that different local probability masses are covered across runs for a given global probability mass cover. Specifically, the shorter runs (hundreds of updates) appear on the left hand side of the plot, while the longer runs (several thousands of updates) appear on the right hand side. This indicates that covering a specific amount of local probability mass for every run may require including a large number of updates from longer runs into the pool.

Using global probability for pooling is more likely to produce much smaller sized pools than using local probability, for a specified global probability mass cover. The effect of pool size, in the case of global and local pooling, for assessment, on the re-usability and robustness of the resulting test collection is a next step in this research.

5. DISCUSSION AND FUTURE WORK

Much of the work in this paper has revolved around exploring the space around a user-model induced probability-based pooling. Research has primarily focused on depth-based pooling using ranked retrieval to varying degrees [4, 5, 8, 10, 13, 14, 15]. We have shown two different methods of generating probabilities for updates as well as two novel methods for pooling based upon those probabilities. Further investigation into the applicability of this new pooling technique is required, especially as it relates to user-oriented evaluation measures, e.g. MSU [3].

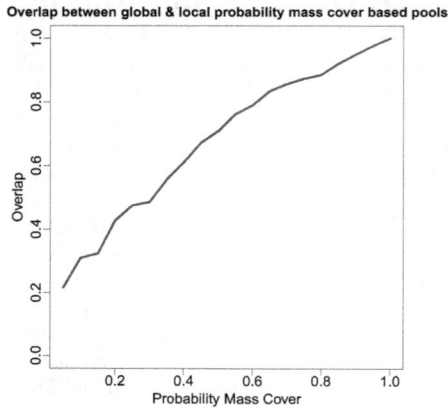

Figure 4: Overlap between pools created using global and local probability mass pooling strategies when both target the same probability mass cover.

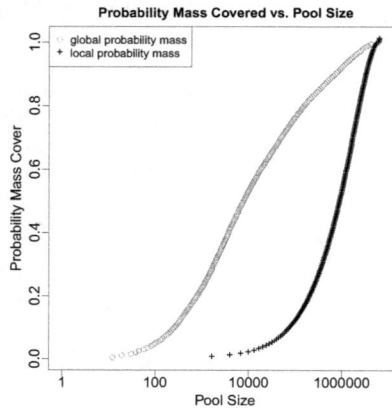

Figure 5: Comparison of pool size and probability mass covered for both local and global probability mass pooling strategies.

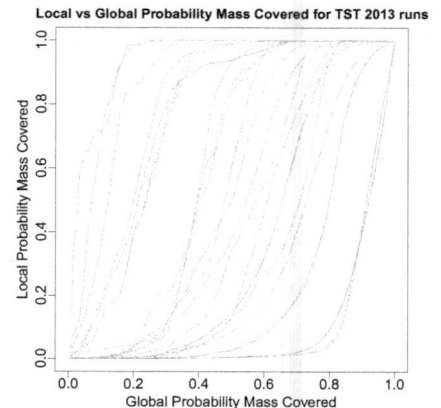

Figure 6: Average local probability mass covered for all 26 runs submitted to TST 2013, when global probability mass pooling is performed.

Additional analysis is required to determine any bias or deficiencies that may be present in this new pooling strategy. The applicability of analyses created for score-based pooling [8, 4] to this new type of pooling remains uncertain. Indeed, pooling is not an end unto itself and further work must be done to verify that the pooling methodology presented herein creates reusable test collections that provides accurate estimates for user-oriented effectiveness measures.

A major limitation of this work is that only a single set of parameters (representing so-called "reasonable users" [3]) is used for this user model. User studies are necessary to observe the behavior of real users and determine parameter settings that reflect actual practice.

6. CONCLUSIONS

We have presented a novel pooling methodology using a probabilistic approach based on a user model. Furthermore, we have shown that the pools based upon the presented methodology are different from scored-based pools constructed as per the TREC standard operating procedure. We have focused, in particular, on two forms of probabilistic pooling, such that, updates that are most likely to be read are included in the pool. By using probabilities tailored to each participant system, we can choose to cover higher (local) probability mass for each system, or a higher global probability mass overall. The trade-off becomes one of size where pools created by global probability mass sampling result in smaller pools and thus less documents to judge. Though it is typically the case that the overlap between local and global tends to be quite high. The effect of these different pooling techniques on various user-centered evaluation measures is left as an interesting avenue of future research.

7. ACKNOWLEDGMENTS

This work was made possible by the facilities of SHARC-NET (www.sharcnet.ca) and Compute/Calcul Canada, and was supported in part by NSERC, in part by a Google Founders Grant, and in part by the University of Waterloo.

8. REFERENCES

[1] J. Allan, R. Gupta, and V. Khandelwal. Temporal Summaries of New Topics. In *SIGIR*, pp. 10–18, 2001.
[2] J. Aslam, F. Diaz, M. Ekstrand-Abueg, V. Pavlu, and T. Sakai. TREC 2013 Temporal Summarization. In *TREC*, 2013.
[3] G. Baruah, M. D. Smucker, and C. L. A. Clarke. Evaluating Streams of Evolving News Events. In *Proc. SIGIR*, 2015.
[4] C. Buckley, D. Dimmick, I. Soboroff, and E. Voorhees. Bias and the Limits of Pooling. In *Proc. SIGIR*, pp. 619–620, 2006.
[5] B. Carterette, J. Allan, and R. Sitaraman. Minimal Test Collections for Retrieval Evaluation. In *Proc. SIGIR*, pp. 268–275, 2006.
[6] C. L. A. Clarke, L. Freund, M. D. Smucker, and E. Yilmaz. Report on the SIGIR 2013 Workshop on Modeling User Behavior for Information Retrieval Evaluation (MUBE 2013). *SIGIR Forum*, 47(2):84–95, Jan. 2013.
[7] C. L. A. Clarke and M. D. Smucker. Time Well Spent. In *IIiX'14*, pp. 205–214, 2014.
[8] G. V. Cormack and T. R. Lynam. Power and Bias of Subset Pooling Strategies. In *Proc. SIGIR*, pp. 837–838, 2007.
[9] M. Johanson. Facebook changes: Users overwhelmingly 'dislike' new news feed and ticker, Sept. 2011. International Business Times.
[10] D. D. Lewis. The TREC-4 Filtering Track. In *Proc. TREC-4*, 1995.
[11] R. McCreadie, C. Macdonald, and I. Ounis. Incremental Update Summarization: Adaptive Sentence Selection Based on Prevalence and Novelty. In *CIKM*, pp. 301–310, 2014.
[12] I. Soboroff, I. Ounis, J. Lin, and I. Soboroff. Overview of the TREC-2012 Microblog Track. In *TREC*, 2012.
[13] K. Sparck-Jones and C. Van Rijsbergen. Report on the need for and provision of an "ideal" Information Retrieval Test Collection. 1975.
[14] E. M. Voorhees and D. K. Harman. *TREC: Experiment and Evaluation in Information Retrieval*. The MIT Press, 2005.
[15] J. Zobel. How Reliable are the Results of Large-scale Information Retrieval experiments? In *SIGIR*, pp. 307–314, 1998.

Predicting Relevance Feedback Effectiveness with the Help of the Principle of Polyrepresentation in MIR

David Zellhöfer
Berlin State Library – Prussian Cultural Heritage
Potsdamer Str. 33
10785 Berlin
david.zellhoefer@sbb.spk-berlin.de

ABSTRACT

The principle of polyrepresentation – a representative of the *cognitive viewpoint* on IR, takes a holistic perspective on interactive IR research.

One of the principle's core hypotheses is that a document is described by different representations such as visual low-level features, textual content, or relational metadata. The conjunctive combination of these representations, the so-called cognitive overlap, is assumed to compensate the inherent insecurity in relevance assessments of documents w.r.t. an information need.

Recently, the cognitively motivated principle of polyrepresentation has been shown to correlate with quantum mechanics-inspired IR models. However, the principle's effectiveness has not been examined in relevance feedback-based interactive MIR. In this work, the principle's utility is studied in interactive MIR in order to investigate whether its main hypothesis can serve as a predictor of retrieval performance during relevance feedback.

In order to obtain resilient results all experiments have been carried out with 6 different standard test sets that provide evidence of the utility of the presented approach and the underlying polyrepresentative hypothesis.

Categories and Subject Descriptors

H.3.3 [**Information Storage and Retrieval**]: Information Search and Retrieval

General Terms

Experimentation; Theory; Human Factors; User Simulation

Keywords

Polyrepresentation; Cognitive IR Model; User Simulation

1. INTRODUCTION

The *cognitive viewpoint* takes a holistic perspective on interactive IR research [11]. From a historical perspective, it can be considered as the first coherent alternative to the system-centric IR viewpoint being predominant in IR.

The most important assumption of the cognitive viewpoint is the dynamic nature of information seeking in combination with the impact of all actors, e.g., users or IR systems, contributing to the retrieval process.

The principle of polyrepresentation (PoP) constitutes a member of the cognitive viewpoint on IR. The central hypothesis of the PoP of the information space (or documents) is that a document is defined by different representations that can be combined to form a conjunctive *cognitive overlap* (CO), in which highly relevant documents are most likely to be contained [12]. In other words, the principle of polyrepresentation (or "multi-evidence" [11]) tries to exploit the uncertainties of the representations proactively by examining how many representations "point" to (or provide simultaneous evidence of relevance [12] of) a document. This evidence can be equalized with the probability of relevance of the document. Although the principle of polyrepresentation is not limited to the *information space*, i.e., the system's perspective on IR, this aspect of polyrepresentation attracted much more attention by the research community [8, 14, 25, 24] than its view on users and their interaction: the *cognitive space*. We believe that this is due to the simpler implementation potential for the PoP of the information space in comparison to the inclusion of cognitive user processes.

The main research questions answered in this paper is: *Does the cognitive overlap hypothesis of the principle of polyrepresentation hold in a preference-based interactive multimodal information retrieval (MIR)?* This investigation is necessary to reveal whether the PoP constitutes a falsifiable theory of IR as suggested by [18, 12, 13]. Hence, this contribution presents an experimental evaluation of the principle of polyrepresentation during relevance feedback.

The paper is structured as follows. In the next section, the principle of polyrepresentation and its implementation using a probabilistic query language combing DB- and IR-based retrieval ideas is sketched. The main part of the paper is formed by the experimental section 3. The last section 4 concludes the paper and recapitulates its core findings.

2. HYPOTHESES OF THE PRINCIPLE OF POLYREPRESENTATION

As said before, multimedia documents are described by a huge amount of different representations. According to the PoP, combining these representations (or features) conjunctively leads to the so-called *cognitive overlap* (CO) which expresses the user's IN and in which relevant documents are expected to be contained. First studies strengthen this hypothesis in the field of IR [18, 12, 13]. For an extensive

Publication rights licensed to ACM. ACM acknowledges that this contribution was authored or co-authored by an employee, contractor or affiliate of a national government. As such, the Government retains a nonexclusive, royalty-free right to publish or reproduce this article, or to allow others to do so, for Government purposes only.

ICTIR'15, September 27–30, Northampton, MA, USA.
© 2015 ACM. ISBN 978-1-4503-3833-2/15/09 ...$15.00.
DOI: http://dx.doi.org/10.1145/2808194.2809485.

discussion of the principle and its relation to other contributions in interactive information retrieval, see [11].

One implementation of the PoP that will be used in this paper is extensively covered in [26]. For the sake of brevity, we will recapitulate the findings and the decision for CQQL as a query language. For details about the query language and its arithmetic evaluation, see [16]. Although we will only utilize CQQL in this paper, the presented findings are not limited to this very query language. Instead, they are transferrable to most probabilistic logic-based approaches that support a weighting of their conditions. The main argument for CQQL's usage to implement the principle is its independence of the retrieval domain and the fact of being a probabilistic logic. CQQL provides means to incorporate traditional similarity scores (such as found in (M)IR) and Boolean attributes. Its second feature allows the formulation of arbitrarily complex queries using Boolean connectors that will be used in the presented experiment.

Furthermore, CQQL supports an explicit relevance feedback (RF) mechanism based on preferences. The RF mechanism (PrefCQQL) has been discussed and its utility has been shown in a number of publications [28, 29, 17]. The core idea of the approach is that the user is given the chance to input an arbitrary number of qualitative preferences (or gradual relevance statements) such as $doc_1 \succ doc_3 \succ doc_2$ which are then transferred to a weighting scheme for a CQQL query with the help of a machine-based learning algorithm.

3. EXPERIMENTS

In order to investigate the utility of the PoP in the domain of MIR, the principle will be compared against other standard matching functions that can be used in an interactive query by example (QBE) scenario typical for this domain. RF is given with the aforementioned PrefCQQL approach for at most 3 RF iterations. A *matching function* in the scope of this paper is a function that will be used to determine the relevance of a document in a collection with respect to a given QBE document. A QBE scenario assumes that a user can state his or her information need (IN) in form of a multimedia document – or an image in the case of this paper. Hence, the MIR system can exploit all (automatically) extractable representations of this *QBE document* to find the best matching documents of a given collection.

3.1 Method

In total, we have examined a total of 7 representative matching functions (see Table 2) based on 15 different representations with varying modalities (see Table 1)[1].

As the PoP *only* makes predictions about the logical form of an effective feature fusion matching function and not the choice of representations, it would not be beneficial for the experimental design presented below and the research question addressed in this paper to include local features although these features are known for their effectiveness.

In any case, this effectiveness comes at the cost of increased computational complexity. Thus, we have not included them in order to limit the computational complexity of the experiments presented below. For instance, the

QBE-based evaluation of the Caltech 101 collection alone consists of 84,584,809 query submissions ($|D_i| * |Q_i|$; see Table 3) multiplied with a varying number of complex similarity calculations per examined matching function[2]. Nevertheless, we decided to investigate such a high number of query/matching function combinations in order to increase the statistical resilience of the presented experiments.

Table 1: Examined features and origin

R#	Name	Type/Origin
1	Auto Color Correlogram	color-related, global [10]
2	BIC	color-related, global [19]
3	CEDD	texture/col.-related, global [2]
4	Color Histogram	global 512 bin RGB histogram
5	Color Layout	color-related, global [4]
6	Color Structure	color-related, global [4]
7	Dominant Color	color-related, global [4]
8	Edge Histogram	edge-related, global [4]
9	FCTH	texture/col.-related, global [3]
10	Scalable Color	color-related, global [4]
11	Tamura	texture-related, global [20]
12	Color Histogram (region based)	color-related, pseudo-local [1]
13	Contour-based Shape	global [4]
14	Region-based Shape	global [4]
15	Gabor	texture-related, global [30]

Table 2: Structure of the matching functions

ID	Matching Function	Structure
1-3	Weighted arithm. mean	$\sum_{i=1}^{n} R_i$
4-6	Conjunction	$\bigwedge_{i=1}^{n} R_i$
7-9	Eidenberger conjction.	$\bigwedge (R_5, R_7, R_8)$
10-12	Eidenberger disjunction	$\bigvee (R_5, R_7, R_8, R_{11})$
13-15	Disjunction	$\bigvee_{i=1}^{n} R_i$
16-18	Q10	$(R_3 \vee R_9) \wedge (R_5 \vee (R_8 \wedge R_{11}))$
19-21	Semantic groups $\bigwedge((\bigvee(R_3, R_9)), (\bigvee(R_2, R_3, R_{10}, R_{12}, R_6, R_1, R_5, R_4, R_7))$	

The matching functions listed in Table 2 have been chosen to reflect the polyrepresentative hypothesis about the (conjunctive) cognitive overlap (# 4; subsequent numbers list RF iterations) and its complementary Boolean operation (the disjunction; # 13), recommendations from others [6] (#7 and #10), considerations about the correlation or redundancy of representations [5] (# 19), and the common baseline matching function weighted arithmetic mean.

Table 2 also shows the formal respectively logical structure of each matching function. To abbreviate the formulas, a general similarity predicate R_i is used. This predicate denotes the similarity regarding one representation (e.g. the color histogram of a document, i.e., R_4) with respect to the QBE document. For instance, matching function #4 denotes a conjunction of all representations which corresponds to a CO[3] of these representations.

Obviously, RF can no longer be given manually with respect to the sheer amount of submitted queries (see Table 3) and RF iterations. Instead, we rely on a user simulation to give RF for at most 3 RF iterations. The actual user simulation strategy is summarized below. The decision whether a document is relevant or not is based on the ground truth of the examined collections.

---

[1] For the sake of reproducibility, all representations have been extracted using the standard parameters of the baseline system offered by the organizers of the ImageCLEF 2013 personal photo retrieval subtask (http://www.imageclef.org/2013/photo/retrieval).

[2] That is, a total of 9,249,189,488 matching operations (1,321,312,784 query submissions with 7 matching function variants per submission in addition to the load caused by the RF algorithm and the user simulation). Each matching operation consists of up to 15 complex similarity calculations (various $\mathcal{L}$-norms in high-dimensional vector spaces because of the vector space representations of the visual low-level features

[3] That is, an intersection of the ranks ordered by each document's similarity w.r.t. a QBE document's representations.

Interaction strategy of the simulated user

1. *Submit query.*

2. *Inspect the 20 top-most retrieved documents. For each of the 20 documents:*

   (a) *Check if an irrelevant document $d_{irrelevant}$ directly precedes a relevant document $d_{relevant}$, i.e., $d_{relevant} < d_{irrelevant}$.*

   (b) *If so, invert the preference into $d_{relevant} > d_{irrelevant}$.*

3. *Resubmit the new preferences to the system.*

4. *Continue with 2. until the maximum number of RF iterations is reached.*

The motivation behind this user simulation is to model an impatient/lazy user in order to assess the effectiveness of PrefCQQL in a sub-optimal[4] setting.

The matching functions and the RF mechanism are tested with 6 test collections aiming at different MIR usage scenarios that are summarized in Table 3 in order to increase the results' resilience as suggested by [21].

3.2 Experimental Results

Because of space constraints, we will not discuss the actual retrieval effectiveness of the investigated matching functions. Instead, we concentrate on the general effectiveness development of the matching functions during 3 RF iterations as it is expected to give evidence of the PoP's validity. Figure 1

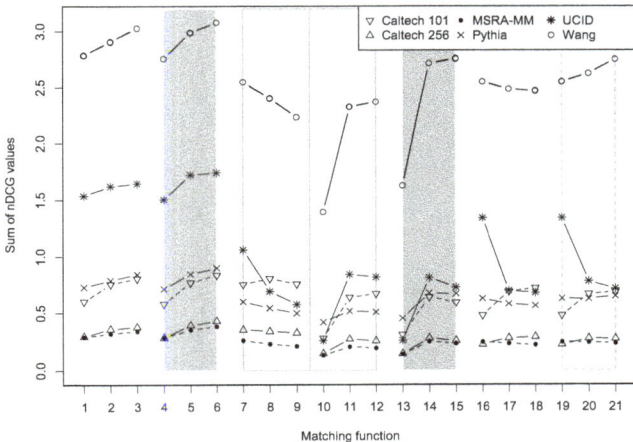

Related RF iterations are grouped visually for the sake of clarity. The labels of the x axis refer to the matching function IDs given in Table 2.

Figure 1: Relevance feedback effectiveness development trends of characteristic matching functions

clearly shows that the retrieval effectiveness of the baseline matching function, the weighted arithmetic mean, gradually increases during the relevance feedback iterations (Fig. 1; 1-3). The conjunction behaves similarly, but reaches a higher effectiveness than the weighted arithmetic mean (4-6) from RF iteration 1 onward.

Albeit the Eidenberger conjunction (7-9) also features conjunctive characteristics, its effectiveness does not increase during the RF iterations as the effectiveness of the conjunction. Instead, its performance falls during the RF iterations for most examined collections.

The disjunctive matching functions, i.e., the Eidenberger disjunction (10-12) and the disjunction (13-15), follow a sim-

---

[4]That is, a potentially sub-optimal setting for the learning algorithm, which is nevertheless realistic because users typically avoid extensive input.

ilar pattern. At the first RF iteration, the effectiveness significantly raises and falls directly thereafter.

The two last matching functions, i.e., Q10 (16-18) and the semantic group conjunction (19-21), act rather unpredictably over all collections. Both matching functions feature conjunctions and disjunctions, while Q10 also relies on a small amount of representations (five in total). Although the use of Q10 might lead to a relatively small increase of the retrieval effectiveness during RF, e.g., for the Caltech collections, there is a trend of decreasing effectiveness. As the results from the UCID collection illustrate (16-18), this trend can become very significant. Roughly speaking, the semantic group conjunction shows an RF performance pattern, which is similar to Q10 and manifests in increases as well as decreases of the performance during RF.

In particular, Figure 1 illustrates that the weighted arithmetic mean and the conjunction have a similar performance development pattern over all collections. That is, the performance plot follows an ascending slope, which is steeper in the case of the conjunction. This means that the conjunction adjusts faster to the user's IN during RF in comparison to the weighted arithmetic mean, which surpasses the conjunction in terms of effectiveness when no RF is used.

Discussion.

As said before, the conjunction (and thus the cognitive overlap) has been shown to be the most effective of the examined matching functions. This is strengthened by its consistent RF performance over all collections. It is followed by the weighted arithmetic mean, which shows a similar RF effectiveness pattern, although at a lower level.

There is evidence showing that the retrieval effectiveness during RF depends on the logical structure of the matching function *and* the number of used representations to model the user's IN. This is in accordance with the hypothesis of the principle of polyrepresentation, which suggests that the most relevant documents will be located in the cognitive overlap – the intersection of different result sets formed by different representations.

In contrast, disjunctions degrade the retrieval effectiveness during RF. In general, disjunctive matching functions improve their effectiveness in the first RF iteration but fall off in quality directly thereafter (the *"disjunctive effect"*). Notwithstanding, these matching functions never reach the same level of effectiveness as their conjunctive counter-parts at RF iteration 1.

Given that the disjunctive effect is also present in the Eidenberger disjunction, which features only four representations and that the effect occurs relatively consistent over all collections, there is no clear evidence that the effect can be explained as being caused by overfitting in case of the disjunction based on 15 representations. Instead, there is evidence that the behavior and effectiveness development are due to the disjunctive characteristics of matching functions.

This claim is supported by the examination of the semantic group conjunctions, which feature both a high number of weighting variables and representations as well as conjunctions and disjunctions. To conclude with, the conjunction and the weighted arithmetic mean can be considered robust.

4. CONCLUSION

In a number of interactive MIR scenarios, which are realized with PrefCQQL in the context of this paper, the data shows that the conjunction (and thus the cognitive overlap of all representations) outperforms all other fusion-based matching functions from RF iteration 1 onward. This includes the arithmetic mean. As a consequence, the predictions of the PoP can be verified in the examined PrefCQQL-based interactive MIR scenario. This finding is important as is forms a step towards the establishment of the principle of polyrepresentation as a holistic, cognitive theory of IR as hinted at by a number of authors [18, 12, 13].

Table 3: Overview over the examined test collections

Collection & Collection Size ($|D_i|$)		No. of QBE Docs. ($|Q_i|$)	Mean QBE Docs. per Topic	Standard Deviation QBE Docs. per Topic	No. of Topics ($|T_i|$)	Disjoint Topics[5]	Primary Usage Scenario
Caltech 101 [7]	9,197	9,197	90.17	125.35	101	✓	Object recognition
Caltech 256 [9]	30,607	30,607	119.14	85.89	256	✓	Object recognition
MSRA-MM [22]	65,443	3,400	100	0	68	✓	Web Image Sample
UCID [15]	904	904	2.45	2.48	262	✓	Personal photos
Wang [23]	1,000	1,057	105.70	16.75	10	✗	Stock photography
Pythia [27]	5,555	13,602	425.38	493.76	32	✗	Personal photos

Disjoint topics states if QBE documents are only associated with one topic.

5. REFERENCES

[1] S. Balko and I. Schmitt. Signature Indexing and Self-Refinement in Metric Spaces. Cottbus, 2012.

[2] A. S. Chatzichristofis and S. Y. Boutalis. CEDD: Color and Edge Directivity Descriptor: A Compact Descriptor for Image Indexing and Retrieval. In *Proc. of the 6th Int. Conference on Computer Vision Systems*, pages 312–322. Springer-Verlag, 2008.

[3] A. S. Chatzichristofis and S. Y. Boutalis. FCTH: Fuzzy Color and Texture Histogram - A Low Level Feature for Accurate Image Retrieval. In *Proc. of the 2008 9th Int. Workshop on Image Analysis for Multimedia Interactive Services*, WIAMIS '08, pages 191–196. IEEE Computer Society, 2008.

[4] L. Cieplinski, S. Jeannin, J.-R. Ohm, M. Kim, M. Pickering, and A. Yamada. MPEG-7 Visual XM version 8.1. Pisa, Italy, 2001.

[5] T. Deselaers, D. Keysers, and H. Ney. Features for Image Retrieval: An Experimental Comparison. *Information Retrieval*, 11:77–107, 2008.

[6] H. Eidenberger. How good are the visual MPEG-7 features? In *SPIE & IEEE Visual Communications & Image Processing Conference*, pages 476–488, 2003.

[7] L. Fei-Fei, R. Fergus, and P. Perona. Learning Generative Visual Models from Few Training Examples an Incremental Bayesian Approach Tested on 101 Object Categories. In *Proc. of the Workshop on Generative-Model Based Vision*, 2004.

[8] I. Frommholz, B. Larsen, B. Piwowarski, M. Lalmas, P. Ingwersen, and C. J. K. van Rijsbergen. Supporting Polyrepresentation in a Quantum-inspired Geometrical Retrieval Framework. In *Proc. of the 2010 Information Interaction in Context Symposium*, pages 115–124. ACM, 2010.

[9] G. Griffin, A. Holub, and P. Perona. Caltech-256 Object Category Dataset, 2007.

[10] J. Huang, R. S. Kumar, M. Mitra, W.-J. Zhu, and R. Zabih. Image Indexing Using Color Correlograms. In *Proc. of the 1997 Conference on Computer Vision and Pattern Recognition*, CVPR '97, pages 762–. IEEE Computer Society, 1997.

[11] P. Ingwersen and K. Järvelin. *The Turn: Integration of Information Seeking and Retrieval in Context*. Springer, Dordrecht, 2005.

[12] B. Larsen, P. Ingwersen, and J. Kekäläinen. The Polyrepresentation Continuum in IR. In *Proc. of the 1st Int. Conference on Information Interaction in Context*, pages 88–96. ACM, 2006.

[13] B. Larsen, P. Ingwersen, and B. Lund. Data Fusion According to the Principle of Polyrepresentation. *J. Am. Soc. Inf. Sci. Technol.*, 60(4):646–654, 2009.

[14] C. Lioma, B. Larsen, and P. Ingwersen. Preliminary Experiments using Subjective Logic for the Polyrepresentation of Information Needs. In *Proc. of the 4th Information Interaction in Context Symposium*, IIIX '12, pages 174–183. ACM, 2012.

[15] G. Schaefer and M. Stich. UCID - An Uncompressed Colour Image Database. In *Proc. SPIE, Storage and Retrieval Methods and Applications for Multimedia*, pages 472–480. San Jose, USA, 2004.

[16] I. Schmitt. QQL: A DB&IR Query Language. *The VLDB Journal*, 17(1):39–56, 2008.

[17] I. Schmitt and D. Zellhöfer. Condition Learning from User Preferences. In *6th IEEE Int. Conference on Research Challenges in Information Science*. Valencia, Spain, 2012.

[18] M. Skov, H. Pedersen, B. Larsen, and P. Ingwersen. Testing the Principle of Polyrepresentation. In P. Ingwersen, C. J. K. van Rijsbergen, and N. Belkin, editors, *Proc. of ACM SIGIR 2004 Workshop on "Information Retrieval in Context"*, pages 47–49, 2004.

[19] O. R. Stehling, A. M. Nascimento, and X. A. Falcão. A Compact and Efficient Image Retrieval Approach Based on Border/Interior Pixel Classification. In *Proc. of the 11th Int. Conference on Information and Knowledge Management*, pages 102–109. ACM, 2002.

[20] H. Tamura, S. Mori, and T. Yamawaki. Texture Features Corresponding to Visual Perception. *IEEE Transactions on System, Man and Cybernatic*, 8(6):460–472, 1978.

[21] M. E. Voorhees. On Test Collections for Adaptive Information Retrieval. *Information Processing & Management*, 44(6):1879–1885, 2008.

[22] M. Wang, L. Yang, and X.-S. Hua. MSRA-MM: Bridging Research and Industrial Societies for Multimedia Information Retrieval, 2009.

[23] Z. J. Wang, J. Li, and G. Wiederhold. SIMPLIcity: Semantics-Sensitive Integrated Matching for Picture LIbraries. *IEEE Transactions on Pattern Analysis and Machine Intelligence*, 23:947–963, 2001.

[24] W. R. White. Using Searcher Simulations to Redesign a Polyrepresentative Implicit Feedback Interface. *Inf. Process. Manage.*, 42(5):1185–1202, 2006.

[25] W. R. White, I. Ruthven, and M. J. Jose. A Study of Factors Affecting the Utility of Implicit Relevance Feedback. In *Proc. of the 28th Annual Int. ACM SIGIR Conference on Research and Development in Information Retrieval*, pages 35–42. ACM, 2005.

[26] D. Zellhöfer. A Permeable Expert Search Strategy Approach to Multimodal Retrieval. In J. Kamps, W. Kraaij, and N. Fuhr, editors, *Proc. of the 4th Information Interaction in Context Symposium*, IIIX '12, pages 62–71. ACM, 2012.

[27] D. Zellhöfer. An Extensible Personal Photograph Collection for Graded Relevance Assessments and User Simulation. In H. S. H. Ip and Y. Rui, editors, *Proc. of the 2nd ACM Int. Conference on Multimedia Retrieval*, ICMR '12. ACM, 2012.

[28] D. Zellhöfer and I. Schmitt. A Poset Based Approach for Condition Weighting. In *6th Int. Workshop on Adaptive Multimedia Retrieval*. 2008.

[29] D. Zellhöfer and I. Schmitt. A Preference-based Approach for Interactive Weight Learning: Learning Weights within a Logic-Based Query Language. *Distributed and Parallel Databases*, 27(1):31–51, 2010.

[30] D. Zhang, A. Wong, M. Indrawan, and G. Lu. Content-based Image Retrieval Using Gabor Texture Features. In *IEEE Transactions PAMI*, pages 13–15, 2000.

A Relationship between the Average Precision and the Area Under the ROC Curve

Wanhua Su
Dept. of Math. & Stat.
MacEwan University
Edmonton, AB
Canada T5J 2P2
suw3@macewan.ca

Yan Yuan
School of Public Health
University of Alberta
Edmonton, AB
Canada T6G 1C9
yyuan@ualberta.ca

Mu Zhu
Dept. of Stat. & Act. Sci.
University of Waterloo
Waterloo, ON
Canada N2L 3G1
mu.zhu@uwaterloo.ca

ABSTRACT

For similar evaluation tasks, the area under the receiver operating characteristic curve (AUC) is often used by researchers in machine learning, whereas the average precision (AP) is used more often by the information retrieval community. We establish some results to explain why this is the case. Specifically, we show that, when both the AUC and the AP are rescaled to lie in [0,1], the AP is approximately the AUC times the initial precision of the system.

Categories and Subject Descriptors

H.3.4 [**Information Storage and Retrieval**]: Systems and Software—*performance evaluation*

General Terms

Theory, Performance

1. INTRODUCTION

We are faced with similar tasks when evaluating binary classifiers or information retrieval systems:

- How effective can the classifier tell if an item has a particular label or not?
- How effective can the retrieval system tell if a document is relevant to a particular query or not?

Metrics such as false positive and false negative rates (or equivalently, sensitivity and specificity) require that we make a binary decision, or commit to a decision threshold. For example, a classifier (or retrieval system) would often produce a numeric score for each item (or document), and we would have to decide that all those with a score above a certain threshold would be classified to have a particular label (or declared to be relevant).

The receiver operating characteristic (ROC) curve [7] traces the tradeoff between false positives and false negatives as the decision threshold varies. Looking at the entire ROC curve is especially useful when we are not ready to commit to a

particular decision threshold. But sometimes we still prefer to have a single, numeric performance metric [3], for example, when we are evaluating a large number of classifiers. Comparing hundreds of ROC curves is simply not practical or efficient. The Area Under the ROC Curve (AUC) is a much widely used choice in this context [4].

While binary classifiers are often evaluated by the AUC, information retrieval systems are more often evaluated by a different metric, namely the average precision (AP) [see, e.g., 6, and references therein]. Like the AUC, the AP is another single, numeric performance metric that does not require us to commit to a decision threshold prior to the analysis; it is the area under the precision-versus-recall (PvR) curve (more on this in §2 below). Why does the information retrieval community prefer the AP to the AUC?

In this article, we provide an answer to this question from a novel perspective. In particular, we show that, when both the AUC and the AP are rescaled to lie between 0 and 1, the AP is approximately the AUC times the initial precision of the system. In other words, the AP explicitly places additional emphasis on the correctness of the few top-ranked items, which makes it particularly suitable for retrieval tasks. As far as we are aware, such a direct relationship between the AUC and the AP has never been revealed, even though the connection between ROC and PvR curves has been explored previously [2]. For example, it was found that, while a system's ROC curve dominates that of another if and only if its PvR curve also dominates the other's, there is no such correspondence between the areas under these two different types of curves, i.e., between the AUC and the AP [2]. Our result crystallizes why this is the case.

2. DEFINITIONS

Suppose that, among a collection of n items, n_1 are relevant, and $n_0 = n - n_1$ are not. For every item i, a retrieval system produces a score, x_i, e.g., a high score means the item is more likely to be relevant, and vice versa. We first define a few necessary concepts using a common set of notations so as to formally define the AUC and the AP in such a way that they can be easily studied side by side. To do so, it is convenient to start with the notion of the hit curve.

Let i denote the *ordered* item index, that is, $x_1 \geq x_2 \geq ... \geq x_n$. If we threshold the scores at x_k, declaring all those with scores $\geq x_k$ to be relevant and all those with scores $< x_k$ to be irrelevant, we will have a confusion matrix as displayed in Tab. 1, where $d(k)$ is the number of items with scores $\geq x_k$, and $g(k)$ is the number of items that are *truly*

ICTIR'15, September 27–30, Northampton, MA, USA.
© 2015 ACM. ISBN 978-1-4503-3833-2/15/09 ...$15.00.
DOI: http://dx.doi.org/10.1145/2808194.2809481.

Table 1: Confusion matrix based on counts.

	Declared R	Declared IR	Total
R	$g(k)$	$n_1 - g(k)$	n_1
IR	$d(k) - g(k)$	$[n - d(k)] - [n_1 - g(k)]$	$n - n_1$
Total	$d(k)$	$n - d(k)$	n

R=relevant; IR=irrelevant.

Table 2: Confusion matrix based on proportions.

	Declared R	Declared IR	Total
R	$h(t)$	$\pi - h(t)$	π
IR	$t - h(t)$	$(1-t) - [\pi - h(t)]$	$1 - \pi$
Total	t	$1 - t$	1

R=relevant; IR=irrelevant.

relevant among those *declared to be* relevant. Clearly, $g(k)$ is a discrete function, defined only on the set of nonnegative integers up to n. We can also represent the confusion matrix (Tab. 1) in terms of *proportions* rather than in terms of *counts*. This is given explicitly in Tab. 2, where

$$t \equiv \frac{d(k)}{n}, \quad \pi \equiv \frac{n_1}{n}, \quad \text{and} \quad h(t) \equiv \frac{g(k)}{n}. \quad (1)$$

When n is relatively large, it is convenient to think of the function $h(t)$, defined on the interval $[0,1]$, as a continuous object. In fact, we will further assume that it is differentiable almost everywhere. This allows us to use the language of calculus — i.e., differentiation and integration — to discuss various concepts. The collection of points, $\{(t, h(t)), t \in [0,1]\}$, traces out a so-called *hit curve*. For simplicity, we will refer to $h(t)$ itself as the hit curve as well. Like the ROC curve, the hit curve also is a signature of the underlying system's effectiveness. Proposition 1 below lists a few properties of the hit curve that will be useful later; proofs are given in the Appendix.

PROPOSITION 1. *Let $h(t)$ be a hit curve (see Tab. 2), assumed to be continuous and differentiable almost everywhere. Then,*

(a) $h(0) = 0$ and $h(1) = \pi$;
(b) $0 \leq h'(t) \leq 1$, for all t;
(c) $\int_0^1 h(t)dh(t) = \pi^2/2$. □

Suppose we threshold the scores at a level such that $t \times 100\%$ of the items are declared relevant. The quantities

$$\text{TPF}(t) = \frac{h(t)}{\pi} \quad \text{and} \quad \text{FPF}(t) = \frac{t - h(t)}{1 - \pi}$$

are called the *true positive fraction* (TPF) and the *false positive fraction* (FPF), respectively; see Tab. 2. The ROC curve refers to the collection of points, $\{(\text{FPF}(t), \text{TPF}(t)), t \in [0,1]\}$. The AUC is simply its area underneath, defined as

$$\text{AUC} \equiv \int \text{TPF}(t) d[\text{FPF}(t)]. \quad (2)$$

Using the definitions of $\text{TPF}(t)$ and $\text{FPF}(t)$ above, it is straight-forward to see that

$$\begin{aligned}
\text{AUC} &= \int \frac{h(t)}{\pi} d\left[\frac{t - h(t)}{1 - \pi}\right] \\
&= \frac{1}{\pi(1 - \pi)} \left[\int h(t)dt - \int h(t)dh(t)\right] \\
&= \frac{1}{\pi(1 - \pi)} \left[\int h(t)dt - \frac{\pi^2}{2}\right], \quad (3)
\end{aligned}$$

where the final step is due to Proposition 1(c).

Instead of the TPF and the FPF, we can also speak of the *recall* and the *precision*. Again, suppose we threshold the scores at a level such that $t \times 100\%$ of the items are declared relevant. Then,

$$\text{Recall}(t) = \frac{h(t)}{\pi} \quad \text{and} \quad \text{Precision}(t) = \frac{h(t)}{t}.$$

The average precision (AP) is defined as

$$\text{AP} \equiv \int \text{Precision}(t) d[\text{Recall}(t)], \quad (4)$$

which can be thought of as the area under the precision-versus-recall (PvR) curve. Using the definitions of $\text{Recall}(t)$ and $\text{Precision}(t)$ above, it is straight-forward to see that

$$\text{AP} = \int \frac{h(t)}{t} \times \frac{dh(t)}{\pi} = \frac{1}{\pi} \int \frac{h(t)}{t} dh(t). \quad (5)$$

For example, if a system picks items at random, then $h(t) = \pi t$. That is, the precision stays constant at π, the overall proportion of relevant items. If, on the other hand, a system is perfect, then

$$h(t) = \begin{cases} t, & t \leq \pi; \\ \pi, & t > \pi. \end{cases}$$

That is, the precision is 100% until all relevant items are identified, after which $h(t)$ necessarily stays constant. Eqs. (3) and (5) easily allow us to derive (steps omitted) that

$$\begin{aligned}
\text{AUC(Random)} &= 1/2, & \text{AP(Random)} &= \pi; \\
\text{AUC(Perfect)} &= 1, & \text{AP(Perfect)} &= 1.
\end{aligned}$$

3. A PIECEWISE LINEAR MODEL

We will now use a simple, piecewise linear model for the hit curve in order to gain important insights about the AUC and the AP. Consider a piecewise linear hit curve (Fig. 1), parameterized as follows:

$$h(t) = \begin{cases} \beta t, & t \in [0, \alpha]; \\ \dfrac{\pi - \alpha\beta}{1 - \alpha}(t - \alpha) + \alpha\beta, & t \in (\alpha, 1]. \end{cases} \quad (6)$$

There are two parameters: $\beta \in [\pi, 1]$, the *initial* precision, $h(t)/t$, of the underlying system; and $\alpha \in [0, \pi/\beta]$, the *change point* at which the system's precision drops. The requirement, $\beta \geq \pi$, ensures that the system is as least as good as random; worse-than-random systems are not interesting and practically irrelevant. The requirement $\beta \leq 1$ is due to Proposition 1(b). Finally, the requirement $\alpha \leq \pi/\beta$ is because, with a precision of β, all relevant items will have been identified by $t = \pi/\beta$, leaving no more for $t > \pi/\beta$. Despite its overwhelming simplicity, there are good reasons why the piecewise linear model (6) is useful.

First, hit curves are typically concave, reflecting the fact that precision typically drops as the scores decrease — that is, higher-ranked items are more likely than lower-ranked ones to be relevant. Eq. (6) is arguably the simplest approximation possible to any concave function. When $\beta > \pi$, the slope of the second segment, $(\pi - \alpha\beta)/(1 - \alpha)$, is smaller than that of the first segment, β — a key feature of any concave function. This idea of using a piecewise linear function to approximate any concave function is inspired by a study [5] that used a quasi-hyperbolic model to approximate any hyperbolic discount function in order to achieve analytic

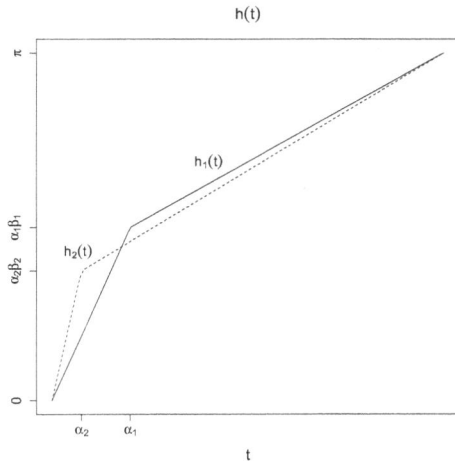

Figure 1: Two piecewise linear hit curves, $h_1(t)$ and $h_2(t)$, parameterized respectively by (α_1, β_1) and (α_2, β_2). In this illustration, the parameters $\alpha_1, \alpha_2, \beta_1, \beta_2$ are configured so that $\mathbf{AUC}(h_1) = \mathbf{AUC}(h_2)$ — see Theorem 1. But since $\beta_2 > \beta_1$, Theorem 2 implies that $\mathbf{AP}(h_2) > \mathbf{AP}(h_1)$.

convenience when studying time-inconsistent intertemporal choices in behavioral economics.

Second, the two parameters, α and β, each capture an essential feature of the underlying retrieval system:

α: As the change point at which the precision drops, this parameter measures the *stamina* of the system — how long can the initial, relatively high precision "last"?

β: As the initial precision, this parameter measures the *momentum* of the system — performing at its best level, how fast can the system "pick up" relevant items?

4. MOMENTUM VERSUS STAMINA

Using the piecewise linear model, we are able to establish two interesting results.

For a piecewise linear hit curve, $h(t)$, given by Eq. (6),

$$\int h(t)dt = \frac{\beta\alpha^2}{2} + \frac{(\pi + \beta\alpha)(1-\alpha)}{2} = \frac{\pi + (\beta - \pi)\alpha}{2}. \quad (7)$$

Then, by Eq. (3),

$$\begin{aligned} AUC &= \frac{1}{2\pi(1-\pi)}\left[\pi + (\beta - \pi)\alpha - \pi^2\right] \\ &= \frac{1}{2\pi(1-\pi)}[(\beta - \pi)\alpha] + \frac{1}{2}, \quad (8) \end{aligned}$$

which immediately implies Theorem 1 below.

THEOREM 1. *If two hit curves, $h_1(t)$ and $h_2(t)$, both belong to the piecewise linear family (6), and are parameterized respectively by (α_1, β_1) and (α_2, β_2), then $AUC(h_1) = AUC(h_2)$ if and only if $(\beta_1 - \pi)\alpha_1 = (\beta_2 - \pi)\alpha_2$.* □

Theorem 1 explains that two retrieval systems h_1 and h_2 can have the same AUC for *different* reasons. The trivial case is when both $\alpha_1 = \alpha_2$ and $\beta_1 = \beta_2$; this is when h_1 and h_2 are identical — same stamina and same momentum. However, if $\beta_1 < \beta_2$, then Theorem 1 implies that we must necessarily have $\alpha_1 > \alpha_2$, and vice versa. That

is, on the AUC-scale, mediocre momentum can be compensated by greater stamina, and vice versa. This result also provides a mathematically explicit explanation for why two qualitatively different systems can sometimes have very similar AUC values.

What about the AP? If $h(t)$ is a piecewise linear hit curve given by Eq. (6), then

$$dh(t) = \begin{cases} \beta dt, & t \in [0, \alpha]; \\ \dfrac{\pi - \alpha\beta}{1-\alpha}dt, & t \in (\alpha, 1]. \end{cases}$$

So,

$$AP = \frac{1}{\pi}\int \frac{h(t)}{t}dh(t) = \frac{1}{\pi}\left[\int_0^\alpha I_1 dt + \int_\alpha^1 I_2 dt\right],$$

where $I_1 = \beta^2$ and

$$I_2 = \left(\frac{\pi - \alpha\beta}{1-\alpha}\right)^2 + \frac{\left(\frac{\pi-\alpha\beta}{1-\alpha}\right)\alpha\beta - \left(\frac{\pi-\alpha\beta}{1-\alpha}\right)^2\alpha}{t}.$$

Hence,

$$AP = \frac{1}{\pi}\left[\beta^2\alpha + \frac{(\pi - \alpha\beta)^2}{1-\alpha} - \left(\frac{\pi - \alpha\beta}{1-\alpha}\right)\frac{(\beta - \pi)\alpha}{1-\alpha}\log\alpha\right].$$

Using the Taylor approximation that $\log(\alpha) \approx \alpha - 1$, the expression above can be simplified to

$$AP \approx \frac{\beta^2\alpha}{\pi} + \pi - \alpha\beta = \frac{\beta}{\pi}[(\beta - \pi)\alpha] + \pi. \quad (9)$$

Recall from §2 that $AP(Random) = \pi$, $AP(Perfect) = 1$, $AUC(Random) = 1/2$, and $AUC(Perfect) = 1$. We can rescale both the AP and the AUC to lie between 0 and 1:

$$\widetilde{AP} \equiv \frac{AP - \pi}{1 - \pi}, \quad \widetilde{AUC} \equiv \frac{AUC - 1/2}{1 - 1/2} = 2AUC - 1. \quad (10)$$

Then,

$$\widetilde{AUC} = \frac{1}{\pi(1-\pi)} \times [(\beta - \pi)\alpha]$$

by Eq. (8) and Eq. (10), while

$$\widetilde{AP} \approx \frac{1}{\pi(1-\pi)} \times \beta \times [(\beta - \pi)\alpha]$$

by Eq. (9) and Eq. (10). These results establish Theorem 2 below.

THEOREM 2. *If a hit curve, $h(t)$, belongs to the piecewise linear family (6), then $\widetilde{AP}(h) \approx \beta \times \widetilde{AUC}(h)$.* □

Theorem 2 suggests that, if two retrieval systems have the same AUC, then the AP will "reward extra points" to the one with larger momentum (larger β). Since momentum is the initial precision, this means the AP places more emphasis on the initial part of the hit curve (and likewise the ROC curve). This explains why the information retrieval community has always preferred the AP to the AUC — because, for information retrieval, the handful of documents ranked at the top are the most important.

Notice that $\alpha < \pi$ necessarily (§3). Although the Taylor approximation, $\log(\alpha) \approx \alpha - 1$, is best for α near 1, our simulation results below (§5) will indicate that the relationship established by Theorem 2 holds for $\alpha < \pi \ll 1$ as well.

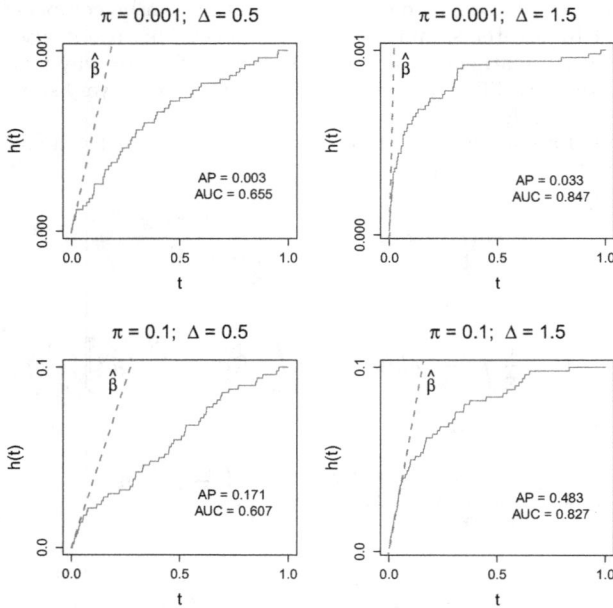

Figure 2: Illustration of $\widehat{\beta}$ [Eq. (11)] under four simulated scenarios, representing different levels of prevalence [high ($\pi = 0.1$) vs. low ($\pi = 0.001$)] and different strengths of the retrieval system [strong ($\Delta = 1.5$) vs. weak ($\Delta = 0.5$)]. Solid lines are hit curves; dashed lines are the function, $f(t) = \widehat{\beta}t$. A total of $n\pi$ scores are simulated from $N(\Delta, 1)$, and the remaining $n(1 - \pi)$ scores are simulated from $N(0, 1)$, with $n = 500$ for $\pi = 0.1$ and $n = 50,000$ for $\pi = 0.001$.

5. BEYOND PIECEWISE LINEARITY

The theoretical insights derived in §4 are based on using a simple, piecewise linear model for the hit curve. We now report a simple simulation study to demonstrate that the approximate relationship established by Theorem 2 appears to hold for general hit curves as well, i.e., those outside the piecewise linear family, Eq. (6).

In the literature [see, e.g., 7], it is customary to simulate retrieval systems (or binary classifiers) in the following manner. Without loss of generality, scores given by the system to irrelevant items are simulated from $f_0(x) \sim N(0, 1)$, and those given by the system to relevant items are simulated from $f_1(x) \sim N(\Delta, 1)$ for some $\Delta > 0$. How well the scores rank the items (in terms of the AP and/or the AUC) is then studied. The parameter, Δ, controls the strength of the simulated system — a large Δ means the system tends to give much higher scores to relevant items than to irrelevant ones; it is thus a more powerful system. Although some recent studies [e.g., 1] have criticised the use of normal-normal models to simulate score distributions for retrieval systems, the simple scheme suffices for our main purpose here, which is to demonstrate that the piecewise linear model is *not* critical to our conclusion.

Given (n, π, Δ), we first generated $n\pi$ scores from $N(\Delta, 1,)$ and $n(1 - \pi)$ scores from $N(0, 1)$. Using these scores, we plotted the resulting hit curve, $h(t)$, as well as computed

AP(h) and AUC(h). Then, we computed

$$\widehat{\beta} = \frac{\widetilde{AP}(h)}{\widetilde{AUC}(h)} = \frac{(AP(h) - \pi)/(1 - \pi)}{2AUC(h) - 1}, \qquad (11)$$

and plotted the line $f(t) = \widehat{\beta}t$ on top of $h(t)$. This procedure was repeated for many combinations of (n, π, Δ).

Fig. 2 shows four representative scenarios, corresponding to different levels of π (low=0.001; high=0.1), and different levels of Δ (low=0.5 for a weak system; high=1.5 for a strong system). Our results, including many that are not shown in Fig. 2, show that the line, $f(t) = \widehat{\beta}t$, is almost always nearly tangent to the hit curve, $h(t)$, at $t = 0$. This suggests that $\widehat{\beta}$, as given by Eq. (11), is a good approximation of

$$\lim_{t \to 0} \frac{h(t)}{t} = h'(0),$$

or the initial precision of the system.

In other words, the relationship established by Theorem 2 — that, when rescaled, the AP is approximately the AUC times the initial precision of the system — is valid even if the hit curve $h(t)$ is *not* assumed to belong to the piecewise linear family (6). This relationship offers some interesting insight into the nature of the two popular metrics. For example, it provides a theoretical justification and explanation for why the information retrieval community has always preferred the AP to the AUC.

APPENDIX

Proof of Proposition 1:

(a) This follows from the very definition of the hit curve. Initially ($t = 0$), no item is declared relevant, so $h(0) = 0$. In the end ($t = 1$), every item is declared relevant, including all the truly relevant ones, so $h(1) = \pi$.

(b) This follows from the fact that, going from t to $t + \Delta t$, the worst case is that no additional relevant item is identified, and the best case is that every identified item is relevant. That is, $0 \leq h(t + \Delta t) - h(t) \leq \Delta t$ for all $\Delta t > 0$. Dividing by Δt and taking the limit as $\Delta t \to 0$, we have $0 \leq h'(t) \leq 1$.

(c) Integration by parts gives $\int h(t)dh(t) = [h^2(t)]_0^1 - \int h(t)dh(t)$. Solving for $\int h(t)dh(t)$ gives $\int h(t)dh(t) = [h^2(1) - h^2(0)]/2 = \pi^2/2$ by Proposition 1(a).

References

[1] A. Arampatzis and S. Robertson. Modeling score distributions in information retrieval. *Information Retrieval*, 14:26–46, 2011.

[2] J. Davis and M. Goadrich. The relationship between precision-recall and ROC curves. In *Proceedings of the 23rd International Conference on Machine learning*, pages 233–240. ACM, 2006.

[3] D. J. Hand. Measuring classifier performance: A coherent alternative to the area under the ROC curve. *Machine learning*, 77(1):103–123, 2009.

[4] J. A. Hanley and B. J. McNeil. The meaning and use of the area under a receiver operating characteristic (ROC) curve. *Radiology*, 143:29–36, 1982.

[5] D. Laibson. Golden eggs and hyperbolic discounting. *Quarterly Journal of Economics*, 112:443–477, 1997.

[6] F. Peng, D. Schuurmans, and S. Wang. Augmenting naïve Bayes classifiers with statistical language models. *Information Retrieval*, 7(3):317–345, 2003.

[7] M. S. Pepe. *The Statistical Evaluation of Medical Tests for Classification and Prediction*. Oxford University Press, New York, 2003.

Revisiting Optimal Rank Aggregation:
A Dynamic Programming Approach

Shayan A. Tabrizi[1]   Javid Dadashkarimi[1]   Mostafa Dehghani[2]
Hassan Nasr Esfahani[3]   Azadeh Shakery[1]

[1]School of ECE, College of Engineering, University of Tehran, Iran
[2]Institute for Logic, Language and Computation, University of Amsterdam, The Netherlands
[3]Department of Computer Engineering, Sharif University of Technology, Iran

{s.tabrizi, dadashkarimi}@ut.ac.ir, dehghani@uva.nl, hnasr@ce.sharif.edu, shakery@ut.ac.ir

ABSTRACT

Rank aggregation, that is merging multiple ranked lists, is a pivotal challenge in many information retrieval (IR) systems, especially in distributed IR and multilingual IR. From the evaluation point of view, being able to calculate the upper-bound of performance of the final aggregated list lays the ground for evaluating different aggregation strategies, independently. In this paper, we propose an algorithm based on dynamic programming which, using relevancy information, obtains the aggregated list with the maximum performance that could be possibly achieved by any aggregation strategy. We also provide a detailed proof for the optimality of the result of the algorithm. Furthermore, we demonstrate that the previous proposed algorithm fails to reach the optimal result in many circumstances, due to its greedy essence.

Categories and Subject Descriptors

H.3.3 [**Information Storage and Retrieval**]: Information Search and Retrieval

Keywords

Rank Aggregation; Information Retrieval; Evaluation

1. INTRODUCTION

One of the most important applications of rank aggregation [6], that is merging multiple ranked lists of objects, is in the field of information retrieval (IR). Typically, rank aggregation in IR is conducted for two different purposes:

1. Aggregating ranked lists of a document set ranked by different ranking methods.
2. Aggregating ranked lists of different document sets ranked by the same ranking method.

Approaches that aim to solve the first kind of aggregation problem, try to take advantage of the strengths of "different methods" and overcome their weaknesses by aggregating (a.k.a. fusing) their results [12, 13]. On the other hand, approaches in the second group try to take advantage of "different sources" by combining their

ICTIR'15, September 27–30, Northampton, MA, USA.
© 2015 ACM. ISBN 978-1-4503-3833-2/15/09 ...$15.00.
DOI: http://dx.doi.org/10.1145/2808194.2809490.

results in a single output (e.g., in distributed IR [3] and multilingual IR [7]). In this paper, by "rank aggregation", we refer to the second problem.

Several merging strategies have been proposed for rank aggregation. Some employ only the information of the initial ranked lists (e.g., round robin, raw scoring, and normalized scoring strategies [6]), while the others use additional information, such as the performance of the underlying ranking methods [8], to provide a better final ranking. In order to evaluate the performance of different strategies, the optimal ranked list can be generated using the relevancy information. Having this optimal ranked list enables us to evaluate different proposed strategies for rank aggregation by measuring their performance as a percentage of the optimal performance [1, 2, 8–11]. This would be an effective way to independently measure the performance of different methods.

As a formal definition, *optimal rank aggregation* refers to a rank aggregation problem in which, with the presence of relevancy information, items from different ranked lists are aggregated into a single final list so that: i) the final ranking has the best possible achievable performance; ii) local ordering of the initial lists are preserved in the final list.

In this paper, we address the problem of optimal rank aggregation. We propose an algorithm based on dynamic programming (DP) that results in an aggregated list whose performance, in terms of average precision (AP), is optimal. We also provide a mathematical proof that shows the result of the proposed method is indeed optimal.

This problem has already been addressed in [4, 5]. In loose terms, the idea of their algorithm is to greedily take segments of documents (named buckets) with the maximum number of relevant documents and the minimum number of irrelevant ones and add them to the final aggregated list. In Section 2 we describe this algorithm in more detail and show that although it is claimed to be optimal [4, 5] and it is employed by several researches [1, 2, 8–11], it does not necessarily result in a globally optimal aggregated list.

The rest of this paper is structured as follows. In Section 2, we discuss the existing algorithm [4, 5] in detail and demonstrate that it fails to find the optimal result in some circumstances. Section 3 presents our proposed method and provides a mathematical proof that shows the optimality of our proposed method. We finally conclude the paper in Section 4.

2. PREVIOUS WORK

In this section we discuss the previous solution for optimal rank aggregation, presented by Chen et al. [4, 5] (hereafter referred to as Chen's algorithm) and demonstrate that it is unable to achieve the global optimum in many cases.

First, we explain Chen's algorithm. This algorithm first segments each initial list into a number of *buckets*. A *bucket* is formally defined as a longest consecutive sequence of zero or more irrelevant documents followed by a consecutive sequence of zero or more relevant ones. A bucket is denoted in the form of $(n^-, n^+)\{d_i, d_{i+1}, \ldots, d_j\}$, in which n^- and n^+ respectively determine the number of irrelevant and relevant documents in the bucket and $\{d_i, d_{i+1}, \ldots, d_j\}$ denotes the documents ranked in positions i to j. For example $(3, 1)\{d_3, d_4, d_5, d_6\}$ has 3 irrelevant documents, d_3, d_4, and d_5 and one relevant document d_6.

Based on the above definition of bucket, the following facts, which will be used throughout the paper, are worth mentioning:

1. Each ranked list has a unique bucket representation;
2. In each bucket, no relevant document can occur before an irrelevant one;
3. In each bucket, no irrelevant document can occur after a relevant one.

After transforming all initial ranked lists into the bucket representation, the algorithm greedily takes the bucket with the least number of irrelevant documents and if two buckets have the same number of irrelevant documents takes the bucket with the most number of relevant ones. The taken bucket is appended to the output list. By repeating this operation until all buckets are added to the output, the final result is obtained. The procedure is illustrated in Algorithm 1 in detail. In this algorithm, l, b_t, and b_t^r refer to the number of ranked lists, the buckets of the t-th list, and the r-th bucket of the t-th list, respectively.

As an example, consider the three ranked lists that are illustrated, along with their relevancy information, in Table 1 as the initial lists. Table 2 shows the corresponding lists in the bucket representation.

In this example, based on Chen's algorithm, the initial *active set* will be: $\{(0, 1)\{A_1\}, (2, 1)\{B_1, B_2, B_3\}, (1, 3)\{C_1, C_2, C_3, C_4\}\}$. Continuing the algorithm, it will produce the following final result: $\{\{A_1\}, \{C_1, C_2, C_3, C_4\}, \{A_2, A_3\}, \{B_1, B_2, B_3\}, \{A_4\}, \{B_4\}\}$.

Although Chen's algorithm is claimed to be optimal [4, 5], its greedy nature prevents it from achieving the global optimum in many cases. To show that, we provide a counterexample which disproves its optimality. Consider the two ranked lists shown in Table 3. In this table, the items in the same bucket are colored similarly. Based on Chen's algorithm, in all but the last iteration, the top bucket of list A is taken and appended to the final ranked list,

---

Algorithm 1 Chen's algorithm [4, 5] for optimal rank aggregation

1: **procedure** CHENAGGREGATOR(Initial Ranked Lists)
2:     **for each** List l_i in the Initial Ranked Lists **do**
3:        $b_i \leftarrow$ BucketRepresentation(l_i);
4:     **end for**
5:     MergedList $\leftarrow \varnothing$
6:     ActiveSet $\leftarrow \{b_i^1 | 1 \leqslant i \leqslant l \wedge n_{b_i^1}^+ \geqslant 1\}$
7:     **repeat**
8:        ActiveSet $\leftarrow$ Sort(ActiveSet)
9:        $b_k^j \leftarrow$ ActiveSet[1]
10:       MergedList.append(b_k^j)
11:       ActiveSet.remove(b_k^j)
12:       **if** $n_{b_k^{j+1}}^+ \geqslant 1$ **then**
13:          ActiveSet.add(b_k^{j+1})
14:       **end if**
15:     **until** *isEmpty*(ActiveSet)
16:     **return** MergedList
17: **end procedure**

Table 1: The results of three different rankings. The relevant and irrelevant documents are marked by '$+$' and '$-$' respectively.

Rank	A	B	C
1	A_1^+	B_1^-	C_1^-
2	A_2^-	B_2^-	C_2^+
3	A_3^+	B_3^+	C_3^+
4	A_4^-	B_4^-	C_4^+

Table 2: Buckets of documents for the ranked lists.

Set	A	B	C
1	$(0, 1)\{A_1\}$	$(2, 1)\{B_1, B_2, B_3\}$	$(1, 3)\{C_1, C_2, C_3, C_4\}$
2	$(1, 1)\{A_2, A_3\}$	$(1, 0)\{B_4\}$	
3	$(1, 0)\{A_4\}$		

because it has less irrelevant items compared to the top bucket in list B. Consequently, the output of Chen's algorithm contains all items in list A followed by all items in list B. However, this is not the optimal ranking, which contains all items in list B followed by all items in list A. The average precision of Chen's algorithm output is 0.5289, while that of the optimal aggregated list is 0.6198.

Table 3: The counterexample that shows that Chen's algorithm does not necessarily generate the optimal aggregated list.

Rank	A	B
1	A_1^-	B_1^-
2	A_2^+	B_2^-
3	A_3^-	B_3^+
4	A_4^+	B_4^+
5	A_5^-	B_5^+
6	A_6^+	B_6^+
7	A_7^-	B_7^+
8	A_8^+	B_8^+

From the provided counterexample, it can be seen that the pitfall of Chen's algorithm is its intention to make its decisions only based on local evidence (only active set). It is noteworthy that we tried to change its bucket selection strategy to other greedy strategies but their optimality were also disproved by counterexamples. This is due to the fact that the *greedy choice property* is not valid in this problem. Therefore, to achieve the optimal AP, it seems necessary to make decisions with a global knowledge of the problem. In the next section, we present our method which is based on dynamic programming and will show that it results in a globally optimal aggregated list.

3. THE PROPOSED METHOD

In the previous section, we showed that Chen's algorithm does not necessarily lead to the optimal aggregated list, due to its greedy essence. On the other hand, a brute-force method could be employed to solve optimal rank aggregation of m ranked lists, split into $|b_1|, |b_2|, \ldots, |b_m|$ buckets, respectively, but the time complexity would be $O\left(\binom{|b_1|+|b_2|+\ldots+|b_m|}{|b_1|, |b_2|, \ldots, |b_m|}\right)$ which is infeasible for many practical purposes. In this section, after a brief introduction of notations, we propose an efficient alternative algorithm based on DP and prove its optimality by mathematical induction. We use the same definition of buckets introduced in Section 2, hereafter.

NOTATION 3.1. *We denote the documents of the final aggregated list by $d(1), d(2), \ldots, d(n)$. The total number of documents and the number of relevant documents of a bucket x, are denoted by n_x and n_x^+, respectively and its documents are shown as $d_x(1)$, $\ldots, d_x(n_x)$. In addition, for a document d, we define $r(d)$ as an indicator function determining if d is relevant, $r(d) = 1$, or irrelevant, $r(d) = 0$. Moreover, the number of relevant documents for the problem and the total number of relevant documents in the lists are denoted by N^+ and n^+, respectively ($N^+ \geqslant n^+$).*

3.1 Dynamic Programming for Optimal Rank Aggregation

In this section, we propose our method which aims to efficiently solve optimal rank aggregation of m ranked lists, split into $|b_1|$, $|b_2|, \ldots, |b_m|$ buckets, respectively. We introduce an m-th order tensor M of size $(|b_1| + 1) \times (|b_2| + 1) \times \ldots \times (|b_m| + 1)$, in which value of an entry $M[i_1, i_2, \ldots, i_m]$ shows the maximum AP obtainable by aggregating top $i_1, i_2, \ldots, i_m$ buckets of the ranked lists $1, 2, \ldots, m$, respectively. We can compute entry $M[i_1, i_2, \ldots, i_m]$ according to Eq. 1, in which index k maximizing the value, shows that the last bucket appended to the output in order to obtain the optimal value is taken from list k.

$$M[i_1, i_2, \ldots, i_m] = \max_k \big(M[i_1, i_2, \ldots, i_k - 1, \ldots, i_m] \\ + \text{AP-GAIN}(k, i_1, i_2, \ldots, i_m) \big). \tag{1}$$

AP-GAIN$(k, i_1, i_2, \ldots, i_m)$ in Eq. 1 is the AP increase after appending $b_k^{i_k}$ at position p (i.e. at the end of the list):

$$p = \sum_{1 \leqslant t \leqslant m} \sum_{\substack{1 \leqslant r \leqslant i_t \wedge \\ \neg(t=k \wedge r=i_k)}} n_{b_t^r}. \tag{2}$$

By storing index k maximizing Eq. 1 for each entry $M[i_1, i_2, \ldots, i_m]$, the optimal solution could be easily generated by starting from entry $M[|b_1|, |b_2|, \ldots, |b_m|]$ and iteratively inserting the bucket indicated by the stored index, at the beginning of the output. Algorithm 2 shows the pseudo-code of the procedure.

Tensor M contains $O(|b_1| \times |b_2| \times \ldots \times |b_m|)$ entries and because a simple computation of each entry requires an average time of

---

Algorithm 2 DP algorithm for optimal rank aggregation

1: **procedure** DPAGGREGATOR(Bucket Representation)
2:     $M \leftarrow [0]_{|b_1| \times \ldots \times |b_m|}$
3:     **for** $i_1 \leftarrow 1$ **to** $|b_1|$ **do**
        $\ddots$
4:         **for** $i_m \leftarrow 1$ **to** $|b_m|$ **do**
5:             $v \leftarrow M[i_1 - 1, \ldots, i_m] + \text{AP-GAIN}(1, i_1, \ldots, i_m)$
6:             $k \leftarrow 1$
7:             **for** $k\prime \leftarrow 2$ **to** m **do**
8:                 $\Delta A_{k\prime} \leftarrow \text{AP-GAIN}(k\prime, i_1, \ldots, i_{k\prime} - 1, \ldots, i_m)$
9:                 $v\prime \leftarrow M[i_1, \ldots, i_{k\prime} - 1, \ldots, i_m] + \Delta A_{k\prime}$
10:                 **if** $v\prime \geqslant v$ **then**
11:                     $v \leftarrow v\prime$
12:                     $k \leftarrow k\prime$
13:                 **end if**
14:             **end for**
15:             $M[i_1, \ldots, i_k - 1, \ldots, i_m] \leftarrow v$
16:         **end for**
        $\ddots$
17:     **end for**
18:     **return** M
19: **end procedure**

$O(mc)$ (c is the average bucket length), the proposed algorithm is of $O(mc \times |b_1| \times |b_2| \times \ldots \times |b_m|)$. In addition, we can calculate AP-GAIN more efficiently to reduce the complexity. To calculate AP-GAIN after adding a bucket x at position p, where there are q relevant documents before, we can use Eq. 3, in which both A and B are functions of $p + n_x^-$ and n_x^+. Considering the equation, we can first fill two $n \times t$ matrices A and B (n and t are total number of documents and the maximum number of relevant documens in all the buckets, respectively) and then use the matrices as lookup tables to calculate AP-GAIN$(k, i_1, i_2, \ldots, i_m)$ in $O(1)$. This results in a time complexity of $O(m \times |b_1| \times |b_2| \times \ldots \times |b_m| + n \times t)$.

$$\sum_{i=0}^{n_x^+ - 1} \frac{q+i+1}{p + n_x^- + i} = q \underbrace{\sum_{i=0}^{n_x^+ - 1} \frac{1}{p + n_x^- + i}}_{A} + \underbrace{\sum_{i=0}^{n_x^+ - 1} \frac{i+1}{p + n_x^- + i}}_{B}. \tag{3}$$

3.2 Proof of Optimality

In this section, we theoretically prove the optimality of the proposed DP solution, named $\mathcal{DP}$. First, we introduce some definitions, notations, and lemmas which will be used in the proof.

LEMMA 3.1. *If i is the position of the first relevant document in bucket x (i.e. $r(d_x(i)) = 1 \wedge \forall k < i : r(d_x(k)) = 0$) and its corresponding rank in the final aggregated list is j, by pushing down documents $d_x(1) \ldots d_x(i-1)$ altogether right above position j (i.e. $\forall k < i : d(j - i + k) = d_x(k)$), AP will not decrease. Similarly, if there are no relevant documents in a bucket, by pushing down all but the last document of the bucket right above the position of its last document in the final ranked list, AP will not decrease.*

PROOF. By pushing down the documents above position j, only the ranks of top j documents might change and since the only documents that are demoted are $d_x(1) \ldots d_x(i - 1)$, which according to the assumption are known to be irrelevant, relevant documents are either promoted or remain unchanged. Thus, with regard to the property of AP that prefers lists with relevant documents at higher ranks, AP will not decrease. The proof is analogous for the case where there is no relevant documents in the bucket. $\square$

LEMMA 3.2. *If we push up a relevant document in the aggregated ranked list, AP will not decrease.*

PROOF. We call the precision at k before and after the promotion $P(k)$ and $P'(k)$, respectively. If we promote a relevant document from position j of the final ranked list to a new position i ($i < j$) and consider $i_1, \ldots, i_{n^+}$ and $i'_1, \ldots, i'_{n^+}$ as the indexes of the relevant documents in the ranked list before and after the promotion, since the promoted document is relevant, for all k: $P'(i'_k) \geqslant P(i_k)$. Therefore, the change of AP is calculated as:

$$\Delta \text{AP} = \frac{P'(1) + \ldots + P'(i'_r)}{N^+} \\ - \frac{P(1) + \ldots + P(i_r)}{N^+} \\ = \frac{1}{N^+} \times \Big(\big(P'(i'_1) - P(i_1)\big) \\ + \big(P'(i'_2) - P(i_2)\big) \\ + \ldots \\ + \big(P'(i'_{n^+}) - P(i_{n^+})\big) \\ \Big) \geqslant 0.$$

$\square$

LEMMA 3.3. *If i is the position of the first relevant document in bucket x (i.e. $r(d_x(i)) = 1 \wedge \forall k < i : r(d_x(k)) = 0$) and its corresponding rank in the final aggregated list is j, by pushing up documents $d_x(i+1) \ldots d_x(n_x)$ altogether right below position j (i.e. $\forall k > i : d(j + k - i) = d_x(k)$), AP will not decrease.*

PROOF. Since all of the moved documents are relevant and their reordering only includes push-ups, Lemma 3.2 implies that AP will not decrease. $\square$

LEMMA 3.4. *For each arbitrary ranking, we can obtain an analogous ranking in which the documents of each bucket are all together (i.e. the ranking can be seen as a list of buckets), with AP of not less than that of the initial one.*

PROOF. Starting from the first document in the ranking, we look for a relevant document or the last document of a bucket without any relevant documents, whichever occurs first. Based on Lemma 3.1 and Lemma 3.3, we can assemble the documents of the bucket that includes that document without decreasing AP by pushing up or down other documents of that bucket. Starting from the first document after the assembled bucket, we perform the above operation again and repeat this for all the buckets. Since such an operation does not disassemble the previously assembled buckets, we can finally reach a ranked list consisting of continuous buckets. Because none of the assembling operations decreases AP, it will be not less than the initial one. $\square$

NOTATION 3.2. *If we have a problem named $\mathscr{P}$, and $\mathcal{M}$ is a method for it, $\mathcal{M}(\mathscr{P})$ is the solution provided by method $\mathcal{M}$ and $\mathcal{O}(\mathscr{P})$ is an optimal solution to it.*

DEFINITION 3.1. *If in problem $\mathscr{P}$ we have m ranked lists and $\{x_1, x_2, \ldots, x_m\}$ are the last buckets of the lists, $\mathscr{T}_1, \mathscr{T}_2, \ldots, \mathscr{T}_m$ are similar problems to $\mathscr{P}$ with the constraint that in the solution to $\mathscr{T}_i$, bucket x_i must be placed at the end of the result. Also, we denote $\mathscr{P}_j$ as the problem $\mathscr{P}$, with the last bucket of list j removed.*

THEOREM 3.1. *$\mathcal{DP}$ finds the optimal solution to $\mathscr{P}$.*

PROOF. We use induction on the number of buckets to prove the theorem. The theorem trivially holds for the base case of just one bucket since according to the constraint of preserving the intra-ordering of the ranked lists, only one solution is possible to the problem and $\mathcal{DP}$ produces it.

For the inductive step, we prove that if the proposed method yields an optimal solution for the problems with k buckets, it will provide an optimal solution for the problems with $k + 1$ buckets. Suppose that $\mathcal{O}(\mathscr{P})$ is an optimal solution to $\mathscr{P}$ with a total number of $k + 1$ buckets. According to Lemma 3.4, we can convert $\mathcal{O}(\mathscr{P})$ into an analogous optimal solution, $\mathcal{O}'(\mathscr{P})$, in which all buckets are uninterrupted. If the last bucket in $\mathcal{O}'(\mathscr{P})$ is from list j, by definition we have:

$$\text{AP}(\mathcal{O}(\mathscr{P})) = \text{AP}(\mathcal{O}'(\mathscr{P})) = \text{AP}(\mathcal{O}(\mathscr{T}_j)). \quad (4)$$

On the other hand, according to the optimal sub-problem property of our problem (as is trivially implied by a simple cut-and-paste reasoning,) the optimal solution to $\mathscr{T}_j$ is obtained by simply appending the last bucket of list j to the optimal solution of $\mathscr{P}_j$. This is equivalent to what $\mathcal{DP}$ does when calculating element $M[i_1, i_2, \ldots, i_m]$ based on $M[i_1, i_2, \ldots, i_j - 1, \ldots, i_m]$; i.e. when $k = j$ in Eq. 1.

It should be noted that the above equivalency holds based on the induction assumption, that is the optimality of $M[i_1, i_2, \ldots, i_k - 1, \ldots, i_m]$ (because the problem corresponding to it has exactly k buckets).

Thus, according to Eq. 4 and Eq. 1 we have:

$$\begin{aligned} \text{AP}(\mathcal{DP}(\mathscr{P})) &= M[i_1, i_2, \ldots, i_m] \\ &\geq M[i_1, i_2, \ldots, i_k - 1, \ldots, i_m] \\ &\quad + \text{AP-GAIN}(k, i_1, i_2, \ldots, i_m) \quad (5) \\ &= \text{AP}(\mathcal{O}(\mathscr{T}_j)) \\ &= \text{AP}(\mathcal{O}(\mathscr{P})). \end{aligned}$$

Since $\mathcal{O}(\mathscr{P})$ is optimal, the above inequality implies that $\mathcal{DP}(\mathscr{P})$ is also optimal. $\square$

4. CONCLUSION

Rank aggregation is a key problem in IR and can considerably influence the performance of many IR systems. Consequently, measuring the performance of different rank aggregation strategies is of great importance. To this end, in this paper, we proposed an algorithm that allows one to independently measure the performance of each aggregation strategy relative to the best possible performance.

The proposed algorithm, using the relevancy information, obtains the optimal aggregated list, and thus yields an upper bound for the performance of the rank aggregation problem. To support the proposed algorithm, we provided a mathematical proof to ensure the optimality of the result. We also demonstrated that the previously available algorithm for the problem of optimal rank aggregation does not necessarily produce the optimum aggregated list. It is noteworthy we have practically employed the previous algorithm, for rank aggregation on several real experiments (on multilingual IR) and observed that in many of the experiments, it did not obtain the optimal performance. This reveals that its failure is not limited to some theoretical and rare cases.

References

[1] M. Braschler. Combination approaches for multilingual text retrieval. *Information Retrieval*, 7(1-2):183–204, 2004.

[2] M. Braschler, A. Göhring, and P. Schäuble. Eurospider at clef 2002. In *CLEF*, pages 164–174, 2003.

[3] J. Callan. *Distributed Information Retrieval*, volume 7. 2000.

[4] A. Chen. Cross-language retrieval experiments at clef-2002. In *CLEF*, pages 28–48, 2002.

[5] A. Chen and F. C. Gey. Multilingual information retrieval using machine translation, relevance feedback and decompounding. *Information Retrieval*, 7(1-2):149–182, 2004.

[6] H. Li. *Learning to Rank for Information Retrieval and Natural Language Processing*. Morgan & Claypool Publishers, second edition, 2014.

[7] W.-C. Lin and H.-H. Chen. Merging mechanisms in multilingual information retrieval. In *CLEF*, pages 175–186, 2003.

[8] W.-C. Lin and H.-H. Chen. Merging results by predicted retrieval effectiveness. In *Comparative Evaluation of Multilingual Information Access Systems*, pages 202–209. 2004.

[9] M. Martín-Valdivia, F. Martínez-Santiago, and L. Ureña-López. Merging strategy for cross-lingual information retrieval systems based on learning vector quantization. *Neural Processing Letters*, 22(2):149–161, 2005.

[10] F. Martínez-Santiago, A. Montejo-Ráez, L. Ureña-López, and M. Díaz-Galiano. Sinai at clef 2003: Decompounding and merging. In *CLEF*, pages 192–201, 2004.

[11] F. Martínez-Santiago, L. Ureña-López, and M. Martín-Valdivia. A merging strategy proposal: The 2-step retrieval status value method. *Information Retrieval*, 9(1):71–93, 2006.

[12] R. Nuray and F. Can. Automatic ranking of information retrieval systems using data fusion. *Information Processing & Management*, 42(3):595–614, 2006.

[13] Y. Tzitzikas. Democratic data fusion for information retrieval mediators. In *AICCSA*, pages 531–537, 2001.

Searching for Twitter Posts by Location

Ariana Minot
Harvard University
School of Engineering and Applied Sciences
Cambridge, MA, USA
minot@fas.harvard.edu

Andrew Heier, Davis King, Olga Simek,
Nick Stanisha
MIT Lincoln Laboratory
Lexington, MA, USA

ABSTRACT

The microblogging service Twitter is an increasingly popular platform for sharing information worldwide. This motivates the potential to mine information from Twitter, which can serve as a valuable resource for applications such as event localization and location-specific recommendation systems. Geolocation of Twitter messages is integral to such applications. However, only a a small percentage of Twitter posts are accompanied by a GPS location. Recent works have begun exploring ways to estimate the unknown location of Twitter users based on the content of their posts and various available metadata. This presents interesting challenges for natural language processing and multi-objective optimization. We propose a new method for estimating the home location of users based on both the content of their posts and their social connections on Twitter. Our method achieves an accuracy of 77% within 10 km in exchange for a reduction in coverage of 76% with respect to techniques which only use social connections.

Categories and Subject Descriptors

H.3.1 [**Information Systems**]: Information Storage and Retrieval—*Content Analysis and Indexing*

Keywords

Social Media Search, Twitter, Geolocation

1. INTRODUCTION

Twitter currently counts 316 million active users. These users broadcast approximately a half billion posts, known as Tweets, daily [10]. Recent interest has centered around

This work is sponsored by the Department of the Air Force under the Air Force Contract #FA8721-05-C-0002. Opinions, interpretations, conclusions and recommendations are those of the author and are not necessarily endorsed by the United States Government.

ICTIR'15, September 27–30, Northampton, MA, USA.
ⓒ 2015 ACM. ISBN 978-1-4503-3833-2/15/09 ...$15.00.
DOI: http://dx.doi.org/10.1145/2808194.2809480.

viewing Twitter as a human-powered sensor network, capable of providing valuable spatiotemporal information in real-time [9]. Relevant applications include detection and localization of news events, such as natural disasters and polical movements, sentiment analysis, and improving recommendation and filtering of information based on location. Knowing the geographic origin of Tweets is key for such efforts.

Twitter allows users to "geotag" their posts with GPS on mobile devices, however only 1-3 % of Tweets are geotagged in this way [6]. If one wanted to search for all Tweets sent from a given area, how can one retrieve those Tweets of interest? In this study, we address this question by proposing an algorithm for estimating the home base of Twitter users for whom the location of their posts is unknown. The resolution of our estimates is at city-level. These estimates are made on the basis of the content of a user's Tweets, as well as metadata on interactions with fellow users.

Analyzing the content of Tweets presents interesting challenges. Tweets are multilingual, with several languages appearing possibly within a single post. In addition, Tweets are limited to 140 characters, often containing abbreviations and misspellings, which complicates applying traditional named entity recognition techniques. We present a new geolocation method based on fusing content-based and social network-based estimates of a user's home location. To the best of our knowledge, our contributions include the first results for improving geolocation by using both Tweet content and social metadata of users.

2. RELATED WORK

A wide range of methods have been studied for the Twitter geolocation problem. We discuss those most relevant to our method and with state of the art results.

2.1 Content Based Geolocation

In [4], Han *et al.* explore a variety of techniques for geolocation based on the words in a user's Tweets, including feature selection methods for learning which words are most predictive for different cities. Determination of "location indicative words" is based on the observed frequency of a given word in a given city. Observed word frequencies also help to inform our estimation algorithm. Among their best results, Han *et al.* achieve a city-level accuracy of 12.6% for English language Tweets sent worldwide. Cheng *et al.* use geotagged Tweets to obtain statistics on which words are most frequently observed in different cities [1]. To improve geotagging performance, the authors study the use of smooth-

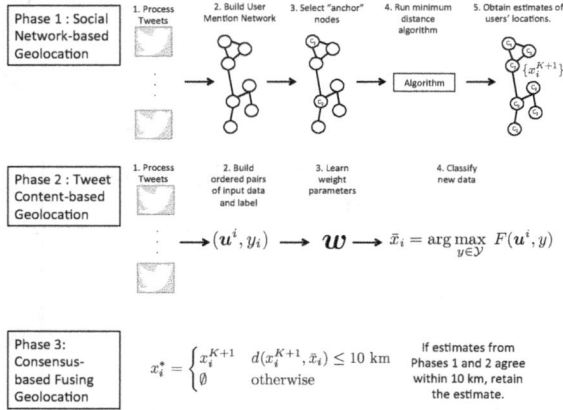

Figure 1: Schematic representation of proposed method described in Section 3.

ing the empirical distributions built from these statistics for cities with only small data samples available.

In contrast to these works, we are interested in further exploring the use of support vector machines (SVM) for this problem. A multi-class SVM can be used to estimate the primary city-level location of users by classifying the set of each user's Tweets as having originated from a particular city. Han *et al.* state that SVM classifiers are found unsuitable because of the many possible classes (*i.e.* cities). We address this by proposing to use structural SVMs in Section 3.2 [5]. Previous works utilizing SVMs for geolocation of Twitter accounts include [7], where a stacked-SVM-based classification algorithm is applied to distinguish between English language Tweets originating from either north or south India. In [8], a SVM classifier is used to geolocate Twitter users with features based on their social connections rather than their Tweet content, which we discuss in the next section.

2.2 Social Network Based Geolocation

The basic principle behind utilizing social connections for geolocation is that people tend to interact with other people in close physical proximity. Evidence of this is shown in [8], where Rout *et al.* geolocate based on the locations of a user's Twitter friends. The authors estimate nearly 70% of their sample of UK-based users within 100 miles of their true location. Twitter provides functionality for users to mention one another in posts. These mentions are referred to as user-mentions. In [2], Compton *et al.* obtain state of the art results for geotagging Twitter profiles based on user-mentions, achieving city-level accuracy of 89.7% of users. Compared to other studies, the authors process a much larger amount of data, specifically 10% of all public Tweets from April 2012 to April 2014, amassing a list of about 111 million users. Of these 111 million users, roughly 25 million of the users' true home locations are revealed via home profile information or GPS. We expand upon this method by exploring how to further improve geotagging using both user-mentions and Tweet content.

3. METHOD

Our method consists of three stages as depicted in Figure 1. In the first stage, users' locations are estimated from their user-mention data. In the second stage, users are geotagged based on the content of their Tweets. In the third stage, we use consensus-based fusing to form an estimate that takes into account both features. To determine the home city of geotagged Twitter users, each geotagged Tweet is labeled as originating from the closest nearby city, and the city with the highest number of associated Tweets is identified as the user's home city.

3.1 Stage 1: Social Network-based Approach

We follow the approach proposed by Compton *et al.* in [2] for constructing a graph $\mathcal{G} = (\mathcal{V}, \mathcal{E})$ from user-mention information. Each node is associated with a user, and there is an edge between a pair of nodes if the users associated with those nodes mutually mention one another. In particular, the edge weight between nodes i and j is given by $w_{ij} = \min(n_{ij}, n_{ji})$, where n_{ij} is the number of times user i mentions user j. Let the total number of nodes in $\mathcal{G}$ be denoted n. To geolocate users, we seek estimates which minimize the distance between users that are neighbors in the user-mention network. Compton *et al.* formulate this as the following optimization problem:

$$\min_{\boldsymbol{x}} \; g(\boldsymbol{x}) \text{ s.t. } x_i = l_i \text{ for } i \in L, \qquad (1)$$

where $\boldsymbol{x}$ are the estimated locations of the users and L is the set of users who have chosen to reveal their locations $\{l_i\}_{i \in L}$ (*e.g.*, via GPS). The objective function is defined as $g(\boldsymbol{x}) = \sum_{i,j} w_{ij} d(x_i, x_j)$. The distance between a pair of locations $d(x_i, x_j)$ is given by the geodesic distance.

Rather than a continuous set of locations in the minimization, we consider a discrete set of cities, ordered with indices $\mathcal{Y} = \{1, \ldots, Y\}$. We refer to the set of nodes corresponding to users with known locations L as "anchor" nodes, because the locations of these users are fixed. The true location of a user is defined to be the city in our chosen set $\mathcal{Y}$ determined by the methods described above. In order to evaluate the performance of our algorithm, we use geotagged data. The algorithm proposed by Compton *et al.* for solving the optimization problem in equation (1) excludes initialization and termination schemes. Location information should propagate from anchor nodes to other users. Let $\{f_i\}$ be a binary-valued set of flags indicating whether or not a user is included in the optimization in (1). We address these issues and present our modified version in Algorithm 1. We have the following result for the convergence of the location estimates.

PROPOSITION 1. *Let $L' = \{i | i \notin L,$ there is no path from i to any node $j \in L\}$. For two nodes connected via a path, let the length of the shortest path between two nodes i and j be denoted d_{ij}. Let*

$$K = \max_{i \notin L' \cup L} \min_{j \in L} d_{ij}, \qquad (2)$$

be the length of a largest minimal distance path between an anchor node and a non-anchor node. Then, using Algorithm 1 to produce the location estimates, we have for each node i

$$\forall k \geq (K+1), \; x_i^{k+1} = x_i^k. \qquad (3)$$

PROOF. First, we show by induction that the number of iterations for any node $i \notin L' \cup L$ required for flag f_i to equal 1 is at most the length of the shortest path from i to any anchor node. Let the closest anchor node to i be denoted j.

Algorithm 1 User-Mention Network Algorithm

Input : Set of pre-geolocated users L and their
locations $\{l_i\}_{i \in L}$. K, the length of longest
path from anchor node to non-anchor node in
graph $\mathcal{G}$.

Output: Set of estimated locations $\{x_i^{K+1}\}_{i \notin L' \cup L}$

Initialization

for $i := 1$ *to* n **do**
  if $i \in L$ **then**
    | $f_i :=$, $x_i^k := l_i$ for $k \in \{0, \ldots, K+1\}$
  else
    | $f_i :=$, $x_i^0 := -1$
  end
end

Main Routine:

for $k := 1$ *to* $K+1$ **do**
  for $i := 1$ *to* n **do**
    if $i \notin L$ *and* $\sum_{j \in \mathcal{N}_i} f_j > 0$ **then**
      | $x_i^k = \operatorname{argmin}_{y \in \mathcal{Y}} \sum_{j \in \mathcal{N}_i} f_j w_{ij} d(y, x_j^{k-1})$
      | $f_i = 1$
    end
  end
end

For the base case, let the path from node i to node j be of length 1. Then, since i is neighbors with an anchor node, we have $\sum_{l \in \mathcal{N}_i} f_l > 0$, and from Algorithm 1, we see that at the first iteration f_i gets assigned to 1. For an inductive hypothesis, let the length of the shortest path from node i to node j be of length $k > 1$, and assume that it takes at most k iterations for f_i to equal 1.

Now suppose that the shortest path, p, from node i to node j is of length $(k+1)$. Consider the neighbor of i that lies on p, and denote it a. Since there is a path of length k from node a to an anchor node, by the inductive hypothesis f_a will equal 1 within at most k iterations. Therefore, at iteration $(k+1)$, node i has a neighbor such that $\sum_{l \in \mathcal{N}_i} f_l > 0$. Thus, Algorithm 1 assigns f_i to 1 at iteration $(k+1)$.

For each node $i' \notin L' \cup L$, let p_i be the shortest path from i to an anchor node. Let $K = \max_{\{i \notin L' \cup L\}} p_i$. By iteration K all of the flags $\{f_i\}_{i \notin L' \cup L}$ will be set to 1, and the values for x_i^k will remain constant for all iterations $k \geq (K+1)$. Therefore the estimates produced by Algorithm 1 will converge within $(K+1)$ iterations. $\square$

The proposition above tells us that the location estimates from Algorithm 1 will have converged within $(K+1)$ iterations. In addition, we note that if a node has no path to an anchor node, then the associated user will never receive a location estimate with this approach. We refer to the percentage of users for which we can obtain an estimate as the coverage of the algorithm. The coverage of the user-mention network algorithm is dependent on the number of anchor nodes and their location relative to the other users.

3.2 Stage 2: Content-based Approach

The principle behind content-based geolocation is that particular words are more indicative of certain cities than others. We propose to automatically learn such words using a structural support vector machine. Structural SVMs were devised by Joachims *et al.* for classification problems with complex structures as categories [5]. In particular, structural SVMs are useful for multi-class learning in a setting with a large number of classes. In our problem, each class refers to a city-level location for a user, yielding on the order of thousands of possible classes. We adapt structural SVMs to the geolocation problem as follows. We consider the discrete, ordered set of cities $\mathcal{Y} = \{1, \ldots, Y\}$ from Section 3.1 as possible locations for users and a discrete set of words $\mathcal{A} = \{a_1, \ldots, a_N\}$. For each user i in the training set of n users, the input data consists of a vector, $\boldsymbol{u}^i$, with its jth entry given by $\log(n_j) + 1$, where n_j is the number of occurrences of word a_j in user i's Tweets (excluding words with $n_j = 0$). The logarithm is used for feature normalization, preventing words and users which occur orders of magnitude more than others from dominating the behavior of the SVM. The score of a proposed city with index y for data $\boldsymbol{u}^i$ is given by

$$F(\boldsymbol{u}^i, y) = \sum_{j=1}^N w_j^y u_j^i, \qquad (4)$$

where w_j^y is the weight associated with word a_j for city y. The training data are used to learn the weights by selecting values for the weights which maximize the score of the correct label, which we denote y_i. As stated in [5], this amounts to the following optimization problem

$$\min_{\boldsymbol{w}, \boldsymbol{\phi}} ||\boldsymbol{w}||^2 + C \sum_{i=1}^n \phi_i$$
$$s.t. \ F(\boldsymbol{u}^i, y_i) > \max_{y \neq y_i} [F(\boldsymbol{u}^i, y) + \Delta_i(y)] - \phi_i. \qquad (5)$$

The parameters ϕ_i serve as slack variables which allow for noisy training samples, and C is a tuneable parameter. The loss function $\Delta_i(y)$ we define to be the geodesic distance from city y to the true location y_i. This is a reasonable choice if we want to penalize misclassification more strongly based on the distance between the estimated and true location. Once we have learned the weights $\boldsymbol{w}$, we estimate the location of a non-geotagged user i by

$$\bar{x}_i = \operatorname*{argmax}_{y \in \mathcal{Y}} F(\boldsymbol{u}^i, y) \qquad (6)$$

3.3 Stage 3: Consensus-based Fusing

We seek an estimate of a user's location which both minimizes the distance to neighbors in the user-mention network as described in Section 3.1 and maximizes the weighted score obtained from the structural SVM described in Section 3.2. To solve this multi-objective problem, we apply consensus-based fusing of the output from the user-mention network algorithm and from the structural SVM. The fused estimate for user i is given as

$$x_i^* = \begin{cases} x_i^{K+1}, & d(x_i^{K+1}, \bar{x}_i) \leq 10 \text{ km} \\ \emptyset, & \text{otherwise}, \end{cases} \qquad (7)$$

where x_i^{K+1} is the user-mention based estimate produced from Algorithm 1, $\bar{x}_i$ is the content-based estimate from equation (6), and $d(x_i^{K+1}, \bar{x}_i)$ is the geodesic distance between the two estimates. Simply put, if the geodesic distance from the city estimated by the user-mention network to the city estimated by the structural SVM is less than 10 km, we retain the estimate from the user-mention network. Otherwise, the user is removed from our sample. We expect that information from user-mentions complements information from vocabulary used in Tweets. Therefore, consensus-based fusing has potential to provide a sample of high accuracy estimates in exchange for a reduction in coverage (*i.e.* the number of users with an estimated geolocation).

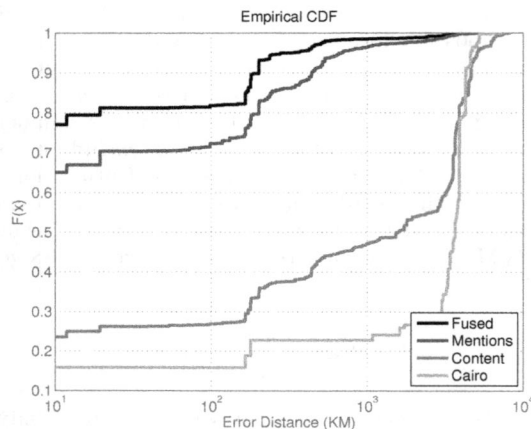

Figure 2: Geolocation results for case study of Tweets originating from sample of users in Africa.

4. APPLICATION: GEOLOCATION OF TWEETS FROM AFRICA

Social media has become an important means for gathering information about the political and social atmosphere in the developing world, where traditional means via surveys can be difficult. In addition, Twitter data is relatively sparse in many cities in Africa compared to other parts of the world such as the US and not as well studied in previous literature [3]. The set of possible home locations for users contains 97 cities in Africa, selected for having a population greater than 500,000. Our data sample contains 29,582 users who we have estimated to live in Africa.

We use geotagged data in order to evaluate the performance of our estimates. We randomly select 20% of these users as anchor nodes with their location revealed. To justify this choice, Compton *et al.* found that using profile information alone results in obtaining a city-level location for 20% of users in their sample [2]. Using the user-mention network method, we observe 60% city-level accuracy with 76% overall coverage. To train the SVM, we gather 5,439,578 Tweets from 220,453 Twitter users from Africa between January and July 2014. On a test set of 2,215,087 Tweets from 94,480 Twitter users, the SVM achieves 22% city-level accuracy. Location information in user profiles and sophisticated data cleaning procedures could further improve SVM performance.

To measure performance of the consensus-based fusion, we study the empirical c.d.f. $F(x)$ of the distance between the estimated and true home city of a user, referred to as the error distance, in Figure 2. At value d on the x-axis, the y-value of each curve is the percentage of users that achieve an error distance less than or equal to d. The performance is shown when basing the estimate on user-mentions alone ("Mentions") and content alone ("Content"). The consensus-based fusing ("Fused") achieves the best performance. As a

benchmark, we report the performance achieved by estimating every user to be in Cairo, Egypt ("Cairo"), the African city with the largest percentage of associated Twitter users in our data. Using consensus-based fusion, the accuracy within 10 km of the user mentions-based approach is increased from 65% to 77%. This is in exchange for a reduction in coverage of 76% with respect to the user mentions-based approach.

5. CONCLUSIONS

In summary, we propose a new method for retrieving Twitter users by location based on both textual content and interactions via user mentions. We are able to achieve significant gains in performance by fusing the two estimates in exchange for a reduction in coverage. In the future, it will be interesting to analyze the use of non-geotagged Tweets in enhancing the structural connectivity of the user-mention network and its potential to improve the coverage property of the consensus-based fusing algorithm. In addition to Twitter data, these methods are of interest for analyzing a variety of online forums and social media sites.

6. REFERENCES

[1] Z. Cheng, J. Caverlee, and K. Lee. You Are Where You Tweet: A Content-Based Approach to Geo-Locating Twitter Users. In *Proc. of the 19th ACM Conference of Information and Knowledge Management*, pages 759–768, 2010.

[2] R. Compton, D. Jurgens, and D. Allen. Geotagging One Hundred Million Twitter Accounts with Total Variation Minimization. *CoRR, abs/1404.7152*, 2014.

[3] C. Fink, J. Kopecky, N. Bos, and M. Thomas. Mapping the Twitterverse in the Developing World: An Analysis of Social Media Use in Nigeria. volume 7227 of *Lecture Notes in Computer Science*, pages 164–171, 2012.

[4] B. Han, P. Cook, and T. Baldwin. Text-based Twitter User Geolocation Prediction. *Journal of Artificial Intelligence Research*, 49:451–500, 2014.

[5] T. Joachims, T. Hofmann, Y. Yue, and C.-N. Yu. Predicting Structured Objects with Support Vector Machines. *Communications of the ACM*, 52(11):97–104, Nov. 2009.

[6] K. Leetaru, S. Wang, G. Cao, A. Padmanabhan, and E. Shook. Mapping the Global Twitter Heartbeat: The Geography of Twitter. *First Monday*, 18(5), 2013.

[7] D. Rao, D. Yarowsky, A. Shreevats, and M. Gupta. Classifying Latent User Attributes in Twitter. In *Proc. of the 2nd Intl. ACM Workshop on Seach and Mining User-Generated Contents*, pages 37–44, 2010.

[8] D. Rout, K. Bontcheva, D. Preoţiuc-Pietro, and T. Cohn. Where's @Wally?: A Classification Approach to Geolocating Users Based on Their Social Ties. In *Proc. of the 24th ACM Conference on Hypertext and Social Media*, pages 11–20, 2013.

[9] T. Sakaki, M. Okazaki, and Y. Matsuo. Earthquake Shakes Twitter Users: Real-Time Event Detection by Social Sensors. In *Proc. of the 19th Intl. Conf. on World Wide Web*, pages 851–860. ACM, 2010.

[10] Twitter Fact Sheet. https://about.twitter.com/company, 2014. Online; accessed 3-August-2015.

A Signaling Game Approach to Databases Querying and Interaction

Arash Termehchy
Oregon State University
termehca@oregonstate.edu

Behrouz Touri
University of Colorado, Boulder
behrouz.touri@colorado.edu

ABSTRACT

As most database users cannot precisely express their information needs, it is challenging for database querying and exploration interfaces to understand them. We propose a novel formal framework for representing and understanding information needs in database querying and exploration. Our framework considers querying as a collaboration between the user and the database system to establish a *mutual language* for representing information needs. We formalize this collaboration as a signaling game, where each mutual language is an equilibrium for the game. A query interface is more effective if it establishes a less ambiguous mutual language faster. We discuss some equilibria, strategies, and the convergence rates in this game. In particular, we propose a reinforcement learning mechanism and analyze it within our framework. We prove that this adaptation mechanism for the query interface improves the effectiveness of answering queries stochastically speaking, and converges almost surely.

Categories and Subject Descriptors

H.2 [**Database Management**]: Query languages

1. INTRODUCTION

Most users do not know the structure and/or content of their databases. Hence, they cannot express their information needs according to how the databases represent their desired information [14, 1, 6]. Hence, it is challenging for database query interfaces to understand and satisfy users' information needs. Database query interface may improve its understanding of how users express their intents through further interaction with users. Similarly, users may gain a better understanding of how the database represent information by submitting queries and exploring their results. For example, to find the answers for a particular information need, the user may submit some initial and ill-specified SQL query, observes its results, and reformulates it according to her observations. Ideally, we would like the user and the database query interface to develop gradually a mutual understanding over the course of several search tasks and interactions: the query interface should better understand how the user expresses her intent and the user

may get more familiar with how the database represents information in the domain of interest. For example, consider a relational database with relation *restaurant* with many attributes including the price level and number of stars for restaurants in the US. Because the user is not aware of the existence *price-level* attribute and/or its values, she may not put any restriction on this attribute in her queries. Given the user's feedback on the results of several information needs, database query interface may infer that the user is more likely to search for high or medium level price restaurants, less likely to seek very high and low level price restaurants, and almost never to ask for restaurant with very low price level. On the other hand, after working with the database for some time and observing the information about her preferred restaurants, user may learn that she can express her preference for nice restaurants using the attribute *number-of-stars*.

Intuitively, both user and query interface may leverage their experiences from the current and the past search tasks to reach a precise mutual understanding fast so they can communicate more effectively. Hence, it is interesting to find the strategies that the query interface and/or the user should follow to achieve a common rapport quickly. Further, one should also explore the properties of this common rapport, e.g. is a perfect and near perfect rapport possible?

To the best of our knowledge, there is not any investigation on the emergence and/or maintenance of such a common representation of information needs between the user and database query interface. In this paper, we propose a novel formal framework that explores the representation of information needs in database querying. It considers the user and query interface as active and potentially rational agents whose goal is to develop a common representation of information needs by communicating certain signals. We formalize this setting as a *signaling game* [7, 15]. We propose a reinforcement learning rule to update the database strategies. We prove that this learning strategy for the query interface improves the effectiveness of answering queries stochastically speaking, and converges almost surely.

2. RELATED WORK

Researchers have proposed querying and exploration interfaces over structured and semi-structured databases that help users to express their information needs and find reasonably accurate results [9, 1, 6, 4]. We extend this body of work by considering users as active and potentially rational agents whose decisions and strategies impact the effectiveness of database exploration. To the best of our knowledge, there is not any game-theoretic approach to database querying and exploration. We also formally explore the information needs representations and the emergence of common representations in database querying and exploration.

Researchers have recently applied game theoretic approaches to model the actions taken by users and document retrieval systems in a single session [13]. In particular, they propose a framework to find out whether the user likes to continue exploring the current topic or move to another topic. We, however, seek a deeper understanding of information need representations and the emergence of common representations between the user and query interface. Further, we investigate the querying and interactions that may span over multiple queries and sessions. A reasonably precise mutual understanding between the user and query interface also improves the effectiveness of ad-hoc and session querying. Moreover, we analyze some equilibria and convergence rates of reaching them for some strategies in the game. Finally, we focus on structured rather than unstructured data.

Researchers in other scientific disciplines, such as economics and sociology, have used signaling games to formally model and explore communications between multiple (rational) agents [12, 7]. Avestani et al. have used signaling games to create a shared lexicon between multiple autonomous systems [3]. We, however, focus on modeling users' information needs and emergence of mutual language between users and database query interfaces. In particular, query interfaces and user may update their information about the interaction in different time scales. We also provide a rigorous analysis of the success of our proposed strategy. Researchers have proposed methods to discover complex search tasks that involve multiple sessions [11, 2, 16]. We focus on establishing a common understanding between the user and query interface in the long run and over a rather large number of possibly simple search tasks.

3. FRAMEWORK

3.1 Basic Definitions

To simplify our model and proofs, we consider a database to be a single relational table. Our results extend for databases with multiple relations. A *database DB* is a finite relation of a fixed arity. Each member of database DB is called an *entity* and shown as $(v_1, \ldots, v_k)$ where $v_1, \ldots, v_k$ are values in DB. Each entity in DB represents information about a single named-entity. To simplify our model, we assume that all values in DB are of type string. A query s over DB is an expression $(u_1, \ldots, u_k)$ where u_i is either a value in DB or a variable. The answer of query $s = (u_1, \ldots, u_k)$ over DB is the set of tuples $(v_1, \ldots, v_k)$ in DB such that if u_i is a value, v_i is lexicographically equal to u_i.

To simplify our model, we assume that users like to find a single entity in the database. Users may submit under-specified queries whose answers contain a lot of non-relevant entities. The query interface may use a ranking function to return top-k entities for the query [5]. Clearly, the set of all under-specified queries over a database is finite. Let $S = \{s_i, 1 \le i \le n\}$ and $I = \{e_i, 1 \le j \le m\}$ be the set of all possible queries and entities, i.e. intents, respectively. We assume that the set of intents have a prior probability π, i.e. $\pi \in \mathbb{R}^m$, $\pi_i \ge 0$ for all i, and $\sum_{i=1}^{m} \pi_i = 1$. In this case π_i is the probability that the user has intent e_i in mind. Without loss of generality we can assume that $\pi_i > 0$ for all $i \in [m]$, otherwise, we can restrict our analysis on the set $\tilde{I} = \{e_i \in I \mid \pi_i > 0\}$.

Throughout this paper, we use the following mathematical notations: For a positive integer $m \ge 1$, we denote $[m] := \{1, \ldots, m\}$. For a vector $u \in \mathbb{R}^m$, we denote the ith entry of u by u_i. Similarly, we denote the (i, j)th entry of an $m \times n$ matrix ($i \in [m], j \in [n]$) by A_{ij}. We also say that A is a row-stochastic matrix (or simply a stochastic matrix) if it is non-negative (i.e. $A_{ij} \ge 0$ for all i, j) and $\sum_{j=1}^{n} A_{ij} = 1$ for all $i \in [m]$. We denote the set of all $m \times n$ stochastic matrices by $\mathcal{L}_{mn}$. For an event A of a probability space

Ω, we use 1_A for the indicator function on the set A, i.e. $1_A(\omega) = 1$ of $\omega \in A$ and $1_A(\omega) = 0$ if $\omega \notin A$.

3.2 A Signaling Game Model

First, let us discuss how we model the interaction between the user and the database as a game. The intent of each user in an interaction is an entity e_i in the database. However, the user does not necessarily know how to formulate the right query for this intent and hence, uses an over- or under-specified query, i.e. signal, s_j to convey her intent. On the other hand, the database is not aware of the intent of the user and it can only base its decision on the signal observed from the user. Therefore, the strategy of the database is also a random mapping from the set of signals to the set of intents to map s_j to an intent e_ℓ. Such an interaction is successful if $e_\ell = e_i$, in other words the database has been successful in decoding the user's signal s_j. Otherwise, the interaction is unsuccessful.

This signaling can be modeled as a signaling game with with identical interests played between the user and the database. In this game, the set of strategies of a user is the set $\mathcal{L}_{mn}$ of row-stochastic matrices and the set of strategies of the database is the set $\mathcal{L}_{nm}$ of $n \times m$ row-stochastic matrices. The payoff of the user and the database in this case are

$$u_1(P, Q) = u_2(P, Q) = \sum_{i=1}^{m} \pi_i \sum_{j=1}^{n} P_{ij} Q_{ji}, \quad (1)$$

where u_1 is the payoff of the user and u_2 is the payoff of the database. The payoff function (1) is an expected payoff of the interaction between the user and the database when the user maps the (random) intent e_i to a signal s_j with probability P_{ij} and the database maps back the signal s_j to e_ℓ with probability $Q_{j\ell}$. The larger the value of this payoff function is, the more likely it is that the query interface returns the desired answers to more users' queries. This payoff structure reflects the widely used performance metric for effective database querying. This setting is very similar to the setting of language games which have been studied extensively in the past [15]. The major difference here is the existence of a none-uniform prior over the intents.

A Nash equilibrium for a game is a combination of strategies where the database system (user) will not do better by unilaterally deviating from its strategy, i.e., $u_1(P, Q) \ge u_1(P, Q')$ for all Q'. A strict Nash equilibrium for a game is a Nash equilibrium in which the database system (user) will do worse by changing its equilibrium strategy, i.e., $u_1(P, Q) > u_1(P, Q')$ for all $Q' \ne Q$. Clearly, the players would like the collaborations to result in equilibria with maximum payoff. The database system and user may adapt some rules and algorithms that update their strategies based on the observed signals to improve their payoff and reach a desired equilibrium. These rules may depend on their degrees of rationalities and/or amount of available resources [12, 7]. Further, the players prefer the collaboration to result in a desired equilibrium in smaller number of interactions.

4. AN ADAPTATION MECHANISM

We consider the case that the user is not adapting to the signaling scheme of the database. In many relevant applications, the user's learning is happening in a much slower time-scale compared to the learning of the database. So, one can assume that the user's strategy is fixed compared to the time-scale of the database adaptation. When dealing with the game introduced in Section 3, many questions arise:

i. How can a database learn or adapt to a user's signaling scheme?

ii. Mathematically, is a given learning rule effective?

iii. What would be the limiting behavior of a given learning rule?

Here, we address the first and the second questions above. Dealing with the third question is far beyond the page limits of this short paper. As in [10], we consider Roth-Erev reinforcement learning mechanism for adaptation of the database adaption. For the case that both the database and the user adapt their strategies, one can use the results in [10]. Let us discuss the database adaptation rule. The learning/adaptation rule happens over discrete time $t = 0, 1, 2, 3, \ldots$ instances where t denoted the tth interaction of the user and the database. We refer to t simply as the iteration of the learning rule. With this, the reinforcement learning mechanism for the database adaptation is as follows:

a. Let $Q(1) = R$ be the initial database strategy with $Q_{j\ell}(0) > 0$ for all $j \in [n]$ and $\ell \in [m]$.

b. For iterations $t = 1, 2, \ldots$, do

   i. If the user's signal at time t is $s(t)$, return a list $E \subseteq I$ of the entities whose cardinality is k with probability:

$$P(E(t) = \{i_1, \ldots, i_k\} \mid s(t)) = Q_{s(t)i_1}(t) \cdots Q_{s(t)i_k}(t).$$

   ii. If the user is satisfied with the list, set

$$R_{ji} = \begin{cases} R_{ji} + 1 & \text{if } j = s(t) \text{ and } j \in E(t) \\ R_{ji} & \text{otherwise} \end{cases} . \quad (2)$$

   iii. Update the database strategy by

$$Q_{ji}(t+1) = \frac{R_{ji}}{\sum_{\ell=1}^{m} R_{j\ell}}, \quad (3)$$

   for all $j \in [n]$ and $i \in [m]$.

In the above scheme R is simply the reward matrix. When the decoding of the signal $s(t)$ using the chosen list $E(t)$ is successful, the database *reinforces* all the pairs $R_{s(t)i}$ for $i \in E(t)$.

Few comments are in order regarding the above adaptation rule:

- One can use available ranking functions, e.g. [5], for the initial conditions $R(1) = Q(1)$ which possibly leads to an intuitive initial point for the learning dynamics. One may normalize and convert the scores returned by these functions to probability values.

- In step b.ii., if the database have the knowledge of the user's intent after the interactions (e.g. through a click), the database set $R_{ji} + 1$ for the known intent e_i. The mathematical analysis of the both cases will be similar.

- In the initial step, as the query interface uses a ranking function to compute the probabilities, it may not materialize the mapping between the intents and queries. As the game progresses, it should maintain the reward values for the seen signals and their returned intents. The number of under-specified queries that return a certain entity is less than to the arity of the database relation, which is normally around 30-50 for most databases. Further, the query interface do not need to store the values in the queries and can store the queries using pointers to the values in their associated entities in the database. Hence, the query interface may efficiently maintain and search the reward table for medium size databases. In practice, the maximum number of under-specified queries is smaller than the arity of the database relation.

5. ANALYSIS OF THE LEARNING RULE

In this section, we provide an analysis of the reinforcement mechanism provided above and will show that, statistically speaking, the adaptation rule leads to improvement of the efficiency of the interaction. The extensive study of this interaction is well beyond the page limits set here. As a result we provide the following simplifying assumption.

ASSUMPTION 5.1. *We assume that the cardinality of the list k is 1.*

Indeed the analytical work provided in this work is extendable to lists with arbitrary cardinality.

For the analysis of the the reinforcement learning mechanism in Section 4 and for simplification, denote

$$u(t) := u_1(P, Q(t)) = u_2(P, Q(t)), \quad (4)$$

where $u_1 = u_2$ is defined in (1).

We recall that a random process $\{X(t)\}$ is a submartingale [8] if

$$E(X(t+1) \mid \mathcal{F}_t) \geq X(t),$$

where $\mathcal{F}_t$ is the σ-algebra generated by $X_1, \ldots, X_t$. In other words, a process $\{X(t)\}$ is a sub-martingale if the expected value of $X(t+1)$ given the past, is not strictly less than the value of X_t.

The main result here is that the random process $u(t)$ defined by (4) is a submartingale when the reinforcement learning rule in Section 4 is utilized. To show this, we discuss an intermediate result. For simplicity of notation, we use superscript $+$ to denote variables at time $(t+1)$ and drop the dependencies at time t for variables depending on time t. Throughout the rest of our discussions, we let $\{\mathcal{F}_t\}$ be the natural filtration for the process $\{Q(t)\}$, i.e. $\mathcal{F}$ is the σ-algebra generated by $P(t)$.

LEMMA 5.2. *For any $i \in [m]$ and $j \in [n]$ (and any time $t \geq 0$), we have*

$$E(Q_{ji}^+ \mid \mathcal{F}_t) - Q_{ji} = \frac{Q_{ji}}{\sum_{\ell'=1}^{m} R_{j\ell'} + 1} \left(\pi_i P_{ij} - u^j(P, Q) \right),$$

where

$$u^j(P, Q) = \sum_{\ell=1}^{m} \pi_\ell P_{\ell j} Q_{j\ell},$$

is the average efficiency of signal j on conveying messages.

PROOF. Fix $i \in [m]$ and $j \in [n]$. Let A be the event that at the t'th iteration, we reinforce a pair (j, ℓ) for some $\ell \in [m]$. Then on the complement A^c of A, $Q_{ji}^+(\omega) = Q_{ji}(\omega)$. Let $A_1 \subseteq A$ be the subset of A such that the pair (j, i) is reinforced and $A_2 = A \setminus A_1$ be the event that some other pair (j, ℓ) is reinforced for $\ell \neq i$.

We note that

$$Q_{ji}^+ = \frac{R_{ji} + 1}{\sum_{\ell=1}^{m} R_{j\ell} + 1} 1_{A_1} + \frac{R_{ji}}{\sum_{\ell=1}^{m} R_{j\ell} + 1} 1_{A_2} + Q_{ji} 1_{A^c}.$$

Therefore, we have

$$E(Q_{ji}^+ \mid \mathcal{F}_t) = \pi_i P_{ij} Q_{ji} \frac{R_{ji} + 1}{\sum_{\ell=1}^{m} R_{j\ell} + 1}$$

$$+ \sum_{\ell \neq j} \pi_\ell P_{\ell j} Q_{j\ell} \frac{R_{ji}}{\sum_{\ell'=1}^{m} R_{j\ell'} + 1} + (1 - p) Q_{ji},$$

where $p = P(A_2 \mid \mathcal{F})$. Note that $Q_{ij} = \frac{R_{ji}}{\sum_{\ell=1}^{m} R_{j\ell}}$ and hence,

$$E(Q_{ji}^{+} \mid \mathcal{F}_t) - Q_{ji} = \frac{1}{\sum_{\ell'=1}^{m} R_{j\ell'} + 1} \left(\pi_i P_{ij} Q_{ji} \sum_{\ell \neq i} Q_{j\ell} \right.$$
$$\left. - \sum_{\ell \neq i} \pi_\ell P_{\ell j} Q_{j\ell} Q_{ji} \right).$$

Replacing $\sum_{\ell \neq i} Q_{j\ell} = 1 - Q_{ji}$ and adding/subtracting $\pi_i P_{ij} Q_{ji} Q_{ji}$ in the term inside the parenthesis in the above equality, we get

$$E(Q_{ji}^{+} \mid \mathcal{F}) - Q_{ji} = \frac{Q_{ji}}{\sum_{\ell'=1}^{m} R_{j\ell'} + 1} \left(\pi_i P_{ij} - u^j(P, Q) \right).$$

$\square$

Using Lemma 5.2, we show that the process $\{u(t)\}$ is a submartingale.

THEOREM 5.3. *Let $\{u(t)\}$ be the sequence given by (4). Then, $\{u(t)\}$ is a submartingale sequence.*

PROOF. Let $u^{+} := u(t+1)$, $u := u(t)$, $u^j := u^j(P(t), Q(t))$ and also define $\tilde{R}^j := \sum_{\ell'=1}^{m} R_{j\ell'} + 1$. Then, using the linearity of conditional expectation and Lemma 5.2, we have:

$$E(u^{+} \mid \mathcal{F}_t) - u = \sum_{i=1}^{m} \sum_{j=1}^{n} \pi_i P_{ij} \left(E(Q_{ji}^{+} \mid \mathcal{F}_t) - Q_{ji} \right)$$

$$= \sum_{i=1}^{m} \sum_{j=1}^{n} \pi_i \frac{P_{ij} Q_{ji}}{\sum_{\ell'=1}^{m} R_{j\ell'} + 1} \left(\pi_i P_{ij} - u^j \right)$$

$$= \sum_{j=1}^{n} \frac{1}{\tilde{R}^j} \left(\sum_{i=1}^{m} Q_{ji} (\pi_i P_{ij})^2 - (u^j)^2 \right). \quad (5)$$

Note that Q is a row-stochastic matrix and hence, $\sum_{i=1}^{m} Q_{ji} = 1$. Therefore, by the Jensen's inequality [8], we have:

$$\sum_{i=1}^{m} Q_{ji} (\pi_i P_{ij})^2 \geq \sum_{i=1}^{m} (Q_{ji} \pi_i P_{ij})^2 = (u^j)^2.$$

Replacing this in the right-hand-side of (5), we conclude that $E(u^{+} \mid \mathcal{F}_t) - u \geq 0$ and hence, the sequence $\{u(t)\}$ is a submartingale. $\square$

The above result implies that the effectiveness of database, stochastically speaking, increases as time progresses when the learning rule in Section 4 is utilized. This is indeed a desirable property for any adapting/learning scheme for database adaptation.

An immediate consequence of Theorem 5.3 is that the efficiency sequence $\{u(t)\}$ is convergent almost surely.

COROLLARY 5.4. *The sequence $\{u(t)\}$ given by (4) converges almost surely.*

PROOF. Note that $0 \leq u(t) \leq mn$ (indeed, a simple application of Hölder's inequality give the bound $u(t) \leq 1$) and hence, $\{u(t)\}$ is a bounded submartingale. Therefore, by the Martingale Convergence Theorem [8], it follows that $\lim_{t \to \infty} u(t)$ exists almost surely. $\square$

6. CONCLUSION & FUTURE WORK

We modeled the interaction between the user and the database query interface as a repeated signaling game, where the players starts with different mapping between signals, i.e. queries, and objects, i.e. desired entities, and like to reach a common mapping. We proposed an adaptation mechanism for the query interface to learn the signaling strategy of the user and prove that this mechanism increases the expected payoff for both user and the query interface in average and converges almost surely. We plan to explore the possible equilibria of this game where the user modifies her signaling strategy with a different rate from the query interface. Further, it may be challenging to efficiently maintain and updated the signaling strategy of the query interface for very large databases. We plan to investigate and address these challenges.

7. ACKNOWLEDGMENTS

We thank anonymous reviewer for useful feedback. Arash Termehchy is supported by the National Science Foundation under grant IIS-1423238.

8. REFERENCES

[1] A. Abouzied, D. Angluin, C. H. Papadimitriou, J. M. Hellerstein, and A. Silberschatz. Learning and verifying quantified boolean queries by example. In *PODS*, pages 49–60, 2013.

[2] E. Agichtein, R. W. White, S. T. Dumais, and P. N. Bennet. Search, interrupted: understanding and predicting search task continuation. In *SIGIR*, 2012.

[3] P. Avesani and M. Cova. Shared lexicon for distributed annotations on the Web. In *WWW*, pages 207–214, 2005.

[4] T. Beckers et al. Report on INEX 2009. *SIGIR Forum*, 44(1):38–57, 2010.

[5] S. Chaudhuri, G. Das, V. Hristidis, and G. Weikum. Probabilistic information retrieval approach for ranking of database query results. *ACM Trans. Database Syst.*, 31(3):1134–1168, 2006.

[6] Y. Chen, W. Wang, Z. Liu, and X. Lin. Keyword search on structured and semi-structured data. In *SIGMOD*, 2009.

[7] I. Cho and D. Kreps. Signaling games and stable equilibria. *Quarterly Journal of Economics*, 102:179–221, 1987.

[8] R. Durrett. *Probability: theory and examples*. Cambridge university press, 2010.

[9] N. Fuhr and T. Rolleke. A probabilistic relational algebra for the integration of information retrieval and database systems. *TOIS*, 15, 1997.

[10] Y. Hu, B. Skyrms, and P. Tarrès. Reinforcement learning in signaling game. *arXiv preprint arXiv:1103.5818*, 2011.

[11] A. Kotov, P. N. Bennett, R. W. White, S. T. Dumais, and J. Teevan. Modeling and analysis of cross-session search tasks. In *SIGIR*, 2011.

[12] D. Lewis. *Convention*. Cambridge: Harvard University Press, 1969.

[13] J. Luo, S. Zhang, and H. Yang. Win-win search: Dual-agent stochastic game in session search. In *SIGIR*, 2014.

[14] A. Nandi and H. V. Jagadish. Guided interaction: Rethinking the query-result paradigm. *PVLDB*, 102, 2011.

[15] M. A. Nowak and D. C. Krakauer. The evolution of language. *Proceedings of the National Academy of Sciences*, 96(14):8028–8033, 1999.

[16] H. Wang, Y. Song, M.-W. Chang, X. He, R. W. White, and W. Chu. Learning to extract cross-session search tasks. In *WWW*, 2013.

Study of Heuristic IR Constraints Under Function Discovery Framework

Parantapa Goswami   Massih-Reza Amini   Eric Gaussier

Université Grenoble Alps,
CNRS - LIG/AMA
Grenoble, France
firstname.lastname@imag.fr

ABSTRACT

In this paper we investigate the effect of the heuristic IR constraints on IR term-document scoring functions within the recently proposed function discovery framework. In the earlier study the constraints were empirically validated as a whole. Moreover, only the group of form constraints was utilized and the other prominent group, the adjustment constraints, was not considered. In this work we will investigate all the constraints individually and study them with two different term frequency normalization, namely normalization scheme used in DFR models and relative term count normalization used in language models.

Categories and Subject Descriptors

H.3 [**Information Storage and Retrieval**]: Information Search and Retrieval - Search process

Keywords

IR Theory; Function Discovery; Heuristic IR Constraints;

1. INTRODUCTION

Fang et. al. [4] proposed a set of constraints which all "good" IR scoring functions should follow. These are divided in two categories, form and adjustment constraints (details are in Section 3). Among them Clinchant and Gaussier [2, 3] expressed the form constraints in terms of first and second order derivatives of the IR scoring function. They also studied these constraints under pseudo-relevance feedback (PRF) framework and derived conditions that PRF models should satisfy. However, these studies did not consider the other important category - the adjustment constraints.

In the recently proposed function discovery approach [6] the form constraints are successfully used as a tool to prune the search space. It is ensured that the generated functions satisfy the form constraints. An experimental validation of these constraints is also provided in light of the proposed framework, which is inline with other empirical validations of these constraints [9, 5].

ICTIR'15, September 27–30, Northampton, MA, USA.
© 2015 ACM. ISBN 978-1-4503-3833-2/15/09 ...$15.00.
DOI: DOI: http://dx.doi.org/10.1145/2808194.2809479.

However, in the original study [6] these constraints are considered together as a single module. In this paper we will investigate the effect of each individual form constraint on the scoring functions through function discovery framework. We will also investigate two adjustment constraints, which were not considered in the original work. We will do so by taking into account two different term frequency normalization techniques, namely the normalization used in divergence from randomness (DFR) models [1] and relative term count normalization used in language models [7].

2. FUNCTION DISCOVERY FRAMEWORK

The general form of retrieval status value or RSV of a document d with respect to a query q can be formulated as:

$$\text{RSV}(q, d) = \sum_{w \in q} a(t_w^q) \ g(w, d)$$

Where, t_w^q is the number of occurrences of term w within query q, $a : \mathbb{R}^+ \to \mathbb{R}^+$ is a positive real-valued function usually set to the identity function and the function $g(w, d)$ is called a scoring function which assigns a score to d for a term $w \in q$. Standard IR models like BM25 [8], language models [7], information based models [2], DFR models [1] etc. all fit in the form of the above equation; and depending on the model in use, the form of the scoring function varies. Table 1 summarizes notations used throughout the paper.

t_w^d	term frequency - # of occurrences of term w in document d
t_w^q	# of occurrences of term w in query q
x_w^d	normalized version of term frequency
$\mathcal{N}_w$	document frequency - # of documents in the collection containing w
y_w	normalized version of document frequency
$\mathcal{N}$	# of documents in a given collection
l_d	Length of document d in # of terms
l_{avg}	Average length of documents in a given collection

Table 1: Notations

The function discovery approach [6] deploys a context free grammar to generate closed form formulas to be used as scoring functions. Two variables are considered in that grammar, normalized term frequency denoted by x_w^d and normalized document frequency denoted by y_w. A real valued constant is also considered, but in experiments it is taken as 1 which we follow here as well. Thus scoring functions in this framework can also be written as $g(x_w^d, y_w)$.

Normalized term frequency can be expressed as a function of t_w^d and l_d, in the form $NTF(t_w^d, l_d)$. [6] considers normalization used in DFR models (DFR normalization) and in this study we also consider relative term count (RTC) normalization, a variation of which is commonly used in language models. Thus one has:

$$NTF(t_w^d, l_d) = \begin{cases} t_w^d \log\left(1 + c\frac{l_{avg}}{l_d}\right) & \text{DFR normalization} \\ t_w^d \left(\frac{l_{avg}}{l_d}\right) & \text{RTC normalization} \end{cases}$$

Here c is a free parameter which is taken as 1, its default value, in this work.

The normalized document frequency of a term w considered in [6], as well as in this study, is the average document frequency of w with respect to the total number of documents in the collection, $y_w = \frac{N_w}{N}$.

3. HEURISTIC IR CONSTRAINTS

Fang et. al. [4] proposed a set of hypothetical constraints which lays a guideline of how a *good* IR scoring function should behave. The constraints are categorized into two groups, four *form constraints* and two *adjustment constraints*.

3.1 Form Constraints

Four form constraints define the general form of the scoring function g. Firstly, the documents with higher term frequency are more important and should get higher score than the documents with less term frequency. This is called *TF effect*. This increase of score with term frequency must be restricted for higher frequency values. As for example, the increase from 100 to 101 (only 1% increase) is much less significant than the increase from 1 to 2 (100% increase). Mathematically this can be ensured by imposing a concave form on the function g, giving the constraint *concavity effect*. Next constraint, known as *IDF effect*, ensures that the scores for very frequent terms in the collection, i.e. the terms with high document frequencies (or low inverse document frequencies), are weighed down as these terms are most commonly used terms, thus have little importance. Lastly the *document length effect* takes into account that for documents of different lengths with same number of occurrences of the term, the longer documents tends to cover additional irrelevant topics than shorter ones, thus the scoring function should penalize the longer documents over the shorter ones. These constraints are expressed in the following analytical forms [2]:

$$\underbrace{\frac{\partial g}{\partial t_w^d} > 0}_{\text{TF Effect}}; \quad \underbrace{\frac{\partial^2 g}{\partial (t_w^d)^2} < 0}_{\text{concavity effect}}; \quad \underbrace{\frac{\partial g}{\partial N_w} < 0}_{\text{IDF effect}}; \quad \underbrace{\frac{\partial g}{\partial l_d} < 0}_{\text{doc. len. effect}}$$

Considering DFR term frequency normalization and $y = \frac{N_w}{N}$, [6] has shown that it is sufficient for a scoring function g to satisfy the following three conditions, denoted by C1, C2 and C3 respectively:

$$\underbrace{\frac{\partial g}{\partial x} > 0}_{\text{C1}}, \quad \underbrace{\frac{\partial^2 g}{\partial x^2} < 0}_{\text{C2}}, \quad \underbrace{\frac{\partial g}{\partial y} < 0}_{\text{C3}}$$

For RTC normalization it is also trivial to show that these three conditions are sufficient for any scoring function to satisfy all the form constraints.

During function generation, it is hence ensured that the generated scoring functions must satisfy C1, C2 and C3. As these constraints are the same for both DFR and RTC normalization, all the generated scoring functions will satisfy the constraints for any of the two normalization schemes.

3.2 Adjustment Constraints

Two *adjustment constraints* aim to adjust the function g satisfying the form constraints by regulating the interaction between term frequency t_w^d and document length l_d. These two constraints are:

C4 Let q be a query. $\forall k > 1$, if d_1 and d_2 are two documents such that $l_{d_1} = k \times l_{d_2}$ and for all terms w, $t_w^{d_1} = k \times t_w^{d_2}$, then $\text{RSV}(q, d_1) \geq \text{RSV}(q, d_2)$.

C5 Let $q = w$ be a single term query, for two documents d_1 and d_2 if $t_w^{d_1} > t_w^{d_2}$ and $l_{d_1} = l_{d_2} + (t_w^{d_1} - t_w^{d_2})$, then $\text{RSV}(q, d_1) \geq \text{RSV}(q, d_2)$.

Document length effect (fourth form constraint) penalizes longer documents, whereas the first adjustment constraint C4 avoids over-penalizing long documents. The second adjustment constraint C5 ensures that a longer document must not be penalized over a shorter document if the excess length is due to the occurrences of the query term.

We present here two properties which will help to study the effect of adjustment constraints over the function discovery framework.

PROPERTY 1. *If a function generated by the function discovery approach using RTC and DFR normalization satisfies* C1, C2 *and* C3, *then the function also satisfies* C4.

PROPERTY 2. *If a function generated by the function discovery approach using RTC normalization satisfies* C1, C2 *and* C3, *then the function satisfies* C5. *If the function is generated using DFR normalization and satisfies* C1, C2 *and* C3, *then it satisfies* C5 *when* $t_w^{d_2} \leq \frac{p.f_1(p)}{f_1(0) - f_1(p)}$ *where* $p = t_w^{d_1} - t_w^{d_2}$, $f_1(u) = \log\left(\frac{l_{d_2} + u + \beta}{l_{d_2} + u}\right)$ *and* $\beta = c.l_{avg}$. *Here* $t_w^{d_1}, t_w^{d_2}, l_{d_2}$ *are as explained in the definition of* C5.

We now proceed to prove these properties. We do so by first proving the two following lemmas.

LEMMA 1. *For a term w if there are two documents d_1 and d_2 such that for any $k > 0$, their normalized term frequencies are $x_w^{d_1} = NTF(k \times t_w^{d_2}, k \times l_{d_2})$ and $x_w^{d_2} = NTF(t_w^{d_2}, l_{d_2})$ respectively, then $x_w^{d_1} \geq x_w^{d_2}$.*

PROOF. Assuming RTC normalization, one has $x_w^{d_1} = x_w^{d_2}$, thus proving the property.
For DFR normalization it can be shown that:

$$x_w^{d_1} - x_w^{d_2} = t_w^{d_2} \log\left(\frac{(k+\alpha)^k}{k(1+\alpha)}\right) \quad \text{assuming } \alpha = c\frac{l_{avg}}{l_{d_2}}$$

Applying binomial expansion:

$$(k+\alpha)^k - k(1+\alpha) = (k^k - k) + (k^k - k)\alpha + \ldots + \alpha > 0$$

This is because the term $(k^k - k) > 0$ as $k > 0$, and all the remaining terms of the expression are positive. Thus we have $\left(\frac{(k+\alpha)^k}{k(1+\alpha)}\right) > 1$ giving that $x_w^{d_1} - x_w^{d_2} \geq 0$ as $t_w^{d_2} \geq 0$, which proves the property for DFR normalization. □

LEMMA 2. *For a term w if there are two documents d_1 and d_2 such that for any integer $p > 1$, their normalized term frequencies are $x_w^{d_1} = NTF(t_w^{d_2} + p, l_{d_2} + p)$ and $x_w^{d_2} = NTF(t_w^{d_2}, l_{d_2})$ respectively, then:*

- *for RTC normalization $x_w^{d_1} \geq x_w^{d_2}$,*

- *for DFR normalization $x_w^{d_1} \geq x_w^{d_2}$ when $t_w^{d_2} \leq \frac{p.f_1(p)}{f_1(0)-f_1(p)}$*

    where $f_1(u) = \log\left(\frac{l_{d_2}+u+\beta}{l_{d_2}+u}\right)$ and $\beta = c.l_{avg}$.

PROOF. For RTC normalization $x_w^{d_1} - x_w^{d_2} = \frac{p(l_{d_2}-t_w^{d_2})}{l_{d_2}(l_{d_2}+p)} \geq 0$ since $l_{d_2} \geq t_w^{d_2}$, which proves the property.
For DFR normalization it can be derived that:

$$x_w^{d_1} - x_w^{d_2} = (t_w^{d_2} + p) \log\left(\frac{l_{d_2}+p+\beta}{l_{d_2}+p}\right) - t_w^{d_2} \log\left(\frac{l_{d_2}+\beta}{l_{d_2}}\right)$$
$$(\text{assuming } \beta = c.l_{avg})$$
$$= (t_w^{d_2}+p)f_1(p) - t_w^{d_2}f_1(0)$$

Let $f_2(t_w^{d_2}) = (t_w^{d_2}+p)f_1(p) - t_w^{d_2}f_1(0)$, then $f_2(t_w^{d_2})$ is a strictly decreasing function with $t_w^{d_2}$ as $f_2'(t_w^{d_2}) < 0$. We have $f_2(0) = p.f_1(p) > 0$, but $f_2(t_w^{d_2}) \to -\infty$ as $t_w^{d_2} \to +\infty$. Thus $f_2(t_w^{d_2})$ crosses zero at $t_w^{d_2} = \frac{p.f_1(p)}{f_1(0)-f_1(p)}$. So $x_w^{d_1} - x_w^{d_2} \geq 0$ when $t_w^{d_2} \leq \frac{p.f_1(p)}{f_1(0)-f_1(p)}$, thus proving the property for DFR normalization. □

Since queries are considered as set of terms and the order is not considered, $RSV(q, d_1) \geq RSV(q, d_2)$ is equivalent to $g(w, d_1) \geq g(w, d_2)$ (here we used the original form of the scoring functions as in Eq. 2). As g is satisfying C1, i. e. $\frac{\partial g}{\partial x_w^d} > 0$, one has $g(x_w^{d_1}, y) \geq g(x_w^{d_2}, y)$ iff $x_w^{d_1} \geq x_w^{d_2}$. Hence the adjustment constraint C4 boils down to the Lemma 1, which is true, as shown above, for all the scoring functions generated using the function discovery approach with both DFR and RTC normalization. Thus all generated scoring functions satisfy C4 proving Property 1.

Suppose $p > 0$ is an integer constant such that $t_w^{d_1} = t_w^{d_2} + p$. Then this constraint can be rewritten as, if $l_{d_1} = l_{d_2} + p$ then $RSV(q, d_1) > RSV(q, d_2)$. Again as g is satisfying C1, one has $g(x_w^{d_1}, y) \geq g(x_w^{d_2}, y)$ iff $x_w^{d_1} \geq x_w^{d_2}$. Thus the adjustment constraint C5 becomes Lemma 2 and is always satisfied by the generated functions if RTC normalization is used. But for DFR normalization C5 is satisfied only when $t_w^{d_2} \leq \frac{p.f_1(p)}{f_1(0)-f_1(p)}$ where $f_1(u) = \log\left(\frac{l_{d_2}+u+\beta}{l_{d_2}+u}\right)$ and $\beta = c.l_{avg}$. This proves Property 2. So for DFR normalization a generated function satisfies C5 for not so high t_w^d values which is the case in most practical scenarios.

4. EXPERIMENTAL EVALUATION

Experiments are performed on six IR collections (Table 2), five from TREC (trec.nist.gov) and one from CLEF (www.clef-campaign.org) campaigns. These collections are indexed using Terrier IR Platform v3.5 (terrier.org). Preprocessing steps in creating an index include stemming using Porter stemmer and removing stop-words using the stopword list provided by Terrier. Generated functions are also implemented in Terrier.

Several sets are created while the functions till a given length[1] are generated. The set of functions which satisfy all

[1] As defined in [6] the *length of a function* is the number of symbols or operators present in that function, e.g. *sqrt(x/y)* has a length 4.

Collection	$\mathcal{N}$	l_{avg}	Index size	#queries
TREC-3	741,856	261	427.7 MB	50
TREC-5	524,929	339	378.0 MB	50
TREC-6,7,8	528,155	296	373.0 MB	50
CLEF-3	169,477	301	126.2 MB	60

Table 2: Statistics of various collections used in our experiments, sorted by size.

the constraints is specified by $\mathcal{C}_V$, whereas the set of functions which satisfy none of the constraints is specified by $\mathcal{C}_N$. Moreover $\mathcal{C}_N^i$ is the set of functions which satisfy only the constraint Ci, e.g. functions of $\mathcal{C}_N^1$ satisfy only C1 and none of C2 and C3. Note that, by Property 1, the conditions C1, C2 and C3 are sufficient for C4 for both RTC and DFR normalization. According to Property 2 same holds for C5 with RTC normalization and for most practical cases with DFR normalization. Thus in these experiments we concentrate on studying C1, C2 and C3.

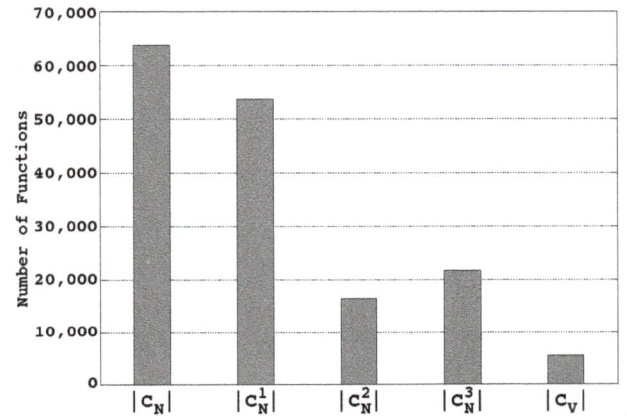

Figure 1: Number of functions in the sets $\mathcal{C}_N$, $\mathcal{C}_N^1$, $\mathcal{C}_N^2$, $\mathcal{C}_N^3$ and $\mathcal{C}_V$ till length 8.

Performances of $\mathcal{C}_V$ and $\mathcal{C}_N$ are compared in [6] to empirically justify the usefulness of the heuristic IR constraints as a whole. Here we study all three conditions separately. An initial intuition can be made by the sizes of the sets $\mathcal{C}_N^1$, $\mathcal{C}_N^2$ and $\mathcal{C}_N^3$. Figure 1 shows the number of functions till length 8 in each of the sets. Clearly the number of functions satisfying C2 is the minimum, whereas the number of functions satisfying C1 is the maximum. Thus the constraint C2 is the harshest one, whereas C1 is the loosest one. Another trivial yet interesting observation is that $\mathcal{C}_N$ is the biggest set and $\mathcal{C}_V$ is the smallest one among all the five sets.

Next, from each of the sets $\mathcal{C}_V$, $\mathcal{C}_N^1$, $\mathcal{C}_N^2$, $\mathcal{C}_N^3$ and $\mathcal{C}_N$, 10 subsets are created. Each subset contains 100 randomly selected sample functions chosen from the initial set. When creating a subset, 100 functions are selected without replacement. When creating another different subset, again all functions are considered for selection. Thus a function may be repeated in different subsets but never within the same subset. These samples are tested on CLEF-3 and TREC-3,5,6,7,8. For each function MAP is noted and it is averaged over all 100 functions within a single sample set. Finally, average performance over 10 sample sets is reported.

Figure 2 shows a plot of average MAP of 10 sample sets from all five sets $\mathcal{C}_N$, $\mathcal{C}_N^1$, $\mathcal{C}_N^2$, $\mathcal{C}_N^3$ and $\mathcal{C}_V$ with DFR and RTC normalization. As expected $\mathcal{C}_V$ is always best and $\mathcal{C}_N$ is always worst among the five sets. Performance of other three sets $\mathcal{C}_N^1$, $\mathcal{C}_N^2$ and $\mathcal{C}_N^3$ are in between $\mathcal{C}_V$ and $\mathcal{C}_N$. Both for DFR

367

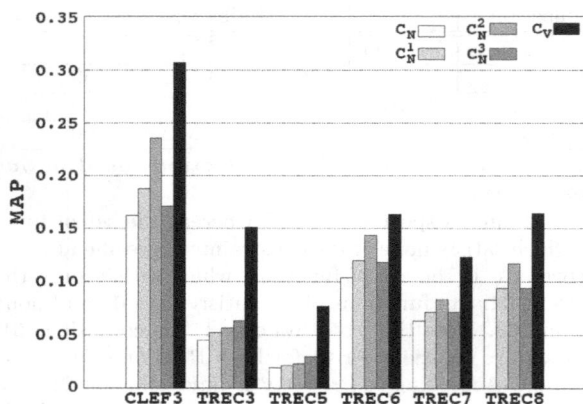

(a) DFR

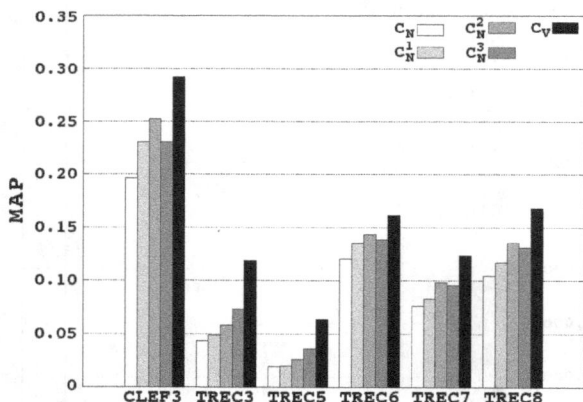

(b) RTC

Figure 2: Average MAP of the sets $\mathcal{C}_N$ ($\square$), $\mathcal{C}_N^1$ ($\blacksquare$), $\mathcal{C}_N^2$ ($\blacksquare$), $\mathcal{C}_N^3$ ($\blacksquare$) **and** $\mathcal{C}_V$ ($\blacksquare$) **till length 8 with (a) DFR and (b) RTC normalization.**

and RTC, C2 is best performing on 4 out of 6 collections. Whereas for TREC-3 and TREC-5 C3 is slightly better than C2. There is no deterministic comparative pattern between C1 and C3. All possible relative orders in terms of performance between C1 and C3 are visible. As for example in case of DFR (Figure 2(a)) C1>C3 on CLEF-3, C1<C3 on TREC-3,5 and C1≈C3 on TREC-6,7,8. But for RTC C1<C3 for 4 out of 6 collections (Figure 2(b)). In summary the general trend is that C2 is the most effective among three constraints although the plots display an inconclusive pattern. Thus it can be said that the relative effectiveness of the constraints is highly dependent on the collection in hand.

Above experiments are performed to study the effects of each constraint. But these experiments also revealed that combination of all the constraints (i.e. set $\mathcal{C}_V$) always performs best. Hence for all practical purposes it is always better to utilize all the constraints together.

5. CONCLUSION

In this paper we showed that the first adjustment constraint is satisfied by all the functions generated using the approach proposed in [6] with both DFR and RTC normalization, as the generation method already ensure that the functions always satisfy C1, C2 and C3. The second adjustment constraint is always satisfied by all the generated functions for RTC normalization, but for DFR normalization it

is satisfied only for not so high t_w^d values which is the case in most practical scenarios. Thus revealing that for most practical purposes it is sufficient for the generated functions to satisfy three conditions C1, C2 and C3. However, a detailed experimental study of C5 for DFR normalization is required to better understand the condition derived in Property 2.

We experimentally studied the effects of each form constraint separately and found that C2 is the harshest among the three as it allows minimum number of functions. According to performances, for both DFR and RTC normalization, on most collections C2 is more effective than C1 and C3 and there is no deterministic pattern between C1 and C3.

Here we have studied the constraints for DFR and RTC normalization, as three constraints C1, C2 and C3 takes the same form with these two normalization schemes. For Okapi, the other popular normalization scheme, the forms of these constraints changes thus generating entirely different sets of valid functions.

Acknowledgment. This work was supported in part by the project AAP18 FUI Smart Support Center.

6. REFERENCES

[1] G. Amati and C. van Rijsbergen. Probabilistic models of information retrieval based on measuring the divergence from randomness. *ACM Transactions on Information Systems (TOIS)*, 20(4):357–389, 2002.

[2] S. Clinchant and E. Gaussier. Information-based models for ad hoc IR. In *Proceedings of the 33rd Annual International ACM SIGIR Conference on Research and Development in Information Retrieval*, pages 234–241. ACM, 2010.

[3] S. Clinchant and E. Gaussier. Retrieval constraints and word frequency distributions a log-logistic model for IR. *Information Retrieval*, 14(1):5–25, 2011.

[4] H. Fang, T. Tao, and C. Zhai. A formal study of information retrieval heuristics. In *Proceedings of the 27th Annual International ACM SIGIR Conference on Research and Development in Information Retrieval*, pages 49–56. ACM, 2004.

[5] H. Fang, T. Tao, and C. Zhai. Diagnostic evaluation of information retrieval models. *ACM Transactions on Information Systems (TOIS)*, 29(2):7:1–7:42, 2011.

[6] P. Goswami, S. Moura, E. Gaussier, M.-R. Amini, and F. Maes. Exploring the space of IR functions. In *Proceedings of the 36th European Conference on Information Retrieval (ECIR)*, pages 372–384. Springer, 2014.

[7] J. Ponte and W. Croft. A language modeling approach to information retrieval. In *Proceedings of the 21st Annual International ACM SIGIR Conference on Research and Development in Information Retrieval*, pages 275–281. ACM, 1998.

[8] S. E. Robertson and H. Zaragoza. The probabilistic relevance framework: Bm25 and beyond. *Foundations and Trends in Information Retrieval*, 3(4):333–389, 2009.

[9] W. Zheng and H. Fang. Axiomatic approaches to information retrieval – university of delaware at TREC 2009 million query and web tracks. In *Proceedings of The Eighteenth Text REtrieval Conference, TREC 2009*. National Institute of Standards and Technology (NIST), 2009.

Theoretical Categorization of Query Performance Predictors

Victor Makarenkov
makarenk@post.bgu.ac.il

Bracha Shapira
bshapira@bgu.ac.il

Lior Rokach
liorrk@bgu.ac.il

Department of Information Systems Engineering
Ben-Gurion University of the Negev
Beer-Sheva, Israel

ABSTRACT

The query-performance prediction task aims at estimating the retrieval effectiveness of queries without obtaining relevance feedback from users. Most of the recently proposed predictors were empirically evaluated with various datasets to demonstrate their merits. We propose a framework for *theoretical* categorization and estimation of the value of query performance predictors (QPP) without empirical evaluation. We demonstrate the application of the proposed framework on four representative selected predictors and show how it emphasizes their strengths and weaknesses. The main contribution of this work is the theoretical grounded categorization of representative QPP.

Categories and Subject Descriptors

H.3.3 [**Information Search and Retrieval**]: Retrieval Models

Keywords

query-performance prediction, categorization, theoretical evaluation

1. INTRODUCTION

The task of query performance prediction without relevance feedback is challenging and has attracted a lot of research attention recently [3]. Pre-retrieval prediction takes place before the retrieval process itself [13, 3, 12], uses query and corpus statistics and is very computationally efficient [12]. Post-retrieval prediction rather operates after the retrieval process and utilizes the result list [20, 3]. Post retrieval prediction is considered to have a superior performance over the pre-retrieval prediction methods [3]. All studies in the field describe empirically evaluated results of different pre-retrieval and post-retrieval QPPs [11, 10, 4, 1]. The reported evaluations are mainly based on TREC datasets along with their existing relevance judgments. An

empirical evaluation is based on applying the predictors on queries[1] and comparing the obtained result list with existing relevance judgments supplied by TREC. Typically [9], the evaluation measures that are being used to evaluate the predictors include:

- Pearson, Kendall-τ, Spearman-Rho or linear correlation between the prediction score of the query and the actual value of this query's average precision [9, 12].

- Root mean squared error (RMSE) between the predicted average precision and the ground truth AP@1000 [13].

A different approach to increase the level of rigor of QPPs evaluation is the theoretical analysis and categorization of the predictors. Applying such analysis, it is possible to compare the relative strengths and weaknesses of predictors and develop different QPP-suites. Theoretical categorization of QPPs can be based on several *properties* that every QPP can either satisfy or not. This analysis would enable the partitioning of the different predictors to a more fine-grained categorization than the common four groups of pre-retrieval predictors: *specificity, coherency, similarity and term relatedness* [3].

Analytical and theoretical evaluation is atypical in the applied field of query performance prediction and estimation. The main contribution of this work is the theoretical framework for QPP that enables categorization of a selected and representative QPP suite.

2. RELATED WORK

Theoretical and analytical evaluation of measures and metrics exists in other fields. For example, such analytics have been associated with software engineering for several decades. Weyuker introduced a formal analytical method to evaluate measures for sequential programs that became popular and very well-known [21]. She proposed addressing software programs as a *sequence* of statements, which altogether create a single program or computational function. Weyuker's properties of the framework were adapted to other fields as well. In particular, Chidamber and Kemerer adapted Weyuker's approach for object-oriented programming metrics [5], and incorporated it with Bunge's [2] view of ontologies to define a class as two *sets* of its attributes and methods and used it to define class equivalence and combination. Later, Makarenkov and Balaban adjusted Weyuker's

---

[1] For example [20, 13] use titles of TREC topics for queries

ICTIR'15, September 27–30, Northampton, MA, USA.
© 2015 ACM. ISBN 978-1-4503-3833-2/15/09 ...$15.00.
DOI: http://dx.doi.org/10.1145/2808194.2809475.

properties-based analytical evaluation for conceptual modeling analysis [16, 17] within UML class diagrams, likewise Chidamber and Kemerer, utilizing the *set-theoretical* approach. In the course of this work, the adapted properties are not required to be necessary nor sufficient. Previously proposed axiomatic approaches and constraints [7, 8] in the information retrieval community are described as *intuitive* and *reasonable* for heuristic capturing of TF and IDF concepts.

3. OUR APPROACH

From the user's point of view, a typical information retrieval scenario is an iterative process during which the user expresses an information need through an initial query. For each iteration, until satisfied, the user reformulates the query and refines the search according to the responses returned from the former iteration. Sometimes, the user completely changes the search topic, i.e., the user might define a new information need, and actually start a new ad-hoc search session resulting in a complete query reformulation and considerably different results list in response. Put otherwise, during a search session the user tries to *predict* which term sequence will most-likely *hit* the desired documents in the collection. In order to formally introduce properties for the QPP categorization with respect to the above information retrieval process, we first define the following notations.

3.1 Notations and Definitions

We define query to be a bag of terms t_i such that $q =< t_1, ..., t_i, ..., t_n >$. We define $D_q^{[k]}$ - the result list of the k most highly ranked documents in response to the query q. D is the document corpus, on which the query is applied.

1. **Semantic Query Near-Equivalence.** Two queries q_1, q_2 are semantically near equivalent if the queries share some percentage α of the top k result lists: $|D_{q_1}^{[k]} \cap D_{q_2}^{[k]}| = \alpha \times k$. For example, by setting $\alpha = 0.99$ we get two results lists that share 99% common documents, making the lists almost identical.

2. **Query Combination.** We define two queries q_1, q_2 to be $q_1 =< t_{11}, ..., t_{1n} >$ and $q_2 =< t_{21}, ..., t_{2m} >$. The combination of these two queries $q_3 = q_1 + q_2$ is a query with $n + m$ terms, defined by a concatenation of the both queries terms. We define $q_3 =< t_{11}, ..., t_{1n}, t_{21}, ..., t_{2m} >$. The limitation of this definition is that adding a term to a query can either raise or reduce the level of query ambiguity, thus not consistently reflecting query effectiveness.

3.2 Query Performance Predictors Properties:

In this work we focus and assume a bag-of-words terms representation under a unigram language model [18]. This implies that some other sensors or dynamics included in other retrieval models are not supported in the framework. We now present seven analytic properties P_1 to P_7 that can be used to evaluate the performance of predictors. These properties are adjustments to properties defined by Weyuker for software development:

- P_1 **Non-Coarseness.** A predictor QPP satisfies non-coarseness if there are two distinct queries $q_1 \neq q_2$ such that $QPP(q_1) \neq QPP(q_2)$. This implies that not

all queries can have the same value for a predictor, otherwise it has no value as a prediction tool.

- P_2 **Finiteness.** A predictor QPP satisfies finiteness if there is a finite number of queries q with the same value of predictor QPP.

- P_3 **Non-Uniqueness.** A predictor QPP satisfies non-uniqueness if there are two distinct queries $q_1 \neq q_2$ such that $QPP(q_1) = QPP(q_2)$. This indicates that semantic query properties are being measured. Two different queries are able to have the same prediction value.

- P_4 **Syntactic Sensitivity.** A predictor QPP satisfies syntactic sensitivity if there are two distinct queries $q_1 \neq q_2$ which are semantically near-equivalent $q_1 \equiv q_2$, having nearly similar result-list, such that $QPP(q_1) \neq QPP(q_2)$. This means that the predictor QPP distinguishes syntactic differences that have little semantic effect.

- P_5 **Monotonicity.** A predictor QPP satisfies monotonicity if for every two queries q_1, q_2 , $QPP(q_1) \leq QPP(q_1 + q_2)$ and $QPP(q_2) \leq QPP(q_1 + q_2)$. Put otherwise, query combination cannot decrease a predictor's value. For example consider the *Query Length* (QL) predictor [12]. QL is defined by the numerosity of its bag-of-terms. Because of triangle inequality which holds for the size of *bag* of terms and *query combination* defined above, QL satisfies this property.

- P_6 **Combination Sensitivity.** A predictor QPP satisfies combination sensitivity if there are three queries q_1, q_2, q_3 such that $QPP(q_1) = QPP(q_2)$ but $QPP(q_1 + q_3) \neq QPP(q_2 + q_3)$.

- P_7 **Interaction Increases Complexity.** A predictor QPP satisfies interaction increases complexity if there are two queries q_1, q_2 such that $QPP(q_1) + QPP(q_2) < QPP(q_1 + q_2)$. The intuitive principle behind this property is that combination of two queries produces an entirely new query, whose performance is different from the two queries apart.

In her original work [21] Weyuker used another *reordering* property. Weyuker did so in order to capture the reordering of computational statements which change the actual function being computed by a sequential program. This property is not useful in the current work due to our bag-of-words unigram retrieval method which disregards the term ordering of a query.

4. THEORETICAL ANALYSIS

We turn to analytical analysis of several predictors. We assume a finite alphabet Σ and a finite lexicon $L \subset \Sigma^*$ such that $|L| >> 1$. The terms t_i of a query belong to L, that is $t_i \in L$. We denote $\{StopWords\} \subset L$ is the set of the stop words. Some properties satisfaction depends on the document collection. In such cases we assume a large collection like TREC GOV2 and the English language.

For the analysis we chose four representative predictors, two are pre-retrieval and two are post-retrieval. We theoretically analyze these predictors, and show how their categorization is further refined.

Table 1: Results of theoretical evaluation of predictors V denotes a satisfied property. X denotes a non-satisfied property. (D) denotes a property whose satisfaction might also depend on a corpus.

Predictor / Property	Non Coarseness	Finiteness	Non Uniqueness	Syntactic Sensitivity	Monotonicity	Combination Sensitivity	Interaction Increases Complexity
Query Length	V	V	V	V	V	X	X
Query Scope	V	V	V(D)	V	X	V	X
LAC	V	V	V	V	V	V	X
Clarity Score	V	V	V	V	X	V	X

- **Query Length(QL)** [12]. QL is defined to be the number of non-stop words in the query[2]. This is probably the simplest pre-retrieval QPP. However, it is theoretically well-grounded, as we refer to Bunge's [2] definition of object's complexity as the numerosity of its composition.
  Theoretical analysis: Obviously QL satisfies non-coarseness for $q_1 =< t_1 >$ and $q_2 =< t_2, t_3 >$ such that $t_1, t_2, t_3 \in L$ and $t_1, t_2, t_3 \notin \{StopWords\}$. It also satisfies finiteness because of the assumptions made for this evaluation[3]. Non-uniqueness is satisfied - for two queries $q_1 =< t_1 >, q_2 =< t_2 >$ and $t_1 \neq t_2$. The combination of syntactic sensitivity depends on the collection D and the specific retrieval method, however, for large collections (like TREC GOV2) this property is satisfied for any $q_1 =< t_1, t_2 >$ and $q_2 =< t_1 >$ such that t_1 does not occur in the collection. Monotonicity holds since for every two queries $QL(q_1) = QL(q_1 + q_2)$ and $QL(q_2) = QL(q_1 + q_2)$. Combination sensitivity is *not* satisfied due to the definition of query combination as a concatenation of query terms. The interaction increases complexity property is *not* satisfied for the same reasons as the combination sensitivity property.

- **Query Scope (QS)** [12]. QS is a post-retrieval QPP which is defined as $QS = -\log \frac{n_Q}{|D|}$ where n_Q is the number of documents containing at least one of the query terms and $|D|$ is the number of documents in the entire collection.
  Theoretical analysis: For a non-trivial L and D, QS satisfies non coarseness. Because of the assumptions regarding the lexicon's size, the finiteness property is satisfied as well. Although satisfaction of the non-uniqueness property strongly depends on the collection D, it is very reasonable to assume that in the course of this work we can state the satisfaction of this property. Syntactic-sensitivity is obviously satisfied for any α. Because QS is a decreasing function of n_Q monotonicity is *not* satisfied. Combination sensitivity holds, if q_1, q_2, q_3 such that q_1 and q_2 have no terms in common, but q_3 is overlapping with q_1 by one term t such that $t \notin q_2$. Then if q_3 has no common terms with q_2, $QS(q_1 + q_3) \neq QS(q_2 + q_3)$. Interaction increases complexity is *not* satisfied.

- **LAC** [13]. LAC is a document collection independent pre-retrieval predictor, which is designed to estimate the *absolute* query difficulty based on Wikipedia. Recall that most common pages on Wikipedia are *entity*

pages, which refer to people, objects, etc. In addition to human-generated categories, almost every page in Wikipedia contains links to related pages. $LAC(q)$ is defined as the overall number of links that contain at least one of q's terms in their anchor text.
Theoretical analysis: Obviously non-coarseness and finiteness are satisfied. Non-uniqueness depends on Wikipedia's structure, but, it is a very *practically sound assumption* that this property is satisfied, for the same reason that syntactic-sensitivity is satisfied. Monotonicity is satisfied by direct implication of the LAC definition. Combination-sensitivity is satisfied in case q_1 and q_2 are overlapping and have terms in common. Consider the following example: $q_1 =< a, b >$, $q_2 =< b, c >$ and $q_3 =< x, y, a >$ while $LAC(q_1) = LAC(q_2)$. In this case $LAC(< a, b, x, y, a >) \neq LAC(< b, c, x, y, a >)$. Interaction increases complexity property is not satisfied as well.

- **Clarity Score (CS)** [6]. This post-retrieval predictor is used to quantify the lack of ambiguity of a query with respect to document collection. Clarity score is defined as being the relative entropy between the query language model and the collection language model.
  Theoretical analysis: Non-coarseness is satisfied for two significantly different queries. Because the query length is limited by definition in this work, finiteness is obviously satisfied. Non-uniqueness is satisfied for a large non-trivial document collection, because its language model is complex and non-trivial, so for $q_1 \neq q_2$ the CS score is different. Syntactic sensitivity is satisfied by the very definition of language-model-based retrieval method and clarity CS computation. Consider the queries: $q_1 = <query>$, $q_2 = <index>$ and $q_1 + q_2 = <query, index>$. Computing clarity score[4] in SIGIR-2013 conference proceedings we get $CS(q_1) = 0.03$, $CS(q_2) = 0.0011$ and $CS(q_1 + q_2) = 0.014$, therefore, monotonicity is *not* satisfied. The same goes for interaction increases complexity property, which is *not* satisfied. Combination sensitivity is satisfied by the definition of language-model-based retrieval and the predictor.

The categorization of the four predictors is summarized in Table 1. These results demonstrate a *multi-dimensional* classification and comparison of QPPs. Due to our assumption about the finiteness of alphabet and lexicon, the property P_2 (Finiteness) is satisfied by all predictors in the current analysis. On the contrary, notice that P_7 (Interaction Increases Complexity) is not satisfied by any predictor.

---

[2]For example if $q = $ *The Breaking News* then $QL(q) = 2$, since *the* is considered as a stop word
[3]The assumptions described in the beginning of section 4

[4]We used the Indri (http://www.lemurproject.org) search engine with Krovetz [14] stemmer.

5. CONCLUSIONS AND FUTURE WORK

We have presented a novel theoretical method for query performance predictors' analysis. We sought to demonstrate how this method provides a multi-dimensional classification QPP suite on four representative predictors, and enables rigorous comparison of the suite's members. To date, the query performance prediction task is still unresolved and its multiple implementations and proposed techniques have not revolutionized the IR field as one might expect [19]. Still, many predictors proposed by now have shared common ground as shown by Kurland et al., [15]. In this work we have assumed bag-of-words terms representation under a unigram language model [18]. However, our approach can be extended to support more models and retrieval methods. Such an extension will result in: 1) more sophisticated notations: such as term reordering for n-gram models or capturing term proximity; 2) more properties, like the original Weyuker's [21] *reordering* property.

For future work, we intend on investigating the correlation between the theoretical categorization presented in this work and empirical evaluation of the same predictors [12, 13, 10] and extend our work with more recent proposed state-of-the-art predictors like NQC [20] and WIG [22]. We intend to develop a criterion to map the satisfaction of a group of properties, or lack thereof, to the quality of prediction. We further intend to suggest accordingly which query performance predictors should be developed to enhance retrieval. One immediate example is a predictor that will satisfy P_7 (Interaction Increases Complexity) property suggested in this work that is not yet satisfied by any analyzed representative predictor.

6. REFERENCES

[1] Z. Bar-Yossef and N. Kraus. Context-sensitive query auto-completion. In *Proceedings of the 20th international conference on World wide web*, WWW '11, pages 107–116, New York, NY, USA, 2011. ACM.

[2] M. Bunge. *Treatise on Basic Philosophy: Ontology 1: The Furniture of the World*. Riedel, Boston, 1977.

[3] D. Carmel and E. Y. Tov. *Estimating the Query Difficulty for Information Retrieval*. Synthesis Lectures on Information Concepts, Retrieval, and Services. Morgan & Claypool Publishers, 2010.

[4] D. Carmel, E. Yom-Tov, A. Darlow, and D. Pelleg. What makes a query difficult? In *ACM SIGIR*, SIGIR '06, pages 390–397, New York, NY, USA, 2006. ACM.

[5] S. Chidamber and C. Kemerer. A metrics suite for object oriented design. *Software Engineering, IEEE Transactions on*, 20(6):476–493, 1994.

[6] S. Cronen-Townsend and W. B. Croft. Quantifying query ambiguity. In *Proceedings of the Second International Conference on Human Language Technology Research*, HLT '02, pages 104–109, San Francisco, CA, USA, 2002. Morgan Kaufmann Publishers Inc.

[7] H. Fang, T. Tao, and C. Zhai. A formal study of information retrieval heuristics. In *ACM SIGIR*, SIGIR '04, pages 49–56, 2011.

[8] H. Fang and C. Zhai. An exploration of axiomatic approaches to information retrieval. In *ACM SIGIR*, SIGIR '05, pages 480–487, New York, NY, USA, 2005. ACM.

[9] C. Hauff, L. Azzopardi, and D. Hiemstra. The combination and evaluation of query performance prediction methods. In *Proceedings of the 31st European Conference on IR Research on Advances in Information Retrieval*, volume 5478 of *Lecture Notes In Computer Science*, pages 301–312, London, 2009. Springer Verlag.

[10] C. Hauff, D. Hiemstra, and F. de Jong. A survey of pre-retrieval query performance predictors. In *Proceedings of the 17th ACM conference on Information and knowledge management*, CIKM '08, pages 1419–1420, New York, NY, USA, 2008. ACM.

[11] C. Hauff, D. Kelly, and L. Azzopardi. A comparison of user and system query performance predictions. CIKM '10, pages 979–988, New York, NY, USA, 2010. ACM.

[12] B. He and I. Ounis. Query performance prediction. *Inf. Syst.*, 31(7):585–594, Nov. 2006.

[13] G. Katz, A. Shtok, O. Kurland, B. Shapira, and L. Rokach. Wikipedia-based query performance prediction. In *ACM SIGIR*, SIGIR '14, pages 1235–1238, 2014.

[14] R. Krovetz. Viewing morphology as an inference process. In *ACM SIGIR*, SIGIR '93, pages 191–202, New York, NY, USA, 1993. ACM.

[15] O. Kurland, A. Shtok, D. Carmel, and S. Hummel. A unified framework for post-retrieval query-performance prediction. ICTIR'11, pages 15–26, Berlin, Heidelberg, 2011. Springer-Verlag.

[16] V. Makarenkov. Metric driven approach to benchmarking model correctness algorithms. In *Masters Thesis*, Ben Gurion University of the Negev, 2011.

[17] V. Makarenkov and M. Balaban. Metric driven approach for automatic creation of model benchmarks. *Technical Report, Ben-Gurion University of the Negev*, 2011.

[18] C. D. Manning, P. Raghavan, and H. Schütze. *Introduction to Information Retrieval*. Cambridge University Press, New York, NY, USA, 2008.

[19] F. Raiber and O. Kurland. Query-performance prediction: Setting the expectations straight. In *ACM SIGIR*, SIGIR '14, pages 13–22, New York, NY, USA, 2014. ACM.

[20] A. Shtok, O. Kurland, D. Carmel, F. Raiber, and G. Markovits. Predicting query performance by query-drift estimation. *ACM Trans. Inf. Syst.*, 30(2):11:1–11:35, May 2012.

[21] E. J. Weyuker. Evaluating software complexity measures. *IEEE Trans. Softw. Eng.*, 14(9):1357–1365, Sept. 1988.

[22] Y. Zhou and W. B. Croft. Query performance prediction in web search environments. In *ACM SIGIR*, SIGIR '07, pages 543–550, New York, NY, USA, 2007. ACM.

Towards Less Biased Web Search

Xitong Liu
University of Delaware
Newark, DE, USA
xtliu@udel.edu

Hui Fang
University of Delaware
Newark, DE, USA
hfang@udel.edu

Deng Cai
The State Key Lab of
CAD&CG
Zhejiang University, China
dengcai@cad.zju.edu.cn

ABSTRACT

Web search engines now serve as essential assistant to help users make decisions in different aspects. Delivering correct and impartial information is a crucial functionality for search engines as any false information may lead to unwise decision and thus undesirable consequences. Unfortunately, a recent study revealed that Web search engines tend to provide biased information with most results supporting users' beliefs conveyed in queries regardless of the truth.

In this paper we propose to alleviate bias in Web search through predicting the topical polarity of documents, which is the overall tendency of one document regarding whether it supports or disapproves the belief in query. By applying the prediction to balance search results, users would receive less biased information and therefore make wiser decision. To achieve this goal, we propose a novel textual segment extraction method to distill and generate document feature representation, and leverage convolution neural network, an effective deep learning approach, to predict topical polarity of documents. We conduct extensive experiments on a set of queries with medical indents and demonstrate that our model performs empirically well on identifying topical polarity with satisfying accuracy. To our best knowledge, our work is the first on investigating the mitigation of bias in Web search and could provide directions on future research.

Categories and Subject Descriptors: H.3.3 [Information Storage and Retrieval]: Information Search and Retrieval

General Terms: Algorithm

Keywords: topical polarity, search bias

1. INTRODUCTION

The advance of Web search engines provides much easier access to huge volume of information with coverage of remarkably wide spectrum. Delivering accurate information clearly is the crucial functionality of Web search engine, as the results may have direct impacts on people's decisions and actions thereafter. However, an existing study [9] reveals that biases are observed during search, as the informa-tion users seek or search engine returns significantly deviates from the truth in two aspects: (1) Most results support the query while only a few disapprove it. (2) Results supporting the query are ranked higher than results disapproving it.

This search bias problem is particularly crucial in medical domain, as any incorrect decision after search may lead to undesirable consequences on the health condition of users. White et al. [10] found that about 3% of search queries have medical intent on Bing, reflecting the high demand of delivering accurate information to end users. Consider the query "can aspirin cause blood in urine" which is expressed in a question, the user may have symptom of "blood in urine" already and have taken "aspirin" before. She wants to confirm whether taking "aspirin" would be the cause under the preconception that "aspirin" caused her symptom. Such process is described as *confirmation bias*, a common psychological tendency which most people have in the interpretation of information. On the other side, Web search engines would return biased results which favor user's preconception. Among the top 10 results from Google, 8 documents are considered as relevant based on our manual assessment, and 6 documents support the belief while only 2 documents disapprove it. Figure 1 presents two relevant documents. The #1 ranked document in Figure 1(a) lists aspirin as one possible cause. Conversely, the #8 ranked document in Figure 1(b) shows that baby aspirin (i.e., low-dose aspirin) would probably not cause blood in urine, and it is the first document against the query. Due to the fact that user is much more likely to click top ranked results while disregarding lower ranked ones, such bias would lead her to believe that aspirin *caused* blood in urine, even though she only took low-dosage.

In this paper, we propose to alleviate the bias in Web search through predicting the topical polarity of documents to balance search results. The topical polarity represents the overall tendency of one document about whether it supports (e.g., Figure 1(a)) or disapproves (e.g., Figure 1(b)) the belief in query. When presented with balanced results, users would have deeper and wider perspective about the topic, seek for answer in a comprehensive approach and make wiser decision thereafter. To reach our goal, we propose to perform binary classification over retrieved documents to predict the topical polarity in a supervised learning approach. In particular, we first extract query-representative textual segments from documents, and train a learning model on convolutional neural network [5], an effective deep learning approach which can unfold useful features automatically. The ultimate document-level prediction is derived based on the aggregation of prediction from textual segments. Exper-

ICTIR'15, September 27–30, Northampton, MA, USA.
© 2015 ACM. ISBN 978-1-4503-3833-2/15/09 ...$15.00.
DOI: http://dx.doi.org/10.1145/2808194.2809476.

Blood in the Urine

The sight of blood in your urine – the toilet water turned a shade of red – is understandably an alarming one.

...

What causes it?

...

- Medications such as antibiotics (rifampin), analgesics (aspirin), phenytoin, quinine, and blood-thinning drugs like warfarin.

`consumer.healthday.com/...-urine-644311.html`

(a) support (rank #1)

Top 10 Doctor insights on ...

Please tell me, could a baby aspirin a day cause blood in urine?

Blood in urine, ASA: Probably not, but you need to be checked for other causes of blood in urine. ...

Could blood in urine be from daily baby aspirin?

No: A daily baby Aspirin would not directly cause blood in the urine but it may make an underlying abnormality more prone to bleed (e.g. Stone, tumor, infection).

`www.healthtap.com/...aspirin-cause-blood-in-urine`

(b) disapprove (rank #8)

Figure 1: Excerpts of two documents for query "*can aspirin cause blood in urine*".

imental evaluation over a set of question-like queries with medical intents demonstrates that our model could predict topical polarity with satisfying accuracy. Although we evaluate on queries in medical domain only, our model is not limited to any specific domain and can be generalized to other domains (e.g., political domain) which require less biased and more impartial results.

2. RELATED WORK

Biases have been a constant problem on Web search engine and received considerable attention from different aspects. Ieong et al. [3] investigated domain bias, a phenomenon in Web search that users' tendency to prefer a search result just because it is from a reputable domain, and found that domains can flip a user's preference about 25% of the time under a blind domain test. White [9] found that users show biases by favoring information confirming their belief when conducting search, and they are subject to the bias of search engine which usually returns more results to support the belief in query regardless of the truth. However, none of them studied how to reduce the bias in search results.

Motivated from sentiment analysis [7], opinion retrieval aims at retrieving documents with subjectively inclined opinion (positively or negatively) towards the query. Most approaches fall into two categories: (1) Lexicon-based, which builds a list of terms with known sentiment orientation [1]. (2) Classification-based, which builds a classifier from training data with opinionated labels and apply the classifier on the testing data thereafter to estimate the opinion score. Representative work include Zhang et al. [11], He et al. [2]. Different from sentiments which are people's subjective attitude (e.g., like or dislike), topical polarity is the tendency about whether one document supports or disapproves the belief in query (e.g., something can cause some symptom), and therefore requires comprehensive understanding to identify it, making the prediction more challenging.

Our research is related to search result diversification [8], which tackles ambiguity in query and redundancy in search results to achieve both high coverage and novelty at the same time. However, there is a clear distinction: they identify subtopics for each query as different aspects and rank documents to balance coverage and novelty based on them, we aim to balance result coverage on two aspects only: supporting and disapproving the belief in query.

3. TOPICAL POLARITY PREDICTION

The topical polarity of a document can be modeled as a binary flag indicating whether the document supports the belief in query, or conversely, disapproves it. Predicting topical polarity of a document is not a trivial problem. We propose to perform supervised classification to solve the problem. There are three major challenges: (1) How to generate the feature representation of a document? (2) How to unfold latent patterns in the feature representations? (3) How to determine the topical polarity based on feature representations? We would discuss our approach to tackle each of them from Section 3.1 to 3.3.

3.1 Textual Segment Extraction

Generating the feature representation for documents is the first step in many IR applications. Language model has been proved to be a simple yet effective representation in many document retrieval models. However, it could not work well in our case as it drops the sequential dependence between terms, making it impossible for comprehensive understanding of documents.

We propose to extract query-related textual segments as the feature representation of documents. By textual segments, we mean any term sequences from the documents, which could include title, sub-title, sentence, etc. The advantages for textual segment over language model include: (1) It retains the term sequential dependence, which is vital for document comprehension. (2) It filters out noises in documents. While language model is estimated based on all the terms in the document, we only select the textual segments which are most relevant to the query, since empirical observation reveals that the relevance of a document is mainly determined by a few textual segments. Consider the example in Figure 1, only the textual segments shown in the excerpt would suffice to determine the relevance.

Algorithm 1 ExtractTextualSegments

Input: query q, document d

Output: Textual segment list seg_list

$PL(q) = GeneratePostingList(q)$

$PL(d) = GeneratePostingList(d)$

$JPL = PL(q) \cap PL(d)$ /* The joint posting list */

$PQ \leftarrow [\,]$ /* A priority queue of term-position pairs */

for $term \in JPL$ **do**

    $pair = MakePair(term, Pop(JPL(term)))$

    $Push(PQ, pair)$

end for

$upper = Max(JPL)$ /* The upper bound */

$coord_list = LocateSegments(JPL, PQ, upper)$

$seg_list = GenerateSegments(d, coord_list)$

return seg_list

Clearly, a representative textual segment should be relevant to the query. We propose a novel segment extraction algorithm based on the snippet generation algorithm in search engine result page. The details are described in Algorithm 1, which consists of several major steps:

1. Generate the joint posting list at line 3. It covers all the terms shared by query and document.

2. Prepare a priority queue as segment window at line 7. The postings of each term serve as anchors for the window to be shifted from beginning to the end.

3. Locate all the valid segments in *LocateSegments* at line 10.

4. Generate all the segments by *GenerateSegments* function based on the coordinates of segments at line 11.

The details of function *LocateSegments* are illustrated in Algorithm 2. We have a segment window covering at least two query terms, and shift the window from the beginning of document to the end. The priority queue is employed to ensure we always have the valid anchors for the window. If the window length exceeds the length constraints, we exclude the last term to shrink the window and find segments via a recursive call at line 18.

Algorithm 2 LocateSegments

Input: joint posting list JPL, priority queue PQ, upper bound of position *upper*
Output: List of segment coordinates *coord_list*

1: $coord\_list \leftarrow [\ ]$
2: **while** True **do**
3:    $Sort(PQ)$ /* Sort the priority queue by position */
4:    /* A valid segment should cover at least 2 terms */
5:    **if** $Len(PQ) < 2$ **then**
6:       **break**
7:    **end if**
8:    **if** $Tail(PQ)[1] > upper$ **then**
9:       **break**/* We reached the upper bound and stop */
10:   **end if**
11:   $seg\_len = Tail(PQ)[1] - Head(PQ)[1]$
12:   **if** $seg\_len > MIN\_SEG\_LEN$ **then**
13:      **if** $seg\_len < MAX\_SEG\_LEN$ **then**
14:         $Push(coord\_list, PQ)$ /* It is a valid segment */
15:      **else**
16:         /* The window is too long, we exclude the last term to shrink it and find segments recursively */
17:         $PQ^* = PQ \setminus Tail(PQ)$
18:         $ext = LocateSegments(JPL, PQ^*, Tail(PQ)[1])$
19:         $coord\_list = coord\_list \cup ext$
20:      **end if**
21:   **end if**
22:   $Pop(PQ)$ /* Shift segment window to the next term*/
23:   $pos\_list = JPL(Head(PQ)[0])$
24:   **if** $len(pos\_list) > 0$ **then**
25:      $pair = MakePair(Head(PQ)[0], Pop(pos\_list))$
26:      $Push(PQ, pair)$
27:   **end if**
28: **end while**
29: **return** $coord\_list$

Due to the fact that *LocateSegments* will only find segments which start and end with query terms, it would break the integrity of sentences as in most cases query terms are spread in the middle of sentences. For example, a possible segment in Figure 1(b) would be "aspirin a day cause blood in urine". The missing of head and tail terms would cause

the loss of useful information, and sometimes the meaning would be totally different. To mitigate such information loss, we extend the segments to the boundaries in the original document based on HTML tags, punctuation marks to make sure the segments consists of whole sentences in function *GenerateSegments* at line 11 in Algorithm 1. In the example we mentioned before, the segment would be extended to "Please tell me, could a baby aspirin a day cause blood in urine" to retain its original meaning.

After the segments are extracted, we need to choose the most relevant ones as feature representation. Since segments are essentially short documents, existing document retrieval models could be employed to rank them. We choose query likelihood, an effective and robust retrieval model:

$$p(q|s) = \prod_{w \in q} p(w|\theta_s)^{n(w,q)}, \qquad (1)$$

where $n(w, q)$ denotes the number of w in q, θ_s is language model of segment s. To reach better performance, Dirichlet smoothing is applied for θ_s. The smoothing parameter μ is set to 250 based on preliminary results. Top k segments will be chosen for training and testing later on, denoted as $S(d)$.

3.2 Learning to Predict Topical Polarity

Recent advances in deep learning have produced remarkable results on pattern recognition in different areas. One advantage of deep learning is the capability of unfolding useful features from data automatically, which fits our task well. Convolutional Neural Network (CNN) [5], which is a type of feed-forward artificial neural network, has been extensively applied in pattern recognition on image data. There have been some pioneer efforts on adapting CNN on textual data with promising results. Kim [4] proposed an effective CNN framework for sentence classification. Word vectors [6] are leveraged to transform sentences to two dimensional matrices similar to image data with fixed width and variable height. The intrinsic characteristic of convolution make it independent of absolute position of terms and capable of capturing latent semantic relations as patterns.

We simply adopt the framework by Kim and use the 300-dimensional word vectors trained from Google News corpus. The shape of filters include 3×300, 4×300 and 5×300, and for each shape we have 100 filters. More technical details can be found in Kim's paper [4].

3.3 Aggregative Prediction

As multiple textual segments are extracted as feature representation of one document, different segments from one document may not share the same polarity, we formalize the problem as regression by predicting how strongly it supports or disapproves the query. To simplify the training process, we assume that all the textual segments share the same topical polarity of the document. We feed CNN with top k segments for document d, aggregate the predictions for all textual segments $s \in S(d)$ and apply majority vote to perform prediction. Formally, we have:

$$p(T = i|q, d) = \sum_{s \in S(d)} w(s|q) \cdot \mathbb{1}(l(s|q) = i), \qquad (2)$$

where $T \in \{-1, 1\}$ is a binary variable for topical polarity (1 for support and -1 for disapproval), $l(s|q)$ is the prediction for s from CNN, and $\mathbb{1}(l(s|q) = i)$ is an indicator function to select segments with same prediction as i. $w(s|q)$ is the weight function for s with regard to q. We use the query likelihood in Equation (1) to approximate it: $w(s|q) = p(q|s)$.

Table 1: Performance Comparison by Precision

Method	k = 5		k = 10	
	Macro-Avg	Micro-Avg	Macro-Avg	Micro-Avg
Sent	0.6806	0.6834	0.6772	0.6812
Seg	0.7134	0.7132	0.7115*	0.7132
Seg-Ext	0.7190*	0.7239	0.7207*	0.7260
Seg-Exp	**0.7376***	**0.7441**	**0.7429*†**	**0.7484**

* and † denote improvements over **Sent** and **Seg** are statistically significant based on two-tailed paired t-test with $p < 0.05$.

4. EXPERIMENTS

There are 50 queries in our data set. 7 queries are from White's paper [9] as they are representative queries with bias. The other 43 queries are selected from topics of medical forums (e.g., drugs.com) with intensive debates. All queries are question-like inquiries (e.g., "Can I take tylenol during pregnancy") covering general usage and side-effects in medical domain. For each query, we retrieved top 20 documents from Bing and Google, and removed duplicated documents. We manually labelled the relevance of documents. For relevant documents, we further labelled the topic polarity (i.e., support or disapprove). For documents with controversial debates, we label it based on the dominant argument. Only relevant documents are used for evaluation. The average number of relevant documents per query is 18.34 and the average number of documents which disapprove the query is 7.40. The data set is available for download.[1]

We use the same setting for CNN throughout the experiments, and focus on the comparison of different textual segment extraction methods, as the quality of segments are crucial to the ultimate prediction accuracy. To evaluate the effectiveness of our segment extraction method in Section 3.1, we use top k sentences from a document as feature representation. Sentence candidates are generated based on HTML tags and punctuation marks, and ranked by query likelihood as in Equation (1) with the same Dirichlet smoothing as for text segments. We denote this method as **Sent**. Based on Algorithm 1, we implement three variations:

- No segment extension is applied in *GenerateSegments* function at line 11, and denote it as **Seg**.

- Segment boundary extension is applied to make sure all segments consist of whole sentences without marginal loss. It is denoted as **Seg-Ext**.

- For medicines with synonyms in knowledge base, we add them to the query to perform expansion for segment ranking. This is common for medicines with different band and chemical names. For example, "Tylenol" is the band name for "Acetaminophen". Same segment boundary extension is applied as above, and we denote it as **Seg-Exp**.

We conduct 10-fold cross-validation over the data and report both the macro and micro-average precision over the 50 queries. Results are reported with k set to 5 and 10. MIN_SEG_LEN is set to 10 and MAX_SEG_LEN is set to 100 in Algorithm 2 to limit segment length in $(10, 100)$.

The performance of all the methods are summarized in Table 1. We observe that our segment based extraction methods deliver significant better performance over **Sent**, implying that segments could provide higher quality feature representation than sentences. In-depth analyses show that relevant information may spread across multiple sentences, and our methods could extract the useful segments covering

[1] http://infolab.ece.udel.edu/~xliu/data/bias/

most relevant information, while **Sent** could only extract partial relevant information.

Furthermore, the superior performance of **Seg-Ext** over **Seg** reveals that the extension over segment boundaries does help as it could retain the useful information in its original context by mitigating the marginal loss. Besides, **Seg-Exp** could deliver further improvements over **Seg-Ext**, demonstrating that simple query expansion based on knowledge base could contribute more useful segments. We expect that more advanced query expansion method would bring further improvements. Note that the best prediction accuracy could be reached at 0.75, showing that CNN could effectively learn latent patterns from textual segments.

5. CONCLUSIONS AND FUTURE WORK

In this paper we proposed a novel model to perform topical polarity prediction on documents. It consists of textual segment extraction to generate feature representations for documents, an existing Convolutional Neural Network framework to unfold latent patterns from textual segments, and aggregative prediction of document based on segment predictions. Experimental evaluations on a real world data set demonstrate that our model could extract useful textual segments and reach promising prediction accuracy. The open availability of data set would help future research work on alleviation of Web search bias.

There are many directions for future work. We would like to study how to leverage topical polarity predictions to balance search results and mitigate search bias. Moreover, we would like to extend convolutional neural networks to better fit topical polarity prediction. Applying our model on Web-scale data and evaluate the impacts on Web search would also be interesting to explore.

Acknowledgments
This material is based upon work supported by the National Science Foundation under Grant Number IIS-1423002 and the National Basic Research Program of China (973 Program) under Grant 20113CB336500. We thank the anonymous reviewers for their useful comments.

6. REFERENCES

[1] B. He, C. Macdonald, J. He, and I. Ounis. An Effective Statistical Approach to Blog Post Opinion Retrieval. In *CIKM*, pages 1063–1072, 2008.

[2] B. He, C. Macdonald, and I. Ounis. Ranking Opinionated Blog Posts using OpinionFinder. In *SIGIR*, pages 727–728, 2008.

[3] S. Ieong, N. Mishra, E. Sadikov, and L. Zhang. Domain Bias in Web Search. In *WSDM*, pages 413–422, 2012.

[4] Y. Kim. Convolutional Neural Networks for Sentence Classification. In *EMNLP*, pages 1746–1751, 2014.

[5] Y. LeCun, L. Bottou, Y. Bengio, and P. Haffner. Gradient-based Learning Applied to Document Recognition. *Proceedings of the IEEE*, 86(11):2278–2324, 1998.

[6] T. Mikolov, I. Sutskever, K. Chen, G. S. Corrado, and J. Dean. Distributed Representations of Words and Phrases and Their Compositionality. In *NIPS*, pages 3111–3119, 2013.

[7] B. Pang and L. Lee. Opinion Mining and Sentiment Analysis. *Foundations and Trends in Information Retrieval*, 2(1-2):1–135, 2008.

[8] R. L. T. Santos, C. Macdonald, and I. Ounis. Search Result Diversification. *Foundations and Trends in Information Retrieval*, 9(1):1–90, 2015.

[9] R. White. Beliefs and Biases in Web Search. In *SIGIR*, pages 3–12, 2013.

[10] R. W. White and E. Horvitz. Studies of the Onset and Persistence of Medical Concerns in Search Logs. In *SIGIR*, pages 265–274, 2012.

[11] W. Zhang, C. Yu, and W. Meng. Opinion Retrieval from Blogs. In *CIKM*, pages 831–840, 2007.

Two Operators to Define and Manipulate Themes of a Document Collection

Emanuele Di Buccio
University of Padua
Department of Information Engineering
dibuccio@dei.unipd.it

Massimo Melucci
University of Padua
Department of Information Engineering
massimo.melucci@unipd.it

ABSTRACT

In this paper, we propose the theme model, which will provide the end user with join and meet operators to define and manipulate themes. These operators have properties that cannot be reduced to the classical logic operators, thus allowing the researchers to model the informative content of documents in a novel way and to rank documents in ways other than those provided by the classical logic. To this end, we introduce the main definitions and properties of the theme model and we link the model to a number of related techniques, thus suggesting how the model can be implemented and applied.

Categories and Subject Descriptors

H.3.3 [**Information Search and Retrieval**]: Retrieval models

General Terms

Theory

Keywords

Query Language; Abstract Vector Spaces; Quantum Mechanics; Exploratory Search; Multi-modal Search

1. INTRODUCTION

In this paper, we propose the theme model. The theme model aims to provide the end user with a language for expressing themes, combining themes through operators and evaluating the degree to which a document is relevant to a theme. In particular, the theme model aims to allow the end user to express the fact that a theme can be joined with another theme and that the result is spanned by both themes. Moreover, the theme model aims to allow the end user to express the fact that two themes are met together and that the result spans both themes.

Technically speaking, the theme model will provide the end user with join and meet operators such that, if t_1 and

t_2 indicate themes, the join of two themes can be expressed by $t_1 \wedge t_2$ and the meet of two themes can be expressed by $t_1 \vee t_2$.

If an artificial language has to be defined, the following artificial commands of this language may give an adequate correspondence so that the join and the meet of `nuclear power` and `green economy` can be written `nuclear power join green economy` and `nuclear power meet green economy`. Informally, the meet is the "smallest" theme spanning both themes and the join is the "largest" theme spanned by both themes. For example, `java join computing` would be "largest" theme spanned by both themes and, if a name is needed, `java programming language` may work since it spans `java`, which is an aspect of the Java language, and `programming language`, which is more general than the Java language; as an another example, `abstract data type meet inheritance` would be the "smallest" theme spanning both themes and `object-oriented programming` may be a name of this theme since `abstract data type` and `inheritance` are aspects of the object-oriented paradigm.

The analogy between join and meet, from the one hand, and intersection and union, on the other hand, may be promptly noted – the crucial difference is that when themes are implemented by constructs other than the sets used to implement union and intersection, the classical distributive law fails [16, 17] as shown in Section 3.

2. RELATED WORK

Automatic Query Expansion (AQE) techniques [3] were proposed in order to obtain a better description of the user's information need, specifically to modify the initial query submitted by the user by extracting additional terms to improve the information need representation; the result of most of these approaches is a new weighted set of related terms that is adopted as a new information need representation for document (re)ranking.

Latent Semantic Analysis (LSA) [4] was proposed to extract descriptors able to capture word correlation. The research in LSA led to topic models which aim at automatically discovering the main "themes" in a document corpus. A well known topic model is Latent Dirichlet Allocation (LDA) [1] where documents are modelled as a distribution over a shared set of topics, which are themselves distributions over words; each word in a document is assumed to be generated by one of these topics. Topics and themes can be visualised and their meaning can be made explicit to the end user using LDA-based techniques; using these techniques, temporal topic evolution can be used to summarise

ICTIR'15, September 27–30, Northampton, MA, USA.
© 2015 ACM. ISBN 978-1-4503-3833-2/15/09 ...$15.00.
DOI: http://dx.doi.org/10.1145/2808194.2809482.

the content of large text collections [9]. In [15] Quantum Interference is adopted to model interaction among topics extracted by LDA. Our work differs since it concentrates on operators designed to generate complex themes and can be integrated with LDA to extract basic themes and with visualisation to visualise themes.

The theme model introduced in this paper relies on some concepts of the mathematical formalism of Quantum Mechanics (QM). The idea of using the mathematical formalism of QM in Information Retrieval (IR) was originally introduced in [16]. Later, a survey on IR system design inspired to QM can be found in [11] while some applications were investigated in some papers as follows. Recently, the intersection between IR and QM has been illustrated in [10].

The user's Information Need (IN) can be represented as a particle (e.g. a photon) subject to measurement through a suite of observables such as document relevance [13]. The user's IN is described by a unit vector in a complex vector space and evolves while the user is interacting with the IR system. The pure state vector determines a probability distribution over the different observables (e.g. relevance). A query algebra with two operators, i.e. mixture and mixture of superpositions are reported in [13] and [2]. This framework is different from our model since it concentrates on superposition and therefore on the probabilistic properties of the abstract vector spaces – our interest is in operators which allow us to define themes.

The principle of polyrepresentation [7] of documents aims to generate and exploit the cognitive overlap between different representations of documents to estimate an accurate representation of the usefulness of the document. The quantum mechanical framework appears to provide a mathematical language of poly-representation. The key idea is to define a series of bases of a complex vector space where each basis refers to an observable applicable to documents and INs. If these bases lie in the same vector space, they can be combined by linear combination so that each vector of a basis can be a linear combination of the vectors of another basis. If these bases lie in different spaces, they can be combined by tensor products so that additional larger bases can be constructed using tensor products between smaller bases together; the probability of relevance is computed as the distance between the information need vector and the document subspace. Our contribution differs from the proposal reported in [5] because we concentrate on a language to combine themes using meet and join.

Quantum Query Language (QQL) aims to interrelate concepts from database query processing to concepts from QM and Quantum Logic [14]. For instance, given a relation and an attribute with values in a domain, the set of possible values can be represented as multidimensional vectors of the canonical basis. In [19] the authors suggested the combinations of the approaches proposed in [5] and [14] since the former lacks in the capability of expressing highly structured queries, while Commuting Quantum Query Language (CQQL) offers the possibility to include complex boolean structure in the query model. In the latter, the concept of superposition/entanglement that is adopted to model IN relationships is not used; a machine learning approach based on relevance feedback is used instead. Our focus is in contrast on IR rather than on databases.

It is known that negative Relevance Feedback (RF) is problematic since the non-relevant documents are noisy and the query resulting from the subtraction of the vectors of the non-relevant documents is not an effective proxy to retrieve relevant documents. In [17, 18], a principled approach to finding the "right" β parameters of negative RF is proposed. Since negative RF might harm retrieval effectiveness although the parameters are optimal, we address operators other than negation and aim to find ways to combine vectorial representation of themes using meet and join.

3. THEME MODEL

Consider a set of features for building themes; it needs an implementation, and, to implement a feature known to most of us, a word of a natural language is an example that may work. In general features are not necessarily required to be textual features: chroma-based descriptors [12] can be used for content-based music representation or *codewords* to describe images; the latter have been used in conjunction with topic models to categorize natural scenes [8]. Since the main focus of our work is on modelling themes and operators, in the following, we assume that a feature is a word, leaving applications to other media for future investigations.

Terms consist of words; for example, "Java language" is a term made of two words. A term is a theme, in particular, it is the simplest form of theme and is the seed of a recursive definition of theme.

Words, terms and themes are represented in a vector space. Words and terms are represented by vectors spanning a one-dimensional subspace (i.e. a ray). Term vectors result from the linear combination of word vectors; the coefficients of these linear combinations measure the role of the word in the term. Themes are multi-dimensional subspaces (e.g. planes) and are spanned by one or more term vectors. It follows that a word is a term because they are both vectors and a term is a theme because a term vector is a one-dimensional subspace; it follows that a word is also a theme. In this way, terms and themes can be represented in a uniform way within a single vector space; for example, the theme about "Java language compiler" can be represented by the bi-dimensional subspace (i.e. the plane) spanned by the vector of the term "Java language" and the vector of the term "compiler"; the vector of the term "Java language" might result from the linear combination of the word vector of "Java" with the word vector of "language".

The subspace that represents a theme can *meet* the subspace of another theme and the result of this meet is a subspace that represents another theme; for example, the ray that represents a theme (e.g. "Java language") can be met with the ray that represents another theme (e.g. "programming") and the result is a bi-dimensional subspace that represents something about Java as programming language.

The subspace that represents a theme can *join* the subspace of another theme and the result of this join is a subspace that represents another theme; for example, the plane that represents a theme (e.g. Java as language) can join the plane that represents another theme (e.g. Java as island) and the result is a one-dimensional subspace that represents something about Java, *tout court*.

Consider the following mathematical description of themes. For starters, a representation of a term is necessary and useful for making the illustration of the theme model effective. A word is represented as a vector of a special kind, that is, a canonical basis vector. In particular, suppose the vocabulary of the words used to build terms contains k distinct words. This number is also the dimension of the vector space in which the canonical basis vectors which represent the words are placed; indeed, the number of the basis vectors of a vector space is also the dimension of the space. The definition of *word vector* follows: The canonical basis vector of the i-th word has k elements, the i-th element is 1 and the other elements are zeros. For example, the row canonical basis vector of the i-th word can be written as[1] $|w_i\rangle = (0, \ldots, 1, \ldots, 0)'$ where $|w_i\rangle \in \mathbb{R}^k$.

Given k coefficients $a_i \in \mathbb{R}, i = 1, \ldots, k$ and the k word vectors $|w_i\rangle \in \mathbb{R}^k, i = 1, \ldots, k$, a term vector is defined as $|t\rangle = a_1|w_1\rangle + \cdots + a_k|w_k\rangle$.

Given m term vectors $|t_1\rangle, \ldots, |t_m\rangle, m \leq k$, a theme is represented by the subspace of all vectors $|t\rangle$ such that $|t\rangle = b_1|t_1\rangle + \cdots + b_m|t_m\rangle$ $b_i \in \mathbb{R}$. For example, a theme can be represented by a one-dimensional subspace (i.e. a ray) in the k-dimensional space as follows; if t_1 is a term represented by $|t_1\rangle$, we have that $|t\rangle = |t_1\rangle$ spans a one-dimensional subspace representing a theme.

Moreover, a theme can be represented by a bi-dimensional subspace (i.e. a plane) in the k-dimensional space as follows; if t_1, t_2 are terms represented by $|t_1\rangle, |t_2\rangle$, respectively, we have that $b_1|t_1\rangle + b_2|t_2\rangle$ spans a bi-dimensional subspace representing a theme. Note that this bi-dimensional subspace differs from the one-dimensional subspace spanned by the sum $a_1|t_1\rangle + a_2|t_2\rangle$, which represents another theme but as a ray. The difference is that, when themes are met (i.e. linearly combined), a subspace of all the linear combinations of the two term vectors is obtained, in contrast, when the term vectors are summed using certain coefficients, one theme vector is obtained.

Any subspace has at least one projector; for example, the subspace spanned by the term vector $|t\rangle$ is one-to-one correspondence with a *projector* written as $\mathbf{T} = |t\rangle\langle t|$; this is an operator that projects a vector of its subspace to itself, that is, $\mathbf{T}|t\rangle = |t\rangle\langle t|t\rangle = |t\rangle$. Each space has two special projectors: $\mathbf{0}$ projects every vector to the null vector and $\mathbf{1}$ projects every vector to itself. A plane may have more than one projector.

If t_1, t_2 are themes and $\mathbf{T}_1, \mathbf{T}_2$ are the projectors of the subspaces corresponding to these two themes, the *meet* $t_1 \vee t_2$ is a theme which corresponds to the smallest subspace containing the subspaces determined by $\mathbf{T}_1$ and $\mathbf{T}_2$; for example, if $\mathbf{T}_1, \mathbf{T}_2$ are the projectors of two rays (i.e. one-dimensional subspaces), the meet corresponds to the plane (i.e. the bi-dimensional subspace) which contains both rays.

THEOREM 1. $\mathbf{T}_1 + \mathbf{T}_2$ *is a projector if and only if* $\mathbf{T}_1 \mathbf{T}_2 = \mathbf{T}_2 \mathbf{T}_1 = \mathbf{0}$ *(i.e. they are mutually orthogonal). When* $\mathbf{T}_1 + \mathbf{T}_2$ *is a projector, it projects a vector* $|t_1\rangle + |t_2\rangle$. *[6]*

When the projectors that are summed are mutually orthogonal, the composition of a theme from the constituent keywords of a term or query is a special case of meet; for example, suppose a user is expressing his query using the words w_1, w_2; as these words are represented by canonical vectors, the corresponding projectors are mutually orthogonal. One term t_i can be defined by each word and can considered a theme. Suppose that these themes are represented by one ray spanned by the vector $|t_i\rangle$; it follows that each theme is represented by a projector $\mathbf{T}_i$ and that $\mathbf{T}_1 + \mathbf{T}_2$ is a pro-

jector of the bi-dimensional subspace corresponding to the theme which results from the meet $t_1 \vee t_2$.

When the projectors that are summed are not mutually orthogonal, it is possible to find two alternative projectors of the same subspaces such that this constraint holds; for example, the Gram-Schmidt orthogonalisation process can be applied to this end. As the dimension of the subspace of $\mathbf{T}_1 + \mathbf{T}_2$ is the sum of the dimensions of the two projectors being summed, this is the projector of the smallest subspace containing both subspaces and therefore it corresponds to the subspace of $t_1 \vee t_2$. In particular, if $\mathbf{T}_1, \mathbf{T}_2$ are the projectors of two rays, their sum is the projector of one plane.

If t_1, t_2 are themes and $\mathbf{T}_1, \mathbf{T}_2$ are the projectors of the subspaces corresponding to these two themes, the *join* $t_1 \wedge t_2$ is a theme which corresponds to the largest subspace contained by the subspaces determined by $\mathbf{T}_1$ and $\mathbf{T}_2$; for example, if $\mathbf{T}_1, \mathbf{T}_2$ are the projectors of two planes (i.e. bi-dimensional subspaces), the join corresponds to the ray (i.e. the one-dimensional subspace) which is contained by both planes.

THEOREM 2. $\mathbf{T}_1 \mathbf{T}_2$ *is a projector if* $\mathbf{T}_1 \mathbf{T}_2 = \mathbf{T}_2 \mathbf{T}_1$. *When* $\mathbf{T}_1 \mathbf{T}_2$ *is a projector, it projects a vector of the largest subspace contained by the subspaces determined by* $\mathbf{T}_1$ *and* $\mathbf{T}_2$. *[6]*

Note that the commutativity of the projectors is only a sufficient condition and it is not necessary. When they do not commute, it is anyway possible to find the projector of the join. Consider two planes. One plane is spanned by $|t_1\rangle$ and $|t_2\rangle$ and the other is spanned by $|u_1\rangle$ and $|u_2\rangle$. A plane is associated to its normal vector, that is, the vector orthogonal to the plane. A normal vector is given by the vector product, in particular, the normal vector of the plane spanned by $|t_1\rangle$ and $|t_2\rangle$ is given their vector product.[2] The join corresponds to the ray passing through both planes and representing the intersection between the planes. This ray is spanned by a vector. This vector is orthogonal to both normal vectors and it spans the ray passing through both planes. This ray is the subspace corresponding to the join of two themes. Figure 1 illustrates how themes are represented by vector subspaces.

The key feature of the theme model is the violation of the distributive law of meet and join. Consider the subspace given by $t_2 \wedge (t_4 \vee t_5)$. Since $t_4 \vee t_5$ corresponds to the subspace represented by $\mathbf{T}_4 + \mathbf{T}_5$ and t_2 corresponds to the subspace represented by $\mathbf{T}_2$, we have that the join between t_2 and $t_4 \vee t_5$ corresponds to the subspace represented by $\mathbf{T}_2$. However, suppose the join is distributed and the following theme is then expressed: $(t_2 \wedge t_4) \vee (t_2 \wedge t_5)$. The join of t_2 and t_4 (first term of the join above) is a theme corresponding to the null subspace (i.e. the zero-dimensional subspace); the same holds for the join of t_2 and t_5 (second term of the join above). It follows that the meet of two null subspaces is the null subspace, that is $t_2 \wedge (t_4 \vee t_5) \neq (t_2 \wedge t_4) \vee (t_2 \wedge t_5)$ and the distributive law fails.

The violation of the distributive law is important since it adds a degree of freedom to the definition of themes. It may be that expressing a theme using $t_2 \wedge (t_4 \vee t_5)$ is more

---

[1] Dirac's notation is at `http://en.wikipedia.org/wiki/Bra-ket_notation`.

[2] The vector product between $|t_1\rangle = (t_{11}, t_{12}, t_{13})'$ and $|t_2\rangle = (t_{21}, t_{22}, t_{23})'$ in the three-dimensional space is the vector $(t_{12}t_{23} - t_{13}t_{22}, t_{13}t_{21} - t_{11}t_{23}, t_{11}t_{22} - t_{12}t_{21})'$.

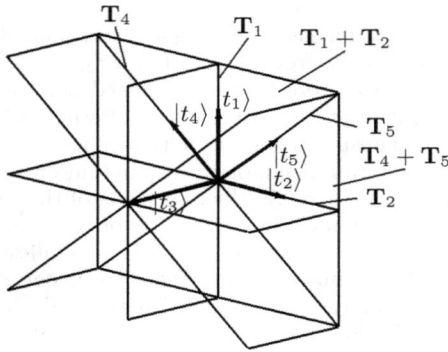

Figure 1: The vectors $|t_1\rangle, |t_2\rangle, |t_3\rangle$ may be term vectors spanning subspaces represented by $\mathbf{T}_1, \mathbf{T}_2, \mathbf{T}_3$, respectively. These term vectors can be used to define themes; for example $|t_4\rangle = \frac{1}{\sqrt{2}}|t_1\rangle - \frac{1}{\sqrt{2}}|t_2\rangle$ and $|t_5\rangle = \frac{1}{\sqrt{2}}|t_1\rangle + \frac{1}{\sqrt{2}}|t_2\rangle$ are two orthogonal theme vectors spanning one one-dimensional subspace each, respectively, represented by the projectors $\mathbf{T}_4$ and $\mathbf{T}_5$. The meet $t_1 \vee t_2$ corresponds to the subspace represented by $\mathbf{T}_1 + \mathbf{T}_2$ which is incidentally the same subspace corresponding to $\mathbf{T}_4 + \mathbf{T}_5$. The join of the subspaces represented by $\mathbf{T}_1 + \mathbf{T}_2$ and $\mathbf{T}_3 + \mathbf{T}_5$ corresponds to the ray represented by $\mathbf{T}_5$.

effective than expressing a theme using $(t_2 \wedge t_4) \vee (t_2 \wedge t_5)$ since the semantics behind these two expressions are different; for example, `java meet (programming join language)` is not equivalent to `(java meet programming) join (java meet language)` when these themes are represented by subspaces, thus providing alternative means for expressing themes and retrieving more relevant documents.

As the theme model is based on the formalism of the quantum mechanical framework, a vector representing a theme encodes a probability distribution of the features. A document is represented by a vector $|\phi\rangle = (c_1, \ldots, c_k)', c_i \in \mathbb{R}, |\langle\phi|\phi\rangle|^2 = 1$ such that c_i^2 is the probability that the document that is represented by the vector is about the theme of term i. The probability that a document ϕ is about a theme represented by $\mathbf{T}$ is defined as $\langle\phi|\mathbf{T}|\phi\rangle$. For example, if $|t_i\rangle$ is a term vector and $\mathbf{T}_i = |t_i\rangle\langle t_i|$ is the projector, the probability that a document ϕ is about a theme represented by $\mathbf{T}_i$ is defined as $\langle\phi|\mathbf{T}_i|\phi\rangle = \langle\phi|t_i\rangle\langle t_i|\phi\rangle = |\langle\phi|t_i\rangle|^2$.

4. FUTURE WORK

Experiments are underway and aim to experimentally evaluate if these operators allow for more effective description of the user information need. An experiment will start with a query, will then extract a set of pertinent themes, and will finally compare the effectiveness of the ranked list obtained by the representation based only on the query terms, on all the distinct terms associated to the extracted themes, or on themes through meet and join. We will use the subtopics of the TREC 2010 Web Track Test Collection as themes.[3]

5. REFERENCES

[1] D. M. Blei, A. Y. Ng, and M. I. Jordan. Latent dirichlet allocation. *JMLR*, 3:993–1022, 2003.

[2] A. Caputo, B. Piwowarski, and M. Lalmas. A Query Algebra for Quantum Information Retrieval. In *Proceedings of the IIR Workshop*, 2011.

[3] C. Carpineto and G. Romano. A survey of automatic query expansion in information retrieval. *ACM Computing Surveys*, 44(1):1:1–1:50, 2012.

[4] S. Deerwester, S. T. Dumais, G. W. Furnas, T. K. Landauer, and R. Harshman. Indexing by latent semantic analysis. *JASIST*, 41(6):391–407, 1990.

[5] I. Frommholz, B. Larsen, B. Piwowarski, M. Lalmas, P. Ingwersen, and K. van Rijsbergen. Supporting Polyrepresentation in a Quantum-inspired Geometrical Retrieval Framework. In *Proceedings of IIiX*, pages 115–124, 2010.

[6] P. Halmos. *Finite-Dimensional Vector Spaces*. Undergraduate Texts in Mathematics. Springer, 1987.

[7] P. Ingwersen. Polyrepresentation of information needs and semantic entities: Elements of a cognitive theory for information retrieval interaction. In *Proceedings of SIGIR*, pages 101–110, 1994.

[8] F.-F. Li and P. Perona. A bayesian hierarchical model for learning natural scene categories. In *Proceedings of CVPR*, pages 524–531. IEEE Computer Society, 2005.

[9] S. Liu, M. X. Zhou, S. Pan, Y. Song, W. Qian, W. Cai, and X. Lian. Tiara: Interactive, topic-based visual text summarization and analysis. *ACM Transactions on Intelligent Systems and Technology*, 3(2):25:1–25:28, 2012.

[10] M. Melucci. *Introduction to Information Retrieval and Quantum Mechanics*. Springer, In print.

[11] M. Melucci and C. J. van Rijsbergen. *Quantum Mechanics and Information Retrieval*, chapter 6, pages 125–155. Springer, 2011.

[12] R. Miotto and N. Orio. A music identification system based on chroma indexing and statistical modeling. In *Proceedings of ISMIR*, Philadelphia, PA, USA, 2008.

[13] B. Piwowarski, I. Frommholz, M. Lalmas, and K. van Rijsbergen. What Can Quantum Theory Bring to Information Retrieval. In *Proceedings of CIKM*, pages 59–68, 2010.

[14] I. Schmitt. QQL: A DB&IR Query Language. *The VLDB Journal*, 17(1):39–56, Jan. 2008.

[15] A. Sordoni, J. He, and J.-Y. Nie. Modeling latent topic interactions using quantum interference for information retrieval. In *Proceedings of CIKM*, pages 1197–1200, 2013.

[16] C. J. Van Rijsbergen. *The Geometry of Information Retrieval*. Cambridge University Press, UK, 2004.

[17] D. Widdows. *Geometry and Meaning*. CSLI Publications, USA, 2004.

[18] D. Widdows and S. Peters. Word vectors and quantum logic: Experiments with negation and disjunction. In R. T. Oehrle and J. Rogers, editors, *Proceedings of the Mathematics of Language Conference*, volume 141–154, 2003.

[19] D. Zellhöfer, I. Frommholz, I. Schmitt, M. Lalmas, and K. van Rijsbergen. Towards Quantum-based DB+IR Processing Based on the Principle of Polyrepresentation. In *Proceedings of ECIR*, pages 729–732. Springer-Verlag, 2011.

[3] http://trec.nist.gov/data/web/10/wt2010-topics.xml

Using Part-of-Speech N-grams for Sensitive-Text Classification

Graham McDonald
University of Glasgow
Scotland, UK
g.mcdonald.1@
research.gla.ac.uk

Craig Macdonald
University of Glasgow
Scotland, UK
craig.macdonald@
glasgow.ac.uk

Iadh Ounis
University of Glasgow
Scotland, UK
iadh.ounis@
glasgow.ac.uk

ABSTRACT

Freedom of Information legislations in many western democracies, including the United Kingdom (UK) and the United States of America (USA), state that citizens have typically the right to access government documents. However, certain sensitive information is exempt from release into the public domain. For example, in the UK, FOIA Exemption 27 (International Relations) excludes the release of Information that might damage the interests of the UK abroad. Therefore, the process of reviewing government documents for sensitivity is essential to determine if a document must be redacted before it is archived, or closed until the information is no longer sensitive. With the increased volume of digital government documents in recent years, there is a need for new tools to assist the digital sensitivity review process. Therefore, in this paper we propose an automatic approach for identifying sensitive text in documents by measuring the amount of sensitivity in sequences of text. Using government documents reviewed by trained sensitivity reviewers, we focus on an aspect of FOIA Exemption 27 which can have a major impact on international relations, namely *information supplied in confidence*. We show that our approach leads to markedly increased recall of sensitive text, while achieving a very high level of precision, when compared to a baseline that has been shown to be effective at identifying sensitive text in other domains.

1. INTRODUCTION

Freedom of Information (FOI) laws exist in many countries around the world, including the United Kingdom (UK)[1] and the United States of America (USA)[2]. FOI states that government documents should be open to the public. However, many government documents contain *sensitive* information, such as *personal* or *confidential* information. Therefore, FOI laws make provisions that exempt sensitive information from being open. To avoid the accidental release

---

[1] http://www.legislation.gov.uk/ukpga/2000/36/contents
[2] http://www.foia.gov

of sensitive information, it is essential that all government documents are *sensitivity reviewed* prior to release.

Sensitivity reviewers are required to identify any *sequences* of sensitive text in a document, for example individual terms, sentences, paragraphs or the full content of the document, so that the sensitive text can be *redacted* or the document can be *closed*. However, the recent increase in volume of digital government documents means that the traditional manual review process is not feasible for digital government documents. Therefore, the UK and the USA governments have recently recognised the need for automatic tools to assist the sensitivity review process [2, 3].

In this work, we address the problem of automatically identifying sensitive information in government documents by directly classifying the text *within* documents. We present an approach that uses POS n-grams to measure the amount of sensitivity contained within a sequence of text, i.e. its *sensitivity load*. Moreover, we show how our approach can be used to deploy an effective sensitivity classifier that classifies sensitivity at the *term-level*.

We propose to perform classification at the term-level because correctly identifying partial sensitive sequences will be beneficial to a sensitivity reviewer. For example, by drawing a reviewer's attention to the positions of sensitivities within a document it will likely reduce the time taken to review the document.

We initially focus on an aspect of FOIA Exemption 27 *International Relations*, namely "information supplied in confidence", since this sensitivity has a clear potential to cause damage to international relations if inadvertently released into the public domain. We show that our approach can markedly improve recall of *in confidence* sensitivities compared to a baseline approach that has been shown to achieve high levels of recall for sensitive text in other domains [11].

The remainder of this paper is as follows. We present related work in Section 2. We present our approach in Section 3, before presenting two classification methods, in Section 4 and Section 5, that implement our approach. In Section 6 we present a baseline approach that we compare our results against. We present our experimental setup in Section 7 and our results in Section 8. Finally, we present our conclusions and future work in Section 9.

2. RELATED WORK

Gollins *et al.* [5] provided an overview of the challenges presented by digital sensitivity review and how these challenges can be addressed by Information Retrieval (IR) techniques. In that work, they noted that although the *type* of sensitivity can be identified, for example *personal information*, the existence of many sensitivities rely not only on the terms or entities in the document but also on the context of the information, i.e. *what* is said about an entity, *how* it is said and *who* said it.

In [9], we presented an initial approach to address the issue of context dependent sensitivity, highlighted by Gollins *et al.*, by deploying a text classification approach with additional features such as the entities in the document, a country *risk* score and a subjective sentences count to identify documents that contained *personal information* and *international relations* sensitivities. Differently from that work, in this paper we investigate automatically identifying sequences of sensitive text, *within* documents, that relates to information supplied in confidence.

Outwith the field of sensitivity review, most work on automatically identifying sensitive text in documents is in the field of document sanitization [1, 4]. Document sanitization tries to automatically *mask* personal information, or information that could reveal the identity of the person the document is about. A popular approach for this is Named Entity Recognition (NER). NER typically identifies *person, location* and *organisation* entities in text and NER approaches to document sanitization typically assume that all named entities in a document are sensitive. However, in this work we try to automatically identify information that has been supplied in confidence and, as such, we need a more general solution that can identify sensitivities in what is said about, or by, an entity.

Sánchez *et al.* [11] presented an approach to sensitive text identification that is more general than NER. They assumed that sensitive text is likely to be more specific than non-sensitive text, and used the Information Content (IC) of noun phrases as a measure of how sensitive the phrase is. Sánchez *et al.* focused on identifying *personal information* sensitivities. However, they also identified textual phrases that are potentially *confidential*. Therefore, their work is more closely aligned to identifying FOIA Exemption 27 sensitivities than NER approaches. Moreover, identifying all potential sensitivities in government documents is the first stage of the sensitivity review process and Sánchez *et al.* found that approach achieved higher recall for sensitive information when compared to NER. For these reasons, we use that approach as a baseline for comparing our work against and we describe our implementation of it in Section 6.

3. IDENTIFYING SENSITIVITY LOADED PART-OF-SPEECH N-GRAMS

The approach we present in this paper uses the *sensitivity load* of POS n-grams to identify sequences of sensitive text in documents. The approach is inspired by Lioma and Ounis [8] who showed that the distribution of POS n-grams in a corpus can indicate the amount of information they contain. More specifically, Lioma and Ounis showed that high frequency POS n-grams are typically *content rich* and removing *content poor* POS n-grams from search engine queries results in an improved overall retrieval performance. Differently from their work, we use the content load of POS n-grams to try to measure the sensitivity load of specific sequences of text.

Our intuition is that certain POS sequences might be more frequent in specific sensitivities. For example, sensitivities relating to information supplied in confidence would likely contain variations of the sequence *noun - verb - pronoun*, indicating that someone has supplied information to someone else. Our approach uses the distribution of POS n-grams to try to identify sequences that are specific to this sensitivity.

To do this, we first represent documents by the POS n-grams they contain. For example, the sequence "The envoy will report on Tuesday" results in the POS tags "DT NN MD VB IN NN". Representing this sequence as POS 3-grams results in the following "DTNNMD NNMDVB MD-VBIN VBINNN"

Having represented the documents by their POS n-grams, we then use a probabilistic method to measure the sensitivity load of a POS n-gram. More specifically, following the work of Li *et al.* [7], we first construct a 2-way contingency table as shown in Table 1, where pos, s is the number of documents in which the POS n-gram appears in sensitive text, $pos, \neg s$ is the number of documents in which the POS n-gram appears in non-sensitive text, $\neg pos, s$ is the number of documents that do not contain the POS n-gram in sensitive text and $\neg pos, \neg s$ is the number of documents that do not contain the POS n-gram in non-sensitive text.

Table 1: 2-way contingency table used to calculate the Chi-square statistic of a part-of-speech n-gram.

	sensitive	non-sensitive
Containing POS	pos, s	$pos, \neg s$
Not Containing POS	$\neg pos, s$	$\neg pos, \neg s$

Having constructed the contingency table, we use the Chi-Square test of independence to measure the degree of dependency between a POS n-gram and sensitive text. The Chi-square score for a POS n-gram, (X^2_{pos}) is calculated as follows,

$$X^2_{pos} = \frac{N_d(p(pos,s)p(\neg pos,\neg s) - p(pos,\neg s)p(\neg pos,s))^2}{p(pos)p(\neg pos)p(\neg s)p(s)} \quad (1)$$

where $p(pos, s)$ is the probability that the sensitive text of a document contains the POS n-gram, $p(pos, \neg s)$ is the probability that the non-sensitive text of a document contains the POS n-gram, $p(\neg pos, s)$ is the probability that the sensitive text of a document does not contain the POS n-gram, $p(\neg pos, \neg s)$ is the probability that the non-sensitive text of a document does not contain the POS n-gram, $p(pos)$ is the probability that a document contains the POS n-gram, $p(\neg pos)$ is the probability that a document does not contain the POS n-gram, $p(s)$ is the probability that text in the collection is sensitive, $p(\neg s)$ is the probability that text in the collection is not sensitive and N_d is the total number of documents in the collection.

The Chi-square test of independence measures how much the observed frequency of a POS n-gram diverges from its expected frequency within a corpus. If a POS n-gram's Chi-Square score is greater than the Chi-Square distribution's critical value for a 95% confidence level with one degree of freedom, then we assume that the distribution of the POS n-gram in the corpus is related to sensitive text. We refer to these n-grams as being *sensitivity loaded*.

By applying our approach, the identified sensitivity loaded POS n-grams can then be used as features in any method for automatic sensitive-text classification. In Section 4 and Section 5, we present two such methods that integrate our approach.

4. SENSITIVITY LOAD FILTERING

Confidential information in documents is rare. Indeed, 95% of terms in our collection are in fact part of sequences that the reviewers did not believe to be sensitive. Moreover, many documents adhere to template structures in which certain sections of a document are particularly unlikely to contain confidential information, for example the header section of an email stating the *sender*, *recipients* and a *subject title*.

Therefore, we can use the sensitivity loaded POS n-grams identified by our approach, presented in Section 3, to filter out sequences of text that are most likely to contain non-sensitive information.

To do this, we count the number of times a sensitivity loaded POS n-gram appears in sensitive and non-sensitive text and use the ratio of sensitive and non-sensitive occurrences to identify POS n-grams that are representative of non-sensitive sequences. Equation 2 shows how we calculate the ratio, $lRatio_{pos,s}$, where Sensitive correspondes to when $lRatio_{pos,s} > 1$ and Non-Sensitive corresponds to when $lRatio_{pos,s} < 1$.

$$lRatio_{pos,s} = \frac{p(pos,s)p(\neg pos, \neg s) - p(pos, \neg s)p(\neg pos, s)}{p(pos)p(s)} + 1 \quad (2)$$

To classify terms in a given sequence of text k, we represent k by its POS n-grams k_{pos}. Then, for any k_{pos} in the set of previously identified non-sensitive POS n-grams, each term t in k_{pos} is classified as being *Non-sensitive*, all other terms are classified as *sensitive*. We refer to this method as the *Filtering* method.

5. SENSITIVITY LOAD SEQUENCES

The identified sensitivity loaded POS n-grams can be used to generate features for a Conditional Random Fields (CRF) sequence tagger [6]. A CRF is a probabilistic framework that models the conditional distribution $p(y|x)$ in sequential data, where x is a sequence of observations, an observation is a term with a set of features that describe the term and y is a sequence of class labels.

To deploy the CRF method we use two term features. The first feature we use is the term's POS tag. Additionally, we use the sensitivity loaded POS n-grams identified by our approach to generate a feature *tag* that indicates whether the term is part of a sequence that maps to a sensitivity loaded POS n-gram.

To generate the feature tag, we look at a sequence of n (POS tagged) terms at a time and check if the sequence maps to a sensitivity loaded POS n-gram. If a mapping exists, we tag each term in the sequence. We then move the sliding window by one term to the next sequence and repeat the process.

To illustrate this, we return to our example from Section 3. Recall that the sequence "The envoy will report on Tuesday" is represented by the POS 3-grams "DTNNMD NNMDVB MDVBIN VBINNN". If our approach identifies "NNMDVB"

as the only sensitivity loaded n-gram, this would result in the sequence being tagged as shown in Figure 1.

When the learned CRF model is deployed, it predicts class labels for each term in a sequence based on its previous observations. We refer to this method as $CRF+POS+TAG$. We also present the results for the CRF method without the sensitivity loaded feature tag, $CRF+POS$, and the simple CRF (i.e. using just the term) as CRF.

6. INFORMATION CONTENT

As previously mentioned in Section 2, we compare our approach against a baseline from the literature that uses the Information Content (IC) of a noun phrase as a measure of the phrase's sensitivity [11]. A noun phrase is a sequence of terms that has a *noun* or *indefinite pronoun* at the *head* of the phrase. IC measures the amount of information provided by the sequence of terms, within the context of a background corpus. More *specific* term sequences are considered as having a higher likelihood of being sensitive.

To calculate the IC of noun phrases in a document, the document is first parsed to extract its syntactic structure. Noun phrases are then extracted from the resulting syntax tree and submitted to a Web search engine as a query. The IC of the noun phrase is calculated using the number of returned results as an indication of the phrase's specificity. Formally, the IC of a noun phrase, np, is computed as $IC_{(np)} = -\log_2 p(np) = -\log_2 \frac{res(np)}{totalpages}$, where $res(np)$ is the number of returned search results and $totalpages$ is the number of sites indexed by the search engine. For our experiments, each term within a noun phrases with an IC score greater than an empirically defined threshold, β, is classified as being sensitive. All other terms are classified as non-sensitive. This baseline is referred to as *InfContent*.

7. EXPERIMENTAL SETUP

Collection: The collection consists of government documents with "information supplied in confidence" sensitivities. The documents have been sensitivity reviewed by trained sensitivity reviewers. Reviewers were asked to annotate the sensitive sequences within the documents, therefore the documents have term-level class labels i.e. each term within a sensitive sequence is labelled *sensitive* and all terms that were not annotated are labelled *non-sensitive*. There are a total of 231893 terms in the collection with 10838 sensitive terms and 221055 non-sensitive terms, in a set of 143 documents. For our experiments, we split the collection at the document level to retain the context of the terms and perform a 5-fold Cross Validation.

Baselines: We compare our approach against the IC baseline presented in Section 6. We use Open NLP[3] to extract noun phrases from documents and for calculating the IC score of noun phrases we use the Bing search engine[4] and set the total number of sites indexed, $totalpages$, to 3.5 billion. For our experiments we test IC threshold values of $\beta = \{1, 2, 3, 4, 5, 6, 7, 8, 9, 10, 20, 30, 40, 50, 75, 100\}$. In future work, we intend to investigate learning the β parameter.

We also report the results of a simple classifier that classifies all terms as the majority class, referred to as *All Non-Sensitive*. Conversely, we also report a classifier that classifies all terms as sensitive, referred to as *All Sensitive*.

```
The       DT
envoy     NN   Sensload
will      MD   Sensload
report    VB   Sensload
on        IN
Tuesday   NN
```

Figure 1: Illustration showing the POS tag and generated sensitivity loaded feature tags for a sequence.

[3]https://opennlp.apache.org
[4]http://www.bing.com/

Sensitivity Load: For identifying sensitivity loaded POS n-grams in Section 3, we use the TreeTagger[5] for POS tagging and, following Lioma and Ounis [8], we use a reduced set of 15 POS tags. We calculate the Chi-Square statistic on the training data for $n = \{1, 2, 3, 4, 5, 6, 7, 8, 9, 10\}$. In future work, we intend learning the optimum value for n.

Classification: For Sensitivity Load Filtering (Section 4) and Sensitivity Load Sequences (Section 5), we test the methods for each value of $n = \{1, 2, 3, 4, 5, 6, 7, 8, 9, 10\}$. For the Sensitivity Load Sequences classification method, we use the Mallet[6] linear chain CRF tagger.

Metrics: We report balanced accuracy (BAC) due to the imbalanced nature of our collection. Moreover, sensitivity review is a recall-oriented task since reviewers must identify all sensitivities to avoid inadvertent release. Therefore, we report the F2 measure that provides a weighted average of precision and recall where recall is attributed more importance and, therefore, a greater weight. We also report the standard accuracy, precision and recall metrics.

8. RESULTS

Table 2 shows the best achieved performance for the Filtering method (*Filtering*), the CRF method using the POS tag and sensitivity load as features (*CRF+POS+TAG*), the CRF method with the POS tag only (*CRF+POS*) and the simple CRF (*CRF*). Table 2 also shows the best performance for the Information Content baseline (*InfContent*) and the *All Sensitive* and *All Non-Sensitive* classifiers scores.

The first thing we note from Table 2 is that the CRF classification metod using the sensitivity loaded POS n-grams identified by our approach outperforms the IC baseline for all metrics. The CRF method using sensitivity loaded 10-grams ($CRF+POS+TAG_{n=10}$) achieves 0.4573 recall. Importantly, the method also achieves 0.9992 precision and, therefore, achieves a balanced accuracy of 0.7282. On closer inspection of the results we found that the CRF method with this setting identified 99% of sensitive text in 67% of the documents and, therefore, we believe this method would be useful in assisting the sensitivity review process. Moreover, we note that the CRF method without the sensitivity loaded POS n-gram feature (*CRF+POS*) correctly identified less than 5% of the sensitive text. This further demonstrates the effectiveness of our approach.

The next point we note from Table 2 is that the Filtering approach also achieves its highest recall (0.9129) when n is set to 10. However, the approach achieves a low precision score (0.0563) resulting in an F2 score of (0.2257). This low level of precision shows that, on this collection, this method is markedly over-predicting sensitivity.

We also see from Table 2 that the CRF and the Filtering methods achieve their best recall scores using POS 10-grams.

Finally, we note that the IC baseline, $InfContent_{ic>7}$, achieved 0.0116 recall and 0.2564 precision. The IC baseline identifies syntacticly complex phrases and specific terms as being sensitive. However, not all complex or specific phrases are confidential and, moreover, not all sensitivities are noun phrases. We also note that the classification methods that use our approach for identifying sensitive sequences of text achieve markedly better recall, and notably better balanced accuracy, than the IC baseline.

---

[5]http://www.cis.uni-muenchen.de/ schmid/tools/TreeTagger
[6]http://mallet.cs.umass.edu

Table 2: Results for the Filtering and CRF methods. The table also shows the performance of the *All Sensitive*, *All Non-Sensitive* and Information Content baselines.

	accuracy	balanced Acc	precision	recall	F2
all Non-Sensitive	0.9533	0.0000	0.0000	0.0000	0.0000
all Sensitive	0.0467	0.5234	0.0467	1.0000	0.1969
$InfContent_{ic>7}$	0.9457	0.1340	0.2564	0.0116	0.0143
$InfContent_{ic>8}$	0.9457	0.1245	0.2388	0.0103	0.0127
$InfContent_{ic>9}$	0.9457	0.1188	0.2281	0.0094	0.0116
$InfContent_{ic>10}$	0.9458	0.1279	0.2466	0.0093	0.0115
$InfContent_{ic>20}$	0.9459	0.0983	0.1911	0.0055	0.0069
$Filtering_{n=7}$	0.3763	0.3805	0.0579	0.7032	0.2178
$Filtering_{n=8}$	0.3360	0.4007	0.0573	0.7441	0.2191
$Filtering_{n=9}$	0.2616	0.4434	0.0570	0.8298	0.2236
$Filtering_{n=10}$	0.1815	0.4846	0.0563	0.9129	0.2257
CRF	0.9226	0.0390	0.0179	0.0283	0.0201
$CRF+POS$	0.9221	0.0647	0.0856	0.0446	0.0494
$CRF+POS+TAG_{n=7}$	0.9600	0.5702	0.8310	0.3094	0.3539
$CRF+POS+TAG_{n=8}$	0.9637	0.6264	0.8932	0.3595	0.4083
$CRF+POS+TAG_{n=9}$	0.9657	0.6608	0.9454	0.3762	0.4277
$CRF+POS+TAG_{n=10}$	**0.9712**	**0.7282**	**0.9992**	0.4573	**0.5129**

9. CONCLUSIONS AND FUTURE WORK

In this work, we proposed an approach for automatically detecting *information supplied in confidence* in government documents. Our approach uses part-of-speech n-grams to measure the *sensitivity load* of sequences of text. On a collection of sensitivity-reviewed government documents, we showed that the sensitivity load of these sequences can be used to accurately classify *in confidence* sensitivities within government documents. In particular, using a CRF sequence tagger with the sensitivity load of POS n-grams as features, this approach achieved over 0.45% recall and 0.99% precision, markedly outperforming a baseline approach from the literature that has been shown to achieve high levels of recall for sensitive text in other domains. As future work, we intend to conduct a user study to quantify the benefits of our approach for assisting in the sensitivity review of digital government documents.

10. ACKNOWLEDGMENTS

The authors would like to thank the sensitivity reviewers for their help in constructing the test collection.

11. REFERENCES

[1] D. Abril, G. Navarro-Arribas, and V. Torra. On the declassification of confidential documents. In *Mod. Dec. for Art. Intel.*. 6820:235–246, 2011.
[2] D. A. R. P. Agency. Darpa, new technologies to support declassification. *Request for Information*, DARPA-SN-10-73, 2010.
[3] A. Allan. Records Review. *UK Government*. 2014.
[4] J. R. Finkel, T. Grenager, and C. Manning. Incorporating non-local information into information extraction systems by gibbs sampling. In *Proc. of ACL*, 2005.
[5] T. Gollins, G. McDonald, C. Macdonald, and I. Ounis. On using information retrieval for the selection and sensitivity review of digital public records. In *Proc. of PIR at CIKM*, 2014.
[6] J. D. Lafferty, A. McCallum, and F. C. N. Pereira. Conditional random fields: Probabilistic models for segmenting and labeling sequence data. In *Proc. of ICML*, 2001.
[7] Y. Li, C. Luo, and S. Chung. Text clustering with feature selection by using statistical data. In *Trans. on Knowledge and Data Engineering*, 20(5):641–652, 2008.
[8] C. Lioma and I. Ounis. Examining the Content Load of Part-of-Speech Blocks for Information Retrieval. In *Proc. of COLING/ACL*, 2006.
[9] G. McDonald, C. Macdonald, I. Ounis, and T. Gollins. Towards a classifier for digital sensitivity review. In *Proc. of ECIR*, 2014.
[10] T. Mendel. *Freedom of information: a comparative legal survey.* Paris: Unesco, 2008.
[11] D. Sánchez, M. Batet, and A. Viejo. Detecting sensitive information from textual documents: an information-theoretic approach. In *Mod. Dec. for Art. Intel.*, 7647:173-184, 2012.

Verboseness Fission for BM25 Document Length Normalization

Aldo Lipani[1]   Mihai Lupu[2]

[1]National Institute of Informatics
2-1-2 Hitotsubashi, Chiyoda-ku
Tokyo, Japan
{surname}@nii.ac.jp

Allan Hanbury[2]   Akiko Aizawa[1]

[2]Inst. of Software Technology & Interactive Systems
Vienna University of Technology
Vienna, Austria
{surname}@ifs.tuwien.ac.at

ABSTRACT

BM25 is probably the most well known term weighting model in Information Retrieval. It has, depending on the formula variant at hand, 2 or 3 parameters (k_1, b, and k_3). This paper addresses b—the document length normalization parameter. Based on the observation that the two cases previously discussed for length normalization (multi-topicality and verboseness) are actually three: multi-topicality, verboseness with word repetition (repetitiveness) and verboseness with synonyms, we propose and test a new length normalization method that removes the need for a b parameter in BM25. Testing the new method on a set of purposefully varied test collections, we observe that we can obtain results statistically indistinguishable from the optimal results, therefore removing the need for ground-truth based optimization.

1. INTRODUCTION

BM25 is the most longevous weighting schema in Information Retrieval (IR), still widely used in industry and studied in research. The peculiarity of this weighting schema is its probabilistic root that is based on the 2-Poisson model of term frequencies in documents [13]. In its classic version, a document d is scored by the function:

$$S(q,d) = \sum_{t \in T_q \cap T_d} \frac{(k_3+1)tf_q}{k_3+tf_q} \frac{(k_1+1)\overline{tf_d}}{k_1+\overline{tf_d}} \log \frac{|D|+0.5}{df_t+0.5}$$

with

$$\overline{tf_d}(t) = \frac{tf_d(t)}{B} \quad B = (1-b)+b\frac{L_d}{avgdl}$$

where q is the query, D is the set of documents, $d \in D$ is a document, T_d and T_q are the sets of document terms and query terms, $\overline{tf_d}$ is the normalized term frequency of the term t within the document d, tf_q is the term frequency of the term t within the query, df_t is the document frequency of the term t, L_d the length of the document d, $avgdl$ the average document length over the collection D of documents,

ICTIR'15, September 27 - 30, 2015, Northampton, MA, USA.
Copyright is held by the owner/author(s). Publication rights licensed to ACM.
ACM 978-1-4503-3833-2/15/09 ...$15.00.
DOI: http://dx.doi.org/10.1145/2808194.2809486 .

and k_1, b and k_3 the three parameters with domains $[0, \infty[$, $[0, 1]$ and $[0, \infty[$.

This semi-parametric retrieval function [10] has 3 degrees of freedom, each with a specific meaning: k_1 and k_3 tune how fast the respective *tf* component saturates, expressing the importance of the presence of an additional occurrence of the term t in the document or query. The parameter b controls the normalization of the *tf* component, varying between the two extremes of non normalized, when $b = 0$, and fully normalized by the coefficient of variation of the document length, when $b = 1$.

The tuning of the three parameters is not an easy problem, nor a resource free task, due to the required development of a test collection. Hence, in most cases, the suggested values are used: $k_1 = 1.2$, $b = 0.75$ [14] and $k_3 = 8$ [12] . Still, as shown by Chowdhury et al. [2], tuning the parameters can lead to a considerable improvement in the effectiveness of the retrieval system. However, tuning is only possible if ground truth is available, and another, more analytical approach can be taken. This consists in trying to better understand the geometry of the information space, in order to extend and improve the current model.

In this paper, we focus on the term frequency normalization, reopening the discussion described by Robertson and Zaragoza [13] about the verboseness and scope hypotheses. We propose a new parameter-free normalization, based on the features of the document collection. We test this model using a sample of five test collections from TREC and CLEF, selected on purpose from different domains: Web, News, Medical, and Patent, in order to verify experimentally the dependency between the normalization factor and the features of the document collection.

The remainder of the paper is structured as follows: in Section 2 we provide a very brief summary of the extensive work already done on the study and understanding of the term frequency normalization. Section 3 provides the intuition of our method and introduces the required concepts and the method itself. In Section 4 we present and discuss our experimental results. We conclude in Section 5.

2. RELATED WORK

The initiators of the discussion about the term frequency normalization are the early participants in TREC, with first insights appearing after TREC-3, and the first efforts on document length normalization showing improved results in TREC-4 [3]. To understand why a document is long, Robertson and Zaragoza [13, p. 358] describe two hypotheses: a) verboseness, to convey the same information using more words than needed; and b) scope, to convey information containing more topics, details, or aspects. These hypotheses have a conflicting effect when treating the normalization in terms of length, because while the first suggests to normalize the *tf* by the length, the second suggests the opposite. Hence, the introduction of a soft normalization based on the coefficient of variation of the document length and the introduction of the *b* parameter that controls the slope of the normalization factor. This is of course not the only way for length normalization. Among others, Singhal et al. [17] studied it extensively for the TF-IDF model.

Not much work has been done on the scope hypothesis, except perhaps the effort spent in passage retrieval. Here, document length is circumvented by viewing the document as a collection of concatenated shorter documents to be retrieved individually.

More work has been done to tackle the verboseness issue. Na et al. [11] briefly introduce the concept of verboseness given by repetitiveness of terms. They compare it with multi-topicality under the language modeling framework. The normalization factors are corrected based on the assumption that the vocabulary size can be used to estimate the number of topics contained in the document. He and Ounis [5] introduced a new term frequency normalization following the idea of Amati [1], who introduced the use of Dirichlet Priors. He and Ounis point out the relationship between test collection features on term frequency normalization, and introduce a new parameter, learned from the test collection. They defined the normalization effect and hypothesized that the optimal parameter is the value that makes the normalization factor give similar normalization results across different corpora [4, 6]. Lv and Zhai pointed out that the retrieval pattern of BM25 does not follow the relevancy pattern, biasing the system against long documents, and introduced a boosting parameter δ that summed to the normalized term frequency in a first version [9] and then summed to the term frequency component in a second version [8] to correct the pattern discrepancy.

Rousseau and Varzirgiannis [15] analyze the problem in terms of function composition, comparing BM25 with TF-IDF and combining the two works previously mentioned, to gain a better understanding of the similarity across the models. Some efforts have been directed towards understanding and removing the parameters of BM25: Lv and Zhai [7] pointed out that it is more effective to use a term-specific k_1, and that it is possible to estimate it using an information gain measure to quantify the contributions of repeated term occurrences. They do not address *b*.

Overall, a criticism of all of these works is that the studies of and experiments with new models of the term frequency normalization always use the same kind of test collection, News and Web corpora.

3. THE NORMALIZATION HYPOTHESES

Document length normalization is based on the observation that documents are long either because they are verbose, or because they cover more aspects, as discussed.

The insight at the base of this study is that we can distinguish two kinds of verboseness: a) *repetitiveness*, in which the same terms are repeated many times (e.g. legal or patent texts); and b) *non-repetitiveness*, where the writer uses different terms to describe the same thing (e.g. over-descriptive narration in Balzac's novels). In the first case, *tf* is expected

to be higher, so it should be normalized more than in the second case, where it is naturally low because of the use of different terms. While non-repetitiveness implies a more semantic analysis of the text, repetitiveness can be easily identified by counting the number of times terms are repeated on average. We define this in an obvious way as the average term frequency:

$$avgtf_d = \frac{1}{|T_d|} \sum_{t \in T_d} tf_d(t) = \frac{L_d}{|T_d|} \qquad (1)$$

However, we should observe that while a high $avgtf_d$ is indicative of repetitiveness, a low $avgtf_d$ would indicate either a broader document that would fall into the scope hypothesis, or a verbose, non-repetitive document. From the observation that *tf* is expected to be higher, we have the chance to better discern the sets of elite and non-elite documents described in the 2-Poisson model. Embedding this new knowledge in the model would take into account the fact that observing a high *tf* can be due either to its relevance in the document, as an elite term, or because of its repetitiveness, as boilerplate, non-elite term.

Our intuition is that it is possible to differentiate the two kinds of verboseness for a specific document based in part on collection statistics. We can then diminish the effect of the *tf* for each document by comparing the average *tf* of a document with *mavgtf*, the mean average term frequency of the collection:

$$mavgtf = \frac{1}{|D|} \sum_{d \in D} avgtf_d \qquad (2)$$

First, a few observations on these new indicators. The average term frequency of a document d ($avgtf_d$) is an indicator of how many times the same term is repeated in the document. If a document does not have any repetitions, $avgtf_d$ is equal to 1. The average term frequency is simply document length over number of unique terms, and this makes it easy to verify that *avgtf* has domain $[1, \infty[$, assuming documents of finite length $[1, maxL]$, where $maxL$ is the length of the longest document. Since *mavgtf* is the average of the *avgtf*, it has the same domain. If the test collection is made on average of documents with a low level of repetition, then the *mavgtf* is very close to 1. The *mavgtf* is a collection specific value that summarizes the repetitiveness of the language in a specific corpus.

From the intuition above we infer first that if the language of a collection is repetitive (high *mavgtf*), we expect to need more length normalization. Therefore we define the BM25 document length normalization factor *b* as:

$$b = 1 - mavgtf^{-1} \qquad (3)$$

This definition of *b* has the required domain $[0, 1[$ and increases monotonically with *mavgtf*.

With this normalization parameter, we can define a new normalization factor, B_{-b} to be used in BM25:

$$B_{-b} = mavgtf^{-1} + (1 - mavgtf^{-1}) \frac{L_d}{avgdl} \qquad (4)$$

However, the reader may have already noticed a potential issue with this new *b*: while in theory it has domain $[0, 1[$, it will only reach 1 as $mavgtf \to \infty$. In practice the *mavgtf* is actually small, in the range of the low single digits, and this will limit the values of *b* to the lower half of the normalization spectrum. The normalization factor B_{-b}

Corpus	EC	Challenge	$|D|$	$mavgtf$
Aquaint	TREC	Hard 2005	1,033,461	1.519
Disks 4&5	TREC	Ad Hoc 8	528,155	1.574
eHealth'13	CLEF	eHealth 2013	1,102,848	2.205
.GOV	TREC	Web 2002	1,247,753	2.481
CLEF-IP'10	CLEF	CLEF-IP 2010	2,670,678	3.008

Table 1: Corpora used, with information about the challenge and evaluation campaign (EC) to which it belongs, number of documents, and mean average term frequency.

will therefore tend to be very conservative in its document length normalization. This is partially by design: as we said before – we do not want to do strong length normalization if the collection is not using repetitive language. Even more, at this point we are still not making a distinction between repetitiveness and non-repetitiveness at document level. To do so, and at the same time to control the $(1-b)$ component in B, we need to introduce another factor in B:

$$B_{\text{VA}} = (1-b)\frac{avgtf_d}{mavgtf} + b\frac{L_d}{avgdl} \qquad (5)$$

This new factor, $\frac{avgtf_d}{mavgtf}$, boosts the normalization factor B when the document at hand is repetitive.

The new formulation for B can also be seen as a re-interpretation of document length normalization: it is now no longer a linear combination between doing or not doing length normalization, but rather a linear combination between normalizing for repetitiveness or length (non-repetitiveness), controlled by a parameter b bound to the general repetitiveness of the language of the collection. For collections that are generally repetitive, it will tend to do length normalization, and the newly added factor will reduce this normalization only for those documents that are not repetitive. For collections that are generally non-repetitive, it will tend to not do length normalization, and the newly added factor will increase this normalization only for those documents that are repetitive. Intuitively, the method compares the repetitiveness of the document with that of the collection. The proposed variant makes the repetitiveness of the document no longer a good indicator of verboseness if the collection is generally repetitive.

Finally, using our b from Eq. 3, our variant of BM25 normalization factor is:

$$B_{\text{VA}} = mavgtf^{-2}\frac{L_d}{|T_d|} + (1 - mavgtf^{-1})\frac{L_d}{avgdl} \qquad (6)$$

4. EXPERIMENTS

To test our predictions we selected five ad hoc test collections from TREC and CLEF, with the aim to observe differences in the use of language, in different domains. We selected from News, Web, Medical, and Patent corpora, listed in Table 1, where we can observe how the average term frequency varies across the corpora. To assess the different experiments, we used the condensed version [16] of mean average precision (MAP') and precision at 10 (P@10') because of their better stability in case of incomplete judgments. We tested the new normalization factors, B_{-b} and B_{VA}, against two different configurations of the classic BM25: standard and ideal. The BM25 standard is characterized by having the suggested configuration of the parameters, k_1 and b. In the ideal BM25, the two parameters have been optimized

Track	P.	k1	b	MAP'	P@10'
		Standard Case			
Hard 2005	CL	1.20	0.75	0.2144‡	0.3600‡
	CL-b	1.20	-	0.2325†	0.4360†
	VA	1.20	-	0.2318†	0.4360†
Ad Hoc 8	CL	1.20	0.75	0.2504‡	0.4720
	CL-b	1.20	-	0.2578	0.4600
	VA	1.20	-	0.2677†	0.4940
eHealth'14	CL	1.20	0.75	0.5565	0.7694
	CL-b	1.20	-	0.5636‡	0.7878‡
	VA	1.20	-	0.5718‡	0.7694
Web'02	CL	1.20	0.75	0.2022	0.2460
	CL-b	1.20	-	0.1972	0.2440
	VA	1.20	-	0.2010	0.2520
CLEF-IP'10	CL	1.20	0.75	0.3562‡	0.6423‡
	CL-b	1.20	-	0.3537‡	0.6371‡
	VA	1.20	-	0.3556‡	0.6371‡
		Ideal Case			
Hard 2005	CL	1.65	0.25	0.2346†	0.4440†
	CL-b	1.70	-	0.2335†	0.4360†
	VA	1.80	-	0.2332†	0.4140†‡
Ad Hoc 8	CL	0.45	0.40	0.2715†	0.4600
	CL-b	0.45	-	0.2713†	0.4520
	VA	0.55	-	0.2744†	0.4900
eHealth'14	CL	2.30	0.55	0.5849	0.8143
	CL-b	2.30	-	0.5844†	0.8143
	VA	2.40	-	0.5922	0.7959†
Web'02	CL	2.40	0.70	0.2062	0.2460
	CL-b	2.05	-	0.2012	0.2420
	VA	2.50	-	0.2056	0.2360
CLEF-IP'10	CL	2.50	1.0	0.3713†	0.6540†
	CL-b	2.50	-	0.3615	0.6536
	VA	2.25	-	0.3643	0.6567

Table 2: Scores obtained with the classic BM25 (CL), classic BM25 with b as in Eq. 3 (CL-b), and our variant (VA). † indicates statistical significance (t-test, p<0.05) against the standard classic BM25 (CL) and ‡ against the ideal classic BM25 (CL).

using as training set and test set the same set of topics, which of course makes it an unrealistic scenario, but an interesting upper limit. In this case, k_1 varies between 0.5 and 2.5. In all experiments we set $k_3 = 0$ to avoid any potential interferences of the tf_q in the scoring of the document.

We used the search engine Terrier[1] 4.0 for the classic BM25 and developed and integrated in it our BM25 variants[2]. All the documents have been preprocessed using the English tokenizer and Porter stemmer of the Terrier search engine. The queries are extracted from the title only, except for the CLEF-IP 2010 where the abstract has been included.

Table 2 shows the performance of each weighting scheme in the two configurations mentioned above. In only two of the five collections (eHealth and CLEF-IP) the standard VA is lower and statistically significantly different from the ideal classic BM25 (CL). This can be explained by the combination of two effects: the large influence k_1 has on the results, as shown in Fig. 1 by the size of the gray areas, and the large difference between the standard k_1 and the ideal k_1.

---

[1] http://www.terrier.org
[2] Code available on the website of the first author

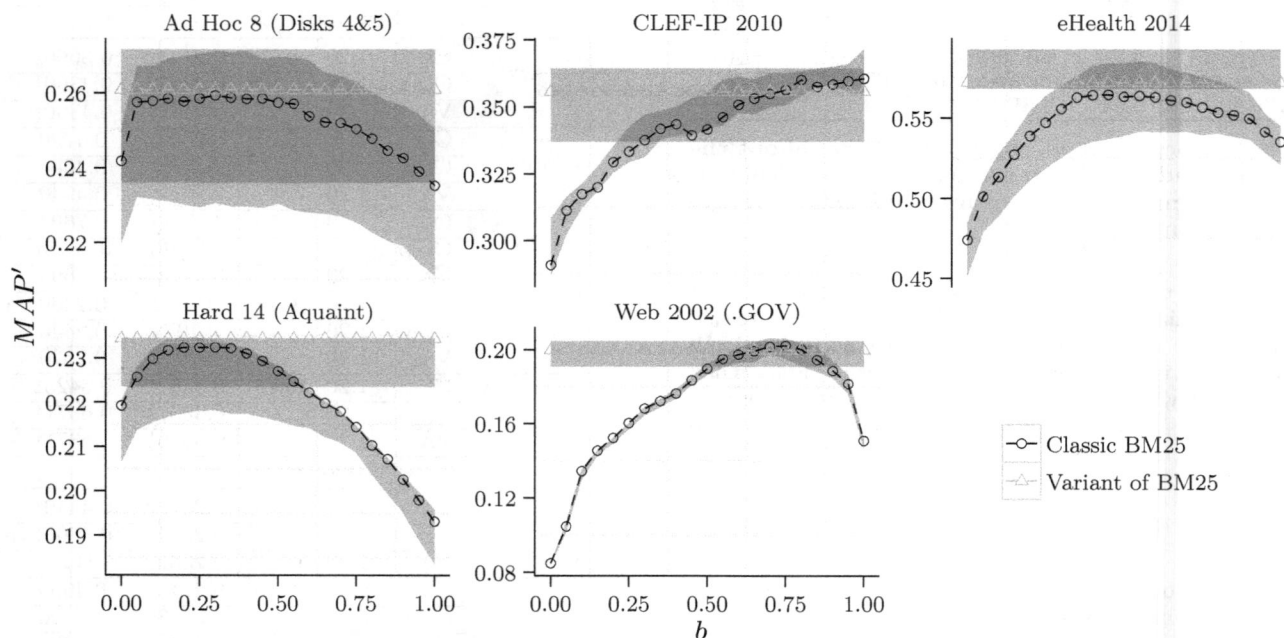

Figure 1: Performance sensitivity of the classic BM25 (CL) and our variant (VA) across all the test collections, with standard $k_1 = 1.2$. The gray area represents the range of values obtainable varying k_1 in the range $[0.5, 2.5]$.

5. CONCLUSION

We continued a discussion started 20 years ago in the context of TREC about the need for document length normalization and the nature of the document length itself. Previous studies, working on test collections of web and news corpora, failed to observe what in legal and patent collections is patently obvious: document length verbosity, in a bag-of-words model, can be expressed via repetition or via synonyms. We proposed a new factor B, including a specific value for the parameter b, and showed that, across different domains, the results are generally statistically indistinguishable from those obtained with ideal b values, without having to identify these ideal values. Together with previous works on estimation of the k_1 parameter, this brings us a step closer to a parameter-free, stable, BM25.

6. REFERENCES

[1] G. Amati and J. C. C. Van Rijsbergen. Probabilistic models for information retrieval based on divergence from randomness. *TOIS*, 20(4), 2002.

[2] A. Chowdhury, M. C. McCabe, D. Grossman, and O. Frieder. Document Normalization Revisited. In *Proc. of SIGIR*, 2002.

[3] D. Harman. Overview of the Fourth Text REtrieval Conference (TREC-4). In *Proc. of TREC 4*, 1995.

[4] B. He and I. Ounis. A Study of Parameter Tuning for Term Frequency Normalization. In *Proc. of CIKM*, 2003.

[5] B. He and I. Ounis. A Study of the Dirichlet Priors for Term Frequency Normalisation. In *Proc. of SIGIR*, 2005.

[6] B. He and I. Ounis. Term Frequency Normalisation Tuning for BM25 and DFR Models. In *Proc. of ECIR*, 2005.

[7] Y. Lv and C. Zhai. Adaptive Term Frequency Normalization for BM25. In *Proc. of CIKM*, 2011.

[8] Y. Lv and C. Zhai. Lower-bounding Term Frequency Normalization. In *Proc. of CIKM*, 2011.

[9] Y. Lv and C. Zhai. When Documents Are Very Long, BM25 Fails! In *Proc. of SIGIR*, 2011.

[10] D. Metzler and H. Zaragoza. Semi-parametric and non-parametric term weighting for information retrieval. In *Proc. of ICTIR*, 2009.

[11] S.-H. Na, I.-S. Kang, and J.-H. Lee. Improving term frequency normalization for multi-topical documents and application to language modeling approaches. In *Proc. of ECIR*, 2008.

[12] S. Robertson, S. Walker, M. Beaulieu, M. Gatford, and A. Payne. Okapi at TREC-4. In *Proc. of TREC 4*, 1995.

[13] S. Robertson and H. Zaragoza. The probabilistic relevance framework: Bm25 and beyond. *Foundations and Trends in Information Retrieval*, 3(4), 2009.

[14] S. E. Robertson, S. Walker, S. Jones, M. Hancock-Beaulieu, and M. Gatford. Okapi at TREC-3. In *Proc. of TREC-3*, 1994.

[15] F. Rousseau and M. Vazirgiannis. Composition of TF Normalizations: New Insights on Scoring Functions for Ad Hoc IR. In *Proc. of SIGIR*, 2013.

[16] T. Sakai. Alternatives to Bpref. In *Proc. of SIGIR*, 2007.

[17] A. Singhal, C. Buckley, and M. Mitra. Pivoted Document Length Normalization. In *Proc. of SIGIR*, 1996.

Author Index

www.ingramcontent.com/pod-product-compliance
Lightning Source LLC
Chambersburg PA
CBHW080702220326
41598CB00033B/5276